SELECTED LETTERS
OF RICHARD WAGNER

SELECTED LETTERS
OF
RICHARD WAGNER

Translated and edited by
Stewart Spencer and Barry Millington

*with original texts of passages
omitted from existing printed editions*

W · W · NORTON & COMPANY
New York   London

Printed in the United States of America.

Library of Congress Cataloging in Publication Data

Wagner, Richard, 1813-1883.
[Correspondence. English. Selections]
Selected letters of Richard Wagner / translated and edited by
Stewart Spencer and Barry Millington; with original texts of
passages omitted from existing printed editions.
p. cm.
Bibliography: p.
Includes index.
1. Wagner, Richard, 1813-1883—Correspondence. 2. Composers—
Germany—Correspondence. I. Spencer, Stewart. II. Millington, Barry.
III. Title
ML410.W1A317 1987
782.1′092′4—dc19

87-32470
ISBN 0-393-02500-4

W. W. Norton & Company, Inc., 500 Fifth Avenue, New York, N.Y. 10110
W. W. Norton & Company Ltd., 37 Great Russell Street,
London WC1B 3NU

1 2 3 4 5 6 7 8 9 0

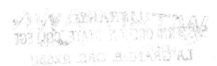

CONTENTS

PREFACE

Sixty years have elapsed since Wilhelm Altmann's selection of Wagner's letters appeared in English, and during that time the number of letters available for selection has almost doubled, among the more important additions being the letters to Hans Richter (100, of which only nine had been previously published), Mathilde Maier (129, all previously unpublished), King Ludwig II of Bavaria (473 previously unpublished letters, telegrams and poems), and Lorenz Düfflipp (73 letters, of which 70 were previously unpublished), together with the letters written during Wagner's years in Switzerland and edited by Max Fehr (156 previously unpublished), and the Burrell Collection edited by John N. Burk (440 letters, telegrams and receipts).

The sheer bulk of the available material and the task of locating it (a bibliography of Wagner's letters runs to nearly one hundred separate publications) present any new editor with problems of such magnitude that, out of a projected thirty volumes, only four volumes of the *Sämtliche Briefe* (Complete Letters) have appeared at the time of writing.

The editors of the present volume have attempted to provide a selection of letters which illustrates Wagner's intellectual and artistic development, rather than one which offers merely factual – or anecdotal – information. To this end, whole letters have been included wherever possible, not least in an endeavour to avoid the fault that seems to us to beset Altmann's selection, namely that of reducing Wagner's letters to a series of epistolary aphorisms. On the other hand, it would not have been sensible to insist on including only complete letters if – for reasons of space – such a policy had entailed the exclusion of paragraphs of interest elsewhere. Where cuts have been made, they generally involve the beginnings and endings of letters, and have been undertaken because the information they contain is either covered elsewhere or of no more than trivial concern. Omissions are indicated by square brackets [...].

Any selection of Wagner's letters must necessarily involve an act of interpretation which runs the risk of precluding all other interpretative possibilities. The editors have been conscious of this risk and, rather than reduce the composer to more manageable proportions, have allowed him to speak freely in all his contradictory roles. (The only exception was the decision to omit all of the Open Letters which Wagner wrote, many of which he himself published in his Collected Writings.)

Earlier attempts to limit our view of Wagner met with undeniable success, involving as they did the wholesale destruction of almost all of his letters to Cosima and to Mathilde Wesendonck. (Cosima also destroyed Peter Cornelius's letters to Wagner, and Nietzsche's letters to her.) Even letters which did not fall prey to Cosima's pyromania were mutilated beyond repair: not even the most up-to-date scientific methods can salvage the deleted passages in Wagner's letters to Mathilde Maier (see p. 414). And a number of letters available to earlier editors have since disappeared without trace.

In other cases, however, the original autographs – or drafts or copies of them – are still extant, and wherever possible, these have been consulted in preparing the present edition. In this way a number of passages have been reinstated which Cosima's team of editors in the years around the turn of the century had seen fit to suppress. The most egregious example concerns the letter of 12 April 1858 to Princess Carolyne Sayn-Wittgenstein [209], in which the printed edition reproduced barely a quarter of Wagner's original. The text of this frank letter written immediately after the crisis of the Mathilde Wesendonck affair is thus – as with similar cases elsewhere in the book – published in its entirety here for the first time in any language. Passages such as these lacking in the printed editions are indicated in the translation by square brackets; the original texts are given in Appendix B.

The translation attempts to steer a mid-course between the legitimate respect that is due to "authoritative texts"[1] and the freedom that is necessary if the translations are to be read and understood without reference to the original. Modern idioms have thus been eschewed; rather, the translation aims to reproduce a nineteenth-century literary style in keeping with Wagner's own ornate and and often highly poetical language. To have ignored this aspect of his correspondence would have been a disservice both to Wagner and to the reader. Wagner's somewhat idiosyncratic punctuation has been retained, except in those cases where to have done so would have impaired understanding. All the translations have been specially prepared for the present volume, even in the case of the Pusinelli letters, of which a number have been available hitherto only in English. None the less, it would have been short-sighted (and ungracious) not to have borrowed the occasional felicity of style from existing translations, and the present translator gratefully acknowledges his debt to those of his forerunners who have blazed a trail through the thicket of Wagner's prose, and in doing so made his own task somewhat easier. The purpose of the introductory essays is not to provide a self-contained biography of Wagner, rather to sketch in the historical background and set the letters in a biographical context. In the essays, as well as in the annotation, we have endeavoured to correct misrepresentations, where appropriate, and to supply something of what is inevitably missing from a unilateral presentation of Wagner's correspondence. The translations are the work of Stewart Spencer, and the introductory essays and glossary of names are by Barry Millington; the editors are responsible jointly for the annotation.

1 See Peter Newmark, *Approaches to Translation* (Oxford 1981).

For permission to transcribe and translate archival material, the editors are grateful to The Curators of the Bodleian Library, Oxford (letter to Felix Mendelssohn of 8 June 1843), The Memorial Library of Music (Department of Special Collections and University Archives), Stanford University (letter to August Röckel of 25/26 January 1854), the Bayerische Staatsbibliothek (letter to Carolyne Sayn-Wittgenstein of 12 April 1858), and Herr Dipl.-Kfm. Walter Just (letter of 25 March 1864 to Eduard Liszt). For answering individual queries we must thank Dr Bauer of the Munich Stadtarchiv, Dr Karl Dachs and Dr Sigrid von Moisy of the Bayerische Staatsbibliothek, Munich, Dr John Deathridge, Dr Manfred Eger of the Nationalarchiv der Richard-Wagner-Stiftung in Bayreuth, Frau Ottermann of the Mainz Stadtbibliothek, Professor Gerhard Schmid of the Goethe-und Schiller-Archiv in Weimar, Wayne D. Shirley of the Library of Congress, Washington, D.C., Professor Alan Walker and Peter A. Ward Jones, Music Librarian of the Bodleian Library, Oxford.

For specialist help and advice on various matters we are especially grateful to Dr Judith Black, David Britt and Dr Konrad Bund (the last of whom braved two freezing Bavarian winters to examine manuscripts with us); the second of these trips was assisted by a grant from *Music & Letters*, which we also acknowledge with gratitude. We are, further, deeply indebted to Dr Isolde Vetter of the Richard Wagner-Gesamtausgabe, Munich, who has generously put her vast knowledge of the sources at our disposal. Particular thanks are due to Herr Günter Fischer of the Nationalarchiv in Bayreuth, without whose willing assistance this book would have been much the poorer. Pauline Baseley, Michael Hall and Harry Haskell gave much welcome help in the daunting task of proof-reading. And our final debt is to our publishers, J. M. Dent & Sons Ltd, who have accommodated our steadily expanding project – and the accompanying schedule – with truly stoical patience. To the staff of Dent we record our grateful thanks.

Barry Millington
Stewart Spencer

Spring 1987

A NOTE ON CURRENCIES

The following information may be found useful in understanding the various currencies which occur in the course of the text and accompanying annotation:

1 thaler = 3 marks
1 florin *or* gulden = 2 marks
1 friedrichsdor = 17 marks
1 franc = 0.81 marks
1 dollar = 4.2 marks
1 louis d'or = 14 marks
1 pound = 20 marks

Wagner's salary in Dresden was 1500 thalers p.a.; the allowance of 3000 francs (800 thalers) made by Julie Ritter in 1851 was thus approximately half of his salary as Kapellmeister. The rent of his second lodging in the Zeltweg, Zurich (1853–7), was 800 francs p.a., while that of the house in Brienner-strasse, Munich (1864–5), was 3000 florins.

YOUTH AND EARLY CAREER
1813–1839

INTRODUCTORY ESSAY 1813–1839

The artist's own testimony is rarely a reliable source of biographical information. In the case of Wagner it is necessary to regard a good deal of it with some scepticism. Scholarly research into the source material relating to his compositions is continuing to contradict the image projected by Wagner himself and enthusiastically promulgated by his followers. His tendency to reconstruct a personal history in accordance with an idealized view of himself provided those intent on posthumous sanctification with precisely the raw material they required; even now, more than a century after his death, the icon is still being dismantled. Wagner's letters – of which at least 12,000 are known to have existed – are an invaluable aid in the process of assembling a more objective profile.

It is unfortunate that there are no letters extant from before 1830, Wagner's seventeenth year, since such documents might have thrown a good deal of light on the composer's psychological constitution as moulded by the formative influences of his infancy: his birth into a war-torn country and frequently uprooted family, the uncertainty of his paternity, his weakness and sickliness as a child. Even so, there are many revealing clues, in the letters that have survived, as to his relations with his mother, sisters, friends, teachers, benefactors and enemies. Treated with due caution, such evidence can usefully be put alongside the accounts of Wagner and of others, as a corrective and as a supplement.

It will probably never be established definitively whether Wagner's father was the police actuary Carl Friedrich Wagner or the actor-painter Ludwig Geyer. The latter was a close friend of the family and he married Friedrich's wife Johanna a respectable nine months after she was widowed by an outbreak of typhus following the Battle of the Nations. What is important is that the boy himself was never to know the truth. He was loved by his adoptive father and took his name until some years after Geyer's death, but he suffered from a lifelong, tormenting suspicion (in fact groundless) that Geyer was of Jewish birth. The fear of belonging to a race considered almost universally at the time as inferior (though redeemable through assimilation) was aggravated by the awkward facts that he was born in Brühl, the Jewish quarter of Leipzig, and that he had the prominent nose and high forehead generally associated with the Jewish physiognomy. It was the perceived necessity of proving to the world that he was without taint that underlay the virulence of his later anti-Semitism.

His frequent ill health as a child, and the slightness of his physical frame, gave his mother much cause for concern. He suffered from hallucinations, nightmares, a recurrent skin complaint (erysipelas) and mild depression, some or all of which may well have been connected with his psychological insecurity: the itinerant career of his step-father Geyer caused the family more than one upheaval and sometimes this involved an unnerving proximity to war zones.

In spite of the professions, in his autobiography *Mein Leben* (My Life), of tender love for his mother, there is evidence here too of emotional deprivation. Wagner's letters are equally contradictory on the subject: the affectionate tone of his infrequent and irregular letters to his mother [12] has to be put alongside the harshly critical comments in a letter to his half-sister Cäcilie and her husband [48].

At the age of seven Wagner was sent for some elementary schooling to Pastor Christian Wetzel at Possendorf, near Dresden; it was at this time that he learned to play some simple tunes on the piano, though his family did everything they could to discourage his musical inclinations. His earliest enthusiasm was for Weber, especially *Der Freischütz*, and, later, the music of Beethoven. At first it was the theatre that chiefly fired him and that inspired the writing, between 1826 and 1828, of a "vast tragic drama" called *Leubald* (WWV 1), but he soon conceived the plan of writing incidental music for his play in the style of Beethoven's *Egmont*. He conscientiously acquired from the library a suitable composition treatise by Johann Bernhard Logier[1] and in the autumn of 1828 began to take harmony lessons (initially in secret) with a local musician, Christian Gottlieb Müller. When he came some years later to write the first account of his early years in the *Autobiographische Skizze* (Autobiographical Sketch) of 1843, Wagner made light of his earlier tuition. In language doubtless calculated to appeal to the dilettantish readers of Laube's *Zeitung für die elegante Welt* (the periodical in which the *Sketch* was published) he reduced the period of his study with Müller to an artistic-sounding inability to cope with the rules of textbook harmony and a despairing shake of his teacher's head. In fact, the lessons with Müller lasted for the best part of three years, in which time Wagner absorbed the primary principles of harmonic style. Moreover, as is shown by the penitent letter [2], recently published for the first time, and by [7], his demanding teacher had clearly earned from his pupil a degree of respect and loyalty.

The tuition with Müller was followed by a short but intense period of study (about six months from October 1831) with Christian Theodor Weinlig, the

---

1 Wagner mentions only a thoroughbass (i.e. continuo) tutor. Logier, a German pianist, composer and teacher who lived and worked in Ireland from 1791, published a work called *Logier's Thorough-Bass* in London in 1818; a German edition appeared in Berlin the following year. His more celebrated treatise, *System der Musik-Wissenschaft und der praktischen Composition*, was published in German, English and French editions in 1827.

Kantor of St Thomas's, Leipzig. Here again Wagner later chose to belittle the significance of this study, preferring to present himself as a composer for whom the stream of inspiration rendered unnecessary the conventional drudgery of apprenticeship. And again his letters of the time provide a truer picture: [3] and [7] indicate that not only did Weinlig help him to acquire a soundly based technique of harmony and counterpoint, but that a firm bond developed between master and pupil on account of the latter's diligence and responsiveness. For Weinlig he wrote the Piano Sonata in B flat (WWV 21), a piece of competent pastiche, followed by the more individual Fantaisie in F sharp minor (WWV 22), also for piano. Other keyboard works from the same time are the four-handed Polonaise (a revised version of a two-handed original) (WWV 23a and 23b), and the Grosse Sonate in A major (WWV 26).

By the spring of 1832 he also had a string of orchestral works to his credit: some eight overtures (only three have survived complete), two *Entreactes tragiques* (WWV 25) and some incidental music to Ernst Raupach's play *König Enzio* (WWV 24). The first of the overtures, the "Drumbeat Overture" in B flat (WWV 10), was performed in Leipzig, an experience that caused the young composer acute embarrassment. The work's nickname refers to a highly innovative feature: after each four-bar melodic phrase a fifth bar was inserted consisting simply of a loud stroke of the timpani on the second beat. As the piece progressed and the drumbeat persisted, the audience's wonderment and hilarity grew; neither were they diminished by the overture's unusually abrupt conclusion. Wagner fled the theatre humiliated, but as letter [2] makes clear, his discomfiture was aggravated by the fear that Müller would regard the whole episode as an act of unpardonable disloyalty.

The fruits of his tuition under Müller and Weinlig are to be seen in the work which he completed immediately after Weinlig had discharged him with his much-valued commendation [7]. It was the Symphony in C major (WWV 29), closely modelled on the Third, Fifth and Seventh symphonies of Beethoven but displaying an assurance of technique that forms its own tribute to the thoroughness of the years of apprenticeship.

These years were also important ones in Wagner's emotional development. He twice suffered the agonies of unrequited love: first with Leah David, the daughter of a Jewish banker, and then with Jenny Raymann. Jenny and her sister Auguste were the illegitimate daughters of Count Johann Joseph Pachta. Wagner had already made the family's acquaintance back in 1827; now, five years later, as a bearded nineteen-year-old visiting the Pachta estate at Pravonin, near Prague, he fell passionately in love with Jenny. Groomed to attract aristocratic admirers, both sisters passed over the serious young musician. In a letter to a friend [5], Wagner describes the mental torture he underwent; his account, though tinged with arrogance ("she was not worthy of my love!"), contains a revealing passage on his tendency to idealize lovers in his imagination – a moment of mature self-awareness.

His confidant on this occasion, and on many others at the period, was Theodor Apel. Two years older than Wagner, Apel had been a close friend of his since they had studied together, first at the Nicolaischule and then at the University in Leipzig. Apel's subject had been Law, but a generous inheritance from his deceased father enabled him to cultivate his poetic and dramatic talents.

While in Pravonin Wagner began to sketch an opera, *Die Hochzeit* (The Wedding) (WWV 31), hardly less grisly than his earlier epic *Leubald*. Of the music, only an introduction, chorus and septet were written; the poem is lost. According to Wagner's account he deferred to his beloved sister Rosalie's critical opinion of the scenario and destroyed the manuscript on the spot.

With his training behind him, Wagner was now ready to take up his first professional appointment. In January 1833 he moved to Würzburg where his brother Albert was able to secure for him the post of chorus-master at the theatre. Here, under the influence of Marschner and Weber, whose works were among those it was his duty to prepare for performance, he completed his first opera, *Die Feen* (The Fairies) (WWV 32) [6]. Other composers whose works he encountered at close quarters during his year at Würzburg were Beethoven, Paer, Cherubini, Rossini and Auber, but the operas that stimulated the most interest locally were Meyerbeer's *Robert le Diable* (which had received its première in Paris as recently as November 1831) and two by Marschner, *Der Vampyr* (premièred in Leipzig in March 1828) and *Hans Heiling* (heard for the first time in Berlin just a few months before its Würzburg performance). *Robert le Diable* in particular was a novelty for a provincial theatre like Würzburg's: the grand operas of Meyerbeer and Spontini were not normally given in Germany outside the Court Theatres in Berlin, Dresden and Munich, or the larger state theatres such as Leipzig and Hamburg. For Wagner, if his later account in *Mein Leben* is to be believed, *Robert* was a disappointment: he found the score unoriginal and superficial. *Der Vampyr* he was prepared to acknowledge as a model for *Die Feen*, at least as much as it was the genre, that of German Romantic opera, that appealed to him. He is much less forthcoming about the influence of *Hans Heiling*; indeed, in a letter to Rosalie [6] he is dismissive of what he finds its many weaknesses. John Warrack has shown that his debt to it was in fact considerable,[2] although that debt should not be overrated. The tragic conflict arising from the love of a mortal for a fairy, which is central to *Hans Heiling*, was hardly a new notion: traceable back to the Middle Ages, it was firmly established in the Romantic imagination by the treatment of Friedrich de la Motte Fouqué in his novella *Undine* (1811), a tale made into an opera by E. T. A. Hoffmann in 1816. Moreover, the Bohemian legend of Hans Heiling itself had been

---

2 "The Musical Background", chapter in *The Wagner Companion*, ed. by Peter Burbidge and Richard Sutton (London 1979), 110.

given both narrative and verse form by Theodor Körner (1791–1813). The fateful interplay of the human and spirit worlds, the mortal and immortal, has indeed many resonances in later works of Wagner (notably *Der fliegende Holländer*, *Tannhäuser* and *Lohengrin*), and on the evening before he died Wagner was musing on the similarity between the Undine water-spirits "who long to have souls" and his own Rhinemaidens. In 1833, however, Wagner was already well on the way to giving the story dramatic expression when he encountered Marschner's *Hans Heiling*. He had fashioned *La donna serpente* into a suitable libretto in January and February of that year, and by the time *Hans Heiling* was given in Würzburg in the autumn,[3] the first act of *Die Feen* was already complete in full score.[4] What he did take from *Hans Heiling* were some important technical devices and the main theme of the Annunciation of Death (*Die Walküre*).[5]

Although his contract in Würzburg did not expire until Palm Sunday 1834, Wagner returned to Leipzig in January and came under a new set of influences, in many respects diametrically opposed to the *Schauerromantik* of Hoffmann, Weber and Marschner. These ideas were those associated with Young Germany, one of the leading figures of which was Heinrich Laube, whose acquaintance Wagner had already made through Rosalie. Young Germany was not a "school", scarcely even a movement: a Bundestag resolution of 10 December 1835 proscribing the writings emanating from what it described as a "literary school" attributed to it a greater degree of co-ordination than actually existed. The resolution mentioned Laube, Heinrich Heine, Karl Gutzkow, Ludolf Wienbarg and Theodor Mundt, to which should be added at least the names of Ludwig Börne, Gustav Kühne and Ernst Willkomm.

But in spite of some fundamental differences of outlook among the Young Germans, there was a good deal of common ground. They rejected not only the Classicism epitomized by such former idols as Goethe and Mozart, but also Romanticism, which they regarded as sentimentally conceived, unduly preoccupied with the sovereignty of aesthetic judgements ("art for art's sake") and unwarrantably remote from the social and political issues of the day. The radicalism of the adherents of Young Germany was a response to the repressive policies of Metternich; more specifically, it took inspiration from the French Utopian Socialists, especially the Saint-Simonists, and from the

3 Glasenapp/Ellis gives 15 October.
4 The Berlin première of *Hans Heiling* was on 24 May 1833, by coincidence the very day that Wagner finished the complete draft of Act I of *Die Feen*, but there is no evidence that he had heard the work before it came to Würzburg.
5 John Warrack, *op. cit.* Among the devices he mentions are "the use of sequences as well as reiterated figures to generate tension, the effect of plunging an audience straight into the centre of a drama, and a heightened dramatic use of orchestration" (p.110).

July Revolution of 1830 which spread from Paris to various German cities, including Leipzig. Progressive ideas such as the unification of Germany, abolition of censorship, constitutional rule, and the emancipation of women were entertained by the Young Germans – in sharp contradistinction to the prevailing climate even among intellectuals, who were generally content with the political and cultural stagnation of the Biedermeier era. They attacked the established orders of the State and Church (in particular Catholic mysticism) and rejected reactionary morality in favour of a hedonistic, sensual enjoyment of life. In this respect, they saw themselves as heirs of the *Sturm und Drang* writers of the 1770s with their Rousseauesque exaltation of freedom and nature.

It was a writer from that period, Wilhelm Heinse, whose novel *Ardinghello und die glückseeligen Inseln* (Ardinghello and the Blessed Isles) made a decisive impact on Wagner. *Ardinghello*, which appeared in 1787, advocated free love and common ownership as the basis for the full realization of human potential. The glorification of sensuality and indulgence became the keynote of a holiday Wagner took with Apel in Bohemia in the summer of 1834 [9]; the artistic product was his next opera, *Das Liebesverbot* (WWV 38), composed over the following eighteen months in a style quite different from the German Romanticism of *Die Feen*, one more in keeping with the sunny Mediterranean voluptuousness of the subject. *Das Liebesverbot* (The Ban on Love) was Wagner's own reworking of Shakespeare's *Measure for Measure*, with the action transferred to Sicily and the target of attack made not simply hypocritical puritanism but bourgeois morality *per se*.

The other major influence on the composition of *Das Liebesverbot*, according to Wagner, was Heinrich Laube's *Das junge Europa* (Young Europe), a trilogy of novels of which the first part appeared in 1833. Laube's work propounded liberty in the erotic and political spheres as two inseparable aspects of the same idealistic vision; it also advocated religious toleration and national emancipation, women's liberation and equal rights for Jews. In Laube's radical periodical *Zeitung für die elegante Welt* Wagner had his first piece of aesthetic criticism published. *German Opera*, which appeared in June 1834, condemns the stultifying effect of Teutonic "erudition" and "pedantry": affected counterpoint and an excessive show of learning have stifled the genuine inspiration that can best be expressed in a single vibrant melodic line (an argument pursued in the essay *Bellini* of 1837: "Song, song, and yet again song, you Germans!" [SS XII,20; PW VIII,68]). Even his idol Weber did not escape censure: in *Euryanthe*, according to Wagner, the overall emotional effect was destroyed by being chopped up into little pieces. Wagner is not uncritical of the Italian style, in which he finds tiresome mannerisms, and in *German Opera* in particular he commends the true element in each style, whether it be German, Italian or French: a convincing dramatic representation for the modern era must transcend national boundaries. In contrast to the increasing nationalism of Wagner's later operas, his outlook at this time, under the influence of Laube, Heinse and others, is one of cosmopolitanism and universalism. In stylistic terms, this mood was reflected in *Das Liebesverbot* by the adoption of Italian and French models, especially Bellini and Auber.

On returning from the holiday in Bohemia, Wagner took up the post of musical director of a theatre company run by Heinrich Bethmann. The crucial factor in his decision to take the job was, according to *Mein Leben*, an encounter with one of the company's leading actresses, Christine Wilhelmine ("Minna") Planer, for whom he felt an immediate attraction. Their ensuing relationship was far from trouble-free, even before their marriage in November 1836; for much of their married life they tormented each other, Minna sharing few of Wagner's intellectual or political enthusiasms. At first, she seemed to provide everything he required: a stable, mature, attractive partner and a loving companion prepared to minister to his bodily needs. If Minna was somewhat cautious in her dealings with the many eligible young men who paid court to her, this could be explained by the bitter experience suffered in her youth: at the age of fifteen she had been seduced and then abandoned by a guards captain, Ernst Rudolph von Einsiedel. The resulting pregnancy had been concealed and the child, Natalie, was raised as her sister – a charade sustained throughout Natalie's life (and only latterly with her knowledge). But such a reserve only fuelled Wagner's infatuation: in life as in art, it was always the pursuit of the unattainable that stimulated his imagination.

In order to penetrate to Wagner's real feelings towards Minna in the years before their marriage, it is necessary to balance his letters to her against those to his friend Apel; both contain aspects of the truth. In letter [8] the allusion to Minna should presumably be taken to signify physical consummation of their relationship. At the same time, he adopts a remarkably offhand tone about his sexual activities: for the mysterious Toni (about whom nothing further is known) "I simply haven't the time". It may be reasonable to suppose that such unconcern is feigned, concealing, perhaps, lack of opportunity. In the last months of 1834 there was a temporary rift between Wagner and Minna, but by May of the following year he is writing to her in a passionate vein [10]. There is an element of theatricality here, in the lovesick sighs, the repetitions, the fragmented punctuation (see also [16] and [21]). But an authentic note of anxiety and insecurity is also present. A few months later, in October 1835, Wagner is to be found putting the affair in a different perspective in his letter to Apel [14]. He explains that it was his "modern attitude towards love" which drew him to Minna; in other words, the liaison began as pure sensual gratification. Gradually he was overtaken by his "wretched bourgeois outlook", and now the desire for a secure, respectable relationship has converted his feelings into love. Meanwhile, Minna, according to Wagner, has fallen irredeemably in love with him and longs for marriage.

Since none of Minna's letters to Wagner from this time survives, it is impossible to determine whether, and if so how much, he is exaggerating. However, it seems likely that to some extent at least he is projecting his own passion on to her. Minna was unwilling to be rushed into marriage: she had her own theatrical career to pursue and, indeed, took up further posts, first at the Königstadt Theatre in Berlin, and then in Königsberg. Such an interpretation would seem to be supported by the distraught series of letters Wagner fired off to her, beginning on the day she left for Berlin [16, 17]. Every day, from 4 to 12 November, he abased himself before her in like manner, making wild promises. Yielding under such pressure, Minna returned to Magdeburg within a fortnight of leaving.

Following *Das Liebesverbot*, Wagner's next scheme for a dramatic work was *Die hohe Braut* (The High-Born Bride) (WWV 40). He sketched a prose scenario from the novel of that name by Heinrich Koenig and sent it to Eugène Scribe in Paris (see [23]), in the hope that the celebrated dramatist and librettist might work it into a text for a grand opera which Wagner could then be commissioned to set to music for the Opéra. *Die hohe Braut* was later fashioned into a libretto not by Scribe but by Wagner himself in Dresden; it was offered first to Reissiger and then to Ferdinand Hiller, but was eventually set by Jan Kittl.[6] Among the instrumental works composed by Wagner during his years with the Bethmann company was the overture and incidental music to a play by Apel; only the overture of *Columbus* survives (WWV 37).

Bethmann went bankrupt in 1836 and after a short, unsatisfactory tenure of the musical directorship of the Königsberg Theatre, beginning on 1 April 1837, Wagner moved to the theatre in Riga, a Lithuanian town (part of the Russian Empire) colonized by Germans. He travelled alone, as Minna had recently confirmed his worst fears by absconding with a merchant called Dietrich. Minna wrote apologizing for her conduct, and Wagner, acknowledging his share of the blame, invited her to come to Riga. The cramped conditions at the theatre, coupled with the unenlightened tastes of the management, soon had a depressive effect. As far as his career and the gaining of experience were concerned, Riga was not without its compensations: he proposed [24] and instituted a series of subscription concerts to be given by the theatre orchestra – evidence of the enterprise and administrative skills that were later to stand him in good stead. But the provincial theatrical life became increasingly intolerable, and when he was eased out of his job in 1839 he turned his attention to Paris and the Opéra which, he supposed, would bring him both success and fortune.

6 For the full history of Wagner's libretto and its setting see Isolde Vetter, "Wagner and Kittl" in *Wagner*, v (1984), 20–30.

1. B. Schott's Söhne, Mainz

Leipzig, 6 October [1830]

Sir,

For some time past, Beethoven's final, glorious symphony has been the object of my most profound study, and the more I have become conscious of the considerable merit of this work, the more I have been saddened to find how misunderstood and how neglected it is by the majority of the musical public. It occurred to me that the way to make this masterpiece more readily accessible would be an effective piano arrangement, but to my great regret I have not yet been able to discover such an arrangement (since Czerny's version for four hands can never really suffice). In my enthusiasm I have therefore myself attempted to arrange this symphony for *two hands*, and have so far succeeded in producing a version of the first, and perhaps the most difficult, of the work's four movements; the result, I venture to add, displays the greatest possible clarity and wealth of detail. Accordingly, I am now writing to your resp. publishing house to enquire whether you might be interested in publishing such an arrangement (since I should, of course, not wish to subject myself any further to such a laborious task without the certainty of your acceptance). As soon as I am assured of the same, I shall set to work without delay, and thus complete what has already been started. For that reason I must humbly entreat a prompt reply: as for myself, you may be assured, Sir, that I shall always show the greatest diligence.[1]

My address:
Leipzig, Pichhof by
the Hallisches Thor, 1st floor.

I am, Sir,
your obedient servant,
Richard Wagner.

SB I,117.

2. Christian Gottlieb Müller, Leipzig

Leipzig, [25 December 1830]

Dear Herr Müller,

How indignant and annoyed you must be with me is something I can all too readily imagine; and, in truth, I cannot blame you for it. You will accuse me of having acted deceitfully towards you, as my teacher, and of having

1 In the absence of a reply, Wagner completed the piano arrangement (WWV 9) and presented it to the publisher in person the following Easter. See also letter [4], p. 15.

insulted you in the most grievous fashion, in order to flatter my own self-conceit. But you may be assured that in many respects the situation is other than you suppose. Let me explain: – about 9 months ago I made the acquaintance of the local director of music, Herr Dorn, and I have to say that he has shown himself a most well-meaning friend towards me. Amongst other things he asked me whether I should like to have some of my music performed, suggesting that I might attempt an orchestral composition, – an idea which led me in my youthful enthusiasm to knock together this overture.[1] I did not dare show it to you, because I thought that, as my *teacher*, you would make fun of me because of it; and although Herr Dorn did just that, he none the less promised to perform the work, should a suitable opportunity arise, so that I could hear what it really sounded like. Such an opportunity, however, did not present itself, and so I forgot about the overture, together with all my other orchestral scribblings, and had not even seen Herr Dorn since last summer; then, quite recently, he sent word via my sister, asking whether I should like to hear my overture performed this Christmas. So surprised was I by this that, unfortunately, I did not think of asking *you*, but took my overture post-haste to Herr Dorn – and not until yesterday did it occur to me how unfairly I had acted towards you, my teacher, and how imprudently towards myself. But there was not enough time to make good my mistake. All I can do now is to ask you most sincerely for your forgiveness, and hope that you will regard what has happened not as an intentional slight on my part but rather as an act of thoughtlessness; the whole thing should be seen as a youthful transgression which does not, however, merit serious punishment. You may be assured that the only thing this performance can teach me is not to attempt anything similar for at least another twelve months. Moreover, I am relying upon the fact that no one in the audience knows my name, so that the whole affair will pass off without attracting attention, as indeed it deserves to do. Be assured of my continuing and most affectionate obedience, and please forget this act of folly on my part: the best Christmas present you could give me would be your sincere forgiveness.

Your
grateful pupil
Richard Wagner

John Deathridge, "Wagner und sein erster Lehrmeister. Mit einem unveröffentlichten Brief Richard Wagners", in Bayerische Staatsoper. Die Meistersinger von Nürnberg: Programmheft zur Neuinszenierung (Munich 1979), 71–5.

---

1 The "Drumbeat Overture" in B flat major (WWV 10). See introductory essay, p. 5; also *Mein Leben* 59–61; English trans. 51–3.

3. OTTILIE WAGNER, COPENHAGEN   Leipzig, 3 March [1832]

My dear, kind Otilie [*sic*],

I, too, have finally got round to sending you a couple of lines to remotest Denmark[1] – it is now so long since I last saw you that I feel a very real need to speak to you again, at least in writing; and yet there is *so much* I should like to tell you about these last twelve months – which have seen such decisive changes in my life – that I am afraid that a single sheet of paper will not be sufficient for my needs; and so, for the time being, I shall tell you only what concerns me most. – How much it saddened me not to be able to say goodbye to you when you left! It was this that has upset me most during the whole of the time you have been away; I felt particularly sad, staying in the inn at Culm, where, according to our mother, you had said goodbye for the last time; – well, I expect it will not be long now before we see each other again; for however much you may be enjoying yourself at present, I still hope that you will one day want to return to us, when your feelings towards us have changed. – But now let me tell you about myself, it may give you pleasure to learn how things stand with me, since you showed such care and concern for me in one of your recent letters. – Oh, how it grieves me to have to admit that, for a time, I led a thoroughly dissolute life, and that mixing with students distracted me from my purpose, with the result that I caused our good mother a great deal of worry and distress, until I finally took a firm hold of myself, and was given such encouragement in this resolve by my new teacher that I have now reached the point when I feel I have already embarked upon the course which I now intend to follow in life. I should have explained that for more than six months I have been a pupil of the local cantor Theodor *Weinlig*, who, with some justification, may be regarded as the *greatest living contrapuntalist* and who, at the same time, is so excellent a fellow that I am as fond of him as if he were my own father. Such is the affection with which he has encouraged me to develop that, as he himself has remarked, I can already consider my period of apprenticeship to be over, so that the advice he continues to offer me is merely that of a friend. The extent to which he cares for me is proved by the fact that when, at the end of half-a-year's lessons, our mother asked him what his fee was, he replied that it would be unreasonable of him to accept any payment, such was the pleasure it had given him to teach me: my hard work and his hopes for my future were sufficient of a reward for him. – You can well imagine that all this has borne ample fruit: – last Christmas an overture of mine[2] was performed at the theatre here, and last week I even had one performed at one of the *main*

---

1 In the spring of 1831 Ottilie had left Leipzig for Copenhagen, where she lived in the house of the Danish poet Adam Gottlob Oehlenschläger.

2 Concert Overture in D minor (WWV 20), first performed in the Royal Saxon Court Theatre on 25 December 1831, probably under the baton of Heinrich Dorn.

concerts;[1] – let me tell you that this latter is no mean achievement; before any work by a young composer is accepted for such a concert, it has to be deemed worthy of performance by all the musical experts on the board of concert directors; the fact that my own overture was accepted in this way proves that it must have something in its favour. – But now I must report on the performance itself, since it was such an important occasion for me: – Rosalie and Luise were there. I could certainly not have anticipated a lively success, firstly because overtures are rarely applauded at these concerts, and secondly because, shortly beforehand, two new overtures by *Marschner* and *Lindpaintner* had been performed without anyone so much as lifting a finger to acknowledge them; – in spite of this I was unbelievably nervous, and I almost died of fear and trepidation; (ah, if only you had been there!). You can imagine, then, my joyful amazement when at the end of my overture, the whole house began to applaud as if they had been listening to the greatest masterpiece – I did not know what was happening to me, I can assure you! – Luise was so moved by it all that she burst into tears: – how I wished you had been there, I am sure that even you would have shared ever so slightly in our pleasure! –

Enough of this! – – Something else that's new: – a piano sonata of mine[2] has appeared in print this week, and I have dedicated it to my teacher *Weinlig*. I have received sheet music to the value of 20 thalers in payment for it. – I would gladly send you a copy, if I did not suspect that the cost of forwarding it to you would be almost as much as the price you would have to pay for it in Copenhagen; all you have to do is go into any music shop and ask them to order it for you from Leipzig, stating the title: "Sonata for the Pianoforte by Richard Wagner 1st work, published by Breitkopf and Haertel" of Leipzig. It is not very difficult, but in the event of your not being able to play it at sight, I suggest that, in my name, you ask Fräulein Lotte[3] to play it for you; it would give me great pleasure to know that you liked it. – In addition, I recently composed an overture to *König Enzio*, a new tragedy by Raupach;[4] it is performed in the theatre here each time the play is given. Everyone likes it. – But that's enough on my various compositions, as soon as you are here with us again, it will give me endless pleasure to tell you all of my news, my good sister.

[. . .]

SB I, 125–8.

---

1 Although Wagner gives the impression that two separate works were performed, the overture mentioned here is again the D minor Concert Overture (WWV 20), revived at a Gewandhaus concert on 23 February 1832.
2 Piano Sonata in B flat major, op. 1 (WWV 21).
3 Charlotte Oehlenschläger, daughter of Ottilie's host in Copenhagen.
4 Overture in E minor to Raupach's tragedy *König Enzio*, in which Wagner's sister Rosalie played the role of Lucia di Viadagoli (WWV 24).

4. B. Schott's Söhne, Mainz   Leipzig, 15 June [1832]

Sir,

I am sending you herewith a piano arrangement for 2 *hands* of Beethoven's Symphony No. 9, which you had in your possession last year, but which, being at that time inundated with manuscripts, you returned to me. I am once again offering you this same piece, which you may put to whatsoever use you wish; I relinquish it to you in perpetuity to dispose of as you think fit. I am not asking for any fee; but if you were to offer me in return some items of sheet music, I should be most deeply indebted to you.[1] Might I therefore ask you to send me, via Herr *Wilhelm Härtel*: Beethoven's: 1.) Missa Solennis (D major) full score and *vocal score*. 2.) Beethoven's Symphony No. 9. Full score; 3.) Idem: 2 Quartets:[2] full score; and 4.) Hummel's arrangement of Beethoven's symphonies?[3] The sooner you were able to fulfil this request, the happier I should be.

I am, Sir,
your most obedient servant,
Richard Wagner.

SB I, 129–30.

5. Theodor Apel, Heidelberg   Leipzig, 16 December [1832]

[. . .] My dear friend, after you had left me, everything seemed dreary and lifeless: I felt totally shut off from the world around me – all the more powerfully did it live *within* me. My mother and sister had gone to stay in Vienna: – I was totally abandoned! My godlike music was bound to come, and you may believe me when I tell you that it was in this state that I wrote what is my most powerful work to date, a symphony[4] which I completed within the space of 6 weeks. – It was finished, and now it was time for life around me to start up again. – I travelled to Vienna, spent four weeks there, and everything was fine. But then . . . ! – From Vienna I travelled to *Pravonin*, one of Count *Pachta*'s estates in Bohemia. There, within the glorious bosom of nature, I spent the next 5 weeks. Oh, what glorious days! For not only nature but (out with it!) love, too, ennobled me. But how? – Imagine in Jenny[5]

1 In 1872 Franz Schott donated the manuscript to the Wagner Family Archives and, in return, Wagner wrote the Albumblatt in E flat major (WWV 108) for Schott's wife, Betty.
2 Op. 127 in E flat major and op. 131 in C sharp minor, both of which works Schott had recently published.
3 Hummel had arranged Beethoven's Symphonies Nos. 1–7 for piano, flute, violin and cello, as well as for piano alone.
4 Symphony in C major (WWV 29).
5 Jenny Raymann, one of Count Pachta's two illegitimate daughters.

an ideal of beauty, and my burning imagination – and there you have it all. In her beauty my passion thought it could see everything that might raise her up to the status of a glorious apparition. My idealizing gaze descried in her all that it desired to behold, and that was my misfortune! – I thought that she returned my love; indeed, it required only a bold advance on my part, and she would have returned my feelings! But what kind of a response? – Some fearful apprehension held me in check; – and yet, what a struggle it cost me to overcome my violent passion. My dreams each night were troubled; – I repeatedly awoke, dreaming that I was confessing my love to her, and yet each time I was aware only of the night around me, suffocating me with a sense of grievous foreboding. – Then at last, – for it could not have continued much longer! – at last the truth was bound to dawn on me! – We travelled to Prague, ah and – you can well imagine the wounds that ardent love may leave behind; – but what such love can kill is more terrible than aught else! – Hear me then, and grant me your compassionate understanding: – she was not worthy of my love! –

A deathly chill once more took possession of my heart. Oh, had I only been able to renounce at once all beautiful hopes, had I grown numb with cold, I should have deemed myself happy indeed! – But to feel every spark of that once refulgent flame dying out by and by, to see every atom of a once burgeoning hope gradually disappear, to see hour by hour the halo of spiritual beauty fading from sight, ah! that wrings from me tears whose bitterness can only be felt but never expressed! – When I tried to warm myself by the dying embers of that love, I felt only death's icy blast blowing over me; I stood there paralyzed, my eyes staring vacantly into a torrent of fire from the past, and the frozen wastes of the future! – Enough, – enough, I have already said too much! – For, despite the infinite void within my breast, I still feel within me a desire for love; – and what shocks me most of all is that I look so hale and healthy! – – –

It was in these circumstances that I drafted the poem of my opera[1] and returned with it completed to Leipzig some 2 weeks ago.

3rd January [1833]

I have rescinded and destroyed the libretto. You'll be hearing from me again soon. – Adieu, adieu!

Yours,
Richard Wagner.

SB I,132–4.

---

1 The libretto of *Die Hochzeit* was written in Pravonin and Prague in October/November 1832. It was destroyed (with the exception of the opening number, which had already been set to music), supposedly because Wagner's sister, Rosalie, found the subject matter too gruesome.

6. ROSALIE WAGNER, LEIPZIG   Würzburg, 11 December 1833

[. . .] Your letter – how shall I put it? – your letter has worked miracles, freeing me from many disquieting worries, while, at the same time, causing me renewed unrest, – for, once having read it, I was unable to work for a number of days. – I intended answering it at once, – but – – I was still missing the last-act finale of my opera; – two days ago¹ – I completed it – and with it the whole opera; – it was just midday – 12 o'clock, and bells were ringing in all the church towers as I wrote *finis* at the foot of the very last page; – – what pleasure it gave me to do so! – Now, my dearest Rosalie, I have completed the *composition* of my opera, and have only the final act to score! My somewhat pedantic manner of writing out the full score immediately as neatly & clearly as possible is what has held me up most of all in scoring the work; – yet I believe that, if I work hard, it will take me about 3 weeks² to complete this last remaining task, so that I shall be able to leave here in around 4 weeks' time. – But how can I describe to you the mood I have been in throughout the whole of this period! – Each time I wrote down a note, it was my family that I thought of, – and of you, Rosalie, most of all: – it was a feeling which often encouraged me to go on, – but which often so overwhelmed me that I could not continue, but had to go outside into the open air. I often felt like that, and it seemed to me a joyful presentiment, so that, oh, how happy I was to discover that your letter bore witness to the same understanding! – May God grant that I do not disappoint you in your joyful expectations; – but I know that this will not be so, for the whole work has poured from my innermost soul – and people say that, if that is so, the work will pass into the souls of others. – – [. . .] But tell me, you wrote amongst other things that *Hans Heiling*³ was extremely popular, and that it was continuing to play to full houses; – I must confess that in one respect this news is most welcome to me. We performed the opera here in Würzburg, and I certainly found the music very pretty, especially the individual numbers; but in no other opera by Marschner have I come across such a complete lack of any overall effect. I don't know, but he has totally failed to exploit the best effects; – and what weak endings to each of the acts! – What an absence of melody in the choruses! In the finale to the 2nd act he treats the culmination of the whole work – "he hails from the realm of gnomes and dwarfs, and is the mountains' spirit lord!" – so nonchalantly and gives such little weight to the climax that one assumes something quite insignificant is taking place! – In a word, not a single number can really hold the listener's imagination! –

1 The complete draft of Act III of *Die Feen* was finished on 7 December 1833.
2 The full score of the opera was completed on 6 January 1834.
3 Heinrich Marschner's *Hans Heiling* had been first performed in Berlin on 24 May 1833 and was quickly taken up by other German theatres.

I must confess that this might almost encourage me to entertain vain hopes about my own opera! – – – [. . .]

SB I, 136–42.

7. FRANZ HAUSER, LEIPZIG   [Leipzig, March 1834]

Dear Sir,

In writing to you, I am choosing the course which you yourself recently suggested when you advised me to submit in written form (thus ensuring a greater degree of calm & clarity) my ideas, counter-arguments and decisions concerning your remarks about my opera which you have imparted to me during the last 3 days, a communication marked, it must be said, by the same sagacious judgement as your advice was warm and sincere. I can begin in no other way than by expressing my most cordial and profound gratitude for these same excellent judgements and demonstrations of your most candid and affectionate friendship, which will for ever bind me to you in a debt of the deepest obligation; – believe me, I know the value of that sincerity, though it may momentarily produce the most painful feelings of disappointed hope, and I esteem it the more, as I grow the more familiar with it & with all that is bound up with it, for this is the very school which I myself have gone through; – believe me, I certainly did not do so because I was misled by flattery; – I had the good fortune of being taught by the most sincere & strict of teachers; my lessons with Herr Müller proved to be a series of almost oppressive demonstrations of an almost pedantically strict sincerity; he inured me to the most injurious & discouraging attacks on my youthful endeavours, teaching me to see in such criticism only instructive demonstrations of sincerity, even when these latter did not always spring from the purest of sources. By the time I had completed my studies in harmony with Herr Müller, and embarked upon the area of counterpoint, both I and all those whom I asked for advice felt that I had outgrown this particular teacher, and so I changed teachers, and began studying with Herr Weinlig. This man, to whom I owe more than I shall ever be able adequately to repay by my own achievements alone, realized where my most immediate deficiencies lay; – he advised me first of all not to continue studying any actual counterpoint, but to gain a thorough grounding in harmony; he began by taking me through the strict *gebundener Styl*[1] of harmony, persevering until he felt I had a completely firm grasp of it, for, in his view, this learned style was the one

---

1 This term has no equivalent in English. It is used to describe the strict style employed in such forms as the fugue or chorale prelude, and is also known as "der gelehrte Styl" (the learned style).

and only basis for a correct handling of free and rich harmonies, as well as being essential for learning any counterpoint. We then set about studying counterpoint along the strictest lines and in accordance with the most basic principles, and then, believing he had laid the most solid foundations by perfecting my knowledge of this final & most difficult part of my general musical education and that, having learned this, I was ready to venture into the most difficult areas of composition, he discharged me with the following words: "I hereby release you from your apprenticeship, as any master should release his apprentice when the latter has learned all that the former can teach him."

I felt uncommonly strengthened by this profound and serious study; I felt myself in possession of those means by which I believed I might now progress and gain a freer, more universal education. In order to achieve this, both my teacher and I believed I must set forth on the road to public recognition, since it is precisely here that the formative principle is to be found. Thus, even during the course of my studies with him, not only was Herr Weinlig not opposed to the performance of any of the orchestral compositions on which I was working at the time, he desired and even encouraged their performance in the liveliest manner. As a result, both during that period & subsequently, several of my overtures, and finally a symphony were performed at our subscription concerts, and I am pleased to be able to say that they have not done me any harm, and that, apart from the great advantage of allowing me to hear the works in question and to realize more clearly the means that are necessary in order for me to achieve my aims, I have also enjoyed the additional benefit of having the sympathetic gaze of the general public directed at me & my music. This same opinion & this same desire are what I now cherish with regard to my opera. You, my most honoured friend, as far as I can see, wish only, in accord with your innermost conviction, to rob me of that opinion & that desire. You do not like my opera, and, more than that, you do not like the general direction which my art has taken, since you see it as incompatible with your own artistic outlook. Of course, the first of these objections is necessarily rooted in the second of them. Our position is now such that it would serve no useful purpose for me to go into detail, since any detailed criticism follows logically from your own general criticism, and, if you will forgive me for saying so, it was precisely that general criticism of yours which seemed to me so unshakeable, even before you had examined my work, since it concerns the general direction of my art – and, I might add, the direction of the age. You could have predicted each of the details which it contains, and you more or less said as much even before you had looked at the work in detail. You find in it all the failings of our age, and at the same time declare it futile to appeal to that age. If I might give expression to your innermost conviction, it is that you consider only that form permissible in which the unattainable models of an earlier age were expressed, and even in Mozart you find an over-ornate use of superficial devices, so that I suspect you would regard only Gluck's music as suitable. You ask me why my instrumentation is not like Haydn's. And what is more: – in all that runs counter to this you not only detect the influence of what is nowadays regarded as the accepted norm (although I believe I have striven to distance myself as far as possible from the excesses of our age, and have, for example, abstained from what *Marschner*, for example, would have permitted himself here), – as I say, – you ascribe all this not merely to that selfsame influence, but to a lack of any inner support; – you reproach me with total ignorance of how to handle the means at my disposal, ignorance of harmony, and a lack of thorough study; – you find nothing that might have come from the heart, you do not examine what might be the result of genuine inspiration. – – If I am not mistaken, this – as far as the value of the *work* is concerned – more or less sums up your reproaches, which seem to me the logical outcome of your opinion of it. I have tried in the course of the foregoing to give some order to these reproaches, – and I can find nothing by way of a counter-argument! This is the position of the man who is criticized vis-à-vis his critic & the criticism itself. It is inadmissible & indeed impossible for the person who has been criticized in this way to attempt to refute the said criticism, or even to defend himself against it! – I shall say nothing, – since any opposition would seem to me to be a sign of arrogance on my part.

None the less, although I remain determined not to interfere with the course already taken by negotiations concerning the performance of my opera, nay, since it is my conviction that only a performance of the same can achieve the goal I have set myself, I feel that I may, in a spirit of extreme diffidence, remonstrate as best I can about your views on the practicability of the work. I am struck by a letter from my brother,[1] who asks with some concern how things stand with the performance of my opera, and I am reminded of a number of things which, to a certain extent, give me encouragement and consolation. In my brother, whom I consider here only as a performing artist, I had my most severe and, I may say, my most ruthless critic: he energetically resisted the occasional impracticability of the vocal line, under his watchful eye I corrected and rewrote what I could, and I assure you herewith that I am prepared to make any changes in this respect which the singers may wish me to make; the fact that, in spite of everything, I shall still not be able to restore to the opera the beauty of Italian melody, goes without saying; – yet I derive considerable consolation here from my brother's final assessment, which ran somewhat along the following lines: "The singers will complain a good deal about their music, and however much he has to alter it for them, they will still find it difficult; – but whoever can grasp it intellectually will always create an effect with it." – That the opera will be difficult to rehearse

1 Albert Wagner.

is clear; but whether it will be more difficult than Marschner's operas, which are staged in many places, I venture to dispute. Indeed, I rather think one could make certain assumptions about the one on the basis of the other. I too have already had some slight experience here; – as a favour I took over as chorus master at the Würzburg Theatre; and in that role I was often involved in rehearsing the whole of a particular opera; – we performed Marschner's Vampire, Hans Heiling, Meierbeer's Robert among others, – where, I must say, I found uncommon difficulties of a sort certainly not exceeded by those of my own opera, – at least a dispassionate comparison appears to tell me so. But I have also already rehearsed & performed a few of the numbers of my opera, – a trio & an aria,[1] – we gave a concert performance of the pieces with some success and brought the whole thing off without undue effort. – I wrote an additional aria[2] for my brother which is certainly no better or easier than any of the numbers of my own opera, – and it flatters me not only to have been witness to its effectiveness but once again to have received word from Würzburg that it continues to be performed to great acclaim! – My most worthy friend, you will surely not choose to see signs of some contemptible vanity in this detailed account of what little experience I have had; – but now that my relationship towards you concerns the very survival of my opera, you can surely not hold it against me if, like a drowning man, I clutch at the merest straw in order to preserve my life & hope. However slight & insignificant these few experiences may be, they nevertheless allow me, by turning from the specific to the general, to derive a certain amount of hope from all this and to consider a performance of my opera as not being totally out of the question.[3] – Were you to dismiss as foolish & pernicious my desire and my attempts to prosecute this aim, then I fear that such an attitude on your part would for ever after dog my endeavours like a curse, – in order to avert that curse, I can only entreat you to take a less serious view of the matter, and, moreover, not to withhold from me your kind and considerate feelings towards me. For the sake of my own position and the path which I must carve out for myself, I and my family feel that it is absolutely necessary for me to adopt this course, and – self-delusion admittedly triumphs everywhere, – but I believe that it will not lead wholly to my ruin. I would ask you not to place any significant obstacle in the way of the negotiations which have already been started, but, so that I may

1 Excerpts from Die Feen were performed by the Würzburg Music Society on 12 December 1833.
2 The piece in question is an allegro section for Aubry's aria in Marschner's Der Vampyr (WWV 33). Wagner wrote both words and music at Albert's request, completing the score on 23 September 1833 in time for its first performance six days later.
3 The opera was not performed during Wagner's lifetime. By mid-July 1834 his interest had turned away from German Romanticism to the Young German idealism of Laube and Gutzkow, and he abandoned his attempts to encourage the Leipzig administration in its half-hearted plans to stage Die Feen.

continue calmly along, as it were, the proper channels, permit me to collect the score from you and deliver it into the official hands of Herr Kapellmeister Stegmeyer. Allow me on this occasion to tempt God.

Yet it would grieve me deeply if you believed that I was thoughtlessly brushing aside everything you have imparted to me with such sincere conviction, – I have taken it all in, and I hope that, on the basis of what you have said, there may now open up before me a completely new, secure and purer course of artistic endeavour. I should be disconsolate to think of your misinterpreting the views I have expressed here and the candour which I was encourage to show by the sincerity that you yourself have taught me. I regard these lines as a foundation on which to build a candid relationship of mutual advice and of a willing eagerness to accept the same. Only in that hope & conviction do I dare to send you this letter, and remain[1]

W

SB I, 149–55.

8. THEODOR APEL, LEIPZIG   Rudolstadt, 13 September 1834

Best of friends, I have been on the point of writing to you on a number of occasions, though I should have preferred any other moment to the present one; although I now have an hour free, I am on the whole so depressed, empty-headed, dull-witted & uninspired that I simply do not know how I might appear before you with the requisite poise & dignity. God has created music purely to spite me, and I find it a real tonic to turn now & again to reading; pounding out music gives me no satisfaction, and when I have to do it, as was the case last week, then it must be the Creator's intentional aim to add to my sense of wretchedness. You know I like Bellini's opera Romeo & Juliet,[2] all right – but now I find myself working for an idiot of a manager who demands that I rehearse the opera in 5 days, since I once had the misfortune to express the view that it is a very easy work to put on. I have now achieved the impossible, and between last Monday and yesterday I managed to drum the opera into 2 of the most unmusical singers on the face of God's earth, so that by yesterday we were even able to have an orchestral rehearsal; – but I've lost all sense of humour in the process, and my soul is awash in emptiness and idiocy, – in addition to which I've allowed all my love affairs to grow cold, I've been gambling and lost regularly, have no money into the bargain, and, above all, am caught up in the composition of a

1 This letter, like many others, survives only in draft form; hence the repetitions, abbreviations and stylistic inelegancies which it contains.
2 Bellini's *I Capuleti e i Montecchi*, first performed at La Fenice, Venice, on 11 March 1830.

symphony[1] about which I have already written to Pohlenz, and which I am completely incapable of finishing. [...]

the 15th Sept.

[...] I've had a fearful amount of work to do; – tomorrow we start all over again, this time on *The Eagle's Nest*;[2] – you'll be here in time to see it. You should also get Fräulein *Planer*, – she has given me a couple of moments of sensual transfiguration, – it was marvellous. – I don't really have a mistress at present, – I simply haven't the time; – I'm still seeing something of Toni – but that's all; – the only thing I feel passionately sentimental about at the moment is the fact that tomorrow is pay-day! [...]

SB I, 161–4.

9. THEODOR APEL, LEIPZIG   Magdeburg, 27 October 1834

[...] Oh, with what wanton delight do I look back on our journey together;[3] – you can have no idea of the pleasure it gives me to think of it! However peevish you were at the time & however much I felt the same, it is all completely outweighed by so many individual memories of the journey & by the whole of the atmosphere surrounding it. The visible signs of fortune's favours which we encountered on every side are such as to make a man happy and proud. The ride home each evening to Teplitz filled me with a sense of poetry which even now continues to reverberate within me. What is there to compare with my comic relationship with the Reimans,[4] the ridiculous jokes in the Black Horse, the journey to Görkau, and the divine boredom of Carlsbad? Yet it is not these individual memories, but everything taken together, and, most of all, the sense of divine licentiousness, which takes on so attractive a form in my mind's eye. And this after just 6 weeks in Bohemia – imagine what a couple of years in Italy would be like! Yes, my dearest Theodor, my plan is now firmly & irrevocably made. My Fairies must be performed in 3 or 4 good theatres in order to lay the ground for my Ban on Love, which I am at present in the process of completing:[5] I am bound to make a name for myself with this opera, and acquire both fame & fortune; and if I am lucky enough to achieve these two things, I shall go to Italy, taking

1 Unfinished Symphony in E major (WWV 35).
2 *Des Adlers Horst* (The Eagle's Nest) by Franz Gläser (1798–1861), first performed at the Königstadt Theatre in Berlin on 29 December 1832.
3 Between mid-June and the end of July 1834 Wagner and Apel had been in Bohemia on holiday together.
4 Jenny and Auguste Raymann; see introductory essay, p. 5.
5 The prose draft of *Das Liebesverbot* had been sketched in Teplitz (modern Teplice) during the summer of 1834; the libretto was completed by December 1834.

both them and you with me; this, I should add, will be in the spring of 1836. In Italy I shall then write an Italian opera, & – depending upon how things turn out – several more besides; when we are sun-tanned & strong again, we shall turn our gaze towards France, I'll write a French opera in Paris, and God alone knows where I'll end up then! But at least I know *who* I shall be – no longer a German philistine. This career of mine must be yours as well. The only thing that can destroy this plan is ill fortune, i.e. lack of good fortune; but I am now resolved to place my trust in good fortune.

[. . .]

SB I, 167–8.

10. MINNA PLANER, MAGDEBURG   Leipzig, 6 May [1835]

My dear, dear & only girl, it is now more than twenty-four hours since I last saw you, I who once craved for even a minute of your time. What is to become of me? I am filled through and through with melancholy and tears, and can find pleasure in nothing, in nothing, – nothing! I have grown too fond of you, – I now realize that all too well, you most excellent, dear child! How can I accustom myself so soon to being parted from you, how could it be possible for me to live without you! You have become a part of me, and I feel mutilated in every limb when you are not here beside me! – Ah, if you could share but half my sense of melancholy, you would be overcome by love and thoughts of me.

I broke down and wept all over again, – tell me, were you angry with me for being so slow in forwarding the letter to you? – Oh, I would have come in person soon enough, – but I would then have remained with you, – I know that for certain, – and I would have abandoned my journey & everything else! – Ah, – who can describe my lonely state! – Yes, my Minna, – I love you, – and in doing so I am a little conceited, – you see – I imagine that it was I who breathed into you the life and soul you had earlier lacked, – or which I had at least not previously noticed in you; – also, I often believed you did not love me, – but now I know otherwise, – yes, when I kissed you that last time, – your love entered into me twice over, nay, a thousand times over! – Oh, my life, – never forget me, – never betray me, – remain true to me, – remain my own Minna, and if you ever felt the emotion of love, bestow it all on me, – and *never* force me to share you with another man, – for you yourself have my whole heart! – Do you hear? Do you hear? Never betray me! – You cannot imagine how painful it is to look back on you all in Magdeburg; – it cuts me to the quick to think of you living in such wretched, humiliating conditions; – I shall do all I can to help Fräulein Haas, – for you refused my offer to help you yourself. – You must both get away from there, – that goes without saying! – I have come to hate Leipzig & Magdeburg & everything else, – I love only you, – oh, come here soon, so that I may see you & convince myself – that you still love me! – Write to me by return of post, and tell me whether you love me, whether you are thinking of me! Write! Write! and console me, my angel! I shall write again soon! Soon! Adieu! Adieu! Think of me, think of

Your
Richard.

c/o Rosalie Wagner,
Reichel's garden, at the back of the building.
SB I, 198–9.

11. THEODOR APEL, FRANKFURT   Leipzig, 6 June 1835

[...] Things are quiet here, I am working and have been very busy, – it's all been very successful. The Columbus Overture[1] was recently performed at Gerhardt's concert, – it was applauded, but appears not to have found favour with the clique which happened to comprise the greater part of the audience that evening; – I was unhappy with the performance; – I myself conducted, but it proved impossible to rouse the players to any warmth of feeling; – the ending went at least as slow again as it had done in Magdeburg. If your mother is telling the truth, the overture was to her liking. I have the most dreadful opposition here; – those who are impartial are all, I think, behind me [...];[2] – but the real *race* is dead-set against me & I am glad to have had a chance to get to know who they are; – it is the Stegmaier-Hauser[3] clique. – I am resolved to have my opera[4] whistled off the stage here first of all – but I shall have it translated into French, adapted by Scribe and performed at the Opéra-Comique, since that is where it belongs & since I, too, belong outside Germany, – which is why I intend returning to Magdeburg in the autumn, it is the quickest way out of here, alas! – All is well – the committee has taken over the theatre, – Bethman as director on a fixed salary & our wages guaranteed; – it's actually happening. –

I am now off to the music festival at Dessau, – then for a few days to

---

1 The *Columbus* Overture (WWV 37), first performed in Magdeburg on 16 February 1835, was revived at a Gewandhaus concert in Leipzig, when the programme also included soprano arias sung by Livia Frege (*née* Gerhard).
2 A phrase has been omitted here since the manuscript is damaged.
3 Ferdinand Stegmayer was Kapellmeister at the Leipzig Theatre, where Franz Hauser was resident producer; see also letter [7], pp. 18–22.
4 *Das Liebesverbot.*

Magdeburg, – from there to Naumburg & Kösen, where I intend spending about 2 weeks with Laube. His "Love-Letters" gave me a lot of pleasure, – the book is very stimulating, – every page has something fresh to say! –

Minna was here – she came for 3 days, during the worst possible weather, without knowing another soul & without once setting foot outside the house, simply to enjoy my company: – things like that move me; – it is remarkable what influence I now have on the girl, – you should read her letters, – they burn with passionate desire, & we both know that that is not a quality she was born with. – She asks to be remembered to you. – [. . .]

Enjoy life & remain cheerful, – I am resolved to become a perfect epicure in respect of my art, nothing for posterity, but everything for our contemporaries & for the present moment: – if I succeed in capturing these people's imagination, posterity will take care of itself; – but *I* shall ignore it. Adieu! A thousand thanks for your love! Adieu! [. . .]

SB I,205–7.

12. JOHANNA ROSINE GEYER, LEIPZIG   Carlsbad, 25 July 1835

Only you, dearest mother, do I still recall with feelings of the most heartfelt love and deepest emotion; – I know only too well that children go their own way, – they think only of themselves & their future, and of the people around them who provide a link between the two; that is how it is & it is something I feel myself, there is a time when separation becomes inevitable; – we then conduct our reciprocal relationships solely from a standpoint of superficiality; we become diplomats joined together by ties of friendship, – we remain silent where it seems politic to do so, – and speak when our view of the affair demands it, and we speak most of all when we are separated from each other. Ah, but how greatly a mother's love transcends all that! I think I, too, am one of those people who cannot always say what they feel in their hearts at a given moment, – otherwise you would often have encountered a more tender-hearted side to my nature. But my feelings remain the same, – & look mother, now that I am no longer beside you, I am overcome by feelings of gratitude for the glorious love of which you recently gave your son such heartfelt and earnest proofs, so much so that I might well be tempted to write and speak of them in the most tender tones of a lover addressing his beloved. Ah, but far greater – is not a mother's love far greater, far more unsullied than that other love? – No, I do not intend to wax philosophical here, – I wish only to thank you, & to thank you yet again, – I wish I could enumerate all the individual tokens of your love for which I have cause to be grateful, – but it would take too long to do so. Yet I know that there is no heart which follows my every move with such sincere interest & such solicitous concern as does your own, – nay, it is perhaps the only heart that watches over my every step, – & not with the intention of passing unfeeling judgement on all that I do, – no, rather is it your wish to include me in your prayers. Were you not the only one to remain unflinchingly loyal to me, when others, judging me simply by external events, turned their back on me with a philosophical gesture of dismissal? I should be intemperately presumptuous if I were to demand the same degree of love from everyone, I know well enough that that is not possible – I know that for myself. – Everything comes straight from your heart, from your dear, kind heart, which I pray God may always remain well disposed towards me, – for I know that if all else fails, it will always remain my final & dearest refuge. Oh mother, if you were to die prematurely, before I could give you adequate proof that your love had been bestowed upon a noble recipient, whose gratitude knows no bounds! No, that cannot be, you must live to enjoy many more fine fruits of your love! – Ah, when I recall the final week we spent together! It is a source of perfect consolation & comfort to me to recall to mind the many demonstrations of your loving kindness! My dear, dear mother, – how pitiable I should be if my feelings towards you were ever to grow cold! –

[. . .]

SB I,209–11.

13. THEODOR APEL, LEIPZIG   Frankfurt, 21 August 1835

My Theodor,

Although I am on the point of coming to Leipzig myself & shall be seeing & speaking to you in person, I can no longer ignore the feelings of pain & fear which clamour incessantly for expression, – I must write to you today, – this very hour. Tears are flowing freely down my cheeks, as they once did during my childhood when I had sinned against someone I loved & had to beg his forgiveness. – My Theodor, what has become of me? Where now is that free & noble courage to face life with which we once inspired each other? Where is that future to which we once aspired, proud in the certainty of victory? – Perhaps you have retained it all, – even developed and improved it; – I do not know, – since we have had no contact with each other for half a year now, – but I assume – & hope – & wish that that is so; – you have found a better friend, – a friend for whom you can feel more respect, – more esteem, – who must needs mean more to you than your old Richard! – Oh, my tears prevent me from going on; – why this soft-heartedness in addition to everything else? – –

I was in Teplitz again, Theodor, & celebrated a sad anniversary; – I was also in Prague where I spoke with the mistresses of Count Baar & Baron Bethman, – whom we once knew as Jenni and Auguste;[1] – I was also in Carlsbad; – ah, and I was also in Würzburg; – my girl[2] has been delivered of a child in the mean time, a boorish farmhand was my fortunate rival. Theodor, Theodor, – how is it that good fortune has abandoned me the moment that *you* abandoned me! Oh, if only fortune were to give me some sign that she still favours me, I would try to conceive an affection for life once again. Everything, but everything has disappeared, – all sense of poetry flees before me, and a worthlessly naked truth spreads out endlessly in front of me! – My God, I feel as though the flower of my youth has withered, as though the cold reality of life has settled on my brow like frost, depriving me of all warmth & love! Oh, have I already enjoyed all that fate has decreed for my enjoyment? Was that my life? – – Yes, – I have sinned; – and yet not! Can one sin if one is mad? – I have fallen out with my family & am bound to regard our relationship as being at an end;[3] – it was I myself who brought things to that pass! I no longer know Leipzig: I shall not go near the town again for a long time to come! A mother who loves me dearly is all I have left, – nothing else! – Theodor, – do I still have your friendship? Do I still possess your love, your trust? – Oh tell me, tell me, – what are your feelings towards me? To have lost so noble & splendid a mind as yours means a great deal to me, – it means I have lost everything! If you, too, were capable of misjudging me – & God knows, Theodor, it would not be beyond the bounds of possibility – for it requires infinite perseverance on your part & from your point of view not to misunderstand me! – Ah, to feel like that, & yet be dependent upon you! – – If you, too, part company with me, it's goodbye to the world! – – –

Ah, how much better that feels – to have wept openly; I have not been able to do so for such a long time; the tears flowed freely, like some magnificent, refreshing storm after a long & persistent drought & heatwave. I now feel somewhat calmer & shall try to write more calmly to you. – My life until now has been squandered away; – my dearest of friends, I was not wicked, – I was insane; that is the only expression I have to describe my actions, – it was a conventional form of madness! I now see only too well that money is not a chimera, not some contemptible & worthless trifle of little account; – I have now come to the conclusion that money has taken on flesh & blood just like the society to which men are subjected. I was insane, I tell

1 Jenny and Auguste Raymann.
2 During his appointment as chorus-master in Würzburg, Wagner had fallen in love with the singer Friederike Galvani, but the liaison had lapsed following his departure from the town. According to the later account in *Mein Leben* 84–6; English trans. 76-7, his rival was not a farmhand but an oboist in the theatre orchestra.
3 In particular Wagner was jealous of his sister Luise's marriage to Friedrich Brockhaus.

you, since I did not understand either myself or my position in the world; – I knew I had not the least solid support & nothing to fall back on, & yet I behaved like a madman, living beyond my means in every conceivable respect, in addition to showing the uncertainty & inexperience of a man who has no justifiable claim to money; other people, & especially rich people, do not squander their money as I do. The result was a whirlpool of chaos & misery whose complexities I can look on only with horror. Not even I can reconstruct all the individual details, – it is scandalous & inexplicable into what an abyss I have fallen. Your immense & persistent efforts to help me out of it only emboldened me, & led me to believe in some blind force which I could not account for but which struck my eyes with increasing blindness. My life in Leipzig, the wretched position I held there, were an intolerable burden; I felt the urge to indulge in what people call independent shows of strength; I went on various jaunts & gave myself up to excesses which, taken together with the lasting effects of my earlier follies, led me to cut myself off completely from my family, & a total breakdown of all my other relationships. What my better nature, my artistic genius, suffered throughout all this is indescribable! This is my standpoint; I see it clearly. I could be satisfied with this newly acquired insight & strive for something better. – If I were now free of the consequences of my continued foolishness, I could now look my fate calmly in the eyes; – I have managed to acquire a secure & decent position at least for the immediate future, & on the basis of my recent experiences & the conviction I have now gained that from now on I am thrown back on my own resources if I want to make everything good again, I may well be justified in hoping to be able to set out on a new course. But I cannot set foot in Magdeburg again until I have shifted a debt of 400 thalers.[1] That is how I stand, – abandoned & cut off from everything, everything I once counted on, accompanied only by the anxious, fearful worries of my mother; – she can give me nothing. *You* are the only person to whom I can still turn, & I have the courage to say so without feeling that in doing so I may anger & alienate you from me; – every other support, every other hope has disappointed me, & it is precisely this sense of disappointment which I have now finally become aware of & which drives me to the extremity of appealing to you once again. Perhaps I have now reached the point where I shall finally sink without trace; – perhaps you will turn coldly away from me, pained by the self-delusion under which I continue to labour in my friendship towards you; it may be that I have now stretched to the limit your faith in my honesty, & that your patience is finally exhausted; – if this were to be the case, then my misery would drive me to the stage where I could no longer consider myself worthy of you. – But, first of all, I turn to you with the words: – do not regard

1 By way of comparison, it may be noted that Wagner's salary in Dresden ten years later was 1500 thalers a year.

our present standpoint as one of life's mere accidents; see it as an *event* of the greatest import in both our lives – & indeed that is what it is, – it is my rebirth. Believe me, – if my spirit is again to unfold in profusion & beauty, – which at present I doubt, – the whole world shall learn who was its saviour. Consider, Theodor, what is at stake! I should add that I am not forcing you to act against your own conviction; – a swift end is better than a slow one. – That would be this year's profit! –

I began this letter suffering the most violent mental turmoil, – & more tears flowed from my eyes than words from my pen; – it has brought comfort to me: – I now feel at peace with myself; – I have confessed my sins, my absolution is in your hands. –

I hope to be able to leave here tomorrow; & I shall reach you a day later than this letter; – what sort of a welcome will you give me? – I am expected in Magdeburg on the 28th inst.; – whether I can be there depends on you! My God, my God, what a state have I been reduced to! – But if you turn away from me now, I shall not be able to sink any lower! –

Farewell, farewell! Remember me!

Your
Richard.

SB I,213–17.

14. THEODOR APEL, LEIPZIG   Magdeburg, 2 October 1835

Dear Theodor, you will at least have received my letter by now, presumably on the same day I received yours; & I hope that this circumstance will have put paid to several of your reproaches, or at least have caused you to modify them a little. I have become caught up here in a fearful whirl of work & drudgery; the whole responsibility for the opera here was unloaded on to me; we finally got going yesterday with Zampa,[1] & the event may be said to have met with considerable success. And so I do not need to worry any more about that side of things; and in every other respect, too, I feel a much greater sense of stability; only in one respect shall I probably turn out to be a knave, – & *you* are the only person I shall tell this to. You know my modern attitude towards love, which is what first brought me together with Minna; my wretched bourgeois outlook soon usurped my more modern views, & all that was left was love; – I reached the stage of feeling jealous, took offence at Minna's reputation, & finally convinced myself, to my own happy misfortune, that Minna has never been wicked, nor is she now; in a word, I am now convinced & fully persuaded of that fact. This once so cold, unapproach-

1 *Zampa*, opera by Louis Joseph Ferdinand Hérold, first produced in Paris on 3 May 1831.

able, & indifferent creature has given me her boundless trust, – I know every feature of her life: – I have fired her to the very marrow of her being, I have transformed her into a tender, devoted woman, – she loves me to the point of sickness, I have become her tyrant; – not a soul crosses her threshold if I do not wish it; she sacrifices everything to me; she is totally unrecognizable on stage, she has life, warmth, ardour. She has rejected *Barby's* hand for my sake; a fellow like *Lauer* pines away, stricken by his platonic love for her, & becomes a poet; the more she understood my pitiful bourgeois outlook, the more she felt drawn towards me; – she has only one wish, there is only one thing that will make her happy, – to be joined together with me in marriage, – an aim she would like to achieve whatever the sacrifice involved. She is tender withal; crying her heart out, she once said to me, "Richard, be honest; – don't entertain any false hopes about me which you may not intend to fulfil; – if you tell me you love me but that you don't want to marry me, I shall bewail & bemoan the fact that my finest hopes & desires have been irretrievably blighted & destroyed by your will, & I shall only be happy in your love as long as you bestow it on me, – but I shall never give my love to anyone else. But now, if you flatter these hopes of mine, & encourage me to believe myself secure in entertaining them, & if at the same time you yourself do not take them seriously any longer, you would be committing the most dreadful sin!" And what do you think my reply was? In order not to hurt the dear girl, I nodded in silent approval, and she believes me, whereas all I can think of is how best to go about betraying her. And I rejoice in my own inner strength, whereby I never give her a serious hearing; – it's a kind of knavery. She is completely free with her favours with me, almost to the point of excess, so that I feel increasingly strong & well; the pleasure I have of her, far from sating & wearying me, binds me even more tightly & warmly to her. What do you say to all this? If I were to deceive her intentionally, would that not be a masterpiece of behaviour on my part? Or should I become a philistine? You lot in Leipzig will have to decide!

This love, with its beginning and its end, will turn into a short story, – a modern condition; – add to it the whole sorry state of my affairs, not to mention the lessons I'm learning along the way, & you'll have a novel.

Adieu.   Your
                                                                                    Richard.

SB I, 222–4.

15. THEODOR APEL, LEIPZIG   Magdeburg, 26/27 October 1835

You will no doubt be surprised at not yet having received a reply to your last two letters; – in fact I had already written to you with an enclosure for F. Mendelsohn-Bartholdy, and had ordered some oil-cloth so that you would be able to forward to him a whole load of my compositions; – I have already sealed the letter, so I shall give it to you when you get here. – I have completely changed my mind, & am not sending you anything since, for the time being, I am taking my definitive leave of the concert hall. I can certainly do without your suggestion that I should send some finely worked overture of mine to Leipzig; I have no wish to be a mere hanger-on; & your praise for Mendelsohn is the final discouragement. Farewell to unalloyed splendour, for I intend to abandon myself to the trumpery of the stage; from now on I shall be exclusively an opera composer, & am throwing myself body & soul – with all my hopes as well – into this opera of mine[1] on which I am now busily working. – Practical music-making is now my chief pleasure in life, – in the short time I have been here it has brought me a considerable sense of reward. The opera company here is now completely my own work, & I have managed, as a result of skilful discernment, to draw a couple of young talented singers to public attention, who may well have something to say to the theatrical world in years to come. Who had previously given serious consideration to Minna's sister,[2] until then a quite insignificant member of the Brunswick ensemble? I engaged the girl on account of her beautiful contralto voice, & have gone through the part of Romeo[3] with her; – rarely can a débutante have caused such a great sensation as she did; – people were beside themselves with enthusiasm; the opera had to be repeated immediately afterwards, & the house was once again packed to the rafters, & the noise was as deafening as that which normally greets Devrient; – I have also discovered a tenor by the name of Schreiber & am giving him a proper musical training, much to the satisfaction of our local audiences. It gives me a real sense of pleasure! And it is all my own work! – Let me tell you, I have also reason to be proud of my achievements as a conductor. The operas I have given are performed promptly & as written; we are rehearsing several new operas – *Jessonda*[4] (completely new here!) – *Norma*,[5] *Lestocq*,[6] I'm determined that everything shall proceed smoothly. In addition, we've now put our affairs in proper order; – our wages are now paid on the dot; – everything's fine, – fine! And I have unlimited control over the company, something which gives me a lot of satisfaction! Perhaps I shall achieve the same sort of high standards as Mendelsohn, – but I am only in Magdeburg, while he is in Leipzig, – that's the difference. Well, this is the road I intend to take! – I feel strong & energetic enough to face what's ahead! I'll not worry about Leipzig, – I'm at present in the process of opening up a completely different line of approach, –

1 *Das Liebesverbot*, first performed in Magdeburg on 29 March 1836.
2 Amalie Planer.
3 In Bellini's opera *I Capuleti e i Montecchi*.
4 *Jessonda*, opera by Louis Spohr, first produced in Cassel on 28 July 1823.
5 *Norma*, opera by Vincenzo Bellini, first produced in Milan on 26 December 1831.
6 *Lestocq*, opera by Daniel-François-Esprit Auber, first produced in Paris on 24 May 1834.

Berlin, where I'm intending to have my Ban on Love first performed; – I'll tell you more about this another time; – all I need say now is that I do not in the least hanker after you lot & the sort of fame you enjoy in Leipzig.

The 27th. I was interrupted yesterday. – It is odd: you, too, have suggested in your recent letters that we should aim at revising our modern ideas; modern attitudes towards love etc. no longer suit you, Theodor, & may perhaps never have suited you; my present middle-class attitude weighs somewhat heavily on me, I admit, & I might even be weak enough to give way once again to a number of obsolete ideas; but my unshakeable views on the present status of art continue to exert the most stimulating & powerful influence upon my middle-class outlook. The same is true of my music; – neither now nor in the future shall I ever pay lip-service to things German, & none of your classical Leipzig *gloire* is going to make me change my mind. We have stuffed our bellies full of too much unhealthy food. It seemed to me highly appropriate that I should concern myself once again with a work by a German composer; – I am at present rehearsing Jessonda, & how violently I *shy away* from every revisionist idea! The opera again fills me with a sense of utter revulsion; the effeminate Bellini is a veritable Hercules in comparison to this great, lengthy & pedantically sentimental Spohr; – I recently had the idea of writing an overture on Romeo & Juliet; I thought of a suitable plan, & would you believe it? – quite spontaneously I hit upon the same basic plan as Bellini's dull & insipid overture, with its battleground of a crescendo.[1] –

Fraülein Haas is very ill, – she is said to be pregnant, & will probably go the way of all flesh.[2] – Don't worry unduly about Minna, – I am leaving it all to fate. She loves me, & her love now means very much to me; – she is now the centre of my life, she gives me a sense of consistency & warmth; – I cannot renounce her. One thing I know for certain, my dear Theodor, is that you yourself have not yet discovered the sweetness of such a relationship; there is nothing vulgar, unworthy or enervating about it; our epicureanism is pure & strong; – none of your miserable affairs on the side; – we love each other & believe in each other, the rest we leave to fate; – that is something you have never experienced, but one can only live like that with an actress; – this disregard for middle-class values is something you can find only when the whole basis is one of imaginative freedom & poetic licence. [. . .]

SB I,225–8.

1 Nothing came of Wagner's plans for an overture on this subject, although he later returned to the theme in April/May 1868 (WWV 98).
2 The German text reads "*himmeln*"; there seems no precedent for the suggestion made by the editors of the *Sämtliche Briefe* (I, 227, fn. 3) that the word means "to have an abortion". In the event, Mathilde Haas died on 19 August 1837.

16. MINNA PLANER, BERLIN   Magdeburg, 4 November 1835

8.30 a.m.

Minna, I cannot begin to describe the state I'm reduced to, you have left me, and my heart is broken; I am sitting here, scarcely in possession of my senses, weeping & sobbing like a child. Dear God, what am I to do; how & where shall I ever find consolation & peace of mind! – When I saw you leaving, every feeling & every emotion broke forth painfully within me; the morning mist which swallowed you up shimmered before me as my eyes filled with tears; Minna, Minna, – the dreadful certainty dawned upon me all at once that the carriage you were travelling in was tearing you away from me for ever & ever. Minna, my child, you are making a terrible mistake if that is what you really intend. I am attached to you by a hundred thousand chains, but I feel as though you have thrown them all round my neck & that you are strangling me with them. – Minna, Minna, what have you done to me! – I am at present sitting in my room, with my thoughts buzzing round in my head; – an emptiness which is hideous, – nothing but tears, grief & misery. – How are you feeling yourself? – A large beautiful city, – – – – oh – I can't go on! –

And yet I must continue, my heart is full to overflowing; what has shaken me so deeply & what is eating away at my innermost soul is the fact that you have so totally misunderstood how important is the present turning point in our lives. Minna, you must realize that we are now going through a very sensitive phase in our love; the slightest disturbance that gets in the way of our amorous moods irritates us both beyond measure. I feel stirred to the very depths of my soul by the thought of being separated from you for even the space of 12 days, – and, – merciful God! – you consider a six-month separation as of little account, but instead slip insensitively away; – you did not even use it as the basis for some agreement between us! – Well, all right, – but I would remind you once again of something I have already urged upon you: – in May of this year I left Magdeburg, cherishing in my heart my deep love for you. I no longer felt free, I felt myself to be chained to you; – our brief separation made it clear to me that I could not live without you; – how could I gain possession of you? By marrying you. In order to achieve that aim it was necessary for me to change the entire course of my life, which I had by then already sketched out with a view to making my name as a composer; – bearing in mind my circumstances, I had planned this career as follows; I intended remaining in Leipzig for the time being in order to complete my new opera,[1] which I intended should be performed there this winter; had I been successful in that, I should then have gone on to visit Berlin, Dresden, Munich, Prague, Frankfurt etc., in order to have my opera

1 *Das Liebesverbot.*

performed there, too. In the event of being successful in all this, I should have visited Paris next summer, & from there would have hurried off to Italy with Apel the winter after next. This was firmly fixed in my mind as my artistic career; – but this is a course which could never, ever have allowed me to marry you; – *one* person could no doubt make good his escape along this route; – *two* require a more settled existence. In order to achieve this, I had to revoke my earlier decisions & take up a practical career, since only this can lead me to my goal. Accordingly, I threw everything aside & got myself re-engaged in Magdeburg, for two reasons, partly to set myself up on my intended course, partly so as to be near you all the time. How happy I was, Minna! Only now did I believe I could explain myself fully to you, & to make our marriage the sole aim of our existence together. We have a whole six months ahead of us to prepare for it; by then I shall either have succeeded *alone* in achieving a sufficiently secure position for myself, or, in the event of my being less fortunate, we shall *together* have saved enough to be able to justify our getting married. – Minna, this is a splendid thought to which I am sacrificing a good many other splendid things; – I am young, & if fortune favours me, my future as a composer will not be inglorious – I am abandoning a colourful & attractive lifestyle in order to be able to possess you, since I can achieve this only by a totally different course; – and you?? – Minna, my faith fails me utterly; – a wretched & inevitably short-lived theatrical intrigue is sufficient grounds for you to destroy our life together, which I have bought at the price of so many sacrifices. Do you feel no grief, no pain, at the prospect of so long a separation, which must necessarily separate us for ever? Minna, did I not entreat you: "grant me these six months, do not leave me, & I swear to you that I shall regard this period as a sacrifice on your part which will bind me to you irrevocably & leave me for ever in your debt; – offer up this small sacrifice to me & to my self-conceit, & in return I shall sacrifice my entire life to you!" – And you said nothing, & answered coldly, "I have no choice – I must have my parts!" – Does a human heart not beat within your breast? Have you but *one* sense of noble love & loyalty? Minna, Minna, – does this voice of mine not find its way to your heart? – My God, my God, what else should I say, – my heart is breaking! – Once more: – I sacrifice to you all the other relationships in my life, – & you cannot even give up two of your roles for my sake? – – – I am beside myself! – Once again I have poured out my heart to you: – if you choose to ignore it, it will be the last time I address you with such warmth of feeling. In future I shall write only when I am calm. – I cannot go on!

Your
Richard.

SB I, 229–31.

17. MINNA PLANER, BERLIN   Magdeburg, 9 November 1835

Minna, Minna, what is it? This is my sixth letter, & I am still waiting in vain for a second one from you; do you consider my letters & what they contain to be unworthy of a reply, – or are you still hesitating to impart the *right* answer? My God, if I were not plagued by even greater worries on your account, I should be jealous, & think that Otterstedt[1] was preventing you from replying. – No, you are now betrothed to me, & infidelity is out of the question, decency demands that I should place total trust in you. – But why do you not write? – I demand that you write once a day, & starting from the day you read this demand, I shall regard every day that passes without a letter from you as an act of infidelity on your part. – Oh my Minna, is this how you try my patience? Is our separation not punishment enough for whatever failing you think me guilty of; do you have to insult me into the bargain?

There are so many points which I cannot discuss properly with you here, since I still do not know what your present standpoint is; let only these words be branded once more on your heart: do not abandon me, & do not degrade me to the point of ignoring all my unhappiness, my entreaties, my remonstrances, my offers. You would lower me in my own self-esteem if you were to dismiss as a mere trifle my most sacred feelings towards you & my most manly resolves, & if you were to abide by this unilateral resolve which you have taken. No, that cannot be! – These are & remain my first & last words, my dear & destined bride, – you will hear only different ones in future, or else none at all.

Love and kisses from
                                                        Your
                                                        Richard.

SB I,243-4.

18. FELIX MENDELSSOHN, LEIPZIG   Magdeburg, 11 April 1836

Dear Sir,
    Here you find me carrying out the trick which you were kind enough to describe in advance as a clever one: I would ask you to accept as a present the enclosed symphony,[2] which I wrote when I was 18; I can think of no finer

---

1 A portrait painter whom Wagner appears to have believed Minna's lover. No further details are known.
2 The Symphony in C major (WWV 29) had been written during the early summer of 1832 and first performed at the Prague Conservatorium under Dionys Weber in November of that year. The full score of the work was not among Mendelssohn's papers when he died, but there seems no truth in the suggestion that he destroyed it "because he detected in it a talent that was disagreeable to him" (MECW I,692; *cf* CT for 15 June 1872).

destination for it. I ask for nothing in return except that you might look through it in some idle moment, it may perhaps serve to furnish you with proof of my honest efforts and industry, for I require you to be favourably predisposed towards me, since you might otherwise condemn me if you were to judge my more recent compositions without first knowing the basis on which my studies were built. But what I desire most of all is that the knowledge of me which you might gain through this symphony might lead to a rapprochement between us.

In admiration,
I am, Sir, your
most devoted servant,
Richard Wagner,
Musical Director.

SB I,259–60.

19. ROBERT SCHUMANN, LEIPZIG   Berlin, 28 May 1836

Dearest friend,

Please find enclosed a further article which I am sending from Berlin for inclusion in your journal;[1] it is not finished, and has neither a proper beginning nor end, – but we have no choice nowadays but to write aphorisms. Bank[2] will presumably be happy with such an article, – there is something about Rellstab in it; – he needs to be attacked occasionally, – you wouldn't believe the harm this man causes here in Berlin. My name, however, must not appear, I intend contributing other articles from time to time as Wilhelm Drach. It really is a crying shame that a composer should feel impelled to try his hand at writing, – but we Germans have no alternative, we are all driven back into speculative regions; – it certainly isn't to our advantage.

A few additional words about myself. I shall be remaining here for a few months, and under the terms of an agreement I have made with Cerf, shall be taking over Gläser's position here at the Königstadt Opera for a brief period, as soon as the latter goes on leave; during my period of appointment I shall perform my opera[3] here, and if you think it worth announcing the fact, you could perhaps include a short piece to that effect in your paper, if you would be so kind. Assuming you have no objections, I shall shortly be sending you something else. I shall be without employment for a time; if you know of anything suitable which at the same time would enable me to earn some

1 Schumann had earlier published Wagner's articles *Pasticcio* and *Aus Magdeburg* but the present article did not appear, and is no longer extant.
2 Karl Banck was Schumann's co-editor of the *Neue Zeitschrift für Musik*.
3 *Das Liebesverbot*. None of these plans came to anything.

money, both I and my purse would be in your debt. Incidentally, you must not take it amiss that I left Leipzig without saying goodbye to you; I was in a trivial frame of mind and wished to spare you a trivial farewell. Give Banck my very best wishes, and for my own part accept my kindest regards.

Yours,
Richard Wagner.

Berlin. At the Crown Prince

How can I get hold of the Musik. Zeitschrift? I am missing at least the last 6 issues.

SB I, 274–5.

20. MINNA PLANER, KÖNIGSBERG — Berlin, [6/7 June 1836]

Ah, my dear sweet girl, my Minna, my angel, my all, – – what a terrible time this is! Believe me, I shall never be happy, never enjoy even a single moment of happiness until I can enfold you passionately in my arms once more. Rest assured, I am trying every means at my disposal to deaden my pain, that is to say – I have not stopped working, – but it is useless, my strength repeatedly ebbs away again, my heart dissolves into a thousand tears, & today there have even been times when I despaired whether I should live to see tomorrow, – for I feel all the time that everything inside me is about to collapse with a loud crash, and that I shall cease to exist. [. . .]

June the 6th.[1] You can probably imagine, my dear wife, how simple & withdrawn is the life I am leading here, – you know me well enough, after all, & know that ever since I first began to love you, I have been unable to bear a life of glitter, even if such a life were within my grasp; & so that you may know what I am doing every single hour of the day, I shall set out a plan of my simple daily routine: as soon as I wake up from dreaming about you, the first thing I do is write to you, – it is my morning prayer, & you are my God to whom I pray in the hope that you might answer me; fortified by my prayer, I then set about my work & as a rule remain at my desk until 2 o'clock. I then eat, & after the meal generally walk to Friedrichstadt where I meet *Laube, Glasbrenner* & a few others with whom I drive out to Charlotten-burg; – there I generally meet Cerf, – drive back to town & go to one of the theatres, – thence to dinner & to bed at about 10 o'clock. The only change I might make to this routine is if I omit the drive to Charlottenburg, & instead either return to my room or else pay a call on Schwabe or somebody similar. But throughout all this I remain very depressed & sad, – God I miss you!

---

1 A mistake for "June the 7th". Wagner miscalculated the date each day between 5 and 14 June.

Write to me, my angelic Minna, & tell me all that has befallen you, – your life after all must be more eventful than mine; – send me an account of everything that has happened to you, & let me share in it. – Yesterday evening I had a disagreeable incident to contend with; – one of the men sitting at our table was a gentleman from Altenburg who had not been back there for some time; in the course of our conversation, Dedal enquired whether he knew you from previously, & praised you a good deal; the other man said, "ah yes, – Fr: Planer, – she's the one who was abducted, & in Meissen, at the inn, I discovered she was staying there; on retiring to my room for the night, I lost my bearings & found myself in her room; – a most interesting scene followed which lasted a good three quarters of an hour." Of course we were all thunderstruck to hear this, & it was my duty & concern to ask for further particulars, since your name had been mentioned. "Fr: Planer?" he said, – "well, I suppose I may be wrong about the name, – yes, – you're right, – it was Mlle: Wunsch or Christiany, – – – forgive me, etc." – I told him that it was of little concern to me what he might have got up to with Mad: Christiany, – but that I must entreat him most earnestly never again to confuse two women's names in this way & in such circumstances. – He then did everything he could to pacify me & to apologize. – – But you see, my love, what people are like, – without wishing to harm you personally, but only out of disregard for names, – one way or another this man could have given you a dubious reputation – if I myself had not been present. – – Any girl or woman from the theatre is too much exposed to this sort of thing, & I consider it my most solemn duty to do all I can to take you away from the theatre as soon as possible. I refuse to allow you to accompany me to Berlin as an actress, – how much better it would be if I had my dear little wife all to myself, & not for everyone in the theatre to gape at. You will then be much more sacred! – Oh, my Minna, my delight! With *what* rapture do I think of the future when it will be *I* who assists & aids you, – – but who is there now to offer assistance & aid, at this hateful and unhappy time. – A death-like chill causes me to tremble from head to foot each time I think – another *three months*! – Do you know of no remedy? Will no miracle intervene? – Minna, my Minna, – no consolation? –

  [. . .]

SB I,288–92.

21. MINNA PLANER, KÖNIGSBERG   Berlin, 22/26 June [1836]

[. . .] I must see you now, Minna, I must discuss with you our fate; – God will give us courage & strength, & ultimately happiness as well. If not, well then, I don't care if everything collapses in ruins around me; fate can free you from a lover & a bridegroom whose sole purpose in life is to bring you *unhappiness*, grief, torment & distress. – – – Write to me *by return of post*, I shall expect your reply within a week at the latest, see what you can find to tell me in the time that's available, sound out Schuberth & *Hübsch* as briefly as you can, & God be with you! I cannot go on! – Be as gentle as possible towards me, Minna, since I am so dreadfully suspicious of myself, – you see, I'm convinced that I'm nothing but a trouble-maker, an utter nuisance & a burden to others, – that you would gradually grow tired of me etc. – It is true, I *am* a disagreeable person, a grey & black page in your book of life, a man dogged by misfortune, – alas, – & a hypochondriac into the bargain, – it's bad. But it will get better, much better, – it has got to get better; – – happiness, – or – – – You see, I'm back in my favourite mood once more, – how often I am to be found nowadays holding these charming soliloquies with myself; – I have become a serious, melancholy fool, – ah, Minna, life, happiness! – Have pity on me, have pity, my angel, you will make me well again, then my heart will break into a thousand pieces, or else – happiness, – happiness – Minna! Ah, I despair of ever finding happiness on earth; – love me, – keep on loving me, but do not insult me, have pity on a miserable wretch, for he is, after all,

Your
Richard.

SB I,313–14.

22. ROBERT SCHUMANN, LEIPZIG   Königsberg, 3 December 1836

My most honoured friend,

You have had no word from me for a long time, and may perhaps have been labouring under the delightful delusion that I no longer exist. But I do still exist, albeit a hundred miles from the cultural centre of Germany. You can well imagine with what manic desire I cling to everything that the distant world still has to offer me in the way of future hopes. You, too, form a part of those hopes, & you must forgive me if I cling on to your coat sleeve at least. But let me come to the point. I am eager to make a start, in the hope of one day achieving something. You know that at the end of last year I completed an opera: the Ban on Love, or the Novice of Palermo; libretto based upon Shakespeare's Measure for Measure. The d. . . . only knows why, but I consider this opera to be not at all bad, and our friend Banck more or less shared my view when I showed it to him. But the thing isn't suited to German tastes, neither with regard to the subject-matter nor the music, and even if I wished to adapt it to meet local needs, you know what enormous difficulties an unknown German composer has in getting his works accepted in Germany. That, indeed, is the plight from which the whole of German opera suffers. I really do not know at what point to make a start; I burnt my bridges in Leipzig right at the outset, since the great Ringelhardt could not stomach the subject.[1] I shall encounter similar obstacles in every other German opera house, the more so since I am now exiled to Siberia, and my presence is not permitted in those places where only my personal influence could achieve anything. But then, what use would it really serve me if I were to meet with success in places like Breslau and Brunswick, where my hopes are pinned at present? Nothing would come of it. No, what I intend is a bold *démarche* in the direction of Paris. The thing is made for the Opéra-Comique. Some time ago I sent Scribe the outline of a scenario for a grand opera in 5 acts;[2] it's a most splendid subject, and I have asked Scribe to lend me his name, his adaptation and his patronage. I have not yet received a reply from him, presumably he has not got round to answering, since he is always away on business. I am inclined to send my comic opera directly to the director of the Comic Opera, he can ask Auber and God knows who else to look over the music and the scenario; if he likes it, he can have the libretto adapted by anyone he wants and then altered to fit the music. It's not at all a bad idea, I think, – heaven knows, Auber can't turn out a new opera for him every month, and why shouldn't he be impressed by the novelty of the idea? At least there's no harm in trying. But I'm first turning to you once again; after all, you have a great many contacts with the authorities in Paris; could you perhaps recommend the best course for me to adopt in order to reach my goal? Or, if that is not possible, could you at least let me know, via one of your correspondents, the exact address of the *entrepreneur* of the Opéra-Comique, and the easiest way of ensuring that something reaches him? See what can be done here. If you yourself discover some means by which I might best set about this undertaking, I would send the score to you in Leipzig, so that you would have a vague idea of the sort of thing you were dealing with. Tell me, most honoured Patron of the Romantic School, what you think of it, what hopes may be attached to it, and what is to be done. After all, you are at the centre of operations, and will undoubtedly be able to offer me some more sensible advice than would be the case here in Prussian Siberia. At all events, such is my confidence in your cosmopolitanism that I know you will not ignore my request, and I beg you most sincerely to let me know your answer.[3]

    Sobolewski told me yesterday that someone had presented him with one

1 The Leipzig intendant Ringelhardt rejected *Das Liebesverbot* as an immoral piece, opining that as a conscientious father he could never permit any daughter of his to appear in such a work (see *Mein Leben* 127–8; English trans. 118).

2 Wagner had apparently sent Scribe a sketch for *Die hohe Braut* (WWV 40) in August 1836.

3 Nothing came of this idea.

of your sonatas;[1] I intend visiting him today or tomorrow, and getting him to play it for me, since I'm far too incompetent a pianist to wish to murder the piece by attempting it myself. – I have at last received a further batch of copies of the Mus. Zeitschrift; I had lost touch as a result of my various travels; I now have all the copies up to around the end of July; could I ask you, if possible, to let me have the remaining ones as well? – I assume you haven't accepted the article I sent you at the end of May from Berlin;[2] presumably you were embarrassed by the kind of polemical attack it contained on Rellstab? No offence intended!

My very best wishes to Herr Banck and my few other friends in Leipzig. You yourself may rest assured of the sincere respect and friendship with which I remain

Your obedient servant,
Richard Wagner,
Musical Director.

SB I,317–20.

23. GIACOMO MEYERBEER, PARIS   [Königsberg, 4 February 1837]

Dear Sir,

You will not, I hope, think it strange to be importuned by a letter from so remote a region as this & from someone who is undoubtedly as unknown to you as I am; but it is the fate of every man of celebrity such as yourself to be close at hand in even the most uncharted regions, to be stared at by everyone as though he were intimately familiar, & yet to regard himself as utterly unfamiliar. First of all, however, I must hasten to familiarize you with myself & my reasons for writing, & shall begin with a simple description of myself. I am not yet 24 years old, I was born in Leipzig, & about 6 years ago, after I had already begun studying at the University there, chose music as my vocation; I was encouraged to do so by my passionate admiration for Beethoven, as a result of which my first efforts at composition were of an entirely one-sided nature; – since that time, & more especially since I went out into the world & embarked upon a practical career, my views on the present state of music, & above all dramatic music, have undergone a significant change, & it would be futile of me to deny that it was your works which suggested this new direction to me. This is certainly not the place for me to pay my own unskilled tribute to your genius, yet I cannot forbear to add that in you I behold the perfect embodiment of the task that confronts

1 Sonata in F sharp minor, op. 11.
2 See letter [19], pp. 37–8.

the German artist, a task you have solved by dint of your having mastered the merits of the Italian & French Schools in order to give *universal* validity to the products of that genius. This, then, is what more or less set me upon my present course. The scandalous prostration of provincial composers in present-day Germany was what first drew my attention to all that now needs to be done; the fact that our German composers must first travel to Paris before they can return to Germany is a deplorable state of affairs, I admit, but it has its reasons. I was, moreover, struck by a wild idea, indeed you may already know about it. I discovered a splendid subject for a grand opera in a recently published German novel;[1] but I realized at once that it could be far more effectively adapted to suit the requirements of a French opera house, rather than a German one. Accordingly, I drafted a scenario which needs only to be versified in order for me to be able to set it to music, & I sent it in August last year to Herr Scribe in Paris. I asked him if he would deign to peruse the sketch, &, if he liked it & if he believed himself capable of turning it into an effective libretto, to appropriate it for himself, leaving me to set it to music & using his authority to bring about a production of the opera in Paris. I have not yet received a reply, & it occurs to me that my action may perhaps have been ill-considered to the extent that I did not first seek to convince Herr Scribe of my ability to produce a good & effective piece. Accordingly, I have just sent off to him the full score of a grand comic opera of my own composition, The Ban on L., together with the request that he submit it to you for your scrutiny. If your verdict were to turn out in my favour, I should once again commend to him the earlier request that I made. This, Sir, would also furnish me with a suitable opportunity to approach you in person. You may easily judge to what extent the whole of my career & the whole of my life are dependent upon your verdict (in the event, that is, of your considering my feeble work worthy of your attention), when I reveal to you that my most ardent desire & my every effort is aimed at being able to come to Paris, since I sense something within me that must inevitably bear goodly fruit there. The opera that is to be submitted to you is one which I myself have adapted from a Shakespearean play, M. f. M.;[2] even while I was still working on it, the somewhat free & almost frivolous tone of the piece, not to mention *the whole colour of the work*, had already convinced me that it was not really suited to our German tastes; I was already actively thinking of France, & have therefore not yet allowed the opera to be performed in Germany.[3] Would it be possible, therefore, to have the scenario translated into French by some able person, & to offer it in that form to the Opéra-Comique for production there? If you liked the opera, it might indeed be

1 *Die hohe Braut* by Heinrich Koenig, first published in 1833.
2 *Measure for Measure.*
3 Wagner fails to mention the disastrous first performance of *Das Liebesverbot* in Magdeburg on 29 March 1836.

possible for you, rather than anyone else, to bring this about. Your reputation describes you as so noble & generous a person that I might even make so bold as to beg you to devote your concern to me; & what finer action is there left for a man like yourself to take? *Greater* honour as an artist can scarcely still be granted you, for you have already attained to heights of unprecedented fame; wherever people can sing, your melodies are to be heard; you have become a demigod on earth; – how glorious it is for the man who has reached this point to glance round & offer his hand to those whom he has left so far behind, in order to draw them a little closer towards him. This is certainly something that you yourself must feel more nobly & more clearly within you than so insignificant an individual as myself can ever adequately express, & I am convinced that it is simply a question of having to earn your goodwill. Well then, – deign to peruse my work, – if you discover that I have been deluding myself as to its merits, you will be able to explain this fact to me more clearly than anyone else could have done; if, on the other hand, you consider it worthy of your protection, I beg you not to refuse me your help. The sort of opportunity that you are able to offer brings with it not only honour & material prosperity, but may arouse, awaken & fashion within us strengths which would otherwise have withered & died, given the miserable state in which we now find ourselves in our beloved fatherland. It was simply the need to make ends meet that drove me here to this inhospitable & obscure corner of East Prussia; & which holds me here still; what can a man achieve in such a situation? It may perhaps require no more than a declaration of your sympathetic interest in my talent & abilities for you to inspire me to produce something that would otherwise have disappeared without trace; will you deny me this if you consider me worthy of it?

How profoundly must I beg your forgiveness for the liberty of denying you a few precious minutes of your time in order to make this somewhat importunate approach; but if you can place yourself in the mental position of a young man whose every nerve & fibre yearns to be able to develop his powers but as yet lacks the helping hand that will show him what direction that yearning must take, then you will certainly grant me your forgiveness, & perhaps even offer me your hand. – In the event of your not yet having received my score from Herr Scribe, you will, I am sure, be so kind as to request it from him. As soon as I am apprised of his answer, then I may well venture to hope that you yourself will inform me of my fate, which I herewith place in your hands & commend to your heart. Everything depends upon your verdict. In ardent admiration, I am your devoted servant Richard Wagner.

Giacomo Meyerbeer: Briefwechsel und Tagebücher, ed. Heinz and Gudrun Becker. Volume III: 1837–1845. (Berlin 1975), 25–8.

24. THE RIGA THEATRE ORCHESTRA   Riga, 11 September 1838

To the Worshipful Members
of the Orchestra.

It may be assumed at the outset that I am simply meeting the wishes of
the worshipful members of the orchestra if I take this opportunity to suggest
that a series of orchestral concerts be organized in the course of the coming
winter, & that the said series be regarded as a separate undertaking on the
part of the orchestra & arranged for its benefit. I have already sought &
obtained the necessary agreement & consent from Herr von Holtey, which
he was kind enough to give me, & my suggestion, briefly, runs as follows:

The number of concerts, at least during the first year when the undertaking
may perhaps not yet have met with the success it deserves, should be limited
to *six*, which would follow each other at an interval of approximately 3 weeks.
With regard to the day, Herr von Holtey has kindly drawn my attention to
Tuesday, when there are often theatre performances in Mitau, thus leaving
the evening free for the orchestra here. A subscription scheme should now
be started for these 6 concerts, to which the orchestra should invite members
of the public to subscribe by means of several subscription lists. As a subscription price for the 6 performances I would suggest 4 roubles, &, as the
admission price on the evening itself, the usual charge of 1 rouble. Once the
subscription list has been closed, a committee of the 4 senior members of
the orchestra shall be entrusted with running the box office & be responsible
for deducting the total costs, about which I shall have something to say in a
moment, from the monies received & for dividing the balance equally among
the various members of the orchestra. In order to avoid any unpleasantness
over the distribution of the proceeds, such as may arise from the differences
between the first & second desks, I would suggest that the said distribution
take place, as indicated, on an equal basis, & that in doing so no distinction
be drawn between the first & second desks, but that those players who sit at
the first desks, or rather – to avoid any risk of misunderstanding – those
players who may be eligible to perform a solo item or a concerto – may be
given the opportunity to offer their services as a soloist & be entitled to an
additional fee for any concert item performed, payable out of the concert
fund. The term "concert item" shall be taken to include *duets, trios, quartets*
and so on, so that all those who are eligible to play such a piece shall have
every opportunity to do so at least once in the course of the 6 concerts. Each
concert should therefore include on average 2 solo works, & for each of these
pieces a certain sum of money should be set aside in advance according to
the amount received through the subscription scheme. Since, however, it will
be unavoidably necessary to perform vocal numbers, if we are to provide a
varied concert repertory, we shall also have to set aside a fee for the singers
each time they are invited to appear, if we are not to be subjected to the

whims of these people; this should probably be the same as that payable for an instrumental solo, & we must reckon on 2 vocal numbers at each concert. The fees payable each time for 4 solo items (i.e. 2 instrumental & 2 vocal numbers) should be included in the concert expenses right from the outset; if these appear to be very significant, especially when we add the hire of the hall, printing of programmes & posters etc. – (the cheapest options to be agreed on in advance) – , we may nevertheless count on substantial cash receipts on the night, a sum which at the end of the season should be used solely for the purposes of being distributed equally among all the members of the orchestra.

Since the undertaking may appear, in this form, to be somewhat innovatory & for that reason perhaps not immediately find favour with the general public, every member of the orchestra should regard it as his duty to contribute whatever he can to increasing the number of subscription signatures, and it would give me personally the greatest satisfaction if I were to succeed in collecting a fair number of signatures by means of individual invitations. – An audience which, at least as far as the great mass is concerned, is no doubt not yet used to the sort of more serious musical pleasures that we intend offering them during the coming season, must be induced by more superficial attractions, & I am thinking in this context of the Leipzig subscription concerts, of which 24 are given every winter to a packed house. Accordingly, not only must all true lovers of art be offered the prospect of edifying musical delights, but the remaining members of the audience must be given an opportunity to see each other & converse, something they may easily do during the long interval between the first and second parts of the concert. This means, amongst other things, that a Swiss baker should be asked to take charge of the buffet arrangements, so that refreshments may be available for the audience during the interval; in a word, everything must be done to ensure that the greater part of the audience may regard these concerts as an evening of agreeable entertainment, since we all know perfectly well that not every section of the audience has come to worship at the shrine of art.

If, in spite of everything, the pecuniary advantages are relatively few this winter, we may nevertheless hope that, providing we seek to make the concerts as attractive as possible, the success of the undertaking will increase from one year to the next & in time achieve the same sort of distinction as that which characterizes similar concerts in so many other towns in Germany. But even apart from all this, the scheme ought to appeal to every artist among us by virtue of the suggestion that, in this way, we are giving so perfectly organized a body as our orchestra may justifiably be described at present an opportunity to show its strengths in this area & to develop along independent lines; for what true musician would not be dismayed to think of so excellent an ensemble being put to no better use than merely carrying out routine duties, rather than achieving something that was genuinely enjoyable & edifying. It is this consideration alone which, by & large, has induced me to put this suggestion to you, since I may state in advance that for my own part I renounce all claims to any financial gain which the said undertaking may produce, & decline to accept any fee.

This well-meant proposal of mine still leaves a good many points to be raised & discussed, but I offer it to all the members of the orchestra for their consideration and, in the event of its being accepted, for their signature; I hope that it may, when duly signed, serve as the basis for the establishment of a Music Society which in time will certainly not escape general recognition.
Riga, the 11th September 1838[1]   Richard Wagner,
                                                                                Theatre Kapellmeister.

SB I,346–9.

---

1 A further twenty-four signatures were appended, in addition to Wagner's own. The editor of the Burrell Collection is wrong in claiming that the proposed scheme came to nothing. Six subscription concerts were held between 15 November 1838 and 7 May 1839, in addition to a benefit performance for Wagner himself on 14 March 1839; see SB I,349–50, fn. 1.

INDIGENCE IN PARIS:
RECOGNITION IN DRESDEN
1839–1849

INTRODUCTORY ESSAY 1839–1849

In order to elude creditors, and because, as debtors, Wagner's and Minna's passports had been impounded, it was necessary to make the departure from Riga a clandestine one. They were allowed to stow themselves away on board a small merchant vessel called the *Thetis* bound for London, and after a stormy voyage they made the crossing from Gravesend to Boulogne, where, by good fortune, Meyerbeer, the reigning monarch of the Paris Opéra, happened to be. Without delay the *Rienzi* libretto was read to Meyerbeer, who promised to give Wagner introductions to Charles Edmond Duponchel, the director of the Opéra, and François Habeneck, the conductor.

From Boulogne, Wagner wrote to his future brother-in-law Eduard Avenarius [25], who directed the Paris operations of the Brockhaus publishing firm, requesting him to obtain accommodation in Paris. Avenarius was among those whom Wagner called on to support him financially in the first months in Paris. Another obvious source of income was work for music publishers, making arrangements, for various instrumental combinations, of tunes from the popular operas of the day. Contrary to the impression given in *Mein Leben*, it was Wagner himself who took the initiative in this direction, as is proved by [26]. It is not known to how many publishers Wagner offered his services, but it is certainly true that the work undertaken for the Jewish publisher Maurice Schlesinger, described so resentfully in *Mein Leben*, was substantial and arduous. In addition to these transcriptions and vocal scores, Wagner turned to literary work; this was seen primarily as an extra source of income, but it also enabled him to air his opinions on the standards and values of the contemporary musical world. In a series of reviews for the Dresden *Abend-Zeitung* he lambasted the mediocrities served up by the Opéra, though he singled out Halévy, Meyerbeer and Auber as composers worthy of respect, and, initially at least, professed faith in the public who, he maintained, were able to discern real talent where it existed. For Schlesinger's periodical the *Revue et Gazette musicale* Wagner wrote a number of lively articles as well as three novellas, *Eine Pilgerfahrt zu Beethoven* (A Pilgrimage to Beethoven), *Ein Ende in Paris* (An End in Paris) and *Ein glücklicher Abend* (A Happy Evening), which dramatize the aesthetic and social issues of concern to him at the time.

In order to get a complete picture of Wagner's musical predilections and prejudices at this period, it is necessary to read these journalistic pieces alongside his contemporary letters. There, freed from the constraints of courtesy towards a public he was attempting to woo, he could wax indignant: "the greatest evil here is the rampant superficiality to which every composer surrenders in his quest for public approval" [35], "Public taste in Paris has sunk immeasurably" [44], "the real opera public only understands the *cancan*" [44]. In response to the degraded taste dominated purely by fashion, Wagner maintains, both composers and performers have prostituted their art, courting popularity with sheer virtuosity. But it is not a straightforward case of damning French art in comparison with German: as a letter to Ferdinand Heine [35] makes clear, the pedantic, undramatic operas of such German composers as Reissiger and Lobe are vastly inferior, in Wagner's opinion, to comparable works by the French.

Less successful than his belletristic activities were Wagner's attempts to interest the leading Parisian singers in his music. To the celebrated bass Lablache he offered an aria, "Norma il predisse" (WWV 52), as an interpolation for Bellini's *Norma*, but neither this nor the various songs he produced to French texts brought him the attention or commissions he desired. From the start Wagner had presumed that the key to his success was the patronage of Meyerbeer. Back in 1837 he had proposed to him a French version of *Das Liebesverbot* [23], and in March 1840, thanks to Meyerbeer's influence, the work was provisionally accepted for performance by the Théâtre de la Renaissance. Only a few weeks later it became evident that the theatre was heading for bankruptcy, and the plans for *Das Liebesverbot* were dashed. Wagner later suggested that Meyerbeer had foreknowledge of the impending bankruptcy, but on the available evidence this seems unlikely. Nor did Wagner at the time give voice to any suspicion of treachery by Meyerbeer (no evidence of it, at least, survives). On the contrary, in a letter of 15 September of that year to Heinrich Schletter he states that Meyerbeer's help has given him renewed hope that his dealings with the Opéra will lead to a fruitful conclusion; and in the same month he assures Apel, "Meyerbeer has remained untiringly loyal to my interests" [31].

The harshness of Wagner's later attacks on Meyerbeer [44, 55 and 76], when seen against the effusive flattery of the earlier desperate pleas for help, must surely be interpreted as the working of a psychological mechanism. So exaggerated had been Wagner's obsequiousness, so low had the "servant" prostrated himself before the "deeply revered lord and master" [28, 29], that a normal relationship, given Wagner's naturally proud disposition, was unthinkable. Shame, frustration, jealousy and insecurity are the motivating forces of his later bitterness. In his early days in Paris, Wagner was willing to tailor his talents and inspiration to the demands of French taste. But with his inability to make headway with *Das Liebesverbot* and *Rienzi*, his attitude began to change. By early 1842 his frustration was combining with his increasing loathing of Parisian mediocrity and finding Meyerbeer as its symbolic target. Wagner's description of Meyerbeer as a "trickster" (*Betrüger*) in his letter to Schumann [44] requires some comment. Contemporary observers frequently noted the unwarrantable intimacy of Meyerbeer's relations with the press. Not only did he organize something similar to the modern press conference, but he was known to bestow favours and presents on critics; he saw no reason to court adverse reviews by breaking with the conventions of the time, tinged as they might be with corruption. Nevertheless, in spite of Meyerbeer's dubious reputation, Wagner may not have intended such a description of his benefactor to appear, even in a journal in remote Leipzig. It is not at all clear which passages of his letter Wagner expected Schumann to publish in the *Neue Zeitschrift für Musik* and which not, though these sentences on the subject of Meyerbeer certainly have the appearance of asides: they seem too private to be for general consumption. Whether or not Schumann did misinterpret Wagner's intentions by printing these sentences – albeit in edited form (see note 3, page 88 to [44]) – there is no doubt that the appending of the intitials "H. V." to the article in the newspaper was Schumann's doing rather than Wagner's. Schumann was, of course, echoing the pseudonym "H. Valentino", presumably invented by Wagner himself, and used, either mischievously or maliciously (since Henri Valentino was a conductor in Paris), for his irreverent essay on Rossini's *Stabat Mater*. But it is worth pointing out first that Schumann, as editor, bears some responsibility for permitting, and perpetuating, the pseudonym, and second that far from being exceptional, the practice of adopting pseudonymity or anonymity was ubiquitous; indeed, it was a custom that lingered on in many countries until well into the present century.

It was a measure of Wagner's remoteness from Parisian taste that his proposed opera *Der fliegende Holländer* (The Flying Dutchman) (WWV 63) failed to find favour at the Opéra. On 6 May 1840 he sent a prose draft for the work to Eugène Scribe, and the following month he sent a copy to Meyerbeer in the hope that the latter might use his influence to have it accepted by the Opéra. Meyerbeer responded by introducing Wagner to Léon Pillet, who became Edmond Duponchel's senior partner on 1 June 1840 and who assumed full control of the administration of the Opéra the following year. After much procrastination Pillet persuaded Wagner to sell him the story. Pillet gave the draft to two French librettists, Paul Foucher and Bénédict-Henry Révoil, and Wagner, perhaps not unreasonably, assumed that their opera *Le Vaisseau Fantôme*, based on the Flying Dutchman legend and produced by Foucher and Révoil in collaboration with Pierre-Louis Dietsch, made use of his scenario. The truth is that they drew primarily not on Wagner but on Captain Marryat's *The Phantom Ship* and to a lesser extent on Heine, Sir Walter Scott (from whose novel *The Pirate* they took several names and other details), as well as probably Fenimore Cooper (*The Red Rover*), the tales of Wilhelm Hauff and various poems.[1] *Le Vaisseau Fantôme* was, as Pillet had demanded of his librettists, a confection "selon le goût français" and a marked contrast with the sombre colouring of *Der fliegende Holländer*. By the time it reached the stage of the Opéra in November 1842, Wagner was back in Germany.

The Paris years were a time of extreme hardship for Wagner and Minna. His plaintive appeal [31] to Theodor Apel, the friend of his youth, yielded no result for over a month, and he faced the real threat of imprisonment for debt. The evidence suggests that the threat did not become a reality,[2] in which case the subsequent letters to Apel, sent by Minna but drafted by Wagner, the first [Appendix A, p. 935] stating that he had had to leave her for the debtors' prison that very morning (25 October 1840), were nothing more than a ruse to extract more money from Apel. Letter [32] to Laube would seem to clinch this interpretation: Wagner would hardly have referred to these days in early December as terrible beyond imagination, and to the imminent "loss of personal liberty", if he had already suffered incarceration in October. Moreover, in letter [33] Wagner appears to be justifying to his brother-in-law the ruse of the Apel letters, the truth of which Brockhaus had already discovered.

Wagner's closest friends in Paris were a trio of expatriate Germans: Gottfried Anders, an employee of the Bibliothèque Royale; Ernst Benedikt Kietz, an artist and early portraitist of Wagner; and Samuel Lehrs, a philologist who introduced him to important background material on the *Tannhäuser* and *Lohengrin* legends. Berlioz and Heinrich Heine were among the more distinguished artists whose acquaintance he made at this time.

In November 1840, with the threat of imprisonment hanging over him, Wagner completed *Rienzi* (WWV 49). Expecting nothing from the Opéra, he offered it to the Dresden Court Theatre, by whom it was eventually accepted [40]. He was in early communication, from Paris, with Ferdinand Heine, the costume designer, and Wilhelm Fischer, the stage manager and chorus-master, both of whom became close friends of Wagner's. Letter [43] to Heine is informative as to Wagner's ideas on the staging and casting of *Rienzi*, ([234] is also of interest for Wagner's interpretation of the work), and is evidence of his early appreciation of the need for cuts. In view of his later disparagement of *Rienzi* [65], it is interesting to note Wagner's enthusiasm for the work both before and after its première. As regards the conception of the work itself, letter [31] provides, in a brief rhetorical question, the only indication we have that it was Apel who first saw the feasibility of Bulwer-Lytton's novel as an opera. Something of the flavour of the excitement and frustrations experienced

---

1 For a comparison of plots and full details, see Barry Millington, "Did Wagner really sell his 'Dutchman' story?" in *Wagner*, iv (1983), 114–27.
2 See SB II, 414-16 (note 1) and Barry Millington, *Wagner* (London 1984), 24-5.

in the rehearsals during the weeks leading up to the première is conveyed in [47]. By now Wagner had returned to Dresden, and his pride and happiness at the hugely successful launch of *Rienzi* on 20 October 1842 are unmistakable [49, 50 and 51].

Meanwhile, *Der fliegende Holländer* had been accepted by the Berlin Court Theatre [45], partly through Meyerbeer's influence. However, the intendant there, Count Redern, retired soon after, to be succeeded by Theodor von Küstner, who was less sympathetic to the project, and it was Dresden that followed up its *Rienzi* success with the first production of *Der fliegende Holländer* on 2 January 1843. Wagner's meteoric rise to fame in Dresden made him a strong candidate for the conductor's post at the King of Saxony's Court there which became vacant at this time. His reluctance to accept the constraints of a full-time job in the royal service was balanced and eventually outweighed by the tempting prospect of security and a salary for life. Wagner's negotiations with the Dresden intendant, August von Lüttichau, are retailed in [52] and [53].

The German Opera was founded in Dresden only in 1817, after it became the seat of a royal Court with the establishment of the Kingdom of Saxony at the Vienna Congress of 1814/15. The repertory of the German Opera, favoured by the middle classes, and that of the traditional Italian Opera, the preserve of high society, vied with one another until the Italian company, under Francesco Morlacchi, was disbanded in 1832. Weber, Kapellmeister at Dresden from 1817 to his death in 1826, had done much to establish a tradition of German Romantic opera (though none of his operas received its first performance in Dresden), and it was Wagner who carried on this tradition with his predilection and respect for his native art. The post Wagner eventually accepted on 2 February 1843 was that of a second Kapellmeister. Wagner was led to believe that his status would be equal to that of the other Kapellmeister, Karl Gottlieb Reissiger, though Reissiger's larger salary confirms the older man's apparent marginal seniority. Kapellmeister since 1828, Reissiger had won for Dresden the reputation of the finest opera house in Germany, but by the 1840s he had come to be regarded as "totally ineffectual" [56], even "lazy" [45], and was certainly content to see the more onerous duties taken on by his younger and more industrious colleague. Together they had responsibility for all the musical activities of the Court, including operatic, instrumental and choral performances, as well as being required to provide occasional ceremonial music, e.g. Wagner's *Der Tag erscheint* (The Day Appears) (WWV 68) for the unveiling of a memorial to King Friedrich August I [58].

Another misleading impression given to Wagner was that he was at liberty to institute a radical reorganization of musical life at the Court [56]; the negative attitude shown later towards just such proposals was to lead to an irreconcilable rift between him and the management. Within weeks of his appointment Wagner consolidated his reputation with a highly praised performance of Gluck's *Armide*. On 6 July followed his "biblical scene" for male voices and orchestra, *Das Liebesmahl der Apostel* (The Love-Feast of the Apostles) (WWV 69). Written for a gala concert to be given by all the male choral societies in Saxony, the piece was performed in the Frauenkirche, Dresden, by a chorus of 1200 amateur singers and an orchestra of 100. Wagner's account of the event to Cäcilie Avenarius [58] is notably more enthusiastic than that given later in *Mein Leben*, where he refers to the "comparatively feeble effect" made by the work.

Among the musical personalities of the day he encountered while in Dresden was Louis Spohr. Spohr was Kapellmeister at Cassel from 1822 (Generalmusikdirektor from 1847) and, as an admirer of Wagner's music, was responsible for mounting *Der fliegende Holländer* in 1843 and *Tannhäuser* in 1853. Wagner's attitude to the older composer was more complex. Spohr's musical language and procedures anticipated Wagner's in various ways, notably in his use of chromaticism and leitmotif, and in his innovative method of through-composed operatic construction (i.e. "number" opera giving way to continuous arioso). It has also been pointed out that Wagner's characteristic enharmonic modulations and suspended chords of the seventh and ninth are prominent in Spohr's *Jessonda* (1822/3),[1] and that the opening chromatic sequence of *Tristan und Isolde* is pre-echoed in *Der Alchymist* (1829/30), where Spohr even uses the phrase as a love motif.[2] Often Wagner in later years disparaged the music of composers whom he had earlier admired and by whom he had been influenced. With Spohr, the reverse is the case. When, as a young man in 1835, he encountered *Jessonda* Wagner dismissed it contemptuously as "pedantically sentimental" [15]. This frostiness thawed, however, when he came into personal contact with Spohr in Dresden. By 1859 he was able to write a fulsome eulogy on Spohr's death, and in the last years of his life he is recorded by Cosima Wagner as on more than one occasion playing through music from *Jessonda* on the piano. Wagner's ambivalent attitude to Spohr is typical of his time. By the 1840s Spohr's preeminence as a composer was unquestioned both in Germany and in England, but he was regarded as technically proficient rather than inspired, and already his music was considered somewhat old-fashioned. Accusations of mannerisms and self-repetition continued to be levelled at him even throughout the most triumphant years of his career.[3] The score of Wagner's next opera, *Tannhäuser* (WWV 70), was written in the early Dresden years and completed on 13 April 1845. It was after the première of *Tannhäuser*, on 19 October 1845, that Wagner felt able, indeed obliged, to take three months off to

---

1 See John Warrack, "The Musical Background", chapter in *The Wagner Companion*, ed. by Peter Burbidge and Richard Sutton (London 1979), 107.
2 See Deryck Cooke, "Wagner's Musical Language", *ibid*, 236–8.
3 See Clive Brown, *Louis Spohr: A critical biography* (Cambridge 1985).

prepare a report setting out the changes he deemed necessary in the musical establishment at the Dresden Court. He acknowledged that artistic standards had risen considerably since Weber's day, but he felt that such progress – and with it the reputation of the Dresden Court itself – was threatened by the "philistines" who held key positions in the management [68]. (It is difficult not to sympathize with Wagner when one recalls that Lüttichau's expertise was not in the arts but in forestry.)

Such views were hardly calculated to enhance Wagner's popularity among his senior colleagues, and his letters of this time record the envy he perceived in those around him. He frequently voices his frustration, too, at the lack of enthusiasm, often the hostility, of the press. Critics, he alleged, were failing to discharge their responsibility to promote the best in contemporary music. He even found himself guiltily casting envious glances towards Paris which at least, he reasoned, boasted an international outlook as compared with the provincial one of a typical German city. It is interesting, in this context, to compare the letter to Kietz [45], written immediately after his return to Dresden in 1842, in which he reveals a divided state of mind over his departure from Paris, with that to Karl Gaillard [68] three years later, by which time his frustration is driving him to reconsider the merits and demerits of Paris. In other letters, too [71, 74], he intimates that the time may be ripe for another assault on that citadel.

Wagner's report, *Die Königliche Kapelle betreffend* (Concerning the Royal Orchestra), was dated 1 March 1846 and despatched to Lüttichau with an accompanying letter [72]. Its recommendations included changes in the policy of hiring orchestral players, a rationalization of their work-load, an increase in their salaries, and improvements in the layout of the orchestra so that players could hear each other and see the conductor clearly. He also suggested a series of winter orchestral concerts and the establishment of two concert halls (adaptable for other purposes); such concerts, he argued, could only enhance the stature of the Dresden Court. Practical and rational as Wagner's proposals were, they threatened too many vested interests to be acted upon. After being kept in suspense for a year, he was eventually informed that his proposals were rejected. Not until 1858 were public subscription concerts instituted in Dresden; nor was there to be a regular concert hall until the opening of the Gewerbehaussaal in 1870.

Wagner's dissatisfactions were exacerbated by the behaviour of the man appointed in 1846 to succeed Eduard Devrient as dramaturg at the Court Theatre. It was Karl Gutzkow, who had been one of the Young German writers banned by the Bundestag decree of December 1835. As dramaturg, Gutzkow was nominally in charge of the opera as well as the theatre, but Wagner soon began to categorize his supervision of the administration of the opera as an interference, and complained that this "journalist" was bringing the opera into disrepute by his incompetence and intriguing. In a candid letter to Lüttichau [77], Wagner vented his grievances and asked, if Gutzkow could not be restrained, that he, Wagner, be relieved at least of his responsibilities to the opera. Out of financial necessity the letter falls short of resignation; Wagner's intention – to achieve a major success in Berlin before entering into negotiations with the King over his duties and salary – is revealed in a letter to Ferdinand Heine [78]. In fact *Rienzi* did eventually reach the stage of the Berlin Court Theatre (24 October 1847), but any pleasure Wagner might have taken in the fact was cancelled out by the hostile reception of the Berlin press, and by the insistence of the intendant, Küstner, that the theatre was not required to compensate him for the two months spent there in rehearsals. Nor was Wagner successful in using the production to obtain a commission from the King of Prussia to write his next opera, *Lohengrin*.

With all these disappointments and frustrations bearing down on him, together with continued financial problems, it was scarcely surprising that Wagner began to turn a sympathetic ear to those calling for revolution. Indeed, Wagner was a natural ally of the bourgeois liberals responsible for the uprisings of 1848/9. Many of them were respected academics and lawyers who nevertheless found themselves increasingly downgraded in social terms, and who resented their lack of political influence. They were not anarchists or natural revolutionaries, but, spurred into action by the failure of the autocratic princes to relieve their people's poverty, and by the threat to their own social position, these liberals began to press for freedom from feudal oppression and for the basic demands of constitutional and representative government. Uprisings in Paris (February 1848) and Vienna (March) led to the erection of barricades in some cities and the formation of a German National Assembly in Frankfurt. Wagner's letter to Professor Wigard, delegate for Saxony [80], sets out the measures he considered necessary if disaster were not to ensue.

The following month he aligned himself conspicuously with the revolutionary republican Vaterlandsverein by delivering an address at one of their public meetings (14 June). The speech was published the following day in the *Dresdner Anzeiger* as *Wie verhalten sich republikanische Bestrebungen dem Königthume gegenüber?* (How do Republican Aspirations Stand in Relation to the Monarchy?). In it, money and usury were denounced, and the emancipation of the human race joyfully anticipated. Wagner also warned that the privileges of the Court were coming to an end, and called for the King of Saxony, as "the first and truest republican of all", to head the emergent republic – a reformist proposal in keeping with the aspirations of bourgeois liberals, who desired peaceful, gradual change rather than revolution.

There were demands for Wagner's dismissal, and he defended his action to Lüttichau in a diplomatically worded letter [81]. Lüttichau, in accordance with the King's wishes, allowed the storm to subside, and Wagner carried on with his duties at the Court. He also continued to work on his own projects.

Lohengrin (WWV 75) had been completed in April, and *Der Ring des Nibelungen* (WWV 86) began to take shape with a prose résumé entitled *Der Nibelungen-Mythus. Als Entwurf zu einem Drama* (The Nibelung Myth as Sketch for a Drama): the 1848 manuscript is in fact headed *Die Nibelungensage (Mythus)*. The same autumn Wagner made a libretto for that part of the myth he intended to treat, calling it *Siegfrieds Tod* (Siegfried's Death). The essay *Die Wibelungen. Weltgeschichte aus der Sage* (The Wibelungs. World History from Legend) appears to have followed (not proceeded, as previously supposed) the prose résumé and libretto.[1]

A sketch for the second act of the projected historical drama *Friedrich I.* (WWV 76) also dates from 1848, and in January of the following year another subject, *Jesus von Nazareth* (WWV 80), was begun (like *Friedrich I.*, apparently intended as an opera). Under the cover of anonymity, Wagner contributed, in addition, to the republican journal *Volksblätter*, founded in August 1848 by August Röckel, who had been dismissed, for subversive activities, from his post as assistant conductor at the Court. Wagner's articles were unbridled diatribes against privilege and inequality. The Feuerbachian concept of necessity is given (as in Marx) a social and political dimension in Wagner's poem *Die Noth* (Need), in which the deeds of necessity are proclaimed to be the overthrow of capitalist structures together with the accompanying evils of greed and usury. Significantly, it was at this time that Wagner met Mikhail Bakunin, the Russian anarchist who was personally acquainted with Marx, Engels and other leading socialists. The ideas of Max Stirner (1806-65), another socialist thinker, are recalled in the "anarchistic egoism" of Wagner's blazing proclamation *Die Revolution*, which appeared shortly after King Friedrich Wilhelm IV of Prussia had indignantly and provocatively spurned the imperial crown offered by the Frankfurt Parliament.

Meanwhile, the Saxon King, Friedrich August II, rejected the constitution agreed at Frankfurt and dissolved both chambers of Parliament (30 April 1849). Röckel was obliged to flee to Prague to escape arrest, and Wagner took responsibility for the *Volksblätter* (now banned) in his place. Almost immediately it became clear that Saxony was about to be invaded by the Prussian army, and Wagner wrote to Röckel [85] urging him to return to Dresden. It was this letter, with its reference to "a decisive conflict" and "the revolution [that] may come *too soon*", which was found on Röckel on his arrest and which was used by the Dresden police to incriminate Wagner. His part in the uprising had been a reasonably active one. At least two political gatherings took place in his garden, and the arming of the populace was discussed. It seems also that Wagner was involved in the giving of instructions for the manufacture of hand-grenades. He attempted, further, to turn the King's troops away from the Saxon people and against the invading Prussian

1 See WWV 76.

army. And he reported on the movement of soldiers from the vantage-point of the tower of the Kreuzkirche. By 9 May (only a week after the letter to Röckel) the fighting in Dresden had ceased; the Prussian troops had succeeded in quashing the insurrection. Wagner narrowly escaped arrest, but Röckel was among those who were apprehended; he received a death sentence which was commuted to life imprisonment, a fact to which we owe a series of important letters from Wagner in the 1850s.

Wagner naïvely thought at first that he might be able to return to his Court post. His letters to Minna [86] and Devrient [87] immediately after the uprising minimize the extent of his revolutionary involvement. That to Devrient was intended to facilitate his return to Dresden; he falsely claims to have been no more than a spectator, and attempts to justify his sympathy by representing it as merely the expression of dissatisfaction with artistic standards – an interpretation that, for obvious reasons, was to be sustained throughout his exile and in his autobiography, written at the request of his new royal patron, Ludwig II. Although his bitter resentment at official hostility to artistic reform was undoubtedly what spurred him to action when the opportunity presented itself, Wagner is doing himself an injustice by obscuring his alignment with the leading forces of liberalism and social progress. As to the extent of his involvement, the Dresden police certainly took a different view; they identified him as an activist and issued a warrant for his arrest. Wagner realized that he had no alternative but to leave Germany immediately; he was not to return to his native country for eleven years.

Boulogne, 23 August 1839

Most honoured Sir and friend,

You will, I hope, permit me to address you in this familiar way since, for my own part, I have heard so much said about the kindness and honesty of your character that I already feel well disposed towards you, to the extent that I shall do everything in my power to earn the name and rights of a friend in return. Laying claim to that status in advance, I have already repeatedly pestered you through my good sister Cäcilie, and the willingness which you have shown in performing a somewhat irksome favour for me is sufficient guarantee that I shall not meet with utter rejection in making the following request, which is the immediate object of this letter. Cäcilie has no doubt already apprised you of my somewhat bold, not to say quixotic, plans for Paris; the impertinence with which I am prepared to face the mass of obstacles that await me there is something which you yourself will be able to judge once you have had the kindness to lend an ear to my news and views in Paris; whereby I reckon chiefly upon the sound advice which I know you will be able to give me and which I would entreat you to communicate to me in advance.

I sailed into London about 12 days ago, following a ghastly and particularly hazardous voyage lasting almost 4 weeks, and was then obliged to spend 8 days – 8 ruinous days – on the city's gold-paved streets, thanks to the confusion of my captain, who had caused some stupid mix-up with my luggage. I arrived in Boulogne by steamer on the 20th, and immediately rented the cheapest place I could find for the coming few weeks; it is in the country, i.e. less than half-an-hour from the town, and I have chosen it for several reasons; 1. I believe that a number of people who are important for my plans are not in Paris at the moment; 2. I still have another few weeks' work to do on what I should like to take with me to Paris already *complete*,[1] so as to be able to begin my machinations the moment I arrive; 3. I should, however, first like to recover from the hardships which I have had to endure, before plunging once again into the hurly-burly which undoubtedly awaits me in Paris. Might I therefore ask you in the mean time to obtain lodgings for me in Paris, bearing in mind the following points: an ordinary room with an alcove is of course quite sufficient for me and my wife; a larger room *alone* would ultimately do just as well; – obviously it needs to be furnished

---

1 Wagner had begun to work on *Rienzi* in June/July 1837; the full score of Act II was completed in Boulogne on 12 September 1839. See also letter [32], p. 74, note 3.

accommodation, although we do have our own beds and bedding, table-linen, candlesticks, kitchen utensils, since we have more or less brought our entire household with us, only the least transportable items having been sold in Russia. My wife will run the house herself, i.e. buy provisions, cook etc.; for that reason she will not require any extra help, except for a maid to assist her with manual chores. I can of course only rent the lodgings a month at a time, and since, in addition, I have no real idea of the price that one must pay in Paris for such accommodation, I will not stipulate a price here but leave it to the dictates of circumstance and to your kind discretion. That I should of course be delighted to find myself living not too far away from you, is something I scarcely need assure you of. – [. . .]

SB I,366–8.

26. To an unknown correspondent, Paris   Paris, Winter 1839/40

Sir,
I am a composer of music who is seeking a favourable opportunity to present himself before the Paris public, and, while waiting, am obliged to find some means of supporting myself by undertaking work in the most ordinary sense of the word.

I am therefore writing to you, Sir, in order to ask whether you can provide me with work, making arrangements for every instrument of the orchestra, the piano etc., which work I shall always do promptly and at the price which you yourself shall fix, under the sole condition of anonymity.

Since, unfortunately, my friend and very good patron M. Meyerbeer, who would be kind enough to vouch for my abilities in the event of your agreeing, is not in Paris at the moment, I would offer to do some work for you in advance, free of charge, in order to prove my abilities to you, if you are able to make use of the same.

Yours   May I ask you to be so kind as to honour me
                                                        with a brief word of reply.

Wagner, v (1984), 3–4 (the original is in French).

27. Eduard Avenarius, Paris   Paris, 4 January 1840

My worthy friend and patron,
Please answer with a simple yes or no, and let me know whether it is in your power – (would to God that it depended merely upon your good will –)

to increase by a further fifty francs the sum which, as you know, you have already lent me, this would then make the sum in question a round figure, or rather a square one.[1] I need scarcely add how fully aware I am that this request of mine, as far as things stand at present regarding my debt, borders almost on impertinence; – but – necessity teaches us not only how to pray but also to show a certain degree of impertinence which *you*, perhaps more than anyone else, will know how to excuse. I should explain that, in order to pay this month's rent etc., I visited the pawnbroker's yesterday, and although I took with me everything we could possibly manage without, I was still unable to raise all the money I needed; since what we are talking about is no more than fifty francs net, I am once again (and this will be the *last time*) appealing to you for help. If you are able to enclose with your affirmative answer the actual *nervus rerum*, you will readily be able to imagine how welcome that would be to me.

Yours,
Richard W.

It was impossible for me yesterday to find the words to put this request to you in person.

SB I,375.

28. GIACOMO MEYERBEER, BADEN-BADEN   Paris, 18 January 1840

My deeply revered Lord and Master,
  When you left Paris,[2] you gave me leave to send you news whenever anything of the least importance occurred touching upon my affairs in Paris. That these reports would always reach you accompanied by renewed appeals for your protection and patronage was something you doubtlessly foresaw, and this belief now encourages me to assume, in my own defence, that that general entitlement to send you news of my activities might also include your tacit agreement to receive such an appeal from me now. – You, my beloved master, you who are kindness and goodwill itself, will, I trust, be less angry with me than others would have been, if I now pursue you into your peaceful seclusion with my perhaps somewhat alarming cries for help. Your departure from Paris – ! ah, thereby hangs a tale of woe in the story of my life and struggles which one day, when I have become incredibly famous – as I do not doubt for a moment that I shall – , will be celebrated and lamented in some 24 to 48 cantos by some great poet. You can well imagine how so

---

1 i.e. 400 francs. Avenarius replied the same day, sending Wagner the requested sum of fifty francs.
2 Meyerbeer had left for Baden-Baden on 12 December 1839.

sensitive a creature as I reacted, how I gasped for air and grew downcast. In the end I was no longer in Paris, but continued merely to vegetate in the beautiful Rue de la Tonnellerie.[1] In addition I suffered a great deal of toothache, and in the end it was scarcely to be wondered at if I wrote an Overture to Faust, Part One.[2] Finally, Herr Dumersan's[3] pretty French verses to my opera brought me back to life once again; the man had made me wait a good two months *à la Parisienne*, and would probably never have produced the verses if he had not finally found the words to tell me that he first wanted to hear some of my music; – I then played several excerpts from my opera to him at his house, and fortunately met with such success that the very next day Herr Dumersan was able to hand over to me the prettiest verses in the whole wide world. Dumersan has even taken it upon himself to use every means in his power to expedite the acceptance of my opera at the Renaissance.[4] To begin with, it was his intention to act without me, on his own; – to that end he conferred with the opera-producer Herr Salomé, and, through him, demanded a meeting with Antenor Joly, in order to discuss with him at length an opera by a certain young man who had already been recommended to Herr Joly by Herr Meyerbeer. Once again things dragged on for a fair space of time, with the delightful result that Dumersan finally wrote me a depressing letter, informing me that Herr Salomé had been requested by the director to convey the message that Herr Joly could not agree to the matter, because – 1., I was a German, and young French composers would be highly indignant to see the Renaissance opening its doors to yet another German composer; that – 2., he would not give operas that had not been expressly written for his theatre and its singers, that – 3., he never gave operas in translation, nor was he allowed to do so, – , that 4., German music in general was too heavy and learned for his theatre.

I found all this most amiable, the more so since I could not but be deeply convinced by the profundity of the reasons given. I thought I might do better to resume personal contact with the theatre, but met with no more success than I had done previously. I then produced the kind letter which you had most generously left with me for that purpose, as a result of which Antenor's brother – for I have so far managed to set eyes only on Constantin – could of course no longer refuse me outright; but his familiar manner (: – "come back in 14 days, the singers are now very tired; etc." –) made it abundantly

1 Wagner lived in rooms at 3 Rue de la Tonnellerie between 17 September 1839 and 15 April 1840, when he moved to 25 Rue du Helder.
2 The full score of the *Faust* Overture (originally intended as the first movement of a symphony, WWV 59) was completed on 12 January 1840. The work was revised during the winter of 1854/5: see letter [178], pp. 326–7.
3 Marion Dumersan had been entrusted with the task of translating the libretto of *Das Liebesverbot* into French.
4 The Théâtre de la Renaissance was managed by Anténor Joly until its bankruptcy in May 1840.

clear that his enthusiasm for my cause was not exactly boundless or over-whelming. – That, then, is how things stand: – I am totally convinced that I shall not be granted an audition as long as I live, at least not unless something exceptional happens, – and it is to employ those exceptional means that I now address this importunate entreaty to you.

Antenor thinks: – "God is mighty, the Tsar is far away and Monpou[1] is not at all bad". – What is to be done here? Terrorism is the only means, and you, my revered ruler of all notes, alone can wield it. I hope for no salvation in this world except from you. – Well then, if you still remember who I am, have pity on me, and write the wicked Antenor a letter, a kind of ukase or papal bull, and in order to give it somewhat more weight, you might perhaps be so kind as to send it directly to Joly from your present whereabouts, so that it might reach the director without first having been profaned or defiled by my own hands. Tell him that it is true I am a German, but from Leipzig not from Mainz; – , that he needs only to listen, and that – – ; oh, you must forgive me my foolishness in daring to suggest how you might write to him; – it would of course be best if I were to leave it entirely to you and simply beseech you to be kind enough to take this step on behalf of my poor self.

But I know *one means* which will persuade Antenor to change his mind in an instant and agree to giving operas of mine; – it is a suggestion which would never have occurred to you, and only because of its singularity do I mention it jestingly now: – I can tell you: – Antenor will be pleased to give operas of mine if you offer him even the faintest hope that you may one day devote your leisure hours to composing an opera especially for him. Indeed, I am convinced that the merest hint of such a hope on your part could turn everything to my advantage. But you may be assured, my most revered master, that I am myself too modest to rate this good fortune of mine so highly that I might seriously weigh it against a demand which you may well deem unreasonable on my part. Forgive me, therefore, if I have been overbold in making mention of this *exceptional* means, and attribute the blame less to my importunacy than to my somewhat desperate endeavours to enter the world of make-believe. Without transgressing the bounds of what I may expect of your kindness, I am convinced that what I may hope to receive from you is something you will readily grant a person as destitute of help as I am. You will consider how much *further* you can still go and save at least half my life with whatever you may feel disposed to accord me. At all events, I promise that, by way of thanks, I shall place a light in every window of my lodgings on the day of your return to Paris.[2] Oh – this return – how I long for it and how it will be celebrated! Even Herr *Schlesinger*, who is shortly to give a major

---

1 Hippolyte Monpou (1804–1841) had scored a success with *Le Planteur*, produced at the Opéra-Comique on 1 March 1839.
2 Meyerbeer did not return to Paris until 14 August 1840.

orchestral concert at which nothing of mine will be performed. – yes, even Herr Schlesinger shall that day be clasped with joy to my bosom.

If I might add to all my other indiscretions the final impertinence of cherishing the hope that I might receive a few lines from you yourself, informing me that my honoured master is in good health and that he forgives the foolishness of his *protégé*, then it would almost be a matter of indifference to me what the Dear Lord were to say to all my importunities, as long as you yourself were not to take them amiss.

With all my sins and weaknesses, distress and grief I commend myself respectfully to you, praying to God and yourself that I may be delivered from all evil. As long as you remain favourably disposed towards me, then God too will not be far from me; that is why I ask you to remember, be it ever so briefly,

Your
ardently respectful and obedient servant,
Richard Wagner.

Giacomo Meyerbeer: Briefwechsel und Tagebücher,
ed. by Heinz and Gudrun Becker. Volume III:
1837–1845 (Berlin 1975), 229–32.

29. GIACOMO MEYERBEER, BERLIN   Paris, 3 May 1840

[...] You had in truth taken such excellent & exhaustive steps[1] that at the end of 2 weeks I thought I would be able to write and inform you how well everything had turned out. In the mean time, however, I have discovered afresh that in Paris even the Dear Lord himself would find it difficult to enforce his will quickly & without opposition. The chief problem was Anténor *Joly's* imminent bankruptcy, which he himself had virtually conceded & which robbed him of every desire and every means of becoming involved in such an affair as my own. Wondrous, however, are the workings of fate. With marvellous foresight you had already assigned me your friend Herr *Gouin*. I must confess that, if ever there *had* been any alternative to your own personal intervention, it could only have been through Herr Gouin. How deeply it moved me to discover anew what an admirable person you yourself must be, that a man must feel himself drawn towards you to form the sort of friendship that persuades him to show so generous a sense of self-sacrifice as Herr Gouin has shown in espousing the cause of a total stranger who, did he not

---

1 On Meyerbeer's instructions, Louis Gouin had arranged for an audition of excerpts from *Das Liebesverbot* to be held at the Théâtre de la Renaissance; a number of singers friendly to Meyerbeer were engaged for the occasion.

enjoy the advantage of having been recommended by you, could not otherwise have inspired the remotest interest.

Joly's bankruptcy had already caused me to lose heart when Herr Gouin suggested the idea that, since such admirable measures had already been taken & since I had singers at my disposal who were ready to perform something of my own composition, I could still derive the best possible advantage from this in order to effect an introduction to various persons of influence. Herr Schlesinger had already introduced me briefly to Herr Edouard *Monnaie*;[1] – my singers were those from the Opera; – why, then, not make use of all this? – Herr Gouin asked Herr Monnaie to agree to my holding the audition in the opera house foyer; – the effect which the name Meyerbeer had on him in the course of this exchange is something you will be able to judge when I tell you that Herr Monnaie gave his immediate consent, nay, more than that, – he even prevailed upon Herr *Scribe* to attend the audition. Herr Habeneck had in fact already pointed out to me that, if I were able to impress myself favourably upon an author such as Herr Scribe, this would be my best means of achieving anything; he knew in fact that the Opera administration wishes to have shorter 1-act operas, in order to avoid having to tear out whole acts from existing operas to be performed on ballet evenings; – that, since those people who actually run the Opera could not concern themselves with the additional responsibility for trivialities such as these, I was most likely to succeed in having such an opera accepted for performance if I could win over an *auteur* who would entrust me with a *libretto*. This was clearly a good idea, & so I decided to use the opportunity to introduce myself to these gentlemen; that this would not further the interests of the particular opera of which they had come to hear extracts, goes without saying. However, I thought to myself: if the gentlemen like my music, why should they not thereby gain confidence in my ability to compose a short, one-act opera? This, then, was my intention. I hope to have succeeded in it; Herr Scribe & Herr Monnaie gave me the most unequivocal signs of their approval, and within the last few days I have been given leave to send Herr Scribe the draft of an opera in 1 act.[2] What prospects, what hopes! And what gives me such a profound sense of joy in all this is the conviction that *this* turn of events, too, has been brought about solely & uniquely by you, and you *alone:* yours was the presiding genius. *One* name was sufficient to win over Herr *Monnaie* to my cause: – *Meyerbeer;* when I introduced myself to Herr *Scribe* & alluded to my earlier mystical correspondence with him,[3] he

1 Edouard Monnais (*sic*) was temporarily appointed co-director of the Paris Opéra in 1839 to assist Duponchel. Léon Pillet took over the directorship officially in 1841, although he had been acting director since 1 June 1840.

2 Wagner sent Scribe his prose draft of *Der fliegende Holländer*, entitled "Le Hollandais volant – (nom d'un fantôme de mer.)", on 6 May 1840.

3 See letter [22], pp. 40–42.

interrupted me to say that I need only assume that he had already heard the most glowing reports, – Herr *Meyerbeer* had already spoken to him about me. When Mlle Nau had to leave for London shortly before the audition & I turned to Mme Dorus-Gras in search of a replacement, it was the letter which Herr Meyerbeer had left me which immediately disposed her in my favour. You see, it is *Meyerbeer* & *Meyerbeer* alone, & you will readily understand me when I tell you that I weep tears of the deepest emotion whenever I think of the man who is *everything* to me, *everything*.

And so a deep abyss has now been crossed, – I am already on Scribe's own ground, – but – now my strength fails me; I can go no further, unless it be that God offers me some form of exceptional help. With what, – ah! with *what* sacrifices I have managed to survive until now is something that only *he* can guess who has known the struggles of a fellow creature abandoned by every form of help. The feeling of wondrous exaltation which overwhelms me whenever I think of you may perhaps at *this* moment blind me to the somewhat unseemly nature of my disclosures, and encourage me to add that, even as I write these lines, my final prospect of continuing survival has been completely shut off to me, – at the very moment when, relying upon that prospect, I had been on the point of turning my present lodgings into a somewhat more comfortable place to live. There is no longer any question of help; not even Herr Schlesinger can offer me the least assistance now. I have reached the point of having to sell myself, in order to obtain help in the most material sense of the word. But my head & my heart are no longer mine to give away, – they are your property, my master; – the most that is left to me is my two hands, – do you wish to make use of them? – I realize that I must become your slave, body & soul, in order to find food & strength for my work, which will one day tell you of my gratitude. I shall be a loyal & honest slave, – for I openly admit that I am a slave by nature; it gives me endless pleasure to be able to devote myself unconditionally to another person, recklessly, & in blind trust. The knowledge that I am working & striving for you, & you *alone*, makes that effort & industry seem all the more agreeable & all the more worth while. Buy me, therefore, Sir, it is by no means a wholly worthless purchase! – If I remain free, as I am now, then I shall simply go to ruin, dragging my wife down with me; & that would indeed be a crying shame. Is there not something better to live for? This summer, when you could perhaps derive a healthy income from me – this summer will destroy me utterly, for I have nothing to enable me to survive even till the end of the merry month of May. But if you help me through until next winter, I may already be paying interest by then! – To put it bluntly: – no usurer can help me any longer, not even an ordinary upright citizen can help me now; for he would never be able to understand how I could ever pay him back; the only person who can do so is someone whose far-seeing eye & overflowing heart sees & feels that I may yet produce a goodly tree which, providing there is no lack of rain, may still bear fruit. Göthe is dead, – but he was no musician; there is nobody left but you. Some twenty-five hundred francs will help me to survive next winter; – will you lend this sum to me? –

And shall I not see you again before this winter? I assume & fear that this is so; no one believes that you will reappear before then. There is only one consolation in all this, & that is my firm conviction that you will return to Paris the very picture of health; & I trust in God that the same will be true of your dear wife. I imagine that from time to time every German feels the need to breathe the air of Germany to regain his strength. I hear that you have been travelling, & I deduce from this that your illness, news of which so distressed me in your last letter, must now have eased. How I long to receive your complete reassurance in this regard! You may be certain that kind & loyal hearts are praying for your health & well-being; both my mother & my wife have so earnestly entreated me to assure you of this that I cannot forbear from informing you of the honest effusion of their gratitude. My dear mother, to whom, in an excess of joy, I sent your letter in Leipzig – (forgive me, my beloved master, it was in order to regale her!) – as well as my dear wife have both been too deeply moved by the touching conviction that, in you, God has sent me my most powerful guardian angel for them not to offer you as such their silent sacrifice. – If the rest of the world is filled with your praises, why should these women not pray for you? – Mine is a different task, for I must work for you, i.e. make myself worthy of being able to thank you. – Here I am; here is the head, the heart & here are the hands of

Your property:
Richard Wagner

I am now living at 24[1] Rue du Helder.

SB I,385–9.

30. GIACOMO MEYERBEER, BAD EMS   Paris, 26 July 1840

[. . .] I have just read that Herr Léon Pillet is leaving Paris today with the intention of visiting you, dear Sir, in *Ems*. At the same time, it is generally known what Herr Pillet is hoping to achieve by this visit, although I cannot of course predict whether & in what manner you will fulfil his request. Nor am I in a position to predict whether you might perhaps be inclined to take advantage of this gentleman's indebtedness towards you to make favourable mention of a poor aspirant such as myself. There is but a single request that

---

1 The correct address was 25 Rue du Helder.

I venture to make: – if it were to appear appropriate & acceptable in the light not only of your deeper insight but of the degree of interest which you may yet cherish on my behalf, I would entreat you in all humility to put in a good word for me & my "winged Dutchman" (1 act), of which I have a few numbers ready for audition.[1]

[. . .]

SB I,400–1.

31. THEODOR APEL, LEIPZIG   Paris, 20 September 1840

My Theodor,

in a situation of which you yourself may have no conception, – & in which I regard myself, as it were, as having reached the very brink of utter ruin, it is the friend of my (alas!) lost youth to whom I turn anew, to a man who has himself been tried by the sorest of afflictions.[2] To avoid all semblance of hypocrisy, I shall begin with the most egotistical part of my letter, a section which ought properly to have come at the end but with which I shall preface this letter of mine – the *first* for many years: it is this: – *I am in the depths of misfortune, & you must help me*! – These words will fill you with a sense of gloomy bitterness. But why, oh God, – why do I feel myself capable of braving that bitterness? – How could I fail to do so when what I have to tell you is this: – for a year now, I have been living with my wife without being able to earn a single groschen, without a single pfennig to call my own. Consider what this confession means, & you will understand what it is that makes me begin my first letter to you for years in the way I have chosen. –

More than 4 years have passed since we last saw each other: – during that time *you* have gone *blind*, & *I* must begin my first letter to you in this way: – there you have a stroke of destiny sufficient for the two of us! –

Scarcely had we begun to feel that we had the whole of our lives to live for when we learned how easily we could be trampled under foot; your own career was cut short by blindness, mine by endless want. When we parted company on that last occasion & I travelled northwards, – do you know what a gloomy presentiment flashed through my mind? It was the awareness that two people were shaking hands who would never again meet in similar circumstances. My light-heartedness had long been consumed by the financial

1 The three numbers in question are generally assumed to be Senta's Ballad and the songs of the Scottish (later Norwegian) sailors and Dutchman's crew; see WWV 63. No audition took place.
2 In May 1836 Apel had suffered concussion as a result of falling from his horse; he never fully recovered and in 1838 went permanently blind.

misery that battened on my natural, sanguine resilience. My struggle was a difficult one, filled with bitter consequences, for I had to learn to *renounce* what I wanted, to fight against my very nature. None of my attempts to achieve a more lofty artistic goal met with any success; I had managed to have my opera[1] accepted in Berlin; all it needed was for me to remain there for half a year in order to keep the weak and vacillating director,[2] over whom I had, nevertheless, a certain personal influence, under constant surveillance & control; – but I was poor, no one wanted to support me. I gave it all up, just as I have subsequently given up so much else, & went to *Königsberg*, where a post had been secured for me. There I married; but indigence & hardship pursued me. I could not take up the post that had been promised me, & had to get by as best I could. – It was only then that I received news of you from someone who had recently seen you in Leipzig. From that moment onwards I knew what my foreboding had signified, though I had never believed it would meet with so cruel a fulfilment. – If ever we see each other again, you must ask my wife what sort of a person I became from that moment onwards! – How the poor woman has suffered in consequence! All cheerfulness, all freedom, all openness fled before me; I can describe my state in no better way than by telling you that this was a year in my life when I wrote scarcely a single note, conceived nothing & comprehended nothing. I was deeply unhappy! – At the end of this year of tribulation my situation improved, at least outwardly; I was appointed to a decent & honourable post as musical director in Riga. There I spent two comparatively peaceful years; I might even say that I began to recover there, were I not increasingly forced to realize that I was never intended to earn my living in such a fashion. I sought to dull my senses by dint of the most feverish activity; but I was physically incapable of leading a life to which the northern climate was so utterly unsuited. I fell seriously ill, a nervous fever which threatened to prostrate me completely. Scarcely had I begun to recover when news reached me that my supposed friend *Dorn* had taken advantage of my illness to deprive me of my post by the most perfidious of means![3] – It was terrible; but in my fevered state I sought to interpret the incident as an example of God's will, & to see in it a sign that I should not stand still but continue to strive towards my higher aim in life. I scraped together a few hundred roubles, & explained to my wife that we were going to Paris. She agreed to coming, out of her love for me, although she has never harboured exalted hopes, & foresaw the misery that lay in store. We boarded a sailing ship & after a dreadful voyage lasting 4 whole weeks, in the course of which we were thrice brought close to death by the storms, we landed in London, from where we travelled to Boulogne. By then we were

---

1 *Das Liebesverbot.*
2 Karl Friedrich Cerf.
3 Shortly before leaving Riga, the director of the theatre Karl von Holtei concluded an arrangement with Heinrich Dorn, whereby the latter succeeded Wagner as Kapellmeister.

so short of money that I thought it well-nigh impossible we should be able to survive even a few weeks in Paris. It was at that point that a quirk of fate brought me face to face with *Meyerbeer* in Boulogne; I introduced myself & my compositions to him, & he became my friend & patron. For I knew that only through the patronage of a man such as *Meyerbeer* could my affairs in Paris be expedited; I took my courage in both hands & resolved to risk the journey here. What I have encountered here in Paris, oh, what a mixture of hopes & disappointments it has been! Meyerbeer has remained untiringly loyal to my interests, – but family commitments have unfortunately obliged him to spend most of his time abroad; & since only *personal* influence is of any account here, his absence could not fail but to have the most crippling effect upon my affairs. – What keeps me going is only fresh hope, but otherwise you can easily imagine that my situation with my wife & without a penny to my name – that this situation is bound to be the most terrible one in the world. More than once I have longed for death; at least I have grown utterly indifferent to it. –

I have thought of you constantly, Theodor, with a sense of dull melancholy. I never received any detailed news of you, & what I *was* told – was terrible! – Is it true that you no longer recognized your own friends?! – I was deprived of every means of consoling you; and what could *I* have done, utterly destitute as I was! You were a friend whom I grieved for, but who no longer belonged to me! – – Then, very recently, I received circumstantial news concerning you from a woman from Leipzig, who was visiting Paris. What I heard shook me & moved me deeply, yet it also revived me & filled me with hope! I learned that your illness was purely physical in nature, & that there are excellent grounds for believing that you will recover completely. Oh, believe me, this was the only news capable of snatching me back from the abyss into which I had fallen! My informant added, by way of confirmation, that you had even published a volume of poems. You are still a poet! My poor, poor friend, – now you can sing, – you see, you have suffered the deepest anguish! Just for a moment let me drag myself out of the mire & explain to you that I, too, am still a poet, or perhaps it is only now that we have both become poets. – God, I feel at this very moment as though we were both sitting together again, gazing at some beautiful object, & that you could see once again! – – And you can see to what extent I have lived *in you*, at one *with you*; – the work I have just completed is called: *Rienzi*, the last of the Tribunes! Who was it first thought of the idea? – I believe we have worked together on it! At all events, it is the best opera I have written. – Let me tell you, (– you see, I'm beginning to prattle on again, as though nothing had happened! –) – our *Rienzi* has turned into an opera in five acts. It was half-finished when I brought it here with me to Paris; in planning it, I intended the work for performance here. But I was soon forced to realize that it could take up to 2 to 3 years before I got such a *large-scale* work performed, since I first need to make a name for myself by means of shorter operas; & so, in order that my favourite work should not be lost to the world, I resolved to complete the piece in German & write it for a German theatre. I chose Dresden; it is more or less my home town, & I have already made all kinds of advance preparations, notably with *Meyerbeer's* help, to ensure that the opera is accepted there. In addition, Dresden now has a large & worthy opera house, – Tichatschek & Devrient are well-suited to their parts; all this encourages me to hope that I shall succeed there. I shall be sending off the score in a month's time; by the beginning of next year it may even have been performed, & I shall go there in person for the occasion. – – You see, we are old friends once again; you would never have heard all this, if you had not published a volume of poems! –

You see, Theodor, these, as it were, are lightning flashes which now & again rend the night-sky all around me, but which cannot illumine the surrounding gloom, for God knows what hopes I have not already seen destroyed! I should almost prefer the certainty of death, but it seems one cannot die so quickly here. Paris is too rich, too rich in prospects & too varied for it not to be able to offer fresh hopes all the time. As a result I am once again engaged in fairly optimistic dealings with the *Grand Opera* for a 2- or 3-act opera, – "the flying Dutchman" – the draft of the scenario which I submitted has already met with the greatest approval. – What more could I hope for? –

For the present I should have liked to buy my poor wife some *medicine!* Will she survive this misery, & shall I be able to bear hers? – Lord God, help me! I no longer know how to help myself! – I have exhausted everything, everything, – every last resource of a starving man; wretch that I am, I have only now discovered what people are really like. Money – it is the curse that destroys whatever is noble; how many friends, who would otherwise have been willing to help, have grown coldly indifferent on hearing that word; my relatives turn to stone even before it has been spoken; – but merciful heavens, what is help without this most tangible of all its forms? Whoever knows true hardship must surely feel that it can be relieved by this means alone. In the past, when you made one sacrifice after another for me, I thought I already knew hardship well enough. I was a fool to regard such temporary embarrassment as hardship, I who have now learned what hardship really is. To have to use one's wife's last remaining trinket of jewelry, her last item of household use, in order to buy a crust of bread, & then to have to leave her without help, sick & suffering, because the proceeds from the wedding rings were insufficient for both bread *and* medicine, – how shall I describe this, if I have already spoken of hardship in the past! – In a word – God forgive me for it – I have cursed life itself; – could I have done worse than that? Scarcely have I regained a friend when I greet him with the words: – send me help as soon as possible; my life is in pawn, redeem it! This is how: I am writing to ask you for *three hundred thalers*, & assure you that, if you send me this sum, it will keep me going for over 8 months, as I know from the experience of the last 8 months, for I have not been able to afford anything but bread during the whole of that time. If you, too, turn your back on me, – I know what my fate will be then![1]

[. . .]

SB I,405–11.

32. HEINRICH LAUBE, LEIPZIG   Paris, 3 December 1840

Most excellent Laube,

In following your orders to the letter, I am writing to inform you that Madame Schröder-Devrient has just received the letter I sent her.[2]

The score of my opera[3] is now on its way to Dresden; it came into the world accompanied by the most dreadful pangs of childbirth; no one can imagine a more terrible time than the two days I had to face on the first and second of this unhappy month;[4] as far as was possible, the last remaining pfennigs of my poor friends here have helped me to postpone the threatened blow until the 15th; there is no doubt but that this will involve immediate seizure of my property and loss of personal liberty: I did not believe it could happen, – but I have had the narrowest of escapes; for as a foreigner I do not have the usual means of protest at my disposal. I have until that date to scrape together the necessary sum from whatever quarter I can; if there is anything you yourself can contribute – *whatever it may be*, send it without delay!

God reward you for your kindness and affection!

Your
loyal and obedient servant
Richard Wagner.

SB I,424–5.

1 Apel responded by sending Heinrich Laube six friedrichsdor (= 125 francs), together with the request that the sum be transmitted to Wagner. Laube delayed forwarding the money, hoping to be able to raise an additional sum from other sources. It was over a month before Wagner finally received the money, during which time his financial predicament was growing increasingly serious.

2 No correspondence has survived between Wagner and Wilhelmine Schröder-Devrient.

3 *Rienzi.* The full score was completed on 19 (?) November 1840 and sent off to August von Lüttichau, intendant of the Dresden Court Theatre, on 4 December 1840.

4 See introductory essay, p. 54.

33. Friedrich Brockhaus, Leipzig   [Paris, after 13 March 1841]

Most worthy Herr Brockhaus,

I am very much obliged to you for communicating to me your views on my position & upon my plan in life;[1] rest assured that I am fully capable of appreciating the level-headedness & calmness of the same, & that I, too, should have adopted some similar plan in life, right from the very outset, had I succeeded even once in being able to gain a foothold in the right place & in finding some support on which to hold. If, for example, I were to have been granted the good fortune of obtaining the position of musical director in a town such as Leipzig, I can assure you that I should never have dreamt up such a wild scheme as that of trying my luck in Paris. Even now, the certainty of a similar position could persuade me to return at once to Germany, & thus would enable me to satisfy the wish which you yourself have expressed; but for that to happen I should need to be offered a helping hand, & since I do not know of whom I might reasonably expect such help, plans of this kind must necessarily remain within the realm of fantasy.

At all events, I know that the communication of your view was well meant, & that is why I take this opportunity of expressing my gratitude to you.

The negative response to my offer to provide reports for the Leipz: All: Zeitung[2] is an aspect of your rejoinder which I find so fully & so appositely motivated that I cannot of course but agree with you; I only wish that *you* had understood me better & not considered it necessary to go to special lengths to justify your refusal to pay me an advance, since such a refusal is inevitably bound up with turning down my offer. In particular, the section of your esteemed letter in which you declare that you are unable to agree to paying me an advance until such time as the direction of my life has taken a turn more in accord with your own ideas on the subject leaves me in no doubt whatsoever that you have totally misunderstood me, inasmuch as you presumably believed that I had used my offer simply as a pretext to ask for financial help. Permit me, therefore, to enlighten you as follows as to myself & my present way of thinking: – had any such thought crossed my mind, then I should certainly have had more pressing cause to ask you for help when I really *was* on the brink of utter ruin, when I & my wife were literally without bread, & when, in order to obtain some few days' supply, we were reduced to measures of which you can really have no conception, & when, in dread of heart, I saw myself driven to take a step which you at any rate have found out about & which, the very next day when I was somewhat calmer, I myself

---

1 Wagner had appealed to his brother-in-law for help in the winter of 1839/40, but Brockhaus had replied that any help he might offer was dependent upon Wagner's first finding a job in Germany. See *Mein Leben*, 226; English trans. 215.

2 Friedrich Brockhaus was co-editor of the *Leipziger Allgemeine Zeitung*.

could not conceive how I could ever have been driven into taking.[1] The fact that, at a time when I was motivated by necessity's law of invention, it did not occur to me to appeal to you for support, may be a guarantee, my most worthy Herr Brockhaus, that I should [*scil.* not] have seen myself driven to making a similar appeal now, at a time when you appear sufficiently well apprised of my situation to express your pleasure at the greater satisfaction to which my present situation appears to entitle me. – I believe that in my last letter I gave you even less cause to hold such a mistaken opinion, since I recall intentionally having couched it in terms which were far from calculated to arouse sympathy but rather to depict my offer simply as a business trans-action. This, too, was something I was persuaded to do by a somewhat hastily offered piece of advice on the part of Dr Laube, & I confess that, left to myself, I should probably never have thought of such an idea, since I know well enough how contrary to your nature it is to have dealings with anyone whose direction in life, whether it find its true outlet in France or in Germany, in a fixed or independent post, fails to conform to your own views on the subject, especially when you believe that, directly or indirectly, you are being importuned for financial support.

Your counter-offer to accept occasional reports on various matters of outstanding interest is one which I take up all the more gladly in that I see in it a suitable means of setting about a gradual repayment of my debt to you, – which, if I am not mistaken, must amount to something in excess of 170 thalers, & whose cash repayment is something which I certainly could not contemplate at the moment.

May I finally ask you to pass on my kindest regards to Luise to whom I owe my sincere thanks for the interest which she recently showed in me in her letter to Cäcilie, & who, if I were to make some urgent appeal to her, would treat the affair – which is now at an end – simply as a *business transaction*, of which you no doubt have many similar ones to attend to every day.

Kindly accept my thanks for communicating your views to me & rest assured of the especial devotion of your most respectful brother-in-law

Wagner, v (1984), 11–13.

34. FRANZ LISZT, PARIS   Paris, 24 March 1841

Dear Sir,

If I make so bold as to importune you with these lines, then I must begin by appealing to the great kindness which you showed me during your last

---

1 See introductory essay, p. 54.

brief visit to Paris, in the late autumn of last year, when Herr Schlesinger introduced me to you in passing. There is, however, a further circumstance which encourages me to take this present step of mine: my friend, the writer Heinrich *Laube*, wrote to me last summer from Carlsbad to tell me that he had there made the acquaintance of one of your countrymen who had boasted of being your friend; – he had spoken to this gentleman about me & my plans, & enlisted his sympathies to the extent that he had, of his own accord, promised to recommend me to *you*, since he was on the point of travelling to another watering-place, where he was certain of meeting you.

You see, dear Sir, on what remote & uncertain connections I see myself forced to pin my most sanguine hopes; you see how anxiously I chase after feeble possibilities in the hope of encountering some stroke of inestimable good fortune. – Could – or might – that promise be fulfilled? – My permanently unlucky star almost forbids me from believing it. But I owed it to myself to ask the question, & I would initially beg for but *a single* sign: Yes! or No![1]

In deepest admiration

Your
most obedient servant
Richard Wagner,
25, Rue du Helder.

SB I,460–1.

35. FERDINAND HEINE, DRESDEN   Paris, 27 March 1841

[. . .] Kietz has mentioned on a number of occasions that you would like to hear my views on Berlioz & the modern French school of music associated with him. I intend writing an article on the subject for the Abendzeitung;[2] I hope you will permit me on this occasion, therefore, to say only a few things about the personal impression which my acquaintance with Berlioz has left on me. The first piece of his that I heard was his *Romeo & Juliet* symphony,[3] in which the insipidity of the work's outward economy violently repelled me, for all the composer's evident genius. The truth is that Berlioz is so totally isolated among French musicians that, deprived as he is of the necessary

1 Liszt invited Wagner to visit him at the hotel where he was staying in Paris, and sent him a complimentary ticket for his forthcoming concert.
2 This was the third of Wagner's reports to the Dresden *Abend-Zeitung;* it is reprinted in SS XII,87–95.
3 Berlioz's dramatic symphony *Roméo et Juliette* was first performed in the Salle du Conservatoire in Paris on 24 November 1839 and repeated a week later. It is not known which of the two performances Wagner attended.

point of support, he is obliged to grope around in some fantastic wilderness, so that it is extremely difficult, perhaps even impossible, for him to develop his prodigious powers along lines that are consistent with *beauty*. He is, & remains, an isolated phenomenon, though he is French in the fullest sense of the word. We Germans are fortunate; for we have our Mozart & Beethoven in our blood, & know how our pulses should beat. But Berlioz has no precursor, he is condemned to an eternal fever. None the less, we in Germany do Berlioz the most flagrant disservice if we imagine him, without the least justification, as a charlatan. On the contrary, his outward appearance is strangely at odds with his inner genius. What he has to give comes from his innermost depths, he is inwardly consumed, & is the only French composer who doesn't grow fat on his own success. His is a highly poetical nature, which is all the more remarkable in that he is so very much a Frenchman in every other respect, & can express himself only in the most total extremes. It is only quite recently that I have sorted out my views on Berlioz, – in fact, not until about 3 months ago, when I heard his *Symfonie Fantastique*.[1] But at the same time I discovered that what justifies his eccentric means of outward expression is to be found in the seductive powers of the orchestra for which he writes; he has felt himself involuntarily misled into turning instrumental music into a form of virtuosity. – Vieuxtemps[2] does exactly the same sort of thing, but by different means, inasmuch as he begins at the opposite extreme. He reduces the element of virtuosity, & if I were to venture a view on Vieuxtemps' later works, it is that I foresee them as part of a reductive process, so that his triumph will consist in his *returning* to an original state of chastely pure beauty. Progress & expansion are not something we should look for in Vieuxtemps; his achievements will always be of a negative value. He lacks the *passion* to write creatively; he is only 20 but is already a man; he has had no youth; the realm of presentiment is unknown to him, all he sees around him is daylight, & that is why he is incapable of feeling the rapture of warmth. But he has no choice in the matter if he is to complete the task that is set him, a task which he feels quite clearly & which he solves with complete & calm awareness. Natures such as his must be regarded as wise emissaries of providence, and must be all the stronger in that they have to combat enthusiasm. Vieuxtemps' name is altogether characteristic. His last concerto is a beautiful piece, I should have found it even more edifying if I could have detected a greater intensity in its motifs. You have no need to fear the influence of Berlioz's music on him, for Vieuxtemps is already fully mature & conscious in all that he does. It is possible that you imagine the turmoil of Paris to be more confused & seductive than it actually is. Berlioz, as I say, is

1 First performed under Habeneck on 5 December 1830.
2 Henry Vieuxtemps (1820–1881), the celebrated Belgian virtuoso violinist and composer, was a childhood friend of Wagner's companion Ernst Benedikt Kietz, and was on one occasion entertained at the Wagners' rooms in Paris.

utterly isolated; – the greatest evil here is the rampant superficiality to which every composer surrenders in his quest for public approval; everyone sacrifices his inner worth to it & grows insipid out of a sense of conviction. Even so, I must admit that the dramatic music of the French far surpasses that of the Germans. I was horrified to come across a handful of German operas here by Reissiger, Lobe etc. Is it possible that the views of German composers concerning the art of melody & song are so misguided that they believe they must always give priority to melodic needs, so that even the most ordinary conversational phrases such as "How are you?" & "Where have you come from?" are spun out along thematic lines, producing an apparent continuum of sound where the nature of the thing demands short, pithy strokes? – The melodious outpourings are, of course, just as one would expect; the result is what we aptly call "note-spinning" & a vocal line that turns into mere *singsong*. Dramatic truth is completely lost sight of, & however much the French may become bogged down in a thousand flirtatious details, they nevertheless know where to stop, using a short stroke that is not susceptible to further development.

But I can see that I'm beginning to get carried away. Forgive me for prattling on like this! I am one of those people who always imagines that a question has been put to him, which is why I for ever end up offering uncalled-for opinions.

[. . .]

SB I,465–7.

36. Theodor Winkler, Dresden   Meudon, 1 June 1841

[. . .] Since you have kindly agreed to accept any contributions I might write for the Abendzeitung & since, in the present unmusical season, my only means of making ends meet is through belletristic endeavours whose interest remains valid for all seasons, I am sending you herewith a kind of literary novelette,[1] or rather two interconnected short stories, which, if I am not mistaken, may perhaps be of some interest to readers of your newspaper, too. Moreover, you will discover from the second of these short stories the sort of fate which generally befalls poor musicians here in Paris; and if I may flatter myself with the prospect of a somewhat better fate than the one reserved for the hero of my novelette, it is because there are periods when I am obliged

---

1 *Eine Pilgerfahrt zu Beethoven* (A Pilgrimage to Beethoven) and *Ein Ende in Paris* (An End in Paris). They first appeared in French in the *Revue et Gazette musicale* between 19 November 1840 and 11 February 1841, and were published in Winkler's *Abend-Zeitung* between 30 July and 11 August 1841. See also GS I,90–136; PW VII, 21–68.

occasionally to look eastwards in search of a protecting hand. These periods most often occur during the summer months especially, when a vast lull overtakes the flood of sound that is produced by the Paris Ocean. I have discovered that it only makes things worse during these sultry periods to try to ignore the effects of such scorching calm on my hearth & home. I should have preferred it if I could have avoided mentioning that most contemptible of all questions – the question of money – in a relationship in which I am already so deeply indebted to you, my most honoured Sir; indeed, I had flattered myself that, whatever happened, I should be able to avoid all reference to it; – but a cruel trick that has been played on my present expectations unfortunately obliges me to cast my gaze eastwards once more, & – as fate would have it – it is upon you that my gaze has fallen! On the whole, my request is of the kind you presumably meet with every day; but it is none the less with a certain distaste that I trespass so roughly & clumsily upon our tender relations; yet I have no choice in the matter, if I am to entreat you to be so kind as to forward to me a moderate advance on the articles which I am enclosing herewith & on others still to be delivered. [. . .]

SB I,493–4.

37. GOTTFRIED ENGELBERT ANDERS, PARIS   Meudon, 17 June 1841

My dear Anders,

The time has come when I must decide whether I can obtain a piano through your kind mediation and under favourable terms, or whether I must incur the onerous expense of hiring one.[1] In view of the fact that I did not find you at home when I called yesterday, I assume that you are feeling somewhat better (– upon which I congratulate you most heartily –) and at least are able to leave the house; and this fact, coupled with the fine weather we are enjoying today, encourages me to beg you most earnestly to obtain a piano for me *today*, so that there is a good chance of my receiving it by tomorrow. You know the kind of instrument I would like to have, – make sure that it is a powerful one and as good a quality as possible, for I have noticed that a better instrument inspires me more than a bad one does, and in that way is more likely to inculcate in me a taste for music, which I otherwise *detest*. – [. . .]

SB I,603.

---

1 Anders was presumably unable to supply an instrument, since Wagner mentions in *Mein Leben* (212; English trans. 201) that the hiring of a piano was the first major expense to be met out of the 500 francs received on 5 July 1841 for the *Hollandais volant* sketch.

38. FRIEDRICH WILHELM VON REDERN, BERLIN

[Meudon,] 27 June 1841

My Lord Redern,

May I entreat Your Excellency most humbly to deign to consider the following request concerning an opera of my own composition for which I herewith solicit the honour of a first performance at the Royal Court Theatre in Berlin. It is a relatively short opera, entitled "The flying Dutchman", or rather it is not intended to fill a whole evening in the theatre, but to be given with a short ballet or a short play. The text of the same will be sent to Your Excellency, in accordance with my instructions, in a few days' time, and no asseverations on my part will be necessary to assure Your Excellency how fortunate I should deem myself if both the basic idea of the libretto and the manner of its execution were to seem worthy of your approval.

Since, for the rest, I cannot but suppose that my name as a composer is as yet unknown to Your Excellency, I believe that it would not be prejudicial to my interests to refer Your Excellency to Herr G. Meyerbeer who, as far as I know, is at present staying in Berlin[1] and to whom I have the inestimable good fortune of being known personally. I may flatter myself that Herr Meyerbeer will not refuse Your Excellency any information that you may desire. Should this information prove to be such that Your Excellency could then decide to accord me the honour I have sought for my opera, I would entreat Your Excellency most humbly to assign its performance to the autumn of this year, for which purpose I would then submit the full score of the work, which I intend to have completed by the end of the summer.[2]

In commending myself most respectfully to Your Excellency's inestimable favour, I take the liberty of beseeching Your Excellency most humbly to accept the assurance of the profound admiration with which I venture to sign myself

Your Excellency's
most devoted servant,
Richard Wagner.

SB I,497–8.

---

1 Meyerbeer had arrived in Berlin on 26 May.
2 The full score was not completed until 19 (?) November 1841. It was sent off the following day to Berlin, and accepted on Meyerbeer's recommendation.

39. ERNST BENEDIKT KIETZ, PARIS [Paris, 5 July 1841]

Dear Kietz, – Berlioz has not obtained a ticket for me;[1] – as a result I shall not be remaining in town & shall not be spending the night at your place. I have put my affairs in the hands of God & Meyerbeer,[2] – here are 50 fr. to be going on with, – it's an additional sum I have managed to get hold of, – how? I'll tell you when I next see you[3] – go easy on the pederasty!

Yours,
Richard Wagner.

SB I,500.

40. ERNST BENEDIKT KIETZ, PARIS [Meudon, 8 July 1841]

His Excellency, Baron von Lüttichau, Marshal to the Royal Court, has written to me & formally announced the definitive acceptance of my opera Rienzi by the Dresden Court Theatre.

I thought this might interest you!

Richard Wagner.

SB I,500.

41. JOSEPH TICHATSCHEK, DRESDEN [Meudon, 6/7 September 1841]

[. . .] I assume you will have heard by now that the General Administration of the Dresden Court Theatre recently accepted for performance there a grand opera in 5 acts, written by myself & entitled "Rienzi". In the letter which accompanied the submission at the end of last year, I spoke openly & positively of the reasons which made it so eminently desirable for *this* particular opera to receive its first performance in Dresden. As an *artist* I consider the most important of these reasons to be the fact that the opera's success lies principally in the best possible casting of the 2 main roles, (&

---

1 At the request of Léon Pillet, Berlioz had prepared Weber's *Der Freischütz* for production at the Opéra, composing recitatives and arranging music by Weber himself as a ballet. Since Wagner had already condemned the enterprise in the *Revue et Gazette musicale* of 23 and 30 May 1841 (while acknowledging that Berlioz was the best equipped of composers to undertake such an edition), Berlioz's failure to provide him with a complimentary ticket is not surprising. *Le Freischütz* opened on 7 June 1841, and Wagner reported on the production in the Dresden *Abend-Zeitung* of 20 June. His apparent failure to attend on 5 July did not prevent him from filing another report, dated 6 July 1841, in the *Abend-Zeitung*.
2 Wagner here parodies the German chorale "Ich hab' mein' Sach' Gott heimgestellt".
3 Presumably from the sale of the prose draft of *Le Hollandais volant*.

in no other theatre in the world do I know artists whom I would be more justified in expecting to fulfil the boldest wishes which I entertain for the success of the opera than Mad. Schr. Dev.[1] & you yourself – my very dear Sir.

[. . .] Although I should of course be sensible of the fact that what I have placed before you is not entirely unworthy, I am nevertheless certain that what most concerns the performing artist is quite often the uniqueness of his own particular talent & his individual temperament, which must be taken into account just as much as the general truths of art itself. The figure of *Rienzi*, as I imagined him & attempted to depict him, should be a hero in the full sense of the word, – a visionary dreamer who has appeared like some beacon of light among a depraved & degenerate nation whom he sees it as his calling to enlighten & raise up. It is an historical fact that Rienzi was a young man of about 28[2] at the time he carried out this great undertaking; this – together with my particular views on the multifarious character of the tenor voice has persuaded me to write the part for a tenor, although in doing so I have stepped outside the circle of received opinion which insists that the tenor voice is appropriate solely to the character of a lover.

[. . .]

SB I,506–7.

42. JOHANNA ROSINE GEYER, LEIPZIG   Meudon, 12 September 1841

[. . .] Every individual who wishes to attain to true – inner and outer – autonomy should, as far as this is consistent with his innate sense of right and wrong, pursue the course which his more serious inclination and a certain irresistible inner urge bid him take. The world will readily forgive him the sufferings he brings down upon himself in this way, for it requires no great generosity on their part to do so; but only the person who would wish to alleviate that suffering has the right to offer advice, – and if, in spite of everything, he is *not* able to alleviate it, he must put up with seeing his advice ignored in the end. I am certainly not one of those people who are stubborn and unyielding by nature, on the contrary I am justifiably reproached for having too feminine a fickleness of mind. But I believe I have sufficient perseverance not to abandon a thing once begun until I am fully convinced of its true nature. Thus it was with Paris: – I am now firmly convinced that

1 Wilhelmine Schröder-Devrient, who created the role of Adriano.
2 In fact Cola di Rienzi was 34 in 1347. More significantly, Wagner himself was 28 at the time *Rienzi* was accepted for performance in Dresden.

it is utterly impossible for me to succeed there, at least as long as I am thrown back upon my own resources in fighting this particular battle. [. . .]

SB I,517.

43. FERDINAND HEINE, DRESDEN   [Paris, January 1842]

[. . .] So – *Rienzi* is in hand. Thank God for that, I shall always be grateful to my dear & excellent friends. Merciful heavens, how insignificant this or that depressing experience concerning the unreliability of this or that individual now seems when set beside such demonstrations of the most unselfish & undeserved self-sacrifice on the part of so many noble friends such as you & Fischer! I am reconciled to all the other million inhabitants of this earth if I can number two such excellent fellows as my friends! I can well imagine what a struggle it was! I still do not know what to make of Baron von Lüttichau's remarkable change of attitude:[1] but I think it would be best not to ascribe it to any malevolent influence: it strikes me as entirely natural that this gentleman should begin to harbour doubts about my opera, – what a man like Herr Lüttichau cannot grasp & feel, he does not consider himself justified in believing. Winkler wrote to say that Meyerbeer was expected in Berlin, & that he intended persuading him to badger Herr Lüttichau on my behalf. Did anything come of this?[2] You did not say a word about Reissiger; how are things with him? Do you suspect him? To be honest – Reissiger's position – as both opera composer & conductor – is a matter of genuine & serious concern: he may be the best fellow in the world, but he could still succumb to the temptation to jeopardize the chances of even an imaginary rival. I shall have to behave very diplomatically towards him: if he is genuinely well-disposed towards me, I should be heartily glad of it, & shall certainly not *feign* friendship in return; & I should be genuinely sorry if my diplomacy were to run counter to my true feelings towards him. Herr Lewy, who has been in Paris for the last week & who will probably be leaving us today, spoke of Reissiger, his opera[3] & so on most respectfully & favourably; – but yesterday – as it seemed (– & as I flatter myself –) on a friendly impulse he recommended that I treat Reissiger with great circumspection: – without wishing to be too personal, he said he felt obliged to consider Reissiger weak-

---

1 Wagner blamed Lüttichau for the repeated delays that were preventing *Rienzi* from reaching the stage.

2 Meyerbeer was in Dresden, on family business, between 29 December 1841 and 3 January 1842. He saw Winkler soon after his arrival in the city, and on Sunday, 2 January, visited Lüttichau.

3 *Adèle de Foix*, first performed in Dresden on 26 November 1841.

willed & lacking any firmness of character: – he warned me & recommended most insistently that I should go to Dresden *sooner* rather than later, in order to be present & see for myself. It goes without saying that I shall come to the performance of my opera & in any event shall arrive about a week early: I shall then see what is going on, and hope that your friendly advice may be sufficient to guide me. – –

All that I have heard from various quarters concerning the beauty of the Dresden Theatre, its splendid furnishings, its admirable band & the excellence of its ensemble fills me with a great sense of joy. If Herr Fischer remains unflinchingly loyal to me (as I have every reason to hope), then I certainly have cause to look forward to the performance with keen anticipation.

The thoughtful and conscientious way in which you intend costuming my opera, and which indeed has long been your intention, is an amiable demonstration of your great kindness: as far as these points are concerned, it is clear that, for my own part, I need have no further worries, – for I know that I am in the best of hands! But how do things stand with the scenery? Much of it will have to be built specially,[1] & even though the Dresden stage sets are in good condition, so that it would be senseless of me to demand that the existing stock should not be put to the appropriate use, there are none the less some individual sets, e.g. (Act I) the church of St John Lateran in the background, (Act IV) the same in the foreground & to one side, (Act II) the view of Rome through the main door, & (Act V) the Capitol itself in the background, which cannot be adequately & *characterfully* assembled without new & additional sets being provided. Is anyone thinking about this and working on it? –

My more detailed comments on the performance which I sent to Herr Fischer will in any case have been passed on to you; unfortunately I fear that my suggestions there will not be sufficient. In view of your earlier report, I had expected Herr Fischer to take upon himself the task of working out some scheme for shortening my opera: – this would definitely have been the best, the most expedient & most speedy solution; a judicious & intelligent outsider is in a far better position to do this sort of thing adequately than the author himself, who is naturally very biassed in his own favour. The cuts which I suggested will have little effect on the overall length, and I am afraid that they have often been made in a clumsy & detrimental fashion. – I would therefore ask Herr Fischer to undertake a further series of cuts according to *his own judgement*. – I shall be satisfied with whatever he does. – The best solution as regards shortening the work would be to tackle the *ballet*: if the number & sequence of the individual dances is to be retained as indicated in

1 It was normal practice at this time to use existing sets in staging new works.

my recent letter, I suggest that they all be duly shortened, which will also make them easier to stage.

The ballet should be less of an actual dance, i.e. dancers waving their legs in the air, since this sort of thing is profoundly repugnant to me – even when performed to perfection as it is here in Paris. – The warlike ceremonial dance (Act II) is performed for the most part by soldiers, & the great dance at the end should be more of a festive *round* with groupings & only brief intermittent solos by the male & female dancers. In this way we shall best avoid exposing the *partie honteuse* of the Dresden Court Ballet. But I am still very much attached to the idea of the *pantomime*, & if, as I hope, the opera is performed in Berlin, it (the pantomime) must unquestionably be included, since it would look very odd if it were omitted in Dresden, particularly in view of the fact that it is easier to present than the ballet itself (given the shortcomings of the latter); three or four good actors can surely be found, & that is all that is needed. The question is whether there are 3–4 actors in Dresden who would *enjoy* becoming involved. I discussed the matter with Lewy: he was of the opinion that this type of pantomime is something new to Dresden, and he encouraged me, among other things, to pay a brief visit to Dresden in order to obtain the 3–4 actors I need by dint of personal persuasion. But I have no reason to set any great store by *personal influence*, & am convinced that other means would certainly be more appropriate here. What does *Herr Fischer* say to this? What do you yourself think?

How have the parts been cast? Have my suggestions been taken into account as suitable & sensible? The casting of Fräulein *Marx* in the role of Irene is something which, as the author of the piece, I do not like in the least; a *laughing coloratura soprano*, as I can well imagine the lady to be, will stand out like a sore thumb: I really cannot see where she will find the opportunity to show off her *roulades*, – & where it might occur to *her* to introduce them, I should be certain to object most violently. In fact I imagined Rienzi's sister to be a very touching, *noble* young girl, & am counting on her a good deal in the final act; Fräulein *Wüst* (– apart from her height –) would have been ideal;[1] if Mme Devrient would also prefer this arrangement, perhaps we should see what can still be done to give the part to Fräulein Wüst; – but if Mme Devrient has no strong views on the matter, if the part has already been allotted to Fräulein Marx, & if changes cannot be made without incurring great hostility & possibly with unfortunate repercussions, – I suppose that things will have to be left as they are! – You must be the judge and act in my name as you think fit!

I refuse to back down on a single point as regards the musical pomp on stage; it is far too necessary & in Dresden can be perfectly well staged with the help of the military & other music corps. My demands, admittedly, are

1 Henriette Wüst sang the part of Irene at the first performance of *Rienzi*.

unusual: I require an exceptional body of men, not some ad hoc arrangement assembled after the fashion of our ordinary brass bands; & yet it should be possible to assemble such a group, – especially if Reissiger is well-disposed to the idea. See to it that in the first act the trumpeters & trombonists accompanying Colonna's and Orsini's military expedition are taken from the cavalry & that they ride on horseback: – this is bound to look splendid and characterful (at least that is how I imagine it), & is certainly feasible on the Dresden stage.

The management must not stint any effort or expense here, – with opera like mine, it is a case of *"Either – Or"* – you understand me! –

[. . .]

SB I,585–9.

44. ROBERT SCHUMANN, LEIPZIG   Paris, 5 [February][1] 1842

Most honoured friend,

It grieves me deeply to have taken so long to answer your esteemed letter, and, although I shall attempt to make good that deficiency now, I regret to say that I am not in a position to meet your wishes entirely. Firstly: – although reports have recently reached me from Dresden informing me that, after countless delays, there is no longer sufficient time, before Schröder-Devrient goes on leave, for my opera to have been *properly* rehearsed and performed by then, for which reason it will not now be produced until *after* Schröder-Devrient's return (i.e. this coming August or September),[2] – although – as I say – the immediate reason for my journey thus falls to the ground, I have none the less not altered my plans in this regard, but shall be leaving Paris this coming March,[3] in order to see my German homeland again for the first time in six years, and at the same time to allow my wife to take the waters at Töplitz.[4] I shall remain in Germany at least until the autumn, and shall probably not return to Paris until next winter. In the circumstances I am afraid that I cannot take up your kind offer concerning reports from Paris; I have, however, done what I can to find another correspondent & have discussed the matter with *Anders*, a co-editor on the *Gazette musicale*, and an *employé* at the Library. He is not only an extremely erudite musician, he also

---

1 Wagner's own dating of "5 Jan. 1842" is probably an error for "5 February 1842": see note 5, p. 89 below. On the same day, Wagner similarly misdated a letter to Wilhelm Fischer: see SB I,594.
2 Further delays followed, and *Rienzi* was finally produced on 20 October 1842.
3 Wagner and his wife left Paris on 7 April 1842.
4 i.e. Teplitz. The spa is now in Czechoslovakia and called Teplice.

wields an eloquent pen; unfortunately, his somewhat advanced age (he is 50)[1] means that he has grown somewhat indolent and irresolute, and the only way to persuade him to make regular contributions would be the payment of a regular and fixed honorarium, which I myself – I may add – would have declined to accept. If this friend of mine is acceptable to you, I would ask you to be so kind as to write to him, making a firm and definite offer: since he himself is not a composer, you will find in him a wholly impartial and independent reviewer. His address is G. E. Anders, Rue de Seine St. Germain No 59, Hôtel de France.

I ought really to have made a point of sending you at least a couple more articles, but circumstances have made it impossible for me to do so. I have had to take over a whole pile of subsistence work for *Schlesinger* which, particularly if I intend completing it by March, literally leaves me without a moment's free time. But in order to show you that I had the best of intentions, I am enclosing herewith some notes which I had begun: [...]

And so, to be brief and to the point:[2] Halévy's *Reine de Chypre* is not bad, some parts of it are attractive, but there is a good deal that is trivial – taken as a whole the work has no special significance. The criticism that it is noisy is unjust; he hits the nail on the head in the 4th act (at least by contemporary standards), for the rest there is a noticeable attempt throughout the work to achieve simplicity, especially in the instrumentation. – Do not forget that *Halévy* is not well-to-do. He assures me that, if he were, he would never again write anything for the theatre, but would concentrate instead upon symphonies, oratorios & the like; because at the Opéra he is enslaved by the interests of the director and the singers, and obliged to write intentionally inferior stuff. – He is open and honest, and not a premeditatedly cunning trickster like Meyerbeer.[3] But you must not be rude about Meyerbeer! He is my protector and – joking apart – an amiable person.

[...]

We Germans delude ourselves dreadfully about the liberal tastes of Paris audiences, their apparent fairness, & so on. But Paris is large; why should one not be able to find 200 people who can acquire a taste for Beethoven's symphonies at the Conservatoire? But the real opera public only understands the *cancan*, which in German means refined filth *lacking in warmth and passion* (which is what makes it so shocking)–. In heaven's name, consider Berlioz: this man has been so utterly ruined by France, or rather by *Paris*, that it is no longer possible to tell what he might have achieved in Germany on the

1 *recte* 46; nothing came of the following proposal.
2 The following report, with various changes, appeared pseudonymously in Schumann's *Neue Zeitschrift für Musik* on 22 February 1842.
3 This is the first of Wagner's explicitly critical remarks about Meyerbeer *qua* composer. Schumann altered the word "trickster" to "rogue", abbreviated "Meyerbeer" to "M.", and deleted the following two sentences.

strength of his talent. I used to like him because he possesses a thousand things which mark him out as an *artist*: if only he had become a complete buffoon, being only half of one he is insufferable – and most dreadful of all – infinitely tedious. Not long ago he gave a concert which systematically drove people insane. Those who had not already been driven mad with boredom and *dégout* certainly had been by the end of the apotheosis of his July Symphony[1] – but out of *joy*; that is the remarkable thing: in this last movement there are passages so magnificent and sublime that they can *never* be surpassed. – In all this Berlioz is completely isolated in Paris. Public taste in Paris has sunk immeasurably: cast your mind back to the time of *Boyldieu's* Woman in White[2] – *Auber's* Locksmith and Mason,[3] Silent Woman[4] etc., and compare them with what is being produced now – *Adam* etc. At the Opéra-Comique it is simply dreadful: Auber's tawdry formulas make up the kind of system that is practised today by such young composers as Thomas, Clapisson etc. Everywhere you look you find the most appalling apathy. –

It is the *Italians* who are *chiefly* to blame for debasing what was once the attractive French style of the Opéra-Comique: they are idolized and imitated unquestioningly. The *couplets* which were once so attractive have become a worthless and utterly tuneless clattering of three quavers to a bar, or else they imitate Italian *sentimentalism* (!). But Italian *sentimentalism* is a real calamity, since it misleads even honest people: all they are concerned about is the singers' execution, so that in the end even the composer becomes a member of the audience, applauding the singers and forgetting that it was he who wrote the music in the first place. – This is the story of the Stabat Mater[5] in a nutshell; week in, week out it is performed at the Italian Opera, with Italians singing it, which is what makes it acceptable – it is *fashionable*. To sum up: all that matters here is *virtuosity*! *Liszt* plays the part of the fool here just as well as *Duprez* does on stage. Everything that looms into sight on the Parisian horizon, however good it may be – becomes inferior and foolish: think of Berlioz. – I hear that Mendelssohn is rumoured to have been commissioned to write an opera for Paris: if Mendelssohn is mad enough to accept the

1 Berlioz's *Grande symphonie funèbre et triomphale*, written in memory of the victims of the July Revolution of 1830, was performed in procession on 28 July 1840; the work was subsequently performed in concerts given in the Salle Vivienne on 7 and 14 August 1840, and 1 and 15 February 1842.

2 *La Dame blanche*, opera by François-Adrien Boieldieu, first produced in Paris on 10 December 1825.

3 *Le Maçon*, opera by Daniel-François-Esprit Auber, first performed in Paris on 3 May 1825.

4 *La Muette de Portici*, opera by Auber, first performed in Paris on 29 February 1828.

5 *Stabat Mater* by Gioacchino Rossini, first performed in its original version on Good Friday 1833 in Madrid, and in a revised version at the Théâtre-Italien, Paris, on 7 January 1842. It is the wave of fourteen performances that same season in the revised version to which Wagner refers here and which suggests the redating of this letter proposed in note 1, p. 87. Wagner's irreverent article on the work had already appeared in the *Neue Zeitschrift für Musik* on 28 December 1841. It was reprinted in GS I,186–93; PW VII, 142–9.

commission, he is much to be pitied; my own view is that he is not even capable of achieving a popular success with an opera in Germany; he is too much of an intellectual and totally lacking in any *great passion*; how will he be received in Paris? – If only he had seen *Der Freischütz!*[1] – How happy we should be if we could break *completely* free from Paris! It has had its Grande Epoque, which, admittedly, had a good and salutary effect upon us. But that is now a thing of the past, and we must renounce our faith in Paris! – There is probably no longer any need for me to remind you of this –.

[...]

In the end I have covered a whole sheet of paper, and cannot help wondering whether, had I done it differently, it would have been any better. You have neither a letter nor a report. Forgive me.

If, as long as I am still in Paris, I find further opportunity to write anything sensible for you, you may count upon my doing so. In the mean time I would ask for your indulgence, and assure you of the amiable regard with which I am

> Your most obedient servant,
> Richard Wagner.

[...]

SB I,573–9.

45. ERNST BENEDIKT KIETZ, PARIS   Dresden, 12 May 1842

[...] I remained here for a few days[2] before going on to *Berlin*, & although I have not yet met Küstner, the new intendant, I nevertheless had a number of useful meetings with Meyerbeer, Mendelssohn, Redern, Rellstab etc. *Count Redern* was most friendly & I learned that my opera[3] has been accepted here not simply out of consideration for Meyerbeer, but after it had been subjected to a thorough scrutiny by the resident critics of the Royal Prussian Court Opera;[4] this is very important for me in my relationship with Küstner: the affair, it may be added, cost me 4 valuable days in an inn. I then returned to Leipzig, & delayed there a few days, but only because of money matters;

1 See letter [39], p. 82, note 1.
2 Wagner and Minna arrived in Dresden on 12 April 1842. His visit to Berlin lasted from 19 to 26 April.
3 *Der fliegende Holländer.*
4 The resident producer of the Berlin Court Opera, Karl August Baron von Lichtenstein, complained that the opera belonged to the "genre of operatic horror stories full of magic and ghosts", and objected to a number of musical and dramaturgical aspects of the work. His objections were apparently overruled by a report drawn up by the Kapellmeister Carl Wilhelm Henning, who described the opera as being "as brilliant as it is original", and by the personal intervention of Meyerbeer, who discussed the work with Redern on 7 December 1841.

things have come to a head, but in a way that is really most welcome to me. My two sisters Luise & Ottilie, & my brother-in-law Hermann Brockh, had discussed my affairs among themselves, & decided to make over to me, from their own income, the sum of 30 thalers a month over a period of 6 months: this suits me very well, since it does not involve any third parties, & the money will, on the whole, be sufficient to meet my most pressing needs. I should in any case have *had* to accept this offer, since there was no other way open to me to obtain a loan of any size. You won't believe how much things have changed: the 100 friends I had when I was last here no longer exist, or else they have grown so distant that I could not count upon them in such matters. I have not yet met Laube, he is out of town. You may infer from all this the present state of my finances, & whether I am in a position to manage without a single thaler: – but that's enough of money matters for now! – To resume. – Back in Dresden, I was fully occupied doing the rounds of local dignitaries; everywhere I went, I was received as a man of standing: Lüttichau has once & for all left instructions for me to be given excellent seats whenever my wife & I present ourselves at the box-office etc. *Reissiger* welcomed me with the most unexpected cordiality, kissed me profusely, & immediately played me his new mass; I have been assured on all sides that he has never expressed himself so well disposed towards a new opera as he has towards mine. *Winkler*, well, that goes without saying. – *Tichatschek* (– a singer, incidentally, very much of the kind that I need: admirable –) has shown great enthusiasm for my work, & congratulated me especially on the fact that I shall be here for the rehearsals; he says that although Reissiger is admirably disposed towards me, he is *very* lazy. *Heine* I found very much as I had hoped: he is a kind & affectionate man, & has a sound education into the bargain: – only to *him* could I take my wife. Both she & I were much taken with Mme Heine, & a warm friendship may well be the outcome. My opera is now due to be taken in hand at the beginning of July & it should be performed at the end of August;[1] Heine himself assures me that August is a good month inasmuch as visitors from all the surrounding health resorts pour into Dresden at about this time, with the result that news of my opera will be broadcast across half the world. However that may be, I still think that it will be delayed until the end of September. – [. . .]

[. . .] I may add that my regret at leaving Paris has grown a little less keen, not least as a result of your letter: my friends – that is a different story; otherwise, what I now regret is simply that my friends did not leave Paris with me, – for all its good points, Paris for people like *us* is no more than a resplendent grave in which our youthful energies ebb away, untapped. The devil take it! – This is something I would scarcely have admitted a week ago: the first impression you feel on returning from Paris to any of our larger cities

1 See letter [44], p. 87, note 2.

is dreadful; it is almost impossible to say why this should be so, – but I imagine it must be comparable to what a fish feels on leaving the great ocean & finding itself in a small river: it's true that it still breathes the same water, but the waves, the billowing movement, the immensity of the element, – everything becomes small & pitiful – & yet, basically, it is still the same water, only our imagination reveals to us the depths & breadths which essentially have nothing to do with our own course. – – Here – I feel – is my *homeland*, this is where I belong, & my only desire is to have my friends here with me, since all that has made them dear to me is similarly a part of this homeland. What do you have there? Hunger & – – inducements, yes, but let it be in Germany that you accomplish all that you feel induced to do. Whenever I find myself growing too much enamoured of Paris, all I need do is pick up the latest issue of the Gazette musicale: my love for the place vanishes in an instant – the devil take it! – [. . .]

SB II,82–8.

46. ERNST BENEDIKT KIETZ, PARIS   Teplitz, 13 June/1 July 1842

[. . .] I began by appealing to Schletter,[1] explained your situation with some warmth & in some detail, & found in him a sympathetic listener. He took your case to heart, & he was certainly not looking for lame excuses when he asked to have time to think the matter over. But Schletter is not the millionaire people say he is, & his inclination to do good is hampered by the fact that he is overwhelmed by requests for money: people expect him to make sacrifices far in excess of his means: this is a fact; every day he receives on average between 2 & 5 letters demanding his help, so that, in order to satisfy as many as possible, he has made it his general rule to agree to only relatively *modest* loans or donations.

I am explaining all this to you because [. . .],[2] simply to make me realize that it is purely a question of his comparatively limited means, certainly not any lack of willingness on his part which prompted him to ask for time to think the matter over & to consult his finances to determine whether, & in what way, he might help you. He has promised to send word to me here as soon as he reaches a decision: he will not be able to find out my address until today, when he gets back to Leipzig, so that I cannot expect to have news from him for another day or so. –

1 Heinrich Schletter (1793–1853), a Leipzig merchant and patron of the arts, had given Wagner considerable financial help while he was in Paris. Wagner now appealed to him again, this time on behalf of Kietz.
2 Illegible phrase in the manuscript.

It occurs to me that it would really be rather pointless to post this letter to you today: all that I could tell you today would have to be regarded as provisional, whereas I can probably give you more definite news in a few days' time. It was a mistake to start this letter so prematurely, so I shall set it aside for a few days & return to it when I know what Schletter has decided. – Goodbye for now!

1st *July*

I have waited *so long* in such agonized anticipation of *a letter from Schletter*, only to discover that on this occasion all my efforts have been a complete waste of time! 10 days after starting this letter I had still not received word from Schletter, & since my embarrassment was growing at my continuing inability to write to you, I wrote to him once again in Leipzig in order to remind him of his promise. I have just received a letter from him in which he informs me in detailed & highly deferential terms of his opinion that the sum requested would be excessive even if it were to be regarded merely as a loan, & that he could not deprive others of it who were *really* in need – etc: I had not expected this for the following reasons: each time I met Schletter at Luise's house in Leipzig, he repeatedly praised your "talent" & your "genius" in the most extravagant terms & exclaimed that if ever he wanted his own or anybody else's portrait painted, then you would be the only person he would ask to do it; the result was that it was Schletter himself who gave me the idea of explaining to him that your existence as an artist was in jeopardy, & of turning to him for help. He immediately countered this by saying that he could give only *limited* aid, & so I made it quite clear to him that he should look on *this* transaction with totally different eyes, – it was not a question of deducting the sum requested from *that* part of his income which he had set aside for helping the needy, but, given the fact that every year he spent what was certainly a by no means inconsiderable sum of money on acquiring *objets d'art*, what he should do was to make you an *advance* out of the fund which he used for this purpose & help an artist for whom he was full of such unstinting praise & from whom – by his own admission – he would not fail to commission a goodly number of portraits; he could be sure that the initial advance would be promptly repaid – assuming he demanded the same in cash – since he was doubtless fully aware of the ease with which you had already saved *quite considerable* sums of money in Germany. – *This* was the argument I had to use both in order to pin him down & to ensure the best deal for you, & I based my hopes on this account of the affair; unfortunately, however, the outcome has taught me that I was dealing with a *tradesman* who is in the habit of regarding any sum of money spent in this way as a total write-off, & of not *counting* on its repayment; seen in *this* light, I can well believe that the sum of money I demanded (1000 fr.) was excessive. I hope he drowns in his own shit! Let's say no more on the matter! It would be a waste of breath! There is only *one* consolation I can give you, & that is that nobody in Leipzig knows of the affair; – & Schletter won't breathe a word about it. – [...]

SB II, 117–19.

47. ERNST BENEDIKT KIETZ, PARIS   Dresden, 6 September 1842

[...] I must add a word about my operatic affairs. There is nothing I can do about the Dutchman at present, firstly because the Court Theatre in Berlin is currently in such a disorganized state that, with the best will in the world, Küstner could not begin to rehearse a new piece, & secondly because when Meyerbeer went to Paris, he sent me word that he wanted to rehearse my opera himself, so that it would be the first work to be staged in Berlin under his new direction; he says this will be immediately following his return from Paris – in November.[1] As a result, I can do no more in this matter except wait, particularly since it would be uncivil of me to insist upon the Dutchman being given before Meyerbeer's return. At all events I doubt whether the Paris production will harm me;[2] it would in fact be the *first* opera of *this* kind to come to Germany; in any case things are unlikely to move so *quickly*; it would take at least a year before the work was given in Germany, & with any luck my own opera may already have been staged in several theatres by then.[3] That is why I am presently devoting all my energies to *Rienzi*; & by God it needs it! If I were not here, watching over my interests with the utmost vigilance, God only knows when my opera would see the light of day. And yet I enjoy the great advantage of knowing that the entire company, including the singers, conductor & producer, have set to work with such excellent goodwill that I am generally assured such amiable single-mindedness has never before been met with in the theatre! But these endless muddles which are caused every day by the most extraordinary narrow-mindedness & stupidity of the intendant[4] place constant obstacles in my path, so that clearing them away is like cleansing the Augean stables. It would be a waste of time to enumerate them all; suffice it to say that we have now had 14 piano

1 The first Berlin performance of *Der fliegende Holländer* took place on 7 January 1844, with Wagner himself conducting.
2 *Le Vaisseau fantôme* by Pierre-Louis Dietsch was first performed at the Paris Opéra on 9 November 1842. Contrary to Wagner's claim, the librettists, Paul Foucher and Bénédict-Henry Révoil, drew on his prose draft to only a limited extent.
3 The first performance of *Der fliegende Holländer* took place in Dresden on 2 January 1843; it was subsequently taken up in Riga (3 June 1843), Cassel (5 June 1843) and Berlin (7 January 1844), but then fell into neglect until Wagner himself staged the opera in Zurich in 1852. Dresden did not revive the work until 1865.
4 August Baron von Lüttichau.

rehearsals, & that the first performance will take place in 4 weeks from now, some time during the first half of October: unless I am totally mistaken, it will be an excellent performance: of Devrient I need say only that I am assured she has never studied a role with such enthusiasm, since she almost always finds it uncommonly difficult to familiarize herself with anything new straightaway: at the very end of the opera she intends to come galloping on to the stage on horseback, riding *cross-saddle*! – Tichatschek has given up the holiday in Salzburg on my account: vocally he is made for the part, & regards the role as the most brilliant one he has ever sung. He is having himself a suit of armour made specially for the part – German silver,[1] richly decorated with real solid silver; it is said to be costing him around 400 thalers. [. . .]

Be an artist, an *artist*, not a fool with 100,000 friends. If you really live for your art, you will be happy even in the midst of the most utter penury, especially if, at the same time, you are conscious of having a friend who is steadfast unto death. God! What would have become of me if I had not thrown myself into the arms of art with ever greater loyalty! Before I landed in this slough of suffering, I could as easily have become a charlatan as an artist! But in those hours when art became my sole consolation, my eyes were fully opened to all its pureness & chastity. – I now know who I am, for all the contempt & catcalls I receive! Be with me, friend! –

[. . .] The only thing I have achieved for myself this summer is the detailed stage draft of the "Venusberg".[2] I consider it a complete success & am convinced that this opera will be my most original creation. As soon as I have a free moment to versify the draft – (& I intend to make every effort to do it as well as I can –) I shall send you a copy. I began working out the details of the draft in the course of a short journey which I made on foot from Teplitz to Aussig & beyond in the mountains; I spent the night on the Schreckenstein (– I don't know if you've heard of it) & started work on it there. Children, it is a charming place! Anders, Lehrs & the rest of you, pray for *Rienzi*, & next year we'll all celebrate together on the Schreckenstein! –

In the parish church at Aussig I asked to be shown the Madonna of Carlo Dolci: it is a quite extraordinarily affecting picture, & if *Tannhäuser* had seen it, I could readily understand how it was that he turned away from Venus to Mary without necessarily having been inspired by any great sense of piety. – At all events, I am now firmly set on *Saint Elisabeth*. – – [. . .]

SB II, 146–53.

---

1 A white alloy of nickel, zinc and copper.
2 The original title of *Tannhäuser*. Wagner made his first prose draft between 28 June and 6 July 1842 and completed the second fair copy immediately afterwards, on 8 July. This section of the letter is dated 10 September [1842].

48. EDUARD AND CÄCILIE AVENARIUS, PARIS

Dresden, 11 September 1842

[. . .] Minna has finally begun a thorough & regular course of treatment in which I was recently able to be of possible assistance to her. We were recommended to try Dr *Ulrich*, who specializes in spa treatment & whose diagnosis of Minna's illness is undoubtedly correct: at all events, he said it was high time that she applied herself exclusively to getting better, & in particular he has imposed a very strict diet on her. She took the waters relatively infrequently, & then only in the sulphurated baths: instead she drank a lot, Eger-Franzen-Brunnen.[1] Of course, her illness is of such a kind that there can be no question of a rapid recovery, but in many respects Minna already feels a sense of relief. A major event in her life was her getting to know our mother: I admit that I genuinely admire Minna for her great tact, & above all for her self-control, in all her dealings with mother. To be frank, I must confess right away that Minna, for all her extraordinary sense of justice & fairness, was profoundly embittered & incensed at our mother's infinite lack of principle & utterly wayward capriciousness, but that, out of her love for me, she learned to moderate her behaviour towards her to such an extent that when mother left us, she admitted that she could not understand how anyone could ever quarrel with Minna or fail to like her. If you, my dear Cecilie, & I are both able to get on with mother, that is only to be expected, since we are after all one flesh & blood; we willingly make allowances for her many failings, since we still remember her from the days when she was actively concerned only for the well-being of her children. You must admit that none of these considerations applies to Minna, since all she has to grasp hold of is the bare truth, & the truth, as far as our mother is concerned, is certainly not attractive: you cannot deny that, within our family, she creates nothing but trouble because of her remarkable penchant for misrepresenting & distorting everything, & for indulging in endless gossip; the result is that all our other brothers & sisters avoid her like the plague: well, if that enables them to avoid the resultant problems, it may ultimately be the only solution; but what most annoyed Minna was our mother's really offensive avarice & egoism which we were exposed to *ad nauseam* in various trivial ways, but especially in her treatment of the servants [. . .]; – it is sad & distressing that I am obliged to use such strong language, but our good mama is utter hell for everyone around her – & Minna now fully understands what you, my dear Cecilie, must have suffered during the long period you lived together. – It is fortunate that our mother is content to lead her isolated &, it must be said, thoroughly comfortable life. I always enjoy seeing her once in a while: she has many charming qualities, even if I feel that her endless

1 Spring-water from Franzensbad on the Eger, near Teplitz in Bohemia.

chatter, with all its fine phrases & instructive examples, is for the most part totally mindless, since she has grown completely dulled towards *action*. I may add that the state of her health is most reassuring, – the spa treatment has done her a world of good; – during the brief period when she was with us in Dresden, she regularly accompanied us on our walks, running around like a young roedeer. – Enough of our mother; I have said many harsh things, – but what is the point in deluding ourselves? –

[. . .] As for Cecilie's taunts about our having *children*, there is still *nothing* to report: we are forced to make do with *dogs*, since there is still absolutely no prospect of *human* progeny;[1] we've just got another one, only 6 weeks old, a funny little animal called *Beps* or *Striezel* (because he looks like one of the dogs from the Striezelmarkt). He's better than old *Rober*[2] was; but it's a bad sign that we always have to make do with such stupid creatures. I'd much rather have a little Max[3] – but *that* can only happen *once* in the world. [. . .]

SB II, 155–60.

49. EDUARD AND CÄCILIE AVENARIUS, PARIS Dresden, 21 October 1842

Cecilie's letter arrived this morning. – imagine our feelings when we read your good wishes!!!

Well, my dearest children! Let me – in all haste & in utter exhaustion – at the very least drop you a line to report what happened yesterday. I'd prefer you to learn it from someone else – for I'm bound to tell you – that, as *everyone* assures me, *never* has an opera been given its first performance in Dresden & been received with such enthusiastic acclaim as was the case with my *Rienzi*. The whole town was caught up in the excitement, it was a veritable *revolution*; – I was called on stage *four* times by the tumultuous applause. I am assured that not even the success of Meyerbeer's Huguenots, when it was performed here, was comparable with that of my *Rienzi*. The second performance is the day after tomorrow:[4] – & for the third one, too, all the seats have already been sold. I am dreadfully worn out & exhausted; I'll write *more fully* after the second performance. The performance was *ravishingly* beautiful – Tichatschek – Devrient – everything – everything was more perfect than has ever been seen here previously. Success! Success!

1 According to Natalie, Minna suffered a miscarriage during their flight from Riga. This may have prevented her from subsequently bearing children.
2 Normally spelt "Robber" by Wagner: a Newfoundland dog which had accompanied the Wagners to London and Paris.
3 The son of Eduard and Cäcilie Avenarius.
4 The second performance in fact took place on 26 October 1842.

You good, loyal & dear people! A new day has dawned! May it shine *on you all*!

Your
Richard.

SB II, 167–8.

50. ROBERT SCHUMANN, LEIPZIG   Dresden, 3 November 1842

Most honoured friend,

I was informed yesterday by someone who had just seen the most recent issue of your Zeitschrift für Musik that he had yet to find in it a report on the production of my opera "Rienzi" which is currently being performed in Dresden.[1] I confess that this news saddened me deeply, since I do not know on whose support I might count if not on yours. How has this come about? After all, you carry other reports from Dresden, – why, then, has there been no word about an event which, seen quite impartially – has caused such a stir here from every point of view? Shall I tell you, in support of what I say, that the composer was called on stage four times (unheard of here) at the first performance and twice at the second? That at the third performance the composer had forcibly to decline the thrice repeated calls on him to appear, since he wished this honour to be accorded to the singers alone? Shall I mention the fact that my opera continues to be given at increased prices, and that, notwithstanding this increase, there are no more seats to be had for any of the forthcoming performances? – I know that these are all things which need not necessarily have anything to do with the merit of my work, and it mortifies me to have to enumerate them for your benefit. Inured to suffering at a time when *art* was my only consolation, I am now sufficient of an artist not to see my only salvation in the flattery of my self-esteem; but anyone who is concerned to make ends meet cannot comfort himself solely with the knowledge that he has striven honourably. –

It would, therefore, have been my earnest wish to have seen you at a performance of my opera, and if this desire of mine might yet be realized tomorrow, *Friday*, at the 4th performance of my opera, you would indeed make me very happy. That the expenses which you incur as a result of your visit will be met from my own pocket is something I hope I need not mention.

There is one other point which I must mention, since I consider it to be most extraordinary: the Dresden management has just invited me to deliver

---

1 An extensive and extremely favourable review of *Rienzi*, perhaps submitted by Ferdinand Heine, had appeared in the *Neue Zeitschrift für Musik* dated 1 November 1842. Wagner's informant must therefore have been referring to one of the three previous issues, dated 21, 25 and 28 October.

to them at the earliest opportunity the full score of my other opera – "the flying Dutchman", since they intend to stage this work, too, without delay and immediately after "Rienzi"; since it belongs to a quite different genre (– the purely Romantic –) & can be rehearsed at very short notice, I have agreed to their request, with the result that it will be performed here by the beginning of December, in other words sooner than in Berlin, where *Lachner's* opera has to be given before work can begin on mine.[1] – If only I could transfer the Dresden performances of my operas to Leipzig![2]

Enough! You will gather from all this my present cares and concerns! Do not be angry with me if I appear importunate, but continue to show your usual friendly disposition towards

Your
most obedient servant,
Richard Wagner.

SB II, 169–71.

51. JOHANN PHILIPP SAMUEL SCHMIDT, BERLIN
Dresden, 30 November 1842

[...] To date "Rienzi" has been performed six times, & although the ticket prices have been increased to a level hitherto unknown in Dresden, the house has always been packed to the rafters: I had the pleasure of observing that at the sixth performance the audience's enthusiastic acclaim almost surpassed that of the first night, &, as the best proof of my extraordinary success I am told that the local audiences, who in the past have always shown the most insuperable opposition to long performances, have always remained right to the very end of my opera, which lasts until half-past-ten, & that they have followed it with the most intense interest. – As for the style of my composition, people are in agreement to the extent that they generally concede it to bear an exclusively German stamp, without necessarily attributing to it any particular model. The subject matter, as you will see, is powerfully affecting in its basic outline: notwithstanding that fact, I have succeeded in extracting from it a number of more lyrical moments, & it is these in particular which appear to have won for me the audience's favour. On the whole, however, I

1 In the event, Lachner's *Catarina Cornaro* was not performed in Berlin until 15 October 1845. Wagner's opera was first heard there on 7 January 1844, having received its first performance in Dresden a year earlier, on 2 January 1843.

2 The first of Wagner's operas to be performed in Leipzig was *Tannhäuser*, which entered the repertory on 31 January 1853; *Lohengrin* followed on 7 January 1854, and *Der fliegende Holländer* on 27 September 1862.

am gratified to discover that their applause has been directed less towards individual passages than to the musico-dramatic whole. [. . .]

SB II, 182.

52. ALBERT WAGNER, HALLE   Dresden, 3 December 1842

[. . .] But what has made – and continues to make – particularly strenuous demands on my time is the position forced upon me by the unexpected death of poor Rastrelli.[1] All eyes immediately turned to me as his successor in office: the affair was discussed at court, and Lüttichau had enquiries made about me. It is a most difficult decision for me to have to take: I should of course like to continue to remain free for the next few years. I am now at the prime of my life, when my creative abilities are at their highest pitch of intensity: I already have plans for two new operas[2] and could complete them within a space of two years if I were my own master. I confess that I should gladly pay for this freedom at the cost of a few financial worries, and, in the final analysis, I may after all now reckon on a decent income from the two operas which are already finished. Of course, here in Germany everything moves slowly and cautiously: as far as the totality of our theatres are concerned, I have arrived on the scene completely unexpectedly, and before they find time to include me in their repertoires, I can afford for a while to remain an observer. It is true that, thanks to Schmetzer, I have already signed a provisional contract to provide Brunswick with a copy of the score; and yesterday I received a letter from the director of the theatre in Aachen, asking me for the score:[3] but meanwhile, even though I may snap up the odd thaler here and there, my old debts, especially the ones incurred in Magdeburg, continue to be a millstone round my neck, and I cannot foresee a time when I might be free of financial worries. And so a few days ago – not least because I was reproached for not speaking out – I discussed the matter freely with Lüttichau, and explained to him that, although I should really have preferred to remain my own master, the prospect of having at my command such an extraordinary ensemble as the Dresden Opera now has to offer me, and of preparing superlative performances with it, was something so tempting that I could easily renounce my earlier resolve: but since a subordinate position of the kind held by Rastrelli would not offer me the prospect I desired, I could not consider the vacant post. Lüttichau thereupon explained to me that it was not his intention to refill the post that Rastrelli had held; but that, since he

1 The Dresden staff conductor Joseph Rastrelli had died on 15 November 1842, at the age of forty-three.
2 *Tannhäuser* (not completed until 13 April 1845) and *Die Sarazenin* (which remained a dramatic fragment).
3 Neither of these plans materialized.

no longer had the necessary confidence in Reissiger, on account of the latter's indolence and helplessness, he planned to appoint a second *Kapellmeister* alongside Reissiger, who would, at the very least, enjoy exactly the same rights as Reissiger. – I now find myself standing like Hercules at the parting of the ways: – anyone who simply had my material well-being at heart would of course cry out: "Seize your chance while you can!" But would that really be the end of the matter? – –

[...]

SB II, 186–7.

53. Cäcilie Avenarius, Paris   Dresden, 5 January 1843

[...] Lüttichau notified me very recently that he has it in mind to appoint me Kapellmeister on a salary of 1800 thalers, only I should first have to serve a probationary year as musical director on a salary of 1200 thlr. I have written to him this very afternoon to tell him that I cannot & will not accept the post. What he will decide now, I do not know:[1] but what is certain is that I shall give up my freedom only in exchange for a very important position. I know of course that in the short term I shall be exposing myself to yet more cares & worries: but that should not deter a person such as myself. Although my operas will gain only slowly in popularity – just as everything in Germany moves only slowly – they cannot fail in time to make their way across the whole of Germany, since my local success has caused such a stir. Rienzi will be given first in Prague & Hamburg, – and then, next spring, in Brunswick too.[2] Apart from my Dresden fee, however, I have not yet received a penny, but time will change all that. Publishers are all still hesitating to make me any offers, no doubt because they want to wait & see whether my operas catch on elsewhere: for my own part, I have no intention of demeaning myself by making the first move; again, it is a question of waiting. I continue to hope for better things, but in the mean time it has been extraordinarily important for me to have found someone – without looking – who is willing to lend me 1000 thalers in cash on the sole security of my honest face & the promise that I shall repay the debt as soon as my situation improves. This person is none other than – *Devrient*: she learned of my circumstances, my commitments & my debts, & on several occasions offered me the 1000 thalers, of her own accord, until I finally accepted the sum. It is extraordinary, – & I confess that, even if all this had not come about, I would still respect &

1 Wagner was appointed Royal Kapellmeister for life on 2 February 1843 at an annual salary of 1500 thalers; the regulation probationary year was waived.
2 *Rienzi* was first performed in Hamburg on 21 March 1844 and in Berlin on 24 October 1847. See also letter [47], p. 94, note 3.

admire her unreservedly. She is a truly noble and warm-hearted woman. She has also found a place in her heart for Minna: she gave us both presents at Christmas: Minna has received the most lavish gifts from her: everything she could have wished for has been given her. About half the sum that Devrient has lent me is destined for Paris: I shall write to Eduard more fully on the matter. With the other half I shall attempt to pay off my old debts from Magdeburg. It will not be easy, since the people concerned are out for blood & threaten at every moment to compromise me in my present honourable position. If I were to pay them *everything* they demand, including costs & interest, they could demand 657 thalers from me. Of the 1000 thalers I shall not spend a groschen on myself. –

This is more or less how things stand with me at present: – you can see that things are improving; & if you, dear Cecilie, & Eduard were to visit us here, you would, I hope, find that our situation has taken a turn for the better. Rienzi is now to be divided into two halves & performed on two separate evenings, since too much had had to be left out on account of its length; all these passages will now be restored so as not to deprive the audiences of a single note. You will gather from this how popular the opera is! In Prague, too, I expect they will perform the opera over 2 evenings. It is to be hoped, my dear Cecilie, that you will have an opportunity to see my operas here, – simply try to get here soon. – We have now made up our minds about Natalie, if you will be so kind as to bring her here at our expense, you will then be rid of her, & she may go & stay with her sister[1] in Zwickau, which is the best place for her.

[. . .]

SB II, 204–6.

54. JOHANN PHILIPP SAMUEL SCHMIDT, BERLIN

Dresden, 9 January 1843

Most honoured Sir,

The extent to which I am beholden unto you for the great kindness & sympathetic interest which you have shown me in respect of my opera "Rienzi" was something I felt in a particularly lively fashion when you were good enough to send me a copy of your review in the Spener'sche Zeitung; I scarcely know what I have done to deserve such unselfish interest on your part, & the only reply I can offer is to thank you in the most sincere terms for all that you have done for me.

Since you wish it – & certainly not to tempt you into placing me under a renewed obligation – I hasten to submit a brief & factual report on the success of my "flying Dutchman", which has just received its third performance. I

---

1 Charlotte Tröger, in reality Natalie's aunt.

am enclosing a copy of the libretto, from which you will see how completely this opera differs in style from that of "Rienzi", indeed, how far it diverges in many essential points from all that our audiences have come exclusively to regard as the leading operatic genre. You will find that I have allowed a simple tale to unfold of its own accord, without endowing it with this or that modern operatic ingredient such as is generally considered necessary nowadays. The French versifier[1] who adapted my sketch (the authorship of which is common knowledge) has completely destroyed the marvellous aura of the tale by weaving into it episodes such as are to be found in every contemporary French opera. Although I felt I had solved the problem by simplifying the plot as far as possible, I could not conceal from myself the fact that I was risking a great deal more by appearing before the general public in what is at present so alien a guise, since there is no doubt but that audiences came with totally different expectations of the work. In this opera I have included no pageantry, nor any thunderous finales straining for theatrical effect, etc. For that reason I had prepared myself for the realization that audiences would reconcile themselves to what I was offering them only after several performances. I was all the more surprised to meet with the most brilliant success at the very first performance, and to be assured that I had succeeded in winning over the audience right from the outset. The first act, as you will see from the libretto, is really only an introduction, but once it had put the audience in the right mood of suspense, they were swept along irresistibly by the work, not least because of the highly original & affecting acting of Schröder-Devrient; I & the singers were called on stage & greeted by tumultuous applause, which was repeated at the end of the third act which, moreover, contains the scene with the ghost ship & a rapid unfolding of the dramatic catastrophe. – The second performance was an even greater success (a very rare occurrence here in Dresden), since the audience was now more familiar with certain individual details which had been overlooked in the first overall impression; after the singers had taken their curtain calls, I myself was twice called upon to take a bow, just as on the opening night. There was similar applause at the third performance which took place yesterday.

I confess that I am prouder of this success than of the success of Rienzi, since in this last-named opera I had recourse to far more superficial means, & the work as a whole conforms much more to our current conceptions of a grand opera.[2]

[. . .]

SB II,213–14.

---

1 Paul Foucher, who with Bénédict-Henry Révoil wrote the libretto for Dietsch's *Le Vaisseau fantôme:* see introductory essay, pp. 53–4.

2 Despite the apparent enthusiasm of the public, *Der fliegende Holländer* disappeared from the repertory after four performances and was not heard again in Dresden until 1865.

55. ROBERT SCHUMANN, LEIPZIG   Dresden, 25 February 1843

My most worthy friend,

I am somewhat late in replying to the letter which your dear wife delivered to me, but you will easily guess what manner of onerous demand is currently being placed on my time, so that I scarcely have need of any further excuse.

The visit which your dear wife paid on the townsfolk of Dresden was so brief that I wish only that she might have stayed longer & been accompanied by your good self. I was particularly keen that you should organize some musical entertainment here for the public at large – I mean a public concert at which people would have had an opportunity to hear your works, & especially your new quintet.[1] Such an occasion would enable you to discover that you are labouring under a misapprehension concerning the present trend in public taste, & that your former prejudices are no longer justified. The age of Bellini is quite dead here, and if his mannerisms still cling, then they do so to a certain clique in high society which is no doubt the same the world over in the triviality of its taste – for reasons which I do not need to go into here. In a place where, for many years, there was only an Italian opera company, it is not surprising if a preference for Italian music should linger on, the more so since a singer like Schröder-Devrient, failing to find an outlet for her superb acting talent in our more recent German works, has thrown herself with somewhat forced enthusiasm into the portrayal of Bellini's heroines. She captivated her audiences in these roles wherever she performed them, – including here. But now that our artists have finally succumbed to a sense of disgust at this preference, they have abandoned it of their own accord & now devote themselves with unalloyed pleasure to the study of more serious music, with the result that audiences, too, have willingly and readily accepted this new refinement of taste. In contrast to earlier times, what has emerged here is a genuine & universal longing for aesthetic enjoyment of the highest kind, yet this is precisely the point where it must be admitted that our lovers of art are poorly provided for. We have nothing here to compare with your Gewandhaus concerts, and the only wretched substitute we have on offer are the subscription concerts organized by the director of music of a military band, although it must be said that these concerts are accorded a degree of interest on the part of our audiences which might well find a more worthy outlet elsewhere. That our own orchestra has not yet been able to do anything to meet the public demand for more frequent performances of outstanding orchestral works is due to a difficulty which is soon to be removed. – For the present I can speak only of our opera performances, & as far as these are concerned, a single glance at our repertoire will suffice to show that the age of Bellini is past: compare this, for heavens' sake! with

1 Piano Quintet in E flat major, op. 44.

what is now on offer elsewhere, in Berlin for example. If you go through last winter's repertoire, what you will find on the whole is Iphigenia, Fidelio, Freischütz, Jessonda, Templar,[1] Bluebeard[2] etc. – Permit me to mention at this juncture that it says much for the seriousness of our local audiences that a composition such as my "flying Dutchman" was given such a warm reception here. Your remarks on this piece, after you had perused the score, confirm this observation of mine, & to judge by the reservations which you expressed concerning its excessively sombre colouring – reservations which I admit to be well-founded – one might have expected that such a work would have had no great appeal here. But since audiences have grown increasingly accustomed to the work the more often they have heard it, I believe it not inappropriate to mention this fact in order to encourage you to think more highly of the seriousness of taste which is increasingly gaining ground here. – I may add that I agree with everything which – in the light of your present knowledge of the work – you have found to say on the subject; there is only one point which alarmed me, & – I must confess, because of the issue it raises – which embittered me: that you can tell me quite calmly that there is a good deal in the work that smacks of – Meyerbeer. In the first place I do not know what in the whole wide world is meant by the word "Meyerbeerian", except perhaps a sophisticated striving after superficial popularity: but no existing work can be "Meyerbeerian" since, in this sense, not even Meyerbeer himself is "Meyerbeerian", but Rossinian, Bellinian, Auberian, Spontinian etc. etc. But if there were really some solid reality that could be called "Meyerbeerian", just as we can describe something as "Beethovenian" or, for all I care, as "Rossinian", I confess that it would have required a wonderful freak of nature for me to have drawn my inspiration from *that* particular source, the merest smell of which, wafting in from afar, is sufficient to turn my stomach; this would be the death-knell of my creative powers, & the fact that you have condemned me thus demonstrates clearly that your view of me is far from impartial, a fact which is perhaps attributable to your knowledge of the *external* circumstances of my life, since these, I admit, brought me into contact with Meyerbeer the *man*, to the extent that I now find myself in his debt.

– As for the general public's making up its mind about my work, I am glad that I may now look forward to the prospect of seeing my operas more widely performed: for what the local press has to say about me is unfortunately of very little value for me & my cause. Of those critics who report for the out-of-town papers, half of them are poor devils who cannot afford to go to the theatre and whose reports therefore run along the lines, "although I have not yet seen the opera, it is said to be" etc. – while the others, who are themselves

1 *Der Templer und die Jüdin*, opera by Heinrich Marschner, first performed in Leipzig on 22 December 1829.
2 *Raoul Barbe-bleu*, opéra-comique by André-Ernest-Modeste Grétry, first performed at the Comédie Italienne on 2 March 1789.

practising musicians, can clearly not conceal their professional jealousy, –
I expect you have read friend Bank's masterpiece in the Wiener musik.
Zeitg.[1] And it is entirely to be expected that Härtel's Mus. Ztg., which carries
reports from some of the most God-forsaken places imaginable, has said
practically no word about the appearance of my operas. Since I know that,
hiding behind this newspaper, is an eminent & widely admired composer,[2] I
cannot but hold a far from favourable view of his true character. If I were in
his position, I wouldn't give a damn what this or that journal said about me:
but as things stand at present, it is bound to be a matter of concern to me
that others should recommend me, purely in order for my name to become
better known, since this is as essential for me and my operas as the air I
breathe. – –

Your quintet, my dear Schumann, pleased me greatly: I asked your good
wife to play it to me twice. I still retain a lively memory of the first two
movements in particular. Perhaps I should have listened to the fourth movement first, then I might have liked it better. I can see what you are aiming
at, & I assure you that I am aiming at much the same sort of thing: it is our
only salvation: *beauty*!

Farewell, my most worthy friend, and kindly remember me to your revered
wife. I remain as ever

Your
most obedient servant
Richard Wagner.

SB II, 220–24.

56. SAMUEL LEHRS, PARIS   Dresden, 7 April 1843

Best of friends,

Finally, after more than three months, I have heard from you again! I was
really beginning to be afraid that the news when it came would not be good,[3]
and although what you have to tell me gives me little cause for rejoicing, it
nevertheless encourages me to hope that in time you may yet be fully cured.
I believe your own situation is similar to that of my wife; I hope to see her
fully restored to health and leading a trouble-free and carefree existence as
soon as she is able to devote her attention exclusively to a life of ease and a
strict diet: medicines etc are of little use in a case like hers; she is planning

---

1 A critical report on *Rienzi* and *Der fliegende Holländer* had appeared in the *Allgemeine Wiener Musik-Zeitung* on 18 January 1843, signed "P. B." Wagner suspected Schumann's co-editor Karl Banck of being the author.
2 Felix Mendelssohn.
3 Lehrs died of consumption on 13 April 1843, a few days after receiving this letter.

to go to Teplitz in May and spend at least three months there, less for the sake of any actual treatment than to be able to enjoy the charming surroundings and the clean air in total independence. My only wish is that you could accompany her there and do the same; – what does it need to make this feasible? Think the matter over and let me have a precise answer. – –

I shall be able to make only the odd journey out there this summer now that I have placed myself in harness. But I cannot complain, it is an easy yoke to bear – and where it chafes, it will also yield. I am treated here with some distinction, of a kind that has almost certainly never been accorded anyone else in similar circumstances. Only six months ago I was still a vagabond who would not even have known where to get hold of a passport – whereas I now have tenure for life with a handsome salary and the prospect that it will continue to increase, and I control a sphere of influence such as has been granted to few men. No secret is being made of the fact that I am expected to undertake a thorough artistic reorganization of the musical life here, as a result of which all the proposals I care to make are accepted unconditionally, which increases the respect people have of me, since they have long been accustomed to seeing Reissiger as totally ineffectual. But so as to prevent all my time from being taken up with routine duties, a second musical director[1] has now been appointed. I can ask for no more. – The first unfamiliar opera I rehearsed was Gluck's Armida: everyone went into raptures at my interpretation of the piece, which is so remote musically from our own age, and at the nuances which I persuaded the orchestra and singers to observe: the King – an honest man with none of the usual airs and graces, but totally sincere in his approach to everything – lavished the greatest praise on me and conveyed his thanks to me even while the performance was still in progress. He takes a genuine and good-natured delight in me, and so I am certain, for example, that if I ever want an extended leave of absence, I need only explain that I intend using it to work on some new composition, and it will be given me at once. – – You see what an agreeable position I am in, and I am increasingly conscious of the fact that this was precisely what I most needed in life: however successful my operas, I could not have survived without this security; I note with alarm to what depths our national sense of honour has sunk with respect to dramatic music, too: the long period during which our theatres were exclusively open to French and Italian music continues to have repercussions even today, when the French and Italians have been utterly discredited. If there is one opera which has caused a stir in Germany when it was performed here, it was my "Rienzi": I am constantly receiving new evidence of the fact that this event is being discussed, from both a literary and a personal point of view, in the remotest corners of Germany: yet there is still not a single director from out of town who has

1 August Röckel.

shown serious signs of staging the opera! It appears they are all waiting for each other to make the first move, – and all the time that this is going on, one new French opera after another sinks without trace!! – However, since I know where the root of the problem lies, I am not down-hearted but shall strive all the more vigorously to bring about a radical cure in due course. It will be a slow process, but progress there will and must be: but that is enough about *Paris*! This is something I must now leave behind me for ever: we opera composers cannot be *European*, – so the question is – either *German* or *French*! You can see the damage that a fool like Meyerbeer has caused us; he spends half his time in Berlin and the other half in Paris, with the result that he never achieves anything anywhere, least of all in Berlin; – it is impossible to describe how ghastly it is there: but that is what happens when you try to please everybody as our friend Giacomo does! – God knows when anything will come of my Dutchman there: Meyerbeer wrote yesterday to say that it is due to be staged in May[1] – damn the whole lot of them! Incidentally, I have already sold this opera to two other theatres, Cassel and Riga, to the former for 20 louis d'or, and to the latter for 15; – you see how modestly I have to begin. But things will soon be different! I have still not sorted myself out financially, I often have such ridiculous expenses: I'm now having to have a court uniform made which is costing me around 100 thalers! Is it not absurd? – I have still made no attempt to find a publisher for my operas, I first want to wait for them to make their way to a number of other theatres, then music dealers will have to pay a decent sum for them – but for the time being I must act discreetly. What the good people of Leipzig think of me you can discover by reading the Leipzig music journal: this organ of Mendelssohn's has so far said practically nothing about my operas! I know from a reliable source that Mendelssohn – who is currently planning an opera of his own – is extremely jealous of me: – the Leipzig clique which now obeys Mendelssohn unconditionally does not know what sort of an expression to adopt when dealing with me – the idiots! I hope to God that Mendelssohn produces a respectable opera, then there will be two of us and we shall be able to achieve more than one on his own. – You reproach me for having gone on about Berlioz etc in my autobiography:[2] I must begin by saying that what I wrote was not intended to appear in print: it was supposed to serve as a sketch for my biographer, and in order for him to know where he stood with me, I presented myself to him just as I am, warts and all. I was as surprised as the next man to see what I had written appearing unaltered. But, in any case, why should I make a fuss about Berlioz? He certainly hasn't

1 See letter [47], p. 94, note 3.
2 In his *Autobiographical Sketch*, written for Laube's *Zeitung für die elegante Welt* and published in two instalments on 1 and 8 February 1843, Wagner had dismissed Berlioz as "lacking all sense of beauty; his music, with few exceptions, is a grotesque caricature" (SB I,107).

deserved it of me, as he made clear when he was here in Dresden,[1] it was an abomination for him to have to stand by and see how successful my operas are. He is an unhappy man, and I certainly would not have written anything against him if I had previously attended the concerts which he gave here: – I felt sorry for him! – –

It amused me greatly to learn that you wanted to know all about my domestic arrangements here, you old cotquean! Unfortunately, I can be of no use to you, since we are still living in furnished rooms; not until next autumn shall we be setting up our own home: then you will be welcome to come and stay with us any day. – Only reply soon to the question in the first part of my letter! –

The text of the Venusberg[2] is finished: I shall write the music this summer; everybody here is waiting for this opera. I shall send you a copy of the text within the next few days. The three copies of my portrait are for Kietz, Anders and my sister: – you, I know, are not interested in such things. And quite right, too.

Reply soon, and be of good cheer, my dear brother, sooner or later we shall be together again! Farewell and enjoy the fine spring air as best you can!

Ever yours,
Richard Wagner.

SB II,231–5.

57. FELIX MENDELSSOHN, BERLIN   Dresden, 8 June 1843

My most honoured Sir,

Unfortunately I did not receive your card until late yesterday evening, since I did not return home during the day; as a result I was robbed of the pleasure of being able to see you and speak to you in Dresden, and it was impossible for me to return your score to you sooner than I am doing now.

I have been assured that the aim of your anthem[3] was perfectly clear & that it achieved general understanding: my only cause for regret was that, in spite of the large number of singers, about half the choir – the tenors – were prevented from joining in effectively because of the very low range of the *unisono* singing, & that in consequence the singing did not perhaps emerge

---

1 Berlioz had attended performances of *Rienzi* and *Der fliegende Holländer* in Dresden in the course of a concert tour of Germany. His review appeared in the *Journal des débats* on 12 September 1843.

2 i.e. *Tannhäuser*; see letter [47], p. 95, note 2.

3 "Gott segne Sachsenland" performed in Dresden's Zwinger on 7 June 1843. See also letter [58], below.

sufficiently powerfully. But if, after taking due account of this unfortunate circumstance, you were nevertheless satisfied at least to some degree with the performance, it would be a source of great pleasure to me.

I hope to be able to welcome you soon to Dresden for a longer period, & may therefore close by expressing the hope that we meet again soon on a friendly & permanent footing.

Respectfully yours

Oxford Collection MS. M. D. Mendelssohn. d. 43 (previously unpublished)

58. CÄCILIE AVENARIUS, PARIS   Dresden, 13 July 1843

My very dear Cecilie,

At risk of incurring your bitter reproaches, I have delayed writing until now so that I could write a *full* report of my activities, & not merely a few brief words: as God is my witness, today – the 13th July 1843 – is the first opportunity I have had of doing so since I last saw Eduard. Letters of the sort that I am writing to you now are ones I constantly defer starting, unless I have an entire morning at my disposal: – well then! Today is the first morning I can call my own in the sense I have outlined. I have been given four weeks' leave of absence by my intendant, & I dedicate the first day of it to this long delayed letter to you. – I have been so overwhelmed by work & other commitments during the last 2 months that I have come to look on my present leave as just what the doctor ordered, so that I can recover from all my physical & mental exertions. Reissiger went off on holiday in the middle of May, leaving me practically on my own to carry out all the duties, both in church & in the theatre, in addition to which I received a commission from the King to write a commemorative hymn[1] for the unveiling of the memorial to King Friedrich August; *Mendelssohn* was also commissioned to write a piece:[2] overall control of the performance, which took place in the Zwinger, was entrusted to me: I assembled a choir of 250 singers from local choral societies, & made a great name for myself, in that it was *universally* agreed that my own piece, which was straightforward & uplifting, knocked Mendelssohn's over-elaborate & artificial composition into a cocked hat. I also received a gold snuff-box worth about 100 thalers from the King as a "souvenir". Scarcely had I recovered from all this when I had to make a start

---

1 "Der Tag erscheint" (WWV 68), chorus for men's voices with words by C. C. Hohlfeld, composed in May 1843 and performed *a cappella* in Dresden's Zwinger on 7 June 1843.
2 See letter [57], p. 109, note 3.

on a short oratorio[1] which I had promised to write for the great Festival of Male Voice Choirs here in Dresden; in spite of all my other heavy commitments, I had 2 weeks to produce a major, serious work, for which I also had to write the words: my nerves by then were so much on edge that I often just sat & cried for fifteen minutes on end. I then had to rehearse my piece, which had initially had to be postponed & which in the end was only just completed in time, & my limbs have still not recovered from the after-effects of these exertions: as director of the local choral society, I additionally had to conduct all their remaining rehearsals. But the success of the performance has amply rewarded me: it was a splendid festival in the true sense of the word, especially the performance in the Frauenkirche. Picture to yourself a choir of 1200 men's voices, all perfectly rehearsed, on a platform occupying almost the entire nave of the church, & behind them an orchestra of 100 players, & you can imagine the impression it must have had! There has never been anything like it in any other church. On this day, too, I carried off the prize; my composition, entitled "The Love-Feast of the Apostles", included a passage depicting the descent of the Holy Ghost, which held everyone spellbound. The singers, who had flocked to Dresden from every part of Saxony, greeted me afterwards with shouts of vivat! & hurrah whenever they caught sight of me; there was no end to the general rejoicing. – Things in general have started to gather pace here: my Dutchman was given in *Cassel* & *Riga* at almost the same time & to the most brilliant acclaim: what is particularly remarkable is the way in which *Spohr* has been won over.[2] I am currently in the process of revising *Rienzi* so as to make it suitable for performing on a *single* evening; & then I think it will be the turn of *this* one, too. I have still not been able to write a line of my new work.[3] –

[. . .]

I shall not write to dear old Kietz today! I have prattled on for long enough to you, & left myself nothing else to tell him; would you be so kind as to pass on all my news to him & Anders? To be honest, my delay in writing is largely the result of a strange sense of dejection which fell upon me like a lead weight at the news of Lehrs' death. For a whole week after receiving the news, my head & my entire being felt dull & expressionless: his death lay on me like some calamity, so that I was scarcely able to lift my head. When I think that I stood by – powerlessly – & watched this poor dear friend of ours slowly being destroyed before my very eyes by the fate which pursues all that is

1 *Das Liebesmahl der Apostel*, completed on 29 June 1843 and first performed in Dresden's Frauenkirche on 6 July 1843; see introductory essay, p. 56.
2 See introductory essay, p. 56.
3 *Tannhäuser*; the second verse draft must have been completed before 7 April 1843 (see letter [56]), and Wagner in fact began to make sketches for individual sections of the score while on a short vacation in Teplitz between 19 July and mid-August 1843, although the complete draft was not begun until November.

noble & undemanding! – Children! Children! In what light did I then see that Paris of yours, that great den of assassins where those of us who are motivated by simple & straightforward ambitions are hounded to death, silently & unobserved! [. . .]

SB II, 296–301.

59. ANTON PUSINELLI, DRESDEN   Schönau bei Teplitz, 1 August 1843

My dear friend,

I have a headache, & am not feeling well, but cannot delay any longer replying to your kind & encouraging letter.[1] Believe me, people like us are delicate plants which have great need of a little warmth, & what could be more heart-warming than so generous an approach as the one you have made me? I have few friends since I am so totally lacking in the gift that is necessary to go out & acquire any: I have little to offer them but must rely upon my own good fortune to provide them. But there is a look in their eyes which enables me to recognize them, – then all I need do is call them by name, & they are mine. This is how all good fortune comes, – who then would doubt in your own faith? Let us both trust in it & be friends for life!

And in truth I must thank Heaven for revealing my true friends now! I have now reached a turning point in my life which people call good fortune: nobody asks whether the way here has been easy or whether I suffered a thousand torments in the course of it, and most of those with whom my present good fortune has led me into contact begrudge it to me. I see the way ahead very clearly & feel with a degree of almost painful embarrassment to what extent I must be on my guard & with what care I must watch over my daily routine. But there is much that appals me about such an attitude! Since all I say & do comes straight from my heart, I should much prefer to be rid of such cares. If only the world knew to what extent these cares gnaw away at the pure kernel of the artist's existence. That we have to be both artist and sly-boots at one & the same time has undoubtedly robbed the world of many a thing of innocent beauty. – If I am to find true happiness in the midst of this so-called happiness, then I must be permitted to win *friends*, or rather friends who give themselves to me as you have done: they will be few in number, but that is what is so good about it! Remain loyal to me, – my innermost soul will always be open to you, & always be yours to call your own! –

Your letter is the only agreeable & cheering thing to have happened to me

---

1 Anton Pusinelli, the Wagners' next-door neighbour in Dresden, became a valued and lifelong friend.

here, so you see that without you – my friend – all else that has befallen me here would have left me indifferent or been simply disagreeable. On the whole the weather has been bad & my health is not of the best. I am following your advice & drinking Marienbad Kreuzbrunnen: to begin with, it did me a world of good – but whether it's something I've eaten or whether I've done something else to provoke a relapse, – my old complaint[1] returned yesterday & the day before in a particularly violent form. I think I am not sufficiently relaxed, I am always distracted & in a hurry.

Breitkopf & Härtel have just informed me that, gratified though they were to have been offered the flying Dutchman, now that they have learnt the terms of my offer – I had demanded 1000 thalers (including the grand piano), they prefer for the time being to forgo the pleasure of accepting it. I have replied to the effect that it seems to me inconceivable that anyone would be prepared to risk a not inconsiderable amount of capital on an undertaking for which they were *not* prepared to pay the usual purchase price – a sum which Br. & Härtel have often paid in the past; – until such time as they find this price acceptable (& they should bear in mind that at a later date the price may go even higher), my offer would not be repeated. And this indeed is my firm resolve, a resolve which my secure position here fortunately enables me to maintain, since I now find myself, at the cost of only a small personal sacrifice, in the position of being able to sit back & wait, without denying myself anything in the process, until such time as I no longer need undersell my operas. – But you see how things stand with anyone born in our own city of *Dresden*! –

Apart from this, most of the things that have happened recently have been marked by a degree of stupidity calculated only to put me in a bad mood; one exception to this was a letter I received from *Riga* in which my correspondent wrote to tell me of the impression which my flying Dutchman had had on him, from which I see that its impact was precisely what I had intended it to be. – –

My Tannhäuser is resting & I feel little inclination to rouse him; admittedly, I have begun composing the music, but what I have done is not worth mentioning! Two things are lacking, – *rest* and (I can think of no other word for it) – *contentment*. I am not content, that is to say, my mood is inwardly & outwardly discordant: I am too easily distracted & long for rest, – not the inactivity of an idler but, on the contrary, a concentrated restlessness: I do not wish to have to think of all manner of different things, but only of a few things at once. But I expect that many years will have to slip by before I achieve such a state of harmonious calm, for I have to make up for ten years of my past. In spite of everything I am looking forward to next winter:

1 Wagner was suffering from gastric disorders, constipation and piles, which he attributed to the cramped and penurious life he had led in Paris.

certainly, I hope that I shall at least be able to satisfy my longing for outward contentment; that itself is worth a good deal, since external discontent can cause almost unbearable torment. –

Like a proper egoist, I've again talked only about myself, as if I were a fellow of some importance! But that's how it is, we are all so terribly preoccupied with our own selves. [. . .]

SB II,308–11.

60. FERDINAND HEINE, DRESDEN   [Teplitz, early August 1843]

Dear Heine,

When I wrote my flying Dutchman, I was of the conviction that I could not write it in any other way. It was in the course of my famous sea-voyage and among the Norwegian cliffs that the subject-matter – long familiar to me from your namesake's writings[1] – took on a quite special colour and character, sombre, admittedly, but copied from that same nature of which we are all a part, and not the speculative vision of some gloom-infected dreamer. But the wide wild ocean with its far-flung legends is an element which cannot be reduced compliantly and willingly to a modern opera, and although the legend of the flying Dutchman, filled as it is with the pounding of the sea, now took hold of me in such a way as to demand an artistic reworking, it seemed to me that the legend would have to be dreadfully mutilated and hacked to pieces if it was to be turned into a libretto which would meet modern requirements for piquant situations and unexpected surprises etc. And so I preferred not to alter the subject-matter as it already existed, except in so far as the development of a dramatic plot required it, instead I allowed the whole aura of the legend to spread unchecked over the entire piece, since only in that way did I believe I could hold the listener's attention, inducing in him that strange frame of mind which alone would persuade even the least poetical listener to conceive an affection – nay – even a real fondness for this most sombre of legends. And I ensured that my music was endowed with a similar character: in order to achieve this aim, I refused to look to the right or to the left of me, or to make the least concesssion to modern taste since I knew that to have done otherwise would be not only inartistic but unwise. From the outset I had to abandon the modern arrangement of dividing the work into arias, duets, finales etc., and instead relate the legend in a single breath,

1 Heinrich Heine's first brief account of the legend of the Flying Dutchman had appeared in the *Reisebilder* ("Nordsee") of 1826. A fuller version was published in French in the *Tableaux de voyage I* of 1833: it was a German translation of this text, published in Volume I of *Der Salon* in 1834, which served as the basis for Wagner's scenario.

just as a good poem should be. In this way I produced an opera whose popularity – now that it has been performed – I find impossible to explain since, in all its external details, it is so unlike anything we now understand by the term opera; indeed, only now do I realize what demands I have been placing on audiences, asking them suddenly to forget all that they had previously found entertaining and attractive in the theatre. But the fact that this opera has won so many friends for itself not only in Dresden but, especially, in Cassel and Riga, and that even the wider public has taken the work to heart seems to me to be a very important pointer for us, suggesting that we should henceforth write only what we Germans are inspired to write by our innate sense of poetry, and that we should never again make concessions to any foreign fashions but simply choose and treat those subjects that appeal to us; in that way we shall be quite certain of satisfying our fellow countrymen, too. If we proceed in this way we may yet regain an original German opera, and all who lose heart and who turn in their despair to foreign models may learn from my Dutchman's example – since it is without doubt conceived in a way that no Frenchman or Italian would ever have conceived it. –   .

A straightforward account of the action of the opera is sufficient to etc. etc.[1]

Yours,
Richard Wagner.

SB II,314–15.

61. CÄCILIE AVENARIUS, PARIS   Dresden, 22 October 1843

[. . .] My health is still not of the best: I'm at present suffering a particularly bad attack of piles; my bowels are in ruins, & the result is a permanent feeling of nausea & a rush of blood to my head. I intend undergoing a thorough course of treatment next spring & hope then to be rid once & for all of this tiresome affliction. – As to my lodgings, the earlier problems have now been overcome: we have moved into an extremely attractive & spacious flat in the Ostra-Allee, & have furnished it as tastefully & as well as we could. Although I have, to a certain extent, committed all the revenue from my operas over the next few years to furnishing the flat (an income which of course will continue to increase), my salary is sufficient to enable us to live comfortably during that time; certainly, everything I have acquired is to last *the rest of our lives.* Ah! how happy that thought makes me! You can readily imagine what my poor & sorely tried wife thinks of all this! And you can

---

1 The text of this letter appeared as part of an anonymous article on *Der fliegende Holländer* published in the Leipzig *Illustrirte Zeitung* of 7 October 1843.

equally well imagine how happy I am to be able to offer Minna this permanent reparation! – [. . .]

SB II,333–4.

62. MINNA WAGNER, DRESDEN   Berlin, 8 January [1844]

God knows whether or not you will receive this letter, dear Minna, or whether you received yesterday's letter in time to set off on the journey here. But I shall write to you, none the less, so that at least I have someone to talk to! It was after midnight when I finally got to bed last night, & at 5 in the morning I sent for a light & had the fire lit since it was pointless remaining in bed any longer, unable to sleep. You know, if you had been here, we could have gossiped all night together, – but I was on my own! God, what does one not feel on a night like last night: how many memories came flooding back! It was one of the most decisive evenings of my entire life! – Imagine, – I was appearing before a *completely unknown* audience with this fantastical opera of mine, a work totally remote from anything they had previously heard or grown to enjoy & offering, on the face of it, so little that is appealing or rewarding! I felt their hostility quite keenly: there was not a single person in the audience whom I knew personally, none of them was predisposed in my favour; – they all sat there feeling only their customary cold curiosity & thinking: well, what sort of an affair is this flying Dutchman going to be? – No one lifted a finger at the end of the Overture, – they listened to the melancholy first act in a mood of expectant curiosity & amazement, without knowing what decision to reach: – now & again one of the singers was greeted with effortful applause; – in a word, I realized the position I was in, – but I did not despair, since I could see that the performance was going extraordinarily well. The second act began, & it gradually dawned on me that I had achieved my aim: I had woven a spell around my audience, such that the first act had transported them into that strange mood which forced them to follow me wherever I chose to take them. Their interest grew, tension turned to excitement, heightened involvement – finally to enthusiasm, & even before the curtain had fallen on the second act, I was celebrating a triumph such as few, I am sure, have been granted. Never before – not even with *Rienzi* in Dresden – have I seen & heard such a prolonged outburst of enthusiasm as manifested itself here once the curtain had fallen: – of all the assembled company, there was not a single one of them, be he high or low, prince or pauper, who could not be seen & heard shouting & roaring with the rest of them. When I finally appeared on stage with the singers, I thought the whole house was going to collapse! –

The last act was child's play: the scenery worked a treat & made a splendid impression; the whole thing was played at great speed, & the ending, which was very well staged, came with surprising rapidity. Well before the final curtain fell, the audience's enthusiasm broke out anew & raged for an eternity before I could extricate myself from the orchestra and appear on stage with the singers, who had been waiting for me in the wings. – In short, my dear wife, I have won a remarkable victory: the extraordinary & almost unprecedented nature of it can be appreciated only by those who are in a position accurately to assess all the circumstances involved, & the present state of our operas, as well as understand how totally different & unfamiliar is the direction I have embarked upon with my Dutchman.[1] – [. . .]

[. . .]

Today I am dining with *Meyerbeer*, tomorrow with Küstner. I did not see *Meyerbeer* again after the performance. The King[2] was present, & someone who observed him closely throughout the performance assured me that he had enjoyed it enormously. Mendelssohn, with whom I also dined on one occasion, favoured me by coming on stage after the performance, embracing me & congratulating me most warmly. –

[. . .]

SB II,351–4.

63. FELIX MENDELSSOHN, BERLIN   Berlin, 10 January 1844

My dear, dear Mendelssohn,
    It gave me great pleasure to learn how well-disposed you are towards me. If I have come a little closer to *you* in the process, then that is the most welcome gain of my entire expedition to Berlin.
    Fare you well!

Yours,
Richard Wagner.

SB II,355.

64. KARL GAILLARD, BERLIN   Dresden, 30 January 1844

[. . .] I really have no illusions about my reputation as a poet, & I confess that it was only as a last resort that I adopted the expedient of writing my own libretti, since no decent texts were offered me. But it would now be

---

1 In spite of the public's acclaim, critical press reaction was unfavourable, and the work disappeared from the Berlin repertory after 25 February 1844. It was not revived there until 1868.
2 King Friedrich Wilhelm IV of Prussia.

totally impossible for me to set another's text to music for the following reason: – It is not my practice to choose a subject at random, to versify it & then think of suitable music to write for it; – if I were to proceed in that way I should be exposed to the difficulty of having to work myself up to a pitch of enthusiasm on two separate occasions, something which is impossible. No, my method of production is different from that: – in the first place I am attracted only by those subjects which reveal themselves to me not only as poetically but, at the same time, as musically significant. And so, even before I set about writing a single line of the text or drafting a scene, I am already thoroughly immersed in the musical aura of my new creation, I have the whole sound & all the characteristic motives in my head so that when the poem is finished & the scenes are arranged in their proper order the actual opera is already completed, & its detailed musical treatment is more a question of calm & reflective revision, the moment of actual creativity having already passed. But for this to be so, I must choose only subjects which are capable of an exclusively musical treatment: I would never, for example, choose a subject which a skilled playwright could just as well turn into a spoken drama. But as a musician I can choose subjects & invent situations & contrasts which must always remain outside the province of a dramatic poet who is writing for the theatre. This, however, is the point at which opera & drama part company, each of which calmly follows its own direction. If it is the task of today's dramatic poet to elucidate & intellectualize the material interests of our age from a moralistic point of view, so it falls to the opera librettist and composer to conjure up the unique & characteristic aura of sanctity associated with poetry as it wafts across the centuries in the form of legends & tales from the dawn of history; for music offers us the means to forge links which the poet alone does not have at his command, at least when faced with today's actors. This is the way to raise up opera to a higher plane & restore it to a level from which we ourselves have debased it by expecting composers to derive their inspiration from trivialities, intrigues & so on, which the modern writer of comedies & plays could far more successfully depict *without* the aid of music.

– For my next opera I have chosen the beautiful & highly characteristic legend of *Tannhäuser*, who lingered in the Venusberg & then journeyed to Rome in search of atonement; I have made a connection between this legend & the Wartburg song contest, in which Tannhäuser replaces Heinrich v. Ofterdingen; the result of this connection is a poem which is rich in dramatic life. – I think it will become clear to you when you get to know the subject that only a musician could have treated it adequately.

[. . .]

SB II,357–9.

65. ALWINE FROMMANN, BERLIN   Dresden, 27 October 1844

[. . .] That you have got to know my "Rienzi" is most unwelcome to me: I
feel nothing but dislike for this monster.
[. . .]

SB II,400.

66. ERNST BENEDIKT KIETZ, PARIS   Dresden, 18 December 1844

[. . .] Unfortunately, my constant preoccupations have prevented me until
now from doing any work on my latest compositions. After a long interruption,
caused chiefly by the publication of my two operas, I finally managed to
resume work on my new opera last autumn while staying at the vineyard
mentioned earlier;[1] I have now had to abandon it again, but hope to complete
the score by early next year.[2] The sets are being painted by Desplechin in
Paris, but since he cannot promise to have them ready before next Easter,
my opera cannot be staged before August or September of next year at the
earliest; I aim to produce a great revolution with it, for I feel that, with it, I
have made a gigantic step forward in the direction of my ideal. – But this is
just between the two of us! –
[. . .]

SB II,407–8.

67. LOUIS SPOHR, CASSEL   Dresden, 4 February 1845

[. . .] There could be no more important event in the operatic life of present-
day Germany than the re-emergence of a master such as you yourself.[3] God
knows, I am of the unhappy opinion that our more recent operatic composers
are of total insignificance as far as recreating German opera is concerned. I
regret to have to say that their latest offerings have forced me to the conclusion

1 Wagner spent six weeks at Wilhelm Fischer's vineyards near Loschwitz from early September
  to 15 October 1844.
2 The complete draft of Act I of *Tannhäuser* was begun in November 1843 and finished on 27
  January 1844; Wagner worked on Act II between 7 September and 15 October 1844, and
  on Act III between 19 and 29 December 1844; the full score of the opera was completed
  on 13 April 1845.
3 Spohr's opera *Die Kreuzfahrer* (The Crusaders) was first performed in Cassel on 1 June
  1845; see also introductory essay, p. 56.

that the people of whom I speak have no other thought in mind than that of *pleasing at all costs*. They doubt and despair in the uniqueness of what is German, and believe they have no alternative but to adopt a cosmopolitan outlook. They think that if they blend Auberian piquancy with a Donizettian emphasis upon singing, and add a dash of German thoroughness by way of compensation, they will be certain of creating something that is generally effective. In my own view, almost every aspect of operatic life in present-day Germany suffers from this distasteful striving after superficial success; what these people lack is an unconditional faith in the invincibility of all that is genuine & true, for where can inspiration exist without this faith? & how can a work of art be created without inspiration? – [. . .]

SB II,417–18.

68. KARL GAILLARD, BERLIN   Dresden, 5 June 1845

[. . .] In truth, I now find myself in a crisis which thus far has prevented me from rising far above myself. After a single stroke of good fortune, which brought me overnight fame & employment (something so necessary & important in Germany), my guardian angel has suddenly folded its wings; since I first appeared on the scene in Dresden, it has proved impossible to make any further advance. What I need is a large city, & indeed the largest in Germany, wherein to consolidate my success in Dresden: but Berlin seems to exist only in order to undermine that success. It was in itself a hazardous undertaking to appear before such a wide public with a work like my "flying Dutchman", given the fact that the audience was not previously disposed in my favour: I really should have made my début in Berlin with "Rienzi". But no sooner had my Dutchman seen the light of day in a fairly effective fashion – albeit in the unmusical & unflattering confines of the Schauspielhaus[1] – when the Berlin intendant took it into his head to undermine the impression I had succeeded in making by removing the opera from the repertoire, purely as a concession to slovenly routine. As a result, he has virtually wrecked whatever chances this work of mine may have had, & I may as well give up all hope of seeing it taken up elsewhere, at least for the time being.[2] I am now working hard to see if a production of *Rienzi* might still be possible in Berlin. *Meierbeer,*

1 The Berlin Opera House had burnt down on 18 August 1843, with the result that Wagner's opera was performed in the Schauspielhaus in the Gendarmenmarkt.
2 The next production of *Der fliegende Holländer* took place in Zurich on 25 April 1852 under Wagner's direction.

who last summer attended the 20th performance of this opera,[1] when he had a further opportunity to convince himself of the effectiveness of the piece, not least because the singers were called out in front of the curtain & greeted with tumultuous applause after each of the *five* acts, indeed, at the end of the 4th act the author himself was twice honoured in the same way, – Meierbeer promised to leave no stone unturned in his attempts to present this opera to the Berliners at the earliest available opportunity.[2] I do not yet doubt the honesty of his intentions towards me, the difficulty which still remains to be solved & which makes a performance of my opera an impossibility is the lack of a Heldentenor – this on its own is sufficient to make me despair in general. – This problem of getting my works accepted elsewhere is doubly prejudicial to my cause thanks to the present state of music criticism in Dresden. Dresden is a place which had sunk into utter critical insignificance as a result of a century of slovenly routine: *Weber* discovered a flourishing Italian opera here, a rank & parasitical growth, – he first had to create a German opera & he had to do so under the most difficult conditions in the world, chief of which was the open hostility of the Court. The artistic standards which he was able to introduce remained fairly modest during his own lifetime, – he himself had his own works first performed elsewhere. Since Weber's death, artistic standards have risen considerably, largely as a result of the dissolution of the Italian opera, but the spirit which informs the new administration has succumbed to the crassest philistinism causing the most irreparable damage to *Weber's* incipient attempts to enhance the musical significance of Dresden. Encouraged by the high standards I found here, I have now set about the glorious task of carrying on Weber's work, i.e. helping to emancipate Dresden musically, taking the philistines for a ride, educating public taste so that audiences learn to appreciate what is noble in art, & in that way making Weber's voice heard. And what is the first obstacle I come up against? *Envy*!! As long as I was the poor musician whom nobody had heard of & whose opera brought him overnight success, all was well: but when this success was seen to be rewarded in the form of a life appointment at an annual salary of 1500 thr., the milk of human kindness curdled & turned sour. Fortunately, I have been able to counteract the hostile effects of this envy, at least where it stood in the way of my practical music-making; but it thrives in rank luxuriance in precisely that field which my honour prevents me from entering, namely the field of *criticism*. [...] I know of course that a newspaper report cannot turn a good work into a bad one or a bad one into a good one; – but newspapers can harm a good cause by impeding & delaying

1 Meyerbeer heard *Rienzi* in Dresden on 20 September 1844. He noted in his diary, "Although deafened by the insanely overblown instrumentation, there are nevertheless some genuinely beautiful and excellent things in it" (*Giacomo Meyerbeer: Briefwechsel und Tagebücher.* III,527).
2 *Rienzi* was first performed in Berlin on 24 October 1847. The title role was sung by Julius Pfister.

its progress, – they have a disheartening effect. In point of fact, I must admit that, for my own part, I have not been disheartened in spite of the evident problems in getting my operas accepted elsewhere, but I have begun to vacillate in my resolve – a resolve which might well have had some slight merit if only I were to have carried it out. It was in fact my intention, following the splendid success I had achieved in Dresden, to sever all links with Paris, in the splendid conviction that the time had come when a dramatic musician could influence Germany from within Germany itself. I still think it is extremely important for the whole future of dramatic music in Germany that a phenomenon which issues from the heart of Germany should spread throughout the country, & I confess that it is with a sense of great pain that I occasionally find myself glancing involuntarily in the direction of Paris in an attempt to escape from the mud which is thrown up at me by every step I take, & I say to myself: is Paris unique in its ability to influence Germany? When my thoughts turn to Paris in this way, I feel a sense of woeful disquiet, as though I were planning to betray my own mother! – It is a fine thing, is it not, for a man to be driven to such treasonable thoughts! – Help me to wipe them from my mind! I am enclosing with this letter a copy of my "Tannhäuser" as he lives & breathes, a German from head to toe; kindly accept it as a present. May he be capable of winning me the hearts of my fellow Germans in far greater numbers than my earlier works have thus far succeeded in doing! This work *must* be good, or I am incapable of ever achieving anything good. I felt that a very real spell had been cast upon me as I was writing it; it required the merest contact with the subject-matter & I immediately began to tremble with warmth & passion: – in spite of the long interruptions which kept me away from the score for months on end, I was always able to reimmerse myself in an instant in the characteristic aura of the work, an aura which had so exhilarated me when I first conceived the piece. – [. . .]

Following your advice I have retouched one or two lines in the text, including the "*sable pinions*" in Wolfram's aria on p. 40; this has now been dropped.[1] But I have left unaltered the final rhyme of "God" & "mock",[2] because what I see in this word "mock" has nothing to do with the constraints of rhyme, rather is it the most typical poetical word for the way in which an

1   The lines in question had originally read, "Wie Todesahnung Dämm'rung sinkt hernieder, / umhüllt das Thal mit schwäzlichem Gefieder" (Darkness descends like some deathly foreboding, / enfolds the valley with its sable pinions). At Gaillard's suggestion this was altered to the now familiar "Wie Todesahnung Dämm'rung deckt die Lande, / umhüllt das Thal mit schwäzlichem Gewande" (Darkness shrouds the lands like some deathly foreboding, / enfolds the valley with its sable raiment).
2   "Hoch über aller Welt ist Gott / Und sein Erbarmen ist kein Spott" (High above the world is God / And his mercy is no mockery).

obdurate priesthood has perverted the meaning of divine mercy. So help me God!

At the end of this month I intend going to *Marienbad* in the hope of finding a cure for my unspeakable abdominal disorder, & in *August* I shall return to Dresden to rehearse "Tannhäuser": the piano arrangements etc. are already finished, so that the day after the first performance[1] I shall be completely free to do as I please. I plan to idle away the whole of the coming year, i.e. devouring the contents of my library without producing any work, although I regret to say that I do once again feel the urge to write something now that a new subject has caught my imagination;[2] but I intend to resist that urge, by force if necessary, firstly because there are a number of new things I should like to learn about, & secondly because I have come to the conclusion that if a dramatic work is to possess concentrated significance & originality, it must be the result of a certain step upwards in an artist's life & of a certain important period in his development: but such a step – such a period is not marked off by half-yearly intervals: it takes several years to produce such concentrated maturity. Only *money-grubbers* can be content to produce a single insignificant work – *I* shall *never* earn any money for myself, – I am now fully resigned to that fact. [. . .]

SB II,429–36.

69. GUSTAV KLEMM, DRESDEN[3]   Dresden, 20 June 1845

[. . .] The manner in which I create my dramatic works, whereby I write not only the music but the entire musical drama, is now so much second nature to me that not only could I no longer reconcile myself to the idea of setting another writer's dramatic poem to music but I recognize that this must be my most important goal in the future – & one which I ought to be capable of achieving. I am now fully convinced that if anything of significance & validity for the history of art is to emerge from this particular genre (which I see as diametrically opposed to the "opera industry" of the present day), this can only be so if the poet and musician are one & the same person. By following the old dispensation you will at best produce a decent libretto or decent music, but never a genuine musical drama, indeed I shall never be able to understand how two artists could ever create a single work of art. The

---

1 The first performance of *Tannhäuser* took place in Dresden on 19 October 1845.
2 *Lohengrin;* see also letter [70].
3 Dr Gustav Klemm, a Dresden Court official, had sent Wagner a libretto with a request, from the poetess Louise Otto (?), that he set it. In the present letter Wagner declines, for the reasons given, recommending that Ferdinand Hiller be approached instead.

fact that I have grasped a subject which came to me alone, that I elaborate it in such a way that I myself can no longer say which parts show the influence of the poet & which the influence of the musician, and that I finally complete both words and music just as the subject originally appeared to me in vague outline – all this I find adequate justification for my exclusively creative – and more especially my *musically* creative powers. In addition to which I am always so richly provided for with future ideas that, given the tedious waste of time involved in completing an opera, I am afraid that I shall carry with me to the grave a number of ideas which I have not had the time to elaborate.

[. . .]

SB II,437–8.

70. ALBERT WAGNER, DRESDEN   Marienbad, 4 August 1845

[. . .] And so we shall have completed our course of treatment in 4 days' time, having by then spent five full weeks here![1] All the signs are that it has been a success both for myself & for Minna, whom, as usual, we have kept as far away as possible from all her acquaintances, since they have now become such a regular nuisance wherever we go; conversely, we have rarely been away from the forests & mountains. But my head was in a whirl as always, & it was in this frame of mind yesterday that I finished writing out a very full & detailed scenario for *Lohengrin*; I am delighted with the result, indeed, I freely admit that it fills me with a feeling of proud contentment. You know the worry that often used to beset me, that I should never again find a subject that approached my Tannhäuser in its warmth & uniqueness: – but the more familiar I have become with my new subject & the more profoundly I have grasped its central idea, the more it has dawned upon me how rich & luxurious the seed of this new idea is, a seed which has grown into so full & burgeoning a flower that I feel happy indeed in the knowledge that I possess it. In creating this work, my powers of invention & sense of formal structure have played their biggest part to date: the medieval poem which has preserved this highly poetical legend contains the most inadequate & pedestrian account to have come down to us, and I feel very fortunate to have satisfied my desire to rescue what by now is an almost unrecognizable legend from the rubble & decay to which the medieval poet had reduced the poem as a result of his inferior & prosaic treatment of it, & to have restored it to its rich & highly poetical potential by dint of my own inventiveness & reworking of it. – But quite apart from all this, how felicitous

---

1 Wagner and Minna were in Marienbad, taking the waters, from 3 July to 9 August 1845.

a libretto it has turned out to be! Effective, attractive, impressive & affecting in all its parts! – Johanna's[1] role in it – which is very important & in point of fact the principal role in the work – is bound to turn out the most charming & most moving in the world. – But enough of this. – Out of the abundance of the heart, etc.[2]

[. . .]

SB II,446.

71. GOTTFRIED ENGELBERT ANDERS, PARIS   Dresden, 1 February 1846

[. . .] My dear Anders, things could be a whole lot better! I have found fame and recognition in good measure, but unfortunately *no income*. Germany has so far proved to be a land accursed – a place which drives men to starvation. How could I ever manage here if I did not have a regular appointment?! –

My plans are therefore once again turning towards Paris: it is the only prospect, as far as my external circumstances are concerned, which promises release from my present predicament. It is highly likely, my dear friend, that I shall be seeing you again in Paris: I pray to God that it be soon! very soon!

As soon as the vocal score of my new opera[3] is finished, I shall send you all 3 of my operas.

I am not recommending my *niece*[4] to *Schlesinger* since I really do not know what use he could be to her: in any case he's a lecherous old goat and could easily kick up a stink. If she were ever to need him, I assume you will be able to recommend her?

Adieu, my good and dear old friend! I pray to God that it will not be long before we see each other again!

Yours,
Richard Wagner.

SB II,485–6.

1 Johanna Wagner, Albert's daughter. In the event, the role of Elsa was created by Rosa Agthe.
2 *St Matthew* 11:34.
3 *Tannhäuser*; the three operas mentioned here are *Rienzi*, *Der fliegende Holländer* and *Tannhäuser*.
4 Johanna Wagner; she studied with Manuel García in Paris between February and August 1846.

72. AUGUST VON LÜTTICHAU, DRESDEN   Dresden, 2 March 1846

My Lord Baron,

I do myself the honour of submitting herewith a major and fairly detailed report[1] which I felt my position and sense of duty obliged me to draw up. Three years have now gone by since I was appointed Kapellmeister to the Royal Orchestra on Your Excellency's kind recommendation and through His Majesty's especial favour: – the passage of such a period of time may well provoke the question as to how the institution as a whole has benefited from its latest addition. It is with a sense of sadness that I have to confess that the benefit which I might have offered in my capacity as conductor has been limited to a mere handful of achievements: that I could have been of not inconsiderable influence on the future development of the orchestra is unfortunately something I discovered did not lie within my power to achieve. I have had to accept the fact that the orchestra has always had to give way in the face of a constant conflict of interests with the theatre and the latter's myriad needs, indeed, it was not even possible to attach to its achievements the weight and consideration which the interests of the theatre *alone* could claim as their rightful due. I sought repeatedly, and in formal accord with my colleagues, to protect the orchestra's aforesaid interests, yet each time I did so, my efforts met only with the most limited success, so that it is with great sadness that I have been forced to conclude that the reason for this lies in the fact that the statements and reassurances that have been issued by the orchestra's technical directors have, for what I assume is now some considerable time, not enjoyed the degree of trust on the part of their most esteemed superior that would alone have been capable of giving them the requisite weight of authority. So firmly convinced am I of the necessity of the same that I have taken upon myself the task of reappraising all the experiences and insights gained during the three years of my appointment and of setting them down in the form of a lucid and cogent exposition. I have spent the last three months subjecting everything I thought necessary to the strictest and most detailed scrutiny, and have done so with the greatest circumspection, carefully weighing up each point in turn, for which reason I have reworked and redrafted some of the items two, three or even four times; in this way I have finally completed the enclosed report which I beseech Your Excellency to rest assured is not attributable to any external pressure; rather does it remain, in the form in which I am submitting it, my own closely guarded secret, nor have the points which it contains been forced upon me as a result, perhaps, of any discussion or agreement with the individuals concerned. My only motivation has been the sense of obligation to which, according to the dictates

---

1 *Die Königliche Kapelle betreffend* (Concerning the Royal Orchestra), published in SS,151-204; see introductory essay, p. 57.

of my conscience, I am enjoined by the oath that I swore to His Majesty the King.

[. . .]

SB II, 488–9.

73. ANTON PUSINELLI, DRESDEN   Dresden, 16 March 1846

My dear friend,

You have called upon me to do something to counteract the rumours currently circulating in the town, in which my own affairs have become the subject of such extraordinary interest.[1] Jean Paul once met Goethe and the two men discussed the shameless and malicious rumours which at various times had been spread about each of them; Jean Paul stated that he would take no action against such tales, or at least he would wait until it was claimed he had stolen silver spoons; Goethe said that even then he would do nothing. Although I cannot, alas, compare with a man like Goethe, you will nevertheless, I hope, permit me to follow his example in treating with the most utter contempt this disgusting rumour which, the greater the heights of stupidity it reaches, the sooner it must collapse for want of support. [. . .]

SB II, 496.

74. KARL GAILLARD, BERLIN   Grossgraupa,[2] 21 May 1846

My most worthy friend,

Thank God I am now in the country, three hours' ride from Dresden, in the most charming part of Saxon Switzerland, and can breathe again as man & artist! I have just been through one of the most appalling winters of my entire existence: envy, malice, stupidity – and a fatal slowness in the spread of my works beyond Dresden were the foes I had every day to contend with in that dreadful struggle; it was the kind of struggle, moreover, in which the person under attack must take care to defend himself with only the most extreme & scrupulous self-control, while all the time feeling that he has the strength to defeat his enemies in open battle, if only he were allowed to speak out. I find it

---

1 Rumours were rife concerning Wagner's mounting burden of debt. The text of this letter appeared in the *Dresdner Anzeiger* of 18 March 1846, accompanied by an explanatory note signed A[nton] P[usinelli].

2 Spelt "Gross-Graupe" by Wagner. He and Minna arrived there on 15 May and remained in the village until the beginning of August.

difficult to tell whether my impaired health is the reason for my disgruntled & cheerless mood, or whether the latter is to blame for my indisposition; – one thing aggravates the other. Everything I started went wrong; as I write these lines to you now, I do not have a single guarantee, a single prospect for the future! If I continue for much longer to enjoy only local successes in Dresden, I shall soon have to say goodbye to all my future hopes. – I have some bad news for you, too, my dear friend, which I should have told you long ago: but who the devil takes pleasure in writing such a letter and hastens to break bad news? My efforts on behalf of your play have proved futile,[1] and I would ask you to spare me from going into details which caused me considerable annoyance at the time and which I attempted unsuccessfully to overcome. The whole affair disgusts me. – Shall I return your play to you? There is no more disagreeable task than that! – My dear friend, we are all the most wretched slaves: it is bad enough to have to put up with tyrannical servitude; but what is more shameful than having to dismiss half-wittedness and foolishness with a mere shrug of the shoulders, perhaps sticking out your tongue at the other person once his back is turned? –

Shall I, by way of a pleasant contrast, mention my opera Tannhäuser, whose fine success has found increasingly profound and sincere support? The success of the piece ought to be a cause for great rejoicing, since it offers the finest amends for the direction my art has taken, – but – God knows the reason why – my sense of rejoicing is decidedly lacking! In Germany the opera still remains only a local success![2] – I am glad we sent my niece to Paris;[3] according to all the reports I have received, she will learn a great deal from Garcia. She will be back in Dresden in August, – only then can I give my operas again. – If you visit us in September, you will be able to see Tannhäuser and Rienzi. The management wants to have the Dutchman again next winter – but I shall have to recast it from scratch.

– My dear Gaillard, I am still hoping to score a brilliant success with Rienzi in Berlin[4] (– when?!! –) before launching a frontal attack on Paris; I have no desire to have another new opera produced in Germany. – Do you know what it is to have financial cares? You're a lucky man if you *don't*! – I now hope that the peasant's life I'm leading at present will restore my former spirits and my health. I am living in a completely unspoilt village, – I am *the first townsman* ever to rent rooms here. My King has acted most charitably in

1 Wagner had attempted to have Gaillard's play *Norbert Schreck* accepted for performance in Dresden.
2 The next production of *Tannhäuser* took place in Weimar on 16 February 1849. The work was subsequently staged in Schwerin (26 January 1852), Breslau (6 October 1852) and Wiesbaden (13 November 1852), and was then quickly taken up into the repertoire of more than forty other German opera houses.
3 Johanna Wagner; see also letter [71], p. 125.
4 See letter [68], p. 121, note 2.

granting me extended leave of absence! – I run around and lie in the forest, read, eat and drink, and attempt to put all thoughts of practical music making clean out of my mind! –

It would be utterly absurd if you were to be angry with me for breaking such bad news to you! God knows I have few enough friends, do not desert me on this account. You are so versatile and not easily deterred, I am sure you can take it! Remain true to me, and do not be discouraged by the effort it costs to be one of my friends!

My warmest good wishes to everyone! Fare you well!

Yours,
Richard Wagner.

SB II,508–10.

75. HERMANN FRANCK, BRESLAU   Grossgraupa, 30 May 1846

Most honoured friend,

I do not know your present whereabouts, yet I cannot resist the urge to converse with you. We recently argued a good deal together on the subject of Lohengrin, and it is this work which continues to concern me now; I have gone back to it again with our discussion still fresh in my mind, and am now clear in my *own* mind what to think: when I looked at my poem again after a period of some time had elapsed, I did so, as far as was possible, as an impartial observer, and I would express its poetic message as follows: atonement for Elsa's failing must necessarily involve her punishment, and rarely can a failing have been followed by a more logical and therefore more inevitable punishment than is expressed here in her *separation* from Lohengrin: neither chastisement nor death (immediately) can be her punishment, – any other form of punishment would be arbitrary and arouse indignation, only the punishment of separation – albeit the harshest of all penalties – appears as utterly inevitable, and it can never appear *too* harsh, precisely because it is the most just and most consequential. *Elsa* has forfeited *Lohengrin*, it is impossible for them to remain man and wife any longer, for the moment Elsa asks the forbidden question, their marriage is already void: right from the outset, from the time I first became familiar with the subject, *separation*, the idea of separation, struck me as being its most characteristic and uniquely distinguishing feature, and now that I have considered every other possible solution, I return with increasing certainty to this idea of their separation, – which, if it were to be left out, would require a total transformation of the subject and probably allow no more than its most superficial externals to be retained. The symbolic meaning of the tale I can best sum up as follows: contact between a metaphysical phenomenon and human nature, and the

impossibility that such contact will last. The moral would be: the good Lord*
would do better to spare us His revelations since He is not permitted to annul
the laws of nature: nature – in this case human nature – is bound to take her
revenge and destroy the revelation. This seems to me to be the meaning of
most of those wonderful legends which are not the work of priests. What
happened to *Semele* in the case of *Zeus*? – Of course, we are bound to ask
ourselves the question whether, on this basis, my poem is capable of being
dramatically effective in a unified way, and this, I know, was what worried
you most. I confess that I am in no doubt about the answer, however rash I
might appear to be in leaving the obvious conclusion to the action to the
audience's imagination, as happens here with the departure of *Lohengrin:* yet
here we must risk enacting the final moment of separation, and this must be
made possible by our being perfectly clear in our minds what is the fate which
ultimately befalls *both* the lovers once they are separated. On this point the
doubt which you raised was of great help to me in forcing me to consider
ways of making *Lohengrin's* involvement in the tragic outcome clearer than
had previously been the case.

I now believe that I have made it perfectly self-evident what Lohengrin's
great (and passive) role is in the course which fate adopts: – in the first scene
in which he appears, I have altered nothing, – it would be wrong to detract
from the splendid privilege which music enjoys of making up for what the
poet hesitates to put into words: surprise at the sight of Elsa, and the *unexpected*
and swiftly kindled flames of love. – Nor do I wish to make any changes to
Lohengrin's rejoinder when Elsa asks him for the second time whence he
has come; his reply, following a stern reproof, was:

> O let my arm, sweet love, enfold thee!
> Unto my beating heart draw nigh,
> By thine own light let me behold thee,
> In whom the world for me doth lie!
> Let me then tenderly caress thee,
> Thy breath upon my cheek to feel!
> Nearer and nearer let me press thee,
> Till bliss complete shall o'er me steal!
> Thy love's to me sufficient treasure;
> To pay for all that it has cost;
> For who upon God's earth can measure
> A prouder lot than I have lost?
> Kings at my feet a crown might lay me,
> I should with scorn the gift disown.

* I mean: the Christian God. –
(I am afraid I have talked a lot of nonsense on this occasion: I lack the means to express
myself.) [*added by Wagner in the margin*]

> But one thing can for all repay me,
> Thy confidence, thy love alone etc.[1]

Here, too, I am reluctant to be more explicit, and I expressly intend to use music here to complement the meaning of this passage, so that no one will be in any doubt as to what Lohengrin feels. It is precisely this which seems to me to be the great advantage to be gained from combining the expressive possibilities of the poem on the one hand with those of its musical composition on the other, namely that the characters who express themselves through these two means can reveal themselves with a certain fixed plasticity and wholeness which would inevitably be weakened by too much secondary motivation. (God knows whether I am expressing myself clearly!) – However, after I have had Lohengrin announce his lofty calling in a calm and solemn tone – instead of turning to Elsa with a bitter reproach, as he did in the earlier version, I now have him speak the following lines with the greatest possible emotion:

> Oh Elsa! Think what thou hast done to me!
> When at the first my glances turned on thee,
> I felt love to my heart straightway had flown,[2]
> The Grail's chaste service did my heart disown.
> But having turned from God in love's excess,
> Atonement and remorse must I endure,
> For ah! the shameful sin must I confess
> Of deeming woman's love divinely pure! –

Do you still think it necessary for him to mention the specific rule associated with the Grail which, although not expressly forbidding the Grail knights from committing such excesses, nevertheless discourages them from acting in this way? I think it should be sufficient for the audience to deduce from what Lohengrin says that the bonds of earthly love are, strictly speaking, unbecoming for a knight of the Grail. (I might add that I have not invented any part of this varying stipulation, – this is exactly how it is in Wolfram.) When *Elsa* now calls on Lohengrin to punish her for her failing, the latter replies:

> No other sentence may suffice for thee!
> My heart and thine equally pain has rent!
> Apart, asunder ever doomed to be,
> This is our sentence, this our punishment!

---

1 GS II,104; verse translation by the Corders.
2 GS II,110; the following five lines were altered in the libretto and not set to music.

Elsa: Ah woe, no harsher sentence can there be![1]
            But death alone remains when reft of thee!

Lohengrin: The Grail's fair knight must *live* in godly fane,
            Thy husband, ah! is prey to parting's pain. –

But enough of this, my most honoured friend, otherwise I shall find myself retelling the whole story all over again. – If your conscience permits you to do so, give me and my work your blessing; I cannot tell you how happy and optimistic I feel on resuming work on the score: – this time my music shall please you, – I believe I have again learned a great deal. –

I hope you will devote a few lines to me so that I may discover where you are at present, and whether you are content or not. God knows why I always become so garrulous when I'm with you: you've already had to put up with a good deal of stupidity from me! When you tear open this letter, will you be shocked and think that I've also been singing it? But you can see I've spared you that! –

May I ask you to convey my kindest good wishes to your very dear wife?

I am, Sir, your respectful and most obedient servant,

Richard Wagner.

SB II,511–15.

76. EDUARD HANSLICK, VIENNA   Dresden, 1 January 1847

Please accept my most sincere thanks, my dear Herr Hanslick, for sending me your article,[2] which I received this morning on New Year's Day. Your review of my "Tannhäuser" is so comprehensive, and its thrust as flattering to me as it is welcome, that I am left in no doubt as to the impression which my work has had on you. I cannot of course pass judgement upon your own judgement, as you so modestly invite me to do, since there can surely be no judgement as biassed as my own. If you wish to know the feeling that I experienced on reading through your article, then I must confess since the truth demands it – that it was one of extreme anxiety. Whether I read praise or censure concerning myself, I always feel as though the reviewer had thrust his hand into my entrails in his attempt to examine them; on this point I cannot suppress a certain maidenly shyness in which I think of my body as my soul: any performance of my operas in the presence of an audience is for me a constant battle against such boundless inner turmoil that there have

---

1 GS II,111; the following three lines were altered in the libretto and not set to music.
2 Hanslick had sent Wagner a copy of his review of *Tannhäuser* which had appeared in the *Allgemeine Wiener Musik-Zeitung* at the end of 1846.

often been times when I have sought to prevent performances from taking place if I did not feel myself equal to that struggle. I am fully convinced that criticism is far more useful to an artist than praise: the artist who is destroyed by such criticism deserves to go under, – only the one whom such criticism encourages has any true inner strength: but that praise, like censure, is bound to affect the artist very deeply, inasmuch as nature has given him the keenest spur of passion, must be seen as self-evident.

The more the works I create are marked by an increasingly well-defined artistic consciousness, the more I am attracted by the *whole* man; I wish to create men of flesh & blood & bones, I wish my characters to walk & move about freely & truthfully, – and I often marvel that so many people perceive only the flesh & examine its softness or hardness. Let me express myself more clearly & consider only a single limb of the body: – nothing has given me greater satisfaction than the effect produced upon audiences by the Song Contest, taken as a whole, in the majority of performances of *Tannhäuser* (– whether this was also true of the performance which you attended, I do not clearly recall –): what I discovered was that each of the individual songs was greeted with lively applause, & that the applause rose to the most unwonted pitch of excitement during the final songs & at the concluding outburst of horror on the part of the assembled company; – I say that this observation gratified me greatly, since this observation of extreme *naïveté*[1] on the audience's part confirms me in my belief that it is possible to achieve a noble aim. Very few people could be certain whether they had the musician or the poet to thank for their response, & my sole concern must be to leave this issue unresolved. I have no special ambition to see my poetry overshadowed by my music, but I should be guilty of dismembering myself & exposing an untruth if I were to insist upon doing violence to the music for the sake of the poem. I cannot broach a poetic subject if it is not already conditioned by music: it follows, however, from this higher purpose of mine that my Song Contest, although dominated by the poetic element, would not have been feasible without music. – But a work of art does not exist until such time as it takes on visible form: in the case of a drama this moment is its representation on stage, – and as far as it lies within my power to do so, I mean to master this aspect, too; indeed, working towards this goal is something which I regard as almost on a par with the remaining aspects of my creativity. In this sense, success is expressed only in terms of the immediate success of the performance itself – once the great mass of the people has come to accept what is so strange & unusual about the work; & it consoles me to know that in achieving this noble end only noble means are permissible. Each time I

---

1 Used here in the Schillerian sense: the naïve poet is at one with nature, whereas the "sentimental" or reflective poet is conscious of his separation from nature, and of his longing to return to it.

have fallen short of this ideal, I have recognized that the flaw lay not in the individual means but in the essential features of the subject as a whole.

There is perhaps one other aspect to bear in mind where music is involved, its powerfully sensorial element forces its way so far into the foreground that the conditions for its effectiveness must appear almost uniquely determinative. But whether the unique quality of music enables it in every case to do justice to what poetry – however musical – has to offer, whether it is capable of giving wholly adequate expression in every case to the claims of dramatic passion, this is something I do not yet venture to decide. Gluck's poems certainly made no exhaustive demands upon music's affective potential, being more or less confined to a certain circumscribed & conventional pathos – that of Racinean tragedy – & in those instances where such pathos should have been transcended, Gluck's music is unmistakably deficient. The poems of Mozart's operas had even less in common with these fundamental truths of human nature: the one exception is "Donna Anna", but even here the possibilities are far from exhausted. What Spontini offers us in the second act of his Vestal Virgin (Julia's scene) & what Weber offers on rare occasions in Euryanthe (e.g. the moment after she has betrayed the secret to Eglantine etc.) is limited to that object of general censure, "diminished-seventh music", & for my own part at least I feel bound to point out how restricted in this respect are the achievements of our predecessors. That we have fallen so far short of the highest & truest potential of opera in employing such devices – & I speak not of their purely musical aspect but of the dramatic work of art as a whole – is incontestable: & it is in this sense & from the standpoint of my own creative abilities – which I am more inclined to doubt in than I am to overestimate – that I regard my present & forthcoming works as attempts to prove whether opera is still feasible.

Do not underestimate the power of reflection; the unconsciously created work of art belongs to periods remote from our own: the work of art of the most advanced period of culture can be produced only by a process of conscious creation. The Christian poetry of the Middle Ages, for ex., was immediate & unconscious: but no fully authentic work of art was produced at that time, – that was something reserved for Goethe in our own age of objectivity. That only the most fertile human nature can effect this wondrous combination between the power of the reflective intellect, on the one hand, & the fecundity of the more direct creative power on the other – this is what makes these highest manifestations of art such rare phenomena, & although we have good reason to doubt whether such giftedness will reveal itself in the immediate future in the area of art we have been discussing, a more or less happy blend of the two intellectual qualities outlined above must even now be assumed to exist in every artist who serves the true cause of art, – and the separation of these two gifts must be regarded – strictly speaking – as unconducive to attaining this higher goal.

That a world of difference separates us is revealed by your high opinion of Meyerbeer; I say this without the least embarrassment, since Meyerbeer is a very close personal friend of mine, & I have every reason to value him as a kind & sympathetic man. But if I were to try to sum up precisely what it is that I find so offensive about the lack of inner concentration & the outer effortfulness of the opera industry today, I would lump it all together under the heading "Meyerbeer", & I should be all the keener to do so because I see in Meyerbeer's music a great skill at achieving superficial effects which prevents his art from attaining a noble maturity, & the reason for this is that it denies the essential inwardness of art & strives instead to gratify the listener in every way possible: – the man who strays into the realm of triviality must pay for his transgression at the cost of his own more noble nature; – but he who seeks it deliberately, that man is – fortunate, for he has *nothing* worth losing. – –

You see how talkative you have made me! I hope that in the process you will not forget the main brunt of my argument but will allow me to express once again my thanks for the great effort you have made on my behalf, & for the generous intention which lay behind that effort; now that I have prattled on to my heart's content, I too feel how useful it was for you to have achieved that intention in every conceivable respect.

Fare you well & be so good as to write to me again soon.

Yours,
Richard Wagner.

SB II,535–9.

77. August von Lüttichau, Dresden   Dresden, 9 July 1847

Your Excellency,

Wearisome as my letters must be, I must regrettably inflict yet another written communication upon you.

My position vis-à-vis the opera at the Royal Court Theatre has inevitably caused me repeated distress on more than one occasion, and I have frequently felt how impossible it was for me to continue to discharge the duties I deemed necessary, given the prevailing circumstances and the rivalry felt by my various colleagues all of whom enjoy the same rights as I do; the result of all this is that I have often felt discouraged and seen my native enthusiasm undermined; – in moods such as these I have often considered in what way I might extricate myself from all responsibility for a business which several parties believe me to be actively involved in, in consequence of which I am now exposed to opinions and attacks which affect me the more keenly, the greater my influence is mistakenly thought to be.

That my own voice carries little weight of authority is something of which Herr Dr Gutzkow, among others, is no doubt fully aware: all the more shameful, therefore, is the course of action which he is currently embarked upon. I shall begin by drawing Your Excellency's attention to the Dresden theatre reports which have recently appeared in the Deutsche Allgemeine Zeitung. – If, in itself, it was humiliating to think that a man who until very recently was a mere journalist and who has subsequently taken a superficial interest in the theatre (– except in the case of the latter's *chronique scandaleuse*, where his interest has been far from superficial –), but who has yet to give any real proof that he knows the first thing about the subject – to think that such a man was suddenly entrusted with supreme technical and almost administrative control over an institution which had managed in the past to achieve splendid things without him, I nevertheless had no reason to register any personal complaints as far as the interests of the opera were concerned, as long as I was able to assume that his instructions were confined in the first instance to the field of spoken drama. Although I noticed in what a short space of time this man had succeeded in bringing down upon himself the ridicule and contempt of the entire company, thanks to his pretentious behaviour and his tasteless instructions – all of which betrayed the most extreme ignorance – , I could no longer remain indifferent when I discovered that this same man was to be made responsible for the administration of the opera. It was this discovery that prompted me to avoid Your Excellency at the beginning of this year: I have never denied that I did so out of annoyance. What has come to light in the mean time is well known to Your Excellency: Herr Gutzkow's achievement, so to speak, was *The Queen's Musketeers*[1] – mine: *Iphigenia in Aulis*. – But this dramatist's meddling in the affairs of the opera finally reached a peak of what I can only call the most shameless vexatiousness when his reports first started to appear in the above-mentioned newspaper; I trust he will not take it into his head to deny that he is the author of these reports, since I should have no difficulty in proving the contrary. Your Excellency will now see the man for what he is and as he has long since appeared most plainly to people who knew him previously, namely a newspaper hack and a creator of cliques who, in the present instance, is quite clearly concerned not for the welfare of our opera but for extending his own sphere of power by seeking to have members of his clique appointed to positions within the opera. – [. . .]

This evil genius, whose intrigues and calumnies are destroying the mutual trust which we need if we are to work together, is leading our institution towards the brink of certain moral collapse; no one is more concerned about

---

1 *Les Mousquetaires de la reine*, opera by Jacques Fromental Elie Halévy, first produced at the Opéra-Comique on 3 February 1846. Gutzkow had brought the work to Dresden and insisted on producing it himself.

this than I, who strives openly, warmly and enthusiastically to achieve the highest goal and yet who so often has cause to regret the manner in which he is misunderstood and rewarded only with a lack of trust. The pain that I feel upon seeing myself condemned in such circumstances to ever increasing disgust and hence to a state of complete inaction, and thus to stand by while the expectations which were once placed in me and in my abilities are increasingly unfulfilled – this pain is so great and so genuine that, if only my present circumstances were somewhat happier, I should without doubt have asked His Majesty to relieve me of my official duties. [. . .]

SB II,548–52.

78. FERDINAND HEINE, MARBACH   Dresden, 6 August 1847

[. . .] I am so full of utter contempt for everything connected with the theatre as it stands at present that – being unable to do anything about it – I have no more ardent desire than to sever all links with it, and I regard it as a veritable curse that my entire creative urge is directed towards the field of drama, since all I find in the miserable conditions which characterize our theatres today is the most abject scorn for all that I do. – You may already have heard that I broke definitively with Lüttichau about 3 weeks ago, such that any thought of reconciliation is now completely out of the question, at least from my own side: Gutzkow was the cause of it. The circumstances are really of no importance: it is the age-old struggle between knowledge and conviction on the one hand and the brutal despotism of crass stupidity on the other; there can be no question of any agreement between the two sides, but when the conflict reaches the stage that our most recent conflict has now reached, even coexistence finally becomes impossible, which is why I am now sticking firmly to my resolve to put an end to the whole affair. However, I have consulted the dictates of prudence and realized that, if I have a major success in Berlin to add to my list of achievements, this can only be to my advantage: and so, if I can keep out of Lüttichau's way long enough to gain this advantage and *then* go to the King, I should much prefer to do so: if, on the other hand, he refuses to leave me in peace, well then, I shall have to take this step sooner than I should otherwise have done: of course I have no particular desire to sacrifice any part of my salary, – but if I have no choice in the matter, I am prepared to reconcile myself even to that. – (Doesn't all this make you want to continue working here for years to come?) –

But now for some more agreeable news! Life at Marcolini's[1] is doing me

---

1 Wagner had moved from the Ostra-Allee in April 1847 and taken rooms in the much cheaper Marcolini-Palais; as a result he now had further to walk to work.

a world of good: – the continuing improvement in my health has enabled me to complete the remaining two acts of my Lohengrin,[1] so that I have now finished the opera and feel pleased and happy as a result, since I am well satisfied with what I have done. If Rienzi turns out a success in Berlin, as I hope it will, Lohengrin will follow immediately afterwards.[2] The King of Prussia spent a week in Pillnitz (unfortunately Lüttichau did not take advantage of the opportunity!) but the former must have spoken to him, and presumably the whole Court must have discussed me at length; – for the day after a great banquet had been given, Lüttichau came running into town and ordered us to drop everything, so that Rienzi could be staged forthwith: (and all this, of course, *after* my catastrophe with L.) Last Sunday we gave Tannhäuser again to a *packed* house: the new ending[3] went well, and even the foreigners, who normally only ever open their mouths on such occasions but never lift a hand, became quite animated.

[. . .]

SB II,554–6.

79. ERNST KOSSAK, BERLIN   Dresden, 23 November 1847

[. . .] Best of friends, what is the point of our preaching to audiences? How sorry I am to see you making such an effort, especially when I myself am the cause of it! There is a dam that must be broken down here, and the means we must use is Revolution! A positive basis must be found; what we ourselves consider good and right must become a firm and immutable reality, so that all that is bad and at present in power shall be transformed, as of itself, to become a stupid and easily vanquishable opposition. A single sensible decision by the King of Prussia with regard to his opera house, and all would be well again!

[. . .]

SB II,578.

---

1 The second complete draft of Act I was composed between 12 May and 8 June 1847, and that of Act II between 18 June and 2 August 1847. Prior to this, the second complete draft of Act III had been finished on 5 March 1847.
2 The Berlin première of *Rienzi* on 24 October 1847 was not a success. *Lohengrin* was not seen in Berlin until 1859.
3 Stage 2 of the opera, first performed on 1 August 1847 (see WWV 70).

80. FRANZ JACOB WIGARD, DRESDEN   Dresden, 19 May 1848

Dear Sir,

Though I should deem my cares needless, especially when addressing such a man as you, you yourself may perhaps concede that patriotic cares, in themselves, are not superfluous. That is why I share those cares with you now:

I fear disaster will ensue if the German Parliament does not take the following immediate decisions:

1. The existing German Federal Diet must be dissolved: Parliament will thus assume all constituent power, together with the authority to appoint a provisional committee from within its ranks to hold executive power.

2. Immediate issue of arms to the whole country in accordance with the usual method.

3. *Offensive and defensive alliance with France.* – These three measures will be sufficient to give a definite sense of direction to the struggle which has now become inevitable: two distinct parties will emerge in every region and in every town: the Frankfurt (German) Party and the Special Government Party. This will bring things to a head.

The fourth step will then be the territorial question of the German states. If the Frankfurt Assembly has the task of producing a constitution which will unite Germany, its first priority must be to deal with the inequality which exists among the individual German states; it must appoint a commission whose task it will be to propose a rational and natural basis for the setting up of a German state on the principle that states will not be admitted with a population of below 3 million and above 6 million inhabitants.

This, finally, is the decisive moment: indeed, if this reform is not introduced, all our work will simply be piecemeal. *It depends then upon the attitude of the princes as to the fate which befalls them: if they begin by opposing us and by protesting, they shall without exception stand accused on a charge which can be perfectly justified from an historical point of view.*

Only when these questions have been resolved and when these battles have been fought shall the assembly proceed to the task of drawing up a constitution, since this task cannot be taken in hand until such time as we have *cleared the ground.* How useless would a new constitution be, given the present state of Germany! *Parliament must first revolutionize the individual states*, and it shall do so by means of the first laws it enacts, since these laws will give the parties the support they need and which has been lacking until now.

If you were to find yourself able to share my views and thus to do all you can to influence the assembly in this way, it would be to your eternal credit. *If you seek less rigorous means, you will not achieve your goal!*

I wish you every success!

Your
devoted servant
Richard Wagner.

SB II,589–91.

81. AUGUST VON LÜTTICHAU, DRESDEN   Dresden, 18 June 1848

Your Excellency,

I beeseech your Excellency most humbly to grant me the favour of allowing me to take 14 days' leave of absence in order that, by observing a suitable diet, I might ward off a gastric complaint which, to judge by my symptoms, is currently threatening my health.

At the same time I consider it my personal duty to justify a step which, although unrelated to the nature of my artistic appointment, is one in which I should not wish to be misunderstood, least of all by Your Excellency.

At a time when even the most uneducated among us is conceded the right to express his views on the current state of our nation's affairs, the educated citizen recognizes how much more it is incumbent upon *him* to take equal advantage of that right. The factional differences among the inhabitants of the town during the last 14 days have forced those with opposing views to adopt such an extreme position that no outside observer can escape the resultant sense of uneasy tension. I myself have joined that society in which the progressive party finds its most decisive expression: partly because I recognize that the progressive party is the party of the future, and partly in consideration of the fact that this party more than any other needs men of intelligence and mildness of disposition to discourage it from crude excesses. I have attended their meetings on only rare occasions, and have never taken part in their debates but stood by merely as an observer: thus I have recently come to realize that it is precisely because of the violent attacks of the so-called monarchists that a spirit of defiance has emerged there with increasingly disturbing consequences: according to current thinking, it is not in itself a crime to declare a republic to be the best form of government: but in most people's minds the thought of a republic necessarily leads on to a belief in the need to abolish the monarchy. Nowhere have I met an orator or a political writer who has paid heed to the idea that the monarchy could continue to remain the sacred focus around which every conceivable popular institution might then be set up; no, rather has the idea of a republic always been directly associated with the assumption that the monarchy will thereby cease to exist: it is this assumption alone which has prevented the mass of the people & their leaders from deciding in favour of the immediate introduction of that form of government; they linked it instead to all manner of conditions which, while not expressing any criminal intent, can only & indeed *must* only lead to every conceivable misinterpretation. My concern, therefore, was to make it perfectly clear to people that, whatever our aims might be, the monarchy itself has never been directly opposed to such aspirations; and that all our aims could very well be achieved on a more permanent basis *with* the monarchy. – The popular party regards the existing form of the Court, with all its outdated and external characteristics, as something of a scandal: I have heard remarks on this subject from people who are far from belonging exclusively to the lowest orders, and these remarks have given me profound insights into the spirit of the people; what they say is more or less that, "once the King has gone, the Court, too, will cease to exist." Now I ask myself: should we encroach upon the monarchy simply because of these external characteristics? No! These external features may disappear, & with them will go a source of discontent which is now directed against the king himself. It was in this context & proceeding along these lines that I considered what is under attack & finally came to the conclusion that, if this could disappear, then everything else would disappear which makes us disaffected with the monarchy. At this point it was only natural that I should feel the desire to convince both parties, monarchists as well as republicans, of the truth of the view I had now arrived at, in order that, were I to be successful, I might lead both parties forwards towards a common goal: retention of the monarchy & with it internal peace. At the same time I was inevitably concerned to shed light on the meaning of the word "republic" – a noble concept which has been so misunderstood even by its own party – & thus to show how the monarchy could for the first time find its true justification within it. It was this desire alone which prompted me to draw up that essay:[1] if, in order to reach my intended goal, I was obliged now & again to attack existing institutions, the fear of making enemies could not be allowed to deter me from giving expression to a deeply felt conviction whose intended aim was not disharmony, but harmony & concord. The warmth of this conviction is to blame for my personal intervention in support of this cause. When I recently attended a meeting of the society, it was to be greeted by those very same speeches which make a direct connection between the concept of a republic – which it cannot be denied is now the main thought occupying the minds of the majority of the people – and the abolition of the monarchy: fully conscious that I was expressing a sound & salutary thought very much for the benefit of this assembly, I resolved there & then to read out my essay, & even if this step had failed to achieve any worthwhile aim, there is *one* aim which it has undeniably fulfilled: never before in this society has our King been accorded such enthusiastic praise, never before has his name been taken up with animated acclaim as was the case when I read out the passage in my speech in praise of his sterling virtues. – [. . .]

SB II, 594–6.

---

1 *Wie verhalten sich republikanische Bestrebungen dem Königthume gegenüber?* (How do Republican Aspirations Stand in Relation to the Monarchy?), published anonymously in the *Dresdner Anzeiger* of 15 June 1848, having been delivered the previous day to the Dresden Vaterlandsverein.

82. Eduard Devrient, Dresden   Dresden, 19 June 1848

My worthy friend,

I sincerely regret having been misled by the heat of the moment into speaking out in public in defence of my recent article. I seem to have been dreadfully misunderstood, and there are many indications that certain people are making serious attempts to discredit me with the King. I hereby confer on you the office of true friendship: I would ask you to use the force of your personality – which is uncommonly suited to such matters – and your gift of words to intercede on my behalf at Court and with the King! Seek as far as it lies within the power of intellectual weapons and unsullied virtue to explain my good intentions to the parties concerned and restrain them if possible from taking steps which could be injurious not only to me (which I do not doubt) but very possibly to themselves as well.

What else can I say: I beg your help as a friend! You will not deny it to me!

Yours,
Richard Wagner.

SB II,598.

83. Ferdinand von Biedenfeld, Weimar   Dresden, 17 January 1849

My very dear Sir,

It is with the most profound gratitude that I acknowledge your kind offer;[1] and my only regret is that it may not prove possible to afford you the desired support.

The work itself which we are discussing here is one from which I have already grown estranged, and I recall only that it was in the course of writing it that I first became fully conscious of my own artistic method. I have always objected to seeing the whole vast apparatus of action, plot and history, supported by the liveliest additions of all the available arts, including painting, sculpture, gymnastics and so on, put to no better use than to drum so many ingratiating tunes into the audience's heads; I convinced myself that the only goal commensurate with such expenditure of effort could be nothing less than the dramatic art-work itself, and that opera is superior to the spoken drama in that to all other means of artistic expression it adds the richest, most varied and most exhaustive of all, namely music. The Greeks, and perhaps also a handful of our own medieval dramatists, were able to bestow upon drama the

---

1 Biedenfeld had offered to write an article on *Tannhäuser*, which received its first performance in Weimar, under Liszt's baton, on 16 February 1849.

advantages of musical expression without thereby altering the drama in any substantial way: in our own day, by contrast, the heroes of absolute music (i.e. music divorced from the art of poetry), and especially Beethoven, have raised the expressive potential of music, notably through their handling of the orchestra, to the level of a completely new artistic force which had earlier scarcely been dreamt of, even by Gluck himself; yet throughout this development, music was bound to have an important influence on drama, since it is in the nature of music to seek to express its own potential. Drama itself had therefore to extend its range of expression and it seemed to me that the musician alone was capable of discovering and developing this quality – a quality which matched the expressive potential of music. Although in this way I elevated the musician to the status of a poet, I could never have allowed him to lose sight of what is very much the central object of drama, not least because his own especial art – music – was now merely being pressed into service in support of a higher – and indeed the highest – artistic goal; and so the musician's true task was bound to appear as follows: to be fully aware and inwardly conscious of the expressive potential of music and yet desire nothing but the drama itself, albeit a drama which could not come into being without the musical consciousness of the poet. In an attempt to make myself perfectly clear, I would refer you to one of the main scenes in my Tannhäuser, namely the Song Contest; it is evident that it is the poetic intent which should predominate here, indeed I had no choice in the matter, not least because this scene is required to precipitate the ensuing catastrophe; to have had the singers rival each other's vocal skills with ornaments and cadenzas might have provided the basis for a competition in a concert hall, but it could never have produced a dramatic conflict of ideas and feelings; on the other hand, a contest involving poets, in which the participants are prepared to risk their very souls, could not be made dramatically effective without this highest and most varied potential which music has of expressing itself; and I have discovered to my satisfaction that it is precisely this scene, in which I have taken so many risks, that has claimed the liveliest and most intense interest on the part of the audience at each of the work's performances: in this way I may triumph in the knowledge that I was able to hold the attention of an audience unaccustomed to such things, and that my appeal was *conceptual* and not merely *emotional*.

Let me sum up briefly: the course I am now embarked upon is that of a musician who, setting out from a convinced belief in the most inexhaustible riches of music, wishes to create the highest of all art forms, namely *drama*. I say *wishes*, in order to indicate that this is something I am striving towards; whether I *can* achieve this ideal is not for me to judge, but, if I stray from this ideal, it will be in consequence of my inferior abilities, not because I lack the necessary resolve.

If, on the basis of this brief communication, it is possible for you to gain some idea of the nature of my achievements, it can only be welcome to me: I could send you more words, but not more substance. Please be satisfied with this, and, if possible, continue to show me your kind concern.

Requesting that you convey my very best wishes to Liszt, I am, Sir,

Your most respectful and obedient servant,
Richard Wagner.

SB II,636–8.

84. CÄCILIE AVENARIUS, LEIPZIG   Dresden, 25 February 1849

[. . .] My Tannhäuser has recently enjoyed the most unparalleled success in Weimar, a fact confirmed by all the reports I have received: the Grand Duke has written almost imploringly to invite me to visit him there next May; though I myself set little store by all this grand-ducal business, his invitation happily coincides with my own desire to pay a brief visit to Thuringia and the Harz at about that time: if an opportunity presents itself to come to Leipzig, I may well bring Minna with me so that the two of you can then travel to Dresden together: that is, if the world has not been destroyed before then, since our noble princes, one and all, seem to have but a single aim in mind at present, namely to destroy the world.

[. . .]

SB II,645.

85. AUGUST RÖCKEL, PRAGUE   Dresden, 2 May 1849

My dearest friend,

I hope you reached Prague safely. I am very overwrought & distracted at the moment thanks to the constant & intense annoyance I have had to suffer from Römpler & Katz,[1] who have still not received any proper instructions from Minckwitz: even so, I hope I can set your mind at rest by assuring you that, in the light of the precautionary measures I have undertaken on your behalf, there will be no further interruptions to our progress.[2]

My dearest friend, come back as soon as your patient allows! things are very unsettled here, all the unions, & this afternoon the entire Communal

1 The printers of the Volksblätter, whose editorship Wagner had assumed during Röckel's absence. See introductory essay, p. 59.
2 Here and elsewhere Wagner uses circumlocutions, on account of surveillance and censorship by the authorities.

Guard & even Prince Albert's regiment which is stationed here have declared their most energetic support for the German constitution: the town council, too. People are preparing for a decisive conflict, if not with the King at least with the Prussian troops; there is only *one* thing they are afraid of, namely that the revolution may come *too soon*. In such circumstances there would be no question of reactionary measures on the part of the government, certainly there has nowhere been any hint of such an attempt so far. – Hungarian Hussars have arrived in Freiberg from Bohemia: everyone has declared his allegiance to them in political addresses. In a word, the air here is filled with the greatest excitement, and I would advise you from the bottom of my heart to return here *very soon*, since your wife & children are in a state of great unease, given the circumstances in which they find themselves. I should add that your wife is well & in good health, Schubert is certainly not pressing his demands, so that all is in order; only the political unrest makes her anxious, and the protection of a husband is something your wife longs for dearly. – No doubt your patients in Limbach[1] are equally anxious to see you. –

Not until today was your wife able to obtain the things you wanted, they will be sent off this evening. I have not let her include what you particularly asked for, for reasons I believe I can justify.

There is nothing else I can write to you at the moment except to say: come back as soon as possible.

Yours,
R.W.

SB II,651–2.

86. MINNA WAGNER, DRESDEN   [Weimar, 14 May 1849]

[. . .] How unfathomable are the ways of fate! I have just survived the most dreadful catastrophe & this, together with yesterday's experiences in Weimar, has made a different man of me & pointed me in a new direction. – Consider, my dear Minna, how during all the years of my appointment in Dresden I have nursed the corpse of the most bitter resentment: the new path I embarked on in my art proved to be fraught with difficulties, causing me to stumble at every turn: consumed with an inner rage, I finally turned my back on my art, which now brought me little else but suffering – , you know that I almost regretted the ink & paper which I felt I was wasting on writing a new opera. Deeply dissatisfied with my position & finding little pleasure in my art, sighing beneath a burden which you unfortunately refused entirely to understand, so

1 Röckel's constituency.

deeply in debt that my regular income would have satisfied my creditors only after many years & the most shameful constraints, – I was at odds with the world, I ceased to be an artist, frittered away my creative abilities & became – in thought, if not in deed – a revolutionary plain & simple, in other words I sought fresh ground for my mind's latest artistic creations in a radically transformed world. The Dresden revolution & all its consequences have now taught me that I am by no means made out to be a real revolutionary: I realized from the unhappy outcome of the uprising that a true, victorious revolutionary must act in total disregard for others, – he must not think of his wife & child, nor of his hearth & home, – his single aim is: – annihilation & if our noble *Heubner* had chosen to act in this way in Freiberg or Chemnitz, the revolution would have triumphed. But it is not people like us who are destined to carry out this fearful task: we are only revolutionaries in order to be able to *build* on new ground; what attracts us is not to *destroy* things but to *refashion* them, & that is why we are not the people that fate needs – these people will arise from within the lowest ranks of society; – we and others like us can have nothing in common with them. Look! *I herewith sever my links with the Revolution....*

[...]

SB II,653–4.

87. EDUARD DEVRIENT, DRESDEN   Weimar, [17 May 1849]

My dearest friend,

I turn to you today with a heavy heart but a firm resolve – once more to ask your help in word and deed. After a long period of tormentingly sultry heat, the storm which finally broke was of such violence and force that all who were close to its centre must have been affected by it, each according to his character and essential disposition. I hope – and it would reassure me to receive confirmation of the fact as soon as possible – that you and your family escaped unharmed from the catastrophe in Dresden. It has affected me deeply in many respects, as chance and sympathy willed it. As long as I was able to follow the Dresden uprising from close quarters, I was in total sympathy with it right from the outset, a sympathy which I expressed quite openly not in deeds, it is true, but in my attitude towards certain individuals – though never (in public speeches, for example) towards the masses. I observed nothing to confirm tales of the Red Republic, but what I saw clear-sightedly and with open eyes, under the banner of the "German constitution" (and I'll be the first to admit that the masses didn't line up to be shot for *that*!), was the entirely natural indignation of the burghers and common people towards a prince[1] who called in foreign troops to coerce public opinion, not to mention the local patriotic anger at seeing "Prussia" of all countries – to whom Saxony has already lost so much – occupying what was left of the region. No sensible person will believe that the revolution was deliberately planned, if it had been, the most important positions around the square would not have been abandoned to the military at the outset. Storming the arsenal was the impetuous act of an unarmed people who believed themselves betrayed when the parade of the city militia was prevented from taking place. With what unbearable tension I followed at close quarters every public act, most notably the setting up of the committee of public safety at the town hall; after the hideous incidents which had earlier taken place, I hoped that these acts would provide a suitable focus for the movement, in the sense that concerted action on the part of the collective authorities and the common people would not only make further bloodshed impossible, but might finally lead to a timely surrender on the part of the King. This was the aim which lay behind my desultory attempts on the second day, after the town had been barricaded off, to do what it was in my power as an individual to do – without placing myself in the public gaze – in order to prevent further conflict between the people and the military. I met a couple of soldiers who were barracked at the arsenal and suggested to them that – in the event of a renewed confrontation with the people – all they had to do was explain to the latter that they would both be on the same side if it were a question of facing foreign troops; I said much the same sort of thing to various individuals whom I met as I was walking past the barricades and I warned them not to provoke the military but rather to ask them the simple question whether they would side with them against foreign troops. This question was even written on a piece of paper and pinned to the barricades, since it seemed to me to be of paramount importance to effect some sort of alliance between the troops and the people, whether by this means or any other, not only so that we could offer proper resistance to the Prussian invasion when it came, but, more particularly, so as to prevent the local movement from straying beyond its original course. A genuine alliance between the Saxon troops and the people of Saxony could in any case only have come into being for the sole purpose of ensuring common resistance to the Prussian invasion and support for the German constitution. If the military and the people had made combined representations to this effect to the King of Saxony, they would inevitably have achieved the desired aim of freeing the latter from stifling Prussian influence, and in this way the whole movement would have been prevented by the most energetic measures from being side-tracked into other areas. I explained to one of the town councillors whom I have known quite well for some time that it was my most earnest wish to see negotiations established

1 Friedrich August II of Saxony.

with the military governor with a view to admitting a number of military members to the committee of public safety. The election of a provisional government did not at first alarm me, since Heubner and Todt offered guarantees not to allow the movement to stray from its true goal and to conduct negotiations with the King accordingly. I felt blissfully happy when I discovered that half the arsenal had been made over to the city militia, and I even hoped that the Prussian cabinet conspiracy would be disclaimed by Saxony – perhaps even without blood being spilt. The third day, however, was to see all my hopes dashed: the truce was announced, Prussian troops arrived, and *in league with them* our troops attacked the people. The resentment which this provoked knew no bounds and, little as I remained close to the centre of action from then on, I can nevertheless assure you quite truthfully that from that moment onwards it was neither the Red nor the Blue Republic, neither Poles nor Russians that provided a spur to the most embittered and ruthless resistance on the part of those fighting on the barricades, but an entirely subjective and personal rage on the part of the burghers and common people directed against the military, a rage which was fed by a particular hatred of the riflemen who had arrived from Leipzig and who, as a body, were motivated by an old personal rancour towards the townspeople of Dresden to whom they had once had to give way in 1830 – a sense of rancour, finally, which had been nurtured by the riflemen's commanding officers in a most unnatural way. As a calm observer of the fighting, I maintained throughout Saturday and Sunday the most objective outlook in the world – from the top of the Kreuzkirche tower, since I found it impossible to sit around at home – in spite of my wife's entreaties. On Monday morning I once again went to the town hall in an attempt to discover what was going on, and there at least I found a great deal had altered: force of circumstances and the need to conduct the defence along strictly military lines had led to a search for strategists, since the commander of the city militia seemed to be lacking in insight and energy: a man from Poland who had studied tactics was recommended, and he was earnestly entreated to assume responsibility for preparing a military plan of defence. It is not true that Poland was involved from the outset. Irresolute and unsure of my present subjective outlook on the movement, I left the city at 8 o'clock on Monday morning and together with my wife, who had already packed, travelled to Chemnitz to stay with one of my married sisters[1] there. On the way we met countless bands of reinforcements from the remotest corners of the land: their great sense of commitment, their courage and endurance which I encountered at every turn left an overwhelming impression on me: in answer to their enquiries I told them what I knew of the state of the fighting in Dresden, and this confirmation of the naked truth served to spur them on and hasten their march. Towards

1 Clara Wolfram.

evening I met the whole of the Chemnitz communal guard in Oederan: they surrounded our carriage and demanded news from Dresden; on hearing what I had to report, some of them retorted that they had heard a different account, namely that Dresden had already surrendered to the Prussians. They forced me to accompany them to the town hall in order to verify my statement: it was there that I discovered I was dealing with people who had been *coerced* into marching to Dresden and who had eagerly seized on every scrap of false information as a pretext for returning at once to their own country. My news upset their plans, and they wanted to arrest me, since they suspected me of being a deserter. I managed to extricate myself from all this by promising to return to Dresden the following morning, after I had taken my wife to Chemnitz; they demanded my word of honour, and I considered it prudent not to deny it to them. What additionally persuaded me to return to Dresden was the concern I felt for a number of my relatives whom I had left behind there, together with the desire to find out exactly what was going on there. The mail-coach took me as far as the Feldschlösschen, and there I discovered that it was safe to go to the town hall but not to any other part of the town. Having reached the town hall, I had an opportunity to discover more details about how things stood: the timorous Todt and cowardly Tzschirner had fled, and Heubner, the man of the centre left, had remained in the square, showing dignity, endurance and presence of mind. An affecting incident gave me an opportunity to get to know Heubner somewhat better: a member of the communal guard who worked for the theatre turned to me with the request that I might intercede on behalf of the young Fürstenau who, having been suspected of firing on the people from his window, had been taken prisoner by them and placed under arrest. I immediately sought an audience with Heubner, and by dint of various reasons known to me attempted to convince him that the prisoner, in my own estimation, was innocent: Heubner set my mind at rest and assured me that the matter would be brought to a satisfactory conclusion. After an hour's delay I sought an opportunity to return to Chemnitz, the more so since the road to my relatives was blocked: but how could I do so at night and given the impossibility of finding a carriage or mail-coach? An old university friend of mine, who is now adjutant with the city militia commando, received a commission to go as courier to Freiberg as quickly as possible and instruct the Chemnitz communal guard to set out without delay; for this purpose he was empowered to commandeer a mail-coach and horses, and I used the opportunity to get away from the city. The next day I used the mail-coach which was travelling empty from Freiberg to Tharand in order to return there once more and discover further details about the night's events: I was half-way there when I was suddenly met by a perfectly ordered withdrawal of around 2000 volunteers from the barricades: I alighted, made my way over to Heubner's carriage and discovered that it was their intention to turn Freiberg into the seat of the provisional government. Outside Freiberg *Heubner* was met by a delegate from the Chemnitz militia, inviting him to establish the seat of the provisional government in Chemnitz: assailed by wealthy Freibergers beseeching him not to ruin their town, Heubner gave in and ordered the volunteer corps to proceed to Chemnitz after a brief rest, while he himself – in order to get a few hours' sleep – rode on ahead to Chemnitz, gave his name at the city gate – since it seemed, in part, unnecessary and, in part, underhand to deny who he was – and found a bed for himself and a few companions at the inn. The wealthy mill-owners of Chemnitz, meanwhile, thought it a good idea to have Heubner woken by the police, taken to Altenburg and handed over to the Prussian military authorities.

However brief the acquaintanceship I struck up with Heubner, I was attracted to him by the greatest sense of personal interest: he was the noblest, most resolute, most honourable – and most unfortunate hero of the revolution. I feel desperately sorry for him. Bakunin – a man of terrible energy – was thrust upon him by force of circumstances at a time when everything was falling apart around him: at moments when energy and energy alone was called for, he could not bring himself to reject him, although Bakunin's goal lay far beyond his own. Had Heubner been a revolutionary pure and simple, bent on victory and victory alone – the only type of revolutionary who will be victorious in the future! – he would have paid no heed to the whimperings of the wealthy burghers of Freiberg or Chemnitz but simply have allowed the terrible wisdom of the revolutioń to take its course, – he would not have fallen and the affair would not have been lost. It was at this point that I realized that we are none of us revolutionaries, least of all myself: we want the revolution in order to be able to build something good on it without delay, – and this consideration causes us to misjudge it totally: the true, victorious revolutionary can desire only destruction, and his unique strength will be his *hatred*, not the *love* which guides us. –

I have prefaced my remarks with this detailed account of recent events in order to give you an accurate picture of my involvement in them. I was initially in total sympathy with the uprising, but what I felt on the middle two days was, rather, embitterment, and on the two final days the most intense excitability and curiosity. But at no point did I take an active part in the proceedings, either with weapons or with public oratory: at no point did I adopt an official stance towards the provisional government. But the extent to which the reactionary party will be capable of committing acts of baseness and villainy once it enjoys the protection of Prussian bayonets on Saxon soil is something I have no difficulty in guessing: not even in Chemnitz with my relatives did I feel safe, my encounter with the town's militia was construed as an act of high treason by the more vocal section of the same. Reports received from my relatives in Leipzig force me to the conclusion that in Dresden, too, I am being slandered and denounced. If only for reasons of safety it is therefore impossible for me at the moment to contemplate a return to Dresden in the present circumstances, circumstances which I expect will prevail for some time. But there are other considerations, too, which now compel me to reach a definitive decision as regards my future life. You know how fraught with difficulties is the path I have embarked upon in my art: I would not mind the wounds I have suffered, but I cannot stand idly by while my entire artistic nature crumbles away. My abhorrence at my official position, the burden beneath which I have languished as a result, the futility of attempting any undertaking within the ambit of theatrical officialdom – all this reduced me long ago to a state of the most bitter resentment, a mood which could only increase in intensity as the years passed. The only thing that kept me alive – or at any rate the purpose of my existence – was my artistic creativity: but time and circumstances have conspired to disenchant me even with this: for two years now I have had a new opera completed:[1] but from no quarter have I received any encouragement to have it staged; the result is that for two years I have been frittering away my artistic abilities without pleasure or satisfaction. And so I finally became a revolutionary – in thought, if not in deed – , and no longer find any pleasure in creative work. The recent catastrophe brought me to my senses again, to the extent that I became fully conscious of this sad and blighted state, and the only hope and the only desire that remained was simply to eke out my existence with my poor and sorely tried wife in quiet seclusion, away from the world, without doing anything, but at the same time without feeling guilty. – Having arrived in Weimar, I was immediately persuaded to adopt a different course by the friends whom my Tannhäuser has won for me here. Liszt, acting in concord with the Grand Duchess, immediately announced that I was to go to Paris and London: that was where I must work for the future and put my energies to good use in the present, too, not in Germany where I would be destroyed, at least as an artist – something I myself had proved by my recent past. The means to do this, and every other influential support have already been offered to me, so that I may pursue my goal there and, to judge by the prospects, it will not be long before I achieve it. Difficult though I find it to occupy myself with things that lie essentially outside Germany, I feel that my life must consist of only the most intense artistic activity: Germany, in its present appalling disorder, can offer the artist only a barren and inhospitable waste-land, and this state of affairs may well last for many years to come: it is a sad consolation, but a consolation none the less, that one may at least preserve our country's art in the safety of a foreign land. There is also the question of my ruined finances, and here, too, I feel that only an energetic assessment of my talent can offer me the prospect of a better future. I am resolved, accordingly, to comply with the invitations and offers of my friends here: a

1 *Lohengrin*, first performed in Weimar on 28 August 1850.

few precautions are all that I need to take before I set off on my journey –
in all probability I shall go first to London. And so the only question that
remains to be answered concerns my continuing attitude towards Dresden. I
would even now consider it necessary to make a complete break with Dresden
if I could not assume that – however harshly I may perhaps stand accused at
present – the matter was bound to be cleared up, since I am after all not
guilty of any actual criminal offence; I have every confidence that, if it is
thought necessary to treat me as a criminal, even according to the ideas of
the party which has now emerged victorious, then half the inhabitants of
Saxony would have to be brought to book with equal severity. And so I would
ask you to attempt to find out indirectly, on the basis of the foregoing
information, which I swear is a truthful account, whether there are sufficient
grounds for instituting legal proceedings against me. You alone, my dear
friend, are in a position to follow the correct procedure in these matters and
take whatever steps are necessary to enable me to return to my own country,
and perhaps even justify the retention of my appointment there. If everything
were to go well and turn out in my favour, the phrasing of any agreement we
reached would have to run somewhat along the lines that I was initially to be
granted six months' leave of absence in order to be able to go to London and
Paris, both to superintend the production of my operas in the local theatres
and also to obtain commissions to write a new opera for one of these two
cities. My present intention is to have my latest opera Lohengrin translated
into English and given its first performance in London. – Let us assume that
the present storms will blow over and that it will not be long before I appear
much less compromised politically than may now be the case, – why should
one of Dresden's artistic institutions remove me for ever from its midst when
it might not be entirely to its discredit to have one of its members win fame
for himself in the greatest cities of the world? – I at least am prepared to
hold out my hand in all sincerity, if it will assist me in my return to Dresden
at a later date, and perhaps the city will have no cause to regret having
accepted the hand that is offered: I have no need to emphasize how beneficial
and consoling this would be to me: only now, now you must let me remain
free, – free in every respect.

God knows if all these proposals may not come far too late! Perhaps I
have already been foolishly condemned as a traitor, or the like; – I have
had no news at all from Dresden, and have heard nothing concerning my
wife, either, for 4 days now, something which is a source of great worry to
me.

Ah, my dear Devrient, do not now be angry with me on account of this
wildly unsettling friendship into which I have drawn you! Help me to become
an artist again, nothing but an artist and a man – you will then have greater
cause to be content with me.

Write to me under cover to Liszt here in Weimar: the letter will either find me here or else be forwarded to me. But soon – send news soon!

I pray that God has kept you safe, my noble friend, and that He will continue to keep you and your dear ones safe – for the sake of your friends!

Adieu, best of men!

Yours,
Richard Wagner.

SB II,660–9.

EXILE IN SWITZERLAND
1849–1858

INTRODUCTORY ESSAY 1849–1858

Acceding to the wishes of Liszt and Minna, who believed that it was time for him to try his luck again in Paris, Wagner made his way there via Switzerland, arriving on 2 June 1849. Revisiting the scene of his former unhappy failure rapidly confirmed him in his own opinion that Parisian soil was for him, artistically speaking, infertile ground [89, 90, 91]. He retraced his steps to Zurich and lodged there with an old friend from his Würzburg days, Alexander Müller. Müller introduced him to some influential local people, including one of the cantonal secretaries, Jakob Sulzer, who became a close and valued friend. Befriended and financially aided by a circle of cultured intellectuals who took an unprecedented interest in his work, Wagner determined to make Zurich his home, even though Minna for a time refused to join him on account of his inability to support her by his own means.

Musical composition initially seemed of less importance to him than a resolution of the crucial social and aesthetic issues that had been brought to a head by the recent revolutionary upheavals. In a series of essays, beginning with *Die Kunst und die Revolution* (Art and Revolution) in July 1849, he addressed himself to the fundamental questions of the social role of art, which most composers, whether successful or unsuccessful with their publics, had been content to ignore. *Art and Revolution* was outspoken and polemical, advocating an "art-work of the future" in which emancipated humanity would express itself through artistic structures that had at last been divorced from capitalist speculation and profit-making. These ideas, and in particular the concept of the reunification of the arts into a comprehensive *Gesamtkunstwerk* ("total work of art") on the ancient Greek model, were developed in two longer essays, *Das Kunstwerk der Zukunft* (The Art-work of the Future) and *Oper und Drama* (Opera and Drama), completed in November 1849 and January 1851 respectively.

If in *Art and Revolution* Wagner's perception of the worthlessness of artistic endeavour within the framework of the existing social structures is influenced by Proudhon and Feuerbach, both of whom he had recently been reading, in *The Art-work of the Future* it is Marx and other revolutionary thinkers, as well as Feuerbach (to whom the essay was dedicated), whose ideas are taken up. As part of an inevitable historical process (cf Feuerbach's concept of *Noth*, "necessity" or "need" – the title given by Wagner to a poem mentioned earlier; see p.59) the new work of art was to emerge as the creation of the

Volk. The product not of the individual genius but of a fellowship of artists, it was to be a communal response to prevailing historical conditions.

During the winter of 1850/51 Wagner was preoccupied with the writing of his major theoretical work, *Opera and Drama*. It is the third and final part of this vast essay (consisting, in all, of some 100,000 words) that is of most interest, for Wagner develops there the principles underlying his concept of the music drama. Essentially the argument centres on the relationship of poetry to music[1] and although Wagner subsequently felt under no obligation to adhere rigidly to the principles he had laid down, there can be no doubt that their formulation enabled him to come to terms with the creative dilemma he faced as a composer in mid-century: namely, how as an inheritor of the classical symphonic tradition reaching its apogee in Beethoven, but as one whose inspirations were fundamentally literary and dramatic, he was to find a vehicle appropriate for those inspirations. The study of the relationship between Wagner's theories and his practice in the *Ring*, *Tristan*, *Die Meistersinger* and *Parsifal*, is a fascinating and complex one;[2] suffice to mention here that Wagner was wont to emphasize that the art form embodying these new ideas and techniques had "already matured" within him before the theory was formulated [122, 143].

Wagner was by no means alone in his dissatisfaction with the state of German opera. Shortly after taking over as editor of the *Neue Zeitschrift für Musik*, Franz Brendel had written and published, in instalments between July 1845 and February 1846, a long, influential essay entitled *Vergangenheit, Gegenwart und Zukunft der Oper* (The Past, Present and Future of Opera).[3] Brendel had argued for the creation of a national opera, one that would express the aspirations of the people in those pre-revolutionary years. He recommended in particular that libretti should be more relevant to the dramatic conception, that large organic structures should replace the traditional set-piece numbers, and that vocal virtuosity and spoken dialogue be abandoned. If these ideas coincide exactly with those propounded by Wagner a few years later in his theoretical writings, there is a further point of special interest: Brendel's proposal of the Nibelung legend as the most appropriate subject matter for the German national opera. That subject had already been suggested by Friedrich Theodor Vischer, the aesthetician-philosopher, in his *Vorschlag zu einer Oper* (Proposal for an Opera) of 1844, and in the following year the idea had been taken further when Louise Otto

---

1 For more detailed expositions of *Opera and Drama* see Frank W. Glass, *The Fertilizing Seed* (Ann Arbor 1983), Bryan Magee, *Aspects of Wagner* (London 1968), and Jack M. Stein, *Richard Wagner & the Synthesis of the Arts* (Detroit 1960).
2 See Glass and Stein, *opp. cit.*, and Barry Millington, *Wagner* (London 1984), chapters 16–19.
3 *Neue Zeitschrift für Musik*, xxiii (1845), 33–5, 37–9, 41–3, 105–8, 109–12, 121–4 and 149–51; xxiv (1846), 57–60 and 61–4.

published a partial libretto on the subject in the *Neue Zeitschrift für Musik*. It is assumed, but unproven, that Wagner was acquainted with the writings of Vischer and Otto. But it is even more tempting to speculate whether he might not have read and responded to Brendel's exhortation, also of 1845: "In my view a setting of the Nibelung opera would indeed be a step forward, and I believe that the composer who could accomplish this task in an adequate manner would become the man of his era."[1]

Another essay from the *Opera and Drama* period, *Das Judenthum in der Musik* (Judaism in Music), caused concern within the circle of his friends and considerable anger beyond. It should be seen as Wagner's contribution to a debate on a theme increasingly exercising the minds of his contemporaries: the extent to which Jews affected the artistic climate of the country in which they lived. Wagner's argument – that the rootlessness of Jews in Germany and their historical role as usurers and entrepreneurs condemned them to cultural sterility – was overlaid with uncompromisingly anti-Semitic observations. A letter to Liszt [120] makes clear too how far personal animus was responsible for the tirade: Meyerbeer, he tells Liszt, reminds him of the "darkest" period of his life, one in which the necessity for recognition led inevitably to insincere, dishonest relationships. Above all, the frequently voiced opinion that he was in some ways indebted also musically to Meyerbeer goaded Wagner beyond endurance: with *Das Judenthum in der Musik* he intended to make clear once and for all how Meyerbeer and everything he stood for were the very antithesis of his own ideals.

Shortly before this, his personal circumstances had been dramatically transformed by two female admirers, Frau Julie Ritter, a widow from Dresden, and Jessie Laussot (née Taylor), an Englishwoman married to a Bordeaux wine merchant. Their proposal that he be granted an annual allowance of 3000 francs, for an indefinite period, gratified him no less as an expression of disinterested generosity and goodwill than as the means whereby he might devote himself to those artistic ends in which he believed [99]. Accepting an invitation to Bordeaux, where he stayed with the Laussots from 16 March to 5 April 1850, Wagner found there a congenial and friendly environment in which he felt himself at last understood and appreciated. Jessie, a mere 21, was a passionate admirer of Wagner's music; she spoke fluent German, was musical, and listened and discussed intelligently. Her marriage was, Wagner had observed, an unhappy one: indeed, she subsequently left her husband and went to live in Florence with the historian Karl Hillebrand. At any rate, she and Wagner fell in love and when he talked about putting his troubled, exiled existence behind him and seeking refuge in Greece or Asia Minor,

---

1 *Neue Zeitschrift für Musik*, xxiii (1845), 124. Quoted in Jon W. Finson and R. Larry Todd (eds), *Mendelssohn and Schumann: Essays on Their Music and Its Context* (Durham, North Carolina 1984), 25. Jurgen Thym's article, *op. cit.*, 21–36, is of much interest for the background to the most influential music criticism of the period.

Jessie responded with enthusiasm. Returning to Paris, Wagner wrote Minna a long letter [106] retracing the vicissitudes of their life together, and recalling the sacrifices they had each made for the other. Wagner gives Minna credit as a "woman of honour", acting reasonably within her own lights, but he concludes that the marriage has irretrievably broken down and that the only solution is for them to live apart. He makes no reference to his affair with Jessie and none to the Orient; indeed, he claims that what has precipitated matters is a letter from Minna demanding once again that he seek his fortune in Paris. To some, the dissemblance and hypocrisy of [106] will appear unforgivable; even his pressing on Minna of half the annual allowance may be read as the salvaging of a conscience. To others, the letter may suggest the acknowledgment of a painful truth, the expressions of sorrow at parting from Minna appear genuine; he had felt himself "bound to her by a thousand chains of old and mutual suffering" was how Wagner later put it to Julie Ritter [110]. Perhaps it is too much to expect any letter written in such circumstances to be totally truthful.

Minna immediately sought Wagner in Paris. He eluded her and travelled south-east to Lake Geneva, booking into a hotel there at Villeneuve. Having already heard from Jessie that she was resolved to join him and share his fate, Wagner conceived a plan whereby they sail on 7 May from Marseilles, initially for Malta and thence eastwards. On 4 May he wrote to tell Minna of his impending voyage. Minna's reply, full of reproaches and self-pity, was a none-too-realistic appraisal of their marital situation, though she accepted his decision to depart as unalterable. She was not at this stage fully aware of Wagner's intentions vis-à-vis Jessie, but she had always resented the bond between them and had scolded him for contemplating acceptance of the allowance rather than working respectably to keep her himself [102]. Just as Wagner was about to leave for Marseilles, he learnt that Jessie had rashly apprised her mother, Ann Taylor, of the plan. The husband, Eugène, had been told and was threatening to kill Wagner, while Jessie herself was forbidden to communicate with him. Wagner set out for Bordeaux, intent on reasoning with Eugène; he was intercepted by the local police and forced to leave the town, his mission unaccomplished. Jessie's mother informed Minna about the whole affair and caused Wagner considerable disquiet in that she appeared to have cast his actions and motives in the worst possible light to both Minna and Jessie [110, 111].

Wagner's conduct throughout the episode can be traced in the letters selected [99, 102, 103, 105, 106, 108, 110, 111]. It remains to point out the connection between the affair and two dramatic projects of the time, eventually abandoned uncomposed. The first, *Wieland der Schmied* (Wieland the Smith), for which Wagner made prose drafts between December 1849 and March 1850 (WWV 82), concerns a smith who, yearning for freedom, forges himself a pair of wings with which he soars above the world united with his lover

Schwanhilde. The story symbolizes on one level the German nationalist aspirations (the *Volk* rising above their oppressors). But it is at the same time expressive of Wagner's personal desire to be liberated from the shackles imposed by exile, a broken marriage and stultifying artistic conventions. The plan to escape from present conditions to some Oriental utopia, accompanied by a woman idealized beyond belief, was prefigured by a matter of only a few weeks in *Wieland der Schmied*.

The other project, *Jesus von Nazareth* (WWV 80), dating from the early part of 1849, is in three sections, of which the second is a series of commentaries on themes arising from the dramatic sketch. While the historical treatment draws on the thesis advanced by David Friedrich Strauss in *Das Leben Jesu* (1835/6), the commentaries, especially those on love and marriage, owe much to writers such as Proudhon and Feuerbach. The ideas promulgated in Feuerbach's *Das Wesen des Christenthums* (The Essence of Christianity) of 1841 included the assertion of the supremacy of love over the law, and the proclamation of a new religion of humanity, that is, a theological outlook in which God was perceived as a projection of the hopes and needs of men and women themselves. All of this, blended with the anarchism characteristic of Wagner's own thinking at this time, is to be found in *Jesus von Nazareth*. There, love is elevated to a position of paramount importance: when subjugated to the law or to the institution of marriage (seen as the mere establishment and perpetuation of property rights), the inevitable result is misery. That Wagner saw the whole Laussot affair in this light is evident from his letters; the sentiments and vocabulary of [110] in particular, in which he rails against bourgeois respectability, loveless marriage and conventional propriety, are remarkably close to those of *Jesus von Nazareth*.

At the height of the affair Wagner wrote to Liszt [107] imploring him to have *Lohengrin* (WWV 75) produced on stage, even if only in Weimar (where he was Kapellmeister). Liszt responded with alacrity and in [112] Wagner makes clear his view on cuts in the work. After the performance, which was the world première of *Lohengrin* and which the composer was of course unable to attend, Wagner wrote expressing his gratitude [115] but also his concern that by all accounts the performance was unwarrantably protracted and somewhat lacking in dramatic impact. He diplomatically attributes the shortcomings to the singers – his comments on the rendering of the "recitatives" are of some interest here – and "the slovenliness and stiffness of the performers" is also blamed in a letter to Kietz [116]. In the latter is floated the idea of a temporary wooden theatre to be erected for the sole purpose of performing the Nibelung dramas, at a free-admission festival taking place within a single week, after which the construction would be destroyed.

Wagner's conviction that his new drama could never be adequately realized on the stage and within the conditions of any existing theatre is frequently expressed, generally in terms of disillusionment about the current political situation. His despair at the failure of the uprising and the consequent lack of will to engage in revolutionary struggle provokes him, in the period 1849–52, to outbursts of ruthless aggression [90, 98, 99, 117]. But if this "terrorism" is the product of the anarchist outlook he shared with men like Mikhail Bakunin and Max Stirner, as well as Proudhon, there is also evidence of a grasp of the Marxist concepts of alienation and false consciousness. In [117] he speaks of "enslaved human nature" and again in [133] of the "slave mentality" under which oppressed working men and women labour, deliberately denied the knowledge that would bring them enlightenment and eventually liberation. These glimpses of understanding should be seen alongside Wagner's elitism and denigration of the masses in his writings elsewhere; his espousal of the *Volk* was an essentially Romantic notion in tune with the limited objectives of the bourgeois liberals who led the 1848–9 uprisings. From time to time, also, Wagner is undecided about the extent to which he will take refuge in his art from the futilities of the world around him: [131] is enigmatically ambivalent on the question of commitment. This letter was written shortly after the *coup d'état* of Louis Napoléon on 2 December 1851, an event which led to a dictatorial suppression of the opposition and dissolution of the Assembly. Although it also led to the proclamation, a year later, of the Second Empire, the coup did not at first seem to be a matter of great moment and Wagner was even able to refer to it in a lighthearted manner the following month (see the jocular postscript to [135]). There is little doubt that Wagner's political views at this time are given their most forthright expression in the letters to Theodor Uhlig, a friend and sympathizer from the Dresden period. A large proportion of these letters (70 out of 93) were censored by Cosima Wagner when she prepared the correspondence for publication in 1888; the relevant passages are given in full in the present edition.

One of the most fascinating themes to trace in Wagner's correspondence is that of the development of *Der Ring des Nibelungen* (WWV 86), from the scenario for *Siegfrieds Tod* (later to become *Götterdämmerung*) in autumn 1848, through its amplification *Der junge Siegfried* (later *Siegfried*) in 1851, and the gradual construction of the whole tetralogy. The first musical sketches are those for *Siegfrieds Tod* dating from the summer of 1850, but it was November 1853 before Wagner embarked on the first complete draft from the *Ring*, namely that for *Das Rheingold*. According to *Mein Leben* the inspiration for the opening of *Rheingold* is supposed to have come to him in a state of half-sleep in an inn at La Spezia, the sound of rushing water gradually resolving into a chord of E flat major, repeated incessantly in arpeggio figurations. Doubt has been cast on this story, however. A close examination of the relevant composition sketches suggests that the genesis of the *Ring* may have occurred rather differently.[1] Nor does a single surviving letter of Wagner's

1 See WWV 86.

from the ensuing months mention any such "vision". The letter to Minna of 5 September 1853 [166], the day of the supposed experience, was written, it is true, in the morning (the "vision" is supposed to have occurred in the afternoon). It certainly reveals Wagner in a state of acute indecision as to whether to return home or to continue his Italian holiday. Possibly it suggests a desire to return to his work desk again – the reasons given Minna, incidentally, are ill-health and a yearning to see her once more – but that could support the argument that the opening of *Das Rheingold* was already working itself out in his head. More significantly, later letters, for example those to Ferdinand Heine [167] and Röckel [171], even where they mention La Spezia or *Rheingold*, make no reference to any "vision". Wagner may indeed have had an experience of some kind, but his subsequent accounts of it seem to have been coloured by his enthusiasm for Schopenhauer, who discusses the connection of dreams and creativity. The first mention of a "vision" at La Spezia is in a letter to Emilie Ritter of 19 December 1854, shortly after Wagner had read the book in question: *Parerga und Paralipomena*.

The discovery of Schopenhauer and in particular his major work, *Die Welt als Wille und Vorstellung* (The World as Will and Representation), was for Wagner, as is well known, a critical one. His impact was felt in two ways: his aesthetics and his philosophy of life. The former, which amounted to an elevation of music over the other media, provided Wagner with precisely the intellectual justification he needed to adjust the balance of the constituent parts in his reunification of the arts. No longer did the reunification have to be on the basis of equality, as laid down in his theoretical writings; though it must be said that the process of adjustment was already under way during the composition of *Das Rheingold* and *Die Walküre*, before the encounter with Schopenhauer.[1]

Schopenhauer's other major influence on Wagner was in his philosophy of pessimism, according to which existence is a constant round of suffering alleviated occasionally by pleasure, which, however, is a mere release from pain. Suffering is the inevitable consequence of the "will to live"; only denial of the will, in annihilation or the Buddhist state of nirvana, can effect deliverance. Wagner's letters subsequent to his reading of Schopenhauer in October 1854 speak unequivocally of joy in the discovery of a kindred spirit; for a long time after, too, concepts such as denial of the will and renunciation are found throughout Wagner's correspondence [187, 193 etc]. No less interesting are the intimations of Schopenhauer's ideas from the period before October 1854. This should not surprise us: not only was Wagner ripe in his outlook on life for this revelation, but also Schopenhauer was already being read and discussed within Wagner's circle of friends (notably by the revol-

---

1 For detailed discussions of the shift of emphasis in music and drama in Wagner's works see Jack M. Stein and Barry Millington, *opp. cit.*

utionary German poet Georg Herwegh and François Wille at the latter's house at Mariafeld, near Zurich).

The other philosophy central to Wagner's thinking at this time and indeed, it could be argued, throughout his life, is that of Ludwig Feuerbach, whose name has been mentioned more than once earlier in this essay. Feuerbach's impact on nineteenth-century German literature and philosophy was immense, since he was instrumental in turning attention away from the abstract metaphysics of Hegelianism towards the moral, religious and social issues of everyday life.[1] Among the many who were greatly influenced by Feuerbach were the Swiss writer Gottfried Keller and (once again) Georg Herwegh, both of whom were among Wagner's Zurich acquaintances.

For Feuerbach the essence of human nature, and the source of its morality, is the "I – you" relationship. Morality is inconceivable for the solitary being; only in conjunction with another, by creating a mutual drive to happiness, does an individual develop any consciousness of social responsibility.[2] Passages in [171] could not have been better put by Feuerbach himself, while the experience described in [161] – a state of lovelessness leading to a recognition of "the glorious necessity of love" – is also evidence of the debt that Wagner acknowledges explicitly in [97].

For Schopenhauer, on the other hand, love was a potentially negative force. Affection or goodness towards others serves only to alleviate the essential condition of suffering. Sexual activity is an explicit affirmation of the will to live and should therefore be shunned. Love in the sense of *eros* is selfish and destructive; only *agape* is acceptable, since that is tantamount to compassion or fellow-suffering. At certain times, the emotional and artistic vacuum in Wagner's life impelled him to a Schopenhauerian formulation, such as the "utterly and completely devastating" nature of love [193]. But in his mature music dramas he never pursued that pessimistic philosophy to its extreme conclusion. Always, and especially in *Parsifal*, there is the hope of deliverance, of redemption, and for this optimism Feuerbach may be regarded as responsible. Wagner's Schopenhauerian outlook throughout his later life, then, was constantly to be modified by his understanding of Feuerbach.

Connected with Wagner's reading of Schopenhauer, and partly stemming from it – though once again the idea was very much in the air and Wagner himself was already responsive to oriental culture [150] – is his interest in Buddhism. In April 1855 he reported to Mathilde Wesendonck from London that he was reading Adolf Holtzmann's *Indische Sagen* (Indian Sagas). Eugène Burnouf's *Introduction à l'histoire du buddhisme indien* soon after provided him with a Buddhist legend of passion and renunciation that he was to toy with

1 See J.G. Robertson, "Richard Wagner as poet and thinker (2)" in *Wagner*, vi (1985), 41–55 for a discussion of the influence of Feuerbach and the cultural background.

2 See E. Kamenka, *The Philosophy of Feuerbach* (London 1970) for a lucid exposition of Feuerbach's philosophy.

for the rest of his life, but which never proceeded beyond the stage of a prose sketch *Die Sieger* (The Victors, WWV 89). And in 1857 he read Count Schack's *Stimmen vom Ganges* (Voices from the Ganges) as soon as it appeared [197]. Letters [185] and [187] testify to Wagner's immersion in Buddhist thinking at this time.

Purely musical influences of this period are harder to determine, but there is no doubt that the compositions of Liszt are of primary importance in this respect. For Wagner, who in his exile throughout the 1850s was acutely conscious of his enforced separation from "real music" [197], Liszt provided a point of contact both with the world of performance and with developments in the techniques of musical composition. Liszt's boldly adventurous harmonic style and method of thematic transformation made a considerable impression on Wagner, and the potential of these and other processes for the "art-work of the future" was not lost on him. In particular it was the symphonic poems that caught Wagner's imagination, as is evident both from his own testimony [192, 197] and from the scores themselves, notably from *Die Walküre* onwards.

Several commentators have pointed out how the opening of *Tristan und Isolde*, and even the epoch-making "*Tristan* chord" itself, were presaged (though never given in that precise form) by composers as various as Mozart (K428, slow movement), Spohr (String Quartet in C, op.4 no.1, and *Der Alchymist*), Gottschalk (*The Last Hope*) and Liszt (the songs *Die Loreley* and *Ich möchte hingehn*).[1] Another critical, but previously overlooked influence on *Tristan* is the orchestral fantasy *Nirwana* by Hans von Bülow. In this work can be found not only a prefiguration of the rising chromatic phrase of bars 2–3 of *Tristan* (mentioned by Wagner, incidentally, in the context of nirvana in [256]: "you know the Buddhist theory of the origin of the world. A breath clouds the clear expanse of heaven") but also a parallel sublimation of it at the close. Letter [176] indicates that Wagner had been studying Bülow's *Nirwana* (originally conceived as an overture to a tragedy of the same name by Karl Ritter) immediately before making his first prose sketch for *Tristan* late in October 1854 (dating from the Annals; see also WWV 90). When he subsequently came to write the music for *Tristan* (the earliest dated sketches to survive are from 19 December 1856) Wagner evidently recalled, probably subconsciously, Bülow's *Nirwana*. Certainly he had admired the work (see his extravagant praise in [176][2]), as indeed he had other music of Bülow's (as long before as September 1847 Wagner had returned to Bülow a batch of his compositions with a congratulatory letter that gave the young man much

1 See, for example, Deryck Cooke, "Wagner's Musical Language" in *The Wagner Companion*, ed. Peter Burbidge and Richard Sutton (London 1979), esp. 236–8; Leon Plantinga, *Romantic Music* (New York [1984]), 287–90 and 408–9, and Ian Beresford Gleaves, "Liszt and Wagner" in *Wagner*, vi (1985), 77–99.

2 See also CT for 11 March 1879, 24 October 1879, 25 October 1879, and 16 June 1882.

encouragement). And the subject matter of *Nirwana* – it was also familiarly known as the "Suicide Fantasia" – with its Buddhist overtones was no doubt a contributory factor. Karl Ritter, it may be recalled, later concluded an abortive suicide pact with Cosima von Bülow, and the circle of associations may be completed by mention of the fact that according to *Mein Leben* it was Ritter's flawed attempt to dramatize the Tristan legend that led Wagner to make his 1854 scenario.

With other contemporaries his relationships were more ambivalent. The originality of Berlioz he admired, had even imitated. When they met in London in 1855, they struck up a sympathetic understanding based on fellow-suffering, but in [206] Wagner speaks of his frustration at a later meeting when Berlioz failed to impress him with a reading of the libretto of *Les Troyens*. Wagner here contrasts the embarrassment of maintaining a polite exterior with the genuine, open friendship he has with Liszt, where no dissemblance is necessary. A lack of affinity with less innovatory composers is exemplified by the brusque dismissal of Schumann's symphonies in [179]; it has to be remembered, of course, that musical opinion in Germany generally was dividing composers into two camps, the New German School (spear-headed by Wagner and Liszt) on the one side and, on the other, the more conservative musicians such as Brahms and Joachim, who were supported publicly by Schumann.

Wagner's visit to London was brought about by an invitation from the Philharmonic Society to conduct their 1855 series of concerts; his acceptance resulted in a four-month stay in England. The story of the London venture will not be recounted in detail here, as a more immediate picture emerges from the relevant letters [178–189] and is supplemented by the annotation. In these letters are to be found all the significant themes: Wagner's reasons for accepting the engagement, his cynicism about the programmes and English concertgoers, the reaction of orchestral players and audiences to his conducting, the hostile press campaign and the reception by Queen Victoria.

Wagner arrived back in Zurich on 30 June 1855, with only 1000 francs (£40) remaining from his fee of 5000 francs: as he had complained to Minna, the cost of living in London was prohibitively high. Appeals to the King of Saxony for an amnesty, for the first time acknowledging his "reckless action" in joining with the insurrectionists in 1849, were rejected [192, 193, 197]. His work on the scoring of *Die Walküre* had been badly hampered during the London visit and continued to be painfully slow, the more so as it became difficult to recall the original inspiration. Domestic ructions, together with repeated attacks of his skin complaint erysipelas, added to his misery.

Then, at the beginning of 1857, his wealthy friend Otto Wesendonck offered him, apparently at the urgent insistence of his wife Mathilde [216], the tenancy of a small house and garden adjoining the villa that was being built for him in the Zurich suburb of Enge. The annual rent of 800 francs was the same as that Wagner had been paying in his previous lodging in the Zeltweg, but now, with a view from his desk over Lake Zurich and the Alps, he had the tranquillity and seclusion he longed for to make progress with his work. Mathilde called it his "Asyl" (Refuge) and Wagner adopted the name.

When the Wesendoncks moved into their villa in August 1857 the closeness of Wagner to Mathilde caused the tender feelings they had long held for each other to develop into a more serious relationship. Immediately before this, Wagner had diverted his creative energies from *Siegfried* to *Tristan und Isolde*, and the two lovers idealized their passion by identifying it with that portrayed in the latter music drama. Whether such a definitive expression of yearning and unfulfilled longing can be reconciled with a physically consummated love affair is doubtful. It may well be that Wagner was telling the truth when he insisted on the "purity of these relations" that "never offended against morality" [210, 216]; see also his vehement protestation of innocence in [270]. Nevertheless, according to [216], Otto Wesendonck was "consumed by jealousy", though his love for his wife forced him to maintain an equable exterior. Minna, on the other hand, had less motivation and less capacity for self-control. In a letter of 23 April 1862 to an unnamed Zurich acquaintance[1] she claims to have been hurt not by any extra-marital liaison of her husband – which she took for granted – but by his insensitivity in flaunting it before her.

However that may be, the simmering jealousy and undercurrents of tension came suddenly to the surface when Minna intercepted the letter headed "Morning confession" [208]. The letter was in fact Wagner's attempt to atone for some ill-mannered behaviour the evening before, when he had taken violent issue with Mathilde's Italian teacher de Sanctis, whose intimate proximity with her he resented. The "Morning confession" addressed itself primarily and at length to the topic of discussion on that occasion – Goethe's *Faust*. But Minna noticed only the flowery expressions of devotion. She confronted first Wagner and subsequently Mathilde with the letter, and Mathilde, insulted by the suggestion that she had secrets from Otto, promptly informed him. Wagner's account of the "Morning confession", in what appears to be a frank letter of explanation to his sister Clara [216], is that it betokens the resignation by which the relationship had always been characterized. Both here and elsewhere Wagner states that he and Mathilde had from the beginning understood and accepted that a "union" between them was out of the question, though [214] reveals that in the aftermath of the incident Wagner entertained at least a passing hope of a permanent union (the suggestion that they both leave their spouses and marry was not a serious one, he later told Cosima: CT for 14 March 1873). As soon after as July 1858 Wagner was expressing to a trusted friend, Eliza Wille [215], his annoyance at Mathilde's vacillation. It may be that Mathilde was torn between her husband

1 Sammlung Burrell 499–500; English trans. 376–7.

and Wagner; on the other hand, the annoyance could be a projection of Wagner's own guilty indecision.

After the catastrophe with the "Morning confession" incident, it gradually became evident to Wagner that he had no alternative but to leave the Asyl. In mid-August 1858 he finally left Zurich and it was in Venice that he was to continue his work on *Tristan*, a composition which on account of its "modest dimensions" [201] he fully expected to see staged in Strasbourg within twelve months.

88. MINNA WAGNER, DRESDEN   Rorschach, [28] May [1849]

My dear, faithful wife,

I am safely arrived on Swiss soil! I had hoped to be able to write to you
from here a day sooner, but the journey was unfortunately a very slow one,
with frequent stops etc. – In Lindau they asked to see only my passport &
gave me a visa for Switzerland without any difficulty.

I left Lindau this morning, crossing Lake Constance to get here, & in half
an hour shall be continuing my journey to St Gall & Zurich. In Zurich I
intend to allow myself a brief rest, which will also enable me to write to you
at greater length. I must stop now.

Safe at last!

May God keep you in good spirits! I have suffered a great deal of anxiety
on your behalf, but – my old vitality has once more returned in full measure!

Fare you well! my dearest Minna, best of wives! More tomorrow from
Zurich!

Yours,
R.W.

SB III,55.

89. MINNA WAGNER, DRESDEN   Paris, 4 June 1849

My dear Minna,

Here I am, sitting in this same city of Paris where we arrived once before,
ten years ago, & where we spent a joyless existence living a life of anxious
care from one day to the next! No words can describe what is going on
inside me! The long journey, the terrible heat – memory, present & future,
everything weighs heavily upon me. I loathe almost all towns, so why should
Paris be able to exercise a more favourable impression on me? – I thought I
had moved to a relatively quiet part of the city, instead of which I find the
noise here as great as in the densest hubbub of city life. And the heat, the
excitement, the commotion, – my mind is utterly confused, – for how long is
it since I last heard from you! Ah, my Swiss courage has already failed me &
the only desire I have left is to be reunited with you & with the familiar
remains of our former household in some quiet secluded spot! I want to
work, & to work creatively, to write verses & compose music, whatever else
the world may demand of me: but to have to run after it & hunt it down, to
be expected to submit myself to all this din, – why? – I should have preferred

to leave it all to other people who like loud noise & bustle! – You see, my
dear, Paris for me is not a city of pleasure & delight! But in Switzerland, in
the glorious & comforting bosom of nature, in a small & friendly town, in
the company of a handful of friends, there could I sooner seize on the notion
of finding happiness with you! But here? here I have no other thought in
mind than of coming *back* to you & to a quiet home! But I know only too
well, – I must first earn this happiness, & so I shall shrink from no effort, no
step – however repugnant I may find it – which may bring me to the point
where I can choose freely, & *what* I shall choose – I already know – : always
to remain at your side! [. . .] But everything that has now to be done here
can only be by way of preparation: my real purpose can probably not be
realized until the autumn, when the Paris season begins. All I can do in the
mean time is to make a decent name for myself through the newspapers &
journals, & prepare to face the countless intrigues to which I shall be exposed
and whose threads for the most part are held by Meierbeer. Now that Liszt's
article on Tannhäuser has appeared in print, Meierbeer must have a pretty
clear idea where things are heading: when I went into Schlesinger's shop, I
was given a very friendly reception; Meierbeer was there, too, but he happened
to be concealed by a screen, where he remained hidden when he heard my
voice, so that it looked as if what was holding him back was his shock at my
sudden appearance & a guilty conscience at his intrigues in Berlin: when I
finally discovered he was there, I went behind the screen, all affability &
smiles, & drew him forth: he was embarrassed & at a loss for words, but I
know enough to be on my guard against him.[1]
   [. . .]

SB III,65–8.

90. Franz Liszt, Weimar   Paris, 5 June 1849

[. . .] I tell you in all honesty: I am totally incapable of taking part in an
intrigue à la "verre d'eau";[2] if my only hope lay in such a course of action,
I should pack my bags tomorrow and decamp to some village in Germany: I

---

1 Not until 1985, with the publication of Meyerbeer's correspondence for this period, was it
  possible to discover the other side of the story: "I happened to meet *Richard Wagner* a few
  days ago. Is it true what I read in the German newspapers, that he is no longer in the service
  of the Saxon Court because he compromised himself during the Dresden uprising, or is it
  merely one of the usual stories fabricated by the newspapers? Of course, I didn't like to ask
  him about it, out of delicacy, but could I prevail on you to let me know whether or not the
  report is true?" (*Giacomo Meyerbeer: Briefwechsel und Tagebücher*, edited by Heinz and Gudrun
  Becker [Berlin 1985], IV,503; letter to Carl Kaskel of [10 June 1849]).
2 *Le Verre d'eau*, comedy by Eugène Scribe, first performed in 1841.

want to work, as I know I can, but to sell my wares in *this market* – that is something I cannot do. This local trafficking in art is so contemptible, so rotten and so moribund that all it needs is a man of courage who knows where to strike at it with his scythe. My dearest Liszt, – far from all political speculation, I none the less feel impelled to speak out: art will not grow in the soil of the counter-revolution; initially, it may not even grow in the soil of the revolution, unless we take steps in good time to see that it does. Out with it! tomorrow I intend sitting down and writing a decent article on the theatre of the future for one or other leading political journal. I promise you that, as far as possible, I shall leave politics out of it and in that way compromise neither you nor anyone else: but as far as art and the theatre are concerned, I shall – with all possible decorum – permit myself to be as red as possible, since no other shade will help us except this one particular primary colour. But I believe this is also the most prudent procedure, and the man who, for reasons of prudence, urged this course of action upon me as the one most likely to succeed is none other than your representative – Belloni. He says that I must have money here, like Meierbeer, or, rather, more than Meierbeer, or: – I must make people afraid of me. Well, I have no money, but what I do have is an enormous desire to commit acts of artistic terrorism. Give me your blessing, – or even better: give me your support! Come to Paris and lead the hunt; let's fire away, and leave a trail of dead rabbits to the right and to the left of us. –

[. . .]

SB III,73–4.

91. Minna Wagner, Dresden   Paris, 8 June 1849

Praise be to God, my dear wife! I feel a new man thanks to a decision I finally took after three of the most agonizing days! I have found myself once again, & now know the means of my salvation. Listen, my own dear wife! I hope we shall be together again within 2 weeks at the latest & I shall not be so easily separated from you in the future. Does that shock you? Well, examine the facts & you will find that I am not acting overhastily, but that my plan is the most natural & most sensible I could have thought of, when I considered the facts more closely & looked calmly, & without exaggeration, into the future. I beg you to listen & to help me with all the love you are capable of feeling for me.

I cannot remain here in Paris any longer: there is nothing else I can be doing here for the time being. I have made a few necessary contacts, notably with a poet,[1] together with whom – albeit at a distance – I can attend to my opera text for Paris. Everything else lies in the distant future, & there is absolutely nothing that can be done here now before next winter: Paris is deserted, notably as a result of the cholera. I have given you only a brief indication of the appalling sense of disgust I feel at this whole Paris business, so as to make it clear that there is no way I could be induced to remain in this ghastly, noisy, expensive & vast prison unless I had a particular purpose in mind. That purpose has now been achieved: there is nothing else that can be done for at least 6 months: so I shall quit Paris & its suffocating atmosphere. Shall I go now to London? I have made detailed enquiries and discovered that if I do not mind spending a small fortune with as little likelihood of accomplishing anything there as I have in Paris, then I can certainly go to London, but otherwise there is no reason for me to do so. The season there is already half finished: all the musicians of Europe have been flocking there, offering themselves like stale beer without accomplishing anything: but there is absolutely no English Opera there at present, only an inferior German one which would be of no use to me whatsoever. I have convinced myself that for London, too, I must make plans well in advance: that is something I can equally well do from a distance, and it will not be possible for me to achieve my goal there until the summer of next year: should I now squander 100 thalers in pursuit of that aim? No, I shall take what steps are necessary *without* going to London, – that is sensible! – What shall I do now? – My dearest thought & wish in all the world is to be reunited with my dear wife for good & to set up house with her in one of the most splendid spots on earth! – Listen carefully: I cannot *at present* return to Weimar as we discussed; but what I *can* offer you is a place where you can recover your health of body & mind, & that place is the splendid town of Zurich in Switzerland. A highly agreeable friendly well-to-do town, in a location such as scarcely any other city can boast: we shall live there in a simple little house just outside the town on Lake Zurich, with a view of the snow-covered Alps. What you need is not Teplitz but the lake baths at Zurich, they are the healthiest in the world & will strengthen & invigorate you, restore your energy & revive your spirits. There in the German-speaking part of Switzerland we shall feel at home: I have a dear friend[2] there, & he & his family & friends are all completely devoted to me; they will gladly serve me in whatever ways they can, simply to have me there in their midst, so that I can write my works *there*. Then – you see, my dear Minna! if I then have you beside me, with Nette, Peps & Papo![3] – then I shall finally pursue my true calling once more, & write an opera. I feel a great urge to write a new work,

1 Gustave Vaëz; see also letter [94], p. 175, note 2.
2 Alexander Müller.
3 Natalie Planer, together with the Wagners' dog and parrot; they arrived in Zurich with Minna
  at the beginning of September 1849.

but my mind must first be calmer, & that will only happen when I am near you!

[...]

SB III,76–8.

92. FRANZ LISZT, WEIMAR   Reuil,[1] 19 June 1849

[...] My wife, who considers it necessary to continue to live among the dregs of vulgar society in Dresden, has reported a thousand repugnant things which make me appear far more compromised by the uprising in the eyes of those pitiful wretches than is in fact the case: their mood towards me is now presumably widespread, and the Weimar Court will itself not have been untouched by it. And so I can imagine that you, too, would not now deem it appropriate to speak out on my behalf at a Court which, in its natural confusion, sees in me first and foremost only a political revolutionary, and in doing so forgets the artistic revolutionary whom it had basically come to like.

[...]

SB III,87.

93. FRANZ LISZT, WEIMAR   Zurich, 4 August 1849

Dear Liszt,

I am sending you herewith my latest piece of work[2] which I have just completed: it is a revised version of the original text which I sent to Paris last week to be translated into French for the arts pages of the National. Whether it is to your liking, I do not know: but one thing I am certain of is that, to judge by your temperament, you and I are of the same mind. I hope you will find nothing in it of the political commonplaces, socialist rigmarole or personal insults which you warned me against: – but the fact that I see what I do see in the deepest recesses of the affair is attributable purely and simply to the circumstance that, as a result of my own artistic nature and the sufferings I have had to endure, my eyes have been opened in such a way that death

---

1 Wagner went to stay with Belloni at La Ferté sous Jouarre near Reuil east of Paris, to escape from the cholera which was raging in Paris.
2 *Die Kunst und die Revolution* (Art and Revolution), originally intended to appear in instalments in the Paris newspaper *Le National*. In the event, it was published as a monograph by Otto Wigand of Leipzig in 1850.

alone will be able to close them again. Ahead of me I see either a totally useless existence or else the sort of activity that accords with my innermost nature, even though such activity may be practised far from the world of glitter: in the former instance I shall endeavour to bear in mind the need to be brief.

May I ask you to readdress the enclosed manuscript and accompanying letter and forward them to the publisher *Otto Wigand* in Leipzig: perhaps I shall succeed in deriving some small financial support from my inferior abilities as a writer.

I have had no news from my wife since my last letter to her[1] which I posted at the same time that I assailed you with my recent petition; her silence causes me no little torment.

From a letter from Baron Schober to Eck in Zurich I discovered to my great delight that your prospects are excellent and that you are resolved to settle in Weimar for good.[2] I presume that our splendid princess[3] is equally pleased and in good spirits: God be praised! – Whether you should show her my manuscript, I do not rightly know: I appear here very much as a *Greek*, so much so that I could not rightly be converted to Christianity. But why do I prattle on as if you were not the people to understand me? Forgive me!

Fare you well, my dear and only friend! Think of me kindly!

Yours,
Richard Wagner.

[. . .]

SB III,106–7.

94. THEODOR UHLIG, DRESDEN   Zurich, 9 August 1849

[. . .] My friend Liszt is damnably keen for me to write an opera for Paris: I even visited the place and have come to an arrangement with a well-known poet[4] to the effect that I shall provide him with a complete draft for an opera libretto, in return for which he will undertake to execute the same in French and ensure that I receive a commission to compose the music from the Grand Opera (forgive me if I have expressed myself somewhat unclearly!). Apart

---

1 Dated 23 July 1849, SB III,100–104.
2 Liszt accepted the post of Court Kapellmeister in Weimar in 1842 (though not taking up the full duties until some years later); he resigned in December 1858, but remained in the post for a few months longer.
3 Princess Carolyne Sayn-Wittgenstein.
4 Gustave Vaëz.

from my Siegfried[1] I currently have 2 tragic operatic subjects and 2 comic ones[2] in my head, but none of them is suitable for a production in French: I now have a 5th one, of which it is a matter of indifference to me in what language it first sees the light of day: "Jesus of Nazareth". I intend offering this subject to my French associate and in this way hope to be rid of the whole affair, since I can well imagine the look of horror on his face when he sees the poem: if he plucks up enough courage to fight alongside me in the thousand battles which must necessarily ensue once he resolves to stage such a subject, – well, I shall consider that fate has willed it so and I shall throw myself into the affair; if, on the other hand, he stands me up, – so much the better, I shall no longer be exposed to the temptation of working in the detestable gibberish of the French language, since you know my basic temperament well enough to be able to imagine that only with the greatest reluctance would I set about composing such a mishmash: if I do so at all, it is simply out of consideration for my creditors, to whom I shall send my French receipts. – [. . .]

SB III, 109–10.

95. THEODOR UHLIG, DRESDEN   Zurich, 16 September 1849

[. . .] God only knows why, but I really cannot feel downhearted! Particularly since my wife is now here with me[3] and I have no reason to worry about my livelihood for the next few months, I continue to feel as complacently self-satisfied as a dog when its master stops beating it. My only regret is that I have not done a stroke of work during the last few weeks: not until next week shall we move into a small apartment here which will enable me to have my own room for working in; until now I have had only a common-room in which to sit and get on with my scribblings, and it is to this circumstance that you must attribute the fact that I have satisfied your demand and prepared my nibelistic essay[4] for publication, although I re-edited it extensively at the

---

1 *Siegfrieds Tod.*
2 The two tragic subjects may be *Achilleus* (WWV 81) and *Alexander der Grosse* (thus, at least, the suggestion of Curt von Westernhagen, *Richard Wagner* [Zurich 1956], pp. 142ff). The generally accepted suggestion that Wagner is referring here to *Wieland der Schmied* (WWV 82) is called into question by the fact that the first mention of this work in Wagner's correspondence is in a letter to Ferdinand Heine of 4 December 1849, SB III,175–85. The two comic subjects are *Die Meistersinger von Nürnberg* and (?) *Der junge Siegfried.*
3 See letter [91], p. 172, note 3.
4 *Die Wibelungen. Weltgeschichte aus der Sage* (The Wibelungs. World History from Legend), written in Dresden in the early months of 1849 and revised in Zurich in late August/early September; see also introductory essay, p. 59.

same time as copying it out, so that it may be of interest to you to compare the enclosed manuscript with the older version, whereby I would draw your attention in particular to the 3rd section about the Wibelungs and then to the 12th and final section about actual possessions, where you will be struck by my more economic handling of the material.

You will find the pamphlet enclosed herewith, and I would ask you to forward it to the publisher Wigand in Leipzig, together with the enclosed letter: the cost of forwarding them both will not, I trust, be exorbitant, but I would suggest that, in order to raise the sum, you should if necessary organize a subscription among the more radical members of the orchestra.

Wigand is already publishing another brochure of mine: Art & Revolution,[1] of whose French fate in the National I have had no news at the time of writing. Get hold of this pamphlet as soon as it appears: it will be only the forerunner, – as soon as I can resume my work, I shall follow it up with a more detailed piece: the art-work of the future, – of which a third essay: the Artists of the Future[2] will later form the conclusion. I shall refrain from giving you any information concerning the approximate content of these essays, since it is not something which can be given in approximate form, but only in its actual, complete form.

But it is absolutely necessary for me to write these essays and send them out into the world before I continue with my more immediate artistic creations: I myself and all who are interested in me as an artist must be forced once and for all to come to a precise understanding of the issues involved, otherwise we shall all spend the rest of our lives groping around in a loathsome world of half-lit forms, which is worse than a state of total obscurity in which the benighted traveller can see nothing at all but where he continues to clutch desperately and piously at long familiar objects to guide him on his way.

If all turns out as I hope it will, once I have finished these essays, I shall write the music for my Siegfried: I long to do so from the very depths of my soul. The same strength of feeling lies behind my desire to evade the operatic plans which have been foisted upon me against my will in Paris. Basically, it is Liszt who is to blame for setting me on this collision course. He's a modern man of the world who may have many admirable qualities, but he loves me in a way which makes him want me to enjoy an enormous international success in Paris. Because of the need to think of earning my living, I did not reject the idea out of hand: I let him do as he liked with me, with the result, as I have already told you, I am now in the ridiculous predicament of having

1 *Art and Revolution;* see letter [93], p. 173, note 2.
2 *Die Künstlerschaft der Zukunft* (Artists of the Future) remained a fragment; it was published in 1885 in *Entwürfe, Gedanken, Fragmente* under the title "Das Künstlerthum der Zukunft", and reprinted in SS XII,254–63; PW VIII,343–52.

to decide between genuine offers of help from Paris and my own inner revulsion. [...]

[...] I want to be *happy*, and man can be happy only when he is *free*: but only that man is free who is what he *can* be and therefore what he *must* be. The man, therefore, who satisfies the inner necessity of his being is free, since he feels at one with himself, because everything he does is at one with his nature and his true needs: but the man who follows not his inner but some outer necessity obeys a coercive force, – he is unfree, a slave, unhappy. But the free man scorns the oppression of outer coercion, as long as we do not sacrifice our inner necessity to it: it can cause only flea-bites but never heartfelt anguish. I do not care what becomes of me, as long as I become what my nature dictates I should become, only then shall I become what is right, – even if not a single person notices me as a result. – Well then: – I do *not* believe in my Paris opera! but my wife must know nothing of this yet. –

   [...]

SB III, 122–5.

96. FERDINAND HEINE, DRESDEN   Zurich, 19 November 1849

[...] But let us pause here and ask ourselves the question: what in fact is my present intention? If my most basic livelihood were assured, it would be my intention to do what must be done, and to leave undone what would only destroy me if I had to do it. I have poured out my heart to the world, i.e. to my friends, in my latest essay: the Art-work of the Future. From now on I shall cease to be a writer, and revert to being an artist. Providing the outside world leaves me in peace, I shall create work upon work, – for I am brimming over with subjects and artistic plans. But as long as the outward form of the world stays the same, these works must remain mute and be intended for my friends alone: only when that form changes, as it necessarily must, will they speak out and be exactly what the world is waiting for. My Lohengrin was completed long ago: I now feel an all-consuming urge to delay no longer but to write the music for my Siegfried. My head is teeming with subjects for 5 operas:[1] I feel a very real need to give expression to each of them, one after the other. I shall even keep half an eye on Paris: it is not, however, the conditions currently prevailing there which I have in mind, but the ones which must inevitably replace them, and in the none too distant future. I shall spend the next few days elaborating my sketch for there;[2] it is: *Jesus of Nazareth*. I

1 See letter [94], p. 175, note 2.
2 There is no evidence that Wagner did so.

must first of all attempt to win over my French poet[1] to the idea, so that, encouraged by the hope of a none-too-distant success, he may come to some arrangement with me concerning the plan, in order that we may appear before the public with the finished work when the time comes. – Only when I regard matters in this light can I remain an artist, and create works of art: if not – I shall cease to exist. – My sole concern, therefore, is: *to gain time*, i.e. *gain life*. Wretch that I am, I know no craft which would enable me to earn my daily bread: as things stand at present, it *must* be offered to me, so that I can remain an artist. Who is to do this? Only those who love me, or rather those who love me, my works and my aims and intentions as an artist in such a way that they feel concerned to preserve me for the sake of my art and my aims as an artist. There are *not many* such people, and what characterizes these few individuals – appropriately enough – is that they love me *energetically*. They have given me many fine and refreshing proofs of this over the years. There are not many of them, and they are scattered abroad, – but they are friends of my very essence. The most natural thing for me to do in my present position would be to appeal to these friends of mine, openly and for all the world to see; to lay my case and my aims before them without reserve, and to invite them to join in helping me as best they can and with a concerted effort to survive this difficult period of my life, since *I* am currently prevented by the present state of things from helping myself. They should not see in me an individual in need of help, but an artist and a trend in art which they wish to preserve for the future and not allow to go under. To them shall belong the works I shall unflaggingly create, until such time as they can be handed over to the *people* as the property which has been preserved for them. Though I were mocked and derided for this by all the curs in the world, it would be a matter of indifference to me as long as I knew that at least my friends had understood me. Were I completely on my own, I should take such a step quite openly, – but I cannot do so because of my wife, – she would not understand me and would hear only the baying of the pack. – And so I must look around for someone who – without publicity – will intercede on my behalf and take upon himself the task of achieving in the most meticulous and self-effacing manner the deed which I myself should have done publicly at a single stroke. The question was how to find this somebody. I felt I had to choose the *most influential* of my friends and am now pleased to have hit squarely on the very man who, I know, more than any other wishes me well.

It is *you*, my dear friend, whom I now entreat to accept this special responsibility for me and my art! Without wishing to anticipate your decision, I shall tell you *how* I imagine you must proceed in the circumstances. You may perhaps begin by inviting one or two people who are friendlily disposed

1 Gustave Vaëz.

towards me to form a kind of committee with you: you yourself can best choose whom to approach; possibly *Löwe* would not be entirely unsuitable. (I might mention in passing that a family by the name of Ritter, about whom Uhlig can give you further details and perhaps effect an introduction, – behaved most commendably towards my wife when I left her in Dresden – and *completely* without prompting – indeed, even without knowing her: perhaps this family could give you some *indication* where you might find other friends of my art who are as yet unknown to you.) You would, as far as possible, initiate into your plan (which of course must appear to be your own!) only those whose confidence can be trusted and who share the same beliefs, and encourage them to play an active part in helping you; you could perhaps issue a discreet circular for this purpose. From outside Dresden you should approach *Liszt* in Weimar, similarly Frau *Frommann* in Berlin (behind the Catholic Church, No 2) and invite them to help in a cautious sort of way with any enterprise you might care to undertake. The aim would quite simply be to collect as much money as possible to be handed over *to my wife*, so that she can procure without trouble whatever is necessary for our livelihood, and leave me to get on with my work! What you then choose to do with my works would be your own affair.[1] – [. . .]

I fear I have said more than enough about myself; and yet I cannot lose sight of myself entirely, even when I now turn to speak of you and Wilhelm.[2] The day after I posted my last letter to you, I received a letter from Wilm in New York in which he invited me, among other things, to send him my operas as soon as possible, so that he might do what he could to rouse interest in them and in me. America for me now and always can be of only financial interest: but if circumstances here at home remain such that I finally run out of air to breathe, I might finally cast an eye in the direction of America, but only to become a craftsman there – albeit with a baton in my hand – which would at least ensure me a better income there than it would here. *I have no children:* this is the difference between you and me: as the *father of a family* you are beginning a new and immeasurably long life in the new world: mine would be completely extinguished there with my death; so you will have a future there, I would have none; for me my art alone must be what your family is for you: *together with your family* you form a whole unit wherever you are, *without my art* I am a miserable egoist, whose only concern would be for his stomach, not for the future. – [. . .]

Much as I enjoyed Wilm's letter, what really fascinated me was the news

---

1 Heine's initial reaction to this proposal was one of dismay and embarrassment. However, an approach was made to Julie Ritter in Dresden and to Jessie Laussot in Bordeaux to provide Wagner with financial support. Jessie Laussot withdrew her offer of help following Wagner's *affaire* with her in the summer of 1850, but Julie Ritter continued to subsidize Wagner to the tune of 800 thalers a year from 1851 until 1859.

2 Heine's 22-year-old son.

you sent me about him: it surpasses our wildest dreams! But I was almost less pleased for Wilhelm's sake than for *you old folks*, and for the fact that you have lived to see such happiness! Ah, to perpetuate one's life through the living flesh and blood is something very different from doing so through writing and notes: all hopes which are directed towards a long artistic life rest basically upon the uncreative poverty of mankind: if men were as they ought to be, a work of art would flourish today and die tomorrow, leaving a new one in its place in full fresh bloom. True, physical immortality is indeed a more beautiful thing: it exists only where love is at its greatest; our loveless civilization, however, has had to get by with all manner of other kinds of immortality, none of which is of much value, – and the same is certainly true of the so-called artistic variety. In return for a single year of genuine, true, human existence I should gladly sacrifice a hundred thousand years of immortality in art. You happy man!

I shall write to Wilm before the week is out: if you have any news of him in the mean time – do let me know.

That you intend going to America so soon has not yet properly sunk in: – I simply cannot conceive it is possible, my heart refuses to accept the idea! – The Heines are off to America!! – Perhaps the autumn mists here are to blame for the fact that I no longer see clearly – possibly also the fact that I am so overwrought: I feel a great sense of sadness, – and there are times when I am assailed by morbid thoughts, – morbid or healthy – they are thoughts of an early death, which often does not seem so dreadful. – I feel so useless, – so utterly superfluous – as lonely people do, – and I often feel very lonely, – especially when I think that the Heines will soon be off to America! –

[. . .]

SB III, 149–55.

97. KARL RITTER, LEIPZIG   Zurich, 19 November 1849

[. . .] I expect that by now you will have grown more familiar with Feuerbach. You should probably have begun with his essay on death and immortality. But you will soon find what is right. It's bad enough having to read books in order to become a natural man! All the harm which lies in this lies, in turn, in the books themselves. In order to express the most basic truth, the writer must write God knows how much, and what's worse, he becomes in the process not a human being but merely a writer once more. But Feuerbach ends up by becoming a human being, and on this point he is so weighty an authority, particularly in relation to absolute philosophy in which the human being is completely subsumed by the philosopher. Nowhere have I found the natural healthy process so clearly and so consciously expressed as by Feuerbach, and I confess that I am greatly indebted to him: the same thing will presumably happen to you, too.

You have misunderstood the point of the comparison between the poet and the thaumaturge. The poet's nature finds expression not only in his more immediate verse-making, seen from a practical point of view, but in the whole way in which he acts and views things, a process in which he must, however, exercise a certain self-restraint if he is to submit himself to it, i.e. act and view things as, for ex., the practical necessity of modern life demands. A modern poet may be forced by sheer necessity into becoming a merchant, a carpet-knight, a citizen of the realm etc., but only to the extent that he violates his own true nature.

[. . .]

SB III, 161–2.

98. THEODOR UHLIG, DRESDEN   Zurich, [21/22 November 1849]

[. . .] Since this work[1] in fact contains an account of my entire history up to the present day, I find it virtually unnecessary to add much else to today's letter to you. Above all, however, I must express my sincere thanks for your various letters, although I continue to regret the fact that you are the one whose pocket has had a hole burned in it because of the enormous sums you have had to pay in postage, especially the time before last: you should be more careful! From your last letter I would single out in particular the predicament caused by your need to obtain favourable reviews of my literary writings. Do not trouble yourself unduly about this! There is only one thing that matters to me, and that is that they are read as widely as possible; I welcome anything that contributes to that end; it matters not a whit if they are torn to pieces, because that is something that is entirely to be expected. After all, I am not seeking to be reconciled with worthlessness, but what I do seek is the most ruthless war: and since the sort of worthlessness I have in mind is one of the conditions of public life and above all of the trade which is practised by artists and literary figures, I can find friends only in those areas which are totally removed from the public sphere as it now predominates. It is not a question of convincing other people and winning them over; it is a question purely and simply of extermination: we shall gain the strength to bring this about in the future if we learn to see ourselves as the disciples of

1 The manuscript of *The Art-Work of the Future* which Wagner had completed on 4 November and which he enclosed with the present letter to Uhlig.

a new religion, and consolidate our faith by means of our mutual love: let us stick to the side of youth, – and let the older generation rot in hell, they have nothing to offer us!

[. . .]

SB III, 165–6.

99. THEODOR UHLIG, DRESDEN   Zurich, 27 December 1849

My dear friend,

I kept thinking I might receive a further letter from you, or from one of my other friends, which I could then answer at the same time as the present letter. I assume that at the moment you have nothing especially urgent to tell me, now that you know I am well provided for in one important respect.[1] I was uncommonly touched and affected by the news from Frau Laussot in Bordeaux, and for more than one reason! My art has always found favour with women's hearts, and that is probably because, for all the vulgarity which prevails at present, women still find it more difficult to harden their hearts as effectively as our political menfolk, who have succeeded in doing so to the general satisfaction of all and sundry. Women are very much the music of life; they are more open and unreserved in the way they assimilate things, which they then enhance by virtue of their sympathetic understanding. While waiting for news from Bordeaux, I was surprised to receive some money from Herr Paez in Dresden:[2] I wrote to him at once, as best I could, and described the feelings evoked within me by these tokens of love and concern on the part of people whom I scarcely knew. Experiences such as these would inspire in anyone feelings of goodness, nobility and cheerful serenity, but their effect upon me at the present time has been to make me supremely happy: never has the awareness of freedom felt so beneficial as it does at present, nor have I ever received such clear confirmation of the fact that the only thing that makes us free is a loving association with others. If Frau Laussot's help were wholly to enable me to see the immediate years ahead as free from the anxiety of having to earn my living, then those years would be the most decisive of my entire life, and, above all, of my career as an artist; for now I can face even Paris calmly and with dignity, whereas previously the fear of being forced by practical necessity to make concessions had, from the outset, discouraged me from making any move in the direction of Paris. That has now changed: whereas the message formerly was: deny yourself! become another person,

1 Wagner is referring here to the financial support granted him by Julie Ritter and Jessie Laussot.
2 Johann Cornelius Paez sent Wagner money in December 1849.

become a Parisian in order to win over Paris for your own ends, – my present intention is now: remain entirely the person you are, show the Parisians what you want and what you are capable of producing from within yourself; get that idea across to them and, to enable them to grasp your meaning, speak to them in terms they can understand, since your aim, after all, is that of being *understood* by them *for what you are*. I hope you all agree with this? – And so I shall be going to Paris on the 16th of January 1850; a couple of my overtures are already in rehearsal there,[1] and I shall be taking with me my completed scenario: it is – Wiland the Smith. I shall begin by attacking the 5-act form of opera, then the rule according to which every grand opera *has* to include a special ballet. If I succeed in winning over Gustave Vaez to this idea, and if I can get him to understand my purpose and to share my desire to carry it through, then all is well, – if not, I shall keep on searching until I find the right poet. Every difficulty which I and my associate may encounter in implementing our plan will provide material for attacks which I shall launch in the newspapers, even though it means ruthlessly raking up the entire dunghill and allowing clean water to flow through it: I shall then be in my element, since my business is to bring about revolution wherever I go. If I go under in the process, well then, I shall regard such a defeat as more honourable than any triumph gained by an alternative method: even if I fail to report any personal victory, I shall nevertheless be of use to the cause. Victory here, however, will only be assured us if we persevere: the man who holds out to the end will inevitably win, and to hold out, for me – since I do not doubt in my strength of will – means having enough money to be able to launch an attack without the need to worry about my own existence. Given sufficient money I would, for ex., immediately have my pamphlets on art[2] translated and distributed. Well, that will all become clear when I am there on the spot, and it will depend upon the means which are placed at my disposal. If my money runs out before the end, I can certainly count on help from another quarter, i.e. the social republic, which sooner or later is inevitable and unavoidable in France: once it comes, I shall be ready and waiting for it, having already effectively prepared the way for it in art. – I do not imagine that things will turn out quite as hoped for by my complacent friends who are biased in favour of our present inferior age; no, things will turn out differently and, if all goes well, for the better, since what *they* want is of use only to me, – whereas what *I* want is of benefit to us all. – You should not make such a fuss about my latest piece![3] But I would be a fool to say that I was not pleased to discover how much you had enjoyed it. Wigand has told

1 François Seghers, the conductor of the Société Ste-Cécile, had promised Liszt that he would perform the *Tannhäuser* Overture, but the orchestral parts did not arrive in Paris until March 1850. The performance was delayed until 20 November 1850.
2 *Art and Revolution* and *The Art-Work of the Future.*
3 *The Art-Work of the Future.*

me nothing about it; it is true that I have been sent 10 louis d'or from Leipzig for my earlier pamphlets,[1] but nothing else was said. But I hope it is being printed? – The printing errors in the earlier pieces were dreadful and often completely distorted the sense. Could I ask you to correct the new one for me? I have asked Wigand if he will do the same. After I had completed the article, I was so firmly resolved never again to try my hand at anything similar that I now cannot help laughing at my resolve: I feel the need once again welling up inside me to write something else. If we are entirely honest with ourselves, then we really must admit that this is now the only thing which has any sense or any real purpose: works of art cannot be created at present, they can only be prepared for by means of revolutionary activity, by destroying and crushing everything that is worth destroying and crushing. That is our task, and only people totally different from us will be the true creative artists. It is only in that sense that I can envisage my forthcoming activities in Paris: even the work that I am writing and producing for there can only be a single moment in the revolution, a token of affirmation in the process of destruction. Destruction alone is what is now needed, – to build anything at present can only be arbitrary. [. . .]

SB III, 194–7.

100. JAKOB SULZER, ZURICH   Paris, 22 February 1850

[. . .] There is little that I can write to you from here: I lead a very melancholy existence. The vagueness of the information I was given and delays which have occurred since I arrived here mean that I have come to Paris at least four whole weeks too soon: you can imagine, as a result, my ill temper and deep sense of discontent which, I regret to say, is only made worse by continuing physical indisposition. What I am actually suffering from is Paris, which now fills my entire being with a sense of revulsion: the conflict between my inner aversion and the importunacy of a number of my friends, and especially of my good wife, may perhaps long since have prepared the ground for my present indisposition through intellectual discontent and involuntary discord. O you people! why will you never realize that the only activity which brings satisfaction and happiness and which is therefore at all useful is that which accords with our whole, true being! Paris for me means nothing but constraints and burdensome responsibility. –
   [. . .]

SB III, 236–7.

1 *Art and Revolution* and *The Wibelungs.*

101. THEODOR UHLIG, DRESDEN   Paris, 24 February 1850

[. . .] In the mean time I have seen the Prophet[1] for the first time in this life, in fact I saw it the evening before I received your last letter, enclosing the book,[2] for which I was most grateful. During the last act I was unfortunately distracted by a banker, who was talking in his box in an uncommonly loud voice. Otherwise I was able to convince myself – at the opera's 47th performance – that the work has been accorded a great and lasting – and undeniable – success by the Paris Opera audience: the house is always full to overflowing, and the applause more enthusiastic than anything I've otherwise found here. –

I am happy to be able to inform you that I have now discovered the basic cause of my illness: to a large extent it was an emotional disorder, or rather it was an involuntary affliction of my mind whose physical symptoms increased to such an alarming degree that they finally made themselves felt. I have recently given full expression to the motives which prompted my decision not to write an opera for Paris, and I did so in a fairly detailed letter to Frau Laussot,[3] the contents of which will have been passed on to you by this truly excellent friend; what I said here was that in no circumstances would I write an opera for Paris but that, at most, I would agree to hand over an already completed work, *Lohengrin*, which has since lost its appeal for me, and which may be plucked and woven into the garland that graces the brow of Paris's grand opera whore: but since I am not so naive as to believe that this gift will be seen as a decent offering, and since, moreover, it is impossible for me even so much as to lift my pen in furtherance of this business of selling myself, I assume that I shall have to deny my dear friends Heine and Fischer (to whom I do not yet dare to communicate this decision) the pleasure of seeing a Wagnerian swan-knight swimming across the Rhine. – What was useful about all this for me was that I began to feel better the moment I sent off the letter, an improvement in my condition which continued yesterday when I received my friend's reply containing her sincere congratulations on my decision. So as not to have wasted my time altogether, I intend waiting for the performance of my *Tannhäuser* Overture[4] before travelling south, taking in Bordeaux, in an attempt to regain perfect health. That, my dear friend, is how the horse cures itself in the wilderness, by biting open one of its veins; in my case the vein is the Paris opera: I delight in feeling this unhealthy blood oozing from the veins in which it had begun to thicken.
[. . .]

SB III,240–1.

1 *Le Prophète* by Giacomo Meyerbeer, first performed at the Paris Opéra on 16 April 1849.
2 *The Art-Work of the Future,* which had just appeared in print.
3 No correspondence with Jessie Laussot has survived.
4 See letter [99], p.183, note 1.

102. MINNA WAGNER, ZURICH   Paris, 2 March 1850

My good Minna,

I received your letter around midday: I wasted no time in drafting a reply for you[1] and, since it must reach the post by 5 o'clock at the latest – which is why I cannot frank it – , I have left myself very little time on this occasion to address even a couple of lines to you yourself. It is impossible for anyone to act more kindly, nobly and more delicately than our friend Frau Laussot! I should have thought, my dear wife, that you would find it most edifying to see the deep impression which your husband's works are capable of producing on healthy, unperverted and noble hearts, and to know that he is able to persuade others to take such selfless decisions, decisions, moreover, which are prompted by the most heartfelt concern! Can you find it in your heart to despise this success which I owe to my art – *for this alone* has produced it – or even to rate it lower than these so-called "brilliant" successes as are nowadays achieved, thanks to speculation and cunning, by the stupid, slovenly, heartless mass of our great theatre-going public? You see now what these faint-hearted, sluggish people are like – people whom I once appeared to please, but who now treat me so shabbily. Shall we despise these people and think only about money? All right, here is money, as much as we need for a quiet, not to say comfortable, life, – it has not been extorted from the scurvy masses, but was offered to me in the most delicate fashion by a noble heart which rejoiced in my works – just as I have created them in accord with my true inner nature! What more do you want? – Of course, my poor good wife, I understand you, I know you and can see what the basic problem is, for all the differences between us: I hope that in replying to Frau Laussot I have hit upon your true and innermost thoughts! – –

 [. . .]

SB III,243–4.

103. THEODOR UHLIG, DRESDEN   Bordeaux, 26 March 1850[2]

[. . .] Everything that I find so attractive about your letters – and especially the first of them – everything in which I rejoice from the very bottom of my heart and to which I can respond only with the warmest affection – these are

---

1 To Jessie Laussot, who, at Wagner's request, had written to Minna in Zurich to explain the motivation behind her proposed financial support. For a brief account of the Laussot *affaire*, see introduction, pp. 159–60.
2 Wagner arrived in Bordeaux on 16 March, at the invitation of Jessie Laussot and her husband. He remained there as their house-guest until 5 April.

points I shall not enumerate in detail, for they concern you, so to speak, as a whole person, and to treat the matter adequately I should need a great deal, a very great deal of time; but, above all, I lack the inclination which it would require to dispose of the matter with the aid of ink, pen and paper. But I shall tell you right out what it is that *dis*pleases me about your letters, or rather I shall *write* it down for you: since this can be quickly disposed of and may possibly be better written than said.

Listen then! –

You are still *incomplete*, i.e. the royal court musician is still too much a part of you, that same court musician who performs his duty, is elected to serve on the widows' pensions committee, and who seeks to reach agreement with Müller about the "procedure" necessary to deal with this or that passage in a particular application. Your concern for increased salaries for the assistants was noble and kind: but the fact that you see the whole world as made up of assistants whose salaries ought to be a cause for your concern, that you regard this concern for salaries as more vital than your concern for *me*, and that you only accept me and my decisions once you feel yourself rid of this concern, – this is something about you which straightway *annoyed* me. Your pleasure when you finally discovered that I was receiving an annuity from Frau Laussot, – this pleasure which only now has given you the courage to accept me as I am – it struck me as being very unworthy of you, for I begrudge you no pleasure save that of the *philistine*, – for you are my brother. I read your most recent – enclosed – letter sitting by the hearth in the company of my friend, Jessie, and found myself growing so dreadfully depressed at it that I finally felt obliged to break off in the middle of reading out a letter from my closest friend in order that this dear woman should not be offended by a philistine's haggling over questions of money; I was – as I say – so embittered and enraged by the unworthy pleasure you took in my "being provided for" that when Jessie insisted upon reading the letter herself after I had hesitated to go on with it, I threw it into the fire that was burning on the hearth. My dear brother, you should be glad that I acted in this way: you have been absolved by this sacrificial gesture: this letter was the final product of the vestigial court musician in you – this letter has now been scattered to the four winds, and since I know that it was the final act on the part of the court musician – his final sign of life, I hope that the latter, too, has similarly ceased to exist, at least within the soul of my brother Theodor! –

What placed this letter of yours in so glaring and disagreeable a light was the fact that it arrived enclosed with a letter from Emilie[1] which I opened and read immediately prior to your own. Ask Emilie what I mean, she will explain and make it clear in two words, – for – believe me – this girl is far ahead of you, – and in what way? – By birth, because she is a woman. She

1 Emilie Ritter, daughter of Julie.

was *born a human being*, – you, and all other men, are nowadays born as *philistines* and only slowly and effortfully do we poor creatures succeed in becoming human. Women have remained entirely what they were at birth and alone are capable of educating us; were it not for them, we men would be hopelessly lost in no time at all. – [. . .]

SB III,263–4.

104. MIKHAIL BAKUNIN AND AUGUST RÖCKEL, KÖNIGSTEIN[1]
Bordeaux, March 1850

Dear fr. & bro. –

It has never been my intention to write to you offering consolation, for I knew you had no need of consolation. But now that I learn that the King of S. has confirmed the death sentence on you both, I should like to give you pleasure by conveying to you a most devoted brother's greeting. I am, however, far away from you: I scarcely dare hope that these lines will reach you, and so I can only wish that you receive them in time.

Whether I was awake or dreaming, you were always close to me: you stood before me strong and suffering, a source of both envy and pity. Now I see you both ready to receive the fatal blow at the hand of that same executioner for whose humanization you once fought. My brothers, let me confess to you the frailty of my love which allowed me to *hope* that I should see your lives spared. I now understand that, just as you are great and strong, so the fate which your enemies inflict upon you must in turn be decisive and violent: they dare not fail to counter your bold strength with their most daring resolves, and thus to honour you. Therefore be proud of yourselves! Dear brethren! what was it seemed to us most necessary to transform men into true human beings? – That they should be forced by adversity into becoming *heroes*. We now see two heroes before us: driven by the holy need of human love, they have developed into joyful heroes: accept our greeting, dearest of men! You show us what we may all become. Die then, happy to rejoice in the highest standards which you know yourselves to have set us!

If, from afar, your brother may mingle a drop of sweetness in the draught of deadly earnest which you are about to drink, let it be to share with you the news that, cared for by the most blissful friendship and love, I can face

---

1 Bakunin and Röckel had been imprisoned in Waldheim for their part in the Dresden uprising of May 1849. Bakunin was later handed over to the Russians, and Röckel was released in March 1862. This letter did not reach its destination (see letter [105]) but is included here to indicate how deeply Wagner was indebted at this time to the ideals of Ludwig Feuerbach. Only the draft of the letter has survived, hence the abbreviations and absence of a signature.

the future in freedom and serenity, and that, with strength renewed and keenly fired, I for my own part and according to my own capabilities, am working away at that same task for which you heroes are now laying down your lives. Mikhail! August! my dear and beloved brethren whom I shall never forget! Your lives will live on. Like the ripples on a pond, your memory will spread in ever widening circles, forming a token of love destined to bring happiness to future humanity! Thus you may die, then, envied, admired and – loved! –

If I might be granted the ineffable pleasure of yet receiving a final word from you, then you must needs know where it will reach me: at M. J. L.[1] – If this greeting should find you still of this world, I doubt not but that my most heartfelt desire may yet be fulfilled.

And so, my dear brethren! I embrace you with all the fervour of a man whose love comes from his innermost soul. Accept this kiss and this final tear! Allow me to share with you the strength with which I see you now standing serenely before me! Happy and proud – that is how you will appear before me until the end of time – allow me thus to dedicate my life to the glory of our friendship!

Yours —

SB III,270–1.

105. THEODOR UHLIG, DRESDEN   Paris, 15 April 1850

Dear Theodor,

It is 10 days now since I left Bordeaux. I had to travel via Paris: a great deal still continues to detain me here.

Emilie's[2] letters were forwarded from Bordeaux, so I did not receive them until I arrived here: I intended to reply either to her, or to Frau Ritter, who has also written to me, but I am still not able to do so, even today. If I do not have a moment's peace to write to Emilie tomorrow, I would ask you kindly to remember me to her for the time being, and to tell her that she is to retain the letter to Bakunin and Röckel,[3] since it would now only serve to cause them the same unnecessary alarm as I myself felt on reading in the French newspapers the explicit but mistaken statement that the King had finally confirmed the death sentence on them. I am most profoundly grateful to Frau Ritter for her splendid letter: there is at present no one who needs the consolation of love more than I. –

1 Mme Jessie Laussot.
2 Emilie Ritter.
3 See letter [104], pp. 188–9.

Among those who have been most implacably displeased by the decision I have taken concerning my future activities and by the consequent abandonment of all my plans for Paris, I must unfortunately number – my poor wife. I can now see quite clearly that it was only the prospect of Paris which persuaded her to join me last year, – a prospect which she regrettably interpreted and announced to others as being far more definite than I ever gave her cause to understand. The sense of disharmony between us which began on both sides at precisely the moment when I started to become the man I am now, goes to the deepest roots of our nature: there is not a single aspect of my nature in which my wife now understands me. The letter informing her that our future had been assured by my friends[1] was marked by a most sisterly affection, yet that letter aroused in her only a sense of humiliation: she does not understand what is involved here. She has written of what appears to her to be a necessary separation from a man "who can no longer support his wife in a way which the world would regard as decent and honourable". I hoped that, following my reunion with her in Switzerland, I might gradually bring her round to my own point of view: in place of any fulfilment of that hope, I soon saw that only silence and the repression of my true nature could enable us to live together without daily scenes of the most violent nature. Beneath this all-consuming constraint, with no means of communicating what I felt to those in my immediate vicinity, and having constantly to deny whatever I thought and conceived, I finally began to pine away and my thoughts turned increasingly towards death. I was on the point of returning to Zurich when I was again beset by my old complaint: I am paralyzed, overcome by melancholy and unhappiness: – only love can cure me, I feel certain of that, but love is not something I shall find in my own house. I no longer feel equal to the task of conducting the most unprofitable daily arguments with the one woman who ought to be closest to me, and yet whom I shall never be able to convince. I can no longer bear this torment which weighs upon me all the more oppressively in that I can communicate it to no one: if I were to live another year like this, I should die the most shameful of deaths. After all that my wife has endured and suffered during our long years of marriage together, I have only one duty towards her: – to make her happy. She tells me that she is incapable of loving me as I am and if I do not change: and so my love for her can consist only in the wish – to make her happy. I now feel that I cannot do so living under the same roof with her: it is not simply that I am worn out by it all, – she, too, suffers as a result, since – being a woman of honour – she does not want a superficial kind of love, but rather one that is basic, i.e. one which involves a basic change in my whole nature. –

Ahead of me I see only gloom, for I feel that it is better for me to speak

1 Julie Ritter and Jessie Laussot.

the plain truth about my loneliness, rather than attempt to cover it up by means of an effortful lie, which would only result in our destroying each other. I am determined that no profitless or misguided effort on my part shall prevent my wife from becoming independent of my own fate, since that is what she desires. What this means, in the light of all that we have been fated to go through together – and how fearfully my heart suffers beneath the burden of this decision – is something which only those who know me well can judge. I shall remain behind, naked and exposed, without the least token of our love, cut off from a world which would have been my ruin. Never again shall I see my dog and parrot – it must be so!

– Next week – the most decisive of my life, I shall spend in the most secluded isolation: – in Montmorency, near Paris. Let the Ritters know what I have told you today: if you all feel and understand what I must suffer in the week of torment that lies ahead, send me a token of your love, from your own hand, by way of consolation: tell me that I have found a new world, now that I have at last released my final hold on the old world. How blissful I was until recently in the thought that my wife might share in the bond which, tighter and tighter and ever more beautifully, was closing around me: but how hopelessly misunderstood this all is by this most wretched of women, whom I sincerely pity because she – cannot feel love. – –

If Wigand still intends sending me the 10 louis d'or, let him send the money at once to my wife in Zurich – through Orell and Fuessli, only be quick about it. –

Fare you well, my brother! Do you feel what it means to love me? Do you feel the pain of this love? If you do not feel it, then you do not love me! Fare you well!

Yours,
Richard W.

[. . .]

SB III,272–5.

106. Minna Wagner, Zurich   Paris, 16 April 1850

Dear Minna,

Thus I address you still, in spite of your signature on the last letter which I received from you and in which you asked that in future I should refer to you as *Sie*.[1] "Dear Minna": that is how I address you in this difficult hour as I appear before you today, – that is how I addressed you in the past, before

---

1 *Sie* is the pronoun used in formal relationships with acquaintances; close friends and married couples would prefer the informal *du*.

the most terrible and irreparable discord divided us, and that is how – if you do not begrudge me this favour – you shall continue for ever to live in my memory! – –

Your letters to me in Bordeaux came as a violent jolt and roused me from a beautiful and last remaining delusion concerning ourselves: I thought that I had finally won you, I wrongly imagined I had seen you yield to the power of true love – and with terrible pain now felt more than ever before the unerring certainty that we no longer belong to each other. From that moment I could take no more: I could no longer speak to a soul, – I wanted to leave quickly – to join you; I hurriedly took my leave of my friends[1] and hastened to Paris in order to return at once to Zurich. I have now been here for 2 weeks: my old nervous disorder has returned; it lies on me like a spectre, – I must shake it off, I must do so for my own sake – and for yours. – Listen to me!

The fundamental differences between us have proved, to a greater or lesser extent, to be a torment both for me and, more especially, for you, ever since the time we first became acquainted. *I* at least have no need to remind you of the countless scenes which have passed between us since the earliest days of our marriage, – for I have no doubt but that you have a livelier memory of them than I do. Yet what bound me so irresistibly to you then was love, a love which was blind to all the differences between us, – a love, however, which you did not share, at least not to the extent that it governed me. It was really only through sheer necessity that you yielded to my insistent demands that we should be married: perhaps you felt everything for me that you were capable of feeling. – But the one emotion which really mattered, and which enables us to bear all our sufferings with a smile – unconditional love, the love with which we love the other person as he is and love him, moreover, for *the man he is*, – this love was something you could never feel, for you have never understood me, even in the past when you always wanted me to be other than the man I in fact am. Ever since we were reunited, following that first disruption to our marriage,[2] your only guiding principle has been your sense of duty towards me, – duty which bade you suffer with me all the hardships we bore in Paris, and even in the last but one letter you sent me, you wrote simply of *duty* with reference to that period, – not of love. If you had felt any genuine love in your heart at that time, you would not now boast of having endured those sufferings; no, rather should your firm belief in me and in what I am have encouraged you to see in those sufferings a necessary evil of the kind people willingly accept for the sake of some higher goal, whereby they think only of that higher goal, are happy in their consciousness of that higher goal, and in that way forget the baser sufferings which they

1 In Bordeaux.
2 In the summer of 1837, when Minna had run off with a merchant called Dietrich.

have to endure as a result. But you – being the woman you are – have subsequently found no compensation, – all you can ever think of is your suffering!

Ever since I first took up my appointment in Dresden, your growing dissatisfaction with me has made itself increasingly felt each time that I – ignoring my personal advantages – refused, in the interests of my art and my independence as man and artist, to submit any longer to the wretched conditions imposed by the management of that cultural institution, but chose, instead, to rebel against them. Anyone who observed me at that decisive period of my life and who attempted to understand me will be bound to admit that everything I did was the inevitable and rightful consequence of my own artistic nature to which I ever remained loyal – in spite of all personal dangers. That I finally rebelled not only as an artist but as a *man* against all those wicked conditions which – given my passionate nature – were bound to inflict greater torment upon me than on anyone else: all this must seem readily explicable – and hence entirely justifiable in the sight of any impartial observer who had followed my progress closely and seen how step by step – not by leaps and bounds – I had reached my present standpoint as man and artist: such an observer would be bound to admit that my actions here were not arbitrary or the result of vanity on my part, for he would have seen how I *suffered* in the process; he would, accordingly, have spoken words of comfort and encouragement, and my wife would have done the same if she had taken the trouble to understand me, for which she would certainly not have required any book-learning, but only *love!* – Each time I returned home, out of humour & irritated by some new vexation, some new insult or some new disaster, what did this wife of mine bestow upon me instead of the comfort and consoling sympathy I sought? Reproaches, new reproaches, nothing but reproaches! Domestically inclined, I nevertheless remained at home, but, finally, it was not to express my thoughts, to communicate my feelings or receive consolation, but to suffer in silence, to be eaten away by cares, and – to be alone! This eternal constraint beneath which I had already lived so long, and which never allowed me to let myself go without incurring the most violent scenes – this constraint, I say, weighed upon me and destroyed my health. What comparison is there between the physical care which you admittedly lavished on me in abundance, and the *intellectual* care needed to nurse a man of my inner excitability? I expect my wife still recalls how she once forced herself to nurse me on my sickbed for a whole week, coldly & unlovingly, because she could not forgive me for a hasty remark I had made before I fell ill?

Enough! The hour of decision struck: I had to flee and leave everything behind. I had only a single wish before leaving Germany for good, and that was to see my wife again! Nothing else mattered, I would have allowed myself to be taken prisoner, – I refused to leave without this one consolation. But when my wife finally made up her mind to yield to my entreaties, it was not to offer me consolation or to receive consolation from my embrace, – but simply to enable an obstinate individual to go on his way at last – albeit to save his own life. I can never forget the night[1] when I was awoken in my place of refuge in order to receive my wife: she stood before me cold and reproachful & spoke the words: "well, I've come, just as you demanded: I expect you're content now! Continue your journey, I shall be setting off back home this very night!" – I finally succeeded in persuading you to stay with me in Jena for a sincere and warm farewell. This farewell was my consolation from afar. I had but a single thought: a prompt and immediate reunion. I begged this of you in my letters in fiery and emotional terms. It was then that I received from you that unfortunate letter, while I was staying in the country near Paris; its loveless, heartless contents turned my blood to ice. In it you declared that you would not come back to me until such time as I could support you in foreign parts by means of *a regular income*: you also said quite clearly that you no longer felt any love for me. – All that has happened since then will still be fresh in your memory. You wrote to me again and announced your decision to join me in Zurich: I was permitted to hope once more! Yes, I cherished the hope that I might still be able to win you over to my own point of view, to convince you of the validity of my ideas, and finally to make you more familiar with my outlook. I was at constant pains to spare you from material cares. You came, – how happy I was! And yet – wretch that I am! you had not come to share both joy & sorrow with me as I was, – but you had come to visit the Wagner whom you assumed was *shortly to compose an opera for Paris!* In Dresden you were too ashamed to say that you were coming to join me in Switzerland, – and so you pretended you were going to Paris and that your husband – as you yourself probably believed – already had a firm commission in his pocket. Oh, the monstrous delusion under which we both laboured could only become clearer as the days passed! All my views & ideas remained an abomination to you – you detested my writings, in spite of the fact that I tried to make clear to you that they were now more necessary to me than all my useless attempts to write operas. You leapt to the defence of every one who did *not* share my views, – and you condemned all those who *did*, – I was not even allowed to speak out in their favour. Your only regret was our earlier life together, – whereas all that you looked for in the future was to be reconciled with that way of life, or else – a success in Paris. My entire being you saw as an object of loathing and contempt: every moment, ah! almost every movement I made seemed calculated to cause you offence. – In a word, it was only now that I first felt so *boundlessly alone* in your company, because I now saw that it was impossible to win you over. If I took up my plans for Paris again with greater seriousness than had formerly been the

1 On 21 May 1849 at Magdala near Weimar.

case, it was simply to escape from you, and to find peace and quiet elsewhere. The inner constraints which I had felt in doing so, the loathsome struggle against my real convictions, the impossibility of explaining my actions to those in my immediate vicinity or of finding consolation, help and advice there, – all these factors produced in me a state of mind which could only aggravate my physical indisposition through an additional mental disorder. I continued to wrestle with the question as to whether I should set off for Paris in *this* frame of mind: weak & frail as I was, I approached you that final Sunday[1] & asked: "Minna, should I not at least wait for a letter from Belloni!" But you had already grown tired of the long delay – for all you ever talked about was *Paris* – ; you were also waiting to scrub down the parlour and have the whole apartment cleaned; – in a word – *you did not understand your wretch of a husband on this occasion either*, but replied to my question in a tone of vexation, so that, tired & ill, I left the house, regardless of the weather, booked my ticket there & then, & was now resolved at least to act, since I knew the life I would lead if I chose to remain. –

It was here in Paris – prompted by the sight of the most contemptible trafficking in art – that, suffering torments of every description, I seized upon the firm resolve once & for all of renouncing what it was impossible for me to do, & of turning my back irrevocably on this whole miserable business. I had only *one* care – not for myself, but for you, for the sake of the lives we had led together. Look! A bond of friendship[2] of the rarest & most ennobling kind had been forged, – my cares had suddenly been lifted: you yourself had been informed of this. I wrote to you from Bordeaux to tell you that I know only *one* happiness, to be able to live peacefully with you in Zurich for the sake of our mutual health, and in that way create my operas to my heart's content.

Your letter has now destroyed all that! You now stand implacably before me, – you look for honour where I must needs see what almost amounts to shame, and are humiliated by all that I regard as most welcome. As I say: it was *not to me* that you came to Zurich, but to the composer of a new opera commissioned for Paris. Yes, now I understand everything! You refer me to an earlier letter – I know the one, it is the letter you wrote last year! You haven't changed! – The fact that you do not love me emerges clearly and unambiguously from every line you wrote, for you ridicule everything I hold most dear, even my use of the word "du"[3] with which – in accordance with my innermost feelings – I choose to address those whom I do not wish to alienate. – In what then can *my* love consist? Only in the wish to requite you for your youth, which you have wasted with me, and for the hardships you

1 On 27 January 1850, two days before Wagner's departure for Paris.
2 With Julie Ritter and Jessie Laussot.
3 See note 1 above, p. 191.

have undergone with me, and to make you *happy*. Can I still hope to achieve this by *living together* with you? – Impossible!

If I can only be unhappy living with you, I must ask you whether our living together makes *you* happy? No! certainly not! and you may perhaps be much more unhappy than I am, for, in spite of all my suffering and self-wasting, I have a great transcending faith in myself, faith in the truth and splendour of the cause for which I suffer & struggle. You, most wretched of women, do not share that faith. I am a total stranger to you, you see only my warts and excrescences, you see only what you find inexplicable about me, and nowhere find compensation for the injuries you suffer at my hands. You hanker after peace and permanence in relationships – I must break them down in order to satisfy my inner being; you are capable of sacrificing everything to have a "respectable position" in the bourgeois world, a world I despise and refuse to associate with; you hanker exclusively after goods & chattels, hearth & home, – I relinquish all that in order to be a human being. You think of the past only with longing and regret, – I abandon it and think only of the future. All your desires are directed at a reconciliation with what is old, at compromise and conformism, and at re-establishing old ties, – I have broken with all that is old, and fight against it with every ounce of my strength. You cling to people, I to causes; you to individual human beings, I to the whole of humanity. Thus there is only disunity between us, irreconcilable disunity: thus we can only wear each other down, without ever bringing each other happiness: and perhaps you are the unhappier of us two, – you, – for I understand you well enough, whereas you do not understand me! Would it satisfy you if I were to force myself to live with you and lead a life in which I was always concealing myself from you, deceiving you as to my true nature, in a word, seeking to lie to you about myself? Of course not! For you are above all else a woman of *honour*, a woman who wishes to belong entirely to her husband, just as she wishes her husband to belong entirely to her! Do you think that my only reason for writing this letter is to shower you with reproaches? No! It was *I* who wished to defend myself against reproaches. Everything you do and think, and the way in which you act and think, is perfectly correct & consistent in terms of your character as a whole: you are a whole woman, a wife whom I would advise other people fully to respect, a wife who could have brought happiness to thousands, and who even now could bring happiness to a husband who shared her views, – but who is bound to be unhappy with me inasmuch as her views are so totally dissimilar from mine. With me you are unhappy, you are wasting away, you imagine yourself constantly exposed to sufferings whose cause is to be found in a nature totally alien to your own – in mine; and so you are dissatisfied & will always remain so, and my strength would daily ebb away if I had to feign a final remnant of happiness in these circumstances. – Our only salvation is:

To live apart!

Should we be influenced by the consideration that we have been married now for so long and have lived together through such varied adventures? should we therefore watch our declining years slip away, just as we saw our youth fade & wither? We who, at the end of 15 years, understand each other *less* than ever before & who are condemned by our innermost natures to face each other as total strangers, shall we allow this misunderstanding to continue to rankle until our dying day, causing us both increasing torment? I know – alas! alas! – that I cannot bring you happiness, living together with you! More than ever I feel the need to be able to devote myself undisturbed to my ideas and my faith, so that, if need be, I may even defend those ideas with *actions*: I can thrive only in the company of like-minded people. How dreadfully unfeeling would I seem to you – you whom I refuse to condemn for being as you are? I fully recognize your virtues and your other splendid qualities, and for that reason can only hope not to torment and torture you any longer. You often said to me: "when you are like this or like that, or when you behave in a particular way, I hate you!" Dear Minna! what is the point of hating me? If we can retain a memory of those features which we understood & admired in each other, we may continue to love each other even after we are separated. For the sake of what remains of the love which still exists between us, I say to you: *let us remain apart!*

[. . .]

I have only *one* last favour to ask of you! It is the most important request I can put to you in these difficult circumstances. Minna! Minna! dear Minna! fulfil this request of mine, or you will make me boundlessly unhappy! – Whatever you choose to do, wherever you go, do this at least! I beg you, I entreat you most earnestly, as a sign that you still feel the tiniest glimmer of love for me: – *Accept half the yearly allowance which has been allotted me, and use it to support your pitiful existence!* It has been *earned*, believe me, *it has been earned*, you need not feel ashamed to accept it! I could furnish you with proof of the fact that at least the half which falls to your share has been earned in return for an obligation which I have assumed. I know your great pride, your man's self-sufficiency! Oh, do not use it to scourge me! Overcome your inclinations, just this once! If not, you will drive me insane, and certainly hasten my death if you refuse me this final request, if you abandon me to the terrible notion that the most wretched of women, who has sacrificed her youth and everything else to me – in vain! – might suffer starvation in years to come, or go into service with strangers! I entreat you in the name of all you hold dear, grant me this request! Allow me as a provisional arrangement to transfer to your poor good mother in Dresden the sum of 100 thalers each quarter: it shall start with the first of July! On the death of your parents, I shall continue to have this sum transferred to you, directly, or in whatever way you desire! With the other half I shall retire to a place of the greatest seclusion, where I shall get by all the more easily in that I shall easily be able to earn a little extra from time to time. – I shall take it for granted, my dear Minna, that you will not deny me this final, most solemn request! I acknowledge your acceptance as the final token of our love which you have to send me. – – What you need to keep you going until the first of July will be provided for you by Baumgartner to whom I intend writing in this matter! The grand piano is yours! – In addition, 10 – well-earned – louis d'or will be sent to you from Wigand in Leipzig. –

Following this final request, I have a final piece of advice, although you may not be inclined to accept advice from me. – If you wish to avoid notice, conceal what has happened between us from our more superficial acquaintances in Zurich: tell them, when you leave, that your departure from Zurich is the result of a message you have received from me according to which I am remaining in Paris and that I have sent for you to join me there. In that way you will best avoid notice. – If you go to Dresden, all you need do is stick to your old story in conversation with your acquaintances there: since I am no longer of any fixed abode and do not intend writing an opera for Paris, you can say that you have not changed your mind but that for the moment – of your own choice – you intend to enjoy the society of your various friends there, which you have indeed been hankering after – separated from me.

And if you were to suggest a *divorce?* Why that? Why should we be divorced? We cannot *live* together any more, but we can always continue to belong to each other in the eyes of the world. In the eyes of the world you will always be my wife, as long as you wish, – only when you no longer wish it, when a complete divorce could be of use to you, – if you were perhaps to find a husband who was more capable than I of making you happy – only then would our divorce make sense, only then would I find it necessary to accept this final dreadful and painful step. –

Oh Minna! Minna! Separated from you, I am now separated from an entire world! From a world in which I suffered, and where I received little respect or appreciation for my anguish, yet a world which had grown familiar to me, & which I had come to love & cherish. Yes, I can feel it! The man who wishes wholly to follow his inner calling must be endowed with iron courage, for he has terrible sacrifices to make: whether I have such courage I do not yet know, – all I do know is that I could delay no longer in destroying our relationship, openly & honestly, a relationship in which we two companions in adversity had long since ceased to belong to each other, & in which we could bind ourselves to each other only by artificial means, to our mutual and most consuming torment. I pray that my courage will not fail me! But I pray that you, too, may find the courage – without growing angry with me, without hating me – to start a new life in which happiness may yet smile upon you, especially if you have the courage! Fare you well! Fare you well! My wife! My old, dear companion in adversity! Oh, if only I could have shared with you the joys I derive from *my great faith*, how happy you would have been with me in spite of all our hardships! It was not granted to me to requite you in that way! I pray that I may now succeed – through our separation – in reconciling you once more with your life, and in bringing you peace & contentment! Fare you well! Fare you well! I have wept a thousand bitter tears during the last 2 weeks because of this most grievous separation! But it must be so! Every delay would betray a fatal weakness! Fatal for you & me! – Fare you well! Fare you well! Minna! My good Minna, fare you well. Think only of the happiest hours we have spent together, & you will also be happy in your memory of me, just as, when parted from you, I shall remember you only with melancholy & with love! Fare you well! Fare you well! Let me kiss you passionately this one last time.

Your
Richard W.

SB III, 275–88.

107. FRANZ LISZT, WEIMAR   Paris, 21 April 1850

My dear Liszt,

I expect you have already heard how things turned out for me this time in Paris: the performance of my Overture[1] came to nothing; here, too, your efforts on my behalf have been in vain, you poor man!

Decisive events have recently taken place in my life: the last fetters have fallen away which bound me to a world in which I would very shortly have perished – not intellectually – but physically. Labouring under eternal constraints – imposed upon me by those who were closest to me – I have lost my health, my nerves are shattered. For the present I shall devote myself almost solely to my recovery: my livelihood is provided for; you shall hear from me from time to time. –

My dear friend, I have just been looking through the score of my Lohengrin – normally I never look at what I have written. An immense desire has flared up within me to see this work performed. I urge this plea upon you: perform my Lohengrin![2] *You are the only man* to whom I would address this plea: to no one but you do I entrust the first performance of this opera: but to you I commend it in total confidence and peace of mind. Perform it wherever you like: I do not care if it is only in Weimar: I am certain that you will obtain all possible and all necessary means, and that you will be denied nothing. Perform Lohengrin and let it be *your* work to give it birth. – [. . .]

SB III, 291.

1 The *Tannhäuser* Overture; see letter [99], p. 183, note 1.
2 The opera received its first performance under Liszt at Weimar on 28 August 1850.

108. JULIE RITTER, DRESDEN   Geneva, 11 May [1850]

My dear, beloved Frau Ritter,
    You will already have received a letter from Karl[1] a day earlier than these
lines from me. Scarcely had I found Karl when I had to leave him again for
a short time: I am summoning up the last remaining ounce of strength in my
ailing body in order to travel with all speed to Bordeaux, – to see not Jessie
but Eugène. Regard me as a dying man, for imminent death – or a new life
awaits me: my strength is at an end, only the miracle of love can restore me
to life.
    [. . .]

SB III,300.

109. FRANZISKA WAGNER, SCHWERIN   [Villeneuve,] 4 June 1850

[. . .] I have no better advice to offer you than this, since I have discovered
in my own case that I was truly unhappy only as long as I was not a *whole*
person, but sought the impossible, and strove to reconcile fire and water,
good and evil. – Now – however much I suffer and however violent the pains
I bear – I yet do not suffer any longer; I face death at every moment, and in
that way regain my love of life, for I can be contented and proud – because
I despise a life which has no true content. –
    [. . .]

SB III,310.

110. JULIE RITTER, DRESDEN   Thun, 26/27 June 1850

My dear, beloved Frau Ritter,
    Five days ago Karl received a letter from Bordeaux in which Jessie indicated
in the briefest of terms that she intended – as she herself expressed it – "to
break with the immediate past and throw into the fire, unread, any letters
written in my hand; he was to burn these lines of hers at once, and inform
me only briefly of the gist of their content." –
    If, in response to such summarily brief proceedings against me, I had been
permitted to express my feelings towards her with similar conciseness, I
should have done so somewhat as follows: – that I gather from this, at least,

1 Karl Ritter.

that I was not able to instil in Jessie *love* as I understand it, but that I am distressed to find that I could not even inspire in this woman the most necessary *respect* for me.

In writing to you now, however, I am placing in your hands the testament of a love of which I shall never be ashamed and which, although physically dead, may perhaps be a source of joyful memory and consoling recollection until my dying day. You must therefore understand me aright, my dear Frau Ritter, when I report with somewhat *less* stoic brevity the course of the catastrophe of which I stand accused with such childish conclusiveness. At least you understood me when, in the course of your sojourn on Lake Geneva, I explained to you my feelings on receipt of that letter which decided me to travel at once to Bordeaux. Even then I thought I could see from the turn which events had taken that Jessie had taken upon herself more than she had the strength to manage, and that she was not equal to her resolve. Never for a moment did it escape me that her decision could be realized only by the boldest revolutionary force, – that this decision and her feelings could only be justified to the extent that they appeared to be of such an insuperably strong nature that all other conceivable considerations must by contrast seem weak and unavailing. – In accordance with my general views on human nature, I am always disposed to welcome such decisions and feelings with the greatest joy because, given the circumstances which determine our lives at present, I see in them only an expression of true, unperverted human nature. The woman who *rebels out of love*, though she were destroyed in the process, is *mine*, and inasmuch as this love was directed at me personally, it could have brought me only happiness, though I *too* were destroyed by it. Thus and thus alone – following the declaration of her love – did I regard my relationship with Jessie: and to other prospect save this alone could have enabled me to ignore all other considerations, however keenly they may have affected me.

But only as a *rebel* could Jessie have carried out her decision, not through treaties and agreements with those who could never, ever treat with her or enter into any agreement with her. (Can a prince decree a republic?) – And so the news that Jessie was incapable of facing up to the force of circumstances, – that she suddenly found it better to treat with others, and to allow them to do as they pleased with her and with her decisions, – that was bound to evoke in me more than a mere doubt in Jessie's strength and in the infallibility of her awareness of love. Our relationship had suddenly become something quite different. Whereas I could previously have trusted not only in my ability to defend Jessie's decision before the whole world *once that decision had been carried out*, but, more especially, in my capacity to propitiate those hearts most bitterly offended by it, – I now knew that I was entirely lacking the skill which it would require, in the course of our negotiations, to win a mistress whom I should not have had to woo from anyone, but whose actual conquest I should simply have had to defend. I was now forced to realize that only personal intervention would protect my honour against the most brutal attacks, and that I should have to act in this matter with total candour, openly confessing my love and the inexpressibly high value I placed upon its fulfilment, – yet, for her own part, Jessie could only ever be left to rely upon her own strength alone, since she was held in chains from which she, and she alone, had to prove herself capable of breaking free. In the light of my recent experiences I had almost every reason to doubt whether I could, indeed, impute to her the necessary strength. However, I did what it was incumbent upon me to do, and confess that I acted in utter indifference to the risk I was running of being shot through the head by her injured husband. –

You will recall our conversations in Villeneuve, when I expressed myself in complete agreement with your view that there was little or no outside help that could be offered to Jessie at present, – that she alone was in a position to help herself, and that the only way she could do so was by dint of her unswerving persistence and power to frustrate all the intrigues to which, quite understandably, she would now be exposed by those around her in their desire to undermine her feelings towards me. – Well, the only power which could have helped her – the power of her love – she has abandoned and betrayed! She is lost to herself, for – *she is* **weak!!**

The woman who wished to bring me redemption has proved herself a *child*! – Forgive me – but I can regard her only as worthy of pity! – What stupid frailty in the consciousness that she had to treat with the enemies of her love, and give these enemies of hers her promise that she would deny her lover all means of communication! Thus to abandon herself totally to the power of people who would clearly use that power for no other purpose than that of systematically stamping out the love she felt in her heart, – such a move would certainly have shown great boldness and strength on Jessie's part, if only her faith had been unshakeable, and if, under cover of her promise, she had worked the more openly and candidly to gain her freedom as quickly as possible. But since, at the same time, she wrote that this relationship might last a year or more, I must sadly admit that this very undertaking on her part was bound to seem the very essence of her frailty, embodying a weakness which was already completely felt as such, but which still sought to disguise itself beneath the semblance of strength. Oh, how strong would Jessie's faith in me have had to be, if it had had to sustain her love in the face of attacks from both her own frailty and the malice of others! –

I do not know what lies she has been told concerning me, or whether she herself might suddenly have been so foolish – forgive the expression! – as to misinterpret certain passages in my letter to Mme Tailor? I finally wrote to this lady to tell her that, great as was my love for Jessie and immeasurably valuable as its fulfilment would have been in my life, I was none the less capable, in the pride of my soul, of renouncing all hope of it the moment I discovered that Jessie's love for me did not have the irresistible power necessary to decide her – her mother – in her favour: for I would not woo her, but would only receive her from her own hand as an unexpected stroke of supreme good fortune. – Could Jessie's understanding of love suddenly have become so befuddled as to place such a gross misinterpretation on the sentiments I had expressed in that letter? But this was the inexpressible charm of Jessie's love that she understood everything about me so quickly, so clearly and surely – that I could not detect in her even a trace of old-fashioned, narrow-minded prejudice, or – if I did – the slightest breath from my lips was all that it required to disperse it! – Or might they – and it is this surmise which gives me the strength to act! – might they have approached my poor wife[1] in an attempt to discover whether we had been legally separated by priests and lawyers? Might they have received from her the very information they desired, namely that I had not yet revealed to her that I was wooing a woman of means, and was therefore asking her to stand down? Might they have gone to Jessie, armed with this evidence, and suddenly confronted her with the idea that my intentions towards her were not "respectable and decent"? – But had it not been Jessie's total frankness in such repugnant matters as bourgeois honour that had pleased me so much about her? Who understood better than she that I love my unhappy wife, that I was bound to her by a thousand chains of old and mutual suffering, and that only with a bleeding heart could I tear myself away from the unhappy woman in order to release her from a fate whose implications she could not grasp but which could cause her only pain and torment, without her ever knowing or under- standing why? Who felt more keenly than Jessie how utterly miserable I was following our separation, since the most candid proof which I gave her of my misery inspired in her that marvellous resolve to break with the world in order to be with me, to requite me for everything and to cure all the wounds I have suffered in my life, including these most recent wounds of mine? Who realized more clearly than Jessie that I no doubt *had* to be separated from that poor woman, but that I could never injure her, never offend or mistreat her? After all, she was prepared to accompany me to the remotest corners of the world, in order to spare the unhappy woman the sight of our love, nay, even the knowledge that we were happy in our love! – How delighted I was to discover in her letters not a single trace of that barbarous and unworthy bourgeois hypocrisy! She was nothing but *love*: we dedicated ourselves to the *God of love*, and scorned all the idols of this miserable world so vehemently that we did not even deign to mention them. Could one of these *idols* have taken possession of Jessie so suddenly that she was forced to sacrifice her *God* to it with such insanely swift and willing eagerness? Could it be possible

1 A surviving letter from Ann Taylor to Minna indicates that the two women were indeed in communication at this period (Sammlung Burrell 412–13; English trans. 307–8).

that this wretched bourgeois consideration had suddenly seized control of her heart? – If she had been forced by present circumstances and by her mother's disciplinary measures to agree that I should be asked to explain myself on this point, – very well then! they should have addressed this demand to me and I would have understood that – painful though it would inevitably have been to submit to such heartless and repugnant pedantries – it was nevertheless now necessary for me to pacify a mother and set her mind at rest. – However, my Jessie simply did not think of this entirely natural expedient: instead, she suddenly took it into her head to see in the information which had presumably come from my wife an ostensible reason for breaking off her relationship with me! In a trice she felt I had offended her, – she suddenly saw that the happiness of love lay in bourgeois respectability, and was so inspired by that thought that she did not even consider it necessary to demand an explanation from me, rather was she suddenly so outraged by what she assumed to be my attitude in this matter that she thought it appropriate to deny me even a modicum of respect, but to send word by my young friend that "she would henceforth burn all my letters unread" etc. How was this possible? What force could so suddenly have dethroned the most glorious love and driven it out into the world like some old cur? – Oh, everything – even the basest action – is possible for the heart which has abandoned to *cowardice* the key to its *innermost chamber*! – Alas! alas for the *weak and the cowardly!!* – –

And yet! How pitiable is the unhappy girl! My heart is broken in twain with grief at how far she has fallen! – Mother! my dear, beloved Frau Ritter! If only you could have witnessed this triumph of love as it burst forth from every sinew of this rich and blessed woman, when she revealed to me that she was mine – not through any spoken confession – but entirely through her own self, through the involuntary, radiant and naked manifestation of love! If only you could have seen this joy, this rapturous delight which animated every fibre of her being, from the movement of her fingertips to the most subtle workings of her mind, when this youthful woman cast her lustrous radiance on me, – sorely tried as I was, unhappy with life and devoid in truth of all those gifts considered necessary to work such wonders as flourished here for my benefit, allowing me to taste the heady intoxication of love! Do not ask me to describe what she was to me, and what she still is in the rapturous memory which I yet have of her! But feel the beauty and the fullness of the love which drove this highly gifted and glorious young woman to take such bold and exultantly audacious decisions, – and then share with me the deep, deep despair provoked within me by the happy success of a course of treatment prescribed by her prudent mother and a solicitous husband in order to cure her heart of its "indecent" passion for me!

Oh, you must believe as I do that love dwells within her heart, and that I did not dream it: it lives, it lives, – and loving nature puts forth her buds of happiness in this most wretched of worlds, with all the unimpaired fullness of her truest nature! But her mortal foe continues to wield a terrible power: its agents are education, marriage, decorum, and business, – and its mask is the deceptive likeness of that love; ruthlessly and murderously it wages war against love's simple unaffectedness, – but always with a smile of loving concern! – Well! Here it can boast of success! – They can be proud of their victory, these clever physicians: it is a beautiful corpse which they have captured as their booty! They are going now to bury it amid pomp and solemn circumstance, – let us, my dear friends, scatter sweetly smelling flowers upon her grave! –

No! we shall not insult her, the dead woman – cut down by the hand of those murderers, – for she was – love itself! Never, dear mother, shall I be ashamed of this love: though it has faded and though I am firmly convinced that none can revive it, her kiss was yet the greatest pleasure I have known in my life! Neither honour, glory nor fame could ever outweigh that pleasure! – Farewell, you blessed beauty! You were dearer to me than all else, and I shall never forget you! Farewell! – –

[. . .]

In Montmorency,[1] at precisely the same time as Jessie was openly revealing her feelings for me, I perceived from a sign that I was being sought out in Paris by certain friends from Zurich[2] who – as I supposed – had been apprised of my affairs. It was impossible – I might almost say physically impossible – to engage in a detailed discussion of the reasons for my recent move with any of my friends – however well-meaning they may have been. Whereas I was already resolved upon a policy of self-preservation, should the need arise, and to avoid all such attempts at reconciliation, the result of Jessie's communication and my consequent excitability was to render me even more incapable of facing embarrassing explanations. I left Montmorency and Paris suddenly, without taking leave of a single one of my friends there. In Geneva, where I turned my steps, I was informed by a friend from Paris[3] – who had written to me poste restante in half a dozen towns in the hope that one of his letters would eventually reach me – that my poor wife had herself arrived in Paris in order to seek me out and explain herself to me. Although I was bound to suppose that my wife had undertaken this step only at the insistence of my friends in Zurich, and although I believed it safe to assume that she was entirely in error if she thought that, by attempting to clarify the contents of her latest letters, she could heal dissensions which were infinitely older

1 Wagner retired to Montmorency in mid-April for "the most decisive week of my life" (letter [105], p. 191). He remained there until the night of 25 April when he set off for Geneva in order to avoid meeting Minna, who had arrived in the French capital the previous day.
2 Wilhelm Baumgartner and Jakob Sulzer.
3 Ernst Benedikt Kietz. It is clear, however, from the Annals (BB 118; English trans. 99) that Wagner knew of Minna's presence in Paris *before* he left Montmorency.

and more deeply rooted, – yet my simple discovery of the very fact that she had sought me out and wished to be reconciled with me was bound to produce a deep and touching impression upon me. Although, as I say, I was bound to recognize that she was mistaken about the two of us, even this very mistake of hers touched me, since it was the unequivocal expression of a love which was stronger than her mistaken understanding of my own nature. For my wife is by no means weak by nature, and I had far rather expected her to turn her back on me, proudly and coldly, on receiving my parting letter, – indeed, I was afraid of her pride inasmuch as it led me to worry that she would refuse any financial help which I offered her, – a refusal which, as I wrote to tell her,[1] would have made me unspeakably unhappy. In these circumstances, the news I now received affected me most profoundly, and certain details which I was told about her filled me with the deepest and most poignant sympathy for a woman who *in any case* was unhappy. It was now impossible for me to strike the final and hardest blow of all while her mind was in torment: on the contrary, I now felt a deep sense of duty to offer her comfort in the immediate future, to show myself a humane physician, and hence I saw myself having recourse to whatever remedies might seem suitable for my immediate purpose. I had to help her survive the immediate weeks ahead, give her some glimmer of consolation, and in that way at least accustom her to the idea of our separation, but at the same time make this separation as bearable as possible in the short term, and thus take advantage of the great healing power of time before informing her, after a certain period had elapsed, of what in the mean time would have become inevitable. And so I wrote to my wife[2] and told her of my decision – which had only then been firmly taken – to go to Greece and the Orient. I knew the beneficial effect this news would have on her; it would give her a kind of satisfaction, especially in the sight of my friends in Zurich, who might now believe that I wished to shake myself free not only from my wife but from present conditions as a whole. Although I insisted expressly upon the contents of my previous letter and once more made it clear to my wife that I regarded our separation as necessary, I did not omit to underline my most sympathetic concern for her well-being: I promised that in the future I would not leave her uninformed as to my activities, and I expressed the wish that she might remain in Zurich, draw a small garden plot, look after our dog and bird and, as far as possible, live a life of hope: – "who knows – I concluded – if God grants us long life, we may one day see each other again."

[. . .]

I pray that I may soon be able to work again! How welcome that would be to me, for I know what pleasure my work gives you. I pray that my imagination

1 Letter of 16 April 1850, see [106] above.
2 Letter of 4 May 1850, SB III,295–8.

may shortly come to my aid once more, now that reality and imagination have again become blurred in my mind! – I shall not complete my Wiland: the faults of this poem are too clear to be hidden from me now by my tired and subjective feelings. Wiland is dead: he will not fly! – I think what I shall do next is compose my thoughts for an essay on genius – the communal and the solitary.[1] Then, when I have regained my strength, I shall make a start on Achilles![2] –

Do what you can to visit us soon, otherwise all will be far from well. –

Fare you well, my dear and much loved Frau Ritter! Remain loyal and well-disposed towards me! –

Remember me kindly to my darling Emilie, and give my love to all your family.

Yours,
Richard Wagner.

SB III,315–31.

111. Minna Wagner, Zurich   [Thun, end of June 1850]

My poor, dear wife,

Not until yesterday evening did Karl[3] arrive here, bringing your letter with him. Now that I have read it, I scarcely need assure you that I shall return home *in any case*, and certainly during the next few days: I can add nothing to this assurance except to say that already in early May, when news reached me in Geneva of your journey to Paris and of your attempts to seek me out,[4] I would not have concealed myself from you but would have given you an opportunity to speak to me if *at that precise moment* – and *not until that precise moment* – I had not had to take account of another person, so that it was quite impossible for me to act as openly during that period as would otherwise have been desirable, or to follow the dictates of a heart which was deeply concerned for your own well-being. The moment that various indications had driven me to suppose that you had received a *thoroughly distorted* account of all that had happened during recent weeks, the only thing that mattered to me was to explain to you the *true* course of events, less for the sake of my own self-justification than to spare you the deep offence and mortification to which

---

1 *Das Genie der Gemeinschaft* (Communal Genius), first mooted in a letter to Uhlig of 27 December 1849 (SB III,198), published in fragmentary form in SS XII,266–71; PW VIII, 355–61.

2 *Achilleus* (WWV 81), variously described by Wagner as an opera and as a "purely dramatic poem" (Königsbriefe I, 183), remained no more than an idea.

3 Karl Ritter.

4 See letter [110], p. 205, note 3.

you must have been subjected as a result of that monstrously inaccurate report. In order to be informed as to its precise details, I sent Karl to Zurich. From your letter I now see that my fears were well grounded, and, even worse, that you have given credence to the most stupid distortions of the truth on the part of a mother who was concerned only for questions of superficial decorum, and of a vindictive but cowardly husband, and that you thus condemned me as wholly guilty, and *yet* had no more ardent wish than that I should return to you, since – separated from me – you felt the only prospect ahead of you was death. If I am now clear in my own mind that you have been labouring under every kind of the most grievous error concerning not only this one specific point but concerning me in general, I see at the same time that your love for me is stronger and more powerful than all your error, – and this alone is sufficient to leave me in no doubt as to what I must now do. I have *never* said that I no longer loved you, – and now I know that all that remains is for me to return to you. –

[...]

SB III,332–3.

112. FRANZ LISZT, WEIMAR   Thun, 2 July 1850

[...] Since I discover that you intend performing Lohengrin as early as 28 August, I shall make haste not to delay any longer sending you the enclosed, and shall reserve the right to return to any outstanding points in a later letter.[1]

My first consideration in drawing up the enclosed notes was to express my thoughts on the staging and scenery. The sketches which I have drawn for this purpose will amuse you greatly:[2] I number them among the most successful creations of my genius; where my technique has let me down, you will be able to deduce my intentions from the accompanying literary explanation. The foliage caused me insuperable difficulties, and if every artist sweats as much blood as I did in trying to achieve a sense of perspective, no one could ever call painting an easy profession. – I should add that in my remarks I have persistently referred to the full score, where the stage action has been indicated in far greater detail and with greater precision than in the libretto, so that it appears there in accord with the music. The producer must therefore work in the closest possible consultation with the score – perhaps using a piano reduction of the same.

I have similarly drawn up for you a few remarks concerning the orchestra. First and foremost, however, I have a great favour to ask of you:

1 See letter [113], pp. 209–11.
2 Reproduced in SS XVI,63–73.

Give the opera as it stands, without cuts!
There is only one cut which I myself would suggest, and indeed I would insist that the passage indicated be omitted, namely the second half of Lohengrin's narration in the great closing scene of the third act. After Lohengrin's words:
"his knight am I and Lohengrin my – " ∧ name
a whole 56 bars should be cut:
"where all of you with God did see me – " ∧ "land"
in other words: – "name" instead of: "land". –
I have often gone through the whole thing on my own, and become convinced that this second section of the narration is bound to produce something of an anticlimax. This passage should therefore also be removed at once from the libretti.
[. . .]

SB III,344–5.

113. FRANZ LISZT, WEIMAR   [Zurich, 20 July 1850]

My dear Liszt,
I have to say it – *you are a true friend!*
Let me say no more than this! for, whereas I have always recognized friendship between men as the noblest and most splendid of all human relationships, only now have I found that ideal so completely realized, for you have allowed me not only to imagine what a friend is, but to feel and grasp it, too. –
I shall not thank you, – for you alone can thank yourself adequately by dint of the pleasure you derive from being what you are. It is ennobling to have a friend, – but far more ennobling – to be a friend. –
The fact that I have found you enables me not only to bear with fortitude my banishment from Germany but to regard my exile almost as a stroke of good fortune, since *I* could not possibly have advanced my own cause in Germany as effectively as *you* have done. But – it could only have been *you*! – Yet I cannot *write* in praise of you: only when we meet shall I be able to *tell* you to your face how I feel. As much as your dealings with me have been marked by thoughtfulness and consideration, so much, you may rest assured, am I able to grasp and value the nature of your concern for me. I know that you had no choice but to act as you have done, and I am especially grateful to you for the *way* in which you have shown your concern for me. – There is only one thing that worries me in all this, namely that you neglect *yourself* in helping me, since I cannot replace that part of you which is lost in the process. Think well on this!

– Your letter left a deep impression on me in a variety of ways. I hold certain convictions which you yourself will perhaps never share but which you will not deem it necessary to oppose when you discover that in no way do they impede me in my artistic activities. I have felt the pulse of modern art and know that it will die! This knowledge, however, fills me not with despondency but with joy, for I know at the same time that it is not *art in general* which will perish but only *our own* particular type of art – which stands remote from real life – , whereas true – imperishable – constantly renewed art is still to be born. The monumental character of our art will disappear, we shall abandon our habit of clinging firmly to the past, our egotistical concern for permanence and immortality at any price: we shall let the past remain the past, the future – the future, and we shall live only in the present, in the here and now and create works for the present age alone. Remember how fortunate I once considered you were in the practice of your own particular art, precisely because you were a performing artist, a real, actual artist whose every performance was clearly an act of giving: the fact that you could do so only upon a musical instrument was not your fault but the involuntary constraint of our age which compels the individual to depend entirely upon his own resources and renders impossible that sense of fellow-ship through which the individual artist, with the greatest possible deployment of his powers, might become part of a communal – immediate and actual – work of art. It was certainly not any wish to flatter you which made me say those things, rather was I – half-consciously – expressing my belief that only the *performer* is the real, true artist. All that we create as poets and composers expresses a *wish* but not an *ability*: only the performance itself reveals that ability or *art*.[1] Believe me, I should be ten times happier if I were a *dramatic performer* instead of a dramatic poet and composer. – Now that I have come to hold this conviction, it can no longer be of interest to me to create works which I know in advance must be denied all life in the present in return for the flattering prospect of future immortality: what cannot be true *today* will remain untrue in the future as well. No longer do I abandon myself to the delusive idea of creating works for a future beyond the present: but if I am to create works for the present age, that age must offer me a less repellent aspect than is now the case. I renounce all fame, and more especially the insane spectre of posthumous fame, because I love humankind far too dearly to condemn them, out of self-love, to the kind of poverty of ideas which alone sustains the fame of dead composers. – As things stand at present, what attracts me to artistic creativity is no longer ambition, but the desire to communicate to my friends, and the wish to give them pleasure: when I know that I have satisfied this desire and this wish of mine, I myself shall be happy

---

1 There is an untranslatable play on words here: the German word for "art" (*Kunst*) is cognate with the verb "to be able" (*können*).

and utterly contented. If you now perform my Lohengrin in your tiny town of Weimar, and if you do so with pleasure and affection, joy and success, – and even if this were only for the two performances of which you write – I shall feel so happy at knowing that my intentions have been so perfectly realized that all my cares concerning this work will be wholly at an end, and I shall be able to devote myself solely to the new task of offering you some other new work in a similar vein. You must be the judge! Can you reproach me for holding these convictions, since they relieve me of all feelings of egotism and all petty ambition? Of course not! – Ah, if only I could communicate to you the inspiriting power of my convictions!

Listen while I tell you the impression your letter has had on me!

Last May I sent the poem of my *Siegfried* to a bookseller for him to publish – as it stands. In a brief introduction I explained that I have no hopes of ever seeing the work completed and performed, and that I am therefore communicating it to my friends simply to show them my *purpose*. In fact, I have no intention of composing my Siegfried in an empty void – for the reasons given above. – Now you offer me the artistic fellowship which might enable Siegfried to see the light of day: – I demand performers for my heroes such as have never yet been seen on our stage; where are they to come from? Well, not out of thin air, but from the soil beneath our feet: I believe that *you* are in the best position to make them grow out of the ground, at least through your enthusiastic support. Irredeemably degenerate as the acting profession now is, the best foundations for all art are still to be found among these foolish actors and singers of ours: their nature, assuming they have not lost heart, is incorruptible: by dint of enthusiasm they can be turned into anything and everything. In a word, once you have produced Lohengrin to your own satisfaction, I shall set about completing Siegfried – but only for *you* and for *Weimar*! – Even as recently as 2 days ago I would not have believed I would reach such a decision. – It is *you* I have to thank for that!

[. . .]

SB III,353–6.

114. THEODOR UHLIG, DRESDEN   Zurich, 27 July 1850

[. . .] I assume that Frau Ritter has informed you as to the latest developments in my domestic circumstances:[1] allow me to draw a veil of silence over the most recent past and report in brief only that I have returned home to find a new wife: although she has remained the same in everything else, I

---

1 i.e. Wagner's return to Minna following his abortive affair with Jessie Laussot.

now know that – whatever might befall me or come to pass – she will remain beside me until her dying day. For my own part, I certainly did not think simply of testing her: but as events have turned out, she has survived an ordeal by fire such as all women must submit to nowadays if they desire consciously to support those of us who acknowledge the future and who strive to meet it. My friends here have proved their worth. – I have grown much older: I now know for certain that I have entered the second half of my life and that all idle hopes are now behind me. –

[. . .]

You see what a great change has taken place within me as a result of this configuration of external events. The moment one knows oneself dependent upon others, one becomes more certain, calmer and freer than if one is left entirely to oneself and has the power to choose – a power which is inhibiting rather than liberating. I, too, was tormented by the choice of what I wished to do next: should I draft a new opera libretto, or write a book or some essays? It all seemed so arbitrary, and all my actions seemed so useless and unnecessary. Once this indecision had enabled me to sort out these ideas in my mind, – the very clarity of that realization was bound to make me appear quite pitiful in my own eyes, and this view of myself was confirmed when I perceived what effect my writings have had. That they would in general receive no further attention was something I had assumed in advance: but that they were for the most part not even understood by the few members of our own party who took the trouble to read them was something I was finally compelled to acknowledge with a deep sigh of regret. Prejudice is so deeply rooted that only life itself can break it down: only a true artist and, indeed, an artistic human being can grasp what is at stake here – no other person can do so with the best will in the world. And who, for ex., shall grasp the natural relationship between plastic art and a direct and purely human art, given the artistic egotism of today's manufacturers of reproductive art? I shall pass over in silence what a sculptor or an historical painter would have to say to all this, but the fact that an otherwise well-disposed writer on aesthetics such as the contributor to the deutsche monatsschrift[1] (for whom it is certainly not simply a question of money) should have sunk to such depths of the most utter mindlessness and been reduced to such artificial and loquacious drivel as he has there succumbed to, well, that is sad. But I also read a review of my latest piece in the Berlin abendpost by the young Bülow:[2] at least he still has the fresh sensitivity of youth, and I believed he would have been able to follow my line of thought with relatively few qualifications: well: at least he was not openly critical – but when the discussion turns to sculpture, lo and

1 A review of Wagner's *The Art-Work of the Future* had appeared in the June edition of the *Deutsche Monatsschrift für Politik, Wissenschaft, Kunst und Leben*.
2 Hans von Bülow's review of *The Art-Work of the Future*, published in the Berlin *Abend-Post* (see Newman, *Life*, II,222).

behold – he suddenly observes that the author has lost his otherwise so laudable clarity and "*appears* to proclaim the decline of sculpture". – At that point I returned home with Karl,[1] read aloud the section on sculpture and painting for his benefit and for mine and – we both found that, however hard we tried to discern some ambiguity in the said passage, the turning point in the whole history of humankind and of art was clearly and explicitly stated to lie with sculpture, a point I intentionally laboured in great detail and underlined with especial emphasis, so that those critics who did not even notice this *importance* but who seemed only to assume that I had stumbled unawares into an area of vagueness and uncertainty out of ignorance and because I insisted upon having my say concerning these other types of art as well could on no account claim to have understood anything at all about the book as a whole, since they interpreted as a marginal aberration on my part the central point of the argument, which I had strenuously emphasized, namely the decline of the egotistically *monumental* aspect of art in contrast to the communally *present* element, which is full of movement. – [. . .]

SB III,360–4.

115. Franz Liszt, Weimar   Zurich, 8 September 1850

Best of friends,

I cannot delay writing to you a moment longer, though I should have preferred to have waited first for a letter from you in order to be able to answer any possible questions you may have had for me.

As far as I am able to judge from the reports which have reached me concerning the character of the performance of my Lohengrin in Weimar, the first thing to strike me most clearly and indubitably was the testimony to your most unprecedented efforts and self-sacrifice on behalf of my work, your touching affection for me, and the confirmation of your genius for rendering the impossible as good as possible. Only subsequently did it really become clear to me what an enormous task you had undertaken and carried through. I really do not know how I can ever repay you!

[. . .]

This much, above all, is clear: the performance proved wearisome as a result of the length of time it lasted. I confess that I was alarmed to discover that the opera played until very nearly 11 o'clock at night. I had played the whole work through to myself, immediately after completing it, and timed it exactly, calculating it on the assumption that the 1st act would not last much

1 Karl Ritter.

more than an hour, the 2nd act 1¼ hours, and the final act once again a little over an hour, so that, taking into account the two intervals, I reckoned the opera would last from 6 o'clock until a quarter to ten at the latest. I would have questioned whether you had correctly followed the suggested tempo markings, if I had not been expressly informed by my musical friends who know the opera that you had consistently followed the markings as they knew them from me, indeed that here and there you had been somewhat quicker rather than slower. I was accordingly forced to assume that the opera had begun to drag whenever you lost direct control as conductor, – namely *in the recitatives*. Indeed, my friends confirm that the singers did not pick up the recitatives as I had performed them for them at the piano. Permit me to explain myself somewhat more fully on this point, and forgive me for acting wrongly in not having done so before now.

As a result of the fatal circumstance that virtually the only operas given in German theatres are ones translated from a foreign language, our dramatic singers have been reduced to a state of the most unspeakable demoralization. The translations of French and Italian operas are for the most part the work of bunglers and almost never of people who might have been in a position to restore the sense of harmony between the words and music which had been the case with the original text, and as *I*, for ex., was at pains to achieve in the most important passages of Gluck's Iphigenia. The result of all this is that, as time passed, singers have grown accustomed to ignoring the connection between words and music; instead, they articulate an indifferent syllable on the accented note of a melody, and, conversely, they sing the most important word on a rhythmically weak beat, as a result of which they have gradually become used to singing the most utter nonsense, to the extent that it is often a matter of total indifference whether they articulate the text clearly or not. It is now highly amusing to find German critics boasting that only the Germans understand dramatic music, whereas experience proves that even an inferior Italian singer in the wretchedest Italian opera declaims the text more healthily and more expressively than the best German singers can do. – It is the recitative that has come off worst in all this: singers have grown accustomed to seeing in a passage of recitative only a certain traditional sequence of scales which they can distort and draw out at pleasure, just as much as they like. Each time a recitative begins in an opera, what that means for the singers is as much as: "Thank God, that's the end of those infernal tempo markings which force us every now and then to adopt a certain sensible style of delivery: now we can relax and hold on to the first note that takes our fancy until the prompter shouts out the next phrase; and since the conductor has nothing more to say to us at this point, we can now get our own back for his pretensions by dictating to *him* when he should stop beating time! etc." Although not all singers are fully conscious of this sovereign attitude of theirs towards the recitative, they generally follow this routine involuntarily and as a result are confirmed in their natural indolence and flaccidity. The composer who now writes for German singers has therefore to pay particular attention to counteracting this indolent levity by means of certain artistic constraints. Nowhere in my score to Lohengrin have I written the word "Recitative" above a vocal passage; the singers ought not to know that it contains any recitatives. On the contrary, I have been at pains to take account of the spoken emphasis of the words and to denote such emphases so unerringly and so precisely that it should be necessary for the singers simply *to sing the notes exactly according to their written value at the given tempo* in order to gain control of the correct spoken inflection. I would therefore entreat the singers most earnestly to begin by singing these parlando sections in my opera exactly in tempo – as written; they should perform them in a consistently lively fashion, with clear pronunciation, and in that way we shall achieve *much*; if they then proceed on this basis with discretionary freedom, showing animation rather than reserve, and if they can then forget what it was they found so awkward about the tempo and produce instead the impression of an impassioned and poetical mode of delivery, – then we shall have achieved *everything*.

Dingelstedt's affectionate and witty article[1] on the performance of Lohengrin made a great impression on me. He admits that he previously knew nothing of my work and believes that it is to this circumstance that he must attribute the sense of confusion which this first performance of Lohengrin aroused in him. He transfers this sense of confusion to the nature of the work itself, speaks of countless contradictory aims which he imputes to me, but nowhere do I see him divining the one aim which was my guiding principle, namely the simple unadorned aim – *of the drama*: he speaks of the impression made on him by flutes, fiddles, kettle-drums and trumpets, but not of the dramatic performers, – in whose stead, as he himself puts it, those very instruments had spoken. From this I gather that in your performance the *purely musical* achievement was by far the more preponderant, that the orchestra was admirable – as I was indeed assured to have been the case by various experts – and that friend Liszt – and all those directly dependent upon him – was the real hero of the performance. But if we think honestly and unegotistically of the essence of music, we must admit that, on the largest scale, it is only a means to an end: but this end, in any reasonable opera, is the *drama*, and it lies, most unequivocally, in the hands of *the performers on stage*. That these performers disappeared before Dingelstedt's gaze to such an extent that what he heard was not them but the instruments of the orchestra saddens me, for I gather from this that in the warmth and expressiveness of their performances they lagged behind the support which was given them by

---

1 Franz Dingelstedt's notice appeared in a supplement to the Augsburg *Allgemeine Zeitung* on 4 September 1850.

the orchestra. I admit that a singer who is supported by an orchestra in the way that is the case here needs to be of the very highest and finest quality, and I also believe that such performers may not be easy to find, not just in Weimar but in Germany as a whole. But what in fact is the most basic and central issue here? Is it the voice alone? – indeed, no! It is *life and warmth* – and, in addition, earnestness of purpose and a powerful strength of will.

[. . .]

SB III, 384–9.

116. ERNST BENEDIKT KIETZ, PARIS   Zurich, 14 September 1850

[. . .] You will recall that in Montmorency I gave you a letter[1] to be forwarded to Liszt: as a direct result of that letter – as I discovered much later – Liszt had the score of the opera[2] sent to him from Dresden, and proceeded to perform the same. The first performance took place on the 28th of August: – I sent Karl Ritter to Weimar in order for him to report back to me all that happened. Karl had heard me play it – the opera, I mean – on the piano, and the performance was not to his liking, chiefly on account of the slovenliness and stiffness of the performers. Apart from that, everything possible is said to have been done, and on the whole it left a most striking impression. But you know me well enough by now to realize that I no longer expect any results either from this or from similar efforts made on behalf of our cause in general or of me in particular. But since I am still alive, and since, with the best will in the world, I can live only in the *here and now*, I must needs do something that accords with my temperament. I am genuinely thinking of setting Siegfried to music,[3] only I cannot reconcile myself with the idea of trusting to luck and of having the work performed by the very first theatre that comes along: on the contrary, I am toying with the boldest of plans, which it will require no less a sum than 10,000 thalers to bring out. According to this plan of mine, I would have a theatre erected here on the spot, made of planks, and have the most suitable singers join me here, and arrange everything necessary for this one special occasion, so that I could be certain of an outstanding performance of the opera. I would then send out invitations far and wide to all who were interested in my works, ensure that the auditorium was decently filled, and give three performances – free, of course –

1 Letter [107], p. 199.
2 *Lohengrin.*
3 The earliest sketches for *Siegfrieds Tod* appear to predate this letter by some weeks; see Robert Bailey, "Wagner's Musical Sketches for *Siegfrieds Tod*" in *Studies in Music History: Essays for Oliver Strunk* (Princeton 1968), 459–94.

one after the other in the space of a week, after which the theatre would then be demolished and the whole affair would be over and done with. Only something of this nature can still appeal to me. I shall receive the sum when Karl Ritter's uncle dies.[1]

[...]

SB III,404–5.

117. THEODOR UHLIG, DRESDEN   Zurich, 22 October 1850

[...] But permit me to say something on the subject of water![2] – I admit right away that you do well to follow your present diet, and that I am indescribably happy to know that it has been so beneficial for your health of body. That we can all be redeemed from the current state of so thoroughly unnatural a condition only by means of this radical element is certain. Lack of healthy food, on the one hand, an excess of lavish enjoyment, on the other, but, above all, our way of life in general, which is entirely contrary to nature, all this has reduced us to a level of degeneracy which we can transcend only by means of a complete renewal of our twisted organism. Superfluity and deprivation, these are the two destructive enemies of present-day humanity. But if you take the trouble to ask yourself the basic question of what we mean by the word "superfluous", you will find – as find you *must* – that everything is superfluous that encloses the walls of a town – and not only what consumes this superfluity, but what produces it, too. All of us who live in towns are condemned to the most joyless suicide. But how do things stand with the population of our villages? Do not all their efforts similarly pass merely from deprivation to superfluity? Here, too, as much as in the towns, excessive work corrupts people to the extent that all they cherish is that selfsame desire for superfluity which makes them think of idle repose as something desirable, being the only contrast to excessive work they can understand. Only universal activity is in itself enjoyable, and a pleasure *per se*: but we are all bound to a specific activity by *the laws of property*, an activity which finds an outlet only in the direction of *one* profession, which absorbs only *one* of our faculties, and which does so to such a violent degree that our total capacity is consumed by it, so that we see in this one daily preoccupation our physical ruin and moral undoing – in other words, our enemy, disgusting, loathsome and wearying work which we finally confuse with activity in general, wishing therefore only to be able to exchange it for absolute and idle repose. In the

1 In the event the inheritance passed to Julie Ritter who supported Wagner with an annual subsidy of 800 thalers between 1851 and 1859.
2 Hydrotherapy, a form of spa treatment which Uhlig recommended to Wagner.

country, such work has the additionally loathsome aspect that, as a result of their *total and exclusive preoccupation* with beasts of the field and with dung, people are themselves turned into beasts of the dunghill! Wherever we turn in the civilized world, we see how degenerate man has become for the reasons given above – but we are justified in despairing of this world only if we consider these *reasons* to be eternally binding. But it is precisely these reasons against which the true spirit of revolution rebels: and what we need to recognize this fact is certainly not a training in metaphysics but the destruction of these misleading teachings in favour of a quite simple natural need. But what, then, is the purport of socialism? Those who preach it no longer understand what it is, because their desire is for organization. Its sole purport is to make superfluity and deprivation impossible. Thus the people do not need to be taught, but simply told they are right! And, indeed, they are telling themselves this with increasing conviction, now that they have seen how trust in their *leaders* has led to their own unhappiness. Do they not need merely to observe the present *political* muddle to know what to think of politics? If ever there was a period in history conducive to remedying an error with the speed of lightning, it is the period of today's reactionism! Do you believe that a human being will still fight *for politics?* Indeed you do, for you have said that you can imagine victory for the revolution only through a new and compulsory association of constitutional and democratic thinkers. I tell you – no one will lift a finger in support of democracy, since every political revolution has become utterly impossible. In politics there is no one who is still blind to the facts: everyone *knows* how disreputable our political conditions are: only the fact that behind them lies the social question gives people enough feeble courage to hold out. We no longer have a movement, apart from the one that is decidedly socialist, but socialist in a quite different sense from the one that our socialists dream of: everything else will remain weak and power-less till then. – You ask me now: "Where are these people hiding who will bring about this necessary overthrow? I see nothing but the most pitiful of people around me, philistines and cowards, and even in the lower reaches I see only obtuseness and a pack-horse mentality!" My dearest Uhlig, recall that day during the Dresden uprising when you met me on the Zwinger promenade and asked me in trepidation and with some concern whether I was not afraid that, at best, the result would be mob-rule? – You had been alarmed by the sight of those same people you now appear to seek in vain! The fact that these people were still tied to the apron-strings of politics, that they bowed their heads in respectful silence before higher political aims which they saw embodied in their leaders, that they were not yet the people they really are nor their actions those that they will one day be, that they showed obedience where they should have acted – it was this alone that subjugated them and made them appear to you as they did – men who were drunk on politics, and who blustered their way through the streets of the town – which they might have set fire to, with all the judicial splendour of our fair city of Dresden, had it only been granted them to act in accord with the fury they felt in their hearts. I have seen these people again in Paris and Lyons, and now know the future course of the world. – Until now we have encountered expressions of enslaved human nature only in *crimes* that disgust and appal us! – Whenever murderers and thieves now set fire to a house, the deed rightly strikes us as base and repugnant: – but how shall it seem to us if the monster that is Paris is burned to the ground, if the conflagration spreads from town to town, and if we ourselves, in our wild enthusiasm, finally set fire to these uncleansable Augean stables for the sake of a breath of fresh air? – With complete level-headedness and with no sense of dizziness, I assure you that I no longer believe in any other revolution save that which begins with the burning down of Paris: – no more June battles will be fought there, – for men now hold themselves in reverence, but these are no longer the prison cells in which they are turned into beasts. – Does that alarm you? – Think on these things calmly and honestly, – you will come to the same conclusion! Strong nerves will be needed, and only true human beings will survive the revolution, i.e. those whose humanity is the product of need and the most grandiose terror. – "Can anything useful emerge from all this?" – Just wait and see how we recover from this fire-cure: if necessary I could finish painting this picture, I could even imagine how a man of enthusiasm might here and there summon together the living remnants of our former art and how he might say to them – who among you desires to help me perform a drama? Only those people will answer who genuinely share that desire, for there will no longer be money available, but those who respond will at once reveal to the world, in a rapidly erected wooden structure, what art is. – At all events, it will all happen quickly, for you can see there is no question here of gradual progress: our redeemer will destroy with furious speed all that stands in our way! – When? – I do not know, for nothing is being achieved here, – but one thing I do know is that the coming storm will exceed all earlier ones to the same degree that the February Revolution exceeded our expectations of 1847. – There is only *one* step still to be taken, and that step is imperatively necessary.

– Look, just as we need a water-cure to heal our bodies, so we need a fire-cure in order to remedy (i.e. destroy) the cause of our illness – a cause that is all around us. Shall we return then to a state of nature, shall we reacquire the human animal's ability to live to be 200 years old? God forbid! Man is a social, all-powerful being only through *culture*. Let us not forget that culture alone grants us the power to enjoy life to the full as only mankind can enjoy it. True enjoyment, however, consists in distilling a specific concentrate out of the general fund of things worth enjoying, so that we can assimilate in an instant what time and the elements have to offer us in a widely divergent context. Who, at the moment of enjoyment, thinks of the permanence of that enjoyment? If we think of permanence, the enjoyment itself immediately fades. Let us fill our lives with true substance, let us delight in our activities, whether those activities involve the giving or the receiving of pleasure, and we shall never be frightened by the thought of those activities coming to an end, for that end will itself be a form of action. Why should we worry whether we live to be 100 or only 30, as long as we live a life of enjoyment: – life *per se* is a mere abstraction, active enjoyment is what matters. Believe me – water will restore us to our former health, but we shall not be truly healthy until we can also drink wine without harm to ourselves! –

My companions are coming; I must close now!

I hope you have had enough this time! Fare you well, and don't try juggling with the lamp or you'll set your bed alight!

Fare you well, and my very best wishes from

Yours,
R.W.

SB III,457–62.

118. FRANZ LISZT, EILSEN   Zurich, 25 November 1850

[. . .] Yes, indeed, my dear, kind Liszt! It is to you that I owe the fact that I can soon become a complete artist once more. I regard the final resumption of my artistic plans to which I am now turning as one of the most decisive moments of my life: between the musical composition of my Lohengrin and that of my Siegfried there lies a world of tumult, but a world – I know – which has also been fruitful. I had to put my entire previous life behind me, while giving conscious expression to the new ideas that had begun to dawn in it, but resisting the inevitable temptation to reflect upon it – which I was able to do by thinking intently about the object in question – before throwing myself once again, in clear and calm self-consciousness, into the blissful unconsciousness of artistic creation. I shall spend this winter, then, clearing everything away that lies behind me: I wish to enter into a new world, free and unencumbered, without any burden to weigh me down, a world to which I bring naught but a cheerful artistic conscience. – My essay on the nature of opera,[1] the final fruits of my deliberations, has assumed greater dimensions than I had first supposed: but if I wish to demonstrate that music (as a woman) must necessarily be impregnated by a poet (as a man), then I must ensure that this glorious woman is not abandoned to the first passing libertine, but that she is made pregnant only by the man who yearns for womankind with

1 *Oper und Drama* (Opera and Drama), written during the winter of 1850/51 and published by Weber in November 1851.

true, irresistible love. The necessity of this union between poetry and music in its fullness and entirety (a union desired by the poet himself) was something I could not demonstrate simply by means of abstract and aesthetic definitions – which generally fail to be understood or to make any impression: I had to attempt to show, with the most manifest clarity, that it derives from the state of modern dramatic poetry itself. And I hope to be fully successful in this. – [. . .]

SB III,467.

119. FRANZ LISZT, EILSEN   Zurich, 18 February 1851

[. . .] My very thick book is finished; it has the title: "Opera and Drama". I do not yet have a publisher: but since I must see to it this time that I get some money for it, I feel almost afraid of the whole affair.

I shall spend next month editing my 3 romantic opera poems:[1] a substantial introduction will extend to cover the genesis of these poems and their relationship to the music. –

With the arrival of spring I then hope to begin work on the composition of Siegfried[2] and stick continuously to the task in hand. –

I might add that my love of life is not great. It is very quiet and lonely here – and I often think of myself as having died and been forgotten.
  [. . .]

SB III,514.

120. FRANZ LISZT, WEIMAR   Zurich, 18 April 1851

[. . .] You ask me about "Judaism".[3] You know of course that the article is by me: so why do you ask? It was not out of fear, but to prevent the question from being dragged down by the Jews to a purely personal level that I appeared in print pseudonymously. I harboured a long suppressed resentment against

1 The libretti of *Der fliegende Holländer, Tannhäuser* and *Lohengrin* were published by Breitkopf & Härtel in December 1851, together with a preface drafted between mid-July and mid-August 1851. The full title, *Drei Operndichtungen nebst einer Mittheilung an meine Freunde als Vorwort* (Three Opera Poems, together with a Communication to my Friends as Preface), is generally abbreviated to *A Communication to my Friends.*
2 See letter [121], p. 223, and [129], pp. 232–4.
3 *Das Judenthum in der Musik* (Judaism in Music), published under the pseudonym of R. Freigedank in the *Neue Zeitschrift für Musik* in two instalments dated 3 and 6 September 1850.

this Jewish business, and this resentment is as necessary to my nature as gall is to the blood. The immediate cause of my intense annoyance was their damned scribblings, so that I finally let fly: I seem to have struck home with terrible force, which suits my purpose admirably, since that is precisely the sort of shock that I wanted to give them. For they will always remain our masters – that much is as certain as the fact that it is not our princes who are now our masters, but bankers and philistines. – Meyerbeer is a special case, as far as I am concerned: it is not that I hate him, but that I find him infinitely repugnant. This perpetually kind and obliging man reminds me of the darkest – I might almost say the most wicked – period of my life, when he still made a show of protecting me; it was a period of connections and back-staircases, when we were treated like fools by patrons whom we inwardly deeply despised. That is a relationship of the most utter dishonesty: neither party is sincere in its dealings with the other; each assumes an air of devotion, but they use each other only so long as it profits them to do so. I do not reproach Meierbeer in the least for the intentional ineffectiveness of his kindness towards me, – on the contrary, I am glad that I am not as deeply in his debt as is Berlioz, for ex. But it was time for me to break away completely from so dishonest a relationship: superficially, I did not have the least occasion for doing so, for even the discovery that he was playing me false could not surprise me or, indeed, justify my action, since it was basically I who had to reproach myself for having wilfully allowed myself to be deceived concerning him. No, it was for more deep-seated reasons that I felt the need to abandon all the usual considerations of common sense in my dealings with him: I cannot exist as an artist in my own eyes or in those of my friends, I cannot think or feel anything without sensing in Meyerbeer my total antithesis, a contrast I am driven loudly to proclaim by the genuine despair that I feel whenever I encounter, even among many of my friends, the mistaken view that I have something in common with Meyerbeer. With all that I want and feel, I cannot appear before any of these friends with the requisite pureness and clarity until such time as I distance myself completely from this vague image with which so many people still associate me. This is a necessary act if my mature self is to be fully born, – and – if God wills it – I think I shall have been of service to many another person in having performed this act with such zeal!

[. . .]

SB III,544–6.

121. THEODOR UHLIG, DRESDEN   Zurich, 10 May 1851

[. . .] From Weimar I have now also received offers for a new opera: I am to deliver it by 1 July 1852, by which time I shall have been paid a total of 500 thalers. – I have now reached a number of new conclusions concerning my plans for this work. When I took a closer look at "Siegfried's death" with a serious view to having it performed in Weimar next year, the whole thing inevitably struck me as utterly impossible. Where would I find the necessary performers and an audience for it? – But throughout the whole of this past winter I have been plagued by an idea which finally took possession of me in a sudden flash of inspiration, so much so that I now intend carrying it out. Have I not already written to you[1] concerning a non-serious subject? It was the one about the lad who leaves home "to learn fear" and who is so stupid that he never learns what it is. Imagine my shock when I suddenly discovered that the lad in question is none other than – young Siegfried who wins the hoard and awakens Brünnhilde! – The matter is now resolved. Next month I shall do the text for "young Siegfried", for which I am now collecting my thoughts. In July I shall tackle the music, – and I have such shameless confidence in the warmth of the subject-matter and in my own endurance that next year, with my strength unimpaired, I plan to get as far as the composition of "Siegfried's death". – "Young Siegfried" has the enormous advantage of conveying the important myth to an audience by means of actions on stage, just as children are taught fairy-tales. It will all imprint itself graphically by means of sharply defined physical images, it will all be under-stood, – so that by the time they hear the more serious "Siegfried's death", the audience will know all the things that are taken for granted or simply hinted at there – and – I shall be home and dry, – the more so in that a far more popular work, which is much closer to people's perception and which deals less with an heroic subject-matter than with the high-spirited and youthfully human "Young Siegfried", will give the *performers* a practical oppor-tunity to train and prepare themselves for solving the much greater task presented by "Siegfried's death". – Both works, however, will form totally independent pieces, which only on their first airing will be presented to the public in this particular order, but which can thereafter be given on their own – according to individual preferences and abilities. And never again shall I have to envisage a general, abstract audience, but a specific public to whom I can communicate my intentions directly in order that I may be understood by them. –
     [. . .]

SB IV,43–4.

1 See letter [94], pp. 174–5.

122. ADOLF STAHR, WEIMAR   Zurich, 31 May 1851

My most honoured friend,

You can most readily conceive of the impression produced upon me by your verdict on "*Lohengrin*"[1] – a verdict which has just been brought to my attention – , if I report that I have discovered, with a certain smile I find it hard to define, that in none of the reviews of the work which I have seen so far, has there been the least mention of the *one* point which I most expected to find there and which you *yourself* have now emphasized with such striking precision.

It is impossible for me to go into detail on this point at present: I am at this very moment engaged in a creative process[2] which renders any critical distraction impossible. Forgive me, therefore, for the brevity with which I intend to make the following important remarks. –

Between my "Lohengrin" and my present plans there lies a whole world. What is so dreadfully distressing for the likes of us is to see our cast-off skin held out involuntarily as our true self. If all were as I wished it to be, "Lohengrin" – the poem of which dates back to 1845 – would long ago have been *forgotten* in favour of my more recent works which have given even me satisfactory evidence of the progress I have made.

Let me explain. In 1847 the music was completely finished. In 1848 there came the revolution: the mists parted. In 1849 I had to flee: with a feeling of rejoicing I turned my back on the whole damn business: I vented my feelings in a brochure: "Art and Revolution", and collected my thoughts earnestly together for a thin volume: "The Art-Work of the Future". I was even close to breaking with the world on a *domestic* level, too. Then one day my glance fell on the abandoned score of "Lohengrin": I regretted that it had never been heard; good-naturedly I wrote a few lines to Liszt, saying that if it amused him to do so, he should stage the work in *Weimar*. – Well, it had to be Liszt who always takes everything so seriously. – As I say, when nobody else made the point you did, I felt like laughing out loud: – but I have stopped laughing now and might almost feel angry that "Lohengrin" has finally seen the light of day after all. If you get to know my present poems, you will understand why. –

This much I will say! I am glad that I once insisted so obstinately on the Christian standpoint, and that I did so as an artist – with the greatest *naïveté*. When I had finished the poem of "Tannhäuser", somebody[3] demanded that I should let Venus triumph over St Elisabeth: – I found it an admirable

---

1 A review of the fifth performance of *Lohengrin* in Weimar on 11 May 1851, published in the Berlin *National-Zeitung* of 27 and 28 May, Nos. 243 and 245.

2 Wagner was currently working on the prose draft of *Der junge Siegfried* (24 May – 1 June 1851). The poem followed between 3 and 24 June.

3 Perhaps Gottfried Semper; see *Mein Leben* 327; English trans. 314.

suggestion, only I had to say that, in that case, it would not be "Tannhäuser" that I wrote. When "Lohengrin" appeared in print, it met with the most fundamental objection on the part of one of my most intelligent friends:[1] Lohengrin, he said, must finally become human. It was this same objection which comprises your own reproach. I actually began to think the matter over and to avail myself of various suggestions that had been made for changing the work: I made every effort to delude myself into believing in a mortified God etc. – fortunately none of these changes was thought adequate by my friend; if I wished to leave Lohengrin to his fate, I had to send him out into the world just as he was, i.e. as the Christian folk had once made him – if I was not to commit one inconsistency after another. It was with a sense of total intoxication that I plunged into the music: there was nothing else to be done; at least I prevented myself in this way from writing a rationalistic opera.

I know what you mean when you speak of monotonous, unrhythmical melody: the solution to the underlying question here is one which I think I have given, theoretically, in the third part of my book "Opera and Drama", which is shortly to appear in print. The reason lies not in the music but – since music after all can only ever be language developed to its fullest potential – in the language itself, in the verse. At present we have only inadequately formed verse, not the real thing. My musical expression, moreover, continues to be related only supersensually to language: a substantial, sensual relationship between the two has escaped me until now. But this is not something I have worked out theoretically – in spite of the fact that you will set eyes on my theory before you encounter the practical demonstration from which it derives: the theory came to me through my poem, *"Siegfried's Death"*, in which I chanced quite spontaneously upon the language necessary for the music.

There is *one* point on which you perhaps do me an injustice: you call my "Lohengrin" an actual polemic against modern opera; you attribute to me a puritanical zeal in my having written it. So be it! but do not call it an *intentional* polemic: when I wrote this opera, I was so obsessed by the subject that my only aim was to bring to light a work that was full and luxuriant, and loudly resonant: and this aim was so far removed from all idea of protest that, on the contrary, I failed to see what it was in reality that turned this work into a form of protest.

Enough! I cannot now criticize, and perhaps can never criticize. – But – if only you knew how I felt today when I read your article! For the last 6 days I have been writing away at a "Young Siegfried", today I finally drafted a complete sketch (in dialogue form) of the closing scene – Brünnhilde's awakening. When you get to know this scene, think of me and of how I felt when I heard you speaking about me.

Well then, let me conclude by thanking you and by expressing the hope

1 Hermann Franck; see letter [75], pp. 129–32.

that we shall remain friends! Do you accept? – *Liszt* wants "Young Siegfried"
to be kept a *secret* for the time being. Once I have finished the poem, I shall
send it to Weimar – Liszt will communicate it to you immediately, and I shall
then have a moment's rest to write more and – I hope – better.

Fare you well, and accept once again the most sincere thanks of

Your most obedient servant
Richard Wagner.

SB IV,57–60.

123. ERNST BENEDIKT KIETZ, PARIS   Zurich, 2 July 1851

Dear Kietz,

Very many thanks for your recent letter: it was as welcome for its contents
as for the friendly zeal with which you conveyed the same to me. In accordance
with your wishes, I am enclosing a brief note to Seghers:[1] will you be so good
as to pass it on to him?

The reason I am so late in replying is that I have only just got round to
writing all the letters I owe: I have been so engrossed in my work until now
that I could not allow myself any distractions. – I have just written the poem
for a "Young Siegfried" which I am planning to compose for Weimar – where
it has been commissioned: it is intended to precede "Siegfried's death", and
is of a non-serious character. – I am now giving people lots to talk and write
about in Germany: Härtels are publishing the vocal score of Lohengrin and
even plan to have the full score engraved. Can you not get hold of the Leipzig
"Illustrirte Zeitung"? The issue of 12 April contains a splendid article on
Lohengrin by Liszt.

My book: Opera and Drama, will be appearing in about 2 months' time.
As for the rest, life here is tolerable: tomorrow I intend setting out for Lake
Constance to meet one of the old faithfuls from Dresden[2] who has skimped
and saved in order to be able to visit me here: we plan to return by way of
the Appenzell alps.

So you ran out of ink again? – God, on the whole I wouldn't care whether
I had any ink or not! What we now do with ink is mere masturbation! – If I
were completely free – I should not mind the least privation: in my present
wretched condition that might even hold some appeal for me. –

I long passionately for the revolution, and the only thing that gives me the
will to live is the hope of surviving long enough to see it and to take part in

1 Letter to François Seghers of 2 July 1851 (SB IV,71), thanking him for arranging the Paris
première of the *Tannhäuser* Overture on 24 November 1850.
2 Theodor Uhlig, whom Wagner met in Rorschach on 5 July and who remained with Wagner
until 10 August.

it. – That Paris must be the starting-point is natural enough! – In the mean time we do what we do in order to blind ourselves to the non-lives that we lead. Art alone, as always, helps us in our self-deception. –

[. . .]

SB IV,69–70.

124. AUGUST RÖCKEL, WALDHEIM[1]   Zurich, 24 August 1851

My dear friend,

Only recently did I discover for certain that you and your companions in misfortune were allowed to receive letters not only from your immediate dependents but from acquaintances as well, provided that such letters touched only on matters of personal interest, or at least that they were unconnected with political issues. [. . .]

[. . .] I have recently given renewed and detailed expression to my feelings as an artistic being: on the subject of art itself in a fairly substantial book, "Opera and Drama", and on the relationship between myself as an individual and the subject of my art in a "Communication to my Friends", which I am having published as the foreword to an edition of my three poems, "The flying Dutchman", "Tannhäuser" and "Lohengrin". The first of these will be published by *Weber*, the second by *Breitkopf and Härtel*. How I wish I might be allowed to send you these books! *Härtels* are now having the vocal score of Lohengrin engraved, too, and – this will really surprise you – they intend doing the same with the *full score* of this opera. You will gather from this that the general feeling towards me as an "artist" has now become much more favourable: but – in the "communication" already mentioned – I have most emphatically rejected any suggestion that I might agree with the view that the "man" be distinguished from the "artist"; indeed, I have drawn attention to the folly of such a distinction. How disreputable and, to be frank, how worthless the whole of our present-day "art" has become has only recently become clear to me now that that art has cast aside the last vestige of its shame and publicly admitted that it is concerned at all costs simply for its own survival. How unhappy a man of my stamp must feel in these circumstances I scarcely need tell you: I am compelled to resign myself open-eyed to a life of illusion in order to be able to justify an activity which, conversely, is still capable of blinding me to how bad things are in general. All further theorizing now disgusts me: Liszt has inspired me to write a new work. And so I have written the poem of a "Young Siegfried" which, I may say, afforded a good

1 Röckel was serving a life sentence for his part in the Dresden uprising.

deal of pleasure. My hero grew up, untamed, in the forest, and was reared by a dwarf (the Nibelung "Mime") in order to kill the dragon which watches over the hoard. This Nibelung hoard constitutes an uncommonly crucial element in the work: crimes of every description are associated with it. Siegfried is more or less the same young lad as the one who is to be found in the fairy-tale, and who leaves home "to learn fear" – which he will never succeed in doing since his intense feeling for nature means that he only ever sees things as they are. He despatches the dragon and kills the dwarf who brought him up – and who secretly plans to slay him to obtain the hoard for himself. Siegfried, longing passionately for an end to his loneliness, now hears the voice of a woodbird – having acquired the gift to do so when he acciden-tally tasted the blood of the dragon –, and the bird directs him to Brünnhilde who – surrounded by fire – lies asleep on a rock. Siegfried passes through the fire and awakens Brünnhilde – *womankind* – in the most blissful of love's embraces. – I cannot intimate any further details here: but perhaps I may be allowed to send you the poem itself. – Only one other thing: – in our animated conversations we already touched on the subject: – we shall not become what we can and must be until such time as – *womankind* has been *wakened*. –
   [. . .]

SB IV,90–5.

125. THEODOR UHLIG, DRESDEN   [Zurich, 3 September 1851]

[. . .] I have again been working very hard since you left:[1] it finally affected my health, – but although I do want to get better finally, I simply do not know *how* to go about it! The most terrible times are those when I am expected to convalesce and relax: for only then do I really notice how things stand with me! Every spark of enjoyment has first to be struck from a whole pile of flint-stones. As long as I work, I can *delude* myself, – but as soon as I have to convalesce, I can no longer delude myself, and immediately I feel – dreadfully miserable! – My only salvation is to keep on thinking of work, and my only pleasure, on resuming that work, is to wear myself out! What a splendid life for an artist to live! how gladly I'd throw it all away in return for a single week of *life*! – I feel a dreadful lack of stimulation from my surroundings. With men I am now completely incapable of getting on – and – a woman! – Yes – a woman! –
   [. . .] – For Liszt I have similarly prepared a copy of my new "comic opera libretto":[2] but whether I shall send it to him, I do not yet know. – I

1 On 10 August; see letter [123], p. 226.
2 *Der junge Siegfried.*

am now making a start on the music and intend to enjoy myself greatly. Things you simply cannot imagine turn up of their own accord: I tell you, the musical phrases turn up around these verses and periods without my needing to make the least effort; everything springs up out of the ground like rank vegetation. The beginning is already in my head; also a few graphic motifs such as *Fafner*. I am looking forward to working on it uninterruptedly. – – [. . .]

SB IV,96–9.

126. CHRISTIAN JULIUS DANIEL STOCKS, SCHWERIN
Albisbrunn,[1] 6 October 1851

Dear Sir,

I learned from Frau Moritz that, since it was you who persuaded the Schwerin Court Theatre administration to concern itself with my Tannhäuser, it was you to whom I should most conveniently address myself if I desired further information about the theatre's plans for its intended performance of my opera.[2]

First allow me to express my sense of pleasure that, having made the acquaintance of this work of mine, you have now developed so lively an interest in it, as I must assume to be the case in view of the course which events have taken. In the light of my concern that the performance should be a *good* one, nothing could reassure me more than to learn that you yourself were responsible for rehearsing the singers. Experience has taught me that this is the most important part of the preparations: for the singers must, above all, accustom themselves to the fact that they are not supposed to be "singing an opera" but "performing a drama". – The next most important thing is the staging of the work: I draw your attention most particularly to the fact that the stage directions, as indicated with great precision in the full score, are to be followed with scrupulous fidelity. Other theatres have assured me that this would most certainly be done: but the performances in question have convinced me how wantonly producers behave in this respect. It is absolutely essential that the producer should have a most detailed knowledge of the full score. My orchestral accompaniment never expresses anything for the ear to hear which is not also intended to be expressed on stage for the eye to see, be it by means of actions on stage, gestures or simply by facial expressions: if these are either omitted or fail to coincide exactly with the appropriate

1 Wagner went to take the waters at Albisbrunn on 15 September, remaining there until 23 November.
2 The local première of *Tannhäuser* took place on 26 January 1852.

passage in the orchestra, an understanding of my intentions is rendered impossible. For his own part, the conductor of the orchestra will therefore have the following task to perform. First of all he must, by dint of assiduous practice alone, ensure that the orchestra is complete master of the work's technical difficulties. Once he has succeeded in this, the conductor has from then on to deal exclusively with the performers on stage, taking his instructions solely from what happens on stage, in whose spirit and movement the orchestra must accompany the drama.

[. . .]

SB IV, 124–5.

127. THEODOR UHLIG, DRESDEN   Albisbrunn, [7/11 October 1851]

[. . .] What I want: a tiny little house, with a meadow and garden! – To work with enjoyment and pleasure, – but not just now. Great plans for Siegfried: three dramas, with a three-act prelude. – When all the German theatres collapse in ruins, I shall run up a new one on the Rhine, summon people together and perform the whole thing in the space of a week. – Rest! Rest! Rest! – Countryside! Countryside! a cow, a goat, etc. – then – sound health – cheerful high spirits – hope! – otherwise – Everything's lost! I don't *want* to go on! – You *must* come here! –

Yours,
R.W.

[. . .]

SB IV, 131–2.

128. THEODOR UHLIG, DRESDEN   [Albisbrunn, 11 November 1851]

[. . .] Last Friday evening I had just climbed out of my hip-bath when the director of the posts from Hausen came rushing into my room, out of breath, to show me a copy of Friday's newspaper, which carried the report:[1]

"Richard Wagner, at present living in Zurich, has been granted a complete pardon by the King of Saxony. (He had been condemned to a long prison sentence for his part in the May uprising.)"

Much to the fellow's amazement, I remained dreadfully indifferent to the news. Nor have I yet received confirmation of the report: I expect for that

---

1 The report was without foundation.

reason it is untrue. The first thing I would do if there *were* any truth in the matter would simply be to apply to the authorities in Saxony for my denaturalization, so that I could become a Swiss citizen: with a Swiss passport I could then travel wherever I wanted: I should probably *not* come to Germany, and even Weimar with its Lohengrin would not really encourage me to commit an act which might give the impression that I accepted the pardon. – However – it is all merely gossip at present, and I do not intend making a fool of myself by crowing in public. All I wish to say here is that my *own* pardon would be a flagrant demonstration of the most abject arbitrariness. – –

Now something about my treatment. For the sake of my wife I have now agreed to return home on Sunday, 23 November: the 24th is our 15th wedding anniversary. My daily routine is now as follows, 1st, half-past-five in the morning wet pack until 7 o'clock; then a cold bath and a walk. 8 o'clock breakfast: dry bread and milk or water. 2nd, immediately afterwards a first and then a second clyster; another short walk; then a cold compress on my abdomen. 3rd, around 12 o'clock: wet rub-down; short walk; fresh compress. Then lunch in my room with Karl,[1] to prevent insubordination. Then an hour spent in idleness: brisk two-hour walk – alone. 4th, around 5 o'clock: another wet rub-down, and a short walk. 5th, hip-bath for a quarter of an hour around 6 o'clock, followed by a walk to warm me up. Fresh compress. Around 7 o'clock dinner: dry bread and water. 6th immediately followed by a first and then a second clyster; then a game of whist until after nine o'clock, after which another compress, and then around 10 o'clock we all retire to bed. – I am now bearing up quite well under this regimen: I may even intensify it. For a month I sweated sulphur: after that my damp towel turned a bright reddish colour; they assure me this comes from mercury.[2] Intense perspiration at high body temperatures. My skin came out in a rash again, which is now gradually going away again. – When I am back in Zurich, I shall continue with the treatment: I shall work very little: only the occasional drafts and sketches. If necessary, my wife will have to apply the packs herself. Very strict diet. – The devil himself must have a hand in it if I cannot then sit back and observe the ways of the world *in sound health* for a while: I shall – I think – again perform something soon; – but probably not in Weimar, where there is absolutely nothing that can be achieved – not even with the help of royal pardons. –

   [. . .]

SB IV, 170–2.

1 Karl Ritter.
2 Mercuric sulphide or cinnabar.

129. THEODOR UHLIG, DRESDEN   [Albisbrunn, 12 November 1851]

I am writing to you again today so that I do not forget a matter of some importance to me. – While I was still in Dresden I made every conceivable effort to buy a book which no longer existed in the booktrade. I finally found it in the royal library. It is a thin little volume in small octavo or maybe even duodecimo, and is entitled: *"The Völsungasaga"* – translated from the Old Norse by *H. von der Hagen.* It comprises (I believe) a part of the Old Norse "courtly romances" which – if I am not mistaken – Hagen published in Breslau between 1812 and 1816. I now need this book in order to glance briefly through it again: there is no possibility of obtaining it here. There is nothing for it, I am afraid, but for you, my good friend, to borrow this book from the royal library, in your own name, and, as a favour, send it to me here for a fairly short period. You could perhaps parcel it up with something else (Figaro?)[1] and I shall then send it back to you – within 2 weeks at the latest – with your Rausse books.[2] Everything by *post* of course. – My music scores[3] can easily go as freight – when you have finished looking through them. – I don't think you would be risking anything with the book: for – even if the worst came to the worst and it went missing or was stolen, you would only have to answer for its loss, i.e. pay the library the cost of the book. But it won't come to that.[4]

With regard to the planned completion of the great drama which I now have in mind, there is little I can tell you at present. You must remember that – before I wrote the poem of "Siegfried's death" – I sketched out the entire myth in its imposing overall context: that poem was an attempt – which I thought of as being feasible on our modern stage – to present a crucial turning-point in the myth by *hinting* at the overall context. But when I turned to its musical execution and was finally obliged to fix my sights firmly on our modern stage, I felt how incomplete was the product I had planned: all that remained of the vast overall context – which alone can give the characters their enormous, striking significance – was epic narration and a retelling of events on a purely conceptual level. In order, therefore, to render "Siegfried's death" feasible, I wrote "Young Siegfried": but the more imposing a structure the whole thing assumed, the more it was bound to dawn on me, as I began the scenico-musical realization of "Young Siegfried", that all I had done was

1 In order to save postage, Wagner and Uhlig used a copy of Beaumarchais' *Le Mariage de Figaro* to conceal their correspondence. The book was franked as printed matter.
2 On hydrotherapy.
3 Left behind in Dresden, these scores included the manuscripts of his early operas, and printed scores of Beethoven's Sixth and Ninth Symphonies, Bach motets and a Schumann Symphony (see letter to Uhlig of [21 October 1851], SB IV,140–2).
4 Wagner acknowledged receipt of the book on 3 December 1851 (SB IV,206) and on [24 December 1851] admitted that, having finally found time to reread it, he "really had had no further need for it in the first place" (SB IV,236).

to increase the need for a clearer presentation *to the senses* of the whole of the overall context. I now see that, in order to be fully understood from the stage, I must present the entire myth in visual terms. It was not only this concentration which persuaded me to adopt my new plan, but, more especially, the overwhelming pathos of the material which I shall in this way be able to present on stage and which offers me a wealth of ideas for an artistic reworking which it would be a sin for me not to use. Imagine the contents of Brünnhilde's narration – in the final scene of "Young Siegfried" – the fate of Siegmund and Siegelind, Wodan's struggle with his own inclination and with custom (Fricka); the Valkyrie's glorious defiance, Wodan's tragic anger with which he punishes that defiance: imagine this as *I* intend it, with the enormous wealth of moments such as these, drawn together into a coherent drama, and what shall be created is a tragedy of the most shattering effectiveness which, at the same time, will make a clear impression on the senses of all that my audience needs to have absorbed if they are to have no difficulty in understanding "Young Siegfr." and "S.'s death" – in their widest sense. I am now planning to preface these three dramas with a fairly substantial prelude which will have to be performed on its own on a special introductory festival day: it begins with Alberich, fired by erotic desire, pursuing the three watermaidens of the Rhine and being spurned by each of them in turn (in playful high spirits), so that he finally steals the Rhinegold in his fury: – in itself this gold is only a glittering trinket in the watery depths (Siegfr. death, Act III, Sc. I), but another power resides within it which can be coaxed from it only by *the man who* renounces *love.* – (here you have the structural motif which leads up to Siegf.'s death: imagine the wealth of consequences!) The capture of Alberich, the allocation of the gold to the two giant brothers, the swift fulfilment of Alberich's curse as embodied in these two characters, one of whom immediately kills the other – all this forms the subject of the prelude. – But I have already said too much, precisely because it is bound to be too little for me to give you an intelligible account of the enormous wealth of material here. – But I should like to have the "Völsungasaga" again; not to model my own work on it (you will easily discover how my poem is related to this legend), but to call to mind again all that I had once before worked out in individual detail. –

But there is something *else* which persuaded me to expand this plan: the impossibility I felt of being able to perform even "Young Siegfried" in Weimar – or anywhere else – at all adequately. I do not care to suffer – and, indeed, can no longer suffer – the torments of *half-measures.* – With this new conception of mine I am moving *completely* out of touch with our present-day theatre and its audiences: I am breaking decisively and for ever with the formal present. You now ask what I intend to do with my plan? – To begin with, I plan to *carry it through* as far as it lies within my poetic and musical powers to do so: this will occupy me for at least *three full years.* I am thus placing myself entirely in the Ritters' hands: I pray to God that they *remain unswervingly loyal to me*!

– A *performance* is something I can conceive of only *after the Revolution*; only the Revolution can offer me the artists and listeners I need. The coming Revolution must necessarily put an end to this whole *theatrical business* of ours: they must all perish, and will certainly do so, it is inevitable. Out of the ruins I shall then summon together what I need: I shall *then* find what I require. I shall then run up a theatre on the Rhine and send out invitations to a great dramatic festival: after a year's preparations I shall then perform my entire work within the space of *four days*: *with it* I shall then make clear to the men of the Revolution the *meaning* of that Revolution, in its noblest sense. *This audience* will understand me: present-day audiences cannot. –

However extravagant this plan may be, it is the only one on which I stake my life, my heart and my every thought. If I survive to witness its execution, I shall have lived a glorious life; if not, I shall have died for a beautiful ideal. Only this thought can still cheer me. –

Fare you well!

Yours,
R.W.

[. . .]

SB IV, 173–6.

130. FRANZ LISZT, WEIMAR   Albisbrunn, 20 November 1851

My dear friend,

I have finally reached the point when I can at long last break my silence towards you. The contents of this letter will show you how many issues – and relatively important issues at that – I had to sort out in my own mind before I could write to you with the decisiveness which is now both necessary and possible.

A large part of the blame for my silence must be borne by my poor state of health. I have now spent over two whole months on my water-cure, and during this period especially it has been quite impossible for me to write to you as fully as I felt increasingly constrained to do, as each day passed. The most pressing reason for writing, and the one most difficult to resist, sprang from my reading of your brochure on my two operas[1] which reached me here at the hydropathic establishment. Your rare friendship, the energetic love you

---

1 *Lohengrin et Tannhäuser de R. Wagner*, published by Brockhaus in August 1851.

feel for my works, your untiring eagerness to propagate those works, and, above all, the glorious intensity, the spirit, the delicacy and the boldness with which you express yourself in your eagerness to help me, – these qualities of yours moved me far too deeply and far too violently for me to be able to address you earlier to express my thanks, at a time when I was already in so agitated a state; I had to postpone doing so until such time as I had recovered my health and collected my thoughts sufficiently to be able to communicate my feelings more fully. – I hope that I have now reached that point, and my first words to you therefore are to say that the sacrifice which you have once more made for me in the name of our most beautiful and loving friendship has stirred me to the very depths of my being, bringing me joy and great happiness. You have moved me most profoundly each time you found yourself in complete agreement with me, since this sense of agreement is not something that already existed between us, rather was it necessary for us both to discover it first; above all, you have aroused my attention, interest and curiosity each time I have seen my original intentions reflected in the mirror of your unique and individual outlook, for it was precisely here that I was able to judge the impression which I was fortunate enough to have made on your over-generous artistic sensitivity.

What you have become to me in this way I recently sought to make publicly known and I did so – precisely because it was for public consumption – in terms of suitable sobriety, sticking closely to the purely factual aspects of our relationship in order to depict it for the benefit of those people who nowadays may not be able to conceive of such a friendship. I did so – urged on by an irresistible and heartfelt desire – in a "Communication to my Friends", which I am publishing as a preface to the edition of my "three opera poems". In this same piece I have said quite candidly that I already despaired of ever again undertaking another artistic venture and that it was to *you* alone and to your so successful intercession on my behalf that credit was due if I had now once again found the courage and will necessary for an artistic undertaking which I am dedicating to *you* and to those of my friends whom I epitomize as "the local concept: Weimar". Timidity on the part of the good Messrs Härtel, the intended publishers of this edition, has caused them to take exception to certain passages in the preface, to which I myself certainly did not wish to attach any demonstrative meaning and which I could equally well have expressed differently, but, as a result of their objections, the appearance of the book has now been delayed to an extent which I find most vexatious for a number of very particular reasons. The public declaration which I have made here in respect of the fate of my forthcoming dramatic work now requires substantial modification, in accordance with my latest resolves, if it is to remain an accurate reflection of the true nature of my present thinking. However, even if this foreword – which I completed at the beginning of last August – is out of date by the time it finally appears in print, I nevertheless

hope that the declaration in question will reach the general public unaltered:[1]
if the promise contained therein cannot be fulfilled by me in the way I have
indicated there, it may none the less be interpreted by you and by my Weimar
friends as an open demonstration of the sincere honesty of my intention as I
then planned it; and I should like to think that in this public declaration I
had offered some token of my gratitude for their feelings towards me, even
if – as I say – I cannot show my gratitude in the way I had earlier promised.

But to you, my dear Liszt, I am now forced to reveal that my resolve to
write a new opera for Weimar has assumed so fundamentally different an
aspect that I can scarcely allow it to stand any longer as such. Let me inform
you, in accord with the strictest truth, of the history of the artistic project on
which I have been engaged for some time now, and the change which this
plan had necessarily to undergo. –

In the autumn of 1848 I first sketched out the complete myth of the
Nibelungs such as henceforth belongs to me as my own poetic property. My
next attempt to present a crucial turning-point in the whole vast action, and
to present it as a drama suited to our present-day stage, was "Siegfried's
Death": after much uncertainty I finally reached the point in the autumn of
1850 of sketching the music for this drama, when I once again recognized
the impossibility of ever seeing it adequately performed, and so I broke off
the undertaking there and then. It was in order to rid myself of this mood of
despondency that I wrote the book "Opera and Drama". Then, last spring,
your article on Lohengrin made such an inspiriting impression upon me that –
for your sake – I quickly and cheerfully resumed my plans to complete a
drama; I wrote to tell you this at the time.[2] But I knew that "Siegfried's
Death" was for the moment impossible; I realized that I should first have to
prepare the way for it with another drama, and so I took up a plan I had
already been cherishing for some time, and began by making *"Young Siegfried"*
the subject of an opera poem; in it, everything that is either retold in "Siegfried's Death" or else assumed to be half-familiar to the audience was meant
to be presented by means of actual events on stage and given a fresh and
light-hearted treatment. The poem was soon sketched and completed. – I
was on the point of sending it to you when I began to feel a strange sense of
unease: I felt unable to send it to you as it stood without further ado; it was
as if I had to explain to you much more – infinitely more – about it, partly
concerning the manner of its execution and partly your necessary response
to the poem itself. The first thing to emerge here was that, before appearing
with this poem in the presence of my friends, I should first have to communi-

---

1 In its original formulation, the Preface had ended with the announcement that *Der junge
Siegfried* and *Siegfrieds Tod* would be produced in Weimar. Following Wagner's decision to
expand the work, he cancelled his contract with Weimar and rewrote the ending of the
Preface. It was this amended form which was published by Breitkopf & Härtel.
2 On 18 April 1851; see SB III,542–4.

cate a great many other things to them besides: that was why I wrote the extensive preface to my three older opera poems which I have already mentioned. I now planned to set about the musical composition of the work: and, to my delight, I observed that the music to these verses came quite naturally and easily, entirely of its own accord. But my initial start on the work reminded me that I would undermine my health completely if, without first having taken proper care of it, I yielded at once to my impulse, and – presumably without interruption – completed what I had begun at a single stroke. Only when I moved to the hydropathic establishment did I feel the need finally to send you the poem: – but, strangely enough, something continued to hold me back; I continued to hesitate, sensing that, on becoming acquainted with the poem, you would initially feel a certain embarrassment at not knowing for certain what you should make of it, nor whether you should place your hopes on it or your mistrust. – Now that I have considered the matter calmly, my plan has finally become clear to me in all its logical consistency. Listen! –

Even this "Young Siegfried" is only a fragment and, as an *individual* whole, it can only make its rightful and indubitable impression when it assumes its necessary place within the *completed* whole, a place which – in accordance with the plan I have now conceived – I am now assigning to it, together with "Siegfried's Death". In both these dramas a wealth of necessary allusions was left simply in narrative form or else had to be worked out for himself by the listener: everything that gives the intrigue and the characters of these two dramas their infinitely moving and far-reaching significance would have had to be omitted from the stage action and communicated on a merely conceptual level. According to my newly acquired and innermost conviction, however, a work of art – and hence the basic drama – can only make its rightful impression if the poetic intent is fully presented to the senses in every one of its important moments; and *I* least of all can now afford to sin against this insight which I now recognize as true. In order to be perfectly understood, I must therefore communicate my entire myth, in its deepest and widest significance, with total artistic clarity; no part of it should have to be supplied by the audience's having to think about it or reflect on it; every unbiased human feeling must be able to grasp *the whole* through its organs of artistic perception, because only then can it properly absorb the *least detail*. There are, accordingly, two principal moments in my myth which still remain to be depicted on stage, and these are both alluded to in "Young Siegfried": the first in Brünnhilde's lengthy narration following her awakening (third act); the second in the scene between Alberich and the Wanderer in the second, and between the Wanderer and Mime in the first act. – That my mind was made up in this matter not only as a result of artistic reflection but, more particularly, as a result of the splendid nature of the material, which lends itself uncommonly well to presentation on stage, you will readily understand once you have taken a closer look at that material. Imagine the wondrously ill-starred love of Siegmund and Siegelind; Wodan[1] in his deeply mysterious relationship to that love; then the discord between him and Fricka, his furious self-mastery when – for the sake of custom – he decrees Siegmund's death; finally, the glorious Valkyrie, Brünnhilde, divining Wodan's innermost thought, defying the god and being punished by him: imagine the wealth of incentive as indicated in the scene between the Wanderer and the Wala, but then – more fully – in Brünnhilde's narration which I have already mentioned – imagine all this as the material for a drama which will precede the two Siegfrieds, and you will conceive that it is not mere reflection but, more particularly, inspiration which has encouraged me to adopt my latest plan!

This plan will now comprise three dramas: 1st, *The Valkyrie.* 2nd, *Young Siegfried.* 3rd, *Siegfried's Death.* In order to present everything complete, these three dramas must additionally be preceded by a great prelude: *The Rape of the Rhinegold.* It takes as its subject the detailed depiction of all that occurs in "Young Siegfried" in narrative form, as it relates to the theft of the gold, the origins of the Nibelung hoard, the abduction of this hoard by Wodan, and Alberich's curse. –

Thanks to the clarity of presentation which will thus have been made possible, I shall now – by discarding, at the same time, all the narration-like passages which are now so extensive or else by compressing them into a number of much more concise moments – acquire sufficient space to exploit to the full the wealth of emotive associations contained in the work, whereas previously, with my earlier, half-epic mode of presentation, I was obliged to prune everything laboriously and thus to weaken its impact. I mention only one episode: –

> *Alberich* comes up out of the depths of the earth to the three daughters of the Rhine; he pursues them with his loathsome attentions; rejected by the first, he turns to the second: joking and teasing him, they all spurn the goblin. Then the Rhinegold begins to gleam; it attracts Alberich; he asks what use it serves? The girls declare that it serves for their enjoyment and sport; its gleam illumines the depths of the floodwaters with its rapturous shimmering: but many are the wonders that could be wrought by means of the gold, great are the power and the might, the riches and the dominion that could be won by the man who knew how to forge it into a ring: but only he *who renounces love* could understand that! but so that none may steal the gold, they themselves are appointed its guardians: the man who approaches them has indeed no desire for the gold; Alberich, at least, does not seem to desire it, since he behaves like a man in

1 Wagner preferred the form Wodan until *c*1860: see his letter to B. Schott's Söhne of 7 July 1860.

love. They laugh at him anew. The Nibelung then grows angry: he
forswears love, steals the gold and carries it off into the depths. –

Enough of this individual detail! now my plan for the practical realization of
the whole!

I cannot contemplate a division of the constituent parts of this great whole
without ruining my intention in advance. The whole complex of dramas must
be staged at the same time in rapid succession, and for that reason I can
envisage only the following circumstances as being favourable to the outward
feasibility of the plan: – the performance of my Nibelung dramas must take
place at a great festival which may perhaps be organized for the unique
purpose of this performance. It must then be given on three successive days,
with the introductory prelude being performed on the preceding evening.
Once I have achieved such a performance under these conditions, the whole
work may then be repeated on another occasion, and only after that may the
individual dramas, which in themselves are intended as entirely independent
pieces, be performed as people wish: but, whatever happens, these performances must be preceded by an impression of the complete production which
I myself shall have prepared.

Where and in what circumstances such a performance may be feasible is
something I do not need to worry about for now; for I must first of all
complete this great work of mine, and this task will take me at least three
years, from the time I have paid some heed to my health. A fortunate accretion
of wealth in the Ritter family, who are such good friends of mine, has meant
that I can now apply myself to my artistic work calmly and undisturbed by
material cares throughout the period in question, and, indeed, for the rest of
my life. But once I have completed my great work, the rest – I hope – will
follow as a matter of course, so that it is staged in accordance with my wishes.
If Weimar is still standing then, and if you yourself have been more fortunate
in your efforts to produce something decent than now, alas, appears to be
the case (and more than simply "appears"!), we shall then see what is to be
done in the matter. –

However bold, unusual, nay, even fanciful this plan of mine may strike you,
you may nevertheless be assured that it is not the result of some superficial and
calculating whim, but that it has impressed itself upon me as a necessary
consequence of the nature and content of the subject which now occupies
my mind and drives me to carry it through to its completion. To complete it
as only I, as poet and musician, may be allowed to do is for now the only
thing I see ahead of me: nothing else must disturb me at present. Knowing
the way you think, I do not doubt for a moment that you will agree with me
in this and, indeed, encourage me in my resolve, even though in this way a
wish which I find deeply flattering! – your wish to perform a new work of
mine so soon after the last one – must necessarily be left unfulfilled. –

But only *now* do I confess that, at the same time as deciding on this definitive change of plan, I also felt relieved of an almost oppressive sense of embarrassment, – my embarrassment at expecting the present Weimar Theatre to stage Young Siegfried. Only now, together with this explanation, can I send you the poem of "Young Siegfried" with a light heart, – only now that I know you will not read it through with the sense of concern which it would necessarily have caused you, if you had had to think of how I was going to complete it and, more especially, of its performance at the Weimar Theatre – such as it is at present and such as it must inevitably remain. Let us not delude ourselves in this matter! What you – and *you* alone – have so far done for me in Weimar is astounding. But it was even more successful from my own point of view: without you I should by now have disappeared without trace, instead of which you have, by dint of means which you alone had at your command, ensured that I now enjoy the attention of all lovers of art; indeed, you have acted with such energy and such success that these efforts of yours on behalf of me and my reputation are solely and uniquely to thank for the fact that I am now able even to think of realizing the plans which I have just communicated to you. I can see all this with total clarity and have no hesitation in describing you as the creator of my present position, a position which is perhaps not entirely lacking in future prospects.

But I now go on to ask: – do you *still* place your hopes in Weimar?

With sad sincerity I tell you that I am bound to regard your efforts in Weimar as – fruitless. You know from your own experience that you have only to turn your back for a moment and the most rank baseness springs up from the very ground where you have striven to plant the choicest fruits; you return, and have scarcely reploughed half the ground when you see weeds shooting up again more brazenly than before. – You are in Weimar: you praise the Court's love of art – ? Do you not recall the most illustrious *Karl August* allowing his friend *Göthe* to be hounded from the same stage by – a poodle,[1] – that same stage on which, in far less favourable circumstances, you now intend to plant the banner of an art for which almost all means of presentation, all use of habit, nay, all hopes of a *true* (as opposed to artificial) success are missing? – Indeed, I can look on only in sadness! Beside you I see only stupidity, narrow-mindedness, baseness and – the empty conceit of jealous courtiers who are envious – with such lamentable right – of genius's every success! –

But – – that is more than enough on this loathsome subject! For my *own* part, it no longer troubles me, for I have sorted out my own feelings in the matter: but – it troubles me on *your* account! I hope that, for the sake

---

1 Guilbert de Pixérécourt's *Le Chien de Montargis ou la Forêt de Bondy* (1814), performed in Weimar in 1817 at the instance of Duke Karl August, was popularly believed to have led to Goethe's resignation as intendant of the Weimar Court Theatre.

of your own good humour, you are not too late in reaching the same conclusion! – –

[. . .]

SB IV, 183–91.

131. THEODOR UHLIG, DRESDEN   [Zurich, 18 December 1851]

[. . .] You will, my dear friend, shortly be hearing of things which will make it clear to you why I have now completely abandoned every attempt to combat the prevailing mood of stupidity, dullness of mind and utter wretchedness, – why I intend to let what is rotten continue to rot and not waste my remaining powers of production and enjoyment on a painful and utterly futile effort to galvanize the corpse of European civilization. I intend only to live, to enjoy life, i.e. as an artist – to create and see my works performed: but not for the critical shit-heads of today's populations. – Since I cannot communicate my ideas to you here as fully as would be necessary, I must conceal from you for today the key to my intentions – and, I hope, of the common intentions of many others – , lest I cause any misunderstanding. Recent political events,[1] however, have played a decisive part here, but only in a positive way. Only this much for today: yesterday (17 December 1851), in the presence of Karl[2] and with his support, Herwegh and I between us reached a decision which – I believe – may become the starting-point of a new phase in world history. We promised each other that we should do everything in our power, and use all the means of persuasion and conviction at our command to ensure that our decision spreads in ever wider circles, in order finally – and I hope in the not too distant future – to come to fruition. From henceforth – except when I am writing my poems and composing music – I shall devote my entire literary activity to this end, an activity whose goal for once is an entirely positive and practical end of incalculable consequence, and at the same time a goal which no reactionary power on earth will be able to impede. – So fare you well for today! Karl will have lots to tell you.

Yours,
R.W.

SB IV, 233–4.

1 Louis Napoléon's *coup d'état* in Paris on 2 December 1851; see introductory essay, p. 162.
2 Karl Ritter.

132. THEODOR UHLIG, DRESDEN   [Zurich, 28 December 1851]

Dear Uhlig,

I also received the 3 Opera Poems yesterday. The preface had almost slipped my memory, and I practically devoured it whole in such a neat and lavish (– and fabulously *correct*!!) edition. God knows what other people will think, – but *I* found this preface enormously interesting, – I can say that without reservation! *This* was really the most important thing I had to tell the world, since it was indispensably necessary as a supplement to "Opera and Drama". But I really do think that I have now written enough as a journalist: *what* is there left to say if my friends do not see things clearly now, and why should I care *now* if they have still got dirt in their eyes. As for what's been done, *I* at least am completely satisfied with myself, for I have certainly spared no effort in making myself understood. The rest is solely the concern of those who take an interest in me!

[. . .]

Apropos of the vocal score, I have again been glancing briefly through the music of Lohengrin: – might it not be of interest to you – since you do, after all, write such things[1] – to expatiate upon the work's formal thematic web, and explain how it is bound to lead to ever new formal structures along the road which I myself have opened up? This struck me at various points in the score, including the opening scene of the second act. Right at the beginning of the second scene of this same act – Elsa's appearance on the balcony – in the woodwind prelude – it struck me that a motif is heard here for the first time in the 7th, 8th and 9th bars of Elsa's nocturnal appearance, which is later developed, and broadly and brilliantly executed, when, in broad daylight and in all her glory, Elsa makes her way to church. I realized from this that the themes that I write always originate in the context of, and according to the character of, some visual phenomenon on stage. But perhaps you can express yourself better on this matter than I can. –

[. . .]

SB IV, 239–41.

133. ERNST BENEDIKT KIETZ, PARIS   Zurich, 30 December [1851]

Dear Kietz,

Thank you very much for your letter, but not for sending me my old clothes, which cost me 6 frc . . . – But nowhere among all these clothes was

---

1 Uhlig published a series of articles on Wagner's theoretical writings in Schumann's *Neue Zeitschrift für Musik*; his premature death prevented him from following up the idea suggested here.

there any sign of a letter!! You failed to understand my reminder to you to write: when all hell breaks loose in Paris, I at least expect a sign of life, do you understand?

Your long and heartfelt litany gave me a good deal of pleasure and amused me in many ways: what I found especially admirable was the musical composition drawn from your imagination by the sorcery of events. For the rest, permit me to refrain from prattling on about politics or anything similar. My entire political outlook no longer consists in anything but the bloodiest hatred of our entire civilization, contempt for all that it has produced, and a passionate longing for nature. But that is not something anyone will understand who felt so enchanted by the industrial exhibition. Well, you've got your exhibition, an exhibition in the pillory, with all your industrious workers! That I ever set store by the workers as workers is something I must now atone for grievously: with the noises they make, these workers are the wretchedest slaves, whom anyone can control nowadays if he promises them plenty of "work". A slave mentality has taken root in everything with us: that we are *human* is something nobody knows in the whole of France except perhaps Proudhon at most – and even he is only dimly aware of the fact! – in the whole of Europe, however, I prefer dogs to these doglike men. However, I do not despair of the *future*; only the most terrible and destructive revolution can make our civilized beasts "human" again.

I am now thinking a good deal of America! Not because I might find what I am looking for there, but because the ground there is easier to plant –

Have you received from Härtel a copy of the *Three Opera Poems* with the preface? –

I am planning to make a start soon on my great Nibelung trilogy. But I shall *perform* it only on the banks of the Mississipi.

Otherwise we are as well as can be expected. When do you intend to come and visit us? I have already said I would pay your fare for you. You'd have to paint my mug in oils for my friends here. – But now you are working on Johanna,[1] whom heaven has blessed and who is kind enough never to reply to me whenever I write to her. – Fare you well, old fellow! Minna sends her warmest wishes! If you like the preface, write and tell me!

Adieu!

Yours,
R.W.

Sammlung Burrell 257–8.

---

1 Johanna Wagner.

134. THEODOR UHLIG, DRESDEN   [Zurich, 12 January 1852]

My dear friend,

I am more or less back where I started, and the devil has me in his clutches again.[1] No treatment on earth has the power to preserve me from the loathsomeness of outside impressions: their evil influence continues to cloud the well-spring of my inspiration and cause it to run painfully dry. Here I sit with all my wishes, hopes and endeavours: I see – and feel – with unbearable clearness that they must all remain unsatisfied and futile! Insensitivity wherever I turn! Each of my plans is bound to strike me at once in all its grey and desolate impossibility! I can no longer flatter myself with self-delusion. The only thing that could sustain me in a happy state of self-deception is denied me: – *sympathy*, words of true sympathy falling on my ears! Everyone I approach hangs his head, sighs, falls silent and, having made this effort, reverts to his old insensitivity. You, in fact, are now the only person I can still turn to for sympathy, for you are the only person who has the energy at least to answer me, – although I cannot help noticing that your letters are now written in as prolix a style as possible with the disturbing aim of filling as much space as possible: often, such as after your last two letters, I ask myself: "is it after all so difficult for him to fill the page with characters?" – Others simply do not answer at all, I asked Liszt to send me his medallion for Christmas: no answer. Bülow has even sunk to such depths of sheer impropriety that he has not uttered a single sound in reply to two letters, the second of which, in particular, contained a number of requests which required prompt attention. And so I always think of myself as a beggar running after all and sundry in the hope of picking up the odd penny! It is not quite the same with Karl:[2] he broods interminably on the great suffering caused him by his stomach, which he has ruined visiting the confectioner's; he has no time to worry himself over trifles such as I foolishly allow to trouble me: and every now and then he does what he can; in the 3 weeks[3] he has been away from here, he has finally written a total of twenty-one words to me, which actually makes one word a day! Ah! the unhappy Ritters, what a bad way they are in!!

In such circumstances – which I shall not go into but which you will infer from the nature of my present mood – I do not know whether it comes from inside me, or from outside, if I am again unwell. As far as my bodily functions

1 Possibly an allusion to Faust's famous cry, "Die Erde hat mich wieder" in *Faust*, Part I, l. 784.
2 Karl Ritter.
3 SB IV,246 reads "13 Wochen", but this is clearly incorrect, as the remainder of the sentence indicates. An earlier letter to Uhlig of [24 December 1851] (SB IV,238) had announced Ritter's departure for Germany the previous evening.

are concerned, I must say that I am still tolerably healthy: but – my nerves! I admit that I overdid things towards the end of my stay at the hydropathic establishment: it was unfortunate that I had no doctor in whom to confide: my cheerful frame of mind was probably a result of nervous irritability, since, in spite of my cheerful high spirits, I was uncommonly over-excitable; yet it was a most agreeable sense of over-excitability. It was inevitable that a release of tension should follow: but it could assume a different aspect – an agreeable sense of repose – if some pleasure, some external influence inviting a feeling of contentment, were to come my way. But – oh my God! what stubbornness, what tediousness and obtuseness people show in their reluctance to break free from the outside world, – so that the only feeling I have left is regret at ever having counted on the world outside! and this regret is a dreadful torment to me. I am once more tearing at my own flesh, consuming more and more until there will be nothing left to appease my hunger!

Indeed, I have long been inwardly consumed! when I look back on my life, I am bound to say that little sustenance from outside has ever been offered to a mind as needy as my own. Nor have I ever for a moment lived in comfort or at ease: nothing but sharp corners to knock against, – nothing but spikes to tread on! And now, for my recovery – I do not say for my reward (for there is nothing here to reward!) – no! only to regain the ability to consume myself for the sake of *others* – which, in turn, can be my only form of refreshment! – I desire nothing more than – – ah! why should I have to repeat it! – Go to concerts, and to the theatre – to – – amuse yourselves!!

Nothing will come of *my* concert:[1] I have abandoned the idea! I can no longer persuade myself to engage in half-measures and undertake a botched piece of work! The futility, and the impossibility of finding self-satisfaction, emerges all too clearly from this. All further plans which were bound up with this idea have been ruined in advance by the insensitivity of my friends. When I first thought of this concert, my only wish was to be able to hear the Prelude to Lohengrin, but I now renounce the expensive apparatus necessary for realizing this wish. How strange that I must feel as Beethoven did: *he* could not hear his own music because he was *deaf* (nothing else could have prevented *him!*) I cannot hear mine because I am more than deaf, because I do not exist in my own time, because I wander around among you like a ghost, because the whole wide world is full of shits! – Ah, my dear friend! at least *write* as much as you can about me and fill the music journals, so that *I* at least shall become very *famous*: then I may after all get something out of it! Remember

1 See letter [159], p. 281, note 1.

me to my niece *Johanna*, Emilie's[1] dear friend: ah, if only she would put in a good word for me! if she only asks properly, she will certainly succeed, she's a good girl: just tell her how badly off her poor devil of an uncle is! She now has it in her power to help me achieve recognition; for I discover to my very great delight that she has taken a *Prussian Prince* as her lover, and that he has already accomplished a good deal for her – including her contract: perhaps if she is particularly complaisant and if her Mama has no objections, she may obtain what I want! Ah, how happy that would make me, and how blissfully contented the Ritters would then be, watching Tannhäuser in Berlin, where I could ensure a performance if only people were to show some sense, and a little indulgence!! –

Ah! if I were not to get up from my bed tomorrow, if I were no longer to wake up to a life that disgusts me, yes – I should be even more blissfully contented than the Ritters at Tannhäuser!!! – Adieu for today!!

———

Past 11 o'clock! again nothing! – Very well! this letter must go off today, I cannot leave such outpourings lying around in the letterbox. –

It is true, is it not, that it is very unmanly of me to pour out my complaints in this way? that I should do better to imitate the Stoics and smile sweetly when in pain, play the insensate, and pretend I have no feelings, i.e. tell lies and dissemble, in order to be – if not a *true human being* – at least as great a man as possible, one who is "above fate", i.e. someone who wants to play a role, be other than he is, "represent" something, some phantasm, some idea such as L. Bonaparte, for ex., "society"? – and all for the sake of those dear sweet philistines who can say "goodness gracious! what a man!" – No, I want everyone to know – everyone who can take pleasure in my works, i.e. my *life* and what I do, that what gives them pleasure is my *suffering*, my *extreme misfortune*! – My dear friend! I am often now beset by strange thoughts on "art", and on the whole I cannot help finding that, if we had *life*, we should have no need of *art*. Art begins at precisely the point where life breaks off: where nothing more is present, we call out in art, "I wish". I simply do not understand how a *truly happy* individual could ever hit upon the idea of producing "art": only in life can we "achieve" anything, – is our "art" therefore not simply a confession of our impotence?[2] – Indeed! or such at least is *our* art, and all the art which springs from our present dissatisfaction with life. It is no more than "a desire expressed with the utmost clarity"! I should give up *all my art* if, by doing so, I could regain my youth, find health,

1 Emilie Ritter. Negotiations to stage *Tannhäuser* in Berlin were in the process of foundering on Wagner's insistence that Liszt should help prepare the production. Wagner accused Johanna, now leading soprano in Berlin, of not using her influence to have the opera accepted. The Berlin première of *Tannhäuser* finally took place on 7 January 1856.
2 See letter [113], p. 210, note 1 for a similar play on words.

nature, a woman who loved me unreservedly, and fine children! Take it! Give me the rest in return! – Ah, how ludicrous it would be if, with all our enthusiasm for art, what we were fighting over were simply thin air! All right, goodbye for today! You will have had enough!

Yours,
R.W.

SB IV,245–9.

135. THEODOR UHLIG, DRESDEN   [Zurich, 22 January 1852]

[...] Now to the business of who is to be godfather.¹ It is disgraceful that you have to have your child baptized: but if you wish to make this act less demeaning in its symbolical influence, and if you think my acting as godfather will help, take me and I shall gladly assist; I also regard *Karl*² as the *only* rightful person to represent me. Concerning the boy's education, I should be glad to hear the programme you have planned for him: do you intend to inoculate him with the poison of religion and modern education and in that way leave it to the vagaries of fate as to whether he spits out the poison again or whether it in fact destroys him? I do not regard this question as a joke. We hold the future in our hands: shall we be so cowardly and base as to hand over our children to the same butchery which (let us be frank!) has made *us* incapable, incomplete and wicked? In the interests of truth, we have reached a period of our lives when we have now grown unsuited to deriving pleasure from it: is this – at best – to be the fate of our children, too? – [...]

To you and Karl I commend a new friend of mine, the English poet *Shelley*. There is only one German translation of his works in existence, by Seybt, which you must get hold of. He and his friend *Byron* together form a single complete and glorious human being.

You will soon learn that I am in the midst of my Nibelung poem: it is my only salvation.

Fare you well! Greetings to all at home and at the Ritters'.

Yours,
R.W.

53(!) December
1851.³

---

1 Uhlig's son Siegfried had been born in December 1851.
2 Karl Ritter.
3 Wagner hoped that 1852 would witness revolutionary change in Europe, in spite of the set-back of Louis Napoléon's *coup d'état* in Paris on 2 December 1851.

(I shall continue to refer to the month of the *coup d'état* until the hoped-for year of 1852 finally comes.)

SB IV, 254–6.

136. FRANZ LISZT, WEIMAR   Zurich, 30 January 1852

[. . .] May I ask you to convey to the Princess v. Wittgenstein, whose most friendly letter I found so cheering, my warmest thanks for her kindness in writing? The sincere interest which she has again accorded my Lohengrin, especially at its last performance, is of inestimable value to me. What especially enthralled me were her intelligent remarks on the role of Ortrud, and the comparison which she draws between the performance of the earlier interpreter[1] of the part and the present one.[2] To which side I *myself* incline will at once become clear to your honoured friend if I indicate my views on this character simply by saying that Ortrud is a woman who – *does not know love*. This says it all – and a most terrible thing it is to say. Her nature is politics. A *male* politician disgusts us, a *female* politician appals us: it was this appallingness which I had to portray. There is one love which this woman feels, love of the past, of departed generations, the dreadfully insane love of ancestral pride which can express itself only as hatred towards all that lives, all that really exists. In a man such love becomes ludicrous, but in a woman it is terrible, because women – given their powerful and natural need for love – *must* love something, and ancestral pride, a hankering after the past, thus becomes a murderous fanaticism. We know of no more appalling phenomena in the whole of history than women politicians. And so it is not jealousy of Elsa – on Friedrich's account, for example – which motivates Ortrud, rather does her entire passion reveal itself in the scene in Act II when – following Elsa's disappearance from the balcony – she leaps up from the minster steps and calls out to her old, long-vanished gods. She is a reactionary, a woman concerned only for what is outdated and for that reason is hostile to all that is new – and hostile, moreover, in the most rabid sense of the word: she would like to eradicate the world and nature, simply in order to breathe new life into her decaying gods. But this is no idiosyncratic, sickly whim on the part of Ortrud, rather does this passion consume her with the whole weight of a woman's longing for love – a longing which is stunted, undeveloped and deprived of an object: and that is why she is so fearfully

---

1 Josephine Fastlinger sang Ortrud in the first five performances of *Lohengrin* on 28 August, 14 September, 9 October 1850, 12 April and 11 May 1851.
2 For the sixth performance of *Lohengrin* on 4 January 1852, Agathe Auguste Knopp-Fehringer took over the role of Ortrud.

impressive. For that reason, there must be nothing in the least trivial about her portrayal: she must never appear to be simply malicious or spiteful; every expression of her scorn, of her malice, must allow us to glimpse the full force of her terrible madness, which can be satisfied only with the destruction of others, or – of herself.

[. . .]

SB IV,273–4.

137. HANS VON BÜLOW, WEIMAR   Zurich, 30 January 1852

[. . .] I have no particular desire to influence you in your plans for an overture to Romeo & Juliet: but I should like to intimate what virtually amounts to a wish, namely that, before proceeding any further, you read an account of the Coriolanus Overture which I have written to assist our audience's understanding of this work when it is next performed here,[1] and which I shall send you as soon as it is printed. I was delighted to observe that this entire piece of music is no more and no less than the accompaniment to a graphic – almost mimic – scene between C. and his mother and wife in the camp outside Rome. You, too, should conflate the whole of the poem of R. & J. to produce a similar moment of graphic intensity: if you continue to plan the work along philosophical lines, your music can only become increasingly incomprehensible. For – once again – absolute music can express only feelings, passions and moods in their antitheses and degrees of intensity, but not relationships of a social or political nature. Beethoven has a splendid instinct for this: I almost prefer *his* poem of Coriolanus to Shakespeare's, at least as regards its artistic conception, since it has a graphic unity and succinctness which almost allows the subject-matter to achieve the sensuality of myth.

[. . .]

SB IV,275–6.

138. THEODOR UHLIG, DRESDEN   Zurich, [13] February 1852

My dear friend,

I am enclosing my account of the Coriolanus Overture. I have decided against writing a report on the performance for the Zeitung f. Musik:[2] it is

---

1 Wagner conducted Beethoven's *Coriolan* Overture at a subscription concert in Zurich on 17 February 1852. His programme note is reprinted in GS V,173–6; PW III,225–8.

2 *Neue Zeitschrift für Musik.* Uhlig wrote up the following observations and submitted them in the form of a four-part article to the journal in question.

better if I keep my mouth shut for a while there. But what I would have chosen to say on that occasion, I shall now communicate to you with the utmost brevity, in the hope of persuading you to devote a proper article to the subject in question.

The conductor of works such as those of Beethoven has until now rarely understood his true task. Clearly what he must do is transmit to the layman an understanding of these same works: since ultimately this is the outcome of a performance which is in perfect accord with the work, the first question to be asked is how such a performance may be achieved? – What is character-istic about Beethoven's great orchestral works is that they are real poems in which an attempt is made to represent a real object. The difficulty as far as our understanding is concerned lies in accurately identifying the object thus represented. Beethoven was completely imbued with each particular object, his most important tonal creations owe their existence almost exclusively to the individuality of the object which thus imbued him: given this awareness, it seemed to him wholly superfluous to describe this object in further detail, except in his tonal creations themselves. Just as our poets of literature really only communicate themselves to another poet of literature, so Beethoven, involuntarily but in like manner, communicated himself only to the tone-poet. Indeed, the truly absolute musician, i.e. the variationalist of absolute music, could not understand Beethoven any longer, since he was concerned only with the "How?" and not with the "What?": the layman, however, could not help but be totally confused by these tonal creations, or at best he was misled into enjoying what served the tone-poet merely as his expressive material. – Until now the layman has heard Beethoven's tone-poems performed only by absolute musicians: and it goes without saying that this could result only in his failing to understand what he was listening to. For the absolute musician it seemed necessary only to identify the "How?": but it was impossible for him to identify even this correctly, chiefly because he did not understand the "What" that ought to be expressed by this "How". As a result, all contact between conductor and orchestra foundered on a complete lack of under-standing between them: the conductor strove solely to articulate musical phrases which he himself did not understand and which he had made his own rather as one learns melodious verses by heart according to their sound alone when the verses in question are written in a foreign language unknown to the person reciting the poem. In the process, of course, only the most superficial aspects of the work can be taken into account: the speaker can never articulate and emphasize the words according to his own conviction, but must stick strictly and slavishly to the most random superficiality of sound as represented by the phrase he has learned by heart. Judge then what our understanding of a poet would turn out to be if only the sound of the language were to be reproduced and perceived by reciter and listener, as must inevitably be the case if the poem is delivered in a language which neither the reciter (who has learned it by heart on the basis of its sound) nor the listener can understand. This comparison with the character of traditional performances of Beethoven's works will be regarded as an exaggeration only if the language of music – being general – is granted a greater and more immediate intelligibility than a rational language of words. But it is precisely on this point that we delude ourselves as regards what is considered to be "understanding": as long as no actual poetic object is expressed by the language of music, that language may of course be regarded as readily intelligible, since there can be no question here of any real understanding; but if what is expressed by the language of music is determined by a poetic object, this language especially will be utterly unintelligible as long as the poetic object itself is not at the same time precisely described by other means of expression than those of absolute music. – Now, in a piece of music by Beethoven, the poetic object can only be conjectured by the tone-poet himself because – as I remarked previously – Beethoven communicated himself, involuntarily, only to the tone-poet who feels exactly as he does, who shares the same training, and who has almost the same creative powers; this man alone is capable of giving the layman an understanding of these works, and the principal way he can do so is by offering a clear indication of the object of the tone-poem to both the performers and the audience, thus making good an unintentional defect in the technique of the tone-poet who had omitted to make this indication clear. Any other performance of the true Beethoven tone-poems, however technically perfect it may be, must remain correspondingly unintelligible as long as the conductor's understanding of it is not communicated in the way described. The most striking proof of this fact readily emerges from a closer examination of the attitude of our modern concert-going public towards Beethoven's tone-poems. If these works were really understood by the audience, i.e. in accordance with the poetic object, how is it possible for this same audience to accept a modern concert programme? How is it possible, at one and the same concert, to offer the audience of a Beethoven symphony other musical compositions of the most unmitigated vacuousness? But the fact that present-day conductors and composers, for the very reason given (namely their inability to recognize the poetic object of these tonal creations), have remained lacking in any real understanding of the same is proved, is it not, by the works which they nowadays compose, and their manner of composition, in spite of Beethoven's admonitory precedent? Would the vague and disjointed note-spinning of modern instrumental music be possible if composers had understood the true essence of Beethoven's tone-poems? And what this essence entails is that Beethoven's longer compositions are only secondarily music, but that first and foremost they contain a poetic object. Or might it be argued that this *object* was perhaps taken simply from the music? Would that not be the same as if the poet were to take his theme from language, the painter his from colour? – But the conductor who perceives only music in a piece by Beethoven is just like the reciter who sticks only to the language of a poem, or like a person interpreting a painting who sticks only to the colours on the canvas. In the case of present-day conductors (many of whom do not even understand the music), the situation at best is as follows: – they can identify the key, the theme, the part-writing, the instrumentation etc. and with that they think they have identified everything that is present in the piece of music.

It is the non-musician who has led the way to a true understanding of Beethoven's works: quite involuntarily he desired to know what the composer had actually had in mind when writing the music. This led to the first difficulty. Imagination, in its search for understanding, fell back upon all manner of arbitrary inventions of bizarre features and romantic images. The grotesque and generally trivial nature of the ideas imputed in this way to Beethoven's compositions was soon sensed by those whose feelings in the matter were more refined, and thus such ideas came to be rejected. Since these images were inappropriate, it was thought better to reject all such ideas entirely. And yet a perfectly legitimate feeling lay behind this urge to create such images: but the only person capable of identifying the desired object (an object which the tone-poet himself had had in mind – without necessarily knowing it) was the one man who, in turn, was entirely familiar with the characteristic essence of the work in question. Certainly, the great difficulty in making such an identification once again lay in the character of the object itself, which the tone-poet presented to us in the tone-painting alone: only those who fully recognized this difficulty, too, might successfully hazard an attempt to foster in others a true and necessary understanding. Here you can tell the story of the Ninth Symphony in Dresden[1] – and what really matters – the striking success I had in placing this work in the correct light, in spite of its reputation for being so extremely difficult. – You can also mention here that I never again agreed to performing Beethoven's compositions without in some way influencing people's understanding in the way described, and that what drove me to do so was simply my inescapable awareness of the need for such an understanding. What always struck me above all else was the effect which my approach had on practising musicians themselves. Here in Zurich I have enabled the most hidebound dance musicians to achieve things of which neither their audiences nor they themselves had previously had the least idea. Pretend all this is based upon private conversations – as though K.,[2] for ex., had told it to you. – Now you can adduce the "Eroica

---

1 Conducted by Wagner on 5 April 1846 and revived on 28 March 1847. His programme note, based upon quotations from Goethe's *Faust*, appears in GS II,56–64; PW VII,247–55.
2 Karl Ritter.

Symphony",[1] and report what a great impression was made, especially upon the musicians, as a result of their understanding the work. I must add that my principal remarks were made by word of mouth at the rehearsals – at the relevant points in the score. My most notable success in describing any poetic object was in the case of the "Coriolanus Overture". I may say that those who have read carefully my interpretation of this work and who have followed the argument through, stage by stage, must admit that, without this interpretation of mine, they would *never* have understood this uniquely graphic piece of music unless they themselves had already succeeded in isolating this one particular scene on the basis of the general description "Overture to Coriolanus", as I myself succeeded in doing. Given such an understanding, the enjoyment of such a piece of music then becomes overwhelmingly sublime: almost all our musicians now share it. – etc. – etc. –

The aim of this endeavour?? – *Drama!!*

It is in this sense, my good friend, and in this sense alone that the Zeitung für Musik must henceforth report matters: you see how much there is to say here. But you must all stick to the maxim which I advanced in my letter to Brendel,[2] "music must be singled out, emphasized and encouraged wherever it develops in the direction of poetry, but where it diverges from that direction, the misguided and erroneous nature of the same must be pointed out and condemned." Nothing further shall be done for now. –

If nothing happens, I shall not be too concerned – for, in the final analysis, my salvation scarcely depends upon the Zeitung für Musik. – Adieu for today! –

[. . .]

SB IV,285–9.

139. HANS VON BÜLOW, WEIMAR   Zurich, 15 February 1852

Dear Hans,

Today I want to send you my account of the Coriolanus Overture and to accompany it with a few lines: I do not suppose it will be much, since my nerves are giving me a devil of a time; I keep having to flatter and cajole them to stop them from growing rebellious.

---

1 Conducted by Wagner in Zurich on 25 February 1851. His programme note was published in the *Eidgenössische Zeitung* of 23 February 1851 and reprinted in GS V,169–72; PW III,221–4.

2 Letter of [25] January 1852 (SB IV,257–68) to Franz Brendel, published in the *Neue Zeitschrift für Musik*, xxxvi (1852), 57ff and reprinted, in slightly revised form, in GS V,53–65 under the title *Über musikalische Kritik* (On Musical Criticism); PW III,59–74.

I have recently written to Uhlig[1] concerning a practice I have adopted in performing Beethoven's instrumental works and which I consider uniquely suited to the spread of *understanding*; I hope my letter will induce him to write an article on this extremely important subject. – If you undertake a detailed comparison, feature by feature, of my own account of the graphic and poetic content of the Coriolanus Overture with the composition itself, you will, I am sure, admit the justice of my view, and at the same time be bound to concede that all attempts to convey an understanding of such works, although hitherto regarded as the absolute preserve of the absolute musician, have so far met with total failure on the latter's part. Only now have *I* been able to perform this work in such a way that what the poetic composer intended is conveyed clearly and intelligibly at all times: the effect that this has had on the purely musical execution of the work is unbelievable. By the way! – the figure in the middle section must always be executed as follows:

 etc.

without this accent, the whole phrase remains expressionless. –

The scene you are looking for in Romeo & Juliet you will not, I think, find anywhere in Shakespeare's play: Shakespeare is an out and out historian, who constructs his plays entirely out of historical detail. You will best find it – for all its superficiality – in the Italian libretto,[2] for necessity has here forced the librettist to concentrate his material against his will. I am thinking of the "famous" finale (E flat major). Here you have the whole graphic subject-matter of the poem encapsulated in a single moment: treat the theme nobly where in Bellini it was trivial. *Hatred* as an all-pervasive element: enthusiastic *love* springing up as a surprising offshoot of this element. But no "fatal/political" motif – instead, *hatred* as pure passion: love, tender in its beginnings, growing ardent, reaching its jubilant climax, – finally consumed by the element of hatred which, inwardly consumed, fades into a lament. Thus: the triumphs of love! –

But this is your own affair, and I do you a great injustice by speaking out so passionately against you; once before I did the same thing – with your suggestion for an Oresteia Symphony:[3] and who did not even reply to me on this point? – my good friend Hans! –

Why provoke me with your architect? – Do you not see that all our plastic arts derive from architecture and that they are all parts of it? – In the architect,

1 See letter [138], pp. 249–53.
2 Bellini's *I Capuleti e i Montecchi*, to a libretto by Felice Romani.
3 Bülow had been contemplating an overture on the subject of the *Oresteia*, but Wagner (in a letter of 12 May 1851) had urged him to make the work a symphony. Neither this project nor Bülow's proposed Romeo and Juliet Overture came to anything.

purely human needs (initially: somewhere to live) generate an artistic intent, just as, in the case of the poet, the artistic intent grows out of the need of life itself; in order to realize this intent, what the architect needs is first a sculptor and finally a painter in order, as far as possible, to give his mathematical straight lines, angles and corners the instinctive shapes of amorphous nature. However – this is not something I can express here quite so succinctly. Only this much: the architect comes into the most direct contact with life's innermost necessity: not only in building a house, but in designing every bench, table and crate, it is the *architect* (the constructor of naked form) who acts first: he is inspired to create his *greatest* work of art by the *greatest* of human needs, and that is the poetic need; and here he comes into direct contact with the poet; prior to that contact, he grows independently out of life. Certainly, a completely independent work of architectural art, unconditioned either by the needs of everyday life or, ultimately, by any poetic need, is unknown to me, though not to King Ludwig of Bavaria etc. This work of art can rest only upon *imitation*, in other words – an imitation of architectonic works of art which, at another time and in different circumstances, met some real, if intrinsically exaggerated and luxurious, need. In its time, however, the Greek temple was a real, religious necessity to the Hellene; no less, in their way, were the churches of the Middle Ages etc. These sprang from an almost artistic need. We *ourselves* shall have only our theatres to meet this need in the future, since our greatest artistic need can no longer be of an ecclesiastically religious nor of a princely luxurious nature. I know not a single work of absolute art, and therefore no absolute work of architectural art. –

[. . .]

SB IV,292–4.

140. THEODOR UHLIG, DRESDEN   [Zurich, 26 February 1852]

[. . .] A few new acquaintances have forced themselves upon me: as far as the spear side is concerned, I am utterly indifferent, but rather less so as regards the distaff side. A rich young merchant, Wesendonk – brother of the Reichstag member – settled here some time ago, and did so with a great show of luxury: his wife is very pretty, and seems to have taken a fancy to me thanks to the Preface to my 3 opera poems. The same is true of a number of Swiss families from the local aristocracy (I speak only of the women – for the men are dreadful.) It astonishes me to find so much liveliness and even charm among them. – Let me take this opportunity to reassure you that there is nothing to fear! There will be no more "scandals"![1] – It is true that I can no longer find any pleasure in other people's company, not even in that of women: yet this latter element continues to be the only thing that now and again helps me to maintain my illusions, for I can no longer entertain any illusions about men. [...]

SB IV,301.

141. THEODOR UHLIG, DRESDEN   [Zurich, 6/7 May 1852]

[...] As regards the role of man of letters which I have been playing in recent years, I have to say that this role has now begun to irk me greatly. If I look back on it with any satisfaction, it is only because I feel that in the process my own thoughts on the subject have become perfectly clear. But it can only fill me with a sense of indignation and depress me to the very depths of my being to observe the impression which my writings have made on the outside world. Tell me, among all the voices which have so far been raised on the subject, is there a single person who might be thought capable of understanding what is at issue here? It is true, I had a low opinion of present-day writers on art, but I never expected to find such unmitigated wretchedness! People have grown so dreadfully stupid that they – literally – no longer know how to *read*: am I now expected to have to teach them how to read as well? – – [...]

SB IV,355–6.

142. FRANZ LISZT, WEIMAR   Zurich, 29 May 1852

[...] As regards your (future!) plans for a *complete* performance of Tannhäuser, there are still a number of things on my mind which it will not be easy to unload. Firstly: some minor points! I do not know for certain whether in your performances Walther von der Vogelweide sang his aria in the Tournament of Song in B flat major (as in the original) or in C major? There is an inconsistency here. I know that B flat major does not accord with the remaining tessitura of his (fairly high-lying) role, and a singer who has the voice for the rest of the part will therefore be ineffectual in the lower key of B flat major: that is why I was obliged in Dresden to have the piece transposed up to C major. This C major, however, ill accords with the key-

---

1 A reference to Wagner's affair with Jessie Laussot in the summer of 1850; see letters [106] – [111], pp. 191–208.

relationships of the arias on either side of it in the Tournament of Song; in particular, the transition to the brighter key of Tannhäuser's ensuing aria in C major loses its intensity. At the same time, the higher key of C major means that Walther's aria suffers a grievous loss of that sense of calm dignity which constitutes its characteristic tone. This conflict can be resolved only by having the role of Walther sung by a *low* tenor, while that of *Heinrich der Schreiber* is sung by a *high* tenor. Both parts will then have to be re-written so that *in all the ensemble passages* the vocal line which in the score is allotted to *Heinrich d. Schr.* must be given to Walther and, conversely, the former must sing the vocal line which *Walther* has there. But Walther must retain all the *solo passages* (in the first finale.) This is something I should gladly have seen to myself! Next! – You'll now be giving the scene between Tannhäuser and Venus complete? I think I have already explained the necessity for retaining all *three* verses of Tannhäuser's song? –

But now to the main point! i.e. – *the great adagio of the second finale*!! When I made a cut in this adagio following the first performance of Tannhäuser in Dresden, I was in a state of utter despair, and in my heart I wrote off all my hopes for Tannhäuser, because I saw that *Tichatschek* could not understand it and that he was thus even less capable of playing the part! The fact that I had to make *this* cut was tantamount to renouncing any aim I might have had of ensuring a true understanding of the work! I beg you, my dearest friend, to look closely at the passage which was cut and convince yourself as to what it contains! After everyone on stage has formed a group around the intercessional figure of Elisabeth and after *she* has assumed the central position, leaving the others merely to listen to her or else to repeat what she says and sings, Tannhäuser, suddenly aware of his dreadful crime, succumbs to the most dreadful contrition, and – on finally finding the words to express himself – words which initially fail him as he lies on the ground as though unconscious, – it is now *he* who becomes the only person that matters, so that the others all now form a group around *him*, as they had done previously around Elisabeth. Everything else recedes in importance, so that it is, as it were, he alone whom the others accompany when he sings:

> To save my soul from loss eternal
> An angel came from heav'n above;
> Ah, why in madness was I driven
> So to profane her spotless love?
> Great God, thron'd in the starry heights of heaven,
> Who sent'st Thine angel from her lofty place,
> Oh pity me who, sunk so deep in evil,
> Dar'd to reject the herald of Thy grace![1]

1 GS II,28; verse translation by Paul England.

In this verse and in the music to which it is sung lies the entire meaning of Tannhäuser's catastrophe, nay, it is the unique expression of Tannhäuser's entire being, which made him such a moving figure for me. All his suffering, his bloody pilgrimage, everything stems from the sense contained within these strophes: unless we hear them at this point, and precisely at this point, and unless we hear them, moreover, as they must be heard, Tannhäuser as a whole remains incomprehensible, an arbitrary, vacillating – pitiful figure, (the beginning of his narration in the last act comes too late to make good what must engage our feelings here with all the violence of a storm!) Not only the end of the 2nd act, but the whole of the third act, indeed – in a certain sense – the entire drama will be effective, as regards its true content, only if the central point of the entire drama, around which it develops as though around its own kernel, emerges clearly and distinctly in this particular passage. – And this passage, the key to my entire work, had to be cut in Dresden, – why? – because it turned out that Tichatschek had no inkling of his task as a dramatic performer, but interpreted his entire role as that of a singer endowed with an outstanding voice. It was precisely here, however, that it became clear how ineffectual in the face of his true dramatic task is the mere possession of material means since the latter forsook the singer at the very point where he felt most dependent upon them. Because Tichatschek could neither understand this passage (as a result of his preternaturally small brain capacity!) nor depict its content, he could not sing it either! His voice gave out at the very point where he could have been effective only if he had allowed his entire being to pour itself out – regardless of whether it was by vocal means or any other – in order to vent himself of an overpowering emotion. Our good friend Tichatschek, beaming bemusedly into the footlights with the look of a good-natured sheep, all the while singing (in tender, dulcet tones) the eighth line of a vocal octet, was unable to produce the note A at the words "Oh pity me"!! I do not possess even a fraction of his voice, yet I can produce a splendid *A* at this point! Of course this "A" does not require to be "*sung*", but must be hurled forth by the singer straining every sinew of his breast, like a sword with which Tannhäuser intends to kill himself. – All attempts to parley with my Dresden tenor were useless: he did not know what was at issue, and kept on maintaining that it was a difficult passage, as his throat kept telling him! – Well, I spared his throat, and cut the passage, since no living soul could have guessed – from the way in which Tichatschek was performing it – what was going on here; all that could be heard here was simply Tannhäuser singing an "inner part" which, in itself – as a series of notes – , is no longer ear-catching; the musical *environment* became the important point – so that the whole thing seemed a longueur which could easily be cut, something I proceeded to do, if for no other reason than because I could not bring myself to listen to it performed in this way. – But – I shall now say *this*: no performance of Tannhäuser accords with my intentions *if this passage* has to be omitted! For the sake of this passage I agree, if need be, to the cut in the allegro of the finale, where what is omitted is really only a continuation of the earlier passage, i.e. where Elisabeth takes up the B major theme as a canto fermo, and Tannhäuser, in his wild despair, pours out his feelings in such passionate terms. If ever a performance of this opera is to meet with complete satisfaction on my part, Tannhäuser must sing *this* passage, too, and in such a way that it does not seem over-long. –

You will now want to know what is to be done about this? can we demand of a lesser singer what a man like Tichatschek was incapable of bringing off? – To this I would say that, in spite of his voice, Tichatschek – given the obstinacy of his temperament and the smallness of his brain – was incapable of bringing off a great many things of which many less gifted singers were capable, provided they were able to understand what was at issue. At the Tannhäuser rehearsal which I attended in Weimar,[1] *Götze*, who was otherwise quite useless, brought off certain passages and clarified certain intentions which Tichatschek had repeatedly failed to do for me. The latter, you see, has a voice which is brilliant and tender by turns, but which lacks any genuine *accent of suffering*. Our local singer in the role of the Flying Dutchman[2] achieved far more for me than the performers in Dresden[3] and Berlin,[4] in spite of their having superior voices. – See what you can do with Herr Beck, and make clear to him what is at issue. – If this passage comes off, your Weimar audience will be the first to understand what is going on here! – (A further technical observation at this point: – if the singer is certain of himself during this passage, leave him free to determine the tempo, the others will have to follow him, – he alone is in command!)

If a performance of Tannh. is to be wholly perfect, the definitive ending of the opera must be given complete as it appears in the new edition of the vocal score, *with* the chorus of younger pilgrims.[5] –

But that's enough of that! I imagine your head is already spinning! –

All you have to do is send your own score of the flying Dutchman to Uhlig: he has in his possession the revised score and will prepare your own copy from it.[6] Once the rehearsal period draws closer, I shall write to you again concerning individual details: but for now it reassures me to know that the parts have all been written out on the basis of Uhlig's copy of the score, and

---

1 On 14 May 1849. The tenor was Franz Götze.
2 Franz Pichon. Wagner conducted four performances of *Der fliegende Holländer* in Zurich in a revised orchestration on 25, 28 and 30 April, and 2 May 1852.
3 Michael Wächter.
4 Louis Böttiger.
5 See letter [78], p. 138, note 3.
6 The Weimar première of *Der fliegende Holländer* took place on 16 February 1853, with Liszt conducting.

that scenery and sets will be based on the sketches which I hope you will be receiving from Caëssmann.[1]

The flying Dutchman *here* has left an indescribable impression: philistines who could otherwise never be persuaded to set foot in the theatre or concert-hall attended each of the 4 performances within the space of a single week, and are now regarded as being insane. I myself am now very much in favour with all the *women* here. Vocal scores are being ordered by the half-dozen.

I have now moved to the country[2] and feel to be in tolerably high spirits. In addition my work is again giving me pleasure: my entire Nibelung-tetralogy is finished in complete draft form,[3] and in a few months the verses should be ready too. From then on I shall once again become solely and exclusively a "music maker", – since this work will no doubt be my last poem, and I hope I shall never again return to journalism. My head is filled only with plans to stage the work: nothing more shall be written, but only performed. I hope you will help me in this! –

[. . .]

SB IV,375–9.

143. THEODOR UHLIG, DRESDEN   Zurich, 31 May 1852

[. . .] I have now made a proper start on my course of treatment: apart from my diet – from which I do not exclude the occasional glass of good wine – it consists of a cold bath in the morning and a fifteen-minute warm one (22 degrees) in the evening. Its effect on me is most soothing and gently invigorating. Above all, it does me good to get out into the open air, where I wander around for 2 – 3 hours every morning before settling down to my work. The time I spend at work never lasts more than 2 hours: through working for 5 – 6 hours, as I often used to do in the past, I seriously overtaxed my nerves. – I have now finished the complete draft of the "Valkyrie" (I): tomorrow I shall make a start on the verses.

I am again more than ever moved by the comprehensive grandeur and beauty of my subject: my entire philosophy of life has found its most perfect artistic expression here. How I wish you were here so that we might often

1 The Hamburg set-builder Ludwig Caëssmann prepared design sketches for the Zurich production of *Der fliegende Holländer*, based upon Wagner's own instructions.
2 Wagner and Minna rented rooms at the Pension Rinderknecht on the Zürichberg from 12 May until 7 July 1852.
3 The prose draft of *Der Raub des Rheingolds* was written down between 23 and 31 March 1852, that of *Die Walküre* between 17 and 26 May. *Die Walküre* was versified between 1 June and 1 July 1852, *Das Rheingold* between 15 September and 3 November.

talk together, and I could tell you things which I now have to save for such time as I can submit them to you in written form. – After this work I do not suppose I shall ever write another opera poem! it is the finest and most perfect work ever to have flowed from my pen. Once the verses are finished, I shall then return to being a musician once more, and then be only – a *performing artist!* I almost hope that I live – or be allowed to live – long enough to do so. –

There were many things I had to tell you, arising from various essays about myself which I have read: I may tell you what these things are at a later date. I have just read the first two articles by Julius Schäffer in the N.B.M.Z.,[1] and it was once more a matter for regret that the man has not yet read my "Preface".[2] What he says, for ex., about alliterative verse (which he cannot find in Lohengrin!) would then have been impossible. But what he says about the "dissolution of the individuality of the various tonalities" could be the starting-point for an interesting discussion. In the IIIrd volume of "Opera & Drama" I demonstrated that harmony becomes something *real* (rather than purely imaginary) only in the polyphonic symphony, i.e. in the orchestra, so that the purely imaginary individuality of tonalities (apologies to Hitzschold)[3] must merge into the reality of the individuality of the different instruments, their manifold colouring and, finally, their style of execution. By clinging to the "individuality" of tonalities, people were clinging to a chimera which, it must be said, had earlier become just as much of a dogma with us as the Dear Lord above. On the contrary, it is the instruments themselves and, ultimately, the human voice *when singing words* which give a particular character to the tonality and to notes in general; thus, for ex., the characteristic individuality of a key such as E major or E flat major emerges most distinctively when played on a violin or a wind instrument, and so it would be a case of doing things by halves if I were to use a key for its own sake and thereby ignore the instrument, or, conversely, to use the instrument for its own sake alone. The instrumental musicians of the earlier century did not know this, they still proceeded on the basis of harmonic dogma: but compare their instrumentation with that of Beethoven and, finally, with mine! – The person who, in judging my music, divorces the harmony from the instrumentation does me as great an injustice as the one who divorces my music from my poem, my vocal line from the words! – Yet in all these matters I have committed the error of having communicated my theories prematurely: I still owe the world what really matters, namely the work of art which, I may add,

---

1 *Neue Berliner Musikzeitung*, xx (12 May 1852), 153ff and 161ff.
2 *A Communication to my Friends.*
3 August Hitzschold, like Wagner, had settled in Zurich after the failure of the Dresden uprising. Three of his notices on the musical life of Zurich appeared in the *Neue Zeitschrift für Musik* between August 1851 and January 1852.

had already matured within me before the theory was ever formulated. –
[. . .]

SB IV,384–6.

144. FRANZ LISZT, WEIMAR   [Zurich,] 16 June 1852

Dearest of friends,
  A request!
  I am hard at work and am hoping to have finished the poem of my
"Valkyrie" within the next 2 weeks.[1] I shall then be in urgent need of some
form of relaxation such as a holiday, the more so since I should prefer not
to finish my final poetic work, the great prelude, here in Zurich, where the
monotony of these familiar surroundings oppresses me, and tiresome visits
generally put me out of humour. I must go up into the Alps and get at least
a taste of Italy's frontier where I may be able to stay for a while. But I cannot
afford such extravagances on my ordinary income. For next winter I have a
few extra receipts to look forward to: (Tannhäuser in Leipzig and presumably
also in Breslau.)[2] Above all, however, I am counting on the receipts which
you will provide me with from the *flying Dutchman* in Weimar.[3] No doubt I
may reckon on 20 to 25 louis d'or? How would it be if you provided me with
this sum *by way of an advance?*
  If Ziegesar is not yet back in charge of business, I should prefer not to
approach the box-office directly for this advance on my fee: but there may
perhaps be some well-meaning individual who would not refuse you this sum
by way of an advance? At the same time you yourself would be the best
guarantee that the revenues in question would actually accrue, since your
enthusiastic zeal will certainly ensure that the flying Dutchman is performed
this coming winter in Weimar. – This advance would be a source of *great
pleasure* to me!! – But – I need the money before the *end* of the month at the
latest! See if it is possible to arrange this![4]
  My *Valkyrie* (1st drama) is turning out to be terribly beautiful! – I hope to
be able to submit the *entire* poem of the tetralogy to you before the end of
the summer. The music will then proceed very easily and quickly: for it is
simply a question of *carrying out* what is already *finished*.

1 See letter [142], p. 260, note 3.
2 The first performance of *Tannhäuser* in Leipzig took place on 31 January 1853; Breslau had
  earlier heard the work on 6 October 1852.
3 *Der fliegende Holländer* was first produced in Weimar on 16 February 1853; see also letter
  [142], p. 259.
4 Liszt sent Wagner a bill of exchange for 100 thalers. Wagner set off on a walking tour of the
  Alps on 10 July, returning to Zurich on 5 August.

Fare you well! Send me word soon about how you are! Has the Imperial Russian Tannhäuser come off yet?[1] Are you now having great problems with your music festival?[2] I wish you every success, and hope that it gives you pleasure!

As ever

yours

Richard W.

Is it true that it will be the turn of Tannhäuser in *Munich* next winter?[3] It is news to me. It would certainly not be to Herr Dingelstedt's discredit if he had such a plan in mind! –

SB IV,392–3.

145. THEODOR UHLIG, DRESDEN   Meiringen, 15 July [1852]

[...] I have now been away for 6 days:[4] I can tell how long it has been from my purse, since each day regularly costs me a 20-franc piece. It is glorious here, and I have often thought about you in the course of my travels. Yesterday I came down from the Faulhorn (8261 feet high): there I had an awesomely sublime view of the mountain ice, the snow and the glacier world of the Bernese Alps, which seem to lie so close in front of you that you could almost reach out and touch them. – I am walking a lot, and am very good on my feet; only my head continues to be a source of dissatisfaction; my cerebral nerves are in an appalling state: overexcitement or lassitude – but no real sense of calm! I do not suppose I shall ever get much better: no treatment in the world can help where there is only one true remedy – and that is for me to be someone other than I am. The real reason for my suffering lies in my extraordinary relationship with the world and my surroundings, neither of which is capable of giving me any pleasure any longer: everything is a torture and a torment to me – a sense of inadequacy! How worthless people are, and how they have vexed me time and again in the course of this journey, amidst the wonders of nature: I am always repulsed by a sense of disgust, and yet – how I long to be with people! – But this worthless rabble! ugh!! –
[...]

SB IV,408–9.

1 A performance of *Tannhäuser* was announced to mark a visit to Weimar by the Tsarina Alexandra Feodorovna on 31 May 1852.
2 A festival held in Ballenstedt on 22 and 23 June 1852, when Liszt conducted the *Tannhäuser* Overture and the duet from Act II of *Der fliegende Holländer*.
3 Tannhäuser was not performed in Munich until 12 August 1855.
4 See letter [144], p. 262, note 4.

146. THEODOR UHLIG, DRESDEN   Lugano, 22 July 1852

[. . .] My first Italian conversation was a delightful affair: try as I might, I could not remember the Italian for *milk*, since it is a well-known fact that this word never appears in any of the Italian operas from which I draw my knowledge of the language. But you soon couldn't have told me apart from *Vestri*,[1] and you'll have a clear picture of me if you imagine this hot-blooded son of the south. – I drove back that same evening by coach from Domodossola to Baveno on Lago Maggiore: this journey crowned the whole day; I felt blissfully happy returning from the wilds to such a charming spot. Unfortunately, the very next day this peaceful mood of mine was shattered by the rabble of humanity: on board the steamer – full of Italian philistines, though no worse for that – poor creatures, chickens and ducks (which were being transported) were so abjectly tormented and left to starve in such terrible fashion that I was once again filled with a sense of raging fury at the appalling insensitivity of those people who countenanced such a sight. To think that one would only be ridiculed if one tried to intervene!! – In general, my dear friend, my views on the human race are growing increasingly gloomy: on the whole I cannot help feeling that this race of ours has no alternative but to perish utterly. –
    [. . .]

SB IV,419.

147. JAKOB SULZER, ZURICH   Lugano, 26 July [1852]

My dearest friend,
    It will no doubt cost me my entire Frankfurt "Tannhäuser",[2] but you are going to have to forward to me another 5 louis d'or (i.e. 100 fr.), which I would ask you to send to me in *Geneva*, poste restante. I should add that my wife and I began making plans this morning, and it was decided to go via the Borromean Islands, Domodossola, Simplon, Wallis etc. as far as *Chamonny*,[3] so that we shall then fetch up in Geneva, where there is the possibility of our arriving without a sou to our name. It was stupid of me not to have asked for 500 fr. all at once, since it amounted to the same thing. Now you must swallow another bitter pill and further deplete the finances of the canton of

1 Giovanni Vestri had been a member of the Dresden Opera ensemble.
2 i.e. the fee of 25 louis d'or which Wagner was to receive for *Tannhäuser* in Frankfurt. The work was first performed there on 15 February 1853.
3 Chamonix in the French Alps.

Zurich for our benefit: but do not worry, "Tannhäuser" will help you out of the frying pan – into the Venusberg of a satisfied conscience.[1]

I was delighted at Minna's arrival.[2] I shall reward her by showing her things that are really worth seeing. And we shall certainly bring back some charming memento for you as well.

Fare you well, and may it please you to convey my very best wishes to all our friends. Kind regards from my wife and from

Yours,
R. Wagner.

SB IV,425–6.

148. JULIE RITTER, DRESDEN   Zurich, 7 August 1852

Most honoured friend,

I have once again thought so much about you, concerned myself so much with you, and, at the same time, had so much cause to feel grateful for all you have done for me that I now, more than ever before, feel impelled to converse with you for a moment.

I have just returned from a journey which must certainly have been unique of its kind. I expect you will already have been informed by Uhlig of all the places I visited: from Lugano I went with my wife (whom I summoned to join me there) back to Lago Maggiore, across the Simplon to Wallis and Chammonix, and via Geneva back to Zurich. I was away for around 4 weeks. The cost of this wonderful journey was met through your own kindness inasmuch as I was able to use certain revenues which are due to me for the purposes of this holiday rather than for my immediate livelihood. I needed a holiday. I had previously completed the poem of the "Valkyrie" in the space of a month, without any interruption, and I could tell only too well from the results of this exertion how things really stood with me. My cerebral nerves were so badly affected that I found myself (other people of course can understand none of this) in a desperate state, but this much at least was clear, namely that if I am to produce anything else, it can only be achieved by subjecting my entire nervous system to a most elaborate course of treatment. Above all, I need a will of iron to keep a close check on myself, more especially to be able to break off completely from my work, both quickly and at frequent intervals, so that, by dint of regular outings, I may distract my cerebral nerves from their present self-destructive course. I had hoped initially that an

---

1 Sulzer, who was cantonal secretary in Zurich, lent Wagner 25 louis d'or on this occasion. The following year he was instrumental in obtaining Otto Wesendonck's help for Wagner.
2 Minna joined Wagner in Lugano on 24 July 1852.

extended holiday would help me to recover my health: the very thought of being able to savour the pleasures of Italy's border had something uncommonly refreshing about it for me. But this journey has radically altered my view of myself, and its effect upon me has been to rob me of my last remaining illusions. I cannot of course deny that, on entering Italy, I was overcome by a sense of genuine delight; but I can no longer suppress the admission that – life no longer has any happiness to offer me. It was precisely there that I realized I am no longer capable of enjoying life, now that I have lost my youth. Yes, indeed – my dear Frau Ritter, I remained young until a certain event[1] in my life with which you are already very familiar: then I became old over night. I now know that I have no more hopes for the future! On one unique and decisive occasion I tried to seize hold of life as it really is, to hold it tight, and to find in it my salvation: it passed me by, I sank back into the world of my own imaginings, and was forced to seek sustenance not in my heart but in my head, a furious effort which now consumes me, – and which will finally destroy me! There is nothing, nothing that I can conceal from myself in the long term by dint of my own imaginings; again and again I am *forced* to see through this elaborate illusion, no dream can gain hold of me, no theoretical pleasure can give me true enjoyment, and so I have finally lost all capacity for any enjoyment, with the result that I was soon bound to feel utterly alone and unhappy in Italy. – I returned via Geneva! well, I was calm, and I was pleased that it all gave my good wife a great deal of pleasure: indeed, I myself no longer felt any sense of pain, but only astonishment that I had to remain in the land of the living! – –

Since I am, after all, an artist, I shall continue to lead this artificial life of mine as long as I can. Of course, only my art can still sustain me and disguise from me how insipid my life has become. The enormous effort it takes to do so is something I must seek to lessen as best I can. What this principally means is that I must at least spare myself the feelings of pain occasioned by over-frequent contact with the foolish world: a little house with a little garden, far off on the lake, in such a place I now believe I have discovered the surest means which art can offer of keeping myself alive. And it almost seems as though this final wish of mine, as it relates to my life, might yet be fulfilled: the German theatres are gradually helping themselves to my operas, and even the King of Prussia has recently commanded a performance of Tannhäuser to mark his birthday: however, nothing may come of it, for I have made so bold as to demand a very considerable fee from them in Berlin;[2] and yet, if

1 Wagner's affair with Jessie Laussot in the summer of 1850; see also letters [106]-[111] and [140], pp. 191–208 and 255–6.
2 The first performance of *Tannhäuser* in the Prussian capital was delayed until 7 January 1856, a delay caused partly by Wagner's insistence upon a fee of 1000 thalers. See also letter [134], p. 246, note 1.

you remain loyal to me, it now looks as though I might still think of fulfilling the only wish which I have left in life. –

[. . .]

SB IV,431–3.

149. FRANZ LISZT, WEIMAR   Zurich, 8 September 1852

A thousand thanks to you, best of friends, for your recent letter! Unfortunately, I cannot respond to it in the way I should like: my cerebral nerves are again causing me so much pain that for some time now I have been instructed to give up reading and writing – I might almost say all intellectual life! Even the briefest letter exhausts me dreadfully, and only a complete rest can – or could – really restore me to health (but where and how shall I find it?). – This is not intended as a complaint, but simply as an explanation of why it is that, in all that I have to tell you today, I shall be short and to the point, and stick only to essentials. Do not, therefore, be angry with me if I do not write to you with the cheerful circumstantiality with which I generally seek to make amends for the impossibility of our personal dealings. –

I am still not entirely clear as to how things stand with Berlin: *Hülsen* regards my demand[1] as a vote of no-confidence in his personal opinion; I had to disabuse him of this error by burdening his conscience with the assurance that I have the most unquestioning faith in him. I now ask no more from him than that he proves by means of a few well-chosen words that he is perfectly aware of the difficult situation in which I find myself with regard to Tannhäuser in Berlin, and that he undertakes to perform the work with the firm intention of overcoming this same difficult situation. I shall then leave him to deal with the whole question of my fee. – *Something* at least has served to reassure me in recent weeks: I drew up a fairly detailed set of instructions for performing Tannhäuser,[2] and had it printed, and have sent sufficient copies of the brochure to all the theatres which have ordered copies of the full score. I hope it will be of some use. I am enclosing half a dozen copies herewith. The piece will not contain much that is new to you, since I have already conveyed most of its contents to you by letter: yet you may find it useful in supporting you in your plans to mount a new production of Tannhäuser, especially if you communicate its contents to the producer and singers. That was really what I wanted to ask of you. (I might add that, as

1 That Liszt should conduct the rehearsals of *Tannhäuser;* see letter [134], p. 246, note 1, and [148], p. 266, note 2.
2 *Über die Aufführung des "Tannhäuser"*, completed on 23 August 1852, published in brochure form the same month, and later taken up into GS V,123–59; PW III,167–205.

always, it was a perfect torment for me to have to write this piece! this endless correspondence with printers is dreadful, the more so when what is at issue is something whose significance I have long since outgrown! Indeed, if I still concern myself with my earlier operas, it is simply because of force of circumstances, certainly not because of any inclination on my part to make reparations for the past.)

This brings me on to *Berlioz* and *Raff*. To be frank, it saddens me that Berlioz is still intending to revise his Cellini,[1] or rather that he has to do so at all! If I am not mistaken, the work is over 12 years old: has Berlioz not developed in the mean time, in order to produce something quite new now? What pitiful self-confidence if he now has to go back to so comparatively early a work. *Bülow* is quite right in his assessment of what it is that is wrong with Cellini: it is the *poem*, and the unnatural position which the musician was driven to adopt in his attempt to cover up a shortcoming by purely musical means – a shortcoming which the poet *alone* can make good. Berlioz will simply never be able to improve Cellini: but who is worth more, Cellini – or Berlioz? Abandon the former, and throw your weight behind the latter! For me, there is something quite gruesome about having to stand by and observe these galvanizing attempts at resuscitation! For heaven's sake, let Berlioz write *a new opera*; it will be his *supreme misfortune* if he does not, for there is one thing alone that can save him: *drama*, just as there is one thing alone that will drag him further and further down, his *obstinate avoidance of this uniquely valid expedient*, – and this view of mine is only confirmed by his renewed preoccupation with an earlier work in which it was precisely the *poet* who let him down and whom he keeps on trying to replace by means of his music. Believe me, – I *like* Berlioz, even though he distrustfully and obstinately refuses to come near me: he does not *know* me, – but *I* know *him*. If I expect anything of anyone, it is of Berlioz: but not on the road which led him to the insipidities of his Faust symphony, – for if he continues along this road, he is bound to end up looking utterly ridiculous. If ever *a musician* needed *a poet*, it is Berlioz, and it is his misfortune that he always adapts his poet according to his own musical whim, arranging now Shakespeare, now Göthe, to suit his own purpose. He needs a poet to fill him through and through, a poet who is driven by ecstasy to violate him, and who is to him what man is to woman. It is with dismay that I see this incomparably gifted artist destroyed by his own egotistical solitude. Can I help him?? – You do not want *Wiland*:[2] *I* consider it a beautiful poem, but for my own part I can no longer complete

1 *Benvenuto Cellini*, first performed at the Paris Opéra on 10 September 1838, thereafter ignored in France but championed by Liszt in Weimar, where it was performed on 20 March 1852, and again on 18 February 1856.

2 *Wieland der Schmied*; see introduction, pp. 160–61, and letter [110] p. 207; the poem had been offered to Liszt in October 1850 (SB III,440–1).

it. Do you wish to offer it to Berlioz? Henri Blaze might be the man to adapt it into French, do you think?[1] –

How are things with *Raff*? I believe he is working on a new piece? No, he is arranging an old one! Do people really have no *life* left in them? *What* can an artist use to create his works if it is not *life itself*, yet surely this life is only artistically productive if it drives the artist to create new works of art as a reflection of life? Is this artificial reworking of old moments in an artist's life really to be regarded as artistic *creation*? What becomes of the *well-spring of our art* if the new does not gush forth so irresistibly that the old is lost without trace, or else is entirely subsumed by *new* creations? O ye people of God, do not confuse *making* art with creating it! What complacency and, at the same time, what poverty is not made manifest by this desire to touch up earlier efforts! If Raff's opera[2] met with the success that you say it did, he should be pleased, at least he was better rewarded than I for my "Fairies", which I did not even have performed, or for my "Ban on Love", which witnessed only a *single* ghastly performance, or for my "Rienzi", which so little occupies my thoughts at present that I should not allow it to be revived, even if such a performance were to be planned. It is only reluctantly that I trouble myself with the *Dutchman*, with *Tannhäuser* and with *Lohengrin*, – if I do so at all, it is simply because I know that – as a result of imperfect performances – they have still not been perfectly understood: if they had already received their due, the devil himself knows I should not ask any more about things I've outgrown. – Children! create something *new!* something *new!* and again something *new!*[3] – if you cling to the past, the devil of uncreativity will claim you for his own, and you will be the most melancholy of artists!

———

Well, I've got that off my chest! Whoever accuses me of insincerity must answer for it before God; but whoever accuses me of arrogance is a stupid fool! –

I can write no more! Do not be angry with me! my head is fit to burst! – Let me briefly bid you the fondest farewell that I have in my heart; remain true to me, and write to me soon.

Yours,
Richard W.

SB IV,457–61.

1 François Henri Joseph Blaze, known as Castil-Blaze: French translator and arranger of numerous German and Italian operas.
2 *König Alfred* (King Alfred), first performed in Weimar on 9 March 1851.
3 "Kinder! macht *Neues! Neues!* und abermals *Neues!*", frequently misquoted as "Kinder! schafft Neues!"

150. August Röckel, Waldheim   Zurich, 12 September 1852

[. . .] Once you are again permitted to concern yourself with literature, I should like you to send me word whether I might from time to time be allowed to send you books. I am sure you would find Feuerbach's writings uncommonly stimulating reading. I would also introduce you to a poet whom I have recently recognized to be the greatest of all poets; it is the Persian poet "Hafiz", whose poems now exist in a most enjoyable German adaptation by Daumer. Familiarity with this poet has filled me with a very real sense of terror: we with our pompous European intellectual culture must stand abashed in the presence of this product of the Orient, with its self-assured and sublime tranquillity of mind. I expect you would share my astonishment. The only merit of more recent developments in Europe seems to me to lie solely in a kind of *universal* disintegration, whereas I like to see in the person of this Oriental a precocious striving after individualism.
     [. . .]

SB IV,471–2.

151. Robert Franz, Coburg   Zurich, 28 October 1852

My worthy friend,
     Forgive me for having been so slow in attesting how much your letter has gladdened me: Uhlig will, I hope, have already obtained your forgiveness, he knows how ill I am. Please accept the enclosed gift of my Lohengrin score simply as an expression of the pleasure I feel at having found someone who, in spite of such unpropitious circumstances, has taken the trouble to get to know me better. How unsatisfactory it is to conduct such an acquaintanceship merely by means of the written word (for even a printed drama or an engraved opera score is, after all, simply an example of the written word) is something which no one feels more keenly and more clearly than I; it must remain unsatisfactory, but at least this knowledge may help to justify and explain whatever misunderstandings arise between us. The fact that, in writing about my Lohengrin, you could know me only imperfectly was of course obvious to me; all the more touching, then, was it to discover the indefatigable effort with which you had sought to come to terms with my ideas, so that, for my own part, I myself felt a spontaneous wish to draw closer to you, at least as far as my present circumstances allow. You may therefore regard my sending a copy of this score to you as an attempt to do my best by way of satisfying this wish. But you are wrong to speak of any possible desire on my part to shame you: rather should you call it sincere gratitude!
     Unfortunately, this score will be of little help to you in getting to know me

better: if only I could present you with one of my dramatic works in the way I should like, I can assure you that it would be something quite different! What I find so painful is that here, too, I am forced to live at one remove from myself: Lohengrin ought to have been performed long ago and immediately forgotten. If I now feel any desire to present this opera on stage in a decent performance, my only reason for doing so is to make good a past omission, and this involvement with the work is something I can really only relate to the actual performance – as a work of art in itself; for what I ought now to be achieving as a human being, as a poet and as a musician, in accord with my innermost nature, bears little relationship to Lohengrin, except as a sort of historical consequence, so that, if I do now perform it, people will see in it only a certain part of me, but certainly not the whole of me as I now am. This sense of remoteness, or rather this dislocation of the artist from his work of art is a real curse, which I do not think anyone has felt as keenly as I have, since for me true, pure artistic creativity is little other than a surrogate for something which I know to be my most basic need but a need which I am never allowed to satisfy. But that is enough on this dreary subject: yet those who are incapable of discovering this point for themselves and of sympathizing with it from the outset can only ever see me in a false and totally alien light. But whoever deludes himself into thinking that I am seeking satisfaction by inventing a new art-form for opera knows not the first thing about me.

Finally a word of reassurance! I discover to my regret that you are having a bad time of things; I, too, am living a life of despair and continuous, enforced resignation: but there is nothing that could make my life less of a burden to me than to be able to exert some beneficial influence on the lives of my friends. If I can be of help to you in the present case, you may be certain that it will make me very happy to do so.

I hope to hear from you again soon and in the meantime offer you my most sincere good wishes.

Your most obedient servant
Richard Wagner.

Fehr I,379–80.

152. FRANZ LISZT, WEIMAR   Zurich, 9 November 1852

[. . .] You who are all that I have, my dearest friend and prince, you who are the whole world to me and everything rolled into one, have pity on me! – But keep calm! keep calm!

I want to say something about the Faust Overture. You caught me out quite splendidly when I tried to delude myself into thinking I had written an

"Overture to Faust"! You were quite right to feel that something was missing here – and that what was missing is womankind! – But perhaps you would sooner understand my tone-poem if I were to call it "Faust in Solitude"! –

At that time[1] I wanted to write a complete Faust Symphony: the first part (the one I finished) was indeed the "solitary Faust" – in his yearning, despairing and cursing: the "feminine" element is present before his mind's eye as the image of his yearning, but not in its divine reality: and it is precisely this unsatisfying image of his yearning which he shatters in his despair. Only in the second movement was Gretchen – the woman – to be introduced: I already had the theme for her – but it was only a theme – : the whole thing was left to lie – I wrote my "flying Dutchman". – It is as simple as that! – If a vestigial sense of weakness and vanity now makes me want to rescue this Faust composition from total neglect, I shall certainly have to revise certain parts of it – but only as far as the instrumentation goes: it is impossible to introduce the new theme as you wish me to: it would then become a totally different composition, and one which I have no desire to write. But if I publish it, I shall give it its proper title: "Faust in Solitude" or "The solitary Faust" – a tone-poem for orchestra. –

My new poems for the two Siegfrieds were finished last week: but I still have to revise the two earlier pieces, "the young Siegfried" and "Siegfried's Death", since there are now substantial changes that have to be made to them. I shall not have completed them before the end of the year.[2] The full title is: *The Ring of the Nibelung*, a stage festival play in three days and a preliminary evening. Preliminary Evening: *The Rhinegold*. First Day: *The Valkyrie*. Second Day: *The young Siegfried*. Third Day: *Siegfried's Death*. What fate has in store for this poem – the poem of my life and of all that I am and feel – is something I cannot say at present: but one thing at least is certain – if Germany does not open its borders to me in the immediate future, and if I am forced to continue this artist's life of mine without sustenance or incentive, I shall be driven by my animal instinct for self-preservation to the point when I *abandon all art*. What I shall then take up to eke out my life, I do not know: but – I shall not write the music for the Nibelungs, and only somebody totally inhuman could demand that I should remain enslaved by my art a moment longer. –

Ah! I keep on falling back into the mood of self-pity which is the basic key-note of this letter! I may well be guilty of a great incivility in doing so – for you may perhaps – have needed cheering up – ! Forgive me if all I have

1 In the winter of 1839/40; see also letter [28], p. 64, note 2, and [178], p. 325.
2 See letter [142], p. 260, note 3. According to a letter to Robert Franz of 18 December 1852 (*Zeitschrift für Musik*, xci [1924], 242), the revision of *Der junge Siegfried* and *Siegfrieds Tod* had been completed by 17 December 1852. Their more familiar titles, *Siegfried* and *Götterdämmerung*, date from June 1856, although even after that date Wagner continued to use the older forms.

to offer you today is hopelessness: I can no longer pretend, but, whether people despise me for it or not, I shall shout out my grief for all the world to hear and make no secret any longer of my unhappiness! What use would it be if I tried to lie to you? But there is one thing you must not forget, even if all else proves impossible! – you must see to it that we are able to meet next summer! Remember that this is *absolutely necessary*, – that it *must* be so, and that no God must be allowed to prevent you from coming here, especially since the police (fall to the ground when you hear their name mentioned!) prevent me from coming to you! – Promise me for certain when you next write that you will come! Promise![1] –

We shall then see whether I have managed to survive until then!! –

Fare you well!! You must make allowances for me! Regards to Hans[2] – and – be of good cheer – you may soon be rid of me!!

Fare you well and write to me soon.

Yours,
Richard Wagner.

Liszt-Briefe I, 190–1.

153. LUISE BROCKHAUS,[3] DRESDEN   Zurich, 11 November 1852

Dear Luise,

Thank you so much for your kind letter, which certainly came as a great surprise. The impression it made upon me was all the more touching in that the mood which inspired you to write it appeared in every respect to be one of melancholy. I have no really clear notion of your present situation, but I suspect that you must have reason enough to think favourably of those of us who are unhappy. I cannot properly explain what I mean by this, since we have now so few points of contact, and the obvious ones belong rather to the realm of vague feelings than to any real consciousness on my part. And so I see myself obliged to speak almost solely of myself in replying to your letter, the more so since you asked me specifically how I am.

It was about a year ago that I wrote to your Clärchen.[4] I was then staying at a hydropathic establishment with the intention of trying to become a completely healthy human being. Uppermost in my mind was the secret desire to regain my health so as to be able to break totally free from what torments me most in life, namely my art: it was a final, desperate struggle to find happiness, a true and noble zest for life such as is ordained only to those

1 Liszt visited Wagner in Zurich between 2 and 10 July 1853.
2 Hans von Bülow.
3 This is the first surviving letter from Wagner to his sister.
4 Klara Brockhaus, Luise's daughter. The letter in question is dated 23 October 1851 (SB IV, 144–6).

who are fully conscious of their health. That I was deceiving myself in this was soon to become clear: my life is forfeit and, having never enjoyed it, I can now eke it out only by artificial means, in other words – by means of my art. But the despair I feel at confronting the artistic life of Europe with *my* art is something which can be felt only by those who know to what extent art for me is a substitute for a life of unsatisfied desire: and how superficial, on the other hand, is the judgement of those people who advise me to set about acquiring fame! I pour out into my art the violent need I feel for love, a need which life cannot satisfy, and all I find in return is that people at best mistake me for an energetic – opera reformer! And so I drive myself from one moment of dissatisfaction to the next, but through driving myself in this way, my health has finally sunk into an increasingly steep decline from which nothing – no treatment in the world can save me. My nerves are already wasting completely away; perhaps some outward change in my life might enable me to defer my death for a number of years by artificial means: but this could only affect the moment of my death, it can no longer delay the process of dying. – That, in brief, is all I have to say about myself.

Dresden's decision to revive Tannhäuser[1] left me feeling fairly indifferent; I know that as far as the most important point was concerned (the role of Tannhäuser) the performance was a dismal failure: that all this fuss and bother appeals to people can give me little cause for satisfaction.

I think back on Dresden only with feelings of abhorrence: no one person ever sacrificed his entire soul more readily than I did there, – and what walls of indifference the sound simply echoed against! Now I discover that people are reproaching me for "ingratitude" towards the King! As if the futility of sacrificing my life and my artistic activities for the sake of an appointment there and for "acts of charity" such as are lavished indiscriminately on any ragamuffin was *my* fault, rather than the fault of the outdated circumstances which I was finally moved by anger to oppose! – Enough of this! –

Give my kind regards to Marianne,[2] and offer her my warmest congratulations! Will you not visit us some day in this beautiful country of Switzerland? I long with all my heart to see Clärchen and Ottchen sitting at our table again! Give them all my kindest regards, and best wishes to your good husband[3] for his continuing prosperity. My wife asks to add her voice to all these greetings and good wishes. But you, my dear Luise, I would ask above all to write to me again soon and remember with affection

Your brother
Richard.

1 *Tannhäuser* had been revived in Dresden on 26 October 1852 in the face of considerable public opposition but with the blessing of King Friedrich August II. After five performances it disappeared from the repertory.
2 Luise's daughter.
3 Friedrich Brockhaus.

I have now more or less completed my Nibelung poem: whether I shall set it to music must depend entirely upon the state of my health: unless my situation changes substantially, I doubt whether I shall. I shall probably have the poems published soon.[1]

Familienbriefe 190–2.

154. THEODOR UHLIG, DRESDEN   [Zurich, 18 November 1852]

[. . .] I am now working on "young Siegfried", and shall soon have finished it. Then I shall move on to "Siegfried's Death" – that will hold me up longer; there are two scenes there which will have to be newly written (the Norns and Brünhilde's scene with the Valkyries) but above all the ending – in addition to which everything will have to be substantially revised. The whole thing will then be – out with it! I am shameless enough to admit it! – the greatest poem I have ever written! –

I shall tell you about my health some other time: I have to avoid tiring myself, including over-strenuous walks: artist that I am, I can now thrive only in luxurious comfort; who knows, – if I change horses, regard my youth as a thing of the past, and consciously enter upon some entirely new dispensation in life, I may perhaps learn to cope with life for a few more years. (Forget the scrawlings and polemics! Place your hopes – in me!)

Adieu!   Your Nibelung Prince Alberich.

(Next time I must tell you something quite priceless about Munich.)[2]

Uhlig-Briefe 246.

155. JULIE RITTER, DRESDEN   Zurich, 29 December 1852

Best of friends,

I really ought not to write to you today, since I am unwell and out of humour; but it had long been my intention at least to send you my good wishes for the New Year and so I shall see, as best I can, whether I can carry out my resolve. –

Above all I must thank you for your obliging news about Uhlig: I knew that you were the best person to turn to. As to the object in question, there

---

1 In a private edition of fifty copies in February 1853.
2 Franz Lachner conducted the *Tannhäuser* Overture in Munich on 1 November 1852, an unpopular move which Wagner saw as a wilful attempt to prejudice local audiences against him.

is unfortunately little to say: only time will tell how things turn out.¹ Uhlig's illness is a severe blow to me: it robs me of my only link with the outside world; since I exist exclusively through the intermediary of the postal services, Uhlig's enforced silence virtually deprives me of that existence.

The negotiations in which I am now engaged with various German theatres seemed initially as though they might bring some sense of excitement to my life; unfortunately they, too, have proved to be no more than a further source of torment for me. This eternal correspondence on the subject is tiresome to a degree, and the only possibility of my becoming reconciled to my present situation – however superficial such a reconciliation might be – would be if I myself were able to attend the occasional performance of one of my operas. But I was guilty of a gross inconsistency in allowing those performances to take place: what drove me to do so was not only my need to exist in my present circumstances, but also a certain lack of concern about my earlier works in which I can now take only an artificial interest and which I really cannot imagine wanting to save up for the "future", since it is already much too late for that. But on the whole I have retained the right to allow only those performances to take place where I have encountered some friendly soul who is well disposed towards me, in order, so to speak, to make contact with my true friends, undisturbed by the multitude of onlookers. Indeed, I have had a number of most encouraging experiences in this respect: in *Breslau*² especially, I seem to have won many friends; you may have heard that they performed Tannhäuser there for the twelfth time on the 1st December and that the house was as full on that occasion as it had been for the previous eleven performances. On their own initiative, they have now hit on the "Flying Dutchman", which they shortly intend to present there.³ This same opera is also being rehearsed right now in Schwerin.⁴ In Wiesbaden there was – by all accounts – an admirable performance of Tannhäuser.⁵ However, in other places where the full score has been demanded, performances have yet to take place: I now tremble for *Frankfurt* where all the signs are that the performance will be a bad one.⁶ With regard to *Berlin* I wish I could make up my mind to demand the return of my score from there, since I have absolutely no faith in a performance taking place in the city.⁷ – On the whole, the sanguine hopes which were aroused in me last autumn by the sudden rush of orders have now begun to dwindle somewhat: it looks as though

1 Uhlig died of consumption on 3 January 1853.
2 *Tannhäuser* was first performed in Breslau on 6 October 1852. The initial impulse came from the singer Henriette Moritz, sister of August Röckel.
3 *Der fliegende Holländer* was first performed in Breslau on 26 January 1853.
4 Schwerin first heard *Der fliegende Holländer* on 6 April 1853.
5 On 13 November 1852.
6 *Tannhäuser* was first performed in Frankfurt on 15 February 1853.
7 See letters [134], p. 246, note 1 and, [148], p. 266, note 2.

performances of my operas will remain only isolated phenomena, and that I shall certainly not make my "fortune" in this way. It was then that I conceived the idea of using the expected pecuniary benefits from my operas for my own ends and of carrying out a long-cherished ambition of mine to acquire a small plot of land: in consequence of this I had to make enquiries of you to find out what the reaction of your dear family would be to this idea, in view of the annuity which had been granted to me; did they intend to support me with it for only a short period, or for the rest of my life and as long as your financial situation allowed? For it goes without saying that only on the latter assumption could I have thought of using my theatre receipts for the purpose indicated. The answer sounded reassuring. Since that time, however, my hopes in the other direction have once more dwindled to such an extent that I was almost forced to abandon the project, in spite of the fact that a young and well-to-do merchant by the name of *Wesendonk*, who lives in these parts and who is friendly with me, has shown great kindness to me and an almost entirely unprompted willingness to offer me the advance which I need to acquire a plot of land. I feel all too keenly that my acceptance of such an offer would place me in the dreadful position of having to instigate performances of my operas at any price and that, as a result, I should have to renounce the right, which it is necessary for me to retain, of agreeing to *the desire and demand* of only those theatres where I can predict a decent success in *my* sense of the word. In addition – as I say – my operas are by no means selling as well as initially appeared to be the case, and I think I would do well to be equally prepared for total silence on the part of the theatres as for a possible increase in demand.[1] – In such circumstances I feel more keenly than ever before the value of your family's gift: for it is this annuity alone which guarantees my freedom and ensures that I derive the greatest possible pleasure from all that I undertake. Permit me to assure you once again that I regard the product of your concern for me as the greatest boon ever to have befallen me.

[. . .]

Ritter-Briefe 84–7.

---

1 In addition to the performances mentioned here, *Tannhäuser* was heard in Freiburg on 7 November 1852, Riga on 6 January 1853, Düsseldorf on 18 January 1853, Leipzig on 31 January 1853, Cassel on 15 May 1853 and Posen on 25 May 1853. During the following season there were productions of *Tannhäuser* in Danzig, Bremen, Darmstadt, Hamburg, Königsberg, Barmen, Bromberg, Cologne, Stralsund, Stettin, Aachen, Augsburg, Graz, Gumbinnen, Prague and Mainz. However, as Wagner pointed out in a letter to Liszt of 16 November 1853, the monies he received for selling the rights of *Tannhäuser* to all these theatres amounted to no more than 362 louis d'or.

156. CÄCILIE AVENARIUS, LEIPZIG   Zurich, 30 December 1852

Dear Cecilie,

I had intended writing to you yesterday, so that you would receive my letter on New Year's Day; but illness prevented me from doing so, which is why my good wishes will now arrive a day late.

Rest assured that your letter gave me a deal of pleasure; I had been expecting to hear from you for some considerable time and was beginning to suppose that something I had said in my last letter had upset you. All the better that it had not! – Each time you turn to me in this way, I am involuntarily reminded of our youth when we two really belonged to each other more than to any one else: all the memories that I have of that time are inextricably bound up with you. – I expect the same is true of you, and, just as we always look back on our youth as a time of greater happiness, you, too, no doubt yearn to retreat from the squalor of the present and rediscover the person who was then closest to you. The Loschwitz bathing party and my boots, Humann etc. still have their occasional part to play: if we had not placed the key in the pumpkin, everything would then have turned out for the better.[1] Don't you agree? – But it has all turned out quite pitifully: I live surrounded by people who drive me back increasingly into myself, in spite of my lively desire for self-expression; there is no man alive who does not feel a greater need than I do to pour out all his riches without reserve, and yet there is none who is given less in return than I; my outgoings bear no relation to my income: I am unbelievably lacking in agreeable impressions; I am continually forced to fall back on myself. It is a particular misfortune for me that most of my friends are philistines and that they often cling to me with an affection that really has nothing to do with my true nature, so that I am obliged to return it with a certain dishonesty. On the whole it is the men whom I find most repugnant, while women are soonest capable of making an agreeable impression upon me. It is hideously nonsensical that men always go around with men, and women with women; the entire human race will eventually perish as a result of this perversity. If only the majority of women had not already been ruined by it all! Men nowadays are born philistines, and women become so because of them. That is how it is! – I am living a kind of dog's life here: all my illusions about friends to which I abandon myself so readily cannot ultimately last for long: in the end I am the one who is hurt by the effort it takes to maintain my illusions, and I am driven by sheer necessity to expose things as they really are in all their naked truth. And so I continue to

1 Humann was Wagner's piano teacher when he was about twelve (see *Mein Leben* 35–6; English trans. 29). For an account of the incident at Loschwitz and the pumpkin anecdote, see Ellis's *Life* I,79–80.

live my old life of solitude: but I am finally succumbing since my heart is lacking in sustenance. My nerves are in a very bad way and, after many attempts to find a radical cure, I have finally lost all hope of getting better: all that I can do is get as much rest and comfort as possible, in order to be able to hold out a little longer. My work is the only thing that sustains me: but my cerebral nerves are already in such a state that I can never spend more than two hours a day working, and even these two hours are only possible if I can lie down for a further two hours after working and finally sleep a little; if sleep is denied me, the rest of the day is wasted. In this way I have finally completed my great Nibelung poem: if the outside world can offer encouragement, I shall make a start on the music in the spring.

[. . .]

Familienbriefe 193–4.

157. CAROLINE UHLIG, DRESDEN   Zurich, 9 January 1853

My poor dear Frau Uhlig,

How can I possibly console you for the terrible loss[1] you have suffered, since I, too, am so sorely affected by it that I can scarcely conceive of its magnitude! However long I live, I shall always have cause to regard the loss of this one particular friend of mine as irreparable – I feel very much as though I have been robbed of half my very soul! What he was to me you certainly know: what I must feel at his death I certainly have no need to describe to you! Nor, indeed, would I be capable of pouring out my feelings at present!!

But when I compare *your* loss with my own, my immediate feeling is a fervent desire to receive from you some indication as to how I may best show my sympathy. If there is any wish that I may be able to help you fulfil, I would entreat you most beseechingly to tell me what it is.

What will become of the child, my godson – Siegfried? If only I might see your children; if only I could take the place of their father – at least for one of them! – I entreat you, whatever you decide for your own future and that of your family, please remember *me* too: if you do so, I shall always be certain that you are acting according to the wishes of my dear departed friend!! I now beg you with all my heart to lighten my cares and send me word soon about your state of health and an answer to all my questions! – My wife – who truly esteemed Uhlig and loved him – similarly feels the sincerest

---

1 Uhlig died on 3 January 1853.

sympathy for you: she bids me assure you most sincerely of this, and asks you – in the event of your finding it difficult to address yourself to *me* directly – to turn to her for help.

Kindly remember us to your children, and send word soon to reassure

Your most devoted servant
Richard Wagner.

Freunde und Zeitgenossen 114–15.

158. Franz Liszt, Weimar   Zurich, 11 February 1853

My dearest friend,

Here's a pile of new things from me![1] You see, my poem is finished, and even though it has not yet been set to music, it has at least been set in type and printed, and printed, moreover, at my own expense and in a limited edition, which I intend to present to my friends so that – if I die before completing the work – they will have received my testamentary bequest to them in advance. – Those who know my present circumstances will be bound to think this another of my extravagances when they receive so expensive an edition: so be it! The real world now behaves in so niggardly a way towards me that I have not the least desire to imitate it. –

[. . .]

As for the poem itself, there is nothing more I can or wish to say at present: if you find the time to read it through sympathetically, you will say to yourself all that I could possibly tell you. I – shall write no more verse. – But the prospect of setting all this to music now attracts me greatly: as regards the form, it is already fully fashioned in my head, and I have never been so clear in my own mind about the musical execution of a work as I now am in relation to this poem. I need only the necessary *incentive in life* in order to find the indispensable mood of cheerful serenity which will allow the motives to well up inside me freely and gladly. – [. . .]

Good luck with the "flying Dutchman"![2] I cannot get this melancholy hero out of my head! I keep on hearing

"Ah,   spec-tral man,   who   can   tell   when you'll find   her!"

together with:

---

1 Enclosed was a copy of the privately printed edition of the *Ring* poem.
2 First performed in Weimar, under Liszt's direction, on 16 February 1853.

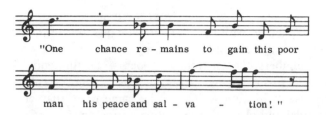

"One   chance re - mains   to   gain this poor

man   his peace and sal - va - tion! "

but it's too late now! for me there is no longer any possibility of redemption, except for – *death*! Oh, how happy I should be to die in a storm at sea, – but not on my sick-bed!!!

Indeed – I should be glad to perish in the flames of *Valhalla*! – Mark well my new poem – it contains the world's beginning and its end! –

I must now set it to music for the Jews of Frankfurt and Leipzig – it is just the thing for them! –

I must stop, this epistle is beginning to get out of hand! – let me conclude briefly! – Adieu! my Franziskus, my only friend – you who tower up to meet me with your giant's heart! Indefatigable man that you are, fare you well! And if you play the Ballad tomorrow – think of me! I am sitting alone on the sofa, staring into the lamp, and brooding on my – great good fortune at having rescued *you* at least from the wretched world! Yes, indeed! It is that which keeps me going! Fare you well, my friend! accept my most tender greetings!!

Yours,

Richard W.

Liszt-Briefe I, 204–9.

159. The Board of Directors of the Concert Committee of the General Music Society of Zurich[1]   Zurich, 22 February 1853

Dear Sirs,

The impossibility of performing any of my musical dramas in the local theatre in a way which would adequately meet the demands of the works in

1 In response to the following proposal, three Wagner concerts were held in Zurich on 18, 20 and 22 May 1853. The programme on each occasion consisted of the Chorus of the Messengers of Peace from *Rienzi*, Senta's Ballad, the Sailors' Chorus and the Overture to *Der fliegende Holländer*, the Entry of Guests into the Hall of Song, the Prelude to Act III, the Pilgrims' Chorus and the Overture to *Tannhäuser*, and substantial excerpts from *Lohengrin*, which gave Wagner an opportunity to hear parts of that work for the first time before he started composing the music of the *Ring*. The orchestra of about seventy players was assembled from towns as far away as Weimar and Frankfurt, and the chorus numbered 110. The festival atmosphere of the occasion was enhanced by Wagner's reading the poems of his operas at public recitals in the Zurich Casino. The loss of 1190 francs was borne by a small number of creditors including Otto Wesendonck, Jakob Sulzer and the President of the Music Society, Konrad Ott-Imhof.

question has not discouraged me from wanting to make Zurich's music lovers better acquainted with the characteristic qualities of my music, but has induced me, rather, to attempt to do so by means of a concert performance of individual numbers chosen from my operas. To this end I have made a selection of pieces from all my operas such as can most easily dispense with a dramatic presentation but which, at the same time, may acquaint people with the essential and characteristic nature of my music – as such – in what may be described as an allusive fashion. My aim of providing a satisfactory notion and, at the same time, a genuine enjoyment of my music can, however, be achieved only if the presentation of these items is of the greatest imaginable perfection, and this in turn will be possible only if a combined effort be made on the part of musical forces such as Zurich can assemble only by the most exceptional means. In wishing, therefore, to present something which is at least perfect of its kind, I am obliged to leave out of consideration all the usual complement of local musical talent, and can regard my plans as feasible only if, as a result of exceptional public interest, I am offered the possibility of bringing in the necessary forces from outside.

According to this design of mine, everything that I have planned in this respect and agreed with expert advisers suggests that the intended performance should take place in our local theatre at the beginning of May of this year and that it should be repeated twice within the space of a week. The full orchestra which I need and which must be entirely suited to the occasion must be made up, for the overwhelmingly greater part, of outside players who would be engaged and invited to Zurich specifically for this purpose; in addition, the stage of the theatre would have to be rebuilt by suitable means so as to form a reverberant space for the orchestra.

I have examined this matter closely and believe that the cost of achieving the foregoing for three performances must be reckoned at 6000 frcs, and that, if the undertaking is to take place at all, we must first elicit an answer to the question whether this sum can be raised out of the proceeds of public interest. In order to ensure that this may be so, the following procedure would seem to me best suited to our purpose. The estimated costs of 6000 fr. must be guaranteed by means of the sale of entrance tickets for all three performances, with the price of all seats in the theatre being raised to the level required by our need to make 2000 fr. an evening. But in order to be certain of bringing in these receipts before any start is made on the actual undertaking itself, a subscription would have to be started straightaway for the better and more expensive seats at the necessary price, and all else would then depend upon the success of this subscription.

I lay these suggestions before the worshipful members of the concert committee of the General Music Society with the intention of persuading them most graciously to take an interest in those aspects of the aforementioned undertaking which are not connected with its purely artistic side but which involve obtaining everything necessary for my own artistic ends, so that in all its purely commercial aspects, including all dealings with those of Zurich's art-lovers on whom claims are to be made, the undertaking may be governed solely by this well-known and highly respected body. In the event of my receiving a favourable response on your part to this wish of mine, I should then confine my demands exclusively to the musico-technical aspect of the undertaking and ultimately see my unique reward as lying in the success of the artistic performance and in a pleasing outcome to the undertaking, since it is my express intention to forgo all share in any pecuniary gain.

In the hope that my request may meet with your kind consideration and that my proposal may receive your gracious consent, I remain your most respectful and obedient servant

Richard Wagner.

Fehr I,381–2.

160. Franz Liszt, Weimar   Zurich, 30 March 1853

[. . .] I entreat you now with the greatest *decisiveness* and *determination*: prevail upon the Weimar Court to take the definitive step of finding out once and for all whether I have any real prospect of seeing Germany open her borders to me again in the near future. I *must* find this out for certain, and soon. Be brutally frank with me! Tell me whether the Weimar Court is prepared to take this step? and – if they take it, and take it quickly – what is their answer? – I am not disposed to compromise myself in the slightest for the sake of this wish: I can assure *you* that I shall remain totally uninvolved in politics, and anyone who is not a fool must see for himself that *I* am no "demagogue" in need of police supervision. (But if they want to, they can have me kept under police surveillance as much as they like!) I ask only that people do not try to shame me into making some confession or other of my remorse. If I may be permitted in this way to return temporarily, well, I do not deny that it would certainly be of use to me to do so! But if it is *not* possible, if the answer is a definitive refusal, – tell me so at once and without further ado: *then I shall know where I stand.* Then – I shall begin a new life. Then I shall set out to make *money*, how and where I can: I shall borrow and – steal – if need be, in order to be able to *travel.* The real Italy, with all its natural beauty, is closed to me (even if I am *not* amnestied); and so I shall go to Spain, Andalusia, look for travelling companions – and try to live again, as best I can. I should like to go round the world! If I *fail* to raise the money – or – if travel does not help me recover my love of life – well then – that will be the end of it, and I would rather kill myself than live on like this!

In truth, my dear friend, it was not until I reached my 35th year that I realized that I have *still not lived*. It was my *art* which was bound to reveal to me the secret of how wretched, joyless and loveless a life I have been leading until now. What will you say when I tell you that I have never enjoyed the true happiness of love? I now spend my life poised between privation and a resigned regard for the limitations of my immediate environment, which is less and less able to understand and comprehend me as each day passes! I cannot and will not cause open offence here (since my own heart would suffer as a result – habit is an undeniably great force!) but I must at least be able to acquire the means to withdraw from this desolation from time to time in order to unfold my wings unhindered and unchecked. Do you understand me? – Only too well, I am certain! –

I must forge for myself a pair of artificial wings, since everything around us is artificial, and nature is everywhere stricken and blighted! –

Hear my prayer, then, and answer it! Let me know very soon, let me know quickly and for certain whether I may be allowed to return to Germany or not! I must now reach a decision on the basis of that information.[1] –

[. . .]

Liszt-Briefe I, 224–5.

161. FRANZ LISZT, WEIMAR   [Zurich,] 13 April 1853

[. . .] You see, my friend, I too am bitterly scorned by our politicians and jurists for my faith: for I believe in the future of the human race, and I derive this faith quite simply from my own essential need; I have succeeded in viewing natural and historical phenomena with love and with total impartiality as regards their true essence, and I have noticed nothing amiss except for – *lovelessness*. – But even this lovelessness I was able to explain as an *aberration*, an aberration which must inevitably lead us away from our state of natural unawareness towards a *knowledge* of the uniquely beautiful necessity of love; to acquire this knowledge by active striving is the task of world history; but the stage on which this knowledge will one day act out its role is none other than the earth and nature herself, which is the seed-bed of all that will lead us to this blissful knowledge. The state of lovelessness is the state of suffering for the human race: an abundance of suffering now envelops us, and torments your friend, as well, with a thousand smarting wounds; but you see, it is precisely here that we *recognize* the glorious necessity of love, *we* call upon it and welcome each other with a force of love which would not be possible were it not for this painful recognition; and so, in this way, we acquire a

---

1 It was not until the summer of 1860 that Wagner received a partial amnesty allowing him to return to Germany.

strength of which natural man had no inkling, and this strength – increased to embrace the whole of humanity – will one day lay the foundations for a state on earth where no one need yearn for the other world (a world which will then have become wholly unnecessary), for they will be happy – to live and to love. For where is the man who yearns to escape from life when he is in love? – Well then! *Now* we suffer, *now* we must lose heart and go mad without any faith in the hereafter: I too believe in a hereafter: – I have just shown you this hereafter: though it lies beyond *my life*, it does not lie beyond the limits of all that I can feel, think, grasp and comprehend, for I believe in *humanity* and – have need of naught else! –

[. . .]

Liszt-Briefe I, 230–1.

162. OTTO WESENDONCK, ZURICH   Zurich, 20 June 1853

Your arrangements, my dear friend, are admirable: I thank you with all my heart!

In order to enter upon my new indebtedness towards you in a way that is worthy and likely to inspire your future confidence, I am today repaying an old debt: give your wife the enclosed sonata,[1] my first composition since the completion of Lohengrin (6 years ago!)[2]

You will soon be hearing from me again: but first you must send me word as to how you are faring.

Yours,
Richard Wagner.

Otto Wesendonck-Briefe 7–8.

163. OTTO WESENDONCK, BAD EMS   Zurich, 13 July 1853

I turn to you today, my honoured friend, with only a few lines in order to thank you for your recent letter, and at the same time to show you some sign of life.

I have just spent a wild, exciting – and yet tremendously beautiful week: Liszt left me only a few days ago.[3] A veritable storm of conversation raged

---

1 Sonata in A flat for piano (WWV 85). The indebtedness refers to a loan (subsequently regarded as a gift) which Wesendonck gave Wagner in May 1853 to help him furnish his new apartment in Zeltweg 13 to which he had moved on 15 April of that year.
2 In fact Wagner had written a Polka in G, also for piano, the previous month (WWV 84).
3 Liszt's visit lasted from 2 to 10 July 1853.

between the two of us: my joy at meeting this indescribably amiable man was all the greater for my finding him so robust and resilient, and in much better health than I would have expected from earlier. We had an incredible amount of things to tell each other: for essentially this was the first time we had really got to know each other, since I had previously only ever spent a few days at a time with him. And so the 8 days which were all he was able to offer me on this occasion were packed so full that I am still well-nigh benumbed by it all. I lost my voice during the first few days, so that Liszt then had to provide for the music himself: his playing was unbelievable! – The two of us then went off on a splendid excursion to Lake Lucerne, and he finally left me with the spontaneous promise that he would return next year for at least four weeks:[1] I hope you yourself will be there then! –

I cannot put up with Zurich a moment longer: and yet this very evening I shall have to submit to yet further celebrations. I am threatened with a vast torch-lit procession with music, singing and honorary awards; rumour has been rife in the town for the whole of last week. – Tomorrow morning, however, I am off to St Moritz: if I survive my course of treatment there, I shall then go to Italy. I have laid in a stock of well-ruled paper for my sketches, and believe that before the year is out, I shall have the score of the Rhinegold fully drafted.[2] To my immense gratification and surprise I discovered that Liszt is in total agreement with my plans for the future presentation of my stage festival play: we have agreed that it shall take place in Zurich between spring and autumn one year; a provisional theatre will be built for the purpose, and all that I need by way of singers etc. will be specially engaged: Liszt will collect contributions for the undertaking from every quarter and from every corner of the earth, and he is confident of raising the necessary money.[3]

You must admit that it was no small thing on which we agreed!

[. . .]

Otto Wesendonck-Briefe 8–9.

164. LOUIS KÖHLER, KÖNIGSBERG   St Moritz, 24 July 1853

Do not be angry with me, my dear friend, for having taken so long to respond to your letter. Shortly after its arrival came Liszt's visit, and immediately after that I travelled here to the mountains of Graubünden to take the waters. In

---

1 Liszt's next visit to Zurich lasted from 13 October to 27 November 1856.
2 The complete draft of *Das Rheingold* was begun on 1 November 1853 and finished on 14 January 1854. The first full score (draft) is dated 1 February – 28 May 1854, and the second full score (fair copy) 15 February – 26 September 1854.
3 Nothing came of this plan.

addition to having little time to spare, I had no great desire to relapse into aesthetic theorizing, which I should have been tempted into doing had I written to you at the time. Now that I have conceived the hope of getting by without doing so, I should like to reply to your letter, even if only briefly, in order to tell you how much pleasure your interest in me has given me and how, in particular, I wish your recent self-sacrificing excursus from Königsberg had met with a better reward than I know was the rather inadequate and uninspired performance of "Tannhäuser" which you attended in Leipzig.

Your book[1] certainly surprised me; much of it so clearly concerns me that it could not remain a secret from me: I had read it even before you sent me a copy.

Your idea of tracing melody through speech is evidence of the great seriousness which you have brought to bear in this matter: you were most fortunate in detecting true melodic and harmonic accents. Basically, I am forced increasingly to realize that what is at issue here is something which each of us does best to come to terms with individually: but since there is such a fearful amount of teaching going on, it is only natural for people to feel a desire to contribute to some more sensible method of teaching. In this respect I have repeatedly drawn Brendel's[2] attention to the fact that he ought to confine himself much more in his journal to what can actually be learned, in other words technique. The content of a work of art is a matter for the individual, and is not a subject for criticism; it is a question here of feeling a sense of liking or disliking for the work under discussion, and that again is a matter for the individual. Technique, however, is the common property of artists of all ages, each inherits it from the next one, every artist adds to it, and forms it as best he can and must. This is something that can be discussed, although only of course among artists: the layman should never find out what is being said. Now, I genuinely believe that my writings have given cause for a great deal of discussion on the principal questions of technique: but I have so far seen little or no evidence that this particular point has been noticed.

If I have raised any important issue in this respect, it is that of the relationship between poetry and music in general, or between spoken verse and melody in particular. I believe it would be a good idea if a precise and intelligible – and exhaustive – attempt were made to examine the essence of modern spoken verse as evolved by our literary poets as their sole preserve, without the least regard for musical melody, and in that way to prove – by means of numerous examples – that such verse as this *cannot* be set to music, because our modern melody has developed out of quite different factors which derive from absolute music and which have not the least thing in

1 *Die Melodie der Sprache in ihrer Anwendung besonders auf das Lied und die Oper* (The Melody of Speech, especially in its Application to Song and Opera) (Leipzig 1853).
2 Franz Brendel was editor of the *Neue Zeitschrift für Musik*.

common with literary verse. On the basis of this one false relationship in artistic technique it ought to be possible to demonstrate convincingly how totally false is the relationship which exists between our literary poetry and our music: but this can be done only by means of a thoroughly detailed exposition of its purely technical aspects. No amount of rhetoric on the problem in all its generality is of the least use here, and Brendel is bound to find himself perpetually assailed by questions such as, "how are we supposed to go about it, should we continue to compose at all, should we compose operas, or what else?" I advised him to take these questions as the basis of a theme for discussion, together with the circumstance that he has received them at all; on closer examination it should then emerge that what we are dealing with here is an outworn and obsolete technique in which there can be absolutely no artistic content, which explains why we should not be surprised if our most skilfully composed music – has nothing to say to us.

I am gratified to discover that you, too, have felt this for yourself: what you have written is proof of this. But I should have preferred it if you had not confined yourself for the most part to those feelings aroused in you by linguistic phrases alone, but had examined more closely the truly melodic linguistic phrase, namely the individual line of verse. If, for ex., you wish to retain the literary verse as it is and sing it simply in accordance with its musically melodic content, what you will get – if you are fortunate – is simply what I have already referred to elsewhere[1] as "prosaic melody" or "musical prose": but it is precisely this prose which must no longer be allowed to occur if we are to remove from our – relatively superior – music the character of unmelodic formlessness. I have – I think – expressed myself sufficiently on this point in the first quarter of the third volume of "Opera and Drama": how little I have been heeded, however, is something I am daily obliged to observe. Many people would have cause to be grateful to you if you were to make this work the object of your studies and examine it, clause by clause, in closest detail. Here alone, and nowhere else, is useful work to be done – instead of which, effort is wasted on insubstantial protestations!

Well, that's enough theory for today: it's not good for me! My illness has been brought on by too much theorizing, and I am now looking to artistic creativity to cure me again. I can no long "write" about art. Perhaps you may one day get something better from me – something to hear and see! Fare you well! I shall be here for another 3 weeks, then, initially, back in Zurich again!

Yours,
Richard Wagner.

Freunde und Zeitgenossen 133–7.

---

1 *Opera and Drama*, especially GS, IV,114; PW II,250.

165. LOUIS SCHINDELMEISSER, WIESBADEN   Zurich, 13 August 1853

[. . .] As for my new poem "the Ring of the Nibelung", it is now a matter of immense regret that I had 50 copies of it printed – quite apart from the cost. Not only was I unable to prevent the book from falling into the hands of people who are totally incompetent to judge it, but I now feel that even my friends ought not to have had a sight of the poem until it had been set to music, I might almost say: until it had been *produced* as well. I now see increasingly clearly that what I envisage must be *done* rather than merely talked about. Instead of concentrating upon the poem before them and on its purely poetic content, people concentrate rather upon the purely technical aspects of what they assume will be its musical execution, as though such poems only came into existence in order to provide run-of-the-mill opera composers with material for musical outpourings, instead of finding their true and necessary justification within themselves, in the life of the poet and in his opinions, offering the musician a new subject for which, and in which, he must discover new music, i.e. music uniquely suited to the subject in question. If, in this way, the musical setting (like the stage setting) necessarily remains my own secret, which I can reveal only when the whole thing is finished, nothing is more distressing to me now than to have to listen to others talking (in public, what's more) about this most intimate secret of my art. – In a word, I wish I could recall all the copies I gave away. Come and visit me here soon, and I shall *read* it aloud to you, *sing* what is already finished, and *talk* to you about it: – only **then** shall you take away a copy, if you wish to have one! But I do not care to contribute to even more misunderstandings – which are so distressing to me. – Do not take this the wrong way! –

As far as Darmstadt[1] is concerned, you also mentioned that the orchestral parts of "Tannhäuser" were already being copied and that you intended beginning rehearsals as early as the 15th of August, etc. Well, that is splendid news, and I cannot tell you how happy you have made me: do not, however, be angry with me if I express a certain surprise at this news. I have still to receive word that the Darmstadt directors have acquired the score of "Tannhäuser": some time ago I received a letter from a certain Herr Tascher; I replied to him and demanded *twenty-five louis d'or*: since then I have heard absolutely nothing. (??) Tell me how things stand! and while I'm on the subject of "business", I must also mention that I have every reason to suspect that the Dresden state police may suddenly take it into their heads to seize my revenues: (all that it needs is for someone who bears me a personal grudge to draw their attention to the fact, and they'll be *forced* to do so!). For this reason I am now insisting upon receiving my fees in *advance*; I would ask you – when you are next in Darmstadt – to remember this notification. – By

1 *Tannhäuser* was first performed in Darmstadt on 23 October 1853.

the way! You will be receiving from Dresden a further alteration to the ending of Tannh.: according to this revised version, the corpse of Elisabeth does *not* appear, neither do the Landgr. & minstrels; conversely, the younger pilgrims, singing their chorus – as in the first revision. Conversely, everything else – necessarily – remains, the whole of Venus's part, etc. up to: "Blessed Elisabeth, pray for me", at which point the earlier ending takes over. The young pilgrims bear the blossoming staff in their midst. – Prior to that, Elisabeth's death is indicated only by the light of torches on the Wartburg, funeral bells and men's voices *coming from there* (in other words, from the top of the hill). –

All this talk about the appearance of a corpse, and prosaic calculations about the socio-physico-anatomical possibility of burying Elisabeth "in so short a space of time" (how fortunate that people have time on these occasions to think about time!) have finally sickened me to such an extent that I have decided on *this* alteration, or restitution. –

[. . .]

Freunde und Zeitgenossen 138–40.

166. MINNA WAGNER, ZURICH   La Spezia, 5 September [1853][1]

Oh my dear Minnikins,

I'd sacrifice the whole of Italy to be with you today! My state of health is indescribable: you know how we once made fun of Eisner[2] in Paris; well, now I feel exactly the same; I have but a single thought: how to get back home to you again as quickly as possible!

To be sure, this change of mood has been brought on by ill health. The trouble is that a drink of fresh water is out of the question here; I may have had too much ice and iced water: in short, at the end of 3 days, I was suddenly struck by diarrhoea and, as a result, am now feeling increasingly weak and dizzy, with a tendency towards feverishness; a very depressed melancholy mood. On Saturday evening – as I told you last time – I set out to sea; I thought the sea air would do me good. We had a strong headwind and heavy seas; it certainly brought back memories! All around me people were being seasick; I too freely threw overboard the entire contents of the meal I had eaten on land at midday; but then I lay down in my berth and thereafter had

1 Wagner left Zurich for Italy on 24 August, returning home on 10 September. The journey was largely financed by Otto Wesendonck. This letter to Minna was written on the day of the so-called La Spezia vision (*Mein Leben* 511–12; English trans. 499); see introductory essay, pp. 162–3.

2 No further details known.

no further trouble from seasickness, spending the entire night stretched out in my bunk. –

We arrived in the Gulf of Spezia early yesterday morning: my diarrhoea had subsided, whereas my dizziness and violent stomach pains had increased. As a result, there was nothing that could cheer or distract me. Although I left quite early in order to spend an hour walking in the mountains wherever the fancy took me, and although everything I saw was quite splendid and beautiful, with strange and surprising vegetation, – nothing sunk in; my mood grew increasingly mawkish, and each time that I thought that it was your birthday tomorrow and that I was five days' journey away from you, I felt like screaming out in my unhappiness. I almost choked with despair. After lunch I took another carriage and instructed the driver to take me along the Gulf for a couple of hours' ride: it was Sunday, everyone dressed up and shorn! But I couldn't stand it there either, and so I went back to my room, swore never again to go on a journey *by myself*, and finally collapsed in exhaustion. However, I became so anxious about falling asleep that I even asked for a doctor: but then I spent a quiet night. Unfortunately, my dizziness and stomach pains this morning are as bad as ever: my mood is unbearable, and the thought of being so far away from you today lies on me like a ton-weight. In addition, I feel so helpless here, and so pitifully alone, that I can scarcely think any longer of continuing my journey. Today, or tomorrow morning at the latest, I shall return to Genoa: I'll see then how I feel! If I still feel as I do today, the only remedy will be to return home immediately; I shall then not bother with Nice but travel by the most direct route possible to Lago Maggiore, in order to return to Zurich across the Gotthardt: in that case, it would be splendid if you were able to come some of the way to meet me – as soon as you feel well enough – , perhaps as far as Flüelen? – However, if my health improves a little, and if I feel able to continue the journey that I had previously planned, I shall certainly go on to Nice after all, and if the problems with my passport can be sorted out, I shall probably also go on to Paris. But I cannot say anything definite about this today – In fact – if you could come to Nice, that would change everything: I invite you to join me there with all my heart and with open arms! But will your state of health allow you to do so? I fear that such a long journey cannot be expected of you at present! However – speak to Dr Rahn, my good Minnikins, he may finally agree to your coming. Dear God, I'd hate to think that I had undertaken this journey to no purpose, and I'd do anything to avoid running away à la Eisner. But the state I am in at present cannot be allowed to last any longer, otherwise there is nothing for me to do but return home. – In order to come to a provisional decision, let's leave things as they are. When you reply to today's letter, write to me in *Nice* (Regno di Sardogna). In the event of my not going to Nice but returning home instead from Genoa, I would telegraph from Genoa to tell you what I was doing, so that you would receive the telegraphic despatch before this letter. If you do *not* receive a telegraphic despatch, but only this letter, you can take that as a sign that I have gone on to Nice. And so, as soon as I telegraph you to say that I am coming home, keep all the letters that arrive for me from that moment onwards, otherwise send them to Nice if, by the time you receive this letter, you have not had a despatch from me. (Unfortunately, there is no telegraph office here, otherwise I should of course have used it to send you my best wishes for today.)

God knows what will become of me today: at the moment, I believe rather that I shall be returning home than continuing my journey. I feel dreadful and cannot describe how much I yearn to be with a friendly soul: I am really too home-loving a person to be able to derive any pleasure in the long term from foreign things. Never again shall I undertake such a long journey without you, or at least without a close friend. Otherwise, I feel such misery suddenly seizing hold of my soul, it is as though I might choke! In such circumstances, introductions to strangers are no use. In Genoa I finally delivered a letter Caronti had given me: I didn't meet the man, and the next day *he* didn't meet me; and so I continued my journey. If only one were younger and had not lived through so many fateful experiences: now only familiar sights can help! –

Today it has finally begun to rain a little; maybe this will help my condition; up to now I've been unlucky since the horizon has never been fully visible but has always been shrouded in a heat haze; as a result I have yet to encounter the beautiful evening light one associates with Italy. –

Here in Spezzia the entire Sardinian court, with the exception of the King himself, is at present in residence, including the Saxon princess who was married here – but I have yet to see them for myself. –

Once again: ah, if only *I were with you today!* I mustn't think of it, otherwise I shall burst with unhappiness! Today, while I am writing this wretched letter to you, I expect you will receive my ecstatic letter from Genoa: what an irony! –

You'll soon learn more about my decision; fare you well my good Minnikins! Be more cheerful than I am! regards to little Peps and get better for when we see each other again! Adieu, Adieu!!

Your very melancholy
Richard

Sammlung Burrell 427–9.

167. FERDINAND HEINE, DRESDEN   [Zurich, 31 October 1853]

Dear Heinemann,

I've just been to Paris[1] – but only for a rendezvous with Liszt; when he left, I sent for my old woman to join me, and spent eight days entertaining her at the scene of our former sufferings. She brought your letter with her; I am most grateful to you for writing. You poor brute, you must really have toiled and sweated over the work[2] – I can well imagine! As a reward you shall one day join me in Paradise! –

Even without having seen the results, I can well believe them to be wholly admirable, and I am certainly looking forward to seeing your work with my own eyes, since it has already so bedazzled Härtels that they intend publishing it against your will in a luxury edition.

Your remarks on the Weimar production showed me that on that occasion you had understood me perfectly in every instance: I have no doubts on that score. But there were a couple of occasions in your recent communication when it seemed as though you had lapsed into your old stage-costume mannerisms, causing me to shake my head in lively disagreement.

You think my stage directions are inadequate to depict Elsa's bridal procession in the 2nd act, given the length of the music (and the artistic effect I aim to achieve here), and you suggest – as a prelude to the actual bridal procession – some kind of courtly ceremony, an idea with which I simply cannot find myself in agreement. There is far too much ceremonial here for the noble and naïve simplicity of that period: Henry the Fowler knew nothing of marshals etc. in the sense in which they are later found: with him a "marshal" is the actual stablelad and so on; it was his son Otto I who (on accepting the Imperial crown) first introduced all this business associated with the Frankish-Byzantine court; he appointed princes as his marshal, butler etc. But what constitutes the local colour of my *Lohengrin* is precisely that we should see before us an old *German* kingdom, in its most beautiful and most ideal essence. Nobody does anything here out of mere routine or courtly custom, rather do the participants take a direct and heartfelt interest in every encounter; there is no despotic ostentation here, with its "bodyguards" (oh! oh!) "forcing the populace back" to form a "guard of honour" for their lordships. No, they are simple boys who provide an escort for a young lady, boys before whom the others all yield cheerfully and entirely of their own accord. I beg you, my dearest Heinemännel, for God's sake get rid of all that dreadful stuff with the masters of ceremony, marshals, bodyguards etc; they

1 Wagner arrived in Paris on 9 October in the company of Liszt, Carolyne Sayn-Wittgenstein and Marie Wittgenstein. On the 10th he dined with Liszt's children, and was introduced to Cosima for the first time. Minna joined him on the 20th, and the two returned to Zurich on 28 October 1853.
2 Heine's design sketches for *Lohengrin*.

must have no further place *here*. Let my Lohengrin be *beautiful*, but not ostentatious and – silly. Look at my "herald", how the fellow sings, as though everything were a matter of personal concern to him: no machines!

It must be said that only a very large stage will be wide enough to allow the bridal procession the architectonic nuances I have in mind: in Paris it would take care of itself. In the case of smaller stages – since the music must not be cut – there is nothing for it but to delay the actual appearance of the main characters who make up the procession. However, on page 130 of the vocal score Elsa must actually pause – on the high ground in front of the knights' quarters: she is touched and moved, and can lean for support on a lady-in-waiting – as though overcome by her feelings of happiness; only after eight bars does she then proceed slowly towards the minster, frequently stopping on the way, returning the greetings of the individual onlookers in her sincere and simple fashion. – In *this* way, not only will this fill *out* the scene, it will also turn it into what I really intended; namely, not a marchlike procession but *Elsa's* infinitely rich and significant progress to the altar: during the music she herself has an uncommonly significant silent role to play, and this must hold our undivided attention.

I know – you will *now* understand me, and would have understood me at once if I had played over the music to you. Do it as best you can: but your gentlemen bodyguards etc. must go. –

Tomorrow I shall begin composition of my *Nibelung* dramas:[1] I'm all ready for it now. Otherwise things are tolerable here: I spent a delightful few days with Liszt and his entourage![2] –

I have bought *Wilhelm's* book:[3] I am now in the process of reading it, and I must say that it gives me a great deal of pleasure to observe this man's development. Give him my best wishes if ever you write to him; give your regards to Mama and Marie; and to the royal producer of the Dresden Opera[4] I would ask you to convey my most brotherly gratitude for his loyalty. Fare you well, dear old fellow: write again soon!

Yours,
R. W.

Sammlung Burrell 444–5.

1 See letter [163], p. 286, note 2.
2 See letter [163].
3 Wilhelm Heine's *Wanderbilder aus Central-Amerika. Skizzen eines deutschen Malers* (Travellers' Tales from Central America: Sketches by a German Painter) (Leipzig 1853); see also letter [96], pp. 179–80.
4 i.e. Heine himself.

168. FRANZ LISZT, WEIMAR   [Zurich, 14 November 1853][1]

My friend! I am in a state of wonderment! A new world stands revealed
before me. The great scene in the Rhinegold is finished: I see before me
riches such as I never dared suspect. I now consider my powers to be
immeasurable: everything seethes within me and makes music. It is –

oh, I am *in love*! – and so divine a faith inspires me that I have no need
any longer – even of *hope*!

Kind regards to the "spectral man"![2] You'll now be receiving a great deal
of things to do for me: prepare yourself. I'll write again soon.

Yours,
Richard W.

Liszt-Briefe I, 277.

169. NATALIE PLANER, LEIPZIG   Zurich, 19 November 1853

Dear Natalie,

We hear that you have left Bachmann's, and accepted an appointment at
the Hotel de Pologne. This is most unwelcome news, and I, in particular,
consider it unsuitable. If you are in need of a *good* home, I should like to
offer you one herewith. It is with us in Zurich. Minna has become very poorly,
and I am seriously concerned about her health, which is why I am anxious
to make everything as easy as possible for her at home: she must no longer
handle anything but always remain quiet, otherwise we shall have much to
fear for her. And so I am firmly resolved to take somebody into the house
who – together with a female cook – will run the house, keep everything in
good order, provide work for the seamstress, oversee the laundry, in a word,
do everything that *Minna* herself has seen to until now. But it would be quite
unthinkable to take a stranger into the house at a time when you, our own
relative, was forced to enter into service in an hotel. I have every confidence
that – if you regard it as a matter of honour – you will be able to do everything
that matters in our house. I am therefore offering you – with Minna's
approval – the said position, and under the following conditions: – you will
receive from me an annual allowance of *two hundred francs*, and of course
appropriate gifts as a member of the family. You will be given a room adjoining
our bedroom, with the bed as it is. Moreover, you will be able to spend your
time as you please, providing always that you maintain the house and household in the state that Minna has kept them until now.

1 Dating suggested by RWA.
2 See letter [158], p. 280.

If you agree to this, I should like you to start in the *New Year* at the latest: I would also ask you to hire a good servant in Leipzig or in Dresden, and bring him with you; we have already spoiled Cathrine to such an extent that she is now quite useless. Perhaps you know of a good maid: she shall be given whatever she demands; I shall send your fares immediately. You must do your best to find a good maid.

First send me an immediate reply so that I know whether I need to look elsewhere or not.[1]

Minna sends her kind regards!

Fare you well!

Yours,
Richard W.

Sammlung Burrell 643–4.

170. Franz Liszt, Weimar   [Zurich,] 15 January 1854

Dearest friend,

The *Rhinegold* is finished – : but *I* am finished as well!!! –

During recent weeks I have necessarily and intentionally rendered myself insensible by means of my work, and in so doing have suppressed every impulse to write to you until such time as I had completed it. This is the first morning that I can no longer find a pretext not to give vent to the wretchedness that I have nourished and restrained for so long! Let it break forth then, – I can no longer contain it! –

Apart from your (so kind!) report on the Leipzig Lohengrin,[2] I also received one from the "Deutsche Allgemeine", and see what a humiliating punishment I must suffer for the crime I committed against my very nature and against my innermost conscience when, two years ago, I was false to a resolve that was so necessary to me, and agreed to performances of my operas taking place! – Ah, how pure I was then, how true to myself when I had only *you* and *Weimar* in mind, and refused to hear of any other theatre, having resolved to forgo all further successes.

Well, it is too late for that now! I have broken my resolve: my pride has been humbled, and it is now a question of meekly submitting to the yoke of the Jews and the philistines!

But how shameful that in return for having sacrificed the most noble thing I own, I have not even received the reward which seemed to have been set

1 Natalie appears to have taken up the offer; see Fehr I,288 and 306.
2 First performed in Leipzig on 7 January 1854. The performance went badly, although Liszt in his letter of 8 January tried to disguise the fact from Wagner. A report carried by the *Deutsche Allgemeine Zeitung* on the 10th served to disabuse him.

aside for me! I still remain the beggar I was before! Dear Franz! not a year of my life has passed recently without my finding myself at least *once* on the very brink of a decision to end my life. Everything about it is so muddled and so hopeless! As a result of a hasty marriage [at¹ the age of 23] to a woman whom I respect but who is totally unsuited to me, I have become an outlaw for life. For a long time the common pressures of my position in life, together with my ambitious plans and wishes to escape those pressures by becoming famous, were the only thing capable of concealing from me my very real emptiness of heart. In truth, I reached the age of 36 before I became fully aware of that terrible emptiness: until then my nature was held in a state of balance between two conflicting elements of desire within me, one of which I sought to appease by means of my art, while periodically giving vent to the other by means of passionate, fantastical [and sensual] extravagances. (You know my Tannhäuser, this idealization of a demeanour which in reality is often quite trivial! –)

But then – in Lohengrin perhaps – I had the feeling, nay the certainty, that these two currents came together as a single unity in true *love*, love which I could know only through yearning but never through actual experience. God, how gladly would I have fled naked into the world and become purely and simply a *happily loving and loved human being*! Well – *that* is something I shall never again be able to be: I shall never be *happy* in love, but only *unhappy* – an "outlaw – an impossible individual"!! –

My dearest friend, – since that time my art has really been no more than of secondary interest to me, a mere *makeshift*, nothing more! Yet time and again it has ended up by becoming a very real makeshift, forcing me literally to make shift with it, simply in order for me to *exist*. But it is really only out of utter despair that I take up my art again: when this happens, and I again have to renounce reality, – if I am obliged once more to plunge into the waves of an artist's imagination in order to find satisfaction in an imaginary world, I must at least help out my imagination and find means of encouraging my imaginative faculties. I cannot then live like a dog, I cannot sleep on straw and drink common gin: mine is an intensely irritable, acute, and hugely voracious, yet uncommonly tender and delicate sensuality which, one way or another, must be flattered if I am to accomplish the cruelly difficult task of creating in my mind a non-existent world.

– Well! once I had resumed my plans for the Nibelungs and for their actual completion, there was much that I needed to inspire in me the requisite mood of artistic sensuality: – it was necessary for me to be able to lead a better life than had recently been the case! The success of *Tannhäuser* (a work I had sacrificed precisely because of that hope) was now intended to help me: – I

---

1 The words in square brackets ("im 23sten Jahre" and "sinnliche") were omitted from the published edition.

reorganized my domestic arrangements, squandered (my God – squandered!!) what money I had on every conceivable article of luxurious necessity: *your* visit last summer, yes – your example – everything contributed to a wilful sense of self-delusion on my part (or rather: gave me the desire for self-delusion) concerning my life. I finally stopped asking what things cost, but simply appropriated everything imaginable, everything that was in any way capable of making a favourable impression on me, or giving me a sense of well-being. The culmination of this whim came in St Moritz, in the midst of my mortification.

– My revenues seemed to be utterly infallible. In this unnatural mood of self-content, I again conceived a desire to write music. But scarcely had I returned from Paris[1] when my situation became critical: the requests for my operas, and for Lohengrin in particular, which I had been counting on, were not forthcoming: as the year drew to a close, it became clear that I should need a very, very large sum of money if I were to survive in my nest of philistines during the weeks which were to follow. And so I considered what to do, wrote to you, and to Härtels – the latter with a view to selling the performing rights of my works; – but nothing came of it. I wrote to Berlin, to my agent[2] there: he offered me the prospect of a good buyer whom I in turn referred to the first performance of Lohengrin in Leipzig. Well, this has now taken place: my agent informs me that it is not possible, in view of the outcome of the performance, to persuade the buyer – in spite of his great willingness – finally to buy the work. –

You must admit, it's a real *"situation"* in which I now find myself!! –

And this torment, distress and concern for a life that I hate, and that I curse! – and for the sake of which I make myself look ridiculous in the eyes of my house-guests, – and at the same time enjoy the wanton pleasure of having abandoned the *most noble work* I have so far created to the predictable stupidity of our theatre rabble and to the philistine's scorn!

God, how do I see myself – ! If only I had the pleasure of knowing that there was someone else who *knew* how I see myself! –

Listen, Franz! You must help me now! Things are bad – *very* bad. If I am to rediscover the means to *survive* (and the full import of this word is not lost on me!), then something *sensible* must be done now that I am embarked on a course which involves the prostitution of my art, – otherwise that's the end of it. Have you not thought any more about *Berlin*?[3] something **must** now be achieved there if this is not to be the end of everything! –

Above all, however, I must also have *money*: – Härtels have been very open-

1 On 28 October 1853.
2 The agent in question, Hermann Michaelson, tried in vain to interest the Berlin firm of Bote & Bock in buying the performing rights of Wagner's operas.
3 See letter [134], p. 246, note 1.

handed,[1] but of what use are hundreds when I need thousands. If the Berlin sale had come off, I could at least have used the *offer* of the same to convince a businessman here of my "capital", so that he would have lent me the necessary sum over a period of three years (with repayment of a third of the sum at the end of each year). I can now say goodbye to all that. The only person who could agree to such a deal must have a private faith in my future (?) successes. Listen, my dearest Franz, you *must* find me such a *man*. Once more: I need – in order to restore me to a state of total calm and equanimity – *three* to *four* thousand thalers. My operas could very easily bring in this amount of money in three years *if* a real effort is now made to save *Lohengrin*: I shall lease my performing rights to the lender, and would relinquish every right to Tannhäuser and Lohengrin in whatever way was thought desirable or necessary. – If nobody considers me worthy of such a service – you'll admit that things will then look very bleak indeed for me, and everything will have been self-delusion!!! – Help me to get over this – for I want to be able to *survive* once more. –

My dear friend, do not be angry with me! I have a just claim on you, as on my *creator*! *You are* the creator of the man I now am: I now live *through you* – that is no exaggeration. Take care of your creature: I call upon you to do so as a duty which you have to perform. –

You see, it is simply a question of *money*: there shouldn't be any problem here. I abandon *love* to take its course – and *art*?? –

Well, the *Rhinegold* is finished – more finished than I thought. With what faith, with what joy did I set to work on the music! But it was in a real rage of despair that I continued the work and finally completed it: I, too, alas, learned what distress is caused by gold! Believe me, no work has ever been composed like this before: I imagine my music must be terrible; it is a morass of horrors and sublimities! –

Soon – (??) I shall prepare a fair copy: – black on white: I expect that is as far as it will go. Or perhaps I shall also have it performed in Leipzig for 20 louis d'or!

I can write no more to you today: *you are the only person* whom I have told *this*: no one else suspects it, least of all those in my immediate vicinity – !

Do not think I have suddenly been plunged into despair by the news from Leipzig. I suspected what would happen and foresaw it all. I can also imagine that the situation in Leipzig will improve, and that "things are not as bad as one thinks" – and all the usual nonsense. Perhaps: – but let me see witnesses! – I no longer have any faith, and only one hope remains: to *sleep*, to *sleep*, so deeply, so deeply – that all sensation of life's anguish fades. I ought after all to be able to achieve that sleep: it is not so difficult. –

1 Breitkopf & Härtel had sent Wagner 300 thalers for nine numbers from *Lohengrin*.

My God, now I'll be causing you bad feeling, too: – what have you done to deserve that! –

The present from the Frau Kapellmeister[1] brought a smile to my lips – a smile that in turn could have brought tears to my eyes. I shall write to her if I survive a few more days: then I shall send you my portrait with a motto which may finally succeed in embarrassing you!

– How are things otherwise? when is the wedding? Burn this letter! it is godless – but I am god-less: be thou one of God's saints, – for I believe in no one but you: Yes, indeed! – and once again: Yes, indeed!

Yours,
R. W.

Something must come of *London*: I myself shall even go to *America* to satisfy my future creditor: I would offer to do even this in order to complete my Nibelungs.

RWA (incompletely published in Liszt-Briefe II, 3–8).

171. AUGUST RÖCKEL, WALDHEIM   Zurich, 25/26 January 1854

How I came to leave your letter unanswered for almost four months is something I can now easily explain to myself, but it will not be so easy to explain the reason to you, my dearest friend! At all events, it was the weightiness of your letter that was chiefly to blame, so that to have answered it at all adequately depended not so much upon my will as, more especially, upon my ability to do so. I was very unsettled last summer. *Liszt* visited me in July; I then went to take the waters at St Moritz in Graubünden (6000 feet above sea-level): at the end of August I repaired to Italy – or at least to such parts as are open to me: Turin, Genoa, Spezzia; I then intended going on to Nice in order to spend some time there; but it was here in this foreign country where such an appalling sense of loneliness preyed upon my mind that I suddenly sank into a deep state of melancholy – which was also the result of a purely physical indisposition – and as a result could not get home quickly enough across Lago maggiore and the Gotthardt. It was while I was recovering here that your letter arrived: but at the same time came an invitation from Liszt to rendezvous with him in Paris. I spent the whole of October there – which led the local newspapers to claim that Liszt and I were planning to perform my operas in Paris: in the midst of all this turmoil, I found it impossible to answer your letter, but fully intended to do so on my return to Zurich. Having arrived back here, I was overwhelmed at last by so violent a

---

1 Carolyne Sayn-Wittgenstein.

desire to set to work on the musical composition of the "Rhinegold" that I was simply not in the right frame of mind to reply to your critical remarks on my poem: it was impossible, I could not! But – after a complete break of 6 years! – I now threw myself passionately into my music, and finally resolved not to write to you until I had finished the composition of the Rhinegold. Well, I have now reached that point; – and I now understand my reluctance to reply to you sooner, for only now that I have finished composing the work do I suddenly find myself in a position to reply to you; and yet my position has changed in the meantime, with the result that I suspect the best course for me is virtually to ignore your criticisms: you are quite right to criticize me, but I, too, am right to have conceived and completed the matter as best I can and may. In other words – I shall not argue with you, but we may well discuss the affair somewhat!

First, however, as regards my present letter, let me tell you how enormously cheered and gratified I was to hear from you and learn how you were faring. I come back to the belief that you strike me as being almost more fortunate in your present position than I am in mine. Every line of your letter attests to your excellent health: I assure you that this news fills me with the most lively admiration! That you were allowed to write me a five-page letter also bears witness to the improvement in your personal situation, an improvement for which I am heartily thankful, although I am bound to admit that I can imagine circumstances in which I might have to forgo each and every alleviation to existence without grieving unduly over what I had given up. One thing counts above all else: freedom! But what is "freedom"? is it – as our politicians believe – "licence?" – of course not! Freedom is: *integrity*. He who is true to himself, i.e. who acts in accord with his own being, and in perfect harmony with his own nature, is *free*; strictly speaking, outward constraint is powerless unless it succeeds in destroying the integrity of its victim, inducing him to dissemble and to persuade himself and others that he is a different person from the one he really is. That is true servitude. But the victim of constraint need never let it come to this: and the man who – even under constraint – preserves his integrity also preserves his basic freedom; certainly more than the person who no longer notices constraints such as the whole world now contains, since he has already accommodated his very being to their power and perverted his nature for their sake.

I believe that this "integrity" is essentially the same as the "truth" of which we read in books on philosophy and theology. "Truth" is a concept and, by its nature, is simply objectified "integrity"; the actual content of this "integrity", however, is "reality" pure and simple, or rather: "the real", "what really is", and only what is "material" is "real", whereas the "immaterial" is certainly also "unreal", in other words merely "thought" or "imagined". If I am therefore justified in calling "integrity" the most comprehensive *feeling* for reality, at the same time as *acknowledging* that feeling, then "truth", in the final analysis, is once again merely the concept of that feeling, or at least has become so in philosophy: it is certain, however, that this concept is as remote from reality as "integrity" – in the sense already indicated – is close to it, which is why people have always deluded themselves as to "truth", so that it has actually become the most deceptive thing in the world; like every concept, it has ended up by becoming no more than a word, and on the basis of such "words" it is of course easy enough to "construct a system", but in doing so one loses hold of reality. Our surest grasp of reality is through feeling, and true feeling is perceived exclusively through the senses. It must be added that what we understand here by "senses" is not what philosophers and theologians mean when they speak with total contempt of the *animal* senses, but the *human* senses which, as is well known, are capable of measuring the stars and imagining their courses. – Now, we shall soon find ourselves in agreement about the "world", inasmuch as it is the object of our feeling of integrity, if we allow ourselves to be guided by our only reliable source of experience, namely feeling, and pay heed solely to the impressions received from that source. The individual, acting in accordance with his own natural temperament, makes use of endless expedients in order to grasp the world as a whole: these expedients, in all their most manifold complexities, are the "concepts" already described: so proud do we deem ourselves in our ability to grasp a whole by means of concepts that, believing we have the whole, we involuntarily forget that what we have is merely a concept, in other words our pleasure comes simply from an instrument of our own making, while in the meantime we have strayed further than ever from the reality of the world. But the man who in the long term can find no real pleasure in the madness of this self-delusion will no doubt end up by realizing how unsatisfactory is his own nature; he will perceive how arrogant and unedifying is his self-delusion, and he will finally recognize the need to approach reality once again in total consciousness and with the aid of feeling. But how is this reality to be grasped once more, since – as an imaginary whole – it had presented itself not to our feelings but solely to our intellect? It can be grasped of course only if we recognize that the essence of reality lies in its endless *multiplicity*. This inexhaustible multiplicity which incessantly reproduces and renews itself can be apprehended, however, by feeling, which perceives it simply as a separate, ever-changing phenomenon: this sense of change is the essence of reality, whereas only what is imagined is changelessly unending. Only what changes is *real*: to be real, to live – what this means is to be created, to grow, to bloom, to wither and to die; without the necessity of death, there is no possibility of life; that alone has no end which has no beginning – but nothing real can be without a beginning, only what has been conceived in the mind. Therefore, to be consumed by truth is to abandon oneself as a sentient human being to total reality: to experience procreation, growth, bloom – withering and decay, to apprehend them unreservedly, in joy and in sorrow, and to choose to live – and die – a life of happiness and suffering. This alone is "to be consumed by truth". – But in order to make such a consummation possible, we must abandon completely our search for the "whole": the whole reveals itself to us only in the individual manifestation, for this alone is capable of being *apprehended*[1] in the true sense of the word; we can *really "grasp"* a phenomenon only if we can allow ourselves to be fully absorbed by it, just as we must in turn be able to assimilate it fully within us. How is this marvellous process most fully achieved? ask nature! Only through *love*! – everything that I cannot love remains outside me, and I remain outside it: the philosopher may no doubt imagine that he can grasp what is going on here, but not the true human being. But the full reality of love is possible only between the sexes: only as *man* and *woman* can we *human beings* really love, whereas all other forms of love are mere derivatives of it, originating in it, related to it or an unnatural imitation of it. It is wrong to regard this love as only *one* manifestation of love in general, and to assume that other and higher forms must therefore exist *alongside* it. Certainly, he who, like the metaphysician, places abstraction before reality and derives sentient reality from ideality – he who thereby prefers logic to genetics – may be right to imagine that the *concept* of love existed before the actual expression of love, and accordingly to speak of the revelation of a pre-existing, non-sensuous love by means of real, sensual love: but he will then do well to despise *this* love as he despises the senses in general. Yet it would be safe to bet that he himself had never loved or been loved in the way that others can love, otherwise he would have realized that in despising this feeling what he had in mind was only animal love, and animal sensuality in general, rather than human love. The highest satisfaction of individual egoism is to be found in its total abandonment, and this is something which human beings can achieve only through love: but the true human being is both man and woman, and only in the union of man and woman does the true human being exist, and only through love, therefore, do man and woman become human. Whenever we speak nowadays of "humankind", it must be admitted that we are so insensately stupid that we always think involuntarily only of men. But it is the union of man and woman, in other words, love, that creates (physically and metaphorically) the human being, and just as the human being can conceive of nothing more creatively brilliant than his own existence and his own life, so he can never again surpass that act whereby he became human through love; he can only repeat it – just as our entire lives are a constant repetition of the multiplicity of details of individual moments in our lives – and it is this repetition which alone makes possible the unique nature of this love whereby it resembles the ebb and flow of the tide, changing, ending and living anew. It is therefore a grievous

---

1 There is an untranslatable play on words here: the German verb *wahrnehmen* (to apprehend) literally means "to take" (*nehmen*) as "true" (*wahr*).

misconception of love to regard as a weakness this quality according to which it can constantly repeat itself and be constantly renewed: whereas conceptual love abstracted from real love, like the love of God-knows-what-universal-abstraction, is imagined as the one genuine form of love precisely because it has permanence. The mere possibility of its indefinite continuance proves how non-essential is this kind of love. "Eternal" – in the true sense of the word – is that which negates finitude (or rather: the concept of finitude): the concept of finitude is unsuited to "reality", for reality, i.e. something that is constantly changing, new and multifarious – is precisely the negation of all that is merely imagined and conceived as finite: the infinitude of metaphysics is eternal unreality. The finite is merely an idea, albeit one that can cause us considerable disquiet; and yet it can do so only when we are unable to apprehend reality through the emotions: if, on the other hand, the reality of love draws upon us with the full force of its presence, it will negate the concept that disquiets us and destroy finitude by preventing all idea of it from entering our minds. Thus only reality is eternal, the most perfect reality, however, comes to us only in the enjoyment of love; it is thus the most eternal of all sentiments. – Egoism, in truth, ceases only when the "I" is subsumed by the "you": this "I" and "you", however, no longer show themselves as such the moment I align myself with the wholeness of the world: "I" and "the world" means nothing less than "I" alone; the world will not become a complete reality for me until it becomes "you", and this is something it can become only in the shape of the individual whom I love. This phenomenon may be repeated in a child or in a friend; but we shall only ever be able to love the child or the friend fully once we have learned to love at all, and this is something that man, for ex., must learn from woman; there is no doubt but that our love for a child or for a friend is merely a kind of makeshift solution, which is most clearly recognized as such by those who have found perfect happiness in sexual love; this is simply one feature of the multiplicity of human nature which allows a place even for abnormalities, abnormalities of the most ridiculous as of the most tragic kind. –

Enough of this! I make so bold as to send this confession of my faith to you in your solitude, without fear of depressing you by sharing my views with you. Not only you, but I, too, – like everyone else – now live in circumstances and conditions which force us to depend upon surrogate measures and make-shift solutions; for you, no less than for me, the truest, most real life can be only something imaginary, something we long for. I had reached the age of 36 before I divined the true reason for my creative impulse: until then I had regarded art as the end and life as a means to that end. But I made this discovery too late, with the result that my new instinct for life was bound to end in tragedy. By taking a broader view of today's world, we can further see that love has now become wholly impossible; one of my friends could call upon the Germans, for ex., with total impunity: "you simply do not know what love is: how can people wish to love who have no initiative of character? – it is quite impossible!" – If it is a question, therefore, of seeking to save ourselves by means of some makeshift solution, I can find none better than a totally honest approach to the above-described state of affairs, and a frank admission of the truth, even if there be no other personal gain to be had from this than the pride of knowing the truth, and, ultimately, the will and the endeavour to pass on that knowledge to the rest of mankind and thus set them on the path that will lead to their redemption. In this way we are certainly working for the whole of mankind, but it is purely as a makeshift solution, since we know that it is not on his own that the individual can be happy, but only when the whole of mankind is happy, for only then may he, too, feel satisfied. You see that in this I share your point of view entirely, except that I regard this point of view not as an end in itself but simply as a means, as a way to achieve my goal: this goal, however, has not yet been recognized as such by the majority of people: but I have indicated above what I understand it to be; it is to render love possible as the most perfect realization of reality – truth; not a conceptual, abstract, non-sensuous love (the only kind possible *now*) but the love of "I" and "you".

Thus I can regard the prodigious efforts of the human race, and hence of each and every present-day science, merely as ways and means whose goal in itself is so infinitely simple and yet so divine an outcome. Thus I respect every one of these exertions, and acknowledge that every step is necessary, rejoicing heartily when each new step is taken: I myself, however, have this simple goal so clearly in sight that I find it impossible to tear my eyes away from it in order to participate in this striving (which is basically unconscious of its goal): only the pressure of a great movement could bring about such an act of self-denial on my part; I shall welcome it, if and when it comes, as the sole means of redemption for me. – But will you now hold it against me if I simply shrug off with a smile your advice to abandon my dreams and egotistical fancies, and devote myself instead to what alone is real, life itself and its aspirations, and if I prefer to believe that I may devote myself to total reality much more decisively, more consciously and more immediately by applying every expression of my life, including the most anguished, solely to that goal and to publicizing it? You will, I hope, agree with me if, for ex., I deny "Robespierre" the tragic significance which he has hitherto had for you, or admit it only with considerable reservations. This type of character is so deeply unsympathetic to me because in none of the individuals who take after him can I find the least idea of what constitutes the true import of man's striving since the time of our degeneracy from nature. What is tragic about Robespierre is really the unbelievable wretchedness which this man displayed when, having reached the goal of his ambitions, he stood there totally ignorant of what he should do with the power he had achieved. He only becomes tragic because he admits as much to himself and because he was destroyed by his inability to do anything or to bring any happiness to people's lives. That is why I find his case the exact opposite of what you conceive it to be: he was not conscious of any higher purpose in the attainment of which he had recourse to unworthy means; no, it was in order to conceal his lack of any such purpose and his very real want of resource that he had recourse to the whole terrible machinery of the guillotine; for it has been shown that the "terreur" was manipulated purely as a means of governing and of maintaining power, without any real passion, but purely for political – i.e. ambitious and selfish reasons. And so this deeply pitiful man – who ended up having to make an ostentatious display of his tasteless "vertu" – really had no other aim than the means he adopted, as is always the case with purely political heroes who are quite justifiably destroyed by their own impotence, so that it is to be hoped that this entire class of men will soon disappear completely from history. – On the other hand, I remain convinced that my Lohengrin (according to my own conception of it) symbolizes the most profoundly tragic situation of the present day, namely man's desire to descend from the most intellectual heights to the depths of love, the longing to be understood instinctively, a longing which modern reality cannot yet satisfy.

But I have held forth on this matter at sufficient length in my preface.[1] All that remains for me to indicate here is what, given my present standpoint, I must now feel urged to do if I and the rest of mankind are to draw nearer the goal which I know has been set for mankind – but from which I, as an individual, must necessarily remain cut off as long as others continue to cut themselves off from it – without having recourse to means of which I can no longer avail myself. This is where my art must come to the rescue: and the work of art that I had no choice but to conceive in this sense is none other than my *Nibelung poem*. I am almost inclined to believe that it was less the lack of clarity of the present version of the poem than your own point of view (which you have adopted with such earnestness and which is really quite remote from my own) which is to blame for your failure to understand a number of points in it. Such errors are of course possible only in the case of a reader who is himself a creative artist and who recreates the work from within himself: whereas the naïve individual assimilates the matter as it is, without any clear consciousness but at least with greater ease. For me my poem has only the following meaning: –

Depiction of reality in the sense indicated above. – Instead of the words: "a gloomy day dawns on the gods: in shame shall end your noble race, if you do not give up the ring!" I now make *Erda* say merely: "All that is – ends: a gloomy day dawns on the gods: I counsel you, shun the ring!" – We must learn *to die*, and *to die* in the fullest sense of the word; fear of the end is the source of all lovelessness, and this fear is generated only when love itself is

1 i.e. *A Communication to my Friends.*

already beginning to wane. How did it come about that a feeling which imparts the highest bliss to all living things was so far lost sight of by the human race that everything that the latter did, ordered and established was finally conceived only out of a fear of the end? My poem shows the reason why. It shows nature in all its undistorted truth and essential contradictions, contradictions which in their infinitely varied manifestations embrace even what is mutually repellent. But it is not the fact that Alberich was repulsed by the Rhine-daughters which is the definitive source of all evil – for it was entirely natural for them to repulse him; no, Alberich and his ring could not have harmed the gods unless the latter had already been susceptible to evil. Where, then, is the germ of this evil to be found? Look at the first scene between Wodan[1] and Fricka – which leads ultimately to the scene in the 2nd act of the Valkyrie. The firm bond which binds them both, sprung from the involuntary error of a love that seeks to prolong itself beyond the stage of necessary change and to obtain mutual guarantees in contravention of what is eternally new and subject to change in the phenomenal world – this bond constrains them both to the mutual torment of a loveless union. As a result, the remainder of the poem is concerned to show how necessary it is to acknowledge change, variety, multiplicity and the eternal newness of reality and of life, and to yield to that necessity. Wodan rises to the tragic heights of *willing* his own destruction. This is all that we need to learn from the history of mankind: *to will what is necessary* and to bring it about ourselves. The final creative product of this supreme, self-destructive will is a *fearless* human being, one who never ceases to *love*: *Siegfried*. – That is all. – It may be added as a matter of detail that the pernicious power that poisons love is concentrated in the *gold* that is stolen from nature and put to ill use, the Nibelung's ring: the curse that clings to it is not lifted until it is restored to nature and until the gold has been returned to the Rhine. This, too, becomes clear to Wodan only at the very end, once he has reached the final goal of his tragic career; in his lust for power, he had utterly ignored what *Loge* had so frequently and so movingly warned him of at the beginning of the poem; initially – thanks to Fafner's deed – he learned to recognize the power of the curse; but not until the ring proves the ruin of Siegfried, too, does he see that only by restoring to the Rhine what had been stolen from its depths can evil be destroyed, and that is why he makes his own longed-for downfall a pre-condition of the extirpation of a most ancient wrong. *Experience* is every- thing. Not even Siegfried alone (man alone) is the complete "human being": he is merely the half, only with *Brünnhilde* does he become the redeemer; *one* man alone cannot do everything; many are needed, and a suffering, self- immolating woman finally becomes the true, conscious redeemer: for it is love which is really "the eternal feminine" itself. – So much for the broadest

1 See letter [130], p. 238, note 1.

and most general aspects of the poem: they contain within them all the individual and more specific details. –

I cannot but think that you have taken this to be my meaning: only it seems to me that you have placed more weight on the middle and intermediary links in this great chain than is due to them as such; it is as though you had to do so in order to justify your own preconceived interpretation of my poem. On the whole I am out of sympathy with the specific objections which you have levelled against any ostensible lack of clarity in individual episodes. On the contrary, I believe it was a true instinct that led me to guard against an excessive eagerness to make things plain, for I have learned to feel that to make one's intentions too obvious risks impairing a proper understanding of the work in question; in drama – as in any work of art – , it is a question of making an impression not by parading one's opinions but by setting forth what is instinctive. It is precisely this that distinguishes my poetic material from the political material which is virtually all that is current today. By insisting, for ex., that Wodan's appearance in "Young Siegfried" should be invested with a greater sense of motivation than is at present the case, you risk destroying the intentional sense of instinctiveness in the development of the whole which I have been at pains to achieve. Following his farewell to Brünnhilde, Wodan is in truth no more than a departed spirit: true to his supreme resolve, he must now allow events *to take their course*, leave things as they are, and nowhere interfere in any decisive way; that is why he has now become the "Wanderer": observe him closely! he resembles *us* to a tee; he is the sum total of present-day intelligence, whereas Siegfried is the man of the future whom we desire and long for but who cannot be made by us, since he must create himself on the basis of *our own annihilation*. In such a guise, Wodan – you must admit – is of extreme interest to us, whereas he would inevitably seem unworthy if he were merely a subtle intriguer, which is what he would be if he gave advice which was *apparently* meant to harm Siegfried but which in truth was intended to help not only Siegfried but, first and foremost, himself: that would be an example of deceit worthy of our political heroes, but not of my jovial god who stands in need of self-annihilation. See how he confronts Siegfried in the third act! Faced with the prospect of his own annihilation, he finally becomes so instinctively human that – in spite of his supreme resolve – his ancient pride is once more stirred, provoked more-over (mark this well!) by – his jealousy of Brünnhilde; for she it is who has become his most vulnerable spot. He refuses, so to speak, to be thrust aside, but prefers to fall – to be conquered: but even this is so little premeditated on his part that, in a sudden burst of passion, he even aspires to victory, a victory which – as he says – could only make him more wretched than ever. – In announcing my intentions I was obliged to keep within extremely narrow bounds in accordance with my own feelings on the matter: none the less, my hero should not leave behind the impression of a totally unconscious individual: on the contrary, in Siegfried I have tried to depict what I understand to be the most perfect human being, whose highest consciousness expresses itself in the fact that all consciousness manifests itself solely in the most immediate vitality and action: the enormous significance I attach to this consciousness – *which can almost never be stated in words* – will become clear to you from Siegfried's scene with the Rhine-daughters; here we learn that Siegfried is infinitely wise, for he knows the highest truth, that death is better than a life of fear: he, too, knows all about the ring, but pays no heed to its power, because he has better things to do; he keeps it simply as a token of the fact that he has not learned the meaning of fear. You will admit that all the splendour of the gods must inevitably grow pale in the presence of this man. Above all, I am struck by your question why, since the Rhinegold is returned to the Rhine, the gods nevertheless perish? – I believe that, at a good performance, even the most naïve spectator will be left in no doubt on this point. It must be said, however, that the gods' downfall is not the result of points in a contract which can of course be interpreted and twisted and turned at will – for which one would need only the services of a legally qualified politician acting as a lawyer; no, the necessity of this downfall arises from our innermost feelings – just as it arises from Wodan's feelings. Thus it was important to justify this sense of necessity *emotionally*, and this comes about as a matter of course providing only that the spectator follow the course of the entire action through each of its simple and natural motives, and that he follow it, moreover, from beginning to end with complete sympathy: when Wodan finally gives expression to this sense of necessity, he is merely repeating what we ourselves already deem to be necessary. When, at the end of the Rhinegold, *Loge* calls after the gods as they enter Valhalla: "They are hurrying to meet their end who think their might will last", he is simply expressing our own feelings at this moment, for anyone who follows the prelude sympathetically, rather than hypercritically and analytically, and who allows the events to work upon his emotions will be bound to admit the truth of *Loge*'s remark. –

Let me now say something about *Brünnhilde*. This figure, too, you have misunderstood inasmuch as you find her refusal to hand over the ring to Wodan harsh and unyielding. Did you not feel that Brünnhilde has cut herself off from Wodan and all the other gods for the sake of – *love*, because – where Wodan clung to plans – she only – *loved?* Moreover, from the moment *Siegfr.* awakens her, she has no longer any other knowledge save that of love. Now – the symbol of this love – after Siegfried has left her – is the *ring*: when Wodan demands it back from her, all she can think of is the reason for having left Wodan (when she acted out of love), and there is only one thing that she now knows, namely that she had renounced her divinity for the sake of love. But she knows that love is uniquely divine: Valhalla's splendour may fall in ruins, but she will not sacrifice the ring – (love –). I ask you, would she not stand before us as pitiful, mean and common if she were to refuse to return the ring because she had learned (from Siegfried, say) of its magic spell and of the power of its gold? You cannot seriously believe such a thing of this glorious woman? – But if you shudder at the thought that this woman should cling to this *accursèd ring* as a symbol of love, you will feel exactly as I intended you to feel, and herein you will recognize the power of the Nibelung curse raised to its most terrible and most tragic heights: only then will you recognize the need for the whole of the final drama, "Siegfried's Death". This is something we must experience for ourselves if we are to be made fully conscious of the evil of gold. Why does Brünnhilde yield so quickly to Siegfried when he comes to her in disguise? precisely because the latter has torn the *ring* from her finger, since it was here alone that her whole strength lay. The terrible and daemonic nature of this whole scene has escaped you entirely: a "stranger" passes – effortlessly – through the fire which, in accord with his destiny and our own experience, none but Siegfried should or could traverse: everything collapses at Br.'s feet, everything is out of joint; she is overpowered in a terrible struggle, she is "God-forsaken". And it is *Siegfried*, moreover, who in fact orders her to share his couch with him – *Siegfried* whom she (unconsciously – and therefore all the more bewilderingly) almost recognizes, by his gleaming eye, in spite of his disguise. (You feel that something "inexpressible" is happening here, and so it is very wrong of you to ask me to speak out on the subject!)

Well, I have certainly allowed my pen to run away with me: indeed, the fear of that happening was the reason why I delayed writing. It worried me that you could have so totally misunderstood certain aspects. But it certainly made clear to me that only when completed could the work hope to avoid being misunderstood: having then been seized by a violent desire to begin the music, I cheerfully abandoned myself to that urge before finally starting this letter. The completion of the Rhinegold (a task as difficult as it was important) has restored my sense of self-assurance, as you can see. I have once again realized how much of the work's meaning (given the nature of my poetic intent) is only made clear by the music: I can now no longer bear to look at the poem without music. In time I believe I shall be able to tell you about its composition. For now let me add merely that it has become a close-knit unity: there is scarcely a bar in the orchestra which does not develop out of preceding motifs. But it is impossible to explain this in a letter.

What you say with regard to completing and performing the whole has my complete support: you are fully aware of what is at issue here. I shall certainly heed your advice in everything. How I shall finally bring off a *performance* admittedly remains an enormous problem. But I shall tackle it when the time comes, since I can envisage no other aim that would be appropriate to my life. I am fairly certain that all the purely mechanical aspects of the enterprise can be brought off: but – my performers?! The very thought provokes a deep sigh from me. I must of course stick to young artists who have not already been totally ruined by our operatic stage: I am certainly not thinking of so-called "celebrities". But I shall have to wait and see how best to train my young people; what I should like is to keep my troupe together for a year without allowing them to perform in public; during that time I would work with them every day, giving them both a humane and an artistic training and gradually allowing them to ripen into their task. Even under the most favour-able conditions I could not count on a first performance before the summer of 1858. But no matter how long it takes, I continue to be attracted by the idea of giving myself a reason for living in the form of concentrated activity in pursuance of an object that is unique to me. As for the rest, I must remain deaf to all your advice concerning my life in general: there is nothing to be done here, where everything comes about of its own accord. Believe me, I have already contemplated "a life in the country": two years ago I visited a hydropathic establishment with the intention of becoming a radically healthy human being; I was prepared to give up my art and everything else if only I could return to being a child of nature. My dear friend, how I was forced to laugh at this naïve wish of mine, when I found myself on the verge of madness! None of us shall see the promised land: we shall all die in the wilderness. We are ripe for the madhouse, as the saying goes: we'll never recover. Since life is as it now is, nature permits only abnormalities to thrive, at best we are forced to be martyrs; he who wishes to avoid this vocation in life thereby rails against the possibilities of his existence. I can no longer exist except as an artist: everything else – now that I can no longer encompass love and life – disgusts me, or else is of interest only inasmuch as it has a bearing on art. The result of course is a life of torment, but it is the only possible life. I may add in this context that I have had some strange experiences with my nerves: when I suffer pain (which is now my normal state), I am bound to regard my nerves as completely shattered: wondrous to tell, however, these nerves of mine have performed a wonderful service whenever the need has arisen, inspiring me with beautiful and apt ideas, so that I then experience a clear-sightedness and an agreeable sensation of receptivity and creativity such as I have never previously known. Shall I then say that my nerves are shattered? No, I cannot. I see only that my normal condition – given the way my temperament has now developed – is a state of exaltation, whereas ordinary peace and quiet is its abnormal state. Indeed, I feel well only when I am "beside myself": only then do I feel to be myself. – If Göthe was different, I do not envy him for it, just as I have no wish to change places with anyone else, not even *Humboldt*, whom you consider a genius, an opinion I cannot share. In the final analysis, I am sure you feel as I do: for I do not suppose you would change places with anyone, and you would perhaps be right not to do so – at least you have my sincere admiration.

I am not so out of touch with nature as you suppose, even though I myself am no longer in a position to have scientific dealings with it. In these matters I look to *Herwegh*, who is also living here and who for some time now has been engaged in a most thorough study of nature: through this friend of mine I have learned some of the most beautiful and important things about nature, which influences me on many vital points. It is only when nature is expected to replace real life – love – that I ignore it. In this respect I resemble Brünnhilde with the ring. I would rather perish or be denied all enjoyment than renounce my belief.

You must not think me ungrateful if I respond to your advice in this way: how could I not be grateful to you for the love which inspires that advice? You see, it gives me infinite delight: I cannot tell you how deeply it touches me. This emotion is equalled only by my admiration for you, for your strength – and, at the same time, for your tenderness of spirit. If there is any one thing I should most care to learn it is that you had completed the work[1] which you wrote to tell me about. Is it possible? What do you need to be able to do so? Tell me precisely what it is, in case I can be of help. – Have you not heard anything from the publisher *Avenarius* in Leipzig? Unfortunately, he is the only person I thought I might be able to influence, since my dealings with my own publishers have always been through a third party, and totally unsatisfactory at that. I wrote to him immediately after receiving your last letter[2] and asked him to contact you directly with possible commissions and so on. In spite of a renewed appeal,[3] I have still not received an answer from him.(?)

I really do not know what to send you now that would interest you: I myself have now lost the habit of reading. But as soon as I find anything, I shall let you know. – My *Tannhäuser* is now being given almost everywhere in Germany;[4] the smaller theatres, especially, have had a go at it, whereas the largest ones – for obvious reasons – are still holding back. As for the performances themselves, I hear for the most part that they are wretched affairs, so that I cannot understand where people's pleasure lies: since I cannot see them, I have grown indifferent to this prostitution of my works, except for the recent performance of *Lohengrin* in Leipzig, which left a most painful impression on me:[5] it is said to have been unprecedentedly bad; among other things it was impossible to hear a single word – except for the herald – all evening! – As a result I have come to regret ever having released my works. In *Boston* they are now even holding *Wagner Nights*, evening concerts at which

1 A translation of works by Ralph Waldo Emerson.
2 Wagner wrote to Eduard Avenarius on 28 September 1853, asking him if he could offer Röckel work as a translator; nothing seems to have come of this.
3 In a letter to Cäcilie Avenarius of 22 December 1853.
4 See letter [155], p. 277, note 1.
5 See letter [170], p. 296.

nothing but my own compositions are performed.[1] I have been encouraged to go to America; but no one can expect me to tour around giving concerts, not even for a good deal of money! –

And now, my dearest friend, I shall come to an end. If necessary I could fill a whole ream of paper; I'd have no shortage of material: but we must keep something back for another occasion. I hope that – if you are *able* – you will not keep *me* waiting as long for a letter as I kept *you* waiting for an answer. Write and tell me, above all, about what you are working on. Anything I may have forgotten can be included then. For now – fare you well, my dear and worthy friend! Do not lose hope – for even I have not lost hope.

Yours,
Richard Wagner,

The Memorial Library of Music, Department of Special Collections
and University Archives, Stanford University
(published with minor variants in Röckel-Briefe 21–47).

172. Franz Liszt, Weimar   Zurich, 7 February 1854

My dear friend,

You were going to send me your "Artists":[2] why have they not arrived? –
How are you getting on with the Faust Symphony?[3]

I am now writing the "Rhinegold" straight out in full score, with the instrumentation: I could not find any other way of writing out the prelude (the depths of the Rhine) as a sketch so that it was clear; that is why I had recourse straightaway to the full score. The only problem is that it will now take much longer to complete: in addition, my head feels somewhat confused.

The Frau Kapellmeister[4] has done admirably well: give her my kind regards and tell her how very grateful I am to her. Who knows what will become of it? For myself I do not wish to know.

Please send me an answer soon in reply to this sign of life on my part.

Yours,
Richard W.

Liszt-Briefe II,11.

1 The Germania Musical Society, founded in 1849, gave Boston its first all-Wagner concert on 3 December 1853.
2 *An die Künstler* (words by Schiller), for male voice soloists, male chorus and orchestra, composed in 1853, orchestrated by Joachim Raff, and revised by Liszt late in 1853 and again in 1856. Liszt sent Wagner a copy of the score on 21 February 1854. See also following letter.
3 *Eine Faust-Symphonie in drei Charakterbildern*, composed between 1854 and 1857.
4 Carolyne Sayn-Wittgenstein.

173. FRANZ LISZT, WEIMAR   Zurich, 4 March 1854

Dear Franz,

Many thanks for your "Artists".[1] You had to overcome a good deal of resistance on my part to this composition, or perhaps I should say rather that I was not in the mood for it. I have grown so unused to passing judgement – in the objective sense – that I tend now to be influenced purely by my own inclinations and to concern myself only with those things that really arouse my sympathy, with the result that I simply enjoy the works I listen to, without seeking any critical justification for the enjoyment that they give me. Imagine what contradictory feelings you were bound to rouse in me by your choice of this of all poems! It is more or less a didactic poem: what we hear is the voice of a philosopher finally reverting to art and doing so with the most emphatic resolve imaginable – Schiller, to the life! – And then a concert chorus – : I have no mind for that sort of thing any longer and could not compose anything similar at any price; I would not know where to find the incentive to do so. – And then – another thing! As a musician, I find that my attitude to spoken verse has changed enormously from what it used to be; not at any price could I produce a melody to fit Schiller's verses, which are clearly intended only to be read. With lines like these one can *only* proceed in a somewhat arbitrary fashion musically, and, since the melody can never really flow freely, such arbitrariness will inevitably drive us to eccentricities of harmony and prodigious efforts to produce artificial waves on the surface of an unmelodic well-spring. – I have already been through all this, and have now reached a stage of development where I have adopted a totally different approach: thus – just think of it! – the *whole* of the instrumental introduction to the "Rhinegold" is constructed on the single triad of *E flat*! Imagine, then, how sensitive I am on all these points, and how taken aback I was on opening your "Artists" to run full tilt against an example of a procedure which is the total opposite of my *present* procedure! I cannot deny that I shook my head as I continued to peruse the score, and stupidly began by examining only what alienated me, i.e. individual details, for all I could see were individual details. But then again many of these details helped me to get over my ill-humour; at the end of the piece I was again taken aback, and so I hit on the sensible idea of letting the *whole* thing pass through me at a single sitting – and this time I was fortunately able to get *into* it! I suddenly saw you on the rostrum – saw, heard and understood you! In this way I gained further proof of the fact that it is simply our *own* fault if we are incapable of accepting what is offered in a spirit of generosity. This call of yours to artists represents a great and beautiful and splendid aspect of your own existence as an artist. I was deeply stirred by the force of your intention. [. . .]

1 See previous letter, p. 313, note 2.

I am hard at work. Do you know of anyone who would be suitable for writing out a fair copy of the full score on the basis of my disorderly pencil sketches? On this occasion I have adopted a completely different method of working. But the fair copy will be the death of me! It is taking up time that could be more profitably spent on other things, in addition to which I am so exhausted by all this writing that it is making me ill and taking away my inclination for any real work. Without such a skilled person I am lost; *with* him I could complete *everything* in *two years*. That is how long I would need the man; any periods during which he was not occupied writing out the full score could be filled copying out the *parts*. Have a good look round! There is nobody here. – I must say it sounds somewhat ridiculous wishing to keep a secretary when I can scarcely afford to keep myself![1] – You have asked me, my dearest friend, how much my most pressing debts amount to. Since you ask, I shall tell you frankly that my only way out has been to present *bills of exchange* to artisans etc. (who were most in need of money). These bills of exchange fall due in the middle of April. God knows how I shall pay them! if only I could *keep going* until the *autumn*, when I shall again receive monies from the various theatres. If you were able to obtain *five thousand francs* in the form of a loan (till the end of the year), you would indeed deliver me from the torments of hell! I have borrowed all I can from the only person I could approach here – poor Sulzer, whom I have reduced to a state of extreme embarrassment by my inability to repay him. This is a further source of torment – I can scarcely bring myself to look him in the eyes.[2] – This is what happens when one is luxury-loving by nature, and yet is condemned to sackcloth and ashes. –

If you can help me, it would be an act of divine mercy.[3] Is there no German music-enthusiast at home who considers me worth a few thousand thalers for half a year? I can refer him directly to my autumn revenues. –

[...]

Liszt-Briefe II, 13-16.

174. JAKOB SULZER, ZURICH   Zurich, 14 September 1854

My dear friend,

Some time ago you asked me whether my situation was desperate? I denied that it was, since I had just then reached the point when I hoped that revenues

---

1 Nothing came of this. On [14 June 1854] Wagner wrote to inform Liszt that "Mme Wesendonck has presented me with a gold pen – of indestructible writing power – which once again has turned me into a pedant of calligraphy".
2 But see letter [174], below.
3 Liszt replied on 4 April to say that his own finances were in a precarious state and that he was unable to help.

from the German theatres would set me afloat. On the basis of last year's experiences, and in response to favourable indications that I had already received, I believed that during the months of August and September, when theatres are normally planning novelties for the winter season, I would receive at least sufficient monies to pay off my most pressing debts during that time, and that I should easily be able to discharge the others in the course of the ensuing months. The period that I had fixed for the fulfilment of these hopes has now elapsed, and I can no longer conceal from myself the fact that my calculations have been proved wrong. The hope that I might now receive considerable revenues as a result of the confluence of a large number of orders has most decidedly not been fulfilled. The reason for this, however, is the result of chance and will not last: all theatres are now going through a bad patch; and, in the short term, I expect I have a rival in the new Meyerbeer opera.[1] You know my relations with Berlin.[2] Since my operas have always been successful and have made money wherever they were given, I may not be altogether wrong in supposing that my hope that, in the course of time, all theatres will acquire the performing rights to them rests upon reasonable assumptions, so that I do not in fact need to regard my financial circumstances as being in any way reduced as a result of the delay that I have now had to suffer. In other words, if I had the time and leisure to wait, this autumn's unfortunate outcome might not have had too serious repercussions on my present situation. But things are quite different here: I simply cannot hold out at the present time nor in the immediate future, unless I receive a large sum of money in cash.

My debts are the result of furnishing my rooms here[3] in the course of last year. The silent or spoken reproaches which I have brought upon myself in consequence of the nature of these furnishings are something which – now that it has come to this – I am incapable of refuting except by appealing to certain processes within me which I fear I shall never be able to explain to anyone who cannot himself sympathize with the essential character of my nature and of my present situation under the impressions of that period and in the face of an incipient artistic task of the kind and extent that I then had in mind. I shall therefore say nothing on the subject, but freely admit that anyone who accuses me of folly may well be right. I am also quite prepared to atone for this act of folly, as I have indeed already atoned for it with some harshness through suffering the most disgusting cares and worries. And I am also willing to give up my new furnishings: since I can no longer afford to maintain them, I attach so little importance to them that I could sell them all

1 *L'Etoile du nord*, first performed at the Opéra-Comique on 16 February 1854. In the event, there was only one production in Germany during the 1854/5 season, at Stuttgart, where the work was first heard on 27 September 1854.
2 See letter [134], p.246, note 1.
3 At Zeltweg 13, where the Wagners lived from 15 April 1853 until 20 April 1857.

and feel only the most utter indifference. Indeed, unless I receive special help, there seems to be no other way of appeasing my creditors, except by offering them the proceeds of my entire household, which would then have to be immediately given up. But it goes without saying that, if I am not to suffer appalling humiliation, such a sale must inevitably entail my definitive departure from Zurich: by way of an excuse, I would have to plead the need to change my place of residence and go away from here – and go, moreover, as far away as possible. However much I have come to like Zurich, especially through the friends I have made here, I am nevertheless willing to atone for my carelessness by leaving, – whether with bitterness and pain? – that must be for me to say. But – my wife would not be able to bear such a move; I know she would succumb, indeed, I believe it could be the death of her.

I must therefore do everything possible to prevent this from happening. That is why I am now turning to you. Here you have an account of my position.

I have made a precise reckoning, and find that I need "ten thousand francs" in order to discharge all my debts – but not including my debt to you.[1] I owe around seven thousand francs here for unpaid bills, most of which have been repeatedly demanded and which I have now promised to settle within the course of this month. The remainder is a more recent debt which I owe Karl Ritter, who was able to advance me the money only on condition that he receives it back by the end of this coming October. (I may add in passing that I still owe you an explanation of certain recent statements of mine concerning my debts.)

If some means were to be offered me now whereby I could obtain this sum, I would surrender the revenues due to me from the various German theatres until such time as the sum is repaid. I have indicated on the accompanying sheet what I may expect here:[2] in drawing up the list I have relied solely on past experience and not reckoned on the fees being as high as some that have already been paid me in similar circumstances, so that the total may easily be more – particularly if we are able to proceed with all due calm. The minimum sum which I expect to receive for my two operas "Tannhäuser" and "Lohengrin" may therefore be reckoned, without the least exaggeration, at 21,000 frs., which ignores – for reasons I do not need to go into – the revenues which I hope one day to receive from Berlin.

If some agreement could be reached, I should be glad to see you yourself placed in charge of these receipts. But since it would be as difficult for you as it would for anyone else to superintend the sale of my operas, I myself

---

1 At least a further 600 francs, borrowed in October 1853 to finance his trip to Paris.
2 Wagner listed thirty-four German and Austrian theatres which he thought might be interested in *Tannhäuser* and *Lohengrin*. In the event, a number were discouraged by the reputed difficulties of staging these works, and by the Saxon authorities' reissue of the 1849 arrest warrant in June 1853.

would have to function more or less as a secretary, seeing to all the correspondence and ensuring that all remittances were simply addressed to you,
possibly under the pretext that the monies would be safer if sent that
way.

There is only one condition I would make here: a yearly allowance of 2000
frs., paid in quarterly instalments over a period of three years, would have to
be deducted from these revenues and made available to me to pay for my
household expenses, since I could not get by otherwise; and in order to
prevent me from falling straightaway into further disorganization, these
advances would have to begin this coming 1st of October.

(I ought also to draw your attention to the fact that I have not included in
the aforementioned sum of 10,000 fr. a further figure of 500 fr. which I am
obliged to pay tomorrow (the 15th September) and for which I am daily
awaiting the necessary money from Breslau, as honorarium for my Lohengrin[1]
(which is why I have not included it in the accompanying list). Since, at the
time of writing, this money has still not arrived, I now find myself in the
embarrassing position of having to ask you, if possible, to advance me the
necessary 500 fr. until such time as I am in receipt of the same.)

Now, my dear friend, you must consider how best to go about helping me
in order to avert what would otherwise be a terrible catastrophe, particularly
as regards my wife. From Germany I cannot – and will not – look for anything
at present, in spite of a few vague prospects that have been opened up to
me there: if anything is to be done to help me, it can spring forth only
from dealings with friends such as exist only in one's immediate surroundings.

Look at me! *I* can no longer help myself, since everything is now so
pressing, and since I cannot, in the immediate future, abandon myself to the
random chance of agreeable surprises.

You may be assured, finally, that I am heartily sorry for the trouble which
I know I must be causing you herewith.[2]

Yours,
Richard Wagner.

Fehr I,309-11.

---

1 *Lohengrin* was first performed in Breslau on 31 October 1854.
2 Sulzer prevailed upon Otto Wesendonck to provide Wagner with the sum of 7000 francs
   against the promise of whatever fees might accrue from future sales of his works. The debt
   of 1000 thalers owed to Karl Ritter was discharged by his mother's withholding her annual
   subsidy of 800 thalers from November 1854 to November 1855.

175. FRANZ LISZT, WEIMAR   [Zurich, 7 October 1854]

[. . .] – For me the "world's" last song has faded into silence.

And do you know what – to my renewed boast – has once again confirmed me in this frame of mind?? It was *your essay on the flying Dutchman*.[1] In these articles I have finally rediscovered myself with the utmost clarity, and recognized that we have nothing in common with this world. *For who was there who understood me*?? – *You* – and no one else! And who now understands *you*? *I* – and no one else! You can be certain of that. It was *you* who, for the first and only time, revealed to me the joy of being completely understood: you see, I have been totally consumed by you, there is not a single fibre of my being, nor even the slightest quivering of my heart-strings which you yourself have not also felt. But now I see that only *this* is true understanding, whereas everything else is pure misunderstanding, a tasteless and unedifying error. But what is there left for me to do now that I have found this out? And what use do *you* still have of me now that you have found this out about me! Let me, as a dear friend, shed a womanly tear in my joy – but what then? – Oh, let us not mutilate ourselves like this: let us treat the world only with contempt; for it deserves no better: but let no hopes be placed in it, that our hearts be not deluded! It is evil, *evil, fundamentally evil*, only the heart of a friend and a woman's tears can redeem it from its curse. – But nor can we respect it like this, and certainly in nothing that resembles honour, fame – or whatever else these foolish things are called. – It belongs to *Alberich*: no one else!! Away with it! Enough – you now know my present mood: it is not a passing whim: it is as firm and solid as a diamond. It is this alone that gives me the strength to continue dragging life's burden after me: but I must henceforth be implacable. I hate all *appearances* with lethal fury: I'll have no truck with hope, since it is a form of self-lying. But – I shall work – you shall have my scores: they will belong *to us*, and to no one else. That is enough. –

Do you now have the *Rhinegold*?

I am in the second act of the *Valkyrie*:[2] Wodan and Fricka: as you can see, it is bound to succeed. –

Fare you well! –

---

1 Ironically, the essay, though printed under Liszt's name, was written partly, possibly even predominantly, by Princess Carolyne Sayn-Wittgenstein. Composed originally in French, for publication in the *Weymar'sche Offizielle Zeitung* in June 1854, it appeared, in a translation by Peter Cornelius, under the title "Wagner's Fliegender Holländer", in a series of five issues of the *Neue Zeitschrift für Musik* commencing on 15 September 1854.

2 The complete draft of Act I is dated 28 June – 1 September 1854; that of Act II 4 September – 18 November 1854; and that of Act III 20 November – 27 December 1854.

Will you write to my wife?[1]

Cordial greetings! –

(I can no longer read what other people write. All that I can still read is your Dutchman essay: that is my life's reward, and its boast!)

Fare you well!

Yours,

R. W.

Liszt-Briefe II,40-1.

176. HANS VON BÜLOW, CHOCIESZWICE   [Zurich, 26 October 1854]

My very dear Hans,

Many thanks for your letters, and more especially for your enclosures.[2] Your works have occupied and stimulated me a good deal: but from the moment of my first acquaintance with them I found myself in the difficult position of knowing that you expect me to pass judgement on them, which is something I cannot possibly do. In the first place, how am I to arrive at a clear idea of the thing? You know how notoriously badly I play the piano and that I am incapable of mastering anything unless I already have a clear idea of it; and that, in comparison to what I demand of a work, what I can pick up simply by looking at it is not enough to give me any proper conception of it. [...]

But if I am to pass judgement on what, in my naïve way, I believe I have managed to make sense of, you will have to make do with the following purely personal opinion. –

I was immediately struck by your inventiveness: you have an unmistakable gift here, which reveals itself above all in the more recent composition, the orchestral Fantasy. In both design and execution, the thematic structure is imposing and clear, and especially in the Fantasy is really quite novel, inasmuch as it emerges entirely from the subject. The characterization of the motifs is clear, although not as decisively so in the Caesar Overture as in the Fantasy: without being merely wilful, I cannot decide – at least on the basis of a single meagre impression – whether all the motifs can be related to specific objects, but no doubt the subject-matter is to blame for this, for it must be said that it does not exactly lend itself to such treatment; indeed, it

1 Minna Wagner was in Dresden, visiting relatives, from early September to early November 1854.

2 *Nirwana*, an "orchestral fantasy in overture form", published as op. 20, and music for *Julius Caesar*, op. 10. Bülow's Overture and March for *Julius Caesar* (Shakespeare, arr. Genast and others) had been performed with the play on 13 December 1851. For *Nirwana*, see introductory essay, pp. 165–6.

even seems to me to have contributed to the fact that the themes appear less original – i.e. always *eloquent* – in the way you have formed them: thus the main theme in the brass, for ex., does not strike me as being in any way remarkable, but seems rather bombastic, after the fashion in which composers regularly write when they are not really sure what to make of a given poetic motif. The situation is quite different – and advantageously so – in the Fantasy: here you were more sure of yourself, and if ever a piece had *atmosphere*, this is it; that it is a quite dreadful atmosphere is a different matter. You are certainly much more independent in this work, everything about it is unmistakable. But in both pieces I admire your technique where, as regards difficulties of form both in detail and in the overall design, it would – in my opinion – be hard to surpass you. I cannot deny your mastery, indeed, I believe you could accomplish anything you set out to achieve. If, conversely, I have any serious reservations – as regards the rules – they concern your attitude towards harmonic euphony: I confess that the only impression I have been able to form here is that of highly meaningful music performed on instruments that are out of tune, for it is precisely here that I most look for the determinative sensuous impression of an outstanding performance before I can rid myself of the fear that now besets me. I know only too well from experience that there are objects which can be depicted in music but which can be expressed only if the composer invents harmonies that will grate upon the ear of the musical philistine. But, having recognized this in the course of my own compositions, I nevertheless found myself constantly guided by a quite specific instinct which led me to conceal the harmonic dissonances as much as possible and finally to place them in such a way that (to my own mind) they were finally no longer felt as such. Now, I cannot avoid the feeling that you yourself have adopted an almost opposite approach, in other words you believe it is important that the dissonance be felt as a dissonance, and the worst example of this seems to me where all your powers ·of invention are concentrated upon expressing just such a dissonance. Whether or not you think me a philistine, I must confess that on no account would I care to have written, for ex.,

at the end of the Fantasy, simply because it is a cheap effect: and what you hope to achieve with the D ♮ in

– except to make people think it is a wrong note – I simply cannot imagine.
I have used all my ingenuity in an attempt to reconcile myself to this

because I saw how much importance you attach to it: and there were moments
when I succeeded in doing so, especially when I was able to picture in my
mind a feeling of suicidal madness. But it did not last long, and I soon
fell back into my old weakness of believing that art consists precisely in
communicating the strangest and most unusual feelings to a listener in such
a way that his attention is not distracted by the material that he is listening
to, but that he yields unresistingly, as it were, to an ingratiating allurement
and thus involuntarily assimilates even what is most alien to his nature. –

You see, Hans, I have been through similar experiences myself during my
earliest period as a composer, when I regarded everything as being of
secondary importance to the discovery of some such harmonic joke. At that
time I could do nothing properly and would certainly not have been capable
of writing a piece of music that was as well-constructed and that attested to
such mastery as does your Fantasy. But in your own case it astonishes me:
certainly, you are mistaken about yourself, you are far too inventive to take
any serious pleasure in such antics.

You see, there is something typically Jewish about the cold and indifferent
way in which others invariably pay heed only to what is different about the
things we have to tell them, and about the way they talk to us as though what
really mattered did not exist. –

You see what a low opinion I have of all this, and how I am convinced that
my objection to your works touches on only inessential points, and not on the
essential ones. And so you should regard my verdict – although I refuse to
have it seen as such – as entirely favourable to you. I do not recall ever having
been so deeply affected in my mood by a recent piece of music, in spite of
my comparative ignorance of the field, as was the case with your Fantasy. –
Have you heard it yourself? You do not say so. –

[. . .]

Bülow-Briefe 59–63.

177. FRANZ LISZT, WEIMAR   [Zurich, 16? December 1854]

Dear Franz,

I am coming increasingly to see that you are really a great *philosopher*! – by contrast I often think of myself as a proper cheapjack. Apart from making – slow – progress on my music,[1] I have now become exclusively preoccupied with a man who – albeit only in literary form – has entered my lonely life like a gift from heaven. It is *Arthur Schopenhauer*, the greatest philosopher since *Kant*, whose ideas – as he himself puts it – he is the first person to think through to their logical conclusion. The German professors have – very wisely – ignored him for 40 years: he was recently rediscovered – to Germany's shame – by an English critic.[2] What charlatans all these Hegels etc. are beside him! His principal idea, the final denial of the will to live, is of terrible seriousness, but it is uniquely redeeming. Of course, it did not strike me as anything new, and nobody can think such a thought if he has not already lived it. But it was this philosopher who first awakened the idea in me with such clarity. When I think back on the storms that have buffeted my heart and on its convulsive efforts to cling to some hope in life – against my own better judgement – , indeed, now that these storms have swelled so often to the fury of a tempest, – I have yet found a sedative which has finally helped me to sleep at night; it is the sincere and heartfelt yearning for death: total unconsciousness, complete annihilation, the end of all dreams – the only ultimate redemption! –

How strange that I have often found your own thoughts here: although you express them differently because you are religious, I nevertheless know that you think exactly the same thing. How profound you are! In your essay on the Dutchman[3] you often struck home with the force of lightning. When I read Schoppenhauer [*sic*] I was mostly in your presence: you simply did not notice. – And so I find myself growing increasingly mature: if I still toy with art, it is only as a way of passing the time. You will see from the accompanying sheet how I now seek to amuse myself. –

For the sake of young Siegfried, the fairest of my life's dreams, I expect that I must still complete the Nibelung pieces: the Valkyrie has exhausted me too much for me to begrudge myself this relaxation; I have now reached the second half of the last act. But it will be 1856 before I have completed the whole thing, and 1858, the tenth year of my hegira, before I can perform it, – if fate so decrees. But since I have never in my life enjoyed the true happiness of love, I intend to erect a further monument to this most beautiful of dreams, a monument in which this love will be properly sated from beginning to end:

1 See letter [175], p. 319, note 2.
2 John Oxenford, "Iconoclasm in German Philosophy" in *Westminster and Foreign Quarterly Review* of April 1853.
3 See letter [175], p. 319, note 1.

I have planned in my head a *Tristan* and *Isolde*, the simplest, but most full-blooded musical conception; with the "black flag"[1] which flutters at the end, I shall then cover myself over, in order – to die. –

[. . .]

Liszt-Briefe II, 42–3.

178. Franz Liszt, Weimar　　　　　　Zurich, 19 January 1855

Dear Franz, I can at last tell you something definite about London.[2] A Mr *Anderson*, treasurer of the Philharmonic (director of the Queen's Band) came especially to Zurich to arrange the matter. I felt uneasy about it: it is really not my business to go to London and conduct Philharmonic concerts, even if – as is their wish – I am to perform excerpts from my own compositions, (since I have written nothing for the concert-hall).[3] But I felt quite clearly that it was a question here of definitively turning my back once and for all on every prospect and every attempt to influence present-day audiences, – or else of grasping the hand that has been held out to me here on this occasion.

London is the only place in the world where it might still be possible for *me* to perform my Lohengrin,[4] at least as long as these foolish kings and princes in Germany have better things to do with their time than to offer me an amnesty. It might be an interesting idea to see if I can win over the English to the extent of their establishing an exquisite German opera for me next year, under Court patronage, where I could perform my own works under my own leadership. I freely admit that I could receive no better introduction than as conductor of the Philharmonic (the *old*[5] one!), and so I ended up having no further objections to selling myself in this way, albeit at a very low price (two hundred pounds for four months). As a result I shall arrive in London at the beginning of March for eight concerts, of which the first takes place on the 12th of March, the last on the 25th of June. At the beginning

---

1 In certain versions of the *Tristan* legend, Iseult's vessel bears a white flag as a token of her imminent arrival at her lover's sick-bed; Tristan's wife falsely gives out the colour as black, with the result that Tristan dies of grief. This motif was not used in the opera.

2 Wagner had been invited to conduct the Philharmonic Society of London's 1855 season of concerts.

3 Three extracts from *Lohengrin* were performed at the second concert on 26 March, and the Overture to *Tannhäuser* was played at the fifth concert on 14 May and repeated by royal command at the seventh concert on 11 June 1855.

4 This hope proved unfounded. London had to wait until 1875 to hear *Lohengrin* (in Italian).

5 In contrast to the New Philharmonic Society founded in 1852 and conducted during its 1855 season by Hector Berlioz and Henry Wylde.

of *July* I shall be on the *Seelisberg*. – It would be splendid if you were to visit me in London: at all events I shall have to perform something of yours there.[1] Think about it.

I am also thinking of Joachim and Hans Bülow: once I am in London I intend to ensure that Bülow, especially, joins me there.[2] –

That you have finished your *Faust*[3] is wonderful news: and that I am incredibly keen to see it, you can well imagine; but that you do not intend showing it to me until much later is terrible. However – if I cannot hear you perform it properly immediately – I shall not scorn an opportunity to play through it at the piano *with you* at least to begin with, and get to know it in that way: there is nothing even to approach the powers of lively communication which you yourself are able to muster. And I set increasing store by the need to acquire a proper impression right from the very outset, so much do I distrust a merely abstract acquaintance with the notes. –

Funnily enough, I too have just been overwhelmed by a great desire to revise my old Faust overture:[4] I have written a whole new score, revised the instrumentation throughout, completely altered much of it, and given it somewhat greater amplification and significance (2nd motif) in the middle. In a few days' time I shall be performing it at a concert here, and shall call it – "A Faust Overture".

Motto:

The god who dwells enthroned within my breast
Can stir my inner vision's deepest springs,
But he who binds my strength to his behest
Brings no command to sway external things.
Thus life has taught me, with its weary weight,
To long for death, and the dear light to hate.[5]

On no account, however, shall I publish it.[6]

1 In a letter dated 25 January 1855 Liszt suggested that Wagner should delay introducing any of his works to London until the 1856 season.
2 Neither Joseph Joachim nor Hans von Bülow was invited to join Wagner in London.
3 See letter [172], p. 313, note 3. In his letter of 1 January 1855 Liszt had announced the completion of this piece, although it continued to occupy his attention until its first performance in Weimar on 5 September 1857.
4 WWV 59. The end of the full score is dated 17 January 1855. In its revised form the Overture was performed at the Casino in Zurich on 23 January 1855.
5 Goethe, *Faust: erster Theil*, ll. 1566–71; translation by Philip Wayne.
6 On [16 February 1855] Wagner asked Liszt to use his influence with Breitkopf & Härtel to have the score published. The Leipzig publishing house accepted it on 31 March 1855 in payment of a fee of 20 louis d'or.

Your New Year's article alarmed me.[1] But here, too, I soon realized that I had reason to be grateful to you simply for your increasing interest in me. And yet, when you hold out my works as something tremendous, I feel you must be confusing the basic standard: what strikes *me* as utterly insignificant and pitiful are present-day audiences and the spirit of our means of presentation etc., whereas *my* works are simply of decent human proportions and appear gigantic only when we attempt to force them into so unworthy a framework. Thus, whenever we claim that our intentions are chimerical and eccentric, we are really only flattering the current worthlessness of present-day audiences, and ultimately giving them the seal of respectability. – We should not impose upon people in this way! –

Dearest Franz, each of your letters is like gold to me – nay, they are worth far more than that! – but – I receive very few actual answers from you: – many of my questions you treat as though they had never been asked. On the other hand, you always have something new to tell me, which is splendid – : but – an answer is sometimes no bad thing either! –

Well, let me have a proper letter from you: and let me *see* you in London. I shall be taking my work with me: I hope to complete the instrumentation of the Valkyrie there.[2] –

Adieu, dearest Franz!

But how are you? – Kind regards from my wife: and best wishes from me to you both.

Yours,

R. W.

Liszt-Briefe II,45–8.

179. HANS VON BÜLOW, CHOCIESZWICE   Paris, 3 March 1855

Dear Hans,

You will be surprised not to have heard from me for so long; so surprised, it seems, that you have forgotten to reply to my last letter. I had resolved to spend my free time in Paris discharging my epistolary debts, and so I shall now discharge my debt to you. –

[. . .]

1 In his letter of 1 January 1855 Liszt had announced that he had committed "a small indiscretion" by submitting "a couple of columns" on *Das Rheingold* to Brendel's *Neue Zeitschrift für Musik*. The article may be found in Volume 2 of the *Volksausgabe in vier Bänden* (Leipzig 1910), 237-42.
2 The first full score of Act I was completed on 3 April 1855; that of Act II is dated 7 April – 20 September 1855; and that of Act III 8 October 1855 – 20 March 1856.

I have almost finished scoring the first act of the Valkyrie: I have never written anything like it before: it is very beautiful! – Liszt was very generous in his remarks on the London affair inasmuch as he, too, discouraged me from any thought of financial speculation: – the Brendel clique[1] etc. seem to think differently and even appears to have had their beloved coterie in mind. But I took another close look at Schumann's symphonies with the honest hope of finding them beautiful and worth propagating. Well, I have now made up my mind about them and am fully convinced that it is *not* worth troubling myself with them: they are simply another kind of jargon which has the appearance of being *profound* but which, in my own opinion, is the same sort of empty nonsense as Hegel's philosophic rubbish, which is always at its most trivial where it seems most profound. Wherever there is a glimmer of light or a real melody, it is Beethoven to the letter, who reveals himself as father and mother in one. May I be spared all further dealings with this stuff! I am more rigid than ever in my views and would prefer it if people ignored me when they talk of the heroes of music of the "present day". How horrified Brendel's clique would be if I suddenly took it into my head to tell them what I really think. – Will you arrange things better? *I hope so!!*

Liszt has been dreadfully slow in returning the "Rhinegold": I hope it is now back in Dresden, where Wölfel is supposed to be finishing off a copy of it: I'll then send it to you in Berlin; let me have your address. – How are you getting on with the piano score of Tannhäuser without W.?[2] – What else are you up to? are you well? Are you reading Schopenhauer? – Remember me with affection! Fare you well.

Bülow-Briefe 64-7.

180. MINNA WAGNER, ZURICH   London, 6 March 1855

At last I have sorted myself out, my dear little Minnikins! This is the first morning I have spent in peace and quiet – for several days – and I intend using it straightaway to write you a far more sensible letter than has been the case up to now. I have lots to tell, though nothing in the least extraordinary.

1 The *Neue Zeitschrift für Musik* had announced, "This step on the part of England is surprising and may have important results. For Wagner will not undertake the conductorship of the Philharmonic Society without making artistic demands on that Society the fulfilment of which will exercise a most salutory influence on its programme" (quoted Altmann/Bozman II,276).
2 The publication by Meser of Bülow's arrangement of *Tannhäuser* for four hands (i.e. "without words") (originally as a series of individual scenes) was announced in the *Neue Zeitschrift für Musik* of 25 January 1856.

You know that it was not Friday but Saturday that I planned to continue my journey from Paris: it was not until very late that I first saw our old friends again. Kietz appears not to be getting on very well with his *concierge*: he did not look in on her on the next day either, so that he never received my note; only when I had again failed to meet him did I issue stricter orders. It was the evening of my second day there that I finally set eyes on the stupid boy, with Lindemann in tow: needless to say, he was again having trouble meeting his tailor's bills! – But he and Lindemann insisted upon inviting Anders and me to a restaurant on my last evening. *Anders* has become incredibly childish: he can no longer trust himself to cross the road on foot, but each time waits for a passing 'bus and then has himself driven across the street in it; a few days earlier he had fallen over in the library, and broken his spectacles etc. in short it was all very distressing.

This time I also saw Rachel, in *Cinna*,[1] but it was a strange experience seeing this kind of virtuosity in action; it pained me very much. Even if the woman were to sing like a goddess while acting, I'd have no use for her in any of my operas. More on this in person when I am back. –

The journey to London finally passed off quite well; since the weather was fine, the crossing from Calais to Dover lasted only two hours, although by the end of it I was beginning to feel somewhat ill, so that I had to lie down, in Dover we stupidly had to wait 2½ hours for the train.

It was odd that in Paris I had to put up with bad weather and fog, whereas I arrived in London – which is notorious for its weather – under a beautiful, cloudless sky. It took the cabman a full hour to drive at a brisk trot from the station to Praeger's house:[2] in the same time I could as easily have driven from Zurich to Dr Wille's house at Mariafeld. It is a dreadfully large city, and, in terms of its area, Paris is simply a village in comparison! – As I told you yesterday, Praeger was very obliging and friendly: but he explained straightaway that if I wanted any peace of mind, I must first of all pay a few quick visits on various people; I complied, and so we then drove all round London until I thought we were never going to finish; Praeger accompanied me everywhere and thus sacrificed his valuable time to helping me. By midday yesterday we had finally finished; we then looked for somewhere for me to stay and indeed found rooms[3] that appeal to me greatly and where I now hope to be able to work in peace and undisturbed – which remains my main

1 By Corneille. Rachel (the stage name of Elisabeth Félix) was the leading *tragédienne* of her day.
2 Wagner arrived at London Bridge station on 4 March and was driven to Ferdinand Praeger's house at 31 Milton Street (now 65 Balcombe Street, NW1), where he spent his first night in the capital.
3 22 Portland Terrace, demolished in the early years of the twentieth century to make way for a block of service flats. The address is now North Gate, Prince Albert Road, NW1.

concern, whereas the concerts are really of only secondary importance. I am living close to one of the most beautiful parts of the Regent's Park, not at all far from the zoological gardens. Between the front of the house and the road is a tiny little garden, and across the road there are the beautiful trees of the park, so that I can really look forward to the springtime when everything will be green. God knows, I need something to look forward to if I am to tolerate the prospect of spending four whole months here engaging in activities that are totally alien to my nature. If only I can complete my work[1] everything will be well, so that I can then make an immediate start on Young Siegfried on my beloved Seelisberg. But, of course, the rooms are not cheap: they cost *two pounds* a week. But really, the main thing is that they are pleasant rooms; otherwise I could not last out here. I intend saving money in other ways. For the time being I dine at Praeger's, who lives only a quarter of an hour away: a stone's throw by local standards; we shall see what happens later. Mr *Anderson* immediately invited me to a great banquet which the Queen's Musicians are holding this Thursday; I thanked him kindly, but declined. I intend to start as I mean to go on: I shall conduct my concerts, and that's all! People must learn to see that I am even more English than they are themselves. But I am very much afraid of the concerts themselves: although the orchestra is said to be very good, I am told that they are incapable of playing *piano*; only *forte*, without any variety. They actually do have only one rehearsal,[2] at which I am expected to play through *two* symphonies, *two* overtures, and the remaining concert items. How do they expect me to manage? – When I asked about the programme for the first concert, the first agreeable surprise they sprang on me was *Lachner's* "Prize Symphony",[3] which had been chosen as a novelty! Well, I wasted no time in throwing it out and told the gentlemen concerned that they could not expect me to trouble myself with such things. Of course, the stupid devils immediately realized they were in the wrong and invited me to attend their committee today, when they will arrange the repertoire entirely to suit my own wishes. And so I think we shall perform a symphony by Haydn and the *Eroica* or else the C minor Symphony by Beethoven;[4] as overtures they have already decided upon the Magic Flute (so as to have something by Mozart) and Fingal's Cave (so as to have something by Mendelssohn). I have no objection to this. *Ernst* will play a

1 The instrumentation of *Die Walküre*; see letter [178], p. 326, note 2.
2 Before accepting the appointment to conduct the season of concerts, Wagner had requested as many rehearsals as he deemed necessary for each concert, together with the appointment of a sub-conductor for the makeweight items. The Philharmonic's treasurer, Anderson, however, was able to secure Wagner's services without either of these conditions being met.
3 *Preis-Symphonie*, No. 5 in C minor, op. 52: see also letter [154], p. 275, note 2.
4 The first concert on 12 March included one of Haydn's "London" symphonies and Beethoven's No. 3, "Eroica".

concerto by Spohr.[1] I do not yet know who will be singing.[2] Unless anything untoward happens, I shall not write to you again until after the rehearsal (on Saturday). But in the mean time I shall expect a letter from you with impatience. I pray to God that you have only good news to send me, especially as regards your health and your attitude of mind: I am sure it is a bad thing that I have had to leave you alone again!

Believe me, my love, although we do not always think alike and now and then express differing views on this or that, neither of us can look back on life without seeing how close we are to each other and what great demonstrations of love and endurance we have shown each other in the most difficult and often the most terrible situations. Just imagine the memories that come flooding back as I step forth in London once again, where 16 years ago we once wandered the streets in such fear and distress. All that you have had to go through with me has been very hard for you. And in truth, if I could now make things any easier for you, it would certainly give me the most heartfelt satisfaction to do so. But the fact that I do not rightly know how to go about this and really only ever continue to cause you distress and worry, well, that is my curious fate which I often sincerely regret for your sake more than mine. It moved me deeply to see how difficult you again found it to say goodbye to me this last time; whatever I can do at a distance to make the period of our separation as agreeable as possible you may be assured that I shall do it. I know that what you would like best of all is to receive good news from me: but this is something I can really only give you if I feel completely free and at ease in my work, now that this work has become my only reward in life. It pleases me to know that you yourself expect no more from here than honour and a successful outcome to my artistic activities, however limited these activities may be in scope. My art will never make me *rich*, and only the knowledge of being able to find a few loyal and totally devoted souls can constitute the riches of my life. For them alone can I remain active in this world. It is in *this sense* that I hope I shall always be able to send you good news; but only when I have nothing else on my mind. I am heartily glad to know that you *now* think exactly the same as I do. And so – expect only good news, and in that way make the period of our separation seem shorter, just as I plan to do the same by means of my beloved work!

[. . .]

Minna-Briefe I, 139-42.

---

1 The Violin Concerto No. 8 in A minor "in modo di scena cantante".
2 Clara Novello sang Weber's "Ocean, thou mighty monster" from *Oberon*, and Willoughby Hunter Weiss and his wife Georgina Ansell (née Barrett) sang a number from Marschner's *Der Vampyr*. All three singers came together for the terzettino "Soave sia il vento" from *Cosi fan tutte*.

181. MINNA WAGNER, ZURICH   London, 13 March 1855

Only another 7 concerts to conduct: then I shall return home! And ultimately that is the most sensible thing for me to do – don't you agree, my dear Minna?

There – in a few words – you have my entire frame of mind. –

By the time the rehearsal had finished last Saturday, it was too late for me to write to you, and so I decided to wait until after the performance on Monday. In fact it was the rehearsal that gave me the greatest pleasure: the orchestra is excellent both in accomplishment and tone, only in its manner of execution has it been utterly ruined by bad conductors. When I began rehearsing the Beethoven symphony[1] in my usual manner, they were all completely speechless: I kept stopping them, and insisted particularly upon their playing *piano*: and I had the pleasure of seeing how quickly the players got used to me; each movement went better than the one before, and in the end it needed only brief indications to make them understand what I wanted of them. These musicians have the *ability* to do anything: the wind section, in particular, is very good, and there is of course no question of my suffering the sort of torment I had to put up with in Zurich, since the *bassoons*, too, are excellent.

And so it turned out that the rehearsal was over sooner than they had all feared. – When I was first introduced to the orchestra, they welcomed me with sustained applause: I got *Sainton*, the first violin, to thank them for me. The applause broke out again after the symphonies and, finally, at the end of the rehearsal. –

The directors of the Society were beside themselves with delight, and assured me that the orchestra had *never* played even remotely like it before. Although I resisted the idea, I was immediately forced to agree to some of my pieces being performed at the very next concert: I chose the 3 pieces from Lohengrin (Overture, Bridal Procession, Wedding Music and Bridal Chorus) *with chorus*. They are already being translated. In addition they are already demanding Beethoven's *Ninth Symphony*, and I finally agreed, partly because the choirs will be there in any case and partly because on this occasion – on account of my own pieces – I shall be given *two* rehearsals, which, I must admit, is most welcome news, on account of the symphony. –

It emerged that people have all grown very expansive, and that they are now placing great hopes in me for an exceptional success to their whole season of concerts. They intend striking while the iron is hot. – Well, the performance was yesterday evening at 8 o'clock, and I was allowed to appear wearing a *black* tie: only when the Queen comes, which happens only *once* in the course of the entire season, do I have to wear a white tie. During the performance the orchestra began by falling back into their old habits, so that I felt how

1 Symphony No. 3, "Eroica".

much hard work I am going to have to put in before they are completely transformed. However, the *Eroica*, and especially the Funeral March, went much better: – of course, I speak only for myself here; as far as all the others are concerned, they felt they were witnessing a miracle. The audience received me with great warmth and at some length – much better than in Zurich! – The orchestra added their own loud applause: every movement was applauded, and at the end there were cries of bravo on every side, so that I scarcely knew in which direction to bow next. The orchestra especially has taken me to heart; many of them assured me that everything I conducted had been *utterly new*; they said they had never previously understood the works, in spite of the fact that they knew nearly all of them by heart; and so I need show them only a little more forbearance. – But it is also my relationship with the orchestra which is my real source of pleasure here: everything else leaves me very cold, especially the audience which, admittedly, treated me with marks of great distinction, but I could not help noticing, thanks to my special feeling for this sort of thing, that they are really incapable of being *moved*; everything seems to be simply empty words and a question of fashion for them.

Basically the same is true of any audience *en masse*, with the result that there are only ever a few people among them who are more intimately familiar with my works and for whom I am sincerely glad to make music. I very much missed these people here; and only when I imagined myself back in Zurich during the Eroica did I warm to my task and become Richard Wagner through and through. But I seem to have made a great impression: Praeger has just been here, and he assured me that all those people who know anything about music are greatly excited and really quite beside themselves. Well, we shall see! –

In my next letter I shall tell you in more detail about how things are otherwise. Unfortunately, I am still suffering from a bad cold: quite apart from the terrible, cold damp fog, the weather is very bad for my health; at home I can never really get warm; the rooms here are so badly insulated, and the hearth heats things only in its immediate vicinity. It costs a *fortune*! A shilling a day almost on coal alone! Places are so dreadfully far apart that I simply have to take a cab everywhere. Half a bottle of Bordeaux in the worst restaurant costs 3 shillings etc. But, as I say, more on this in my next letter. I am now awaiting news from you: I hoped I might have heard something by yesterday. I was pleased and touched by your first letter: very many thanks for writing, you're a good wife! Even here I still feel, and shall always feel, that I am really at home with you and our dear friends. I intend writing to each of them in turn. For today please give them all my sincere good wishes. My home is with you and nowhere else! Fare you well, my dear good Minna! You'll soon hear more about my life! Fare you well, my good old wife!

Yours,
Richard.

Although I don't have a wife here, I've a mother and sister: Praeger mothers me, and *Klindworth*, a pleasant young man who is just like *Uhlich* and whom Liszt recommended to me, sisters me, so that I'm well looked after by the two of them!

Semper and Klindworth came back home with me yesterday evening: they brought wine and champagne with them, and we sat up until 2 in the morning. I'm very tired today. – Forgive me!

On Sunday I dined with Mr *Anderson* en famille: there was a toast to *you*, which moved me very much, so that I swallowed an enormous mouthful. – Liszt still has not sent me an introduction to Erard, so that I am still without a piano and – unfortunately – have not yet done any work.

And so – once again; fare well, dear old Minna! Send me *really good* news about yourself, so that I feel relieved when I think of home. – I have been intending to use Wesendonck's introduction for a day or so – although I do not *need* anyone.

RWA (published with minor errors of transcription in Minna-Briefe I, 143-6).

182. OTTO WESENDONCK, ZURICH   London, [21 March 1855]

[. . .] My dearest friend, give up your attempts to make me "independent"; as long as I live I shall remain a knave – at least in the sense that the English understand the term – so that my only hope is that no one is dependent upon *me*, since anyone who depends on me will not escape so easily. But that's how it is. However, I may soon abandon my art, and then all will be well. It is this alone that encourages periods of self-delusion which in the long term can have only serious repercussions for me. There are times when it induces in me a sense of frivolity, and you know that frivolity never did anyone any good, least of all the person who abandoned himself to it. But there is no doubt about it – it will take very little to bring me to the point of putting a final stop to this source of all my life's folly: I have reason enough to do so; the pain which my art has caused me far outweighs the rare pleasures that it offers. It requires very little, indeed, a single event, and I shall abandon this game as well: – then – I shall no doubt do so, albeit in other ways than most people would have expected. –

I visited Herr *Benecke*[1] in the City: the day after tomorrow his driver will collect me and take me to his home outside the town. At all events it was a

1 Otto Wesendonck had provided Wagner with a letter of introduction to Frederick William Benecke, who worked in the City (for Schunck, Souchay & Co., at 63 Moorgate Street) and whose home in Denmark Hill (now demolished) was a shrine devoted to the worship of Mendelssohn.

very good letter of introduction which you gave me. In fact, he and his family belong to the Times faction, in musical matters, too: his wife is a relation of Mendelssohn's, whose rival people now consider me to be, in spite of the fact that they all assure me that they have never heard his Hebrides Overture as well played as conducted by me. I may add that the *Beneckes* are also famous here as a wealthy and art(?)loving household. We shall see. But I am certainly grateful to you for your kind thought.

Apart from this, my favourite London acquaintance up until now has been the first violinist here, *Sainton*, a native of Toulouse, passionate by nature, kind-hearted and amiable. He alone is the reason for my having been invited to London.[1] He has been living here for several years with a German by the name of *Lüders*, with whom he is on terms of the most intimate friendship; the latter had read my aesthetic writings and been so prejudiced in my favour as a result that he told Sainton all about them, as best he could, whereupon the two of them concluded that I must be a splendid fellow; and so, when Sainton proposed my name to the directors and was asked to explain how he knew me, he told them a lie, and said he had seen me conduct, since – as he explained to me – these people would never have understood his real reason for believing in me as he did. At the end of the first rehearsal, when Sainton embraced me in his enchantment, I could not help but call him a "téméraire" who should count himself lucky that, on this occasion at least, he had not made a fool of himself. I like this man very much. Yesterday, after the rehearsal, when he saw how exhausted and out of humour I was, he did not balk at driving home with me and waiting until I had changed, whereupon he cancelled the meal I had ordered to be served in my rooms, and took me back to his own house,[2] where I dined *en garçon*, in the most pleasant surroundings, with him and Lüders, until I felt somewhat better disposed. –

Such a man as he, in London, among the English, is a perfect oasis in the desert: by contrast, I find it impossible to imagine anything more repugnant than the real genuine Englishman; without exception they are all like sheep, and the Englishman's practical intelligence is about as reliable as a sheep's instinct for finding its food in the open fields; of course, it finds its food, but the whole of the beautiful fields and the blue sky above might as well not exist, such are its organs of perception. How unhappy, by contrast, must a man feel who sees only the fields and the sky but finds it hard to make out the yarrow! –

I have also taken a great liking to a young musician whom Liszt recommended, a man by the name of Klindworth: if the man had a tenor voice, I'd not shrink from abducting him; he's got everything else, especially

1 This *canard*, released by Sainton and repeated by Wagner in *Mein Leben* (528; English trans. 515), is untrue; see Barry Millington, *Wagner* (London 1984), 57–8.
2 8 Hinde Street, off Manchester Square, London W1.

the physical appearance, that it takes to be Siegfried. – I may add that I now have a fine Erard grand piano in the house: I had to have a writing desk specially built by a carpenter; it was impossible to obtain one otherwise. And so I am now all set up for work, and have been so for some days now; but I have little to show for it; the interruption that I suffered was both long and violent: to begin with, my work felt utterly alien. Let's hope I can find my way back to it again: – or shall I abandon it altogether? –

   [. . .]

Otto Wesendonck-Briefe 14-16.

183. OTTO WESENDONCK, ZURICH   London, 5 April 1855

[. . .] You want me to send you some newspapers? Very well, but what do you want to read in them? Something to help you throw sand in people's eyes concerning my local successes? For that only the *Illustrated News* and *Daily News* would be of any use: these are provided with appreciative reports on the Philharmonic's concerts, and hence on my own achievements, by Mr Hogarth, the Society's full-time secretary. A few other critics find the tone of Messrs Dawison[1] and Chorley over-impertinent, and so they write conciliatory reports, in which they concede that some point or other was good, but do not deny that some other point was bad. I am bound to question whether anyone can judge me, or, indeed, whether they can even listen impartially to what I am giving them to listen to. But it is the two gentlemen named above who know best what they want: they are paid to keep me in my place, and in that way they earn their daily bread, which is not as cheap in London as many Americans think.[2] – Everyone who lives here is so deeply convinced of the worthlessness, insolence, venality and vulgarity of the local press that – to be honest – I prefer not to dirty my hands by so much as touching a newspaper. Anyone who understands anything and has a really independent opinion does not mix with this Jewish rabble. Indeed, I have been assured that after the *second* concert it was possible to predict a certain change of bias on the part of the reporter of the *Morning Post*, because the *Times* etc. had attacked me so mercilessly that the former was forced to be more cautious, since no reporter wishes to fall foul of any other: for there may be occasions later on when they have need of each other's services. Only the editorship of the *Times* itself seems to have found *Dawison*'s invective too strong and coarse, which is said to be the reason why his report on the second concert did not

1 James William Davison [*sic*] was music critic of *The Times* from 1846 to 1879, as well as editor of the *Musical World*. Henry Fothergill Chorley wrote for *The Athenaeum*.
2 Possibly a reference to the Wesendoncks' years in America.

appear.[1] It is possible that this unexpected turn of events may have an encouraging effect on the other papers next time, and that a shift in my favour may be noticeable; it is possible, too, that, if things go on like this and if the real audience continues to be favourably disposed towards me, everybody may end up by becoming converted to my cause, a move to which the Philharmonic itself – which is fighting for its survival – could contribute a good deal if it were to undertake certain manoeuvres: and so it is possible that you were right to say: "that's how things are, that's the way of the world, and in this way you'll finally come to be – recognized!" – Everything is possible! But what about me – ? What is the point of my being here? To perform symphonies, which – to be honest – I made my métier in Zurich only by way of an exception and as a favour to you – : and what else? The Tannhäuser March and one of my overtures? And then?? – Yes, I know. –

As you can see my present mood is not exactly one of sweetness and light, but it is certainly not the result of *my* having harboured expectations which have subsequently been disappointed: no, it is that others continue to expect something to emerge from a quite futile conflict between my own innermost nature and a nature that is totally alien to me. For my own part, I have already found the necessary peace and quiet to be able to see things in an ironical light and to treat them with indifference, and in that way to wait for the affair to run its course. The weather will improve, I shall often visit the wild animals, and ultimately I shall return home having saved a few odd pfennigs. What more can one wish for? –

Ah, the lovely music they have here! I was recently at a concert of the New Ph. S.[2] There was an endless series of overtures, symphonies, concertos, choruses, arias, etc., one after the other – it was sheer delight: they were all conducted in a slip-slop fashion by Dr Wylde until the whole thing was over, which was fairly late: the public applauded as always; and the next day all the papers said that this was the finest concert of the whole season: immediately after the second of the concerts that I conducted, those same reporters who had written favourably about me accorded this other concert the very same praise they had given mine. Shall I not send you these newspapers? –

But the real delight of the English is the oratorio: here their music becomes the interpreter of their religion – passez-moi le mot! – For four hours they sit in Exeter Hall,[3] and listen to one fugue after another, secure in the belief that they have done a good deed for which they will one day be rewarded in heaven by hearing nothing but the most beautiful arias from Italian opera. It is this deeply religious fervour on the part of English audiences which

1 Ellis (V,219) thinks it more likely that there simply was not room for Davison's review.
2 The New Philharmonic Society, whose concert on 28 March had been conducted by Henry Wylde.
3 Exeter Hall in the Strand was opened in 1831 and closed in 1882. The building was demolished in 1907, and the site is now occupied by the Strand Palace Hotel.

Mendelssohn understood to perfection, encouraging him to compose and conduct oratorios for them with the result that he became the true saviour of the English musical world. Mendelssohn is to the English what Jehovah is to the Jews. And Jehovah's wrath now strikes me down for being one of the unbelievers; for you know that among the qualities attributed to the dear God of the Jews is a very real thirst for vengeance: Dawison is the high priest of this divine wrath. – What would Auntie[1] say if I were to write an oratorio for Exeter Hall? –

[. . .]

Otto Wesendonck-Briefe 20–3.

184. FRANZ LISZT, WEIMAR   London, 5 April 1855

Klindworth has just played me your great Sonata![2] –

We spent the day alone together: he dined with me, and afterwards I made him play for me. My dearest Franz! you, too, were here in the room with me – . The Sonata is beautiful beyond belief; great, lovable, deep and noble, – as sublime as you yourself. I was most profoundly moved by it, and all my troubles here in London have suddenly been forgotten. There is nothing more I can say at the moment – immediately after listening to this work, but I am as full of what I could say to you as is humanly possible. Once again: you were here beside me: – oh, if only you could be here in the flesh, and soon: only thus would life be tolerable!! –

Klindworth has amazed me with his playing: no lesser a man than he could have dared perform your work for me for the first time. He is worthy of you: indeed he is! – It was wonderful! –

Good night: many many thanks for such infinite enjoyment!

Your
R. W.

Liszt-Briefe II,65.

185. JAKOB SULZER, ZURICH   London, [10/12 May 1855]

[. . .] As far as the real nature of my London expedition is concerned, my wife has no doubt kept you sufficiently informed on the subject, and you will know that it is basically a matter only for regret that I ever accepted this

---

1 Mathilde Wesendonck.
2 Sonata in B minor, composed in 1852/3 and published in 1854.

engagement. The odd thing about it is that my experiences here have certainly not destroyed any hopes or illusions that I might once have had, but that what I find here is simply confirmation of something I already knew perfectly clearly in advance. That I again allowed myself to be seduced into consorting with a world with which I had in fact broken off all relations long ago rests upon an inconsistency in my nature which, to my great regret, has existed for as long as I can remember. My dealings with the public world of art have necessarily brought me to the point where all I can feel for it is contempt, a contempt which every serious thinking person must feel nowadays. The repeated discovery that I can only besmirch myself, i.e. insult my conscience, through contact with this art has already inspired in me the wish to shuffle off the artist in me, in order to stifle a yearning which I can never seek to appease without suffering renewed torments. But all I could probably then become, were I really able to break free from my art, would be a Schopenhauerian saint! Well, I need not worry on that score, since as long as there is a glimmer of life in me, these artist's illusions of mine will almost certainly not release their hold on me; they are really a kind of decoy with which my instinct for self-preservation repeatedly lures my better judgement into its service. I can really imagine nothing pure and clear that is not immediately contaminated by such images and which, once my insight has passed, repeatedly makes me an artistic visionary once again. The stupidest thing of all is that I can see all this quite clearly and know that I am always the victim of a certain delusion, but, instead of perceiving this delusion as such and protecting myself against it, I allow this, too, to become an image which provides me with the outline and colour I need to portray it, at which point I then turn round to face life once more in all its most sensual and captivating impressions and connections, in order that the dance may start up all over again.

And so this artistic nature of mine is very much a daemon which repeatedly blinds me to the clearest insights and draws me into a maelstrom of confusion, passion and folly, and, finally, restores me to a world which I had really overcome long ago and whose nullity and emptiness is perhaps more obvious to me than it is to many others, since, ultimately – given the lively sensitivity of my own feelings – , it must necessarily reveal itself to me as utterly pitiful. And so there are often moments in my life when I feel so completely annihilated by this insight that I suddenly begin to ask myself whether I can go on living. You will perhaps laugh when I tell you that such moments occur above all when I see an animal being tormented: I cannot begin to describe what I then feel and how, as if by magic, I am suddenly permitted an insight into the essence of life itself in all its undivided coherency, an insight which I no longer see as mawkish sentimentality but which I recognize as the most genuine and most profound way of looking at things, which is why I have taken such a great liking to Schopenhauer in particular, because he has instructed me on these matters to my total satisfaction (?).

It is at moments such as these that I see the "veil of Maya"[1] completely lifted, and what my eyes then see is terrible, so dreadful that – as I say – I suddenly ask myself whether I can go on living; but it is at this moment that another veil descends, a veil which – however dissimilar it may appear – is ultimately always the same "veil of Maya", in all its artistic forms, which casts me back into the world of self-deception where – gladly (because necessarily), I freely admit, – I then allow myself to become entangled, often to the point of utter distraction.

Well, it really is a pretty awful business! There is no doubt but that I cause many people pain in this way; but it is equally certain that I cause nobody such hellish torments as I inflict upon myself; it is the artist in me who is almost entirely to blame for this; and so, if there is anyone who can derive any pleasure from what I have created, he really has nothing to complain about if I cause him distress, since I certainly suffer more as a result than he himself.

I scarcely think you will understand all that I am saying, for – do not be alarmed – I am bound to think of you as far more worldly than I know myself to be; for you even set store by honour and reputation, i.e. recognition by those very people who are simply not in a position to recognize us, since they are incapable of knowing us. And so I really had to smile when you asked for a good article about me in some English newspaper or other. Fortunately, I know you well enough to suppose that you attach less importance to the article itself than to the effect which you hope it will have in Switzerland. As long as my head is filled with such an insane project as the completion and performance of my Nibelung plays, I can feel only gratitude that I have friends who wish outward successes upon me: if only these outward successes had a little more meaning and sense! That is what is so insane about this whole affair, namely that we must always speculate with counterfeit money, if we have to speculate at all – which is precisely what is so stupid!

My dearest Sulzer, best of friends! Everything here is so full of lies and deceit that one can really only concern oneself with it by maintaining one's illusions about it and, at the same time, remaining totally remote from it all. I would gladly treat you to a longish stay in England, for I should be keen to hear your verdict on the things of this world. That I, as an artist, feel very much as though I am living in hell here does not mean a great deal: but I should like to know what would happen, as time passed, to your respect for "public opinion". There is something to be said for observing people at first hand, even if one cannot see into the deepest recesses of their privy councils; but the physiognomy of this entire race has something most decidedly eloquent about it. I am astonished here to see the way in which the boundless

---

1 In Buddhist philosophy Māyā is illusion, the source of all evil; see introductory essay, pp. 164–5 and letter [187], pp. 342–7.

emptiness, dullness of intellect and narrow-mindedness of all national and civic dealings are treated simply as though they were self-evident. When one discovers the public secrets of parliamentary life (especially its elections and partisan electioneering, and hears that nobody imagines even for a moment that the people who govern the country take their business in the least bit seriously but follow a traditional routine with the most frivolous coldness – a routine which has the advantage of giving themselves and their private interests an air of respectability and which does not prevent them from having the most sprightly and self-satisfied appearance even at the age of 70 or 80 – , one is no doubt struck by it all, and certainly not with admiration. I may add that England and her sublime political wisdom seem to have reached a critical point in their history: all that one hears points to a period of deep decline, of which the hitherto unemancipated lower orders have only the vaguest premonition but which – one hears it openly said in railway carriages etc. – will lead to a total revolution. What is at issue here is something I cannot go into; to be honest, I have become dashed indifferent to politics and expect nothing from either the continued existence or from the overthrow of existing conditions.

Well, I seem to have got somewhat carried away, so I shall now bring these improvised ramblings to a rapid conclusion. In fact, for some time I have been wanting an opportunity to talk to you at length by letter, since we have always had problems when talking in person, problems which have often proved a sticking point in the past and which, on occasion, have even caused us considerable pain and embarrassment. But what seems to me beyond question is that on the most serious matters we think increasingly alike, indeed, I am sure we are already in total agreement as far as the main issue is concerned. Of course it was not so easy for me to come round to your way of thinking: for a long time my artistic nature forced me to live a life of *hope*, a hope which was unique to me only insofar as I could hope on behalf of the whole world; the monstrous shapes of this great universal hope I once reduced to the form of certain demands, on which we could of course never agree. Well, I have now renounced this hope, together with all of my demands: what remains is a certain insight and the sincere wish not to be distracted too often from this insight by various kinds of new, but very fleeting, delusions, – but what I feel above all is a desire to be able to return as soon as possible from this splendid city of London to the beauties of Switzerland and to be with my friends again. Well, this final hope is one I may soon see fulfilled, so – fare you well, until we meet again soon,

Yours,
R. W.

[...]

Fehr II,344-7.

186. FRANZ LISZT, WEIMAR   London, 16 May 1855

I am most sincerely grateful to you, my dearest Franz, for your kind letter, for which I had been waiting for some considerable time. The prospect which you hold out to me of finally visiting me again in September[1] is the only glimmer of hope to lighten the darkness of this sad year. I am living here like a damned soul in hell. I did not think I should ever again be obliged to sink so low! I cannot begin to describe what a wretched opinion I have of myself for putting up with such appalling conditions, and I realize that it was an absolute sin, a crime, to accept this London engagement which, however well things had turned out, could only have led me further away than ever from my true course. There is certainly no need for me to open my heart to you and tell you at length about my position here: it is the logical outcome of an act of the greatest illogicality which I have ever committed. It has reduced me to the point of having to conduct an English concert programme (!): that says it all! I have stepped right into a morass of etiquette and custom and am in it up to my ears, unable to channel even a drop of fresh water in my direction in order to revive myself. "Sir, we are not used to that sort of thing here", – that is all I ever hear, perpetually echoed back at me!. – Not even the orchestra can offer me any compensation: it consists almost entirely of Englishmen, i.e. skilled machines whom I can never really get going: trade and business stifle every other emotion. Added to this is a public which – I am generally assured – is very well-disposed towards me but which can never be drawn out of itself: it sits through the most moving music as it does through the most boring, without ever betraying the fact that it has received any real impression. And then there is this ridiculous Mendelssohn-cult, the whole brazen hypocrisy of this absurd nation.

– But even if things were not as bad as they are, – what am I doing here conducting concerts such as these? It is no business of mine to be here! It is something *entirely* different if now and again I perform a Beethoven symphony for some of my friends: but to be a formally appointed concert conductor who has the scores of concert items etc. sent to him at his home so that he can beat time to them – this is something that is bound to fill me with the most profound sense of shame! In fact, it was this awareness of the total unsuitability of my appointment which, at the end of the 4th concert, finally forced upon me the decision to demand that I be released from my contract. Of course, I was immediately dissuaded from doing so, and it was principally out of consideration for my wife, who would have received the news of my sudden departure from London, and all that would have been written about

1 In his letter to Wagner of 2 May, Liszt had expressed his intention of visiting Wagner in Zurich on his return from Hungary. The visit was postponed several times and did not take place until the autumn of the following year (1856).

it, with utter dismay, that I resolved to stick it out until the final concert. But what hellish torment this means for me, I can scarcely tell you: all desire for work is fast fading away, I had intended finishing the score of the "Valkyrie" during the four months I am here, but there is no longer any question of that now; I shall not even finish the second act, so dreadfully dispiriting is the whole of this burdensome situation. In July I intended beginning Young Siegfried on the Seelisberg by the shores of Lake Lucerne; but I am already thinking of postponing this start until next spring! –

This disinclination for work is the worst part of it all: I feel as though eternal night were closing in on me as a result: for what else is there for me to do in the world if I cannot work?

– I am being accompanied throughout this hell by "Dante", a work I had never previously got round to reading. I have passed through his Inferno, and now find myself at the gates of Purgatory. In truth, I have need of this Purgatory: for, if I consider the matter aright, it was an act of truly sinful frivolity which brought me to London, an act for which I must now fervently atone. I must be resigned, indeed I must: this knowledge led me long ago to admit the necessity of resignation – in its widest sense; but I still have to overcome this wild and terrible instinct for survival which continues to cloud my vision and to cast me into a chaos of contradictions. And so I hope one day to pass from Purgatory into Paradise: the fresh clear air of my Seelisberg may perhaps help me to do so. I do not deny that I would be happy to find my Beatrice there!

[. . .]

Liszt-Briefe II,67-9.

187. FRANZ LISZT, WEIMAR   London, 7 June 1855

Allow me, best of men, to begin by expressing my amazement at your *immense creativity*! So you are planning a Dante Symphony?[1] And you hope to show it to me, already completed, this autumn? Do not take it amiss if I sound amazed at this marvel. When I look back on your activities during recent years, you strike me as being quite superhuman! there must indeed be something quite unique about it. But it is entirely natural that we should find pleasure only in creative work, indeed only in that way can we make life at all tolerable: only when we create do we become what we really are, all the other vital functions are quite meaningless for us and are basically only concessions to the vulgarity of everyday human existence, concessions which always leave us

1 *Eine Symphonie zu Dantes Divina Commedia*, composed in 1855/6 and first performed in Dresden on 7 November 1857.

with a feeling of disquiet. All that *I* at least still hope for in this world is a whim and the right frame of mind to be able to work: and how difficult it is for me to preserve these moods when beset by such vulgarity. It is entirely the same with you: but what amazes me in your case is that you are so creative, so that I always see you in an enviable light. –

And so – a "Divina Comedia"? It is certainly a most splendid idea, and I am already looking forward to enjoying your music. But I must discuss certain details of it with you. That the "Inferno" and "Purgatorio" will be a success I do not doubt for a moment: but I have misgivings about the "Paradiso", and you yourself confirm these misgivings when you tell me that you are planning to include choruses in the work. In the Ninth Symphony (as a work of art), it is the last movement with its chorus which is without doubt the weakest section, it is important only from the point of view of the history of art since it reveals to us, in its very naïve way, the embarrassment felt by a real tone-poet who (after Hell and Purgatory) does not know how finally to represent Paradise. And indeed, my dearest Franz, there is a considerable difficulty with this "Paradise", and if there is anyone who can confirm this for us, it is – remarkably enough – *Dante* himself, the singer of a Paradiso which I have no doubt is similarly the weakest part of his Divine Comedy. I have followed *Dante* through Hell and Purgatory with the deepest fellow-feeling; having emerged from the pit of hell, I washed myself with fervent emotion, together with the poet, at the foot of Mount Purgatory – in the waters of the sea, I then savoured the divine morn, the pure air, rose up from one cornice to the next, mortified one passion after another, struggled to subdue my wild instinct for survival, until I finally stood before the flames, abandoned my final wish to live and threw myself into the fiery glow in order that, sinking into rapt contemplation of Beatrice, I might cast aside my entire personality, devoid of will. But that I was roused once more from this ultimate self-liberation in order, basically, to revert to being what I had been before, simply in order that, on the basis of the most laboured sophisms unworthy of a great mind, and of what I can call only the most infantile inventions, the Catholic doctrine of a God who, for his own self-glorification, has created the existential hell that I have had to suffer should be confirmed in this highly problematical and, for my own part, utterly unacceptable way – this has left me feeling very unsatisfied. In order to do justice to Dante (as with Beethoven), I had to revert to an historical standpoint; I had to imagine myself living at the time of Dante and bear in mind the actual aim of his poem, which clearly sets out to produce a specific effect upon his contemporaries, and in particular upon Church reform; I was forced to admit that in this sense he had the uncommon knack of expressing generally valid, popular ideas with unfailing accuracy, and where I most agreed with him was in his praise of those saints who voluntarily chose a life of poverty. And even in his sophistry I was forced to admire his profound poetic imagination and power of presentation (just as

I admire Beethoven's musical skill in the last movement of his Ninth Symphony); I was finally forced to feel the most profound and sublime emotion by virtue of his splendidly inspired idea of turning his childhood sweetheart Beatrice into the figure in whom divine teachings are revealed to him, and, inasmuch as this teaching is designed to encourage the emancipation of personal egoism through love, I am delighted to acknowledge this teaching of Beatrice. But the fact that Beatrice emerges from a car in a Church pageant and, instead of offering us this pure and simple teaching, makes an ostentatious display of all the subtleties of Church scholasticism – this, in spite of the poet's assurances that she grows increasingly radiant and glowing, makes me regard her as increasingly cold and, finally, as an object of such indifference that, as a plain reader, I may well acknowledge that Dante proceeds here entirely in accordance with his own age and his own aims, but, as a sympathetic fellow-poet, I wish that I could have lost my private consciousness, and hence *consciousness in general*, in that refining fire, for, had I done so, I should have felt undeniably better than I do in the company of a Catholic God, even if Dante portrays Him with the same degree of skill as you yourself will no doubt show in attempting to celebrate Him in your choruses.

What I am offering you here is simply an accurate reflection of the impression which the Divine Comedy has had upon me, since, in the "Paradiso", the poem seems to me to amount to no more than a "divine comedy" which is ruined for me both as a participant and as a spectator. The really perplexing problem among all these other questions is always how, in this terrible world of ours, beyond which there is only nothingness, it might be possible to infer the existence of a God who would make life's immense sufferings merely something *apparent*, while the redemption we long for is seen as something entirely real that may be consciously enjoyed. This may not be a problem for philistines – especially for the English variety: the reason they get on so splendidly with their God is because they enter into a contract with Him, according to whose terms they have to fulfil a certain number of contractual points, so that, finally, as a reward for various shortcomings in this world, they may enjoy eternal bliss in the world to come. But what do *we* have in common with such vulgar ideas? – You once told me your views on human nature, which were that mankind was "une intelligence, servie par des organes". If that were so, the overwhelming majority of people would be very badly off, having only "organs" but as good as no "intelligence" (at least in your sense of the word). I, on the other hand, see the question in a different light; it is like this: man (like any other animal) is a will to live; his organs are created to meet various needs, and one of these organs is his intellect, i.e. the organ for comprehending whatever is external to it, with the aim of using such objects to satisfy life's need, according to its strength and ability. A *normal* man is therefore one in whom this organ – which is directed outwards and whose function is to perceive things, just as the stomach's function is to digest food – is equipped with sufficient ability to satisfy a need that is external to it, and – for the *normal* person – this need is exactly the same as that of the most common beast, namely the instinct to eat and to reproduce; for this will to live, which is the actual metaphysical basis of all existence, demands solely to live, i.e. to eat and reproduce itself perpetually, and this tendency is demonstrably one and the same whether it be found in the dull rock, in the more delicate plant, or, finally, in the human animal; the only difference lies in the organs which man, having reached the higher stages of his objectification, must use in order to satisfy more complicated needs which, for that reason, are increasingly contested and harder to meet. Once we have gained this insight (and it is an insight which has been confirmed by the tremendous findings of modern science), we shall suddenly understand what it is that is characteristic about the lives of by far the greater part of mankind of all ages, and we shall no longer be surprised if we always think of them as beasts: for this is the normal human condition. But just as the vast majority of people remain *below* this *norm*, inasmuch as their complex cognitive organ is not even developed to the point where it can adequately meet their normal needs, so we also find (albeit only rarely, of course) *abnormal* individuals in whom the cognitive organ, i.e. the brain, has evolved beyond the ordinary and adequate level of development found in the rest of humanity, just as nature, after all, often creates monsters in which *one* organ is much more developed than any other. Such a *monstrosity* – if it reaches its highest level of development – is *genius*, which essentially rests upon no more than an abnormally fertile and capacious brain. This cognitive organ, which orig-inally and in normal circumstances looks beyond itself in order to meet the needs of the will to live, gains such lively and fascinating impressions from outside – in the case, that is, of abnormal development – that there are times when it breaks free from its role of serving the will – which had after all created it solely for that purpose – and is thus able to perceive the world *undistorted by the will*, i.e. aesthetically; the objects of the world of external phenomena are thus seen undistorted by the will and are its ideal images, which it is the *artist's* task to capture and set down, as it were. In the case of a strong individual, his interest in the world of external phenomena is necess-arily encouraged by this act of observation, and it grows to the point where he permanently forgets the original needs of his own personal will, in other words he begins to *sympathize* with the things outside him, and he does so for their own sake and not because of any personal interest in them. The question must then be asked *what* we see in this abnormal state, and whether our sympathy can be regarded as participating in the *joy* of others or, rather, in their *suffering?* The answer to this question is provided by the true *geniuses* and the true *saints* of all ages, who tell us that they have seen only *suffering* and felt only *fellow-suffering*. In other words, they have recognized the *normal* condition of all living things and seen the cruel, eternally contradictory nature of the *will* to live, which is common to all living things and which, in eternal self-mutilation, is blindly self-regarding; the appalling cruelty of this will, which even in sexual love wills only its own reproduction, first appeared here reflected in that particular cognitive organ which, *in its normal* state, recognized itself as having been created by the will and therefore as being subservient to it; and so, in its abnormal, sympathetic state, it developed to the point of seeking lasting and, finally, permanent freedom from its shameful servitude, a freedom which it ultimately achieved only by means of a *complete denial* of the will to live.

This act of denying the will is the true action of the saint: that it is ultimately accomplished only in a total end to individual consciousness – for there is no other consciousness except that which is personal and individual – was lost sight of by the naïve saints of Christianity, confused, as they were, by Jewish dogma, and they were able to deceive their confused imagination by seeing that longed-for state as a perpetual continuation of a new state of life freed from nature, without our judgement as to the moral significance of their renunciation being impaired in the process, since in truth they were striving only to achieve the destruction of their own individuality, i.e. – their existence. This most profound of all instincts finds purer and more meaningful expression in the oldest and most sacred religion known to man, in Brahman teaching, and especially in its final transfiguration in Buddhism, where it achieves its most perfect form. Admittedly, it puts forward a myth in which the world is created by God; but it does not praise this act as a boon, but presents it as a sin committed by Brahma for which the latter atones *by transforming himself into the world* and by taking upon himself the immense sufferings of the world; he is redeemed in those saints who, by totally denying the will to live, pass over into "nirvana", i.e. the land of non-being, as a result of their consuming sympathy for all that suffers. The *Buddha* was just such a saint; according to his doctrine of metempsychosis, every living creature will be reborn in the shape of that being to which he caused pain, however pure his life may otherwise have been, so that he himself may learn to know pain; his suffering soul continues to migrate in this way, and he himself continues to be reborn until such time as he causes no more pain to any living creature in the course of some new incarnation but, out of fellow-suffering, completely denies himself and his own will to live. – How sublime and uniquely satisfying is this teaching in contrast to the Christian-Judaic dogma according to which each human being – for in this case, of course, the suffering *beast* exists only to serve man!! – merely has to behave himself in the eyes of the Church throughout the short space of his life on earth, in order to lead an extremely easy life for the rest of eternity, whereas those who have not followed the teachings of the Church in this brief life will suffer equally eternal torment as a result! – We may allow that Christianity is such a contradictory phenomenon because we know it only through its contamination by narrow-minded Judaism and through its resultant distortion, whereas modern research has succeeded in proving that pure, uncontaminated Christianity is no more and no less than a branch of that venerable Buddhist religion which, following Alexander's Indian campaign, found its way, among other places, to the shores of the Mediterranean. In early Christianity we can still see clear traces of a total denial of the will to live, and a longing for the end of the world, i.e. the cessation of all life. The unfortunate part about it, however, is that such profound insights into the nature of things are vouchsafed only to those individuals who are totally *abnormal* in the sense described above, as a result of which they can be fully understood by them and by them alone; in order to convey these insights to others, the sublime founders of the world's religions must therefore speak in such images as are accessible to people's ordinary – normal – powers of comprehension; whereas much is distorted in this way (although the Buddha's teaching relating to the transmigration of souls almost certainly expresses the truth), the vulgarity and licentiousness of general egoism that characterizes normal people means that, in the end, the image is necessarily distorted to the point of grotesqueness, and – I feel sorry for the poet who takes it upon himself to restore this grotesque distortion to its original form. It seems to me that *Dante*, especially in the Paradiso, has not entirely succeeded in this: in his account of the divine natures he often strikes *me* at least like a childish Jesuit. But you, my worthy friend, may have more success here, and since you are planning to depict this image in *music*, I can almost predict your success in advance, since music is the real artistic original likeness of the world itself, for those who are initiated into its mysteries no error is possible here. Only for the Paradiso, and especially for the choruses, do I feel a friendly concern. – You will, I trust, excuse me from adding anything of comparative insignificance to these somewhat weighty considerations?

I shall write again soon: I leave here on the 26th, and that knowledge will help me to last out until then! –

Fare you well, my dear dear Franz.

Yours,
R. W.

Liszt-Briefe II, 73-80.

188. MINNA WAGNER, ZURICH   London, 12 June 1855

Gracious me, dear Minnikins, I am quite hoarse from so much talking with –
the – Queen![1] First she asked me what Peps[2] has been up to? then, if
Knackerchen was behaving himself? then, if I was taking anything back for
my wife? – finally she asked after Sulzer, and whether Baumgartner had really
come to grief the other day? and so it went on. Well, you can imagine all the
answers I had to give her; in short, I'm incapable of uttering another word
today.

Do not think that I am joking: I'm deadly serious – the Queen of England
spoke with me at great length. And I can assure you that she is *not* fat, but
very small and not at all pretty, with, I am sorry to say, a rather red nose: but
there is something uncommonly friendly and confiding about her, and
although she is by no means imposing, she is nevertheless a delightful and
kind person. She does not like instrumental music, and whenever she attends
such a long concert – which is certainly not the case every year – she does
so only as a favour to her husband, who is rather more musical and who
enjoys listening to German instrumental music. On this occasion, however,
she really seems to have been impressed: Sainton, who was able to keep a
constant eye on her from where he was sitting, assured me afterwards that
she had followed my conducting and the performances with quite exceptional
and intense interest: during the Tannhäuser Overture, especially, she and
Prince Albert are said to have got quite worked up. But what is certain is
that at the end of the Overture *both* of them applauded me most warmly when
I turned towards them and that they smiled at me in a most friendly fashion;
of course the audience followed their lead and honoured me on this occasion
with a very marked and unanimous and prolonged round of applause. This
was at the end of the first part of the concert, and the Court then withdrew
to a refreshment room whither I was immediately summoned and where I
was handed over to the Lord Chamberlain[3] to be formally introduced. I
treated His Lordship very triflingly; on the other hand, I must confess that I
felt extremely touched when this friendly and homely Queen assured me in
all confidence that she was pleased to make my acquaintance, because I was
involuntarily reminded of the position in which she must have seen me, a
position which could really not be more awkward or embarrassing. Here was
I, a man pursued by the police in Germany like some common thief and who
has had problems obtaining a passport in France, now being received in the
presence of the most aristocratic Court in the whole world by the Queen of

1 Queen Victoria and Prince Albert attended the seventh Philharmonic Society concert on
  Monday 11 June.
2 The Wagners' dog, which died on 10 July 1855. Knackerchen, alias Monsieur Jacquot, was
  a replacement for Papo who had died on 12 February 1851.
3 Spelt "Lord-Chambelan" by Wagner.

England herself and treated with the most uninhibited friendliness: that really is quite something! I did not scruple to tell her so, whereupon quite a lengthy conversation developed on the subject of my operas, a conversation in which Prince Albert – a very handsome man! – joined with the most gratifying interest. When the Queen ventured the opinion that my things could perhaps be translated into Italian in order to be given here at the Italian Opera, the Prince retorted, very sensibly, that my libretti were unsuited to this, and, in particular, Italian singers would have absolutely no idea how to sing them. In reply to this the Queen said, very naïvely – "but most of the singers at the Italian Opera are now German, so they would only need to sing in their native language." We could not help laughing at this, and I retorted that, unfortunately, German singers had deteriorated a good deal, and that – if ever I planned to perform the great work on which I was now engaged – I should have to give serious thought to training my people first. I do not think they understood me entirely, but they expressed a concerned interest in what I was saying, and added that they were quite enchanted by the Overture; whereupon I thanked them for having asked to hear it, and assured them both that they had given me the liveliest pleasure through this demonstration of interest on their part. –

And so it was indeed: for although this evening can bring me no further outward success, it has given me a most agreeable sense of satisfaction, so that I can leave London feeling somewhat more reconciled than I did before. At the end of the concert both of them applauded me once again, in a most friendly fashion, directing their applause straight at me (they were sitting at the front, right next to the orchestra), and in that way encouraged the rest of the audience to add a fairly lengthy round of applause to their own. – My few friends here, who later joined me in my rooms, were beside themselves with delight. Präger had loaned me a white tie: he now intends keeping it as a memento of the occasion when a German demagogue wore it to conduct "God Save the Queen" in the presence of the Queen of England. You must understand that when the Queen entered the hall, the national anthem had to be played, and I had to beat time to it. It occurs to me that the German police should now let me in without a fuss! –

Basically, if this event has given me any pleasure, it is chiefly on your account, since I knew that my report of it would have a most cheering effect upon you: if you are eager for me to win honour, then on this occasion it has certainly been bestowed upon me in full measure, and there is no doubt but that I am much envied today. The press will not find it easy to swallow the idea that I have been revenged on them in this way: the critics' fury may well know no bounds. I am making you a present herewith of this whole incident; do with it what you will; if it would give you satisfaction to do so, you may pass on some of the details of the report to Marschall or Spyri, so that they can put something about it in their newspaper. But I am inclined to doubt whether the papers will report much of what has happened.[1] –

I am still planning to conduct my last concert (a hellish task on each occasion that I would not wish to go through again for all the money in the world.) – and then take my leave with the greatest possible sense of contentment. In 14 days' time, at 8 o'clock in the evening, my train leaves London-bridge!!! May my journey's end be a joyful reunion with you! Fare you well, Muzius;[2] be of good cheer! Cordial greetings to all our dear friends from your

Knight of the Order of the Garter.

[The Queen had already heard of my beautiful satin trousers: I'm having to send them to the Palace for her, so that she can have a pair made for Prince Albert. But I doubt whether they'll turn out a success without Mistress *Poseck*.][3]

RWA (published with omission of postscript in Minna-Briefe I, 213–15).

189. MINNA WAGNER, ZURICH   London, 26 June 1855

Dear Minnikins,

They are trying to make it hard for me to leave. Yesterday evening[4] the orchestra and the whole of the very large audience gave me a brilliant ovation. I was warmly received the moment I appeared, and the Beethoven symphony[5] caused a sensation, but then, right at the very end – after the Oberon Overture – the orchestra rose to their feet and gave me a tremendously long and loud round of applause, and, at the same time, the entire hall burst into applause that went on and on, so that, caught between the orchestra's increasingly loud clapping and the audience's ever more furious applause, I scarcely knew which way to turn. Finally, I had to resort to a dumb-show in which I entreated people to stop clapping and go home.

I finally made my point, albeit with great difficulty. But now the hand-shaking began: the entire orchestra of around 100 players insisted upon shaking hands with me individually, and as they filed past me, many affectionate scenes took place. But there were also members of the audience who

1 The *Eidgenössische Zeitung* of 17 June and the *Tagblatt* of 18 June contained detailed reports of Wagner's meeting with Queen Victoria.
2 Another of Wagner's pet names for Minna; possibly cognate with *Mietze* ("pussy") and *mutzig* ("short" or "stumpy").
3 The postscript was suppressed from the printed edition.
4 The final Philharmonic Society concert had taken place on Monday 25 June.
5 Symphony No. 4 in B flat. In the course of the season, Wagner conducted all the Beethoven symphonies with the exception of Nos. 1 and 2.

crowded around me, and I had to let them all shake me by the hand, men and women, it was utter confusion. In short – I was moved by it all, because I was finally made to realize that people have come to like me very much. I am inclined to think that the behaviour of my little Queen contributed a good deal to this undisguised outburst of emotion. Indeed, there was really nothing in the least affected about it. It was a *tremendous demonstration* against the *Times* and the other critics. And that has *never happened before*; *never* have the audience and orchestra shown such *independence*. – And so I am really leaving London as a hero after all, and much honoured into the bargain. –

The Prägers, Sainton, Lüders, Klindworth and – *Berlioz* with his wife drove back home with me, and we remained together, over a bowl of champagne punch, until *3 o'clock* in the morning. – I have finally got to know Berlioz very well, and I am delighted to be able to say that we are now the best of friends. He is really an amiable – but very unhappy man. –

Today I have the very devil of a headache, and I now have to start packing. I shall be meeting my friends once again for dinner at Präger's house; then, at 8 o'clock, I shall be off. –

And so – dear Minnikins, – until we *meet again*, – when I hope we shall both be in a good mood. Fare you well, and may you share in my feeling of satisfaction!

Your
good Richard

Sammlung Burrell 478–9.

190. FRANZ LISZT, WEIMAR   [Zurich,] 3 October 1855

So, my dearest Franz! Today I am sending you the completed first two acts of the "Valkyrie"; it gives me a profound sense of satisfaction to know that they will soon be in your hands, since I know that there is no one who is more sympathetic to my work than you are. I am worried that the second act contains so much material; there are two crises here of such import and such power that there is really enough material for two acts; but they are both so interdependent, and the one follows so immediately upon the other that it would be quite impossible to keep them apart. If it is presented as I require – and if all my intentions are fully understood – it is bound to produce a sense of shock beyond anything previously experienced. But a thing like this is written only for those people who can bear up under a certain strain (that is for no one!): the fact that the incompetent and the infirm will complain will certainly not be allowed to affect my decision. But whether it has all turned out satisfactorily – even according to my own intentions – only you can say; I can simply not do it any differently. In disconsolate and dispassionate hours what I was most afraid of was Wodan's great scene, and especially the revelation of his fate to Brünnhilde, indeed, in London I was once on the point of discarding this scene entirely; in order to resolve the matter, I went back to my sketch once again and declaimed the scene to myself, bringing to it all the necessary expression; fortunately I discovered in this way that my spleen was unjustified, and that, on the contrary, a proper rendition produces a most musical and riveting effect. In certain passages I have given more precise indications as to how I intend them to be played, but there is a great deal still to be done, and it will one day be a major task to initiate some talented singer and actor into the very heart of my intentions by conveying my ideas to him in person. I am confident that *you* will see what is needed immediately. This is the most important scene for the development of the whole of the great four-part drama and, as such, will presumably soon receive the necessary interest and attention.

[. . .]

Liszt-Briefe II, 95–6.

191. IGNAZ HEIM, ZURICH   Mornex,[1] 13 July 1856

My most excellent friend,

Here is something for you! It is the long-awaited vocal score of the "Rhinegold".[2] May I ask you to be so kind as to have a word straightaway with our friend Schmidt[3] and give him the manuscript for him to copy? He should not be angry with me for having ignored him for so long: after all, he has already paid me back in advance by keeping *me* waiting just as long. But tell him he should now drop everything else in order to make a start on the vocal score. At the same time I would ask you to hand over to him the accompanying full score of this same operetta,[4] so that he can copy the *stage directions* straight into the vocal score, and do so, moreover, at exactly the same points as they appear in the full score: tell him, finally, to make a decent job of it, and to take special care over the spacing. You will see to this for me, will you?

1 Wagner arrived in Mornex near Geneva on 10 June and remained there, taking the waters, until 16 August.
2 Eventually made by Klindworth, rather than Bülow as originally intended, the vocal score of *Das Rheingold* was published by Schott in 1861.
3 The Zurich oboist Karl Schmidt, who was to copy Klindworth's arrangement of the score.
4 An ironical reference to *Das Rheingold*.

As far as my course of treatment is concerned, it has taken a somewhat unexpected turn, so that I am not yet certain how I am going to tell my dear Dr Rahn about it, which is why I would ask you not to say anything more about it to him for the time being. It must be said that *Dr Coindet*, to whom Rahn himself had recommended me, was the first to shake his head when he heard of the sulphur baths which I was to take, and he recommended me, without further ado, to *Dr Vaillant*, the director of a hydropathic establishment in Mornex. In spite of his advice, I dutifully began with the sulphur baths, difficult though they were to take, and as a result found myself feeling so ill and excitable that I was glad to follow Vaillant's advice to desist from them, and to entrust myself instead to the treatment of this wholly admirable doctor. And so I am now undergoing a course of hydrotherapy, something I would never had believed possible, so prejudiced had I become towards hydropathic doctors, most of whom are down-at-heel medics. But I soon convinced myself that I was dealing here with an exceptionally intelligent and cautious individual, and fortunately I have had no cause to regret my trust in him. I shall tell you more about it on my return, for it is well worth the effort: for today let me say only that I had never had an inkling previously that water could have such a *calming* effect on one's nerves and, at the same time, such a restorative effect as my ingenious doctor has managed to produce. He is uncommonly cautious in his method: he observes me almost hourly and, on the basis of what he sees to be my condition at any one time, he prescribes a suitable type of treatment which, generally speaking, has a calming effect upon my entire nervous system, while at the same time stimulating my bowels and haemorrhoidal tumours, though even here nothing is forced but, after each moderately vigorous stimulation, the effect of the treatment is again such as to calm me. As a result, I have now reached the point at the end of the first 4 weeks of treatment where, with the aid of the clear air here and a good diet, I am now aware of openings (if you'll forgive the expression) which I had completely forgotten about. Here is the source of all the colds I have suffered from and, ultimately, of the awful erysipelas which I now no longer think about, since the action of my skin has already changed so much that I have now completely stopped sweating, for ex., which I used to do – from nervous exhaustion – at the least exertion. Vaillant promises me that at the end of another 4 weeks I shall be completely cured and – I believe him. The only medicine that I have taken internally – with Vaillant's permission – is Carlsbad salt!! Long live Ignaz!

But no coffee! – coffee with milk, in particular, is a thoroughly unhealthy drink! More on this later.

Of course I must not think of work at present: but I hope to return home in the second half of August, and if there is still any warm gruel left by then, I shall see if it will inspire me to new exploits.

But now, most blessed of heroes, give my very best wishes to your wife Sieglinde:[1] tell her to practise, and to forget the distress which her godless brother Siegmund has caused her! Remember me also to Frau Stokar,[2] whose offer relating to the *Allgemeine Zeitung* touched me very much: I shall be scrupulous in returning the issues which I have received! If I receive any further copies, I shall do the same with them, too.

Baumgartner is a knave!

Keller is better-behaved – give him my best wishes!

And now – may God the most merciful bless, protect and preserve you!

Yours,

R. W. Fips.[3]

Fehr II,360–2.

192. FRANZ LISZT, WEIMAR   Mornex, 20 July 1856

[. . .] Your symphonic poems[4] are now much more familiar to me: they are the only music that occupies me at present, since I myself am not allowed to think of work during the course of my treatment here. Every day I read through one or other of the scores, just as I would read through a poem, fluently and uninhibitedly. On each occasion I feel as though I were diving down into some crystal flood, in order to be quite alone there, to leave behind the whole of this world, and to live my own life for an hour. Refreshed and fortified I then swim back to the surface and long for your presence. – Yes, my friend, *you can do it*! *You can*!

Well, there is really not much that can be said here; even the noblest expressions could well appear somewhat trivial. Enough – you will soon be here, and you will be bringing *my Dante*[5] with you. What a splendid, glorious prospect! – How can I ever thank you!! –

Yesterday I sent you a parcel: it was the original scores of the *Rhinegold* and the *Valkyrie*, which will now suffer whatever fate has in store for them. Let me be brief! –

I am slowly dying, and shall become incapable of going on with my work

1 On 22 October, to mark Liszt's forty-fifth birthday, Wagner arranged a performance of Act I of *Die Walküre* at the Hotel Baur au lac in Zurich. Emilie Heim sang the part of Sieglinde and Wagner sang both Siegmund and Hunding. Liszt played the piano.

2 Clementine Stockar-Escher, Wagner's landlady and portraitist.

3 Fips was Wagner's dog, a present from Mathilde Wesendonck following the death of Peps in July 1855.

4 On 5 May 1856 Liszt had sent Wagner copies of the recently published scores of *Tasso*, *Les Préludes*, *Orpheus*, *Prometheus*, *Mazeppa* and *Festklänge*.

5 See letter [187], p. 342, note 1. The work was dedicated to Wagner.

unless I find the kind of home I need, in other words, a small house all to myself, with a garden, far away from all noise, and especially from the noise of all these damned pianos which – even here – I am condemned to put up with wherever I turn, and which get on my nerves so much that the mere thought of them prevents me from working. For four years now I have sought in vain to fulfil this wish, and only by buying some land and building a house for myself can I hope to find what I long for. Like a man distracted, I have been brooding on ways of making this possible, and it finally struck me quite recently that I could offer my Nibelungs to *Härtels* and obtain the necessary money from them. They have now informed me of their willingness to take this exceptional step in order to acquire the rights to my works, so that I have now formally made my request, whereby they will buy from me now the two dramas already completed, and expect to receive "Siegfried" in the course of next year and "Siegfried's Death" at the end of 1858, paying me an honorarium on each occasion; and they will then publish the whole thing in 1859 – the year of performance. It is sheer despair which has driven me to take this step, for in this way I hope that Härtels will provide me with the means of acquiring the plot of land that I have in mind. If we agree – and I shall soon know their decision[1] – I shall first have to deliver my two scores to them so that they are in possession of the same ready for publication at some future date: but for now they are simply to make a copy of them as quickly as possible, and then return the originals to me straightaway. At all events – if I wanted the money immediately – I was obliged to offer them an act of seisin: for the duration of your visit here they must of course loan me the scores if they have not already been copied – that goes without saying. But since you yourself do not yet even know the last act of the Valkyrie, I am sending you the full score first, so that you – and no one else – shall be the first to learn of its contents. If you have time, read through the act as quickly as you can; but keep the whole lot ready to send to Härtels as soon as I ask you to do so. –

We must come to some better arrangement concerning this whole affair when we next speak. –

I must say that, during my course of treatment here, I have grown utterly indifferent to my work: God knows, if other people do not encourage me in my work, I shall abandon it. Poor devil that I am, why should I sweat and toil beneath the weight of such terrible burdens, if my contemporaries cannot even provide me with a place to work? I have said as much to Härtels: if they cannot help me acquire a quiet, freehold house such as I need, I shall give up writing such rubbish. –

---

1 In their letter of 30 August 1856 Breitkopf & Härtel withdrew from the deal; see Newman's *Life*, II,503–7.

I am beginning more and more to regret my letter to the King of Saxony.[1] The scandalous behaviour of the Saxon Government towards *Semper*[2] leads me to expect only the very worst from them, namely scorn and derision: they are knaves of the most shameless sort! Do you not agree? –

Well, if *you* come, I shall be glad to forget Saxony and the whole of Germany for quite some time. Bring the Frau Kapellmeister with you, do you hear! And Marie must come, too. If you put me in a really good mood, I may well inflict my "Victors"[3] upon you; the great difficulty here is that I have been toying with the idea for this piece for some time now, whereas the means by which to realize it has only just dawned on me like a flash of lightning, so that *for me* it is extremely clear and definite, but it is not yet ready to be imparted to other people. You first need to digest my *Tristan*, especially its third act, with the black and white flags.[4] Only then will the "Victors" become clearer.

But why am I going on in this way! –

Come to Zurich! and bring me the Divine Comedy – then we shall see whether we can agree on the divine tragedy.

Ever yours,

R. W.

[. . .]

Liszt-Briefe II, 130–2.

193. AUGUST RÖCKEL, WALDHEIM   Zurich, 23 August 1856

My dearest friend, your letter, far from making me feel argumentative, has rather served to confirm me in my belief that in this world nothing is ever gained by disputation. That which is most unique to us as individuals we owe not to our conceptualizations but to our intuitions: but these latter are so much our own that we can never fully express them nor adequately communicate them, for even the most complete attempt to do so – in what the artist

1 Wagner had asked Liszt to request an audience with King Johann of Saxony, whom he suggested approaching through a letter of introduction from Grand Duke Karl Alexander of Weimar. Liszt persuaded the Grand Duke to write to King Johann, but the latter rejected the appeal. At Liszt's suggestion, Wagner also addressed a personal appeal to the King, in which he attributed his behaviour at the time of the Dresden uprising to artistic disillusionment rather than political idealism; this was likewise rejected.

2 Like Wagner, Semper was denied an amnesty because of his part in the 1849 revolution.

3 *Die Sieger* (WWV 89), based on the Buddhist legend of Ananda and Prakriti (later renamed Savitri); the prose sketch is dated 16 May 1856 and was published in SS XI,325; PW VIII,385–6.

4 See letter [177], p. 324, note 1.

does, namely his work of art – is ultimately apprehended by others, in turn, purely in accordance with their own particular way of apprehending things. But how can an artist hope to find his own intuitions perfectly reproduced in those of another person, since he himself stands before his own work of art – if it really *is* a work of art – as though before some puzzle, which is just as capable of misleading *him* as it can mislead the other person. And how, in turn, can we reach a clearer understanding of this singular state of affairs except, at best, by falling back on our own intuitions? I can speak with some authority on this subject since I have made the most surprising discoveries on this very point. Rarely, I believe, has anyone suffered so remarkable a sense of alienation from self and so great a contradiction between his intuitions and his conceptions as I have done, for I must confess that only now have I really understood my own works of art (i.e. grasped them conceptually and explained them rationally to myself), and I have done so with the help of another person, who has furnished me with conceptions that are perfectly congruent with my own intuitions. The period during which I worked in obedience to the dictates of my inner intuitions began with the flying Dutchman; Tannhäuser and Lohengrin followed, and if there is any single poetic feature underlying these works, it is the high tragedy of renunciation, the well-motivated, ultimately inevitable and uniquely redeeming denial of the will. It is this profound feature that gives sanction to my poem and to my music, without which they would have no ability to stir us. Now, nothing is more striking in this context than the fact that, in all the conceptions that I held and which were devoted to speculating upon and reaching an understanding of life, I was working in direct opposition to my own underlying intuitions. While, as an artist, my intuitions were of such compelling certainty that all I created was influenced by them, as a philosopher, I was attempting to find a totally contrasting explanation of the world which, though forcibly upheld, was repeatedly – and much to my own amazement – undermined by my instinctive and purely objective artistic intuitions. My most striking experience in this respect came, finally, through my Nibelung poem; it had taken shape at a time when, relying upon my conceptions, I had constructed a Hellenistically optimistic world for myself which I held to be entirely realizable if only people wished it to exist, while at the same time seeking somewhat ingeniously to get round the problem why they did not in fact wish it to exist. I recall now having singled out the character of my Siegfried with this particular aim in mind, intending to put forward here the idea of a life free from pain; more than that, I believed I could express this idea even more clearly by presenting the whole of the Nibelung myth, and by showing how a whole world of injustice arises from the first injustice, a world which is destroyed in order – – to teach us to recognize injustice, root it out and establish a just world in its place. Well, I scarcely noticed how, in working out this plan, nay, basically even in its very design, I was unconsciously following a quite different, and much more profound, intuition, and that, instead of a single phase in the world's evolution, what I had glimpsed was the essence of the world itself in all its conceivable phases, and that I had thereby recognized its nothingness, with the result, of course – since I remained faithful to my intuitions rather than to my conceptions – , what emerged was something totally different from what I had originally intended. But I also recall once having sought forcibly to assert my meaning – the only time I ever did so – in the tendentious closing words which Brünhilde addresses to those around her, a speech in which she turns their attention away from the reprehensibility of ownership to the love which alone brings happiness; and yet I had (unfortunately!) never really sorted out in my own mind what I meant by this "love" which, in the course of the myth, we saw appearing as something utterly and completely devastating. What blinded me in the case of this one particular passage was the interference of my conceptual meaning. Strange to relate, this passage[1] continued to torment me, and it required a complete revolution in my rational outlook, such as was finally brought about by Schopenhauer, to reveal to me the cause of my difficulty and provide me with a truly fitting key-stone for my poem, which consists in an honest recognition of the true and profound nature of things, without the need to be in any way tendentious.

This sequence of events is by no means without interest, and my reason for telling you of it now is to make clear to you, at least, how I have come to interpret the problem of differentiating between intuitions and concepts – a problem resolved for me by Schopenhauer's profound and happy solution – not simply as a conception but as an experience, the truth of which has now impressed itself upon me with such compelling conviction that, especially now that I have admitted to myself the true nature of the situation, I am perfectly content to accept it for myself and not be misled into presuming to force it upon others by a process of dialectic reasoning. I myself recognize all too well that such a conviction could never have been forced upon me if it had not already corresponded to my own deepest intuitions; equally, I recognize that it cannot be forced upon anyone else either, unless he has grasped it intuitively before he recognizes its conceptual validity. We cannot accept a thing conceptually if we have not already grasped it intuitively: this state of affairs is too self-evident for anyone who has seen it clearly for himself, especially if he feels as little of a philosopher as I do, to expose himself in public as a dialectician. I can speak only in works of art. – Nevertheless, I ask you, in order to bring the matter to a summary conclusion: – can you conceive of a *moral action* except in the sense of *renunciation?* And what is the greatest holiness, i.e. the most perfect redemption, if this principle is not acknowledged as the basis for all our actions? – But even with such simple

---

1 The so-called Feuerbach ending of the *Ring*, printed in GS VI,254–5; see also Barry Millington, *Wagner* (London 1984), 225–7.

questions as these I am already straying too far from my purpose, and becoming more abstract than is good for me. Let me tell you, therefore, something about my concrete existence. –

I am only an artist: – that is my blessing and my curse; otherwise I should gladly become a saint and know that my life was settled for me in the simplest way possible; as it is, I run round in circles, fool that I am, in search of peace and quiet, i.e. the complicated peace of an undisturbed and tolerably comfortable existence, in order – to be able to work, and to be only an artist. But it is so difficult for me to achieve this end that, in my perpetual pursuit of peace and quiet, I am often obliged to laugh out loud at myself. [. . .]

As far as the external events of my life are concerned, the German theatres continue to perform my operas badly, albeit with lasting success, a fact that fills me with amused astonishment. Efforts are being made to obtain permission for me to return to Germany, the Grand Duke of Weimar in particular has taken a most active interest in the affair, but without so far having received a favourable reply.[1] For my own part, what I chiefly desire for myself is the soundness of health necessary to complete all the plans of which I am still full; unfortunately, I am fuller than I need be, since, in addition to the Nibelung dramas, I have in my head a Tristan and Isolde (love as fearful torment) and my latest subject "the Victors" (supreme redemption, Buddhist legend), both of which are clamouring for attention, so that it requires great obstinacy on my part to suppress them in favour of the Nibelungs. –

Here, my dearest August, you have in black and white all that I – a man in great need of rest – could produce at a single go. Remain cheerful and clear-headed, and suit your philosophy to your needs: ultimately we know only what we want to know, for this much at least you will admit, namely that, for all our knowledge, we are nothing but the will incarnate and, as such, the most powerful but certainly not the wisest, of all beings. Fare you well, and remember me with affection,

Yours,
R. W.

Röckel-Briefe 65–72.

194. JULIE RITTER, DRESDEN   Zurich, 30 November 1856

My dear, kind Frau Ritter,

So rarely do you receive any sign of life from me; and yet there is no one for whom I feel a more inviolable sense of veneration than for you, my most

---

1 See letter [192], p. 356, note 1. A negative reply had been sent by the King to the Grand Duke on 25 April 1856.

loyal benefactress! At the passing of each new phase in my life, when, searchingly and silently, I finally feel at peace with myself again, I then look round for you as though for the source of some better life, in order to compose my thoughts and ask myself whether I am worthy of such great love. The sense of yearning that drives me to seek refreshment in your sight and in the tender words that speak directly to my heart then turns to deepest sadness, and tears flow freely down my face when I recall that final fearful glance with which your eyes met mine when we said farewell to each other,[1] such that I must now feel cut off for ever from the elevating power of your concern for me! – As things stand at present, it now seems likely that sooner or later the Grand Duke of Weimar will procure permission for me to visit my friends there.[2] I hope that when this happens I may finally be able to greet you again! Indeed, this hope is one of my most important reasons for wishing to receive the Grand Duke's dispensation as soon as possible. Otherwise there is little for me to do in Germany, especially now that Liszt has promised to visit me again each year without fail. It must be said that my only desire is for peace of mind, something which I need from every point of view if I am to prosper. I can never again belong to the real world; I gladly regard myself as dead; all that I long for is the undisturbed leisure for artistic work. Even Liszt's visit, which on this occasion was noisier and more turbulent than I would have wished as a result of the presence of the Princess,[3] tired me almost as much as it raised my spirits. In addition I had to put up with a certain unpleasantness right at the outset, when Liszt's extraordinarily violent behaviour so offended Karl[4] that the latter – in spite of Liszt's propitiatory advances – could not get over the insult, but avoided our company for the rest of the visit. This saddened me very much. [. . .]

I have an important favour to ask of *Emilie*.[5] *Liszt* has told me certain things about Jessie[6] which have greatly aroused my interest. She is in the process of reordering her life along independent lines by setting up an educational establishment, and she has even appealed to Liszt to help her in achieving this aim. What I would now ask Emilie to do is to let me have precise

---

1 In May 1850 when the two had met in Villeneuve following the breakdown of Wagner's affair with Jessie Laussot.
2 See letter [192], p. 356, note 1.
3 Carolyne Sayn-Wittgenstein.
4 Karl Ritter. According to the later account in *Mein Leben* (550–54; English trans. 538–41) Liszt "almost seemed to be looking for trouble": a remark about baboons was taken as a personal insult by Ritter; when Julie Ritter heard of the incident, she blamed Wagner for it, with the result that the latter felt obliged to renounce (albeit temporarily) the pension he had been receiving from her since 1851.
5 Emilie Ritter.
6 Jessie Laussot. She subsequently established a Società Cherubini in Florence which she used to promote the music of Liszt and others, frequently conducting herself. She remained a fond friend of Liszt and Bülow.

information about J.'s most recent past and this surprising turn of events which seems to have taken place in her life. If it were possible that J. might have developed sufficient strength to break free from an unworthy dependence (as far as this concerns her husband), there would be no one who owed her more heartfelt sympathy than I myself; indeed, I might even claim to have been put to shame by her. I am still not entirely clear in my own mind about the tenor of her unfortunate letter to Karl (in June 1850) which was bound, of course, to turn me against her. It would be very consoling for me to be able to offer J. my hand as a friend, now that violent passion no longer clouds our relationship. You will, of course, see in this request to my dear Emilie no more than an honest wish on the part of a man in need of peace and desirous of reconciliation, who would like to be able to reap the fruits of a lasting friendship from a passing storm of passion! – A thousand greetings to Emilie! And to you, my glorious, incomparable friend, all the blessings in the world for your noble heart! Fare you well, and remember with all your old affection your eternally grateful

Richard Wagner.

My wife, whose health is often a cause of great concern to me, asks to be remembered to you with the most dutiful affection & gratitude.

Has Karl told you of my future "Tristan" and "Victors"?

Ritter-Briefe 102–5.

195. FRANZ LISZT, MUNICH   Zurich, 6 December 1856

[...] Things are so-so here! During the next few days I shall finish the first scene.[1] It is strange, but only in the course of composing the music does the essential meaning of my poem dawn upon me: secrets are continually being revealed to me which had previously been hidden from me. In this way everything becomes much more passionate and more urgent. But on the whole it requires a good deal of obstinacy on my part if I am ever to finish it all: and you yourself have not exactly inspired me with any great desire to do so. –

But I also believe I am doing all this only for myself, as a means of getting through life. So be it! –

Well, you may believe it or not, but I know of no other desire at present than to be able to visit you soon! Keep on telling me what sort of prospects there are for me here! I also lack music – and, God knows! that is something

---

1 Of *Siegfried*. The first complete draft of Act I was finished on 20 January 1857; the second complete draft is dated 22 September 1856 – 5 February 1857; the first full score 11 October 1856 – 31 March 1857; and the second full score was begun on 12 May 1857.

only you can give me: as a musician I feel utterly wretched, whereas I now believe I have discovered that you are the greatest musician of all time. I am sure that will come as a great surprise to you! –

Adieu! Tell Marie that I have again been working on the old red pocket-book,[1] and that I have sorted out my biography up until the 1st of December 1856. –

[. . .]

Liszt-Briefe II, 138.

196. OTTO WESENDONCK, PARIS   [Zurich, *c*5 January 1857][2]

> My father's sword yields to his son:
> and I'll forge it myself.[3]

I had just reached this passage, and was brooding over the motif that is to describe the sudden turn of events which marks the beginning of Siegfried's marvellous feat of forging his sword anew, when I was interrupted by your letter with its *confidential* news,[4] so that you may now judge what progress I shall make on my work for the rest of *today*! But I can easily sacrifice "today", since I now see before me such a long and beautiful "tomorrow" that will encourage me to work, and which I now owe to the rarest friendship and most loyal concern!

You know what you have given me with this news; all else that I lack in life must be denied me; I feel that my only course is renunciation, and that I must seek the unattainable things I desire within myself, and within my own nature. When this awareness began to dawn upon me with increasing clarity, and I was able to seek my solitary consolation and exaltation as far as possible in the uninterrupted practice of my art, all my wishes and desires, inasmuch as they relate to this world, came to assume the single purpose of providing me with undisturbed peace and leisure in order that I might carry out my artistic plans. You know that I told you of this great wish of mine some 5 years ago, when I described it as the longing for a pleasant and peaceful place in the country with a little garden attached. [. . .] Do you now want to know how I received *today's* – totally unexpected – news of the success of your efforts to obtain this plot of land? – A deep, deep sense of calm took hold of

1 Begun in mid-August 1835, the *Rothe Brieftasche* or Red Pocket-Book was used for making autobiographical notes at least until 12 November 1864. (Only the first four sides survive, covering the period 1813–39.)
2 Dating from Ellis.
3 GS VI,114; Andrew Porter's translation.
4 The purchase of the "Asyl". The Wagners moved in on 28 April.

me; a feeling of salutary warmth suffused me to the very depths of my being, without, however, causing the least flush of violent emotion. A vision of sunlit brightness suddenly appeared before my eyes, in which I saw the whole world lying before me in calm transfiguration, until a solemn tear fragmented the image into a thousand wondrous refractions. My dearest friend, I have never known anything like it! never before has the force of friendship brought such fundamental encouragement to my life: for what I felt was less a sense of joy at having acquired property than a glorious feeling of warmth which the knowledge of your friendship has given me, the consciousness of being held aloft, which has suddenly lifted every pressure and every burden from me. – Oh, you good, dear people! *What* am I to say to you? As though by magic, everything around me has suddenly been transformed! All sense of wavering must come to an end: I know *where* I now belong, *where* I can work and create, *where* I shall now find comfort and consolation, recovery and relief, and where I can now face, in total confidence, all the vicissitudes of my artistic career and all the efforts and labours that it brings with it, for I know where I can again find peace and relaxation in their truest sense, in the bosom of such loyal and loving friends! Oh children! You shall be well satisfied with me – indeed you shall! – For – as long as I live – I belong to you, and my successes, like my cheerful good humour and my creative genius, shall now give me pleasure, I shall cultivate and cherish them, that they may give you pleasure in turn! –

Oh, it is wonderful! It has resolved *many, many* uncertainties! If only I could describe to you the marvellous and profound sense of peace which fills me today! –

Now you must see to it that we meet again soon; I long for that moment with all my heart, and would do so even if my life here were not so isolated. Happily, I do not think we need fear war[1] any longer, but, even in the event of this happening, I believe I can remain protected here. I shall write to you again.

A thousand greetings!

Your R. W.

Otto Wesendonck-Briefe 45–7.

197. Marie Wittgenstein, Weimar   [Zurich, 4 March 1857][2]

Have you completely forgotten me, my dear child? Did you not receive my little note, which I addressed to you in Weimar some time ago? – I have spent such a miserable day today that I have been unable to work, but I should like

1 A royalist conspiracy in the principality of Neuchâtel, which was ruled by Prussia, was brought to a peaceful conclusion through the mediation of Napoleon III.
2 Dating from Altmann/Bozman II,325.

at least to be able to wish *you* a good day. I am a poor tormented creature who will never again find peace of mind: I now know only tension and apathy, brief intense periods of well-being, and long persistent periods of misery; the agreeable sensation of repose that lies between these two extremes is denied me.

Frau Herwegh gave me news of your Mama, and also of your long journey home.[1] How are you both now? Poor Franz is ill again! I am sorry to hear it; I feel something of a reproach here, for it was while he was with me that he first began to feel unwell, or at any rate was unable to stand the pace here. – And so I am not to be permitted to visit you so soon? Liszt's report sounds fairly hopeless.[2] It has disheartened me very much. Indeed, if I have to live without Liszt for any length of time, I shall pine away completely.

I simply cannot tell you of my longing to hear all his works performed by a decent orchestra. However badly things went for me in St Gall,[3] the concert there has left an unforgettable impression upon me. I should now like to hear *everything*, especially *Hamlet* and *Dante*; but I do not even have the scores![4] I have just read a report from St Gall in Brendel's journal, claiming that I had spoken out "most appreciatively" on the subject of Liszt's compositions!! This annoyed me so much that I was on the point of writing to Br. to protest. All this talk of "appreciation" makes me feel a complete fool. As if there could be any question of appreciation when I was beside myself with admiration and so deeply imbued by all that I heard that I could do nothing but revel in this most rare and supreme moment! – But, good heavens, I can never again bring myself to write to a newspaper. I would not know where to begin or where to end. And, ultimately, *whom* would I be speaking to? You know my poor opinion of the readership of these music journals, my disgust is insurmountable!

But how shall I set about ever hearing all these works? Everything passed me by here like some momentary intoxication, and what I gained from it all was not a sense of satisfaction but only one of longing. – Just imagine what my life here is like!! My poor ears are constantly exposed to every form of torment; I would rather be deaf! I suffer the most appalling torments purely as a result of this wretched sense of hearing, with which I am yet so keen to hear real music. –

Since your departure I have been greedily devouring the Goethe-Schiller

---

1 Following their stay in Zurich from mid-October until 27 November 1856.
2 See letter [192], p. 356, note 1.
3 Wagner and Liszt took part in a concert in St Gall on 23 November 1856, when Liszt conducted his *Orpheus* and *Les Préludes*, and Wagner conducted Beethoven's "Eroica" Symphony.
4 Wagner was evidently under a misapprehension with regard to the progress of Liszt's symphonic poem *Hamlet*: it was not completed until the following year (the autograph is dated June 1858).

correspondence. Whenever I read a book, it is rarely the actual words on the page that I read, but rather what I read into them. And what I read into these letters was all the things that Liszt and I could promote, instigate and propagate, if only we were nearer each other! I also read here of our rare friendship, written in letters of gold – and the speaker at the St Gall festival, whom Liszt can tell you about, may well be partly to blame for this. And so this book became a very real celebration of the time we spent together. – Since then I have been unable to read anything else. Whenever I am tired in the evenings and wish to avoid over-exciting myself before going to bed, I take up – Walter Scott. On the whole I avoid reading things that will over-excite me since, whenever I do so, I always stumble involuntarily upon ideas for future works, so that I am afraid of being interrupted in my present task. However, I have also read Schack's *"Voices from the Ganges"*,[1] which has just appeared. You must read it yourself, even though the poems are not from the noblest period of Indian poetry. Pay particular attention to the IIIrd "Bharata": – if, while reading it, you recall a certain conversation which we had in St Gall, you will soon see why this poem was bound to have such a passionate appeal for me.

I am struggling to make progress with *Siegfried*. The scene with the Wanderer[2] has turned out magnificently, and I am now in the process of forging the sword: today – in the midst of my misery – Mime cried out:

> though I grew as old
> as cave and wood,
> no sight like this would I see![3]

at which I couldn't help laughing out loud, with the result that my wife came hurrying over in amazement, thinking that I was stretched out on the sofa nursing a sore head. – Well, that's how it is! A sudden burst of laughter, and then a long period of pain! –

Well, I have prattled on enough about myself. . . . [4] My wife is well. Fips[5] is growing very fat, and the parrot is making more noise than is good for us both. I use the dolls' tea service every day. – Now you know all my news. What else shall I tell you? Yes – in the "Victors", what will happen is as follows: the girl (presumably Savitri)[6] who, while waiting for Ananda in the second act, rolls in the flowers in utter ecstasy, absorbing the sun, the woods, the birds and the water – everything – the whole of nature in her wanton pleasure, is challenged by Cakya, after she has taken her fateful vow, to look around her and above her, and is then asked what she thinks of it all? – "Not

---

1 Adolf Friedrich von Schack's *Stimmen vom Ganges* (Berlin 1857, 2/1877).
2 In Act I; see letter [195], p. 361, note 1.
3 GS VI,115; Andrew Porter's translation.
4 Suspension points as in printed text; the whereabouts of the autograph are unknown.
5 Wagner's dog.
6 See letter [192], p. 356, note 3.

very beautiful" – she then says gravely and sadly, for she now sees the other side of the world. In the 2nd act of *Tristan* – but you shall not hear any more about this for the present. It is all still only music. –

Adieu, my dear child! Write soon, do you hear, and tell me how things are at the Altenburg; you know that Liszt is always so brief. Did you have any more problems on your journey home? And how is your mother now? Is she in good health, spirited and fiery, and does she still have a place in her kind, indulgent heart for a wicked and stupid person like me?

A thousand cordial greetings!

Be good to your

R. W.

Freunde und Zeitgenossen 199–202.

198. JULIE RITTER, DRESDEN   Zurich, 6 May 1857

[. . .] If you would like to hear another piece of good news, it is that, although I have completed only the first act of "Siegfried"[1] this winter (when I was frequently interrupted in my work, firstly by Liszt's visit and later by a great feeling of exhaustion), it has turned out better than I could ever have expected. It was completely new ground for me, and, after the terrible tragedy of the "Valkyrie", I entered upon it feeling fresher than I have ever done before: now that this act has turned out as it has done, I am convinced that Young "Siegfried" will be my most popular work, spreading quickly and successfully, and drawing all the other dramas after it, so that it is *he* who will most likely become the founder of a whole Nibelung dynasty. But it seems increasingly probable that the first performance of the whole thing will not take place before 1860; for even when I have completed the whole of the music, I shall still need a full 12 months for the preparations, although these should be made simpler for me by the fact that I have already come across a number of felicitously talented performers.[2]

[. . .]

Ritter-Briefe 122.

1 See letter [195], p. 361, note 1.
2 Following a reconciliation with his niece, Johanna Wagner, Wagner was confident that the role of Brünnhilde was no longer a problem. Other singers who had been provisionally cast were Joseph Tichatschek (Siegmund), Albert Niemann (Siegfried) and Luise Meyer (Sieglinde).

199. FRANZ LISZT, WEIMAR   Zurich, 8 May 1857

I have finally got round to writing to you, my dearest Franz! I have just come
through a very bad period, but one which now seems as though it could well
make way for a much more agreeable state. 10 days ago we moved into the
little country house that you know about, near the Wesendoncks' villa, and
for that I have to thank the truly sympathetic interest that these friends of
ours have shown in me. But I first had to contend with another round of
affliction; furnishing the little house – which, I must say, has turned out to
be very nice and entirely suited to my needs – took a lot of time, so that we
were under pressure to move out of our old rooms before there was any
possibility of our being able to move into the new house. In addition, my wife
was ill, so that I kept having to stop her from interfering, and, instead, had
to take upon myself, single-handedly and alone, the whole effortful burden
of moving. For ten[1] days we lived in an hotel, and when we finally moved in
here, the weather was so dreadful and so cold that it was really only the
thought of our definitive move that enabled me to remain even-tempered.
But that is now all in the past; the whole house has been laid out and
furnished to meet our long-term wishes and requirements; everything is in
the place it will occupy until my death. [And[2] the bed on which I shall one
day breathe my last has been set up on the very spot where I shall eventually
be carried out.] My work-room has been laid out with all my well-known
pedantry and need for elegant comfort; the desk is next to the large window
with a splendid view over the lake and the Alps; peace and tranquillity
surround me. A pretty and already very well-kept garden offers me space for
short walks and little resting-places, and it will provide my wife with a most
agreeable way of occupying her time and distracting her from worrying about
me; in particular, there is quite a large vegetable garden which will lay claim
to her most tender cares. You see, I have acquired a most charming spot
where I can live in seclusion, and when I reflect upon how long I have been
demanding such a place and how difficult it had become to find even the
merest prospect of acquiring it, I feel compelled to acknowledge this good
fellow Wesendonck as one of my greatest benefactors. By way of compensation, his wife gave birth to another son 3 weeks ago,[3] who is said to boast
a high forehead, and whom I have provisionally called the youngest Siegfried.
The Wesendoncks hope to be able to move into residence early in July;[4] their
proximity promises to be both welcome and agreeable. – Well then, that's

1 In fact only eight days, during which time the Wagners lived not at the Hotel Baur au lac
  (*Mein Leben*) but at the Hotel Zum Sternen (see Fehr II, 80).
2 This sentence was omitted from the published edition.
3 Karl Wesendonck, born on 18 April 1857. He was the fourth of the Wesendoncks' five
  children, though the first, Paul, died in infancy.
4 This did not in fact happen until 22 August.

settled! – I hope shortly to be able to resume my long-interrupted work,[1] and at all events I shall not leave my charming refuge (not even for the odd excursion) until Siegfried has sorted out his relationship with Brünnhild. So far I have finished only the first act; but it is all cut and dried, a great success, and more beautiful than all the rest: even I was astonished at my ability to bring it off; for ever since we were last together, I have again come to think of myself as an appallingly bungling musician. But I have been able to win back my self-confidence by degrees; together with one of the singers from the theatre here, whom you heard in the Jewess,[2] I went through the last great scene from the Valkyrie; Kirchner accompanied us; I scored a direct hit, and this scene, which caused you such vexation, completely fulfilled all the hopes that I had placed in it. We went over it three times at home, and I am now completely satisfied. The problem is that everything about this scene is so fine, so deep, and so gentle that it requires a conscious rendition of the greatest delicacy and perfection to make its meaning clear; but if this succeeds, I have no doubt what impression it will make. But anything like this is bound of course to hover on the brink of extreme tedium if the audience is not made to feel the most perfect, solemn and conscious composure; – to rattle through the piece, as we attempted briefly to do, is simply not possible; in my own case, at least, all aptitude and intelligence desert me – as though instinctively; I become totally mindless. But I have now settled this matter to my own satisfaction, and when – one day – you hear Siegfried's smelting and forging songs, you will discover something new. But it is a crying shame that I cannot play it over to myself; and I have no real hopes that your next visit will be any better; there is always so much for us to do that we can really only do things in a hurry, and that always works to my disadvantage; I really only exist when I can concentrate completely; the slightest distraction is the death of me. – [. . .]

I am also most grateful to you for Lohengrin![3] It now leads such a shadowy existence for me, I scarcely know what to make of it any longer; I no longer know it. You arrange these things on your own and never seem to think that I might like to have been present myself. But I respect the secretive silence which my distinguished, nay my *most* distinguished patrons are so conscientiously observing on the critical question of my return to Germany, and I

---

1 *Siegfried;* see letter [195], p. 361, note 1. The first complete draft of Act II is dated 22 May – 30 July 1857; the second complete draft occupied Wagner from 18 June to 9 August 1857, whereupon he laid the work aside until 1864: see letter [201], pp. 370–72.

2 Halévy's *La Juive*, performed at the Aktientheater in Zurich on 20 October 1856 in the presence of Wagner and Liszt. The singer in question was Karoline Dressler-Pollert, who had sung in the ill-fated première of *Das Liebesverbot* twenty years previously. The pianist was Theodor Kirchner of Winterthur.

3 *Lohengrin* had been revived in Weimar the previous month in a performance which Liszt described as "the best we have had so far".

shall be content simply to despise them. The Grand Duke[1] should not imagine that I am writing my Nibelungs for him, so that he can claim all the glory for himself, when, given half a chance, he would allow the person who did all the work to waste away without a single thought. There are other ways for me to achieve my aim than through this weak-willed prince who, in the course of recent years, has given me sufficient reason to thank him for precisely *nothing*. – Well, that is by the way! – But, joking apart! the Emperor of Brazil[2] has just sent me an invitation to visit him in Rio Janeiro; I am to be given everything I could possibly need there. And so – if not Weimar, then *Rio*!!

[. . .]

RWA (incompletely published in Liszt-Briefe II,158–61).

200. KARL KLINDWORTH, LONDON   Zurich, 18 May 1857

[. . .] As far as your allusions to Präger are concerned, there is only one thing I can say. You over-estimate the importance of my dealings with him. It must surely have been clear to you that I had only the most superficial contact with him: if we met comparatively often, it was because, given my passionate and earnest nature, what I sought above all else from this particular relationship was to satisfy a need of mine to let myself go in a nonchalant sort of way, and a desire for homely relaxation. What I seek on such occasions is comfort, and I am easily won over by helpfulness and flexibility: and I also like to have someone at hand whom I can tease a little, since it does me a world of good to fool around in this way. This, my dearest friend, was the extent of my dealings with Pr., and you can judge for yourself that it is utterly impossible for me ever to find myself in the position of being betrayed by Präger![3] I have never had any occasion to think more deeply about him; I am sincerely sorry if Gerber[4] has been obliged to do so. But I have no inkling as to what can have happened there, but as soon as I discover what has taken place, I shall certainly not suspend judgement. But for now you need have no fear on my account. Pr. cannot possibly abuse my "confidence"; he is simply not in a position to do so. – At all events, I am most grateful to you

1 Karl Alexander; see also letter [192], p. 356, note 1.
2 Dom Pedro II of Brazil. Nothing came of this idea.
3 This remark is placed in an ironical light by Praeger's somewhat fanciful memoir, *Wagner as I Knew Him*, published by Breitkopf & Härtel in 1892 and withdrawn from circulation two years later.
4 A Saxon exile, like Wagner, Gerber had a medical practice in London. It appears to have been he who alerted Wagner to Praeger's alleged breach of confidence.

for this warning. Every good wish to Gerber, and cordial greetings for when we next meet!

Yours,
R. W.

Freunde und Zeitgenossen 211–12.

201. FRANZ LISZT, WEIMAR   Zurich, 28 June 1857

[...] The Wesendoncks, it may be added, are still labouring under their inability to move in; things are not going at all smoothly for them. That my relationship with this couple is a fairly artificial one and not at all easy for me is something I have hinted at sufficiently often in the past: it may continue to be bearable as long as I can preserve my independence from its business aspect, a task which I shall henceforth regard as my strictest duty. But given the extraordinary loneliness of my life here, (for Semper, Herwegh etc. live only for their own troubles and cares), I suppose I must put up with whatever burdens I choose to drag around with me, since at least they remind me of the fact that I am still alive. Enough of this; and now to something rather different. –

I shall not have any more trouble with Härtels,[1] since I have finally decided to abandon my obstinate attempts to complete my Nibelungs. I have led my young Siegfried into the beautiful forest solitude; there I have left him beneath a linden tree and have said farewell to him with tears of heartfelt sorrow: – he is better there than anywhere else. – If I am ever to take up this work again, it must either be made easier for me, or else I myself must in the meantime make it possible to *bestow* this work on the world in the fullest sense of the word. Indeed, it finally needed no more than this altercation with Härtels – my first contact with a world which is supposed to enable me to realize my plan – , in order to bring me to my senses and make me see the totally chimerical nature of this undertaking. You are the only person (of any importance) who has shared my belief in this possibility, but perhaps you did so only because you had not a sufficiently clear idea of the difficulties involved: but Härtels, who would have been expected to pay out real money without delay, looked at the matter more closely, and are doubtless quite right to regard any future performance of this work as impossible, especially if –

1 See letter [192], p. 355.
2 In fact Wagner finished the complete draft of Act II before laying aside the score. See letter [199], p. 368, note 1.

without *their* help – the author is not even going to get as far as completing it.

As for my present plans, there was a time when even without the prospect of ever living to see the work performed, I was able to conceive and begin it, and to complete one half of it. Even as recently as last winter the assurance with which you left me and your confidence that I would soon be released from my mute and silent refuge gave me the courage to continue – courage which by then had become very necessary; I needed encouragement because, having lived for eight years without the inducement that a good performance of a single one of my works would have given me, my situation had finally become unbearable. Our attempts to make music at the piano further contributed to an increasing awareness on my part that my music is simply a pitiful way of getting by; indeed, I felt that there were many things I myself could make clear to you only through a satisfactory performance. – Since this fateful silence from Weimar means that my last hope has now been completely dashed, all I can now feel is an uncontrollable sense of bitterness, such that I no longer find it possible to believe in any future prospects. As the rarest of friends, you do what you can to set me on my feet again in whatever ways you are able, and to keep me cheerful and eager for work: but I know that you are bound to regard this merely as an end in itself. And so – I am now resolved upon a course of self-help. – I have conceived a plan to complete Tristan and Isolde without further delay; its modest dimensions will facilitate a performance of it, and I shall produce it in Strasbourg a year from today with Niemann and Meyer. There is an attractive theatre there, the orchestra and the rest of the (relatively unimportant) cast will be provided by one of the neighbouring German Court theatres (Karlsruhe perhaps), and so I think that, with the help of God and without the Grand Duke of Weimar, I may again present something of mine, in my own way and on my own terms, that will help to provide me with some feeling of freshness and restore my self-awareness. At the same time this undertaking offers me the only possible chance I have of keeping my head above water; only a somewhat frivolous act on my part – the sale of my Tannhäuser to the Josephstadt Theatre in Vienna[1] – has enabled me to maintain a necessary state of balance, but my position will shortly be under threat again, or at least is by no means secure, so that – in this respect too – I have been obliged to think of ways of freeing myself from my worries. For – I think I may safely assume that a thoroughly practicable work such as Tristan will be will soon bring in decent revenues and keep me afloat for a while. In addition, I am planning to do something rather curious with it. I am thinking of having this work translated into Italian and offering it to the theatre in Rio Janeiro – which by then will probably

---

1 *Tannhäuser* was first performed in Vienna at the Thalia Theatre, the summer home of the Josephstadt Theatre, on 28 August 1857.

have presented Tannhäuser[1] – where it will receive its first performance in Italian; but I shall dedicate it to the Emperor of Brazil, who will shortly be receiving copies of my last three operas, and I think that there should be enough pickings from all this to enable me to be left in peace for a while. Whether I shall then feel attracted by my Nibelungs again, I cannot tell: it will depend on moods over which I have no control. On this occasion I had to exercise considerable self-restraint; while feeling in the best possible mood I had to wrench Siegfried away from my heart and place him under lock and key as though I were burying him alive. I shall leave him there, and no one shall have a glimpse of him as long as he has to remain locked away like this. Well, perhaps the rest will do him good; I have no plans for waking him, and neither Härtels, nor your Grand Duke – nor even Councillor Müller – shall be allowed to waken him without my bon plaisir. – It has cost me a hard and bitter struggle to reach this point! – Let us now regard the matter as closed! –

[. . .]

Liszt-Briefe II, 170–73.

202. JULIE RITTER, DRESDEN   [Zurich,] 8 October 1857

[. . .] The visit of the young Bülows[2] was the best thing that happened to me all summer. They stayed in our little house for three weeks – in the very spot that we have prepared for you and Emilie! – I have rarely felt so agreeably and pleasantly stimulated as I was by this intimate visit of theirs. During each morning they had to remain quiet, since I was then busy working on Tristan,[3] of which I read a new act to them each week. For the rest of the day we almost always made music, to which end Frau Wesendonck would faithfully come over to us, so that we had a most appreciative little audience already to hand. Bülow's mastery of the instrument is quite exceptional; not only his infallible musical intuition, his incredible memory and this amazing dexterity of his, but his indestructibility and constant readiness to play all came in extremely handy.

Once you get to know Cosima, you will no doubt agree with me in thinking the young couple most happily matched: for all their profound understanding and true genius, there is something so carefree and vibrant about these young

---

1 Nothing came of this plan. The first performance of *Tannhäuser* in Rio de Janeiro took place on 30 September 1892; *Tristan und Isolde* was first heard there on 27 May 1910; both performances were given in Italian.
2 Hans von Bülow had married Cosima Liszt on 18 August 1857. They stayed with the Wagners in Zurich from 5 to 28 September.
3 The prose draft was begun on 20 August, and the verse draft completed on 18 September 1857.

people that one cannot but feel at ease in their company. It was with great sadness that I finally let them go, but only on the firm understanding that they would return next year.[1] –

[. . .]

Ritter-Briefe 127–8.

203. FRANZ LISZT, WEIMAR   [Zurich, 11 January 1858]

My dear Franz,

Now it is my *friend's* turn to help – : without him I do not know where to turn! –

What was it, when I visited you that last time in Weimar,[2] that persuaded you to go to Karlsruhe, in spite of so many obstacles? I do not know; but you felt it necessary to fulfil the obligations of friendship, and so – you had to go there. – This time it is I whom you must help, and quickly. I am at the end of a crisis that involves everything sacred to man: I must make a decision, and every choice that is open to me is so cruel that, in reaching it, I must have beside me the one *friend* that heaven has granted me.

But I would prefer it if you did not come here to *Zurich*, since my decision must necessarily take me away from here for the present. Since I hope to find a way of causing the least possible harm, I plan for now to go to Paris, where – in the eyes of the world and especially of my good wife – I may claim to have been taken by certain interests that need protecting.[3] It is there that I should like to meet you. If this is too far for you, or if Paris is totally inconvenient, we could also arrange a rendezvous in Strasbourg. I should like to discuss my entire position *with you*, in order that the only friend I have may give his complete consent to whatever course I decide to adopt. You will see quite plainly that I am *not* acting unthinkingly. I shall forbear to go into detail in these lines, but you will have no difficulty in imagining what has happened without any need for explanation on my part: it is sufficient to say that it involves me as a complete human being and that what is at issue is all that is most sacred and noble in life. – But chance has dealt me another bitter blow. I would set off at once, were it not for the fact that I am at present waiting for some money to arrive; just when I need their help, everyone

---

1 The Bülows returned to Zurich on 15 July 1858, and were house-guests of Wagner's from 21 July to 16 August 1858.
2 From 13 to 20 May 1849.
3 Wagner left for Paris on 14 January, ostensibly to protect the French copyright of his operas. The real reason seems to have been a "neighbourly confusion" (BB 128; English trans. 107) caused by his increasing involvement with Mathilde Wesendonck; see introductory essay, pp. 167–8.

abandons me; I have had to send a letter of attorney to Haslinger in Vienna in order to force my director[1] there to pay me quite a large sum of money that he owes me: I cannot reckon with any certainty upon a successful outcome here for at least a month. From Berlin, where Tannhäuser was performed precisely once during the last quarter, I received precious little for a change, whereas I had come to expect large sums of money from there during the winter months. Only within the last few days have I been able to write to Härtels and offer them Tristan on certain conditions,[2] so that – even in the event of their acceptance – I cannot demand an immediate advance from them, since I cannot send them any of the manuscript until the end of February. My wife's purse is nearly exhausted; she is anxiously awaiting money from me to pay a pile of New Year's bills. In such circumstances – since I am completely without resources here – I find myself in the painful position of not being able to effect my necessary departure, which I would not be able to do even if I were to receive the necessary fare, since I cannot leave my wife, even for a short time, without any means. Accordingly, I need at least 1000 fr. in order to be able to leave. Since I expect Härtels to send me a sizeable advance on the first act by Easter at the latest, if, indeed, I am not able to ask for it sooner, I can certainly promise to pay back the money by then. In heaven's name look around to see from whom and by what means you can get hold of this money: it is most dreadfully important for me to be able to get away from here during this time.[3] Think where I am *living*! – Send me the money, even if it is from the most Jewish of Jews, – and at the same time let me know where you want to meet me – in Strasbourg or in Paris. I am sure that *you* will have no objection to a meeting taking place. As for me, I believe the time of my **friend** is now at hand.

I do not dare ask to be remembered to your circle. Fare you well! Until *we meet again very soon*.

Yours,
Richard.

Liszt-Briefe II, 184–5.

1 Johann Hoffmann; see letter [201], p. 371, note 1.
2 Wagner had written to Hermann Härtel on 4 January, demanding a fee of 600 louis d'or, payable in three instalments upon receipt of each of the three acts of the work. Breitkopf & Härtel beat him down to 200 louis d'or.
3 Liszt wrote on 15 January to say that the money would be available through his son-in-law Emile Ollivier. In the mean time Wagner had telegraphed to say that it was no longer necessary for Liszt to meet him in person.

204. HANS VON BÜLOW, BERLIN   Paris, 18 January 1858

My dear Hans,

I am most sincerely grateful to you for your loyalty and love. I received your gifts while I was still in Zurich: your red Calderon has remained with me. Many thanks, too, for looking after my affairs for me.

I suppose you must have had a lot of work with your concert, otherwise I should have received the letter you promised me recently? I cannot at present recall the various points which you raised and which I had intended to reply to today, so I shall tell you only the most important things that have happened to me. First, however, I must say that Cosima's reserve towards me saddened me very much, now that I am certain that her excuse about the language[1] is simply a pretext, and that she really feels rather embarrassed in my presence. If my manner appeared strange to her, and if the occasional blunt remark or my tendency to ridicule others (such as the Herweghs etc.) hurt her in any way, I should very much regret having been over-familiar: this is a failing that I am always ready to admit and regret whenever I find that I have alienated some person whom I sincerely respect. But I am certain that on this occasion it amounts to no more than a misunderstanding. My entirely unthinking familiarity towards people whom I find sympathetic has already lost me many friends: I hope that your dear young wife will not be estranged from me for any length of time.

[...]

Bülow-Briefe 83–4.

205. FRANZ LISZT, WEIMAR   [Paris, 23/4 January 1858]

Dearest Franz, a kind fate has brought me another friend to stand beside me during this curious period when I must reach the final and most important decisions of my life. How comforting it is to make the acquaintance of a poet like *Calderon* at a mature stage of life. He has accompanied me here, too, and I have just finished reading his "Apollo and Clymene", together with its sequel, "Phaeton". Have you ever felt drawn towards Calderon? In my own case, my utter lack of linguistic (and musical!) talent means that he is available to me only in the form of translation. But Schlegel, Griess (the most important pieces), von der Malsburg and Martin, too, (published by Brockhaus) have all done much to open up to us the poet's mind, and even his indescribable subtlety. I am tempted to place Calderon in a class of his own. Through him,

---

1 Cosima had apparently claimed that her knowledge of German was not good enough for her to write to Wagner. See also letter [207], pp. 379–81.

the essential significance of the Spanish character has been revealed to me: a unique and incomparable bloom, showing such speed of development that it was soon bound to end in the destruction of matter and – in denial of the world. The fine and deeply passionate spirit of this nation has seized upon the concept of "honour" to express an idea in which all that is most noble and, at the same time, most terrifying assumes the form of a second religion. The most terrible selfishness and, at the same time, the greatest self-sacrifice seek satisfaction here. Never could the nature of the real "world" find a more sharply defined, more blinding and more commanding, but – at the same time – a more crushing and more terrifying expression than it does here. The poet's most affecting portrayals take as their starting-point the conflict between "honour" and a deeply human sense of fellow-suffering; "honour" determines those actions which are acknowledged and praised by the world; injured fellow-feeling seeks refuge in an almost unspoken melancholy which, for that very reason, is the more deeply embracing and the more truly sublime: in it we see how terrible and how empty is the world's true essence. It is this strangely affecting awareness that confronts us in Calderon in such enchantingly and creatively formative a way, and there is no other poet in the world to equal him in this. Now, it is the Catholic religion that seeks to bridge this deep divide, and nowhere could it achieve a more profound significance than here, where the contrast between the world and fellow-feeling assumes so clear, distinct and vivid an outline, in a way that is true of no other nation. How significant it is that almost all the great Spanish poets took holy orders during the second half of their lives. And how singular that, following their complete spiritual victory over life, these poets were then able to depict this self-same life with a certainty, purity, warmth and clarity that they never had in the hurly-burly of life; indeed, they produced their most gracious and witty creations against a background of spiritual seclusion. Faced by this wonderfully significant figure, I now find every other national literature deeply insignificant by contrast; and if nature produced only one such individual as Shakespeare among the English, we can now see how unique this poet was; indeed, the fact that the glorious English nation continues to thrive and prosper so splendidly by exploiting the world for financial gain, whereas the Spanish nation has gone to rack and ruin, this fact, I say, affects me very deeply because this phenomenon, too, clearly reveals what it is that the world regards as important! – –

[. . .]

Liszt-Briefe II, 190–1.

206. MARIE WITTGENSTEIN, WEIMAR   Zurich, 8 February 1858

[. . .] On the day of my departure[1] I had to spend some time with Ollivier at the Palais de justice: I walked up and down there for an hour in the Salle des pas perdus with advocates dressed in cap and gown, explaining Tannhäuser to them at their request, an explanation which they received with great warmth. Altogether, it has been a most salutary experience, not least as a result of my observations this time in Paris: people like me very much! This may be because of my incredible outspokenness and self-abandon in all that I say, so that, given their common attitude to life, people can respond only with an almost apprehensive concern which more or less expresses their belief that such a man as I, who thinks so little of himself but only of the object that absorbs him, must necessarily have to put up with a great deal of suffering, which invites them to feel compassionate towards me, a sentiment that is very close to love. In consequence, the admiration which great artists inspire is almost entirely lacking with me; for pre-eminent and exceptional talents are similarly lacking in me. I have only the bond that concentrates more ordinary gifts into a single forceful action, so that, when this action finally ensues, these gifts of mine produce things that are technically beyond the individual talent. This, I believe, is total self-oblivion, obliviousness to the world around me, complete absorption by the object in question, an object which must be vast and profound simply because any lesser object could not produce this effect upon me. This was brought home to me by Berlioz, who is my opposite in this respect. This man undoubtedly has all the gifts of genius, without its spirit, which is the bond of which I spoke. He sees only the detail of his subject before him, and is significant because of his ability to master this detail in such a lively fashion. He read me his libretto,[2] and in doing so increased my concern for him to the extent that I almost hope I may never meet him again, since my distress at not being able to help a friend would finally become painfully unbearable. This libretto is clearly the pinnacle of his misfortune, for nothing else can ever come near it. To see this unfortunate fabrication (which is bound to strike every listener as such) regarded by him as the ultimate and finest achievement of his artistic career, a career to which he intends to sacrifice everything since he means this to be his final work, is bound to fill me with more than a sense of sadness. The way he recited the text was significant; he read it very effortfully, with strong emphasis and with a great show of enthusiasm, but without ever revealing the least sign of any real enthusiasm, so that his delivery often reminded me of bad actors who have been given the wrong role to play. There was no sense of passion, apart from the obstinacy of his outlook which, in turn, nowhere appeared truly sure

1 On 3 February 1858. Wagner arrived back in Zurich on the 6th.
2 *Les Troyens*. See Newman's *Life*, II,537.

of itself. I had great difficulty explaining to him my painful bemusement at
the curious nature of the whole thing, which I did by expressing doubts and
misgivings about individual details; but it is never possible to make oneself
understood in this way, if the work as a whole has to be spared from criticism.
I left with a feeling of great sorrow, but at least he spared me the possible
embarrassment of my having to tell him how I felt since, for his own part, he
never shows any genuine interest or fellow-feeling: I do not think he knows
what love is; that is the key to the tormenting riddle of his nature. And so it
is hard for his friends to satisfy him. He places us in the embarrassing position
of having to deceive ourselves and, ultimately, the world as well, lest we
destroy *his* illusions about himself and about us: it is clear at a glance that
any attempt to disillusion him would immediately bring about a breach and
the loss of his friendship, for there has never been anyone in the world to
whom he might be capable of sacrificing himself and his outlook. In certain
circumstances, and if one remains completely silent, one may well resolve to
leave the world to its illusions simply by being silent, but it is more difficult
to try to delude *oneself*, and this elaborate exercise is one that is totally
repugnant to me; but since there is no other way of preserving Berlioz's
delusions about himself, I can only hope that I never again find myself in the
painful position of having to serve a friend in *this* way. God, what a blessing
is my relationship with Liszt by contrast! I freely admit that I believe that the
highest ideal attainable in life is to be able to be boundlessly true and honest.
Every relationship that I value has this meaning for me, and I measure the
extent of its value simply by whether I feel I can be outspokenly honest or
not; whereas the greatest torment I know consists in having to leave people
in a state of uncertainty about me, if not by dissembling to them, at least by
self-restraint; and it is this sense of compulsion that characterizes all our
relationships in life, for the only gift that nature has given us is the gift of
reason as a defence mechanism with which to deceive others. Indeed, the
constant growth of my friendship for Liszt is based almost solely on an
increasing lack of constraint in our honesty and outspokenness towards each
other; love is a prime requirement here, but so, too, with natures like our
own, are intellectual breadth and constitutional productiveness, for it is only
as a result of these qualities that love gains that undaunted power which, in
the case of paltry intellects, inevitably soon falls short. And so, with us, the
one complements the other; where we appear to differ utterly, it needs only
total honesty in order to produce an immediate understanding. You are
therefore quite right to idolize our friendship: you will not soon see its like
again. –
    [. . .]

Freunde und Zeitgenossen 215–18.

207. Cosima von Bülow, Berlin   Zurich, 1 March 1858

Dear Cosima,

As a change from one of my normally quite wretched days, I have today spent an utterly miserable day, which at least has the advantage of not sending me straight to the medicine bottle, namely my work. And so I shall see whether I may not improve my situation a little by paying back old debts, and lighten my cares by telling of my sadness to one who is happy. – Yes, indeed! all you have to do is tell me the reason for your hostility; I shall not allow it to intimidate me: my misery assures me that no one can seriously hate me except when they are mistaken about me, – which ultimately tickles my sense of humour and thus affords me the only pleasure of which I am capable. I feel as though you, too, have been led somewhat astray by the cheerful good humour which I showed you while you were here;[1] this is the only explanation I can find for a number of things. What a strange time it was! Each morning I put my misery into verse, and spent the rest of the day making fun of it with you. And yet it gave me immeasurable comfort to be able to do so; but I could do so only because I had you there, dear young couple that you are. For only then did I feel the genuine joy which I am still able to feel! And when Hans played me to sleep in the evenings, and you listened so splendidly, I felt I had spent one of the best days of my life. – I am now spending the mornings setting my misery to music,[2] but now I have no one with whom to make fun of it; with my good wife that is simply not possible; – and so I remain hard at it all day, and by the evening my own music is mute; I cannot find even the least pleasure in it. And so I feel miserable throughout the whole day, which puts me out of humour, – but it usually happens then that a wonderful power transforms my wretchedness into the most ineffable joy; I then feel so immeasurably sublime and happy that an incredible sense of pride comes over me, causing the whole world to seem wretched beside me. Well, I then have to atone for this of course, and my old sense of misery then comes flooding back. And it won't get any better until you and Hans return here; but I do not really believe you will, since you are for ever talking about it; each time that your Papa promised most faithfully to visit me, I could be certain he would not come. I really cannot rely very much on you two either. But time will tell! In the mean time I shall spice the joys of anticipation with

---

1 Between 5 and 28 September 1857.
2 The music of the three acts of *Tristan und Isolde* was written in Zurich, Venice and Lucerne. The first complete draft of Act I (with the Prelude) is dated 1 October – 31 December 1857, and the second complete draft 5 November 1857 – 13 January 1858; the first complete draft of Act II is dated 4 May – 1 July 1858, and the second complete draft 5 July 1858 – 9 March 1859; the first complete draft of Act III is dated 9 April – 16 July 1859, and the second complete draft 1 May – 19 July 1859. The full score of the whole work was completed on 6 August 1859.

a little doubt. – That the Olliviers will come, too, I simply refuse to believe any longer: their "Yes" to the question that I have repeatedly put to them sounded so downright pitiful. – I shall write my next letter to Blandine on the next miserable day that I have. She had a most salutary effect upon me in Paris, and will do so each time that my star guides her to my vicinity. If only you good children had an inkling of how I felt in Paris! Blandine must often have thought of me as very foolish; the only thing that kept up my spirits was noticing this. But I was very amiable at Mme Erard's, as Blandine can no doubt attest: for it was a question of capturing an "Erard" for myself. It is on this grand piano, which I am shortly expecting here, that I immediately pinned all my hopes of future enjoyment; for it is on this instrument that Hans shall play to me in the evenings when you are next here and when I have again spent the day feeling cheerful. Above all, I hope that skating runs will no longer cause Hans's fingers to trip over each other.

Well, if you bring Blandine with you, do not forget to bring Ollivier as well; it is true that the French he requires of me is often beyond my means, but I am heartily glad to make an effort for the sake of the first Frenchman to have affected me with such very real sympathy. You could also bring the Hérolds; but I hope we already have the pick of the Erards here: at a pinch, you could leave them with the "Dumb Girl".[1]

And so that you, my dear child, may also come in total trust, I must tell you that, ultimately, I really do like the Herweghs, and that he in particular is my favourite person here of the male sex. I have often – as on a certain recent occasion – been obliged to turn to him as the only person who can understand certain difficult aspects of my character, which the world may perhaps regard as unfathomable. His wife, too, has often been our guest here, and I always offer her a cigar with a great show of courtesy, then look away while she smokes it in her excessively charmless fashion. Between the two of us, she is a thoroughly decent, highly intelligent and very gifted wife, in addition to being an incomparable friend. My God, if only I had a wife who took such care of my money as she does for her husband! – I hope, my dear Cosima, that your feelings are now much less ruffled as a result of this greeting of mine, and although I may perhaps be expecting a good deal if I ask you to remember with my affection, it is not, I trust, more than lies within your power, if you wish to be at all fair to me?

Fare you well, and think of me.

Yours,
Richard Wagner

Hans will shortly be receiving the full score of Tristan for him to arrange. If he has no particular inclination to work on it, I have temporarily spared

1 *La Muette de Portici*, literally "The Dumb Girl of Portici", but usually known as *Masaniello* in English.

him the arrangement for 4 hands: his name – it goes without saying – will also appear on the title page, although he will still receive only 3 thlr. a sheet. Tell him, therefore, to work on both the large vocal score and the piano score for 2 hands at the same time.

Eger I, 12–15.

208. MATHILDE WESENDONCK, ZURICH [Zurich, 7 April 1858]

Just out of bed.[1]
Morning confession.

Oh no! no! it is not De Sanctis[2] that I hate but *myself* for repeatedly finding my poor heart guilty of such weakness! – Shall I offer as an excuse my ill health and the sensitivity and irritability that it fosters in me? Let us see what happens. Two days ago at noon an angel came to me, blessed and refreshed me; this made me feel so much better, and cheered me so much that in the evening I felt a sincere need to be among friends, in order that they might be allowed to share my inner happiness: I know I would have been most amiable and friendly. I then heard that no one in your house had dared hand you my letter, since De Sanctis was with you. Your husband was of the same opinion. I waited in vain, and finally had the pleasure of receiving Herr v. Marschall, who settled down here for the evening and, with every word he spoke, filled me with a terrible hatred of all the De Sanctises in the world. The lucky man – he kept her away from me! And by means of what gift? Simply by dint of her patience. I could not hold it against him for being so much in earnest; for everyone who has dealings with you is most certainly in earnest! I, too, am in earnest! to the point of tormenting you! But why does she encourage this burdensome pedant? What does she care about Italian? Well, I soon found the answer to that. But the better I understood the reason why, the more annoyed I became with that tiresome man; in my dreams I confused him with Marshall, and from this confusion there emerged a figure in whom I recognized all the misery that the world has in store for me. – And so it went on throughout the night. In the morning I regained my senses, and was able to pray to my angel from the very depths of my heart; and this prayer is love! Love! My soul rejoices in this love, which is the well-spring of my redemption. Then the day came, with its miserable weather, the pleasures of your garden were denied me; nor could I get on with my work. And so the whole of my day was a struggle between ill-humour and my

1 Enclosed with this letter was the pencil sketch of the Prelude to *Tristan und Isolde*; see introductory essay, pp. 167–8.
2 Mathilde's Italian teacher, Professor Francesco de Sanctis.

longing to be with you; and whenever I yearned with all my heart to be with you, our tedious pedant kept on coming between us and stealing you from me, and I could not help admitting to myself that I hated him. Oh, what a wretch I am! I had to tell you; there was no alternative. But it was very petty of me, and I deserve to be properly punished. What is my punishment to be? – I shall come to tea next Monday after your lesson: I shall spend the entire evening being utterly charming to De Sanctis, and shall speak French in a manner that will be a joy to hear. –

What was that foolish quarrel about Göthe yesterday? That Göthe can be adapted by philistines to suit the world rests ultimately upon a misunderstanding of the poet; but the fact that such a misunderstanding was *possible* makes me somewhat wary of him, and especially of his interpreters and apologists. Well, as you know, I accepted all of this yesterday, including your great delight in Faust; but finally having to listen to people saying time after time that Faust was the most significant human type ever created by a poet, this – (very foolishly!) – made me angry. I cannot allow my friends to delude themselves on this point. Faust's despair about the world rests initially either upon his knowledge of the world, – in which case he is to be pitied, following his transformation, for rushing headlong into the world he despises and for living it up, and he is, in my view, one of those people who despise their fellow men while at the same time knowing of no other ambition throughout their lives than to delude others and enjoy their admiration; – or else, and this is how it is, Faust is simply a scholar with fanciful ideas who has yet to experience the real world, in which case he is simply cripplingly immature, and we may regard it as a good thing that he is sent out into the world in order to learn what he can from it. But it would have been even better if he really *had* learned all that there was to learn, and learned it, moreover, at the first, wonderful, opportunity, through Gretchen's love. But, ah, how happy the poet is when he has removed Faust from the soulful depths of this love and allowed him to wake up one fine morning with not a trace of the whole affair to cloud his memory, so that the real world, the world of classical art, the practical world of industry can now be *acted out* before his highly objective gaze in the greatest possible comfort. As a result I can regard this Faust really only as a missed opportunity; and the opportunity that has been missed is nothing less than the unique chance of salvation and redemption. This is something that the grey-haired sinner feels for himself in the end, when he seeks, somewhat obviously, to make good his earlier omission in the final tableau, – so extraneous, after death, when it no longer embarrasses him but where it can only be an agreeable experience to let the angel draw him to its breast and no doubt waken him to a new life. – Well, I thoroughly approve of all this, and Göthe is certainly no less great as a poet, since he always remains true to life, indeed, he cannot be otherwise; people may after all call it objective if the individual never succeeds in absorbing the object, i.e. the world (which can be achieved only by the most active *fellow*-suffering), but instead simply imagines the object, and loses himself in it by contemplating and perceiving it rather than by sympathizing with it (for in that way he would become the world itself – and this identification of the individual with the world is the business of the saint, not of the Faust poet, who has ended up as a model for philistines to emulate); finally, what I always like about Göthe is that he always felt the inappropriateness of his behaviour and yet found no comfort in expressly avoiding all contact with fellow-suffering, – as I say, Göthe for me is a gift of nature by means of which I learn to understand the world, and in this he is almost unique. He did what he could, and – all honour to him! – But why attempt to turn his pitiful Faust into one of the noblest types of humankind? It is because the world grows fearful when it stands before the abyss that is the great problem of why we exist; how grateful people are when Faust finally steps back from the void and, having refused to quit the world, resolves to accept it as it is. Yes, if only you knew that from now on his only guide is Mephistopheles, you could prepare yourselves for the eternal torments of the father of lies, after the blessed redemptress, the glorious figure of Gretchen, has turned her back on you, she who is exalted by suffering. Göthe knew this very well; but you should know it, too! –

What nonsense I'm talking! Is it the pleasure of talking to myself, or the joy of talking to you? – Yes, to you! But when I look into your eyes, I am lost for words; everything that I might say then becomes meaningless! You see, everything then becomes so indisputably true, I am then so sure of myself, whenever these wonderful, hallowed eyes rest upon me and I grow lost in contemplation of them! Then there is no longer any object nor any subject; everything then becomes a single entity, deep, immeasurable harmony! There I find peace, and in that peace the highest and most perfect life! He is a fool who would seek to win the world and a feeling of peace from outside himself! A blind man who would not have recognized your glance nor found his soul within it![1] Only inside, within us, only deep down does salvation dwell! – Only when I do not see you – or may not see you – can I speak to you and explain myself. –

Be good to me, and forgive me, and forgive my childishness yesterday: you were quite right to call it that! –

The weather seems quite mild. I shall come into the garden today; as soon as I see you, I hope I may find you alone for a moment! –

Take my whole soul as a morning salutation! –

Sammlung Burrell 490–3.

---

1 There is an implied parallel here between the ageing Faust who, though physically blind, looks beyond himself to the world around him and, by helping others, gives meaning to his own existence, and Wagner himself.

209. CAROLYNE SAYN-WITTGENSTEIN, WEIMAR [Zurich,] 12 April 1858

Your letter, my dear Frau Kapellmeister, was almost a source of embarrassment to me on this occasion, for, having sent me this reminder, you will certainly not believe me when I assure you that I would have written to you today in any case, and of my own free will. [But¹ because of your kindness you have robbed me of even this one slight reward which I should otherwise have merited by having finally written to you without being asked; for – I have no doubt that you will not believe my assurance, eager though you are to believe most things. Very well then, let this, too, be an exercise in humility! –]

Yes indeed, my dear, kind friend! You would have received a letter from me today in any case; not because I had anything to report, but precisely because I wanted to tell you that nothing happens in my life any longer; [and I should then have done so after my own fashion, and managed to turn it into a letter for you, – a letter of the kind that I have been wanting to write to you for quite some time. In fact, I could also say that I needed only to tell you why I have not written for so long; in that way I should have finished up at more or less the same point, and you would have discovered more about me than it is good for my friends to know. I was extremely relieved to have you write and tell me about the concert at the Wesendoncks',² since I discovered in that way that you already knew about it, and because I can imagine that I could easily have omitted to say a single word to you about it – but to have done so entirely unpremeditatedly and without intending to convey anything particular in the process. At all events, the brilliant report which reached you – perhaps from Herwegh's pen – absolves me from offering you any further description of the event, so that,] in informing you of my news, I may confine myself to the otherwise uneventful nature of my life. All that goes on in the world is of no particular appeal to me; the more intimate side of life – which is all that people like us are concerned about any longer – is always lost sight of here; the more people I show my face to, the less I am understood. In public it is only the mask that counts, for even if one were to appear before them without a mask, people would still see it as a mask, since this is all they have ever known. What increasingly attracts me to great poets is what they conceal by their silence rather than what they express, indeed, it is almost more from a poet's silence than from what he says that I learn to acknowledge his greatness: and it is this that makes Calderon so great and so precious for me. What makes me love music with such inexpressible joy is that it conceals

---

1 The passages in square brackets have not previously been published.
2 A serenade organized by Mathilde Wesendonck for her husband's birthday and held on 31 March. Some thirty musicians from Zurich, under Wagner's baton, played excerpts from Beethoven's third, fourth, fifth, seventh, eighth and ninth symphonies in the spacious vestibule of the Wesendonck villa; a hundred guests were accommodated in the surrounding rooms.

everything, while expressing what is least imaginable: it is thus, strictly speaking, the only true art, the other arts being merely adjuncts. [What I concealed that evening I revealed to the assembled guests in loud and sonorous tones by means of my Beethoven: you have been told that it was not my silence that was understood but only the sounds that I made. And you wish me well for this feast of sound, just as the whole of the world rejoiced in it. And so all I should now need to tell you is what I concealed: but it will be far from easy to do so. Let us attempt to explain this by means of similes! What an absurd word – : similes! What did I want to express by using it? There it is on the written page: let it stand; you yourself must think of the most sensible interpretation here! –

And so I shall tell you a little of how I felt before and after this concert.

About 2 weeks before these celebrations I had come to the point where I was ready to grab my hat at the first opportunity and set out into the world, intending to disappear for ever from the sight of a certain three people. This seemed to me the only solution to a situation which had grown to be utterly intolerable. What held me back? – the realization that to have done so would have been the death of one at least of these three people, and perhaps of all three of us. And one recoils from being the cause of so sudden a death in others, even though, for oneself, it must appear the ultimate boon. – I remained. It was then, as you know, that I brought off a really first-rate concert. However, this brilliantly festive and cheerful occasion left me feeling somewhat exhausted; I fell ill, and was annoyed at not being able to write to you about it immediately, since, with the best will in the world, I could not have done so, a fever of several days' duration having left me somewhat weak. And on the very day that I was first able to go out into the fresh air again,[1] my dear wife fell prey to a temptation of the devil's which I sincerely hope she may one day come to see as a test that God has set her. What made this incident particularly painful for me was that for some time now the poor woman has been suffering from a serious relapse of an illness dating back some considerable time.

The enjoyment afforded by our tiny garden and her preoccupation with it, together with the pleasures of our new-found domesticity, had done her a power of good last summer, and her terribly excited state, involving, as it did, often lengthy periods when she could not breathe and all kinds of other worrying symptoms which had become increasingly noticeable over the years, seemed to have disappeared altogether. During the second half of this last winter, however, her illness suddenly returned, and (you may be assured) entirely without any obvious outside cause (for she knew nothing of that catastrophe), indeed, it did so with such violence and forcefulness that these last few months have been absolute hell for the two of us. Heart ailments of

1 7 April 1858; see introductory essay, p. 167–8.

this kind typically express themselves in permanent insomnia in particular, and in a terrible excitability, in violence, melancholy, oversensitivity, a fanciful determination to take everything amiss, and often total confusion when it comes to rational thinking and thought. All the remedies which the doctor has tried have so far led only to a worsening of the problem, and since I was so pleased with the results of the treatment which I received at the time with Dr Vaillant outside Geneva, I finally attempted to persuade my poor wife to undertake a similar course of treatment for herself. Fortunately, a friend was able to draw my attention to a hydropathic establishment very near Zurich, run by an excellent doctor who has already been successful in treating a notorious case entirely similar to my wife's (only more critical). We paid a call together on this doctor two days ago, and *both* of us immediately felt total trust in him, and my poor tormented wife is now resolved to begin her treatment in Brestenberg the day after tomorrow. This marks a temporary halt in the increasing decline from which I am suffering. I shall be on my own for some time – a good two months no doubt – and shall at least have peace and quiet at home, in addition, I hope, to having the leisure to work. During this time my wife's illness will reach a turning-point: I am fully confident, and have every hope that she will find complete relief from her suffering. How happy I should be if she were to enable me to devote to her what I can sacrifice to her future welfare and the peace and quiet of her declining years! But *you* must not be angry with me, my dear Frau Kapellmeister, if it is not until today that I have finally found time to write to you. –

I shall shake friend Wesendonck's hand for you, but shall take good care not to convey your real meaning to him when I do so; it might easily confuse him to discover that people had too high an opinion of him. He is very good-natured; but his behaviour – which in many respects is thoroughly respectable – no doubt rests for the most part simply upon the fact that he is at his wits' end. He is quite incapable of rising to the level of true, manly resignation. He stands in awe of me, and feels profound respect; indeed, he often shows me the most loving affection. None the less, the crux of my dealings with him remains the fact that there is nothing for which he can ever reproach me. With what sacrifices this has had to be achieved, not only on my part but, more especially, on the part of his wife, you can well enough imagine. She is fading away, and is kept alive only by the sight of me. And yet on that festive evening we were able and, indeed, obliged to admit to each other that there was no one else with whom we would wish to change places. Consciousness of our suffering is the source of our solace. –]

I have again been thinking a great deal about my amnesty of late; it alone could make our position substantially easier to bear. Trips to Germany, periodic artistic ventures would offer a worthy diversion, and appease the canker that eats away inside me. I tried to do something about it recently in

Dresden; but, as it appears so far, once again without success. No doubt my cup must be drunk to the bitter dregs. May heaven grant me a noble end! Amen! –

I am making slow progress on my work.[1] I have signed a contract with Härtels for publishing "Tristan" [in return for very slight financial advantages]; the full score is to be engraved, and, in order to make a start, I have begun by scoring the first act. I finally intended to start the second act at the beginning of this month [but it was impossible to do any work]. I hope I shall soon be able to get back to it. [– By the way, the rumour that I was writing my new opera for a first performance in *Prague* was so stupid as not to need refuting; it rested upon the fact that a certain theatre director[2] was giving himself airs, having thought that he could interpret a jocular remark of mine in this way. –] For the rest, dearest of friends, things are as wretched as ever with me. But I mention this [too] only in passing! –

[And so, you now have a whole bundle of good news from me, including some in advance, so that none of you shall forestall me with anything better.] I am following Liszt's campaigns step by step in the musical journals; I am genuinely pleased for his sake [but for a long time now I have felt so utterly remote from the feeling that guides him that I can regard it all only as though it were a dream; there is no firm reality about it for me, and I do not know, when I look at Franz, whether he is in the light and I in the shadow, or the other way round. It all strikes me as an insubstantial and inaudible play of shadowy figures whose once clear outlines grow gradually more and more indistinguishable. But you are standing in the midst of the fire, and for you the world's approval is a fixed and tangible reality which does you good. I no longer have any feeling for it, and so you must not regard it as a lack of interest on my part if I do not announce my pleasure at Liszt's triumphant successes in more energetic terms than these; my voice fails me, like that of the man who tries to speak in a dream to the phantoms of his dreams.

Nor will the announcement of your future visit assume the form of a genuine hope for me yet: you know I have no faith, but only courage. You must instruct me, unbeliever that I am: however, I need to be with you face to face, for that to be possible. But, if I may make a confession, I am resolved to *hope*. –]

And now a thousand sincere thanks for your generous, unshakeably loyal friendship! Never think of me as ungrateful, but only as unhappy; never as despairing but only as resigned! And give Marie[3] my very best wishes! [My

---

1 *Tristan und Isolde;* see letter [203], p. 374, note 2 and [207], p. 379, note 2.
2 František Jan Škroup (1801–62), director of the Estates Theatre in Prague; *Tannhäuser* was first heard in Prague on 25 November 1854, *Lohengrin* on 23 February 1856, and *Der fliegende Holländer* on 7 September 1856; it was not until 29 April 1886 that *Tristan und Isolde* was first performed there.
3 Marie Wittgenstein, described as "das Kind" (the child) in the published text.

dear friend, if you were able to send her to Zurich in advance, as a pledge of your own intending visit, you would be doing us a tremendous service. She could live very comfortably at the Wesendoncks', *and what she would be to us* is something I doubtless have no need to intimate! After all, you are great and unusual in all that you think and do. Do something unusual, for what is at issue is out of the ordinary! – But enough of this, too! I know that unusual things happen to *me* only as a part of the most painful crown of thorns that adorns my brow; I am not fated to enjoy any pure and refreshing happiness. That is why I am more religious than you! –]

Fare you well, dear kind Frau Kapellmeister! And once again a thousand thanks for your love! Give my best wishes to Franz, and tell him that all is well with me!

Yours,
Richard Wagner.

Bayerische Staatsbibliothek Autog. Cim. Wagner, Richard (published incompletely in Freunde und Zeitgenossen 220–1).

210. MINNA WAGNER, BRESTENBERG[1]   Zurich, 23 April 1858

Poor dear Minna,

Once again I entreat you and repeat my appeal a thousand times over, have *patience*, and above all: have **trust**! If only you knew how much you torment me by your lack of trust, you would regret it, I am sure. Recently, when you assured me that you did indeed still love me, I implored you to prove as much by avoiding all further scenes and by giving up your demands for an explanation on my part, at least until after your treatment, whereupon I, *for my own part*, promised to do all that you wished me to do to set your mind at rest. But the old tempter has got the better of you for a second time, and this time you have openly violated your love and faith in me. I forgive you, partly because of your dreadful state of health which has made you almost irresponsible for your actions, but more than that: I forgive you all future lapses. But I now beseech you to summon up all your strength of mind and continue to *maintain, firmly* and *inviolably*, your belief in my sincere and lifelong concern for you, in my heartfelt wish to ensure your well-being, and in my firm resolve not to give in to any other, additional hopes for my life. If you are unable to do so, you will make *both* of us unhappy! It would not be necessary for me to beseech you in this way, if you yourself had had the

---

1 In the wake of the crisis precipitated by her interception of the "Morning confession" [208] (see introductory essay, pp. 167–8), Minna was persuaded to take the waters at Brestenberg, where she remained from 15 April to 15 July 1858.

calmness of mind to judge me fairly from the beginning, and, especially, to form a clear idea of the relationship which, as I now see, continues to fill you with needless anxiety, even after you took the law into your own hands. There is only *one* reproach I have had to suffer from the other side, and that concerns my failure to inform you at the outset of the *purity of these relations*, so that it would have been impossible for you to insult the woman in question in the way you did. These reproaches have been made by the woman's *husband*, by the man who, having been drawn from the outset into his wife's confidences, has been able to behave towards me in a way that has always been noble and amicable, precisely *because* he was convinced of the purity of our relations. The only excuse I could offer him here was that I considered it utterly impossible to convince *you* of such a thing, – a conviction which, sadly, in spite of all my assurances, now appears to be proving all too true. –

And so I ask you once again, and for the last time (for if you continue as you have done, you will destroy *yourself*!) – *trust me*; forget what appears to you to be inexplicable about all that has happened, – (like the familiar expressions I used in that letter,[1] and stick simply to the explanations that I have repeated here today! And I include here the wish that I may soon find in you a really *sensible* wife, a wish which, I hope, you will no longer take amiss.

I may add simply that I was indeed Wesendonck's guest on Sunday, but that I went *alone*. I have spent two days at the Willes. Next week the Wesendoncks are going away for a while. I long to get back to my work[2] again, and plan to take it up again tomorrow. For the moment there is nothing else of note for me to add to this grave and truly well-intentioned letter.

Your recent *suffering* has again shocked and stirred me deeply; as God is my witness, I pray for your speedy recovery with all honesty and sincerity. Persevere! only when you begin to get better will you see everything in a calmer light, and recognize that the cause of life's suffering lies not only *outside* us but, generally, also *within* us.

And so! Get well soon!

We shall soon be seeing each other again!

Your
faithful husband
Richard.

Minna-Briefe I,265–6.

---

1 See letter [208], pp. 381–3.
2 *Tristan und Isolde*; see letter [207], p. 379, note 2.

211. MINNA WAGNER, BRESTENBERG   Zurich, 27 April 1858

Today is the day, dear Minna, on which I have decided to have myself committed not to a hydropathic establishment but to a madhouse; – since this seems to be the only place for me! Whatever I say or write, and however good my intentions, I cause nothing but misfortune and misunderstanding. If I am silent about certain things, I make you mistrustful and you suspect that I am planning to go behind your back; if I then write in a serious and candid vein, and – as I was stupid enough to think – in a way that would at the same time reassure you, I discover that I have been plotting some subtle villainy calculated to drive you to an early grave! But at the same time I am told to be a *man*! Very well then, but I want to be *your* man, not just *any* man: you have only to tell me exactly how to speak, think and view the things of this world, and I shall always do exactly as you say, and never speak, think or look at anything of which you do not approve: – will that satisfy you? You can also tell me how and what I am to compose, write and conduct, and I shall be governed by you in everything, so that you will not be able to doubt in me a moment longer. For whatever I do of my own accord and in my *own* way you believe comes ultimately not from me but from someone else who has certain designs on me. Very well! This, too, shall no longer be so. I shall no longer look to the left or to the right of me, and if you can *still* doubt the fact that I live only for you, that I love you and worship you, then *I* at least shall no longer be responsible for what happens.

God knows if what I have said has put you in a good mood, as was my intention, or whether I again appear subtly villainous to you. I am so confused about all that I say and do that I shall soon be reduced to having myself carried round like a child. But none of this will matter if only you will abandon these terrible fancies of yours and recognize that I at least have the best and most honourable intentions of showing myself to be a good, grateful, loyal and devoted, loving and concerned husband. Or shall I end up like Sulzer before he married, hating all "women" without exception and wishing only that there were none but men in the world? –

God in heaven, what shall I do to satisfy you? –

Now listen! On Thursday I shall write to you and tell you precisely *when* you are to fetch me from the station on Saturday; then we shall see what we can achieve between us. Until then think only the *best* you can of me, and you will be pleasantly surprised by what you then find.

Nothing has happened. I shall bring with me a letter to you from the Princess.[1] It is well meant: she was very moved by the description I gave her of your state of health and mind.

Today I am going with Herwegh to the Willes. In fact I regretted having

1 Carolyne Sayn-Wittgenstein.

agreed to go, since I felt like working; but today's letter from you has so bewildered me that the distraction will be most welcome. – I pray to God that this letter does not cause you to get worked up all over again: I simply do not know any longer what I am doing! Whatever I say, you read only the blackest of intentions into it. Well, we shall see, and hope for the best that your mind will soon be somewhat calmer.

I have been on some killing walks with Fips, yesterday, for ex., we went via Kilchberg, Sihlwald etc. He eats very little. But he is pining. He, too, will be pleased to see you again. Once the railway has been opened, I, too, shall be able to visit you more frequently, and all in all I now feel as though the worst is over in every respect. Things can only get better: if they were to go on like this, neither of us would survive.

And so, on Thursday I shall send you more details about our meeting! – The best, the most sincere, and the most reassuring wishes from

Your
decrepit
husband.

Minna-Briefe I, 266–8.

212. JULIE RITTER, DRESDEN   Zurich, 11 May 1858

Oh, you dear and precious friend! – To see your handwriting again was a great comfort to me; no more welcome or more beautiful gift could have been bestowed upon me than these blessed lines of yours. You can have no idea of the suffering I have been through, – and how sad, in spite of the smiling spring, everything around me seems; but I shall not torment your dear affectionate heart by giving you a glimpse into the hopelessness of my situation! – It is sufficient for me to tell you that my wife, too, is now suffering from the most agonizing ill health; as a result of receiving the wrong treatment from her doctor – a treatment that I had repeatedly but vainly warned her against – , a recurring illness from which she has suffered for many years has finally developed into a heart disease which, last winter, assumed so painful a character that she has finally abandoned our little house and garden and embarked upon a thorough course of treatment. For the last four weeks she has been in Brestenberg with Dr Erismann, whose acquaintance has also been made by Frau Julie[1] in the company of her husband. In view of my success with Dr Vaillant of Geneva,[2] which for the last two years has freed me from the need for any other form of medical treatment, I attempted to

1 Julie Kummer.
2 See letter [191], p. 353.

persuade my wife to undertake a similar course of treatment under the supervision of this admirable doctor; however, since a friend of ours had recommended Dr Erismann particularly warmly to us, she preferred the proximity of Zurich, and, to judge by her progress so far (a progress which, in the case of such a dreadfully advanced nervous complaint, is bound of course to be very slow), we believe we have chosen the right course. And so, for the present at least, I now have outward calm, even though I continue to be plagued by worries of every description. But what I have had to put up with this winter from this quarter alone is something that can be understood only by those who know the character of such heart complaints. Continual sleeplessness finally induces a terrible degree of excitability, a determination to see only the black side of everything, and such passionate outbursts that I freely admit that I – a man who is happy never to set foot outside his own back door – felt my home had become an absolute hell. Instead of being met by the forbearance and charitableness which I need, given my irritability and the continually exhausting nature of my work, I had the additional task of having to think of this other worry, too, in each of my words and glances, without, however, generally managing to achieve what I was forcing myself to attempt. – In any case, my wife, too, finds it impossible to tolerate this lonely life of ours in winter; she cannot adequately entertain herself, but needs outside distractions. Next winter she will in any case live in Germany – Dresden, Berlin, Weimar – , while I expect that I myself shall go to Paris. How passionately I, too, long for my amnesty[1] in these circumstances is something you can easily imagine; all desire to work finally deserts me if I am obliged for ever to work only for the written page; and since I am resolved never again to allow any new work of mine to receive its first performance *without me*, the result of all this is a feeling of paralysis and a sense of faltering inspiration of the most worrying kind. In addition, I have had to countenance the grievous loss of any kind of income during recent months, not to mention my anxiety and the perpetual uncertainty that I suffer, so that you can understand with what a singular and wonderful feeling I receive the continuing tokens of your loyalty and concern. Now more than ever before, the calm and eternal sameness of your friendship for me reveals to me the *most genuine* boon that has ever been granted to me. I cannot tell you how it moves me!

[. . .]

Finally, let me tell you of a most cheering and edifying adventure. On my journey to Paris last winter, I missed my connection in Basle, and was obliged to spend half a day and a night in Strasbourg; as I was sauntering through the streets, I noticed a theatre playbill announcing a play and, beneath it, in large letters, the overture to Tannhäuser with which the performance was to begin. Quite by chance I was given a seat near the orchestra, and some of

1 See letter [192], p. 356, note 1.

the musicians recognized me from Zurich, quickly informing their colleagues and the conductor[1] of my presence. I waited for the performance to begin with a feeling of tense trepidation: it was the first time for ages that I had been able to hear an orchestra again, or, indeed, any composition of mine conducted by another person. To my most agreeable surprise it was played very well, indeed, much of it was excellent, finely detailed and the whole piece enthusiastically executed, so that I was intensely moved and deeply shaken by it; the melancholy chorus of pilgrims at the end had an especially profound and solemn significance for me. At the end, when the piece was applauded, the orchestra rose to their feet and, with their conductor at their head, turned to me with loud applause and gave me an ovation, whereupon the audience became aware of my presence and quickly realized who I must be, so that, with tears streaming down my cheeks, I found myself subjected to an act of public homage such as I have never before experienced. I had to leave the auditorium at once. –

You see, that's how it is with me: always right down in the depths, and – suddenly – high up, on wondrous heights! –

A thousand sincere regards to your dear, beloved family. My thanks, my heartfelt thanks for your heaven-sent friendship, and every good wish for your continuing health!

Yours,
Richard Wagner.

I do not know where Karl[2] is staying, and so I would ask you to forward the enclosed note to him as quickly as possible: it contains nothing but a sincere invitation to him to visit me soon. –

Ritter-Briefe 130–4.

213. MINNA WAGNER, BRESTENBERG   Zurich, 31 May 1858

My dear Minna,

I have had an excellent night's sleep, which has calmed and fortified me. What a godsend! May you yourself be granted the same in ample measure! – And so I now feel calm again, lucid and fortified. My view of the beautiful garden and this charming refuge stirs me deeply; that you were suddenly forced to lose all your appreciation of it, after that difficult night, pained me very much. Judge for yourself what *I* had gone through up to that time; I

---

1 Josef H. Hasselmans.
2 Karl Ritter. Wagner had not seen him since October 1856, when Liszt's unfortunate remark about baboons (see letter [194], p. 360) had driven him from Zurich in a fit of injured pride. He returned to Zurich early in August 1858.

who had the garden tended in order to spare you now, during your treatment! but – , I am calm and rational; let us not regard anything as having been finally decided. God will help to make our hearts lucid and rational; and everything comes from the heart, both good and bad. Take heart; and whatever may prove inevitable in days to come, never forget, however harsh the trials that lie in store, that within me beats a kind and grateful and loving heart that lives for you alone; be just, and admit that during what for me, too, has been a terrible time, I have ultimately been guided in each and every one of my actions by this heart of mine. But what I have suffered you can judge from the fact that I felt and suffered not only my own afflictions but those of others, too. So I now regard myself as thoroughly purged, and, although I have been unable to spare you many harsh blows of late, my sense of peace has now returned more calming than before, and I can feel nothing but charitableness. But a sense of great solemnity has come over me, and it will for ever remain a part of me. If you yourself are able to gain this same sense of noble solemnity which constitutes true human dignity, we shall have no difficulty in finding ourselves in total agreement on every question. If I may be permitted to draw inferences from my own inner frame of mind, I may indeed hope that the trials which we are yet destined to suffer may assume a salutary form. For now, however, I am firmly and irrevocably resolved to give up all personal contact with our neighbours:[1] only in this way have I found it possible to keep the Asyl as long as we need it. In the end, this will, and *must*, be agreeable to all the parties concerned.

Well, every good wish! I hope that these few lines may have helped to reassure you!

Fare you well! Take good care of yourself! I shall visit you very soon.

Yours,
R

Minna Briefe I 278–9.

214. MATHILDE WESENDONCK, ZURICH   [Zurich, 6 July 1858]

Tuesday morning.

You did not of course expect me to leave your wonderful, glorious letter unanswered? Or was I supposed to deny myself the splendid right of reply to this noblest of words? But how could I reply, except in a way that is worthy of you? –

The tremendous struggles that we have surmounted, how could they end, except in our victory over every wish and desire?

---

1 Otto and Mathilde Wesendonck. They returned to Zurich from Italy on 1 June.

Did we not know, as we drew closer to each other in our moments of greatest warmth, that this was our goal? –

Of course we did! Only because it was so unheard-of and so difficult could it be attained only through the hardest of struggles. But have we not now fought our last battle? What others might still lie before us? – Indeed, I feel profoundly that they are at an end! –

A month ago, when I informed your husband of my decision to break off all personal contact with you, I had already – renounced you. But in this my feelings were not yet entirely pure. You see, I felt that only total separation, or – total union could save our love from the terrible contagions to which we had seen it exposed in recent months. And so, while, on the one hand, I felt the necessity of our separation, I also felt, on the other, if not a voluntary – at least an imaginary – possibility of our union. Herein lay the sense of tension and strain which neither of us could bear. I came to see you, and it became clear at once to us both that that other alternative was a sin that we should not even contemplate.

As a result, the need for us to renounce each other necessarily assumed a different character: the sense of strain gave way to a gently conciliatory release of tension. The final traces of egoism disappeared from my heart, and my decision to visit you again was now a victory of the most pure humanity over the final stirrings of selfish desire. I wanted only to reconcile, to soothe, to console – to cheer, and thus to find the only happiness that may yet be mine. –

Never before in my life have I felt anything as profoundly or as terribly as in these last few months. All earlier impressions were meaningless by contrast. Such violent shocks as that catastrophe caused me were bound to leave deep scars; and if there was anything calculated to increase the profound serious-ness of my frame of mind, it was the state of my wife's health. For two months I have lived in daily fear of the possible news of her sudden death; for the doctor had felt it necessary to hint that this was a real possibility. Everything around me breathed an aura of death; whether I looked forwards or back-wards, all I saw was images of death, and life – as such – lost its final appeal for me. Required, as I was, to show extreme indulgence towards that unhappy woman, I had, nevertheless, not only to take the decision to destroy our latest hearth and home, which we had only just set up, but finally to tell her, much to her own dismay, of the decision that I had taken. –

What do you think I felt when, in the course of these wonderful summer months, I surveyed this charming refuge, which is so uniquely suited to all my wishes and future aspirations, when I wandered through the dear little garden in the morning, saw the abundance of flowers in bloom, and listened to the garden-warbler that had built its nest in the little rose-tree? And what it meant for me to tear myself away from this last anchor-hold, you alone can tell, who know my deepest thoughts!

Do you think that I, who fled from the world once before, could now return to it? Now that I have grown so extraordinarily delicate and sensitive, as a result of my increasing lack of contact with it? My recent meeting with the Grand Duke of Weimar[1] showed me more clearly than ever that I can thrive only in the most unequivocal independence, so that I was obliged to reject from the very depths of my being any suggestion that I might enter into a firm commitment, even with this genuinely amiable prince. I can never, ever return to the world; to settle permanently in a large town is unthinkable; and – must I, instead, think of establishing some new refuge, some new hearth, now that I have been forced to destroy my present one, almost before I had enjoyed it, a refuge which friendship and the noblest love have built for me in this charming paradise? Oh no! – To go away from here means the same for me as to go under!

With these wounds in my heart I can never again attempt to build a home for myself!

My child, I can conceive of only one salvation, and this can come only from the innermost depths of the heart, not from any outer event. It is rest! Rest from longing! The stilling of every desire! Noble, worthy resignation! To live for others, for others – as a comfort to ourselves! –

Now you know the full extent of the solemn and resolute mood that fills my soul; it embraces my entire philosophy of life, the whole of the future, all that is close to me – including yourself, you who are the most precious thing I have! Upon the ruins of this world of longing, let me now – make you happy! –

You see, never in my life, in any relationship, have I ever been importunate but always revealed an almost exaggerated sensitivity. But now I mean to appear importunate to you for the first time, and ask you to be inwardly calm on my account. I shall not often visit you both, and from now on you shall see me only when I am certain of being able to show you a calm and cheerful aspect. – I used to visit your house in suffering and in longing: I brought unrest and suffering to the place where I came seeking comfort. That shall no longer be the case. And so, if you do not see me for some time, – pray for me in silence! – For then you will know I am suffering! But whenever I do come, you may be certain that what I bring to your home is the gracious gift of my very being, a gift such as it is perhaps granted to me alone to bestow upon you, to me who has suffered so much and so willingly. –

Probably, nay – certainly, the time will shortly come, presumably at the beginning of next winter, when I leave Zurich for a relatively long period. My amnesty,[2] which I am now expecting soon, will open up Germany to me

---

1 On 23 June 1858. In the course of the meeting, which took place in Lucerne, the Grand Duke Karl Alexander repeated his hope that the *Ring* might receive its first performance in Weimar.

2 Not until July 1860 was Wagner granted a partial amnesty.

again, and I shall return there periodically in order to make up for the one thing that I have been unable to achieve here. Then I shall not see you both for long periods. But then to return once more to the Asyl which has now grown so dear to me, to rest from torments and unavoidable vexations, to breathe pure air, and find renewed enthusiasm for my old work which nature, after all, has chosen me for, – this, if you will not begrudge it me, will always be the gentle beam of light that will sustain me there, the sweet comfort that will beckon me back here.

And – have you not conferred upon me the highest boon that life can give? Did I not thank you for the one thing on earth that can still seem worthy of thanks? And should I not seek to requite you for all that you achieved for me by dint of such unspeakable sacrifices and suffering? –

My child, these last few months have turned the hair at my temples noticeably whiter; there is a voice inside me which calls longingly for rest, – for the rest which, long years ago, I made my flying Dutchman feel. It was a longing for "home" – , not for the wanton pleasures of love! Only a loyal and glorious woman could win this home for him. Let us consecrate ourselves to this beautiful death which contains within it and assuages all our longings and desires! Let us pass away in bliss, with a calmly transfigured gaze and the hallowed smile of fair resignation! And – no one shall *lose* if we – – are *victorious!*

Fare well, my dear and hallowed angel!

Mathilde Wesendonck-Briefe 78–82.

215. ELIZA WILLE, MARIAFELD   [Zurich, 21 or 28 July 1858]

My dear and honoured friend,

I discovered to my regret that during my absence yesterday you favoured us with your kind visit. At the same time I heard that you still wish to go ahead with the musical soirée which we discussed on one occasion. I must ask you to give up this plan, at least insofar as I myself was to have been involved. I can regard my continuing presence here only as a form of damnation from which I long every day to be released. All the shame and torment that I have suffered during the last three months arose from the fact that, immediately after that first catastrophe, I did not then carry out the resolve which I have now, finally and irrevocably, taken. If I vacillated, I may perhaps be forgiven for doing so by that same woman[1] who had reduced me to a state of not knowing any longer what she wanted. I am bound in turn to

1 Mathilde Wesendonck.

forgive her for her refusal to understand that all the consideration that I showed my wife derived principally and decisively from my consideration for her, since I can see to what extent she labours under her own mistaken ideas. But that, only a few days after our recent farewell, she was able to bring herself to torment me by her childish and senseless reproaches concerning my alleged relationship with my wife, reproaches which she conveyed to my friend[1] by way of remonstration, this makes me painfully aware that she can scarcely be capable of appreciating what I suffer for her sake.

Enough, I feel that I can no longer be of any comfort to her by remaining here (a closeness which has probably been made possible only by dint of unspeakable sacrifices), and so I am reverting to my original resolve, in which I was shaken for a time by *her* alone. I am separating from her, in order to withdraw henceforth into the strictest seclusion. All that now delays the execution of my resolve is the extreme difficulty of my situation, which does not permit me to act as freely as I would wish at any given moment. Yet I cannot describe to you just how unbearable my present situation feels to me. As a final consideration to my wife, I had guaranteed that I would hold out here until September, so that she has until then to make whatever arrangements she deems to be necessary to deal with our furniture, and to deal with it, moreover, with the propriety that she thinks is expected of her, since, as far as is practicable, she hopes to take the furniture back to Germany with her. But I do not believe that I can bear to see our bourgeois circumstances sorted out in such a normal way. If I *could*, I should be more worthy of your admiration than I believe I deserve to be. I shall attempt to ensure that I am able to leave by the middle of August;[2] but it is not impossible that I shall leave Zurich for ever within the next few days, since I fear that I cannot bear the torment of these days any longer. At all events, my honoured and dear friend, you will realize that I can now hold out here only by dint of "total self-denial, and negation of my existence"; any attempt at amusement or distraction can seem only sinful. And so – please: have no further regard for me! However satisfied I once was with my own company, I must now learn to live with it for its own sake alone. But since I do not know how long I shall be able to hold out like this, and cannot promise for certain that I shall not disappear sooner than I have indicated, I am telling you all of this *now*, and, in the event of my going under, I reserve for myself the right to inform you in writing of my subsequent fate, of which I shall say only that not even an amnesty will be able to draw me out of the lonely state into which I am now withdrawing. –

Accept my most sincere and heartfelt thanks for your noble friendship

1 Hans von Bülow.
2 Wagner left the Asyl at dawn on 17 August 1858 (see letter [217]). Minna returned to Germany on 1 September (see Fehr II,143–9).

which has brought me such great happiness. Be always to her what you were to me! Fare you well, and recall with affection your

Richard Wagner.

Fehr II,391–3.

216. CLARA WOLFRAM, CHEMNITZ   Geneva, 20 August 1858

My dear Cläre,

I promised to tell you more about my reasons for taking the decisive step in which you now see me engaged. I shall tell you what you need to know to form a clear idea as to what has happened, and thus be able to counter any further gossip, although I may add that *I* regard such gossip with the utmost indifference.

What has sustained and comforted me during the last six years and what, more especially, has given me the strength to endure living with Minna, in spite of the enormous differences in our character and nature, has been the love of that young woman[1] whose initial response to me was one of diffidence, doubt, hesitation and shyness, but who later approached me with increasing certainty and self-confidence. Since there could never be any question of union between us, our deep and mutual affection assumed that sadly melancholic character that banishes all vulgarity and baseness, and recognizes the source of all joy in the other's well-being. Since first we came to know each other, she has shown the most untiring and tender concern for me, and, in the most courageous manner, obtained from her husband all that could ease my life's burden. Faced with his wife's open candour, the latter could not but fall prey to increasing jealousy. Her greatness lay in the fact that she kept her husband constantly informed of the state of her heart, and gradually persuaded him to resign her completely. It is not difficult to judge the sacrifices and struggles that this must have cost her: what enabled *her* to achieve her success was the depth and sublimity of her affection for me, from which all selfishness was banished and which gave her the strength to appear before her husband as a woman of such account that the latter, finally compelled to countenance the threat of his wife's death, had no choice but to resign her to me, and prove his unshakeable love for her by supporting her in her concern for me. It was a question, ultimately, of not losing the mother of his own children, and so he accepted his renunciatory role for their sake, – indeed, it was they who kept us insuperably apart. And so, although he was consumed by jealousy, she herself was able to enlist his sympathy for me to the extent that – as you know – I often enjoyed his support; when it

1 Mathilde Wesendonck.

finally became a question of providing me with the little house and garden that I desired, it was she who prevailed upon him, by dint of the most unheard-of struggles, to buy me the beautiful piece of land next to his. But the most wonderful part about it is that I never had any inkling of the struggles that she underwent for my sake: because of her, her husband had always to appear friendly and uninhibited towards me; not a single black look was allowed to enlighten me, nor was he allowed to touch a single hair of my head: the very skies above me were made to seem clear and cloudless, every step I took was to be soft and yielding. Such was the unheard-of success brought about by the glorious love of the purest and most noble of women; and it was this love, to which we never gave expression, that was bound at last to reveal itself when I wrote the *Tristan* poem a year ago and gave it to her. Then, for the first time, her strength failed her, and she told me she would die!

Consider, dear sister, what this love must have meant for me after a lifetime of cares and suffering, of turmoil and sacrifice, such as my life has been! – But we both recognized at once that a union between us was unthinkable: and so we grew resigned, renouncing every selfish desire; we suffered, and we endured, but – we loved each other! –

Thanks to her shrewd woman's instinct, my wife seemed to understand what was going on here: although she behaved in a way that often bespoke jealousy, scorn and condescension, she none the less tolerated our meetings, since they never offended against morality but were calculated, rather, to assure us of each other's presence. And so I assumed we had Minna's consent, and that she understood that there was really nothing here for her to fear, for the simple reason that, as I say, a union between us was unthinkable, and that forbearance on her part was therefore the most advisable and best course for her. Well, I was soon to discover that I had deluded myself on this point: gossip reached her ears, and she finally lost her head to the extent of intercepting a letter from me[1] and – breaking it open. This letter, had she been at all capable of understanding it, ought in fact to have given her the reassurance she so desperately wanted; for here, too, our resignation formed the burden of its theme. But she saw no further than the expressions of intimacy that it contained, and lost her reason. Furious, she came to see me and forced me to explain to her, calmly and clearly, how she had managed to bring unhappiness upon herself by breaking open such a letter, and that, if she did not know how to control herself, we should have to part. On this point we were in agreement, I calmly, she passionately. But the next day I felt sorry for her. I went to see her, and said: "Minna, you are very ill! Get better, and *then* let us speak of the matter again." We conceived the idea of sending her away on a course of treatment; she appeared to grow calmer, the

1 Letter [208], pp. 381–3.

day of her departure for the health resort drew nearer. She was bent on speaking to Frau Wesendonck before leaving. I forbade her explicitly from doing so. My sole concern was to acquaint Minna gradually with the character of my relationship with that woman, in order to convince her in that way that there was nothing for her to fear, as far as the continuation of our marriage was concerned, but that she should behave sensibly, reasonably and nobly, renounce all foolish thoughts of revenge, and avoid any kind of a scene. She finally vowed to do so. But she could not rest. Instead, she went over to the other house, behind my back, and – probably without understanding what she was doing – insulted that woman's tender sensibilities in the coarsest imaginable manner. When she said to her: "If I were an ordinary woman, I should go to your husband with this letter!", Frau Wesendonck, who was conscious of never having kept anything secret from her husband, (something that a woman like Minna cannot of course understand!), was left with no alternative but to go to her husband and report this scene and the cause of it to him. – Such crude and common interference in our pure and tender relationship was bound to have many repercussions. It took me a long time to explain to my friend that a nature like my wife's could never be made to understand a relationship of the loftiness and disinterestedness that had existed between the two of us; for I felt most keenly her grave and deep reproach that I had neglected to attempt any such explanation, whereas she had always treated her husband as her confidant. – Anyone who can understand what I have suffered since then (it was then the middle of April) must also understand how I felt when I was finally forced to admit that my constant efforts to maintain things as they had been were totally fruitless. For three months I looked after Minna with the greatest care during her course of treatment; in order to reassure her, I finally stopped seeing our neighbours during this time; concerned only for her health, I tried everything possible to make her see reason and to do what was befitting for her, or for any woman of her age: it was all in vain! She persisted in the most trivial remonstrations, claimed to have been insulted, and scarcely had I calmed her when her old fury broke forth anew. Throughout the whole of the month that Minna was back – and while we had visitors[1] – a final decision became increasingly inevitable. To have the two women living in such proximity to each other could not go on; for even Frau Wesendonck could not forget that, as a reward for her supreme self-sacrifice and the most tender considerations, she had been so rudely and offensively treated by me, in the person of my wife. Moreover, people had begun to talk. Enough; the most unheard-of scenes and torments showed no sign of abating, and out of consideration for the one

1 Minna returned from Brestenberg on 15 July. The visitors in question were, variously, Joseph Tichatschek, Hans and Cosima von Bülow, Karl Klindworth and Karl Ritter.

woman as for the other I was finally forced to make up my mind to abandon that beautiful refuge that had been prepared for me with such tender affection.

What I now need, however, is rest and the most total seclusion: for there is much that I have to get over. – Minna is incapable of understanding how unhappy our marriage has been from the very beginning; she has a totally distorted view of the past, and, although I found consolation, distraction and oblivion in my art, she has even come to believe in the end that I never had need of such things. Enough, I have now made up my mind on the matter: I cannot endure these everlasting quarrels and suspicious moods of hers any longer if I am to fulfil my life's task with any enthusiasm. Anyone who has observed me closely must have marvelled at my patience, kindness and, indeed, my weakness, and, although I may now be condemned by superficial critics, their criticisms can no longer hurt me; but Minna never had a better opportunity than this to show herself worthy of being my wife, when it was a question of rescuing the one thing that I held most highly and most dearly: it lay within her grasp to show me whether she truly loved me. But she does not even understand what true love is, and her fury blinds her to everything! –

Yet I forgive her because of her illness; although this illness, too, would have assumed a different, and milder, character if she herself had acted differently and more mildly. The many adverse adventures which she has lived through with me and which my inner genius (which, alas, I could never explain to her!) easily helped me to overcome make me feel considerate towards her; I should like to cause even *her* as little pain as is possible, for, ultimately, I continue to feel very sorry for her! But I feel incapable any longer of living under the same roof with her; nor can I be of any use to her in this way: I shall always be incomprehensible to her, and an object of suspicion. And so – we have separated! But in kindness and love! I do not want her to suffer shame because of me. I would wish only that she herself might realize in the course of time that it is better if we do not see much of each other in future. For the present I shall leave her with the prospect of my joining her in Germany as soon as my amnesty is announced; that is why she ought to take all our effects and furniture with her. After all, I do not want to break any promises, but prefer it if everything can be left to depend on my future state of mind. May I ask you, too, to stick to the story that it is to be only a temporary separation? I would also ask you not to neglect any means at your disposal to calm her and make her see sense! For – as I say – she is very unhappy; with a lesser husband she would have been happier. You, too, should feel sorry for her, as I do! I shall be more than grateful to you if you are, my dear sister! –

I am waiting here in Geneva for a little while longer until I can go to Italy, where I plan to spend the winter, probably in Venice. I already feel somewhat refreshed by my solitude and by the absence of such tormenting company. By the end it was impossible to think of work any longer. As soon as I feel in the right frame of mind to continue my work on Tristan, I shall know that salvation is at hand. This, indeed, is how I must seek to help myself: I ask nothing of the world but that it leave me in peace to write the works that shall one day belong to it. May I therefore not be judged too harshly by it! – Feel free to use the contents of this letter, dear Cläre, in order to provide whatever explanations may be necessary. On the whole, however, I should of course prefer it if little were to be said about all that has happened. Very few people will *understand* what is at issue here; in order to do so they would have to be intimately acquainted with the parties concerned.

Fare you well, dear sister: and, once again, accept my sincere thanks for the discreet question which, as you can see, I have answered for you in total trust. Treat Minna indulgently, but make her understand by degrees what sort of a man she is dealing with! Fare you well!

Your brother
Richard W.

RWG (published with minor errors of transcription in Mathilde Wesendonck-Briefe 31–7).

THE WANDERER
1858–1864

INTRODUCTORY ESSAY 1858–1864

Wagner's decision to seek refuge in Venice was an impulsive one, made on the recommendation of Karl Ritter, who accompanied him there. Prevented, in the wake of the scandal on the Green Hill, from communicating direct with Mathilde Wesendonck, he gave expression to his feelings in the so-called Venice Diary [217, 219, 221, 222, 223, 224, 227]. This collection of letters, sent in instalments to Mathilde but not read by her until later, can be interpreted as either deeply intimate or as the working out of yet another artistic fantasy. The roles now allotted Wagner and Mathilde are no longer Tristan and Isolde but Ananda and Savitri: the Buddhist tale of the lovers who find salvation by joyfully embracing renunciation continued to appeal throughout Wagner's life as a possible subject for operatic treatment, but *Die Sieger* (The Victors) never proceeded beyond the stage of a prose sketch. *Die Sieger* was eventually superseded by *Parsifal* (WWV 111), and it is fascinating to witness, in the letters of this period, the tentative exposition of the philosophical ideas that were later to be given such rich and ambiguous expression in the final music drama. The themes of fellow-suffering, renunciation and redemption are of primary importance in these letters; already the dramaturgical implications are evident, but the significance of the themes is seen to grow directly out of Wagner's personal circumstances and preoccupations. Letters [221] [222] and [242] are especially important for an understanding of *Parsifal*; at this time (1858/9) the work existed only in the form of a prose sketch (now lost), but it is clear from these letters that various characters and scenes were already taking shape in the composer's mind. Letter [221], for example, moves from an account of human maltreatment of animals, through philosophical meditations on the subject, to a transfiguring perception of the role of suffering in human existence: "This meaning will one day become clearer to you from the Good Friday morning scene in the third act of Parzival."

The letter (which thus prefigures the structure of *Parsifal* itself) is also revealing for the light it throws on a different, but – as we now see – related matter. Suffering, according to Wagner's Schopenhauerian/Buddhist-influenced view of life, is the inescapable condition of existence. So essential is the function of suffering, he tells Mathilde, that when he sees "evident contentment, or the intention of ensuring the same", he recoils in horror. This, and not envy, he is convinced, is the motivation for his "instinctive hatred of the rich". Freedom from material cares, he acknowledges, does not necessarily ensure happiness; what he despises is the attempt to obtain contentment and exclude suffering. When he observes such behaviour in an individual it renders him "capable of going to lengths of great cruelty in order to make him conscious of the need to suffer". When one remembers that the husband of this letter's recipient was an extremely affluent man who having made his fortune as a businessman in New York had retired to Zurich to live out his days in luxury and carefree contentment, one is tempted to suggest that the letter may be read as a philosophical justification for the suffering caused Otto Wesendonck by the intimacy with his wife.

However that may be, relations had been sufficiently restored by August 1859 for Wesendonck to make Wagner an unsolicited offer of financial help to finish the *Ring*. Wagner felt unable to accept either a loan or a gift [244] but instead he proposed a business deal [245] by which Wesendonck would buy the copyright in the four scores for 6000 francs each and enjoy the proceeds while Wagner would receive the revenues from public performances. As for suffering, Wagner had plenty of opportunity in Venice to test its efficacy as a stimulant to the imagination. His ailments, which included gastritis and a painful leg ulcer, caused him to be confined to his room [227, 228]; when he was active, he was, as a former revolutionary, kept under close police supervision.

On a more personal level his relationship with Liszt sustained a damaging blow from which it never fully recovered. Wagner's financial affairs were once again in a desperate state and he was forced to haggle with the new intendant at Weimar, Franz Dingelstedt, over the terms for a forthcoming production of *Rienzi* there. Dingelstedt was meanwhile causing Liszt grave distress as he was determined to see the theatre prosper in Weimar even if it was at the expense of the opera. The production, in December 1858, of Cornelius's *Der Barbier von Bagdad* brought matters to a head: a demonstration, directed primarily at Liszt, persuaded him that he should move on. The bitterly ironic tone of Wagner's letter [229], arriving at the very time of this crisis, was unfortunately misinterpreted by Liszt. His reply of 4 January 1859 [Appendix A, p. 937] shows that he was offended by what he took to be Wagner's rejection of his congratulations on Act I of *Tristan* (which Härtels had just sent him in proof).[1] Wagner's letter of 7 January [230] cleared up the mis-understanding, but the damage was done; from now on, Wagner observed to Bülow [233], he would have to exercise caution in his relations with Liszt.

Such a failure of communication came about, Wagner assured Bülow, through their lack of personal contact and because Wagner's sense of humour was "completely foreign" to Liszt. "I can no longer find the right words to

---

[1] Wagner's letter of 31 December 1858 and Liszt's reply of 4 January 1859 were both omitted from the first and second editions of their correspondence, and hence from the standard English translation by Francis Hueffer (rev. edn, New York 1897, R1973).

write to Liszt" [249], he was still lamenting in October of that year, and yet artistically they had as much to offer each other as before (see p. 165). Wagner's embarrassment at the public advertisement of his debt to Liszt has often been quoted: "After all, there are many things we willingly admit to between ourselves – for ex., that I have become a totally different fellow in matters of harmony as a result of getting to know Liszt's compositions; but when friend Pohl blurts out this secret for the whole world to hear, right at the head of a short notice on the Tristan Prelude, it is indiscreet to say the least" [249]. The protest is nearly always cited as evidence of Wagner's disloyalty and ingratitude towards Liszt. But a reading of this sentence in its context throws a rather different light on the matter. Wagner begins by telling Bülow that it was ill-advised of him to publicize his doubts as to the likely popularity of *Tristan und Isolde* (WWV 90). (Brendel had printed in his *Neue Zeitschrift für Musik*, apparently without authority, an extract from a private letter written him by Bülow.) Ironically, Bülow was well aware of the need for discretion: in a letter addressed to Julius Stern just a few days before the appearance of the relevant issue of *Neue Zeitschrift für Musik*, he had written "What you said this morning, as to the difficulties of Wagner's work, has made me fearful lest you innocently should drop a similar remark in presence of some ill-natured musician or theatrical who would immediately pass on the alarm to the bigwigs of dramatic music-institutes, and scare them off in advance . . . ".[1] Wagner then passes from this incident to the question of what he and Liszt owe each other artistically. Liszt had recently dedicated his *Dante* Symphony to Wagner in glowing terms ("As Virgil guided Dante, so have you guided me through the mysterious regions of those worlds of sound that are steeped in life . . . "), but Wagner had begged Liszt not to make the dedication public as it embarrassed him in the extreme. In the face of Liszt's own compositions, Wagner had told him, he felt "an absolute bungler": "And now *you* come along exuding music from every pore in streams, springs and waterfalls, – and I have to listen while you say things like this to me" [241]. This is the context of the protest about Pohl's indiscretion. Liszt may think he owes Wagner a great deal, and Wagner "can accept that as an excess of friendship", he tells Bülow [249]. But it would be just as foolish to proclaim such an obligation to the world as it was for Pohl to draw attention to Wagner's debt to Liszt, or for Bülow himself to cast doubt on the popular appeal of *Tristan*. Such things may be discussed in private, but in the public realm they are liable to be seized upon by one's enemies.

Wagner certainly needed all the friends he could find for his renewed assault on Paris (1859-61). This time the path was cleared to some extent by Auguste de Gasperini, who made it his business to introduce him into influential Parisian musical circles. Unlike the previous occasion, of course, Wagner

1 Letter of 31 August 1859, quoted in Ellis, VI,408-9; trans. by Ellis.

had by now a considerable reputation; it was no longer to be the public's indifference to him that was to be the cause of his suffering. The initial response was encouraging. In a series of three concerts in the Salle Ventadour of the Théâtre-Italien on 25 January, 1 and 8 February 1860 Wagner conducted excerpts from his own compositions. The programme on each occasion was the Overture to *Der fliegende Holländer*; the March and Chorus from Act II of *Tannhäuser*, together with the Introduction to Act III, the Pilgrims' Chorus and the Overture; the Prelude to *Tristan und Isolde* (with Wagner's own concert ending); and the Prelude to Act I, Bridal Procession, Prelude to Act III and Bridal Chorus from *Lohengrin*. Wolfram's "O Star of Eve" was added in the second and third concerts.

Many distinguished figures were in the audience, including Berlioz, Meyerbeer, Auber, Gounod, the novelist Champfleury and the poet Baudelaire. The last named was overwhelmed by Wagner's music and wrote to thank him for the experience, which he described as that "of being engulfed, overcome, a really voluptuous sensual pleasure, like rising into the air or being rocked on the sea".[1] Baudelaire was subsequently among those who were invited to Wagner's weekly salons held at his home in Rue Newton. (After the *Tannhäuser* débâcle the following year, Baudelaire wrote another appreciative letter which Wagner gratefully acknowledges in [267].) The Théâtre-Italien concerts were reviewed savagely by the press (whom Wagner had disdained to invite). Berlioz, reporting in the *Journal des débats*, wrote enthusiastically about the *Holländer*, *Tannhäuser* and *Lohengrin* excerpts, but admitted to total non-comprehension of the *Tristan* Prelude.[2] As for the audience generally, Wagner himself was convinced that there had been a large measure of appreciation and understanding, even of the *Tristan* Prelude.

But whether or not the concerts could be counted an artistic success, they were irrefutably a financial disaster. The deficit of 10,500 or 11,000 francs (the amount is variously computed in different sources) added to Wagner's existing debts, necessitated urgent action. At the end of the previous year Wagner had responded to Schott's approach to publish a score of his, by offering him *Das Rheingold* for 10,000 francs [253], on the understanding that Otto Wesendonck, who had previously bought rights in the score for 6000 francs, would be reimbursed by Schott [254]. Now Wagner resorted to the ingenious device of asking Wesendonck to regard his 6000 francs as an advance payment for the fourth work in the tetralogy, as yet unwritten. Wesendonck's agreement helped to ease the new burden of debt, as did an

1 Letter of 17 February 1860, reproduced in H. Barth, D. Mack and E. Voss (eds), *Wagner: A Documentary Study* (London 1975), 193.
2 Berlioz's review and Wagner's published reply are reproduced in H. Barth, D. Mack and E. Voss, *op. cit.*, 189–93.

unsolicited gift of 10,000 francs from Marie Kalergis and a further 5000[1] from Julie Salis-Schwabe. The latter, the Jewish widow of a Mancunian industrialist, hoped, together with Malwida von Meysenbug, to raise a subscription for Wagner among the music-lovers of Paris, in order that he might not have to repay the loan. In fact, the bill of receipt which Wagner insisted on giving her was to cause no little distress a few years later, during the preparations for *Tristan* in Munich. Hearing how Wagner's debts were then being paid off by King Ludwig, she presented, through her lawyer, the bill of receipt with a demand for repayment. Legal proceedings were instituted, and timed to coincide with what should have been the day of the first performance of *Tristan*, 15 May 1865. The bill was settled immediately by the Treasury.

The chief motivation of the Paris venture had been to pave the way for a possible performance of *Tristan* in France by German singers, but Wagner was now forced to reappraise his plans [256]. To the extent that the concerts were an artistic success, however, they were probably a contributory factor in the finally satisfactory outcome of Wagner's applications for an amnesty. In July 1860 he was granted a partial amnesty, allowing him to enter all the German states except Saxony – the regulations and their frustrating effect are spelt out in [262] – and the following month he did once again set foot on his native soil for the first time in eleven years. In September, though, he was back in Paris for the start of rehearsals for *Tannhäuser*, the performance of which at the Opéra had been decreed by the Emperor himself, largely in response to lobbying by Princess Pauline Metternich.

At first, things augured well for the performance. "Never before have I been so fully and unconditionally provided for with whatever material I need for an outstanding performance", Wagner told Liszt on 13 September [262]. The following February (1861) the rehearsals were progressing well and Wagner was confident that "the forthcoming performance will be altogether exceptional"; his Tannhäuser, Albert Niemann, was "altogether sublime . . . a great artist of the rarest kind" [263]. Niemann, however, had from the start been slow to respond to Wagner's wishes and now, hearing rumours that the production was to be sabotaged, he gave thought only to salvaging what he could of his reputation. Determined to save his voice for the last act, he demanded the cut in the Act II finale which Wagner had been forced to allow Tichatschek and other interpreters of the role. Wagner had written most of his long, persuasively argued letter to Niemann of 21 February [264], begging him to put his trust in the composer, when he received Niemann's ultimatum

---

1 Sometimes, following *Mein Leben*, given as 3000 francs. But 5000 francs is the figure given in Dr von Schauss's letter to Moritz von Schwind of 1865 (see Königsbriefe V,229-30). The bill as finally presented and paid was for 2400 gulden.

written the previous day: Wagner must either cut the passage in question or find himself another Tannhäuser.[1]

In a postscript to [264] Wagner conceded the demand, but by now it had become clear that the conductor, Pierre-Louis-Philippe Dietsch (the very man who twenty years earlier had set to music a rival version of the Flying Dutchman legend), was simply inadequate to the task; his rank incompetence was attested also by Bülow, among others. As the resident conductor of the Opéra, Dietsch could not be replaced. Wagner's letter to Royer, the Opéra director [265], insisted that he be allowed to conduct both the final rehearsal and the first three performances. But he did not get his way and on 13 March 1861, after no fewer than 164 rehearsals, the curtain at last rose on the Paris *Tannhäuser*. The ensuing débâcle is a familiar story; the essential point is that it was generated neither by Dietsch's incompetence, nor by audience dissatisfaction, but by way of a political demonstration against the unpopular Princess Pauline Metternich, who had supported the production. The perpetrators were the members of the aristocratic Jockey Club and their organized whistling and jeering annihilated the three performances that were attempted before Wagner was finally allowed to withdraw the work.

He now turned his attention to *Tristan und Isolde* and the possibility of a performance in Vienna, rather than Karlsruhe as earlier intended. But only a few months later he was immersed in a new work, one for which he had sketched out a prose scenario back in July 1845: *Die Meistersinger von Nürnberg* (WWV 96). This, he informed Schott [271], was to be a "thoroughly light and popular" opera, one calling, moreover, for only modest resources and thus remaining within the reach of smaller houses. For all that Wagner did restrict himself to an orchestra of double wind (as opposed to the triple of *Tristan* or the quadruple of the *Ring*), eliminating also the bass trumpet and contrabass trombone, the work that eventually emerged was anything but modest in scale; nor did it, in spite of his forecast to Schott, dispense with the need for "a so-called leading tenor". Indeed, it was not long before the breadth of his conception moved the composer to assert: "It has now become clear to me that this work will be my most perfect masterpeice" [278].

The previously quoted letter to Schott [271], incidentally, gives the lie to Wagner's account in *Mein Leben* of the aesthetic experience that inspired him to start work. According to his autobiography the impetus was provided by his viewing of Titian's *Assumption of the Virgin* while visiting the Wesendoncks in Venice at the beginning of November. In the letter to Schott, however, which is dated 30 October, Wagner had already announced his intention of beginning work on *Die Meistersinger*. The letter is also interesting for Wagner's statement that the idea of embarking on this new subject has given him "pleasant relief from my burden of sorrow". The mood was only a temporary

1 Sammlung Burrell 512–13; English trans. 387.

one: letter after letter from these years testifies to that "burden of sorrow". Financial worries were still pressing, but the trouble went deeper. Wagner was in a continual state of depression about the likelihood, or lack of it, of seeing his major works (especially *Tristan*) on stage; the *Ring* remained unfinished and unrealizable; he was, until 1860, unable to return to his native country; and above all at the centre of his emotional existence there was a vacuum. Without the company of one prepared to love and care for him, life, he frequently lamented, was scarcely worth living; only artistic creativity drove him along.

Wagner's letters of this period to Minna reveal a touching optimism about the possibility of salvaging at least something from their broken marriage. Settling down in Paris in September 1859 he invited Minna to join him there [246] with a view to making a new life together. That the optimism was genuine and that he was capable of tender feelings and concern for Minna we know from many letters to other correspondents (see, for example, [225]). Even the request to Pusinelli [248], their doctor and friend, to forbid sexual relations between them, supposedly on the grounds of her health, is expressed in the most delicate and sensitive terms. Minna joined him in Paris, but two years later he was again writing to her, holding out the prospect of their being able to "settle down for good in some pleasant spot" [270]. By this time (October 1861) Minna was raking back over the Wesendonck affair. Inevitably one's view of Wagner's stance of moral rectitude and tolerance here must be coloured by one's judgement of his conduct during the affair. But it is difficult to resist the force of his repeated assertions of innocence, vis-à-vis Mathilde Wesendonck, both in this letter and elsewhere.

Another crisis was to decide the matter once and for all. From Biebrich in February 1862 Wagner informed Minna of his intention of making his home in that town, once again proposing that she consider joining him. Minna arrived forthwith, unannounced, and Wagner's account of the ensuing "ten days in hell", as he described them, is given in full in his letter to Cornelius [276]. Minna's account[1] is very different and frankly difficult to believe: according to her, Wagner lost his head and began raving at her, on the arrival of the fateful present from Mathilde, even before she had opened her mouth. Whoever's version we choose to believe, the couple's incompatibility was now beyond doubt. But even after this, Wagner's concern for his wife, suffering as she was with heart disease, is amply documented (see, for example, [282], [287], [288] and all the letters to Minna herself). His intention not to divorce her, since such an announcement might prove a fatal shock to the ailing woman, was occasionally reappraised, but in the event honoured. Instead he suggests to her that she retire to Dresden, setting aside a room for him to make periodic visits. The allowance he settled on her to do this was not

1 Sammlung Burrell 539–40; English trans. 408–9.

ungenerous, and in fact contributed to his financial problems in the months remaining before his "rescue" by Ludwig II.

It is not necessarily proof of duplicity on Wagner's part that during the years following the enforced departure from the Asyl he was constantly casting around for female companionship and/or sexual gratification, even a permanent partner. There is no evidence that his intimate friendship with Blandine Ollivier (the wife of the French lawyer and politician Emile Ollivier) amounted to anything more than that. On the other hand the young Seraphine Mauro, niece of his friend and occasional host, Dr Joseph Standhartner, almost certainly acted as more than just housekeeper when the doctor was away, much to the chagrin of Peter Cornelius, who was Seraphine's lover. The "sweet-tempered, obliging" seventeen-year-old girl mentioned in [291] perhaps fulfilled a similar role, while her elder sister, Marie Völkl [292], was the individual urged to have ready the "pink drawers" (the ownership of which remains a matter of scholarly debate).

Wagner was also attracted to the twenty-eight-year-old Mathilde Maier, the daughter of a notary. Mathilde was apprehensive about getting too closely involved with him, realizing that the incipient deafness from which she suffered would prove even more of a disability in the company of a musician. But Wagner was not so easily discouraged. She seemed to play the role of the perfect Eva to his Sachs in the music drama still taking shape, and he tried on several occasions to persuade her to join him in co-residence as housekeeper-cum-consoling angel. Many of his letters to Mathilde Maier are rambling and incoherent; many, too, were censored on first publication. The autograph manuscripts of sixteen of the surviving letters to her were tampered with, excisions, made with thick black lines, ranging from a few words to whole paragraphs. These presumably embarrassing passages can no longer be reconstructed.[1] (Only two of the Maier letters included here, [286] and [295], are affected.)

To this roll-call of female admirers could be added the names of Friederike Meyer, the sister of the soprano Luise Dustmann (at one time intended for the role of Isolde in Vienna), and of course Cosima von Bülow, who with her husband visited Wagner in Biebrich in July 1862 and thereafter became steadily more closely acquainted. But the memory of Mathilde Wesendonck lingered on. After re-establishing contact, both by correspondence and by occasional visits (legitimized by Otto's presence), they continued to express their feelings for each other in the most tender and affectionate terms. Wagner even went so far as to inform his confidante Eliza Wille that "she is, and remains, my first and only love!" [287] Nor was the devotion merely one-sided. Few of Mathilde's letters to Wagner survive, but occasionally in those

1 The originals are now in the Bayerische Staatsbibliothek, Munich.

that do,[1] there is a hint of dissatisfaction or unhappiness in her life, possibly in her marital situation. And sentences such as the following certainly imply a closeness and dependency similar to that frequently proclaimed by Wagner: "The weft of the mysterious weaver who intertwined the threads of our mutual fate is not to be unravelled, but only to be torn asunder".[2] It is evident from the original printed edition of Wagner's letters to Mathilde Wesendonck that numerous passages, doubtless of a compromising nature, were excised. The originals of these letters were copied by Mathilde herself – whether in full it is not possible to say, because the originals have not survived. This is the background to Minna's apparent discovery in 1861 that "the pair *remain* in love"[3] and to her continuing suspicion that was to erupt finally and irrevocably in the "ten days in hell" of February/March 1862.

1 See W. A. Ellis (ed.), *Richard Wagner to Mathilde Wesendonck* (London 3/1911), 343–66.
2 W. A. Ellis, (ed.), *op. cit.*, 362; trans. by Ellis.
3 See W. A. Ellis, (ed.), *op. cit.*, 372.

On my last night in the Asyl[2] I retired to bed after 11 o'clock: I was due to depart at 5 o'clock the next morning. Before I closed my eyes, the same thought flashed through my mind that had always done each time I wanted to lull myself to sleep with the idea that, one day, I would die here: this is how I would lie when you came to me for the last time, when, openly and before the whole world, you enfolded my head in your arms, and received my soul with a final kiss! To die in this way was the fairest of my imaginings, and it had taken shape entirely within the locality of my bedroom: the door leading to the stairs was closed, you entered through the study curtains; thus you wrapped your arm around me; thus I died, gazing at you. – And what now? Has even this chance of dying been snatched away from me? Coldly, like some hunted animal, I left the house in which I had been entombed with a daemon which I could no longer exorcise except by flight. – Where – where now shall I die? – – And so I fell asleep. –

I was roused from my uneasy dreams by a strange rushing noise: on awakening I was sure I felt a kiss upon my brow: – a shrill sigh followed. It was so real that I started up and looked round me. All was silent. I turned up the light: it was shortly before 1 o'clock, the end of the hour when ghosts are said to walk. Had some spirit stood watch beside me during this anxious hour? Were you awake or asleep at that hour? – What were your feelings? – I could not get to sleep again. For a long time I tossed and turned in bed, until I finally got up, got fully dressed, closed the last of my trunks, and now, pacing up and down or else stretched out on my bed, I anxiously waited for the day to break. This time it came later than I had grown used to during the sleepless nights of the previous summer. Reddened with shame the sun crept forth from behind the mountain. – Once more I gazed lingeringly across to you. – Oh heavens! Not a single tear moistened my eye; but I felt that the hair at my temples had all turned white! – Now I had said my last farewell. Now everything inside me was cold and certain. – I went downstairs. My wife was waiting for me there. She offered me a drink of tea. It was an hour of utter misery. – She saw me off. We went down through the garden. It was a glorious morning. I did not look back. – As we said farewell for the last time, my wife was overcome by wretchedness and burst into tears. For the first

1 Letters [217], [219], [221], [222] and [223] are from the first part of the Venice Diary, which was despatched to Mathilde Wesendonck on 12 October 1858.
2 The night of 16/17 August 1858.

time I remained dry-eyed. Once again I exhorted her to appear calm and noble, and to strive for Christian comfort. Her old vindictive fury flared up once more. – She is irredeemable! I was forced to tell myself. And yet – I have no desire to be avenged on the unhappy woman. She herself must carry out her own sentence. – And so I was dreadfully earnest, bitter and sad. Yet – no tears came. – And so I left. And behold! – I do not deny it: I felt better, I breathed more freely. – I sought solitude: that is where I am at home; there in a state of solitude, where I may love you with every breath! – –

[. . .]

Mathilde Wesendonck-Briefe 85–6.

218. MINNA WAGNER, ZWICKAU   Venice, 1 September 1858

My dear good old Mutz,[1]

I am sitting here in Venice. Where are you? I assume you must be in Zwickau.[2] But I find it very worrying that I have still not had any news from you. Could you not have written at least a couple of lines to me in Venice *poste restante*, as I told you to, when I telegraphed to you from Geneva? I arrived here on the 29th of August, and was really hoping for a letter from you. I have been to ask every day, but in vain. Today I have finally begun to get very anxious. You now have to face a very difficult period, and one which will certainly be of great sadness for you; I asked you to ensure that it was as brief as possible. And so I continue to suppose that you left after all on the 29th, since you still remembered that day from when you arrived in Zurich.[3] I pray to God that I receive a letter from you tomorrow which will confirm this, and, at the same time, tell me that you summoned up all your strength and successfully overcame all obstacles. There is nothing I can say to you in addition to what I have already said that will comfort and sustain you. All I can do is call out to you: hope, and do not lose heart! You see, you poor woman, your fate should have granted you a calmer and more uniform existence, but it was bound up with the fate of a man who, however much he, too, desired tranquil happiness, was nevertheless destined in each and every respect to develop in such an extraordinary way that he himself now believes it necessary to renounce his wishes, simply in order to fulfil his life's task. All that I now seek is inner composure in order to be able to complete my works: fame no longer has any effect upon me, and I despair

1 See letter [188], p. 350, note 2.
2 Minna left Zurich on 1 (not 2) September and stayed with her sister Charlotte Tröger in Zwickau, before moving to Dresden on 4 November 1859 (see Fehr II, 147).
3 i.e. in August 1849.

of ever seeing my works successfully performed, – nothing, nothing – save for work, creative work itself, can keep me alive. That such an extraordinary fate must necessarily inspire extraordinary sympathy is entirely natural; there are many people who have felt a deep and sincere devotion for me. If you have been made to suffer as a result, these sufferings will one day be taken into account, and your reward shall be – my prosperity, and the prosperity of my works. But for now – let us not think only of the future. Let us seek to surmount the present, and hope to find peace of mind, reconciliation and charitableness, which we may then enjoy. –

Do not ask me to tell you much about Venice today. I am dreadfully over-wrought as a result of the journey and, especially, of looking for an apartment. I shall not recover my senses until I have established myself here as well and as comfortably as is necessary if I am to hold out; you know that where I live counts for a good deal with me; and I *must* now set my sights on settling down in one place in order to be able to continue my work. I am of course living in furnished accommodation: there is no other kind. My landlord, who is Austrian,[1] was delighted to house such a famous name. All such apartments here are in large palaces that have been abandoned by their former aristocratic owners; speculators have now turned them into apartments for foreigners. But I shall tell you all about this next time. For today let me say only that I hope to be able to hold out in Venice; this town is exceedingly interesting, and the actual stillness – one never hears a carriage – is indispensable for me. I receive no visitors, and hope to live here totally withdrawn into myself. For the moment I am seeing Karl[2] every day for lunch, for which we always arrange to meet at a restaurant in St Mark's Square. If ever this arrangement should no longer suit me, I can have the meal brought to my apartment. It really does not seem at all expensive; only the apartment is relatively not cheap. I am about to write to *Heim* to tell him to send me the grand piano at once; he will have no import duty to pay for the simple reason that Venice is a free port. I do not think I shall need the bed linen and beds; I must of course make do with something inferior.

And now, my dear old Minna, accept my most sincere and heartfelt congratulations on your birthday![3] You poor thing, if only it could have been a better one! But it consoles me to think that you will at least spend it with your relatives, as you did 4 years ago. On that occasion it did you a lot of good; may it be of some comfort to you this time, too! Give them my very best wishes; get better during the time you are with them, and try to forget as best you can! Look on the bright side, and hope that we may soon see

1 In *Mein Leben* he is described as Hungarian. Venice remained part of the Austro-Hungarian Empire until Prussia's defeat of Austria in 1866, when the city became a part of United Italy.
2 Karl Ritter.
3 On 5 September.

each other again in Germany.[1] I am sending you a genuine Venetian present as a souvenir for your birthday: I hope it arrives in time. And so, take heart! Remain calm! Look after your health! If you want to send a really fine present to me in exile, send me word that you are feeling somewhat better, and are hoping to get over your sufferings! Fare you well! A thousand heartfelt, heartfelt greetings! And give my regards to good old Fipps, and even that stupid parrot, Mr. Jacquot! I, by contrast, am now in a totally strange world! Nothing around me except my manuscripts, which show me what I still have to do and – to suffer! You have taken our household goblins with you: look after them, they mean a lot to me as well! Adieu! Adieu! Do not stop loving me!

Your
Richard.

Here is my address, which you must always get someone to write out for you in a very clear hand.

Herr Richard Wagner
Canale Grande, Palazzo Giustiniani
Campiello Squillini No. 3228
in Venice.

Minna-Briefe I,302–4.

219. MATHILDE WESENDONCK, ZURICH   Venice, 3 September 1858

[. . .] Yes! I hope to get better for your sake! To keep you for myself means the same to me as keeping myself alive for my art. To live with it – as a comfort for you – that is my task, and one that accords with my nature, my fate, my will, – and with my love. So am I yours; so shall you, too, get better through me! Here shall Tristan be completed[2] – in spite of all the world's rantings. And – if I may – I shall return with it to see you, to console you, and to make you happy! Thus it stands before me, as my most beautiful and most solemn wish. To work then! Tristan the hero, Isolde the heroine! help me! help my angel! Here shall you bleed to death, here shall your wounds be healed and closed. From here the world shall learn of the sublime and noble distress of supreme love, the lamentations of most sorrowful bliss. And, like some august god, sound in body and clear-eyed, you shall see me again, your humble friend! [. . .]

Mathilde Wesendonck-Briefe 90.

1 The couple next met in Paris on 17 November 1859.
2 See letter [207], p. 379, note 2.

220. HANS VON BÜLOW, BERLIN   Venice, 27 September 1858

My dearest Hans, best of friends,

Do not be angry with me for having given you only common tasks to perform for me since we last parted,[1] and for having not yet told you anything sensible about myself. Today will not be much better, in spite of the fact that I have the best of intentions. For a time I was entirely preoccupied with worries about my material existence. My sudden departure from Zurich caused me a good deal of annoyance and increased my outgoings considerably, so that I must now take steps to exploit the success of Rienzi in Dresden[2] and acquire the means to lead as carefree a life as possible at least until such time as I have completed Tristan. Because of this I have had to write letters upon letters, with the result that my head is now in a complete whirl: I hope that the effort will at least bear fruit, although there has unfortunately been no sign of any so far.

But what I *do* see is that Venice was a happy choice, for which I have to thank Karl:[3] I am greatly attracted by the place, which is so unique and melancholy: I desire the most absolute privacy, and I can certainly find this better here than anywhere else. And so I am hoping for a calm and undisturbed frame of mind with which to resume my work. My grand piano, which has been held up in Zurich until now,[4] is expected to arrive within the next day or so. My recent, heart-rending experiences of life have made me feel even more negative in my attitude to the world: I now feel almost totally free of all wishes and desires. All I want is to cause as little suffering to others as possible: if I know that their sufferings have eased, then mine, too, will disappear. Everything tells me in clear and decisive terms what I must do in order to stop vacillating: were I not an artist, I could become a saint, but I am not destined for that kind of redemption: nor can I take my own life, for if I wished to do so, this will of mine would similarly become an object of art for me, and draw me back towards life at least until I had turned the object into reality, and thus returned once more to the whole circle of grief and misery that is connected to it. That's how it is with me; it is fate, it cannot be altered. And so I act it out, and put up with it, as long as people now and again put me in the right frame of mind for it. What I mean by this is the glance of a friend, a sympathetic and heartfelt appeal, and a joint profession of fellow-feeling and love! What more do I want! All other desires make us common, and draw us back into the common circle. Let all who have anything worth saving flee from it!

1 On 16 August 1858.
2 From 1858 onwards Wagner's operas began to play an increasingly prominent part in the Dresden repertoire; see Newman's *Life*, II,501 (note).
3 Karl Ritter.
4 The Erard grand was temporarily impounded by Wagner's creditors in Zurich.

When will Cosima learn to understand that misery is a part of existence, and to discover where redemption alone is to be found.[1] A single day, an hour, brings more maturity than do entire years. – As for myself, the only thing that amazes me is that my hair is still the same colour: there were moments when I thought I would become an old man! –

My poor wife has had another hard time of things: but it appears that the trouble and effort of moving house, which the stupid woman was determined not to spare herself, have in fact helped to sustain her. She is still with her relations in Zwickau, where she at least enjoys peace and comfort. Her resignation now seems to be deep and in earnest: she thinks only of death. Strange how strong is my sense of fellow-suffering. We can bestow our fellow-suffering on even the commonest object, but fellow-love is reserved only for the noble being whom we love. But since the world exists not for joy but for suffering, compassion always gains the upper hand, since it addresses itself to the very core of our existence.

And so I feel that I belong to him who suffers most, at least as long as he continues to suffer: only when I am expected to share his joys do I turn away from him, unless those joys are the joys of a noble being. And what can these joys be? Agreement in our recognition of the world's condition: sympathy, comfort through fellow-feeling. – How many people could I make happy if only they were to make it possible for me, and for themselves! – Well then – that is why I work, write and compose! Accept it as best you can, and – leave me in peace! – But – no one shall die of grief because of me: – I cannot allow that to happen! –

Fare you well! You see, I am incapable of saying anything sensible! – As soon as I have completed any more of Tristan, you shall learn from that the best I can tell you!

Kind regards to Cosima! And tell her only good things about me. But she should inform her Mama[2] that I was inconsolable "de l'avoir voulu entraîner vers les Wille." My God, whatever made me think of that? –

Adieu! A thousand greetings from

Your
R. W.

RWA (published with suppression of Wille's name in Bülow-Briefe 106–8).

---

1 See introductory essay, p. 407.
2 Countess Marie d'Agoult, who had stayed at the Hotel Baur au lac in Zurich from 22 June to 18 August 1858; for an account of this minor episode, see Fehr II,141–2.

221. MATHILDE WESENDONCK, ZURICH   Venice, 1 October 1858

Recently, while I was in the street, my eye was caught by a poulterer's shop; I stared unthinkingly at his piled-up wares, neatly and appetizingly laid out, when I became aware of a man at the side busily plucking a hen, while another man was just putting his hand in a cage, where he seized a live hen and tore its head off. The hideous scream of the animal, and the pitiful, weaker sounds of complaint that it made while being overpowered transfixed my soul with horror. – Ever since then I have been unable to rid myself of this impression, although I had experienced it often before. – It is dreadful to see how our lives – which, on the whole, remain addicted to pleasure – rest upon such a bottomless pit of the cruellest misery! This has been so self-evident to me from the very beginning, and has become even more central to my thinking as my sensibility has increased that I really do believe that the legitimate reason for all my sufferings lies in the fact that I still cannot positively abandon my life and all its aspirations. The consequence of this is bound to make itself felt in everything, indeed, only on the basis of this discord can one explain my behaviour with its often incomprehensible vicissitudes and not infrequent tendency to treat with bitterness even what is most dear to me. Wherever I perceive evident contentment, or the intention of ensuring the same, I turn away with a certain sense of inner horror. As soon as another's existence seems to me to be lacking in suffering and carefully calculated to keep all suffering at bay, I can follow it only with unsmotherable bitterness, so remote is it from what I regard as the real solution to man's task. And so, without feeling any envy, I have nevertheless felt an instinctive hatred of the rich: I admit that not even they can be called happy, in spite of their possessions; but they have the quite obvious intention of wishing to be so; and it is this which alienates me from them. With subtle intent they avoid anything that could possibly make them feel sympathetic towards the misery upon which all their longed-for contentment rests, and it is this alone that keeps me a world apart from them. I have observed the way in which I am drawn in the other direction with a force that inspires me with sympathy, and that everything touches me deeply only insofar as it arouses fellow-feeling in me, i.e. fellow-suffering. I see in this fellow-suffering the most salient feature of my moral being, and presumably it is this that is the well-spring of my art.

But what characterizes fellow-suffering is that it is by no means conditioned in its affections by the individual qualities of the suffering object but rather by the perception of suffering itself. In love it is otherwise: here we advance to a feeling of fellow-joy, and we can share the joy of an individual only if we find the latter's particular characteristics acceptable in the highest degree, and homogeneous. This is more likely in the case of common types, since here it is purely sexual relations which are almost exclusively at work. The more noble the nature, the more difficult it is to achieve fellow-joy through redintegration: but, if we suceed, there is nothing to equal it! – Fellow-suffering, by contrast, is something we can feel for even the commonest and least of beings, a being which, apart from its suffering, is totally unsympathetic towards us, indeed, may even be antipathetic in what it is capable of enjoying. The reason for this, at all events, is infinitely profound and, if we recognize it, we shall thereby see ourselves raised above the very real barriers of our personality. For what we encounter when we exercise fellow-suffering in this way is suffering as such, divorced from all personality.

In order to steel themselves against the power of fellow-suffering, people commonly assert that it is demonstrably the case that lower natures feel suffering far less keenly than a higher organism: they argue that, as the sensibility that first makes fellow-suffering possible increases, so, proportionately, does suffering gain in reality: in other words, the fellow-suffering that we expend on lower natures is a waste of emotional effort, being an exaggeration, and even a pampering of feeling. – This opinion, however, rests upon a fundamental error which is at the basis of every realistic philosophy; for it is precisely here that we see idealism in its truly moral stature inasmuch as it reveals the former as an example of egotistical narrow-mindedness. The question here is not what the other person suffers but what *I* suffer when I know him to be suffering. After all, we know what exists around us only inasmuch as we picture it in our imagination, and how *I* imagine it is how it is for *me*. If I ennoble it, it is because I myself am noble, if I feel the other man's suffering to be deep, it is because I myself feel deeply when I imagine his suffering, and whoever, by contrast, imagines it to be insignificant reveals in doing so that he himself is insignificant. Thus my fellow-suffering makes the other person's suffering an actual reality, and the more insignificant the being with which I can suffer, the wider and more embracing is the circle which suggests itself to my feelings. – But here lies an aspect of my nature which others may see as a weakness. I admit that unilateral actions are much impeded by it; but I am certain that when I act, I then act in accordance with my essential nature, and certainly never cause pain to anyone intentionally. This consideration alone can influence me in all my actions: to cause others as little suffering as possible. On this point I am totally at one with myself, for only in this way can I hope to give others joy, as well: for the only true, genuine joy is to be found in the conformity of fellow-suffering. But I cannot obtain this by force: it must be granted me by the other person's friendly nature, which is why I have only ever encountered a single perfect example of this phenomenon! –

But I am also clear in my own mind why I can even feel greater fellow-suffering for lower natures than for higher ones. A higher nature is what it is precisely because it has been raised by its own suffering to the heights of resignation, or else has within it – and cultivates – the capacity for such a development. Such a nature is extremely close to mine, is indeed similar to it, and with it I attain to fellow-joy. That is why, basically, I feel less fellow-suffering for people than for animals. For I can see that the latter are totally denied the capacity to rise above suffering, and to achieve a state of resignation and deep, divine calm. And so, in the event of their suffering, as happens when they are tormented, all I see – with a sense of my own tormented despair – is their absolute, redemption-less suffering without any higher purpose, their only release being death, which confirms my belief that it would have been better for them never to have entered upon life. And so, if this suffering can have a purpose, it is simply to awaken a sense of fellow-suffering in man, who thereby absorbs the animal's defective existence, and becomes the redeemer of the world by recognizing the error of all existence. (This meaning will one day become clearer to you from the Good Friday morning scene in the third act of Parzival.)[1] But to see the individual's capacity for redeeming the world through fellow-suffering atrophy, undeveloped and most assiduously neglected, makes me regard people with utter loathing, and weakens my sense of fellow-suffering to the point where I feel only total insensitivity towards their distress. It is in his distress that the individual's road to salvation is to be found, a road which is not open to animals; if he does not recognize this to be so but insists upon considering it to be locked and barred to him, I feel an instinctive urge to throw this door wide open for him, and am capable of going to lengths of great cruelty in order to make him conscious of the need to suffer. Nothing leaves me colder than the philistine's complaint that he has been disturbed in his contentment: any compassion here would be pure complicity. Just as my entire nature involves shaking people out of their common condition, here, too, I feel an urge simply to spur them on in order to make them feel life's great anguish! –

[. . .]

Mathilde Wesendonck-Briefe 101–5.

222. MATHILDE WESENDONCK, ZURICH   Venice, 5 October 1858

[. . .] Çakyamuni[2] was initially totally opposed to the idea of admitting women into the community of saints. He repeatedly expresses the view of them that, by nature, women are far too subject to their sexual identity, and hence to whim and caprice, and far too attached to worldly existence to be able to achieve the composure and deep contemplativeness necessary for the individual to renounce his natural inclinations and achieve redemption. It was

1 The familiar spelling of Parsifal was not adopted until March 1877 (see CT for 14 March 1877).
2 One of the names of Gotama, the Buddha.

his favourite pupil, Ananda, – that same Ananda to whom I have already allotted a part in my "Victors" – who was finally able to persuade the master to relent and open up the community to women. – With this I gained something uncommonly important. Without any sense of unnaturalness, my plan has been vastly and hugely expanded. The difficulty here was to make the Buddha himself – a figure totally liberated and above all passion – suitable for dramatic and, more especially, musical treatment. But I have now solved the problem by having him reach one last remaining stage in his development whereby he is seen to acquire a new insight, which – like every insight – is conveyed not by abstract associations of ideas but by intuitive emotional experience, in other words, by a process of shock and agitation suffered by his inner self; as a result, this insight reveals him in his final progress towards a state of supreme enlightenment. Ananda, who is closer to life and directly affected by the violent love of the Chandala girl, becomes the agent of this ultimate enlightenment. – Deeply stirred and shaken, Ananda can return this love only in his own, supreme, sense, as a desire to draw his beloved to him in order to share with her his ultimate salvation. The master responds to this without harshness but as though lamenting an error, an impossibility. Finally, however, when Ananda begins to think in his deepest sadness that he must abandon all hope, Çakya, drawn to him by his fellow-suffering and as though by some new and ultimate problem whose solution detains him in life, feels called upon to test the girl. The latter now arrives to appeal to the master in her deepest grief, begging him to marry her to Ananda. He expounds the conditions, renunciation of the world, and withdrawal from all the bonds of nature; on hearing the principal commandment, she is sincere enough in her resolve to collapse in a faint; after which there unfolds (perhaps you recall it?) the colourful scene with the Brahmans who reproach him for his dealings with such a girl, claiming that this is proof of the error of his teaching. In rejecting all human pride, his growing sympathy with the girl, whose earlier existences he reveals to himself and his opponents, grows so strong that, when she herself – having recognized the whole vast complex of universal suffering on the basis of her own individual suffering – declares herself ready to swear that oath, he accepts her into the number of the saints, as though by way of his own final transfiguration, and thus regards his own course through life – which has been one of redemption and devotion to all living things – as now complete, since he has been able to promise that womankind, too, may now be – directly – redeemed. –

Happy Savitri! You may now follow your lover everywhere, be around him and with him constantly! Happy Ananda! she is now close to you, you have won her, never to lose her!

My child, the glorious Buddha was no doubt right when he strictly excluded art. Is there anyone who feels more clearly than I that it is this unhappy art that everlastingly restores me to life's torment and all the contradictions of existence? If I did not have this wondrous gift of an over-predominant visual imagination, I could follow my heart's instinctive urge, in accordance with my own clear-eyed insight, – and become a saint; and as a saint I could say to you: come here, leave behind you all that holds you back, burst the bonds of nature: in return for this I will show you the road to salvation! – Then we should be free: Ananda and Savitri! [. . .]

Mathilde Wesendonck-Briefe 108–10.

223. Mathilde Wesendonck, Zurich   Venice, 12 October 1858

[. . .] The world has been overcome: in our love, as in our suffering, it has overcome itself. No longer do I see it as a foe from whom I must flcc, but as an insubstantial object indifferent to my will, an object I may now regard without shyness and pain, and therefore without any real aversion. This do I feel with increasing clarity, now that, in theory, I am less aware of the urge for total seclusion. Until now this urge has had for me the meaning of yearning, of seeking and of longing: but this – I feel right now! – has at last been wholly stilled. The recent decisions that we reached together have made me clearly aware that I have nothing more to search for, nothing more to desire. So abundantly did you give yourself to me that I cannot call this feeling resignation, least of all despair. This mood of recklessness used once to be the outcome of my searching and of my yearning: but I am relieved of its necessity now that you have made me feel so profoundly happy. A sense of inviolable satiety has taken hold of me. The urge I once felt has been deadened now it is fully satisfied. – Inspired by this awareness, I gaze anew at a world which thus appears in a wholly different light. For I no longer have anything to look for here, no longer have to seek out the spot in which I may hide away from it. It has now become a wholly objective spectacle, like nature in which I see the days coming and going, and see the seeds of life blossom and die, without feeling that my innermost self is itself dependent upon this coming and going, this blossoming and this dying. My attitude towards it is almost entirely that of an artist who perceives and portrays what he sees, a man who feels for himself and for others, without himself wanting or seeking or striving for anything. [. . .]

[. . .] No doubt we shall see one another again: but I think that, initially, it will be as – in a dream, like two departed spirits who meet at the scene of their sufferings in order to refresh themselves by recalling the glance and the clasp of hands that once delivered them from this world in order that they might find a place in heaven. If ever – perhaps on the strength of my new-found tranquillity – I may be granted a beautiful and unclouded old age, it may yet be possible for me to return once again and to be beside you, when suffering and jealousy are all overcome. The "Asyl" could then become a reality once more, after all. Perhaps I might even need to be cared for then. I hope such care would not be denied me. Perhaps – one morning – you would come to my bedside through the green study, in order to receive my soul in your arms with a parting kiss. – And my diary would then end as it began. – Yes, my child! Let my diary end here! It brings you my sufferings, my exaltation, my struggles, my glimpses of the world, and throughout – my eternal love for you! Accept it graciously, and forgive me if at any point it opens up old wounds. –

I am now returning to "Tristan", that it may speak to you of the profound art of resonant silence. What gives me new life at present is the great solitude and state of withdrawal in which I live: it enables me to summon up my vital strengths which have been so painfully squandered. For some time now I have been able to enjoy a thing I had almost never known before, the benefits of a deep and restful night's sleep: if only I could give it to everyone! I shall enjoy it until my wondrous work is finished and completed. Only then shall I see what an aspect the world presents to me. The Grand Duke of Baden has managed to obtain permission for me to visit Germany for a time in order that I may superintend the performance of some new work of mine. I may perhaps use this opportunity to perform Tristan.[1] Until then I shall remain alone with it in this dream-world of mine which has now come to life here.

[. . .]

Mathilde Wesendonck-Briefe 115–19.

224. MATHILDE WESENDONCK, ZURICH   Venice, 1 November 1858[2]

Today is All Souls' Day![3] –

I have woken up from a brief, but deep, sleep after long and terrible sufferings such as I have never previously suffered. I stood on the balcony and gazed down into the black depths of the Canal; the storm wind was raging. Had I jumped and fallen in, no one would have heard me. I would

---

1 See p. 356, note 1. *Tristan und Isolde* was finally performed for the first time in Munich on 10 June 1865.

2 Letters [224] and [227] are taken from the second part of the Venice Diary, which Wagner kept, with increasing infrequency, from 18 October 1858 to 4 April 1859. The depressed tone of letter [224] was caused in part by confirmation of Minna's illness (see letter [225], pp. 428–9), and in part by news of the death of Guido Wesendonck, Mathilde's three-year-old son, on 13 October 1858. According to Fehr (II,151–4), the news of Guido's death led to a resurgence of Wagner's longing for Mathilde.

3 All Souls' Day is in fact celebrated on 2 November; 1 November is All Saints' Day.

have been free of all torment the moment I jumped. And I clenched my fist in order to lift myself up on to the parapet. – Could I – with my eyes upon you, – upon your children? –

Now All Souls' Day has dawned! –

All Souls! May you rest in peace! –

Now I know that it will yet be granted to me to die in your arms! Now I know! – – I shall soon see you again: no doubt in the spring; perhaps even in the midst of this coming winter.[1] –

You see, my child! The final thorn has gone from my soul! [. . .][2] Now I can do anything. We shall soon meet again! –

Pay no heed to my art! I now feel quite clearly that it is not a consolation for me, nor a form of compensation; it merely accompanies the deep harmony I feel with you, it nurtures my wish to die in your arms. When the Erard arrived,[3] it could only seduce me because your deep and unshakeable love had flared up more unerringly and more brightly than ever, after the storm. *With* you I can do anything: – *without* you nothing! Nothing! [. . .]

Mathilde Wesendonck-Briefe 124–5.

225. ANTON PUSINELLI, DRESDEN   Venice, 1 November 1858

My dear and faithful friend,

I am turning to you today in a matter that touches me deeply. – My wife will be spending this winter in Dresden. She has probably already arrived, and may perhaps already have visited you. I recall the cordial and comforting information concerning the state of her health, which you so touchingly sent me last summer in response to my description of her condition. I now entrust the poor patient to you in person. Be her doctor, her adviser, her helper – if you can; her comforter, if you cannot. – The sincere conviction that a change of scene and company, and even her temporary removal from my vicinity, which has always tended to make her somewhat irritable, would at all events serve to offer the sick woman at least a chance of recovery – this conviction has contributed in no small way to my belief that we should live apart for a period. On the whole, I have no doubt but that Dresden will appeal to her as being both homely and, ultimately, restful; she will be moving into a small ground-floor apartment in the Rottdorf house where we first lived in Dresden, but before then will be staying at the Tichatscheks'. –

1 Wagner saw Mathilde Wesendonck in Zurich on 3 April 1859.
2 Suspension marks in the printed German edition; the original letters from Wagner to Mathilde Wesendonck have all been destroyed, with the exception of the musical examples which they contain. The culprit was presumably Cosima.
3 The Erard grand arrived in Venice in mid-October 1858.

She was recently at her brother-in-law's,[1] who is himself a doctor. Since I wanted some reassurance about her condition, I addressed myself to him, and am now enclosing his reply, which I received yesterday. You see what little comfort I can draw from her condition. The news has affected me deeply! –

As for the origins of her condition, she herself will be able to give you little clear information. A weakness in one of her organs (perhaps originating in her glandular system – for her mother died of dropsy of the chest) has probably been developing ever since, and certainly during, our time in Dresden. But the increasingly shattered state of her nerves dates chiefly from the many violent and sorrowful incidents in our lives. By 1853 her nervous irritability and sleeplessness were already very pronounced; a doctor treated her for gout; using hot baths and douches which almost drove her insane. She then learned of the pleasures of laudanum, which was incautiously prescribed to her in small doses for her insomnia; unable to detect any improvement in her condition, she increased the doses to a score more drops at a time, as she later confessed to me. As her irritability increasingly got the better of her, it became impossible for us to avoid frequent quarrels; and – as I freely admit – this was the reason why our living together finally became intolerable for us. – You will soon find out more about her physical condition for yourself. I beg you to be honest with me, dear Anton, and tell me everything, so that I may do everything possible to support you in your treatment as scrupulously as I can. My conduct and future attitude towards her will be determined by no other thought in the world than the sincere wish to contribute to her recovery and her relief, and to showing her every consideration. I shall make it my most pressing concern to do everything that may serve this end. If we can prolong her life, and make it as painless and as comfortable as possible, my most heartfelt wish will have been fulfilled, and I am prepared to make whatever sacrifices are necessary to achieve this end. – For the present I hear, much to my relief, that – as was to be expected – she is already somewhat calmer; and she is said to be looking better. Let the poor woman, whom I pity from the depths of my soul, be commended to your noble heart! Be to her whatever you can, and count upon my most ardent thanks! –

As for myself and my extremely secluded life, you will learn something about all this from my wife; I myself shall tell you more about it the next time I write, which I most urgently hope you will very shortly give me occasion to do by kindly informing me as to my wife's health, and, at the same time, allowing me to express my gratitude towards you. –

Fare you well, best of friends! Accept the good wishes and blessings of

Your
Richard Wagner

RWA (published complete in Freunde und Zeitgenossen 232–5).

1 Adam Tröger.

226. JULIE RITTER, DRESDEN　　　　　　　Venice, 19 November 1858

My dear and deeply revered friend,

Karl is leaving tomorrow to convey his best wishes to you on your birthday. It makes me very happy to think of his return; I feel as though he will then be bringing you yourself back with him, so greatly do I value the power of personal contact! Get him to tell you all about me. He brings with him a thousand heartfelt wishes from me.

Your kind letter caused me a great deal of embarrassment,[1] since it made me see how embarrassing you yourself must have found it to tell me something I ought no doubt to have spared you. That you had suffered losses I had no means of knowing. But even without this information, I had been hoping from one half-year to the next that I might find myself in a position to send you satisfactory news about myself and ask you, of my own accord, to put an end to the sacrifices which your dear family has been making on my behalf. When you renewed your remittance at Easter last year, I naturally took it as a token of your unshakeable concern for me, but it was also of great value inasmuch as I was then having to defray the costs of occupying the little plot of land which I had desired so much up to that time, and on which I had used up all my resources. I had a difficult year up to last Easter; my revenues, which unfortunately are always a matter of chance and impossible to calculate, failed me completely for a time, and furnishing the house, in addition to laying out and maintaining the garden, cost so much more than I had estimated that it was not until last summer, when some decent revenues came in, that I regained my balance, so to speak, discharged all that I owed and, with good prospects ahead of me, was looking forward to the time when I would be able to set something aside for less auspicious times and thus ask you, gratefully, to withhold your subsidies for the present. I confidently predicted being able to do so by the beginning of next year, and was genuinely looking forward to announcing as much to you. My sudden departure from Zurich has again placed me in a much altered position. The fittings and furnishings that we had just finished paying for were now completely useless; several thousand francs which I had set aside for living expenses now had to be used to pay for these unforeseen changes; current bills that fall due in the New Year now became a matter of urgency, and my dream of a well-ordered existence quickly turned into what – for a time – was a most disagreeable reality. Next year, however, I am expecting decent returns which should more than meet my needs, notably as a result of the appearance of Tristan; but just at present I am very hard-pressed, the more so since my hopes that Rienzi would spread rapidly have now been dashed. This, then, was the moment to help, and your

---

1 Julie Ritter had written to say that, having suffered serious financial losses, she could continue her annuity for only another twelve months.

most kind offer to make the annuity available to me once again next year has helped me – thanks to Karl's mediation – out of my present predicament. And so for next year I shall again make demands on your kind help, and believe that in return I may give you the well-founded assurance that by next year you will see me in a position where I can thank you for evermore.

Thus, my dearest of friends, the sacrifices which you have made, thanks to your unique and enthusiastic concern for me, will have achieved their intended aim in the noblest sense of the word. You have not only protected me and kept me personally independent, but, more especially, you have preserved the mood of courage, freedom and, I may add, of aesthetic content-ment that I need to work creatively, irrespective of whether my works bring me rewards or not. During this time my attitude towards the outside world has been shaped by the increasing recognition that has been shown me, to the point where all that is now required is my amnesty for me to be fully conscious of the fact that I am master of my own fate and, more especially, of my external circumstances. Here, too, I have every hope that a decisive change will take place next year, and that this will then provide me with the good fortune of being able to see you again and to tell you in person, face to face, what you have been to me during this long and fateful period, what you have contributed to the development of my character as a whole, and how I shall be eternally grateful to you for all that you have done. –

My most sincere and heartfelt congratulations on your birthday!

A thousand good wishes from

Your most loyally devoted
Richard Wagner.

Ritter-Briefe 137–40.

227. MATHILDE WESENDONCK, ZURICH   Venice, 1 December 1858

Here I am, poor soul that I am, confined to my room again for the last eight days, and this time even confined to my chair, from which I am not allowed to get up, so that in the evening I have to be carried to bed.[1] Yet it is only an outward affliction, which I have even come to regard as decisive for my general health, inasmuch as my condition even fills me with the hope that, from now on, I may be able to continue with my work undisturbed, whereas it was above all the interruption that I suffered which made my recent bouts of illness so unbearable. – At such periods my intellect is always very active; plans and ideas occupy my imagination in the liveliest fashion. This time it

---

1 Soon after his arrival in Venice Wagner succumbed to gastritis, and was subsequently laid up for a month with a painful ulcer on his leg.

was philosophical problems which engaged my attention. During recent weeks I have been slowly rereading friend Schopenhauer's principal work, and this time it has inspired me, quite extraordinarily, to expand and – in certain details – even to correct his system. The subject is uncommonly important, and it must, I think, have been reserved for a man of my own particular nature, at this particular period of his life, to gain insights here of a kind that could never have disclosed themselves to anyone else. It is a question, you see, of pointing out the path to salvation, which has not been recognized by any philosopher, and especially not by Sch., but which involves a total pacific-ation of the will through love, and not through any abstract human love, but a love engendered on the basis of sexual love, i.e. the attraction between man and woman. It is significant that in reaching this conclusion (as a philosopher, not as a poet, for as such I have my own material) I have been able to use the material of the concepts which Sch. himself provides. The presentation of this argument will take me very deep and very far; it involves a more detailed explanation of the state in which we become capable of recognizing ideas, and of genius in general, which I no longer conceive of as a state in which the intellect is divorced from the will, but rather as an intensification of the individual intellect to the point where it becomes the organ of perception of the genus or species, and thus of the will itself, which is the thing in itself; herein lies the only possible explanation for that marvellous and enthusiastic joy and ecstasy felt by any genius at the highest moments of perception, moments which Sch. seems scarcely to recognize, since he is able to find them only in a state of calm and in the silencing of the individual affects of the will. Entirely analogous to this view, however, I have succeeded in demonstrating beyond doubt that in love there lies the possibility of raising oneself above the individual impulse of the will to a point where total mastery over the latter is achieved, and the generic will becomes fully conscious of itself, a consciousness which, at this level, is necessarily synonymous with total pacification. All this will become clear even to the inexperienced person, provided that my presentation of it proves successful. The result, however, will inevitably be very important, and fill in the gaps in Schopenhauer's system in a thorough and satisfactory fashion. We shall see if ever I feel inclined to do anything about it.[1] –

Mathilde Wesendonck-Briefe 130–1.

---

[1] Wagner got no further than drafting a letter to Schopenhauer (SS XII,291), although the idea adumbrated here continued to influence his thinking for the remainder of his life and helps to explain his ability to reconcile the otherwise conflicting philosophies of Feuerbach and Schopenhauer.

228. MATHILDE WESENDONCK, ZURICH
[Venice, around 20 December 1858]

Our letters crossed in the post: yours arrived just after I had posted mine! –
I have been on my own for some time now. Karl Ritter left me to visit his sick mother and to wish her well on her birthday. When he went, I was just on the point of recovering from an illness which had interrupted me in the work I had but recently begun.[1] I promised that by the time he got back I should have completed another large section of Tristan. But once again I had to consent to remaining in my room – and, as a result of an injury to the outside of my leg, I was on this occasion even confined to my chair, in which I had to have myself carried to bed. This lasted more or less until now; only within the last day or so have I been out again by gondola. I am telling you this tale of woe by way of introducing the information that never for a moment have I lost my patience but that, although I have had to abandon my work again, I have kept my mind constantly active and unclouded. During this time I saw no one save my doctor, Louisa – my donna di servente, who looked after me very well and bandaged me up, – and Pietro, who had to heat the room a good deal, bring me my meals and, in the morning and at night, with the help of a gondolier, carry me on my chair out of and into bed – a process I always called a "traghetto", accompanying it with a loud shout of "poppéh", which people regularly call out in Venice. Louisa and Pietro were always surprised and pleased to find me in such a good humour; one thing they particularly liked was my explanation of why I had such difficulty conversing with them, which I told them was because they had a Venetian dialect, whereas I spoke and understood only pure Tuscan. –

On one occasion I was visited by a good-natured highly cultivated and intelligent man, a Prince Dolgorucki;[2] I was pleased when he came, but even more pleased when he went away again. I feel perfectly content not to be entertained and distracted. – Nor did I do much reading; in any event I read very little at times like this. But I had W. v. Humboldt's letters sent to me; they were not especially satisfying, indeed, I found it difficult to read much of them. I already knew the best bits in an abridged version: four lines of them were preferable, I thought, to all the rest with its diffuseness and lack of clarity. No doubt you can guess which four lines I mean? –

I am more interested in Schiller, and am now reading him with uncommon pleasure: it was difficult for Göthe to hold his own beside this uncommonly sympathetic type. What a passion for knowledge there is here! You would think this man had never existed, but that he was always on the look-out for intellectual light and warmth. His poor health apparently did not stand in his

1 See letter [227], p. 431, note 1.
2 Peter Vladimirovich Dolgorukov or Dolgoruki.

way: and during his years of maturity he seems to have been totally free of any overwhelming moral afflictions. Things seem to have been quite tolerable for him. And then there was so much for him to know, knowledge that was difficult to acquire at a time when Kant had left so much that was unclear, indeed, it was particularly hard for a poet, since the latter wishes to be perfectly clear in his ideas, too. One thing is missing in all these men: music! But they felt it as a need, as a presentiment. This often finds quite clear expression in their writings, notably in their extremely felicitous substitution of a contrast between "visual" and "musical" poetry for the one between "epic" and "lyric". With music, however, a position of omnipotence has now been achieved in contrast to which the poets of that wonderfully questing and aspiring age of evolutionary change produced works that are merely sketches. But that is why I feel so close to them: they are my living heirloom. Yet they were happy – happier without music! A concept cannot cause suffering; but in music every concept turns into a feeling; it consumes and burns till it becomes a bright flame, and the new and wondrous light can laugh out loud! –

I then studied a good deal of philosophy and reached conclusions which complement and correct my friend Schopenhauer. But I prefer to ruminate on such matters rather than to write them down. On the other hand, poetic projects are again crowding into my mind in a most lively fashion. Parzival[1] has preoccupied me very much: in particular, there is a curious creature, a strangely world-demonic woman (the messenger of the grail) who strikes me with increasing vitality and fascination. If ever I manage to write this poem, I am sure to produce something very original. But I simply cannot imagine how long I shall have to remain alive if I am ever to realize all my plans. If I were really attached to life, I might suppose that all these many projects would guarantee me a really long life. But it won't necessarily happen. – Humboldt reports that Kant planned to elaborate a whole series of ideas in greater detail, but that his death, at a ripe old age, naturally prevented him from doing so. –

I notice on this occasion a quite fatalistic resistance even to the completion of Tristan; but this cannot persuade me to work any faster. On the contrary, I compose as though I had no plans to work on anything else for the rest of my life. By way of compensation, it will be more beautiful than anything I have yet done; the smallest phrase takes on the meaning of an entire act, so carefully do I execute it. And while on the subject of Tristan, I must tell you how happy I am at having received a first copy of the newly printed poem in time to send it to you as a gift. –

Mathilde Wesendonck-Briefe 157–60.

1 See letter [221], p. 424, note 1.

229. FRANZ LISZT, WEIMAR   [Venice, 31 December 1858]

Oh dearest! dearest Franz! –

Your answer was far too emotional! Let me add a humorously realistic commentary to my last letter! – What of Dingelstedt! What of the Grand Duke! What of Rienzi![1] – Stupid things, the lot of them! – I need money. If only that wretched night-watchman had sent me his miserable 25 l. d'ors[2] at once, I wouldn't have minded. But then to receive a promise to pay me "after the first performance" – (idiot!). You speak far too nicely about me with other people. Tell them "Wagner doesn't give a damn about you, your theatres, and his own operas; what he needs is money; that's all!" Did *you* not understand me either? Did I not say to you, clearly and distinctly, that I was trying to scrape together some money at all costs? Did I not ask you to put in a word for my operas (Lohengrin or flying Dut.) in Coburg etc? What in God's name am I supposed to do with Diana de Solange?[3] Why should I put up with such open contempt on your part? – Not a word? No money? –

All right! I haven't even 10 gulden left; I can't pay the rent, and can't send my wife anything, although she wrote to me a fortnight ago to say she had very little left. – But all of this is only temporary. Next Easter, when Tristan is finished, I'll have more than I need. But now everyone leaves me in the lurch. Everyone! Everyone! Not a single prospect of a definite receipt. – And what I now get is – – Diana de Solanges! It's enough to drive a person insane! I can see you simply do not *know* what hardship is – you lucky man! –

Or is this a way of reproaching me for living too well? My Franz, when you see the second act of Tristan, you'll admit that I need a lot of money. I'm a great spend-thrift; but, really, it does produce results. – You know that. But just think about it. And never believe that I take seriously any of the complaints that I have about Dingelstedt, the Duke or anyone else. All that I need from the world is money: apart from that I have *everything*. – It is *you* and your delight in the 1st act of Tristan that are to blame for this fit of high spirits on my part. When you get to know the second act, you'll even be able to forgive me for doing nothing today except to shout out for – money! Money! – How and from whom doesn't matter. Tristan will repay it all! –

1 Liszt had written to Wagner on 26 December rhapsodizing over the first act of *Tristan und Isolde* which Härtels had just sent him, and adding that his influence with the Grand Duke of Weimar and with the new intendant Franz Dingelstedt was insufficient to persuade them to expedite plans for a new production of *Rienzi*; the opera was finally performed in Weimar on 26 December 1860.
2 The honorarium offered by Dingelstedt for *Rienzi*.
3 Opera by Duke Ernst II of Saxe-Coburg-Gotha, which the Duke was planning to dedicate to Wagner. It was first performed in Coburg on 5 December 1858; productions followed in Gotha, Dresden, Vienna, Rotterdam, Prague, Brünn, Riga, Reval, Berlin and New York.

When I'm completely insane, I'll telegraph you with my last remaining napoleon! –

Adieu! Happy New Year!

Send Dante and the Mass![1] But first send me – money! A fee – for God knows what! Tell Dingelstedt he is a fool as long as he lives! And tell the Grand Duke that his snuff-box has been pawned – it's true! It's up to him to redeem it for me. –

Never again write to me in such a serious and emotional tone! God! I told you last time that you all bore me. Was it to no avail?

Get better in the New Year! A fine how-do-you-do *that* will be! Oh! Oh! Good night!

Yours,
R.W.[2]

Liszt-Briefe II, 237–8.

230. FRANZ LISZT, WEIMAR   Venice, 7 January 1859

My dear Franz,

You will presumably have reread my letter and discovered what I was jokingly referring to with my reproach that "your answer was far too emotional and serious". It cannot have escaped your notice, given the precise terms of my – admittedly somewhat loosely worded – letter that what I understood by your reply was the way you had interpreted my attitude towards Dingelstedt in the matter of Rienzi. Since this section of my letter appears at all events to have remained unclear to you, I hope that the following will serve as an explanation. My letter to you on the subject of my withdrawing Rienzi was intended to be shown to others, since I had referred Dingelstedt to you. But I thought *you* would see through it and realize that what particularly annoyed me was his obstinacy concerning my fee, and the prospect of its being paid out so late. I hoped that, by raising the question of my withdrawing the entire opera, my letter would have the effect of producing the fee sooner rather than later, and perhaps even increase the amount that I received. I had – alas! – set my hopes on receiving this sum before the New Year, and thought I could count even more firmly on it inasmuch as I had already confided to you how difficult my position is at present. In sending you Dingelstedt's recent letter, I had no other thought in mind than to complain about his pedantic instruction: "The fee will be paid out to you after the first perform-

---

1 *Eine Symphonie zu Dantes Divina Commedia*, published in 1859 and dedicated to Wagner, and *Missa solemnis zur Einweihung der Basilika in Gran*, first performed at Esztergom on 31 August 1856 and published in Vienna in 1859.
2 For Liszt's reply, see Appendix A, p. 937.

ance" (an instruction which I am no longer accustomed to receiving from any other theatre), and to persuade you – as I made perfectly clear – at least to ensure that my fee was paid out to me without further delay. Since it was designed to be shown to others, my letter concerning the withdrawal of Rienzi may well have been unclear and difficult to interpret aright; but I know that I had intended it as a warning shot aimed at Dingelstedt and as a weapon for you – to obtain prompt and decent treatment for me. With this thought in mind, I hoped that the success of this little manoeuvre would be to secure the receipt of these wretched 25 l. d'or before the New Year, since I was obliged to regard this sum as the only revenue I could count on for the very good reason that you yourself could pursue the matter on the spot, whereas the other remittances that I could imagine receiving from all the various quarters were simply potential hopes which were just as likely to turn out to be vain. Thus I reached New Year's Eve. My money was all gone; I had already pledged my watch, the Grand Duke's snuff-box, and the Frau Kapellmeister's bonbonnière (my only objects of value), and of the money obtained in this way I had only about one-and-a-half napoleons left. – When I returned that evening to my lonely New Year's Eve apartment, I found your letter, and I admit my weakness in hoping that it would announce the imminent despatch of the 25 l. d'or, in consequence, moreover, of a successful demonstration against Dingelstedt which, I believed, I myself had set in train. Instead of which, I found, in respect of this matter, a serious explanation of your relations with Dingelstedt which, as I see from your letter, have already become a matter of bitter and worrying experience for you. I had foreseen this, and at the time – when Dingelstedt was called to Weimar at your instigation – I reproached you silently on the matter. I now understood, too, that, since you had already been feeling annoyed for some time, you were, on receipt of my last letter, in a mood that misled you as to the nature of my threat to withdraw Rienzi. All you saw in me was my annoyance – with which you sympathized – at all the unworthy things we have both had to face, and, in doing so, you *failed* to see that, poor devil that I am, I had not been entirely serious on this occasion. As a result you agreed, gravely and bitterly, to my withdrawal of Rienzi which, after the insults you had suffered, must finally have been most welcome to you, and I, in the situation I have described to you on New Year's Eve, saw that my final, secret, but all the more certain, hope of being sent some money had now been dashed. At any other time, the great anguish of the moment would probably have reduced me to total silence and a feeling of reserve. But I had been waiting and longing for some sign of your sympathy for Tristan for such a long time and with such incredible suspense that when this boon finally arrived, it provoked a quite convulsive outburst of petulance on my part. Once again, your delight in my first act had suddenly brought you so close to my innermost soul that at such a moment I felt I could make the most insane demands on you. I said as much, if I am not mistaken, when I wrote that "your delight in Tristan is to blame for my fit of high spirits" –. My dearest Franz, at such a moment I could not conceive of the possibility of a misunderstanding. Since I thought that everything, but everything, was so certain and infallible between us, I launched out in the opposite direction and reproached you for having left me in the lurch over the money, for having interpreted my political gesture or demonstration against Dingelstedt far too seriously and emotionally, in the context of whom I said I cared for nothing in the whole world but a little money: and I went on to say that everything which, at close hand and in your present position etc., appears to you to be grave and critical simply does not exist for me, since the only justification that these theatres have, with all their public art, is that of providing me with money. –

That of money – ! yes. – And will you reproach me for this? What? Do you not *pity* me because of it? Do you believe I would not prefer *your* attitude towards performances of my own works, whereby you do not have to worry about money? – My first letter to you this year will have taught you that I *too* am capable of regarding the matter more seriously and with genuine emotion, i.e. *suffering.*

Enough! Today's letter from you, you will no doubt have realized, has left me feeling deeply shaken. I am, nevertheless, calm and confident. Your strange misunderstanding whereby you assumed that my reproach concerning your "grave and emotional reply" referred to your delight at Tristan must soon become perfectly obvious to you as such. I am in no doubt on that point, since any unprejudiced and intimate friend, were you to grant him a sight of our recent correspondence, would be able to persuade you, however prejudiced your own attitude, that my reproach (which, I may add, was intended to be merely humorous in its half-joking high-spiritedness) was directed at your interpretation of my intended withdrawal of Rienzi, and at the general point concerning my expectations of Dingelstedt, the Grand Duke and the whole shitting business of German opera houses in general. You now know the position which inspired this mood of desperate humour, and I hope it will be a long time before I again have to change my last napoleon at the telegraph office.

It is you, my friend, whom I see suffering and in need of comfort, for the extraordinary lines which you have now found it possible to send me must have sprung from a terrible inner resentment. I hope that you may draw some comfort from the detailed explanation that I have attempted here and from my disclosure of this misunderstanding of which you are guilty; I have no other comfort to offer you at present. If your ill-humour was directed at me alone, it ought to have been entirely dispelled by these lines. But I can further reassure you that you have in no way hurt me, since your arrows were wide of the mark, indeed, they remain embedded in your own heart with their barbs. May this help you to tear them out!

There is only one other favour that I have to ask of you today: –

Do not answer my letter of the 2nd of January, now or ever! Regard it as though it had never been written and never received.[1] – I know now that you are not capable of putting yourself in my position with enough understanding and goodwill to do justice to that letter. I beg you – pay absolutely no heed to it! I will then forgive you the reproach you made me [concerning[2] my joint-stock artistic enterprises], you strange and dear, dear friend! –

And now, fare you well for today!

I am sure that I have not lost you!

Yours,
Richard Wagner.

RWA (incompletely published in Liszt-Briefe II, 245–8).

231. MINNA WAGNER, DRESDEN   Venice, 16 January 1859

[. . .] Do you know how I managed to get Rienzi accepted in Hanover? Since you wrote to tell me that, having heard Tichatscheck in the part, *Niemann* was afraid of not being able to sustain it, I wrote to the latter and asked him whether it had not occurred to him that T. was simply trying to cover up his true weakness by letting loose such a tremendous, and often totally unnecessary, volume of sound and by showing off his powers of vocal endurance in this way, or whether he believed that there was really nothing else to Rienzi than merrily bawling away at the top of his voice for hours on end? Certainly, T. was impressive in this, I told Niemann, but his only real concern was to demonstrate that he was inimitable in the part; purely out of malice he showed Niemann what he was capable of, although Niemann is still young and not such a distinguished singer. I then went on to demonstrate how the role ought to be interpreted in order to meet the challenge that I have set here, instead of the singer's simply solving it by his powers of vocal endurance. I went on to say that if he performed the role with the requisite originality, and according to my own interpretation, he would be able to show Tich. what Rienzi really involves. This is my honest opinion, and I can tell you, too, that T. is far from being my ideal as Rienzi. In a role like this, where his only assets are his vocal stamina and volume of sound, he does me

---

1 In his letter of 2 January 1859 Wagner had asked Liszt to arrange for a consortium of princes, headed by the Grand Dukes of Weimar and Baden, to provide him with an annual pension which would allow him to devote himself in future exclusively to composing new works.

2 The phrase in parentheses was omitted from the published edition: "der Kunst-Actien-Unternehmungen".

incalculable harm, and I am keen to see a more intelligent performer meet this challenge in order to show, at the same time, that T. is not alone in being able to sustain the part. – This suggested a different concept to Niemann; and only now has a date been set for the opera in H. – You may perhaps reproach me to some extent for betraying T. But, my dear child, you must remember that all my life I have been afflicted by the intimacies of these superficial and obstinate people,[1] although in reality we are worlds apart, and that I have always found myself at odds with them. I cannot deny that I set little store by friendships of this nature. His attachment to me touches me: that is why I am ultimately prepared to put up with a great deal from him. –

In general, my long exile has made me fairly touchy as far as Dresden's art-world is concerned. I am beginning to find certain tiresome gossip extremely annoying. So even *Devrient*[2] could find nothing better to say about Tristan than to remark on the long death-scene in the third act? This act, then, is nothing but people popping off? Well, I see a good deal else here, and even the practical aspects of the performance are well thought-out. The woman really belongs in the theatre, to which – as I hear from you with some astonishment – she would like to return. Can she not conceive of art as art, instead of always as theatrical routine?

– Tell Papa Fischer, whoever heard of a poet who has written a drama while in love? It is as though Schiller needed to live with a band of robbers in order to write the "Robbers", or Shakespeare to have been a jealous husband to write "Othello". One cannot write anything that is true to life, more especially in drama, unless one stands apart from it and sees it, as it were, facing one; the poet is incapable of writing clearly if he is in the thick of things. But not everyone can understand this, least of all that the poet, precisely because he is a poet, portrays a world he has never seen, just as Jean Paul described Italy without ever having travelled there. – I still recall how surprised Count Redern was in Berlin when he made my acquaintance after the flying Dutchman: "My God – he said – you're such a friendly, agreeable person; to judge by your opera, I'd have expected a gloomy, sombre and gruff individual." – Oh dear, – I suppose I shall have to listen to a good deal of such nonsense when I start seeing people again! Well, I shall soon grow indifferent to it! For the present I suppose I am somewhat melancholy on the whole; I admit that my secludedness has its disadvantages. In addition, I am never fully fit; my sensitivity continues to increase. My long lack of exercise played havoc with my bowels. [I am again suffering badly from a haemorrhoidal complaint, and in order to deal with it have again attacked my stomach with clysters.][3] Above all I suffer from colds. I have never been so

1 "Flachköpfe und Eigensinne": the published text merely reads "of this kind of person".
2 Wilhelmine Schröder-Devrient.
3 This sentence has not previously been published.

frozen as in Italy. It must be said that my apartment is really intended only for the summer, since it does not see the sun, the bedroom never. It makes my hair stand on end to think of what I have spent on heating these pitiful stoves, so badly insulated are the doors and windows. My hopes remained pinned on an early spring, when I intend to enjoy the apartment properly at long last. But it will then be time for me to move out!! – [...]

RWA (incompletely published in Minna-Briefe II, 30–2).

232. MATHILDE WESENDONCK, ZURICH Venice, 19 January 1859

Thank you, my friend, for your beautiful tale![1] No doubt one can readily explain why everything I receive from you always arrives as though with some symbolic significance. Yesterday of all days, to the very hour and minute, your greetings arrived as though necessarily constrained by some magic charm. I was sitting at the piano; the old, gold pen was spinning its final web over the second act of Tristan and, hesitatingly and lingeringly, was just describing the fleeting joys of my lovers' first tryst. When I am calm at last and can abandon myself to the enjoyment of my own creations, as happens when I am scoring a work, I often sink, at the same time, into an infinity of thoughts which involuntarily represent for me the entirely characteristic and, as far as the world is concerned, perpetually unfathomable nature of the poet or artist. I then perceive quite clearly what it is that is so wonderful and so completely contrary to people's normal view of life, namely the fact that, whereas the world gets by and is held together solely by dint of experience, the poet's intuition precedes all experience and, on the basis of his own unique poten-tiality, comprehends what it is that gives all experience its significance and its meaning. If you were a well-practised philosopher, I should refer you to the fact that what we have here is the best possible example of that same phenomenon which alone makes cognition possible, whereby the entire frame-work of space, time and causality in which the world is represented to us is prefigured in our brain as the latter's most characteristic functions, so that these conditional qualities of all objects, namely their spatiality, temporality and causality, are already contained within our heads before we recognize these objects, since without them we should have no means of recognizing them at all. –

But what is raised above space, time and causality, and what does not require these expedients for us to recognize it, in other words, what is unconditioned by finality, of which Schiller says so memorably that it is

1 *Der fremde Vogel* by Mathilde Wesendonck.

uniquely *true* because it has never *existed*;[1] this is something that can never be grasped by any common philosophy but is perceived by the poet with that same prefiguredness that lies within him, conditioning all that he creates and enabling him to represent this something with infallible certainty, – this something, I say, is more definite and more certain than any other object of our cognition, in spite of the fact that it involves no property of the world as we apprehend it through experience. –

It must inevitably strike him as an absolute miracle when this previously glimpsed, substantial something finally becomes a part of his own experience. His idea of it will then play a large part in his shaping of the experience; the purer and loftier the former, the more remote from the world and the more incomparable will be the latter. It will purify his will; his aesthetic interest will become a moral one; and his supreme poetic idea will be joined by a supreme moral consciousness. It will then be his task to put it to the test in the moral world, where he will be guided by that same foreknowledge which, in the form of his recognition of the aesthetic idea, persuaded him to represent the idea in a work of art, and which made it possible for him to experience it. –

The common world, which is entirely subjected to the influence of experience forced upon it from without, and which can grasp nothing that has not been more or less physically and palpably suggested to it, can never understand the poet's attitude towards the world of his own experience. Such people will never be able to explain to themselves the striking certainty of his creations except by supposing him to have encountered them in his experience with the same immediacy with which they note everything down in their memory.

This is a phenomenon which I have perceived most strikingly in the case of my own works. My poetic conceptions have constantly been so far in advance of my experiences that I can regard my moral education as having been almost entirely determined and brought about by these conceptions. Flying Dutchman, Tannhäuser, Lohengrin, Nibelungs, Wodan, – they were all in my head before they were part of my experience. It will no doubt be easy for you to appreciate the curious relationship in which I now stand to Tristan. I can say so quite openly – since this is a phenomenon that belongs if not to the world then to the votive spirit – : never has an idea so clearly become a part of experience. How far the two were mutually predeterminative is such a strange and subtle question that every ordinary mode of perception will conceive of it only in the most inadequate and distorted form. Now that Savitri – and Parzival – fill my mind with a sense of presentiment and strive

1 Schiller's *An die Freunde* contains the lines "was sich nie und nirgends hat begeben, / das allein veraltet nie" (What has never anywhere come to pass, / That alone never grows old), quoted by Schopenhauer in Para. 51 of *The World as Will and Representation*.

initially to form themselves into a poetic idea – : now, given my artistically completed work, to bend over my Tristan with a sense of calm that thinks in visual images, – now, who can guess what miracle must imbue me as I do so and wrest me from the world so that I can almost think of it as having been overcome? You can guess it, you know it! Yes, and in that you are no doubt alone! –

[. . .]

Mathilde Wesendonck-Briefe 145–8.

233. HANS VON BÜLOW, BERLIN   Venice, 23 January 1859

[. . .] Liszt gave me a sad start to the New Year. I wrote him a whole letter[1] that was aimed solely at Dingelstedt and couched, moreover, in terms that bespoke a certain humour, of a kind that all my friends readily understand, but he misunderstood it and replied to it in such a hurtful way[2] that for a long time neither I nor Karl[3] – who knew the facts very well – could get over our amazement. I did all I could subsequently to help him reach a proper understanding of this letter, for I was most sincerely anxious to rid him of his erroneous belief that I had been mocking him and his delight in Tristan. But he has not yet replied to me; I should be sorry if his pride were to prevent him from admitting at once that he had allowed himself to be misled in such a striking fashion on a decisive point like this as a result of his misunderstanding a friend of his. I do not doubt for a moment, however, that he will see this for himself, and I feel certain that his friendship will last, although I cannot help wishing to see an end to the evil from which our friendship evidently suffers, namely the lack of any real personal contact and dealings between us. I now realize more than ever that I cannot entirely let myself go with Liszt and that I must always exercise a certain caution in my relations with him. My humour is completely foreign to him. –

[. . .]

I am still rather unwell, and am constantly in pain. But I am again working eagerly. Tomorrow I shall be sending part of the second act[4] to Härtels. They will have the whole of it by the end of February. When you get to know it, you will feel what an effort it has required and how rarely I was able to find the hours in my present life to make a success of such a work. I hope you

---

1 Letter [229], pp. 435–6.
2 See Appendix A, p. 937.
3 Karl Ritter.
4 Of *Tristan und Isolde*, the second act of which was completed on 18 March 1859 and sent off to Breitkopf & Härtel the same day.

will be pleased with it. If my daemon allows me to do so, I plan to outlast the third act with the coming spring months of March April May: if I remain undisturbed from without and within, I know that I shall not need much time for something like this. The performance has been provisionally fixed for the 6th of Sept. – the Grand Duke's birthday – in Karlsruhe.[1] Whether I shall have been amnestied by then is open to question, but the G.D. wants me to go there and stay with him at his discretion, but he asks me not to let a word of this leak out *beforehand*, otherwise this bold plan of his will become impossible. I earnestly entreat you to do as he asks. –

My sincere thanks to Cosima for the news she sent to Zurich, and for enclosing your recent letter, which I assume I am to keep? – I have to put up with a good deal of hardship, worry, and various discouraging afflictions, but my work keeps me afloat; and a little high-spiritedness can help me now and then, except when I cause myself renewed harm as a result, as is generally the case.

Remain true to me then, and *never* take anything that I say amiss. It is quite the stupidest thing anyone can do with me. I am much too tender-hearted and sensitive to want to cause anyone serious harm. – Fare you well! A thousand good wishes to Cosima!

Yours,
R.W.

[. . .]

Bülow-Briefe 110–12.

234. ALBERT NIEMANN, HANOVER   Venice, 25 January 1859

My most worthy friend,

This time it has taken me rather longer to get round to answering your kind letter. I am often overwhelmed by such a mass of correspondence that I am obliged to postpone writing letters for which I need to be in the right frame of mind. I am sorry that you took exception to my report of the rumour concerning your alleged fear of "Rienzi". You are quite right to suppose that it is mere actors' gossip; but I knew of no better expedient than to mention the matter to you openly. I hope that this has had the advantage of allowing us to come to a *proper understanding*, so that we may achieve something really original here. Truth to tell, I had already given up *this "Rienzi"* altogether. Thanks to *Tichatscheck's* tremendous vocal achievement – perhaps also (excusably!) thanks to the work itself – the piece had gained the reputation of being

---

1 See letter [223], p. 427, note 1.

a speciality that could be unearthed uniquely and solely by Tichatscheck. Now that I find myself dealing with *you*, the object *itself* has taken on a new lease of life for me, and it gives me pleasure to go through the work once again with you, as far as is feasible by letter.

And so, with regard more especially to the character's chief feature, the following – as already indicated – is to be borne in mind.

Nothing affected Rienzi so deeply in his youth as the brutal killing of his little brother by the soldiers of the *nobili*, against whom he was unable to obtain justice. Starting out from a desire for vengeance, but failing to find satisfaction anywhere, he began to ponder the matter and learned to recognize its causes in the *general* misery of his age and, more especially, of his own fatherland. In order to account for this, he familiarized himself with his country's history; going back from one source to another, he finally reached Roman antiquity and immersed himself enthusiastically in contemplation of the grandeur and greatness of ancient Rome, and, on turning back to the present, became conscious of a tremendous decline, so that, where he had previously brooded only on the reasons for his own unsatisfied vengeance, he now saw the general decay of the entire world, a decay from which he resolved to free it. And so the original motive of "vendetta" became a purified patriotism of visionary sublimity which, once he had suppressed all memory of the injury he himself had suffered, gave him the wonderful power which, for a time, he exercised over his people. – His counterpart is the figure of *Adriano*. In the latter's case it is his enthusiasm which is the starting-point for his actions, an enthusiasm which Rienzi is able to inspire in him on the strength of the young man's love of Irene. But instead of maintaining this enthusiasm, which in Rienzi finally overrides all natural and personal relationships, Adriano sinks back down to the level from which Rienzi had set out in order to rise to his present greatness. "Blood" comes between them, and Adriano cannot rise above the feeling of "vendetta"; he remains ensnared in mere family ties, whereas Rienzi has only the state as a whole in mind, with the result that, fired by his passionate thirst for vengeance and scarcely restrained by his love, Adriano perishes powerless and demented, while Rienzi, launching into the battle hymn, allows himself and the Capitol to be destroyed by an ungrateful and misguided populace. –

Setting aside the remaining brilliance of the stage-picture, this is Rienzi's essential characteristic, and one which must be clearly brought home by the performer.

When Rienzi first appears among the people, it is, as it were, simply as a peace-maker, in all his deeply conscious dignity. He then sees the ladder at the window of his house; a glance at Irene and the *nobili* tells him everything. "And so yet another encroachment upon my family, then it was murder, today an attempted abduction!" Carried away by deadly hatred and almost seething with fury, he acts over-precipitately at the beginning of his recitative against the *nobili*. Entirely spontaneously, however, his injured personal interests quickly expand to embrace his violated fatherland; he grows in stature and becomes ever greater, and with the words: "are you yet Romans?" he stands before the degenerate assembly like the god of vengeance himself. From now on he regains his full sublime calm and dignity. He scornfully dismisses the mockery of the *nobili* and is concerned only to dissuade the people from their ill-considered attack. – The more terribly worked up he is in his first speech to the *nobili*, when he catches sight of the ladder, the more sublime must now be the impression left by his self-assurance and calm, with which he finally invites the people to assemble the next morning at the *sound* of the trumpet's note, to pray for freedom.

He now speaks to Adriano in a mild and serious tone; he is above all prejudice, and rejoices in the possibility of winning over a son of his mortal enemy to his righteous cause, rather than exacting vengeance upon him. But it is precisely *this* which reminds him of the blood that has been spilt: it then *flares* up, more terribly than before. In his account of his brother's death, he reveals to us, as though himself bleeding, the mysterious origins of the demon he has subdued. Let him be terribly moved. The more awful his suffering appears to us here, the quicker we shall recognize Rienzi's entire great, fully purified nature when Adriano asks him: "what shall I do to expiate our shame?" and, suddenly raising himself to his full height, he replies with the inspiriting exhortation: "be mine! be a Roman!" – This must create such a powerful impression that it strikes the youth like a lightning flash, so that he calls out to Rienzi, beside himself with emotion: "let me be a Roman". –

After this rough outline, I shall now single out for you all that relates to this one principal motive. – When the *nobili* (in the 2nd act) trespass against his person and against the freedom of the state, he is assured and firm in dealing with them; no inner reproach clouds his judgement, which he pronounces briefly and grimly. But when he is alone for a moment, his first thought is "my poor brother! not by me but by Rome herself are you now avenged!" And so his desire for personal vengeance has not yet been entirely suppressed, and when *Adriano* rushes in, beside himself, in order to save his father's life, he touches on a spot that Rienzi himself has left uncovered. It is through this feeling that Rienzi is really reformed once more, in order, as it were, to destroy the last remaining seeds of personal vengeance. And so he quickly resolves, at the risk of his own safety, to pardon the *nobili*. – He is now completely stainless. But woe betide them if they relapse! For then he may no longer be the avenging brother but only the avenging godhead! – Thus the third act finds him resolute and unswerving in the face of their repeated betrayal. Here he is of annihilating greatness and terribleness in contrast to Adriano, for, while the latter increasingly forgets Rome, his father-land and freedom simply in order to see his slain father once more, Rienzi now puts all thought of fraternal vengeance behind him and is now fully conscious *in himself* of representing only Rome, his fatherland and freedom.

But Rome, the fatherland and freedom now exist in him and in him alone. The populace itself knows none of this; they stand in a state of half-awareness on the side of Adriano, for they, too, can see only their own brothers and sons who have fallen in battle and for whose deaths they now make Rienzi responsible. His downfall is therefore certain. The great purity that he has now gained and his transfigured majesty help to delay it, but they cannot prevent it from happening. Scarcely has he won over the conspirators outside the church by his all-powerful grandeur and enthusiasm when everyone recoils before him, stupidly and aghast at his excommunication. For he now sees that only his idea was real, not the common people. He remains great and noble, but as rigid as a statue, his gaze fixed firmly in front of him in sublime and rapt contemplation, just like his idea, which has similarly grown petrified like some monument and which the world cannot grasp. But once again the marble melts; Irene throws herself upon his breast. He sees that he is not alone; smiling gently he recognizes his sister and now knows that there is, after all, "a Rome". – In his prayer in the 5th act he communes alone with the God who once spoke to him and who has always spoken to him, of that noble idea. It is, as it were, the "idea" which the whole world has failed to understand that now speaks to itself. Nobility, purity, deeply felt religious fervour, the desire for dissemination, finally to be lost entirely within himself, to be totally self-absorbed: – during the postlude to the prayer, therefore, he should incline his head and whole body towards the ground. –

Final, painfully animated enjoyment of this idea in his scene with Irene. An exalted and sublime joy in the overall mood here. Profound delight in his sister who has renounced her love and thus, like her brother, has enabled the idea to triumph over passion. If, by dint of prudent economy, your vocal powers are undiminished by the time you reach this scene, it is bound to be one of the most enthralling in the whole piece. –

The ending is self-explanatory. –

Whether I have made myself clear, I do not know, but I have certainly warmed to this youthful subject of mine, which only now do I myself properly understand. I hope that I have conveyed this warmth to you; only if you accept it in this spirit will you hit upon the right course, which involves genuine seriousness and profound sympathy with the part, qualities which I could never demand of the good and splendid *Tichatscheck*. – I do not doubt your success. You must then propagate this opera, too.[1]

1 Niemann, already a noted Tannhäuser and Lohengrin, first sang Rienzi in Hanover on 11 December 1859.

My most respectful greetings to your dear *betrothed*,[1] and allow me to assure you of the sincere friendship of

Your own
Richard Wagner

Niemann-Briefe 81–7.

235. ELIZA WILLE, HAMBURG   Venice, 21 February 1859

And so, my dear and honoured friend, I am seeking you out in Hamburg, as you gave me leave to do!

How often have I felt the urge to tell you how much your noble, loyal and thoughtful interest in me constantly fills me with renewed warmth whenever I gaze upon the great desolation of my present and future, and, feeling as though I have been chilled to the bone by freezing fog, look round in search of some sunny spot! It is very difficult to tell you how things stand with me. I am almost obliged to say nothing to those who understand me well, because in addition to my old affliction I then have the new one of increasing their cares about me. For a long time I was very ill;[2] and I must confess that I still consider these periods to have been the happiest of all: my sense of resignation, which is often no more than an ideal, then becomes a humble reality; the knowledge that one *cannot* do a certain thing helps one see that it *must* be so. But the endless pain of this intermediate state, when desire stirs again and each time comes up against the same old obstacle, has a deeply depressing effect upon me. Then work is the only answer. But what work! I feel as though I shall never have done with it; as though I wanted to force death to catch me in the act! Never before have I worked so intimately; every stroke of my pen has the significance of an eternity for me; and I do not continue until I feel attracted by what I have written. It is a strange feeling to survey the thing as a whole and realize that never before have I written anything of such musical unity, of such inexhaustible fluency. Tristan will be beautiful! But it is eating into me. Who knows whether there will be any part of me left? –

And that is now my only amusement! For the rest, I have never before lived such a hermit's life as at present. Venice makes it very easy for me to do so. Right from the outset I declined to make any new acquaintances: and that is how it has remained. In the evening Karl Ritter often comes here. Whenever I dine out at the restaurant, I see a very good-natured and extremely

1 Marie Seebach.
2 See letter [227], p. 431, note 1.

intelligent Russian prince,[1] who has settled here because of me. For the rest, I am frozen stiff in my vast room, I take my morning walk along the *riva* as far as the public park, and spend the evenings from 6 o'clock onwards at home. I have not been to the theatre,[2] and have not even seen the Fenice.

All the more do I live away from here. What a varied life there is out there! I have a pile of correspondence that drives me to distraction. My opera performances abroad melt into insignificance; I no longer feel anything for them. All the more have I been kept busy again by the question of my home in Germany; they want me to stand trial in Dresden, since only in that way may I reckon on being pardoned. I have declared in the strongest possible terms that I shall never do this on any condition, and – as was to be expected – I believe I have now closed my country's doors to me for good.[3] Where shall I settle now? That is the question. I am – very tired, and long for a final haven of rest. I still hope that, if I find it, I shall also be able to offer it to my poor wife. There is said to have been a not unmarked improvement in her state of health, although there can never be any question of a complete recovery (as her doctor[4] has explained to me). I am told that her course of treatment this coming summer in the country outside Dresden will have a decisive effect on what happens next. If only the woman would enable me to look after her there as comfortably as possible! She keeps such sad company, torments herself and me as well, and seems determined never to find any real peace of mind. I continue to look upon her with great and heavy care! –

I do not suppose I need tell you that our friend,[5] that dear child of God, is the sole source of my exaltation and solace. We are now writing to each other quite regularly. Her letters always fall like drops of fragrant springtime showers in the barrenness of my existence. Her poetic soul continues to grow ever richer. She sees and hits upon everything with a thoughtful sagacity that is entirely typical of genius. She is melancholic, but, it seems to me, profoundly calm. What a great comfort that is to me. – Yes, my friend! It is love! – If I complain to her too candidly, she is almost beside herself with joy at the prospect of being able to console me. Yes! Indeed! she shall have much joy of me yet! – And – She deserves it; believe me! –

A short time ago the Saxon government tried to have me extradited. I had to resort to the expedient of a medical certificate in order to be able to extend my stay here. I should like to delay any new interruption to my work until I

1 Peter Vladimirovich Dolgorukov or Dolgoruki. The restaurant in question was the Albergo San Marco.
2 At least not since September 1858, when Wagner had been to the theatre on at least three occasions.
3 See introductory essay, p. 411.
4 Anton Pusinelli.
5 Mathilde Wesendonck.

have completed the last act of Tristan in outline. But I do not think I shall manage to do so before the end of May.[1] I pray to God that I remain undisturbed until then. Where next? To Switzerland, at all events: I must have mountain air again. Perhaps to Lucerne. If I were not afraid of the wicked doctor,[2] I should come straight to you and finish off Tristan for good and all in Frau von Bissing's room. What would your sister say to that? If war is declared,[3] I shall leave somewhat sooner: I have not the least inclination to become involved in Italian freedom. My final refuge will no doubt be Paris. I feel as though I cannot escape the absurd fate of dying there. For I have come to the end of the road with Germany.

Well, my dear friend! here you have a little pile of news from me. May I hope for a reply from you and for a report on your own activities? Are all of you assembled in the paternal home? And how goes it with those loyal and clear bright eyes that always seem to want to cause you pain? Do wish them a full recovery on my behalf. And a thousand good wishes from Venice to your sons. And if you write to Wille, tell him that I am really not as bad as all that! Perhaps he will believe you! And many sincere greetings to the entire household! In eternal and heartfelt gratitude I remain

Your Richard Wagner.

Fehr II, 411–13.

236. KARL KLINDWORTH, LONDON   Venice, 4 March 1859

My dear Klindworth,

I am to go to New York for 5 months next winter. German elite opera. Performances of my operas. They seem to want to pay well. I am gradually taking a more serious view of the matter, and have submitted my conditions, one of the chief of which is that apart from me – who will conduct *only* my own operas – *you* yourself are to be appointed as second conductor on 10,000 francs = 2000 dollars for the five months.[4]

Think it over and let me know whether you would accept if they agree. The crossing – 1st class – is free, and one month's salary will be paid in advance in Europe. For the rest of our wages, I shall insist upon their being

---

1 Wagner began the first complete draft of Act III on 9 April (see also letter [207], p. 379, note 2). He left Venice on 24 March, and arrived in Lucerne on the 28th.
2 François Wille.
3 Cavour's avowed desire to expel Austria and form a North Italian kingdom had gained in urgency following Victor Emmanuel's memorable words, on opening the Piedmontese parliament on 10 January 1859, that he could not remain insensible to the *grido di dolore* which reached him from all parts of Italy.
4 Nothing came of these plans.

deposited with a firm with which I am on friendly terms in New York. You could save at least 5 to 6000 francs; but, in addition to that, you could establish a position for yourself which would at least be more profitable than the one you have in London.

I should enjoy working together with you; and even the journey would be more tolerable. If this central issue can be settled, I shall genuinely look forward to accepting the business.

Write soon.

Keep the orchestral sketches to Siegfried[1] for the time being. I am leaving Venice at the end of this month. I shall tell you beforehand exactly where I am going and shall then ask for the sketches to be sent on to me. Give me a good excuse for writing to you by letting me have an affirmative answer.

Best wishes from

Your very letter-weary
Rich. Wagner.

Freunde und Zeitgenossen 248–9.

237. MINNA WAGNER, DRESDEN   Venice, 23 March 1859

[...] I have now declined the *Ritters'* subsidies once and for all. I learned from Karl, having been prompted to make enquiries following hints from you, that during the last war the Ritters suffered serious losses to the money that they had invested in Russia, and that Frau Ritter had not informed me of her difficulties only because it was precisely then that the quarrel with Karl had arisen[2] and because she wished at all costs to avoid giving the impression that that was the reason why the subsidy had ended. This was sufficient to persuade me to address myself to Frau Ritter last November[3] and assure her that my prospects for the coming year and for my future in general were so good that it would be unjust of me to lay any further claim on her money. I accompanied this with a word of sincere and genuinely heartfelt recognition of her uncommon generosity, for which I should never be able to thank her enough, etc. She was very moved by this and thanked me so warmly for my "kindness" and "delicacy" that I may regard the ending of this relationship as almost more beautiful than its beginning. She is an extraordinary woman, and the whole family, for all its peculiarities, remains a great and welcome exception. Do give them all my very best wishes today!

[...]

Minna-Briefe II, 62.

1 Klindworth was arranging *Siegfried* for the piano.
2 See letter [194], p. 360, note 4.
3 Letter [226], pp. 430–31.

238. MATHILDE WESENDONCK, ZURICH   [Lucerne, mid-April 1859]

Child! This Tristan is turning into something *terrible*!
    This final act!!! – – – – – – –
    I fear the opera will be banned – unless the whole thing is parodied in a
bad performance – : only mediocre performances can save me! Perfectly *good*
ones will be bound to drive people mad, – I cannot imagine it otherwise.
This is how far I have gone!! Oh dear! –
    I was just in full career!
                    Adieu!

                                                        R.W.

Mathilde Wesendonck-Briefe 169–70.

239. MINNA WAGNER, DRESDEN   Lucerne, 18 April 1859

[. . .] In this context, my dearest Minna, I have some news for you which I
hope will not be entirely unwelcome. Listen! I have long felt that it was
important to put a forceful and decisive end to the mischief that has been
caused by certain idle tongues, affecting the honour of many of the parties
concerned, including of course your own, and started, admittedly, by my own
conspicuous departure from Zurich. I was glad that the possibility of doing
so was gradually opened up to me. Last autumn Wesendonck informed me
of his Guido's death in a very touching letter; I answered him in kind, and
since that time we have written to each other on occasion, and always in a
friendly tone. However, it was none of this that persuaded me to settle in
Lucerne, indeed, I was planning not to go near Zurich, in spite of the fact
that I had mentioned to the Heims that I might visit them this summer. But
then, a few days ago, I received an invitation from Wesendonck; I was to stay
at his house, he would send his carriage to the station, and he gave me to
understand that he was anxious to put an end to all these exaggerated and
distorted reports by means of his open and friendly dealings with me. And
so I accepted, travelled to Zurich last Saturday,[1] got into Wesendonck's
carriage, spent the night at his house, and returned on Sunday afternoon,
having driven that morning, again in W.'s carriage, to the Zeltweg, where I
visited the Heims on my own. This was, as we both hope, a very salutary
demonstration, and everyone will of course infer from it my present standing
with this family; the servants are naturally all very impressed. He was very
pleased and happy, and I, no less, have been relieved of a great source of

1 The 15th. In fact Wagner had already visited Mathilde Wesendonck on 3 April. He returned,
  at Otto's invitation, on the 15th and this time stayed the night.

embarrassment. You, too, I hope, will draw from all this the same conclusions as have helped to reassure Wesendonck. Before I leave Switzerland altogether, I think I shall accept a further invitation to go there, when a larger gathering is to be held.[1] –

I do not suppose that I need tell you that this will not make the least difference to my own or to our mutual arrangements for the future. Everything remains just as we agreed. However, what is behind me – & behind you, too, I hope – is now all clear, and bright and plain for all to see, and there are no longer any mists & clouds to be dispersed. –

[. . .]

Minna-Briefe II, 74–5.

240. MATHILDE WESENDONCK, ZURICH   [Lucerne, 26 April 1859]

[. . .] On the whole I am feeling somewhat dull-witted and morose. I have been engaged on this work too long, and I feel very much as though my creative powers are still feeding on the shoots and blossoms which were produced over a short period as though by some fructifying storm. As a result I cannot really get down to any truly creative work; the longer it takes, the more favourable my mood must remain if my inner resources are to be kept alert, and these moods cannot be provoked at will on the strength of mere reflection, as so much else can, especially in relation to the world. It is true that I work every day, but only briefly and there is little to show for it, just as the flashes of inspiration are brief and few in number; often I would prefer to do nothing at all, were it not that I am spurred on by my dread of a totally empty day.

[. . .]

Mathilde Wesendonck-Briefe 175.

241. FRANZ LISZT, LÖWENBERG   Lucerne, 8 May 1859

I should really prefer not to write to you today, my dearest Franz, since I am not in the mood for it. But since it is impossible to think of work, I may as well attempt *some* kind of activity, although I do not know what the result will be. If you were suddenly to enter my solitude, it would be my only chance of finding even the possibility of such a possibility. However, it seems as

---

1 Wagner later stayed with the Wesendoncks on 16/17 May and between 6 and 10 September 1859. See Fehr II,162–76.

though you have already disposed of your summer, so that Löwenberg and Leipzig have come out of it very well, while the third L (Lucerne) has been totally forgotten. Well, I'm stuck here in Lucerne, and, looked at closely, it is the only place in the world where I can possibly stay at present. That this is no "life" that I am living, you already know, or can imagine; the only thing that could help, art, art to the point of drowning and forgetting the world, – well, I have even less of that than I do of life, and this, moreover, has been going on for quite some time, so that I shall soon be counting it in decades! Apart from the servants, I see and speak to no one. Just think occasionally how I must feel. – Children! Children! I fear I have been left in the lurch far too long, and that you will suddenly be made to feel that, in my case, it is "too late". People are now saying to me: "Finish Tristan, then we shall see!" – That is all very well. But what would happen if I were not to finish Tristan, because I could not finish it? I feel as though I am now about to pine away finally and collapse within sight of my – goal (?). At least I look at my book once a day with a right good will, but my head remains confused, my heart empty, and I stare outside at the mists and rain-clouds which, ever since my arrival here, have prevented me from enjoying even the prospect of stirring up my lifeless blood by means of a few refreshing excursions. And so people say: – well, why don't you work, then things will get going again! Admirable advice; but, poor devil that I am, I have absolutely no routine, and if things do not happen of their own accord, I cannot make them happen. A delightful state of affairs! And, at the same time, absolutely no chance of helping myself in any other way. Everything barred and bolted! Only work is said to help me: but what will help me to be able to work? – Clearly I have too little of what you have too much! –

Oh, what enthusiasm I feel for the German Confederation of the Germanic Nation! For God's sake do not let that criminal L. Napoleon get his hands on my dear German Confederation:[1] I should be too deeply distressed if there were any changes here! – For the rest, I am curious to know what will become of my projected move to Paris. It is after all terribly unpatriotic of me to want to make myself at home in the principal haunt of the enemy of the Germanic Nation. The good Germans really ought to do something to spare their most Germanic of all Germanic opera composers from this grim ordeal. – In addition, I may find myself pretty well completely cut off in Paris from my German resources; and yet, once in Paris, I shall be in a position to appeal to the very highest quarter in order to ensure my permanent settlement there, for my stay in Switzerland is of course coming to an end. So Germany is bent on driving me into the arms of her enemy! That too, is all right by

---

1 On 3 May 1859 Napoleon III had declared his intention of making Italy "free from the Alps to the Adriatic". His Italian expedition was brought to a rapid conclusion by the Peace of Villafranca signed on 9 July and forced upon him by the allied states of Austria and the German Confederation.

me!! – But there is now also the possibility that I shall go to America for six months in the autumn, since I have received offers from there which, in view of the German Confederation's present interest in me, I cannot reasonably ignore. This ought to be decided before long.[1] What makes me hesitate is the fact that it would interfere with my plan for Tristan in Karlsruhe, because I would have to abandon it for the present and would probably never again take it up again at any future date. Having reached the last act of this child of sorrow, I am at the very brink of "to be or not to be"[2] – slight pressure on some spring of common chance, to which I am so pitilessly exposed, and this child may perish in the final throes of birth. With me everything can change in the twinkling of an eye; I may go on, or I may come to a complete standstill. For you see, Franz, I am in a bad way! –

I have heard nothing from any of my friends for a long time; no doubt they all assume I am perfectly happy in my beloved Switzerland, in such splendid solitude, oblivious to the world in the joy of composing. –

I do not blame them for deluding themselves in this way. But if only they knew that it was I who had to point a pistol at your head in order to get you to send me the Dante[3] you had dedicated to me, they would have grounds for concluding that all was not as it seemed. What do you say to that? – And so I find myself talking about Dante after all, although I had absolutely no desire to speak of it today, since I care for it too much to implicate it in my present mood. But I do want to say at least this, that we had better keep to ourselves the words of dedication[4] which you wrote in my copy; I, at least, shall not divulge them to a living soul. They have made me positively blush for shame, believe me! I cannot tell you forcibly enough how pitiful I feel as a musician; from the bottom of my heart I consider myself an absolute bungler. You ought to see me sitting here on occasion, thinking to myself, "that will do" – and then going over to the piano to put together some miserable rubbish which I am then stupid enough to abandon. Can you imagine what I feel then – ! It is the sincere conviction that I am musically worthless! And now *you* come along exuding music from every pore in streams, springs and waterfalls, – and I have to listen while you say things like this to me. I find it very difficult to believe that this is not the purest irony, and I have to recall your friendship for me very clearly and very fully in order to convince myself that it was not your wish simply to make fun of me. – My

1 See letter [236], pp. 450–51.
2 Quoted in English in the original.
3 *Eine Symphonie zu Dantes Divina Commedia.*
4 "As Virgil guided Dante, so have you guided me through the mysterious regions of those worlds of sound that are steeped in life. – / From my innermost heart I call out to you: / 'Tu se lo mio maestro, e il mio autore!' / and dedicate this work to you in steadfast loyal love" (Liszt-Briefe II, 264). The score of Liszt's symphonic poem *Hamlet* (autograph dated June 1858) contains some marked resemblances to that of *Tristan und Isolde*; see also introductory essay, p. 409.

dearest friend, it is an odd story, but, believe me, I am worth very little. I do now believe quite genuinely that Reissiger helped me with Tannhäuser and Lohengrin. And *you* have certainly helped me on my new works; but now that you leave me in the lurch, I can write no more.

Of Dante only this much today, that my chief pleasure was to discover how perfect a memory I had retained of it, from your first playing it to me. Now that I have studied it in more detail I see that not a single important feature had escaped me; indeed, it is as though the smallest and finest detail had remained entirely familiar from that first hearing; I might almost regard it as pleasing evidence of my receptive faculties; but I think the credit is due to the characteristic greatness and properties of your work.

[...]

For the present I am squandering all the good humour I can summon up on my wife! I pamper her and look after her as though she were a honeymoon bride. By way of compensation I have the satisfaction of knowing that she is getting on well; her health has improved visibly, she is convalescing and I hope she may even acquire a little sense in her old age; I recently wrote to her, shortly after I had received your Dante, to tell her that we had passed through *Hell*; that I hoped that *Purgatory* would do her good, and that we may finally, perhaps, enjoy a little *Paradise*. It is all quite splendid! – Now give my kind regards to the Prince of Löwenberg or whatever he is called, and tell him that if the German Confederation does not recall me soon, I shall go to Paris and betray the length and breadth of Germany!

God be with you! You will, I hope, forgive me this insane letter!

Ever yours,
R.W.

Liszt-Briefe II, 264–8.

242. MATHILDE WESENDONCK, ZURICH   Lucerne, 30 May 1859

[...] I am now engaged in working out the first half of the act.[1] The passages which describe suffering always hold me up a great deal; at best I can only ever complete a very little at a single sitting. The fresh, lively and fiery sections then go incomparably faster; and so, even during the technical working out, I live through every moment "in suffering and in joy",[2] and become entirely dependent upon the object in hand. This last act is now a

---

1 Act III of *Tristan und Isolde*; see also letter [207], p. 379, note 2.
2 "Leidvoll und freudvoll", the opening words of Klärchen's song from Act III, Scene 2 of Goethe's *Egmont*; it ends with the words, "Happy alone / Is the soul that loves".

real intermittent fever: – the deepest and most unprecedented suffering and yearning, and, immediately afterwards, the most unprecedented triumph and jubilation. God knows, no one has ever taken the matter so seriously before, and Semper is right. It is this thought that has most recently turned me against Parzival again. You see, it has again dawned upon me of late that this would again be a fundamentally evil task. Looked at closely, it is *Anfortas*[1] who is the centre of attention and principal subject. Of course, it is not at all a bad story. Consider, in heaven's name, all that goes on there! It suddenly became dreadfully clear to me: it is my third-act Tristan inconceivably intensified. With the spear-wound and perhaps another wound, too, – in his heart – , the wretched man knows of no other longing in his terrible pain than the longing to die; in order to attain this supreme solace, he demands repeatedly to be allowed a glimpse of the Grail in the hope that it might at least close his wounds, for everything else is useless, nothing – nothing can help him: – but the Grail can give him one thing only, which is precisely that he *cannot* die; its very sight increases his torments by conferring immortality upon them. The Grail, according to my *own* interpretation is the goblet used at the Last Supper in which Joseph of Arimathea caught the Saviour's blood on the Cross. What terrible significance the connection between Anfortas and this miraculous chalice now acquires; *he*, infected by the same wound as was dealt him by a rival's spear in a passionate love intrigue, – his only solace lies in the benediction of the blood that once flowed from the Saviour's own, similar, spear-wound as He languished upon the Cross, world-renouncing, world-redeeming and world-suffering! Blood for blood, wound for wound – but what a gulf between the blood of the one and that of the other, between the one wound and the other! Wholly enraptured, he is all devotion and all ecstasy at the miraculous proximity of the chalice which glows red in its gentle, blissful radiance, pouring out new life – so that death cannot come near him! He lives, lives anew, and more terribly than ever the sinful wound flares up in him – *His* wound! His very devotions become a torment! Where is the end to it, where is redemption? The sufferings of humanity endlessly drawn out! – Would he, in the madness of his despair, wish to turn away for ever from the Grail and close his eyes to it? He would fain do so in order to die. But – he himself was appointed guardian of the Grail; and it was no blind, superficial power which appointed him, – no! it was because he was so worthy, because there was no one who knew the Grail's miraculous nature as profoundly and as intimately as he knew it, just as his whole soul now yearns, again and

---

1 The forms Anfortas and Amfortas coexist in the manuscript tradition of Wolfram's *Parzivâl*. Wagner later settled on the second alternative and shifted the stress from the first to the second syllable. On the orthography of Parzival, see letter [221], p. 424, note 1.

again, to behold the vision that destroys him in the very act of worship, vouchsafing heavenly salvation and eternal damnation! –

And you expect me to carry through something like this? and set it to music, into the bargain? – No thank you very much! I leave that to anyone who has a mind for such things; *I* shall do all I can to keep my distance from it! –

Let someone do it who will carry it through à la Wolfram; it will then cause little offence, and in the end may perhaps sound like something, maybe even something quite pretty. But *I* take such things far too seriously. Yet just look at the extent to which Master Wolfram has made light of it, by contrast! That he has understood absolutely nothing of the actual content is of no great matter. He tacks one event on to the next, one adventure to another, links together the Grail motif with all manner of strange and curious episodes and images, gropes around and leaves any serious reader wondering whatever his intention can have been? To which he is bound to reply that he himself in fact knows no more about what he is doing than the priest understands the Christianity that he serves up at the altar without knowing what is involved. – That's how it is. Wolfram is a thoroughly immature phenomenon, although it must be said that his barbaric and utterly confused age is largely to blame for this, fluctuating as it did between early Christianity and a more modern political economy. Nothing could ever come to fruition at such a period; poetic profundity was immediately submerged in insubstantial caprice. I almost agree now with Frederick the Great who, on being presented with a copy of Wolfram, told the publisher not to bother him with such stuff![1] – Indeed, it is sufficient to have given new life to such a subject on the basis of the genuine features of the legend, as I have now done with this Grail legend, and then to take a quick look at how such a poet as Wolfram has depicted the very same thing – as I have now done by leafing through your book[2] – in order to be utterly repelled by the poet's incompetence. (The same thing happened to me with Gottfried v. Strassburg in the context of Tristan). Consider only this one point, that, of all the interpretations to which the Grail has been subjected in the various legends, this superficial "deep thinker" should have chosen the most meaningless of all. That this miraculous object should be a precious stone is a feature which, admittedly, can be traced back

---

1 Wagner appears to have remembered the anecdote incorrectly, inasmuch as it was medieval texts in general rather than Wolfram's *Parzivâl* specifically of which Frederick was so dismissive: on 22 January 1784 he wrote to the publisher C. H. Myller telling him that the medieval works which he had published were "not worth a rap and do not deserve to be dragged up from the dust of oblivion" (quoted in *Der grosse König: Friedrich der Einzige in seinen Werken, Briefen, Erlassen und Berichten seiner Zeitgenossen*, edited by Heinrich Schierbaum [Bielefeld/Leipzig 1920], 119).

2 A copy of Wolfram's *Parzivâl* which Mathilde Wesendonck had sent Wagner in the second (1858) edition of San-Marte (Albert Schulz).

to the earliest sources, namely the Arabic texts of the Spanish Moors.[1] One notices, unfortunately, that all our Christian legends have a foreign, pagan origin. As they gazed on in amazement, the early Christians learned, namely, that the Moors in the Caaba at Mecca (deriving from the pre-Muhammadan religion) venerated a miraculous stone (a sunstone – or meteoric stone – but at all events one that had fallen from heaven). However, the legends of its miraculous power were soon interpreted by the Christians after their *own* fashion, by their associating the sacred object with Christian myth, a process which, in turn, was made easier by the fact that an old legend existed in southern France telling how Joseph of Arimathea had once fled there with the sacred chalice that had been used at the Last Supper, a version entirely consonant with the early Christian Church's enthusiasm for relics. Only now did sense and reason enter into it, and I feel a very real admiration and sense of rapture at this splendid feature of Christian mythogenesis, which invented the most profound symbol that could ever have been invented as the content of the physical-spiritual kernel of any religion. Who does not shudder with a sense of the most touching and sublime emotion to hear that this same goblet, from which the Saviour drank a last farewell to His disciples and in which the Redeemer's indestructible blood was caught and preserved, still exists, and that he who is pure in heart is destined to behold it and worship it himself. Incomparable! And then the double significance of this one vessel which also served as a chalice at the Last Supper – , without doubt the most beautiful sacrament of Christian worship! Whence, also, the legend that the Grail (Sang Réal)[2] (whence San(ct) Gral) alone sustains the pious knights, vouchsafing them food and drink for their repasts. – And all of this has been so senselessly misinterpreted by our poet, who took only the inferior French chivalric romances as his subject-matter and repeated them like a parrot! You can infer from this what the rest must be like! Only individual descriptions are in any way attractive, but this is the forte of all medieval poets, for whom the predominant mood is a finely felt pictoriality. But each work *as a whole* always remains confused and silly. I would have to make a completely fresh start with Parzival! For Wolfram hadn't the first idea of what he was doing: his[3] despair in God is stupid and unmotivated, and his conversion is even more unsatisfactory. The thing about the "question" is that it is *so* utterly preposterous and totally meaningless.[4] I should simply have to invent everything here. And then there is a further difficulty with Parzival. He is indispensably necessary as the redeemer whom Anfortas longs for: but if Anfortas is to be placed in his true and appropriate light, he will become of such immense

1 On the origins of the Grail see, for example, Konrad Burdach, *Der Gral* (Stuttgart 1938, R1974).
2 lit. "royal blood", an etymology which Wagner owed, indirectly, to Malory.
3 i.e. Parzivâl's.
4 In Wolfram's *Parzivâl* the hero is required to ask the question, "What ails thee, uncle?"

tragic interest that it will be almost impossible to introduce a second focus
of attention, and yet this focus of attention must centre upon Parzival if the
latter is not simply to enter at the end as a deus ex machina who leaves us
completely cold. Thus Parzival's development and the profound sublimity of
his purification, although entirely predestined by his thoughtful and deeply
compassionate nature, must again be brought into the foreground. But I
cannot choose to work on such a broad scale as Wolfram was able to do: I
have to compress everything into *three* climactic situations of violent intensity,
so that the work's profound and ramified content emerges clearly and
distinctly; for *my* art consists in working and representing things in *this* way.
And – am I to undertake such a task? God forbid! Today I take my leave of
this insane project; Geibel can write about it and Liszt can compose it! –
When my old friend Brünnhilde leaps into the funeral pyre, I shall plunge in
after her, and hope to die a Christian! So be it! Amen!
  [. . .]

Mathilde Wesendonck-Briefe 190–5.

243. MATHILDE WESENDONCK, ZURICH   Lucerne, 24 August 1859

But child, whatever possesses you to think of me as a "philosopher", or even
to wish to do so? Am I not after all the stupidest person imaginable? Judged
by the standards of a wise man, I must straightway seem criminal, simply
because I know so much and so many things, and, more especially, know that
wisdom is so desirable and so wholly admirable. But this, in turn, gives me
my characteristic ability to leap over abysses which the wisest of men are not
even aware of. That is why I am a poet, and – what's worse – a musician.
Just consider my music, with its delicate, oh so delicate, mysteriously flowing
humours[1] penetrating the most subtle pores of feeling to reach the very
marrow of life, where it overwhelms everything that looks like sagacity and
the self-interested powers of self-preservation, sweeping away all that belongs
to the delusive madness of personality and leaving only that wondrously
sublime sigh with which we confess to our sense of powerlessness – : how
shall *I* be a wise man when it is only in such a state of raving madness that
I am totally at home?
  [. . .]

Mathilde Wesendonck-Briefe 216–17.

1 Used here in the sense of the cardinal humours or temperaments.

244. OTTO WESENDONCK, ZURICH   Lucerne, 24 August 1859

My dearest friend, for God's sake do not interpret it as an insult if I entreat you to take back the money[1] you have offered me! –

I cannot, in all honesty, accept a loan when I know my own situation and constitution as well as I do, and that neither of them can ever be expected to change.

Even less can I accept a gift, and this, you may rest assured, from *no one*, not just because it is you, to whom I already owe so many notable sacrifices.

Please accept my warmest thanks for your kind sentiment and my most sincere good wishes.

Yours,
Richard Wagner.

Otto Wesendonck-Briefe 53–4.

245. OTTO WESENDONCK, ZURICH   Lucerne, 28 August 1859

My dearest friend,

Can we not do *business* together?

You know that I have so far been unable to ask anything more of Härtels for the publication of my Nibelungs than a declaration of their willingness to assume responsibility for producing the edition, together with the offer to share with me any profits that may result from its sale. Six months ago I enquired whether the Grand Duke of Weimar was interested in acquiring the publishing rights of my scores: he was to pay the same for each of the scores as Härtels had agreed to pay me for Tristan[2] and, in return, he, for his part, would acquire my rights to a financial share in the edition. In response to this enquiry, I received a carping and evasive reply (which Liszt attributed to Dingelstedt's influence), and so I let the matter rest.

However, the possibility of being paid a fee for these scores is now of such pressing importance, and my inclination to complete the whole work now depends so much upon my receiving the encouragement to do so in the form of some outside interest in this work that, in my present mood of cheerful confidence, the thought has occurred to me to address to you today the same offer that Weimar has rejected.

Let me begin by mentioning briefly all that can be said in favour of such an arrangement – quite apart from the friendly relations between us without

---

1 Following the breakdown of negotiations with Breitkopf & Härtel over the publication of the *Ring*, Otto Wesendonck had offered Wagner a loan to enable him to complete the tetralogy.
2 200 louis d'or.

which the deal could not of course be brought about. As soon as the performance has taken place and the possibility has emerged that the work will be
taken up elsewhere, Härtels would not hesitate for a moment to offer me the
fee I have demanded for its publication. But I cannot expect them, purely as
businessmen, to regard all the difficulties which stand in the way of a
successful outcome to this venture, as having already been surmounted. None
the less, I know for certain that I shall surmount them all, and the forthcoming
production of Tristan[1] is the first step in that direction. My attitude towards
this work shall be exactly the same as towards all my other works: I shall do
all I can to ensure the success of the first performance, but after that I shall
trouble myself no further with it, but abandon it to other theatres in the
confident expectation that they will begin with the most popular pieces, such
as young Siegfried, and gradually prepare all the others, a process in which
they will be helped by their intensely national subject-matter. Quite apart
from this later increase in popularity, however, I cannot think of a first
performance as being in any way possible except in circumstances that attract
the eyes and interest of the entire world to this work such that its success
and, consequently, the sale of the edition will bear no relation to anything
previously seen in this field.

Since, moreover, I have paid only scant attention to the present age in
writing this work, but am appealing rather to the next generation and to
posterity (and certainly with more justification than anyone before me), it
follows that, if I had children and were additionally able to afford it, I should
certainly not part with this work except on condition that I received a share
in its proceeds. Thus, if I surrender my rights to a third party who has not
only the means to afford to await a gradual and perhaps long-delayed success
but also heirs who might benefit from that success, I believe I may enter into
an acceptable relationship with the intended third party. I can of course draw
the other person's attention to the chances of long-term profits offered by
his ownership of such works; within the last few days I have come across
confirmation of this in the fact that the fortune which Schiller left to his heirs
consisted solely in the continuing profits from his own works, which even
today still provide his successors with a handsome income.

– These are the considerations which persuade me, in the case of my
present offer to you, to emphasize the beneficial nature of this proffered sale,
even if it be one that becomes profitable only with the passage of time. If you
accept my proposal, I shall enjoy the satisfaction of knowing that I have made
you an honest offer, however unfavourable the circumstances may initially
seem, and, even as I lie dying, I shall be conscious of the fact that, although

1 Negotiations with Karlsruhe broke down in the second half of October 1859 because –
Wagner believed (BB 131; English trans. 110) – King Johann of Saxony had exerted pressure
upon the Grand Duke of Baden not to sponsor the work. Contemporary gossip blamed the
"unperformability" of the piece.

it may not be the case by then, the capital that you have invested will return to you or your family not only with interest but also, perhaps, with a corresponding profit.

None the less, I can speak here only of my *own* personal satisfaction. The fact that, for your own part, quite different motives must be involved in persuading you to agree to such a hazardous transaction is something that I understand better than anyone need tell me; and here I hope it will be sufficient for me to assure you that I should have no difficulty in valuing your acceptance at its true worth. – The favourable outcome of your agreeing to this proposal would be most heartening for me. I should then find myself in a position that would encourage me in my future work, a position I believed (in silent despair – as you can well imagine!) I had to work to achieve for myself by means of the American adventure we discussed,[1] – in other words: I could set aside all forthcoming theatre receipts for some time to come and thus know that my future was progressively assured in advance. But the most cheering aspect of this whole affair would be to know that this pleasure would derive directly from a work to which I could now devote myself uninterruptedly and undistractedly. No other course could offer me this same benefit, especially now that I am firmly resolved to accept no further resources other than those that result from my own labours, just as I have no longer been accepting the Ritters' annuity for some time now (I mention this only in passing), in spite of the most moving protests on the part of my noble friends.[2]

If you wished to accept my offer, I should insist upon a legally binding deed of sale, somewhat along the lines of the accompanying draft. In fixing the price of each score, I have referred to what I am receiving from Härtels for Tristan. They are paying me 200 louis d'or for the score now, and have assigned to me a share in the proceeds of up to an additional 100 louis d'or, so that, bearing in mind the fact that I am surrendering my copyright in perpetuity, I would stipulate 300 louis d'or, or rather 6000 francs, for each score. Accordingly, you would have to pay me 12,000 fr. immediately for the two completed works, 1., the Rhinegold. 2., the Valkyrie, a further 6000 fr. on completion of "Young Siegfried", and a similar amount on completion of the last of the 4 pieces. – Moreover, once your copyright had been established, the finished scores would be handed over to Härtels as soon as possible (say, after the appearance of Tristan), so that the task of engraving and publishing them can then be taken in hand. As you know, I set great store by this edition, and the fact that it will take such a long time is yet another reason why your acceptance of my offer would be so welcome to me, since I should otherwise consider it necessary to hesitate before handing over the scores to Härtels. It

1 See letter [236], pp. 450–51.
2 See letter [226], pp. 430–31 and [237], p. 451.

goes without saying that I shall assume responsibility, in your name, for whatever steps need to be taken with the publishers in this respect. –

Let me know what you think of this proposal, which I refuse to regard on this occasion as a request or favour.

When I consider the sacrifices you have already made in order to encourage me and my works, I believe I am right in thinking that it is not expecting too much either of your means or of your kindness towards me. The only thing that makes me hesitate is the fact that, as a result of your earlier sacrifices, you have already acquired a right to my works: and this – I really cannot deny, but would have to throw myself on your mercy.

I look forward to your early reply and assure you, whatever happens, of my most sincere and appreciative thanks.

Yours,
Richard Wagner.

Draft.

1. Herr Rich. Wagner hereby surrenders to Herr Otto Wesendonck in perpetuity the copyright of the stage festival play: the Ring of the Nibelung, written and composed by the first-named party and consisting of the following four pieces 1., The Rhinegold. 2., The Valkyrie. 3., The Young Siegfried. 4., Siegfried's Death, such that Herr Ot. Wes., his heirs and other assignees shall be granted all fees and profits in perpetuity which shall accrue to the author under the terms of an agreement to be signed with the publishers of the said works for the publication and reproduction of the same whether engraved or printed.

The author himself shall retain only such revenues as shall result from public performances of the said works.

2. In return for the surrender of the copyright, Herr O.W. shall pay to R.W. the sum of 24,000 fr., in instalments of 6000 fr. for each completed 4th part of the total work.

Separate receipts for the payments received are attached.[1]

Otto Wesendonck-Briefe 54–9.

246. MINNA WAGNER, DRESDEN   Paris, 19 September 1859

My good old Mutz,[2]

Everything finally looks more certain, and I now have a more secure hold on fate. You must accustom yourself to the idea of coming with me to Paris

1 The contract was signed on 7 September while Wagner was in Zurich, and the first instalment of 6000 francs was paid to him in cash the following day.
2 See letter [188], p. 350, note 2.

from Karlsruhe, for I now see increasingly clearly that we must live here for at least a few years in order for me to lay the foundations for our whole future, foundations which I can establish in no other way than this. This much at least is certain, that I now need to remain in Paris for an uninterrupted period in order to ensure that my operas are performed here within the near future. The Théâtre lyrique[1] seems destined by Providence to pave the way for me here: the operas of Mozart and Weber are performed there, with great success, before a select audience, and the charlatanism that is typical of Paris is almost entirely absent there. The director is a well-educated, pleasant and noble-hearted man, and totally independent; he was already waiting for me here in order that the two of us may reach a serious and definitive agreement. There is talk of starting with Tannhäuser, and for good reason: show-pieces like Rienzi belong in the *Grand* Opera, and once we have gained our first success, this other work will follow as a matter of course. All the French people who have travelled in Germany know only Tannhäuser, but they all rave about it, precisely because it is so new and so unusual, and whenever my name is mentioned in Paris now, it is in the same breath as "Tannhäuser". There are still great difficulties in the way of Rienzi, and these can be removed only when Tannhäuser has proved a success. I, too, prefer to start with Tannhäuser. After all, I still remember all too clearly what happened in Berlin 12 years ago when I thought I could force the issue better with Rienzi; Franck[2] and many other people were quite right to reproach me for not having insisted upon Tannh. since this work is more original and makes me appear as an exceptional figure, whereas Rienzi does not really meet the specific expectations of me that have now been roused in people. –

My first priority has been to take in hand the necessary arrangements for a good translation. I can see that I shall have an incredible amount of work to do here: no Frenchman can do it on his own; and absolutely no one has helped me, rather have my commissions been carried out badly or not at all. There is no one who can be relied on, unless I myself take energetic action; and that is why it is now a question of remaining in Paris, at least for a few years. And so I have instructed my translator[3] to come to my house every morning, in order for me to work on the text with him, line by line: only in that way can we achieve anything. This translation, however, is the most important thing initially; only when it has turned out a success can a proper start be made on the rest. Yet even as things stand, I may still hope for a

1 The Théâtre Lyrique was the most important rival company to the Opéra and Opéra-Comique from its inception in 1851 until around 1870. Its director from 1855 until 1868 (apart from a brief period in 1860/61) was Léon Carvalho. Wagner's plans to stage his operas at the Théâtre Lyrique were side-tracked by the Imperial decree to mount *Tannhäuser* at the Opéra.
2 Hermann Franck.
3 Stanislas de Charnal.

performance this winter. I shall be meeting the director within the next few days to decide on the matter. –

Now that I have explained to you, dear Minna, why it will be necessary to spend some time in Paris, at least initially, it is a pleasant task to be able to put you in good spirits for such a stay. The area in which I am now living[1] shows me Paris from a totally different angle: splendid walks in the immediate neighbourhood, pure clear air, peace and quiet, and yet life as well; the *Bois de Boulogne*, which has now become utterly enchanting, close at hand; and if one wants to relax, it is such a remarkable town, with the heavenly Conservatoire Orchestra, and excellent quartets etc. behind one: I confess that there is nothing better I could ask for in the foreseeable future, nor anything more agreeable that I could offer you. In addition, we can live quietly on our own, just as we like: Fipps[2] can be taken out without a lead, and can run about and chase things to his heart's content. In addition, there is the firm prospect of *considerable* revenues. And all this will be ours simply for the asking. I have excellent hopes of finding a pleasant apartment: but I want to have a good look round before deciding. All our acquaintances are still in the country, even Monsieur Kietz. Only Grandmother Herold was there: an uncommonly kind and good-hearted old lady. These people are to lend me a helping hand, especially in my search for a good maid-servant. I visited her son's apartment; it was quite new, and had large attractive rooms and an uninterrupted view of the Luxembourg Gardens, but it is on the 3rd floor and costs 2500 fr. I imagine I shall get everything I want for 3000 fr. at most. Well, more on this next time.

In such circumstances, you will no doubt realize, dear Minna, that I am in no hurry to send a new appeal for clemency to the King of Saxony, unless he himself expressly invites me to do so and agrees to an amnesty. At least there is no immediate urgency here, so that I shall leave this question unresolved at least until such time as I have conferrred with my friends in Karlsruhe, including the Grand Duke and you yourself. There is not long to go until then: and now that we have waited so long, we can afford to let the matter rest a little longer. –

I have considered what would have to be done if you were to conceive of an insurmountable aversion to Paris. If the Grand Duke were to offer me permanent asylum with him, I should ultimately have to think about settling down there, and *I* should have to come to Paris on my own for months at a time. This, too, might work out in the end. But what would we gain by it?

I received your Strasbourg letter on the same day that I wrote to you. I am grateful to you for welcoming me to French soil; I hope your good wishes

1 Wagner was living at 4 Avenue Matignon off the Champs-Elysées (near the Rond-Point). He then moved to 16 Rue Newton, close to the Etoile, where Minna joined him on 17 November.

2 The Wagners' dog which Minna had taken with her back to Germany.

are fulfilled. I expect to hear from you again soon, and am confident that you will have good news to tell me concerning your state of health? I still have a dreadful number of letters to write, as always happens when I change my address. But I am already expecting an answer from Berne concerning Natalie.[1] You, too, should look round for a female companion and nurse whom you would find acceptable. I assure you there will be no lack of means by which to lead a life that is free from cares; otherwise, I should not suggest Paris to you. And so, fare you well for today, my good old wife! Take care of yourself, and hope for all that is best in everything. Adieu! A thousand cordial greetings from

Richard.

I gave Frau Cl. Stockar a kiss, so deeply was I touched and affected by the care she continues to lavish on the grave of our good Peps. A most beautiful, fenced-in bed of flowers over the grave, with a fresh bunch of flowers in the middle! Really most touching! –

I am expecting a detailed report from Devrient during the next day of so, including the date:[2] you shall be told everything as soon as I hear from him. –

By the way! If you do not wish to go to Kaskel in person, it is sufficient for you simply to write to him, since he already *knows* you, and ask him to send you the money that I have transferred to you through Rothschild.

RWA (published with suppression of Natalie Planer's name in Minna-Briefe II, 139–42).

247. COSIMA VON BÜLOW, BERLIN   Paris, 19 September 1859

Dear Cosima,

The beautiful letter you wrote to me in French and for which I must thank you most warmly has aroused in me a new reproach. You claim to like me and to wish to be of help in whatever way you can, yet it occurs to none of you that, if an attempt is to be made to perform Tannhäuser in Paris, no one who is a Frenchman through and through can possibly understand the poem and translate it properly. I have heard both from the Altenburg and from the Anhaltstrasse[3] that some Pole or other was intending to translate my operas, or Tannh. in particular. Now that I am in a position to take the matter more seriously, I find myself standing here utterly helpless, although I know of a

---

1 Natalie Planer. Wagner had written to Professor Georg August Fröhlich in Berne asking him to employ Natalie at his institute. Nothing came of the idea.
2 Regarding *Tristan und Isolde* in Karlsruhe; see letter [245], p. 462, note 1.
3 The Altenburg was Liszt's residence in Weimar; Hans and Cosima von Bülow lived in the Anhaltstrasse in Berlin.

young and enthusiastic female friend[1] who has produced a very fine translation of Hebbel's Magdalene, but who has of course never given a thought to translating Tannhäuser. And so I sit here abandoned by all who claim to be my friends. –

As you know, a young French aspirant by the name of de Charnal has set about the task of translating Tannh. I read through the first act, and my first thought on doing so was – : it's impossible! The young man has a female relative who knows German, and who has provided him with a literal translation; it is on the basis of this that he has produced the French verses which in themselves may not be at all bad. He did not have a vocal score. A year-and-a-half ago, shortly after my last visit to Paris,[2] I asked Blandine to buy a vocal score on my account and to give it to de Charnal; I received the reply that this had been done, and so I assumed that the poor man had been adequately provided for in his work. [This, however, was not true. Blandine lied to me, which now explains various other statements in your recent letters where certain things were claimed to be true.][3] At all events, the Olliviers have done nothing for me, nothing at all: well, I cannot force them against their will. – But back to the point! – I am persevering with a translation of Tannhäuser. What has persuaded me to do so is less the consideration of any financial advantages than the fear that it will presumably be possible only after my death to transplant my operas to France, but that by that time I shall no longer be in a position to exert any influence on the translation, which I know would be exposed to the most absurd distortions. And so, as a good father, I am making provision for my children in perpetuity. For my own part, I intend, with the help of my little author, to attempt to beat some sense into the translation, but I am bound to doubt in our success. That is why I am now inviting you, my dear child, to set about producing your *own* translation of Tannh., as you ought to have done long ago. You and Hans together are bound to produce the best version. In doing so, you would, I believe, do well to observe the following maxims. It will be quite impossible to produce a translation which follows the nuance of expression from phrase to phrase if, in doing so, you intend to retain the rhyme throughout. De Charnal's work has convinced me that the greatest evils are due to this, and this alone; the use of rhyme serves no purpose whatsoever and is completely inaudible in my music, which is why it is now disappearing; worse than that, it generally distorts the structure of the free periods. The French of course cannot conceive of a line of verse that does not rhyme: very well! The unrhymed lines can be published as prose, and an explanation can be appended to the libretto – to forestall any possible criticism – announcing that, at the compo-

1 Cosima von Bülow, who had translated Friedrich Hebbel's *Maria Magdalene* into French.
2 From 16 January to 3 February 1858.
3 The passage in square brackets was crossed out by Eva Chamberlain in an attempt to render it illegible.

ser's insistence, the translator, when confronted by a choice between rhyming verse which does not conform to the music and unrhymed lines which fit the music perfectly, decided in favour of the latter. It would, moreover, be a matter of complete indifference to me if these "verses" were to be criticized, providing that the dramatic effectiveness of the music, together with the words, turned out a complete success. – Furthermore: wherever the rhythm of the melody is of decisive importance, as in the Pilgrims' Chorus etc., you must try as far as possible to adapt the words to the musical phrase: where, by contrast, the delivery is freer, I am perfectly prepared to conform to the verbal phrase in the musical declamation, too. I insist only that you follow the exact nuance of the phrase, since there can never be *inversions* of this nuance without destroying the character of the music. – Now see what you can produce.[1] But work hard, and then I shall be satisifed!

Daniel's illness worries me very much.[2] Tell him to look after himself. Give him my very kind regards and every good wish for his recovery.

All my acquaintances are still à la campagne. Only Mme. d'Agoult was there, but could not receive me since she was just on the point of leaving pour chercher le soleil d'Italie. – I am now looking for an apartment where I can stay for some time, and I am feeling tolerably well. Give my regards to Hans, remember me with affection, believe in my friendship, and work hard, so that I can believe in yours!

Yours,
Richard Wagner

Eger I, 17–20.

248. ANTON PUSINELLI, DRESDEN   Paris, 3 October 1859

Dear Anton,

A deep sense of well-being and of reconciliation with the whole of human-kind overcomes me whenever I am reminded of your inestimable friendship. Accept my most sincere thanks, and may you enjoy, untroubled, the splendid self-awareness which your noble-hearted loyalty must needs afford you! –

Your news concerning my wife does not find me unprepared. From her letters and from her own confessions, it is quite clear to me that the poor soul must be in a very bad way. In particular, however, I can see that your own efforts to help her as a doctor have been prevented from enjoying any real success simply because my wife continues to associate with the kind of people whose company can have only a detrimental effect upon her. I am not

---

1 After making a start on the translation, Cosima abandoned the attempt.
2 Daniel Liszt, Cosima's brother, who died on 13 December 1859 at the age of 20.

speaking here of malign influences, but merely of the thoughtless behaviour of women in general, and of women of a certain inferior education in particular. She consorts with all manner of old spinsters etc., who – since women in general lack the most basic common sense – stand on a very low level of moral and intellectual breeding among the real Dresden element (well-known for being among the most miserable!). If it is not one thing that alarms her, it is something else: nothing but gossip, and yet more gossip! And then she is visited by Frau Tichatscheck who travels out from Dresden[1] with the express intention of worrying my wife all over again concerning the matter of my pardon; all the calm which I have brought to bear and sought to communicate to my wife is again being destroyed; people are urging her to entreat me anew to take this or that step (totally unconsidered on her part), and so it goes on. Or else she goes to a performance of one of my operas in Dresden and then simply *has* to run from one person to the next, telling everyone she meets some delightful bit of gossip, with the result that she then returns home once again with her heart more violently agitated than ever. And then there are her endless worries about me, her expectations and her curiosity. Thus one thing is clear to me: the fact that my wife found *you* as her doctor was a stroke of great good fortune for her, but that it had to be in *Dresden* of all places was a misfortune. In any other place she would have been less exposed to all the influences that I have indicated here in brief. There, my dearest Anton, she cannot improve, for what she needs most of all, apart from medical help, is constant male supervision and to be moved to a place where it is easy to keep her away from all contact with pernicious female gossip.

As for Paris, you are mistaken. My wife will live with me here in the greatest seclusion. I have rented a most pleasant apartment, almost outside the town, in a new and extremely quiet quarter, in an elevated position, with the purest air, near the most delightful walks, the bois de Boulogne etc. I, too, can survive only by leading a quiet life, without the buzz of society but with the greatest peace and quiet and the delights of domestic comfort. As for all the enterprises that lie ahead of me here, I shall involve myself in them only to the extent that they are strictly related to my own affairs and, conversely, I shall keep myself completely aloof from the kind of coterie that others seem to find necessary; fortunately, my reputation is so great even in Paris that I do not need to worry about considerations of this kind, but can go my own way in peace. My wife will lead a most agreeable and peaceful life with me here, without either of us causing the other the least inconvenience. [. . .]

This, then, is my plan. I hope, my dear friend, that it has your approval. For consider one thing! Decisive medical intervention was indispensable for

1 Minna was now living in Schandau, some nine miles to the south-east of Dresden.

my wife: but, in the last resort and in spite of all the skill and care which a doctor can give, it is moral influences that are the most important in an illness of this sort, and – as I well know – the life and death of my wife depend solely upon me! I can destroy her, but I can also save her: and so, since I know that her fate rests in my hands, my future behaviour towards her will be determined in advance with the greatest possible certainty. Trust me. There is another point that I have to communicate to you. It is of such a delicate nature that I can scarcely speak of it to a friend, but only to a doctor who is friendly towards me. One of the main reasons for my wife's unsettled condition lies in my having ceased to have sexual intercourse with her, something which gradually came about of itself simply as a result of her poor state of health. I do not believe that I have to accuse her of a passionately sensual nature (although I cannot judge to what extent her extreme excitability and nervous tension may have influenced her in this respect); but what unsettled her more than ever before was the jealousy she began to feel at this time. She really does not know me well enough, and has no proper idea of the true seriousness of my nature. I now hope that, in time, she will find every reason to recognize how foolish her jealousy is; none the less, in view of the fact that her mental condition means that she is no longer responsible for her actions, I consider it important that you, as her doctor, should impose a strict prohibition upon her in this respect – indeed, you can turn it against me, half-jokingly – a ban whereby she must consider not only herself but me as well. I hope I have said all I need; unfortunately, things of this kind are of undeniable importance! –

And now once more, my sincere and deeply felt thanks, you loyal, noble and true friend! I shall give you no more news concerning myself, since this is always available to you from my wife. It is sufficient to say that I feel within me a sense of calm, and patience enough to deal with each and everyone. I am still hoping to bring about a performance of Tannh. this winter in Paris. I hope I may then succeed in selling the opera to a Paris publisher, and thus enjoy the satisfaction of conscientiously carrying out my promise of a prompt repayment of a not insignificant part of the money that I owe you.[1]

Fare you well, then, give my best wishes to your dear little wife and your· many many children, and be ever assured of my constant love and gratitude.

Yours,
Richard Wagner

RWA (incompletely published in Freunde und Zeitgenossen 254–7).

---

1 Nothing came of this.

249. HANS VON BÜLOW, BERLIN   Paris, 7 October 1859

[. . .] I have read the extract from your letter about Tristan.[1] It is bound to be held against you. The beautiful and tremendous things you have to say about it I shall ignore: they are your own affair. But I do condemn as impractical your doubts as to the opera's likely popularity. Such things are never said in *confidence*, but are always retailed to strangers and to people who are more or less permanently hostile towards us: and this must always be borne in mind when it comes to publications. Härtels are already proving difficult on account of this doubt that has been expressed by one of my own friends. But why should you, or I, or any of our few genuine friends worry about this tiresome question of popularity? Why should we even allude to it? After all, there are many things we willingly admit to between ourselves – for ex., that I have become a totally different fellow in matters of harmony as a result of getting to know Liszt's compositions; but when friend Pohl blurts out this secret for the whole world to hear, right at the head of a short notice on the Tristan Prelude, it is indiscreet to say the least, and am I not supposed to assume that he was authorized to commit such an indiscretion? Liszt, for ex., may well write in ink on the dedication page of his Dante[2] that he thinks he owes me a great deal; I can accept that as an excess of friendship. But it would be foolish of me to insist that something of the kind should be printed and added to the dedication for all the world to read. The very suggestion would have provoked an immediate public protest on my part. We'd both do well to recommend that Herr Pohl show a little more discretion in future, for I believe he is compromising Liszt, though he may also be pleasing the Princess. – Well, this is merely by the way. –

In all confidence, however, I must lament the fact that I can no longer find the right words to write to Liszt. I have been tormenting myself for weeks now with the intention of writing a letter to him. No doubt I could make things easier for myself, since *I* never really receive a letter from Liszt but, at best, answers to my letters, and even these are only a half or even a quarter of the length of my own letters. He clearly feels no great urge to write to me. If I make the first move, he is the most admirable friend you could wish for, but – *he* never makes the first move. What is the point of my continuing to make such a move? Admittedly, my situation very frequently gives me cause to address myself to my friends, but I must see if I cannot gradually break free of this habit. How things stand between Liszt and me, or rather – *what* stands between us – is something you can explain well enough from his attitude. His Dante (dedicated to me) appeared in print over a month

---

1 On 9 September 1859 Brendel had printed in his *Neue Zeitschrift für Musik* an extract from a private letter written to him by Bülow; quoted in Ellis, VI,409–10.
2 *Eine Symphonie zu Dantes Divina Commedia.*

previously; I waited for him to send me a dedication copy and assumed that the reason for the long delay was because Liszt, after his extravagant fashion, had wanted to outdo me in my efforts to send him his dedication copy of Lohengrin in a *de luxe* binding. Finally, my impatience got the better of me: in an offended tone I complained to him about the delay and begged him to let me have a copy. Well, he sent it to me, but I realized to my shame that I had been mistaken as to the reason for the delay: the copy was as it came from Härtels. Liszt, however, had written a few over-exuberant lines in it, to corroborate the dedication, lines which R. Pohl would not have allowed to be printed;[1] but not a single friendly word of apology was enclosed. – I now discover that his Mass[2] has been out for some time; Cosima asks whether I have read his piece on music in Hungary.[3] Liszt knows that I set great store by his being the first to provide me with his new works; but I have not so much as seen either his Mass or his book.

I know that Liszt's generous nature ultimately triumphs in any conflict; the lines he wrote in Dante were evidence of a fine impulse and a sense of noble shame at an earlier weakness in which he had presumably yielded to insinuations that he should treat me in a more lukewarm manner. In consequence, Liszt will always remain a sublime and deeply sympathetic individual whom I love and admire greatly; but – it is impossible to think very much longer of the benefits of cultivating his friendship. He has already set me a striking example of how to neglect such a friendship: I *cannot* do other than follow that example; I should otherwise have to *conceal too much* from him in future, and that makes it impossible to cultivate any friendship.

I can no longer *find* the right words to address to him; my warmth has too often been met by empty phrases. Phrases, however, are something I cannot write to him: I am too fond of him for that. – And so I would ask you to tell him all about me and my present whereabouts. I hope that in this way he may recognize what it is that governs him, very much to his disadvantage, so that it may dawn on him what it is that he must necessarily lose as a result.[4]

[...]

I spent 4 days in Zurich,[5] staying with the Wesendoncks as their guest: the husband is very devoted to me, and is to be admired in the truest sense of the word. What has developed here is a beautiful and almost certainly unique relationship which has proved what true seriousness of purpose can achieve in the case of even the least gifted natures. Thus the husband stands between

1 On 8 May 1859 (see letter, [241], p. 455, note 4) Wagner had asked Liszt that the dedication be kept between themselves.
2 See letter [229], p. 436, note 1.
3 *Des Bohémiens et de leur musique en Hongrie*, written as an introduction to the *Hungarian Rhapsodies* and expanded into book-form by Carolyne Sayn-Wittgenstein.
4 Bülow forwarded the present letter to Liszt.
5 From 6 to 10 September 1859 (dating from Fehr).

me and his wife – whom he had to forswear utterly – as what I can only call the truest of mutual friends.[1] I regard this development as the occasion for extreme pride on my part: I was guided only by the most earnest desire not to deprive the poor woman of my company. I have now succeeded in this almost unprecedented task. We visited each other repeatedly between Lucerne and Zurich: I always stayed at their house, and I am doing all that I can to help this loyal woman in her difficult life, while her husband feels only a sincere delight in my comings and goings. It is a splendid achievement that you see here! Can you emulate it? –

I am again taking back my unhappy wife: she is somewhat improved but can prosper only if her care and treatment are of the greatest forbearance. Only *I* can bestow this upon her: her very life and death depend upon me, and in consequence my attitude towards her is clearly determined in advance.

Now, fare you well! Give my very best wishes to Cosmus; ignore my objection to your effusions concerning Tristan, since I am sure they were intended only as gossip, and write again soon, for even from you I never receive proper letters! –

Adieu!

Yours,
R.W.

Bülow-Briefe 125–9.

250. Mathilde Wesendonck, Zurich   Paris, 29 October 1859

I am now becoming increasingly aware of a quality which I have acquired in my art, since it also determines me in my life. From the very beginning it has been a part of my nature for my moods to change rapidly and abruptly from one extreme to another: states of extreme tension, after all, can scarcely do otherwise than impinge on each other; indeed, it is because of this that we are so often able to preserve our own lives. By the same token, true art has basically no other object than to show these heightened moods in their extreme relation to each other: the only thing that can matter here – the important decision – is the result solely of these extreme contrasts. In the case of art, however, the material use of these extremes may well result in a pernicious mannerism which may degenerate to the level of a straining after superficial effects. I have noticed how the newer French school in particular, with Victor Hugo at its head, is clearly caught up in this. . . .[2] I recognize

1 The language of this sentence is deeply indebted to the poetic diction of *Tristan und Isolde*, especially Marke's lament in Act II, Scene 3 (GS VII,52–5).
2 Suspension points in printed edition; see letter [224], p. 428, note 2.

now that the characteristic fabric of my music (always of course in the closest association with the poetic design), which my friends now regard as so new and so significant, owes its construction above all to the extreme sensitivity which guides me in the direction of mediating and providing an intimate bond between all the different moments of transition that separate the extremes of mood. I should now like to call my most delicate and profound art the art of transition, for the whole fabric of my art is made up of such transitions: all that is abrupt and sudden is now repugnant to me; it is often unavoidable and necessary, but even then it may not occur unless the mood has been clearly prepared in advance, so that the suddenness of the transition appears to come as a matter of course. My greatest masterpiece in the art of the most delicate and gradual transition is without doubt the great scene in the second act of Tristan and Isolde. The opening of this scene presents a life overflowing with all the most violent emotions, – its ending the most solemn and heartfelt longing for death. These are the pillars: and now you see, child, how I have joined these pillars together, and how the one of them leads over into the other. This, after all, is the secret of my musical form, which, in its unity and clarity over an expanse that encompasses every detail, I may be bold enough to claim has never before been dreamt of. If only you knew how that guiding emotion has inspired me to invent musical devices that would never have occurred to me previously (devices in terms of rhythm, as well as harmonic and melodic development), you would realize that even in the most specialized branches of art no truth is ever invented that does not derive from such grand primary motives. – That, then, is art! But this art is very much bound up with my own life. Extreme moods in a state of violent conflict will no doubt always remain a part of my nature: but it is embarrassing to have to consider their effects upon others. To be understood is so indispensably important. Just as, in art, it is the most extreme and the grandest of life's moods that must be made intelligible (moods which on the whole remain unknown in ordinary people's lives, except in rare times of war and revolution), this understanding can be achieved only through the most well-defined and most compelling motivation of these transitions, and my entire work of art consists very much in producing the necessary and willing emotional mood by means of this motivation. Nothing has horrified me more than when cuts have been made in my operas, as, for ex., in Tannhäuser, the opera in which I first worked with a growing sense of the beautiful and convincing need for transitions, and where, between the outburst of horror at Tannhäuser's dreadful confession and the devout attention with which Elisabeth's intercession is finally heard, I had composed a most significantly (and musically) motivated transition of which I have always been proud and which has never failed to make a convincing impression. You can well imagine how I felt when I discovered that (as in Berlin) people saw nothing here but long-windedness and straightway struck out one of the most essential sections of my work of art? –

That is how it is with me in art. And in life? Did you not often witness the way in which people found that what I had to say was presumptuous, tiresome and unending whenever I was guided by the very same instinct, and wished only to guide the conversation gradually round, after some agitated or unusual remark, towards some conciliatory and conscious understanding? –

Do you still recall that last evening with Semper?[1] I had suddenly lost my temper and insulted my adversary in a strongly worded attack. Scarcely had the words left my lips when my anger immediately abated, and all I could see – and feel – was the need for reconciliation and to restore a proper sense of composure to the conversation. At the same time, however, I was guided by a very clear feeling that this could not be sensibly achieved by suddenly falling silent, but only by a gradual and conscious transition; I recall, even while I was still speaking my mind quite forcefully, that I was already conducting the conversation with a certain artistic consciousness which, had I been allowed to have my way, would most certainly have led to an intellectually and conciliatory conclusion and have ended on a note of understanding and appeasement. I admit that I am asking too much here since, once real emotions have been aroused, everyone always insists upon being in the right and even prefers to be seen as the injured party rather than be made to see reason. On this as on many other occasions I have succeeded only in bringing down upon myself the reproach and rebuff of self-complacency when speaking. Even you yourself, I believe, were misled for a moment that evening and were afraid that the fact that I was continuing to speak as forcefully as before was the result of my persistent excitedness: and yet I also remember retorting, very calmly: "just allow me to guide the conversation back to its earlier point, that is something that takes time!" –

Do you perhaps think that experiences like these are very painful to me? – In truth, I love my fellow humans, and it is no timid, egotistical instinct which increasingly drives me from their society. It is not injured vanity that makes me sensitive to reproaches that I talk too much, but the sad feeling – what can I be to people and what can they be to me if, in my dealings with them, I seek not to achieve an understanding but only to maintain my opinion unaltered? On subjects that are alien to me and of which I have neither experience nor an unerring feeling, I would certainly never expatiate unless it were to learn more about them: but whenever I feel that I have something sensible and coherent to say on a subject that is familiar to me, simply to allow the other person to destroy the development of my argument so as to give him the appearance of being in the right by holding the opposite view –

1 This episode is recounted in *Mein Leben* 605; English trans. 591–2.

well, that really invalidates every word that might ever be spoken in society in general. I now decline all real society – and feel much better for it.

But perhaps I am again talking too much today, and making too many connections between things that ought to remain apart? – Do you understand me when, in talking to you on this occasion, my feelings strive in the direction of a "transition" and I attempt to guide the conversation round in such a way as to accommodate the rough edges of my moods, rather than suddenly falling silent and suddenly announcing all at once that I am calm and serenely cheerful? Could this possibly seem natural to you? no! Today, as before, you should follow the course along which I should like to guide your sympathetic interest in me in order that you may arrive at a calmer feeling towards me! There can be no more painful emotion in my heart than to arouse in others an interest that causes them torment: though it has fled from me, you may yet grant me the fair freedom to bring about a gradual and gentle sense of calm. Everything with me is so very much linked together within an overall context: this has its grievous disadvantages, since it means that common afflictions that may (possibly) be easy enough to remove can often exert a quite disproportionate influence upon me; but it also has the advantage that I acquire from within this same context the means by which to reassure myself; just as everything flows towards my ultimate task in life, my art, so, in turn, this art is the source of that clear spring which bedews the parched byways of my life. As a result of my sincere wish to exercise a calming and conciliatory influence upon your feelings of sympathy for me. I have today been enabled to gain an awareness of this supreme artistic quality of mine which I find developed in my new works to increasing advantage, and thus I have been allowed to address you as though from the sanctuary of my art, without the least constraint and without even the least friendly deception, but entirely truthfully and unaffectedly. –

[. . .]

Mathilde Wesendonck-Briefe 232–6.

251. MATHILDE WESENDONCK, ZURICH   Paris, 11 November 1859

My dear child,

You have given me much pleasure! I fully intended to write to you yesterday – so much have I been delayed! – with the letter to Wesendonck, in order to tell you how much pleasure your recent letter had given me: I was interrupted yet again, but then today came, bringing with it Schiller's Dithyramb.[1] I have

1 Schiller's poem *Dithyrambe* (1796), which Mathilde Wesendonck had sent Wagner to mark the centenary of the poet's birth on 10 November 1759.

never understood this poem as well as I did today: you teach me how to see ever-new beauties. How pleased I was to see from all this that you are feeling better again! –

I, too, am now slowly getting better, and – I can now admit it – from a serious illness. 10 years ago – also in Paris – I suffered from severe rheumatism; the doctor advised me, in particular, to do all I could to conduct it off to the outside lest the attacks should find their way to my heart. And so all my life's sufferings now came together and threatened to terminate at my heart. This time I really thought I would succumb. But everything is once again to be driven to the outside: I shall attempt to divert this pressure on my heart by means of some nobly distracting activity. You will help me in this? Won't you, my good people? –

My first piece of good news came from myself. The proofs of the third act of Tristan suddenly arrived. You will, I know, understand how I felt when my gaze fell upon this last completed work of mine, a glance that brought renewed life and strength to me, a sense of fulfilment and – of inspiration. Scarcely can a father have felt such joy at the sight of his child! In a flood of tears – why deny my weakness? – I heard a voice calling out: no! You shall not end yet; you must complete what you have begun! He who has just created *such* a work is still full to overflowing! –

So be it! –

Well, your letter pleased me, too, not least when I saw that your child, who has grown to be very intelligent, is occasionally guilty of a trivial mistake concerning me. I then say to myself: she will soon have the pleasure of reaching a clearer understanding of this point, too; for ex., that when I argue about politics, I have something quite different in mind from the apparent subject etc. But how it pleases me to be in the wrong whenever I argue with you: I always learn something new in the process. –

A most melancholy duty of love then came my way. I suddenly learned of the fatal illness of dear father Fischer in Dresden. You will recall that I often spoke of his wonderful loyalty and devotion. A – heart disease finally brought the old man to the brink of death: when my wife went in to see him, he was racked by the most terrible heart spasms and struggled to utter the pitiful cry: "Oh, Richard! Richard has forgotten me and cast me aside!" I had been expecting him in Lucerne this summer, and then not written to him again. I immediately wrote to him now. I then received news of his death, he had not been able to have my letter read to him.

I have spent the last few days writing a piece in his memory:[1] as soon as I receive a copy of it, I shall send it to you! – What a business! –

And the workmen have still not left the house: these Parisians are no

---

1 Originally published in the *Konstitutionelle Zeitung* of 25 November 1859 and reprinted in GX V,105–110 where it is wrongly dated "1860"; PW III,145–52.

different from the people you had in. I have finally got my *own* little apartment in order. Were you to set foot in it, you would almost think you were entering the Asyl. The same furniture, the old desk, the same green carpets: engravings, everything – just as you know it. The only difference is that the rooms are smaller, so that I have had to divide things up: my small salon contains the Erard, the green sofa and both the armchairs that used to be in the tea-room; on the wall are the Kaulbach, the Cornelius and the two Murillos. To one side is a small cabinet with shelves for books, a desk, and the famous causeuse (a souvenir of Lucerne). I have had my bedroom decorated with a plain pale-purple paper with a border made up of a few green stripes: the Madonna della Sedia is the only ornament. A tiny little room next to it is fitted out as a bathroom. And so I am now finally ensconced, for the last time, I hope. You know I can stick to decisions that are made in earnest: well – : never, ever again shall I set up house! God knows *what* may bring an end to this final move: but I know that it, too, will come to an end before I die: but I also know that I shall not establish another haunt for myself but, totally dispossessed, shall simply wait until someone closes my eyes for me. –

On this occasion, too, I was again overcome by an absurd eagerness to arrange everything as quickly as possible, so that I might again have some peace and quiet: I always undertake too much at such times, not through any pleasure in what I am doing but in order to arrive at the intended goal as soon as possible, so that certain needs, often satisfied down to the tiniest detail, shall no longer have a disruptive effect upon me. That is how it must be: for there is no other way that I can explain to myself the absurd eagerness with which I devote myself to such activities when, on the other hand, I know how little attached I am to such things and how carelessly I can cast everything behind me. Yes, you may well laugh! It does not bother me. –

A few days ago I was invited to a musical soirée at which sonatas, trios etc. from Beethoven's later period were played. Both the interpretation and the execution put me in a very bad mood, and I shall not be caught out again so soon. Still, I had some memorable experiences. I sat next to Berlioz, who immediately introduced me to the composer Gounod who was sitting next to him – an artist of amiable appearance and honest aspirations, but not, I think, very talented. Scarcely had word got round that I was there when everybody crowded round Berlioz, demanding to be introduced to me; strangely enough, they were all admirers of mine, having studied my scores without understanding German. This is something that often puzzles me greatly. I now fear that I shall have a large number of visitors, and I shall have to be somewhat on my guard. I have neglected the young Mme Charnacé quite shamelessly so far. As for Paris, I have not yet recovered my senses. But on the whole it amuses me to undertake something purely in order to keep my "rheumatism" at bay.

I am reading Liszt's Gypsy Music.[1] Somewhat over-inflated and hackneyed: but the prominence given to the gypsy character (unmistakably the Chandalas of India) has again brought Prakriti (or Savitri) vividly to mind. More on this another time.[2] –

And now for today – a thousand thanks! Ah! Does that really say it all!! I shall soon be gossiping again with the child! –

R.W.

Mathilde Wesendonck-Briefe 238–41.

252. FRANZ LISZT, WEIMAR   Paris, 23 November 1859

Believe me, my dear Franz, it is becoming very difficult for me to give you news about myself. We spend too little time together, and must inevitably become strangers in one important aspect of friendship. You wrote to me in Venice and Lucerne to say that you would welcome my move to Paris if for no other reason than that you could visit me there more often. Just as I have often assured you that an amnesty would be particularly welcome to me since I could then visit you more often and for longer periods, so I now gave you to understand that your assurance was one of the arguments that had persuaded me to look upon my stay in Paris in a more favourable light. My first request that you should visit me here has now met with an immediate refusal: you say you cannot come to Paris. By way of compensation you suggest a two-day rendezvous in Strasbourg. What are we – indeed, what am *I* – to do during these two days in Strasbourg? I have nothing urgent to tell you, I am not planning anything that needs to be discussed with you. I simply want to enjoy your company, and to spend some time with you, since we have spent so little time with each other in the past. Why has Paris suddenly become such an impossibility? Paris where – if you *wish* it so – virtually no one need know of your presence; I can find rooms for you near where I am living – very much out-of-the-way; we can spend the days at my apartment; you can see whom you want while you are with me. Or do you always have to be a public figure in addition to being an intimate friend? Look! I do not understand; the whole of my poor abandoned life has made me incapable of conceiving of an existence which keeps one eye on the world at every step that it takes. Forgive me! – However – I must decline the Strasbourg rendezvous, greatly as I appreciate the sacrifice that you are prepared to make for me: but this sacrifice is too high a price to pay in return for a few hurried days in a Strasbourg inn.

1 See letter [249], p. 473, note 3.
2 See letter [261] p. 499.

That the Princess was unable to call on me pained me grievously. Nor do I understand her most valued letter. She would have realized immediately we met what she means to me by the spontaneity of my joyful and cordial encounter with her. She has often experienced this, and will certainly never have harboured the suspicion that it is simply affectation on my part. I do not know what I should say to all this, – and so I shall say nothing! –

And so I shall say nothing about anything that I might otherwise wish to tell you about myself. If there is anything to tell, it is better that I say nothing about it. You are no doubt already sufficiently well informed about the Karlsruhe enterprise.[1] Devrient has found it expedient to excuse the consequences of his totally inept and negligent handling of the idea that Tristan should receive its first performance in his theatre by declaring that the work is impossible to perform. I shall not answer him either. What shall I say? *I* know my lot and my position – and say nothing. It is more serious when I consider the effect upon my livelihood of crossing off this new work of mine from the roll of life. But – why should *I* be the person who has to point this out? Anyone who has all his senses about him must realize what my position is. I can no longer complain, since this would amount to an accusation. And I do not wish to accuse anyone, not even friend Devrient: I have not said a word to him. – No doubt you now know enough, and more than will please you!

My wife is now staying with me. She is feeling somewhat better, and I hope things will work out tolerably well with her. She told me, without a murmur of complaint, that you had been in Dresden, but that you did not visit her: I tried to console her as best I could. –

Fare you well, my dear Franz! Do not misunderstand me: I had to write to you, and for a long time did not know how to go about it. God knows whether I have done the right thing! Rest assured that you will always remain dearer and closer to me than aught else, even though I no longer understand many of the things that determine your actions.

Fare you well! Give my very best wishes to the Princess, and tell her that her letter, even if I did not understand it, gave me a great deal of pleasure. Give my good wishes, too, to Princess Hohenlohe! May you all remember me with affection!

Fare you well!

Yours, R.W.

Liszt-Briefe II, 276–8.

1 See letter [245] p. 462, note 1.

253. B. Schott's Söhne, Mainz   Paris, 11 December 1859

Dear Sirs,

Your offer to publish a dramatic work of my own composition is as flattering to me as it is gratifying, and arrives at a time which I must call both favourable and unfavourable at once. Favourable – because I do indeed have a work available which I should like to see published soon; unfavourable – because I am still prevented from entering *Germany*, a state of affairs which not only places obstacles in the way of the first theatrical performance of my new works, at which it is essential that I be present in person, but is bound to place limits on my publisher's eagerness to take on a work of mine. As long as conditions continue to remain unfavourable, I find it difficult to decide whether or not to press ahead with the fulfilment of my wish to see my works published in the near future if, in doing so, I forfeit the advantages which I am convinced will accrue if I wait for the time when I can personally breathe life into the first performances of these works.

I could come to an agreement only with a publisher who, like me, had faith in the fate of my most mature works, who could look beyond the immediate obstacles and, as a guarantee of later success, would rely upon the experience that we have all had with my earlier works, which for a long time were deemed impracticable before finally achieving a degree of general acceptance that even I did not expect. If, in addition, I consider what at present, even given the most difficult circumstances, speaks in favour of the publication of my more recent works, and if I may assume that interest in them is so great that they will be in exceptional demand even before a theatrical performance has taken place, I may now consider that the moment has come to discuss the matter seriously with a publisher of your standing.

Given the preconditions herein indicated, I would respond to your kind offer by making the counter-offer of a dramatic composition of mine, entitled "the Rhinegold". I now set particular store by the publication of this work, rather than any other, since, now that the publication of my "Tristan and Isolde" marks my first reappearance as a creative artist after a considerable interval of time, I am anxious to present myself to our educated audiences in as popular a light as possible, and "the Rhinegold", especially, belongs to a genre which is very unlike that of "Tristan" but which reveals an entirely new aspect of my creative art – one that I may call the characteristically popular aspect – of a kind that I have never touched upon in any of my earlier works. As a result, I should attach great importance to the appearance of this work especially – *alongside* "Tristan".

If you were to have the patience to allow me one to two years before the first theatrical performance of this work, I would briefly indicate the conditions under which I might now relinquish it to you as follows:

In consideration of the sum of *Ten thousand Francs*, payable immediately, I shall sell you the full score and the completed, and highly successful, piano arrangement of my dramatic composition "the Rhinegold", with the right to publish the said work in any form in *Germany, France* and *England*, while I myself retain only the right of performance to it. The vocal score has been arranged by Herr Charles *Klindworth* of London, whom you would need to pay only the usual fee, to be reckoned by the page. As for the text, you would have the right to produce a cheap edition for sale at theatrical performances, but with the express reservation that you would have to come to some arrangement on this point with the bookseller[1] to whom I, in turn, reserved the right to offer my longer dramatic poem "the Ring of the Nibelung", in order that it may be published separately as a work of literature, in an expensive *de luxe* edition. The "Rhinegold" forms a self-contained and independent part of this dramatic poem, which I shortly intend to have published by a leading bookseller. – It would finally be left to your own judgement whether you preferred to engrave the full score and publish it straightaway, or to wait until such time as the first theatrical performance of the work had been assured – which I undertake to effect within two years at most.[2]

My dear Sirs, if it is now possible for you to share my confidence in the interest with which a new work of mine of this kind is now likely to be met on the part of an educated audience not only – I may well say – in *Germany*, but also in *France, England* and even *Russia*, I would ask you to honour me with a prompt reply, and, in the event of your agreeing to my proposal, to be for ever assured of my genuine appreciation of the greatness of mind with which you have viewed this matter. All the manuscripts are ready to be handed over immediately in order for you to undertake the necessary instructions.[3]

In the hope of receiving a favourable reply and in sincere gratitude for your flattering enquiry, I remain your most respectful and obedient servant

Richard Wagner.

Verleger-Briefe II, 2–4.

254. OTTO WESENDONCK, ZURICH   Paris, 12 December 1859

[. . .] I shall say nothing today about my Parisian enterprises: everything still hangs in the balance, although a number of important points will shortly be resolved.

On the other hand, I have a question to put to you and a favour to ask.

1 Following an abortive approach to Eduard Avenarius, the libretto of the *Ring* was published by J. J. Weber of Leipzig in 1863.
2 The first performance of *Das Rheingold* took place in Munich on 22 September 1869.
3 After attempting to beat Wagner down to 7500 francs, Schott finally agreed to publish *Das Rheingold* on Wagner's terms.

The great music publishers B. Schott and Sons in Mainz, who have hitherto been hostile towards me, have now approached me with the desire to publish one of my major dramatic compositions. Without further ado, I offered them the "Rhinegold", with the sole reservation that I myself retain the right to have a complete edition of the entire poem of "the Ring of the Nibelung" published by a bookseller of my choice; and at the same time I asked them what they would pay for it. I am now writing to ask your consent in the event of Schotts' paying at least 6000 fr. and, in the event of your agreeing – as I hope you will – I would beg you to empower and allow me to undertake a definitive sale of the publishing rights of the "Rhinegold", on condition that the firm of Schotts pay 6000 fr. to you or your firm without delay. I believe it would be sufficient for you to declare your agreement by letter.
[. . .]

Otto Wesendonck-Briefe 75–6.

255. MATHILDE WESENDONCK, ROME   Paris, 28 January 1860

[. . .] All my past experiences are as nothing compared to an observation or, rather a discovery which I made yesterday during the first orchestral rehearsal for my concert,[1] since it has decided the entire course of my future life, and its consequences will now govern me with a tyrannical sway. I had the Prelude to Tristan played to me for the first time; and it was as though the scales had fallen from my eyes, allowing me to see how immeasurably far I have travelled from the world during the last 8 years. This short Prelude was so incomprehensibly *new* to the musicians that I had to guide my people through the piece note by note, as if to discover precious stones in a mine.

Bülow, who was present, admitted to me that whenever this piece has been attempted in Germany the public have simply accepted it on trust, but that in itself it has remained totally unintelligible. I succeeded in making this Prelude intelligible to the orchestra and audience, indeed – people assure me that it produced the deepest imaginable impression: but do not ask me *how* I brought it off! Sufficient to say that it is now perfectly clear to me that I cannot think of any further creative work until I have filled in this terrible gulf behind me. I *must* perform my works first. And *What does that mean?* –

Child, it means plunging into a slough of suffering and self-sacrifice in which I shall probably perish. Everything, but everything *may* be possible; but only if I have sufficient time and leisure for it; if I can advance step by step with singers and musicians; if I do not have to hurry or break off anything

[1] For Wagner's three Paris concerts in January and February 1860 see introductory essay, p. 410.

through lack of time, and if I have everything constantly ready. And what does that mean? The experiences of this concert, for which I was allowed so little time, have told me the answer: I must be *rich*; I must be able to sacrifice thousands upon thousands in total disregard for the consequences, in order to buy space, time and goodwill. Since I am not rich, I must seek to make myself rich: I must give my older operas here in French, so that the not inconsiderable profits that accrue to me in this way will enable me to reveal my newer works to the world.[1] – That is what the future holds: I have no other choice! And so – come death and destruction, that is my task, and that is no doubt why my daemon has kept me alive! It would be folly to think of anything else! I see nothing ahead of me but the terrible throes of bringing my latest works into the world. –

[. . .]

Mathilde Wesendonck-Briefe 249–51.

256. MATHILDE WESENDONCK, ROME   Paris, 3 March 1860

[. . .] – When it recently struck me how indispensably necessary it is to risk everything on a first performance of Tristan, I said to myself: with this goal in mind, you will be spared all further humiliation! Each and every step that you take in pursuance of the necessary power and means cannot involve you in any shame, and to anyone who does not understand you when he sees you travelling these untrodden pathways, you may call out: "What do you know of my goal?" – For only he who understands this can understand me. –

Every day gives birth to new plans; I see now one possibility and now another before my mind's eye. So inextricably am I bound up with this work that – in all seriousness – I could willingly lay down my life and swear that I should not wish to live a day longer once I had had the work performed. And so it is only natural that the thought which now preoccupies me is to forgo all the struggles and humiliations which I should have to face in order that "Parisian" successes might furnish me with the means I need, and, instead, incur the utter torment of going to Dresden, submitting to a formal examination and judgement, and – for all I care – receiving a pardon, so that I could then be left alone to look round, on the spot, for the very best theatre in Germany where I could perform Tristan, and in that way exorcise the spell that now has hold of me. There is nothing else that seems to me to be worth my effort! It almost strikes me as being the most sensible thing to do, and I cannot but regard it as an act of unpardonable egotism to reject all idea of

1 Nothing came of this plan.

torment and shame, if this might lead to the redemption of my work. For what am *I* – without my work? – And then there is something else! I *do not believe* in my opera in *French*. Everything I do in furtherance of this aim contradicts the inner voice that I can silence only by levity or by force. I believe in neither a French Tannhäuser, nor a French Lohengrin, to say nothing of a French *Tristan*. In any case, all my steps in this direction remain doomed: a daemon, – no doubt *my* daemon – is against me in everything. Only a despot's command could sweep aside all the personal obstacles that prevent me from making headway in the Paris Opera. But I have no real desire to obtain that command. Above all, what interest do I still have in my old works, works to which I have grown almost indifferent in the meantime? I regularly catch myself out feeling only the most total disinterest in them. And now the French translations! I must regard them as utterly impossible. The few lines that were translated for my concert cost me unspeakable effort, and were insufferable. Nor – in spite of endless labours – has a single act of any of my operas been translated yet, and the little that I have in front of me here disgusts me. It is because of the language that everything here remains so alien to me. The torment of a conversation in French is uncommonly wearying for me, and I often break off in the middle of a discussion, like a man racked by utter despair, who tells himself: "it really isn't possible after all, everything is futile!" I then feel quite wretched and homeless. And I ask myself: where do you belong? There is no country, no town, no village that I can call my own. Everything is alien to me, and I often gaze around me, yearning for a glimpse of the land of nirvana. But nirvana quickly turns back into Tristan; you know the Buddhist theory of the origin of the world. A breath clouds the clear expanse of heaven:

it swells and grows denser, and finally the whole world stands before me again in all its impenetrable solidity. That is my age-old destiny, as long as I continue to have such unexorcized ghosts around me! –

[...]

Mathilde Wesendonck-Briefe 259–60.

257. MATHILDE WESENDONCK, ROME   Paris, 10 April 1860

But, my dearest and most precious child, why no news? Do I have to draw all information out of you by force? Can people not write to me, wretch that I am, instead of merely answering my questions? It is really most unsettling.

I wrote to Otto recently: no answer from him either! Now there is nothing left but to dream: and that helps me to get by. I dream a great deal and often: but even pleasant dreams have something disquietening about them, since, according to the rules that govern the interpretation of dreams, one must never forget that, even though the object that arouses our worries may appear harmless enough, it will reveal its opposite facet at the least sign of excess. But what a poor makeshift our dreams are! Though we may know a great deal about what each person dreams, all that this indicates is the emptiness of our existence in a waking state. I keep on remembering der grüne Heinrich[1] and how he ended up only dreaming. –

[...]

I almost feel as though I should say nothing about myself on this occasion: but, then, what do I know about you! Nothing, except that I know nothing: genuinely philosophical knowledge! And about myself?? Dearest child, nothing sensible will become of me as long as I live, and, above all, no one of any intelligence will be any the more sensible as a result. At present, for ex., I am being fêted by all intelligent people, and the whole world imagines that I must be beside myself with joy and self-contentment, since I have finally achieved the incredible good fortune of having one of my operas accepted for performance in Paris.[2] "What *more* can he want?" people are saying. As you can imagine, – I have never been more weary of the whole affair than at present, and to everyone who congratulates me, I bare my teeth in anger. That is how I am! –

[...]

Anyone who can calmly observe the life of such a talented but incredibly decadent nation as the French and who can summon up an interest in everything that may be seen as useful in developing and ennobling this race can scarcely be blamed for regarding the acceptance of a French Tannhäuser as a matter of the most vital concern for the educability of these people. Just think of the miserable state of all French art, and how poetry is in fact completely alien to a race that knows only rhetoric and eloquence. Given the total exclusivity of the French language and its inability to absorb the poetic element that is alien to it by means of translations from another language, the only means by which poetry may influence the French is through *music*. The Frenchman, however, is really not musical, all his music having reached him from abroad: from the very beginning, the style of French music has been moulded by contact with Italian and German music, and is really nothing more than the crossing point between both these styles. –

Strictly speaking, Gluck taught the French only how to reconcile music

1 *Der grüne Heinrich* (1851–53) by the Zurich writer Gottfried Keller.
2 On 12 February Wagner had written to Otto Wesendonck announcing his intention of approaching Napoleon III in order to have *Tannhäuser* accepted at the Opéra. Within a month the Emperor had issued instructions for the production to go ahead.

with the rhetorical style of French tragédie; basically, there was no question here of true poetry. That is why the Italians have had virtually the whole field to themselves ever since, for it was only ever a question of a rhetorical mannerism, but otherwise it had as little to do with music as it did with poetry. The resultant neglect, which has grown increasingly worse right up to the present day, is unbelievable. In order to get to know the singers at the Opera, I was recently obliged to listen to the latest offering of a certain Prince Poniatowski.[1] Imagine how I felt there!! What a longing seized hold of me to return to the simple mountain valleys of Switzerland!! I felt completely done in when I arrived home, and all possibility of work disappeared without trace. What I did learn, however, is that hideous impressions serve only to provoke more intense counter-reactions and to increase the significance of these latter for us. "You can see", they told me, "*how* things stand, and *what* we expect and demand of you!" The people who told me this are men who have not set foot inside the Opera for 20 years and who knew only the Conservatoire concerts and quartets, and who finally – without knowing me personally – studied my scores, and not only musicians but painters, scholars, indeed – statesmen. They say to me, "what you have brought us is not even remotely like anything that has been offered here before, since you bring the whole of poetry with your music; you bring a complete whole, and bring it, moreover, entirely independently and free of the influence that was earlier exerted by our institutes upon any artist who wished to create anything for us. You, however, bring us something that is both perfect in form and supremely forceful in expression: not even the most ignorant Frenchman could wish to alter any of it; he must accept it as a whole, or else reject it as a whole. And herein lies the great importance that we attach to the forthcoming event: if your work is rejected, we shall know at least where we stand, and shall abandon all hope; if it is accepted, and accepted, moreover, at a stroke (for the French can be influenced in no other way), we shall all breathe a sigh of relief; for neither science nor literature, but only the art of the theatre, which is the most immediate and most general in its effectiveness, can impress the mind of the nation and alter its views. However, – we remain convinced that the greatest and most lasting success will be yours!" –

Indeed, even the director,[2] who has now made a more detailed acquaintance of the subject, boasts in public that, with Tannhäuser, he can at last reckon on a real "succés d'argent".

I talked at great length in Brussels[3] with a remarkable man, an old, very

---

1 *Pierre de Médicis*, by Józef Poniatowski, performed 47 times at the Paris Opéra following its première there on 9 March 1860, and subsequently heard in Madrid (1863) and Milan (1869).
2 Alphonse Royer.
3 Wagner visited Brussels between 19 and 29 March to conduct two concerts at the Théâtre de la Monnaie.

shrewd, witty and uncommonly knowledgeable diplomat,[1] who advised me most warmly not to ignore the French: whatever one might say and think about them, one thing was indisputable, he went on, namely that the French now represented the real prototype of European civilization, and that to make a decisive impression upon them meant influencing the whole of Europe. –

All this really sounds most encouraging, and it is clear that I shall not be able to escape from the position of importance that people expect me to occupy in the world. But it is strange that I really feel so little concern for Europe or, indeed, for the world at large: and at the bottom of my heart I ask myself, what concern is all this of mine? But, as I say, I can see that I shall not escape from all this: oh, my daemon will see to that. The surest guarantee of my unfailing influence upon Europe is – my present hardship!

[...]

In the meantime I must put myself in the right frame of mind to write a great ballet. What do you say to that? Do you doubt my ability to do so? Well, you shall beg my forgiveness for that once you have heard and seen it. For now only this much: not a note, not a word of Tannhäuser will be altered. But a "ballet" was said to be imperative, and this ballet was supposed to occur in the second act, since the subscribers to the Opera always arrive at the theatre somewhat later, after a heavy dinner, never at the beginning. Well, I declared that I would not take my orders from the Jockey Club, but that I would withdraw my work. But now I intend to help them out of their difficulty: the opera does not need to begin until 8 o'clock, and then I shall have another go at the unholy Venusberg, and this time I'll do it properly.

This court of Frau Venus was clearly the weak point in my work: lacking a good ballet, I resorted at the time to a few coarse brush-strokes, and in that way spoiled a great deal: in particular, the Venusberg left a very dull and indecisive impression, and, as a result, I lost an important foundation upon which the whole of the subsequent tragedy should have been built to shattering effect. All those decisive reminiscences and reminders whose aim is to fill us with a powerful sense of horror (since only in this way can we explain the course of the action) lost almost all their effectiveness and significance: fear and a constant sense of unease failed to make themselves felt. But I now also recognize that at the time that I wrote Tannhäuser I was not yet able to do the sort of thing that is necessary here: for this I should have required a far greater mastery such as I have only now acquired: only now that I have written Isolde's final transfiguration have I been able to find the right ending for the Flying Dutchman Overture, as well as – the horrors of the Venusberg. One becomes all-powerful only by playing with the world. Of course, I shall have to invent everything here myself in order to be able to prescribe every last nuance to the ballet-master: but it is certain that only dance can be effective

1 Georg Friedrich Klindworth.

here and complete the sense: but what a dance! People will be amazed at all that I have hatched here. I have not yet got round to writing anything down: but I intend to attempt a few preliminary indications here. Do not be surprised if I do so in a letter to Elisabeth.

Venus and *Tannhäuser* linger behind in the way originally indicated: now, however, the three Graces are discovered reclining at their feet, their limbs enchantingly entwined. A tight-knit group of childish limbs surrounds the couch: they are sleeping cupids who, as though in some children's game, have fallen upon each other, fighting, and fallen asleep.

All around, on the ledges of the grotto, loving couples recline at ease. Only in their midst are to be seen dancing nymphs, teased by fauns from whom they attempt to flee. This group becomes more animated in its movements: the fauns grow more wanton, the teasing flight of nymphs invites the menfolk from among the reclining couples to come to their defence. Jealousy on the part of the deserted women: the fauns' increasing impudence. Tumult. The Graces rise to their feet and enter the fray, demanding that charm and composure be restored: they, too, are teased, but the fauns are driven off by the young men: the Graces reconcile the couples. – Sirens can be heard singing. – Then the sounds of tumult are heard in the distance. The fauns, bent on revenge, have summoned up the Bacchantes. The Wild Huntsmen come storming along, after the Graces have resumed their position at Venus's feet. The triumphant procession brings all manner of monstrous beasts with it: among others, they seek out a black ram, which is carefully examined lest it be found to have a white mark upon it: to cries of jubilation it is dragged towards a waterfall; a priest strikes it down and sacrifices it to the accompaniment of hideous gestures.

Suddenly, to the sounds of wild rejoicing, there emerges from the whirlpool your old friend, the Nordic Strömkarl[1] with his strange and over-large fiddle. He now plays to the dance, and you can imagine what I shall have to invent here in order to give this dance its appropriate quality; more and more of the mythological rabble are drawn in. All the animals sacred to the gods. Finally centaurs galloping around among the raging throng. The Graces despair of quelling the tumult. They throw themselves in desperation upon the raging host; in vain! They look round in search of help in the direction of Venus: with a beckoning gesture she arouses the cupids who now fire off a regular hail of arrows at the raging host, more and ever more of them; their quivers are constantly refilled. Now the figures begin increasingly to pair off with each other; wounded men-folk stagger into their lovers' arms: a raging desire

---

[1] Jacob Grimm mentions the Strömkarl in his *Deutsche Mythologie* (1835 edition, p. 461) and also notes that black lambs were traditionally sacrificed to this Nordic water-sprite. The Strömkarl was also the subject of a poem by Mathilde Wesendonck.

seizes hold of them all. The arrows, wildly whirring all around them, have struck even the Graces. They no longer have any control over them.

Fauns and Bacchantes rush away in pairs: the Graces are abducted on the backs of the centaurs; the others all reel away towards the background: the couples sink down to the ground: the cupids, still shooting their arrows, have run after the Wild Hunt. Growing weariness. Mists descend. The sirens can be heard further and further away. All are protected. Calm. –

Finally – – Tannhäuser starts up from his reverie. – Something like that. What do you think? It amuses me to have used my Strömkarl with the eleventh variation. This also explains why Venus and her court have travelled northwards: only there could they find the fiddler to play for the old gods. I also like the black ram. But I could perhaps replace it by something else. Jubilant maenads ought to carry in the murdered *Orpheus*: they would toss his head into the waterfall, – and then the Strömkarl would spring up. But this is not so easy to understand without words. What do you think? –

I wish I had access to Genelli's water-colours: he really brought these mythological excesses to life. Ultimately I shall have to help myself out here. But there is still a great deal for me to invent.

Well, this is another proper Kapellmeister letter that I have written you. Don't you think so? And this time it is even a ballet-master letter. I hope it puts you in a good mood?

And yet you do not write to me? Nor Otto, either. Oh you wicked, wicked people! Where shall I find the letters to cheer me up? You know very well that there is nothing else that gives me such genuine pleasure. But only when it is you I am dealing with.

[. . .]

Mathilde Wesendonck-Briefe 261–70.

258. JULIE RITTER, DRESDEN   Paris, 8 June 1860

[. . .] As for my direct relations with Germany, I find my progress persistently impeded by one difficulty after another, the most discouraging of which is the discovery of how incredibly little people in Germany can be bothered about me and my new works. It seems very much as though they are basically quite satisfied to think that my Tristan is really a failed and unperformable work, as my Karlsruhe friends have very wisely given it out to be: this saves them a great deal of trouble and spares them every kind of effort; it also allows them to forget the matter, an attitude which I myself might even end up by accepting since my earlier works are now fairly widely accepted. More or less the whole of my German fatherland replies to me in this vein, a few foolish young admirers excepted. But anyone who now approaches me in person will no doubt end up feeling a sense of shame, and will come to see for himself the humiliation that is inflicted upon me: that is why so many people are wary of approaching me in person; ignorance is so much to be preferred at a kind of abstract distance. As chance would have it, I recently came into contact with the Saxon ambassador here,[1] an extremely good-natured man whose initial reaction to me was very much the one described. He is now in Dresden, and I almost believe that when he confers in person with the King, he will find a way of settling this business of mine. At least *he* hoped as much! – If I am to be allowed to set foot on German soil once again, I expect that only then will the full extent of my misery finally become clear to me and many of my last-remaining illusions will disappear: I can more or less see it in advance: and yet my curious destiny drives me to seek understanding at the breast of one of the stupidest of all nations, simply because I happen to speak that nation's language.

In the mean time, however, this same destiny will guide me in other directions. Just when Germany makes things difficult for me, the glorious prospect of France suddenly opens up to me – as though out of the blue. Although I did not have an inkling of what was going on,[2] it appears that at a court ball the Emperor Napoleon III made the young Princess Metternich the chivalrous gift of ordering a performance of my Tannhäuser to be given at the Grand Opera. At the same time, everything I require for this purpose is to be placed at my disposal: I shall be able to command the services of the entire institute, just as I think fit. So far I have felt insuperably indifferent to the whole affair, and the director[3] is having some difficulty in spurring me on. However, the thing I had least believed in – a good translation – has now in fact come off, at least as far as such a thing is possible; admittedly, it cost me a good deal of effort and trouble, and involved many a smiling concession on my part. But it is now done. I still have a great deal to do, especially the first scene in the Venusberg (which was always rather weak): it needs significant changes for which I have already worked out a satisfactory plan. I expect that by degrees I shall rediscover my desire for work and, with it, regain my enthusiasm for the whole affair, since I am gradually coming to understand the wisdom of my fate's decrees behind its apparently arbitrary whims. – I feel clearly that Tristan and the Nibelungs are the only works that now concern me, and every plan that distracts me from them leaves me cold. But given the quite singular nature of these works, their uncommon difficulties, and the unbelievably impoverished state of our opera houses, I

1 Albin Leo von Seebach.
2 But see letter [257], p. 487, note 2.
3 Alphonse Royer.

could regard it only as a misfortune if, ignoring all this, I chose to surrender these works to these same theatres just as they were, and to arrange a first performance, here or there, as the occasion arose. For this, as for my principal task in life, I must be given total and unconditional freedom to do as I please; I must be able to regard these performances as something quite out of the ordinary and exceptional, and bring them off as such, otherwise – Karlsruhe will be proved right.[1] And so I must be able to move around as freely as possible, to renounce all monetary advantage, and even be in a position to make sacrifices: and – – the Paris Tannhäuser now offers me the chance to do all this. This, it is true, is a round-about means, but – it appears – it is the only certain route to my goal! And so I shall no doubt have to comply and be patient. Do you not think so, too? – Ah, how fortunate the Germans are that Napoleon takes such good care of them: they themselves are certainly incapable of doing so! –

For the rest, I can assure you that I have no reason to be dissatisfied with Parisian audiences. When I think, for ex., of the bewilderment which my dear Dresdeners felt at Tannhäuser, and contrast it with the swift and instantaneous impression that my music has sparked off in the French, who immediately greeted certain of my melodies and phrases with the greatest enthusiasm, I am bound to ask myself whether the conceited notion of the Germans' alleged intelligence is not straight out of one of the Grimms' fairy-tales? Even the press wasted no time in declaring itself much more emphatically in my favour than was ever the case in Germany: the fact that many of the local hacks are paid, and therefore predisposed to slander, means nothing: everyone knows as much here, and, however voluble their abuse, it has no effect; but the fact that all the unbiased critics quickly and decisively declared their recognition and admiration is something I never encountered in Germany. If, in addition, I consider the uncommon importance that many intelligent French men and women who have made my acquaintance now attach to what they regard as the wholly predictable success of my Tannhäuser, I may well have good grounds for observing the forthcoming undertaking with a great deal of interest. And yet I am childish enough not to want to tear myself away, even for a moment, from Tristan and my Nibelungs! How foolish one can be at times! –

[. . .]

Ritter-Briefe 150–4.

---

1 See letter [245], p. 462, note 1.

259. MALWIDA VON MEYSENBUG, LONDON   Paris, 22 June 1860

Best of friends,

I am most grateful to you for your kind letter. You were quite right to suppose that my long silence was attributable to my ill humour. Throughout my life I have had to contend with a great many vexations, and the mocking combination of total impecuniousness and such an obstinate disposition as mine has at all times been the cause of bitter conflicts for me. No one really understands this, and yet it is plain for all to see if only people would look closely enough at me now, for ex. – now that I have everything within arm's length that promises to lighten my life's burden, and yet am so little capable of making concessions that I told the director of the Opera[1] yesterday that Tannhäuser will be given as it is (without a ballet in the 2nd act) or else it will not be given at all. Quite what this obstinacy means is something which you yourself are in the best position to judge, since you know what my present position is. For I must confess that in all the 8 years that my operas have been given in Germany, I have never before known a situation like the present one: I used always to have some form of income and could survive in the way that I had chosen to lead my life. Now, however, my older operas are completely exhausted, my new ones are thwarted, enormous losses, and – no one to help me – !

All I ask for is credit during a slack period! Impossible! I unburden myself, and in return reap nothing but ridicule: – I read in the papers that I have received 10,000 fr., but the mockery that accompanies the article is all I have got for it.[2] My Russian general[3] arrives: it turns out that there can be no question of Petersburg next winter since I would have had to be there at the same time that I am needed here: and so – silence! – Now I have had to stave off claims from one day to the next: the most embarrassing shortages at home. My wife overwrought and sleepless. She is supposed to be going to Soden to take the waters there: but I cannot provide her with the money to do so. And so it goes on, and will continue to do so for at least another 6 months, assuming it can *go on* at all. And this happens to *me* of all people, of whom it is repeatedly being said on all sides that I inspire enthusiasm wherever I go etc. – Of all the people to whom I have turned, it is Mme Schwabe[4] whom I am most justified in regarding as the one person who has really made an effort to help me. As things now stand, and as they have turned out, I can assure you quite truthfully that I have learned a great deal of respect for Mme

---

1 Alphonse Royer.
2 Wagner had in fact received 10,000 francs from Marie Kalergis to set against the deficit of his Paris concerts (see introductory essay, p. 411).
3 General Saburoff, who had invited Wagner to direct *Tannhäuser* in St Petersburg.
4 For the loan from Julie Salis-Schwabe, and the proposed subscription, see introductory essay, p. 411.

Schwabe. When I recall how you came to me on that day of the most pressing need and how you were able to hand over to me the not inconsiderable sum that I required, I am bound to acknowledge her as the only person who has proved her worth. Tell her that! I wrote to her yesterday to tell her myself. – I now have no alternative: I must keep her waiting: But she will *certainly* get the money back. Do not be surprised if I do not shower praise on *you*, although I know well enough that what Mme Schwabe did was *your* doing alone: this, however, goes without saying, whereas the same cannot be said of Mme Schwabe. – There can no longer be any question of a subscription; everything here is completely and utterly unsuited to such an undertaking; what ought to have been the work of two days at most has dragged on for two indiscreet months, so that it has now not only got into the papers but, unfortunately, has also fallen into Fould's hands,[1] which itself is sufficient reason for me to decline my benefit. I have not yet seen Frau v. Pourtalès:[2] at all events, she has not understood what is involved here, and I have little desire to enlighten her. –

Let us forget the whole affair: all that remains is my debt, my gratitude and my apologies to Mme Schwabe; also – the hell from which I have not the remotest inkling how I am to escape. The only solution would be for you to interest Fr. Burdett's rich heiress[3] in my fate, of whom it is said that she has so much money that she does not know what to do with it; all I need is 5000 fr., the remainder of my deficit, in order to last out until such time as Tannh. has been performed. –

In spite of all this, I have been able to devote my sympathetic attentions of late to Garibaldi: and I confess that it is always with great eagerness that I have the evening newspaper brought to me: as you very rightly remark, this is the only thing that can even begin to cheer me up at present, since the artistic element is incapable of doing so, most of all in situations like my own: for this one must *be* free, not simply wish to be free. In moods like this I cannot find the freedom to read about art, so that Plutarch has again been providing me with the distraction that I need at present. I had previously been deeply impressed by his life of Timoleon which I came across quite by chance. This life has the unprecedentedly rare distinction of ending on a note of perfect happiness: a quite exceptional case in history. It really does one good to see that such a thing was once possible: but, with regard to all else that is noble, it cannot prevent me from recognizing that such a case has really only been set up by the world daemon as a decoy. This *possibility* had

1 Achille Fould was Secretary of State and Minister of the Household to Napoleon III; as such, he was responsible for the finances of the Paris Opéra.
2 Countess Pourtalès was the wife of the Prussian ambassador in Paris. Wagner was in fact to receive 1200 thalers from her in 1862.
3 Angela Georgina Burdett-Coutts was the daughter of Sir Francis Burdett and grand-daughter of Sir Thomas Coutts, from whom she had inherited the sum of £1.8 million in 1837.

to remain open in order to be able to mislead countless individuals as to the true nature of the world: if this possibility had never existed, one could almost have assumed that it ought to be possible for us to take a shorter route to reach the point which – as it appears – we westerners can get to only by means of a very long detour. How many points of contact there were that even now could be drawn between Garibaldi and Timoleon. He is still fortunate: might it yet be possible for him to be spared a very real sense of the most terrible embitterment? I sincerely hope so: but I often tremble to see him like some fly caught in the great spider's web of Europe. Many possibilities remain open, however. Perhaps the fly is too big & strong. He should not count too much on his *people*, but a great deal on his mountain infantry! For the rest, let treason, and the skill to direct it, help him. Through the baseness of those who are base, one occasionally conquers the insolence of the base. –

That you are coming to Paris is a great comfort to me. It is impossible for me to leave here, and I shall thank my stars if only I can get my poor wife to the spa. – Fare you well!

‹ Every good wish from

Yours,
Rich. Wagner

Meysenbug-Briefe 72–3.

260. MATHILDE WESENDONCK, ZURICH   Paris, 22 July 1860

[...] – There is certainly no one who has less pleasure, enjoyment, or even relaxation and passing stimulus of any kind than I. Whatever I do, I have never for a moment considered giving myself enjoyment or pleasure, since I have learned to realize with increasing certainty that whatever I have sought has never come to pass but always turned into the opposite of what I was seeking. This is so certain for me that, after an excursion which I recently undertook to Fontainebleau, where I was drawn by the promise of the beautiful trees there, I am now firmly resolved not to think of any further kind of distraction, for ex., throughout the rest of this summer, since I have now grown so extremely sensitive that even an outing such as this one ultimately revealed itself to me as an occasion for torment rather than pleasure. No one enters my lonely life whom I am not glad to see the back of when he leaves.

Whenever I feel the stirrings of an unquenchable desire for familiar contact or even for the slightest change, I tell myself, with increasing certainty, that every potential fulfilment of that desire would cause me only pain, and so I remain quietly at home, conscious of the fact that I would not find even the least relaxation that I was hoping for. This perfect and total sense of resignation is something which I have no doubt will be understood by scarcely any one, least of all by those who have children! –

The fact that I not only lead this unspeakably joyless existence, but that I live in a world of exigence and consideration for others which, in *their* eyes, almost always make me appear in the kind of light that they covet for themselves ultimately leads, on my part, to the strangest sensations of this world. I tell you quite openly that the bitterness which I often admitted to you is growing less and less a part of me, and in its place has come contempt. This is not a violent emotion, rather does it give me an increasing sense of peace: for my own part, I no longer have a relation with anyone in which this feeling does not have the upper hand now: and this places far fewer demands on my heart, which is now a good deal less vulnerable: – I can now feel contempt where I once felt embittered! –

And so I express myself much less frequently, too, and assume that I am not here to be judged by my actions, but rather do I hope that some, at least, of my works will be understood one day. But this much I *shall* say: only the feeling of my own purity gives me this strength. I feel that I am pure: I know in my innermost soul that I have constantly worked for others, never for myself; and my constant sufferings are my witness. –

But joy? Joy no longer interests me! And that is my consolation: each joy that I caught myself feeling would be a form of self-accusation, and that would be the end of my proud right to feel contempt. –

And so it is with an odd sense of satisfaction that I can tell you today that the disclosure which I received a few days ago from Germany, informing me that my exile had been lifted, has left me thoroughly cold and indifferent. Telegraphic despatches arrived here, jubilantly bearing their senders' congratulations: I have not replied to a single one of them. Who would understand me if I told them that this news has merely opened up a new field of suffering for me, suffering that so outweighs all possibility of my feeling contentment that I see before me only sacrifices on my part? Anyone who happens to come too close to me suddenly seems to understand this: but it is no more than the faintest trace of understanding; once he has turned his back, it is not long before he ends up thinking that it is mere affectation on my part! And these are some of the better kind! But as for the rest! – I feel only disgust! –

But I have a friend to whom I am growing more and more attached. It is my old friend Schopenhauer, so sullen in appearance and yet so deeply affectionate a person. Whenever my feelings have ranged most widely and deeply, a unique sense of self-renewal overcomes me each time I open that book of his, for here I find myself a whole person once more and see myself fully understood and clearly expressed, but in a quite different language, which soon transforms my suffering into an object of understanding, and, on the basis of what I feel, soon changes everything into marmoreal, cool and comforting intellect, an intellectual understanding which, by revealing me to myself, at the same time reveals the whole world to me! It is a quite wonderful reciprocal action, an exchange of the most supremely inspiriting kind: and its effect is always fresh, since it continues to grow in strength. It is this that restores my sense of peace, and even contempt resolves itself as love: for all flattery is at an end; clear understanding makes my suffering less intense: the folds are smoothed away, and sleep again assumes its restorative power. And how good it is that the old man knows nothing at all of what he is to me, nor what I am through him.

And let me also remind you of a quite different friend. You may laugh, but I am speaking of a true angel whom I always have about me: a creature of unshakeable kindness that never so much as looks at me without lavishing upon me a veritable torrent of joy and caresses. It is the little dog that you once sent me on my sick-bed! I cannot tell you how affectionate this incomparable animal is to me. Every evening I lose my way with him in the Bois de Boulogne! I often think then of my peaceful Sihlthal! Fare you well, you kind soul! And accept my most grateful thanks! –

Mathilde Wesendonck-Briefe 281–4.

261. MATHILDE WESENDONCK, ZURICH   [Paris, early August 1860]

What a poet I am! Heaven help me, I am growing quite presumptuous! – It is this interminable translation of Tannhäuser that has made me so conceited: not until I had to go through the work word by word did I finally realize how concise and unalterable this poem already is. Take away a word or a meaning, and both I and my translators[1] were forced to admit that an essential element would be lost. Initially I believed that it would be possible to make small alterations: we were forced to abandon each and every one of them as impossible. I was most surprised at this, and then found, in comparison, that I really know of very little else to which I can ascribe this same quality. In a word, I soon had no choice but to admit to myself that the poem could simply not be improved on. What do you say to that? I can better improve on the music. The orchestra in particular will be given a number of more expressive and richer passages. Only the scene with Venus will be completely rewritten. I found Frau Venus somewhat stiff; a few good qualities, but no real life. Here I have added quite a number of new verses: the goddess of joy will be almost touching, and Tannhäuser's torment will be real, so that his cry of

1 Edmond Roche and Richard Lindau, assisted latterly by Charles Truinet (Nuitter).

Mary bursts forth from his soul like a cry of deepest anguish. This is something I could not have done previously. In order to compose the music, I shall need to be in a very good mood indeed, and have no idea as yet where I shall find it! –

A prose translation of the four pieces: Dutchman, Tannhäuser, Lohengrin and Tristan is soon to be published, and I plan to write a preface[1] for it which I chiefly intend shall give my friends here some information concerning the formal aspect of my art. I have just been through these translations, and was again obliged to relive these poems of mine in every detail. Lohengrin affected me very deeply yesterday, and I cannot help thinking it the most tragic of all poems, since reconciliation is really to be found only if one casts a terribly wide-ranging glance at the world.

Only a profound acceptance of the doctrine of metempsychosis has been able to console me by revealing the point at which all things finally converge at the same level of redemption, after the various individual existences – which run alongside each other in time – have come together in a meaningful way outside time. According to the beautiful Buddhist doctrine, the spotless purity of Lohengrin is easily explicable in terms of his being the continuation of Parzifal – who was the first to strive towards purity. Elsa, similarly, would reach the level of Lohengrin through being reborn. Thus my plan for the "Victors" struck me as being the concluding section of Lohengrin. Here "Savitri" (Elsa) entirely reaches the level of "Ananda". In this way, all the terrible tragedy of life would be attributable to our dislocation in time and space: but since time and space are merely *our* way of perceiving things, but otherwise have no reality, even the greatest tragic pain must be explicable to those who are truly clear-sighted as no more than an individual error: I believe it is so! And, in all truth, it is a question simply of what is pure and noble, something which, in itself, is painless. –

I can do nothing but prattle when writing to you: nothing else is worth the effort! And only with you do I enjoy prattling on about such things! Time and space – which, after all, bring nothing but torment and distress – then disappear for me! And – ah! how rarely do I feel in the mood for such prattle! –

Tristan is and remains a miracle to me! I find it more and more difficult to understand how I could have done such a thing: when I read through it again, my eyes and ears fell open with amazement! How terribly I shall have to atone for this work one day, if ever I plan to perform it complete: I can see quite clearly the most unspeakable sufferings ahead of me; for if I am

---

1 The preface, dated September 1860, was translated into French by Paul Challemel-Lacour. It is more familiar under its German title *"Zukunftsmusik": An einen französischen Freund (Fr. Villot) als Vorwort zu einer Prosa-Übersetzung meiner Operndichtungen* ("Music of the Future": To a French friend [Frédéric Villot] as Preface to a Prose Translation of my Opera Poems), published by Weber in 1861, and reprinted in GS VII,87–137; PW III,293–345.

honest with myself, I have far overstepped the limits of what we are capable
of achieving in this field; uniquely gifted performers, who alone would be
equal to the task, are incredibly rare in the world. And yet I cannot resist the
temptation: if only I could hear the orchestra!! –

Parzival has again been stirring within me a good deal; I can see more and
more in it, and with ever-increasing clarity; one day, when everything has
matured within me, it will be an unprecedented pleasure to complete this
poem. But many a long year may pass before then! And I should like to be
satisfied for once with the poem alone. I shall keep my distance from it as
long as I can, and occupy myself with it only when it really *forces* itself on my
attention. This strange creative process will then allow me to forget just how
wretched I am. – Shall I prattle on about this? Did I not tell you once before
that the fabulously wild messenger of the grail is to be one and the same
person as the enchantress of the second act. Since this dawned on me, almost
everything clsc about the subject has become clear to me. This strangely
horrifying creature who, slave-like, serves the Knights of the Grail with
untiring eagerness, who carries out the most unheard-of tasks, and who lies
in a corner waiting only until such time as she is given some unusual and
arduous task to perform – and who at times disappears completely, no one
knows how or where? –

Then all at once we meet her again, fearfully tired, wretched, pale and an
object of horror: but once again untiring in serving the Holy Grail with doglike devotion, while all the time revealing a secret contempt for its knights:
her eye seems always to be seeking the right one, – and she has already
deceived herself once – but did not find him. But not even she herself knows
what she is searching for: it is purely instinctive. –

When Parzival, the foolish lad, arrives in the land, she cannot avert her
eyes from him: strange are the things that must go on inside her; she does
not know it, but she clings to him. Hc is appalled – but he, too, feels drawn
to her: he understands nothing. (Here it is a question of the poet having to
invent everything!) Only the manner of execution can say anything here! –
But you can gain an idea of what I mean if you listen to the way that
Brünnhilde listened to Wotan. – This woman suffers unspeakable restlessness
and excitement: the old esquire had noticed this on previous occasions, each
time that she had shortly afterwards disappeared. This time she is in the
tensest possible state. What is going on inside her? Is she appalled at the
thought of renewed flight, does she long to be freed from it? Does she hope –
for an end to it all? What hopes does she have of Parzival? Clearly she
attaches unprecedented importance to him! – But all is gloomy and vague: no
knowledge, only instinct and dusky twilight? – Cowering in a corner, she
witnesses Anfortas's agonized scene: she gazes with a strangely inquisitive
look (sphinx-like) at Parzival. He, too, is – stupid, understands nothing, stares
in amazement – says nothing. He is driven out. The messenger of the Grail

sinks to the ground with a shriek; she then disappears. (She is forced to wander again.)

Now can you guess who this wonderfully enchanting woman is whom Parzival finds in the strange castle where his chivalrous spirit leads him? Guess what happens here, and how it all turns out. I shall say no more today! –

Mathilde Wesendonck-Briefe 284–7.

262. FRANZ LISZT, WEIMAR　　　　　　Paris, 13 September 1860

[...] My position with regard to Germany, moreover, remains very obscure. As you know, I am neither amnestied nor pardoned, and all I have been promised is that the right of extradition will not be invoked in cases where, for the purposes of a performance of my works, I wish to enter any of the German federal territories whose government has consented to my doing so and which will first have sought permission for such consent from the Saxon government. I would not even have been able to extend my six-day journey to the Rhine[1] in order to take in Weimar without first having seen to the fulfilment of these conditions, assuming, of course, that I did not wish to begin by insulting the Saxon government. None of our German potentates can deal directly with me in any way at present, since I remain as before a political outlaw. And so I still cannot expect any Court to take any significant or adequate measures on my behalf, with the result that plans for the performances of my latest works have really made very little progress. And this is all the more evident in that, on the other hand, our greatest opera houses are in such a shocking state: Berlin, for ex., is quite out of the question, unless one were to envisage the possibility of a complete revolution of the theatrical and administrative conditions there. I cannot say that I was so bold as to appear before the Princess of Pr.[2] with any hope of making a significant impression on her in this respect: I know that what I am thinking of cannot be even remotely understood by anyone from that region, simply because there is no possibility there of any really serious interest in me. And so I was perfectly content to find in the Princess the expected intelligent, shrewd and lively woman that I had imagined; it was sufficient to express my appreciation and gratitude for her uninterrupted pleasure in my works, without my being in

---

1 Wagner was absent from Paris between 11 and 19 August 1860, visiting Minna in Bad Soden, his brother Albert in Frankfurt, Louis Schindelmeisser in Darmstadt and Princess Augusta of Prussia in Baden-Baden.
2 Prussia.

any way misled into informing her of any particular plans or wishes that I might have.

And so, for the moment, it remains a mysterious secret *where* my Tristan will first see the light of day. Its birth would be simplest – it seems – if I were to entrust its confinement to the King of Hanover. *Niemann* claims that the King would immediately engage any singer, male or female, whom I needed for a model performance of my work, as long as the performance were to take place in Hanover. That would be something. This King appears to be liberal and munificent in his passion for the arts: nothing else is any use to me. Let us hope that he sees no obstacle in my political situation.

For the present I am fully preoccupied with my Paris venture, which mercifully obscures the prospect of my future misery in Germany. I do not know what rumours are circulating with you in respect of the difficulties placed in my way: they may be well meant, but they are erroneous. *Never before have I been so fully and unconditionally provided for with whatever material I need for an outstanding performance* as is the case here in Paris with the performance of Tannhäuser at the Grand Opera; my only wish is that a German prince might one day offer me the same kind of thing for my new works as has been offered me here. It is the only triumph of my art so far that I myself have experienced in person: I owe it to the success of my works in Germany which have brought me such warm admirers that, on the strength of their word, the emperor[1] resolved to issue a truly imperial *decree* which now makes me master over all the material I need and which protects me against all intrigues. The translation has finally turned out the greatest possible success and encourages me to hope for a favourable outcome in every other respect: I am assured of getting the best possible singers; in every one of the backstage areas there is a prevailing mood of eagerness and care to which Germany has little accustomed me. The entire administrative staff is delighted to undertake such a task which promises a more interesting occupation than their usual work. I, too, am taking the matter seriously: weaknesses that I have recognized in the score are to be removed; it is with a great deal of pleasure that I am reworking Venus's big scene, and I plan to improve the whole work in this way. The ballet scene, too, will be completely redone according to a more elaborate plan that I have devised.[2] –

Unfortunately I have not yet been able to make an actual start on any of these essential tasks. Up until my recent excursion to the Rhine, I was fully occupied with the translation. On my return I first had to write a short literary piece which I have only just completed. M. Frédéric Villot, about whom Hans will no doubt have spoken to you, invited me to publish my opera poems in a prose translation, and to add a preface explaining my ideas. I have now

1 Napoleon III.
2 See letter [257], pp. 489-91.

done this. I believe the piece will appear at the beginning of October at the latest. – We are now all ready for the rehearsals: unfortunately, I finally had to object to the baritone.[1] Fould was immediately obliged to issue instructions for a new singer to be engaged: but the right man has yet to be found, and although this has resulted in a slight delay, there is no trace of any ill-will on anyone's part. Meyerbeer, who is now behaving in his usual coy manner, is ultimately powerless to influence the emperor and, indeed, the whole affair: on the contrary, he is seeking to avail himself of the talents that have been engaged for my benefit and use them for his own future advantage. Well, I do not begrudge him that. The fellow never had any initiative.

There, my dearest Franz, you have a more or less clear idea of my present position and activities. You will not, I imagine, expect me to feel happy here: but what I do feel is the peace of mind of the fatalist who abandons himself to his fate, surprised, perhaps, at the strange manner in which it ordains my actions and guides me along unexpected channels – telling me in secret: this is ultimately how it must be!

It is with a real sense of horror that I now think of Germany and of the future plans I reckon on undertaking there. May God forgive me, but all I see there is pettiness and meanness, the semblance and conceit of solidity, but without any real ground or basis. Half-heartedness in everyone and everything, so that I would ultimately prefer to see the Pardon de Ploërmel[2] here in Paris than in the shade of the famous, glorious German oak! I must also confess that setting foot on German soil again made not the slightest impression upon me, except, at most, a sense of surprise at the foolishness and unmannerliness of the language that was being spoken all around me. Believe me, we have no fatherland! And if I am "German", it is no doubt because I carry my Germany around with me; and that is fortunate, since the garrison at Mainz did not exactly inspire me. –

[. . .]

Liszt-Briefe II, 292–5.

---

1 According to the much later account of Charles Truinet, published in the *Bayreuther Festblätter* of 1886 (translated by Elizabeth Forbes in *About the House* [Summer 1975], 34–7), Wagner wanted the part of Wolfram to be sung by Jean-Baptiste Faure (1830–1914); when Faure demanded a fee of 8000 francs a month, the part was offered instead to Morelli at the end of September 1860. Morelli's fee was 3000 francs.
2 *Le Pardon de Ploërmel*, an *opéra comique* in 3 acts by Giacomo Meyerbeer, which was first heard at the Opéra-Comique on 4 April 1859.

263. MATHILDE WESENDONCK, ZURICH   [Paris, 12 February 1861]

I hope that fat Tuesday[1] will finally grant me a quiet morning in which to tell my friend a little about myself.

Whenever my head is crammed full of the hundred or so details that my present undertaking brings with it, I find that there is really no sense in talking about myself. For what was always so remarkable about our relationship was precisely the fact that the essential import of our actions and thoughts seemed quite spontaneously to engage our attention in a purified form, allowing us, as it were, to feel emancipated from our real lives the moment we met. If I empty my mind of all the rubbish that it contains in order to make it completely free for you, what remains there can be only the very best, and there can no longer be any question of torment: on the contrary, a vague melancholy settles around my soul, revealing all else to us in an appropriately worthless light: for nothing has any real value for the person who feels how much he must sacrifice whenever he wants to give meaning to the semblance of reality. –

What consoles me, in spite of all the torment that my art causes me, is the fact that it can always appear to you in a serenely cheerful light. You own and like paintings, you read and study and attend lectures: you assimilate whatever seems worthy and noble, untouched by the things that you are able to disregard. All the news you have sent me, including your latest news from this winter, agrees on this one point, namely that you have been granted the happiness of enjoying life calmly and gently. The significance of this enjoyment will now have dawned upon you in full: perhaps it means the same to you as my activities, and perhaps also my distress, mean to me. Yet I often flatter myself that I, too, might be capable of such enjoyment, and that only my mission prevents me from being able to do so. When I consider what I am capable of enduring, I cannot but be amazed, and the longing that so often consumes me for calm and peaceful seclusion is bound to seem totally unjustified. And yet I am always attended by a certain inner calm: that of the deepest and fullest resignation. A thoroughly unmalicious but all the more unerring lack of any belief has taken possession of me: as a result I have not only abandoned all hope but, more especially, all my relations to those who approach me are founded upon so insubstantial a base – in spite of the periodic airing of my often highly communicative nature – that there is no longer any possibility of my ever being shaken in this lack of belief.

Even if weeks or entire months were to pass by before I met someone again who had today made a lively impression upon me, not a single speck of dust would cloud our relationship in consequence. I am never unkind, only incredibly indifferent. Habit has no part of me.

---

1 "Der fette Dienstag", a literal translation of the French *mardi gras*, or Shrove Tuesday, which in 1861 fell on 12 February.

You asked me about the women of my acquaintance. I have got to know a good many, but am not in habitual contact with any of them. Madame Ollivier is very talented and even dazzling by nature, albeit gentler than her sister.[1] When I ask myself why it is that we see each other so rarely, I find above all that it is a certain lack of truthfulness on her part that has driven me away from her, so to speak, and I do not feel sufficiently attracted by her to take Ollivier into the bargain since, for all the kindness that he has shown me, he has one unbelievable quality, which is that of an over-excited and over-excitable barrister. The same is true of all my acquaintances: however much I cultivate their friendship, the chances of any profit on my part are so unequal that I prefer to resign the struggle and – as the mood takes me – put up with whatever fate brings my way.

Among others, these acquaintances include a democratic old maid, a certain Fräulein von Meysenbug, who is at present staying here as governess to some Russian children. She is unbelievably ugly, but she has this in her favour, that when she was first introduced to me some years ago in London, I treated her very badly in a fit of ill-temper provoked by her effusive ideas on improving the world.[2] This memory stirred me now, and, as a result of my remorse, she now feels more at ease in my presence. My own writings had made the unhappy woman somewhat overwrought, but she is now more subdued, and is enjoying the Tannhäuser rehearsals. From the so-called upper class there is a lady whom I used to know only superficially but who has now engaged a greater measure of my attention than was previously the case: it is the Countess Kalergis, a niece of Nesselrode, the Russian Chancellor of State, whom I have no doubt already mentioned to you. As a well-known diplomatic intriguer, she used to excite open loathing on my part. However, she spent part of last summer in Paris, and she visited me here and persuaded me to summon Klindworth from London in order to make music with her. I sang Act II of Tristan with Garcia-Viardot, just the two of us, with Berlioz the only other person present. We also performed part of the Nibelungs. It was the very first time I had done so since leaving you. What drew this women to my attention was the observation of a strange feeling of satiety on her part, a contempt for the world and a loathing which might have left me indifferent if I had not at the same time observed her quite evident and profound longing for music and poetry, a longing which in the circumstances seemed to me significant. Since she is not without talent in this respect, the woman ended up by engaging my interest. She was also the first person I met who, quite spontaneously, surprised me by her truly magnificent understanding of the position I was in. But even her I was on the whole glad to see the back of again: I simply have no need of all this.

1 Cosima von Bülow.
2 See *Mein Leben* 621; English trans. 607.

I have already expressed my views on the Princess Metternich. She is certainly a strange creature. I was told that her dancing is utterly enchanting, and that she sings with a most original accent. She asked me recently whether I had written any fugues. She said she would enjoy playing them! I looked at her wide-eyed with amazement, and recalled how her wretched Viennese piano was perpetually out of tune and how she always asks the most incredibly naïve questions. But – I told myself, everything is possible here! However, I have not yet had an opportunity to convince myself of her talents. I have had to decline all her invitations so far, and have put in an appearance only when I was obliged to entreat her to issue some command or other on my behalf, an appeal that I always preferred to address to her rather than to anyone else since I always seemed to give her great pleasure by doing so. Her husband, the young prince, is quiet and genuinely good-natured, but without any real warmth. He, too, is a composer, and has asked my permission to dedicate something to me.

Frau von Pourtalès, the wife of the Prussian ambassador, seems to be not without a certain depth, and certainly appears to have refined tastes. I have discovered that the wife of the Saxon ambassador, Frau von Seebach, is a woman of real substance. She is very ugly and coarse in her appearance, but I was surprised by a certain gentle fire glowing here beneath the lava. She could not understand how anyone could fail to see the tremendous passion of my conceptions, and thought it a risky business to take her young daughter with her to see Tannhäuser. One makes such curious acquaintanceships here! But that is all they are – acquaintanceships that I need to remind myself periodically of ever having made! The husbands of the afore-mentioned women are distinguished by their good-naturedness and by their very slender talent. I believe, however, that they lead a much more brutal life on the whole than the women. On the contrary, it is a common experience here, too, to find that intelligent men generally have very uninteresting wives. It is they whom I like best, namely the husbands. Their wives are not an embarrassment, and my dealings with them pass off without any difficulty, but ultimately very little hinges upon them.

Ah! child – let us speak no more of such things! Believe me, only in this way can one drag oneself along, effortfully, effortfully – and scarcely pleased to have to account for the way one does so. It is vain to wish for anything: to act and to torment oneself is the only way to forget one's misery.

Your decision, my child, not to come to Tannhäuser saddened me deeply – as you can well imagine! – simply because it robbed me of the pleasure of seeing you again in the near future. The reasons that combined to produce this decision I was obliged to accept as the promptings of your innermost heart, for it was always the safest course for me to adopt when I strove to understand you, enriching and often correcting my own feelings by appropriating yours. I was sad – and said nothing. –

Then Otto wrote to me recently to say that you would be attending the event after all. Believe me, my pleasure at this news was painfully intense! I knew that you had done yourself an injustice, and this news made me so happy that I scarcely dared hope that its promise would be fulfilled. – Now Otto has written to me again – you will not be coming with him. I find this unspeakably unsettling! Can you not see that? –

For all that your friend has had a hard struggle recently, let him now say to you quite calmly: –

The first few weeks of Tannhäuser will involve me in a great deal of work: I do not think that this is an auspicious time for answering the silent needs of our souls. A good deal of unnecessary work will be unavoidable, and everything will tend to be superficial and unedifying. I would therefore do better to agree to your own suggestion and wait for a more settled period when I can present the first performance of a complete new work of mine with the same degree of meticulous preparation as has been the case here with Tannhäuser: the performance itself must, and indeed will, have much to offer you then, when the atmosphere is calmer, and we ourselves can enjoy it calmly. –

I say all this and admit it quite openly. But should I make a secret of the fact that everyone and everything fades into insignificance beside the thought of finally being able to see you again – even for an hour? – No! My child, I shall not keep this a secret from you. And – if, in spite of everything, you were to come and risk finding little of me and my true self, I would neverthe- less – egoist that I am! – give thanks for the hour that enabled me to gaze once more in your eyes! –

Enough! You know all this better than I! – At present I have a certain peace and quiet, since there are not rehearsals every day. But I have a great deal of extra work which continues to make extreme demands upon my time. The rehearsals are progressing, and receiving an unprecedented degree of care which often strikes me as incomprehensible; at all events, the forthcoming performance will be altogether exceptional. Niemann is altogether sublime; he is a great artist of the rarest kind. The success of the other parts will owe rather more to artifice: but I hope that the extreme care that has been expended here will succeed in covering up the joins. –

And now, a thousand sincere good wishes! Give Otto my warmest thanks for his loyal perseverance: whatever he finds when he arrives here, I am sure he will endure it and will certainly take away with him a significant impression.

Adieu, my friend!

The performance is still fixed for Friday the 22nd. But Otto should also be prepared for Monday the 25th![1]

Kesting 425–30.

1 The first performance took place on Wednesday 13 March 1861.

264. ALBERT NIEMANN, PARIS   Paris, 21 February 1861

Please read the last page first and then, depending upon your inclination and mood, read the whole letter through from the beginning, or else not at all! My friend,

I hear it said that you are continuing to feel increasingly disheartened, and that this sense of discouragement is driving you to expect yet further sacrifices of me. No one would ever forgive me if I flattered this weakness a moment longer! –

During the six months that we have been rehearsing our "Tannhäuser", I have had the satisfaction of exercising so beneficial an effect upon singers who had previously no idea of how to sing my music that people are amazed at this success, a success which has finally left its mark on their performances. While everything else here is growing in stature and filling me with joy and hope, you yourself appear increasingly small and, by gradually receding into the distance, rob me of the satisfaction of knowing that I had gained some influence over you, too. Whereas someone like *Tedesco*[1] surprises me at every turn and achieves things which she previously claimed she was incapable of achieving, – and whereas *Sax*,[2] for ex., has at my insistence acquired a degree of breath control of which she previously seemed to have no notion, so that she now sings passages such as the end of the adagio section of the 2nd-act finale with such perfect beauty as you yourself heard at yesterday's rehearsal, I have not succeeded in persuading you even so much as to breathe at a different place in order to link together the two parts of the first verse of Tannhäuser's song and thus achieve a beautiful, heartfelt and grateful effect at this point!

Although I honoured you not only in the eyes of all Germany, where you were previously but little known, but also in the sight of France and Europe, too, by having you – and you alone – summoned to Paris as the only singer in whom I had complete – and blind – trust, I have failed – from the very moment of your arrival in Paris – to elicit even the least trust from you in return. You have maintained what I am bound to call an almost insulting reserve towards me, and have shown an equally meticulous care in refusing to accept any of the advice that I might have given you. You commit the indelicacy of telling me, very prematurely, that at the end of May you intend leaving the Paris "Tannhäuser" in the lurch once and for all; you declare that in future you do not intend to have much to do with any of my operas, and in that way you effectively nip in the bud my hopes of finally having found the longed-for interpreter of my heroic roles, knowing full well the importance that I attach to you for my own future and that of my works. –

1 Fortunata Tedesco, the Paris Venus.
2 Marie Sax, the Paris Elisabeth.

I shall have to learn to get over this blow, and make my future plans accordingly. –

Our immediate concern, however, continues to be this Paris "Tannhäuser". I cannot conceal from you what it is that weighs heavy on my heart in this regard. –

Although you made it clear from the very outset that you were not disposed to accept any attempts on my part to rationalize your interpretation for you, I nevertheless hoped that your sound artistic susceptibility would enable us to come to some understanding on various points of detail. Although you proved most inflexible in this respect, I was nevertheless able to hope that you had heeded the odd hint in matters of detail. I now realize that after six months of working with me your own object ultimately has been to reduce the achievement that I expected of you to the level of your previous achievements in this role, since it seems that you believe that only in this way can you find any peace of mind. My warm appreciation even of such an achievement as this, as far as I can draw conclusions from what I have seen so far, is something that I have repeatedly and sincerely made known to you, and you would be doing me the most grievous injustice if you were to doubt for a moment in the sincerity of even the most flattering protestations on my part. Notwithstanding this fact, I have realized that your previous achievement was not altogether perfect; it was the product of an immense talent on the basis of your first youthful conception of the part: to hallow this with the name of full artistic maturity was the task reserved for you during your long course of study here under the guidance of the author himself. It remains for you to place a universally correct interpretation upon the first and second acts in particular, to put the finishing touches to your vocal training, especially where the question is one of tenderness of expression, and to forge a complementary link with the individual moments of vocal brilliance. I hope you will not respond to this by quoting the usual theatrical jargon about effects and bravura passages, a jargon that becomes *you* least of all: you would then leave me with no choice but to ignore you completely. Building to some extent upon this idea, however, I now consider it necessary to say the following.

That it was possible for you to sing only the third act in Germany is in itself sufficient to disclose the weak point in your previous achievement. Even the most mediocre singers have known how to be relatively effective in this third act: they were able to do so as a matter of course, in much the same way that Masaniello's mad scene[1] was effective, making every tenor seem better than he was. I tell you, by contrast, that you can keep the whole of this third act if you can give me a proper rendering of the finale to the second act. It is here that the dramatic crisis lies, and here, too, that Tannhäuser must enlist and maintain the greatest interest: if he fails in this, the 3rd act,

1 In Auber's *La Muette de Portici*.

however successful, will remain a mere play for actors by which I set no store whatsoever, – and then – it would at least be entirely consistent to omit the whole of the first two acts. But let us not do that here! This is why I insist that the finale of the 2nd act must be given complete, and given, moreover, with all the weight of utterance that you can muster! Do not refer me here to the fact that I cut the adagio passage for *Tichatscheck*:[1] if I had had *you* then, you may rest assured that I would not have shortened it. Nor should you believe that I took this passage away from *Tichatscheck* because it might have tired his voice: on the contrary, as far as his voice is concerned, *Tichatscheck* could have sung six such passages, for the longer he had been singing, the richer his voice became and the greater his powers of endurance, so that I was totally unused to hearing *Tichatscheck* complaining in the way that I constantly hear you complain, you who are a veritable Hercules in terms of strength and talent; which is why I cannot pay any real heed to these complaints of yours. The deficiency which ruined this important passage at the time of the Dresden performances was as follows: – a glance at the score will show you that the entire ensemble of minstrels continues to sing at the same time as Tannhäuser himself; their voices cover his to the extent that Tannhäuser's solo gives the impression of being simply an inner part which might, however, have stood out if *Tichatscheck* had been capable of expressing any real sense of tragic pain: but we know that this was precisely where his weak point lay. The inspired idea of omitting the ensemble and having Tannhäuser sing on his own did not occur to me at the time, and only recently have I hit upon the right solution. On that occasion I had no alternative but to strike out the passage, since, as a result of its being mixed up with the ensemble singing, it remained unclear, and thus appeared to be a meaningless *longueur*. Now *Tichatscheck* too will once again sing this passage (as a solo) with all his old power. – Well, you have doubtless realized how important this passage is, and know not only how effective it can be in itself but also how important it is for our interest in Tannhäuser. You are concerned only for your voice, and your anxiety is increased by the belief that *Tichatscheck* himself had not been able to sing this passage. It was to refute this belief and to restore your confidence that I have just recounted this entire incident all over again, and repeated the reason why I cut it on that occasion and why I am now restoring it for *Tichatscheck*, too.

You should therefore abandon this fear of yours and take a more courageous view of the matter. Do not think about the third act: this is not a problem for you. Think only of this finale to the second act and throw yourself into it body and soul, as though you did not have another note to sing after this finale. The gain will then be certain: at the most crucial point in the opera – where everything has reached the highest pitch of intensity, and the slightest

[1] Joseph Tichatschek had created the role in Dresden in 1845.

sound will be picked up with breathless suspense – here it is that the course of the *entire evening* will be decided! Believe *me* and trust in me just this *once*! You shall never hear from me again as long as you live!! – If you produce this "pitié pour moi" as I have already heard you sing it on repeated occasions and as I know you can, and if you produce it, moreover, in such a way that everyone's hair stands on end and their hearts tremble, *everything*, but *everything* will have been achieved, the immediate effect will be immeasurable, and everything that follows will be – child's play; for an immense faith will then exist, a faith that you will not be able to undermine, even if your intonation begins to falter in the 3rd act. If, however, you fail to maintain interest in your person at the end of the second act (in other words at the point of crisis), the third act will simply be rated as a brilliant episode, but the performance as a whole will be regarded – instinctively – as a failure. (Do not counter this by telling me of your previous successes in Germany's 2nd- and 3rd-rate theatres;[1] the fact that you were able to give only the 3rd act there confirms my own opinion!)

Once more: – sing the 2nd-act finale as if you were to end the evening with it – and rest assured – only then will you sing the third act entirely to my liking. In a word: I find you far too fresh in the third act, too physically powerful, and I have waited in vain so far for the nuances that I demand. I do not *want* an exhibition of sensual vocal strength in this scene: everything about your interpretation is still far too solid. If I wanted to keep pace with you, I should have to re-score the entire orchestra at your entrance. Everything here is calculated to produce a ghostly tonelessness which gradually rises to the level of a touching tenderness, but no further. There is too much physical strength in your rendering of the narration up to your arrival in Rome: that is not how a man would speak who had just been roused from madness to a few minutes' lucidity, a being from whom others shy away when they meet him, who for months has gone almost entirely without food, and whose life is sustained only by the glimmer of an insane desire. On your lips the papal ban has an energy which, admittedly, is shatteringly effective: but if this energy were to be somewhat less substantial, the scene would certainly not fail to make its proper effect, quite the opposite, only now will it produce the appropriate effect, when backed by a suitable rhetorical delivery. Well, far be it from me to desire anything *different* here; all I wanted to say was that you should not sacrifice the passage in the 2nd-act finale for the sake of this one here. And I wanted to indicate that, even if Tannhäuser were to be somewhat hoarse in the 3rd act, this would be no great misfortune, whereas I should consider it unfortunate, in the true sense of the word, if, in the 3rd act,

1 Niemann had sung Tannhäuser in Insterburg and Gumbinnen (1854), Hanover (1855), Wiesbaden (1856), Hamburg (1857) and Frankfurt (1858).

Tannhäuser were forced to resort to a physical expedient in order to restore an interest which he had lost in the crucial 2nd act. –

There is something else that I have to say to you concerning this third act. Whereas, in the course of the rehearsals, you have given marked emphasis, at least in certain passages, to the nuances with which you had previously invested your acting, nuances, indeed, which you have generally endowed with a certain degree of violence, it saddens me to find that there are certain instructions which I have given you which have yet to be adequately rendered by you. I do not know whether you will perform the scene resting on your staff in the way that I have asked you, or not? And so I repeat once more:

act out the horn accompaniment

clearly and vividly: doubling up in anguish on the last note. And you must not move a single step. This is repeated four times: it will produce the most horrifying effect when, on the final occasion, he says – : "but I am seeking him who can show me the way to the Venusberg". Do you understand what I am saying? This alone will give you the right tone for the whole scene. "Speak not of Rome!" has a harsh enough effect. – Your voice is too powerful during the first part of the narration: only moving tenderness, – without any bitterness. You are spoiling the twofold ending in F major by not dropping smoothly in the diminuendo – p – etc.

"To sweeten the tear that my angel once wept for me
(p.)   (più p.)

"My angel's tears to sweeten!"

Since you are so bent on being effective, believe me, you will achieve this aim here only through the *p.*, through moving and mellifluous tenderness.

Similarly, the passage in the 1st act where you take up the phrase of the Pilgrims' Chorus is too harsh, too immediately expressive: more tender; as though choked by tears at the end. –

You see my friend, I have not yet given up my attempts to persuade you to heed my advice: my tremendously high opinion of what you have achieved and are capable of achieving pursues you, perhaps to the point of importuning you. – Your present agitation is something I can readily understand: without this profound excitability and even a momentary sense of discouragement – no real eagerness to see victory, no genuine awareness of a great task. But let us beware of allowing this situation to continue, and indeed of allowing it to seduce our strength of purpose. Who – in the devil's name! shall finally be bold and daring enough to accomplish this task if it is not you yourself, whom nature has equipped for the part in a way that I had previously only dreamt of but certainly never thought possible? My destiny has led you to me – and am I now, at the moment of recognition, to lose you through some imaginary weakness? You saw the sacrifice I was prepared to make for you. I can say in all confidence that you were wrong not to attempt the new verse in the Song Contest: it means losing a great deal of brilliance and a most necessary part of the whole. It is, however, quite impossible for me to sacrifice the passage in the 2nd-act finale to your momentary faint-heartedness! Even you, the young and stalwart hero, would find it strange to return to Germany and there discover from old *Tichatscheck* just how effective this passage is: for – the latter still sings it.

Courage, courage, my friend! Do not allow yourself to be overwhelmed by a faint-heartedness that so ill becomes you! Perform this passage at the final dress rehearsal with *all* your might, and let us then see its effect on your third act.

This is the last request which I, as author, shall make of you. You have made it sufficiently clear that, however much it pains me to admit it, I shall be obliged to manage without you in the more distant future.

11.30 o'clock.

I had reached this point when your letter arrived.[1]

I now see how far you are prepared to go with me. You address me in a language which I can really understand only by casting my mind back to the earliest days of my arduous career.

I believe I may say, however, that you are mistaken when you say that I have exposed you to public ridicule, and I am amazed that anyone should have brought such boulevard gossip to your attention.

I ask myself with some hesitation whether this letter can still serve any purpose, or whether it can only make matters worse. I do not intend, however, to cut myself off quite so abruptly from my last remaining hope as an artist.

You will see from this letter what an immensely high opinion I have of you, and this certain knowledge must surely preserve you from a superficial misunderstanding of the spirit in which I address myself to you here.

On one point, however, I take back the foregoing protestations.

I declare my readiness to cut the passage in question.

Calm down! Take care of yourself, and – if possible – revise your opinion

---

1 Niemann's note of 20 February 1861 (Burrell Cat. 377) announced that if Wagner was not prepared to cut the passage in question, he would have to find another Tannhäuser.

of me so that in future it encompasses somewhat greater respect on your part
than you have shown me by the tone of your lines to me today. –
   Keep calm!
   With the most sincere appreciation,

Yours,
Richard Wagner

Niemann-Briefe 118–30.

265. ALPHONSE ROYER, PARIS   Paris, 25 February 1861

My dear Monsieur Royer,
   I really cannot allow the result of such tremendous hard work on the part of
so many artists and répétiteurs to be abandoned to the mercy of a conductor[1]
incapable of supervising a definitive performance of my work.
   Without wishing to restate all the grievances that I might well lay at the
door of the musical director, who has misunderstood the friendly nature of
the proposal that I put to him whereby I myself might be permitted to conduct
one of the rehearsals; and without insisting, either, upon the outcome to be
expected from such a rehearsal, which would have allowed me to indicate to
him, and to a certain extent to demonstrate, all the essential nuances that he
has not been able to grasp for himself, I see myself obliged, as a result of his
resistance, to increase the sum total of my demands, and to lay before you
the irrevocable decision that I have taken in the light of yesterday's rehearsal.
   I am writing to you today, therefore, to ask not merely that I be allowed to
take the final rehearsal but, in addition, to conduct the first three performances
of a work whose execution I consider impossible unless you find the means
to satisfy my legitimate demands.
   It is not for me to examine the difficulties which may lie in the way of your
taking this step, but simply to make you understand its inescapable necessity.
   Whatever the outcome, the very question as to whether my Tannhäuser is
to be performed at all at the Opéra can no longer be regarded as a separate
issue. And I may also remind you, my dear Monsieur Royer, that there is an
urgent need for you, in turn, to come to a decision and make one last effort
in support of a task in whose accomplishment you have so far assisted me
with so much goodwill.
   You will understand that, as things stand, a prompt solution is necessary.
It is impossible to prolong the rehearsals any longer, even allowing for any
improvement on the part of the musical director; the artists are exhausted,
and, as for myself, I no longer feel the courage necessary to set about

1 Pierre-Louis-Philippe Dietsch.

educating the conductor, except by inviting him to be present at the final rehearsal and the first three performances, conducted by myself.

I have the honour, Sir, to be your most obedient servant,

Richard Wagner

Paris Opéra Archives (published, with corrected orthography, in Tiersot 231-2) (the original is in French).

266. JOSEPH TICHATSCHEK, DRESDEN   Paris, 23 March 1861

God, how much I have thought of you recently, my dearest Tscheckel! How often have I told people the story of how you forbade the copyists, following the first performance of *Rienzi*, to make the cuts that I had indicated and how, when I took you to task for this, you retorted: "No, I won't allow any cuts! it's too divine!" How the hot tears ran down my cheeks. –

I couldn't help recalling this now that I find myself dealing with a coward who runs around whining loudly that he is ruining his voice with my Tannhäuser. You can imagine how I feel!

Sammlung Burrell 515.

267. CHARLES BAUDELAIRE, PARIS   [Paris, April 1861]

Monsieur,

No, I did not judge it necessary to reply to the editor of the *Papillon*,[1] who began by sending me several somewhat vulgar letters and who finished up writing that my *Tannhäuser* was as stupid as it was bad. You know that I am beholden to M. Victor Cochinat, editor of the *Causerie*;[2] I got to know him through the kindness of M. Leroy. The last time that we spoke about it was at Tortoni's, and what I was promised was fairly interesting. You know better than anyone how much money I need to earn in order to live. For these unhappy and disagreeable days have been worse then merely sad for me from this point of view. I have earned seven hundred francs in all. You can well imagine that this is not enough to repay me for all this wasted time, and for this opera. Among my friends, there are some who reproach me for the fact that the Opéra has spent more than 300,000 francs on me. I am accused of ingratitude. But these young people who came to welcome me and console

1 No details known.
2 Cochinat had taken Wagner's part and offered him the columns of *La Causerie* to answer his critics.

me have comforted me, and I am perfectly contented. I number you among them. M. Auber is astonished. Not I, for I have always been attracted by young people, and I love all that is young, all that is beautiful. Oh! yes, all that is beautiful. In this regard, I have had some very fine experiences with the young people of this town. I like them because I feel friendly towards them. And one cannot be another person's friend unless one loves him.

Ah! love and friendship! It is this that makes up for all I have suffered. I have emerged victorious; I have triumphed over the misfortune which this society of jockeys[1] has caused me. What have I done to them? I sinned, oh! yes how many times have I been told that I sinned against the sacred spirit of this society, which was unable to come at the agreed time. And the ballet had ended. This ballet which had been written for them. Yes, this ballet without any stars. It is the fault of these young people that I failed to be crowned. And you know how much I have suffered because of this idea. But other young people were behind me. And that is why I am infinitely grateful to those among you who are so good. M. Leroy was no less kind. I confess that M. Catulle Mendès immediately opened up his review to me.[2] I bless this beautiful child whom God created in a moment of great happiness. And he promises me a great deal. I need it all, monsieur. M. Auber would not understand me, any more than all those other old men, not to mention D . . . ,[3] who maltreated my poor *Tannhäuser*.

I see that youth, if it does not belong to the jockeys, has a great deal of good sense. It understands me. And you, you devote some very fine pages[4] to my work. You are in the vanguard of these dear and devoted young people. Yes it is necessary to be beautiful to be loved. I never understood this as well as I do now. Beauty and friendship are the two most beautiful things in the world, and one cannot love what is unattractive. All these young people are a society of honest friends distinguished by their beauty. And that is why I believe it was the old men who whistled.

Love is a grandiose bond for intelligence, and love binds friendship, as one of your youngest colleagues says. For there is love in every friendship. There is certainly love, for I cannot explain how one might be truly loyal to a man unless one loved him sincerely. And that is why I am happy to have met you.

May I thank both you and, especially, M. Leroy once again. He came running to meet me on my arrival in Paris. That is what I call love and friendship. If one could not love a friend, one could not be an honest friend. And how sad life would be then! It would be worthless. Men and women

---

1 i.e. the Jockey Club, which had sabotaged the production of *Tannhäuser* at the Opéra (see introductory essay, p. 412).
2 Mendès invited Wagner to contribute an article to the *Revue fantaisiste*.
3 Pierre-Louis-Philippe Dietsch.
4 "Richard Wagner et Tannhauser à Paris", originally published in the *Revue européenne* of 1 April 1861.

have a mutual need of this love. I love you because you are my friend, and that is why I am writing to you.

Yours, etc ...
Richard Wagner.

Leroy 177-80 (the original is in French).

268. MINNA WAGNER, PARIS   Vienna,[1] 13 May 1861

My dear Mutz,

The performance of Lohengrin is not until Wednesday.[2] Frau Ortrud has been given a short break. This delay was most welcome to me, since the excitement of the performance would have followed too soon upon the emotions of the rehearsal. This rehearsal took place last Saturday: I sat on the stage, and did not stir from my chair, and yet I could scarcely stand up at the end. This rehearsal far surpassed *all* my expectations, and for the first time in this artist's life of toil and suffering I felt the most total sense of enjoyment, a feeling that has reconciled me to everything. I cannot begin to tell you how deep and unalloyed my pleasure was. Orchestra, singers, chorus – everything admirable, unbelievably beautiful! It is possible that the emotion and solemn mood of everyone involved in performing my work for the first time contributed a good deal to the incomparably delicate, noble and enthusiastically fiery performance: everything was strictly ordered, and yet there was not the least sense of constraint; there was something touchingly sincere about it. I sat quite still the whole time, without moving: but one tear after another ran down my face. The dear people then came up to me and embraced me in silence. Only the orchestra and chorus finally broke into loud cheers. You can imagine how I thanked them! But it was Kapellmeister Esser to whom I gave the greatest pleasure: the poor man had previously been immensely anxious lest I be dissatisfied and wished to change a number of things. And so he stood there without uttering a sound, as though thunderstruck, while I explained that anyone who had just received such a gift from heaven as this performance was incapable of voicing any kind of objection: and that it was all so admirable that I felt nothing but joy, gratitude and profound emotion. And indeed this came literally from my heart: never have I cast such amorous glances at a man as at this good and honest Kapellmeister at his desk. – In a word, dearest Mutz! it is a heavenly opera here: a mass of splendid voices, each more beautiful than the next, – chorus – orchestra – enchanting! *Ander* – the tenor – quite perfect; his voice, too, is not merely adequate but, where it

---

1 Wagner arrived in Vienna on 9 May in search of singers for *Tristan und Isolde.*

2 i.e. 15 May. *Lohengrin* had first been performed in Vienna on 19 August 1858, but it was not until the dress rehearsal on 11 May 1861 that Wagner heard his opera for the first time.

matters, of brilliant vitality: at the same time a thoroughly conscientious artist, admirable in his vocal delivery and in his acting, entirely involved, full of life and fire. *Dustmann*, with her divinely expressive voice that lacks for *nothing* but always sounds gentle and tender, has a splendid dramatic style of delivery: she brings out each nuance so naturally and so clearly, so movingly and yet so correctly that I did not need to say a single word to her. – With these two – Tristan and Isolde – no question of it! –

My God, it really does me a power of good to be here! There is nothing more that I can report to your ladyship today. Whether I can prise these people away from here for August and September is a question I am bound to doubt. I fear it will be quite impossible. – Today – I have – just this very moment – been introduced to Count Lanskoronski,[1] the *Court* intendant of the Imperial Theatres: to this man, who is said to take an interest in every little detail concerning the theatre, I was able, with a clear conscience, to say only the most flattering things; for my own part, *I* had the advantage over him of having been enthusiastically received here as a composer. And so we parted, I believe, as the best of friends. He has placed his theatre at my disposal for each and every one of my operas: and I am told that he is not joking, but that he means exactly what he says, and that he will keep his word. – At all events, I now feel slightly ridiculous with my laborious attempts to arrange a model performance in Karlsruhe, where I would first have to assemble all that I needed, and believe I would do better to seize the opportunity offered me here, where *everything*, but *everything* that I need is ready to hand, with a large and enthusiastic public to back me up. – On the other hand, I remain wedded to Karlsruhe as somewhere to settle down. On this point, my dear Minna, I shall soon have further and better particulars to report! At all events, a favourable and lasting change is now taking place in the circumstances of our lives: may heaven grant us the peace and reflective calm to make the right choice, and that our choice will finally bring us security and permanence. –

Fare well for today! I am afraid that I am already under siege here, and feel permanently exhausted: Tausig – and Cornelius are also here! The confounded boy is just as amusing as ever; [he is no longer as insolent.][2] –

But that's enough! – I look forward to hearing from you, and hope it will be good news! Kindest regards to our friends, and all manner of tender greetings to our fellow lodgers![3] Adieu. Keep well, and be of good cheer!

Yours,

R.

RWA (incompletely published in Minna-Briefe II, 178–80).

1 *recte* Lanckoronski.
2 "er ist nicht mehr so frech." This sentence was omitted from the published text.
3 Fips the dog and M. Jacquot the parrot.

269. MALWIDA VON MEYSENBUG, LONDON   Paris,[1] 25 July 1861

My sincere thanks, you dear kind soul! – Your second letter was more than usually welcome – since it brought me your new address. Your first letter arrived in the midst of the most appalling weeks of my life: I soon forgot where I had put it, and as a result lost your address.

The worst is over. I shall not waste time describing the events of last month;[2] that kind of thing is best forgotten! I had finally no alternative but to importune my diplomatic friends here: though it cost much effort and distress – and a great deal of goodwill besides (as I am only too ready to attest) – we managed to scrape together the barest essentials; and it consoles me to think that my wife really noticed very little of my distress. After we had spent four more ghastly days in the house together, she left here with the parrot 2 weeks ago to the day.[3] She, too, has made an incredible effort, after her fashion. No doubt she will now have a chance to recover.

The Prussian ambassador invited me to stay with him as long as I have to remain in Paris, an invitation which I was glad to accept – not least on account of his beautiful garden with its tall trees and black swans. I am treated as a member of the family, I have my grand piano in one of the beautiful high-ceilinged rooms, and might even be prepared to put up with it all if only so many of the more agreeable things that might yet befall me were not so late in coming: apart from the briefest moment of contentment – brought about more especially by a pleasant lack of noise – I am now utterly unaffected by any kind of agreeable sensation. – My eyes are always filled with tears, and the whole affair strikes me as increasingly distressing and meaningless! – To be alone, – to be completely alone – is ultimately the only thing that still appeals to me!

The Flying Dutchman is making only slow progress in French:[4] finished or not, I am resolved to leave here on Monday evening. I intend spending a day in Soden with my wife and saying goodbye to her. I'd have preferred to have done without Liszt: I learn, however, that if I do not come, I shall make him unspeakably miserable.[5] Then on to Vienna, where I shall no doubt remain somewhat longer. Whenever my glance falls on my Tristan score, I still cannot think of it as a real possibility!! –

1 Wagner returned to Paris on 26 May and moved into the Prussian Embassy in mid-July, as guest of the Count and Countess Pourtalès.
2 Presumably a reference to Wagner's renewed financial difficulties in the aftermath of the *Tannhäuser* fiasco.
3 Minna went to take the waters in Bad Soden.
4 Wagner and Charles Truinet were translating the libretto into French for Gustave Alexandre Flaxland, to whom Wagner had sold the French performing rights of his works.
5 In his letter of 7 July 1861 Liszt had announced how much he was looking forward to Wagner's visit to Weimar, where he was to attend a meeting of the Tonkünstlerverein at which some of Liszt's works were to be performed.

Gaspérini is also coming to Vienna. And so, my kind, dear friend, it may console you to know that I have once again escaped from the final extremity: that I have lost a good deal in the process is unfortunately something I feel more and more; two precious years have been utterly wasted – and I feel extraordinarily tired. What I have lost in art I may perhaps have gained in life: one final lesson, deeply inscribed, not to try to force things to happen that are not decreed by fate!

You can see now how to get by in future, now that you know what fools we all are to grope and wallow in vain! – I often think of you, so you must not think me insensitive to your fate! Let us talk of it some other time!

Kind regards to Klindworth: when shall I see him again? –

Fare you well, and remain ever friendly towards your

Rich. W.

(Weimar until the 6th of August. Then Vienna, Imperial and Royal Court Theatre.)

Meysenbug-Briefe 75.

270. MINNA WAGNER, WEIMAR   Vienna, 19 October 1861

My dear Minna,

You are tormenting yourself needlessly, – you can be certain of that! Your letter, admittedly, is too well-meant for me to dismiss it with this brief rejoinder, but – believe me – however much I endeavour to enlighten you, I shall not be able to achieve much more than simply by saying: you are tormenting yourself needlessly. Of all the incidents and explanations that date from that difficult time, you continue to cling to only a few of them, and ignore both the context in which they occurred and other events which were more extenuating and less unsettling, and, on the basis of your extremely deficient recollections of what happened, you continue to weave for yourself a veil through which, to your own mortification, you gaze dimly and erroneously at events which, in consequence, are always bound to appear to you in a hopeless light. I realized long ago that it would be impossible ever to make you see that relationship in its true light; I also admit that, at the time in question, there were such violent excesses on every side that even the most sober-minded among us began to vacillate in his position, and I, too, will not attempt to defend myself against the charge that I occasionally lost my head. It was precisely for that reason that an end had to be put to the whole affair, so that our rows could not go on endlessly repeating themselves. For your part, of course, my dear Minna, you can always find excuses for each of the mistakes which you committed, not only for having broken open that letter,[1] which was bound to make you so unhappy, but also for the fact that, in spite of my well-founded pleas and entreaties, you paid that fatal visit[2] which was bound to rob me of my refuge and make us both homeless for long years to come – who knows for how long? – But I know the intractable nature of women's hearts: they are simply incapable of sober-mindedness in such matters. – For our more distant future, however, a more serious consequence was that it has never been possible for me, even by letter, to enlighten you as to the nature of that relationship; that it would be equally impossible for me to do so today is again clear to me from your letter. I felt as a result that, if ever we wished to see each other again and live together, we should have to come to some agreement between us on *one* basic and essential point: *never* to mention *that relationship and those events in any way*. Only by strictly observing this agreement would we find any possibility of living together in peace in the future: it was simply *to make this possible*, and certainly not to decide the rights and wrongs of the matter, that I had to insist upon this agreement. But the moment that you showed even the slightest sign of acting in disregard of this agreement, when we were living together again, I lost all control over myself, for I recognized that an understanding was impossible, and that everything hinged solely upon complete mutual discretion. You will scarcely wish to recall how often sentiment got the better of you and betrayed you into openly breaking our agreement. I was soon bound to realize that I was expecting too much of so violently suffering a woman's heart, indeed, my only cause for complaint was that your *own* life was becoming embittered in consequence. On the other hand, I still hoped to be able to carry out my firm resolution and confront you with a display of tranquil calm and silence each time that you showed any inclination to act in disregard of our agreement. The fact that I was not always able to carry out this resolve and, indeed, was less and less able to do so in the end, this, I admit, is to be regretted. When I credited myself with the strength to do so, I reckoned upon being able to lead a quiet life with fewer cares and excitements. It is with a real sense of horror that I now look back on that ghastly period that we went through again in Paris, when care, worry, annoyance, toil, and sufferings of every description finally reduced me to a state of such misery and over-sensitivity that I am amazed that I survived it at all and that I did not once lose my self-command. Could there be anything worse, in addition to the countless vexations that I had daily to endure, than inopportune reminders of earlier events that you have perpetually misunderstood? I now regard your entire view of that relationship as utterly erroneous, and am conscious of the fact that everything was

1 The "Morning confession", letter [208], pp. 381–3.
2 Minna's confrontation with Mathilde Wesendonck on 7 April 1858.

quite different, and infinitely calmer and more decorous than you imagine it to have been: the slightest scorn, the least abusiveness on your part – I was as racked by torment then as ever I was before – was bound to provoke my anger. The fact that you refuse to understand this, and that, each time my violence erupts, you choose only to vent your pent-up self-hatred, or else to see me burning with passion for another woman, this – you can well imagine! – can only make me more furious, so that at moments such as these I really wish I were dead, – for there seems no remedy against such misery, and confusion adds to confusion. It was for *that* reason that I resolved always to remain calm and silent in such cases: the fact that my fate in Paris was again so sad and contrary, and that, perpetually tormented and stung, I was unable to retain my self-command; and the fact that there were again such useless and dreadful scenes between us, – *this* it is that suggests the need for caution in the future. – The extent to which you *continue* to labour under the most erroneous illusion concerning this relationship is again clear to me from your letter. It has become an obsession with you that I desired to possess another woman and for that reason hated you and often treated you badly, since you stood between me and my goal. The fact that, following those appalling rumours which compromised the honour of an entire family and encouraged people to believe in God-knows-what criminal goings-on, I was able to regain and keep for ever the complete and devoted friendship of a man whom those rumours had dishonoured in the eyes of the whole world – not only this but the conduct that I was required to show in order to win back this man's total trust as a friend, – this is something about which you have not had the least misgivings, since you do not deem it necessary to imagine *what* must have happened here and *how* well-founded this man's opinion of me and my relationship to his wife must have been, in order for him calmly to accept me in his house and allow me to remain under his roof as a guest! And do you deem me capable of availing myself of his hospitality – a hospitality that is open to me at any time under these conditions and with these assurances – in order that, by availing myself of all the advantages of complete domestic trust, I might sue for the hand of this man's wife? Tell me, Minna, is not this the very stuff of madness? Can you not infer from the relationship which I have formed with her husband – *following* these events – what must be the nature of my relationship with the woman herself? If ever passion entered into what was originally a tender and pure relationship – which, to my sad regret, I cannot deny – can you not infer from the way in which, following such violent onslaughts against his honour, this relationship finally took a turn whereby the husband, in spite of his having been so grievously affected, has now, to his own reassurance, found his rightful place as a third party, – can you not infer from this the channels into which this relationship has now been restored, – nay, can you blame me for feeling deeply and sincerely aggrieved to see you – as the fourth person involved – bent upon excluding yourself for ever from it? I cannot overcome your obstinate desire to remain excluded from this relationship (because you continue to see this relationship in a false light), and so I have abandoned every attempt to do so. However, your blindness will never persuade me, simply in order to pander to your prejudice, to abandon my close and intimate commerce with this family which – both husband and wife – is devoted to me in its unswerving friendship: to do so would be tantamount to an admission that there was any truth in your erroneous ideas. As a result, I am resolved once and for all that, if you are not prepared to change your views, you will at least not place any obstacle in the way of my seeing these people; by this I necessarily mean that you will refrain from remarking on these relations, and, indeed, from ever mentioning them: for your continual mistrust is an insulting humiliation which I cannot admit to without making myself party to that insult. – And so, for your own part: total silence! Total avoidance of the subject! Not because there is anything dubious or suspicious here, but because you cannot or will not accept it *as it is*.

Will you be able to carry out this undertaking, and stick to your resolve in future – for the sake of your own peace of mind?? – Although you will deny that you have not done so already, I know from the experiences of recent years that it will not be entirely possible for you to do so in future! Of course, I feel sorry for you on that account, and am angry with you only because you cause *yourself* such unnecessary distress in consequence! Since, on the other hand, I feel only too well what I owe you in return and what a deep-seated obligation requires me to provide for your peace of mind and your greatest possible comfort, and since not even the view of genuinely well-intentioned mutual friends can ever persuade me that the best solution, as far as your own peace of mind is concerned, lies in our living apart: nothing grieves me as much as the helplessness in which I find myself with regard to your future fate. Truly, Minna, I am fond of you; you do me the greatest possible wrong, especially when you abandon yourself to such erroneous ideas concerning me. I myself would gladly contribute to your reassurance, and not even now do I intend giving up my attempts to provide you with a carefree and contented old age at my side, which is something you so richly deserve: you ought to realize that I, too, desire only peace and quiet, and not any new possessions. But how can I make you see this? The experiences of our recent stay in Paris have shown me how little I can trust myself, however good and calm my resolutions, whenever the endless agitations of a tempestuous and often desperately worrying outward situation cause me to be torn apart by secret inner divisions. And yet, as long as I remain fully conscious of my best intentions always to treat you gently and kindly, I have no difficulty in imagining how the two of us will learn to get along quite famously in the course of time, and how we shall be able to enjoy a life of relative comfort; but only on condition that my position in life is completely assured, and that we can settle down for good in some pleasant spot where I am assured of some suitable occupation and where a means of adequate subsistence will be placed at my disposal once and for all. If I achieve this – and I am working towards this goal with every ounce of my strength (for I, too, need these things if I am to survive), I would be the most heartless of men if, after so many storms and tribulations, I did not offer to share this longed-for refuge with you, my poor and sorely tested wife: indeed, it is with the most heartfelt joy that I should then call out to you: come on, you old thing! Let's finally make ourselves comfortable! – And indeed, I do not doubt but that – after so many painful experiences – good fortune, peace and contentment will then be ours. What satisfaction that will give me, what heartfelt pleasure to be able to offer you all this at last. My old spirits, my delight in domestic comforts would then return: if you grow crotchety again, and if your old whimsical ideas start to prey on your mind again, – why, I shall leave you in peace on your own, until you have got over it once more! –

This much may be regarded as settled! I may even be able to offer you something quite soon!

But now, my dear wife! – now you must help me to bear my *misery*! Take a dispassionate look at my present situation and you will see how, in addition to all the terrible cares and afflictions that have almost done for me, you are acting most unjustly in bringing down on both our heads yet further torments and useless agonies, as you have just been doing – however good your intentions. Consider how things stand with me! Not one of my attempts to find a fixed appointment has yet received the least attention: an ordinary Kapellmeister's post would be the death of me. My older operas are everywhere to be heard: with my new works I encounter almost insuperable difficulties. In writing these new works I have moved far – far ahead of my time and of what our theatres are capable of achieving. Karlsruhe has already harmed my chances for Tristan: it is with malicious glee that my enemies are spreading the report, "that it is my best work, but unperformable". I arrive in Vienna. Ander ill; it finally emerges that it will be difficult to count on him for the rest of this winter. This misfortune is again being used to broach the subject of the opera's unperformable nature. The new tenor Morini, whose début I am now awaiting, first has to relearn all his operas in German: if he is to be of any use to the repertoire, it will be difficult to release him for a new opera for 2 months in the middle of winter. I am having to accustom myself to the idea of waiting until the autumn of next year for the work to be performed. In the circumstances, even the administration is racked by uncertainty: I find it difficult to ask for a larger fee: but nor do I intend to give anything away. To put on new productions of Tannhäuser and Lohengrin here, and in that way gain attention for my accomplishments as a conductor (which would then have made it easier to raise the question of my being appointed general music director), was also impossible. So that there is nothing – nothing that I can do in Vienna at the moment. How do things fare elsewhere?

Not a soul asks after me. I am having to start all over again from the beginning. There is nowhere any demand for my art, for the age we live in is very unfavourable to artistic interests in general. I want to go to Berlin and see what sort of an impression I can make there in person. But what hopes do I have there? Very few. Nothing encouraging from Paris. The director of the *Théâtre lyrique*[1] is an irresolute, faint-hearted man, for ever pursued by financial ruin. At the *Opéra comique* all the regulations are against Tannhäuser: Royer was allowed to perform the work only *once*. There is again talk of *Perrin* and a new theatre under him. *Rienzi* – in the distant future.[2] For the moment everything is problematical. As a result of my departure from Paris all I could expect by way of help is exhausted. And so – my poor Mutzi – my outward position really *is* helpless and desperate. – And what do you think my inner self must be suffering? For years I have again been wrenched away from my works which alone sustained me in the past: everything that I might yet produce, if I still felt any inclination to do so, must now strike me as chimerical. How could I ever perform it, given the miserable state of our existing opera houses? Deep down inside me, I feel that if things continue like this, I shall be finished. I no longer have any hope or trust in anything. This makes me bitter: nor am I spared vexation upon vexation. I often say to myself: oh! if only I could disappear from the world! I also see in all seriousness that only if I can devote myself permanently to superintending a theatre can the ground be prepared for my future as an artist – assuming that I have any prospects at all in this direction. – For this, however, I need the very position which I am now striving to achieve but for which I still have absolutely no prospects. I cannot expect anything from Vienna for another year. Where shall I find the patience? Where shall I find the courage and inclination to lead a life in which I am perpetually thwarted? – Oh! I could go on like this for hours and still would not have exhausted all the reasons for a mood which I can truthfully call one of profound despair. It is true that my head is still above water; I have neglected nothing that might be of any use to me. I have already written to *Seebach* recently: my amnesty, my *amnesty*[3] is far too important. Yesterday I also wrote to *Pourtalès* again. I want people at least to know how abandoned I am, so that when I die they cannot say that they did not know what was happening! –

But what can I now offer you, my poor wife, in such a sad situation and with such a sad consciousness? – In God's name, do not add to my burden of care! – You may rest assured that I shall not lose sight of my concern for

1 Léon Carvalho.
2 *Rienzi* was first heard in Paris at the Théâtre Lyrique on 6 April 1869.
3 i.e. permission to return to Saxony, which was finally granted on 28 March 1862.

you: I hope to achieve something in Berlin which may serve to reassure you, too. I intend going there shortly.[1] Whether I then go on to Paris will depend upon the news I receive. If Tristan (with Morini) were to come about this winter in Vienna, I would regard it as a stroke of great good fortune which might well have important repercussions for the future. But – everything is so vague and unsettled, and all one can do is struggle to get by from one day to the next. – You must admit – – *fair auspices indeed for a silver wedding!*[2] – Ah, my child! therein lies my sadness! I almost believe that we would do well to ignore this day on this occasion! Fate, after all, is dreadfully against us. But there is still some time to go before then: perhaps some good will come our way! If this be the case, we'll try to celebrate on our own! I expect I shall not be far away from you at the time: – we'll see! But – for heaven's sake, do not add another imaginary worry to our existing cares! We have enough to put up with already! I can really add nothing to what I have already said! –

Well! Fare well as best you can for today! And – though fate should decree whatever it may think fit, I entreat you to say nothing, absolutely nothing about that other matter! It seems as though you will now have to remain for ever in doubt!

Once again, fare well – and be kind to your

Husband R.

Minna-Briefe II, 213–20.

271. B. Schott's Söhne, Mainz   Vienna, 30 October 1861

[. . .] The desire to make a start upon some easier work,[3] which will be less exhausting and therefore quicker to complete, has been brought back to mind not least by my present situation in which I am still having to struggle against the difficulty of performing my more serious works, and I regard it therefore as an inspired idea that happily accords with my present mood and circumstances to take in hand the immediate execution of an earlier[4] plan of mine for a popular comic opera. I have already drawn up a complete draft.[5] The opera is called "the Mastersingers of Nuremberg", and the main hero is the –

---

1 Nothing came of this.
2 The Wagners had been married for twenty-five years on 24 November 1861. They spent the day apart.
3 i.e. easier than *Tristan und Isolde*.
4 The first prose draft is dated 16 July 1845 (SS XI, 344–55).
5 The second draft, undated, may be found in SS XI, 356–78. It was followed immediately afterwards by the third prose draft, completed in Vienna on 18 November 1861 (SS XI, 379–94).

jovially poetic – "Hans Sachs". The subject is exceptionally rich in good-natured drollery, and I pride myself that with this original plan, which is entirely my own invention, I have hit upon something quite unexpected and singular. The style of the piece, both in the poem and the music, shall be thoroughly light and popular, and a guarantee of its rapid diffusion to all the other theatres is the fact that on this occasion I need neither a so-called leading tenor nor a great tragic soprano.

I must confess that not only does this plan flatter to perfection my present mood, which is very much in need of relaxation and preoccupation with some lighter subject, but this resolve of mine has suddenly become especially attractive as a result of my relations with you, my dear Herr Schott. I undertake to deliver this work "the Mastersingers of Nuremberg, grand comic opera in 3 acts" complete and ready for performance by next winter.[1] As soon as the poem is finished, I promise that I shall submit it to you at once; you will then be able to see from its character whether you yourself wish to undertake publication of the opera. For the present, I shall retain the 3000 fr. which you kindly sent me as an advance on my fee, the receipt of which I hereby acknowledge.[2]

It is my sincere wish, my dearest Herr Schott, that, just as I – in a moment of gloom – have found pleasant relief from my burden of sorrow by means of this newly conceived plan, so, in turn, I may have brought you pleasure, and so I would beg you to have the kindness to agree to my proposal!

I feel that I need a break from the very real gravity of my everyday preoccupations in order to create something quickly which will bring me into more immediate contact with the practicalities of our present-day theatres. In this way I believe I shall make some beneficial contribution to the future realization of my more substantial and more serious plans. When things are difficult, it is often necessary to proceed by round-about means! To you all thanks are due for having favoured me with your encouragement in the course of this round-about journey!

But now one final *urgent* request, namely that, for the time being, you observe the strictest silence concerning the plan I have communicated to you here. Premature discussion has already been highly prejudicial to me in the past! I *myself* am firmly resolved not to confide in even my closest friends, in

1 Wagner began work on the Prelude to Act I in April (?) 1862; the full score of Act I was not completed until 23 March 1866. The first complete draft of Act II is dated 15 May – 6 September 1866; the second complete draft 8 June – 23 September 1866; and the full score 22 March – 22 June 1867. The first complete draft of Act III is dated 2 October 1866 – 7 February 1867; the second complete draft 8 October 1866 – 5 March 1867; and the full score 26 June – 24 October 1867. The opera was first performed in Munich on 21 June 1868.

2 The sum was an advance on *Die Walküre* which Wagner had offered Schotts in a letter of 17 October 1861.

order that I may work the more uninterruptedly on the realization of this plan.

I would ask you, finally, to convey my regards to your very dear *wife*, and to accept the assurance of the deepest respect with which I remain

Your most obedient servant
Richard Wagner.

Verleger-Briefe II, 23–4.

272. MATHILDE WESENDONCK, ZURICH [Paris, end of December 1861][1]

Accept my most grateful and heartfelt thanks, my child! –

I shall respond with a confession. It will be futile to speak it out loud: everything about you tells me that you know everything, and yet I still feel the urge to confirm what you already know. –

Only now am I fully resigned!

One thing I never abandoned, and, indeed, I believed I had regained it again with difficulty: it was the belief that I had found my Asyl once more, and that I could again live near you. – An hour together in Venice[2] was sufficient to destroy this last fair delusion of mine!

I was soon forced to see that the freedom which you need and on which your very existence depends is something which you cannot maintain when I am near you: only my absence can give you the power freely to obey the dictates of your will; only when you have nothing to buy do you not have to admit to any price.

I cannot bear to see you constrained and oppressed, dominated and dependent as the price of my presence: I cannot make good this sacrifice, since my presence can offer you nothing in return, and the thought that I would mean so pitifully little to you in such circumstances makes me regard a presence that is bought at the price of freedom and true human dignity as a form of torment.

There is no point in flattering myself any longer. – I can see that you feel and know this yourself: indeed, you should be the first to do so! You realized it long ago, sooner than I, who for a long time afterwards continued to remain a secret and incurable optimist. –

It was this, and this alone, that in Venice lay on my soul like lead. It was not my situation nor my other misfortunes: I am, and always have been, indifferent to these ever since I first met you. You can scarcely believe with what total lack of feeling I decide all these matters which, in truth, do not

1 Wagner arrived in Paris on 4 December 1861 and remained there until 1 February 1862.
2 Wagner was guest of the Wesendoncks in Venice between 7 and 11 November 1861.

affect my feelings at all, or, if they do, it is only in passing and then only in respect of a situation which might be worthy of me and in which there would be no question of success or failure for me.

I remain true to my assertion that it consoles me to know that the dispositions with which you are endowed and the bourgeois circumstances in which you find yourself make it possible for you to invest your suffering with an idyllic and gentle character. For my own part, I aspire only to ordering my outer life in such a way that I can abandon myself, unmolested, to my inner creative urge which has been preserved as good as new. What I need above all else is to settle down in a place of my own: I shall accept anything, no matter what the conditions. For I shall then be able to endure everything, but everything, since nothing can then oppress me. Life and all that relates to it no longer has any meaning for me. The questions "where?" and "how?" – are a matter of infinite indifference to me. I want to work: nothing more! Only then can I be anything to you, when I am entirely my own master. I know that is so, and you know it, too! The final appalling obstacle has been overcome: Venice, the return journey, and the subsequent three weeks – terrible! – they are now behind me! As long as I do not lose heart, things must work out! –

I shall often send you some of my work. You'll be wide-eyed with amazement when you see my Mastersingers! Steel yourself against *Sachs*: you'll fall in love with him! It is a wholly astonishing work! The old sketch had little or nothing to offer. Yes, one needs to have been in Paradise to know what lies hidden here! –

As for my life, you will hear only what is absolutely necessary – only its superficial aspects. Of my inner life – you may rest assured! – there is *nothing at all* to report; nothing but artistic creativity. Thus you will lose nothing but receive the only thing that has any value, my works. But we shall also see each other now and then. Do you not agree? But without any desire! And thus wholly free! –

Well! What a remarkable letter this is! You will not believe how relieved I am to know that you know that I know what you have known for so long! –

Here, in addition, is a Shoemaker's Song![1] –

Adieu! my child!

The
Master!

Mathilde Wesendonck-Briefe 334–6.

---

1 Enclosed with this letter was a copy of Sachs's *Schusterlied* from Act II of *Die Meistersinger von Nürnberg* (GS VII, 211–13).

273. CÄCILIE AVENARIUS, BERLIN   Paris, 7 January 1862

Dear Cile,

If I don't write even a few lines to you now, I shall not get round to writing at all: a little is therefore better than nothing, however quick! –

If only you knew how strange a feeling comes over me when I see from your letter, too, how infinitely little you all know of my life's troubles! How odd it seems to read that in the great wide world, surrounded by fame, I have forgotten everything unconnected with this!! – How and where shall I begin to disabüse you!!

Suffice it to say that all my fame and all my successes in Germany have not helped me to find a place to compose my thoughts and prepare myself for some new task. An invitation to spend some time in Paris with the Metternich family, leading a life of quiet, carefree seclusion, was bound to strike me as a stroke of great good fortune while I was still in the heart of Germany. It lured me back here: in the mean time the Princess's mother died, and her – deranged – father was brought to Paris and given the rooms intended for me, so that I – was left to look round for a well-furnished room for myself & my work, which is all I have left!! Everything I undertake is a failure – rejection on all sides – no idea what to do with myself wherever I turn! – No security, no income, hardship and care: no home, no family, nothing! –

Ah, what do you know! –

My child, *why* did you never come to visit me in Switzerland in all the 10 long years I was there? Kläre,[1] after all, found the means to do so! –

However, that is how things are!

I shall no doubt come to Berlin one day soon! But Berlin **can** – or **could** be too important for me not to be cautious about paying too hasty a visit there. This, unfortunately, is a question of politics! –

Next month I plan to move to *Wiesbaden* in order to work there in peace for a time.[2] It is crucial that I settle down somewhere soon: however bad it may be, everything else is even worse for me.

Well, take heart, and be of good cheer: you are suffering from your nerves – my child, it won't kill you, however much you may suffer: suffering of this kind gets better with time! On the whole, I *myself* am now feeling better than I would have expected. Take heart! We shall see each other again this year. Nothing is fixed, but there is much that points in the direction of a visit to

---

1 Clara Wolfram, who stayed with Wagner in Zurich from 20 August until early November 1856.
2 Wagner rented rooms in Biebrich, just south of Wiesbaden, on 8 February 1862.

Berlin![1] Be brave, and summon up your courage. I'll give you something to laugh at: you can count on it! –

Fare you well, my dear Cile! Be satisfied with this! There is nothing sensible to be said about me! – Greetings to Eduard. Is he well? Tell him I'm in a bad way. Then all will be fine.

Adieu! Take heart, and remember me with affection!

Your
brother
Richard

RWA (published with minor errors in Familienbriefe 242–3).

274. PETER CORNELIUS, VIENNA   [Paris,] 9 January 1862

I shall now be remaining here until the end of the month, simply in order to complete my poem[2] – without any new interruptions. When I reached the end of the first act, I intended only to wait for Schott's letter before setting out for Wiesbaden without delay, where I planned to settle down for a longer period of time. In my impatience, I finally began the second act; Schott's letter arrived and did not exactly thrill me with its sense of urgency. And so I am now amusing myself with my verses, and have finally succeeded in forgetting how wretched I am. I also have a horror of setting out again so soon in the dead of winter to visit yet another foreign country: and so I have today come to the decision to spend the rest of the winter in Berlin with the Bülows.[3] I cannot survive any longer without a friendly soul beside me. – Then – are you still listening? – Then, at the end of the coming spring, I plan to have a closer look at Wiesbaden. Nor can I survive unless I settle down somewhere in a place of my own: this much is equally clear to me. I am now completely set on the Rhine: neutral. At the same time I ask for somewhere cheap, and a comfortable, pleasant apartment. The rest – including how I shall survive – I leave our Dear Lord to determine. But I shall never again go into service. – I come now to my main point: – *My friend, you must come and live with me, once and for all!* –

Think it over! I have already thought it over.

As far as I am concerned, the matter is settled. If *I* have not yet got to the bottom of what a uniquely true and supreme profit life can yield, I must be a hardened sinner indeed. A friend, a highly prolific individual who is his

1 Wagner next visited Berlin on 19 February 1863, on his way to St Petersburg.
2 The libretto of *Die Meistersinger von Nürnberg* was completed on 25 January 1862.
3 Nothing came of this idea: according to *Mein Leben* (690; English trans. 674), Cosima was "horrified" at the suggestion.

own master, and yet at the same time someone who is utterly sympathetic to me. Anyone who could misjudge such a friend would not be worthy of him.

Hans[1] has often refused to believe how deeply attached I am to him. But there are difficulties with the good fellow! – And you are free – and, as I believe I may assume, you are likely to remain so. If I now ask you to come and live with me as soon as I am settled in again, it goes without saying that this will in no way pre-ordain the future. It is enough that one thinks involuntarily of eternity. I take this to mean that you will belong to me, as my wife does, and that we shall share everything equally together, be it good fortune or failure, everything as a matter of course. If ever ambition moves you, well then, may the devil take you: there is no alternative!

Do not misunderstand me – you'll do what you can, as I shall; but always like two people who really belong to each other like a married couple. It will all work out for the best. If Wiesbaden, for ex., does not appeal to you, we can consider somewhere else. Ultimately my luck is bound to improve, and you will contribute to its doing so. But I believe that you, too, will meet with success. And if not? What does it matter? At all events we shall have each other. –

And so my immediate hope is that we shall see each other at the beginning of the summer on the Rhine, which is really where your home is. – Right then! Think it over! –

God, how I should like to have the poor doll[2] there, too! In such matters my sense of morality is incurably naïve. I should certainly have no objection to the girl's coming here, especially if the pretty little thing were to be what she is capable of being for me. – But how shall I find the right "terminus socialis"? Heavens above! – I am sorry, though I can't help but smile! –

My wife is well; she seems to be recovering and is behaving like a good, sensible girl. Ultimately it is all innate, and the poor woman, who in many respects is totally remote from me, is so bound up with my fate through the misery of her life that I cannot think of spending my old age in tolerable comfort without including her in my plans. And so she could and, indeed, may very well be living with us, too: you'll have an uncommonly salutary effect upon her. I hope so at least!

What a wonderful letter you sent me. No one else has ever written to me like that before. Thank you for everything. As for the melodrama in Heiling,[3] you repeated exactly my own early impressions of it: even at that date I regretted that it was placed at such a dramatically stupid and ineffectual point in the work.

1 Hans von Bülow.
2 Cornelius, fearful for his artistic independence, and unwilling to share his lover Seraphine Mauro (the "poor doll") with Wagner, declined the offer.
3 Heinrich Marschner's *Hans Heiling*; see also letter [6], pp. 17–18.

My thanks to the Standhartners for Christmas Eve!

You can simply have no idea of my poem: I cannot work on it without growing shamelessly arrogant (how right you are!). It will be my most brilliant creation: I shall say no more. I may shortly write out certain passages from it and send them to you. Merciful heavens! If only I had a nest in which to hatch this brood at leisure! – Learn from my example, and come to stay with me once I have another nest! Look! I have written operas and have been successful, I am famous, indeed honoured and loved by many, and – here I sit, and no one cares a fig for me. Five, six days go by without my speaking to anyone except my waiter! And those are the good days: for only then do I work, go out late, dine at the restaurant, come home, and read or write letters. That is what I am doing today. Here's one for you, the next one will be another doll's letter. Then my best wishes to the Standhartners.

Do I hear nothing more from Vienna? Well, it will no doubt not be good news. Adieu my friend, you kind and deep man! Fare well and remember me with affection!

Your Richard.

Freunde und Zeitgenossen 291-4.

275. MINNA WAGNER, DRESDEN   Biebrich, 9 February 1862

Dear Mutz,

Here I am, sitting in yet another inn! What a life! And at the same time to have no other wish than to be able to work in peace and quiet! I must confess that if anyone were to invite *me* to be patient and to show perseverance, I should like to know *who* could then be allowed those qualities! – I was delighted to learn that you have seen *Cornelius* in the meantime; I feel as though I myself was there with you both. As far as I recall, you grew very fond of Cornelius that time that you were staying at the Altenburg. I got to know him only very gradually in Vienna, but finally discovered that in *every* respect he really is an extremely rare and unusual individual, as regards both his character and his intellectual abilities. He is really the only one of my younger friends (although he is well into his thirties) to whom I can attribute true genius. His sense of moderation, modesty, self-sufficiency and immense moral dignity, however, all set him apart. I can only hope that this amiable individual might come and live with us permanently: but he is pursuing his own independent course in life, which I respect. –

He will have told you a good deal about me and my plans. Both he and everyone else consider that it would be much the best idea for me to settle in *Biebrich*. The advantage of this lies in the fact that, since I am resolved never again to take up a fixed appointment in any theatre, it makes all the difference to me to be able to reach every part of the country *by means of periodic excursions*, while retaining my actual place of residence in some quiet and pleasantly secluded spot. Biebrich lies in a quite unique position in this respect. If I take the steamer, I can be in Mainz within 10 minutes: not only do the Schotts hold out their arms to welcome me here, but a tolerable and – outwardly – most imposing theatre offers me a certain amount of interest. *Schmidt* (from Frankfurt) is now Kapellmeister there, and I believe he may be there for some time, which suits me admirably. I can be in Wiesbaden in 10 minutes, where the theatre is very good both in summer and in winter. (I shall be seeing Gounod's Faust there today.) In 1¼ hours in Frankfurt. In ¾ of an hour in Darmstadt. In 1½ hours in Mannheim. (All of them leading theatres) In 3 hours in Karlsruhe; in other words, I am as far from Karlsruhe as Leipzig is from Dresden. And I am almost exactly at the very centre for Vienna, Berlin & Paris. The place itself is charming: there is no pleasanter walk than to go on foot to Mainz, or Wiesbaden. Going down to the right are the most heavenly parts of the Rhine with walking tours at every turn. And attached to the castle is a large and wonderful park with magnificent trees. I have noticed some very pretty apartments directly adjacent to this park. If I were to find one which fully met my needs and which was suited to my settling down here, it would be very difficult for someone like myself, who has been so harshly tossed around and yet who is in such need of domestic routine, to resist the temptation to rent it. For my own part, *I* should be in no two minds as to whether or not it suited my needs to settle down in this way. For – I have now got to know myself somewhat better, and may now organize the remainder of my life according to certain rules. *To work* and create something new: that is my element; to perform my works – all right! if I am *asked* to do so, and if all my wishes are met. Then shorter or longer excursions, but always with the prospect of being able to return to my silent hearth to work, following each such exertion. It is *this* that is most important of all, and *this* that I must always keep in view, since it is something that depends upon *me* alone. Everything external to me is outside my power; such things may happen, or they may not; I cannot depend upon them for my peace of mind. The last 12 months have brought this home in a painful way! –

In Karlsruhe I spoke to the Grand Duke[1] for a whole hour: his wife had been ill; he will invite me back within the next few days, if possible to conduct Lohengrin, too.[2] I must say that when taking my leave of this kind man I

---

1 The Grand Duke Friedrich of Baden.
2 Wagner returned to Karlsruhe between 8 and 10 March, not to conduct *Lohengrin*, but to read the poem of *Die Meistersinger von Nürnberg* and to attend a (heavily cut) performance of *Tannhäuser* staged in his honour.

shook his hand most warmly. It was clear that his relations with me must have been very much on his mind ever since his last letter[1] (which I did not answer). He was genuinely embarrassed, and assumed I was angry with him. I caught him feeling strangely confused with regard to his ideas concerning my present circumstances, and am inclined to suspect our dear over-excited Alwine[2] of causing a certain amount of this confusion. It emerged, for ex., that he had not really understood how straightforward my proposal was, and assumed there were other things (such as large debts etc.) behind it. Nevertheless, I was glad that he [did[3] not relent when, with considerable hesitation, I allowed him to say all he wanted to say, but] kept on repeating how much he felt obliged to answer for my peace of mind and freedom from care. In response to this I said very calmly that I had certainly indicated this to him in my letter, and so I simply repeated to him now that, since I had no inherited wealth, there were only two ways open to me by which to survive: 1st, to produce such works as would in a short space of time provide me with a fortune on whose interest I could then live – something which, given the wretched manner in which people are rewarded for their services in Germany, is impossible, or 2nd, to accept a position as Kapellmeister, something which I hoped *he* would be the last person to demand of me, since there were other people far better suited to serving as Kapellmeisters than creative poets and composers like myself. In response to this the Grand Duke did not raise even the hint of a protest, but maintained that I needed to be given the kind of appointment in which absolutely no obligations of any kind would be imposed upon me; everything must be left entirely to my own discretion as to whether I wished to trouble myself with performances of my works, or not. He knew only that I needed to be able to lead a quiet and carefree existence. Well, I said, that is quite simple: those who recognized this should join forces and pay me an annual pension. But no one seemed willing to understand this: Liszt had told me that he had conveyed this same idea to the GD. of Weimar, but that he had not been given a hearing; I had already conveyed a similar suggestion to him, and he, too, had considered it impossible. What, I asked, was there now left for me to do but fight my way through the world living from hand to mouth and feeling happy whenever I found a publisher who might pay me enough by way of an advance on a piece of work to enable me to survive while working on it? – No, he cried, things must not go on like this. I shall immediately take the lead and hope that, thanks to my example, I may persuade a number of other princes who are friendly towards you to

---

1 The Grand Duke had written to Wagner in (?) August 1861, explaining that he would find it embarrassing to arbitrate in the event of an argument breaking out between Wagner and the Karlsruhe intendant Eduard Devrient over the proposed production of *Tristan und Isolde*.
2 Alwine Frommann (see Burrell cat. 385A).
3 This phrase was omitted from the published text.

join with me and take steps to ensure that you receive a fixed pension. Tell me honestly: how much do you think you need as a fixed annual allowance? – My God, I said, if I can rely upon a fixed income as a matter of certainty, a small amount would be sufficient, and if you were able to assure me of 1500 to 2000 gulden[1] on these conditions, I should know where I stood: I would cut my cloth accordingly, and would be able to survive with the help of my other random receipts. He was delighted to hear this, and undertook to see that my wish was fulfilled at the earliest opportunity. And in order that we should not lose contact again, he asked me to visit him again soon in Karlsruhe in order to attend a rehearsal of Lohengrin, and, if I were entirely satisfied with it, to do them the honour of conducting the work myself. I promised to do so. – He was well pleased, moreover, with my plan to settle in Biebrich: he said he wished me to be entirely independent and that he would then attach even greater value to whatever occasional pleasures I was able to give him. – In spite of this really most gratifying and (I do not doubt) successful renewal of my relations with the Grand Duke, I have now completely abandoned my idea of settling in Karlsruhe, not least because of *Devrient*, whom I did not even visit on this occasion. I should never be able to get on for any length of time with this obstinate old pedant, whose principal concern is how best to maintain a state of mediocrity and who has done me persistent harm, moreover, with his shameless talk about the practicability of Tristan: I should lose my patience, and – God knows! my present motto is peace and quiet. But I might still decide to go on arguing with the old fogy. It will be a different matter to go there now and then at the Grand Duke's invitation. –

These, my dear Mutz, are the affairs that are of outward concern to me. I have told you exactly what my needs and wishes are, and also – in certain circumstances – my resolve. There is only one thing that fills me with trepidation: – Where do you stand in all this? Would you wish to settle in Biebrich? Would it give you pleasure to do so? Would you not prefer somewhere else? – You will understand that, since I have set out here on the basis of my *own* needs, I am bound to be anxious lest my choice does not coincide with yours. It appals me to think of doing anything which I may possibly soon have cause to regret! The place itself is extremely quiet, and in itself – during the winter – offers few resources. Of course, I am very indifferent to this, for I have noticed in Paris and elsewhere that what I really want is simply to feel at home. It is true that even in winter we can live at the same time in Mainz & Wiesbaden, for a visit there is the same as driving in a cab from one end of a moderately large town to the other, except that it is much cheaper and more convenient. It is worth having a try at it. *I* should prefer to make a start here in the winter, in order to see how things turn out. I can have visitors at any

1 i.e. between 1000 and 1335 thalers. Wagner's salary in Dresden had been 1500 thalers a year. Nothing came of this proposal.

time; I need only invite them to Wiesbaden or Mainz. There is always something refreshing about such an excursion. – And so I think that for the time being I shall leave fate to decide the matter, at least to the extent that I am making detailed and careful enquiries to see whether I can find a really suitable apartment that accords with all my needs. *This* must now be the case: for in such circumstances there would be no pleasure in simply seeking some makeshift solution. Whether I find the apartment I want is still very uncertain. Food and everything else is said to be very *cheap*: if we wanted a whole floor to ourselves, I am told that we could have the very best for 250 to 300 fl.[1] – All right then – , I intend setting to work in a quiet way, and not rushing anything, since I have learned a real horror of repentance. – Let us see what happens. If I find something, my need for domestic comfort is now so great as to be absolutely decisive: *you* would then have to see whether it suited you as well.

I shall soon be acquiring a little dog! –

My visit to Berlin will now no doubt be called off completely. My God! There was not a single person in Paris to whom I could have showed a line of my new poem.[2] I thought of spending an evening with you, with Old Fromm-maid[3] and with the Bülows: it would certainly have been a pleasant evening. We would have convinced each other that we were still alive, and would have conferred with each other: it would all have been quite splendid! But I would only have had to waste time looking for somewhere to sleep and spend 2 days; one thing after another: then Albert[4] and his wife – whom I had completely forgotten were living there, Old Fromm-maid and her royalist fears, and, last but not least, the Jews and the critics, and God knows what else! Well, I can certainly do without that! No, it is not this that I wanted! I hope Cecilie[5] will be patient in her sisterly affections, and agree to some other occasion. I am heartily sick of travel, and of living out of a suit-case! Oh! and the money that it costs! I am thinking not of the boarding charges, but simply of what I spend in tips! No! God forbid! – Heavens, yesterday evening, when I arrived here and was again rummaging around in my trunk, looking for some article or other, I began to howl, poor devil that I am, and the tears poured down my cheeks. And all this at a time when I have such a splendid work in my head, for which no one can provide me with a quiet corner into which to retire. It's a crying shame! – I am expecting the Erard in a couple of days' time, and then all hell will be let loose! – Wish me

1 300 florins = 200 thalers.
2 *Die Meistersinger von Nürnberg*.
3 Alwine Frommann.
4 Wagner's brother Albert, who was engaged at the Berlin Court Opera between 1857 and 1865.
5 Wagner's half-sister Cäcilie Avenarius; see also letter [273], pp. 530–31.

good luck, and remember me with a tiny bit of affection, you old woman of Dresden.

Bye-bye for now.

Very best wishes from
Your R.

(You will have some money before the month is out, that goes without saying, Mutz!)

RWA (incompletely published in Minna-Briefe II, 256–61).

276. PETER CORNELIUS, VIENNA   Biebrich, 4 March 1862

My dear Cornelius,

I am very unhappy and need someone to whom I can pour out my sorrows! I cannot turn to a woman's heart: I would only cause it more pain because of its helplessness than I would find comfort for myself. The hardest thing to endure is to know oneself so utterly alone in one's troubles and anxieties, and to have to decide everything on one's own. It then occurred to me, as though by some providential decree, that I have you to turn to! You will understand me, and I can unburden at least some of my heart's anguish on you. –

My dearest friend, it is now clear that I cannot possibly live with my wife any longer. You cannot know what a world of meaning is contained in these few words. My heart bleeds: and yet I realize that I must suppress all feelings of soft-heartedness, since my only salvation lies in firmness and in frankness.

You know how much I yearned for a return to domestic routine, and how I thought that I could achieve that aim only by being reunited with my wife. While I was sadly attempting to order my household arrangements for the winter here in Biebrich, my wife, moved by my distress, suddenly took it into her head to emulate *you*, with the result that, instead of sending me a reply by letter, she herself turned up in my room, where I had just completed my makeshift arrangements. My heart leapt, and she must soon have realized how I felt when she saw my great joy and emotion. I reproached her for not having brought her parrot and come for good, instead of which she had come for only a week in order to help me settle in. But we immediately discussed a permanent arrangement in Wiesbaden. She looked fit and well, which proved how she always recovers her health when she is on her own, pursuing her own inclinations in whom she sees and the life she leads, when undisturbed by me. How I now pondered upon ways of ensuring that our future lives together might be made permanently bearable by means of all manner of sensible conventions and concessions, in spite of our totally opposed inclinations, characters and outlook! The terrible misfortune of having no young children to mediate between us and of being thrown back upon ourselves in consequence of my preference for leading a life apart inevitably led to constant friction between us, a state of affairs that became all too perceptible on the very first day: but I was filled with such good intentions that I willingly addressed her in the same strangely make-believe language that one uses with children, listening with apparent interest to things which are totally remote from me and often downright repellent. I attempted to suppress by force the strange stirrings of that conscience which allows no untruth to flourish, and fell asleep that first night in the calm belief that all things might henceforth be possible. – The next morning fate intervened in a remarkable way, providing such striking proof of its workings that I could not help but be amazed. Listen!

Since our last meeting in Venice[1] there had been an unintentional but lengthy interruption to the correspondence between me and my friend Frau Wk. Everything between us is now so well understood and so well organized on the basis of total resignation that I have continued to write to her only on the occasional friendly impulse, the more especially since my dealings with her most upright but – personal relations apart – tiresome husband have proved so insupportable that I have renounced any more lasting personal contact with them both and remain only in intermittent contact by letter, a form of communication intended to lighten the burden of *her* life especially. At such unsettled and distressing times as these present months have been, I prefer to say nothing at all. And so it happened that my friend had heard nothing at all of my journey to Paris,[2] and had sent a small Christmas present to me in Vienna which, after many wanderings, was eventually returned to her in Zurich. I later wrote to her from Paris and informed her of my plans to move to the Rhine, whereupon she wrote to report the mishap that had befallen her Christmas present, and begged me to let her have my later address on the Rhine, so that she could then send me the gift that she had intended for me. This I did while I was still in Mainz.[3] For a long time I remained without news, until she finally announced in a brief note that she had been in Düsseldorf, attending her mother's funeral, whereupon I immediately sent her my sincere condolences.[4] – She then wrote at some length to thank me both for my letter and for informing her about the Mastersingers, and announced that she had just sent off my belated Christmas present. Her letter arrived here on the *second* day of my wife's visit, her

1 Between 7 and 11 November 1861, when Wagner was a guest of the Wesendoncks in Venice.
2 Wagner had written to Mathilde Wesendonck on 21 December to wish her well on her birthday (the 23rd), and to inform her that he was in Paris. Mathilde replied on the 25th, returning the first draft of *Die Meistersinger von Nürnberg* which Wagner had given her, and lamenting the fact that, in ignorance of his change of address, she had sent to him in Vienna "a small chest containing a few trifles".
3 Wagner wrote from Karlsruhe on [3 February 1862] to inform Mathilde of his latest movements.
4 Letter of 16 February 1862.

Christmas present on the *third* day,[1] and both of them immediately fell into the unhappy woman's hands. Incapable of seeing my relations with that woman in anything but a disgustingly trivial light, she refused to listen to any of the explanations which I offered her simply to calm her down, but vented her feelings in that vulgar tone of voice which again caused me to lose my self-command: she interpreted the violence of my reaction as the result of that woman's continuing and disturbing influence on me, and – the whole insane edifice stood before me once more, bright and unshaken! I felt as though I were losing my reason. Here was this woman at exactly the same point she had been four years ago: word for word precisely the same outbursts, the same vulgar tone! – Having survived these storms, I recovered my self-possession, tried to see what had happened as a final tempestuous outburst of madness, – and tried to continue to hope, and not deny any possibility. But the full extent of our misery now stood revealed more clearly than ever before: suspicion, mistrust; every word ill construed! Added to that, our complete isolation here; to be alone during long winter evenings with a creature who does not understand my own nature in the slightest, and who, as soon as I pick up a book, is unable so much as to follow me in this, since she does not know how to occupy herself. And here I am, wanting nothing but quiet and peace of mind, and yearning to get back to my work, but having to make appalling efforts to overcome the hardships caused by my circumstances and present situation, and disagreeably upset by every contact with the outside world, including gossip & such like! Finally, my wife's worsening heart disease! It was ten days of hell, but at least these ghastly 10 days had the advantage of serving as a final warning, and I could not help but be amazed that this grave warning should have come, in all innocence, from my friend!

You can readily imagine the firm resolve that has now matured within me! Curiously enough, my wife, who after all must suffer her own private hell in my company, always finds it difficult, when she has calmed down, to adhere to views which she appears to acquire only in moments of passion. When I heard her suddenly begin to talk about setting up house again, a very real sense of horror seized hold of me! – Oh, what misery to let such wretchedness go on for so long! My wife will manage, since I shall keep up appearances for her sake! It is, and will remain, impossible for me ever to divorce her: it is too late for that, and the inhumanity of such a procedure revolts me. And so I am resolved on the following expedient. From next autumn my wife is to settle in Dresden on her own with our furniture and effects, apart from the few things that I shall keep with me here, and she will reserve a room "for me" there. Under the – entirely valid – pretext that I need a refuge where I can work in peace, I shall continue to maintain a small permanent lodging such as the one I am now occupying, and – perhaps I shall visit my

1 Minna arrived in Biebrich on 21 February and left on 2 March 1862.

wife occasionally for a few weeks at a time. That is how things shall seem, simply in order that they may seem inoffensive! But how favourable our circumstances would have to be if this arrangement were to be even moderately tolerable! What this means in detail is running two households, – by someone who is scarcely equal to running *one*. For I cannot conceal from myself the fact that my outward situation is rapidly deteriorating! I can be of no further *use* to myself. The gulf between me and the so-called world of art is growing wider and wider. My friend, there is no one I can still talk to! Whenever I meet a Kapellmeister or a theatre manager, or even a man like Raff, I have to cross myself, and try to hide away in some corner where I can be my own master. What shall I do about Schotts? I feel as though I shall have to dupe them all, and that I shall indeed do so! My only refuge continues to be the young Grand Duke of Baden: there is a native nobility of feeling here, happily wedded to an open and free intelligence. The man *knows* how things stand with me, and is entirely of the opinion that I should never have to ask for a penny for my works. Well, he is not rich or powerful enough, but I am certain that I shall shortly be receiving from him the one thing that will be of use to me. Even now it is a pleasure for me to be able to speak with him openly and without dissimulation. What I should like is for him to engage me personally, and provide for my life and works in "naturalibus". I should then assign a small pension to my wife. But however this question of my outward existence may yet be resolved and however favourable the solution, I fear that it will scarcely reassure me as to the one point that really gnaws away at my heart. I am so dreadfully full of regrets. It appals me to think of anyone suffering because of me!

And so it requires an enormous effort to make myself see reason. It is entirely self-evident that, whatever the circumstances, my wife is better away from me than with me: indeed, I can see quite clearly that she has no real feelings of love for me: she recognizes *only* the injustice done to **her** and deep down inside her is incapable of ever forgiving me for it. But – that's how it is: the world we perceive lies within *ourselves*; *I* imagine that things must be different, and that genuine sadness and deep affection alone can cause suffering, and – my own heart bleeds. Ever since the day before yesterday, when I left my unhappy wife in Frankfurt, still angry and thinking only of herself, a gnawing sense of unease has continued to rankle in me, and only the certain knowledge that soft-heartedness would merely serve to prolong the torments that we *both* suffer can finally teach me – resignation. – Oh God! I then grow tearful and say: oh for some kind womanly being to take me gently in her arms! But I am closing my heart to that now! In that way, I believe all my wife's sorrows will be avenged! –

Ah! –

Tell me what has been happening to you? You were not at Esser's on Sunday: did you have an accident on the way?

Your disappearance while we were still taking our leave of each other[1] touched us all very deeply. This whole visit was like something out of a fairy-tale: however did you manage it? Your guardian angel left with you, just as he arrived with you. You left me with some curious people on the whole. One evening recently I asked if your sister could be invited to the Schotts (I wanted to read them something;), but she was unable to come. I am still feeling rather ill-tempered. But I have grown fond of Weissheimer; I like his seriousness and great industry. And I consider him to be not without talent. He often comes out to see me. – Nothing will come of the Raffs. Allow me to pass over in silence an adventure in Darmstadt.[2] –

Life here is very agreeable. You ought to come and enjoy the springtime here with me. Of course, I have not got round to doing any work: it is incredible how our lives are snatched away from us. – I am now busy discharging a pile of epistolary debts. –

Greetings to Esser and the Standhartners. The doll[3] has written me a most wonderful letter. Oh, how I'd like to have her here! – Write and tell me what you are doing. Everything within me and around me is still utterly desolate, like the month of March itself! There is a tremendous feeling of disgust deep down inside me. If I do not get down to work soon, it will all be over. Heavens, if only I had a year of peace and relative comfort! –

Well, take what is of use to you from this pile of news from a man who is utterly worn out! Remain cheerful, remember me with affection, and think up another fairy-tale soon.

Adieu, my friend! It is all very sad!

Your R.W.

(I too feel indebted to O. Bach:[4] he deserves better consideration, the poor man.)

RWA (published with minor errors of transcription and omission of postscript in Freunde und Zeitgenossen 297–304).

277. MINNA WAGNER, DRESDEN   Biebrich, 21 May [1862]

Dearest Minna,

That's how it is! As a result of my eagerness to ensure that my birthday journey could go ahead as planned, I have in fact made it impossible for me

1 Following Wagner's recital of the poem of *Die Meistersinger von Nürnberg* in Mainz on 5 February 1862, for which Cornelius travelled specially from Vienna.
2 A production of *Rienzi* with Niemann in the title role on 21 February 1862.
3 Seraphine Mauro.
4 Otto Bach (1833–93), Austrian conductor, music teacher and composer; an acquaintance of Wagner and Cornelius.

to carry out that plan. I had resolved that, if I managed to sort out the scene with David,[1] I would travel to Frankfurt on Tuesday evening and then continue my journey to Dresden on Wednesday morning. But it so happened that on Sunday I so forgot myself in my eagerness to get on with my work that it was not until half-past-six that I got up from my desk and went out to eat, not having had anything since a drink of tea at breakfast-time. I bolted down the meal and then, in spite of the bad weather, gave myself some vigorous exercise by walking to Wiesbaden, caught a chill on the way back, and on Monday felt thoroughly wretched, with weakness and diarrhoea, which on Tuesday was joined by a mild but debilitating fever. Today, at all events, I already feel better, and my indisposition is at least of no further consequence; but it would have been impossible for me to undertake my journey today without arriving in Dresden feeling genuinely ill. And so I regard it as the workings of fate, which at least has the advantage of allowing me to add a further 100 thalers to what I sent you last time. Would you be kind enough to let me know whether you think you can survive until around the second half of July?

I intend writing to Frau v. Bülow and asking her to send you details about Reichenhall:[2] I believe it is still very cheap there and fairly primitive. –

It would give me great pleasure to be able to collect you from Reichenhall on the 5th of September[3] and accompany you as far, say, as Nuremberg: my work (I hope!) will permit me at least *one* such excursion – especially at around that time. That this work dominates every aspect of my life is something you will by now have learned to appreciate; it renders me indifferent to everything else, e.g. whether I hear Tichatschek or Schnorr. This work alone, and my actual completion of it as soon as possible, is also my excuse for having set up this temporary refuge here: without such a goal I would be forced to regard even this interim arrangement as irresponsible. And I shall remain here only until this goal has been achieved: I hope to have reached that point by the late autumn and, assuming this to be so, I plan to move in with you in Dresden on the 24th of November.

Provisionally, I still think that my decision to regard a home in Dresden as *your* home is a wise and prudent one, and one that best accords with my present circumstances. Looked at closely, *my* position is so abandoned and helpless that I should consider it unjustifiable for *me* to think of settling down on a permanent basis and living a life of comfortable ease. My prospects for the future are provisionally those of complete uncertainty and possibly of total destitution, so that only a major new success may now alter the situation. In

1 *Die Meistersinger von Nürnberg*, Act I, Scene 2.
2 A spa nine miles south-west of Salzburg, one of the most fashionable health resorts in the second half of the nineteenth century.
3 Minna's birthday. Nothing came of this plan. Wagner next saw Minna (for the last time) in Dresden between 3 and 7 November 1862.

much the same way, Countess Pourtalès, who has generously helped me out with much-needed funds, beseeches me to expect very little or, even better, nothing at all from the Court despite the absolute trustworthiness of the Grand Duke of Baden. And so, when my new opera is finished, I see myself helplessly cast out into the world, and only by taking in hand some new work could the idea of settling down temporarily in this way in the future seem necessary and therefore responsible. – In these circumstances my wife would of course have to share my inconstant and uncertain fate. But since she has already shared so many similar upheavals and inconveniences, my first thought is to give *her* at least a sense of security, and offer her a permanent place to live, and I am delighted to discover that a most suitable place has already been found, inasmuch as you yourself have often declared of late that, now that you are there again, you feel happiest living in Dresden. My only thought in all this is to keep your Dresden refuge safe and secure for you, and at all times provide you with the necessary means to lead a decent existence there. For my own part, I plan to think of my home always in terms of a little room in your house, while leaving it entirely to *you* as to how you can best make me feel at home there. In the course of time and, I hope, as the result of a successful new opera, I reserve for myself the right, as soon as I have any firm prospects, of extending the Dresden establishment so that it meets all *my* needs, while ensuring *at all costs* that you yourself remain secure there, since this can be achieved by relatively modest means. –

In the face of these clear and self-evident arrangements, I now have to endure the pain of being told that I am driving you out into the world, and that you regard it as a mercy to be invited to Russia by relatives[1] with whom you were once on a personal standing of open hostility! – There is nothing I can say to this. – –

Following the unfortunate outcome of Tannhäuser in Paris, I was advised (more especially by Liszt) to visit *Rossini*, who had allegedly been told all manner of distressing things about me; indeed, Rossini himself sent word to me one day that he would be pleased if I were to visit him. It seemed to me that a false and, for me, humiliating construction could very easily be placed on this visit, and since I realized that the dear old man would never be able to understand *me*, and that nothing but confusion could ensue, I did *not* visit Rossini, preferring instead to live with the self-reproach of having offended this kind and genial old man.[2] – I have now been brought an article, dated last year, from a German music journal, containing a long and detailed account of a visit that I am said to have paid Rossini following the Tannhäuser affair, in order to win him over & persuade him to intervene on my behalf, whereupon Rossini is said to have dismissed me with a scornful display of

---

1 Minna's sister Amalie von Meck and her husband.
2 Wagner had visited Rossini in March 1860.

his wit. Everyone has naturally taken this to be true, and Weissheimer has urged me belatedly to refute this lie. I have grave – and very melancholy reasons for not doing so, and for letting the matter rest. None the less, this episode will no doubt find its way into my biography. But what will *not* be found there? Anyone who finds letters from *you* in my possession will read there that my wife calls me and my behaviour towards her "heartless" "brutal" & "vulgar". So this will no doubt also find its way into my biography.

There's nothing I can do about that!

But let us say no more about all this – and, above all, complete the *Mastersingers*! I am full of confidence. Then let us see what happens next!

Kindest regards to Madame Huber, and – sincere good wishes to you from your

Birthday Man.

RWA (published with minor errors of transcription in Minna-Briefe II, 284–7).

278. MATHILDE WESENDONCK, ZURICH   Biebrich, 22 May 1862

My dear friend.

It is my birthday today. Flowers have been delivered to my house. I was ill, and not until yesterday did I go out into the park again. I have had little cause to think of you, since I can no longer be of any help to you but only cherish silent hopes for your well-being.

Thus I sat alone.

I was suddenly struck by an idea for the orchestral introduction to the third act of the Mastersingers. This act will be crowned by a most moving climax at the moment when Sachs rises to his feet before the assembled populace and is received by them with a sublime outpouring of enthusiasm. At this point the people sing in bright and solemn tones the first eight lines of Sachs's poem to Luther. The music for this was already written. Now, for the introduction to the 3rd act, when the curtain rises and Sachs is discovered sitting there in deep contemplation, I shall have the bass instruments play a soft, tender and profoundly melancholic passage that bears the imprint of the greatest resignation: then, on the horns and sonorous wind instruments, comes the solemnly joyful bright-toned melody of "Awake! for dawn is drawing near: and from the woodland green I hear a rapture-laden nightingale": the melody adds its voice to what has gone before and is increasingly developed by the orchestra.

It has now become clear to me that this work will be my most perfect masterpiece and – that I shall live to complete it.

But I wanted to give myself a birthday present; I shall do so by sending you this news.

Look after yourself; take good care of yourself, and – if you have to think of me – imagine that you see me always in the mood inspired by this birthday morning hour: this will console you, and you, too, will prosper. Without doubt! –

Kindest regards from

Your,
Richard Wagner.

Mathilde Wesendonck-Briefe 342–3.

279. MALWIDA VON MEYSENBUG, LONDON   Biebrich, 15 June 1862

Many thanks, my dearest friend, for your very beautiful and full letter! Never before can anyone have contemplated and characterized as well as you have done the significant and uniquely important possibility of a political development of the European peoples. Your Roman idea[1] struck me as wholly admirable, and I immediately set about thinking how I could best contribute to its realization! – My dearest Malwida, this much is certain, that the myth of a Messiah is the most profoundly characteristic of all myths for all our earthly striving. The Jews expected someone who would liberate them, a Messiah who was supposed to restore the kingdom of David and bring not only justice but, more especially, greatness, power and safety from oppression. Well, everything went as predicted, his birth in Bethlehem, of the line of David, the prophecy of the three wise men, etc., his triumphant welcome to Jerusalem, palms strewn before him, etc. – there he stood, everyone listened, and he proclaimed to them: "My kingdom is not of this world! Renounce your desires, that is the only way to be redeemed and freed!"[2] – Believe me, all our political freedom fighters strike me as being uncannily like the Jews. – All right, this is something one can say to only a very few people: that goes without saying, and so – let us see what happens! – but I fully recognize the particular charms of Italy. – Your plans to settle in Florence are highly respectable! – Everything is possible with someone like me![3] I no longer like to plan more than a month in advance. There is no doubt but that all I want & all I look for in this world is the leisure to work, since this alone can explain my existence to me and make it seem acceptable. I can renounce performances

1 Malwida had written to Wagner to express her thoughts on current political developments in Europe and to propound her belief that Rome should remain neutral territory, as "a city of the mind".

2 Almost identical ideas to these are expressed in a letter to Mathilde Wesendonck of 9 June 1862. *Cf St John* 18:36.

3 Malwida had invited Wagner to join her in Italy.

entirely. But trying to secure this leisure is what so appallingly difficult. I am working in private on a plan to disappear from the face of the earth and continue only to work on my artistic projects in secret like some departed spirit. I shall otherwise not find rest. My wife is again in a pitiful state and causing me quite unbelievable distress: it is utterly impossible to make her see reason; she is bound to destroy herself, irredeemably – it's heart-breaking! –

Of course, I am thinking of staying here as long as I can afford to do so for the sake of my work.[1] It is making progress and is turning out a success, – but I cannot work quickly: firstly because of the unavoidable outer and inner distractions, then – because there is not a single bar of the music that delights me or gives me pleasure unless it owes its origins to a genuinely inspired idea. But this sort of thing cannot be made to order. –

Klindworth's letter reached me safely while I was still in Paris. Tell him not to worry, if you have an opportunity to see him. There was not much I could add to the unfortunate incident, which I already knew about. I hope he emerges unscathed. Give him my warmest good wishes, and tell him where I am!

Kindest regards to Olga![2] Perhaps – in Italy: everything is possible: only at present have I no time to make any plans, and am glad if I can guarantee even the next month of my existence.

And so, once again: a thousand thanks! Please accept my warmest good wishes from the very bottom of my heart!

Yours,
Rich. Wagner

Meysenbug-Briefe 80.

280. WENDELIN WEISSHEIMER, MAINZ   Biebrich, 5 October 1862

Dearest Wendelin,

It's no good! I am still denied all peace and quiet: there is no point in trying to work! I must first provide a proper basis for my existence if I am to enter upon my fiftieth year with dignity and decency.

And so I am resolved to travel from Leipzig[3] to *Vienna*: "Tristan" with *Ander* is out of the question, but I may rehearse "Tannhäuser" there (with

---

1 *Die Meistersinger von Nürnberg.*
2 Olga Herzen.
3 Wagner conducted the first performance of the Prelude to *Die Meistersinger von Nürnberg* at a Gewandhaus concert in Leipzig on 1 November 1862. He arrived in Vienna on 14 November and returned to Biebrich on 13 February 1863.

the new scenes).[1] Apart from this, I intend to give a big concert there which I may perhaps be able to repeat several times.[2] For this I shall put together a programme from all my as yet unperformed works. I am now busy preparing it. What I need above all is to ensure the services of *good* copyists to write out the parts. As far as I know, there are some excellent copyists in Leipzig, and Härtel, for example, must be able to refer you to some of them. Would you be so good as to engage about three copyists in my name with immediate effect: in the course of October I am having to write out the entire programme for a very large orchestra, so that three will not be too many; I'd prefer one more (but good and reliable). Within the next day or so I shall then send you part of what has to be copied out. I think we shall be able to defray the cost of preparing these copies from the concert receipts, of which you certainly have high expectations. – My subsequent plan is as follows: when I have finished giving the concerts in Vienna, I should like (if possible!) to repeat the same programme in Leipzig. You might therefore make clandestine enquiries as to a suitable time when this plan could be instituted. I had then thought of inflicting myself on *Berlin*, where *Hans*[3] shall give me a helping hand. We shall then see whether I have then earned a period of *profound* peace for myself for a time in Biebrich. –

As far as *our* concert in Leipzig is concerned, I have been assailed by doubts as to whether it will be worth our while – in view of the expectations of what I hope will be a very large audience[4] – to perform only the one piece – the prelude to the "Mastersingers". It strikes me that I ought to offer something else besides. If you – and others – are of the same opinion, I would propose the following.

"Fragment from 'Tristan and Isolde':
    a) Prelude.
    b) Closing section of the opera (without singing)."

This could be done as follows: at the end of the Prelude, as it appears in the theatre score, with the half-cadence in G in the basses, there would follow – without a break – page 425 of the full score – second system "mild and softly". The whole thing would then form two splendid – and complementary – companion-pieces; the ending in particular was uncommonly effective when we rehearsed it in Vienna.

I would give the whole thing something like the following title:
    a)"Love-death". Prelude.

---

1 i.e. the version performed in Paris. Nothing came of this plan until thirteen years later when Wagner revised this version for a new production of *Tannhäuser* in Vienna on 22 November 1875.
2 Three concerts were held in the Theater an der Wien on 26 December 1862, and 1 and 11 January 1863.
3 Hans von Bülow; nothing came of this plan.
4 The hall was barely half full, although the Prelude was encored.

b)"Transfiguration". End of the opera.

Think it over. I am ready to do it. You can obtain the parts from Härtels: ask for them at once.[1]

Well! God be with you! Write soon!

Yours,
Richard Wagner.

Weissheimer-Briefe 176–8.

281. FRANZ SCHOTT, MAINZ   Biebrich, [20] October 1862

You are mistaken, my dear Herr *Schott!* You are greatly mistaken as to the way in which a man like me may be treated.[2] Many things may be extorted by hunger, but not works of a higher nature. Or do you think that when my cares prevent me from sleeping at night, I shall be serenely cheerful the next day, and full of good ideas for my work? The "Mastersingers" would have been very close to completion by now if you had taken due care of me since the date when I first settled here for that very purpose. You had done enough – and I shall never cease to acknowledge it! – to enable me to undertake such a work: – but you should have done more – since it was necessary and there was no alternative – and kept me in a good mood as well. If it meant making sacrifices, here – if anywhere – was the place for them, whereas parsimony and timidity have caused everything to stagnate. Since the end of August – almost two months ago – you have left me very much in the situation of a drowning man. You finally declared yourself ready to offer a certain amount of help: and again you have spent 2 whole weeks forcing yourself to torment me! –

Well, you, too, complain of lack of peace and quiet: I suppose that I might concede that you contribute to your own peace of mind by making mine impossible, but I scarcely think that likely.

Very well, then! You will know how best to act in keeping with your character: I am, and shall remain, mindful of my obligations, but I wish that I could discharge my debt to you in cash rather than manuscripts, – something which you yourself would no doubt ultimately prefer? All that can be done will be done, and if any good can come of torment, some good will no doubt come of *me*, for – I am in torment! –

---

1 On Weissheimer's recommendation, the excerpts from *Tristan und Isolde* were replaced by the Overture to *Tannhäuser*. The concert also included Liszt's Piano Concerto in A major played by Hans von Bülow, and five vocal and orchestral works by Weissheimer.

2 Schott had declined to advance Wagner any more money until the latter had delivered a further section of the score of *Die Meistersinger von Nürnberg*.

I felt that in accordance with the eternal laws of justice I should not spare you the effusion of a sleepless night.

Your most obedient servant
Richard Wagner.

PS. If it had really been your earnest intention to publish the poem of the "Mastersingers", I ought no doubt to have seen a proof-sheet by now. I can scarcely believe that it takes 14 days to produce a printed sheet in *Mainz*.

RW.

Verleger-Briefe II, 56–7.

282. MATHILDE MAIER, MAINZ   Vienna, 4 January 1863

I must not alarm the dear child a moment longer. But I have very little to report that is at all satisfactory, at least as far as I myself am concerned. Rather let me speak of my second concert[1] and the Viennese public: the first was extremely successful (thanks to an expensive and massive sound-board around the entire orchestra!) and the second was hot and brilliant. There was no lack of applause, more, indeed, than the first time; for entire pieces (from the Valkyrie) had to be repeated. But my old complaint keeps on recurring: namely that in the case of undertakings such as this I always have to think at the same time of making a profit – generally as a matter of extreme urgency!! The receipts were greater than anyone had suspected they would be on New Year's Day at midday; and yet they were still not enough to cover the enormous costs. This unfortunate state of affairs has set me against all further undertakings of this kind since, although they will no doubt continue to bring me fame and reputation, they serve only to make my life's burden all the more unbearable. Concerts can no doubt bring me certain advantages, but – they may bring *me* to the point where I would rather forgo all further advantages! It is with some reluctance that I have agreed to the third concert on the 11th inst., which can again be expected to involve a great deal of expense since, for my own part, I simply cannot undertake anything that is at all mediocre! It may be that the receipts on this occasion will reach the maximum possible: that might to some extent make up for everything else. But this game of chance here – when I am so very much in earnest – wears me down and revolts me!

My child, on the 2nd day of the year I was in a dreadful temper, made appreciably worse by extreme indisposition. What is more, I had to attend a piano rehearsal of Tristan on this ill-starred day, a rehearsal which, given the

---

1 The second of Wagner's three concerts in Vienna, on 1 January 1863; see also letter [280], p. 548, note 2.

mood I was in, was bound to reveal to me with irrefutable clarity the irreparable harm which this whole undertaking has caused me. To have such an
utterly incompetent invalid as Ander, with his threadbare voice, as my
Tristan?? Impossible! – All right! they are continuing to rehearse the piece:
I shall let them get on with it, but I'll not trouble myself with it or set any
store by it either. Schnorr *cannot* come after all – and so it looks as though
all my enterprises are once more at an end! You can no doubt imagine, my
child, that these were trying times – very trying times – for me: and they were
the first days of the new year!! Still filled with the seriousness of this mood
I have a question to put to you which you must consider in the first place
as something purely theoretical, rather like a moral dilemma – : nothing
more! –

When I think seriously about myself and ask myself what is going to become
of me, there is only one salvation that I can envisage. I lack a home: – not
in terms of a place to live, but in terms of people. I shall be 50 next May. I
cannot marry as long as my wife is alive: to divorce her, given the state of
her health (dilation of the heart in an advanced stage of development), when
her life might be ended by the slightest blow – I cannot possibly deal her
what might well be a mortal blow. On the other hand, there is nothing she
will not be able to endure if she can retain the semblance of respectability.
You see! I am being destroyed by this situation, and by this present state of
affairs! I lack a womanly being who might resolve – in spite of everything &
everyone – to be to me what only a wife can be in such pitiful circumstances,
and *must* be, I say, if I am to survive. Well, I may perhaps be blinded by an
over-estimation of my own worth if I presume to suppose that a woman who
might resolve to devote herself to me in such precarious circumstances would
thus be prepared to withdraw from all contact with those human relations
that have no useful place in the life and work of a man like me. She would
not even need to reassure herself by recalling that in other countries and
other social circles the situation in which she would find herself is regarded
as by no means offensive, she would need only to tell herself that she was
raised high above all that was customary and usual around her – : these are
more or less the things which I then say to myself! My God! how many
people do I have to say these things to? And yet it gives me no comfort to do
so. My desire only increases all over again; no other solution can be found:
each of them leaves the yawning gulf wide open. Not the Rhine, not Biebrich,
not here, not there! – I want a loving woman at my side, though she be a
child as well! I then think: somewhere there must be a woman who loves you
sufficiently for that. Very well; but how would you provide for her? Here, too,
I have found a way.

In spite of my concerts, in spite of Tristan – I now know that I need look
no further than *Vienna* as the focus of my activities. Everything is possible
here; the ground is extremely fertile; I am held in high regard here: there is

wealth in plenty. I need only to *will* things to happen. But how must I set about being able to do so? I now know. I shall rent a sitting-room and bedroom[1] in the inner city, good and respectable, and shall furnish it in a modest way; and it is here that I shall "live"; people will visit me in the afternoons at set hours; once and for all, I shall *not* admit callers in the mornings, and only in certain rare cases in the evenings. But – where shall I work? where shall I really be at home? – here, too, I have the answer. I shall have a pleasant apartment in some free and attractive suburb, but I shall not live there, no, it will be a dear child (or wife) – call her what you will – who lives there. Additionally, I shall install my Biebrich furnishings and the Erard grand piano there, too. The faithful child will nurse me with her tender loving cares. And when I wake up in the morning, feeling refreshed, the child will come to my bedside; she will attend to my breakfast, and then I shall work, no one will be allowed to see me, except for my friend, who will come and see how my work is progressing. She will then provide me with a good, yet simple, midday meal. But then I shall have to go into town, give audiences, pay various visits and, if all goes well, I shall then return punctually of an evening to the place where I really belong. There is no doubt but that, on an external level, I shall be able to carry out this plan in a large city: everything will fall into place as though of its own accord. – But who is the woman who will live out there? R. W.'s final refuge, his angel, – his wife, – if the unhappy woman who married him in the blindness of her youth were to die before him. –

You see, these are the thoughts of – a desperate man on New Year's Eve and New Year's Day! God knows what you will make of them! None the less, I could not conceal from you the things I was plotting. How will you interpret them?? Yes, – ultimately, it is only a theoretical problem which I have set you. But it is none the less interesting to discuss it. What do you think, my little friend? –

For today, my child, my warmest and most sincere good wishes. You should also read the "Armer Heinrich" of Hartmann von der Aue,[2] in Simrock's translation! – The beautiful violet scarf never leaves my neck, so that it will very soon be threadbare – alas; how you flatter me, my love! –

Best wishes to Mama and your aunts: as for my return? – Oh, who can tell – with me everything is left completely to chance. – And Louise[3] must remain faithful to me, and visit us often in Vienna. Best wishes also to Käth:[4]

1 Nothing came of this. Wagner remained at the Hotel Kaiserin Elisabeth until 12 February 1863, when he returned to Biebrich.
2 Hartmann von Aue's *Der arme Heinrich* (Poor Henry) deals, on one level, with a young girl's willingness to sacrifice herself to save the sinful hero. In his letter to Mathilde Maier of 25 January 1863, Wagner signed himself "Poor Henry".
3 Louise Wagner, Mathilde Maier's friend (and unrelated to Wagner himself).
4 Käthe Maier, Mathilde Maier's sister.

who knows, I may after all have to go to Petersburg in the middle of February.[1] I need to earn enough money to set up house. (we must also have a little dog!) Ah – it's heart-breaking! Believe me! but be good to me in spite of all that, just as you are always kind & dear to me: you must believe that, too! And now a kiss! Adieu!

Yours,
R.W.

Maier-Briefe 48–51.

283. MATHILDE MAIER, MAINZ   St Petersburg,[2] 10 March 1863

I have just received your letter, dearest child, and intend replying immediately, although I cannot tell you about the second concert until tomorrow, since it is not due to take place until this evening. I hope that it will again turn out to my satisfaction.

When your letter was written I cannot rightly say, since it is not dated. My last letter to you, with the enclosed bills of exchange for 2000 fl., will have reached you yesterday, I imagine, or today at the latest. If not, you must let me know at once. Your news is not very consoling. I understand it well enough, since I am used to things appearing very straightforward to begin with, and only recognizing the difficulties when I have to take the matter more seriously, for which the vulgar streak in people is generally to blame, making them seek their own gain in the enthusiastic efforts of others: once upon a time I might have wished for an easier life, for it seems as though everything worth having will come too late, in other words when I am already exhausted by my labours and by the need to be patient. There shall be no lack of money: in accordance with your wishes I shall shortly be sending you another large sum for Schüler. However, since I have now made up my mind to acquire my own plot of land, what has initially decided me in favour of Biebrich – setting aside all additional reasons – is the hope and prospect of being able to remain undisturbed in my present apartment until such time as the building work is completed.[3]

If, however, the difficulties were to increase, more especially on the part of Frickhöffer, the best way of persuading him to agree to the most favourable conditions, in other words to relinquish his own plot of land, would probably be to show him that we were seriously seeking to acquire a plot of land

1 See letter [283], pp. 553–4.
2 Wagner arrived in St Petersburg on 24 February 1863; he gave three concerts on 3, 10 and 18 March, before travelling to Moscow for a further three concerts on 25, 27(?) and 29(?) March; three more concerts in St Petersburg followed.
3 Nothing came of this plan.

elsewhere in the Rhinegau. May I ask you to negotiate with Herr Kraus on the matter? Is it not possible to find a pleasantly situated plot of land in one of the many attractive villages in the outlying area, from Schierstein to Winkel, Geisenheim etc? If this were the case, I would beg Herr Kraus to take over the entire matter at once. I am very much in favour of it. At all events, if we show ourselves to be seriously interested in the idea, we shall have a good chance of overcoming the chicaneries of the Biebrich set. –

My business affairs seem to be taking a favourable turn here: since I have still not heard anything from Vienna that would require me to hurry back there, I have today concluded an engagement with Moscow, under the terms of which I should be able to earn 4000 roubles in the course of a week of, admittedly, hard work. It has been decided provisionally that I shall go there a week on Thursday, in the event of my being able to arrange a benefit concert here next Tuesday, which would bring me in 2000 roubles. I shall no doubt have to put an end to this raiding expedition since – it is dreadfully tiring; not only the performances and rehearsals themselves, but all the fuss & bother connected with them, especially having to talk to so many people. I am already atoning today for having been so indulgent in accepting invitations: I slept badly and feel ill, so that I am afraid for this evening.

I spent one evening in the company of the witty & well-informed Grand Duchess Helene; she wished to get to know the Mastersingers: since I had intentionally not brought a copy of it with me, in order not to be held up at the frontier, she immediately telegraphed to Berlin for one. But the question is whether there will be a copy available even in Berlin; for I found further evidence of Schott's asinine behaviour and pitifully inadequate business sense when, in the course of my journey through Berlin, Bülow assured me that it had been impossible for him to procure a copy of the poem.[1] These are supposed to be "practical" people, and we are the visionaries!

I have sent some more tickets today to Käth;[2] I think she will come this time.

Forgive me, my dearest, but I must close now, since I keep on being interrupted. In addition, my head is all confused, and your news has somewhat shattered the agreeable illusions that I had invested in furnishing my little house. God, when will anyone be able to report a really decisive success for me: how deplorable that one must struggle so hard to wrest everything from the sloth of the world! – Well, that is how it must be! –

Remember me with affection; and learn to put up with Tannhäuser at any rate, and take good care of its author, who has finally had himself photographed in Russian for you, looking in the best possible spirits, and who now

1 The libretto of *Die Meistersinger von Nürnberg* was published by Schott's in January 1863. Wagner had passed through Berlin on 19 February 1863.
2 Käthe Maier.

sends you his very best wishes! Sincere regards to you all! I am fond of every one of you! Fare you well, my sweetheart!

Yours,
R.

Maier-Briefe 72–5.

284. MATHILDE MAIER, MAINZ   Moscow, 21/22 March 1863

Here I am in Asia, my child, actually in Asia!

I have not yet been able to see the Muscovite splendours for myself, and have observed only that I am in a tremendously large village, with an Asiatic castle (the Kremlin) and various Boyar palaces at its centre.

I may add that I can thank my lucky stars that I did not wake up this morning feeling really ill: I went to bed yesterday afraid that I would. My poor throat & chest, especially, were so strained as a result of rehearsing with a couple of unmusical & dreadfully nervous singers that I suffered from violent chest pains for the very first time in my life. Before my departure I had 3 days of endless vexations, with insomnia and all the trimmings. Finally, everything about the concert itself affected me in the most extraordinary way, more especially the enthusiastic response of the whole vast orchestra, which almost overwhelmed me, so that it was a long time after they had welcomed me before I was able to begin, since I had first to regain a certain sense of steadiness.

Only Käth[1] has again caused me a good deal of trouble. She seems to have a fairly stupid person as mistress of her every move. On this occasion the 3 best stalls seats were returned to me, on some pretext or other of impropriety: it was too late to exchange them, since everything else was already sold out. –

But I hope that the poor girl was at the concert, and that she has sent you a report on it. I then spent 20 hours, without rest & sleep, travelling to Moscow, so that I arrived here in a wretched state. But I hope that the exertions of these Moscow concerts will be the last that I have to endure for the present.

As from Sunday (the 28th) I shall again be staying in Petersburg for about another week, but only to conduct something of my own for a charitable cause,[2] and also to rest and make allowance for the numerous personal relationships into which I have entered here. First and foremost is the Grand Duchess Helene. I feel as though she will have a great and decisive influence

---

1 Käthe Maier, who was employed as governess by the Heckler family in St Petersburg.
2 A benefit concert for Carl Schuberth. As a result of indisposition, Wagner's return to St Petersburg was delayed until 1 April.

on the rest of my life. The impression which I made recently in Petersburg has astounded even my most ardent admirers. An hour before I was due to depart, I received a visit from some high-ranking gentleman,[1] and I had to promise that I would speak to him again on my return. People seem to think it impossible that I should be leaving Petersburg for good. Fortunately, they look at everything very closely here and realize that if I am to work here, it should be only very rarely & by way of exception. –

Some people called to take me on a drive through the town, from which I have just got back, but I have only enough time to tell you that it is, after all, a quite astonishingly remarkable "village". The Kremlin is a convoluted mass of the most amazing buildings, straight out of the Arabian Nights: from the top you can look down on a town of 400,000 inhabitants[2] with 800 churches, many of which have up to 5 towers: everything is very colourful, bright, golden, domed – strange & wonderful, – so that I could not help laughing out loud in amazement. How like children we are! – In half-an-hour I have to be at the rehearsal, and *then* I scarcely think I shall get round to writing. And so a brief word now on my present feelings towards the plot of land.[3] I feel as though I ought to leave everything in the balance for another 2 weeks. It is not out of the question that – someone – will have the house built for me, in which case I am attracted by the possibility of a *larger* garden with beautiful trees. – Listen! –

Look out for such a plot of land along the beautiful Rhine! Do not be bound by a particular place. – This is all that I can say for today. –

Everything else now strikes me as being over-hasty. Adieu my dear, sweet child! Sincerely yours,

R.

[...]

Maier-Briefe 78–9.

285. MATHILDE MAIER, MAINZ   Vienna,[4] 5 May 1863

My dear, sweet child,
    I have some important news for you; how will my love receive it?
    God knows how passionately I had contemplated settling down by the

---

1 Possibly Alexander Arkadyevich Suvorov-Rymnikski (see *Mein Leben* 734; English trans. 717–18).
2 Paris at this time had a population of 1¾ millions, Berlin ¾ million, St Petersburg 600,000 and London over three million.
3 See previous letter; nothing came of these plans.
4 Wagner arrived in Vienna on 25 April.

Rhine! The greatest enthusiasm that friendship and love could muster was unable to provide me with what I desired. With what coldness and apathy have I recently been made to wait – in vain – for a reply from Zurich.[1] – Here – it was sufficient to make known my wish, and lo and behold! scarcely have I turned round when – – I have found what I was looking for, at least in terms of space. A certain Baron von Rochow,[2] a great admirer of mine, reckons it a stroke of great good fortune to be able to make available to me his country house in Penzing, half-an-hour from Vienna, with a large, park-like garden and splendid tall trees, and to lease it to me for life, or for as long as I wish to live there, at a relatively very low rent! –

The surrounding area, like everything else in Vienna, is quite delightful; in the immediate neighbourhood I have the large gardens of Schönbrunn, with their splendid zoological garden for my morning walks. In winter, whatever my needs, all the company I might wish for: and the only place where I shall ever concern myself with performances of my works is barely a stone's throw away; travelling for that purpose, living in hotels, etc., will cease. –

Of course, my dear child! only when I think of you could I hesitate for a moment in the face of this offer. But I have indulged this feeling for a whole week now. What finally triumphed was my deep-seated need to attain domestic peace *at any price*: I have rented the place, and telegraphed to Biebrich for my furniture. I am now writing to assure you of my total love! you see, it is so earnest and so sincere that it no longer admits of any substantial obstacle, even in our lasting separation. I have just found an expedient; I have a couple of dear little guest rooms for the summer; my sweetheart will come here often with her Mama or her cousin,[3] and will visit me here. –

Oh, not another word on the subject today! It has – lasted a week.

You dear, noble creature! – Wish me – – good luck! As though anyone could ever be happy! –

Now just let me set up house here, as quick as I can: once everything is in place and all is ready, I shall know where I am and where I am really *at home*, and I shall then set out at once and visit you on the Rhine – no doubt about it!

The fourth page of this letter is reserved for business matters: ask Lieschen for the keys to the cupboards and chests, and send them to me separately. Ask Schüler to settle your expenses, together with Thomas's bills; I am writing to him on the matter today to give him my instructions. And now? –

Accept a sincere and heartfelt kiss from me; look me calmly in the eye! We shall soon see each other again, and one day you will finally come here

1 It appears that one of the reasons for Wagner's visit to the Wesendoncks in November 1861 had been to solicit Otto's financial help (see Newman's *Life*, III, 151–2).
2 Also spelt Rachovin by Wagner (letter to Mathilde Maier of 24 June 1863). Other variants include Rackowitz and Radowitz.
3 Louise Wagner.

for good: my hair is already growing greyer by the hour! – Fare you well! A thousand good wishes to you all!

Yours,
R.W.

[. . .]

Maier-Briefe 90–1.

286. MATHILDE MAIER, MAINZ   [Vienna, 11/12 May 1863]

I have just got back from Penzing. A glorious day, sun, everything wonderfully green, a peaceful garden, beautiful apartment – how wretched I felt! – Only now I am completely worn-out! – Friendly servants,[1] an honest couple with pleasant, gentle faces, – they come with the apartment. And everything new! a fresh start: nothing familiar, none of the sweetness of well-known objects around me! Is it to be here then? – My child, you no longer feel loneliness as *I* do! I am quite ill with it. – And the sun? with you it shines on a sad and lonely man! – – Oh – – !! help is needed here, a further attempt must be made to regain my stability – do not begrudge me my flattering attempts to have you here with me, – here rather than there! –

God knows how deep your bourgeois bigotry goes – : but, what if your entire family with all your aunts were to move here? – Yes, indeed! another Russian campaign is called for, and so I am offering you the equally beautiful ground-floor apartment in my house.

Your family will run my household. And then? What do your aunts say to that? – Ah! get away with you!! You are all quite pitiful – the lot of you! Quite pitiful! You must be prepared to take risks with a man like Wagner![2]

The next day.

I was interrupted: the night brought with it a great sense of weariness. I have slept. – Oh, what poor material we are for the world daemon! In me I recognize Ananda and the Buddha, in you Savitri, the Chandala girl of my "Victors".[3] One must be and become everything oneself: that is how I create my art! Whom do I profit thereby? Ultimately – ourselves alone. That is something we shall have to see about! –

Oh, my child, your letters were too wonderful for words! They were written by an angel. I simply cannot bear to think of them, – you dear, sweet thing! Do not leave me! Do not float away from me! [. . .][4] Write to me as often

1 Franz and Anna Mrazéck.
2 Untranslatable play on words: the German verb "to take risks" is *wagen*.
3 See also letter [197], p. 365.
4 A sentence has been rendered illegible here; see introductory essay, p. 414.

as you can! Especially now: do you hear? Every day! – I would be quite capable of abandoning myself totally to my emotions, of bearing every injury & expense, and of coming to see you now, were my one overwhelming desire not for – rest! – Oh, my child, I am 50! Love knows only one desire now, that of my flying Dutchman: calm after the storm. – But, in view of the way you are made, I have not given up hope of achieving this aim with you in one form or another. –

Fare you well! I am oppressed on every side. For my birthday I shall send you some large & splendid photographs of myself. I shall celebrate it entirely on my own. Yesterday the gardener showed me some rose-bushes which he had bought for me; I burst into tears, and felt only sadness on seeing them. –

But! Patience! It will all soon be different, but, however fate wills it, things can only get better!

Adieu, my darling!

Yours,
R.W.

Maier-Briefe 93–4.

287. ELIZA WILLE, MARIAFELD   Penzing, 5 June 1863

Dear and honoured friend,

I finally intend writing to the Wesendoncks again within the next few days. But – I can write only to *him*. I love his wife too much, I feel so tender-hearted and overcome with emotion whenever I recall her to mind, that it is impossible for me to address her in the form which it is now more imperative than ever that I should be enjoined to use towards her. What I feel in my heart I cannot write to tell her without betraying her husband, whom I sincerely respect and hold in high esteem. What is to be done? Nor can I keep all this locked away in my heart: *one* person at least must know how I feel. That is why I am telling you this: she is, and remains, my first and only love! I feel this now with increasing certainty. It was the high point of my life: the uneasy and agreeably anxious years which I spent in the growing enchantment of her presence and of her affection contain all the sweetness that I have known in my life. It requires only the gentlest reminder to feel myself in its thrall once more, filled with that wonderfully melting mood which even now, as once before, takes my breath away and leaves me the power only to sigh. And if there be no other reminder, then my dreams may have the same effect, dreams which are always welcome and which do me good each time they put me in mind of her. – Now, tell me, my friend! How can I speak to this woman as I should and must speak to her now? –

Impossible! – Yes, I even feel that I must never see her again.[1] Ah, even in Venice[2] it made me deeply unhappy to see her again: only now that this memory has faded completely away is this woman again what she once was to me. I feel that she will always be beautiful in my sight, and that my love for her will never grow cold; but I must never see her again, not under this ghastly constraint which – however necessary I recognize it to be – must mean the death of our love. What shall I do now? Am I to leave my dearest under the illusion that I have grown indifferent to her? Surely that is too harsh! Should you disabuse her of her illusion? Would that do any good? I do not know! – And finally life passes by. It is heart-breaking! –

Since leaving Zurich[3] I have been living the life of a virtual exile: – there is no telling what I have sacrificed! – My only desire is now to regain at least some sense of domestic calm, in order to be able to live for my work alone. Through the most unprecedented exertions I have at least acquired the possibility of establishing another home for myself, which I shall henceforth have to tend entirely on my own. Repeated attempts have convinced me and my friends that it is impossible for me to live together with my wife any longer, and that it would destroy us both if we did so. And so she is living in Dresden, where I am making adequate provision for her, far beyond my means.[4] She cannot fully compose herself, and only by violently suppressing the constant stirrings of pity within me can I force myself to adopt a harshness without which I should merely prolong her suffering and rob myself of all prospect of peace and quiet. I can say quite truthfully that this is the greatest burden I have ever had to bear. By way of compensation, however, I am renouncing everything, and desire only the peace and quiet I need to work, the one thing that absolves my conscience and that can truly set me free! –

But now, my dear Frau Wille! Grant me my request, and let me have occasional news of our friend! I hope you are still fond of her, and that she is equally loyal towards you? It is too hard to know that so infinitely loyal a creature must drag out her existence in so remote and alien a clime, without our ever being able to cast a single glance in her direction. You will understand that what I can discover from her husband does not reveal the friend to whom I can swear eternal love, since I never intend to see her again. Never? – It is hard, – but it must be so! –

I have again opened the green portfolio which she once sent me in Venice;

---

1 Wagner was guest of the Wesendoncks in Zurich from 22 to 24 November 1863 (see Fehr II,194–5). The Annals for April 1864 (BB 140; English trans. 118) record a "visit to the Wesendoncks", but in *Mein Leben* (752; English trans. 735) Wagner claims that it was the Wesendoncks who visited him in Mariafeld. Fehr (II,203) disputes both accounts. Wagner saw Mathilde for the last time at the 1875 Bayreuth rehearsals (CT for 9 and 23 April 1875).
2 Between 7 and 11 November 1861.
3 On 17 August 1858.
4 Wagner gave Minna an allowance of 1000 thalers a year.

how much torment has been suffered since then! And now, suddenly to be in thrall once more to that old, ineffably beautiful spell! In it are sketches to Tristan, to the music of her poems[1] – ! Ah, my dearest friend! We love but once, whatever life may offer to intoxicate and flatter us: yes, only now do I fully realize that I shall never cease to love her, and her alone. You will, I know, respect the innocence of this protestation, and forgive me for placing this confession before you.

Fare you well, and be ever kindly disposed towards

Your
Richard Wagner.

Mathilde Wesendonck-Briefe 347–9.

288. NATALIE PLANER, ZWICKAU   Penzing, 20 June 1863

Dear Natalie,

This time I am sending the money for Minna to you, with the request that you forward it to her at once.

I was already intending to do so: a letter from Minna which I received today confirms me in this decision.

She writes in a vein which, by her own lights, is fair and just, nay, almost charitable and friendly. And ultimately she is quite right to see things as she does: it is simply that I see them differently – and therein lies our misfortune.

Believe me, my dear Natalie, my heart bleeds and has done so for years: for it is now entirely clear to me that I cannot live with Minna any longer. It is not a question of apportioning blame, any more than it is a question of reproaching her: but experience has shown me that it would be the greatest possible misfortune for us to live together again. Although this was bound to become clear to me some time ago, I kept on vacillating over how best to carry out this bitter resolve. It was usually consideration of her health which turned the scales, persuading me to avoid saying anything final and decisive. If I could only hope that in this way I might make up for all that has happened, I would gladly continue to pursue this course. However, I can see that in this way I am prolonging *her* torment and my own as well. In the end she *will* keep clinging to a hope which I cannot fulfil, and in that way is prevented from leading the kind of life which, in the circumstances, could alone help *her* to find peace. I used to think that it would be all right if I were to visit her now and then: but it is easy to think such thoughts, and I am now convinced that such an arrangement would be feasible only in the case of

---

1 *Fünf Gedichte für eine Frauenstimme* (WWV 91a), usually known as the Wesendon(c)k Lieder, composed between November 1857 and October 1858, and published by Schott in 1862.

quite different, more easy-going natures. She has, quite naturally, developed a sense of mistrust and a nervous inhibitedness towards me which make the days we are together an hourly torment. In spite of the fact that I have the best of intentions and feel deeply and sincerely sorry for her, I am now so clearly conscious of this that I constantly shy away from the thought of visiting her. Of course, I do not hate Minna: I should like to be of as much benefit to her as I can; but the differences are too great, and the divisions caused by our unhappy experiences together are too obvious for any attempt to deceive ourselves otherwise ever to succeed.

And so I must now ask myself what purpose it could possibly serve to leave the poor woman in a state of uncertainty any longer, an uncertainty which is a torment both to her and to me. Not even our letters can be completely innocuous: there will always be something that contributes to our misunderstanding and provokes remarks which continue to unsettle us both. I am forced to conclude that it would be better to stop writing, too. When I say this, you may be certain that it has cost me a terrible effort of will, and that my heart suffers more from this apparent harshness than any of you can ever imagine. Better, though, to keep my weakness to myself: if I reveal it to Minna, it will only produce renewed confusion. My only consolation is that there is nobody who knows us both who is not of the opinion that it is better like this for us both.

Minna now writes to say that she wants to give up the large apartment. Of course she should do so, and I shall do what is necessary to give notice for the 1st of October. But she should not think of moving into a furnished apartment! If she cannot use certain of our things in a smaller apartment, she should give them away or sell them, but always keep what she can use. I also wonder whether it would not be better for her to move to Zwickau, where she would be nearer you: she could live there very pleasantly on the money which she will receive from me with scrupulous regularity, and she would then have her relatives with her. In Dresden her position towards me (I fully realize!) is bound to become uncomfortable. Really, she should begin an entirely new life! – But it does not behove me to offer her advice, least of all to prescribe what she should do: oh! I must leave it entirely to her how she manages her life in future. The only contribution I can make is to end the uncertainty which prevents her from achieving any peace of mind. – She is absolute owner and proprietress of all those things which she has with her at present: she may dispose of them as she pleases. But if she wishes to send me something, I would ask for the silver laurel wreath and beaker which were once given to me; perhaps she would also *share* with me the whole of the silver of which she already left me certain pieces in Biebrich. I would also ask her for the fire-screen, if I did not sincerely believe any emotional excitement to be harmful and pernicious at present: but the arrival of this screen would touch me deeply.

Natalie! I write these lines with tear-stained cheeks. Perhaps I should have waited; it is, after all, only right and proper that *both* of us should now show the greatest composure and calm. –

However, if I now express, simply in the form of an *urgent* request, the desire, or, rather, the imperative need to arrange my relations with Minna in such a way that she no longer entertains any more false expectations concerning me, I declare, conversely, that she shall *always remain my wife*. I shall *never think of divorcing her*. I shall remain alone, and no one shall take her place. –

But it is impossible for us to live together any more: it simply will not work. *Anything* must be easier to bear than the sad relationship into which we should inevitably lapse! Let Minna think well on what this declaration of mine means, and I hope she will find in it proof of my true and sincere respect for her. –

My lot is loneliness – : my life – work! –

There is nothing I wish to add to this. I know only too well that discussions of this kind between Minna and me are totally unproductive. There is no question here of right or wrong: the only person who would continue to be in the wrong would be he who thoughtlessly and superficially were to advise a renewed attempt at living together!

With a bleeding heart I ask you to remember me to Minna! May she be reconciled to what is inevitable! It may perhaps be harder for me than for her!

Best wishes to you, too, dear Natalie, as well as to good Tröger and Charlotte!

Your Richard W.

Sammlung Burrell 546–8.

289. MALWIDA VON MEYSENBUG, ROME   Penzing, 22 June 1863

Dearest and best of friends,

You really are one of the few friends I have who are not immediately frightened away if a letter remains unanswered, but who can be counted on to write again! May Heaven, too, reward you for this! –

I received your last letter but one on my return here to Vienna from Russia: I did not know what to say to your assumption that I would not accept the invitation of the Petersburg Philharmonic Society (exclusively German musicians) out of a sense of Polish patriotism,[1] and that I would have preferred to starve in Germany! It must have astonished you to see me go there after all, but I have seen to it in the mean time that you shall have better guarantees

---

1 An attempt by the Poles to cast off the yoke of Russian oppression was crushed in 1863/4.

of my Polish conscientiousness in future. – Oh, best of friends! I am a thoroughly frivolous man: a fanatic for peace, – nothing more. In Petersburg and Moscow, in the midst of my triumphs, in the midst of such genuine delight at the truly unbelievably fine performances which I managed to bring off with the musicians there; – in the midst of all the acclaim which in warmth and enthusiasm exceeded anything I have ever previously known, even in Vienna, – all that I could still see before me in my imagination was the apartment and garden with a few beautiful old trees which everyone in Germany had been given instructions to enquire after for me when I left, and which I was determined to acquire only by dint of my own efforts. In Vienna, where I arrived straight from Petersburg, I visited no one, but scoured the area in search of the apartment and garden that I longed for: from the Rhine came news of delays, – then, all at once, I found what I was looking for in Penzing (in Penzing!) – an apartment & garden, peaceful & pleasant! I am renting it and furnishing it with my money, – or rather with what I have been left of it, – so that it is pleasing to the eye, in accordance with my own ideas on the matter.[1] I am alone, have found some good, sympathetic servants, and am now getting out my work again! –

You must admit that nothing can be done with a man like me! You should give him up for lost! –

While I was still looking, I thought: my God, what if Liszt were suddenly to write to say that he had found a beautiful apartment and garden for me in Rome – , would I go to Rome after all? – – Yes, but reluctantly! – Why? – I cannot bear any further excitements, especially at the moment. It is an utter disgrace that I have lost so many precious years of work and creativity, so much so that I believe that such a mass of new impressions as Italy and Rome would afford me would throw me completely off the rails. Proudhon once said, in contrast to those people who expected the railways to work wonders for the intellectual development of mankind: "Le génie est sédentaire!" – So it is. Believe me. He who cannot create his own world out of little will still less be able to create one out of much. – And yet I say all this with a certain bitterness of renunciation: – heavens, how gladly would I, too, stretch out my limbs and let the wonderful world outside leave its mark upon me! But everyone has his own daemon, and mine is a horribly powerful beast; it completely & utterly subjugates me to its own ends.

Tell me, child! How can I have the poem of my *Mastersingers* forwarded to you? Make enquiries and let me know. – I am living here without any form of social contact, and wish only to be left in peace in order to be able to complete this nonsense on which I am working, without any further interrup-

1 For a diagram of Wagner's Penzing apartment and its furnishings see H. Barth, D. Mack and E. Voss (eds), *Wagner: A Documentary Study* (London 1975), 203.

tions. Whether I shall ever perform any of it is a question to which I have finally grown utterly indifferent. Indeed, the fact that I did not have to go straight back to Tristan again following my Russian exertions (Frau Dustmann is indisposed) suited me admirably. Ultimately one has to live with the person one is: to be allowed a little self-respect is therefore the only thing with which we must be satisfied. –

Of course one should not then have to listen to such warm and *eloquent* accounts of wonders such as Michel Angelo etc.; for then one's heart grows heavy, – it does indeed! – I may add, by way of consolation, that I read an Austrian newspaper every day and that whenever I see reports of the Polish uprising I always feel an involuntary sympathy with them, and even relapse into many of my old weaknesses. But in this I am like Göthe: I do not feel sufficient *hatred* to be capable of any real political fervour: and without it one is insufficient for any party. My God! do you imagine that there is a *single* educated person in Petersburg who does not regard the events in Poland as an abomination, and who does not speak & feel exactly the same as you and I? But "politics", "government" – and all the rest of this confounded business, – yes – that is another matter – ! Well, believe me, you & I, we are not made for things like that: not even Garibaldi,[1] and Bakunin still less; but Louis Napoleon most definitely. Well, just let people compare themselves to him! Ugh! –

Little Tausig is my only contact with the outside world: an intelligent and quite exceptional young man! In all seriousness he enquires most eagerly after his bride, and asks you to convey to Olga his most tender greetings! – If you can make any sense of the present season – (it is ghastly weather outside!) – , I should be heartily glad. *Where* should I begin to write you a sensible letter!

A thousand sincere good wishes!

Yours,
Rich. Wagner

Meysenbug-Briefe 83–4.

290. WENDELIN WEISSHEIMER, MAINZ   Penzing, 10 July 1863

My dear Wendelin,

Better a brief word now than nothing at all!

Once again, my sincere thanks for your kind letter on my birthday. Good

---

1 A type of biscuit containing layers of currants.

luck with your work, in which I take the liveliest interest: I hope it all turns out a success! – you have a lot on!

As for myself, well, thereby hangs a tale: I can't go on. My 50th birthday, which I spent alone, in total isolation, without a single soul to call my own, has left a deep impression upon me, an impression which, in its repercussions, has developed into a decisive turning-point in my courage to face life. I cannot go on, I feel such a total stranger in a world in which I find myself so utterly thwarted in everything, be it art and life, or will and disposition.

I have lost all sense of pleasure: the shocks I have suffered and my recognition of the powerlessness of the individual are too great and decisive. This is something that someone of your age will not really be able to understand. Of me it is true to say quite simply that I am – tired of life. What I lack is nothing less than all that is necessary to live a life of human happiness.

Great as is my need for peace and quiet, what continues to alarm me most of all is the total lack of any future prospects as far as my actual theatrical plans are concerned. In order to rid myself of this fear to some extent, and to see for myself whether this kind of excitement can restore any of my optimism in life, I intend from time to time to undertake concert performances similar to the ones I gave in Vienna. Since I do not care to inflict myself upon Russia again so soon, and since the money I saved there has finally dried up (as a result of my ordering all the furnishings and fittings for an entire house, together with other heavy losses), – thereby reviving my cares concerning the future – , I have again been considering places where I can find decent orchestras and where I know there are people subservient to my wishes. In this context I have also written to Schindelmeisser in Darmstadt, asking him whether Dalwigk might prevail upon the Grand Duke to place his musical institutions at my disposal for a major performance similar to the one in Vienna, and to allow me to keep the receipts, at increased prices. Perhaps at the beginning of September,[1] if the Grand Duke were to act generously in this regard, his action would do honour to both him and me, and might also set a good example for other princes to follow. Sch. has just replied to say that neither of the two people concerned is there at present, but that the matter is not urgent, and that he can raise the question, in accordance with my wishes, as soon as an opportunity arises. –

If it is not too much trouble, I would ask you to seek out Sch. and make things hot for him. I am prepared to appeal directly to Dalwigk or even the Grand Duke as soon as I am given to understand that this will serve any useful purpose. –

1 Wagner conducted two concerts in Karlsruhe on 14 and 19 November. Other concerts were given in Budapest (23 and 28 July), Prague (5 and 8 November), Löwenberg (2 December), Breslau (7 December), and Vienna (27 December).

Please let me hear from you soon in any case. I am living a life of utter seclusion here, and have not yet been able to bring myself to give any further thought to Tristan! – Until now I have been busy scoring the Mastersingers.[1] But progress is very slow: I confess that the luxuriant spring of good humour and the courage to face life, from which all such delight in one's work must flow, has now dried up within me. Nor do I know where I might rediscover it, given the pitiful state of our theatres. In this respect, at least, it would have cheered me to see Tristan launched.

If anything comes of Darmstadt, I promise you that I shall certainly give the *Cobbling Song* an airing there (in other words, for the first time), perhaps also the "Awake!" chorus & so on.

Perhaps all this will revive my sense of enjoyment. At present everything looks so utterly *wretched*. – Well, kind regards to your most admirable Papa and to your kind mother: and remember me, too, to your sisters and brother. – It is always with deep emotion that I recall the sufferings and cares that I caused you in Vienna.

Sincerely and ever yours,

Richard Wagner.

David Salomon Auction Catalogue
(published, with minor errors of transcription,
in Weissheimer-Briefe 244–7).

291. MATHILDE WESENDONCK, ZURICH[2]   Penzing, 3 August 1863

Dearest Meisterin,[3]

To judge by your last kind letter, I should really have waited for "more detailed" news from Schwalbach. I travelled through there on my way to Pest,[4] where I had been invited by the Hungarians to give two "concerts". I got back from there a few days ago, and found that the lamp you had promised me was already waiting for me, a gift which I find as beautiful as it is masterly and for which I wanted to thank you most sincerely. –

As for my refuge, things are only so-so; quite curious really. The need to settle down on a more permanent basis in a suitable and pleasant apartment had become overwhelming. I felt that only from such a base could I face the

1 See letter [271], p. 527, note 1.
2 This letter was sent to Zurich, although the Wesendoncks were staying at the health resort of Schwalbach, twelve miles north-west of Wiesbaden.
3 "Meisterin" is the feminine form of "Meister", a term which Wagner used to describe himself during the *Meistersinger* years and later.
4 See letter [290], p. 566, note 1.

world one more time – the last time – and discover how things stood with it and with me. I now find that it is not in the best of health, and I sincerely regret having spent my poor and dearly earned money in acquiring the costly basis for that step in knowledge. Since no one wishes to take me in, I would have done better to buy myself a place in some Italian poor-house with my few thousand Russian roubles, and to have left the world to go its own way from now on. I really do not know any longer what I am supposed to be doing here. I tell you this in all truth and completely calmly, from the very depths of my soul! If I were to enumerate the strange misfortunes which have dogged me since my departure from Switzerland,[1] even *you* would surely find here an almost systematic attempt on the part of fate to divert me from my plans. I have no luck! And a certain amount of good luck is needed if people like us are to delude ourselves into thinking that we are a part of the world. –

Meisterin, things are not good! – And I am heartily sickened of life. I recently discovered this quite clearly, thanks to an incident in which my very life was in danger. It happened on the Danube in Pest, in the selfsame boat in which two young Hungarian cavalrymen had travelled from Rotterdam to Pest last summer. A charming and intelligent woman by the name of Countess Bethlen, the mother of six children, had taken control of the tiller. There was a violent squall, and she grew anxious and sprang her luff: the waves drove the vessel against a raft, so that it cracked apart. I was seized only by pity for the poor woman, whereas all that I myself could feel was a strange sense of well-being which was so agreeably bracing that the young people around me could only marvel at my behaviour, whereas they had thought that someone as excitable as I am could be counted on to get very worked up. When they applauded me, – for I played a small part in the rescue, – I could scarcely contain my laughter!

But what is the use of it all! Death does not come so easily, especially when our time is not yet to hand. That is how it must be with me. And yet I can no longer perceive any reason why I should have been spared. Is it so that I can be of some help to those who are dear to me?? Can I mean less to them when they know I am dead than when I am cut off on every side and feel only pain? As a person, I can no longer mean anything to anyone: and spiritually? My spirit remains theirs, though it no longer refreshes *my* heart. I have lost all sense of enjoyment, – in everything. I lack all sense of devotional feeling, all composure: a profound and unsettling listlessness governs my inner life. I have no present, and quite clearly no future. Of faith not a vestige. There is no doubt but that true artistic activity, performances of my new works, could have altered a great deal here, and altered it significantly. My return to Germany, on the contrary, has been a fatal blow to me: it is a wretched place, and Ruge is right when he says: "the Germans are an abject

1 On 17 August 1858.

nation".[1] There is not a glimmer of hope here, and how things stand with those august gentlemen I once thought of as my patrons you can deduce from the fact that I was invited by the Czechs in Prague, and by the Russians and the Hungarians, to repeat my Viennese concerts, whereas I am now preparing to face the fact that my worthy Germans, when asked, will almost certainly turn me down. In Berlin the intendant[2] has refused to receive me. Etc. – It has still not been possible for me, ever since my return from Russia, to get to see a single person from the theatre here. My disgust at having to deal with these people is so great that I am incapable any longer of undertaking a single enterprise where I would need them. Everyone who is at all familiar with the situation here finds this entirely natural: but it also explains why my career is now at an end. Believe me, it is a strange feeling to know that even you yourself do not really know my works: I need perform only a fragment of them complete, and even the most talented and experienced of my disciples is forced to admit at once that he had previously as good as no idea at all of the piece. – What, then, is my spirit, my works? – without me they exist for no one. Indeed! that makes me think of my poor person as someone of great importance: yet this selfsame person exists only for me! It's a bad business. No doubt something could be said on the matter, even something comforting and emphatically self-delusive: – but it no longer serves any useful purpose to do so! I hear what is said, what the words are, and, especially when they are written down, I can even see that all my dealings with people are now almost entirely limited to letters.

What shall I now do with my refuge, in spite of the portfolio and lamp?[3] A difficult question, especially in view of my extreme listlessness. – I keep turning over the problem in my mind. Shall I set myself yet another time limit, a certain number of years, say, five? How shall I set about obtaining these years? It will be very difficult, and I really do not understand how. My needs are increasing: I have two households to support, two households alike in their wretchedness! – That is why I have finally fallen back upon myself as a *person*. No one asks after my works: the world acknowledges and respects only the virtuoso. Well, necessity has shown me that I, too, am a virtuoso. I seem to produce this effect upon people whenever I appear at the head of an orchestra. The Hungarians, who had no idea of my music and whose diet at their National Theatre consists solely of Verdi etc., accorded each of my pieces from the Nibelungs, Tristan, Mastersingers the most incredibly lively response, – but it was clear that they did so because *I* was performing and

1 On 23 June 1848 the political writer Arnold Ruge had told the Bundestag in Frankfurt, "at that time [in Paris in 1845] I said, 'the nation that tolerates this is abject'". His words, taken out of context, were later frequently misquoted, not least by Wagner himself in *Das Bühnenfestspielhaus zu Bayreuth* (The Stage Festival Theatre in Bayreuth) (GS IX,334).
2 Botho von Hülsen.
3 Presents from Mathilde Wesendonck.

presenting my works to them. And so I have been telling myself, each time
that I consider how best to gain "time", that I shall have to travel around
and give concerts. And no doubt this is the course of action that I shall adopt.
But the unfortunate thing about it is that I cannot sustain this kind of activity
at frequent intervals and for long periods. The exhaustion I suffer at such
performances and rehearsals is beyond belief. But I shall see what I can do.
Perhaps if I were to approach you on the subject, you might arrange a similar
"concert" of fragments from my newer works for me in Zurich; but there
may be difficulties here, since my poor "person" needs very many other
persons in order to exert any personal influence. However, be that as it may,
you will shortly discover that I am again giving concerts somewhere or other:
some people will say: "oh, he wants to make some money for himself!" – a
few others perhaps: "it is said that he wants to die!" –

But perhaps everything will turn out tolerably well, and my refuge (how
many is it now?) will once again come in useful: the lamp will again light up
the room, the portfolio will be filled, and – a tea-service (my old one is
unobtainable!) will provide agreeable refreshment. My God! everything is
possible, and although I feel constant pain and torment in every limb of my
nerve-racked body, my doctor simply laughs when I ask him whether it is not
bound to prove fatal in the end. This is intended to cheer me up! In truth,
one feels wretched, but at least one feels *something*. Only complete loneliness
is something that I can no longer bear: the old hunting dog that my landlord
has given me[1] is really no substitute. With my 50th year has come a kind of
desire for the company of a daughter. When Bülow recently presented his
little daughter[2] to me in Berlin, regretting that it was *only* a little daughter, I
felt a sudden flash of blinding light, and said to him: be glad, you will have
great joy of this daughter. I was recently recommended a young 17-year-old
girl[3] from a reputable family, who was said to be sweet-tempered, obliging
and completely unspoilt. I took her in, to serve me my tea, to keep my affairs
in order, and to be present at table and in the evenings. My God, what an
embarrassment it was for me to get the poor child out of the house again
without obviously offending her! She was dreadfully bored, and longed to
return to the town, although she made every effort to conceal this from me,
so that only by using my visits abroad as an excuse was I able to get rid of
her and finally able to feel relatively happy once more! – Oh God! It would
be so easy to satisfy me: I know from experience how well I can get by with
my servants. I thought of Vreneli[4] who waited on me in Lucerne, but she

1 Pohl, a cast-off of Baron Rachovin.
2 Blandine von Bülow, born 29 March 1863. Wagner had passed through Berlin, on his return
  to Vienna, on 23/24 April 1863.
3 Lisbeth Völkl, the daughter of a pork butcher from Vienna's Josefstadt; her elder sister,
  mentioned towards the end of this paragraph, is the recipient of letter [292] below.
4 Verena Weidmann, later Stocker.

could not get away. More recently, the elder sister of the girl I sent home turned up here: she is more experienced and reticent, and she seems sweet-tempered and is not unpleasant. I think I may have another try with her.

You see, that is how things are: I simply have to try to acquire everything by means of money, presumably because I have so much of it! – I shall let you know how things turn out.

However, I now see that I must put a stop to this letter-writing. Your husband will be quite right to criticize me for making you over-excited! Indeed, my dear, I find it difficult to write to you. All the sweetness that alone can refresh me from time to time is but a memory which lies in the past: that is why I cannot and may not write about it! What is there left? How glad I would be to be able to tell you of some genuinely innocent pleasure, or some agreeable occurrence in the present; but where might I find such a thing, without inventing it? I have already told you how I nearly drowned, but that is now over and done with! – Shall I write and tell you how I was fêted and applauded by audiences in this place and that? Believe me, I do indeed appreciate what people have done for me, and do not underestimate the ability of my music to inspire in them almost the same degree of enthusiasm as is normally the case with ballerinas and similar artists: but, God forgive me if I am always happy when it is all over, and I do not have to think any further about it. Perhaps it is pure ingratitude, which is demonstrably one of my cardinal vices. Now and again my mood of melancholy is interrupted by an agreeably delusive but fleeting impression of a more attractive kind: in Pest, for ex., I had a very young and beautiful singer[1] with the most expressive and natural voice to perform short extracts of Elsa; she was Hungarian, spoke German in a very correct but charming manner, and had probably never really known anything about music in her life. I was very moved to have someone as innocent and as unspoilt as this girl to sing my music, and the dear child seemed in turn to be so affected by me and my music that she felt genuine emotion for the first time in her life. This outpouring of emotion was indescribably affecting and utterly delightful, so that many people must have gained the impression that the girl had fallen violently in love with me. She, too, is someone to whom I shall now have to "write" again. – You see, I am telling you all the good news I can, but I do not rightly know what else I should add, and do not even know whether you will reckon this latest story to be "good" news or not. – But at least it gives this letter a sense of direction, and you finally have something to tell your husband about me. The poor man seems fated to suffer all manner of torment: quite apart from America (for I have just about had enough of Germany!), it really is bad luck that he is still being plagued by such a dreadful sore throat which (as he amiably confessed to me) often prevents him from contradicting other people. He says he ought

1 Mlle Rabatinsky.

to be placed in a situation where he would simply not be tempted into talking: I intend suggesting that he should change places with me for a couple of months, – that is, when I am in Penzing, not when I am giving concerts, since that would finish him off in a fortnight. – But Otto really must be awfully sick of me: how often has he not tried to help me; how often has he not thought that things must finally work out for me, – and all the time I remain stuck where I am, nothing is of any use – it is all thrown away! Yes, I, too, believe that everything is wasted on me: huntsmen say in such a case that a man is "bewitched", i.e. someone has cast a spell upon him so that he is unable to shoot straight. – That's how it must be! –

I do not know where to send this letter. You wrote to me from Zurich on the 15th of July to say that you would be back there in 3 weeks at the latest. And so I think it safest to assume that these 3 weeks are about to expire, and to write to your old address with this letter.

Fare you well, and a thousand grateful thanks for being alive. You still exist, – and so I, too, must no doubt also exist a little, though my life be no better than it is. Kindest regards to your husband and children; they should always think well of me. I've finished chattering: I only hope that this letter will not make you too unhappy! Console yourself with the thought that I was able to write it at all! – Adieu, my dearest Meisterin!

Yours,
R.W.

Mathilde Wesendonck-Briefe 355–62.

292. MARIE VÖLKL, PENZING   Breslau, 6 December 1863

Dear little Marie, I shall be returning home again next *Wednesday*, arriving at Vienna North station at 7.30 in the evening. Tell *Franz*[1] to bring the carriage and to be there on time, and he should also prepare whatever is necessary for the trunk. Now, my darling, prepare the house for my return, so that I can relax there in comfort, as I long very much to do. Everything must be clean and tidy, and well-heated. See that the best room is really welcoming for me: when you have heated the stove, open the door, so that the temperature in the room warms up. *And plenty of perfume: buy the best bottles, so that it smells really sweet.* Heavens! how I'm looking forward to relaxing with you again at last. *(I hope the pink drawers are ready, too???)* – Yes, indeed! Just be nice and gentle, *I deserve to be well looked after for a change.* We'll have a tree for Christmas and I'll light the candles on it: everyone will

1 Franz Mrazéck.

be given presents, including yourself, my darling! Not everyone needs to be *told* of my arrival until later. But tell Franz to instruct the barber and hair-dresser to present themselves on Thursday morning at eight-thirty. And so: *Wednesday*, at 7.30 in the evening in Vienna, and soon afterwards in Penzing. I leave it to you whether you wish to meet me at the station. But it would be nicer if you welcomed me back in the heated rooms at home. I shall probably need only the coupé. And so, kind regards to Franz and Anna. Tell them to make everything nice for my return. Love and kisses to my darling! Until we meet again!

R. Wagner.

Kapp 236–7.

293. MATHILDE MAIER, MAINZ   Penzing, 5[1] January 1864

It looks bad, does it not, dearest Mathilde, that I have kept you waiting so long for news? – But you once entreated me to count upon your forgiving me such sins of omission. That is what I have done now. In point of fact, my love, I have nothing to tell you, except that I received the presents which you and Louise[2] sent me.

Otherwise nothing at all has happened, – unfortunately – except for yet more exertions – a concert for Tausig which I conducted[3] – and which once again reduced me to that state of exhaustion which has now become so demonically injurious to me. On the other hand, – this gives you a fairly clear idea of my present situation – you know what decisions I now have to reach! While waiting for a solution to the question whether I have to go to Russia, or whether I can settle down permanently to my work, I remain in a state of anxious uncertainty which takes my breath away and robs me of all desire to be cheerful. I have spent the last few months as though half-asleep, and would have been grateful for any distraction. I gave Christmas presents to my servants, and to Peter,[4] Tausig & H. Porges: I wish you could have been there! –

My niece, Ottilie Brockhaus, is still here: we spent New Year's Eve together at Dr Standhartner's. I went there thinking I would not be able to say a word: as usual I ended up by being the only chatterbox present. But I am paying for it now! I always feel miserable, and am developing a very real sense of hypochondria. I am growing more and more remote from the world: but it

1 Incorrectly dated 7 January 1864 in Maier-Briefe 136.
2 Louise Wagner.
3 A concert on 27 December 1863 in Vienna's Redoutensaal.
4 Peter Cornelius; see also Newman's *Life*, III,207–8.

can hardly be otherwise, – I am worlds apart from it. – How often and how much have I thought of the Karthäuserstrasse![1] –

There is now a glimmer of hope inasmuch as I can now get down to my work in peace. I have already given up Kiev for this reason. The miracles which shall save me cannot come from the things of this world; religion can exist only within the heart of the individual. I shall soon know the answer: there is no lack of the noblest intentions on my part. – And so I am leading an interim existence, and keeping warm by wearing Eva's magnificent fur-lined shoes.[2] What shoes they are! I really believe I could have walked to Kiev in them! – The pictures are excellent! Very many thanks! There is nothing of mine from my younger days that is small enough to send you. Except the portrait by Cäsar Willig.[3] Louise[4] has written me a most kind & heartfelt letter, and sent me a magnificent portfolio. Tell her how pleased I was to receive it: unless you have any objections, I shall write to *her* next time, & she can then pass on my news to you. – Kind regards to everyone at home. Did you stay up on New Year's Eve? Peter congratulated me with a beautiful poem which he improvised. Well, verse-making seems to be infectious at present: I have been receiving almost nothing but poems from the Karthäuserstrasse. Kind regards to the charming poetess, and tell her that I, too, hope to write poetry again one day – very calm & tender verses! Oh, how I yearn to write my life's last poem.[5] Compliments of the season from the bottom of my heart! Perhaps some good will come of it after all. Out of sheer necessity I am in an optimistic frame of mind. I shall write again soon, when I hope to have more definite news for you!

Love & kisses from

Yours,
R.W.

Maier-Briefe 136–7.

294. EDUARD LISZT, VIENNA   Munich,[6] 25 March 1864

Dear and honoured friend,

Permit me to confer dispassionately with you on the barest essentials, and to come straight to the point.

Important though it is for me, for obvious reasons, to ensure that my

---

1 The Maiers' house in Mainz, where Wagner had stayed on 26/27 November 1863.
2 A present from Mathilde Maier.
3 *recte* Willich. The portrait was painted in Biebrich in 1862: Wagner thought very little of it (see *Mein Leben* 706; English trans. 689).
4 Louise Wagner; she is also the "poetess" referred to later.
5 *Die Sieger* (see letter to Mathilde Maier of 29 March 1864).
6 Wagner fled from Vienna on 23 March in order to avoid his creditors. He sought refuge first in Munich and then, from 26 March to 28 April, with Eliza Wille in Mariafeld.

departure from Vienna be as unostentatious and as honourable as possible, I am, none the less, particularly anxious that, for reasons connected with my concern for my future as an artist, I should be able to return to Vienna openly and without embarrassment, and, more especially, to appear in public there in the perhaps not too distant future.

Even today I hope that people still regard me as having gone away for only a relatively short period. This measure was aimed above all at facilitating your negotiations with my *rapacious* creditors; if you succeed in reaching an advantageous settlement here, there will no longer be anything to prevent me from returning to Vienna and staying in or near the city, unless, of course, I decide to give up my Penzing apartment in consequence of its having proved too expensive to maintain, and to exchange it for one which promises a more secure haven of peace for my work. If I had sufficient time at my disposal either to give due notice on my apartment, or else to rent it anew, this could be done straightforwardly and privately, without drawing undue attention to myself; more especially, from my apartment in Penzing I would not have any difficulty persuading those of my creditors to whom I still owe money to defer settlement of the same, since, on the one hand, they have already received considerable payments on account from me, and, on the other – as I have, for example, been told – they are only too well accustomed to extremely long delays on the part of certain gentlemen of the highest rank, in addition to which I have enjoyed their complete confidence in the past. My relations with *these* men will immediately change the moment that I move out of my apartment, and leave Penzing and Vienna for good. If only it were possible to gain more time, so that I might succeed in completely appeasing these creditors, by preparing them for such an eventuality, too! You see, it is my intention to present the affair to them as follows, or – proceeding in the proper manner – to beg you, my dear friend, to come, first of all, to the following arrangement with my landlord. You must say that experience has now shown, on the whole, that my Penzing apartment is too expensive to maintain and that in winter it involves intolerable difficulties, which is why I was already disposed in due course to give notice that I was leaving the apartment, and to leave it, moreover, by next winter. Within the last few weeks, however, it has emerged that I shall be abroad for most of this summer, and, as a result, shall not be able to enjoy the last remaining advantage which the retention of my Penzing apartment would have offered me – that of granting me a pleasant place to stay this summer. As a result, I am anxious to find a new tenant who would enter into the terms of my own tenancy at least for the necessary period of a year. And so I empower you to take whatever steps are necessary to find a suitable tenant for my apartment: however, all my furniture, as it comprises at present, will remain in the apartment until such time as it has been let, and in the unfortunate event of your not finding another tenant in time, I shall at least fulfil my obligations to the landlord and pay the necessary rent, –

of this there can be no doubt. – Since, however, I have converted the apartment at great expense into a highly recommendable proposition, we may well assume that you will have no difficulty in finding a tenant for the same from the 1st of April onwards, which is the date on which I should first like it to be made available to be let. –

Once this has been done, I would then give further instructions for my furniture to be taken into temporary storage at some suitable place, in order that I may use it again at some later date, once I have decided to rent a new and convenient apartment in Vienna. –

It is in this spirit that I now intend to appeal to my other creditors, in other words, to tell them that I am *not* leaving Vienna, but that I am in fact thinking only of moving house.*

In truth, I do not think that I am lying when I say this. All things considered, my dear friend, I have repeatedly had to atone in my life for the unfortunate consequences of two mistakes above all: over-haste in choosing an apartment, and over-haste in giving up the same. If, in the present case, I hold a *single* thread in my hand, linking me to the public world of artistic enterprise, it is the one which binds me to the Vienna Opera. Above all: if I really do succeed in completing the Mastersingers in the course of this year, Vienna will continue, as always, to remain the most preferred and most important place for the first performance of the same. It therefore seems very likely that I shall be staying there next winter, indeed – in the case just posited – it would even be completely unavoidable, since I could not agree to the first performance of this work taking place there *without me*. Certain consequences would inevitably be bound up with this, chief of which is that I would remain in continuing contact with Vienna as my place of residence.

How difficult and expensive it was on previous occasions to make do with regard to my lodgings in Vienna is something I have discovered only too well. It therefore seemed sensible in every respect not to give up my Viennese connections entirely. My furniture would therefore have to be put back: perhaps only a few unnecessary items could be sold at once. For I should let you know, my dear friend, in the course of this summer how things were faring with me, and whether, given the above pre-suppositions, I intended to return to Vienna for the winter. In that case I would entreat you to use your experience – as you have already offered to do for me – to seek out and rent a suitable and more modest apartment for me in Vienna itself, which I would then furnish with some of the necessary furniture pending my later return. Past experience would enable me to strike the right balance in furnishing *this* apartment, a task which would be made simpler by the fact that it would not be for

---

* In the enclosed letters, which I would ask you to be so kind as to deliver in person – wherever possible (in the event that disquiet at my departure has already made itself felt) – or else to post, I have not said anything about this, but have simply asked people to be patient and to rest assured that I have the best of intentions. [*Wagner's own marginal note*]

the purposes of leisure that I was settling down there, but simply for the purposes of domestic accommodation at times when I was engaged in business.

And so let us be agreed *that I am not leaving Vienna, but intending only to move house!* –

I hope that you are fully in favour of this idea; if so, I would ask you to submit it to our friend Dr Standhartner for his advice and approval, after which you should both jointly inform the general public of its purport, if need be by means of a notice in the newspapers.

It is in this spirit, too, that I shall now appeal to my creditors, and, if necessary, take the liberty of referring them to you for confirmation of what I have said. – (As already mentioned, I have not yet deemed this necessary.)

This agreement would be undermined only if my creditors, and, more especially, the usurers among them,[1] alarmed at my departure, were to have lost their heads and seized my furniture etc. I suppose I shall discover soon enough whether this is so. This was of course not one of our pre-suppositions: and I hope that, in the course of your negotiations so far, you have succeeded in impressing upon people the need to behave in a decent manner towards me!

In order to be perfectly clear as to the question of which of my debts are founded upon bills of exchange, it is necessary for me to give you the following detailed report.

Through *Emanuel Kellner*, Josephstadt, Schmiedegasse No 4, I negotiated a loan of 7400 fl., for which I received 5000 fl. in cash, i.e. *five thousand gulden* in Austrian currency. [This was in December 1863, for the end of February and the end of April together.] On the 1st of March I gave Herr Kellner 100 fl. in order to obtain the necessary extension.

Further:

Through *Joseph Glauber*, Teinfaltstrasse, No 17, I negotiated 3 loans of 1500 fl. each, totalling 4500 fl. in all. This was at the end of January 1864, and of the 3 bills of exchange (all of which fall due on the 30th of April this year) the first – I happen to know – is now in the hands of a certain Herr *Schwarz*, 13 Opernring. For the first two of these bills I received 2000 fl. in cash, in other words 1000 fl. for each sum of 1500 fl. borrowed; for the third, however, I received only 900 fl. since, although Glauber repeatedly promised to bring me the missing 100 fl., he has not carried out his promise in spite of repeated reminders. (It must be said that Glauber is the one creditor who least deserves our consideration: unfortunately, the three bills which he provided are endorsed by Herr *Tausig*. You know this already.)

In order to redeem the bills which I made out to my upholsterer *Ferdinand Schweikart*, Mariahilfer Hauptstrasse 64/11, and of which you have similarly already been notified, I must ask my friends to be kind enough to take whatever steps are necessary.

1 Some of Wagner's creditors demanded interest at 200 percent per annum.

– Unfortunately, I have only just informed our friend Dr Standhartner that I had forgotten to tell you of a debt of honour, in the form of a bill of exchange for 200 fl., which I owe *Franz Goltsch*, commissionaire at the Hotel Kaiserin Elisabeth. I promised the man that I would redeem his bill of exchange at the end of this month: he did indeed obtain the sum of 200 fl. for me and, because my generosity is sufficiently well-known to him, he expects a gift which cannot really work out at less than 20 fl. –

This brings me to the end of this dreadful confession of my sins! You know, my dearest friend, in what an utterly hopeless position I find myself just now, and how it is not possible for me *at present* to make even the least contribution towards a material ordering of my financial affairs. And so I must place all my hopes for a tolerable degree of prosperity in future upon your succeeding, by dint of your vigorous efforts, in effecting the most advantageous possible arrangement with the above-named creditors in such a way that my reputation does not suffer so much in the process that it becomes impossible for me to return to Vienna in the future. But, ultimately, this aim can be attainable only if other, well-to-do friends of my art, having been apprised of my position and asked for their help, could persuade themselves to hand over to you the necessary pecuniary resources.

If this is not successful, or if it is insufficiently successful for you to achieve the essential aim of all these efforts, I would most certainly have to regard myself as having taken my leave of the world when I last left Vienna, and, in doing so, I should presumably be prevented from embarking, with any prospect of success, upon the last remaining expedient that might yet lead to my future artistic prosperity.

Whatever happens, I shall never for a moment be in any doubt as to the debt of gratitude that I owe you, my dearest friend, for your exceptional kindness! You may always be assured of this fact, and I would ask you, therefore, on this assumption, to remain at least tolerably well-disposed towards

Your
grateful & obedient servant
Richard Wagner

Eger III, 14–71.

295. MATHILDE MAIER, MAINZ   Mariafeld, 5 April 1864

My dear, sweet creature,

Thank you so much for your beautiful and encouraging letter! Whether you may really think of me as having reached the "haven of peace" you imagine must remain open to question, however. When shall *I* ever find peace? Anyone who is abandoned to so wretched a fate as I am, and whose only concern must be to place no further hope in fate or good fortune, such a man can envisage only *one* kind of peace! – I am ill, and utterly bored with everything & everyone. Really, this final abortive attempt to found a purely neutral refuge – remote from all wearying human contact – , the unprecedented instances of misfortune and the unpropitiousness of every circumstance & chance event, the complete absence of even the faintest glimmer of light, and finally having to creep away like a thief from my servants, my dog, and my few possessions – all this, I feel, has left me a broken man. God knows, if I wanted only to vegetate, your little room in the Karthäuserstrasse would have been Elysium itself to me: I could have asked for nothing more. But I needed to complete this ill-starred task.[1] I wanted to finish it in a single breath, without renewed interruptions! – I fear it is all over with me. Life weighs too heavily upon me. – Do you think it is easy for me here? Believe me, our neighbours in Zurich[2] have been more of a hindrance than a help in my flight to Mariafeld of all places. Every contact with them is unspeakably embarrassing, and I who now needs only peace and quiet, to belong to myself, I find myself having to perform a further onerous and difficult task here: really, given our proximity to Zurich, it can be a question only of avoiding the false impression that further discord has developed between us; I should otherwise gladly forgo all contact with this household.

    [. . .][3]

My own rooms here are a delight. I hope *very much* that you will visit Switzerland *this* summer: of course, you must bring Louise[4] with you and give the place a tour of inspection. I'll then take you into the mountains & across the lakes. Well, that's settled, isn't it? –

The only problem is that I am now unwell again, and have been unable to leave my room for 2 days. A mist as grey and impenetrable as my future hangs over the lake, obscuring the mountains from view! My future! I could certainly tell you a story about *that*, the more so since I have had to make it a general rule to regard all hope as sinful. I am strongly advised to get a divorce and marry a woman of means.[5] That sounds very sensible, the more so when one thinks of a proper "mariage de raison". But it strikes me as more or less comparable to the time when *you* hit upon the brilliant idea of marrying a rich husband post-haste in order to be able to help me. Yes, it is easy to say such things; but it scarcely suffices as a subject for conversation. –

1 *Die Meistersinger von Nürnberg.*
2 Otto and Mathilde Wesendonck; see also letter [287], p. 560, note 1.
3 Ten lines have been rendered illegible here.
4 Louise Wagner.
5 An entry in the Annals for this date reads, "Idea of separation from Minna and going for rich marriage" (BB 140; English trans. 118). The woman in question was Harriet (or Henriette) von Bissing, the widowed sister of Eliza Wille.

Listen, child! If it does not involve *any* sacrifices for *you* and, above all, for your mother, to turn your backs on Mainz & its narrow streets and to rent a pleasant apartment somewhere else (wherever it may be, whether on the Rhine or near Darmstadt), and if this apartment were to contain a quiet, well-situated room for me, for which I would pay you a yearly rent of 100 fl., – in other words, if this could be achieved without any sacrifices and without any regrets on the part of your family, I would ask you, completely unconditionally, sincerely and earnestly, to arrange this for me. A room in your house would be a very real possession for me for the whole of my life, come what may, and it would be one of my favourite recreations & consolations to derive what pleasure I could from it. Let me say this in all truth & sincerity, and with total certitude! If this is feasible, act accordingly, & ask no further questions. I would even pay somewhat more – a way can certainly be found; and once I am with you, the rest will follow. – Now ask me no further questions! I am reading a great deal at present,[1] although none of it sticks: I have never felt so listless and weary of life as I do at present. I have the German Christian mystics in front of me: today it is Tauler. The entry of "grace", especially, is always deeply affecting. None the less, everything on the Ganges is more expansive, more peaceful, and more serene than in the cells of these Christian monks. You can see how the weather here is always dull and overcast. – Frau Wille is quite unique: she knows literally *everything*. And at the same time she is able, active and unreservedly generous. You will like her a lot, in spite of her extreme ugliness.

From Vienna I have not yet heard a single word, – which keeps me in fearful suspense! – Oh that I might find peace! Peace! –

But enough of this; it is past four o'clock, and I can feel a slight fever coming on again. – Last night (in my fevered state) I dreamt that Frederick the Great had summoned me to his court, with Voltaire. (I had been reading his diary.) That's how it is with my secret ambition! –

Adieu! Dear sweet child! You give me such great and intense happiness! Believe me! May you always continue to do so!

A thousand good wishes to the Karthäuserstrasse and the fashion warehouse!

Yours,
R.W.

P.S. You no longer need convey my regards to Schindelmeisser! He must have heard by now that you intend renting a room for me in Darmstadt.

Maier-Briefe 147–9.

---

1 According to *Mein Leben* (752; English trans. 736), Wagner's reading matter at this time included Jean Paul's *Siebenkäs*, Frederick the Great's Diary, Johann Tauler, George Sand, Walter Scott, and Eliza Wille's *Felicitas*.

296. PETER CORNELIUS, VIENNA   Mariafeld, 8 April 1864

My dear Peter,

What has really made me so sick and weary of life are the experiences I have had of other people recently, whereby it has become clear how insincere most of them basically are in their protestations of sympathy. I live in hourly torment at present, awaiting the arrival of the postman in the hope of receiving some sort of response to the urgent appeals that I addressed to you and to Standth. asking for news of the state of my abandoned affairs. Standh. has again been kind enough today to forward letters that had arrived for me in Penzing: but he has again not added a single word of his own, not a single word of greeting! – Can you not understand that this is bound to alarm me more than the worst possible news could do? Or does no one write to me simply because you all wish to avoid the pain of telling me something painful? – But cordial friendship ought in the end to triumph over all other considerations! –

What direction my life now takes depends entirely upon how things turn out behind me; it is from this that I must deduce what lies ahead of me. If everything continues to be as irredeemably bad as it has been so far, it would be wrong of me to expect any good to come of it, since I have now reached the point where I regard it as fatal to entertain any hopes for the future: but how I am supposed to derive any pleasure from artistic creation in my present frame of mind, when I am bound to feel so utterly sickened of life, is something which anyone who takes my age and experiences into account must inevitably regard as thoroughly problematical. –

The malignancy with which circumstances now conspire against me may be clear to you from a single example. Among Standth.'s first bundle of letters was one from Moscow informing me that my letter of the 2nd of February had arrived there on the 23rd of March, and that my friend regretted this very much because, had it arrived in time, a cycle of concerts could have been arranged for me, the proceeds of which, to judge by all the signs, would have turned out very much to my advantage.

How it has come about that this letter, which I sent to the lady-in-waiting in Petersburg[1] to deal with, and which I was informed had indeed been correctly forwarded, reached my business friend in Moscow[2] so incredibly late is so utterly incredible that I am almost inclined to believe in a conspiracy. However that may be – if I had sent my letter direct, and if it had arrived in time, I should now be on my way back from Moscow, having earned enough money at least for my departure from Penzing to have passed off with all due propriety. – At all events, there still remains the prospect of my being able

1 Editha von Rhaden.
2 Alexey Fyodorovich L'vov.

to earn enough in Russia next year to pay off my Viennese debts, assuming I can organize a winter campaign there: but only on condition that the affair be managed *at present* in such a way as not to overburden me with feelings of shame and unworthiness. My position is very unsettling; I feel to be on a knife-edge: a single jolt and it will all be over, so that there will be nothing more to be got out of me, nothing, nothing more! – *Some light* must show itself: *Someone* must come forward and *help* me *now* with his energetic support, – only **then** shall I still have the strength to repay him for his help: otherwise, I feel it will be impossible! –

My friend, Switzerland has become a burial ground for me, too: I should have gone anywhere but here, where everything is so bitter and redolent of the grave.

Yet nowhere but here could I have found the one person, the one human being who can be of benefit to me at present. I mean my hostess, Frau Wille, who is quite unique! This woman is beyond praise, she is quite incomparable and utterly unique. Whatever can be done to provide me with a pleasant refuge, well-suited, moreover, to my work, has been done unstintingly: she is even trying to obtain at least sufficient money for me to be able to hope to pay my local creditors something shortly, and thus to do something to improve the humiliating appearance of my departure from Penzing. I hope that in other respects, too, this possibility will remain open to me, although I am totally ignorant of the state of affairs that I left behind me there. The most annoying part of all this is that I have been given notice to quit my apartment: for it is this, more than anything else, which will alarm everyone, with fatal consequences for myself. I would almost have preferred to bear the sacrifice of retaining the apartment as a temporary measure.

If things are to get going again, and – if anything is to come of it all, I shall need you to visit me soon, dear Peter. I have grown very fond of you, and what fills me with the greatest sadness is that you no longer visit me. I am at present engaged in negotiations with a number of theatres concerning the fees that they owe me:[1] I could send you 100 fl. shortly if you wanted to come here, where everything is ready and waiting for you. It's true, believe me! –

But perhaps nothing more can be done to help! Indeed, I feel that, deep down inside me, the end is near. My sickliness contributes what it can to this frame of mind. I am again very weary, and plagued by my old bladder complaint. Standth. does right not to bother with me any more. I asked you to get him to prescribe some drops for me. Tell him that as from today I have been drinking Vichy water in the mornings: I hear that it is also good for bladder complaints; perhaps it is the same as the one he provided me

---

1 According to the Annals (BB 140; English trans. 118), Wagner received 75 francs from Charles Truinet in Paris and "75 Thr!" in royalties from Berlin.

with for a similar purpose. Oh God! All this is done in the hope that things can go on at all: whether this can really be the case is something I shall discover soon enough. As I say: *some good* and truly helpful miracle must now befall me, otherwise it will all be over! –

Your terrible silence seems to indicate that this delightful miracle is already on its way! –

Adio, my friend! Look up my good friend Eduard List,[1] give him my news, – entreat him and – thank him! –

Give Standth. a big hug from me! – The poor man, however strong he is, I am certainly too much for him! And so I can give him absolutely no pleasure! Not him or anyone! – And yet – perhaps Tausig! If all turns out well, he may succeed in being nailed to the cross for my sake. (Cf. his standing bail for me.)[2]

It is heart-breaking – and not even profound! – Fare you well and – if things are to get better, come and see me soon!

Yours, RW.

[...]

RWA (incompletely published in Freunde und Zeitgenossen 371–4).

297. COSIMA VON BÜLOW, BERLIN   Mariafeld, 10 April 1864

Dear Cosima,

Would Hans be kind enough to write to me the moment he returns from Petersburg? I need the advice and the loyal assistance of all who love me, in order that I might reach and carry out certain decisions which, if at all possible, will cure my sick existence to the extent that I may yet be able to achieve something. Death eludes me, but life, too, is impossible, at least the sort of life I have been leading until now. – It is not peace which I have here, but only a refuge. I cannot entertain the thought of work: this says it all.

I beg you: tell Hans to write; for the time being we must stick together.

With a sad heart, sick and wretched

RW

Eger I, 119.

1 Eduard Liszt.
2 See letter [294], pp. 574–8; this phrase was omitted from the printed edition: "(Vergl. Bürgschaft.)"

ROYAL PATRONAGE
1864–1872

INTRODUCTORY ESSAY 1864–1872

On 10 March 1864 a new monarch ascended the throne of Bavaria: Ludwig II was just eighteen years old, an incorrigible Romantic, and a passionate Wagnerian. As soon as he had succeeded in tracking down Wagner, he installed him in the Villa Pellet, overlooking Lake Starnberg (just outside Munich) and opposite the royal castle Schloss Berg, and presented him with 4000 gulden to relieve his most pressing debts – the first of many such gifts.

From the start, Wagner was clearly aware of the dramatic potential in his relationship with the King. About their first encounter, he wrote to Mathilde Maier: "Our meeting yesterday was one great love-scene" [299]. Indeed, it is possible to regard the whole relationship as an essentially literary one, scarcely rooted in reality. Rhetorical flights of fancy and excessively florid turns of phrase are thus employed to disguise what Oswald Bauer has described as a "conceptual vacuum".[1] Certainly, it is often the case that ideas devoid of significance – even, sometimes, of meaning altogether – are wreathed in garlands of circumlocution and flattering hyperbole. For Ludwig, the opportunity to identify with the other-worldly and misunderstood Lohengrin, the longed-for saviour Parsifal, or the heroic Siegfried afforded an escape route from the tribulations of kingship. For Wagner, too, there can be little doubt that the play-acting was conscious. Commenting in later years on his letters to Ludwig, he said: "Oh, those don't sound very good, but it wasn't I who set the tone" (CT for 10 July 1878). A full account of the relationship in its early stages – replete with mutual admiration, trust and confidence in the future – may be found in [300].

In October 1864 Wagner took up residence in Munich itself, in the imposing house at 21 Briennerstrasse, made available to him by Ludwig. The King had already followed up his initial gift with an annual stipend of 4000 gulden (comparable to that of a ministerial councillor), and a further gift of 16,000 gulden in June, to which he now added another 4000 gulden for removal expenses. As the previous year in Penzing, Wagner called on the Viennese milliner and seamstress Bertha Goldwag to furnish his apartment with velvet drapes and portières and to supply him with a wardrobe of silks and satins. His claim [312] to be leading a "modest" existence is scarcely

---

1 "Lost Illusions: Richard Wagner and King Ludwig II", Bayreuth Festival Programme, i (*Tristan und Isolde*), 1986, p.49.

borne out by such letters to her as [309], while [357] – a later order for a satin house-coat – is further evidence of the extent to which Bertha Goldwag was required to pander to Wagner's hedonism.

Physical comfort did not, however, bring spiritual solace. In vain Wagner begged Heinrich Porges to join him as secretary and companion [301]. He turned also to the composer Peter Cornelius [302, 313], who did answer his summons soon after (he arrived in Munich on 30 December 1864), though Cornelius' determination to remain artistically independent led to some intemperate comments on him to Mathilde Maier [320]. Wagner's former love for Mathilde Wesendonck had by now soured; in a passage subsequently suppressed he complained to his confidante Eliza Wille [300] of Mathilde's childish refusal to correspond and of her "unforgiveable" rejection of him. To Mathilde Maier herself he renewed his entreaties for her to join him as companion/housekeeper [305], simultaneously stressing, in a letter to her mother [306] the "honourableness" of his intentions. Whether Frau Maier would have given any credence whatsoever to this proposal – accompanied as it was by assurances of separate sleeping arrangements and renunciation of "sensuality" by Wagner – is not known, because she never received the letter. More puzzling still is the fact that Wagner was attempting to lure Mathilde Maier at the very time he was expecting a visit from Cosima von Bülow and her husband Hans. The full text of *Mein Leben* contains a passage – deleted from the printed edition of 1911 – describing a pledge of mutual commitment sealed by Cosima and Wagner the previous November (1863) "with tears and sobs". It is also known that Cosima's unhappy marriage had induced her, as early as August 1858 (only twelve months after the wedding), to enter an abortive suicide pact with Karl Ritter. What is not generally known is that Cosima made several subsequent attempts to end her life: the relevant passage in the letter to Eliza Wille [310] was suppressed from the printed edition and is published here for the first time. However, in spite of the secret "betrothal" – if, indeed, such a thing took place as early as 1863 – Wagner's invitation to Mathilde Maier suggests that he was not expecting from Cosima at this stage such a positive response as she gave. When, at his invitation, she arrived at Starnberg, accompanied only by her two young daughters and a nurserymaid (Bülow had been detained in Berlin), Wagner hurriedly withdrew his offer to Mathilde. It is virtually certain that the child (Isolde) born on 10 April the following year was conceived by Wagner and Cosima in the week before Bülow's arrival on 7 July.

As often in Wagner's middle years, his spirits at this time were alternately soaring and plummeting. In June 1864 he was mapping out plans for the next decade [303]. By November of the same year he was making secret resolutions to live no longer than the three years he thought he required to finish the *Ring* [314, 330]. The new year two months later brought him renewed confidence and determination [316]: he was now planning a collected edition of his writings (see also [373]), including articles on theatrical reform and drafts for unrealized works such as the "musical dramas" *Jesus of Nazareth* and *Wiland the Smith* (spelt thus). In the same letter he also sets out a programme for the first performances of *Tristan* that year (1865), and in subsequent years revised editions of *Tannhäuser* and *Lohengrin*, as well as the premières of the *Ring, Die Meistersinger, Parsifal* and *Die Sieger* (the last never realized).

It was at the beginning of 1865 that Wagner suffered his first, temporary, fall from royal favour. Judging from the laconic entry in the Brown Book, Wagner appears to have offended the cabinet secretary, Franz von Pfister-meister, by referring to the King as *"Mein Junge"* (My boy). Pfistermeister evidently retailed this indiscretion to Ludwig, who then, on 6 February, refused Wagner an audience. The King's displeasure had been exacerbated by a misunderstanding – again fuelled by Pfistermeister – over the payment for a portrait of the composer by Friedrich Pecht. The local press seized on reports of Wagner's "disgrace", and a flurry of accusations and denials was followed up with an anonymous article in the Augsburg *Allgemeine Zeitung* of 19 February, entitled "Richard Wagner and Public Opinion". The writer (the poet Oskar von Redwitz) reiterated the rumours of a fall from favour and went on to charge Wagner with profligacy, sybaritism and ingratitude (towards his former employer, Friedrich August II of Saxony) and his partisans of arrogance and condescension towards the people and musicians of Munich. Wagner and his followers, Redwitz concluded, were "thrusting themselves between us Bavarians and our beloved King". In a skilfully worded reply, concocted with the aid of Cornelius, Bülow and Pecht, and printed in the *Allgemeine Zeitung* of 22 February, Wagner invoked the privacy of the indi-vidual and the social responsibility of the artist. His creativity required a certain degree of comfort in his surroundings, while monetary advances were to be repaid out of future receipts from performances. If he held a low opinion, he continued, it was of the musical world in general, not of Munich, of which city he entertained great hopes. Finally, he dealt with Redwitz's comments on the reputation of the King: by what was true it could only be enhanced, for what was false only such people as the anonymous author were to be blamed.

Wagner was soon reconciled to Ludwig, who then requested a full, written account of the composer's life so far: the dictation of *Mein Leben* accordingly began on 17 July 1865. For the forthcoming première of *Tristan* Wagner was able to secure the King's agreement to Bülow [319]; he had already engin-eered his appointment as performer to Ludwig – now, at Wagner's request, Bülow was given the title "Court Kapellmeister for special services". On the day appointed for the performance, 15 May, a number of Wagner's creditors, seizing their opportunity, sent in the bailiffs. Although Ludwig was able to come to the rescue, the performance could not in any case proceed because it was discovered in the afternoon that Malvina Schnorr, the Isolde, had lost her voice. To the dismay of Wagner and his associates [324], but to the undisguised delight of his enemies, the first performance had to be postponed until 10 June. The fourth and last performance took place on 1 July; within three weeks the Tristan, Ludwig Schnorr von Carolsfeld, was dead. Wagner's shocked reaction to this double blow – Schnorr was valued as both friend and artist – is recorded in [328], but it was three years before he had recovered sufficiently to pay full tribute in the essay *Recollections of Ludwig Schnorr von Carolsfeld*.

In the same letter Wagner refers to the plans drawn up by Gottfried Semper, on the King's instructions, for a Festival Theatre in Munich. Such a scheme was opposed both by the city's artistic establishment – presumably out of jealousy or fear for their own position – and by court officials responsible for state expenditure, notably Pfistermeister and Ludwig von der Pfordten, the recently appointed prime minister of Bavaria. Wagner particularly resented Pfistermeister's meddling in artistic matters and he tactfully suggested to Ludwig [328] that this loyal minister's talents and experience did not equip him to be the sole intermediary between monarch and composer. Wagner proposed that instead an intendant be appointed to take charge of all artistic matters relating to the Court: the existing theatre, orchestra and chorus, the proposed new theatre and music school (which Ludwig and Wagner had long since agreed to be necessary). For this job Wagner recommended one Baron von Moy, but although the latter was approved by the King, nothing came of the plan. A lengthy report drawn up by Wagner on the need for a music school had been published in March 1865. Advocating an institution geared to national conditions and aspirations, able to cultivate performers for both the classic German repertory of the past and the festival-scale stage works (i.e. Wagnerian music dramas) of the future, the report threatened too many vested interests to achieve implementation. Nevertheless, in October 1865 Wagner was still urging Ludwig [336] to give the necessary command to establish a "German Academy of Music and Dramatic Art" along the lines of the report. In order to free Wagner for his compositional activities, Bülow – who had been instrumental in drawing up the report – was to be appointed director.

The tide was turning, however, against both Bülow and Wagner. Bülow's lack of tact had already won him many enemies in Munich and it had been noticed that Cosima now spent more time at 21 Briennerstrasse than with her husband. Wagner, moreover, had become embroiled in the intrigues of Court politics, and it did not long remain a secret that he had been offering advice to the King on the replacement of certain officials. Matters were brought to a head by an article in the Munich *Volksbote* of 26 November which provocatively suggested that the Wagner camp was aiming to dispose of two prominent members of the cabinet – Pfistermeister and Julius von

Hofmann (the treasury secretary) solely to facilitate the extortion of yet more money from the exchequer. Wagner suspected – no doubt correctly – that the article had been inspired by someone within the cabinet; his response took the form of a pair of letters to Ludwig [337, 338]. The nub of these letters was that the scheming Pfistermeister should be dismissed and a new cabinet formed by the liberal Max von Neumayr. The latter had in fact himself been dismissed by Ludwig only that month, and the King pointed out to Wagner, in his reply of 27 November, that even granted the need to replace Pfistermeister and others, Neumayr was hardly an appropriate choice for prime minister. Two days later, an anonymous article in another Munich newspaper, the *Neueste Nachrichten*, claimed that Wagner was being victimized by individuals who sought only personal gain; the King and the Bavarian people alike would be well served if these individuals were removed from office. A draft of this article survives in Cosima's handwriting and there can be little doubt that it was dictated, or at the very least inspired and approved, by Wagner himself. Pfordten, the threatened prime minister, saw that Wagner had over-reached himself and put it to Ludwig that he had to choose "between the love and esteem of your loyal subjects and the 'friendship' of Richard Wagner". Ludwig, recognizing that he faced a crisis, uncharacteristically took advice from his family, and from state and ecclesiastical dignitaries, and concluded with bitter regret that Wagner must leave Bavaria for an indefinite period. His decision was communicated immediately to Wagner, on the evening of 6 December, by the second cabinet secretary, Johann von Lutz, and confirmed by letter the following day. Wagner accepted the decision philosophically [339] and left Munich early in the morning of 10 December.

Much indignation has been expended on Wagner's supposed abuse of the royal exchequer. However, some sober figures quoted in Manfred Eger's discussion of the relationship between Wagner and Ludwig[1] put the matter into perspective. The total amount received by Wagner over the nineteen years of their acquaintance – including stipend, rent and the cash value of presents – was 562,914 marks. This amount, which is less than one-seventh of the yearly Civil List (4.2 million marks), may be compared with the 652,000 marks spent on the bed-chamber alone of Herrenchiemsee, or with the 1.7 million marks spent on the bridal carriage for the royal wedding that never took place. One further statistic of interest: Meyerbeer received 750,000 marks for a hundred performances of *Le Prophète* in Berlin.

On 25 January of the new year, 1866, came the sad but not unexpected news of his wife Minna's death. They had not seen each other since November 1862 and had had nothing in common in the last years. But Wagner had always taken responsibility for her material comfort, and now, although he

1 "Richard Wagner und König Ludwig II.", *Richard-Wagner-Handbuch*, ed. U. Müller and P. Wapnewski (Stuttgart 1986), 171.

did not attend the funeral, he requested Pusinelli in Dresden to ensure that the appropriate arrangements were made and that he (Wagner) be charged with any excess [344]. Accompanied by Cosima (Bülow was on tour), Wagner travelled from Geneva to Lake Lucerne, where they discovered the house called Tribschen delightfully situated overlooking the lake. (Wagner's spelling of "Triebschen" – an etymological conceit – was a purely personal whim.) Bülow was warmly invited to take up residence with his family there, occupying the bottom of the three floors – the middle was to be for Wagner himself, and the top for the children and servants [347] – but it was without her husband that Cosima and her three daughters (Daniela, Blandine and Isolde) arrived at Tribschen on 12 May. They were still there when, on Wagner's birthday ten days later, Ludwig arrived on the doorstep, announcing himself as Walther von Stolzing. Against Wagner's advice the King was neglecting his official duties – Parliament was due to be opened on that day – in order to be with him. In fact, Ludwig was seriously contemplating abdication – as he had been for some months past – thinking that this would allow him "to be united with him [Wagner] and living at his side".[1] Realizing that Ludwig's abdication would all but bring an end to his munificent support, and that his proximity would make it impossible to conceal the liaison with Cosima, Wagner urged him to stay. Writing a couple of months later on the subject [352], Wagner humours Ludwig by appearing to concur on the question of abdication, but he goes on to make it clear that such a course would spell disaster for the great works of art that alone sustain the King: "if you wished to sacrifice yourself for my sake alone, it is I myself whom you would be sacrificing".

The unpopularity of Ludwig's visit to Tribschen at the expense of his state obligations induced the Munich *Volksbote* to launch another attack. An article on 31 May made reference to " 'Madame Hans de Bülow' ... with her 'friend' (or what?) in Lucerne", a scarcely veiled allusion to an affair, which Bülow (though by now presumably aware of) felt obliged to refute by challenging the paper's editor to a duel (the challenge was ignored); he also tendered his resignation from his posts in Munich. Wagner's letter of 6 June to Ludwig [350] affected outrage at the deplorable treatment of Bülow and of "his noble wife" who was "being dragged publicly through the mire". Enclosed with it was a draft of a letter which Wagner begged Ludwig to send Bülow so that he might publish it. This letter spoke of the King's faith in his conductor and of his disgust at the attacks on his honour; it went on to promise an investigation into "these criminal public libels", in order to ensure "that the culprits are brought to justice with merciless severity". Cosima followed up Wagner's letter with one of her own, protesting her innocence and imploring the King to save them from "shame and ignominy" by writing

---

1 Telegram from King Ludwig to Wagner, 15 May 1866 (Königsbriefe II,34–5).

the requested letter – for the sake of her three children "to whom I owe the duty of transmitting the honourable name of their father free of stain". The full hypocrisy of this appeal to honour can only be appreciated in the light of the knowledge that one of those three children, Isolde, was Wagner's, and that a fourth, Eva, had been conceived by them just three weeks earlier. Nor can Bülow himself be entirely exculpated: he knew of and connived at the approach to the King, and duly published the letter provided. Few were convinced by it, but it temporarily served its purpose since no one could afford to flout the King's authority by persisting with the accusations in public.

The resentment of many Bavarians at Ludwig's devotion to Wagner to the detriment of official business was aggravated by the fact that the state was now faced with political crisis, even war. The continuing struggle between Prussia and Austria for the sovereignty of the emerging national state of Germany was being raised to a pitch by the former under the aggressive prime ministership of Otto von Bismarck. Wagner took the view that Bavaria should not align with either Prussia or Austria, but maintain its own independent line. In this he was influenced by the policies advocated by the conservative federalist Constantin Frantz, which he recommended to Ludwig [343]. Wagner had in fact struck up a correspondence with Frantz [345], who in turn regarded Wagner's music as central to the prosperity of the future German nation. When, in April 1866, a few weeks before the Austro-Prussian War finally broke out on 14 June, Wagner denigrated Bismarck as "an ambitious Junker [who] betrays his imbecile of a King [Wilhelm I of Prussia] in the most brazen manner" [348], he was voicing a widespread mistrust. The outcome of the war, however, caused many – including Wagner – to change their minds. Unable to remain neutral, Bavaria joined other states in the German Confederation in supporting Austria, but with Prussia's decisive victory in July, the Confederation disintegrated and all eyes turned to Bismarck as the potential moulder of the new nation state of Germany. His leadership qualities commanded respect on all sides and many believed that he had opened the way to the long-sought national unification, and even to a liberal administration with increased democratic participation. Against this background Wagner's rapid conversion to Bismarck's cause appears less idiosyncratic than sometimes portrayed.

Hardly had the ripples of the *Volksbote* scandal subsided when the affair erupted again in a most spectacular fashion. Ludwig Schnorr's widow, Malvina, who had sung Isolde in the Munich première of *Tristan*, had taken, in her grief, to communicating with her husband's spirit. Though not herself deranged, her companion and pupil, Isidore von Reutter, does appear to have been mentally unstable. The message transmitted by Isidore from Schnorr's spirit was that she herself must marry King Ludwig, while Malvina's role was to remain at Wagner's side and assist him in the creation of his great artistic work. As Wagner's protectress, Cosima attempted to turn aside the claimants;

her reward, as Wagner told Ludwig [355], was to draw down on to her own head the anger and hatred of the frustrated Frau Schnorr. Accurate as this is, Wagner appears to have been over-hasty in his assumption that Malvina was attempting to lure him into marriage. Malvina's enraged reaction to Cosima's obstruction was to enlighten the King as to Wagner's liaison with Cosima. At first Wagner was able to counter the charge indirectly by professing concern for the effect on the King's own reputation. But as Malvina persisted in informing Ludwig about the truth of the *Volksbote* case, Wagner and Cosima sank deeper into the mire of subterfuge and deceit. They also tried – unsuccessfully in the end – to have Malvina drummed out of Munich and her pension stopped. The affair rumbled on into the new year, 1867, and in November Wagner was to return to the attack [363], protesting "total innocence", complaining that "this criminal woman" was still in Munich, drawing her pension, enjoying her free seat in the theatre and provoking Cosima openly in the street. It was not until the following autumn that Malvina finally left Bavaria and by that time the truth, for so long evident to everyone else, had at last been discerned by Ludwig [p. 722, note 2].

The resurfacing of the Malvina Schnorr affair coincided with another incident that apparently taxed Ludwig's patience with Wagner. A newspaper designed to be the vehicle for Wagner's ideas had for some time been under discussion. The scheme was backed by the King and on 1 October 1867 the first issue of the *Süddeutsche Presse* appeared, its publication guaranteed by state subsidy until at least the end of 1868. The paper's editor, Julius Fröbel, had been approved by Wagner and initially, at least, listened sympathetically to his detailed prescriptions as to its style and content, even though he noted, perceptively, at an early stage that Wagner "saw politics too poetically, I might say theatrically or operatically". Wagner contributed anonymously a series of articles entitled *German Art and German Politics* in which he expanded on some of his favourite themes: the debasement of art, and civilization generally, by materialism; the need for a revival of the folk spirit; and the responsibility of the German people to bring about such a regeneration. The thirteenth of such articles had just appeared when further publication was forthwith banned in the King's name. There being no dramatic change of content in that particular article, it can only be assumed that Ludwig, who had expressed his delight in earlier instalments, was reacting to the latest developments in the Malvina Schnorr affair.

Meanwhile, for all that he shared Wagner's aspirations regarding the ideal performance of his works, Ludwig did not have his patience. His most urgent desire was to have a model performance of the work with which he had from boyhood so strongly identified: *Lohengrin*. Wagner was only half-hearted, but he did agree to supervise the final rehearsals, at the request of the conductor, Bülow. The problem was with the singer of the title role. Schnorr was now dead, and the other likely candidate, Albert Niemann, was refusing to sing either *Lohengrin* or *Tannhäuser* without the cuts that he was accustomed to make. Wagner's next choice was Tichatschek, but he was now sixty, and Ludwig was very dubious that he would be able to create the heroic swan-knight of his fantasies. In the event, his fears were realized. After the dress rehearsal on 11 June, Ludwig complained bitterly that Tichatschek's aging face and body produced a travesty of the youthful knight, that his acting had consisted entirely of grimaces, and that he had not even worn the blue cloak requested by the King. Wagner's reply to this tirade [360] was that Ludwig had observed too closely instead of trusting to his ears. The letter goes on to speak of his fears that their enemies would make political capital out of any postponement of the performance. This was precisely what the King was demanding, in order that a new Lohengrin could be found and he remained unmoved even by Wagner's veiled threat that any succour given to the conspirators might force him, like Lohengrin himself, to retire from the scene. At Ludwig's command the performance took place four days later, on 16 June, with a local tenor, Heinrich Vogl, in the title role.

By the time preparations were under way for the première of *Die Meister-singer* the following year, the rift had been healed. Suitable singers were eventually found for each of the key roles, including Franz Betz (the future Wotan) for Hans Sachs, and a young tenor called Franz Nachbaur for Walther. Under Bülow and Hans Richter, who had taken up a post as répétiteur at Munich, the rehearsals proceeded efficiently, though not without distressing confrontations between conductor, orchestra, composer and management. At the first performance, on 21 June 1868, Ludwig invited Wagner to share the royal box, from where, in a much criticized breach of protocol, he took applause after the second and third acts. For Wagner, that performance "was the best that has ever been given of any of my works" [370] and although it was disliked by the critics, led by Hanslick, it was a huge popular success, so much so that Wagner even withdrew objections to its incomplete performance elsewhere.

Initially, at least, Wagner was also prepared to sanction performances of individual works from the *Ring*, provided they were properly supervised. When, therefore, in February 1869 Ludwig began to press for a production of *Das Rheingold* in Munich, Wagner was not at first opposed to the idea. By March, however, he had begun to express concern about the adequacy of the likely production and was begging the King to restrict the audience to person-ally invited guests only. From Lucerne Wagner attempted to exercise influence over the proceedings. Three French visitors to Tribschen that July – Judith Mendès-Gautier, her husband Catulle Mendès, and the poet Villiers de l'Isle-Adam – were authorized to attend the rehearsals in Munich [380] and Wagner's own ideas on costume design were transmitted direct to Hans Richter, who was in charge of the performance [381]. But it was clear to Richter that justice was not going to be done to *Rheingold* – in particular the

staging – and with Wagner's connivance he attempted to postpone the première by submitting his resignation. The proceedings were delayed, but an
enraged Ludwig insisted that the performance should go ahead. Several
conductors, out of deference to Wagner, declined the invitation to assume
control. Franz Wüllner, however, a local conductor and teacher, was not
deterred, even by Wagner's intemperate admonition [385], and the première
took place on 22 September. Wagner pointedly absented himself, and his
bitterness at what he regarded as Ludwig's betrayal of their common ideals
is still evident in his letter of 20 November [386]: *"Do you want my work as
I want it?"* Wagner bluntly inquired, or was the whole enterprise to be reduced
"to the level of achievement of some wretched operatic repertory performed
for subscribers and critics!"? In fact, a wounded silence might have been
maintained even longer had it not been for reports that Ludwig was now
preparing to produce *Die Walküre* in Munich too.

Meanwhile, Wagner had not allowed his polemical pen to lie idle. Earlier
that year (March, 1869) he had published a new edition of his anti-Semitic
tract *Judaism in Music* with a preface, in the form of a letter to Marie
Muchanoff, explaining that it was intended to account for his hostile treatment
in the press. It was Wagner's conviction that the Jews, who occupied positions
of influence in the artistic establishment and "dominated" the press, had
never forgiven him for the original publication of the essay in 1850; at the
same time he regarded it as virtually a social obligation to warn that true
German culture was being "swamped" by the Jews, who, being aliens, were
incapable of expressing the inner emotions and feelings of the German people.
Such an articulation of the *völkisch* ideology was very much in tune with the
views of German intellectuals, even on the eve of Jewish emancipation. But
Cosima was apprehensive about the possible reaction from Jews themselves,
and rightly so. Within days "the mail brought an anonymous letter from
Breslau 'in the name of 7000 Jews' – full of abuse and threats" (CT for 15
March 1869); there was an outcry in sections of the press, a performance of
Die Meistersinger in Mannheim was hissed, and one of *Lohengrin* in Berlin had
to be postponed [p. 748, note 2].

Cosima was by now living permanently with Wagner at Tribschen, having
moved in on 16 November 1868 with her two younger daughters Isolde and
Eva. Ludwig had been officially informed of their relationship, but was not,
for the time being, told of their cohabitation. Although Wagner wished to
marry her as soon as possible, Cosima was unwilling to press for a divorce
immediately, out of consideration for her husband, Bülow, and her father,
who was now the Abbé Liszt. It was partly to explain her abandonment of
Bülow to their children that Cosima began her Diaries on 1 January 1869
(the opening entry makes as much clear). The original intention had been
for Cosima to continue Wagner's biography from the point at which it broke
off: his summons to Munich in May 1864. In the event, all that exists for the

intervening years, 1864–8, are Wagner's own sketchy notes in the Annals. Preparations were now set in train for the printing of *Mein Leben* – not for general publication but for circulation among his family and a few intimate friends, in order, as he told Pusinelli [388], that they could better refute "all the distortions & calumnies which circulate about me, as they do about nobody else". The proof-reading of *Mein Leben*, and other mechanical tasks, were entrusted to the latest valued recruit to the Wagnerian cause, Friedrich Nietzsche [390, 391]. Appointed Professor of Classical Philology at Basle University in February 1869, at the age of twenty-four, Nietzsche took advantage of the proximity of Lucerne to pay his respects to the composer whose music had long exerted a compelling fascination over him. Having accepted an invitation to stay at Tribschen, he was present there at the birth of Wagner's and Cosima's third child, Siegfried, on 6 June (1869). Wagner's admiration for Nietzsche's erudition and insight is clear from [392], a letter in which it is interesting to note the older man urging the younger to moderate his expression of his radical, unconventional views.

Confirmation that Cosima's marriage to Bülow was finally dissolved permitted, after years of agonized waiting, her marriage with Wagner, which took place on 25 August 1870 in the Protestant church in Lucerne. Wagner's pride and happiness in the anticipated event is evident in [395]. But the new sense of fulfilment and security bore little immediate fruit in terms of artistic creativity. Having finished the second complete draft of Act 1 of *Götterdämmerung* on 2 July (1870), Wagner allowed a whole year to elapse before commencing the drafting of Act 2 (24 June 1871). There are several reasons for this delay. In the first place, Wagner was engaged in another major theoretical disquisition on the relationship of poetry to music in the music drama: the essay, *Beethoven*, was written and published as a contribution to the celebrations organized for Beethoven's centenary. In the second place, he was still putting the finishing touches to *Siegfried*. For some time he had left part of it unscored in order to prevent its premature performance: on 6 October 1870, however, he resumed work on Act 3 and completed the full score on 5 February 1871. Against his will, *Die Walküre* had been put on in Munich at the King's insistence (26 June 1870), Wüllner again conducting. Thus a third reason for the delaying of *Götterdämmerung* seems to have been an unexpressed feeling that the tetralogy was better left unfinished until the problems related to its ideal performance were resolved. The Upper Franconian town of Bayreuth had become a possible venue when, on 5 March 1870, at Cosima's prompting, Wagner looked it up in an encyclopaedia. At first he thought that the existing Margraves' Opera House might prove suitable, and planned a journey to Bayreuth to investigate, as well as one to Berlin to give a lecture at the Prussian Academy of Arts with the aim of promoting the music drama and its appropriate performance [399]. " 'We will try once more with the German fatherland, with Bayreuth; if it doesn't succeed, then farewell the North and art and cold, we shall move to Italy and forget everything' ", was Wagner's proposal as reported by Cosima (CT for 26 September 1870). The journey to Germany was postponed [397] until the following spring, when Wagner informed the Court secretary Düfflipp [400] that the Margraves' Opera House was "the most fantastical roccoco [sic] building that could possibly exist", but that its uniqueness did not permit radical alteration. In the same letter, however, Wagner announced that he was "firmly attached" to the idea of settling in Bayreuth and requested Düfflipp to ascertain whether he could count on Ludwig's support.

Yet another reason for the slow progress on the Ring during 1870 was the shadow cast over Tribschen by the advent of war. The Franco-Prussian War, which finally broke out in July 1870 (Bavaria joining as Prussia's ally), was fought against a background of rising national pride in Germany; the intemperately partisan – not to say rabidly jingoistic – attitude of Wagner and Cosima was a reflection of that prevalent among Germans. Cosima's Diaries reveal the turbulence of their alternating emotions: fierce patriotism, contempt for everything French, horror at their atrocities, and anxiety about the outcome. The entry for 2 August also suggests an explanation for the extremity of Cosima's belligerence. A bad dream caused her to be "robbed ... of the German language", so that she could converse only in French: evidently her roots and upbringing in France were being repressed at some psychical cost. The French were before long obliged to capitulate. The German princes proclaimed the Second Empire, Wilhelm I of Prussia became the Kaiser on 18 January 1871 and ten days later the armistice was signed between France and Prussia.

Wagner's tasteless, lumbering farce, Eine Kapitulation, making capital out of the privations suffered by the French during the siege of Paris, may have been designed to appeal to the prevailing mood of chauvinist hysteria, but in the longer term it did his reputation little good. Indeed, he appears to have had his own doubts about it, at least to the extent of withholding his identity as author [398]. Richter reluctantly set about writing music for it, but abandoned the project on the pretext that no theatre wished to produce it. Beyond the foreground plot based on the capitulation of the Parisians to the German army lies a familiar Wagnerian theme that is also unlikely to have recommended the play to a conventional German theatre: in cultural terms it is the French who have conquered the Germans, especially in opera, where superficial, ear-catching entertainment has become the order of the day.

The German victory in the Franco-Prussian War and the proclamation of the Reich enabled Wagner to say, on 1 February 1871: "My confidence in the future has been revived" [399]. From this letter and others his enthusiasm for the Reich – as a vehicle, and expression of, the revival of the German spirit – is in no doubt. Conditions also seemed favourable for the execution of the long-entertained plan for a production of the Ring at a special festival.

Bayreuth proving suitable, a scheme was devised to raise the 300,000 thalers deemed necessary to construct and equip a theatre: 1000 "Patrons' certificates" were to be issued at 300 thalers each. In Friedrich Feustel, banker and chair of the town council of Bayreuth, and Theodor Muncker, the mayor, Wagner found influential allies. His letter to Feustel of November 1871 [402] enquired about the possibility of a free transfer of a plot of land for the theatre, and sought assurance on such points as the facilities for the accommodation of 2000 visitors during the festival, and a strike-free work-force to undertake the construction. Feustel was able to offer him, with the authority of his council, any site he should choose (though Wagner's first preference, some land adjacent to the palace gardens [402], turned out to be impracticable – the Bürgerreuth was the alternative agreed).

At this stage Wagner had every hope and intention of adhering faithfully to his original ideal conception of the festival: the theatre was to be a provisional construction only, possibly of wood, subsequently to be handed over to the nation [407]; the enterprise was to be strictly non-profitmaking, the performances to be attended only by invited guests and Patrons, with no admission charges and a number of seats to be distributed free of charge to residents of Bayreuth [402]; singers and musicians were to receive expenses only, no fees [407]. While these arrangements and the patronage scheme were intended to grant the festival a measure of independence, Wagner was well aware that he could not afford to alienate the King. Ludwig accepted the idea of the festival being held outside Munich with reluctance but good grace. However, a surprisingly frank passage in a letter to Feustel and Muncker [406] deleted from the printed edition and not previously published is indicative of Wagner's impatience and annoyance with what he regarded as Ludwig's obstructive behaviour.

Plans for the new theatre in Bayreuth progressed sufficiently smoothly for Wagner to arrange a stone-laying ceremony for 22 May (his birthday) 1872. Only one work could serve to lay the foundations for the home of music drama: Beethoven's Ninth Symphony. In letter [405] Franz Betz is urged to undertake the bass solo – a part he accepted. The following letter [406] throws a curious light on Wagner's intentions for the finale of the Beethoven: "I am convinced that the actual audience should join in the singing (just like the congregation in church)." As for his intentions for the festival and the family succession, Wagner was apparently, in 1871, far from convinced that his son Siegfried would necessarily take over in due course. He would not be persuaded even to become a musician; indeed, Siegfried – then aged two – was to be encouraged to become a surgeon [401].

298. KING LUDWIG II OF BAVARIA, MUNICH   Stuttgart, 3 May 1864

My dear and gracious King,

I send you these tears of the most heavenly emotion in order to tell you that the marvels of poesy have entered my poor loveless life as a divine reality! – And this life, with its final outpouring of verse and of music, now belongs to you, my gracious young King: dispose of it as you would of your property!

In the utmost ecstasy, faithful and true

Your
subject
Richard Wagner.

Königsbriefe I,11.

299. MATHILDE MAIER, MAINZ   [Munich, 5 May 1864]

My child,

My heart is bursting, I must share my news with someone dear to me. See here the picture of a wonderful youth whom fate has ordained shall be my redeemer. It is he for whom we were waiting and whose existence was never in doubt, but whom it fills me with awestruck amazement to find so fair of form. He sent out in search of me, no stone was left unturned. Our meeting yesterday was one great love-scene which seemed as though it would never end. He shows the deepest understanding of my nature & of my need. He offers me everything that I need to live, to create, and to perform my works. I am to be his friend, nothing more: no appointment, no functions to fulfil. It is all I ever wished for. – Here, read his letter – but send it *back immediately*: I covet it.

Not a word about our bond is to be given to the newspapers; it is purely an affair of the heart! And so (I implore you) be *discreet*, as though it were some tender love-affair. Not a word to Schott or Städl – no one must know about it, except my friends in the Karthause[1] amongst themselves.

Now my room in your house must be nice and welcoming for me in the future. I often think of living there in friendly, comfortable surroundings, whenever I visit you!

1 See letter [293], p. 574, note 1.

Adieu! A thousand good wishes   R.W.
And for this to have happened now – now – in the blackest night of death
of my whole existence!! I feel as though I have been crushed! – Let me have
the letter back quickly. The picture of my belovèd friend is yours to keep.

Maier-Briefe 155.

300. ELIZA WILLE, MARIAFELD   Starnberg,[1] 26 May 1864

My dear, kind and honoured friend,
   I doubt whether this letter will reach you in Mariafeld, but I assume that
it will be forwarded to you. I am really only writing to stop you from coming
to think of me as ungrateful. It was with you that I had to endure the terrible
throes of child-birth that led to my present good fortune, and it was you who
were my midwife: we saw and felt only the distress and anguish of this birth;
and it may well be that for mothers, too, it is a process of life and death in
which all thought of what is to be born fades completely away, and pain
remains the only reality. Yet I scarcely know how I could have survived all
this and how, finally, without any visible hope ahead of me, I could have been
capable of taking my leave of you in what I can only describe as a composed
and bearable frame of mind, had I not been conscious in my heart of hearts
that, by virtue of my unspeakable sufferings, I had at least *acquired a superior
right*, an entitlement which, even if it had not been acknowledged by the
world, would have raised me far, far above the world and thus, even in the
depths of my misery, would have made me *inwardly* a *hallowed and blessed
human being*.
   [. . .]
   Do not doubt this for a moment, my dear. It is this good fortune which
alone accords with all the sufferings I have had to bear, including the utmost
misery. I feel that even if it had never come, I would still have been worthy
of it: and this gives me the certainty that it will last. But if, in addition, you
desire confirmation that *this* good fortune, too, is of divine provenance, you
shall hear it forthwith. In the year that "Tannhäuser" was first performed[2]
(the work with which I first embarked upon a course that was as novel as it
was fraught with difficulty), and in the very month (August) when I felt so
immensely creative that I conceived both "Lohengrin" and the "Mastersingers" at one and the same time,[3] a mother gave birth to my guardian angel.

1 Wagner moved into the Haus Pellet on Lake Starnberg on 15 May 1864.
2 1845.
3 Strictly speaking, *Lohengrin* and *Die Meistersinger von Nürnberg* were conceived in July 1845.
   Ludwig was born on 25 August 1845.

At the very time when I was completing my "Tristan" in Lucerne,[1] when I was making untold efforts to secure my return to German soil (Baden),[2] and had finally turned in despair to Paris, in order to wear myself out in enterprises repugnant to my nature, – it was then that the 15-year-old youth first attended a performance of my "Lohengrin",[3] a performance which affected him so deeply that from that moment onwards he based his own education upon a study of my works and writings, with the result that, as he openly admits to those around him, and now admits to me, it is *I* who have really been his one and only mentor and teacher. He followed my career and my troubles, my adversities in Paris, my starvation in Germany, and came to cherish but one desire, that he might gain the power to give me proof of his supreme love. One care, however, consumed the youth, his inability to persuade the dullards around him to take the necessary interest in me. At the beginning of March *this* year – I know the day well – it became clear to me that every attempt to remedy the hopelessness of my situation had been a failure: everything that befell me with such awful and degrading inevitability I saw approaching with open and helpless despair. Then – totally unexpectedly – the King of Bavaria died,[4] and filled with compassion – and in the face of destiny – my guardian angel ascended the throne. Four weeks later, his first concern was to send for me: while I, in despite of the help you were able to offer in easing my pain, was draining my cup of sorrow to its very last drop, his emissary was already looking for me in my abandoned apartment in Penzing; he had to take his affectionate monarch a pencil, a pen of mine. – How and when he finally found me you already know. – My dear, there is no doubt about it: – *this* was it, and *this* is it! – Ah! at last a love-affair that brings neither sorrow nor suffering! What it means to me to see this glorious youth before me! For my birthday he gave me the beautiful oil painting for which he had sat especially for me. This wonderful portrait has taught me how I can prove to others that I have "genius": here, look at it, here before you, you can see my "genius" with your very own eyes! –

A close friend of the King assured me that he believed that the only reason why the young man was so serious and strict in his handling of the affairs of government was that he did not wish to fall under alien influence, but to retain complete freedom for himself and, certain and secure of his power, to be able to live, in total independence, for his love for me. He is fully conscious of who I am and of what I need: I did not have to waste a word in describing my position to him. He feels a King's power ought to suffice to protect me from all that is base, to leave me wholly free for my Muse, and to provide me with all the resources I need to perform my works, when and as I wish.

1 August 1859.
2 But see letter [246], p. 466.
3 On 2 February 1861 in Munich.
4 Maximilian II died on 10 March 1864.

He spends most of his time at present in a small castle near here;[1] his carriage takes me there in 10 minutes. He sends for me once or twice a day. I then fly to him as to a lover. He is delightful company. This urge for instruction, this gift of understanding, this trembling and warming to each new subject is something that it has never before been my lot to experience so utterly unreservedly. And then his tender solicitude for me, his enchanting chastity of heart, of his every expression as he assures me how happy he is to possess me; thus we sit for hours on end, lost in each other's gaze. He does not boast about me: we are complete unto ourselves. If I wanted – or so I am told – the whole Court would be open to me, but he would not understand me if I desired to play some ambitious role there. It is all so beautiful and all so genuine. How easy it is for me now to exert a calming influence on every side: no one minds me, and I interfere with no one; all the things that we both inwardly despise go their own way in peace; we do not worry our heads about them. Everyone will come to love me in time; even now the young King's immediate entourage is happy to discover and know the sort of man I am, for they can all see that my immense influence upon the prince's mind can lead only to the common good, and can be to no one's disadvantage. And so everything within us and around us grows better and more beautiful by the day! –

This is my good fortune, my friend! Can you doubt but that it is the right thing for me? The right thing, yes – it must be the right thing: you shall now see how long it lasts, and how everything prospers. Cast aside your doubts! –

If there is one thing in my life which has made me inconsolably sad and ill-humoured, it is a characteristic of the "world" against which the likes of us are powerless to act. It is the philistine's conceited belief in his own "practical wisdom", and his often – sweetly smiling – assumption that it is he who is uniquely clever and wise, in contrast to those rare and profound individuals whose minds he himself cannot fathom. This appalling cleverness, this absurd abstemiousness in grasping and valuing the things of this life, which now and then triumphs even over the madcap visionary, degenerates, in contrast to those who are genuinely more profound, into what is strictly speaking an animal instinct for discovering only what is useful and necessary at the moment in question; since the man whose mind is more profound frequently overlooks what is immediately necessary (an omission which is often intentional, lest it obscure his broader vision of things), he seems, to those who pride themselves upon their practical intelligence, to be lacking in sense and utterly unintelligible. Well, we shall no doubt have to put up with it if the world which *we* understand well enough does not understand us, but takes the liberty of pitying our unpractical nature. If, however, this same situation is transferred to the realm of morality, and if the philistine regards

1 Schloss Berg, a small hunting lodge on Lake Starnberg.

himself as uniquely moral simply because he has not the first idea what true morality is nor the least feeling for it, we shall find it difficult to remain tolerant towards him and to retain our sense of irony in conceding that we are right: but if a *woman* loses all *her* instinct for love to the extent that she judges, pities – and admonishes the object of her love from the standpoint of her own moral philistinism, then her attitude will become unbearable. It was my punitive fate to mar and spoil my own wife to such an extent, as a result of excessive tolerance on my part, that she finally lost the basis on which to do me any kind of justice. The consequence of this was all too plain. *I* do not wish to incur any blame for causing a similar estrangement between myself and our friend from the Enge[1] by similarly spoiling her: I would believe that I wished only to play with her if I did not make her feel the injustice of what she is doing to me and of what she has so often done to me.[2] I am returning her childish little letter to you: no one will have a better opportunity than you, my dear, to inform her that the most shameful adversities which befell me made me neither angry nor bad so that her childish exhortation to me to be *good* is meaningless. –

My last letter, had she not refused it, could have taught her otherwise, and corrected her view of me: it was my final letter to her, a hallowed letter. It remains so, in spite of the good fortune which has so suddenly overtaken me: for it concerned my very being, which fortune cannot alter, and if she had understood it, she would also have realized that I already bore that good fortune within me. – Let her now strive to rediscover me: she had me once and knew me; that she could lose me and misjudge me I can – understand, but not forgive. Let her atone for what she has done! For she means too much to me for me to play with her. –

Where are you now, my dear? Will you write again soon? I am utterly alone here: I miss having people in the house, but perhaps I shall get Cornelius to come.[3] Shall I be able to renounce the "eternal feminine" completely? Sighing deeply, I tell myself that I ought to wish that I could! – A glance at his dear portrait helps me again! Ah, the dear young boy! I suppose he must now be everything to me; world, wife and child! A thousand sincere good wishes!

Ever yours,
RW.

Wille-Briefe 76–82.

---

1 Mathilde Wesendonck, whose Zurich home was Die Enge.
2 Mathilde Wesendonck had returned unopened Wagner's letter to her of April 1864. The letter in question appears not to be extant. See Newman's *Life*, III,211.
3 See letter [302], pp. 607–8: Cornelius did not come until 30 December 1864.

301. HEINRICH PORGES, VIENNA   Starnberg, 28 May 1864

My dear Heinrich,

Now let us be serious! My young King wants me to have everything I need. I need a secretary, but of the kind that *I* need. He must be able to deal with my business correspondence for me, keep my manuscripts in order, make literary and musical fair copies, and make arrangements of my scores etc. – in a word, he must be completely versatile. Do you wish to take this on? I think that, as a start and as a basis on which to build, it might serve you just as well, if not better, than the dreary business of giving lessons. My affairs would occupy you only occasionally, although at certain periods you would no doubt be very busy, but generally you would have sufficient completely free time to be able to do your own work, or even – if you can find talented pupils – to give lessons. I can confidently offer you 400 fl. a year during the periods when you have board and lodging etc. here in my house, and 600 fl. for those periods when you have to provide your own board and lodging (apart from the midday meal). However, except for the 12 months from next autumn until the following autumn, when I assume I shall be moving into my own house, you can live with *me*: here, as in my own house, allowance will be made for your accommodation (**with** piano). Bülow's position in Berlin rested upon the 400 thalers he received from the Conservatoire, a sum which is at least the equivalent there of 400 fl. here. I can easily help you to expand and exploit your literary activity: a good deal can be done here. If you manage to produce any decent artistic work, you will find that the success of your endeavours receives much encouragement from your being here with me. – What does Vienna have to offer you?

If you accept, you will make me very, very happy! You know of course that the secretary is merely an excuse for having my friend here with me. If you wish to bind your life to mine (and how long will this life of mine last?), you will, I hope, never have cause to regret it. And how important, how splendid, and how reassuring it will be for me always to have my witty and friendly companion here beside me! –

And so – shake hands upon it, and have no scruples about accepting. I know what I am doing, for the friendly will which now provides for me wills it so. I would beg you therefore to take up your appointment punctually on the 1st of June. Your room is ready, and I know you will like it here from the moment you arrive. It is utterly delightful! –

I believe I may be right in hoping that you will not need to reflect for long. All the right decisions are swiftly taken. Would you be kind enough to ask Tausig to hand over to you the orchestral parts from my concerts? You can either bring them with you as refundable excess-baggage, or have them sent on ahead as express freight: but the former is better, since it avoids tedious formalities. I would similarly ask you to bring with you the various books of mine which are still scattered around the place at Tausig's & Cornelius's.

Only – do not make me wait beyond the 1st of June. Here in my splendid isolation I yearn desperately for someone of your stamp, and – given the man I am – I suffer from this deprivation.[1]

I dare not say any more on the subject of Cornelius: he has not answered a single letter, or not what I would call "answered" (his delightful birthday poem is a different matter!). There is something about him that often mystifies me: God knows why he often causes me so much worry! I have grown accustomed to regarding him as a gift from heaven, like good fortune, good weather and the like, but I see that I cannot expect fate simply to hand him over to me. It would be splendid if he, too, were to come, and come soon! For it really is divine here at present, and it offends me strangely to think of what I am offering you both, and to see you, for your part, doubtful and hesitant, ignoring my offer in favour of the pitiful lives that you both are leading! –

If Fritz[2] does good business with the various theatres, I should welcome it: tell him to see whether he can extort the 300 fl for Trotter by the 15th of June. On my present secure income[3] I can of course afford to maintain secretaries, but fresh supplies are needed to deal with certain Viennese upholsterers.[4]

Well then! A thousand good wishes to your dear, loyal family in the Praterstrasse! – Let me know soon when you will be arriving! – The fast train will get you to Munich at 5.30 in the morning, and then take you on immediately to Starnberg at 6.30; Franz[5] will collect you in the boat, and bring you across the lake. If an opportunity presents itself, we may then go to Munich together and spend a day there, having a proper look at the place.

Adieu! Come soon! Won't you?

Sincerely yours,

Richard Wagner

RWA (copy not in Wagner's hand; published with minor variants in Freunde und Zeitgenossen 403–5).

1 Porges did not come.
2 Friedrich Porges, who was currently administering the receipts from performances of Wagner's works.
3 In addition to an immediate payment of 4000 gulden in settlement of Wagner's Viennese debts, Ludwig had granted the composer an annual stipend of 4000 gulden (later raised to 6000). A further sum of 16,000 gulden was paid to Wagner on 10 June, and, under the terms of a contract dated 18 October 1864, Wagner sold the *Ring* to Ludwig for 30,000 gulden.
4 See letter [294], p. 575 and [309], pp. 619–20.
5 Franz Mrazéck, Wagner's manservant.

302. PETER CORNELIUS, GENEVA   Starnberg, 31 May 1864

My dear Peter,

I am trying to sort out my affairs, so that I know for certain what I own and what I shall have to resign. I have now reached a stage in my life when this is demanded of me: I must organize my peace of mind, whether it be – as I say – by owning possessions or by resigning them.

I have told you repeatedly that everything has been carefully arranged here for your arrival: the two of us, and anyone else, can live here side by side, completely independent of each other, each free to get on with his own work, or to follow his own inclinations, yet with the possibility of being able to enjoy each other's company whenever we like. Your piano, which will not disturb me, is already here: there is a box full of cigars waiting for you in your room etc. This, dear Peter, is *keenness* for you! It demands a reciprocal gesture, or else – it will turn very sour. – You have not yet sent me a single line in response to all the reports I have sent you, but, instead, you have asked H. Porges to tell me that you are sorry you cannot come, since you are planning to spend the next 3 months revising your "Cid", and must therefore remain in Vienna. –

What would you advise now, dear Peter – that we should discuss this strange behaviour of yours, or that we should say nothing? – I am almost tempted to think that silence is better, since – quite clearly – there is something you wish to hide here which will not become any clearer by being discussed but, on the contrary, can only be distorted and stifled. – All life's decisions are ultimately the result of involuntary impulses: we are attracted and repelled by a thing in spite of all that we may otherwise adduce to the contrary. When I ask myself in what way this impulse has already found expression in your relations with me, the result of my disquisition is not to my liking. Exactly 2 years ago today I was eagerly expecting you in Biebrich: for a long time there was no news, until I suddenly discovered through a third person that you had allowed Tausig to drag you off to Geneva. You never really discovered how deeply that upset me.

I shall not allow anything like that to happen on this occasion, but we must discuss the matter openly as man to man. –

I simply cannot accept your reasons for not wanting to entrust yourself to me, given my concern for your being able to work here in peace. A year ago you left Vienna and went to Munich *in order* to work there in peace. I, *too*, intend to work here now: but I can no more see how my Mastersingers could disturb your Cid than the other way round. Quite the opposite, for what motivates me is my concern for you & your work. And – I can say so quite openly – I should very much like to be able to offer you my advice, sincerely and honestly, when you come to revise your opera. But if you wish to avoid *this*, – well, that is a question of will, and, certainly, there is nothing more that can be said on the matter.

But I was no doubt wrong when I said that you went to Munich a year ago the better to be able to work; perhaps you also went there because you longed to get away from Vienna. I feel as though you have already admitted as much. Perhaps it is for the opposite reason that you now find it difficult to leave Vienna. Well, when our hearts bid us act in a certain way, there is nothing we can do about it. I only hope on this particular point that, in doing as your heart bids you, you at least feel happy and confident. If not, then perhaps you will now heed a friend's advice and, if necessary, not give in so easily in the future.

In any case, I should prefer you to display a more open attitude towards me. In the light of my own keenness, your present behaviour is nothing short of *insulting*, and – I already feel it as such.

And so, dear Peter, you must not hold it against me, now that I am having to sort out my affairs, if I tell you straight out the conclusion to which my conflicting emotions have led me.

Either you accept my invitation without delay, and settle down with me for the rest of your life's days in a kind of genuine domestic union with me.

Or – you scorn me, and thus expressly repudiate my desire to bind you to me. In the latter case I in turn repudiate you completely and utterly, and shall certainly not include you in whatever arrangements I may make for my life in future. –

It will, and must, depend upon the degree of trust you show me in informing me of your reasons, whether we are destined to see each other as friends in the future.[1]–

One thing will be clear to you from all this – how much I need *peace and quiet*. For this I must know for certain where I stand: my present relationship with you torments me dreadfully. It must either become complete, or else break altogether!–

I hope you will see from the seriousness with which I interpret my relations with you that I feel anything but contempt in this matter!

Sincerely yours,
RW.

Freunde und Zeitgenossen 406–9.

303. HANS VON BÜLOW, BERLIN   Starnberg, 1 June 1864

My dear Hans,

And so the most remarkable month of May of my entire life has come to an end! A year earlier and it would have been marvellously in keeping with

1 See letter [300], p. 604, note 3.

the age of "Jupiter" that I had then reached.[1] All that I experienced during this time is utterly beyond compare: the contrasts put me in mind of one of those storms whose most stiflingly oppressive climax is suddenly followed by its complete opposite. This is something you will soon discover for yourself in person: let me say now only that a world has perished behind me, and that, in all truth, I see myself as having died, so that I now think of myself as a departed spirit who no longer has anything really in common with that former world. –

[. . .]

Indeed, my dear Hans, I died a Christian: but, as the price of dying a Christian, I still have a number of vows to fulfil; they *alone* still bind me to the earth. They are as follows:[2]

1864 Summer (during the Court's period of mourning) "Scenes from the Nibelungs" at the piano, with H. v. Bülow.
Late autumn, "Grand Concert of fragments from my works."
1865 Spring. Tristan and Isolde (with Schnorr & Tietjens).
Beginning of winter.
Mastersingers.
1866 Tannhäuser (new) Lohengrin (complete) with Schnorr etc.
1867–68 Grand performance of the entire "Ring of the Nibelung."
1869–70 "The Victors". –
1871–72 "Parzival!"
1873 Final *beautiful death* and redemption of the votary.

___

And so, tell them, one and all, high and low, to expect no more of me, – I'll be finished! –

That's how it is, my Hans! Since you intend coming here soon,[3] you will see my young King for yourself, and make his acquaintance.

You will soon know for certain what no description or assurance of mine could make you believe. There is something godlike about him, something undreamt-of, something incomparably and gloriously beautiful that has come true and entered my life. No one can understand this because it has *never* happened before: for – in truth: – I *alone* could have been favoured in this way. *I* have created this miracle, with my very own yearning and suffering, and a queen had to give birth to this son for *me*. – Well, you will get to know him for yourself! –

But I shall send you a portrait of him. He is my genius incarnate whom I see beside me and whom I can love. –

1 Wagner had been fifty in May 1863.
2 Of these projects only two were realized on time, the "Grand Concert" in Munich on 11 December 1864, and the production of *Tristan und Isolde* in 1865.
3 Bülow arrived at the Haus Pellet on 7 July 1864; Cosima and their children had arrived a week earlier. The whole family returned to Berlin on 3 September 1864.

My dear Hans, do not torment yourself thus throughout the summer! I beg you! – You can stay with me and live here as long as you wish, and it won't cost you a penny. My domestic arrangements are such that you won't disturb me for a moment. Your travelling expenses etc. will be fully reimbursed, at all events (or, rather, made good); I, *too*, still owe you some money, which you can collect while you are here.

I entreat you not to think of Wiesbaden, and other jokes like it. Remain here, enjoy a complete rest, and – if you *must* – exorcize the spirit of Karlsruhe[1] afterwards: ultimately, I should be glad to see you go there, since I still believe that the Grand Duke – if he is finally to achieve anything at all – ought at least to offer you the sort of position you deserve. But it would also be good if you were to remain here as performer to my young King:[2] for we are resolved to create our own intimate world here, away from the theatre and the venal world of public music-making. – Well, this, too, can be discussed later: I wanted only to persuade you in advance not to defile yourself by giving concerts at a time when you ought to be convalescing. Do as I say! –

Schott still hasn't engraved anything.[3] If you want, I can send you the old arrangement of the Valkyrie (which you already know): but do not be so concerned about your own "achievement" – heavens above! –

Adieu, my dear Hans! Write again soon. And tell Cosmus to write for a change. Next year, when the Mastersingers is finished, & Tristan has been performed, we shall all do something nice together, in order to enjoy ourselves and relax! The Bechstein[4] I find thoroughly sympathetic, believe me! – Adieu, my dear Hans! Cordially yours,

RW

[Give Liszt my best wishes & tell him that hearing from his Grand Duke makes me physically ill, as though from some ducal Saxon Swedish punch! – But this is all in the *past*! Dingelstedt has it in black and white!]

RWA (published with omission of postscript in Bülow-Briefe 213–16).

1　The Allgemeiner Deutscher Musikverein met in Karlsruhe between 22 and 26 August 1864; Bülow was too ill to attend. No doubt there is a pun here on the name Karlsruhe = Charles's *rest*.

2　Bülow was appointed *Vorspieler* or performer to the King on 29 July 1864; he took up the appointment on his return to Munich on 20 November 1864.

3　The score of *Die Meistersinger von Nürnberg*.

4　Wagner had persuaded Carl Bechstein to present him with a replacement for the Erard grand which had been impounded by his Viennese creditors. The Erard is now in the museum at Tribschen.

304. COSIMA VON BÜLOW, BERLIN   Starnberg, 16 June 1864

My dear Cosima,

I returned here yesterday[1] to find a letter from Hans which shows in what a very bad way the poor man must be – indeed, I always feared it would come to this, given the unnatural over-exertion of his powers.

Am I to regard it as a matter of chance and of indifference that it is precisely now that, for the first time in my life, fate has placed me in the position of being able to look back upon my long-suffering friends, now that all my own needs have finally fully been met? Of course not! – You will have gathered from my behaviour last month that it was only hesitantly and with reservation that I set about offering you my advice. My increasingly clear understanding of the sublime beauty and purity of my relationship with the young King helped me to overcome all my reservations, and what I proposed to you was properly thought through with all the certainty of a mathematical calculation. That this calculation may contain an error is a possibility I must accept: but this would relate only to my estimation of the character of our dear Hans. However – he is very ill. That is why I am turning to you, my sweet child, and leaving it up to you to apprise him at an opportune moment and in a suitable manner of what I have to say to you.

I first made Hans' acquaintance when he was 12 years old: my affection for him has always had something of the character of an older man's tender concern for someone younger than himself. More especially since I found occasion, at an early date,[2] to exert a decisive influence upon his life, it has always been a reproachful concern of mine to contribute what I can to his successful progress. How sad it was for me that for so very, very long I was never once in the position of being able to devise or carry out a single plan or a single suggestion that would have been to his advantage, or to intercede on his behalf! Or have I ever communicated some practical project to him? Alas, no, – I was never able to do so. On the contrary, my own life was so dissolute and so indigent that I should only have increased the poor man's cares, and dragged him down into the maelstrom of my own seething existence. –

Well, a state of perfect happiness has now revealed itself to me for the first time, and revealed itself, moreover, in such abundance and beauty that it would make me sad and miserable to enjoy it, if I could not share its blessings with those whom I love so dearly, but whom I see suffering and on whom I have never been able to exert even the slightest favourable influence.

Hans's letter and bitter behaviour shall not deter me now from making a

1 From Vienna, where he had been settling his outstanding debts.
2 In 1850 when, with Wagner's encouragement, Bülow had embarked upon his career as a musician.

sincere attempt to persuade him to trust me. – And so, my dearest child, here is my calculation, – the first I have ever put to Hans! –

I have repeatedly heard tell of attempts in Hans's past to escape the daily round of giving lessons: he himself told me of his regret at having failed in his attempts to pursue a career as Kapellmeister even as an interim measure (as in Schwerin), a career which even today remains a sad business after all. Finally Hans even spoke to me on one occasion of his plan to retire to Gotha, where the cost of living is particularly low and where he hoped to get by on your own small income and the profits from periodic concert tours, so that he could then pack in having to give lessons. I have now heard the latest news from Berlin, of his quarrel with Stern and his having given up his appointment there; and, on top of all that, his mood of utter torment which the pressure of such circumstances always produces. – At the same time I can see what my dear young King is lacking here: he lacks a musical education, he knows only my works, but nothing by Beethoven, and almost no other music either. He longs to be able to make good this omission: but he himself cannot, at this stage, start to receive instruction in how to play an instrument. It must all be conveyed to him by means of intelligent conversation; I cannot play for him, however. But how divinely and utterly uniquely Hans can do so! I told him of this: he now yearns for refreshment from this font of instruction. The Cabinet Secretary Pfistermeister, who is very much the basis upon which the security of my relationship rests, is urging me to bring Hans here. I know that all that is required here is for the three of us – the King, Hans and myself – to spend a few pleasant hours together, and things will happen as if of their own accord, without my needing to add much more than the odd word here and there; to my mind, and given my knowledge of the situation here, what this means is simply that Hans will remain here, as performer to the King, at a salary of *at least* 1500 fl. – And that is all. Munich is one of the cheapest places in Germany: it will be a great improvement on your "Gotha". If he wishes, Hans can continue with his concert tours, but he will give *almost* no more lessons in future, and need not trouble himself with anything more, but can get on with his work in peace, and – I shall then have you *both!* – It is all so simple and easy to achieve: only because I have never had anything even remotely like it to offer Hans, nor anything as easy to achieve as this, have I **never** devised any plans for Hans: but I am doing so now. –

One point to bear in mind. – The King is not master of his time: he is having to spend the greater part of the summer away from here and in the company of others.[1] But he has arranged to be free at present in order to spend almost 2 weeks nearby here, completely undisturbed: every day he sends to enquire whether he may expect my friend. And I (poor fool that I

1 Ludwig was in Bad Kissingen between 19 June and 15 July, when he returned to Munich.

am!) good-humouredly resort to high-spirited shock-tactics and telegraphic despatches, and – the rest we know! – But perhaps calm deliberation may still prove successful. According to the latest arrangements, the King is due to arrive in Berg, close by here, on the 25th inst., and to remain there until the 9th of July. I hope that our poor Hans will draw up his own plans accordingly. If he *can* devote himself to us during that time, all well and good: if *not*, he will none the less be welcome here at any other time. –

As far as you yourself and your children are concerned, my dear Cosima, you should be guided in your decision by your doctor and by him alone: if he agrees, you should not allow yourself to be deterred by any other thought from the summer holiday which I am offering you here. Believe me, you will be completely undisturbed here, and will not disturb me in the least: we do not need to see each other for days at a time – indeed – if you wish – not for weeks on end, so large is my house, and so well appointed with servants & all necessities. –

There is nothing else I can say now! Was it enough? – Even this I should prefer to have left unsaid, hence the allusiveness of my remarks, and the appeal to your trust, since I have *never* yet offered the two of you anything, and was thus never able to betray your trust. –

Now, make up your minds, my dear children, and, whatever happens, remember me with at least a little affection.

Yours,
Richard Wagner

We have a beautiful cowshed here with 40 magnificent Swiss cows. What milk for the children!!!

Eger II,3–6.

305. MATHILDE MAIER, MAINZ   Starnberg, 22 June 1864

Child! I am hounding myself to death, and can find no peace of mind! –

I must have someone here to run my house for me! –

I cannot spare you the shock of being shaken out of your peaceful existence by the question:

Will you come here and run my house? –

Can you account for my long silence? – I had to go back to Vienna again; packing and unpacking furniture, sorting things out! And in town again in the autumn! – And *me* – always alone with – servants: me of all people! No womanly being at my side! no educated person to talk to in the house! – It is quite clear that it cannot go on! No king nor emperor can offer me anything if things are not right at home! I can find no peace of mind. I am again looking for a woman to keep my things in order! It comes and goes, I cannot make up my mind. Is there a curse on me that prevents me from managing here? –

Once more; it cannot go on like this.

The Bülows are now coming to stay with me for a couple of months:[1] I have made everything ready for them, so that their stay in this vast house of mine is as comfortable as possible; – this will help in the short term! Certainly, I have people around me, but no one to take over the running of the house.

But how are you yourself? Do I still have to fear upsetting you each time I ask you to come here? Has nothing changed? Everything still as it was? – How it torments me to know you once more surrounded by people from whom you even have to conceal the letters I send you! Ugh! I'm ashamed! – Can you not see that things must change? My needs are not to be gainsaid: they must be met. I speak *only* of my familiar, domestic needs. –

If you were to marry, would you not also have to leave your mother? And were you not once before on the point of accepting an appointment? Regard my own case as the same kind of thing, and call it by the same name! As in Munich I am living on 2 floors here, one above the other: I am on the downstairs floor, and you could live upstairs. My God! My God! always these pitiful petit-bourgeois considerations; – and this where there is so much love! What is it ultimately that one loves more? – You see how it is! I have struggled for a long time to write to you calmly on this matter, but now my patience is at an end, – it is a disgrace that I am for ever expected to manage on my own! I cannot go on, I simply cannot: – a decision must be taken here, for I fear that you will lose me one day if you do not help me now. It is no good here simply talking and writing letters. – Heavens, it terrifies me in advance to think of how worked up I shall again be making you: – but I am incapable any longer of writing anything but this litany of my distress. I can find no peace of mind; my days, my house, my very life will be a source only of sorrow to me if I have to remain like this. This was the chief cause of my distress all last year, and the reason why I was unable to work: I kept this from you, because I know how much this would unsettle you, without inspiring in you the decision to help. I beg you, come in September, examine the matter closely, help me – and impose whatever conditions you wish, only let me have you! –

Well, here you have it, the whole truth, I've done with playing games! – Send me the answer I want, I beg you!

Yours,
R.W.

Maier-Briefe 162-3.

1 See letter [303], p. 609, note 3.

306. JOSEPHINE MAIER,[1] MAINZ   Starnberg, 25 June 1864

My dear, kind friend,

Only to someone like yourself, to whom I am already indebted for so much love & true devotion, can I dare to address a question and a request of the kind that I must necessarily put to you today. –

I must now decide how best to set about making my house sufficiently bearable in the future, so that the splendid security which I now enjoy in my outward situation may bring about a sense of inner well-being, too. You know that I am separated from my wife: the need to entrust my household affairs to some womanly creature has recently grown so great once again that I have seriously considered whether it might not be better to ask my wife to live with me again, rather than my remaining on my own. Only the conviction based upon long experience and confirmed by the observations of all my friends and relations that our reunion would result in a far more intolerable state of affairs for the two of us than our separation could ever be – only this conviction, I say, has again obliged me to abandon the idea. In such circumstances I was obliged to think of divorcing my wife: as a result of all my enquiries, however, I have discovered that this would be impossible, since my wife is resolved never to agree to an actual divorce – although she is obliged, on the other hand, to consent to our living apart. In these circumstances a divorce could be effected only by resorting to the most extreme and distasteful measures which, in turn, would involve the use of force. In view of my wife's state of health (a heart disease which at every moment exposes her to the risk of sudden death), it could never enter my head to commit an act of cruelty which I could never defend before my conscience and the world, no matter what my ultimate aim might be. And so I am obliged to leave the question of my marital relations temporarily unresolved. And yet the resultant indecision is not to be tolerated, preying as it does upon my peace of mind. I need a woman who, in the first place, will take over the running of my household for me, but who, ultimately, is sufficiently close to me in education and character to meet my spiritual and emotional needs with her friendly presence. I am of an age which would certainly allow me to adopt a young girl as my daughter, and I believe that such a relationship would meet my needs quite admirably. But one cannot go out in search of such a relationship: how and where should I find such a girl, whom I do not know and whom I might perhaps be over-hasty in choosing, thereby bringing down upon myself renewed and unbearable sufferings. What I need cannot be sought after but must be found as a gift from heaven. And it is precisely in this way that I have already found the kind, intelligent and good-natured creature that I need so much: you know what your daughter Mathilde means to me. She

---

1 See introductory essay, p. 588.

understands what my need is and what, at my age, can alone be sensible! If she is not quite of an age to be considered my daughter, there are, none the less, other degrees of kinship which she could conveniently assume in order to be able to remain in my company. I myself have nieces of her age who would cheerfully come here, and whom nobody would object to my taking in. Would such a relationship be possible even if no actual kinship could be attributed to it? I do not know how this kind of thing must appear to others: but to a man of *my* intentions and needs it appears so pure and blameless that I find it very difficult not to feel a real sense of bitterness when I think that the kind of relationship that I desire may appear to some people as impermissible and worthy only of blame. – This much is clear, I *must* consider some remedy here. My domestic arrangements for now and the future have already been made with this in mind: I live on 2 floors (not least to ensure peace from the neighbours), and use only *one* of them for my actual apartment, whereas I leave the other to my household staff and whoever is chosen to run the household. I *must* aim, as carefully as possible, to find a relatively young woman whom I can trust to satisfy whatever needs I may have but which will in no way involve any further sensuality. I have every reason to be afraid of not being able to find such a creature; I cannot decide upon any of my nieces, nor, indeed, do I wish to; – for many reasons! What follows from this? –

Would you have the courage to face the world and enough confidence in me to entrust your daughter to me? I know what a difficult question this must be for you, and that you may even be crushed by the weight of it! But I cannot avoid putting it to you. Urgent necessity constrains me to do so, for I must have a decision. Could you bring yourself to see Mathilde leaving your own home in order to be for me what she once was for you – to belong henceforth to a far-off friend in deepest need? Could you accept it (for the sake of the world) if Mathilde were to take up an honourable position and worthy station for the remainder of her life; if this were offered to her, and if it were to be to her advantage for her to accept it, surely you would not choose to oppose her, however much you would miss the dear child? – I understand how difficult and wellnigh impossible all this must seem to you: and yet – I *have* to ask you this question, in all seriousness, and my trust in your splendid loyalty and love gives me the courage to do so, and relieves me of any fear I may have of causing you serious offence. – Or does it require even more definite reassurances on my part before I may risk these questions? Ought I to reassure you that Mathilde will be well and truly cared for here, and that she will be protected in the most explicit and vigorous manner against all suspicion and against all taint? Or might it be possible, without nurturing an impious wish, to adduce the eventuality of my wife's death and, in that case, to sue for your daughter's hand in marriage?–

Whatever you may wish to retort to all this, I hope to receive a frank and amiable answer, even if it prove contrary to my wishes. I am far too fond of you to be able to imagine any change in our relations, or to believe that such a change might mislead me into committing the injustice of undervaluing your love. I have but one excuse to lay before you here for presuming upon your kindness in this way: this request is so exceptional that it can be excused only by the exceptional nature of my whole existence. After all, everything about me is out of the ordinary: thus have I acquired a king as my dearest and kindest son; and thus do I desire, chastely but sincerely, a loving woman by my side. – And so, whatever happens – do not be angry with me! – I remain eternally true and grateful,

Yours,
Richard Wagner.

Maier-Briefe 164–7.

307. Mathilde Maier, Mainz   Starnberg, 29 June 1864

Oh, my dear child! No, not at any price do I want that![1] I can & will bear anything in the world, but not the renewed storms of emotion & conflict which I am bound to foresee if you give my letter to your dear Mama! Yes, I admit it, I am an egoist, – I want peace, gentle relaxation, and tender embraces, – and I intend to renounce everything, but everything, that can be obtained only by desperate and convulsive measures and that can be retained only at the price of some private grief! I must, and shall, manage on my own, without upsetting you further; I cannot possibly wish for anything that can be acquired only at the cost of some catastrophe! Have you no notion of how tired I am, how I yearn for uniformity and peace, & to glide gently away? –

I really flattered myself that your mother was now more prepared to be parted from you. But I see that you did not think the time was at all ripe when you could attempt to acquaint her of such a possibility. Or was it only the questionable nature of the position you might have adopted towards me which constituted the real impossibility? On this point I can only remain silent and strive to understand you: for you alone could know, in the light of your knowledge of the ideas entertained by your family's circle of friends, what is possible here and what is not possible. At all events I am bound to fear the very worst from *every* point of view, otherwise you would not have gained the impression, upon reading through my letter to your mother, that this letter, in spite of its rational tone, would "crush" her! – It is here, my dear creature, that my error lies: I did *not* think that my request to have you here could have had so dreadful a significance & effect.

But you will no doubt realize that it is enough for me to have been apprised

1 See introductory essay, p. 588.

in this manner of how things stand for me to know at once what I must do. It is to beg you most sincerely neither to give the letter to your mother nor to communicate any of its contents to her! – I was – apparently – over-hasty again: your last letter encouraged me to think that it was admissible to take this decisive step with your mother. I was wrong. – There can be *no* question for now of any change in our mutual position. – After all that has happened, it hardly befits me to appeal to you for calm! – but that is all I can do. It is a bad situation I find myself in, and highly unsatisfactory, with my life wasting away like this: but it would be quite dreadful and utterly unbearable if I were suddenly to be swept away by a torrent of emotions to which I am no longer equal and which would rob me of my peace for ever. Whatever may come to redeem me must come in the guise of gentle and peaceful happiness, untainted, without any passion, like the sun after a storm, – just as my gracious King came to me at the blackest hour of my life. I can bear no further convulsions of pain, no more silent grief, for I have already borne more than is humanly possible, and my strength to do so is now at an end. –

You need fear no aberrations on my part either: for the present I shall be having friends[1] to visit me, and for the autumn I may still be able to get Vreneli[2] to come here from Lucerne: at least I shall then be relieved of my *household* responsibilities, – and for the rest I shall perhaps be helped by my work and by becoming involved in performances. And so – calm down! Adieu, my child! I cannot today. After having felt sickly for some time, I was seized by a terribly violent attack of fever a couple of evenings ago – but it was only the result of a chill: the illness I feared has failed to develop. I am all right again! – Fare you well, take care of yourself, and, in spite of everything, do not stop loving me!

Truly yours,
R.W.

Maier-Briefe 168–9.

308. ELIZA WILLE, MARIAFELD   Starnberg, 30 June 1864

Dear, kind friend,

I am very tired, and suffering from all that I have been through: now that the excitement has passed, the pain is beginning to grow, as with wounds. I shall not be able to return to my art as quickly as you might suppose. Even now, I continue to be amazed at the idea of how things would have stood

1 Specifically Hans and Cosima von Bülow, although Wagner's house-guests during the summer also included the sculptor Caspar Zumbusch, the socialist writer Ferdinand Lassalle, Karl Klindworth, Karl Eckert and his family, and, for one night only, Franz Liszt.

2 Vreneli (or Verena) Weidmann, who arrived in Starnberg in September 1864.

with me now if this one unexpected event had not overtaken me; for everything I thought I could count on has, and would have, failed me pitifully! I can see that now, and shudder at the thought of it. – My loneliness is terrible. With this young King I can exist only as if on the highest mountain summit. The abandoned state of my household affairs, the compulsive need to busy myself with things for which I was not really intended paralyses my vital spirits: once again I have had to move, and set up house, and had to worry about knives and forks, pots and pans, bed-linen and so on. I, the glorifier of women! How kind of them to leave me to deal with their errands for them. –

My dearest, the most beautiful thing about your beautiful letter was the intimation of your visit.[1] I am already looking forward to it, and so I do not need to write any more now, which, given my present weariness, suits me admirably. You will be able to live here in splendid fashion: since there was no alternative, I have a large house entirely to myself, and you shall find everything here for your convenience. Bring a secretary with you, and then you can dictate from your portfolio the novel you promised us. And *this* time we must have a proper conversation: who knows when there will be another opportunity? How happy I should be to die now!

Frau v. Bülow arrived yesterday with her children and nursemaid: her husband will follow. It provides a certain amount of animation, but I am so perverse that nothing makes any real impression upon me any longer. Perhaps it is only the bad weather that is to blame – do you not agree? We artists do not normally take things so seriously! Well, we shall see. But come soon, and remain for as long as you can. Let me say only this about my young King, if I am not completely and utterly happy, it is not his fault. I am sure you can have no real idea as yet of how glorious our relationship is. You will gain an idea of this, too, when you are here; in a word – the male sex has been completely rehabilitated in my sight thanks to this particular representative. –

You must see all this for yourself! – Adieu! My dear, kind, anxious, caring, and perceptive friend! – A thousand thanks for your friendship!

Cordially yours,
R. Wagner.

*RWA (copy not in Wagner's hand; published with minor errors
of transcription in Wille-Briefe 82–3).*

309. BERTHA GOLDWAG, VIENNA   [Starnberg, end of June 1864]

When I saw you on the last occasion in Vienna in May, you expressed a willingness to receive further orders from me.

I feel that I am still somewhat in your debt; in addition, you are familiar

1 The visit did not take place.

with the style of the clothes that I wear about the house etc., and the fabrics which I would in any case prefer to have provided for me are difficult to obtain here in a decent variety. And so I should welcome it if you were to provide for my tastes now and in the future, only I would ask that your accounts be rendered annually not only for these but for all other expenses not calculable in advance, and I shall settle these accounts at the year's end. If you are able to comply with these wishes of mine, I should like to place a number of orders with you immediately. You would oblige me, therefore, if you could send me information, in the first instance, concerning the following fabrics.

1. Can you obtain from Szontag a fine heavy satin, *light brown* in colour, to match the enclosed sample?
2. The same in *dark pink*?
3. Is there a good quality fabric obtainable at 4 to 5 florins to match the enclosed *light pink*?
4. – ditto – the *blue*, but preferably *somewhat lighter*, certainly not darker.
5. Has Szontag enough of the *new red* or *crimson*-coloured heavy satin in stock that you used to line my white dressing-gown (with the floral pattern)?
6. Do you still have any of the *dark yellow* which we used to make the curtains for the little tables?

May I ask you to obtain suitable samples (small remnants will do) of these 6 colours and fabrics, and, at the same time, let me know whether you are able to agree to my proposal. I should welcome it not least because this is the most convenient arrangement for *me*, and in this way I can occupy you permanently in future.

I hope you still have the patterns for my house-clothes?

I look forward to hearing from you, and remain

Your respectful and obedient servant
Richard Wagner.

PS: Do not confuse No 2, the dark pink, with the earlier violet pink, which is not what I mean here, but genuine pink, only very dark and fiery.

Library of Congress Music Division (published with minor errors of transcription in Putzmacherin-Briefe 57–9).

310. ELIZA WILLE, MARIAFELD   Starnberg, 9 September 1864

[...] I have been completely on my own again for several days now, and feel as though I am living in a haunted castle. I cannot deny that such utter solitude is very bad for me at present: believe me, it is a wretched state of affairs, and I shall no doubt bleed to death from it. Unfortunately, even while

I had friends to stay, the place still seemed as though it were haunted: there was no sense of benediction or peace. Poor Bülow arrived at the beginning of July utterly exhausted, his nerves overwrought and shattered; he had cold, inclement weather the whole time he was here, and, as a result, had an insalubrious stay, which resulted in his succumbing to one illness after another. And, on top of everything, a tragic marriage; a young and quite unprecedentedly gifted wife, the very image of Liszt but intellectually superior to him, – [who, only a year after their marriage, – when the two of them were visiting me in Zurich for the second time,[1] – tried to take her own life in her despair at having committed the error of marrying; since then she has made repeated, and conscious, attempts to contract various fatal illnesses, but has finally found the strength to persevere and suffer patiently as a result of her visionary tendency towards the sublime. Her husband, sensitive and sufficiently self-aware to see where he stands, curses *himself* for having chained this woman to him; he seeks to dull his pain by striving too hard in the execution of his art, indeed he is deliberately trying to ruin his health in order to forget and – to die. – This, then, is the cruel basis upon which qualities of the greatest kindness have been developed on both sides, revealing the most touching concern for each other's well-being which now binds them both together]. If only I were made in such a way as to be able to obtain my rightful share of pleasure from superficial things and circumstances! But I am not made like that; I am foolish enough to take everything seriously. The most important thing here was to tear Bülow away from his insanely exhausting activities as an artist and find him a nobler field in which to work. It was easy to persuade the young King – for whom, in turn, it was a matter of the first importance – to appoint Bülow his performer. I now hope that I shall soon have the Bülows living here permanently with me. There is only one means of redemption for us all, and I have promised it to both of them: to create works of art and work together with a single common interest. – This will oblige us to persevere and undertake new enterprises, – in spite of the sweetness of feeling so utterly weary of life. – You see, with me nothing goes smoothly! Not even a case like that of Lassalle's death:[2] the unfortunate man was here (because of Bülow) exactly a fortnight prior to his death, appealing to me to intervene with the King of Bavaria against his ambassador in Switzerland (Dönniges). (I am regarded, you see, simply as an all-powerful favourite: my help was recently sought by the surviving relatives of a woman accused of poisoning someone!) What do you say to that? I had never met Lassalle until then; and on that occasion I disliked him immensely: it was a love-story inspired by sheer vanity and false pathos. I saw in him a typical

1 From 15 July to 16 August 1858. The passage in square brackets was suppressed from the published German text.
2 For more on this episode see Newman's *Life*, III,324–6.

example of the great men of the future, a type that I can only call Germanic–Judaic. –

I am still without anywhere to live in town: I should dearly like something that promises to be permanent, but can find nothing. People tell me to have something built specially, but that takes two years. Shall I live as long as that? Yes, I shall. My young King is saving money by suspending his father's building works etc., in order to collect together enough for a performance of the Nibelungs. I have not had a single day of proper peace and quiet so far: I keep on hesitating as to what I should start on first. In the end I expect I shall put everything aside and complete the Nibelungs: if I tell the King this, I shall be even better off. –

But listen now: on the 2nd of October, when the King will be making his first return-visit to the theatre, I shall be presenting a model performance of the "Flying Dutchman"[1] for him (the only one of my operas which can now be given properly here.) We are all set for an outstandingly good performance. For mid-October I have promised a grand concert[2] of pieces from my newer works, as in Karlsruhe. Will you come? – In *May* of next year "Tristan" with Schnorr.[3] – Will you come to that, too?–

How are you getting on with your novel? – How are Wille and your sons? Do give them my very best wishes! – How is the "haunted region"? Are you still fond of me? Do you believe in my gratitude? – Do *you* believe in me? – Answer me properly.

Cordially yours,
Richard Wagner.

RWA (incompletely published in Wille-Briefe 85–7).

311. KING LUDWIG II OF BAVARIA, HOHENSCHWANGAU
Starnberg, 26 September 1864

My august and dearly belovèd King,

That I have been placed in so novel and so auspicious a situation I owe to your Majesty's gracious favour, a favour which I find as totally unexpected as it is undeserved. The resolves which were bound to ripen within me under so benign an influence I now propose to lay before my gracious protector, and to address to Your Majesty a most humble entreaty arising therefrom.

I am now in the fifty-second year of my life, with my powers at their highest

---

1 The performance was delayed until 4 December 1864.
2 The concert, consisting of excerpts from *Tristan und Isolde, Die Walküre, Siegfried*, and *Die Meistersinger von Nürnberg*, together with the *Faust* Overture, was given on 11 December 1864.
3 The première of *Tristan und Isolde* was delayed until 10 June 1865.

pitch: if I may be permitted to believe that the consummation of all my existing achievements is even now in prospect, then it follows that I should not delay in addressing these powers to that selfsame end.

I am resolved to lay aside all other work for the present, however advantageous it might have been to me in view of its greater practicability, and to devote myself, exclusively and without delay, to completing the composition of my great Nibelung work.[1]

In doing so I believe that I shall also be acting in accord with the exalted wishes of my gracious protector, whose thoughts are inspired by the loftiest ideals, and, on this supposition, I would entreat Your Majesty most graciously to commission the completion of my tetralogy "The Ring of the Nibelung", together with the systematical preparation and eventual performance of this work in Munich. May it please Your Majesty to assign to me suitable accommodation in Munich for this purpose, together with the means to live freely and independently during the period necessary to complete this task, without my being obliged to pursue any other trade.[2]

In consequence of this explicit commission – a commission to which, in accord with your own more lofty insight, Your Majesty may deign to attribute the same great and far-reaching national significance that I myself expressed when I published the poem in question[3] – Your Majesty would, in my most humble opinion, proclaim to the whole of the world, in clear and unmistakable terms, a unique and noble design, a work whose performance will be of detriment to no one but which will bring honour to our fatherland; my own position, which is so much envied, will then become understandable and need no longer be concealed in all its beauty, and Your Majesty will have no difficulty in granting me the grace and favour you desire me to have by bestowing upon me whatever privileges may yet be necessary if I am to obtain the total peace and quiet that my work demands.

In the most fervent trust I therefore commend my entreaty to Your Majesty's grace and favour, through which alone I exist as an artist in the eyes of the world, and, assuring Your Majesty of my deepest respect and most inviolable devotion, I remain

Your Majesty's
most loyal subject and servant
Richard Wagner

Königsbriefe I, 25.

1 Wagner resumed work on the fair copy of the full score of Act I, Scene 2 of *Siegfried* on 27 September 1864.
2 See introductory essay, p. 591.
3 *Vorwort zur Herausgabe der Dichtung des Bühnenfestspieles "Der Ring des Nibelungen"* (Preface to the Edition of the Poem of the Stage Festival Drama "The Ring of the Nibelung"), written in Vienna in the winter of 1862/3 and published by Weber of Leipzig in 1863. Reprinted in GS VI,272–81; PW III,274–83.

312. ANTON PUSINELLI, DRESDEN   Starnberg, 2 October 1864

Dear, kind friend,

It seems I shall never cease to encounter difficulties. On every side the most absurd rumours concerning my sudden wealth are having the most unfortunate consequences. Even the official authorities have found it necessary to protest on the spot against such jealous animosities: I have sent my wife this correction which was published in a local newspaper: from it you, too, can see how modestly I am provided for in terms of my outward situation: I have just enough to manage on my own if I live very frugally, and then only because the King is providing for my accommodation. I have taken it upon myself to reduce my personal interests to the most modest dimensions in order to be able to give free rein to the King's admirable arrangements for performing my works. – I would now beg you most earnestly, as an old and trusted friend, to help me remove the difficulties which have arisen as a result of this, as far as it lies within your power to do so. *Firstly*, be so kind as to enlighten poor Frau *Kriete* as to her error; believing that I am rolling in money here, she is demanding 1822 thalers interest on a capital sum of 2000 thr. that has already been repaid. – It is madness to demand such a thing from me now: it *is* possible that the time will come when I am actually rewarded for my works and for my sufferings: but I need a great deal more patience if I am to bring this about. On the other hand, should not Herr Müller, the music-dealer, be persuaded, for honour's sake, to pay out some more money to Frau Kriete? as I now discover, he managed to get Flaxland in Paris to pay him a tidy sum (behind my back) for the Paris edition. He is now doing excellent business with the flying Dutchman. If he wishes to behave decently, I shall give him my new scenes from Tannhäuser[1] to exploit as he likes, and seek no further compensation from him, but *otherwise* I shall **not** publish them. – That's the first point! –

Now my wife! – My monthly income, apart from my free accommodation, is 100 fl.[2] And this satisfies my needs. My wife's annuity of 1000 thalers I can of course pay only out of random receipts from other quarters. As a rule these will be sufficient to cover this, but they are not regular, so that it is difficult for me to be punctual. But if *you*, my dearest friend, were to be kind enough to mediate here! In particular, I would ask you, on my account, to hand over 250 thalers to my wife regularly, every quarter; *I*, by contrast, will send you whatever I receive from abroad as soon as it arrives. Of course, the money you lay out must remain within acceptable limits, and you must in any case have been repaid whatever old amount is still outstanding *before* a new one falls due. However, if such an arrangement were possible, I need hardly

1 i.e. the Paris revisions.
2 But see letter [301], p. 606, note 3.

say how much it would contribute to the peace of mind that is so necessary to me! – At present, for ex., I had twenty louis d'or (110 thalers) coming to me from *Coburg* for the flying Dutchman, and I forwarded this sum directly to my wife. From Berlin I am expecting notification of my percentage of the profits there, which I shall similarly send on to her; from *Brunswick* I can expect 30 louis d'or within the course of the coming months. You see, my dearest Anton! I would forward these receipts to you directly I knew that you had, for ex., been kind enough to deliver to my wife the missing 140 thalers.

Certainly, you ought not to suffer any loss by doing so, and – if ever I really fell into arrears – the King would be only too pleased to help me (and you) in such individual cases. But *only* as a last resort. You must understand this! And so, if you can, do this as a favour for me, and in return you can count on my most scrupulous honesty. –

Only – let me have peace! Peace! – these perpetual cares are undermining all hope of ever setting my spirit free – as I must needs do!

And so – all the best, and let me hear some good news soon.

Write to me at *Munich, Briennerstrasse,* 21.[1]–

Adieu! A thousand good wishes to your family! Remain kindly disposed towards me, and accept my eternal thanks!

Cordially yours,

Richard Wagner

RWA (published only in English in Lenrow 167–9).

313. PETER CORNELIUS, VIENNA   Munich, 7 October 1864

Dear Peter,

By especial order of His Majesty King Ludwig II of Bavaria I am hereby requested to invite you to settle in Munich as soon as you are able, there to live for your art in expectation of the King's especial orders, and, as a friend, to help me, who is your friend.

From the day of your arrival[2] an annual stipend of One Thousand gulden will be assigned to you from His Majesty's exchequer.

Cordially yours,

Your friend
Richard Wagner

Freunde und Zeitgenossen 421.

---

1 Wagner left Starnberg early in October 1864 and stayed in a hotel in Munich, before moving into his new home in the Briennerstrasse on 15 October 1864.
2 Cornelius arrived in Munich on 30 December 1864.

314. KING LUDWIG II OF BAVARIA, HOHENSCHWANGAU
Munich, 6 November 1864

My glorious and dearly belovèd King,

There is a secret which can be revealed to my august and gracious friend only in the hour of my death:[1] but then it will become clear to him what today must seem obscure – that *he* alone is the creator and author of all that the world will attribute to my name from this day on. My sole reason for living is the wondrous love which descends upon me like drops of dew from the heart of my royal friend – as though from the lap of God – fructifying new seeds of life within me! Last All Souls' Day I felt as though I were garlanding my own tomb with the gladsome flowers of this love. In truth, I – am no more! I have endured and suffered too much; life and its increasingly alien aspects have drawn me away for ever from my own inner self towards a state of dissipation which has finally grown too deep for me, and too disturbing. Now that I can finally compose my thoughts once more, – and only the magic power of your love and inspiration has made this possible, – I feel as though I am beginning a new and second life upon the grave of my old existence! And the sole creator of this life is my gracious friend, the saviour who leads me to a new religion, a religion which brings forth a second, new life from deep within me, – a life which knows not of death! –

It is to my royal friend that I dedicate the convalescent's new-found strength in these feeble lines herewith. I may well hope that, as a result of the painful crisis which followed upon an earlier chronic illness, this selfsame illness will now be less afflicting than it has been previously, and that it may indeed be allayed for some time to come; so that I regard it as a good sign that, at the very moment of actually moving into my final refuge,[2] I may look forward to the comforting prospect of an improvement in my health as well. Soon, indeed very shortly, I shall be back at my work again, like a man reborn, and I shall not forsake it again until it is completely finished. It is a marvellous passage where I now have to resume composition,[3] having put the finishing touches to a number of earlier passages! It is the most sublime of all scenes for the most tragic of all my heroes, Wotan, who is the all-powerful will-to-exist and who is resolved upon his own self-sacrifice; greater now in renunciation than he ever was when he coveted power, he now feels all-mighty, as he calls out to the earth's primeval wisdom, to Erda, the mother of nature, who had once taught him to fear for his end, telling her that dismay can no longer hold him in thrall since he now wills his own end with that selfsame will with which he had once desired to live. His end? He knows what Erda's primeval wisdom

1 But see letter [330], p. 658.
2 See letter [312], p. 625, note 1.
3 Act III, Scene 1 of *Siegfried*.

does not know: that he lives on in *Siegfried*. Wotan lives on in Siegfried as the artist lives on in his work of art: the freer and the more autonomous the latter's spontaneous existence and the less trace it bears of the creative artist – so that through it (the work of art), the artist himself is forgotten, – the more perfectly satisfied does the artist himself feel: and so, in a certain higher sense, *his* being forgotten, his disappearance, his death is – the life of the work of art. – This is the frame of mind in which I am now turning once again to the completion of my work: I want to be destroyed by my Siegfried – in order to live for ever! O beauteous death! –

With what awesome solemnity shall I now awaken *Brünnhilde* from her long sleep! She slept while Siegfried grew to young manhood. How significant this must all now seem to me! The last music I wrote was the woodbird's announcement to Siegfried that he would be able to waken Brünnhilde if he had not learnt the meaning of fear: laughing, he ran after the bird which, fluttering away, showed him the way to the magic rock. – This road, my gracious, royal friend! – this road was long and arduous for me. I believed I should never, never reach the rock. But, if I am Wotan, I have now succeeded through Siegfried: it is *he* who awakens the maid, the most precious thing in the world. My work of art will live, – it lives! –

[. . .]

Königsbriefe I, 30–1.

315. MATHILDE MAIER, MAINZ   Munich, 31 December 1864

My dear, kind and poor child! I have had myself wheeled over to my desk again today in order to send you one last greeting before the year is over. An ulcer on my lower shin, which at first seemed unworthy of attention, grew more painful as a result of too much exercise to which I subjected myself on Christmas Eve, so that I have been unable to leave my bed since early on Christmas Day, – at least until now, when I am writing to you. I had to put up with this ordeal as a bitter trial of my patience before finally being allowed to quit this strangely wonderful year! But how slight is this suffering in comparison to your own, of which you sent me such sad tidings in your recent letter![1] You cannot believe how utterly disheartened and world-weary it has made me feel, now that I recognize in what hopeless and disconsolate a state all that is dear and precious to me now languishes. And now to have to see such boundless misfortune inflicted upon you of all people – a misfortune, moreover, which you yourself had feared!

---

1 Mathilde Maier suffered from hereditary deafness, a complaint which she felt would make her an unsuitable companion for a musician.

My soul is increasingly rent by sighs and oppressed by the most fearful anxiety: why make a show of getting by when each day brings with it only new and unforeseen torments! – And yet there may still be room for hope in your case! The fact that deafness is endemic in your family must of course be cause for serious concern, and I do not know whether it would not be more humane to prepare for the worst, rather than regard that possibility as something you could not bear to contemplate. For my own part, I must confess that I have often got used to the idea of being completely cut off from the world through the loss of my hearing. I believe I have suffered far more pain than I have ever known enjoyment as a result of all the shameful & vexatious things I have been forced to listen to. How extremely rarely have I felt genuine pleasure on listening to music, and how often, by contrast, has it caused me torment!

I cannot help recalling at this point that for some time my sole endeavour has been to obtain some respite from this sense; if I have made things difficult for myself in settling down and setting up house, it has generally been with the aim of avoiding all irritating noise, so that for some time now I have often maintained, paradoxically, that Beethoven's misfortune was less great than mine; for I have not been allowed to hear what is beautiful and what I longed to hear, being constantly disturbed, instead, by all that is vulgar and loathsome. As a result, my longing for peace and quiet has grown so extreme that, coupled with my other experiences, I have completely cut myself off from any desire to hear my works performed. Even now this resignation gives me all the strength I need to resist unpreparedness, inadequacy and misrepresentation, so that I tell myself that I should prefer *not* to do something rather than do it inadequately. In spite of the enthusiasm of my young King, and in spite of the fact that he has now summoned Semper here to discuss with him a commission to build *my* theatre, – I still do not believe I shall ever really perform my works for myself and the rest of you, since my lack of faith in suitable performers is too great. Even now I would almost prefer not to fall into the temptation of wanting to hear them performed, but rather to enjoy the hushed silence all around me, and, if possible, not to disturb the peace of God. That, in truth, is how I feel! So you can see that it would not be particularly difficult and that it would require very little effort on my part to console you for what you fear will be the loss of your hearing. It occurred to me that it would be far worse for me if I were to go blind: it was objected to this that blind people are normally of a cheerful, calm and deeply contented disposition, whereas deaf people generally become mistrustful and gloomy. Here, too, I could adduce living proof to the contrary in the shape of your dear mother and aunt: in short, you see that it is within myself that I seek consolation for you in your distress, and that it is by no means impossible for me (and for me especially) to feel this. But does that not tell you everything? I know that what is terrible is not death but dying! – But perhaps you already have better news for me concerning the state of your health, indeed, I hope that this is so, for your news has left me deeply and sorely shaken, you poor, poor girl! How happy I should be to receive this comfort from you! – Would you – you of all people – be made very unhappy by it? I can scarcely think so! The very *fact* that I am working creatively and achieving results must mean more to you than *what* I create. Is that not so? –

The Bülows have been here since the 20th of November, and are now completely settled. Peter Cornelius finally arrived yesterday. In February I am expecting the Schnorrs for a brief preliminary visit. In April, May and June Tristan will be rehearsed and performed: I have every hope of obtaining only the very best performers for it, and that they will be entirely in sympathy with me: Mitterwurzer (Dresden – my old Wolfram – a man of sterling qualities) as Kurwenal, Beck (Vienna) as Marke.[1] The performances are to be given in the small Residenz Theatre, not for the general public but for a select audience invited from far & near. That is the point I have now reached. In order to achieve the purity that my style and ideal demand what I now need above all is to exclude all those elements that have to do with existing opera-house routine. Only when we have reached the point at which my work of art is revealed before us in perfect purity and clarity can the wider public be admitted to the new and special theatre built according to my own designs, and then only on special holidays. Otherwise it is impossible to educate them. – Whether I shall achieve this, God only knows! I doubt in nothing, except in my performers and, ultimately, in my own intentions. Disgust! disgust! – It is stronger than any appetite! and, once again – not to hear at all is infinitely more worthy and more desirable than to hear what I have had to hear until now. –

Adieu! My precious child! Courage and patience in the New Year! A thousand good wishes to your family – who are mine as well! Sincere thanks for all your loyalty and love.

Yours,
R.W.

Maier-Briefe 193–6.

316. KING LUDWIG II OF BAVARIA, MUNICH   Munich, 6 January 1865

My adored and angelic friend,
My belovèd King, –

Again and again it is this sweet and gently constraining enchantment which, as though empowered by God, seizes hold of me, of my heart and of my life,

---

1 The part of King Marke was sung by Ludwig Zottmayer from Hanover.

whenever sadness rears its head, and, snatching me back from the abyss, guides me onwards to my highest calling!

When such wondrous tidings arrive as did so again yesterday evening,[1] I feel as though stunned by an electric shock: ardour suffuses my vision; everything around me grows bright and rosily clear: the future becomes the present, and I am once more master of my strength, and of my faith.

What can the word "gratitude" mean here? Only love and a creative act can speak for me here! In me they are both as one! – The love-begotten act, it shall be done! Indeed! – I am enclosing herewith what my most gracious King has desired of me. – For this, too, I am most deeply grateful to him: for it is incentives such as this which render worthwhile all self-preoccupation. Perhaps it may one day benefit the world. It always makes me blissfully happy to be able to fulfil even the slightest wish of the friend whom I adore! –

From the depths of my heart I yearn to be allowed to set eyes again soon on the face of my august patron. My spirits fail me when I must needs be deprived for so long of this sweet consolation.

> Once every year a dove descends from heaven
> to strengthen and confirm its wondrous power![2]

It is this refection which I desire – only more frequently than the Knights of the Grail! –

Filled with the finest and most noble of wishes, overflowing with ardent desires, ever blessèd and raised on high by the miracle which brought me my angel, I remain, perpetually true and grateful, my august friend's most intimate self,

Richard Wagner

Many years ago I intended to collect and publish my writings in an edition which I later abandoned but for which I had drawn up the following programme.[3]

Volume I.   1.   "Art and Revolution." (published in booklet-form.)
2.   "Art and Climate."
(Essay contained in the "Deutsche Monatsschrift", edited by A. Kolatschek between 1850 and 1852.)
3.   "Letter to Liszt concerning the Goethe Foundation" (Neue Zeitschrift für Musik.)
4.   "A Theatre in Zurich." (published in booklet-form.)
5.   Fragments of a plan to reform the theatres in the Kingdom

---

1 A letter from the King welcoming the news of Wagner's recovery, and looking forward to their future collaboration.
2 *Lohengrin* Act III, Scene 3 (GS II,110).
3 When this project was finally realized during the 1870s and 1880s, Wagner ordered his collected works chronologically rather than thematically.

of Saxony. (Manuscript in the possession of Kammer-
musikus Rühlemann in Dresden.)

Volume II.   1. "Letter to Brendel." (Neue Zeitschrift für Musik.)
          2. "Judaism in Music." (in the same place.)
          3. "On Conducting." – (not yet written up.)
          4. "Gluck's Overture to Iphigenia in Aulis" (Neue Zeitschrift für Musik.)
          5. Programme notes.
             a. Beethoven's Symphony No 9.
             b. Beethoven's Symphony No 3 (Eroica)
             c. Beethoven's Overture to Coriolanus.
             d. Overture to the Flying Dutchman.
             e. Overture to Tannhäuser.
             f. Overture to Lohengrin.
          6. On Performing Tannhäuser. (Booklet.)
          7. On Performing the Flying Dutchman. (Manuscript.)

Volume III.   1. "A Pilgrimage to Beethoven." (Novella.)
          2. "The End of a Musician in Paris." Novella. (Both printed in the Abendzeitung in 1840.)
          3. "Le Freischütz." (in the same place.)
          4. "A Happy Evening." (Manuscript – in the possession of Frau Mathilde Wesendonck in Zurich.)
          5. "Parisian Amusements." (Lewald's Europa 1840.)
          6. "Rossini's Stabat Mater." (1840.)
          6. "Virtuosity & free Art." (in French: Gazette Musicale 1840.)
          8. Letters from Paris. (Abendzeitung 1840–41.)

Volume IV.   1. Draft for a Grand Opera "The Saracen Woman" – (Manuscript in the possession of Karl Ritter in Naples.)
          2. Draft for a Grand Musical Drama "Jesus of Nazareth." – (In the possession of Princess Caroline von Wittgenstein – in Bonn.)
          3. Detailed draft for a musical drama: "Wiland the Smith." – (In the possession of Franz Liszt.)
          4. "The Wibelungs." History from Legend. – Published in booklet-form.

          Published complete:
          1. "The Art-Work of the Future." –

2. "Opera and Drama." –
3. "Three Opera Poems."
4. "Tristan and Isolde."
5. "The Mastersingers of Nuremberg."
6. "Music of the Future." A Preface to the French translation of my earlier opera poems.
7. "The Ring of the Nibelung."
8. "On the Court Opera House in Vienna." –

My programme –
to be realized if my precious
King wills it so and helps. –

May and June 1865.

Tristan and Isolde

In the Residenz Theatre, before an invited audience, three to six performances – with Schnorr & his wife, Mitterwurzer (from Dresden) Beck[1] (from Vienna) – Fräulein Stehle[2] (from Munich)

May and June 1866.

Tannhäuser and *Lohengrin*

Complete, revised and performed absolutely correctly, with the collaboration of the above-named, or perhaps even drawing upon newly trained singers. –

Place: Residenz Theatre, or, in exceptionally favourable circumstances, in the large Court Theatre. –

With a revival of *Tristan*. –

August 1867.

Ring of the Nibelung.

In the newly built Festival Theatre. –

August 1868.

Revival of the *Ring of the Nibelung.*

August 1869.

Smaller Festival:
The Mastersingers.
Also perhaps: Tannhäuser & Lohengrin.

August 1870:

The Victors.
also the *Mastersingers.*

August 1871.

Tristan and Isolde. Victors.
Mastersingers.

1 See letter [315], p. 629, note 1.
2 The part of Brangäne was sung by Anna Deinet.

August 1872.

Parzival. –
With repeats.

August 1873.

Ring of the Nibelung.
Before: Tannhäuser. Lohengrin. Tristan.
After: Mastersingers. Victors. Parzival.
May others then follow!

RW.

Königsbriefe I,46–9.

317. ELIZA WILLE, MARIAFELD   Munich, 26 February 1865

My friend,

Two words to set you straight! – You know my retort:[1] here it is again. It contains an insincerity: the account of the limited nature of my relations with the King. In view of my need for peace, I only wish it *were* so. The King's wonderfully profound, fatalistic affection for me. – Although (for the sake of my own peace of mind) I may renounce the privileges which it gives me, I cannot imagine how I could reconcile it with my heart and my conscience to shirk the duties which it imposes upon me. You can guess that those who have been goaded into attacking me in public are only the instruments of others: it is of no significance, and slander even now is playing its last desperate card. But who are the prime movers? I am bound to tremble at the idea of withdrawing within the bounds that are alone conducive to my peace of mind, if, at the same time, I must leave *him* – to *his* entourage. –

My very soul is seized by dread, and I ask my daemon: may not this cup pass away from me? Why, when I sought only peace and the leisure to work undisturbed, why have I become involved in a responsibility in which the salvation of a divinely gifted man, and perhaps even a country's welfare, has been placed in my hands? – How can I save my heart here? And how then can I remain an artist? – *He lacks the person he most needs!* – It is this – this – which is my real predicament. The superficial game of intrigue, which is calculated purely to drive me frantic and thus to lure me into committing some indiscretion, will soon fall in on itself. But what energy would it require – an energy which would wrest my peace of mind from me for evermore – to wrest my young friend from his entourage! – He remains true to me, with a loyalty that is touching in its beauty, and for the present he denies himself to everyone. –

---

1 An anonymous attack entitled "Richard Wagner und die öffentliche Meinung" (Richard Wagner and Public Opinion) had appeared in the Augsburg *Allgemeine Zeitung* of 19 February 1865, and provoked a riposte from Wagner three days later; see introductory essay, p. 589.

What do you say to my fate? – My longing for ultimate peace is beyond belief: my heart cannot bear any more of these deceitful goings-on! – Sincere good wishes to Wille!

Yours truly,
Rich. Wagner.

Wille-Briefe 87–8.

318. KING LUDWIG II OF BAVARIA, MUNICH   [Munich,] 9 March 1865

My King,
My belovèd friend,
So must I take up my pen, that I may end a situation which cannot be allowed to last a moment longer if my very soul is not to be consumed!

What this state of mine must be my understanding friend may judge for himself! –

On the 6th of February this year, at 1 o'clock, a most terrible thing happened to me: I was turned away from the door of my august friend, having appeared there at his kind invitation, and was led back down to the courtyard. It was not my king's indisposition but his great displeasure at me[1] which was adduced as the reason for this rebuff. Ever since that day more and more rumours have been circulating concerning the disfavour I am said to have incurred. Finally, certain accusations have been clearly levelled at me, accusations which I have no hesitation in declaring complete fabrications and which – if necessary – I shall denounce as such in public. My most gloomy assumptions and most anxious doubts have been countered, finally, by my friend's most gracious words which, in their kingly beauty and dignity, at once attest to the fact that my complete innocence has never for a moment been doubted, indeed – the whole tissue of lies may never even have affected my august friend. And yet no entreaty on the part of one who has suffered so much, nor any promise on that of my friend whose favours have made me supremely happy has so far led to the fulfilment of my most ardent wish, which is that I might approach my noble patron and speak with him face to face.[2] Even the recent heaven-sent opportunity provided by the presence of the artist Schnorr, whom Your Majesty had Yourself summoned to Munich, was transformed – for reasons which I still fail to understand – into a rebuttal, directly involving a demonstrable lie, so that my affable singer, perplexed and saddened, found himself, like me, turned away from your door. –

1 See introductory essay, p. 589.
2 This is untrue. Wagner had been received by Ludwig on 17 February, and had "assured" him of his "innocence" (BB 143; English trans. 120).

During this period of bewilderment, certain written communications and effusions reached me from my august friend, showering me, as it were, with a heavenly radiance whose contents reveal to me a world of wonderment and beauty, a world of which my soul has only ever dreamt but which my astonished gaze has never yet beheld. I admit that the love which is here made manifest gives me no privileges, rather does it impose obligations upon me, sacred and sublime obligations which must render me utterly indifferent to my own well-being. Were I concerned solely for the latter, I should have no compelling reason to regard my situation as at all intolerable, even as things stand at present: – I may well hope that my public declarations are sufficient to defend myself against a repetition of the most unworthy attacks to which I have here been subjected in the most pitiless manner. The advantages of my external position, which I owe to the munificence of my noble patron, remain as before; nor has any perceptible hindrance been placed in the way of my artistic aims, since it must be evident to all that these aims are also those of the sublime friend of my art. And so, were I concerned solely for myself, I could easily follow the advice which I have been given, and allow the affair to run its course. – But I feel that the artist and the man in me, which ignorant fools would seemingly wish to separate, have become inextricably linked. My heart grows weary, and so my spirit, too, begins to sicken. I cannot, and may not, bear to remain apart from my adored friend, while knowing myself so close to him. Were I to tolerate this situation, I should inevitably suffer the self-reproach of believing that in some way I had abused your royal favour: I shudder at the insane falsehood of this reproach, and arm myself against it with the pride which is necessary to face far worse tribulations, rather than silently render myself culpable of so degrading an admission. –

Yet how shall I now express the thought which this pride inspires in me? How shall I explain my necessary resolve to this divinely pure heart which enfolds me in its heavenly goodness, and devotes its own happiness to *my* redemption?

Here is the fearful abyss! –

If everything here were not so profound, so noble and so divinely tender, how simple it might seem to a man as sorely tormented and aweary of life as I myself to call out to his gracious friend: –

"My King! – I have brought you disquiet: – let me go, let me leave you for some distant land, where the gaze of envy and ignorance will not pursue me: –

Apart – who can divide us?

Divided – still we are one![1]–

And yet – how can I bring myself to do this without causing my heart to

---

1 *Cf* Brünnhilde's words to Siegfried in the Prelude to *Götterdämmerung* (GS VI,186).

break asunder, when, deep within that heart, I feel the place which I hold within *your* heart? I, who draws new life and renewed inspiration from a single glance from your eyes, – could I of all men misprize the boundless import of personal contact, of the closeness of one man to another? – Only he who is under a spell can himself cast spells: – I, too, feel what I am to my friend; – he alone can break the spell that lies upon me, – he alone can say to me: – "Be gone." – – – I – cannot! –

What shall I do now? – I have poured out my heart: but how can I have unburdened it when I have merely shifted its burden to the heart of my friend? – What shall I do? What advice shall I give? – –

Well then! – I know that hatred cannot show me the way out: – love alone can do so! My sacred, noble love for my angel! –

I cannot feel hatred! My strongest emotion in this direction is merely – loathing! – If, as a child, I flinched from the spider out of disgust, I have long since learnt to overcome even *this* feeling: I can explain the spider, I recognize its needs, its subjection to toil and suffering, like all living things; I may perhaps side against it to the extent of rescuing the fly which would otherwise be trapped in the predator's web, but I could not possibly crush the spider itself, as I would have done as a child with a sense of passionate loathing! – Here you have my confession, my gracious friend! I can, and shall, forgive all who have had a hand in spinning this loathsome web which on this occasion has fallen apart of its own accord. I can understand the aberrations and fears which fill the ignorant and uninitiated with cares whose motives I would not interpret as wholly impure but which may even, perhaps, in part be justified: the fact that the artist is so little esteemed I am willing to ascribe to the disregard in which art itself is commonly held, a disregard for which there is, alas, justification enough in view of its present effectiveness, as I myself have had cause to realize. How could such people understand the mind of the wondrously gifted prince whom the stars themselves have chosen to see what none but he could see, that, on *this* occasion and in the case of *this* artist, the situation is quite unlike anything they have otherwise encountered, and utterly beyond their grasp? – Of course, it all makes sense to me: I can, and must, be fair. If *I* must impute an action to others, I do not accuse them of it: – I – forgive them, and know that repentance will be my reward. –

And so I declare that no one shall suffer at my hands: let deepest oblivion veil all that has happened! Not another word shall pass my lips on the matter. He who has dealt most perniciously with me shall be the first to see how intense are my efforts to gain his understanding and his respect – perhaps even his love.

This is my solemn declaration. –

I lay it reverently at my redeemer's feet.

May it enable him to gaze into my eyes once more! For there is one thing alone that I seek to obtain, and must indeed do so: the free and unhindered enjoyment of the inspiriting company which my gracious friend and King alone can provide. –

Do I deserve this single privilege, for the sake of which I would gladly forgo all others in the eyes of the world? –

I – hope so!

Faithful unto death,
Richard Wagner[1]

Königsbriefe I,68–71.

319. KING LUDWIG II OF BAVARIA, MUNICH   Munich, 12 March 1865

Your most serene Highness,
Most mighty King and Lord,

I have finally come to believe that Your Majesty's most gracious commission to ensure as exemplary a presentation as possible of my as yet unperformed lyric drama "Tristan and Isolde" may be adequately realized only if I myself assume direction of all the necessary rehearsals. However, experience has shown me that, if I am to superintend not only the purely musical aspect of the rehearsals but also the stage production as well with the necessary degree of circumspection, it is imperative that I should be excused from assuming direct leadership of the orchestra, more especially for the rehearsals, since I know such involvement to be beyond my mental and physical resources. However, I could only contemplate what would be a considerable and highly desirable lightening of my burden of responsibility if I knew that the orchestral direction had been entrusted to a musician who was entirely familiar with the task in hand, right down to its very last details, and who was, moreover, extremely close to me. To expect the highly respected General Music Director F. Lachner to offer me the necessary support would mean placing this eminent maestro in an almost improper position, whereby he would not only be subordinate to me but would have to conform to whatever instructions I might have for him. Since I cannot for a moment suppose that any of the subordinate conductors of the Royal Court Orchestra possess the qualities necessary for my purpose, and more especially a detailed knowledge of my intentions, I find myself in the very situation which Your Majesty foresaw when he most graciously summoned Dr Hans von Bülow here, a man who is particularly close to me, and who is everywhere highly reputed as a consummate musician.

Accordingly I make so bold as to submit this most humble entreaty to Your Majesty, begging that Your Highness might deign to permit and instruct the King's Own Performer Dr Hans von Bülow to conduct the Royal Court

1 For Ludwig's reply, see Appendix A, p. 937.

Orchestra at the rehearsals and, if necessary, also at the performances of my work "Tristan and Isolde". Since custom, moreover, requires that special authority be granted here, an authority granted only to those of Your Majesty's civil servants appointed to conduct Your Majesty's orchestra but which, in special cases, may be additionally vested in the composer of the work to be performed, it will be necessary to provide Dr Hans von Bülow with the requisite authority, for which reason I most humbly beseech Your Majesty most graciously to confer upon my friend the title of Extraordinary Royal Kapellmeister whose duty it will be to conduct the Royal Court Orchestra at Your Majesty's especial command, if and when the occasion arises. –

It gives me great satisfaction to know that, by expressing this wish and submitting my most humble entreaty, I have not only indicated the means whereby the arrangements which my august patron has so generously made in favour of the most perfect possible performance of my work may now be regarded as truly complete, but at the same time to have recommended as our collaborator in this enterprise a man of many parts who is also an artist of such extensive knowledge and especial aptitude for our present requirements that I am now in a position of being able to offer the most complete guarantee for the success of his achievements in every possible respect.

In the expectation of a gracious reply to my most humble entreaty, I remain, in respectful loyalty and devotion,

Your Majesty's
most obedient subject
Richard Wagner

Königsbriefe I, 74–5.

320. MATHILDE MAIER, MAINZ   [Munich,] 17 March 1865

[. . .]'s[1] visit to you is an anachronism: I have long since outlived him; for me he is no more than an occasional diversion. He is one of those whom I construed for my own ends in order to have a share in him: now that I have finally noticed *what* it is that I really have, I see that it is simply what he himself is, and not a whit more. A strange mixture of imagination & shallowness: utterly childish by nature, and belonging only to the present moment.

But he often amuses me with his good ideas [. . .].[1] As a person he is of no value to me whatsoever: I have finally had to admit as much, it has now

1 In spite of attempts to render this and the later passage illegible, it is clear that Wagner's venom is directed here at Cornelius, who had passed through Mainz on his way to Weimar, where *Der Cid* was being rehearsed.

become inevitable, especially now. Bülow has energy and perseverance – if only the poor devil enjoyed better health: but of all men he is the closest to me; and I know that he loves me in a loyal and genuine way. –

None of them has been of any use to me in my present situation, they have only made my sufferings worse.

My dearest child, I am too tired and sensitive to endure much more of the kind of distress that I have just been through. I asked him why, in the name of heaven, I should not entreat the King to allow me to write my works for him in Naples, where I could work just as well, if not better, than here, where envy and ignorance stir things up between us. I must live among people who interest me purely as a spectacle: those with whom I may have to deal I can no longer tolerate. Well, the King will not let me go, and so I am resigned to waiting a few more years before fulfilling my last remaining fond ambition – Italy. –

No one has proved of any lasting worth in the recent storm, except for me and the King. He is my only real friend, – and certainly the stars have destined him for me: he belongs to *me*, he *cannot* do otherwise, – and so – I belong to him. During this recent period, when his mother left no stone unturned in her efforts to tear him away from me, he did not bat an eye: he has survived every test with heavenly purity and loyalty. –

His letters during these weeks have been utterly divine! – My dearest, I *must*, because he – *wills* it so!

That's how it is! –

[. . .]

Maier-Briefe 202–3.

321. KING LUDWIG II OF BAVARIA, MUNICH [Munich,] 21 March 1865

My noble and glorious friend,
My beautiful will and loving providence,

Heartfelt thanks for your inspiriting greeting! – I am at present engaged in writing a great essay[1] which I shortly intend to submit to my august patron: its immediate cause was the invitation which I received to report on the future of the local Conservatoire, whose existence is now so seriously threatened. Once again, and for the last time – but this time in the energetic hope that I shall not have expended any wasted efforts upon it – , I am summarizing

1 *Bericht an Seine Majestät den König Ludwig II. von Bayern über eine in München zu errichtende deutsche Musikschule* (Report to His Majesty King Ludwig II of Bavaria concerning a German School of Music to be established in Munich), dated 31 March 1865 and submitted to Ludwig on 6 April 1865. Printed in GS VIII,125–76; PW IV,171–224.

all my experiences in order to lay at your feet the final fruits of my deliberations, so that the thought therein expressed, fructified by the will of my
glorious friend, may become an act which forms and fosters a noble art.

Fate – which has so fatally obstructed all my creative endeavours – has
imposed this mission upon me: I must strive to establish what my King is
called upon to execute.

Deep within me I feel that, without such a hope, my creativity, too, would
now be paralysed. If I am to execute all my plans in the only way that I now
know how, then I must have before me a constant image of the intended
performance: since my return to Germany, however, I have been so appalled
by my contact with our theatres that I now feel a genuine loathing and a
desperate sense of disgust whenever I look beyond these plans of mine to the
reality of present artistic conditions. My powers of imagination grow paralysed,
and I feel that it is now high time for me to build up my courage and faith
again by means of some fine and cheering experience.

That I may finally look forward to so decisive an improvement I owe to my
beloved guardian angel, an angel made flesh as man and king. To the forthcoming performance of Tristan I attach a value which I see as definitive. It
is now six years since I completed this work, and yet I have until now been
unable to perform it. What has this experience not meant for me! – But now
it is to happen. What will be achieved cannot be properly assessed as yet.
But, whatever happens, the performance will be one of the rarest and most
momentous of all artistic acts: for my ideal will be brought fully to life here,
an ideal which is the dramatico-musical embodiment of the thought of which
I have spoken; what I could previously only hint at will here find lucid
expression. If I had not found so highly gifted an artist as Schnorr, if he had
not been trained entirely by me and for me, and if he had not been completely
devoted to me, the solution of my task would have remained impossible. He
is utterly loyal in his love for me, and his tender-hearted docility in learning
from my most gentle hints has once again completely enchanted me. He –
another *Ludwig* – will be perfect. For Isolde I shall have to make do as best
I can for now: *not one* of the relatively good singers who are available at
present and who are known to me personally has inspired in me the hope of
seeing this exceedingly difficult task overcome. Like her husband, Frau
Schnorr is on the most friendly terms with me: for years she has lived for
this task, and has made it her own with all the enthusiasm of true friendship.
She will surprise everyone, perhaps even my august friend, whose demands
in these matters are justifiably high: I am certain of that. For she is a true
artist, possessing a quality which, most happily, often makes up for the most
dazzling of natural talents which commonly serve only the world's vanity. As
Kurwenal, Mitterwurzer will be just as admirable as Schnorr himself: he
belongs to me, and is my faithful pupil. For Marke it was, alas, not possible
to obtain the admirable Beck from Vienna: but many gratifying observations

during recent weeks allow me to hope that, spurred on by the achievements of my friends, I shall succeed in making the already most commendably talented Kindermann more than adequately effective in this touching role.[1]

My kind master and friend has given me great joy by allowing the loyal Bülow to assume direction of the orchestra: only now do I set about my work without hesitation, and may hope to withstand the great emotions and exertions of the coming rehearsals without any danger to myself. A thousand sincere thanks for such sensitive and thoughtful concern for my needs! –

And so Tristan, this child of my sorrow, shall be born into the world noble and free, to the greater glory of my wondrous redeemer! –

The sweet lord of my life will soon hear more – much more – from me. My great essay shall be in his gracious hands by the end of this month!

Faithful in body and soul to my most glorious friend, and devoted unto death,

Richard Wagner

Königsbriefe I, 76–7.

322. King Ludwig II of Bavaria, Munich Munich, 14 April 1865

My adored and wonderful friend,

How joyful, and how sad, it must make me to think of you! At one moment my heart leaps, and beats more proudly, when I hear how fair, how glorious and how secure is the path which my royal angel treads, arousing amazement and enchantment on every side: but at the next moment I am bound to grow fearful and anxious when I hear that he is ill, unhappy and hindered. And all this close at hand, yet so remote that I feel as though it is merely a dream. – How strange a destiny! How extraordinary, how curious it all is, like a fairytale which, in turn, has actually come to life for me! –

My dearly belovèd, unique and most glorious friend! With tears in my eyes I ask: – How are you? Are you sad? Are you happy? – How does my most gracious monarch feel? –

Today is Good Friday again! – O, blessèd day! Most deeply portentous day in the world! Day of redemption! God's suffering!! Who can grasp the enormity of it? And yet, this same ineffable mystery – is it not the most familiar of mankind's secrets? God, the Creator, – he must remain totally unintelligible to the world: – God, the loving teacher, is dearly belovèd, but not understood: – but the God who suffers, – His name is inscribed in our hearts in letters of fire; all the obstinacy of existence is washed away by our immense pain at seeing God suffering! The teaching which we could not

1 See letter [315] p. 629, note 1.

comprehend, it now affects us: God is within us, – the world has been overcome! Who created it? An idle question! Who overcame it? God within our hearts, – God whom we comprehend in the deepest anguish of fellow-suffering! –

A warm and sunny Good Friday, with its mood of sacred solemnity, once inspired me with the idea of writing "Parzival":[1] since then it has lived on within me and prospered, like a child in its mother's womb. With each Good Friday it grows a year older, and I then celebrate the day of its conception, knowing that its birthday will follow one day. – Last Good Friday[2] I spent as a fugitive in Munich: I was travelling around at the time, but did not wish to continue my journey that day; sick and suffering, I hoped for a good night's rest. I crept through the streets of the town: the weather was raw, and overcast. The townsfolk in mourning surged out of the various churches and over the city squares. In a little side-street, in a picture-dealer's window, I first caught sight of the picture of the youthful successor of the monarch who had just departed this life. I was held enthralled by the ineffable charm of those inconceivably soulful features. I sighed. "Were he not your King, you would no doubt wish to make his acquaintance", – I said to myself. "Now he is King, he cannot find out about you!" Silent and lonely, I wandered on. – Sad though I was, I none the less marked my "Parzival's" day of conception – this Good Friday, too – indeed, the picture in the little side-street had brought me instinctively back to my hero: the young King and Parzival merged into one; a presentiment dimly dawned – I was so utterly lacking in hope! – and soon it became a memory; I recalled the sunny Good Friday of that first conception. A loving and tenderly devoted woman's heart[3] had at that time taken me into its care and protection: the hope that I had cherished for years had now come to pass; I had been able to move into a little house of my own, with its own attractive garden, wonderfully situated with a splendid view over Lake Zurich and the Alps. I sat there – it was the first fine spring day! – on the verandah of my refuge, the bells were ringing, – the birds were singing, the first flowers gazed up at me; it was then, in the depths of my ecstasy, that Parzival was conceived! – I now wanted to return to Lake Zurich, to see whether I could find another little house there, peaceful and isolated. Overcast and cold outside, no hope within me, – tired, longing for death, – what were the thoughts that did not pass through my mind that last Good Friday, here in Munich, – near to the supreme and glorious radiance of my life, the sun which was to illumine my night, my redeemer, the saviour of my existence! –

It is – wonderful, – for it is more wondrous than anything any poet could ever invent! –

1 This myth, perpetuated in *Mein Leben* (561; English trans. 547), has long since proved to be a fabrication; see, for example, Barry Millington, *Wagner* (London 1984), 62–3.
2 25 March 1864.
3 Mathilde Wesendonck.

Yes! *He* found me!
My adored friend! – Could I ever leave him? – –
Enough! – thus did I celebrate Good Friday! –
Now "Tristan" has been born; he is growing and prospering: each day brings us renewed cause for celebration, – a feast of celebration in honour of King "Parzival"! –

> Truly yours for all eternity –
> Richard Wagner

Königsbriefe I, 82–4.

323. ANTON PUSINELLI, DRESDEN   Munich, 6 May 1865

My dear friend,
Impossible to ignore you now! – My dearest Anton, if you can manage it, come to my "Tristan". The performances are definitively fixed for the 15th, 18th & 22nd of May.[1] If you come, spare my wife, and *don't say a word to her about it*. It has now reached the point where all contact with her leaves me feeling hurt and embittered, since she is & remains the one person who will *never* really understand me. See if you can manage it, and – come. You will experience something of which you cannot have even the remotest idea: the performance will be nothing short of *wonderful*. I invite you to stay at the Bayerischer Hof as my guest. I shall see you only infrequently – I am extremely overwrought & need to be shown endless consideration. But you will hear from me. You shall also have my *bust*[2] – in any case. – Write to me! Forgive me for being so brief! remember me with affection! Come and – say nothing! –

> Cordially yours,
> Richard Wagner

RWA (incompletely published in Freunde und Zeitgenossen 441–2).

324. KING LUDWIG II OF BAVARIA, BERG   Munich, 17 May 1865

My noble and august friend,
My fairest, supreme consolation,
May love's most heartfelt greetings go with you to your delightful Berg! – How happy it makes me to know that this change of scene will do you good!

---

1 Four performances were given on 10, 13, 19 June, and 1 July 1865.
2 By Caspar Zumbusch.

I desire only the greatest uniformity and peace: this is the outcome of a life which has always been most severely disturbed when I most needed peace and oblivion. And so I cling to this final refuge, which your heavenly love has provided for me: I tremble at the thought of setting foot outside the house and of walking through my small garden, since I do not know what misfortune might suddenly prevent me from returning to this final haven of peace. Oh! my sweet King! I have *you* – and nothing more in the world. Everything else that I am fond of belongs to me only in the way that the clothes I wear belong to me: only to you can I say: to *you* do *I* belong! –

My most heartfelt need drives me to be totally open with you: I feel as though I would be deceiving myself if for any reason I were to leave you in the dark concerning me. It is impossible for me to pretend to be serenely contented when I am sad at heart. Love was always the final refuge of utter sincerity, a sincerity which – not least for reasons of pride – must so often be hidden from the world. – In reply to your question which yesterday evening impressed itself upon me with such unearthly beauty and gentleness, I said I was calm and serious! – As recently as yesterday I had to suffer the most distressing and – the most elevating of experiences. – My old daemon was roused from his sleep, and put paid to the efforts of all my friends who had come from far and wide, at immense sacrifice to themselves. The news that Tristan cannot now be given before next week had a shattering effect upon all of them, wringing bitter tears from many of the men, and bringing others close to despair. Poor *Klindworth* had come from London *just* for this *one* day, having obtained leave of absence only with the most incredible difficulty, and at the price of the most humiliating sacrifices: he set off back again this morning, naturally without any possibility of returning. Two poor musicians[1] came from Königsberg in Prussia, travelling 3rd-class on a cheap goods-train, with only the prospect of Tristan to sustain them throughout their three-day journey. In Pest a number of poor musicians obtained release from their duties thanks to all manner of sacrifices: others, from Weimar for ex., set off without having been able to obtain leave, at risk of losing their posts. These poor wretches were thunderstruck by the news: – in order to comfort them, I finally had to go and speak with them; they soon came to share my emotion: with genuine enthusiasm I persuaded them that, having already made such sacrifices as these, they should now risk even more; for what I could promise them was – I said – a hitherto unprecedented act of great artistic beauty. Almost all of them – – *are remaining*!!

Is that not wonderful, my King? –

Your heavenly letter reached me while I was with them. They will all be

1 Louis Köhler and Adolf Jensen.

photographed with me today at Albert's:[1] may I send the group photograph to my dearest friend, too? Only poor Klindworth will not be on it! –

Indeed, my belovèd King! I am much loved! The modesty of these loyal friends, who wished to spare me all sight of their pain, has touched me deeply, and once again has made me feel a deep sense of earnest! –

All the love which has here been bestowed on me I lay at the feet of my lord who is loved above all else! May he bring happiness to his people, may he one day raise Germany from her sunken state: the love which so many pure souls bear me is of a quite especial kind: I dedicate it to you as the sweet May-flower of my life. My angel will not, I think, spurn its perfume! –

Uniquely true to the one I worship,

Yours,

Richard W.

Königsbriefe I,99–100.

325. KING LUDWIG II OF BAVARIA, BERG   [Munich,] 13 June 1865

My most beautiful, supreme and only consolation,

The words of Marke[2] which you are kind enough to apply to my work require completion:

"Who (with pride – ??) may call it *his*?!"

Oh, my King! It is yours, it is your work! I no longer have a part in it. It was born in pain such as no mother ever suffered for her child. It no longer belongs to me. But does it belong to the world? To each of us belongs only what he himself can appropriate. I no longer care to think of it. Like the man of religion – I need a symbol in which to comprehend everything. And you are my symbol, – my sacred Parzival!

My supreme and ultimate happiness! My King! My – friend! My consummation! My victorious Siegfried – victor – bringer of peace! – Who can tell you anything about me that I myself cannot tell you? *We* – lack a friend! But – if this friendly soul existed, – how could I approach you? – Should I complain when my belovèd lord has every right to demand only joy and a noble reward? – I cannot, nor will I – : yet I am afraid that much may be left undone. I am afraid my belovèd may not receive the reward which he has so gloriously earned, and for which alone I still care to live, in order that I might bestow it upon him.

---

1 Joseph Albert produced a series of group photographs; see, for example, H. Barth, D. Mack and E. Voss (eds), *Wagner: A Documentary Study* (London 1975), No. 138.

2 In his letter to Wagner of 12 June Ludwig had paraphrased Marke's words in Act II, Scene 3 of *Tristan und Isolde* to describe the "wondrous sublime work which your spirit created" (*cf* GS VII,54).

Yet – one thing has been achieved! This wayward Tristan has been completed. You know that all who have written poems about Tristan have left them incomplete – from Gottfried von Strassburg onwards. It almost seemed as though my own work, too, were to be dogged by the same misfortune: for – it was not complete until it actually came alive for us, as a drama, and spoke directly to our hearts and senses. – This has been achieved. The age-old love-poem, it now lives and speaks aloud to the common folk who bear touching witness to their having been stirred by it. What we – my noble belovèd – have achieved *with* this completion is something which you shall one day judge for yourself! I say so quite boldly: *Our* Tristan, as it will today resound and shudder once more, can be compared to naught of its kind. And this was – your doing! Thus has my gracious King *begun*! – That must mean something, something grave and profound! – All hail to him! – He will find the right people: – what do I myself matter, I the individual! –

The most abundant blessings of all noble hearts to my belovèd, to him who has been chosen by God! What is success, what is failure? To be, to *be* what is right – that is everything! –

Listen! The old yearning melodies are beginning!

Truly yours for all eternity –
Richard Wagner

Königsbriefe I, 106.

326. LUDWIG AND MALVINA SCHNORR VON CAROLSFELD, MUNICH
Munich, 20 June 1865

My dear, kind friends,

So! now you may rest![1] The incomparable has been achieved. And if, one day, the fruits of the most characteristic and German art are really to ripen – an art which I nurture within my spirit and which, in its depth and beauty, must surpass all else that other nations have ever created for their own greater glory, so you may be certain that you dear people will never be forgotten by the world, for your deeds have marked the onset of spring, a spring which gave warmth to my work, and strength and light to my artistic urge! –

We cannot praise ourselves in this way: we put forth shoots, we blossom and flourish together, each of us through the other! Intimately familiar, we work as one! –

And now – rest! You have earned the right to remain silent henceforth, if it pleases you to do so. What you have accomplished must remain imperishable in its influence! –

1 i.e. after the first three performances of *Tristan und Isolde*. In fact the Schnorrs were summoned back from Tegernsee, where they had gone to recover, for a fourth performance on 1 July.

If the weather proves clement, I would suggest that the three of us should set out, tomorrow perhaps, in search of relaxation and recreation!

Let me know whether this is acceptable! –

Wholly yours,
Richard Wagner.

Freunde und Zeitgenossen 447–8.

327. KING LUDWIG II OF BAVARIA, BERG   Munich, 5 July 1865

My dear, belovèd lord and friend,

In response to your wonderfully beautiful letter from Linderhof I could reply in no other way than by – the sounds of my Tristan![1] – My King, I am not well: life has become a burden for me, and my artistic labours are far from easy. The whole effort, moreover, of reviving so strange a work as Tristan has left me very tired. What depresses me is not the malice of the world – but the extreme difficulty of working effectively and creatively, so that I feel like a stranger, almost like a fool, in this world of ours, and in this century. Every step requires the effort of a long and wearisome journey: may I still hope that I shall one day succeed in feeling completely at home in this world and this century? Would it not be better to withdraw from it entirely? If I am to be properly understood, I must always refer to this basic frame of mind whenever I tell you anything about myself – you who are my dearest and most sympathetic listener. Only on this basis do I once more discover the familiar, more light-hearted manner in which, without the need for hypocrisy, I can again discuss what I intend shall give pleasure to my belovèd lord. – Let me now try to strike that note again: how gladly do I do so! –

I am making provisions for the concert which you desire me to give.[2] It shall be performed entirely on the lines which you yourself have indicated. I am having great difficulty in including anything from the "Rhinegold": I need certain resources such as are not yet at my disposal here: but I shall succeed in letting you hear the end of the piece, from Donner's storm incantation onwards. I am also performing something from the Mastersingers which has not previously been heard but which Schnorr's presence has persuaded me to include: Walther before the Masters. I shall shortly be drawing up a detailed programme which I shall submit to my most precious lord.

This concert would be possible as early as Sunday or Monday, if the flying Dutchman had not already been requested in its place. Poor Mitterwurzer

---

1 Ludwig's letter of 29 June 1865 was followed by the fourth, and last, performance of *Tristan und Isolde* on 1 July.

2 A concert of vocal and orchestral excerpts from Wagner's works was given in the Residenz Theatre on 12 July 1865. A performance of *Der fliegende Holländer* had preceded it on 9 July.

seemed really ill; he could not be prevailed upon to perform this role, too. It seems, however, that my noble friend has laid especially kind emphasis upon a presentation of the flying Dutchman: for that reason it must, no doubt, be given, and it certainly affords Schnorr the keenest pleasure to be allowed to meet his royal patron's wishes, and to do so, moreover, with such great eagerness: only I myself feel somewhat mortified in the face of the forthcoming performance, when I think that we must inevitably expect a great step backwards from the point we had so successfully reached with Tristan. –

The concert would then follow a few days after the flying Dutchman. – My gracious King has yet to be kind enough to reply to the anxious request which I addressed to him a few days before the last performance of Tristan;[1] but I live in the hope that it will not be long in coming. – My King! Your love, your favour and your affection for my art, as for my person, impose grave responsibilities upon me. The measure which I resolved to propose to you is an important and powerful link in a chain which must be completely closed if I am to succeed in my mission to redeem a degenerate branch of our great, human art. The choice here means either that music as an art continues to be merely entertaining and, if so wished, pleasantly gratifying, a kind of art which we may occasionally enlist for festive occasions or for our more basic enjoyment, and which we consequently put up with as best we can; or, at very least, it will assume the same importance that was allotted to painting in the 16th century, when the cardinal's mitre could be destined for Raphael, and aristocratic honours awarded to the least of his helpers. Music as *I* intend it can and should mean more to this century and to the people of all ages than painting could ever mean to that century and to humanity in general. This is my belief. Well, there are only two things I can do: – I can go completely quiet and disappear completely; or – in everything that I create and achieve I can strive and take soundings in accordance with this belief of mine. –

I know that you, my glorious friend, have been sent to me by God in order that my belief shall become a religion. To establish ourselves we need to break away entirely from the old way of perceiving things. No one can advise you to do anything that he himself cannot grasp. But I shall never advise my King to do anything that is not also just and fair, in addition to being well-founded in practical terms, and feasible. No one, however, can pass judgement on the practicability and feasibility of measures the sense and significance of which escapes him. There are many demonstrations of my august friend's supreme and unshakeable trust in the unswerving integrity, well-considered suitability and proven feasibility of my proposals which, in the service of my mission, I still have to demand of him. I know exactly what my first request

---

1 In his letter to the King of 29 June 1865 Wagner had proposed the setting up of a commission to improve the conditions of the members of the Court Orchestra.

in this respect is intended to achieve, and I may testify that its aim can be understood only by those who, like my King, feel so deep and noble a sensitivity towards art that, inspired by that love, they will not find it difficult to exercise a sense of justice here, too. Perhaps this justice will be attended by difficulties: all the more necessary, then, to practise it! –

In the most sincere trust and boundless love I greet my august friend as

His most faithful of all friends

Richard Wagner

Königsbriefe I, 117–19.

328. KING LUDWIG II OF BAVARIA, BERG   [Munich, 21/]22 July 1865

Most belovèd of men, dear and glorious friend,

When I received your letter yesterday, I was seized by the liveliest desire to set out at once and visit you in the mountains. How happy you must be! Greater than the poet: the poet's fulfilled ideal!

I am once again reliving my youth with you, save that, in your case, the anxious dream has become a welcome reality. I, too, was fond of roving, of fleeing into the mountains, and of rediscovering myself on lofty heights. No school could teach me the ideas that I formed there. But everything was effortful, cramped and forced: faced by so wretched a reason for living, I often came to look on my rovings, longings and effusive outbursts as a failing worthy only of reproach. I was often in fact subject to censure; it seemed, people said, that "I had been right royally spoilt". – This is now my experience with my friend: see how free and noble everything appears here! Yes, that is why he is King, a King who is equally well suited to being a poet! – How beautiful, how beautiful indeed it is for me to have been granted the miracle of truly witnessing and enjoying the dream which my soul had long cherished! – Beware, my belovèd friend! My works will soon have no real significance left for us; but only for the world to which they can give notice of what we *are* to each other: their substance is now the object of our own experience! –

What was I doing when your letter arrived here yesterday? – To spare you the effort of guessing, I shall tell you what it was: – I was dictating my biography![1] Friend Cosima never tires of reminding me of our King's wish. Every available hour I now fill by faithfully retelling what my friend then carefully writes down. She is amazed that it is all so fluent, as though I were reading aloud from a book. I am still at the stage of my early years, and she often bursts out laughing as I dictate to her: what joy! The poor child will soon have much cause for weeping, for the years are approaching which cost

---

1 *Mein Leben*, which Wagner had begun dictating to Cosima on 17 July.

me ever more melancholy experiences. We have decided to continue the dictation up to the time of my association with you, my dear and glorious King: from then on Cosima shall continue the biography on her own, and, I hope, she will one day complete it. She is best placed to do so, and will bring it to a most splendid conclusion. She has covered 42 sides so far: we have reached my fifteenth year. It will be fairly voluminous, for only now does my real life begin: also, we are constantly interrupted, and the time is now approaching when I hope to be able to devote myself to the resumption of my work with real perseverance. How I yearn to do so: for ultimately I can recover completely and fully from all the misery of the world and all the suffering brought about by my shattered nerves only if I can sit at my desk and work. And yet I create my work for you alone for whom I live! Believe me, even our friend[1] helps me only to live for you! –

What childlike pleasure your gifts have given me, my belovèd! In time, I can see, all of the ornaments which I bought elsewhere will disappear, in order to make room solely for my friend's remembrances, rich in associations as they are. I still had to thank you for the Lohengrin statuette when, much to my genuine amazement, the Tannhäuser painting[2] arrived. I almost regretted having said that I found it interesting, since my dearest friend thought he must deprive himself of it for my sake. Our friend Cosima soon helped me out, however, by claiming that these gifts are valuable and meaningful precisely because they cost the giver such very real sacrifices.

In truth, my dearest friend! The painting enthrals me greatly. It belongs to a style which was created by Cornelius[3] and which is characteristically cultivated in Ille's work: it reproduces and, as it were, complements, the view of the classical Middle Ages in the way one might assume poetic objects would have been depicted in art if painting had developed to the same pitch as medieval poetry. That is why this style will never be free from the reproach of a certain affectation and artistic pretence, and I believe that, with my own poems and stage directions, I have demonstrated that the objects of the Middle Ages can be depicted in a more ideal, more purely human and more generally valid manner than this school of painting sets out to achieve. The painter who can match my own conception is therefore no doubt still to be found. None the less, this water-colour of the Tannhäuser Ballad, for ex., remains an enthralling and characterful work which I, for one, find uncommonly attractive. My most sincere thanks to its most affectionate donor for such a beautiful gift! –

Yesterday – or the day before – I finally received Semper's plans[4] back again. I have now studied them in detail, and find them admirable, original,

1 Cosima.
2 By Eduard Ille (see CT for 14 February 1873).
3 The painter Peter von Cornelius.
4 For the projected Festival Theatre.

beautiful, and highly suited to their purpose. I was saddened by the letter which friend Pfistermeister enclosed with the consignment: even now the poor man does not understand me, and feels offended when nothing could have been further from my thoughts than to cause him offence; but it is precisely this which was so embarrassing about a situation to which I simply had to put an end: God himself cannot bring about an agreement where a true understanding between like-minded individuals is not possible. The confusions which must inevitably arise each time that two people of totally differing views in the realm of beauty are expected to agree upon the means whereby to achieve success in that realm are something I can tolerate only up to a certain point: putting an end to such conditions has finally become an act of self-defence designed to save my very life. That a man of such skill, experience and extreme versatility as your late father's Cabinet Secretary should have become the sole personal link between so wonderful and highly poetical a royal friend and the so-called "opera composer" Richard Wagner – a man whom his fellow contemporaries still fail almost entirely to understand – this, I say, was intended neither by his birth nor his training. For some time now I have suffered in the most painful way from the need to arrive at some understanding with this man: forgive me, my belovèd friend, if I have caused you even the slightest distress in finally disclaiming him! I could not go on! – but I feel the need, now more than ever, to be just towards Pfistermeister. I genuinely believe that it was always a matter of the most sincere concern to him to carry out the wishes and commands of his King, whose love for me he could no longer doubt, and to carry them out, moreover, in an urgent endeavour to see me calm and content. I have too many demonstrations of the sincerity of his intentions not to feel deeply indebted to him for what he has done. And though I had no other reason for doing so, my recollection of our first meeting after he had come in search of me, having been sent out by my angel to find me, would be sufficient excuse for remaining his friend for ever, and always feeling well-disposed towards him. And that is how it shall be! That is why I am happy to forgive him, with all my heart, for having vacillated between two opposing interests – albeit for only a matter of days perhaps – and for having behaved in a confused and suspicious manner on the occasion of that premeditated catastrophe last winter.[1] He simply did not understand the meaning of your love for me, nor the nature of my mission. He subsequently sought as best he could to make up for the errors that had been committed, and I believe that his loyalty and devotion to his most gracious lord are really not in any doubt. And so, if my royal friend were not to find some reason of which I myself were unaware for removing Pfister-meister from his present office, I myself would most certainly not wish him to be removed in this way. But I believe that I must advise my dear friend to

---

1 The events of 6 February 1865 when Wagner was refused an audience with the King.

reduce and limit your future employment of this man to the natural level of his original position. To be honest, I believe that the importance of this position has become more comprehensive and weighty as a result of his having held the office for so many years, to the extent that it can no longer appear conducive to the dignity of the King for the present situation to continue. – Hence the well-considered request which I recently submitted to my adored friend, desiring him to choose a just, loyal and representative nobleman of the royal household, who, worthily and regardless of common personal interests, could carry out, to the letter, all the orders and instructions of a monarch whose understanding of art is as deep as yours. You yourself named Baron von Moy to me. It seems to me that my clairvoyant friend has found the right man in him. As far as it has been possible for me to make enquiries, I am pleased to have received only the most favourable reports concerning the unimpeachable honesty and genuinely aristocratic mind of this already highly-placed courtier. How would it be if my belovèd King were now to offer this gentleman the following commission: –

By his being appointed intendant of all the departments of the royal household relating to art, he shall be entrusted with supreme control of the Court Theatre and Court Orchestra, and given instructions, in the first place, to organize the budgets of the Court Theatre and Court Orchestra in such a way that, once a detailed enquiry into their needs has been conducted, a new budget may be drawn up and agreed, with appropriately improved salaries first for the Court Orchestra and then for the theatre chorus, after which, with these budgets retained unchanged, the subsidy of the Court Theatre itself may then be fixed. In addition, the intendant shall in future assume responsibility for the King's commissions and instructions to artists in the various branches of art. In particular he should at once conduct and conclude those negotiations which are required to reorganize the Conservatoire of Music, as well as to construct a temporary Festival Theatre in the Glaspalast, in accordance with the intentions and especial wishes of the King.[1]

The 22nd of July

I had reached this point yesterday when I received a telegraphic despatch from Dresden announcing that Schnorr had just died, at 11 o'clock in the morning! – –

Now I have only *one* Ludwig left! The only one!! –

I must now try to understand this death and – compose myself! –

In spite of my great weakness, I shall be setting out with Bülow at 12 o'clock today in order to attend the funeral in Dresden tomorrow morning at 9 o'clock.[2] –

---

1 Nothing came of any of these plans.
2 As a result of the body's advanced state of decomposition, the ceremony was brought forward to 7 o'clock; Wagner and Bülow arrived too late.

What I feel at *this* bereavement is almost impossible to fathom!
– My Tristan! my belovèd! for me he lived – for me – he died! What we see before us here has never before been known or felt! –
How shall I look on you when we next meet, you who are all the world to me? –
I hope to be back on Tuesday –
Ah, this last sad journey![1]

Faithful and sad unto death –
Your
Richard

Königsbriefe I, 129–32.

329. OTTO WESENDONCK, ZURICH   Munich, 31 July 1865

Dear Wesendonck,
Although I find little time nowadays to review my past life with any degree of awareness, it is enough for me to mention your name in order to recall one of the most important periods of my life, and to recall it with such clarity that my heart, immediately suffused by the most tender feeling of gratitude for your kindness and friendship, is at once disposed to feel friendly towards you. Why your friendship and the sacrifices you made in providing for my welfare could bring neither peace nor quiet – that is a question I must now seek to answer: I understand the reason when I realize that no relationship in the world, no friendship, nor any love could ever bring me true peace and quiet. I understand the past, in which you, too, were so closely bound up, when I look back on that past from the standpoint of the present, with its strange tensions and excitements, a time into which is so powerfully woven the most visionary, devoted love of a wondrously talented royal youth for an older man who longs for rest. – I am not destined to enjoy peace and quiet: – no doubt there is good reason for that! –
Yet how happy I am if I can at least find peace in my recollection of the past: let me dream of repose in the memory of that time when I lived and worked under your own patronage! – It was a mightily creative period: in spite of the greatest exertions we have not yet reached the point of giving the world what was then created. The disruption which drove me from you six years ago ought to have been avoided: it so estranged me from my life that you yourself did not really recognize me, any more than I recognized myself, when I once again turned to you on that last occasion.[2] I ought to have been

1 *Lohengrin* Act III, Scene 3 (GS II,112).
2 Presumably between 26 March and 28 April 1864, when Wagner was in Mariafeld.

spared this painful experience, too: I felt this should have been possible; it would have been fine, very fine, even sublime, if I could have been spared that experience. But – the sublime is not ours to command, – and I was wrong. –

A great deal has now changed in my life. Everything around me is now fairly new. Yet the new world only animates my attempt to reanimate the old world. The Nibelungs, too, are now to be taken up again, completed and presented to the world. What you could not achieve, for all your most generous and self-sacrificial sympathy, only a King can bring to fruition. I have confessed to you that, following my departure from your neighbourhood, my life was caught up in a current which consumed everything aimed at ensuring that my creative powers continued to flourish. Even the liberal advances which you made me against the publication of the Nibelung works were swallowed up on expenditure that no longer bore any useful relation to these works. As early as a year ago I had to ask you to regard those advances as lost, since there was no possibility of recovering them by publishing the works themselves. I must almost feel happy now at seeing even these works published: for the "Valkyrie", of which I am sending you a copy today, I can obtain from my publisher no more than a very small part of the advance which he made me on the Mastersingers, a work whose completion now lies some time ahead. If I am now obliged, therefore, to ask you to renounce, in their entirety, your claims to my Nibelung works, I *myself* do not intend to abandon the hope of one day being able to pay back your advances in person. This of course can become possible only through the generosity of my royal friend. If, however, I am to think of his paying back even the debts that I owe to friends like yourself, I must necessarily wait for a suitable moment, and ask you in turn to wait. For the present you will understand how cautious I must be here lest I involve my youthful patron, who is scarcely of age yet, in too great a system of expenses on my account. Such is his ardour that what he envisages above all is a performance of the works themselves: we are establishing a school especially to train our performers, and a special theatre shall be built for the festival performances. You will have not failed to notice the disturbing effect that these plans have had on all sides, and what persecutions and threats the young King's schemes have already caused me. I know that you will be the first to advise me to show prudence and self-restraint here, and – since it is within your power to do so – you, especially, will be only too pleased to help me, by dint of your patience and forbearance, to exercise the necessary prudence and self-restraint here. However, since these works can never yield the least profit from any commerce with the general public, they should and must now belong to the King of Bavaria. I shall never allow even Tristan and Isolde to be performed elsewhere, – and now probably not even in

Munich.[1] The Nibelungs can be presented to the nation only in the form of a festival gift bestowed by the King: as for the actual theatre where what is at stake is the need to please or the failure to please, to buy or not to buy, I am finished. I am sure, my dear friend, that you will understand me aright and not misconstrue my sympathetic request if I entreat you most sincerely to allow him who will complete and perform my Nibelung work to have sole possession of that part of it which is *my* work. Please understand me, and do not be displeased with me for asking you to be so kind and generous as to hand over to the King of Bavaria the original full score of the "Rhinegold", which you are safeguarding. The King must, and will, hear of your rights in these works: I am certain that he will not leave you without compensation.[2] If we postpone this reimbursement, it is because we trust in the kindness of an old friend who, by dint of this new demonstration of his nobility of mind, shall contribute to the prosperity of the creator of these works in such a way that he may obtain the peace and leisure he needs to support himself during their completion and performance. I am sure you will not be angry with me, and that you will understand my request?

No doubt it is unnecessary for me to add how much I need only emollient and favourable impressions at present, never, indeed, have I needed them more than now. The powers that govern my life, tormenting my soul and alarming me with the most unheard-of terrors, you will no doubt discover without my needing to tell you about them specially. If, amidst the glorious impressions of rehearsing Tristan, I dreamt for a brief space of a truly successful culmination to my long and painful life as an artist, I need only remind you that I returned a week ago from the body of my noble, glorious singer[3] in order to tell you what I must think of my "success"!! –

Sincere good wishes to your dear wife! She will safeguard for ever what is more precious than the fair copy of the full score which I have requested back.[4] If it grieves her, however, to return this to me, I may perhaps send you something in its place which I hope will seem a fair exchange. What? –

Fare you well, my good Wesendonck! May these lines find you well and of good cheer!

Yours,
Richard Wagner.

Otto Wesendonck-Briefe 117–21.

1 *Tristan und Isolde* was next performed in Munich, with the Vogls, in June 1869; eight further performances were given there between 1872 and 1875. Other theatres which performed the work during Wagner's lifetime were Weimar (14 June 1874), Berlin (20 March 1876), Königsberg (10 December 1881), Leipzig (2 January 1882), London (20 June 1882) and Hamburg (23 November 1882).
2 Wesendonck handed over the score. Ludwig wrote to thank him on 28 August 1865, pointing out that the request was Wagner's, not his; the question of compensation was not raised.
3 Ludwig Schnorr von Carolsfeld.
4 The sketches of *Das Rheingold, Die Walküre*, and the first two acts of *Siegfried*.

330. KING LUDWIG II OF BAVARIA, HOHENSCHWANGAU

Munich, 8 August 1865

My wondrous friend,

What must such a letter mean to me, time and again! Though ardently awaited, it none the less comes as a surprise, falling, as it were, straight from heaven into this earth-bound life of mine! I then relive anew the fairest and most profound of all nations' myths and dogmas; and the noble belief in the transmigration of souls becomes an inwardly experienced truth. How clearly do I feel that I have lived through several lives in me, in you, in her, and in all who are dear to me: and whenever I feel to be living there, I am conscious of the joys of death, of redemption, and of an end to being. What mysterious riddle is this? It is the mystery of love, a love which no longer knows desire, but which only gives, gives of itself in self-liberation.

Beautiful soul[1] in which I live when utterly lost, how I love myself when I see myself in you: then all grief is at an end, and the deepest pain becomes the most joyous sensation! Thus the most unspeakable sadness shall merely extend the infinity of my existence: in me the departed spirit[2] lives on, and with him I live in you! – The chain has expanded, not broken! –

My thanks! My thanks for this fair message, too!

———

My belovèd friend! I am still sitting here, wondering whether or not to go into the mountains. I was held here, rooted to the spot by the most luxurious summer heat, and gazing yearningly towards the mountains. Now, all at once, the summer seems over. I know my old ill-fortune: the moment I arrange things laboriously in terms of time and space, all my calculations miscarry. – And yet – this very moment a sign has come, persuading me, at whatever risk to myself, to set out tomorrow morning. I must do something at once to restore my nerves, since I am wasting away in my melancholy mood from day to day, and can find no remedy for my sorry state. And so I intend to take the hunting-lodge on the Hochkopf as a sign that I must keep my head held high![3] The idea of going there has come through my belovèd, who stayed there: my stay in the lodge shall be welcome, as a demonstration of your gracious kindness; I intend to stay there – with you. – And so I am resolved: I shall set off tomorrow at first light. May wind and weather prove favourable!

---

1 The concept of the "schöne Seele" dates back to the writings of Goethe and Schiller, and refers to an harmonious quality in those people (especially women) who are at one with themselves and the world; see Daniel Farrelly, *Goethe and Inner Harmony* (Shannon 1973).
2 Ludwig Schnorr von Carolsfeld.
3 A pun on the word "Hochkopf", a hunting-lodge which the King had placed at Wagner's disposal. Wagner stayed there between 9 and 21 August 1865.

I need sublime seclusion, mountains and forests in order to restore some tension to my enfeebled and wearisome nerves. –

Shall I soon hear from my belovèd there? I am taking plenty of work with me, and plan to get on with the full score of Siegfried.[1] With love and faith, but – as yet with little hope! –

The vocal score of the "Valkyrie" is finally ready, and moved me deeply when it arrived here: the first thing I looked for was the poem![2] To me – it is the most precious page in the whole volume. Here it is, my belovèd friend! For the first time I can send out into the world a work which bears the noble stamp of love's own true servant: the world shall see naught else of mine that is not ennobled by this mark. This is its import: nothing else! The world shall know that I now work and create for you alone, my gracious King! –

May it please you to receive what is yours! –

Soon there shall follow a work in my own *hand*.[3]

———

My King! For all that we wish to achieve there is but *one* correct and successful starting-point: undisturbed personal understanding! No one can help us, save you and – me! I know the middle course to be useless. It is true, I admit, that I am waiting in a mood of confident composure to discover whether you have already come to a decision, and, if so, what? But if none has yet been reached, I shall take it as a sign from heaven, for I am now of the opinion that in fact – we need no one. You will be able to assure yourself of the loyalty and obedience of your administrative officials by dint of your royal prerogative: but *what* must be carried out is something that *we* alone can grasp and decide. No other way is possible. And so I entreat this one thing of you above all else: *regular, frequent and undisturbed personal contact.* Here, my noble friend, we must reach a basic decision. The whole world knows what I am to you. The secretiveness of this relationship is what makes it so beautiful for me: and only to beautiful souls can it ever be revealed. But the world, although it will never grasp the meaning of this secret, must be given an open and intelligible interpretation of our relationship, lest its trivial judgement be misled. I now believe that, instead of seeking out some court-servant's strange and inappropriate title for me, it would be extremely simple and straightforward if – openly and in full view of the whole world – you were to give me a formal *commission* to carry out, with all their consequences, the suggestions and plans contained in my "Report on the German School

1 Wagner worked on the first full score of Act II between 22 December 1864 and 2 December 1865. The second full score was not completed until 23 February 1869.
2 The dedication to Ludwig.
3 The full score of *Das Rheingold*; see letter [329], p. 655.

of Music", and for this lay down the condition that I should henceforth have to communicate the relevant artistic plans to you in person, and receive your decisions in this artistic matter in like manner. The purely administrative side of the business would simply devolve upon your cabinet officials. In this way the "Intendancy" would disappear, whereas the artistic aspect of the same would be filled in by myself. If a "title" were considered indispensable here, then – I should have to reconcile myself to it, if not – so much the better!!! What I am, and what I can be to you alone, is something which most certainly cannot be summed up in any sort of title. –

And now, my friend, we must also restore order to my personal relations. From a communication from Baron von Moy, whose visit I thought it meet to return, I gathered that, mindful perhaps of my refusal to accept the services of our excellent Councillor of State Pfistermeister, you had proposed that this gentleman, previously considered for the post of Intendant, should also be asked to superintend the relations between ourselves. I realized once again how deeply indebted I was to you for your tender solicitude. And yet I was alarmed at the thought that we might need an intermediary between us. If the King alone can grant me all that I might claim from the world, then only my friend can express what no King has previously felt moved to grant me. That is why I turn to my friend in person, asking him to intercede with himself, the King, and discover what I can, after all, finally receive from the hand of my friend alone. In a quiet moment I have accordingly set down in writing a clear account of what is necessary for such a communication. I am enclosing this document herewith. – I must conclude by describing the frame of mind in which I am submitting this document. It is one of great calm. –

A year ago, when I informed you of my wishes in respect of my plans to settle here for three years in order to complete the Nibelungs, I told you that there was a secret here. It was this: I did not wish to live longer than these three years, and found it criminal to worry about a time *after* the Nibelungs were finished. This has changed. The sacrifice has been made: Tristan is redeemed. I died in my friend! Rest in peace, my noble Ludwig Schnorr! –

Now I know that I shall carry out all my plans as long as I am enabled to do so: – more than the Nibelungs, everything! – But someone else must *will* it so, for my will no longer belongs to me. I have now considered the conditions necessary for my activities on earth. If I am denied them, my will shall have failed me. I can no longer desire anything, as such, for myself. – If you find it difficult, deny me: this will be my fate. But the common people and all the world already believe me far better provided for; this much is certain. Perhaps it is therefore not so difficult. But once again: I – desire nothing! – I say this without the least bitterness: tender-hearted, grave and calm. –

And now, in spite of wind and weather, off to the mountains! My trunk is being packed: my faithful servant and the dear old dog[1] are accompanying me. An old Indian epic, "Ramayana", is coming too: Siegfried, in his manifold guises, shall breathe anew on mountain heights.

When shall I hear from my friend? Shall I see him soon? Shall I disturb him on his birthday? Does my sweet and glorious friend believe me when I say that I love him more than myself and the world, and more than my works, and that I live for him alone?

Soul in soul; truly yours and for ever true,

Your
Richard W.

Report.

The annual salary of 4000 fl. which was most graciously allotted to me at the outset was adequate only on the assumption that I could move into an ordinary residence. A separate house and garden would require greater expense: such a property is very difficult to find here, and in order to be sure of enjoying it at least until such time as I had completed my Nibelung work, I requested special assistance for this special purpose over a period of three years, assistance which was most graciously granted to me by means of a formal contract covering the order and delivery of the work.

Since that time the following changes have taken place in my situation.

The favours which were granted me have been exaggerated and denounced to the general public in an inflammatory fashion: although they failed to achieve the actual aim of their malicious indiscretion, the whole world's attention has now been drawn to the apparent splendour of my situation in what is for me a highly vexatious manner, since my sole intention had been to secure the peace and quiet that I need to work at leisure. In consequence, various claims against me from every period of my extremely difficult past life have now been revived, claims which, as a result more especially of my inhabiting a most attractive property and appearing to enjoy a truly splendid situation, I can no longer dismiss by pointing out what is in fact my total lack of possessions, still less can I do so when it is a question ultimately of compensating genuine friends who once supported me with their sacrifices at a time of great need, and who are themselves now reduced to a state of impoverishment and importunity. Throughout this period, moreover, I have been importuned by all manner of people in need of assistance, people whose appeals have often been so affecting that, after considering the matter closely, I have found it impossible not to admit that what appears to be a well-to-do situation is in truth scarcely adequately endowed, and have thus been unable to deny them the help they begged of me, not least in cases of genuine

1 Franz Mrazéck and Pohl.

hardship which I shall not trouble my august patron by relating here. Even these latter cases involve me in outgoings far in excess of my revenues. –

Moreover, my present experience – which could be gained only in my new surroundings and in my new circumstances – has shown that merely running a household in domestic conditions such as mine is more expensive than I had previously been led to believe, as a result of my having to maintain a garden which has been much neglected of late, of the extreme difficulty of heating the place in winter, and of sundry other complications.

Even by the end of last winter this situation had resulted in my having to think of some fundamental remedy for the troubles that then threatened. Three ways offered themselves here: –

Giving up the property, and leaving Munich completely;

-ditto-, but withdrawing to a small room in the home of the Bülow family: – firstly retaining the prospect of a possible completion of my works; secondly giving up this prospect and limiting myself simply to the superficial activities involved in establishing the School of Music. –

A new adjustment of my revenues, with the aim of creating the means whereby to preserve my present domestic arrangements, would have been the third expedient, but one which I could countenance only with the greatest reluctance, since I could see that I would again be subject to the discretion of those same administrative authorities whose kind indiscretion had recently caused me such unspeakable annoyance and anguish. –

Since then my freedom of choice has been substantially impaired by a certain incident. While I was so enthusiastically occupied in rehearsing Tristan, I was facing the threat of being given notice to quit with immediate effect and of having to move out of my house, all on the basis of a spiteful interpretation of a clause in my rental agreement. Simply in order to keep my choice open, and, above all, to have temporary peace and quiet (especially during that period of wearying activity), I was moved by Councillor of State Pfistermeister's kind concern to entrust him with the care of keeping this disagreeable disruption at bay: with all the eagerness of a true friend – an eagerness which deserves the highest recognition and engages my warmest gratitude – the Councillor of State appears to have reported this unfortunate incident to my royal patron, and to have done so in so solicitous a manner that the gracious command to acquire the property in secret on His Majesty's account was at once obtained, and carried out with great address. – Deeply moved and grateful though I was for this new demonstration of the most self-sacrificial interest in whatever might make my life easier for me, I nevertheless felt renewed embarrassment, since I saw that my earlier freedom of choice was now made much more difficult for me. – Since I had finally agreed with myself that my complete departure from Munich could not lie within my choice, and that my removal would be rendered necessary only if my royal friend desired it so, I had to consider the kind of establishment that would be necessary to secure my permanent residence here, including my retention of the property in which I am now living.

A change in the previous stipulations was bound in any case to seem opportune. The privileges granted me, by way of exception, in the autumn of last year extended over a period of only three years: they were intended to enable me to settle down and establish myself in the house in question, which was leased to me for a relatively short number of years, in addition to enabling me to pay the not inconsiderable rent of 3000 fl. a year. This stipulation, in particular, can no longer make sense now, inasmuch as it covers the rent and specifies a period of only two years.

As a result, and on the basis of my retaining the property which I have furnished and which I at present inhabit, it must now be possible to reach something on the lines of the following agreement.

1. His Majesty the King shall assign to me, rent-free, for the duration of my life, the property which belongs to him at No 21 Briennerstrasse.
2. Use of assets totalling twice one hundred thousand gulden, also for the duration of my life, the said sum to be made over to me in such a way that 40,000 fl. in cash be transferred to me with immediate effect, to be administered as I shall deem fit; 160,000 fl., however, shall be administered by the royal Cabinet Exchequer, with only the interest at five percent being made available to me in quarterly instalments of 2000 fl. each, in return for which all the annuities and subventions previously granted me by His Majesty, together with the stipulations thereto relating, shall be regarded as having been revoked and cancelled. –

In declaring my willingness to recognize not only my wishes but also my need for independence as having been fully and permanently satisfied by this loan, and by the form of this loan, I may add the following information concerning my use of the sum requested.

With the help of the interest on that part of the capital which remains behind in the Cabinet Exchequer I plan to defray my outgoings in such a way as to apply myself, honestly and expeditiously, to looking after and maintaining the property which has been transferred to me, and to supporting the necessary household, servants etc., in addition to meeting, in a dignified and frank manner, all the other lesser and more refined needs of a man who, at the same time, is a creative and productive artist honoured by His Majesty with important and influential commissions.

The sum of 40,000 fl. which will immediately be entrusted to me to be administered as I shall deem fit is intended, on the other hand, to provide me with a fund which would be available at all times and without further ado, enabling me to compensate others, as has proved unavoidable, for the sacrifices they made for me at an earlier date, to discharge pressing obligations from the past, or to facilitate, where appropriate, older contractual agreements (e.g. with a publisher who, in desperate times, obtained from me certain rights to the publication of my compositions which in certain circumstances could now seem oppressive, disadvantageous or even humiliating.) This fund, which I would entrust to a well-tried and experienced friend of relatively long standing[1] for his safe administration, could therefore be reduced by me at certain times, but could equally well be increased by the addition of any revenues from abroad of which, for ex., the revenues which I can certainly expect to receive in time from performances of my works in Paris could easily reach a level not at all disadvantageous to the fund in question.

Since my royal benefactor shall be expressly appointed heir to all that I shall one day leave behind in cash, I may not be entirely unjustified in assuming, somewhat to my own gratification perhaps, that, following my death, this fund of 40,000 fl. may be restored to him unchanged, if not actually increased. At all events, the interest on this sum would enable me, in the frequent cases that arise, to bestow upon all assiduous distressed persons the support which I must now refuse them or which I can grant them only to the very real detriment of my own domestic livelihood. The interest on this sum would also be useful in defraying the costs of such holiday trips and the like as may from time to time become necessary, so that in future, however unpredictable the vicissitudes that befall me, I shall be adequately provided for here, and not be obliged to trouble my gracious patron with individual appeals for his help.

I may note expressly that I am not thinking of maintaining an equipage, nor indeed may I think of doing so. On the contrary, I count myself fortunate that I can take sufficient care of my wife who, alas, lives apart from me, and that I can do so regularly and uninterruptedly, without detriment to my personal livelihood, by means of an annual pension of 1000 thalers.

Richard Wagner[2]

Königsbriefe I, 143–9.

331. BERTHA GOLDWAG, VIENNA   Walchensee, 18 August 1865

Dear Fräulein Bertha,

I asked you last time to come to some arrangement whereby you could wait until the end of August. I still hope to be able to send you everything by the end of this month: but it is *possible* that it will be September. I cannot *possibly* press for payment of the monies which I am expecting around that time; I should only cause myself inestimable harm. However, I have taken account

1 Presumably Anton Pusinelli, although no correspondence has survived on this subject.
2 Wagner's stipend, which had already been raised to 6200 gulden on 1 August 1865, was increased to 8000 gulden on 1 October 1865. On 18 October he received the gift of 40,000 gulden from the King. See Newman's *Life*, III, 466–8.

of all this in my calculations, so that you will receive everything in the very near future: but, as I say it *may* be September, and I should like to prepare you for that possibility. If these delays cause you sacrifices, I shall compensate you for any loss, you can certainly count upon me to do so. I shall be coming to Vienna for a few days around that time[1] and shall see you then. Rely upon it! –

I can also see now that in future I cannot, and may not, expect any further outlay of such magnitude on your part. You yourself misled me here by depicting this as easier for you than it is. – Well, all this shall be sorted out within the next few days, and, I may add, it shall not be allowed to happen again.

And so: I shall be seeing you soon. Until then, I remain, your devoted servant,

Rich. Wagner.

[...]

Putzmacherin-Briefe 63–4.

332. KING LUDWIG II OF BAVARIA, HOHENSCHWANGAU
Munich, 29 August 1865

My wondrously bountiful friend,

Your never-ceasing benevolence imposes upon me the pleasant duty of sending you these few lines before I had originally intended to write, in order that I may make you a surprise. Since you wish it so, I am engaged for the first time in setting down in writing my plan for "Parzival":[2] although I have not once taken up the sources of this subject since the time of my earliest acquaintance with it and although, even now, I must avoid becoming involved in it, except in passing – as on this occasion – the subject – even given such self-command – has swollen in so rich and powerful a way that I cannot complete this elaboration of it in the two days that I had initially thought possible. I need a few more profitable mornings: the draft will then be finished, and he for whom it is uniquely intended shall then receive the work at once.

[...]

Königsbriefe I, 167.

1 Wagner visited Vienna between 23 and 28 October 1865.
2 The prose draft of *Parsifal*, dated 27 – 30 August 1865, was set down in the Brown Book. A fair copy of this draft was sent to Ludwig on 31 August. According to *Mein Leben* (561; English trans. 547), an earlier sketch (now lost) was made in April 1857. On the spelling "Parzival", see letter [221], p. 416, note 1.

333. KING LUDWIG II OF BAVARIA, HOHENSCHWANGAU
Munich, 7 September 1865

[. . .] "What is the significance of *Kundry's* kiss?" – That, my belovèd, is a terrible secret! You know, of course, the serpent of Paradise and its tempting promise: "eritis sicut Deus, scientes bonum et malum."[1] Adam and Eve became "knowing". They became "conscious of sin". The human race had to atone for that consciousness by suffering shame and misery until redeemed by Christ who took upon himself the sin of mankind. My dearest friend, how can I speak of such profound matters except in a simile, by means of a comparison? But only the clairvoyant can say what its inner meaning may be. Adam – Eve: Christ. – How would it be if we were now to add to them: – "Anfortas[2] – Kundry: Parzival?" But with considerable caution! – The kiss which causes Anfortas to fall into sin awakens in Parzival a full awareness of that sin, not as his own sin but as that of the grievously afflicted Anfortas whose lamentations he had previously heard only dully, but the cause of which now dawns upon him in all its brightness, through his sharing the feeling of sin: with the speed of lightning he said to himself, as it were: "ah! that is the poison that causes him to sicken whose grief I did not understand till now!" – Thus he knows more than all the others, more, especially, than the assembled Knights of the Grail who continued to think that Anfortas was complaining merely of the spear-wound! Parzival now sees deeper. – Thus he, too, sees deeper who does not believe what the whole world believes, that *I*, for ex., have suffered as a result of the failure of my Tannhäuser in Paris, that I have suffered through the newspapers' attempts to detract from my fame, or through lack of recognition: Oh no! my suffering goes deeper; he who would know of it must hear in my works themselves what superficial listeners cannot hear. Happily, it is an awareness not of sin but solely of redemption from the sin of the world. But who has divined this redemption in my works? –
   [. . .]

Königsbriefe I,174.

334. KING LUDWIG II OF BAVARIA, HOHENSCHWANGAU
Munich, 23 September 1865

[. . .] Our love, my sweet prince! – so wondrous and unheard-of, what happiness it must bring to the world. Now that I can collect my thoughts with ever greater calm and devotion, I am seeking to fathom the task which we

1 *Genesis* 3:5, "Ye shall be as gods, knowing good and evil".
2 See letter [242], p. 457, note 1.

must solve. What was once bound to fill my heart with despair when I recognized and witnessed it I may now recall with an eagerness full of hope in order that, on the strength of what I have recognized, I may clearly and distinctly define the aim of our efforts, an aim which I now know to be solvable. While weaving the feathery garment of sound of those woodbirds which speak so clearly to Siegfried I think of presenting my life's belovèd hero with a lesson gleaned from an experience of the world which has been bought at the price of manifold sufferings, and of bringing it to his attention in the form that it has now assumed in my mind, – in the shimmering light of a solemn, devotional hope. I may now speak the language of these communications, for what has happened between us constrains me to prophetic clarity and an unerring proclamation of what my hero now can hear, since – he hears it of his own accord. He is like Siegfried with the woodbird. Twice he listens: but the first time he hears only the melody; he would fain understand the sense of that melody, too: how should he set about doing so? He accomplishes a mighty *deed*: he slays Fafner. What is the use of this tremendous deed? Behold! he now *understands* the sense of the bird-song, too. Before him is revealed, in all its clarity, the meaning of his deed, his power, the proclamation of his high-born bride. Thus I proclaim to my life's dear Siegfried the sense of the act of his love for me, his power: his awakening of the high-born bride: Germany – is his Brünnhilde! – I sing the song which awakens this bride. It is a serious, solemn song: and yet dear and heartfelt. It is the thoughtful word of the "German spirit". –

The notes jotted down during recent days[1] expatiate upon this serious theme, and provide, as it were, the text to many a melody which has already forced its way into my belovèd's heart. Unless you find it tiresome, I shall continue, and elaborate the theme over many more pages. In this way I shall be somewhat more reconciled to having been so long deprived of your most earnestly longed-for company! –

[. . .]

Königsbriefe I, 187.

335. ELIZA WILLE, MARIAFELD   Munich, 26 September 1865

Tell me, dear friend, how was it possible for you to pass me by this summer? How often have I wanted to address this question to you! My astonishment

---

1 Between 14 and 27 September 1865 Wagner kept a "Journal", the entries of which were copied out by Cosima and presented to the King in instalments. Excerpts were published in the *Bayreuther Blätter*, i (1878), 29–42, under the title *Was ist deutsch?* and reprinted in GS X,36–53; PW IV,149–69. The complete text was first made available in Volume IV of the Königsbriefe.

has until now prevented me from doing so. – So it was possible for you to
ignore even your husband's exhortation? You have lived, in the closest intimacy, through strange and terrible periods of my life, both in me and with
me, feeling and suffering with me, only to abandon me completely and without
warning at an important high point of my life! – How odd! It certainly gives
me further food for thought! –

What shall I now tell you about myself? –

I spoke of an "important high point": I did not say a "joyful" one. The
fact that even here, at this high point of my life, there was really only pain
and suffering for me to feel, – that is something you perhaps suspected, and
felt in too much pain yourself to offer me your sympathy? –

There was a brief period when I really thought I was dreaming, so marvellously well did I feel. This was the period when I was rehearsing "Tristan".

For the first time in my life, I and the whole of my entire art lay as though
upon a bed of love. It had to be so, just for once. All the workshop arrangements were noble, ample, free and generous: a wonderful pair of artists,[1] sent
to me by heaven itself, intimately familiar with their task, utterly devoted, and
quite astonishingly talented. My faithful guardian angel, hovering over me as
beautiful and beneficent as ever, filled with childlike exultation at my contentment and delight in our increasing success: ordering whatever might serve
my purpose, removing whatever was in my way, and always with an unseen
hand. The work grew like some enchanted dream to become an unsuspected
reality: the first performance – without an audience, just for us – advertised
as a dress rehearsal, it was like the fulfilment of an impossible vision.

The feeling that I was dreaming never left me: I was amazed – utterly
amazed – that it could have all come about! – It was a wonderful high point,
and yet made *bitter* by – *absences*! – Really: bitter! How petty you all seemed
to me for avoiding this – excitement! –

From then on – nothing but sheer suffering. Since I really pay very little
heed to so-called "success", all subsequent experiments before the general
public (for that is how I accounted them) were simply disturbing and humiliating for me. At the fourth performance – during the final act – I was seized
by a sense of the sinful nature of this unprecedented achievement: I cried
out: this is the last performance of Tristan, it must never be given again.
This has now been fulfilled. My glorious singer left us rejoicing, happy and
blissful in his pride and sense of well-being. Eight days later I rushed to
Dresden to be present at his burial: flying gout was the name of the daemonic
illness which passed from his knee-joint to his brain. There he lay. – Since
then I have been in a sorry state. I was lonely in the mountains, and now I
am lonely here. I can no longer speak to anyone, and am still believed to be
out of town. The King's wonderful love keeps me alive: he cares for me as

1 Ludwig and Malvina Schnorr von Carolsfeld.

no man has ever cared for another. I live in him, and intend to go on creating my works for him. I really no longer live for myself. But he keeps at bay everything that reminds me of life and reality: I can continue only to dream and work.

That is how things stand and how they will go on. My pleasure in my work consumes all my memories. The Nibelungs are now being completed:[1] a Parzival has already been sketched.[2] It is all wonderful, dreamlike: otherwise it would all be deadly painful.

Now you must tell me about yourself. –

[I expect to hear from you some time that our friend Mathilde[3] has finally demanded back from you the letter that I wrote to her. You will no doubt understand that I can never write to her again until she has answered *this* letter. –]

A thousand good wishes, dear sweet friend! Do you still recall your prophecies? But it is not a question of that here: what could be fulfilled has been fulfilled as nothing else has ever been fulfilled – more beautiful than any dream. And you did not even wish to come near the place where this dream came true?

How are things with the bundle in the famous portfolio?[4] –

My warmest and very best wishes to you all from your

Richard Wagner.

RWA (copy not in Wagner's hand; incompletely published in Wille-Briefe 90–2).

336. KING LUDWIG II OF BAVARIA, HOHENSCHWANGAU

Munich, 10 October 1865

My friend, who is more precious to me than all else,

I am not well. Yesterday I drew up the accompanying draft of a letter such as I wish you to send me but intended for the public eye. Since I cannot write any more today, I hesitated to send you this draft on its own. Yet I am seized by a longing to hear from you. I believe this draft cannot be unwelcome to you. Without being diffuse it expresses in clear and explicit terms what *must* some day be expressed *in this way* if a start is to be made in the outside world. I regard such a document as a formal decree to establish the necessary work of the future. – That is why I do not hesitate to send you this paper

1 See letter [330], p. 657, note 1.
2 See letter [332], p. 663, note 2.
3 Mathilde Wesendonck; see letter [300], p. 604, note 2. This paragraph has not previously been published.
4 A reference to Eliza Wille's literary endeavours.

today, although I cannot accompany it with any further news. My indisposition is turning out to be a severe chill: it is entirely without danger, but I must avoid all forms of exertion. –

Forgive me, my dear and noble friend! I am so sad if I cannot always be something for you! Life has otherwise no meaning whatsoever, nor any further appeal for me. –

I shall soon have recovered and shall then continue! –

Loving and true unto death

Your

Richard Wagner

The reports which you have communicated to me confirm me in my opinion that it is time to devote particular attention to fostering an important area of German art. You have shown that the German nation has produced perhaps the greatest creative masters in the realm of music, but that nowhere on German soil has an institution been called into being which would have enabled a truly valid performance style to be established for the works of those masters, and ensured that that style was handed down to posterity. At the same time, you base upon the expected success of this institution the hope that a valid German style of music might be developed for performance style in general, and, by demonstrating that the selfsame need exists in the case of our great German poets, you wish to see that institution expanded in such a way that a valid and correct style might also be developed on the dramatic stage, a style in keeping, that is, with the German musical style. Were we to succeed in calling into being an Academy of Art which made good our past failings, with the result that the German nation might one day again produce minds as great as Mozart & Beethoven, Göthe & Schiller, and if these masters were to find the means for their artistic presentation as well-prepared as in Italy & France, which have at all times maintained such means in a state of constant readiness for their own masters, I should inevitably regard such an outcome as an uplifting reward for the most noble exertions. The grandson of him who revived the plastic arts in Germany,[1] and the son of the royal patron of national science & literature[2] need recall only that he is the great-grandson of that German prince[3] who first went out to meet his people with truly German trust, in order that he, too, may set himself a noble task, a task of benefit to the German spirit and for the powerful realization of which he may reckon upon the supportive loyalty of his noble people.

The higher and more worthy of the German spirit I esteem that task, the more clearly do I recognize, however, the great difficulties bound up with its solution. We are entering the realm of an artistic genre here which, like

1 Ludwig I.
2 Maximilian II.
3 Maximilian I.

music & the theatre, has until now generally been accounted a form of entertainment: I have now become conscious of the harmful consequences of exploiting this public prejudice, and I find that real courage is required if I am to proceed here with that seriousness of purpose which has previously been deemed appropriate only to the other branches of art. Herein, especially, do I recognize the need to establish a Royal precedent, and I intend to provide such an example with a resoluteness which has unfortunately not been shown so far elsewhere.

And so, although I am certain that this undertaking will shortly be accorded the seriousness of purpose which it requires, I, like you, must nevertheless recognize the difficulties which have arisen as a result of our having previously been deflected, in our German seriousness of purpose, from this area of art, and which consist in the fact that suitable means of educating people to higher artistic ends are so extremely hard to find here. I realize therefore that the fruits of even our most strenuous labours will ripen only very slowly. Since, however, I do not doubt in the ultimate success of our continuous and serious zeal, I resolved to issue you with instructions to establish and organize the proposed Academy of Art according to the plan which you developed in greater detail in the report which you prepared for me.[1]

One consideration, however, holds me back: I wish you, above all other things, to be able to devote yourself, completely undisturbed, to the completion of your great creative works, and, whereas I may make a point of doing all I can to keep your mind free of all cares, I am bound to doubt in my own ability to carry out this resolve if I am to burden you, at the same time, with the task of setting up & running the Academy of Art.

Fortunately, your destiny has brought you the friend who appears eminently suited to replacing your activities in this one particular direction. Dr Hans v. Bülow, whose outstanding reputation as a virtuoso artist of the first order has recently received the most general recognition & confirmation as a result of his astonishing achievement as the conductor of so very new and difficult a work as your Tristan, seems to me the only man truly suited to take your place in running the proposed school, the more so in that he has also become so very dear to you and so intimately friendly in consequence of his versatile and learned education in other areas, too. I am therefore writing to inform you of my decision to appoint H. v. B. director of the German Academy of Music and Dramatic Art, and assume that in consequence of this appointment the institution will, at the same time, be assured of your most intimate involvement, just as it shall be administered in your spirit alone, in order that your own serious artistic aims may there be realized. May the outcome of my decisions coincide with the intimate wishes which gave rise to them.

Königsbriefe I, 194–7.

1 See introductory essay, p. 590.

337. KING LUDWIG II OF BAVARIA, HOHENSCHWANGAU

Munich, 26 November 1865

My King,

As recently as yesterday I thought I could henceforth leave you without any further advice on my part. Following the latest unfortunate experiences which I made in the course of the day I am now resolved to ask you today to issue no further instructions concerning me either to your cabinet or to the theatre, at least until such time as fundamental changes have taken place here, since the resultant confusions have finally risen to an unbearable pitch for me. – Today, after a sleepless night spent in worry and a restorative sleep this morning, I feel sufficient strength returning to offer you one final piece of forceful advice, which I am moved to give you out of my love for you and my conscience concerning your country. –

Consider, my august friend, in terse outline the state of affairs in which you have become enmeshed.

With the removal from office of your minister *von Neumayr* you have been rendered a grave disservice. He was the only liberal man in your ministry who, as long as he remained there, would have been able to restrain the most extreme of factions. There were two reasons for persuading you to remove him: a purely personal one, inasmuch as he was a conscientious minister who proved unwilling to tolerate Pfistermeister's demands that the latter's creatures be appointed to office; and then a political one, – since blind reaction has of late become Prussia's watchword. The fact that your cabinet, in collusion more especially with Herr von der Pfordten, is of a mind to give in willingly to Bismarck's wishes I have gathered from open remarks made by Herr Lutz, just like the reasons first given for his annoyance when friends of his were not appointed to office. The country openly attests to the inherent importance of the measure which has here been enforced: whereas only the most squalid of parties shows itself more or less satisfied in the unspeakable paper a copy of which I am enclosing herewith,[1] the great general party of hope considers that the welfare of your government is threatened. The storm has turned against the real evil-doers, who have rightly been recognized as such: during my visit to Hohenschwangau[2] you discovered how severely critical liberal opinion is now becoming as a result of its growing indignation. A way has now offered itself for Herr Pfistermeister to divert this sense of indignation away from himself, by abandoning your friend, indeed – by disparaging your own royal inclinations and actions, and to save himself by exposing *me* to popular resentment. In the enclosed article from the "Volksbote", a paper which is fortunately held in general contempt, you will find a clear account

1 The Munich *Volksbote* of 26 November 1865; see introductory essay, pp. 590–1.
2 Between 11 and 18 November 1865.

of his plan to mount such a rescue attempt. You will see that the most monstrous indiscretions contained in this article could issue only from your private cabinet itself, and so I refrain from offering any proof of this; the tissue of lies bound up with these indiscretions you will in any case see through without difficulty: and yet I confirm once again, in explicit terms, that I was totally ignorant of the Ruf affair, that I never in any way suggested writing a newspaper article, including that of the Nuremberg correspondent,[1] and that, since living in Munich, I have never lodged any visitors in my house, least of all Herr "Eckart", whom I do not even know. But I do not think I need reassure you on this point. –

The question now is whether, in such aggravated circumstances, your friend should leave you without advice in the face of such shameless treachery on the part of your most trusted servants. – I admit that I now consider it dangerous to do so, whatever the circumstances, since certain revelations have been made to me following my return which concern Pf.[2] especially and which fill me with genuine horror. The difficulty you would have in appointing a new cabinet gives this man the brazen confidence to mock you openly, since he believes himself to be indispensable. And so you should not delay for a moment longer in depriving him of his confidence. Since I have already discovered in the case of Riedel, whom I suggested to you, how awkward it is for me not to have known the man personally, I have been obliged to consider how best to advise you in choosing someone whom I do not know but who would be the right man for you.

I pride myself on having found such a man, and would advise you therefore, in all seriousness of conscience and of my love for you, to summon back, by means of a hand-written letter unknown to your secretaries, your former minister v. Neumayr, and charge him with the task of forming a new cabinet.

Do not be alarmed! In this way you will achieve all that needs to be done at present. In view of recent events and the reaction which Neumayr's removal from office has met with in the country, everyone will realize that you have, entirely spontaneously, seen through the trick that had been played upon you in his regard, and a splendid, all-inspiriting impression will be left upon the entire country if you appoint the very man whom you had previously been misled into dismissing, in order to surround yourself with servants of greater loyalty than before. At the same time, Pfistermeister's plot to divert on to *me* the hatred which is at present directed towards him will be most fittingly destroyed, in that the course of the intrigue will be traced back to the actual source from which it issued. – –

I would also draw your attention to the fact that Herr v. Neumayr would

1 The *Nürnberger Anzeiger* of 13 November 1865 had printed an article entitled "Plain words to the King of Bavaria and his people concerning the Cabinet Secretariat", condemning the "unconstitutional institution of the Secretariat".
2 Pfistermeister.

presumably seek to guard himself against my "influence" upon you: he, too, will be unable to form any real idea of the relations which bind us together, and he will think he has to regard me as a kind of favourite against whom one must protect oneself. Do not allow yourself to be deterred by this, but acquaint him of our true relationship, as far as he can comprehend it, and remove any suspicion he might entertain that I know anything of the step you have taken. This is necessary: for we are dealing here with people whom we must be glad if they are honest, loyal and obedient, but who will never be able to fathom our innermost selves. –

This, my King, is my final piece of advice, my final word on the matter. I hope you will not shy away from taking the step I advise you to take: it is the only swift and successful way to find salvation. In this instance you must see to it that Neumayr's arrival comes as a complete surprise to Pf.: for the step must *succeed*; if thwarted, it will cause you only renewed embarrassment. Despatch your most devoted groom with the letter! –

Oh heavens! My King, how I suffer! And yet how proud I feel in the consciousness of having performed so important and loyal a service, and of finally being able to prove myself entirely worthy of your love and trust!

I have nothing more to say now. I must lock myself away in my innermost self, and truly hope that I may see my glorious friend freed from the snares of ignoble men! –

God be with you! Bavaria for ever!

From the truest of hearts
Your own
Richard W.

Königsbriefe I, 225–8.

338. KING LUDWIG II OF BAVARIA, HOHENSCHWANGAU

Munich, 27 November 1865

My King,

I told you yesterday that I had given you my final piece of advice and said my last word in this matter. I am writing to you today, after the most mature consideration, in order to underline what I said then, and to confirm that piece of advice.

Whereas, in accord with our most recent arrangements, it was a question of obtaining peace and quiet, and securing the unimpeded execution of such measures as would serve our ideal artistic plans, what we must do now is destroy a full-blown conspiracy against the honour of my royal lord and against his freedom. Consider the means at your enemy's disposal: for 16 years Pfistermeister has exercised his interfering influence on all the offices of state and country in order to fill those positions with such as owe *him* their advancement and good fortune. It was against this bestowal of offices that a number of upright ministers directed their opposition: their resistance was interpreted as disobedience towards the sovereign will, since the secretary could, of course, accommodate his favourites only in the "name" of the King. Incitement of the King and his ministers was the consequence of this: incomprehensible changes often took place of which no one could see the true causes. It was no higher political norm which guided the ambitious secretary here: his talent and his knowledge are so slight that it would be impossible for him to carry out a political order on his own. Only political power and its preservation could be his game; but if he himself pursues no political end, men more perceptive than he usurp his position and his influence in order to exercise a sway over the King's decisions, without the latter's knowledge, a sway which is authorized by neither the laws of the land nor the laws of humanity's intellectual progress. To maintain a state of conflict between a prince and his people is the means adopted by this obscure party which, whatever it may claim to the contrary, aims not at spiritual but at temporal power. I have also gained clear insights into its workings. You now see, my belovèd friend, what power has been entrusted to such people as the result of error and weakness! Your secretary feels he is more powerful than you: he orders the far-flung hordes of those favourites whom he himself maintains to traduce his sovereign lord, – and this is what happens. The most alarming rumours fill the town: it is said that you are neglecting the affairs of government, and merely indulging in fantasies of which *I* in turn make use to further my own shameless demands – , this is the only way in which people deign to understand our relationship. But now it is the "musician", too, who is said to exercise a decisive influence upon your political decisions, and – since they are now suddenly afraid because of this wretched business – they even put it about that I am to blame for Neumayr's dismissal, since he did not wish to appoint Froebel (!!). Yesterday, finally, the whole town was shocked by the rumour that you, my King, were intending to leave the country for seven months and to go to Italy, a rumour which has caused boundless dismay. What the real aim of this may be is as yet incomprehensible to me, as it is also perhaps to the unhappy man himself, a man who thinks only of heaping difficulties upon you because he still hopes to remain the only person at your command who is ultimately able to exorcize them; just like last winter when he finally offered to extinguish the very fire which he himself had started.

How can I think of *my* peace of mind now, and not place all my mental powers at the disposal of my friend? – So be it! God will lend me his strength. – If I feel called upon by fate to perform a great and noble service for you and your country, it must remain *your secret and mine alone*. No one must know that it was I who opened your eyes for you. That is why my advice remains the same as before:

dismiss Pfistermeister immediately and, at the same time, appoint Neumayr to advise you on forming a new cabinet.

The first of these measures will alarm your opponents and paralyze them, the second will show the country what it can expect of you. Prudence and justice come together here: their relationship is pure, conducive to the public good, and typically Bavarian.

I have only one worry now, and it is that, as a result of your enemy's skill, you may feel too strong a personal prejudice against Neumayr. I do not know this man at all, and can judge him only on the basis of the position he has held so far. As a result I see him more as a symbol than as a person: but as such he represents two things clearly and distinctly: "moderate liberalism" for the political situation; and for the particular situation at present, "justice" on the part of the monarch. Oh, be great and high-minded in this matter, as you have always been towards me!

Resist the thought that his appointment might cause you humiliation: the King can never be unjust, especially when he dispenses justice. The injustice was bound up with the whole of this flawed system which, made wise by this experience, you now intend to remedy.

I must also repeat – (forgive me!) – a point to which I had already drawn your attention yesterday, by underlining the advice that I gave you to keep control of your actions and remain benevolent and friendly, even if Neumayr should turn against me. People must clearly entertain the notion – encouraged by our enemies – that I enjoy – God knows what? – "influence", and that this is the result of your friendship for me. You will have no difficulty disabusing him as long as you do not allow yourself to be – understandably – upset by any objections that he may raise. But you must not allow *him*, least of all, to notice that it is *my* advice which has contributed to his appointment. It shall be my supreme pride and joy to have performed so fine a service for Bavaria, a service of which only my friend and I shall know. –

But, my King! act quickly and decisively! – As bold as you are, and as I love you, I almost wish to see you mount your horse, ride merrily to Munich, without a word to anyone, summon Neumayr to you here, and immediately put everything back on the right lines, like a hero! –

But perhaps you are already awaiting Neumayr at the very moment that these lines reach you? In that case – may God give you his blessing! –

Loyal and loving through death and beyond

Your
Richard W.

Königsbriefe I, 230–2.

339. KING LUDWIG II OF BAVARIA, MUNICH

Munich, 7 December 1865

My dear King,

I am sure that you, too, are under no illusion as to the length of time I shall be away.[1] I would ask you therefore to allow me some few days in which to put my house and affairs in order in a dignified manner. Everything I shall do is merely by way of preparation for my departure which, as I say, shall take place in a few days' time. Do not allow me to be hurried in an undignified manner, nor importuned in any other way. Trust in my nobility of mind and, above all, in my love for you, and believe me when I say that I shall not cause you, or anyone else, the least disquiet in any conceivable manner. In return I would ask you most urgently that my departure – as you indeed promised – shall go unnoticed. I shall repair to the gentle shores of Lake Geneva "for the sake of my health". When I depart I shall leave you my temporary legacy. Let me never for a moment doubt in your love. Continue to offer me your protection. Make me happy by faithfully nurturing our ideals!

If you cannot persuade the Court Secretariat to issue the necessary declaration[2] as I desired of you yesterday, I shall consider it necessary to act independently and to issue the same declaration, in more or less the same words, in a wholly unprovocative manner. If my lengthier declaration concerning the truth of the favours which you have shown me is irksome to you, I shall suppress it, just as I have always been ready to do whatever was agreeable to you, and not to do what was disagreeable. I would ask you only to consider how important it is that those gross reproaches to which the declaration I requested from the Court Secretariat would have related should not be allowed to weigh upon your friend once he is removed from your presence. –

A final parting word will follow soon! Until then I entreat your royal protection for my undisturbed peace of mind. In a few days' time I shall write to inform you that I am standing on your country's furthest frontier.

True unto death

Your

Richard Wagner

Königsbriefe I,237–8.

---

1 The previous day Ludwig had communicated his decision that Wagner must forthwith leave Munich for an indefinite period; see introductory essay, p. 591.

2 Wagner had asked for a public declaration to the effect that rumours concerning the sums of money he had received from the Bavarian Exchequer were "totally incorrect and wildly exaggerated" (Königsbriefe I,234).

340. MATHILDE MAIER, MAINZ   Vevey, 17 December 1865

Dear little Mathilde, I really must send word to the Karthäusergasse, too, to reassure you all concerning me. – In order to describe my frame of mind to you, I would ask you only to consider this: last Wednesday evening, 8 days ago, when the King's secretary, Lutz, came to see me and informed me of the King's request that I should leave Bavaria for a few months, I suddenly saw before me, as large as life, one of those pretty villas on Lake Geneva which I have known for so long now, with myself inside it and my servants with me, total peace of mind, Mastersingers, being able to breathe again at last. For a long time I heard nothing more of what the unhappy man was saying. I then worked myself up into a state of unnatural excitement, at which I afterwards had to laugh, and – the very next day I gave instructions for my bags to be packed. I have now told the King as much. No doubt he will bow to his fate. I am already hard on the trail of a villa here: I hope I shall soon be able to work in earnest, something I should never, ever have been able to do again in Munich. I had already told the King this, he knew of my wish to go away. However, they conjured up a fog for his benefit, claiming that I was in great danger & that a terrible revolution, directed specifically at me, was about to break out: the poor man believed that the only means of protecting me was to send me away. Since then he has written me the most heart-rending letter. – That is the position. –

But do you also want to know how it all came about? Children are always inquisitive. The Jesuits wanted to give me 2 Festival Theatres, 2 Academies of Art, villas & a regular income, whatever I wanted, as long as I showed myself to be compliant. Instead of which I simply ended up advising the King to send for a man of honour, and to form a new cabinet. At the eleventh hour they once more tried to gain my support for their plans which involved a complete reaction & the overthrow of the 1848 constitution. Only now did they set the dogs on me: I had had as much as I could take, and denounced the brutes more or less publicly. The King, (artificially) harbouring a personal prejudice against the man whom I had proposed, missed his opportunity, gave himself away, and fell into the trap. Everything I wish for now is for him alone! He must now help himself: if he cannot do so, he was not the right man, and I must grieve at the loss of a glorious hope. –

As far as I am concerned, I regard myself as saved, and am now looking forward to my work. The basic condition here – to be out of the world! All – but *all* – dealings with other people make me excitable, and consume my mental powers. Perfect and pleasant seclusion, in a *foreign land*, in *surroundings unfamiliar to me*, no relationships whatsoever, no contact with others, these are deeply felt preconditions for my ultimate prosperity. I shall visit you, but I can – *live* only in a totally alien land.

You know my instinctive ability to create those elements necessary to cut me off from the world. My servants are following me; Franz & Pohl[1] are already here: Vreneli[2] is coming in a few days; Anna[3] will come with the children when the house is ready. I am hoping to find the right place within the next few days.[4] I may even be working again by the 1st of January.[5] – Now be of good cheer! There is only one grief that could grow any greater, and that would be if the King could not be saved: *I* believe I can reckon on his love as long as he lives. God knows, he may survive after all. My friends are a cause of worry to me. But this impossible situation must come to an end for their sakes, too. I want Bülow to start by taking a year's leave of absence. He will travel around and give concerts: she will perhaps come here with the children, a move which is advisable not least on account of the glorious climate. – Now are you content? – Child! I could take no more of it. To ride out one day with the King in a coach and four, and the next day be torn apart by the priests – and all the time wanting only to work in peace. It was absurd! –

If everything turns out well, as I hope it will, this period of torment will have brought me a great deal, everything that I could have wished for, and – people are right to be amazed at my sprightly appearance. Well, there is a "reason" for that. Believe me. Best wishes to everyone, and continue to remember me kindly! Sincerely yours,

R.W.

(Only Pohl has a bad cough: he is seeing the doctor.)

Maier-Briefe 231–3.

341. KING LUDWIG II OF BAVARIA, MUNICH Vevey, 20 December 1865

Oh my King! My – friend,

No! it will not end like this, with all that has ripened within me slowly and effortfully during half a century falling prey to the boorish whim of the daemon of confusion and misunderstanding the moment that it is warmed by the sun of your love. No! A moment of calm reflection, and everything will disappear like an insubstantial haze! –

1 Franz Mrazéck and Wagner's elderly pointer.
2 Vreneli Weidmann.
3 Anna Mrazéck.
4 Wagner remained at the Pension du Rivage in Vevey from 12 to 20 December 1865; from 20 to 28 December he stayed at the Hotel Metropole in Geneva, and on 28 December moved into the Villa Campagne aux Artichauts near Geneva, which remained his base of operations until 4 April 1866.
5 Wagner resumed work on Act I of *Die Meistersinger von Nürnberg* on 12 January 1866; he finished the second complete draft on 21 February, and the full score on 23 March 1866.

I am ill and wretched. Finally prevented even from leaving the house in order that I might cast my tired eyes around me in search of some quiet apartment, I closed my eyes, worn out by my over-long vigil. What did I then see before me? My dear little house by the Propyläen, the small garden – the peacocks wandering around in it, bathed in sunlight and a sense of calm. "What? is it then my birthday today?" I asked: "after all, it is only the *fourth*[1] of May?" I looked around me then, and – Siegfried laughed aloud: "it *is* your birthday, do you not know it?" – Then I awoke, in tears – and telegraphed to my dear, long-suffering friend! –

Do not be angry now, my belovèd King! I do not wish to alarm you. But – I am not looking for a new place to live, either here or anywhere else. I intend to remain away as long as you think it appropriate, but, if I am never again to return to my little house – and to you, there is nowhere else I shall ever again stay – nowhere! –

I have written to Lutz: also on the unfortunate matter of your "inconstancy": you must believe the assurance I gave him. Not I (oh! I?) – but your people, believe me, your people – form these ideas. – But what does all that matter! After all, there is nothing here but confusion and foolishness. – Yet it will all turn out well in the end. God knows what chaos there was! I could no longer hear or see anything. It must never happen again: no doubt about that! Now you must allow me a couple of years of utter peace and oblivion; you alone shall know of my existence: I shall then complete my works. People shall simply not believe that I am still of this world. I shall do everything, everything that is demanded of me, if only I can come back quietly, oh so quietly, and hide myself away again soon in that little house of yours. Let us forget everything – the Academy of Art and God knows what else – for which we should need other people. We have no one now. Time will tell: it really will! But for now only peace of mind and creative work. Keep the Bülows for me. If he asks, give him a year's gracious leave of absence initially: he will then travel around and get to know people whom we shall later need. – Let us go to ground until the sun comes out again, the beloved Maytime sun! Only remain well-disposed towards me, and never doubt in my faith! But you must also remain in good health for me: bear ill-fortune stoutly and firmly! The days at Hohenschwangau[2] were too beautiful – : my daemon demands his due! Now only be true and dear to me! This is our real test. Ah! What *we* intend to create is so great, so new, so all-embracing: how could it take root so quickly, like common grass seed in the dry earth! – Have courage and patience! Put a bold face on it, most dearly beloved of men! After all, people ultimately do not mean us such harm. I know that he who *knows* me is not my enemy: it is just that I am a difficult person to get to know. *You*

1 Presumably a reference to Wagner's first meeting with Ludwig on 4 May 1864.
2 See letter [337], p. 670, note 2.

know me, and remain true to me! Is that not so? Very well then, when the time is right, I shall steal back once more to my little place of work, silently, oh so silently: not a soul shall know that I still exist.

Is this acceptable to you, my King, my saviour? Forgive me if bitterness overcame me: I have suffered a great deal, a very great deal. But my tears today have washed everything away. – God be with you!

True unto death,
Richard Wagner

Königsbriefe I, 271–3.

342. LUISE BROCKHAUS, DRESDEN   Geneva, 3 January 1866

My sincere thanks, dear sister, not least for your news! – I have had welcome occasion of late to think of my family: in the midst of all the upheavals of my curious existence in Munich I spent the evenings dictating my biography, in which I have now progressed as far as my 21st year: of course you all appear in it, and it moved me deeply to be reminded of my youth, which lay before my mind's eye with such uncommon clarity. Up to this period of my life I have been able to write in an exclusively cheerful vein, even when it came to reporting all my errors: but from now on – (and I have reserved this for later!) my life becomes serious and bitter, and I fear that the note of cheerfulness will now desert me – my marriage comes next! Not a soul knows what I have suffered because of it! –

Of course, what I dictate is not intended for the public eye: only after my death will it serve as a reliable support for whosoever may be called upon to give the world an account of my life.

Believe me, I was deeply upset to hear of dear Fritz's death:[1] you know how much he always meant to me, and how much I liked him. But just at that time I was beset by such unsettling and irritating circumstances that I could not have found a moment to offer you my condolences except with the most unworthy brevity. –

I had in fact daily contemplated leaving Munich: the King knew that he would be doing me a favour by not detaining me any longer; since it served his purpose to do so, he was even able to derive some momentary advantage from it. He will have to grow older, and get to know people a little better; his ardour left me no peace, he injured everyone around him without being able to resolve on any proper resistance. What shall I say? Time will instruct him. If he cannot find strength in himself to take a firm stand, I cannot provide him with any artificial strength. For the present I am insisting upon

---

1 Luise's husband, Friedrich Brockhaus, had died on 24 August 1865.

a few years' complete withdrawal simply to be able to work: all plans for founding schools and performing my works are to be postponed, and indeed *must* be postponed. The King expects me back in Munich at Easter; but – I prefer to live here or elsewhere in secret, since my ultimate salvation demands it. –

I hope these few lines will suffice! It's only a little – but at least I was able to write at once! –

Fare you well, my dear Luise; rest assured of my most sincere condolences on your grievous loss, remember me to your children, and remain well disposed towards

Your
brother
Richard.

Familienbriefe 259–60.

343. KING LUDWIG II OF BAVARIA, MUNICH   Geneva, 8 January 1866

[. . .] My King, I read that you are now being sent deputations from many towns in Bavaria, telling you that people are deceiving you by wanting you to believe that your relations with me are giving the country cause for dissatis-faction, a dissatisfaction which they have a quite different reason for feeling. I would ask you to reply to the first explanation by calmly announcing that it was my own wish that I should leave Bavaria, and that my departure had nothing whatsoever to so with state interests. As for the rest, you should listen calmly to what is said, but without committing yourself any further: but – use the opportunity to converse with these gentlemen, question them in detail and at length, and – note well what they say! What I have in mind here really has nothing whatsoever to do with politics. I am of the opinion that there is something unhealthy and sterile about the very nature of our constitution, and that in the long run it will undergo many changes. I am a royalist through and through. Only the King can will change and make it happen: only the German princes can save Germany. But it is for the most part a question here – as I believe – of *honest, upright men*: and it is these men whom you need.

I told you that only with the proud pain of renunciation in your breast would you become clairvoyant. But I want you to have the right companion on the difficult journey which you must now undertake – a man who will be genuinely instructive. I would ask you therefore to invite our friend[1] to obtain the following two essays for you: 1, "Thirty-three Propositions concerning the German Federation" and 2, "The Restoration of Germany", both of

---

1 Cosima von Bülow.

them by Constantin Frantz. This is the man who approached me recently and revived my hopes for the future. Of all the Germans his is the most sensible and statesmanlike mind yet to have come my way. The second and longer of these two books, more especially, expounds what I, too, had already foreseen as being the only correct and truly German policy; the author wrote to tell me that the harmonies of my music had revealed to him a picture of Germany's future. If you agree with my opinion of these books, I would advise you most affectionately to summon this distinguished gentleman to Munich without delay in order to have him at your side as your reader or your tutor in constitutional law, or in whatever other capacity would bring him into frequent contact with you. I do not think it a good idea to ask your cabinet to deal with this appointment: we know these loyal subjects of yours only too well! You should rather ask our friend to invite C. Frantz to visit you in private in Munich and have a private audience with him. If you like the man, you can decree his immediate appointment.[1] –

So much for today, my King, my friend! I can write no more. I am racked by rheumatism, contracted through living in my present draughty apartment, and writing causes me a great deal of pain.

But one more consoling glance! –

What shall we gain through this terrible renunciation of ours?

First and foremost: you will become a powerful and glorious King, Germany's saviour and Bavaria's idol! –

Though ruling in grave apprehension and silently wishing to hear the sound of my music, you will yet be able to say to yourself: – "There he sits in all calmness of mind, and it is you alone, your generosity and your sacrifice, which he must thank for finally allowing him to proceed with his work, calmly and uninterruptedly!".

And should you call on me to visit you in some lonely, quiet and unobserved spot, a hint is enough, and I shall come at once, however far away I may be, that – *that goes without saying*! –

In May 1867[2] *we* shall perform the "Mastersingers of Nuremberg" in *Nuremberg* – then more work – Siegfried, Twilight of the Gods! Then the ravens will cease to encircle the mountain, the glorious emperor will be redeemed![3] Indeed! Indeed! We shall be victorious – but only in this way! With God, my true and dearly belovèd friend!

Eternally yours,
Richard W.

Königsbriefe I,281–2.

1 Nothing came of this suggestion.
2 *Die Meistersinger von Nürnberg* was first performed in Munich on 21 June 1868.
3 According to popular legend, Frederick Barbarossa sits asleep in the interior of the Kyffhäuser hills in Thuringia, awaiting the day when he will awaken and lead the united peoples of Germany against the country's enemies. See also GS II,155; PW VII,298.

344. ANTON PUSINELLI, DRESDEN.   Marseilles, 26 January 1866

My dear, belovèd friend,

Your telegram with its sad tidings[1] was sent on to me here by telegraph from Geneva; it was impossible for them to do so until yesterday evening since I left Geneva last Monday[2] and have been on the move ever since, with the result that it was not until yesterday afternoon that I was able to send word that, for the time being, I would await all letters and despatches here. In consequence I do not even know the date of your Dresden despatch since it was copied out in Geneva with only the word "Dresden" being added to your name. It is possible therefore that my poor wife died earlier than is suggested by the "last night" of your despatch. I set out for southern France in an attempt to find a place to settle here, somewhere that would meet my most pressing need for the greatest possible seclusion and quiet, and so I have been wandering around, guided only by whatever information I had been given. The need to nurse an injured finger, which I neglected to do on my journey and which is now so inflamed as to have become intolerably painful, obliges me to delay here for several days. I had just retired to bed last night and had been asleep for an hour when I was woken up and given the sad tidings. A number of my friends already knew that I had had a premonition of what was to happen, and that, after all the terrors and cares which have assailed me for so long and which have finally become increasingly intolerable, I had already anticipated that the unhappy news would either destroy me completely or else find me well-nigh indifferent. Up until this morning, after a wretched night, I can describe my condition only as one of utter stupefaction in which I brood gloomily to myself – brood – without knowing what to imagine! –

My cup runneth over: and a nature intended for ceaseless creativity and artistic invention in loving peace and quiet finally finds itself so positively abused and so falsely employed by the kind of use to which life has put it that I am finally forced to smile at all that has happened – which the world may well regard as a kind of madness! – Enough! Let us consider what is to be done next! There is nothing more to be said here – ! –

I shall expect a letter from you in Geneva, in accordance with the telegram I sent you today; perhaps I may expect to receive it there at the beginning of next week. In that way I shall discover more exactly what has happened and how I was represented by you and by my Dresden relatives. I assume that, in your kind concern for my poor, unfortunate wife, you showed her, in my name, the same honours that I myself would have shown her if she had been fortunate enough to pass away at the side of the husband whom she had

1 Minna had died early on 25 January 1866.
2 22 January 1866.

made so happy. It is entirely in this spirit that I beg you to see to her last resting-place. –

At the deceased's request I gave her authority last year to dispose as she might think fit of all the goods in her possession, whether owned jointly or by me alone: I assume therefore that she has made appropriate testamentary arrangements, and believe therefore that there is no need for me to involve myself any further here. I would ask you, my dear friend, to calculate at once the expenses which are now being run up for the funeral, place of burial, etc. and which cannot be met from the deceased's cash in hand, in order that you may receive this sum from me by return. –

May the pitiful woman's fearfully tormented heart finally find rest!! –

All my own plans and designs have but a single aim now, which is to protect me, at all costs, from the most unprecedented disturbances to my peace of mind, and to protect me in such a way that I may finally recover the composure I need to create and complete my works, since I feel in turn that this is all I can and must now do. That is why I now find myself in the position of having to reply in the most unequivocal terms to my young friend, the King of Bavaria, whose passionate desire it is to have me near him again from Easter onwards, since I am resolved to devote myself wholly to my work and not to any further performances. But it is impossible to find the peace and quiet necessary for my work in such direct dealings with a King when I am so terribly exposed to envy and hatred. This is now my struggle. He is inconsolable. I fear that he might get carried away to the point of abdicating. Judge for yourself the agitations to which I am exposed by the only possible alleviation of this affair! – And so, as on each and every other occasion, everything conspires to torment and afflict my heart! It must be healthy and strong indeed to withstand all this. My poor wife succumbed because, organically, she was less well endowed in this respect. What distress! What misery! – Oh, she is to be envied, she who has finally and painlessly cut short the struggle! – When, oh when shall I find – peace? –

Fare you well, dear noble friend! Some day I shall come to Dresden and avail myself of your hospitality, my thanks, my sincere and heartfelt thanks. Your much-tried friend

Richard Wagner

Kesting 525–7.

345. CONSTANTIN FRANTZ, BERLIN   Geneva, 19 March 1866

Dear Sir,

I owe you a more detailed reply to various communications on your part which were as pleasing to me as they were valuable. Given the important subject matter with which we are dealing I cannot seek to excuse this delay by appealing to my indisposition and resultant disinclination to face each and every form of undertaking; but I may perhaps adduce it in order to explain the fact that I was unable to follow up the need I felt to reply to your confidential approach in the requisite manner and to the extent that I would otherwise have desired, which was why I omitted even to inform you of my resolve.

My intention – as long as you yourself, my dear Sir, have no objection – is to discuss the various questions which are of mutual concern to us, at least as far as these questions *can* be of mutual concern, i.e. as far as I may consider myself qualified and justified in expressing my thoughts on such matters, and to discuss them, moreover, in a generally stimulating manner in a short series of open letters to you.[1] I can achieve my desired aim here only if I succeed, as I have every prospect of doing, in persuading the Allgemeine Zeitung to accept my articles, since we have no doubt all learnt from experience that only newspaper articles are still heeded by the public. I feel impelled to undertake this task since I should first like to clarify my own thoughts on the underlying trend of certain enterprises before I embark upon them; but I also realize how necessary it is to attempt in this way to find confederates and sympathizers among those of the nation's scattered intellectuals who share my aims, men whom I can reach only in this way since they are otherwise wholly unknown to me. It would be my aim to encourage these intellectuals to think seriously about the matter, and to prepare them to the extent that, at a given moment, they may be capable of responding, in a well-prepared manner, to a practical appeal to join in certain enterprises. My singular experiences in Bavaria have in fact convinced me that, without a serious and conjoint offensive on the part of like-minded confederates against so well-organized a phalanx of vulgar and corrupting elements, even the most favourable prospects of achieving great ends – if based purely on personality – will in fact achieve nothing, especially if those ends are, alas, as novel as ours. But since the success of my articles can be advantageous to our cause and harmful to our enemy only if I take care to give the most moderate and discreet account of all purely personal aspects of the matter, and to show the most sparing regard in every respect, my reason for communicating with you today is to place at your disposal – in all confidence – the data which you will need to gain a more conscious sense of direction in the matter of my extraordinary relationship with the young King of Bavaria, so that you may understand how indispensable it must seem to me to abandon my strangely isolated position. Since I may assume that you are already familiar with most of what is generally known, as a result of the numerous frank and true accounts of recent "state" events in Munich which have been reported in the

1 Nothing came of this plan.

liberal press, I believe that for the rest, too, it will be sufficient for me to give you only the following brief description. – I continue to regard the youthful King Ludwig as having quite uncommon abilities, as you yourself would be convinced at the very first sight of his highly striking physiognomy. But the great question now is how the qualities necessary to govern will develop within him. An unbelievably senseless education has succeeded in arousing in the youth a profound and hitherto utterly insurmountable aversion to all serious preoccupation with the affairs of state; contemptuously dismissive of all concerned, he simply leaves such matters to be dealt with, as though out of a sense of disgust, by existing officials in accord with existing routine. His family and the entire Court are repugnant to him, he hates everything to do with the army and military life, finds the nobility risible, and despises the great mass of the people; on the priesthood he is clear-sighted and unprejudiced, and in the matter of religion serious and intense. There is only one way to arouse his sympathetic faculties, and that is through me, my works and my art, which he regards as the true, actual world, whereas everything else seems to him to be insubstantial nonsense. Contact with this one element arouses within him the most surprising and truly wondrous abilities; he sees and feels things with astounding certainty and reveals a will to achieve the most far-reaching of my artistic goals, a will which, for as long as it lasts, comprises the man's entire being. I then see before me the most wondrous success ever accorded an artist, and feel rapture and extreme anxiety at one and the same moment! So charming and, indeed, so engaging an ignorance of real life must, as you can well imagine, involve the royal youth in conflicts which, in more pressing circumstances, drive him into open displays of weakness. Since people can get round him only by referring to me, they were able to effect my removal only by pretending that it was his love for me which had brought me into the utmost danger. In the end I could not, for my own part, avoid pointing out to him the seriousness of his royal duties: in this direction, too, there was only one way of achieving any success, and that was to bring into play his love for me. In his eagerness to serve me, he acted with such blind enthusiasm that he even had the sketches of my diary[1] (with which you yourself are in part familiar) copied out and distributed among his various ministries so that the ideas therein contained could be "put into practice". I do not need tell you of the almost comical confusion to which this gave rise! All that now remains for me to discover is how far his sheer understanding of the world can be sharpened and strengthened. I have been quite pitiless in telling him my opinion of his officials, ministers etc; he accepts all I say, and hopes and promises to control his opponents and enemies, but he still does not appear in any way to have reached the point of thinking seriously about what I have said to him, and thus of forming a true verdict concerning

1 See letter [334], p. 665, note 1.

those people and things which are obviously governing *him* at present. As for my wish that he should summon you to Munich, he did not so much as mention it in his reply, but, in general terms, only reconfirmed his intention of placing everything in my hands when the moment is right. The vagueness of his demeanour makes me afraid of seeing him fall into some very real weakness of character. I can now see quite clearly that reason and remonstrations are of no avail, and that ultimately only one means of influencing him continues to remain open to me, namely my art – which influences his ideas, and his love for me – which influences his will. You will see therefore that this quite unique relationship of ours contains within itself, in the most incomparable way, a prefiguration of the means whereby I may influence Germany, inasmuch as Germany, too, is not to be got round by rational means. The fact that, through my art, I am in a position here to render a King lucid and fully clairvoyant who is otherwise incapable of properly appreciating the most everyday aspects of real life; that I may hope to persuade this same King to embrace the grandest and most far-reaching resolves and actions because of his inspired love for me – this must fill me, in my exalted mood, with a well-nigh momentous presentiment of the spirit and manner in which I might yet be called upon to influence Germany itself. I am too experienced to indulge in any vain and cosy self-deception in this matter. This much, however, is now clear to me: my own artistic ideal stands or falls with the salvation of Germany; without Germany's greatness my art was only a dream: if this dream is to find fulfilment, Germany, too, must necessarily attain to her preordained greatness.

I hope you will see here the outlines of an agreement which may bind me to you and to your endeavours: there is something in the fact that you felt drawn to me, and that I of all people found in you what it was that I lacked. Only Germans could be destined to feel this! –

And so – let us hope, and work in harmony! With the most sincere good wishes

Yours
Richard Wagner
(*not* "Kapellmeister" – please!)

Königsbriefe IV, 132–5.

346. KING LUDWIG II OF BAVARIA, MUNICH   Lucerne, 8 April 1866

Oh my friend,

So I have finally plucked up the courage to write to you once more!! – What does that mean? – Everything! Save that I might ever for a moment have ceased to love you! And – that says it all. Does my belovèd friend understand? –

You, too, will have been enlightened by our dear friend[1] as to the strange agonies to which I am incessantly exposed and which would be felt less severely by anyone other than me – at the very evening – of my life! Oh that I had to tell myself by way of consolation: "He did not know what he was doing!" He did it – I suffered – but – he did not know. But why did he not know, since his feelings were so intense and since he knew from the deep and overflowing gratitude that I owed him what unspeakable kindness he had shown me when he gave me a home, a fixed abode, a house and garden, the dearly belovèd companionship of a friend, and a sphere of influence which awakened my greatest hopes? Yet he did not know that he was destroying all this, – no! he did not *know!* Otherwise he would not have allowed himself to take that fatal step until he had summoned his friend to his side once more – though it were for the last time! – and listened to his advice as well, *his* advice above all: he would then have discovered that for less than his most belovèd friend's well-being that same friend would have sacrificed homeland, peace and worldly comforts, and that no sacrifice would have seemed too great to serve his friend's *true* well-being. He should have been certain of that! "Oh Parzival! Parzival" how often have I sighed those words. "What is the point of having had to sacrifice all this since *he* has not gained by it!" It is that – that – , my belovèd friend, which gnaws at my heart: the sacrifice was not only useless, – it was harmful to you. Nothing, but nothing will ever alter this view of mine! – – But it is a question now of turning this sacrifice to your advantage: and this, my belovèd, is now my task. We may not bid each other welcome again until such time as you can welcome me freely and openly before the whole world – and not for my sake – for I have no need of the world's testimony! – but for your own sake. In acting in this way you must feel that you are *master*, and must show Germany – of which I, too, am a part – what it can expect of you. For – *this* is the significance which our relationship has now assumed, and it is in order that this significance may be revealed to the whole world with its promise of hope that I now make this sacrifice, and – thus serve the fame of my glorious friend by continuing unceasingly to sacrifice myself. Only *now* does the sacrifice have any meaning! –

Good Friday brought me – with what deep significance! – safely home to port,[2] a port from which I can, from now on, observe your greatness grow. It was here that I dropped anchor once before, just seven years ago;[3] once again, at the end of this daemonically sacrosanct period, I approach the old coast

---

1 Cosima von Bülow.
2 On Good Friday (30 March 1866) Wagner and Cosima had discovered Tribschen near Lucerne; Wagner rented the villa from 4 April, and moved in on 15 April 1866. See also letter [340], p. 677, note 4.
3 Wagner had arrived in Lucerne on 28 March 1859 to work on Act III of *Tristan und Isolde*.

on my spectral ship, aweary from watching, and once again I hear the crash of the anchor: and here – I shall complete everything! Here I wrote the last act of Tristan, a work which, in its wondrous solitude, shall become the tombstone of a noble and supremely gifted friend,[1] towering up into the distant world as a monument to an ardent belief in love which none will ever understand. Seven years have passed: my breast swells with renewed hope; I feel an urge to be released from a solitude which no one understands. I have heard the old song of a new and glorious love: yearning for youth its sounds wafted gently towards me, borne aloft by your wondrous affection for me. And so this time I intend to create the work which shall redeem us and reconcile us with the world. We need – friends, – believe me, my belovèd lord! I want to create those friends for us and gather them around us. If things were to go on as at present, we should all be destroyed! Trust me! I have learnt something in the course of my Flying Dutchman's travels: – we need friends! They will not be made for us by any "Pfo" of "Pfi":[2] it is *I* who must make them; and, indeed, I can, for I know how. How I shall do so you must for a brief space allow to remain my own private secret. But rest assured, I shall give you something to be pleased about, and more: I shall lay the foundations of a building which shall embrace our Nibelung work! –

And so for now, my belovèd! you must leave me here in all trust: it makes sense for me to remain here a while. In order to avoid the upheaval of another change of address I was resolved only a week ago to accept the great expense of remaining in the Geneva Campagne, which is why I wrote to Herr Lutz, asking for an advance on my salary in order to obtain the wherewithal to rent the villa for a year. In the end, however, the Good Friday thought of "Lucerne" asserted itself, and, since I had encountered new difficulties with regard to the Geneva Campagne, I soon made up my mind to submit myself to the renewed discomforts of a change of address. I am now more or less a day's journey nearer to you than before, no further from Munich than in the Riss[3] where there would have been great difficulties during the colder weather for which I shall now have to prepare myself once more. I can remain here until the star of your great majesty is in the ascendant, the star which will shine forth far beyond me and illuminate the whole of Germany. Also, the terms of the rental agreement, although not easy, are none the less somewhat more reasonable here, and I can get over the difficult periods with somewhat less pressure on me. Even so, I hope that the request which I communicated to Herr Lutz may yet be granted: its fulfilment would provide me with a welcome sense of relief, and rid me for some time to come of my peculiarly painful dealings with your lower officials who, on instructions from their

1 Ludwig Schnorr von Carolsfeld.
2 Ludwig von der Pfordten and Franz von Pfistermeister.
3 Ludwig had offered Wagner accommodation in his hunting lodge in the Riss.

superiors, only ever seem to assume a friendly countenance when they have managed to prove that they have done all they could to make life a misery. – But Parzival prefers not to hear such things! And so I shall say nothing! Yet I know how things stand with him. It is true that he shoots the swan through the heart in flight, so that it sinks down bleeding at his feet: but I know that he alone is fated to understand Anfortas's suffering: it impresses itself upon him like a world-redeeming remembrance of the Saviour; he laughs at the snares which a maliciously short-sighted spell has cast upon him: at the very moment when deceit was most likely to delude him, a tremendous remembrance of fellow-suffering arose from deep within him, sounding its shrill lament: now he *knows*, he recognizes and grasps the sacred lance; as he brandishes it in his hand, the evil spell becomes as dust: his friend sinks to the ground at his feet, redeemed, in godlike radiance the grail illumines his realm and the world. –

That do I know! And – that is why I take this risk! –

There was no need of your wonderful letter to our loyal friend[1] to reveal your greatness to me: you know that I have already praised it in song. – Now, my dear one, you must also spare our friend: if I am "Wotan", she is my "Brünnhild"; this will explain to you all the love which unites us. Who – saving yourself – could understand Wotan and Brünnhild? You must be noble, generous and without reserve in providing for her so highly deserving husband: accord him your full and frank recognition. He is the most important prop in my edifice, a building whose foundations rest upon your love and whose gable is your undying fame! –

God be with you, my noble wonder!

Faithful unto death
Richard Wagner

Königsbriefe II, 17–19.

347. HANS VON BÜLOW, MUNICH   Lucerne, 8 April 1866

Now, my dear Hans, a friendly word to you! – I have just written to the King to tell him that I am now remaining here. To you I say that it is here that I shall complete what will be of benefit to us all. I am in good spirits: you should be, too! Fate has brought us together in the strangest way. Though we berate the "fool", he none the less belongs to us, and will never be able to break free of us. All we need now is a little patience. If we can obtain from him all that he has promised me – intelligible to my innermost self – , just think what an unprecedented and unhoped-for miracle that will be! There is

---

1 Cosima von Bülow.

nothing in the whole history of the world that could compare with this prize for its significance. You, too, know that! And so – be patient! And the signs are good! I have written to him again today, demanding that, by way of making a start on his involvement, he should honour and reward you with his unconditional recognition. I shall see from this whether he is serious. – And so – let us persevere: the prize, if we gain it, is immense. But you must make it possible for me, too, to persevere. I have rented a beautifully situated and spacious villa on Lake Lucerne for a year. My only thought in doing so was that you will live with me here for as long as is possible. For only if you grant me my wish can I bear to be torn away any longer from such good conditions. If you do not grant me my wish, it will all be quite pointless; I shall fall prey to disquiet, which would be fatal to the fulfilment of all my remaining plans. And so, my dear friend, listen!! – My house has 3 floors. The bottom floor with its salon etc. belongs to you – the middle floor to me – the top one to the children and servants. In this way we can live together without disturbing each other in the slightest. My income – more especially since the death of my wife – is perfectly sufficient to provide for everything necessary to support a relatively large family with ease and decency. And so I invite you most earnestly and sincerely to visit me here with your wife, children and servants, to live with me here in the villa, and to be so kind as to put up with my simple hospitality. If you grant me my request, you will contribute in the greatest way possible, nay in the only way possible, to my welfare and the welfare of my work – and of my future activities. Arrange things as you wish, come and go, remain just as you like, but from this spring onwards – as long as is possible – regard my house as your house – my establishment as your establishment, as the domestic base of whatever operations you may be planning. –

Hans! You'll grant my request? – Of course you will![1] For you know that I love you, and that – apart from my dizzying, but wonderful relationship with this young King – nothing, but nothing binds me to life as much as you and your family. That – you know! –

You have my profound thanks and proof of my joy at your stalwart labours. You have *proved* yourself – no doubt about it! Are we not bound to become a thing of wonder in the eyes of the world? And you see, what is so splendid about him is that he understands this wonder. And so we must not break this noble spell. It exists to bring happiness to us all! –

"Midsummer day! Midsummer day!" Hans Sachs – Hans Bülow. – Hansomely does it! – Fare you well, and be infinitely good to me – alors – Sire, vous faites bien! –

Yours,
Richard W.

Bülow-Briefe 245–6.

---

1 Cosima and the children arrived in Tribschen on 12 May 1866 (but see Newman's *Life*, III,520–21); Bülow joined her there on 10 June. They remained until 1 September 1866.

348. KING LUDWIG II OF BAVARIA, MUNICH   Lucerne, 29 April 1866

[. . .] My dearest friend, you are beset on all sides by an association of personal interests which cannot be other than hostile to our productive union; and it takes in everyone from the very least to the very greatest. What is needed is the elaborate spy-glass of all-pervading love to penetrate this haze and make out your star's true and genuine magnitude. I now stand outside, at a distance, and the people are with me: what I can see by dint of my magic they, too, suspect; but what clouds their vision fills me, who sees it clearly, with deep and painful discontent. An atmosphere whose atoms consist only of narrowness of outlook, foolishness, frivolity, superficiality, insincerity and disloyalty of the most miserable kind – who will ever penetrate it? Will the light of your star transcend it? Will the storm-clouds gather and clear the air with a terrible storm? How do you think I feel now, as I observe the course of present events! With what chilling frivolity is sport now being made with the fates of the noblest and greatest nation on earth: see how an ambitious Junker[1] betrays his imbecile of a King[2] in the most brazen manner, forcing him to play a dishonourable game which would appal the honest monarch if only he could see what was happening; and how, in order to save the nation and prevent any harm from befalling the brazen sinner whose fortunes are now being told by the great Gallic intriguer[3] it is not the *princes* of this nation – the natural protectors of the people and the ones most directly affected by all that has happened – who have come together to consult with each other and reach a speedy agreement in order to take steps worthy of princes; no, it is the *diplomats*, "German diplomats" (what an absurdity!) who sit around, no longer able to tell the difference between what is honest and what is deceitful, since their sole concern is the game itself, a game which they assure their masters to be fearfully difficult and to require both skill and experience if others are to be allowed to join in – be it for profit or for loss! Even at best I see only half-heartedness, speciousness and inadequacy in place of all that is right and whole, and, as a consequence of that, I see boundless confusion setting in, of a kind that no prince will finally be able to combat but to which will be added mass chaos – the chaos of a brutal mass in need of help; and then – I see my "Germany" perish – for ever! To what avail shall my life have been then, to what avail my work and my creativity? To what avail the godlike love of my dear redeemer, who has rescued me and my works for the world? My artistic ideal stands and falls with Germany, just as my works will live or die with her. What will follow the downfall of the German princes is that Jewish-Germanic mass which I once described to you

1 Otto von Bismarck.
2 King Wilhelm I of Prussia.
3 Napoleon III, who in order to advance his interests at home encouraged Bismarck in his policies of confrontation.

in my diary:[1] you know what I mean by the word "German". But – your diplomats cannot understand that. Ask any of them what he knows about the German character and what he thinks of it! – And I have to stand by while this happens, saying nothing – : for – what does an "opera composer" understand about politics! But now my heavenly friend is singled out and called upon to act, a prince whom Germany's guardian spirit has fashioned and nurtured to lead our unique, well-preserved and great German fatherland, as though for his own deliverance! Alas! He still does not know that those who tore his dearest friend from his bosom wished only to frighten and humiliate him in order to bring home to him a sense of their own importance – their sad sense of self-importance which, if it were true, would be proof enough that Germany was already lost beyond hope. – But – I have fallen from the ship into the waves of a desert sea! What do I – poor and solitary as I am – want now: wind and storms obey God's will; may He deign to govern the sea: I can do no more than seek to tend the light in my lighthouse. That shall I loyally do: and, as I hope, so may I hope to find the vessel whose fate fills us all with anxiety.

[...]

Königsbriefe II, 26–7.

349. KING LUDWIG II OF BAVARIA, BERG   Lucerne, 1 June 1866

Oh my belovèd, wondrously kindred spirit and friend,

How shall I begin this first letter to you after so intoxicating a reunion, after so blissfully anxious a parting?[2] When I look upon you and upon your love, the world fades from my sight: the highest goal, the most pressing concerns of earthly commerce seem but slight beside the immeasurable concerns of souls that are united in beauty and nobility far beyond men's normal lives, pouring themselves out in ineffable effusions! Alas for our poor contemporaries who have no notion at all of this spiritual outpouring, and for whom our souls' sublimest concern seems but a uselessly futile game! To us it is and will always remain our supreme capacity, as it is our supreme destiny: in it we shall always remain united, even though severance and total separation be our lot for the rest of our earthly lives, even though it were to be my most solemn duty to accomplish that destiny!

My friend! – We are on the very brink of a decision: since our supreme concern is clearly ordered and since it has been recognized with irrefutable

1 *Was ist deutsch?*; see letter [334], p. 665, note 1.
2 Ludwig had visited Wagner at Tribschen from 22 to 24 May 1866; see introductory essay, p. 592.

clarity, as though the result of some primeval destiny, there is no need for a single word to pass between us in that solemn hour which fate decrees for us and which I contemplate today in calm self-recollection: all we need to agree upon is how we may with dignity avoid the ordeal that now awaits us, the fearfully sad ordeal of utter separation for the rest of our lives on earth.

This separation is necessary, and it is imperative that I should carry it into effect if all that the most glorious power of love has achieved within you cannot at the same time arouse your supreme energy as head of state. Fate has willed it so and led its chosen representatives unavoidably along these paths. As greatly as you love me as the poet of all mankind, so great must you yourself be as German prince and monarch: fate wills it so!

Let us glance at our situation! –

In reply to your desperate question as to whether you should abdicate the throne, I retorted by entreating you most sincerely to grant me half a year's supreme indulgence, to forbear all mention of me and my return in your dealings with your officials, to forgo all artistic enterprises in which I myself would have been involved, and calmly to await an excuse for changing your ministers, an excuse which sooner or later would have been provided by the present state of things. – You thought you would not survive this trial of your patience, and so you sent me your newly acquired, loyal friend:[1] he was to bring me to you, since you were resolved to face the consequences attendant upon my return, and to face them, moreover, with a resolute mien. This disclosure broke my heart: I was bound to explain to your confidant that, if the inevitable struggles were directly to involve me and my return, they would give the enemy a fatal ascendancy over us and an advantage which would easily ensure him victory, and bring ruin upon my glorious friend. I informed your confidant of the measures I deemed necessary to purge your environs of the pernicious influence that daily threatens you, something which seemed to me possible only if our relationship could be left completely out of it. Then you yourself came: fair and loving, like a god! All circumspection was put at naught. But – things have now changed. Neither caution nor cunning can help us now, for what is needed is sheer courage, and the most sublime wisdom. – Our love has again been used as a means of stirring things up in the most appalling manner; my friends are being abandoned to their despair, and the accounts with which our enemies have been regaling the people, placing events in the most shameful and deceitful light, have finally dismayed even those who are well-disposed and fair-minded, for – no one can destroy this fabric of lies except me – me alone, and – *I* must remain silent, impenetrably silent, and in that way encourage these calumniators to believe in their own calumnies.

To answer for my honour and for the honour of those of my friends who

---

1 Paul von Thurn und Taxis.

have so loyally sacrificed themselves for my sake – to do so now – at a time when even to show good intentions is a dubious business involving the belief that your love is no more than a frivolous and unkingly disposition – this has now become the most pressing duty of my whole existence. Sweet is the consciousness of being able to portray only the absolute truth in simple outline in order to appear pure and blameless in the eyes of the world. Yet I cannot take even this simplest of steps without naming the authors of those calumnies, however unintentionally, in terms that would be equally clear and explicit: it lies within my power to expose their worthless and treasonable intentions; and – having once been invited to undertake a serious defence of my actions in the sight of my contemporaries and of the posterity of which I, too, am a part – I should have no choice but mercilessly to describe the head-quarters of these criminals as being in your immediate vicinity, among your closest advisers. I cannot do so, my dearest friend, without at the same time throwing back to you all the kindnesses which you have showered upon me in your godlike love and munificence, bringing happiness to one whom the world had abandoned: from that day forth I would be a beggar, and, as far as *this* world were concerned, I should have to pronounce our relationship at an end.

This – *must* I do! –

But what shall I do with this means of deliverance? This, too, I must now tell myself. Perhaps – oh God! – I shall drive you to distraction! You were already close to despair: if you renounce the throne – – our enemies' aim will have been achieved: I shall have helped to destroy Germany's last remaining hope; a terrible reproach, to have awakened this love within you and to have cherished it to your own undoing – such a reproach would drive me, too, to distraction and make me put an end to my life! –

This is the choice that confronts me: for I can *see*, while you, alas! my noble and belovèd friend, are still blind! –

And yet – there *is* one means of deliverance: fate shows us the way clearly and distinctly. What you may not do as a friend, you can and *must* do as – King. – King of Bavaria, the most illustrious of German princes! Look beyond the miserable rabble at the Hofburg and Residenz, and behold your *country*! The envoys of the Bavarian people are assembled around your throne: listen to their voice, and when they express the country's wishes, fulfil those same wishes as the wise monarch that you are! I ask no more. If you do this, we are saved. When new and noble deeds proclaim the royal will, your friend whose honour has been so offended must needs fall silent: then the world will *know* how things stand where the friendship between Ludwig and Richard is concerned, and actions will speak louder than words.

Oh belovèd one! Listen to what I have to say and trust your loving, earnest friend who has severed his links with the world in order to be able to serve you alone in loyalty and love.

The explanations which were intended to reach you by means of extraordinary deputations following my removal from Munich last winter, but which, having been misled by disloyal advice, you did not in fact receive, – these explanations, which will tell you that the people place all their hopes in you and that you have countless friends who can see through the deception that has been practised on you, and who know that my removal from Munich lay not in the country's interest but in that of a worthless band of traitors, – these same explanations – I hope! – will now be communicated to you in the greatest confidence and in spite of the most recent calumnies with which these wretched people have misled the whole world, but this time they will reach you by more strictly constitutional means by being sent to the regional Chamber of Deputies. The larger party, which will have the honesty and courage to tell you that it does not believe in the calumnies of our enemies, calls itself the party of progress! It would be our ultimate misfortune if these vipers were to succeed in stirring up in you an insurmountable prejudice against this name! May the god of our love prevent this from happening! We are on the side of "progress" – it cannot be otherwise! However much vagueness, foolishness and pettiness may predominate in this great party (which encompasses almost all of the people and which has this word emblazoned on its flag), we should nevertheless not permit ourselves to be discouraged from seizing this flag of theirs as our own: what can often degenerate in *their* hands into an unintelligible deception can become a symbol of redemption in the King's right hand, a symbol to redeem this century and, with it, all that is noble and great. In God's name I entreat you: do not be faint-hearted! Trust resolutely in the advice which issues from the hearts of your people! If you have to choose new men to advise the Crown, be bold and trusting, and overcome all prejudice against names, a prejudice which it was the diabolical skill of these traitors to nurture within you! –

In their utter dismay at the latest worthless accounts of your actions,[1] people have turned to me in a discreetly confidential manner, seeking information about these unprecedented goings-on and wanting proper assurance concerning their royal lord. It is with profound emotion that I recognize the hand of fate itself in the trust that has been shown me here: for fate has created this most terrible situation in order to part us for ever – by your own choice – or else to provide us all with the greatest and most sublime satisfaction of seeing the traitors cast into everlasting darkness. And so, dismayed though they were, I have been able to inspire these people with a sense of encouragement, and arouse within them my own inner confidence that your love for me, my glorious prince, will encourage you to agree, without reserve or timidity, to the delegates' wishes, and grant a gracious audience to all that they have to say. –

1 i.e. Ludwig's secret visit to Tribschen.

And now, my august and noble belovèd! Our fate rests in your hand; destiny's decision lies in your boundless trust in my love and in my loyal understanding! Be great as a King, as you are immeasurably great as a friend, – and my most comforting life's work will be accomplished! Peace and calm will be ours for ever!

Truly and eternally yours,
Your
Richard Wagner

Königsbriefe II,48–52.

350. KING LUDWIG II OF BAVARIA, BERG   Lucerne, 6 June 1866

My King! My sublime friend,

A man[1] who, trusting to my star and yielding to my most eager persuasions, gave up the prospect of an exceptionally influential and advantageous position in Berlin after years of patient waiting in order to accept your royal invitation to settle in Munich, today sees himself obliged, in return for this and for the great kindness which you have shown *me*, his friend, to leave the town as a result of a kind of treatment unprecedented in the most sordid history of German Court life, and, with all the apparent signs of disgrace, to abandon a place and a sphere of influence which in any other country he would have graced to general acknowledgement as a result of his spotless integrity and incomparable artistic achievements. His noble wife who, with the most sympathetic devotion and helpful encouragement, has consoled, supported and sacrificed herself to the friend of her father, the mentor of her husband, and the highly regarded protégé of a King whom she reveres with such deep infatuation – this woman is now, as a reward for the love which a kind-hearted monarch has shown towards his friend who, for that very reason, is now being persecuted – this woman, I say, is being dragged publicly through the mire and heaped with a shame which, were it inflicted upon the angel of innocence himself, would stain him with its taint. And all of this – has gone unpunished! – Those who have been abandoned in this way without protection have thus no alternative but to withdraw for ever from the scene of such undeserved shame. Their decision is as necessary as it is irrevocable. –

To you, my King and belovèd friend, I would address but a single request at this time of such great need: break your royal silence, at least on this single occasion: write a letter expressing your sovereign satisfaction with my friend Hans von Bülow and, at the same time, give vent to your royal indignation

---

1 Hans von Bülow; see introductory essay, pp. 592–3.

at the abject treatment which he and his wife have suffered at the hands of some of the newspapers in your capital city of Munich, and allow the recipient to publish it; and, in the event of you yourself recognizing that Bülow's continued stay in the city is no longer possible, at least ensure that your conduct as King towards him and his wife (who has behaved towards you, too, like a devoted friend) gives them both the satisfaction they need in so unheard-of a situation, in order that they may not seem to have been summarily excluded from the enjoyment of your hospitality and dismissed in shame and disgrace.

My King! I beseech you most generously to accede to this request, which I address to you, at the same time, as a duty that friendship imposes; for upon your response to this request may yet depend my own predisposition to regret having made the Bülows homeless, since I shall not be able to count any longer upon finding their house, with its sheltering welcome, open to me as their guest, as was the case in Berlin; so that any future move to Munich would be the total ruin of us all.

Since I am bound to assume that my kind friend is so far removed from the lowly concerns to which the rest of us are exposed that he will be unable to tell the best means by which to express himself in the letter that we are requesting of him, I make so bold as to enclose, by way of a suggestion, a draft which I myself have composed.[1]

My King! My august friend and last refuge! Deign to grant me my request! There is nothing more I can say to you today, so deep is my distress!

Loyally and lovingly

Yours,
Richard Wagner

Königsbriefe II, 52–4.

351. COUNT KARL ENZENBERG, KARLSRUHE   Lucerne, 15 June 1866

My dear Count Enzenberg,

What a beautiful letter! It warmed my heart and gave me such pleasure! Please accept my heartiest thanks for the noble opinion which you have of me. I have long been convinced that my artistic ideal stands or falls with Germany. Only the Germany that we love and desire can help us achieve that ideal.

I, too, envisage a German hymn which, simple and solemn, may inspire us

---

1 Wagner's draft letter to Ludwig, purporting to be addressed by Ludwig to Bülow, appeared with only minor alterations in the *Neueste Nachrichten* of 19 June, and in the *Augsburger Abendzeitung* of 20 June.

all with the will to act: it is not days of contemplative brooding but a single moment of inspiration, need and transcendent rapture that will provide me with what is right. Days of extreme danger are at hand:[1] may our princes see them as such; far better than all their diplomats, the bard will be able to address their appeal to the people.

You may be certain that I shall bear your noble request in mind! Let us hope and strive!

With the most sincere good wishes of the most heartfelt esteem,

I remain Your Honour's most devoted servant

Richard Wagner

RWA (copy not in Wagner's hand; published with minor variants in Freunde und Zeitgenossen 462–3).

352. KING LUDWIG II OF BAVARIA, MUNICH   Lucerne, 24 July 1866

Belovèd,

The heart speaks and ordains: now more than ever it is a question of keeping our heads! –

When I learned from our friend of your latest tidings,[2] I was overcome by such leaden heaviness that I was obliged to lie down for a brief morning sleep. I have now awoken much fortified by it, and feel my mind to be clear and lucid; and as this tells me my heart is right, I have no further doubts about writing to you today and sending you the necessary answer.

Your last letter to me, my precious and beautiful friend! had already refreshed me to the very depths of my soul. For thus do we love each other, and this is what love is! Everything else is politics, and of that God knows nothing. Loved by you, I can write only poetry and music: all other forms of contemplative thinking have to be forced out of me! One thing is certain: – we are alone! The miracle has happened: the fully developed artistic man is now understood only by a royal youth whose visionary enthusiasm has blossomed into life! – It is now a question of settling old scores with the world! – And that is what I am now doing. –

My Ludwig! my august friend! What your heart now tells you with such great certainty my own feelings long since told me was true, a truth that my reason was also obliged to concede. I admit that you are right, perfectly right:

1 War had broken out between Prussia and an Austro-Bavarian coalition on 14 June: it ended with the defeat of Bavaria at Kissingen on 10 July 1866. The "hymn" referred to here and which Enzenberg had called on Wagner to compose remained no more than a vague idea until 1871, when Wagner wrote the *Kaisermarsch* as a prospective national anthem.
2 Ludwig had written to Cosima on 21 July, reaffirming his intention of abdicating.

and so I shall not contradict you. Nor do I require time to think things over and repent, but steel myself to accept the fearful responsibility of not opposing your resolution. I say to you: Yes! there is a nobler fate than that of being King of Bavaria at present. If you wish to abdicate, there is a higher calling that could be yours than as King of Bavaria. But only if you yourself wish it so can I counsel you to carry through this resolution. That is why it is now my duty to show you clearly and distinctly the significance which your abdication would have to have if you wished to prepare the way for this higher existence. And so: there must be no contradicting your resolution, but only the most careful consideration of how to carry it through. It must not appear to express flight or retreat: it must express what the world needs to know. For in this way you can perform a more salutary act by resigning your office than would be possible if you continued in power. You must therefore proceed here with great presence of mind and self-assurance: if a delay is necessary, you must offer one last sacrifice, and offer it, moreover, to *me*. Look at me, and see the immense burden of responsibility that I must bear through agreeing to your resolution. My dear friend, I must begin by making this perfectly clear to you. –

Even though it shall never ultimately rule our innermost lives, what the world thinks of us is not something to be taken lightly: all our efforts must be aimed at coming to an understanding with the world; unneutralized public opinion can turn us into complete strangers upon this earth of ours, and make all further activity so difficult for us that it finally becomes totally impossible. – Public opinion will say: "Our promising young king, to whom we showed so much love, has been spirited away from us by this man Wagner! The man has ensnared him with his magic tricks so that he now rejects his own people, his country and his royal duties!" This will have to be borne, and – it will not be easy. But what affects me more than *this* accusation (which derives ultimately from ignorance of my true nature) is the complaint made by the *real* people, who have conceived a great, if as yet somewhat vague, trust in you, in contrast to other young popular princes – precisely because you were so different from the usual heirs to the throne, and because, half-consciously, they recognized in you an uncommon capacity for a quite exceptional kind of royalty. It is precisely your most independent action – my summons to Munich, and your loyal friendship for me – which has alienated you so much from the powers that now terrorize the town but which encourage the people – for all their vague presentiment of my own significance – to pin their particular hopes upon you and your character: when you apparently repudiated me, they were – I know – utterly appalled, not because of any affection for me but because they believed themselves deceived as to your own resoluteness. What this section of the people – which I shall call the youth of the Bavarian nation – must see going to waste if you abdicate, – this, most belovèd of friends, must indeed weigh heavy on my heart. You have of course taken this into account? – – But what weighs heaviest of all is – your own lot, and your own more distant future! – Oh heavens, my Ludwig! You are so young, and still so inexperienced in this world! With the exception of a handful of castles, almost all you know of your country is Munich: you think that this is Bavaria, and imagine the inhabitants of your Court in Munich to be your people! Forgive me my perhaps indelicate temerity, which may seem to you almost like a reproach. Ascribe it, however, to my deep concern and to the feelings of fearful responsibility which are tearing me apart. Will the world always appear to you as you imagine it at present? Of course not! As you mature into manhood, you will find the world a wider place and become conscious of your claims on it: never – of this much I am certain! – will the tension slacken in you that strives for an ideal, but your feelings as a man will also make you aware of your capacity for royal power: only then may you regret the *power* which now weighs upon you like some restrictive burden: perhaps you will then realize how you should have used this power *now* in pursuit of powerful ends; the longing to make up for past omissions will spur you on, and – you will then feel powerless to act! Kingship – believe me! – is a religion! A King must believe in himself, or else he is no King. But what if it were only now that you were to lack this faith, although it were none the less deeply rooted within you? What if you were only to become fully aware of it when you had already abandoned your right to that faith? If – you were one day to be overcome by *remorse*? – Tell me, my belovèd! If I were ever to perceive a shadow lying over you, what misery would I then feel, knowing that I had not prevented your present resolution, indeed – that I myself had at bottom caused you to take it?

You must admit, my dearest friend, that I have good reason for countering your resolution with most fearful trepidation! And so you must also concede me the right at least of advising extreme caution, and – if it must be so – as an indispensable precondition of my consent (assuming that there can be any question of this) allow me to vindicate the supreme significance of this step.

In what could this significance now consist? – You want to consecrate your life to mine? Well then, allow me to inform you what my wishes and views are in respect of our working together in the future, now that I am clear in my own mind how I myself stand with regard to these points. First and foremost I must confess that I have finally lost all faith in my return to Munich. Of course I might still have to countenance my return and a tolerable existence there because of your supreme authority as King: but since this place has become so utterly repugnant to me, and since I have made a close study of all its worst characteristics and realized that, of all German cities, it stands in a class apart (in the saddest sense of the word), the only purpose which my return could have served would have been to facilitate the commerce with you that is so dear to me. But my commerce with you, more especially in Munich, would have been possible only with the most wearying of interruptions – this much is as plain as day, and it does not surprise me that you, too, now feel the impossibility of this for yourself. Accordingly, necessity had forged for me a pair of Wiland's wings, and the following plan had suggested itself to me. The "Mastersingers" became my saviour in time of need. They point to "Nuremberg", that is where they belong, and that is where they shall first be presented to the world.[1] What a turn of fate! Nuremberg, the old, true seat of German art, German uniqueness and splendour, the powerful old free city, well-preserved like a precious jewel, reborn through the labours of its serenely happy, solid, enlightened and liberal populace under the patronage of the Bavarian throne. It is there, my belovèd, that I wanted to invite you next year; there the townspeople would have welcomed you jubilantly, their numbers reinforced by friends of my art from the whole of Germany, deeming themselves profoundly honoured and fortunate indeed to welcome us within their walls: nothing was against us there; enthusiasm and love would have borne us along, for it was a question, at the same time, of restoring and elevating the dear, old town of Nuremberg. Our success cannot be judged too highly: there – and there alone, the eyes of all Germany would suddenly have been opened to the significance that lies behind our "model performances", performances that would no longer be given as part and parcel of the scandalous repertory productions of our Residenz Theatre, but offered, pure and free of all dross, as a gift to the nation. There we could have asked the town what it would do to have our Conservatoire in its midst, and there it would have had to be established, to the greater glory of the whole of Germany, or all my creative efforts will have been in vain. I was certain that my belovèd King would far prefer to be among the friendly people of Franconia than among the priest-ridden, dull-witted rabble of Munich: there, in nearby Bayreuth, he would have finally found his favourite residence,[2] and – in time – he would no doubt have drawn the whole of his government to this heart of Germany, abandoning Munich to those to whom it already belongs on the strength of its name.[3] –

Thus, dearest of men, did the idea germinate and grow within me, thus did it raise my failing spirits: the Mastersingers gave me new heart; at last, at last – I was once again able to work on this strangely favourite work of mine with feelings of pleasure and love.

At the same time this work was intended to mark your release. Yes! the Mastersingers – "in Nuremberg" – were meant to lure the King of Bavaria away from his "Monkish" Residence to the fresh Franconian air where he

1 See letter [343], p. 681, note 2.
2 i.e. the Eremitage outside Bayreuth. On 20 February 1866 Wagner had written to Hans von Bülow, expressing the hope that Ludwig might offer him (Wagner) accommodation in the grounds of the Eremitage.
3 The name Munich derives from Middle High German *münech* (monk).

could again breathe freely – , to that same "Franconia" where my "Walther" knows he is at home, where he is "master in his own house" – and Hans "Sachs" – the Saxon – was intended to crown Walther in Nuremberg. – That was my quietly well-meaning plan. It would have ensured that Bavaria kept its King, a King on whom alone all the noblest elements among the people continue to place their hopes. But now you are losing your patience: my Walther wants to be off and away, so filled is he with despair. Should I say to myself, like Sachs: "Beware! it may not be!"? – I dare not do so, but instead I shall tell you my plan, cordially and as a friend. If you still feel the courage to carry it through as King – , oh! what great happiness it might yet bring! All that it would cost you is – to be patient until next spring. My life has been so unsettled for such a long time, but if I were to suffer no further kind of interruption or change of circumstances, I would certainly be finished by the end of this coming winter. I would then go to Nuremberg, where advance preparations could already have been made by then. And in the autumn I could then perhaps visit you in Hohenschwangau in order "to strengthen once again my wondrous power."[1]–

I am almost tempted to stop at this point, and end for today by asking, with the most loving entreaty, whether you can master your patience until next summer. – But I have no wish to conceal from you today that, quite apart from your relations with me, I attribute to your resolution a serious motive which, were you to emphasize it with the fullest consciousness and clarity of purpose, would certainly dissuade me forthwith from any desire to wish to see your decision in any way altered. I shall explain what I mean briefly and without reserve. The German Confederation has proved itself a pitiful affair: it cannot be a salutary feeling simply to be numbered among the princes of this Confederation as the equal of men who acknowledge only their dynastic interests, but not the great concerns of the German peoples; for years to come Prussian despotism will exploit Germany for its own ends: if you were openly to admit that the dignity of the King of Germany's oldest state does not permit you to act in this way, you would be offering a powerful and most creditable excuse for your action. Nor can it be given to an inspired and nobly feeling heart to know that, as King of Bavaria, it was being used as the mindless tool of popish intriguers: but, almost without exception, this has been the oft acknowledged fate of the Bavarian royal house for the last three centuries. Munich is famous throughout the world as a breeding-ground for these shameless intrigues: outstanding individuals (among them Rumford, our country's benefactor) have repeatedly been undermined and removed from office, in spite of their uncommon merits, thanks to the power of those formidable priests who stabbed *Thiersch* in the back when he submitted a plan

---

1 *Lohengrin* Act III, Scene 3 (GS II,110). Nothing came of these plans; *Die Meistersinger von Nürnberg* was first heard in Munich on 21 June 1868.

to reform the schools, and who now heap shame upon me and my friends because they know that we are incapable of serving their ends. I now understand why King Max II was so long-suffering, and so difficult and diffident; only by dint of the most obstinate efforts and cautious circumspection, only by dint of appeasement and skill, was it possible for him to keep the power of these people in any kind of check. But Munich belongs to them, they harass and lead the mob, and everyone is afraid of them – everyone: no one dares say who they are, no names are ever mentioned; there is simply a timid shrugging of shoulders. Pfistermeister knows them; his minions serve them. No one can maintain himself in the face of them. I understand everything, and – a free, noble nature like that of my belovèd friend – why, it has a different task in life than simply to squander its energies in this one direction, however sensible and anxious its concern. But these people control the whole of Bavaria's state machinery: no one is appointed who is not beholden unto them. Only great and fundamental changes to the whole history of Germany can provide a remedy here: the individual squanders his energies in a useless struggle with an inaccessible yet omnipresent and sinister power. If you declare openly that you refuse to be called King if you cannot be so in reality, you will indicate a second reason for your resolution which will redound to the welfare of your country and to the fame of you yourself.

The third reason, my belovèd, is one which you will not then need to name: the world will discover it for itself! While, politically, Germany may perhaps be settling down for a long period of hibernation under Prussian guardianship, *we* shall no doubt be calmly and quietly preparing the noble hearth at which the German sun shall one day be rekindled. Such is the great significance which your resolution and choice of purpose could have for the world. But, in order to avoid seeming petty, over-hasty or simply ill-humoured, I entreat you to show the clearest possible presence of mind and circumspection. There is a great deal that must be considered, arranged in advance and marked out in preparation, before you surprise your entourage by telling them of your decision. My only purpose in writing today was to induce you to do this now! You know me fully by now. I *wish* you could remain patient for a whole year: if you cannot, I shall of course understand; but if I am to be allowed to remain your loyal and constant companion, you must stand there in supreme splendour both during and after your abdication: if you wished to sacrifice yourself for my sake alone, it is I myself whom you would be sacrificing; for I should have to fade from your sight completely, were I ever to fear that you had been given grounds for regretting your decision! –

Now, dearest of men! Enough for today! I am utterly exhausted, and could not write another page! – How strangely glorious you are, my soul's guardian angel! Yes, I love you! – Do not doubt in me! Let me have an early reply to my letter! Sincere good wishes to your dear Friedrich:[1] if only he could spend a single day with us now! – Truly and eternally yours,

Richard Wagner

Königsbriefe II, 76–81.

353. KING LUDWIG II OF BAVARIA, MUNICH   Lucerne, 26 July 1866

My king,

I have but a single, great and decisive favour to beg of you!

Appoint Prince Hohenlohe-Schillingsfürst at once,[2] – discuss the matter in detail with him, and seek his advice.

You owe it to yourself and your country to take a decisive and independent step: I declare my willingness to accept whatever emerges from your discussions with the prince. Even the laying down of your Crown will seem easier for my sorely afflicted conscience to bear if it emerges from these discussions and can be arranged with dignity as a result.

Out of your love for me – accede to this request, and in that way keep from despair

Your friend who is faithful unto death

Richard Wagner

Königsbriefe II, 81–2.

354. MATHILDE MAIER, MAINZ   Lucerne, 23 October 1866

It goes without saying that a dear kind soul like you deserves another letter from me! I am sending you 3 choice pages,[3] but shall write something in addition: that's what I'm doing now! – My love, I have nothing whatsoever to tell you, except to say that I have nothing to tell you other than what

---

1 The code name of Paul von Thurn und Taxis.
2 Chlodwig Fürst zu Hohenlohe-Schillingsfürst was appointed Prime Minister on 31 December 1866, following Ludwig von der Pfordten's resignation earlier that month.
3 From *Die Meistersinger von Nürnberg*. Wagner had resumed work on the first complete draft of Act I in February 1866; the full score of Act I was completed on 23 March 1866. The first complete draft of Act II occupied Wagner from 15 May to 6 September 1866; the second complete draft from 8 June to 23 September 1866; and the full score from 22 March to 22 June 1867. The dates for Act III are: first complete draft, 2 October 1866 – 7 February 1867; second complete draft, 8 October 1866 – 5 March 1867; full score, 26 June – 24 October 1867.

concerns my infinitely pedantic and monotonous life. I have Cosima here with me,[1] together with her 3 children, governess and nursemaid, in addition to Vreneli, Steffen, Jost, Marie & Louise – our cook from Toulouse. Also Russumuck, Pohl's successor,[2] a huge Newfoundland, – and also Kos, the famous little pinscher; and the peacocks. We are now settling in for the winter, stoves & fires already laid. Not a soul is admitted. I get up at 7 o'clock: if I am in a good mood, Vreneli dresses me in all my finery, – if not, Steffen has to bring my outdoor clothes at once. Breakfast is taken between 8 & 9 either in my room or in Cosima's; then we go our separate ways, daybreak, – finally work. 1 o'clock mealtime: 3 o'clock long walk. Back home between 5 & 6, half an hour in the nursery; teaching Isoldchen[3] to walk. Then change of clothes: work, while Cosima gives the children a French lesson. 8 o'clock tea in my room; 9 to 10.30 dictation of my biography. And so to bed! That's how it is every day. Cosima is beginning to blossom – which she certainly needed. At the same time the Mastersingers are making good progress: I have reached the 3rd act: still hope to have finished it by the New Year. My finest work: everything is working out well: I laugh & cry while writing it. If all goes according to plan, we shall perform it in Nuremberg in the summer. My little treasure from Mainz will be there as well: she belongs with the Mastersingers. –

Well, while all this has been going on, my young King has been having a good clear-out. It has actually happened, he has got rid of Pfistermeister; it is just as if, in her own day, the Empress of Austria had got rid of Metternich. It has all passed off satisfactorily and promptly, and – just as I predicted – the curs have suddenly fallen silent: the spell is broken, the ghost has been laid. It was necessary for *his* sake, and it makes me deeply happy: perhaps – perhaps he may yet fulfil all my hopes. What he has done now he did simply out of his love for me, entirely of his own free will. But neither he nor anyone will drive me away from my Triebschen at present. Once the Mastersingers are finished – I shall no doubt show my face again, but only so as to make Triebschen seem all the more desirable. – Do you want more? I do not know. I cannot write my music for you. We live in limbo, outside the world – and – deserve to do so.

You are quite unique, a dear kind creature whom we love with all our hearts: believe me! Remain loyal & kind, so that, as happy "human beings", we can all one day enjoy each other's splendid company in perfect consolation.

1 See letter [347], p. 690, note 1. Cosima returned to Tribschen on 28 September and remained there until 16 April 1867.
2 Pohl had died in late January 1866 and been replaced by a Newfoundland also known as Russ.
3 Isolde, Wagner's and Cosima's first daughter, was born on 10 April 1865.

Very best wishes to your Mama, and to your sister and aunts, and especially to your cousin Louise! Fare you well, dear noble child!

Cordially yours,

Rich.

I   see the day approaching that no doubt brings great joy! [1]

Maier-Briefe, 240–1.

355. King Ludwig II of Bavaria, Würzburg

Lucerne, 22 November 1866

My shield and treasure! Dearest of friends!

My belovèd lord,

A thousand good wishes to you in Nuremberg from the haven of Triebschen! What an agreeable surprise it was to learn of your journey to your Franconian provinces! The letter in which you recently announced this intention was full of solemnity and sadness: I understood all that was left unsaid!! The theme of the third act on which I am now working is:

Illusion! Illusion! everywhere illusion!;[2]

this theme is brought out everywhere: even Beckmesser's laughable despair is given this magical background. My glorious friend, it is the theme which dominates my own life and that of all noble hearts; would we have to struggle, to suffer and to deny ourselves, if the world were not ruled by "illusion"? I am now taking care to keep out of its way, and pay the world practically no futher heed, except inasmuch as it involves avoiding illusion, mercilessly and with complete resignation. I am sitting here in my lonely lakeside fortress, like Sachs in his cobbler's shop, observing the world with a view to writing poetry and music about it: but "illusion" knows how to root me out even here, and it recently came in the form of sheer madness; and since, thanks to your bravery, my Siegfried! – it is no longer my *enemies* who now disturb me, it now has to be my "friends". I pray to God that I may succeed in

---

1 *Die Meistersinger von Nürnberg*, Act II (Beckmesser's Serenade) (GS VII,219).

2 "Wahn, Wahn! Überall Wahn!" (GS VII,233): the word *Wahn* means "illusion" or "self-delusion", but, as used by Wagner, it resonates with ideas of madness, folly and fancy, but also self-actualization and determinism; see Iris Gillespie, "The theory and practice of 'Wahn' " in *Wagner*, v (1984), 79–85.

sparing you this latest calamity to befall me, which has left me in the most painful agitation for two weeks now! But in order to give you some indication of what things are always like with me, I must tell you – but this time to amuse you – that it is no longer a question of my having to recommend people to you for every kind of grace and favour – something for which I receive demands almost every day from every quarter of the globe, and which, in spite of their great futility, keep on accumulating: no! This time I am to see to it that you fall in love with and marry a young lady[1] of dragoon-like temperament who has taken it into her head to become your wife! The unhappy girl is a pupil of dear Frau Schnorr and, finding the latter disposed to believe in ghosts, so prejudiced her in her favour and urged her on with alleged appearances and communications from her late husband that I am bound to believe, for many other physiological reasons besides, in the imminent onset of total madness in our poor friend. These unhappy women thrust themselves upon me here: Frau von Bülow, who has made it her rule to take upon herself every kind of self-sacrifice in order to protect me from all disturbances, fended them off as best she could, and in the process drew down upon herself the hatred of the eccentric Frau Schnorr to the extent that we must now fear the most furious outbursts of her anger; which is why we have had to think of taking certain measures which – if necessary – may result in medical precautions having to be taken but which alternatively may involve the police, since what we are dealing with here is a series of blatant criminal intrigues on the part of an impostor in respect of whom – as I know from sad experience – I may not be wrong in assuming the hand of our enemies to be involved, so critical a moment have they chosen! This disturbance has had a most distressing effect upon me, since my soul's most sacred and delicate sinews have been rudely plucked by this violent stirring of memories of our dearly departed friend. In consequence of such experiences I now ask myself with ever greater longing and seriousness how I should best set about fleeing from the world? It is a curious thing, but it really does seem strangely anachronistic that I should have been born at this moment in history. Rather should I have been born in an age of noble endeavour: I should then have spread my wings in boldest flight, instead of which I have been born into an age of decline and decay, which I must first survive before the springtime of my artistic ideal can find the light and air that it needs. But if, in consequence of this understanding, I am now utterly tired of life and weary of the world, if I am often deeply, deeply – oh! so deeply – ! depressed and sad beyond consoling; – lo! the light shines forth once more! Thanks to my friend's great love a portrait of him now smiles down on me from a wall in every room of my house! Oh! my belovèd! my King! my angel! A smile from your lips, a glance of your eye, and my soul is transfixed by a celestial light:

1 Isidore von Reutter; see introductory essay, pp. 593–4.

and all at once I see what a sin it is to feel despair! "You"[1] were born for me; and so I, too, was born at the right time! –

But what is this? Today I am writing to you in – Nuremberg! – Do you know what this strange old town of Nuremberg now means to me? It is the abode of the "art-work of the future", the Archimedes point at which we shall move the world – the inert mass of the stagnating German spirit! – And now, back to my "illusion". –

May I describe for my belovèd's sake the Prelude to the third act of my "Mastersingers"? I often have to play it to our friend:[2] God knows! it seems to have turned out a success. – This is how it is there: – during the third verse of Hans Sachs's Cobbling Song we heard a second, deeply plaintive melody accompanying the tune of the song itself – a melody made up of sustained notes. It now emerges in a lower register at the beginning of the introduction to the third act, quite alone, grave and melancholy, like plaintive brooding: it is taken up by the other string instruments in an interlacing pattern and brought to a sadly resigned conclusion; but at that very moment the strings are joined by the lower wind with "Awake! full soon will dawn the day" – which all the townsfolk will sing at the end of the act, greeting Sachs in a mood of the most solemn emotion. It now rings forth like a blissful premonition: following the first section of this melody the string instruments again add their voices, lifting up their eyes to the sun, as it were, in tender emotion, to a sun which shines clemently through the window on the head of the brooding figure, causing the dust to dance a golden dance, in contemplation of which the rapt figure is lost in a smile of tender melancholy. Once again the lower wind enter with the second section of their glorious proclamation and bring it to its conclusion as though with solemn emotion: the strings add their voices then, as though in a flood of the most sublime tears; it is the same theme as we heard at the beginning, but in a soft and gentle colouring; it sinks down as though with a smile of tender resignation, the only happiness of a noble heart and lofty mind, in order to die away, tenderly and touchingly, as though with a nobler reminiscence of the actual Cobbling Song. – That is the Prelude: the curtain rises. Sachs in a chair reading a chronicle of world history; finally he engages in conversation with David, but without really allowing himself to be interrupted in his meditations: when the young apprentice has left, we hear the earlier plaintive, low-pitched melody once again; to its accompaniment Sachs now begins to sing: "Illusion! Illusion! everywhere illusion!" –

This, my belovèd Parzival, is my daily task, my day's activity, in the best sense of the word. – But – , today I am writing to you in Nuremberg: – what this means is:

1 Here, exceptionally, Wagner uses the form "Du": see letter [106], p. 191, note 1.
2 Cosima von Bülow.

But now has dawned Midsummer's day!
We'll see now how Hans Sachs intends
turning this madness to his ends,
   that good may come of ill;
   for if it plagues us still,
   e'en here in Nuremberg,
   let's make it do such work
as needs a touch of madness in it;
and so let one who's mad begin it.[1]-

This is what I have been telling myself, and this is the meaning of my words of greeting to my belovèd in Nuremberg. Believe me – you, me and Nuremberg – thereby hangs a tale! How everything now falls into place, so strangely, as though woven by our angel in order to master our daemons. Oh, I pray that you may like it there: it is your first triumphal entry, for with this entry into Nuremberg at the end of your first royal tour you will triumph over the worst of your enemies; yes, you will celebrate a victory over yourself; for I believe and know what it has cost you, my dear and incomparably sweet friend: it has cost you a great effort of will to tear yourself away from such a consoling haven of peace in order to perform duties whose harshness can be mitigated by no amount of splendour or magnificence. Oh, I believe and know this to be so! How often have I yearned to be able to hold out a fellow hand to you, even for a moment, when I followed the course of your journey, festivities, speeches, balls etc. in the newspaper! But ah! that is precisely what it was![2] But if you must suffer and bear an intolerable burden, you can at least tell yourself that this suffering will bear fruit! And indeed, it must be so. Most belovèd of men, I should like to see you again soon and speak to you: I have already told you of my deep and sincere desire to do so. But of course, Neumayr must not let himself be embarrassed by this: for – this man has my blessing from the very bottom of my soul. This man, too, I should like to get to know, more especially for his own sake, so that he may form his own opinion of me and learn to get by in a situation in which, I freely admit, the studies of Bavarian statesmen have so far made little progress. I should also like to consult with you on the arrangements necessary for performing the Mastersingers: assuming that no new "madness" overtakes me here and that the wretched world leaves my poor nerves in peace, I hope, with luck, to have finished my (your!) score by the spring, and, if I could now assure myself in good time of the requisite means of performing the piece, there would be nothing to prevent a festive performance of the work from taking place in the course of next summer. I should also like to become

1 Act III, Scene 1 (GS VII,235); verse translation by Ernest Newman.
2 Possibly a punning allusion to the previous sentence, where the verb *verfolgen* (to follow) might also imply "persecution" and "harassment".

personally acquainted with your new Cabinet Secretaries: the unfortunate circumstances in which we have found ourselves until now have meant that a great deal has had to be left undone, and that I shall be cast in a poor light if this situation is not fundamentally and systematically regulated. At all events, if our reunion (albeit for only a brief visit in the first instance!) were to run into difficulties (difficulties which I, for one, have no wish to cause), it would be desirable if my gracious lord were to indicate to me which of his secretaries I could turn to in the cases outlined above. –

I am now on my own for a time, since Frau Cosima has gone to see poor Hans in Basle, in order to offer him what help she can at present. Great, however, is the decline into which we have all sunk – and to what avail? That utter wretchedness may thrive! Oh world! "Illusion! Illusion! Everywhere illusion!" – Which brings me back to where I started! If Hans Sachs did not know a way of using illusion for some nobler end, and if his Walther had not beckoned to him from the royal castle at Nuremberg, – ah, how sad my theme would sound today! – But the music I hear is:

Awake! Full soon will dawn the day! –

Good luck, my King! Good luck, my hero, my saviour! Thus far have we come: – my King prospers and reigns! He loves me, and I live in him! All hail the day! All hail Nuremberg! I am happy!

Sincerest good wishes from the very depths of my soul!

Eternally
Your most loyal servant
Richard Wagner

Königsbriefe II, 101–5.

356. Clara Wolfram, Chemnitz   [Lucerne, 15 January 1867]

My dear Kläre,

It is wrong of me to have delayed so long before replying to your letter: how this has come about will be understandable to anyone who is at all familiar with me and my strangely secluded, yet unceasingly eventful, life. I shall therefore not waste any time in apologizing, but would only ask you to believe me when I say that it was not any lack of sincere concern on my part which prevented me from finding a suitable moment to write to you. In this regard, too, you could easily have formed a true opinon of me if you had been present on those evenings when I have been dictating my biography, &, much to my own surprise, have seen my past life unfold with such vividness and clarity. [The[1] pile of pages has already grown quite large,

---

1 The bracketed passages have not previously been published.

and if ever you were to look through them yourself, you would realize what a vivid & immediate impression I have retained of you, too, dear sister, in my memories of our experiences together, and how tenderly I recall you and with what feelings of emotion. Of course, these pages cannot be published until long after my death; whenever I am in the right mood of an evening, I dictate additional sections for my young friend, the King of Bavaria, who is already receiving them section by section in order to keep them for himself.] I have at present reached the period of my Dresden appointment: it often affects me deeply to look back over my past life.

A further reason for delaying writing was because I was half planning to revisit my birthplace & my relatives. But I have been prevented from doing so until now because of my work on the Mastersingers, which I was finally able to take up again last summer & which I shall not now put down again until I have finished it. But I am counting upon carrying out my plans next summer, when I intend to relax again for a while. I shall then visit you,[1] & tell you how sorry I was to hear of your severe trials & tribulations and how much I sympathize with you. – That Minna did not make better provision for you in her will is a matter of great regret to me for several reasons: but you know that her private feelings were never directed at any of the people with whom *I* was friendly. God knows to whom she assigned much of what was hers, though I have no doubt but that it would have been better looked after in other hands. It would, however, have been a matter of the deepest repugnance for me to have had any dealings whatsoever with her on this point. As for the grand piano I do not believe you have lost very much, apart from what it may have been worth as a souvenir:[2] I hope one day to be able to provide you with a suitable instrument to go in your house. [My latest composing instrument already belongs to the King of Bavaria.] Your report of Minna's death has once again filled me with a very real sense of horror: the poor woman – it was enough to make one weep, but there was nothing that could be done for her. There is something quite hopeless about her fate which casts a shadow over the whole of human existence in my eyes!

Whether you have a clear picture of the curious fate that I myself have suffered in recent years must remain an open question: from time to time I have come across things in the newspapers which came fairly close to the truth. I was forced to make it my general rule to observe only the most absolute silence, since any public utterance could only expose my poor young friend. I had to let everything depend upon the course of events, upon the young King's progressive maturity of judgement & character, and upon his

1 In the event Clara Wolfram came to Munich for the première of *Die Meistersinger*.
2 Wagner's Dresden piano passed into the possession of Natalie Planer. It is now in Wahnfried.

ultimate actions. What was at stake was no more and no less than the ruin of Germany's last, uniquely promising prince; unsuspecting as he is, he was ensnared and betrayed by his own most privy officials; it was no small undertaking for me to make him see things clearly at last, & only his boundless love for me finally gave me the power to persuade him to take the decisive steps that have finally freed him from the most extreme of dangers. I have now every hope that his welfare is assured, and, for my own part, desire only to be left in peace here for a relatively lengthy period of years, now that I am living in another world and have finally found occasion to work again & pleasure in doing so. –

That, in brief, is really all that I can tell you by letter: if I wanted to go into detail, there would be no end to it. Let us hope we may see each other again soon! I number this among the more agreeable prospects open to me at present. Keep well and – be brave & face up to life's ultimate trials! Kind regards to your family, and remember me with affection,

Your loyal brother
Richard.

RWA (copy not in Wagner's hand; incompletely published in Familienbriefe 260–2).

357. Bertha Goldwag, Vienna   Lucerne, 1 February 1867

Dear Fräulein Bertha,

Tell me exactly how much money I would have to send you if you were to supply me with a house-coat based upon the enclosed sketch. It would be *pink* in colour, and be based upon one of the enclosed patterns, which I have numbered 1 and 2, so that you can work out the price of them both, since I assume they will be different. No 2 is somewhat stiff and cut away at the back – presumably an Austrian fabric – but I like the colour. And so – an exact estimate.

As for the blue, I have chosen the sample which I am returning herewith and which I hope is not too expensive. I need 12 yards. In the event of your not being able to get by on the money intended for the new items, I am enclosing herewith a further 25 thalers and shall be grateful if you will credit this sum to my account. In any case I would ask you to include with the blue satin 10 florins' worth of very narrow blonde lace for shirt trimmings (you know the one, about an inch in width).

Frau v. Bülow looks forward to receiving your invoice for the portfolio which she will settle at once.

And so – how much would it cost to make the house-coat described herewith?

Best wishes. Your devoted servant

RW.

Pockets with
puffcd ruche
and bows of same
material.

Pink satin. Quilted with eiderdown and *sewn in squares*, like the grey and red cover which I have of yours; exactly the same thickness, light, not heavy; and of course the outer and inner material must be quilted together. Lined with a light-weight white satin. Width of coat at lower hem *six* lengths, i.e. very wide. Also, sewn on extra, *not* stitched to the quilting! – a puffed ruche of the same fabric, all the way round; from the waist down the ruche should issue in a puffed inset (or trimming) wider towards the bottom and closing off the front.

Examine the drawing closely: this trimming or flounce must be particularly opulent and beautifully worked, and must extend on both sides by a foot in width and then, as it rises to the waist, lose itself in the usual width of the puffed ruche that encloses the waist. At the side of the flounce three or four beautiful bows of the same material. The sleeves, like the ones you recently made for me in Geneva, with puffed trimmings – opulent; a bow at the front and a broader one, opulent, on the inside at the bottom of the part that hangs down. Also a wide sash ten feet long, the full width of the material at either end but somewhat narrower in the middle. The shoulders narrower, so that the sleeves do not pull down: you know. And so six lengths wide at the bottom (quilted) and, *at the front,* a flounce one foot in width on either side. In other words six lengths and two feet wide at the bottom.

Putzmacherin-Briefe (including facsimile) 64–71.

358. OSKAR SCHANZENBACH, MUNICH Lucerne, 20 February 1867

My dear Dr Schanzenbach,[1]

Once again I must thank you for your undaunted *détour* to Lucerne, which gave me the honour and pleasure of making your valuable personal acquaintance. I must also take this opportunity to thank you for your kind letter of some days ago, although the news that it contained was, in essence, far from pleasing.

You tell me in confidence of the awkward atmosphere that surrounds Prince H. as a result of intrigues in the King's entourage and the latter's mistrust of his Prime Minister, a mistrust which is encouraged rather than diminished by such intrigues. I find this very distressing, since I should most certainly regard it as an incalculable misfortune if the prince were to lose the patience necessary to perform his task and if the King were to be deprived of his support in consequence. I cherish this sentiment purely out of love for my exalted friend and out of concern for his welfare.

But how can I make it clear to you that what guides me here is no other interest than the motive that I have just outlined? I can see from your recent letter, well-meaning though it was, that I have failed to convince you on this point, in spite of the highly explicit assurances that I gave you when we spoke together on the subject. It seems to me important that I should once again explain myself and my attitude to these questions in the most explicit terms.

I am unaware of any personal interest in the furtherance of which I should need to call upon anyone in the world to intercede on my behalf with the King or with the state of Bavaria. My strongest personal wish is to be able to live here where I am, in absolute tranquillity, unmolested and forgotten about, for as long a period as is possible, living only for my work: the King's true love for me fulfils this wish of mine as a matter of course.

The artistic plans which I have instigated go beyond all personal interest on my part and can be realized only at the cost of unprecedented personal exertions and sacrifices: they are entirely at the mercy of the King's fiery will and such is his enthusiasm that he is more eager to take them in hand than I myself would wish for the sake of my present peace of mind; all the plans that I had previously sketched out have been ratified and assigned to the Civil List to be put into practice. There is not the least need for any intervention on the part of the Ministry of Education or Herr von Gresser.[2] The only thing that prevents them from being put into practice at present is Bülow's

---

1 Schanzenbach, Ludwig's personal physician, was acting as intermediary between Hohenlohe, the new Prime Minister (see letter [353], p. 704, note 2), and Wagner.
2 The Minister of Education.

delay in accepting the King's highly flattering proposals,[1] since he is ill and out of sorts, and, if possible, has an even greater aversion to returning to Munich than I myself.

Moreover, nothing until now has stood in the way of my own return (which I would certainly not regard as a permanent arrangement) except for the dilemma in which the formerly indispensable Minister von der Pfordten placed the King by declaring that he would resign his portfolio the moment I returned. It would be in Prince H.'s power to exert similar pressure on the King if he were to issue a similar declaration to that given by Herr von der Pfordten. If the Prince is not interested in exerting this kind of pressure on the King, I would consider it important and necessary – and this, my dear Sir, I now make so bold as to emphasize – that he should speak his mind, openly and explicitly, and – as I have already indicated – reassure the King by his doing so.

Of course, I have no clear indication that the King imputes the same kind of quirkishness to the Prince as Herr von der Pfordten was inspired to show when he was a member of the royal cabinet: indeed, he was delighted to be able to inform me that H. is well-disposed towards me. As for the Prince's wish to keep me out of Munich for some time yet, it has already struck me that the King, according to his own testimony, had not heard the Prince express this wish directly, but that the latter's views had merely been passed on and reported to him. I also know that it appears to be in the particular interests of the King's entourage to pander to his remarkable reluctance to discuss delicate questions directly with the highest relevant officials, with the result that they present themselves as mediators and messengers.

These mediators and reporters – my dearest friend – are the devils that currently blight the whole of Bavaria's political life. If the Prince encounters mistrust on the part of the King, he may be certain that this mistrust has been fomented not least by the fact that among the tales conveyed and reported to the King by these worthy gentlemen is the claim that Prince Hohenlohe is suspicious of me, as he is in general, etc.

I say this to you: if you are interested, as a good Bavarian, in seeing Prince H. remain at the helm of government, you should try to persuade him to speak openly and reassuringly about me not with the Minister of Education but with H.R.H. himself. It is not vanity which makes me emphasize my own importance, but only the truth, and my concern for the welfare of my exalted

---

1 On 18 January 1867 Wagner had written to Ludwig demanding that Bülow be appointed director of the projected School of Music, that he be authorized to reorganize the Court Theatre orchestra and engage singers for *Die Meistersinger von Nürnberg*, that he be given overall control of the Court Opera, and that he be invested with a Bavarian decoration. According to his letter to Raff of 16 February 1867, Bülow found these terms "insufficient"; but on 5 April he agreed to being appointed Royal Kapellmeister in Ordinary Service, with the promise of "a further post with a fixed salary", when the School of Music materialized.

friend, whom I love and for whom I predict great misfortune were he to be decisively prejudiced against the Prince for quite insignificant reasons (among which I should be happy to number my own affairs).

And there is something else I must ask you to explain. How is it that your letters and those of the King to me or Frau v. Bülow are sealed, and their envelopes addressed, by the same hand? It is most curious. What is more, the enclosed envelope addressed to Fr. v. B.,[1] which I did not receive until the 17th inst., contained a letter from the King written on the 6th of Feb. The King told me that Count Holstein[2] was now acting as mediator and forwarding all his letters to me. How is it that you now find yourself performing the same function? Please let me know: one word will suffice!

That is enough from me – Sapienti sat![3]

Sincerest good wishes from your devoted servant,

R. Wagner.

RWA (published with minor variants in Freunde und Zeitgenossen 478–82).

359. KING LUDWIG II OF BAVARIA, MUNICH   Lucerne, 25 April 1867

[...] Responsibility for the conspiracy which was intended to bring you to the point of abdicating last summer must be borne by all who did not openly and self-sacrificingly defend and avenge the dignity of their King, a dignity that was defiled in the most unheard-of manner. The whole of your ministerial and secretarial staff at the time bear fellow responsibility: none of them stood up for you; they were all, and still are, mere tools in your enemies' hands. Claims that they acted only out of ignorance or, rather, with a view to helping you, are a lie. The Court in Vienna lived in daily expectation of receiving news of your abdication: Archduchess Sophie enquired openly whether the ... had been sent packing yet. – It is your duty here to clean up properly and clear things out, and then gradually, but decisively and without delay, to surround yourself with entirely new men. –

Listen further to the words of a dying man! –

What you cannot achieve by a change of staff, you must aim at accomplishing by a powerful show of political initiative! Nothing can save Bavaria unless you choose the only right and proper course of action, and carry it through with all your energies.

The German Confederation could have been saved, and it might have led to something significant in a salutary sense, if only Bavaria had taken the

---

1 Cosima von Bülow.
2 *recte* Holnstein.
3 *verbum sapienti sat est* (a word is enough for the wise man).

initiative last spring and acted energetically. Bavaria was called upon to lead the German princes and to arbitrate between Prussia and Austria, but only if every conceivable defensive power had been mustered at once. This opportunity was missed because the Bavarian Minister was already in collusion with Prussia: the shameful semblance of a war that he conducted, and the resultant weakening of Bavaria's position and her humiliation, all created a mood of despair in the country: everyone is openly turning to Prussia, in order at least to partake of a powerful government and organization. Working against this is the influence of Austria and the Jesuits bent upon saving the country for Austria as soon as the latter recovers (as it hopes it will) and takes its revenge on Prussia. In this event Austria will treat Bavaria and Württemberg as Prussia treated Hanover and the Electorate of Hesse: the Main will then divide Austria and Prussia; and there will no longer be any question of Germany or of Bavaria. In the face of this, Bavaria can retain her independence only by forming an allegiance with Prussia; for Prussia can never "annex" Bavaria; but Austria can and *will* do so the moment that it recovers. And so, resolutely and honourably, an allegiance with Prussia: for only in this way will Germany, too, be saved; precisely because Prussia (more especially as "Prussia") can never annex the southern German states; and this, ultimately, is the only way in which it will be possible for Austria to rejoin the German Confederation as an allied power, since it will then be *obliged* to do so by force of circumstances. And so, if Bavaria adopts the right policy and does so unflinchingly, she will at the same time guarantee Germany's continuing existence and powerful reunification, otherwise the country will disintegrate for ever into an Austrian and a Prussian half. Bavaria can be the cement, so to speak, or the heart of this union. Then Germany will *be* something, it will be powerful: the German will feel *himself*, and *we* shall show the world what is German and what the German spirit is, we shall pour new life into the arid veins of the poor, unbelieving German world. Let the flag of the noble German spirit then flutter over Germany from Munich, a flag which I, too, will have helped to weave and which my glorious Siegfried shall flourish high above the German lands. –
    [. . .]

Königsbriefe II, 166–7.

360. KING LUDWIG II OF BAVARIA, BERG   Starnberg, 12 June 1867

My most truly belovèd friend and lord,
    When I spoke to you about Tichatscheck as "Lohengrin"[1] and said that his singing was like a painting by Dürer, but that his outward appearance was

---

1 See introductory essay, p. 595.

more like a picture by Holbein, I ought to have been more explicit and begged you to listen to the singer with your ears open, but not to observe him too keenly: for only in this way would it have been possible for you to gain an impression of him, and understand that, given the quite deplorable quality of all other tenors known to me, he remains the best available. You ignored my warning: you stared at him with redoubled intensity; it was impossible for him to withstand this scrutiny: the vital illusion was lost.

I fear now, my gracious friend, that on this occasion your eye was too keen and that you have destroyed all I had been at such pains to build up; my only wish is that you might now cast in *my* direction the same keen glance as that with which you destroyed this illusion, and see your friend who feels his continuing presence in your proximity, where you had so confidingly bade him appear, to be a source of embarrassment and growing shame. You would also see the advantage which, because of your decision with regard to this performance of Lohengrin, you have given those people who are actively engaged in using my continuing presence in your proximity as an excuse for a new and ominous separation. The Viennese papers have already carried reports of some new disfavour into which I am said to have fallen; the almost inevitable confirmation of this is bound to follow the moment the performance of Lohengrin fails to take place, or else takes place without you; what further consequences may ensue from this we know only too well from experience. All desire on my part, and all ability to exercise a formative and beneficial influence upon so utterly derelict an artistic institution will be paralysed in the cruellest way possible: it will be a victory for the basest theatrical cabal. People will once again ask themselves whether I am really so close to your heart, or even if I enjoy your respect sufficiently for them not to be able to make any impression upon me.

There is but a single means whereby I may avoid these sad but predictable consequences, and this I owe once again to my noble benefactor's boundless grace.

> In distant lands where none of you shall wander
> there lies a burg that Monsalvat is called. –

Thither will the white dove lead me back: – it is Noah's dove which returned to the Ark when it found the world still a desolate expanse: the dove of the Holy Ghost. There you will allow me to create my works for you: I cannot and will not do more. I shall leave you my sword and horn:[1] prevail upon my loyal Hans to fight bravely with them for me. Our friend[2] will keep the ring: loyal as she is, she shall help you remember me.

---

1 In the final scene of *Lohengrin*, the hero bequeathes his sword, horn and ring to Gottfried of Brabant.
2 Cosima von Bülow.

Fare you well, dearly belovèd friend! – Eternally loyal, I remain yours in unbroken love,

Your own
Richard Wagner

Königsbriefe II, 177–8.

361. HANS VON BÜLOW, BASLE   Lucerne, 10 September [1867]

Very many thanks, dear Hans, for your news! Your worries about Beckmesser's lute touch me deeply, but everything that concerns you touches and moves me, from your visit to Graupe near Pillnitz with Lipinski and your debut in Zurich – to these melancholy lines in which the whole purport of our relations in life must now be examined with an earnestness that cannot but cause great pain. Our arrangement in Munich was designed and calculated to transfigure our suffering with the aid of art; what separated us was meant to keep us together, what we sacrificed was meant to enrich us. How deeply and sincerely – and how often – was I moved by you when we stood at the very pinnacle of our task: you, too, then saw things clearly and comprehensibly. But this arrangement has now been taken from us: what enthusiasm alone once illumed with lightning-like intensity must now stand revealed to us, clearly and consciously, in the calm light of day; what is unavoidably necessary must now become part of a rational, conscious plan.

What is it that you want to say when you keep on calling me "honoured Master"?

How often have I appealed to your heart! do you now mean that the friend is sacrificing himself to his "Master"? Indeed, it is only as "Master" that I may lay claim to a friend's sacrifice: shall I continue to work creatively, or am I now finished? – That is the decision that hangs over me. I, too, have already made great sacrifices, – believe me, supreme sacrifices of friendship, in order that I might continue to work: everything now points inexorably in the same direction, – only a friend's sacrifice can ensure that I continue to work in the future. Do you believe in friendship? – love of the master![1] –

And were it to be so – ah! – you need have no fears about getting Beckmesser's lute made! Many thanks for seeing to it! it reminds me of my own duty! If only I could make you really happy! – Let us hope that I can! –

Yours,
R.W.

Bülow-Briefe 258–9.

---

1 Implicit in these lines is the demand that Bülow should sacrifice his wife to Wagner.

362. HEINRICH LAUBE, VIENNA   Lucerne, 4 October 1867

My dear old friend,

This summer I read your great novel, the German War, and, as I did so, I felt a repeated urge to give you some sign of life on my part. I cannot deny that I was especially affected by the Jesuit party in it, and by the poisoning of Bernhard v. W.[1] How you could hope to remain inviolate in your Viennese appointment after writing such a book was quite inconceivable. As soon as I heard of the latest turn of events, I told my friends what the reason was.

On winter evenings I have been dictating my biography, urged to do so by friendly entreaty; many memories have been revived in the process, and, much to my own delight, my gaze grew more intense as I recalled my relations with you, for, in essence, you are the only person whom I can thank for having rendered me true service as a friend; I consider you to be one of the *very* few honest men who have met me. I shall always remember you with sincere warmth.

I knew nothing of the newspaper rumours which – on account of their inaccuracy – persuaded you to write to me: but, as you can well imagine, they would not have made any impression upon me, even if I had known of them. As far as the directorship of the Munich Theatre is concerned, it looks as though things will remain as they are; I doubt whether anything decisive will emerge from it. Given my extremely poor opinion of the activities of Germany's regular theatres and my firm belief that, however these theatres are run, – (a belief which was confirmed when I told the King of my decisive reluctance ever to have anything to do with them) – they can only add to the confusion and corruption that characterize the Germans' taste in art, I have promised myself no further involvement except, where possible, to see to it that, should the case arise and something of mine is to receive a decent performance, I should deal only with a relatively couth and helpful person such as I now find entrusted with running the theatre in Munich.[2] It now seems uniquely difficult to achieve even *this* aim.

For the rest I thank God for being allowed to live here quietly and in the most absolute seclusion, completely cut off from the world and devoting myself to my creative work which has been neglected for so long now: I am so jealous of this good fortune (which I owe to the most wonderful love of a young King) that I tremble at any undertaking that might disturb it.

I am grateful to you, dear Laube, for having remembered me. Give my

1 Bernhard of Saxe-Weimar. According to Emil Heckel, Wagner planned a stage play on the life of Bernhard based upon Laube's nine-volume historical romance *Der deutsche Krieg* (1865–6); *cf* BB 147; English trans. 123.
2 Baron Karl von Perfall.

warmest regards to my admirable friend, your dear wife, and accept the most cordial good wishes of

Your
Richard Wagner

Freunde und Zeitgenossen 487–9.

363. KING LUDWIG II OF BAVARIA, HOHENSCHWANGAU

Lucerne, 30 November 1867

[...] Now that we have reached the point, my true and trusty Siegfried, when we have finally set foot on dry land and can calmly arrange our seed-corn for planting, it is first and foremost the need to secure this new-found calm – without which we who have been so deeply shaken can no longer hope to prosper – which induces me to inform you of a personal matter which has not turned out as we had expected but which, having been inadequately dealt with, continues to threaten not only my own peace of mind but that of my sorely tested friends the Bülows. Frau Schnorr continues to find herself in Munich, drawing a pension of 2000 fl., and possessing a free seat in the theatre, and, whenever she meets Frau v. Bülow there or in the street, she approaches her in a spirit of triumphant provocation, so that our friend has now turned to me, such is her anxious amazement. In response to my enquiries, it has been reported to me that at the time in question Frau v. Schnorr did indeed appeal to you, begging your forgiveness for her behaviour, and that you granted her your kind permission to absent herself from Munich for a time in order to return, as she wished, at some future date. The woman's behaviour now shows how hypocritical was her appeal to you, since all she wanted was to be able to remain in Munich where she would soon find an opportunity to avenge herself, as she had sworn to do, in the most spectacular manner on Fr. v. Bülow. This remark of hers, well-authenticated as it is, has similarly been communicated to my friend Bülow. Imagine the feelings it must have aroused in this poor and painfully sensitive man, who has already been sufficiently tormented, no less than in his wife, who, in her total inno-cence, has shown only kindness to that worthless woman! It appears that this woman is only awaiting the moment of my return to Munich before exacting the vengeance which she has sworn to take on me. My King! In this affair your kindness and perhaps even your worries on our behalf have once again been abused because of the weakness or very real enmity of your inferiors. I would ask you now to put to the test the honesty with which this criminal woman besought your forgiveness: let her address the selfsame appeal to Frau von Bülow, either in person or in writing, and let her confess to having been misled by an impostor[1] into committing not only an act of lese-majesty but into slandering a friend who had done so much on her behalf; in return for evidence that she has received this forgiveness, I for my part would have no further objection to her remaining in Munich in future, but on the condition that, whatever else happens, neither I nor Bülow would ever set eyes on her again. Since all further dealings with this woman are now out of the question as far as we are concerned – and for this she has only her own abject behaviour to blame – there can also be no further question of our using her for our artistic ends, for which purpose Frau v. Bülow had, by dint of her untiring intercession, obtained an increase in the woman's pension from 1200 fl. to 2000 fl. In the name of justice, and in order to spare myself the reproach of misusing the Civil List for totally futile and unmerited expenses, I must therefore insist that Frau v. Schnorr's pension be reduced to the level originally intended by your royal favour; and in doing so you will express your royal acknowledgement and remuneration of a single, passing artistic achievement the like of which had never been seen anywhere previously. If – out of compassion – you were to agree to accede to my request but were to meet with misgivings lest the affair give rise to an unpleasant stir, I would declare in the most explicit terms, both in my own name and in that of my friends, that we are not conscious of having to fear anything, save the exposure of the most abject shamelessness on the part of a person who, on the contrary, by being left in the fullest advantage of her situation, gives *us* the appearance of harbouring the opposite kind of misgivings. – I believe by contrast that, in requesting this favour, I have proposed the least – and therefore the most necessary – level of punishment which, were it not exacted, would inevitably and regrettably encourage her in her base behaviour and in her defiance of your royal decrees.[2] –

[...]

Königsbriefe II, 209–11.

364. GUSTAV HÖLZEL, VIENNA   Munich, 22 January 1868

Dear Sir,

Your letter to Herr v. Perfall has just been passed on to me, and I see from it that, because of the difficulties caused by the very high *tessitura* of the part of "Beckmesser" in my "Mastersingers", you find yourself unable

---

1 Isidore von Reutter.
2 Ludwig forwarded this letter to Düfflipp with the note, "The thread of my patience is at last beginning to break". And he went on, "But I am even more amazed that you believe there is something suspicious in the matter between Wagner, Fr. v. Bülow and Fr. v. Schnorr. If that sorry rumour, which I could never bring myself to believe, should turn out to be true after all, if adultery were *really* involved – then alas!"

to agree to work with us in performing this role. – I should like to try to show you that you have been misled by appearances into falsely succumbing to this fear, as you would realize at once if I were to go through the part with you. It is a comic character part and can in no way be compared with a bass *buffo* role in the old style: the musically high *tessitura* is the result solely of an impassioned, screeching tone of voice intended to bring out as much as possible; I admit that, in order to achieve this forceful intonation, I have completely avoided "singing" in the sense of a normal Italian *buffo* part, and conceived the part instead in such a way that it needs only a good actor, albeit one who must be enormously *musical*, since, although there is very little question here of any actual "singing", the whole style of delivery rests upon a highly complicated musical basis which can be intelligible only to an experienced singer, even though the latter is not really called upon to perform as a normal "singer". If you were prepared to incur the effort of coming to Munich for a few days – in return of course for the assurance that you would be reimbursed – it ought to be possible for me to convince you of what I mean, by performing the part myself, and in that way to dispel your misconception, a misconception which, at first sight, is certainly most understandable. I know that *any bass* could sing this role as soon as he found the necessary intonation: in no circumstances could a normal baritone voice achieve this, because everything would then acquire a false tenderness, whereas what is required here is a harsh and forceful accent.

Please do what you can to fulfil my request by paying us a brief visit, and be so kind as to let me know your reply without delay.

With the greatest esteem I am
Your most devoted servant,
Richard Wagner

Hölzel-Briefe 171–2.

365. LORENZ VON DÜFFLIPP, MUNICH   Munich, 5 February 1868

Most honoured Sir and friend,

Since it can serve no useful purpose for me to remain in Munich during the preliminary rehearsals of my "Mastersingers", I intend to retire to the tranquillity of my Lucerne retreat at the end of this week. – Would you have the goodness to report this to His Majesty the King, in conformity with my duty in this matter, and, at the same time, convey to my exalted benefactor, whose incomparable generosity I shall always have occasion to acknowledge and to praise for granting me a refuge so conducive to my spiritual well-being, my unending and abundant gratitude for all the favours he has shown me? – I am already confident that I shall find sufficient peace of mind there to be able to resume work on the full score of "Siegfried", and thus to ensure its completion within the course of this year.[1]

As regards the future performance of this work, which my exalted benefactor has followed with such keen interest, my attention has been caught by news of a certain wish on the part of Herr von Perfall: this wish relates to the need to obtain sovereign approval for the reconstruction of the stage of the Royal Court Theatre, work which has long been felt to be necessary and which might be carried out in the course of next summer. Not only is this rebuilding work well-nigh indispensable if the Munich Court Theatre is to be put on a level with the better German theatres, it might also – as Herr von Perfall was optimistic enough to intimate to me – enable the stage of the Royal Court Theatre to meet any staging demands such as those which I make in my Nibelung dramas, and to meet them, moreover, tolerably well. In consequence of this it would not be impossible, should His Majesty the King wish it, for the separate parts of the cycle to be provisionally performed there, perhaps at yearly intervals: for ex., a start could be made next year with the "Rhinegold", continuing with the "Valkyrie" the following year, and the whole work could be successfully produced in this way. At all events, these plans would be greatly assisted if the tenor Bachmann were to be offered a firm engagement, since, of all the aspirants to my young heroic roles, he seems to me to be uniquely suitable, which is why I make so bold as to recommend his engagement in such positive terms.

There is another especial favour which I would entreat you most kindly to convey to His Majesty. Two years ago I was most anxious that my exalted benefactor should receive possession of the original score of the "Valkyrie" even before a complete copy of it had been made for practical use; since it is now imperative that this omission be made good, I must entreat His Majesty most humbly to deign to entrust the original score to me once again for such time as is needed to copy it out. My former secretary, Hans Richter, who is now the temporary chorus master here and whom I can trust in every respect, will supervise the task of preparing this necessary copy and, in the hoped-for event of His Majesty's deigning to grant my request, I would beg you, most honoured Sir, to be so kind as to hand over the King's original score to this intimate friend of mine.

At the same time I make so bold as to repeat my most humble request that you send Frau von Bülow the last sheet of my biography which she has been writing down from my dictation and which His Majesty the King was recently kind enough to invite her to continue to communicate to him (in the event

1 Wagner had worked on the first full score of Act II of *Siegfried* between 22 December 1864 and 2 December 1865; the second full score was completed on 23 February 1869. The first complete draft of Act III occupied Wagner from 1 March to 14 June 1869; the second complete draft from 25 June to 5 August 1869; and the first full score from 25 August 1869 to 5 February 1871.

of his retaining his sovereign interest in it), since the point at which it must be taken up again can be discovered only by a comparison with this last sheet. –

I would finally entreat you to commend me to our most gracious lord, my belovèd benefactor and patron, and to convey to him the most heartfelt blessings of one whom his grace has made supremely happy. With the most cordial greetings and good wishes for your own prosperity, I remain

Your most respectful and devoted servant

Richard Wagner

Petzet 793–4.

366. KING LUDWIG II OF BAVARIA, MUNICH   Munich, 30 March 1868

My most gracious King,

Allow me to report in brief today how things stand with regard to the performance of the "Mastersingers" which you were previously kind enough to command. Since your theatre intendancy has not yet succeeded, in the only way open to it, in attracting a suitable interpreter for the principal role of Walther – a role that is as important to me as it is to you, my august and enlightened friend! – and since it is quite impossible for me to entrust so aristocratic, ardent and poetic a figure to such a thoroughly incompetent singer as Vogl,[1] the local tenor, and since, finally, the time is now upon us when we must reach a final decision, I am bound to say that I consider a performance of my work to be out of the question this spring, and, instead, must advise the intendant to seek your kind permission to postpone it until next autumn.[2]

My most gracious benefactor would be right to chide me for insincerity if this insincerity were to concern my innermost frame of mind – the source of my creativity. I shall not conceal from you, therefore, that my misplaced hopes of finding a favourable incentive for renewed creative activity in a successful presentation of my latest work have had a deeply unsettling and depressing effect upon my frame of mind. But I pray that what I have admitted to you here, simply out of my desire for sincerity and because of your exalted concern, may not appear to you an invitation to become involved in extraordinary measures designed to allow an undertaking to go ahead which – it seems to me – should now be abandoned. Far be it from me to expect sacrifices of you which must appear disproportionate to your royal sensitivities. All I wanted to do was describe this new source of sadness that weighs on the

1 The part of Walther von Stolzing was sung by Franz Nachbaur. See Newman's *Life*, IV,132.
2 Preparations nevertheless went ahead, and the first performance took place on 21 June 1868.

mind of your friend, and I ask most graciously for your kind indulgence, should you discover that I have not been wholly successful in resisting the effects of my sorrow.

It is with the most heartfelt concern that I seize upon what few scraps of news that still reach me concerning the health of my belovèd friend and lord: I pray that they may always give me cause to be grateful!

In the holiest loyalty and love for my most exalted friend, I remain until death

Eternally and uniquely yours,
Richard Wagner

Königsbriefe II, 218–19.

367. KING LUDWIG II OF BAVARIA, MUNICH [Munich,] 20 June [1868][1]

All hail to one who is loyal and fondly gracious!

I knew it: *he* understands me!! Impossible for him not to have seen through the strange outer shell of popular humour and felt, in all its clarity, profound and wistful melancholy, that lamentation and cry for help of fettered poesy reborn on earth in human form, the irresistible force of its magic power as it vanquishes all that is vulgar! – So it was! My belovèd's glorious words proclaim it so! And so: God speed! Hand in hand like Walther and Sachs, let us go on telling our century all that we have to say to it!

Eternally and uniquely yours,
Richard Wagner

20 June: a.m.
(Amidst the torment
of countless visitors!)

Königsbriefe II, 232.

368. MALWIDA VON MEYSENBUG, PARIS   Lucerne, 7 July 1868

Best of friends,

You are kindness and loyalty itself, and have the most warm-hearted understanding that I have ever known! – I am sorry that you wrote when you did, since I was intending to do so myself; in addition to which your letter touches

---

1 Ludwig had written to Wagner on the 19th, telling him of the "divine raptures" that "thrilled through" his body following the dress rehearsal of *Die Meistersinger* which had taken place that day.

on a matter which annoys me greatly. You have no notion of my experiences with regard to Mme Laussot, – to whom it was *I* who proffered a friendly hand on this occasion, treating her as an able and intelligent person whom I was pleased to see leading so independent a life thanks to her own vigorous efforts. Unfortunately, her natural disposition had an even more alienating effect upon me than the eighteen years which she has been able to spend without showing the least sign of remorse for the most loathsome act of betrayal ever perpetrated. Well, it is after all 18 years: but *I*, at least, do not wish to be reminded of it in any way: and that – without knowing it – was precisely what you did.[1] –

My dear friend, I have been ill since my return: indeed, almost bedridden for 10 days – a chill took violent possession of my overwrought nerves, and will not let go – But do come and visit me in Triebschen on your return journey, and bring Olga[2] with you; you can both stay here with me as long as you wish, and – it is beautiful here! – And then I can also thank you for your saint-like behaviour towards my old and highly dissolute sister.[3] It was typically Malwidian of you, quite unique! Adieu! Enjoy your cure! Best wishes to Vole![4]

Yours,
Rich. Wagner.

Meysenbug-Briefe 91.

369. King Ludwig II of Bavaria, Hohenschwangau

Lucerne, 16 July 1868

My belovèd King,
My uniquely gracious friend,
　　Since returning to my refuge I have been ill and, in consequence of feverish and violent attacks of night perspiration, have suffered from persistent and increasing lassitude from which I am only slowly recovering, so that I cannot as yet give any thought to beginning my mineral water cure, necessary though this cure is to me. My first moments of new-found spiritual freedom should have been devoted to a solemn letter to my exalted friend: but fate would not

---

1 *cf* CT for 31 January 1869: "a stupid letter from Mme Laussot, who wishes to give him explanations (from 20 years ago!). That annoys him, because it is so utterly useless". See also letter [194], p. 360, note 6.
2 Olga Herzen.
3 Clara Wolfram, whom Malwida had entertained during her visit to Munich for the première of *Die Meistersinger von Nürnberg*.
4 Olga Herzen's pet-name.

have it so. Our friend[1] informed me today of the recent letter which you were so very kind as to address to her; it contains – in addition to an assurance of the generous trust which you place in your friends and which we ourselves would never for a moment have questioned – a piece of news which, precisely because it came from you, has had a deeply dismaying effect upon her great and free-born soul. She begs me to lay her farewell greeting humbly at your feet, and to entreat you to be so kind as to excuse her from having to reply to your letter. In her soul she will always retain her gratitude towards you, but she has now been rendered incapable of giving you any further expression of the feelings which she harbours even for me. I would understand, she believes, how certain protestations must inevitably strike her after the tenderest heart-strings of a woman's nature have been wrenched in so hurtful a way, and after her justifiable pride as a woman has been thus offended for a second time. –

As for the affair itself, what is at issue here, in my own estimation, is a calumny on the part of my old friend Röckel: I shall never believe so worthless a claim, at least until such time as I hold in my hand the most incontrovertible proof. Having lived away from me for so long and having had no dealings with me during that time, Röckel has no doubt begun to associate recently with those of my acquaintances who, on account of their false assessment of my relations with my exalted royal patron and because of the senseless demands they have made on me as a result, have irked me and frequently persuaded me to entrust our uniquely understanding friend with the task of correcting their foolish ideas: sacrificing herself on every side, she has often protected me from these tiresome people and, in her own way, disabused them with forceful candour. As a result these people are now agreed amongst themselves that Frau v. B. holds me in her power, that she is isolating me from my friends, and so on. Many people have also wondered why, since I have been a widower for two years, I have not remarried; indeed, friend Röckel even had one of his daughters lined up for me: since no one knew what to make of me in this respect either, it must have occurred to them quite spontaneously that Frau v. B., who was in any case said to have great power over me, was preventing me from marrying again. Where is the man who is not exposed to such gossip, especially when he finds himself in a position like mine? It is possible that Röckel, too, may on occasion have expressed himself in this thoughtless and foolish vein: but that he might deliberately have accused me of a crime I consider completely out of the question.

---

1 Cosima von Bülow. Ludwig had written to her on 12 July 1868, "As a true friend, I felt myself obliged two years ago to inform you of that letter from Frau v. Schnorr in which she had the impudence to utter the most shameless calumnies against you and our friend; as a true friend, I believe it would be wrong of me on this occasion, too, to conceal from you that I know from an utterly reliable source that a man who until now has always been regarded by Wagner as a true and honest friend has made the selfsame worthless allegations against you and our friend; this man is Röckel".

But it is enough that things have again been stirred up: and to what end? It is as plain as the day: it is not I nor Bülow whom people are now warning of some false friend or other – no, they go straight to the King himself and tell *him* what is going on.

My King! – this is an abject way to behave, and the ill intent is only too clear for there to be any doubt as to the source of the rumour in this instance. There is nothing more for me to say in this matter either: I know how people are getting their own back for the supreme glories of my life. Everything is now lost, and no hope remains. –

My most gracious King! Frau v. B. will leave Munich during the next few days, presumably never to return. Her doctors have insisted that she should seek some milder climate; she will probably choose to stay in Italy next winter, presumably close to her father or other relations. It must then be asked whether artistic conditions in Munich will prove sufficiently promising to persuade Bülow himself to persevere there in a position which will then have become so much more difficult for him; if not, he would of course have to appeal to your generosity to release him from his appointment. –

So much for my friends who, as I realize, are once again being made to pay for the fact that they are the most devoted and self-sacrificing friends of the Master whom you yourself, my glorious monarch, have honoured with such extravagance. –

If we can set aside all these pretexts and grounds for abject and hostile machinations which, although persistently ineffectual, have always gone unpunished, my belovèd friend and I may finally find peace. If all that remains is two individuals, who even now have become almost legendary (for who, even now, could regard Ludwig II and his friend Richard Wagner as a pure reality?), what will soon emerge, clearly and plainly, and entirely in accord with the deep relationship that lies behind our lives together, is the task that we both must needs perform, so that even your courtiers will finally have nothing more to which to object. –

The first Mastersingers evening is behind us: great and beautiful, thanks to your wonderful love, the like of which has never been known in the whole of history. Was it your intention to release me from a vow of mine by dint of your sovereign power? If my vow had included this first Mastersingers evening, I should have had to break it in any case: the need to keep a watch on my performers kept me in the theatre where no one else was supposed to know of my secret presence. But *you* discovered me there, and drew me, stunned as I was, into a realm of splendour such as no poet before me had ever known:[1] and in the midst of such splendour, I felt myself warmed by the heart of my dearest and truest friend. Who can grasp the beauty of your action? – – But I have not broken my vow: if I once swore I would never

1 Ludwig had invited Wagner into his royal box.

attend a first performance of one of my works, it was because of my aversion to the sight of the audience at an ordinary theatre performance and because of my reluctance to deal with them directly.

It is quite a different matter when it comes to my great vow, which I hold sacred because I impute to it a magical power. You know what it is. On the 1st of January last year, when I first saw the model of the Nibelung Theatre in Zurich,[1] I was suddenly struck by what a tremendous potential for guiding the whole of modern art back into its true and sacred path is contained within the idea of actually building this theatre and of realizing the ideal that such a structure implies: in return for so great a gain, great was the sacrifice I had to offer, and so I swore that, if I lived to see the building completed and the Nibelungs performed in it, I would absent myself from the festival, remain deaf to the tremendous impression that its dedication must inevitably have, and silently and in secret, humbly and in fervent prayer, pay homage to my guardian spirit and godlike friend, to him who is my consummation. – This was the oath I swore. Shall I live to see the day when I may be allowed to keep it?? –

No matter! My life belongs to you. I shall now build up my strength in order to devote my new-found powers to serving you alone, and to the completion of my work. This is the other thing that needs no vow. And so: God speed! – I hope I shall always be in a position to tell you news of our matchless friend: she is so profound, so unusual that she – does not belong in this world. That is why she must disappear from the world like all that is noble, which can exist only by dint of its effect on the world. And yet we shall remain as one. "Apart, who shall divide us?"[2] –

Once more: God speed! A thousand good wishes of homage from your eternally grateful, loving friend from afar

Richard Wagner.

Königsbriefe II,234–7.

370. KING LUDWIG II OF BAVARIA, BERG   Lucerne, 14 October 1868

[. . .] Our friend[3] returned to Munich with her children two days ago in order to put her affairs in order, and to carry out, with due dignity, her irrevocable decisions. She has gone with my blessing: I have every reason to

---

1 On 1 January 1867 in Zurich Semper had shown Wagner his model for the proposed festival theatre to be built in Munich for the presentation of the *Ring*; for details of this abortive project see Newman's *Life*, III,409–37.

2 *Götterdämmerung*, Prelude (GS VI,186). Ludwig wrote to Wagner on 25 July, claiming that he did not believe the rumours he had heard, and insisting that Cosima should remain in Munich.

3 Cosima von Bülow, who (apparently) wrote to her husband on 3 October, informing him of her decision to live with Wagner.

honour her as the purest witness to sincerity and inexhaustible profundity that life has had to offer me: she is the most perfect creature ever to enter the realm of my own experience. That is why she belongs to a different world-order. There is nothing I can do except to stand by her: I pray that you, too, my exalted and gracious lord, will loyally support me in this! –

My unique and noble lord will sense from these intimations that I am caught up in a mood of vital import, when final decisions have to be made. It will not be easy to explain exactly what this mood is, nor how it came about. There is much here that I must leave to the future to unravel, perhaps even to posterity: I have done enough to place in the hands of my solicitous friend all that he needs to judge me accurately. My most gracious belovèd, if you have kept all my letters and memoirs, then you will have in your possession all the unique and necessary material for such time in the future when, in advancing and less troubled years, you wish to evoke the spiritual form of him who is your friend. Nowhere have the changes that have taken place in my life, whether outwardly or inwardly, during the four-and-a-half years since I found you, been accorded more complete and clearly intelligible expression than in my communications to you, to which you have at all times given such gracious encouragement. It would therefore be more than superfluous if I were to return here to any of the points contained in those communications: what was built, what was destroyed will all become clear to you one day when you reflect upon your friend with this legacy before you. Only in a few details do these communications require completion: may what follows be a brief attempt at such an undertaking. –

In taking up where I left off before, I can do no more than renew my thanks and declare that the evening of the first performance of the "Master-singers" was the high point of my career as man and artist. Just as it will be found, in time, that this work of mine is the most perfect of all that I have written so far, so must I declare that this performance of it – which I owe to your goodness alone – was the best that has ever been given of any of my works: the inestimable honour which you showed me that evening at your side I declare to be the most deeply-felt reward ever bestowed upon a leading artist. And so I declare that there is nothing more I could ask for here: that no desire for anything greater could remain in my heart. – And now you discover that on that selfsame evening I also felt how utterly and completely wretched my life has become, and that I suffered from my inner wounds to the point of utter exhaustion. To be able to explain *this* to you I would have to have died first! – Last winter, while dining with friends, I drank a toast in which I said that only he would know great success who renounced all joy of it in advance. I was understood by everyone! Well then: such a success was reserved for me; I have just described it, and declared that it could not have been more perfect. How is it then that it was also the very pinnacle of joylessness for me? My most gracious friend, this, too, will become clear to you some day. Here are but a few indications.

The work itself, which I have just described to you as my most perfect, will live on: but how? I expect that all the German theatres will attempt to appropriate it; but not one of them has shown the inclination or intention to give it complete and unmutilated. The utter wretchedness and deep decline into which the German theatre has sunk is something I shall discover to an even fuller extent by what happens to this very work of mine. I resisted every concession, and was determined not to grant permission for any performances of the work to be given: it was impossible to carry this out! Trusting solely in the great popularity of the piece, my publisher[1] made great sacrifices at the time in order to be able to publish it, sacrifices the like of which had not been heard of previously: I am duty-bound to make amends for this by doing nothing to oppose performances of the work. The only thing to which I could have appealed in these circumstances – a sense of honour on the part of German theatre administrators and their staff – but the last spark of all such feeling has been snuffed out in this land of ours! Appalling desolation surrounds me on all sides; no one understands me; many are amazed; the majority deride me. In Munich I had a theatrical success: that is all that will live after me of my work! – It pains me to think of it. –

I declared the performance to have been supremely successful: – but who has the faintest idea of the daily torments and the hopelessness I felt as I conducted these rehearsals? This is something, my King, which I cannot even begin to hint at without describing the most deep-seated discord of a kind you could scarce comprehend.[2] How very deceptive are appearances here, concealing things from our sight with all the greater obscurity in that the noblest hopes and desires inspire us to maintain delusions and errors without which, it seems, the world cannot exist. Who can bear the truth? – Enough: even in the face of a performance which finally turned out such an exemplary success, I knew I was utterly alone, unbefriended, and not understood; all I could do was to smile at the deceptive effects of an illusion which I myself had conjured up with convulsive efforts and which shone forth on every side, but which left my soul untouched. – Never again shall I attend a performance of one of my works!

After all this I must surely have reason to fear and lament that even you will find me inscrutable and enigmatic? Might even *you* be inclined to believe that I was not pleased to receive the most extravagant proof of your favour

1 Franz Schott.
2 Wagner supervised the rehearsals of *Die Meistersinger*, though the performance itself was conducted by Bülow. The Annals for the rehearsal period record "Great confusion of feelings: all the time fresh difficulties. Unspeakably love-sick. Inclined to run away & disappear. [...] Piano rehearsals: oppressive feeling of Hans's deep hostility & alienation" (BB 198; English trans. 166–7).

with which you raised me to an honour which I have already declared to have struck me as unique and unparalleled? Might you think that I did not retain it as a joyful memory? – Oh my King! As little as I could fail to love my work or could misprize it because of all my sufferings, so little could I doubt in the value of your love and favour. But the very greatness of this love and favour was bound to fill me with sadness, nay, with horror, since this was the only air that I breathed. Time and again I saw you appearing before me, shedding upon me the light of your splendour, so that the eyes of the whole world were bound to be drawn in my direction: I saw then the looks of those from whom you had set me so immeasurably far apart, and in them I read only the sufferings that I knew must strike me down. And this time, too, the arrows of vengeance have struck home, and – as before – it is not only I that is wounded. It is the mark of a King not to heed, not to understand what is aimed at those whom he feels called upon and qualified to protect: and so I feel that I should not complain here, nor make any accusations. It is fate that speaks here: a semblance of happiness spares us until the semblance itself must fade. "Against baseness the gods themselves contend in vain."[1] The contest is over. Every hope is dead, and the cry of "Too late!" rings forth with tongue of brass! – May one thing alone remain: your love! –

Thus, my King, may I show you by means of a single example what other life exists apart from the one which the world alone sees and knows. – And now, my exalted and most dearly belovèd! You ask after Siegfried? – What would you say if I were to answer this question with a tale of ill health? –

When I arrived in Munich on my birthday, my doctor hoped that I would be able to travel to Kissingen under his supervision and complete the course of treatment there that I have been in need of for so long now. He soon realized that this was out of the question, such were the agitations caused by the rehearsals for the Mastersingers! The treatment was postponed until July, by which time I would have retired to the tranquillity of Triebschen. I arrived here at the end of June, and during the first week succumbed to a serious illness with a persistent, debilitating fever. The result was that it is now too late to begin my course of treatment this year: in order for it not to have exhausted me, it would have had to have lasted six weeks; it would then have been followed by a period of convalescence in the mountains, for which there was, however, no longer a suitable time. I also consulted my own physician, Dr Standhartner in Vienna: the conclusion was postponement of the treatment until next year. –

I must now entreat my most gracious friend to be allowed, at all costs, to devote next spring and next summer to recovering my health, and not to insist upon anything that would again make it impossible for me to undertake the

[1] A paraphrase of Schiller's "Against stupidity the gods themselves contend in vain" (*Die Jungfrau von Orleans* III,6).

treatment I so badly need. And so: no performance of any new, as yet unperformed, work of mine next year! For even if all my demands were met and if everything were done, according to your royal decree, to enable a performance of part of my Nibelung work to take place, I could not be present in person to co-operate with you on this performance, and, without this, believe me, such a performance would be wholly abortive.

And it is the favour of this self-denial on your part that I must now begin by begging of you![1] –

[. . .]

Königsbriefe II, 244–7.

371. NATALIE PLANER, DRESDEN   Lucerne, 27 November 1868

[. . .] I have a favour to ask you today which I have kept on forgetting until now. Among the objects which remained in Minna's household in Dresden and which were all transferred to her at her request is a present which Countess d'Agoult gave me and which only negligence could have persuaded Minna to regard as one of *her* possessions. It is a small Chinese *Buddha*, a kind of gilt idol, enclosed in a small casket of black wood, the doors of which used to open to reveal the small statue inside. – God knows what Minna did with this piece: at all events it was not right of her if she gave it away. May I ask you to endeavour to obtain the return of this piece for me: if the present owner is indelicate enough not to return this keepsake at once, in return for the above declaration, I am ultimately willing to pay whatever compensation may be necessary to ensure its return. Except for my incomparable friend Pusinelli, my experience with Minna's and my own former acquaintances in Dresden are a source of little credit to the people concerned, and it may well be possible that difficulties will arise which will prevent the return of the piece, difficulties which, at all events, I should like to think may be avoided.

But I must ask *in all seriousness* for the return of my *letters to Minna*. No arrangements can be made to dispose of such letters: as long as the recipient was alive, they belonged to her, and she could either keep them or destroy them. If Minna has definitely and demonstrably done the latter with my letters, there is of course nothing I can say against it: but if she kept them, they must necessarily revert to the sender and, in the event of Minna's having given these letters away, I shall contest this illegal action with every legal means I can, should this become necessary, and insist on these papers' being surrendered. I should be grateful if you would give me some information on

1 See introductory essay, pp. 595–6.

this point, and, if possible, help me regain possession of these letters, which, in any case, I claim as *my* property.[1] –

[. . .]

Sammlung Burrell 729.

372. HANS VON BÜLOW, BASLE   Lucerne, 27 December 1868

I have now received two letters from you for which I have to thank you today, and to which I should like to reply without any further delay. I am also in your debt for sending me Hanslick's brochure[2] (you interpreted my telegram perfectly correctly). Let me say straightaway what the reason was for my asking for this piece. I intend re-editing "Judaism in Music": it will take the following form. A letter to Mme Moukhanoff (Kalergis), who asked with some astonishment how it has come about that the press etc. keeps on attacking *me*, of all people, with such unrelenting hostility? This sense of astonishment – which has also slipped into many another innocent reporter's writings about me – shall not be allowed to continue a moment longer. My initial response is a reprint of my 18-year-old article, only somewhat cleaned up in terms of its style. – It annoys me to have to think of the possibility of dying without first having corrected a good many of the errors of judgement on the part of entirely fair-minded people which have been intentionally maintained. I am anxious to put things straight, and also to recover what has been lost: hence my recent demand that Heim should help me locate a number of musical trifles from my earliest days. –

Of all the news that you were kind enough to send me concerning events in Munich and, more especially, your activities there, it was your speech to the orchestra and the censure of it in the press which gave me greatest pause for thought. Of course, every word you said to the musicians was just and salutary: but perhaps it was not only not entirely right but even perhaps unjust that your warning to the artists became a kind of denunciation of the audience. I believe an audience should never be criticized:[3] it will always retain the sovereignty of a child. How should it be reproached for its taste? After all, it fails utterly and completely to hear or see what strikes us artists as being essential. It clings to the events on stage, and to nothing else, but in these – as you know – it takes a wholly personal interest: but of all that lies behind

---

1 The Buddha and a selection of letters arrived in Tribschen on 16 January 1869, and Wagner acknowledged receipt of them three weeks later. However, a further 128 of Wagner's letters to Minna remained in Natalie's possession, and were later acquired by Mary Burrell.

2 *Wilhelm Lübke und Eduard Hanslick über Richard Wagner* (Berlin 1869).

3 But see letter [374], pp. 737–8.

these events and which we ourselves consider the only true object of art, it knows not a thing. And herein lies our entire consolation: for we can hope to present *ourselves* and our higher aims behind these events on stage; and in that way we shall persuade our audiences, by means of the correct illusion, to acquire, without noticing it, a greater refinement of taste. [. . .]

Bülow-Briefe 270–1.

373. MALWIDA VON MEYSENBUG, FLORENCE   Lucerne, 11 January 1869

My dear friend,

Please accept my warmest thanks for your kind letter, and at the same time my sincerest good wishes both to you and our enthusiastic Olga.[1] –

The floods which caused you so many difficulties on your journey to Italy made my own return from there one of the most spectacular adventures of my life.[2] I was stuck in Ticino at the foot of the Gotthart for a whole week. –

I have authorized the music-dealer Lucca in Milan to approach Frau Laussot with a view to the latter's checking the editions of my operas. Please thank her most sincerely for her amicable readiness to assist me! –

There is another great service that she could render me. *Karl Ritter*, who is completely inaccessible to me, has in his safe-keeping (assuming he has not allowed them to go astray) two old – and in themselves relatively unimportant – manuscripts of mine, both of which are dramatic sketches. 1st The Saracen Woman (5 acts) 2nd Jesus of Nazareth.

I am very anxious to have these two things back, in manuscript or in a copy, since I am planning a complete edition of my literary & poetic works. Frau Laussot ought to be successful in helping me here. –

I shall be sending you a 2nd edition of "Opera & Drama" with a new preface within the next few days.

Yesterday I sent my publisher[3] the manuscript of a new (and pretty desperate) brochure, "Judaism in Music", which you should also receive in due course. –

Do you also want to know how I am? I am resolved never to set foot in Germany again. –

I should very much like to come to Italy. Perhaps I could even do some good there. I discovered that the Crown Princess of Italy was very interested in me, and wanted me to come to Florence to give a new impulse to regener-

1 Olga Herzen.
2 Together with their servant Jakob Stocker, Wagner and Cosima had toured northern Italy between 14 September and 5 October 1868.
3 J. J. Weber of Leipzig.

ating musical taste which has grown so corrupt. It was the young princess's governess who told me this in Munich.[1] If you know this woman, or if you have access to her through others, tell her that I am ready to follow a serious summons to Florence.

You will gather from these disjointed sentences how deeply earnest is my present mood.

I'll have nothing more to do with this world. A final attempt could be made possible only if the circumstances were sufficiently appealing. –

Once again: my sincere good wishes!

Remember with affection

Your loyally devoted friend
Richard Wagner

Meysenbug-Briefe 91–4.

374. LUISE BROCKHAUS, DRESDEN   Lucerne, 28 January 1869

Dearest Luise,

A brief word in answer to your question! – Do me a favour, and the next time that such disastrous restlessness (more especially on the part of the Sunday audience) breaks out at the end,[2] withdraw deep into your box, close your eyes, and simply follow the words of H. Sachs's closing address. If you then find that his words express, in a meaningful way, the real and more serious sense of the whole (a sense which only now emerges), and if, at the moment when the theme of the Nuremberg Mastersingers is directly wedded to that of Walther's Prize Song, you hear this wider significance borne in upon your feelings as an agreeable play of melody, tell me then what you would think of me if, simply as a favour, I were to sacrifice this moment of beauty to the rudeness of a part of the audience (which after all forces itself upon me uninvited) – a moment, moreover, which I offer as a gift to those whom I *have* invited. It is these latter for whom my work is solely intended and who ought therefore to do what they can to retain the beauty of this moment undefiled. After all, if the King of Saxony returned in his coat to applaud, it may of course be that his applause was intended for Kapellmeister Rietz, and perhaps also Mitterwurzer, who similarly claims this honour for himself; I believe that the impulse which persuaded him to show his support must have received its strongest impetus from Sachs's final address; for it is at people such as him that this address is directed. Simply leave those who

1 No further details known.
2 *Die Meistersinger* had received its first Dresden performance on 21 January 1869, when it had met with popular acclaim.

are not called upon in this way to elbow their way to the exit: it happens all the time; at the best concert establishments the audience grows restless at the end of a Beethoven symphony: if you go to the theatre, you must know in advance that, according to the majority, you will end up among the rabble. It is the task of those who are more refined and better educated to maintain and protect what is good and genuine in the face of such bad habits. Instead of appealing to me, you should try to persuade some spirited and sensible person to take audiences to task publicly for their rudeness, and make it clear to them what they are ruining and losing. –

I was genuinely pleased by everything you all had to tell me, rest assured of that; and, of course, it pleases me no less to discover that my work was at least given in such a way that it could not fail to make a fine impression.

Further reports would be most welcome to me, since I am certainly not over-provided with them otherwise. If the theatre administrators were better educated and had more sense of honour, I should no doubt have received news from them as well: but people do not seem to know this any longer.

Fare you well, dearest Luise! Sincere good wishes to you and your family!

Yours,
Richard.

Familienbriefe 272–3.

375. KING LUDWIG II OF BAVARIA, MUNICH

Lucerne, 23/24 February 1869

Most dearly belovèd, gracious lord and friend,

This morning I put the finishing strokes to the second act of Siegfried: this, too, is now ready to pass into the hands of my royal friend, and I can scarcely gainsay my solemn promise to give him an immediate insight into those parts of my work which are now completely finished. But it would make no sense for me to do so; for you are right to demand the *whole* work from me: and – with God's help – I shall be able to acquit myself honourably on your feast-day this year.[1]

But it is a long and, more especially, a laborious task. That so little that is altogether perfect has been achieved in the world is no doubt due in part to the fact that the true genius proves himself not only in the comprehensive speed with which he conceives some great plan, but, more especially, in the impassioned, and even painful, perseverance which is required if his plan is to be fully realized. Nothing can be done here with only superficial indications: for what, from an artistic point of view, convulses us like a flash of lightning

1 25 August, the King's birthday; but see letter [365], p. 724 note 1.

is a miraculously linked and delicately structured piece of jewelry in which each precious stone, each pearl, and each tiny link in the chain is made to fit with painstaking diligence, like a work of art in its very own right. In much the same way, only by making this fair copy for you (which, at the same time, shall serve, in the first place, as the basis for a copy for practical use) have I completely finished with what had been previously sketched.

However, because of my persistent preoccupation with it, this task of developing the sketch has also served to reimmerse me in the spirit of my work and make me feel so completely at home once again that I can now go on with it as though I had never been interrupted. Of course, my great worry was naturally how to pick up where I had left off. An interruption of *twelve* years in any work is of course unheard of in the history of art: and if it now proves that this interruption has made no difference to the freshness of my conception, I may no doubt adduce this as a demonstration of the way in which these conceptions have an everlasting life, that they are not yesterday's, and not for tomorrow alone. The final, highly detailed working-out of the second act often enthralled and attracted me in a way that, so great was my rapturous delight, I often had to take a proper hold of myself. But I once dashed off these lines to our friend:[1] "Siegfried is divine. It is my greatest work!" – Let me describe to you the passage which I was bold enough to find so pleasing and so exhilarating. Siegfried has slain Fafner: the forest murmurs that had earlier captivated him so charmingly now exert their magic spell; he understands the woodbird, and – as though guided by some sweet narcosis and obeying, as it were, some instruction without knowing what he is doing – goes into the dragon's cave to remove the hoard; the Nibelung pair, having lain in wait, now rush at each other, each of them anxious to win the hoard for himself by wresting it from the lad; they wrangle and squabble in unheard-of fury. Siegfried, sunk in thoughtful contemplation of the ring, then re-emerges from the cave on to the high ground in front of it: the Nibelungs notice with horror that he has picked out the ring from the hoard, and they withdraw, each to strive after his own fashion to gain the ring for himself. Siegfried, contemplating the ring and the tarnhelm: "What use you are to me, I do not know." As he emerges, one hears the motif of the ring winding its way eerily through the accompaniment (during the speeches of the two Nibelungs): it now passes, with supreme and ghostlike pliancy, into the theme of the Rhinedaughters from the end of the Rhinegold: "Rhinegold! Purest gold! ah, would that you still lit the watery depths!" (Do you remember this from that last evening in the Residenz Theatre?)[2] To the accompaniment of a gentle *tremolo* on the strings, this theme is now heard on six horns, as

---

1 Cosima von Bülow.
2 A concert performance of excerpts from Wagner's works held in the Residenz Theatre on 12 July 1865.

though from some distant natural dream-world. The sense of expectancy which seizes hold of us here is quite overwhelming! When the woodbird warns Siegfried afresh against Mime's approach, and as the latter now creeps up from afar, wondering who could have told the lad of the ring, we hear gently, oh so gently his mother Sieglinde's loving concern for her son sound forth with tuneful tenderness – the son to whom, dying, she had given birth. The bird continues to hold our attention with its gentle warning phrases, as Mime now turns fawningly to Siegfried. Finally, when Mime too has been slain, a feeling of utter loneliness breaks out in the youth who until now has felt only high spirits: bear, wolf and dragon have been his only associates: the woodbird whose language he now understands is, as it were, the only creature to which he feels akin. And now the terror of ecstasy, as it tells him of Brünnhilde!! Yes, and what does all this mean? It is certainly no scene from family life: the fate of the world hangs upon the boy's godlike simplicity and the uniqueness of a fearless individual! –

Yes! – My Siegfried is beautiful, oh true and noble one! My King! –

The next morning, 24th Feb.

That is as far as I reached yesterday evening! – If I wanted to tell you more about Siegfried today, I should have to speak of a dark, sublime and awesome dread with which I enter the realm of my third act. We come here, like the Hellenes at the reeking crevice at Delphi, to the nub of the great world tragedy: the world is on the brink of destruction; the god seeks to ensure that the world is reborn, for he himself is the world's will to become. Everything here is instinct with sublime terror, and can be spoken of only in riddles. Since the time I returned to Munich after that wonderful week in Hohenschwangau[1] and had to raise such anxious questions about our fate, I have been haunted by a theme which I first conceived then and which greets us now at the very beginning of this act, proclaiming the world-god's decision, his final question and final resolve. Until this moment a sense of dread had prevented me from writing down what had flared up within me with the brightness of lightning on solitary walks through storm and tempest. But the proud exultation of the lovers united for death also found musical expression at this same time:[2] it is like the triumphant shout hurled from a hero's breast, flinging its cry of victory, love and joy across the Alpine heights, to abandon it to eternity's endless echo.

And so I too, like Wotan, must shut off the world of the will, firmly, unopenably and with final resolution: this have I done! Nothing shall open it up again! In it and for it I suffered all I was capable of suffering: I have now

---

1 11–18 November 1865.
2 This theme (set to the words "Sie ist mir ewig", Eulenburg miniature score 1152) first occurred to Wagner in the summer of 1859 (see Curt von Westernhagen, *The Forging of the "Ring"* [Cambridge 1976], 161), and reasserted itself on Midsummer Day 1868 (see Königsbriefe IV,193).

acquired the right no longer to be a part of it! – You, my most gracious friend, will discover some day *what* I am telling you here and what I am hinting at! – And so I am now ready to cast myself into this final horror: for I can already hear the echo from the mountains resounding with the exultant clamour of redemption. – The coming three spring months that are already crowding so forcefully into the world shall help this long-delayed act of my work to grow to final maturity! – Thus it is written in the stars that shine on my lonely house: there to the left, in the north, is the "Plough", the faithful old Pleiades; and to the right here, in the south, is Orion's flaming sword: between them in the north-east: Jupiter, lonely and radiant. –

––––––

But first there are many questions for me to answer. You were kind enough to want to know about my life and health, and how I divide up my day. Well, my life is dominated by a strange stability, or rather a sense of balance in which good and evil are finely poised, leaving only the poet and artist to live their lives within me. Since my brief visit to my relations in Leipzig,[1] I have not set foot outside Triebschen, and not seen a single stranger. No one can understand how I can live like this and many people no doubt cudgel their brains, more especially in Munich, where they no doubt persist in believing that I was not serious when I said goodbye to the place, and that I am no doubt playing fast and loose in order to achieve God knows what ends – perhaps even the government of Bavaria, where I would then abolish both state and religion in order to conduct affairs from a large opera-house. I shall shortly be stirring things up for a hired servant[2] of one of these anxious wise men, since, now that I am departing this life, I have certainly no intention of simply abandoning to scoundrels and knaves the precious inheritance that I am bequeathing to the nation. Mothers take care of their children: mine, too, shall have no cause to complain about their father. The wretched kinsfolk with whom I have had to deal for a quarter of a century; who these people are who have impeded my work and influence at every step, and who, at the end of an unprecedented career, have time and again obliged me to begin afresh – this is something I still have to explain to those who cannot understand any of this. –

However, all this ultimately forms only a brief parenthesis in the current phase of my present activities. What this means, according to the rule of the

1 Wagner had stayed with Hermann and Ottilie Brockhaus between 2(?) and 9 November 1868; it was there, on 8 November, that he first met Friedrich Nietzsche.
2 Eduard Devrient. The article concerned, *Herr Eduard Devrient und sein Stil* (Herr Eduard Devrient and his Style), appeared in the *Norddeutsche Allgemeine Zeitung* of 26 and 28 March 1869 and, pseudonymously under the name Wilhelm Drach, as a separate brochure published by Cäsar Fritsch of Munich. It is reprinted in GS VIII,226–38; PW IV,275–88.

order, is: "nulla dies sine linea!"[1] The rule itself means starting early with a
modest breakfast, after washing in cold water, then a brief look at the newspaper, of which I normally read only the table of contents and only look at
the inside pages in greater detail if I find something about the King of Bavaria
(for so long now the only way to discover news of my exalted friend!):[2] and
then there are the letters, too, often a great many of them, but nearly always
nonsensical, or making foolish demands: very rarely anything cheering! (for –
unfortunately! – not even the reports about the various splendid successes of
the Mastersingers[3] give me any special pleasure; everything is being eaten
away by an evil noxious canker: I no longer have any faith!) Paris is now
causing me the most painful disquiet, since I could not reasonably prevent
them from taking Rienzi in hand: well, I am now firmly resolved to take no
further notice of their project. The editor of the great political journal "La
Liberté" invited me through a third party[4] to send him some biographical
notes for an article intended to welcome me to Paris, where they are confidently awaiting my arrival. In reply I have sent this journal a letter, through
the agency of this same woman, who has spoken up for me in Paris with such
remarkable enthusiasm, and in it I declare that I am *not* coming to Paris, and
that I regard all attempts to introduce my works to the city simply as private
enterprises on the part of the theatre directors in question etc., but that I
myself have nothing in common with them. That will certainly amaze many
people who believe that I am planning to play a leading role in Paris, the
more so since – as rumour once more has it – I am wholly out of favour with
the King of Bavaria, and my earlier relations with him have become the total
opposite of what they once were. Yes, indeed, my exalted friend, this is the
latest news; and it dates from the beginning of last January! – On this point,
too, people will again be much amazed. But there is nothing I can do about
that. – From time to time, however, I also read reports which interest me
because they show some wit and understanding, e.g., the recent report on
the Dresden production of the Mastersingers in the Neue Zeitschr. für Musik.
But on the whole I am glad not to know what is going on in the world. –
And then at 10 o'clock I settle down to my score: this always gives me three

1 "No day without its line", a saying attributed to the Greek artist Apelles (4th century BC).
2 Apart from a coolly worded telegram at New Year, Ludwig had not written to Wagner between
   14 September 1868 and 10 February 1869, by far the longest gap in their correspondence to
   date.
3 The Munich première was followed by productions in Dresden (21 January 1869), Dessau
   (29 January 1869), Karlsruhe (5 February 1869), Mannheim (5 March 1869), Weimar (28
   November 1869), Hanover (26 February 1870), Vienna (27 February 1870), and Berlin (1
   April 1870).
4 Judith Gautier. The letter in question was published in *La Liberté* on 10 March 1869 and
   reprinted in SS XVI,114–15. With the publication of Cosima Wagner's Diaries, however, it
   emerges that the letter was written by Cosima herself (CT for 21 February 1869). *Rienzi* was
   first performed at the Théâtre Lyrique on 6 April 1869.

beautiful, uniquely enjoyable and substantial hours each morning. At 1 o'clock Jacob[1] then calls me to table. I then leave my desk in the green study. This is a remarkable little room which I created as a result of the rebuilding work which I have had done on the whole house: it consists in part of the room which you had the infinite kindness and condescension to make your night-quarters. A window has now been added by removing the kitchen, where I now have a small bedroom; and it gives an extremely welcoming, intimate impression. I have all kinds of keepsakes hanging on the wall here, including the large photographic portrait of my royal friend, and the water-colour of Hohenschwangau. The principal object of my attention in this room is now my library which, so often and so grievously, had been reduced in size by resettlements and the ravages suffered at so many stages of my past life but which I am now gradually supplementing and building up in such a way that, if ever heaven should grant me a serene old age, I might find ultimate refreshment and enjoyment in its collected riches of the mind. The salon is now decorated exclusively with oil paintings: in addition to the portrait of my King there is also – and I owe these treasures to the wonderful thoughtfulness of our noble friend, who has managed to acquire them for me by the most remarkable and round-about means! – a fine copy of my father's portrait, painted by my father,[2] then a portrait of Göthe which the immensely talented Munich artist Franz Lenbach was asked to sketch and paint for me on the model of what seems to me a wholly admirable engraving, and, more recently, a highly successful copy of Tischbein's portrait of Schiller (1803), the original of which is owned by the Schiller Society in Leipzig; their frames have all been made with the greatest possible imaginative skill according to our friend's selection and design; in particular, the frame of the large mirror above the (rebuilt) hearth, based upon the design of an old German frame in the Bavarian Museum, is a real work of art. And there is now – in addition to our busts – a splendid masterpiece in a corner of the salon – an original water-colour by the recently deceased Genelli, showing the Muses educating Dionysos – I maintain it to be the best thing this brilliant artist ever did.[3] It was found among the possessions of my late brother-in-law Friedrich Brock-haus, in whose house I had often contemplated it as a young man with genuine fascination, gaining as I did my first vital insight into the Greek spirit of beauty: when I told our friend this, she managed to persuade my sister to part with the painting, which she then gave me as a present. – From the salon two doors lead into my "gallery", which is what I have christened this long and narrow room, created out of what was once a small closet and the earlier

1 Jakob Stocker.
2 Ludwig Geyer.
3 Genelli's *Dionysos among the Muses* was later seen by Nietzsche and, according to his letter to Erwin Rohde of 16 July 1872, was a formative influence on *Die Geburt der Tragödie* (The Birth of Tragedy).

narrow dining-room by tearing down the partition-wall. The centre of the longer wall is taken up by Ille's water-colour of Tannhäuser, which my gracious friend was once generous enough to make over to me: on both sides of it are the six hand-coloured photographs based upon Echter's Rhinegold: beneath them are my bronze keepsakes, and portfolios containing engravings and photographs. The two shorter walls are decorated with other mementoes, including a recently acquired Indian Buddha[1] which I once received as a present in Venice from Countess d'Agoult and which had found its way into my wife's estate but which I have now succeeded in recovering. It is through this "gallery" that I must pass when called by Jacob at 1 o'clock: it leads into the dining-room, which has been newly created out of the old remains and a part of the former entrance hall, and it is here that I take my by no means sumptuously or elaborately prepared meal, at the end of which I am normally joined by my canine masters; I then withdraw to the salon for coffee and newspapers or any letters that may have arrived, followed by a short sleep or a brief session at the piano, according to my mood and needs. Then, at 3 o'clock, I don my fearsomely large Wotan hat, and, accompanied by Russ and Koss[2] – Falstaff with his page! – set off on my regular walk which, if the weather is bad or the paths muddy, is normally limited to an errand into the town of Lucerne, where I really only look in at the Post Office or often rummage at a second-hand bookseller's in search of interesting books – recently, for ex., I came across some that were extremely rare, namely the 4 volumes of the "Horen", edited by Schiller, in the original edition which is now completely impossible to find. As a rule I return to Triebschen at 5 o'clock, lie down for a brief quarter of an hour, and then return to my score (unless there are letters to be written!!); I work until around 8 o'clock, before retiring to the smaller salon on the upper floor, which once and for all I have set aside for our friend's summer visits;[3] here I have a very light supper and tea, before ending the evening by taking down a book to read, in the doing of which I repeatedly fall back upon our great minds Schiller, Göthe and Shakespeare: but Homer, too, has had his turn, as well as Calderon, less frequently learned writings such as Winckelmann. This gives me my night-time benediction: I am in good company, and know the friends to whom I can cling. At 11 I normally wend my way to my bed in the tiny bedroom next to my study; and now the question is: will the night bring restful sleep? Unfortunately this is not always the case: my abdomen is – and will always be – rebellious, until such time as a good course of treatment enables me to take radical action against this complaint. If sleeplessness sets in as a result, then the night becomes my foe. For care then sets in, too, and anxiety painful

1 See letter [371], pp. 734–5.
2 A Newfoundland and a Dobermann pinscher.
3 Here and later Wagner refuses to admit to Ludwig that Cosima is already living with him at Tribschen: she had moved in on 16 November 1868.

beyond imagining, and dawn will find me tired, gloomy and despondent. It then pains me to receive bad news, or to feel this silence, – this silence! with which my daemon mocks the solicitous impulses of our hearts. How utterly wretched do I then feel, my King! And if, in addition, it is borne in upon me how baseness and worthlessness repeatedly raise their ugly heads, playing with all that is most sacred to me and dragging it through the mire, while all that is good remains silent – silent! – then there are times when it becomes impossible for me to work on my score, and – then I ask myself why this day cannot be my *last*. –

But God knows what strength has been given me that it keeps on springing up again! A good night's sleep, a comforting word, a friendly nod are enough, – and – I'm back at my score again, and – I'd be happy to go on sitting there till the angel of death himself came to take me away! – –

As for our friend, the news that I have to tell my most dearly belovèd lord is far from encouraging. She appears to be suffering much discomfort: according to her own report, the great and painful weakness of her back has now made it impossible for her to write for any length of time, and the doctor has forbidden her to do so in the strictest terms. As a result I am now obliged to look around for a suitable copyist to work on my biography which you are kind enough to ask after; various attempts to find one locally have proved pitifully unsuccessful. I have now made enquiries with Richter in Munich to see whether I might be able to attract a good copyist whom I know there to come to Lucerne for a while;[1] for it is quite out of the question that I should abandon this dictation: the copyist must carry out his work under my direct supervision. Whatever happens, it will be a *most* remarkable book! And so, my most precious and exalted of friends, I must entreat your kind forbearance with regard to new instalments! –

But you then go on to ask about books with which to study the sources of the Siegfried legend? – What I *myself* used as such, in addition to the Nibelungenlied and the Edda itself, were Wilhelm *Grimm's* "German Heroic Legend", and *Mone's* "Investigations into Heroic Legend". In addition, very important, a translation of the "Völsunga Saga", which I tracked down to the Dresden Library, but which can certainly also be found in the Munich Library. I also believe that Franz Müller collected all this information together and drew attention to it in his monograph on my "Ring of the Nibelung".[2] – Oh! if only you had an able private librarian or "secretary" endowed with enthusiasm for this particular subject. What a joy it must be for the right

---

1 Wagner had written to Richter on 19 February to ask if the copyist Waschmitzius would be prepared to come to Lucerne to work on his projected Collected Edition.
2 Franz Müller, *Der Ring des Nibelungen: Eine Studie zur Einführung in die gleichnamige Dichtung Richard Wagners* (Leipzig 1862); see also Stewart Spencer, "The Language and Sources of 'The Ring' " in *ENO/ROH Opera Guide 35: The Rhinegold/Das Rheingold*, edited by Nicholas John (London 1985), 31–8.

person to be able to meet your every enquiry here! But – that is not to be! – Otherwise Nohl could no doubt be recommended, since he has deserved very well of me and – precisely because of that! – has incurred hostilities of every description; – certainly, he could never have dreamed that they would come from the direction they did! I myself got to know him only within recent years, and, to my very real delight, was able to overcome every prejudice against him.[1] – But I should not have said this: I know that I must stop recommending people! –

Finally, however, most precious and gracious of men! I still have to reply to your wishes concerning performances of "Tristan" and the "Rhinegold". My King! Kindly lend an ear! –

In the course of the last two years you have done as much to enable such performances to take place as it was possible to do in the prevailing circumstances: for this I must thank you from the bottom of my heart! Certainly, both this and all the other kindnesses that you have shown me have given you the incontestable right to dispose of my works and their performance as you think fit. And I myself shall lend a faithful hand in every way possible: but I know that you will not demand my personal participation if you believe me when I assure you that this is henceforth impossible. On the other hand, I can easily arrive at an understanding on all the points relating to the musical side of things with those who are appointed to direct the work: for every other arrangement I would simply beg as a favour that you assign Hallwachs as producer; for there is no one else I should care to deal with in this respect. I shall answer for him as soon as he receives full and exclusive authority to superintend the stage presentation of the "Rhinegold" according to my own instructions.

Another point here concerns the circumstances in which the performances of parts of my Nibelungs may be presented to the *general public*. On this point I shall make so bold as to inform you of my exact wishes when the right time comes![2] –

And so, my most belovèd lord! I am yours to command! I shall *only* help, and never get in the way! –

And now a final word in confidence concerning my personal affairs. Quite some time ago I asked Herr Düfflipp as a friend whether he thought that, given his intimate familiarity with the present state of affairs, it would be difficult or easy for him to arrange a relatively large advance on the stipend which has so kindly been decreed for me: in the latter instance I entreated him to lay before my exalted benefactor my particular wish in this regard.[3] In doing this I remained true to my belief or, rather, my feeling that, after

1 But see letter [450], p. 868.
2 On 22 March 1869 Wagner wrote to Ludwig, expressing the hope that the performances would be given "before an invited audience only, and free of charge" (Königsbriefe II,269).
3 On 2 March 1869 Ludwig granted Wagner a new loan of 10,000 gulden.

you had shown me so many kindnesses as a demonstration of your grace and lovingly solicitous favour, I myself could never really address an entreaty to you direct, but that since, on the other hand, you have often asked me lovingly about my needs and wishes, I need only intimate these to you through the intermediacy of a friend. On each occasion your granting of my wish was a glorious act of grace and love. – If I am in error as to your feelings here, I must beg most humbly for your forgiveness. In respect of the wish that was recently communicated to you, I now confirm that, as cheering and consoling as such a subvention would be, the very granting of it has become indispensable to me now that it has developed into a question of your grace and friendship.

I pray that you may be kind enough to understand this, and to show your usual loving tenderness! –

For my fate and final resolution place me in your hands! I will not, nor shall ever, serve another lord! So must you dispose of one who is uniquely yours! –

All hail! Hail! Good luck! – thus do I call out to him whom I love and adore before all else! Always remember with grace and goodness

Your eternally loyal
Richard Wagner

Königsbriefe II, 256–65.

376. HEINRICH LAUBE, LEIPZIG   Lucerne, 6 March 1869

Dear Laube,

I would be sincerely grateful to you if you would use your position with the Leipzig Municipal Theatre to ensure that my operas are never again given there in the future.[1]

In the hope that you will have the kindness to fulfil my request, I remain

Your devoted servant
Richard Wagner

Freunde und Zeitgenossen 496 (facsimile in Walter Lange, Richard Wagner und seine Vaterstadt [Leipzig 1921], 227).

---

1 Wagner was unable to forgive Laube his critique of *Die Meistersinger* in the *Neue Freie Presse* of September 1868.

377. FERDINAND LEUTNER, VIENNA   Lucerne, 6 April 1869

Most honoured Sir,

Accept my sincere thanks for your parcel, and also for your letter. Your little booklet contained much that I found encouraging. As for your letter, I can tell you that it had the same consoling effect upon me, something which very rarely happens, but which, when it does, leaves an even more pleasing impression in that insipidity and malice cannot affect me as adversely as wit and sympathy can cheer me. In the present instance you are the first and only person to have given me this pleasure and, in doing so, happily made up for so much that is bad.

As for the object in question, the brochure[1] itself, you do well to recognize that my only aim could be to ensure that it is read at all: how people interpret it is of course not my affair but theirs. My own view is not that anything can still be done to arrest our present great cultural decline, but that something *must* be done to force us to see what has happened. Just as the poor political economy of the Poles has led to the country's wealth falling into the hands of the Jews, so the boundless neglect, nay, the squandering of the German spirit's cultural capital by German governments has allowed this same capital to be exploited by the selfsame Jews in accordance with entirely similar natural laws. All one can do is admit this: it is no longer possible to fight against it or argue about it. But we should not seek to conceal this from ourselves for the sake of our own convenience. That was my intention, as you yourself recognized it to be. Why should we squabble with our conquerors? It is only ourselves that we have to blame for having caused us to be disinherited. –

May I thank you once again, and ask that you keep in touch?

I remain, Sir, your most respectful and obedient servant

Richard Wagner

Adolf Zinsstag, Die Briefsammlungen des Richard Wagner-Museums in Tribschen bei Luzern (Basle [1961]),40.

378. CARL TAUSIG, BERLIN   [Lucerne, April 1869]

Although somewhat belatedly, I must reply to your splendid telegram,[2] more especially to express my gratitude for it and pleasure at it. A somewhat more detailed description of the performance of Lohengrin would certainly have

1 *Judaism in Music.*
2 A performance of *Lohengrin* in Berlin had had to be postponed because of the furore caused by the republication of *Judaism in Music.* Tausig reported the success of the performance when it finally took place with the telegram, "Huge success of *Lohengrin*, all Jews reconciled, your devoted Karl" (CT for 7 April 1869). Wagner's reply to Tausig found its way into the hands of Julius Lang, who published it, without permission, in his pamphlet *On the Reconciliation of Jewry with Richard Wagner* (Berlin 1869).

been welcome, more particularly to give me some idea of Eckert's merits and his conducting in general.

Of course, your assurance that all Jews are reconciled with me also had its effect on me. It would certainly be no bad thing if my brochure *were actually properly read* by sensible and intelligent Jews, but it seems as though people have forgotten how to read. Only from Vienna did I receive a letter from a young man of letters,[1] attesting to the fact that people do indeed still know how to read. This man found that what was characteristic about my essay was its contemplative quality. And even I, when I reread it, am bound to testify that there is probably no one who has shown more objective calm than I in depicting and discussing the history of such unheard-of persecution and of the disparagement that I have encountered, a disparagement that has been as exhaustive as it has been unrelenting. Of course, I should have had to suffer in silence and say nothing if I had not uncovered the reason for this persecution. This could not be done with the kind of circumlocutions that I should now have to use in expressing my ideas on Judaism (as I call it) as something typically my own – but this is something I have in any case no intention of doing, since I cannot countenance a conflict here (utterly useless as it must be). And so I have simply had to republish the corpus delicti (out of date though it now seems to me) in order to be able to depict and explain the whole unprecedented story. To see this old piece again may have been very painful for many people – and more especially for those who are totally innocent; I could have been spared all this, and they, too, could have been spared it if the article's *latent* potential had finally faded in this respect as well. For a long time I expected that this would happen, but the unprecedented insolence of the Viennese press on the occasion of the "Mastersingers", the continual, brazen lie-mongering about me, and its truly destructive effects have finally persuaded me to take this step, regardless of its consequences, more especially after I had been questioned on the matter.[2] But I have now given some really intelligent Jew all the material he needs to give the whole question a new and, no doubt, beneficial twist, and to assume a highly significant attitude towards this most important of all our cultural concerns. *I know there must be such a person: if he does not dare to do what it is his business to do, then it is with immeasurable sadness that I shall have to concede that I was right to describe Judaism – or more especially modern German Judaism – as I did, and if I leave the description to stand, as I have done.* But one needs courage as well as mere presumption, for I take the matter very seriously. – When you tell me that "Lohengrin" has reconciled the Jews with me, what I understand by this is really only that my brochure is regarded as over-hasty and, as such, is *forgiven* me. I do not find this very comforting. *I have already encountered a*

1 Ferdinand Leutner; see letter [377], p. 748.
2 By Countess Marie Muchanoff; see letter [372], p. 735.

very great deal of good-naturedness, especially on the part of Jews. Let one of them show real courage, only then will I rejoice! –

Richard Wagner.

SS XVI, 102–3.

379. FRIEDRICH NIETZSCHE, BASLE Lucerne, 3 June 1869

Most honoured friend,

Please accept – albeit somewhat belatedly – my profound and heartfelt thanks for your beautiful and thoughtful letter!

Whereas I wished then[1] that you would visit me, I now repeat with all the greater insistence the sincere invitation that I extended to you in person when we said goodbye in front of the "Rössli".

Do come – a single line of advance warning is all I need – Saturday afternoon for example; stay throughout Sunday, and return early on Monday: even a manual worker could manage this, how much easier it must be for a professor.

You will stay with me here, and spend both nights in the Triebschen trust house.

Now let me see the kind of man you are. My experiences with my fellow Germans have been less than wholly delightful so far. Come and restore my not entirely unwavering faith in what I – together with Göthe and a few others – call German freedom. –

Sincere good wishes from your devoted servant Richard Wagner.

Nietzsche-Briefe II, 2 14.

380. HANS RICHTER, MUNICH Lucerne, 25 July 1869

Dear kind Richter,

There are so many demands upon my time at present, but since I wanted to give my Paris friends[2] a letter of introduction to take with them to you, I

---

1 Nietzsche had visited Wagner at Tribschen on 17 May, the second of twenty-three visits there (the first, on 15 May, had been abortive). He returned, in response to Wagner's invitation, for the weekend of 5/6 June, a visit which coincided with the birth of Siegfried Wagner.

2 Judith Gautier, her husband Catulle Mendès, and Philippe-Auguste Villiers de l'Isle-Adam.

shall drop you a brief note today because of the other favours that I have to ask of you.

1. The Mrazeks – should pack separately the crockery that belongs to me, & send it to Frau B. separate from the other things. They should try to sell the double-doors. And could you settle Thierry's trifling account?

2. I have read in Siebert's Journal that there is talk of a "revival" of the fl. Dutchman in Hamburg.[1] This theatre has no right to give this opera; they have never paid me for it & – some 18 months ago – found my claim too high. Would you inform Siebert of this?

Let us stick with Schelper then.[2]

Persist for the present quite definitely in demanding your dismissal.[3] Guarantees must be given for your future independence, guarantees which cannot be obtained by good-natured means; only if you stick firmly to your declaration will they perhaps turn to me, and only then may it be possible for me to obtain the position for you without which it would be sheer hell for you to remain in Munich. Enough for today!

Be good to my friends from Paris: they are quite exceptionally important people who are, moreover, utterly devoted to me.

Sincere good wishes from me and the rest of us!

Yours,
RW.

Richter-Briefe 33–4.

381. HANS RICHTER, MUNICH   [Lucerne, 26 July 1869][4]

Dear Richter,

Costume designs for the "Rhinegold" – presumably from the Royal Court Theatre intendancy – have been sent to me here today, and I make so bold as to return them to you herewith, with the request that you forward these sketches to the Royal Court Theatre intendancy together with the following report.

Once again it is an occasion for regret that the author himself has not been consulted until so late a stage with regard to his wishes in so highly problematical a matter as that of designing costumes for a subject such as this. Had people done so, they would have discovered that the experiments attempted

1 *Der fliegende Holländer* appears to have been first performed in Hamburg on 22 March 1870.
2 See letter [382], p. 753, note 2.
3 See introductory essay, pp. 595–6.
4 Dating from CT.

by Herr Echter in the case of the frescoes in the royal palace[1] could in no way be regarded as a definitive solution to this question, but that it must rather be left to me – when it finally came to arranging for the actual performance of my work to take place – to insist upon more detailed studies with the aim of finding characteristic costumes for this ancient Germanic world of gods. The most imaginative painters and archaeologists would naturally have to be consulted here. In general, my initial objection to the sketches I have been sent is that they show no sense of invention and that (as copies of Echter's frescoes) they include only Greek costumes (accepted there as an expedient, for want of anything better), with peplum etc., a kind of costume which reveals everything except Germanic gods. It would therefore be advisable to enquire into the character of the costumes worn by Germanic gods in Roman times – more especially on the basis of allusions in Tacitus: even some slight allusion would be sufficient to provide an intelligent and inventive mind with analogous forms, which could then lead to other ideas. This would be a task for the Royal Academy of Art. Also, I desire *less nakedness* and more actual clothing, and no savages from the Prussian coat of arms for the giants: the gods should have attributes, e.g. Froh a sickle, Fricka a distaff, Freia as goddess of flowers & fruit similarly correspondingly characterized. No *gold* jewelry! that surely goes without saying in a piece where gold first has to be discovered and made known to the gods, etc.

Would you be so kind as to read out this report – perhaps at the next meeting, and perhaps persuade Herr Hallwachs to send me further information in this matter.

If it were still possible to shelve this entire undertaking for the present, I should welcome this as by far the best solution.

Sincere good wishes from your devoted servant

Richard Wagner.

Richter-Briefe 34–6.

382. HANS RICHTER, MUNICH   Lucerne, 13 August 1869

Poor, dear friend,

It is all most regrettable what you have to tell me! – Not only can I not blame you, I must even advise you to address yourself, as soon as possible, directly and in writing to the King, informing him of your request for dismissal: do this as though you wanted to tell him the plain truth (as is your intention), and hoped to be able to serve the King by carrying out to the

---

1 Thirty frescoes, depicting scenes from the Nibelung legend, in the Theatines' entrance to the Residenz in Munich.

letter my artistic directives and instructions; instead of which you have found it impossible to obey the orders of an intendant[1] whose total ignorance is matched only by his opposition to everything that emanates from *me. Lay the whole emphasis on this!*

I still hope that, in the end, the King will be able to retain you: otherwise, things will certainly not be easy for you in Munich. Entreat his favour and ask that, in recognition of your exceptional and responsible achievement in the case of the "Rhinegold", he should allow you to remain in His Majesty's pay until the vocal score of "Siegfried" is completed. But perhaps it would be even better if you were to say nothing of this for the present, but to leave me to settle this point in person, depending on what the King's reply turns out to be.

As for the rest, however, you have completely misunderstood me, my dear Richter, if you think I did not want you here with the three singers.[2] On the *contrary*, your presence is most important to me. There is only *one* thought that I have in mind with their entire production, namely that the score be performed in a correct, accurate and lively manner. Scenery – and acting – all this I abandon: but the music must be beyond reproach: at least we shall then have saved the most important thing! Most of all I should have preferred it if the whole performance had taken place without scenery and costumes.

And so – I expect you as soon as possible. – There is of course still time, since I have just read that the performance has been postponed until the 29th.[3]

In any case it would be good to see you again and speak to you!

Sincere good wishes for today from your own

Richard Wagner
plus all the hangers-on at Triebschen.

I am reopening this letter in order to bring it into line with the telegraphic despatch[4] that I subsequently decided to send you. For I am of the opinion that you should send your request for dismissal *before* you arrive here: it cannot arrive quickly enough if we are to enjoy any (possible) benefits from it.

Richter-Briefe 36–8.

1 Karl von Perfall.
2 Franz Betz (Wotan), Otto Schelper (Alberich) and Max (Karl) Schlosser (Loge) arrived in Tribschen on 18 August for a coaching session. Betz and Schelper later withdrew from the production, and Schlosser was recast as Mime.
3 The première of *Das Rheingold* finally took place on 22 September 1869.
4 The telegram read, "Meeting with singers here indispensable. Arrange same. Await today's letter. Request release from contract on basis of same. Wagner" (Königsbriefe V,93).

383. KING LUDWIG II OF BAVARIA, BERG   Lucerne, 30 August 1869

My gracious friend! My generous benefactor!

If a proud-spirited undertaking by my exalted patron at which the whole of art-loving Europe now gazes in eager expectation has not become an object of universal mockery, it is due to the courage and self-sacrifice of my outstanding disciple and faithful representative Hans Richter. – From the reports of discriminating friends[1] who came to Munich expressly for my work[2] and who would (as they tell me) gladly have closed an eye to the scenery in order to be able to enjoy it, – from these reports I have been forced to infer that this work of mine was exposed to the immediate risk of appearing ridiculous. I took the liberty of submitting to you a report by the singer Betz, who is himself one of the affected parties, and this report confirms the risk. Liszt, who is accustomed to pay scant heed to the stage and devote his attention, instead, to the musical performance alone, confirms that this performance was beyond reproach, but that, the scenery having turned out as badly as it has, a performance of the work is now impossible.

My reluctance to raise a word of protest against my royal friend, who has desired the Rhinegold to be performed, was in itself an act of painful self-denial, for it was now no longer possible to fulfil the encouraging reassurances that had once been offered me: even so, I believed that I still might accede to your desire, inasmuch as I was able to imagine that the performance which was to be given would at least be decently acceptable. Whereas a perfect and uniquely worthy performance could have been achieved only through my own co-operation and with the aid of knowledge and expertise which I alone possess, I was bound on this occasion to refuse my co-operation, and to refuse it, moreover, for reasons that I wish had been the object of earnest and sincere enquiry. Instead, I had to leave the affair to run its course, relying for a tolerably good outcome upon the certainty of being able to ensure a correct interpretation of the music by a conductor loyally devoted to me, and secondly upon the assumption that the new and most distinguished machinist Brandt would be able to supervise the scenery, at least in the sense of the best modern theatre administrations, if I were able to confer with him in detail. Even this last-stated assumption appeared to be confirmed, inasmuch as I was able to discuss each and every point of the stage presentation with Herr Brandt, who was sent to me at my express wish, accompanied by the producer Hallwachs, and to discuss these points in such a way that I was able to gain the most favourable impression concerning this young man's calm and serious intelligence and to feel very satisfied in this respect, too, now that all

1 Judith Gautier, her husband Catulle Mendès, and Philippe-Auguste Villiers de l'Isle-Adam.
2 i.e. for the rehearsals.

the difficulties appeared to have been solved. About four weeks ago, however,[1] in response to my anxious entreaty, I was visited by the scene-painter Jank, who came to submit his designs for my approval. To my astonishment, I now discovered that the scene-painter had been kept in total ignorance of all my discussions with Brandt, and that, in consequence, orders had been issued without regard for my own instructions. When I asked why this was so, I discovered that the intendant[2] had had no intention of regarding Herr Brandt & Herr Hallwachs as my plenipotentiaries, and that he had refused, in this spirit, to accept their report, but that, on the contrary, he had, at his own discretion, invited both stage-managers, Brandt & Penkmayer, to compete with each other, a competition which he, Herr von Perfall (presumably as an experienced and enlightened expert), reserved for himself the right to judge. He decided in favour of Penkmayer's designs, at least in the main parts, which he distilled together into a kind of compromise which robbed Herr Brandt of all freedom to implement those ideas of his which I myself had praised as sound. – As if this *modus operandi* was not bad enough (and in the end there was nothing I could say to it, except that they should do as they liked), there was the extraordinary delay with which all these tasks were taken in hand, so that I must now concede that a great deal that turned out badly at the dress rehearsal was a question of this alone, and that it could still be put right. None the less, the result of all this was that the scenery at the dress rehearsal turned out in such a way as to render an immediate performance perilous beyond measure, and, indeed, quite out of the question. – Thus determined, I telegraphed to my gracious patron,[3] begging him in the first place to agree to the postponement that seemed to me to be necessary: yesterday I telegraphed my suggestions for improving the scenery to Court Councillor Düfflipp. If these suggestions are met, I would further presume to take it upon myself, without causing any personal anxiety, to bring about a performance next Sunday which will save my work and give Your Majesty some pleasure. It goes without saying that the musical direction of the music director Herr Richter is an indispensable part of this: he is a loyal man who is as enthusiastic as he is vehemently devoted to me, and since – in the circumstances – he could see no other means of preventing inevitable disaster from overtaking my work except by refusing – in complete disregard for his personal well-being – to co-operate on so scandalous a production, the intendant hit upon the idea of casting round for another conductor for my work.[4] Now, I may well assume that my name is sufficiently respected among musicians to discourage them from committing the outrage that is

1 On 14 July 1869.
2 Karl von Perfall.
3 On 28 August. The dress rehearsal had taken place the previous evening.
4 Approaches were made to Eduard Lassen (Weimar), Johann Herbeck (Vienna), Hermann Levi (Karlsruhe), and Camille Saint-Saëns (Paris).

now expected of them: but that such an expedient should have even been attempted fills me with very real dismay. – Why must this happen to me, – to me of all people, why, in the name of the proud-hearted protector of my life and art, a man who has at all times made me supremely happy through the most inspiriting assurances, and whose oft-asserted task in life it has been to be the tutelary genius and guardian spirit of my works, the only man to have helped, in blameless fashion, to give birth to my boldest and most difficult work – why should I yield to men whose incompetence, ill-will, pettiness, and even malice offer up this work to general ridicule? –

I have seen a great deal in my time, and my decisions to withdraw completely have not been taken lightly: however, – this is something I will not and cannot believe. And that is why I have dared to tax your patience today, my most gracious King, with this account of a situation about which you presumably have neither accurate nor honest reports. Unfortunately, I have often, nay almost always, had to suffer the King's enigmatic silence in reply to remonstrations of this kind. I pray that my friend and intimate votary may answer me one more time! I await your telegraphic instructions in order to take immediate steps to fulfil my promise for Sunday.[1]

Eternally and truly yours,
Your own
Richard Wagner

Königsbriefe II,284–6.

384. PETER CORNELIUS, MUNICH   Lucerne, 8 September 1869

Dear friend,

I wrote straightaway to Court Councillor Düfflipp, recommending that he accept your wish.[2] Be so kind as to contact (or, rather, confer with) him on this point. Your decision to leave Munich is one that I am bound to welcome in every respect, even though the reasons behind it are much to be deplored. –

That the confidence which, 2½ years ago, persuaded us all to renew our links with Munich was utterly without foundation I recognized as soon as I returned there for the first time at the end of 1867. I undertook only to perform the Mastersingers, and resolved never again to return to M. None

1 Ludwig did not reply. Instead he wrote to Düfflipp, "The behaviour of 'Wagner' and the theatre rabble is nothing less than a crime and a disgrace; it is open insurrection against my orders, and that is something I cannot tolerate. On no account may 'Richter' conduct, he is to be dismissed at once, and that's final. The theatre people must obey My orders, and not 'Wagner's' whims" (letter of 30 August 1869 in Königsbriefe V,101).
2 Cornelius had written announcing his intention of resigning from the School of Music in Munich.

the less, I hoped that my friends, and more especially Bülow, would be able to hold out there by dint of their talent and in a less highly-charged atmosphere than was bound to be the case when I was there. As was to be feared, however, reaction soon set in against the consequences of my evening in the imperial box,[1] and led to deep cuts. The honour of Fr. v. B.[2] was once again impugned in His Majesty's presence, leaving her with no choice but to break with Munich for ever, and press for a divorce from one whose name and honour she had no wish to sully any further as a result of the hatred that she was made to feel. Only a few months ago[3] she was able, quite justifiably, to recommend that her husband agree to a divorce, in spite of his hesitations, since such a step would also favour his continuing to remain in his Munich appointment, inasmuch that the reproach that he owed that appointment to his services as a husband would then be impossible to sustain; in return for which she was disposed to submit even to the rigours of a divorce. B. thanked her, and conceded that she was right, but declared that, as a result of the worthlessness of conditions in Munich and his never-ending annoyance with them, his position had in any case become insufferable in the highest and final degree, and that, come what may, he was intending to give it up. I have deposited documentary evidence to this effect in an important place, and have reserved for myself the right to refer to it should the need arise. –

So much for today on this for you and my friends! –

What we have all suffered and endured is beyond imagining! –

Be glad you are turning your back on all this! Best wishes to your good wife! Remember me with affection,

Your Richard.

Freunde und Zeitgenossen 499–501.

385. FRANZ WÜLLNER, MUNICH [Lucerne, 11 September 1869][4]

Herr Kapellmeister Wüllner.

Hands off my score![5] Take my advice, Sir, or may the devil take you! – Beat time for music clubs and choral societies, or if you *must* have opera scores, get hold of ones by your friend Perfall! And tell that fine gentleman that if he doesn't openly admit to the King his personal incompetence to give

1 See introductory essay, p. 595.
2 Cosima von Bülow.
3 Cosima had written to Bülow on 15 June. For her letter and Bülow's reply, see Geoffrey Skelton, *Richard and Cosima Wagner* (London 1982), 114–22.
4 Dating from CT.
5 The score of *Das Rheingold*, which Wüllner was to conduct in Munich; see introductory essay, pp. 595–6.

my work, I shall light such a fire under him that not even all the gutter journalists whom he pays for out of the leavings from the Rhinegold expenses will be able to blow it out. I am going to have to teach the pair of you a lot of lessons before you learn how ignorant you are.

RW.

Königsbriefe IV, 201–2.

386. KING LUDWIG II OF BAVARIA, HOHENSCHWANGAU

Lucerne, 20 November 1869

My exalted friend and gracious benefactor,

You see that I cannot bear "not to write" to you![1]

Reason wars with sentiment, feeling struggles with discretion, and what finally reasserts itself ever and anew is what we are and what we cannot but be.

When I received your last letter, so unexpected as it was, and read it, my first reaction was bound to be: "So was it often before!" And it was precisely this that so disheartened me: the last thing I wanted was for everything to be repeated all over again. And yet, with all the foresight of a heart that is fearful of being hurt, I must once again recognize that a fundamental feature of our relations has remained unaltered. In your gracious friendship I continue solely to enjoy the spiritual and temporal benefits of my creative calm, and what this means in terms of my lot in life is quite beyond measure.

Yet I must also live with you in perfect peace. That would always have been possible if our relations had never transcended the ties that bind a gratefully devoted poet to his exalted patron and benefactor. But on this point I have repeatedly and sorrowfully expressed my mind! – It seemed always that I would not be right, until, time and again, I was reminded that ultimately I had been right after all. You know, my most gracious of friends, what I am thinking of here, since your own noble confession attests to that knowledge. It is not the difficulties of the affair itself, nor even those of our situation, which so often appear to divide us utterly; but that it must sometimes seem to me as though you were travelling a quite different path from the one where you hoped to encounter me, as though you wanted something quite different from me. Then you keep aloof, and avoid me – indeed, you join forces with the difficulties which, together, we might so easily have surmounted, so that

1 In his letter of 1 November 1869 Wagner had told Ludwig that he could not address him frankly; but a report in the *Signale* of 2 November, announcing that plans were already in progress to produce *Die Walküre* in Munich, persuaded him to change his mind.

I, a total outlaw, must ask myself whether I merely dreamed that I had a King as my friend.

Yet in order to transcend all the grief and the bitterness that I have had to endure at times such as these, I have need of but one thing alone, namely: to be able to turn once again to the future with great fixity of purpose and in the fullest of confidence. So much pettiness, and a sense of unworthiness little deserving of our regard still clings to recent events that it is impossible to countenance even the least satisfaction within this circle. The whole situation in Munich, with the personalities that it involves, can now be regarded only as an attempt which has simply not turned out to our advantage. I do not wish to return to this situation in any way. In consequence I am loath to give any further consideration to all that has happened. To do so could be of significance for me only inasmuch as I might discover that your own, inner will were involved here. Permit me therefore to indicate with what well-considered level-headedness I lovingly strive to ensure that so wondrously noble a bond as that which unites us both may achieve its fruitful and natural term. It was impossible for me here to fall back upon such expedients as cleverness or mere worldly wisdom (suitable as these may seem to others!), for I can only ever appeal to the great and uncommon feature that is our bond of ideal friendship. And that is why I must enquire closely into your *will*, for in its actions alone can my power lie.

I would ask you therefore to let me know, clearly and definitely, and after mature reflection, whether it was ever your serious and true intent to carry out the great plan according to which we would perform the Nibelungs and hold them up to the German world as the monumental starting-point for a new and noble period of art? Your heart alone can tell you whether this was ever your true intent. The course which events have taken during the last two years – and it is now exactly two years! – has inevitably made it ever clearer to me that you did *not* in fact want to carry out this plan – indeed, that the embarrassment caused you by my assumption that it would be carried out placed a constraint on you and drove us apart. Ever since I first recognized this I have been forced to fall back on myself: these two years were a sad afterglow to the sacred flame which until then had shone forth from our bond. Judge then with what bitter, nay – Godforsaken feelings I had to submit to seeing your commands carried out, as you reduced this tremendous work of mine to the level of achievement of some wretched operatic repertory performed for subscribers and critics! – There is nothing more that I can repeat here; for even before I knew you, when I had no hope of ever meeting a King, I had already sketched out, in clear and definite terms, the one and only plan according to which my work would be presented to the world: I must therefore presume to direct your attention afresh to the foreword to the poem of my Nibelung's Ring, if you now wish to be clear in your mind what I must now be feeling – in regard to my work. – But enough!

Perhaps it was all no more than a case of sad confusion. You demanded to hear something of my work; the confusion of the situation made you forget that I could have enabled you, my King, to hear my work at any time – imperfectly, perhaps, as it could not be otherwise, but none the less sufficiently correct to give you at least some idea: but it could have been only for you, the King; my intimately understanding friend. And now the only question that still matters, for your answer to it will determine our entire future:

Do you want my work as I want it, –

or: *do you not want it like that? –*

If so, then I no less than you and others certainly recognize the uncommon difficulties facing us here: – however, these difficulties should not *separate* us, but *unite* us. – To begin with I would ask of you only *one* sacrifice. It is that you withdraw for a period from all involvement in the theatre, nay – from all regard for the theatre. – Oh, would that you might believe me when I tell you that this theatre is unworthy of your touch, unworthy of my royal friend and of one who completes the work of – Richard Wagner! – If you can bring yourself to accept this, – and you will be able to do so if, as I most passionately desire, you extend your field of vision – in an artistic context, too – beyond the limitations of what, by chance, has offered itself to your gaze so far, and cast your eyes towards Italy, to its wonderful towns and works of art, in order to discover how different are those things that still lie ahead of you – things worthy, indeed, of the regard of an art-loving King and far removed from the importunate pettinesses of a German Court Theatre! – If you were able, I say, to rise for a time above this atmosphere of utter inadequacy, – if you were able to do so, more especially, out of regard for your country's grave situation in which each of your royal resolutions is now of such crucial decisiveness, – this would be the time when all might grow to be worthy of our work. To console you for this deprivation – a consolation which I once described in my essay on "State & Religion" as the sweetest that a King might know – I would, throughout this period, perform all my works *for you alone*, in the manner to which you were accustomed – musical performances at least, with singers and orchestra, and given as often as you wished. During this period we would then calmly and circumspectly work out a plan for performing our great work, preparing its performance, and solving and surmounting every difficulty with sagacity and firmness. But the feat of our ultimate great success will shine forth throughout history in undying splendour, vouchsafing to you immeasurable fame and granting us both the most sublime satisfaction.

This feat is possible if a King wills it so *with* me.

Or will it, conversely, be possible to achieve only what the King wants *in spite of* the poor and helpless artist that I am? – It is this latter that has now been revealed to the world, and those who wished to witness this tawdry miracle will by now have awarded you their approbation.[1] – –

[. . .]

Königsbriefe II,290–3.

387. FRANZ SCHOTT, MAINZ   Lucerne, 4 December 1869

Most honoured Sir,

A few lines in haste to thank you most cordially for the gift of the full score of the "Mastersingers" which arrived today in response to my request and which I intend as a present this Christmas for a friend[2] who is utterly devoted to me and extremely able, but quite without means: it will make him very happy. –

As for *Hamburg*, I entirely agree with you that the fee for performing rights[3] should be reduced to 40 ld'or: but I would ask you to insist on immediate payment, since the Hamburg management is not to be trusted for longer than a week. 18 months ago the management there wrote to me asking for the "flying Dutchman"; I demanded 30 ld'or; they replied, saying that that was too much, and so I let it pass. Last summer I discovered that the "flying Dutchman" was being given in *Hamburg*;[4] my agent however advised against prosecuting the people there, – he said they were always on the brink of bankruptcy, and that I should have to spend so much on powers of attorney etc. that it was questionable whether I should recover even my costs. – And so! forgive me if I repeat my urgent request that you remit a copy of the full score (with your stamp granting them the performing rights) only in return for immediate payment of my fee as well. With so many theatres it is difficult to retain an overall picture. –

A complete edition of the full scores of my operas is something that increasingly preoccupies me. Much has already been lost here. I recently heard from *C. F. Meser's*[5] unfortunate successor in Dresden, who wrote to say that ever-increasing orders for the full scores of "Rienzi" and the "flying Dutchman" were a source of frequent embarrassment to the firm, making

1 The draft of this letter (in RWA) is addressed "To His Majesty von Peabeaudy", a reference to the American banker and philanthropist George Peabody (1795–1869).
2 Possibly Richard Pohl.
3 For *Die Meistersinger von Nürnberg*, first heard in Hamburg on 9 April 1871.
4 See letter [380], p. 751, note 1.
5 The publisher of *Rienzi, Der fliegende Holländer* and *Tannhäuser*. The vocal scores were engraved, but the full scores struck off by an autographic-transfer process which precluded the possibility of making any more copies after the initial printing. On Meser's death in 1856, Hermann Müller was installed as manager.

him regret that they had not had the full scores engraved at the time. On the other hand, the engraving of the full score of "Tannhäuser" came at a bad time for him, since it was taken in hand by the said Herr H. Müller before I had set to work revising some of the scenes (for *Paris*). Since then he has behaved so inconsiderately towards me that I have not yet permitted him to complete the score with the new scenes, and, in consequence, have not yet sent them to him. In other words, if this score were to be completed according to the revised version, I would insist, after my own fashion, that theatres would have to obtain *this* edition. All this is in the air at present, since I should prefer to save it up for a complete collected edition. None the less, it would be of interest to me to know, should you care to make something out of this, what sort of an arrangement you would come to with Herr H. *Müller* (Meser) and *Breitkopf & Härtel*[1] with a view to taking over their publishing interests. I should like to begin, for ex., with a somewhat amended edition of the "flying Dutchman", and then devote the remaining years of my life to the remaining editions, finishing with the "Nibelungs", a task to which I could attend gradually and at my convenience. I believe the best solution would be for you to announce a subscription, since you would then have no difficulty in finding a form in which the King of Bavaria could be persuaded to support the enterprise: he would put his name down for as many copies as you thought necessary to cover more or less all of the costs.[2] –

Well, that is as far as I can go today!

Assuring you of my best wishes, I remain

Your most devoted servant
Richard Wagner.

Verleger-Briefe II, 127–8.

388. ANTON PUSINELLI, DRESDEN   Lucerne, [13][3] January 1870

My dear, good, old friend,

I have often felt the need, when suitably stimulated, to write to you at length about myself. You know that I have kept on meaning to visit you in Dresden: I was once on the point of doing so, but repeatedly failed even to make a start on so brief a trip down memory lane. To explain this properly, I should need to tell you my life-story, since there is little about that life that can be understood ex abrupto, as it were. But help is at hand in finding the right expedient in this sense: for about 5 years now – at various periods – I

1 The publishers of *Lohengrin* and *Tristan und Isolde*.
2 Nothing came of this suggestion.
3 Although the autograph letter bears the date "12 Jan. 1869", emended to "1870", it appears from Cosima Wagner's Diaries that the correct date should be 13 January 1870.

have been dictating my complete life-story to a creature who is closer to me than anyone else, and only the last 10 years are still missing. The true meaning of this exercise will become clear to you when I tell you the purpose for which it is necessarily intended: the material itself cannot be published until long after my death. In the meantime, however, it sheds light on too many incidents for it not to seem very important that my friends should know of the existence of a document which could emphatically refute all the distortions & calumnies which circulate about me, as they do about nobody else. To protect such a manuscript against loss, I am now in the process of having a very small number of copies of it printed at my own expense. These shall in part be left to my family; but even during my lifetime I should like to give a copy each to you and perhaps two other younger and entirely trustworthy friends, in return, of course, for the most faithful pledge never to let it out of their sight, nor to publish it after my death. Against this, it will be of use to these few people even now, since it will enable them to contradict false statements that may be made concerning my life (more especially these absurd biographical sketches that appear from time to time) by relying for whatever corrections may seem necessary upon the dictated material itself.

For the present I have been sent a trial print from the press, which I am sending on to you straightaway with my kindest good wishes.

This life of mine really has been the strangest affair. Anyone who reviews it in detail is bound to find in it the expression of but a single need, a single aim, namely: that of finding peace and tranquillity, albeit endowed with whatever degree of comfort is necessary for artistic creativity. On the other hand, the outward course of my life appears such that not even a lunatic hell-bent upon high adventure could have fashioned a more turbulent and vicissitudinous life for himself. The attentive reader of my biography will soon see the reasons for this contradiction: they are of an ideal & a practical nature. In the first instance, they are to be found in my particular artistic bias, because – as an "opera composer" – I am condemned to the most trivial of all artistic spheres for my life's work, and because it is precisely *here* that I intend to create a work of art that utterly transcends all other artistic genres. The practical reasons reveal two main obstacles in my life: my total lack of financial means, and my premature and utterly unsuitable marriage. But want of property was certainly the worst of all. Inherited wealth may be great or small, but it alone can provide the independence necessary to a man desirous of something serious and genuine: given my own inclinations, and, more especially, given the sphere of my activities, having to earn my money in order to live is an absolute curse. Many great men have felt this already, and many have perished as a result of it. I am convinced that the possession of even moderate means would have made me completely stable as regards the outward aspect of my life, and spared me so much unrest. However, the complete opposite of this has made me, too, indifferent to the value of money, almost as if I had known I could never actually "earn" any money for myself. Given the other bias in my life, towards the ideal, I have had to suffer unspeakably from the consequences of this indifference.

You have seen from my fateful encounter with the young King of Bavaria – at a time when I was already well advanced in years – how extraordinary are the ways along which fate was to lead me before I could find any kind of compensation for my lack of property. Nor will it have escaped your notice that the advantages of this gain have brought down upon my head only renewed and quite unprecedented troubles, not least as a result of envy and the unusual nature of our situation. Only very slowly am I managing to turn to good account the very real advantages of this financial assistance, an assistance which has undeniably freed me, gradually but completely, from actually having to earn my living, and which has helped me pursue my real aim in life. But there will always be an element of extraordinary difficulty and anxiety here, an element that is based very much in the character and destiny of my royal friend, for all that he is devoted to me with such rare affection. – There is only one relationship that has become fully satisfying and truly redeeming for me, but which, at the same time, has brought with it the most painful sufferings. Even though supreme self-sacrifice was shown me here, and the saddest sacrifices had to be made, there was really only one thing that constrained me to accept it all: a deep and unshakeable awareness. If my life thus far has been aimless and storm-tossed, my ship of life has had to suffer the most unprecedented hardships before reaching port. But – I have now reached port. And now I must live gladly and joyfully. A handsome, sturdy son, high of forehead and bright of eye, Siegfried Richard, will inherit his father's name and preserve his works for the world. – Forgive me, my friend, for observing the discreet silence of one who, as long as only his own assurances can speak for him, must await the time when action and a clearly recognizable status speak for him. That time is not far off. You were no doubt enlightened long ago as to your error concerning the bridegroom of my niece Doris Brockhaus: although (as such) it made me smile, it also touched me deeply, and pleased me to think that it had prompted you to send me your heartfelt congratulations.[1] – Almost the same thing happened to me again on the occasion of the false rumour that I had supposedly been taken ill, only this time I was able to reply to your kind concern with a smile of reassurance. God knows what people have to get up to with me! I could straightway publish a newspaper simply to refute all the false and worthless things that are said

---

1 Wagner's niece had announced her engagement to a man called Richard Wagner, "which made us laugh a lot" (CT for 30 November 1869). There seems no truth in Elisabeth Förster-Nietzsche's claim that the announcement of the engagement, followed by news of the fiancé's suicide four months later, led first to a "deluge" of "well-meant congratulations" and then "a repetition of the confusion and vexation of the Tribschen family" (*The Nietzsche-Wagner Correspondence* [London 1922], 44).

about me every day. From what I hear, you all seem to have been splendidly entertained at my expense last summer in Dresden: the source of it was easy to guess in a certain I. Reuter,[1] who, as a friend of Frau Schnorr's (who was absolutely determined to marry me), had for her part taken it into her head a few years ago to have me introduce her to the King of Bavaria. Since that was not possible, I incurred the hatred of both these ladies to a quite unprecedented degree; that this, in part, should have been cooked up in Dresden, where the would-be royal bride is living, was to be expected. Well, on this point there are still various things worth reporting for the last ten years of my life, but most of it I shall have to pass over in sheer disgust! –

As far as my health is concerned, I appear – more especially to the experts – to be an example of a particular species of human being destined for long life and work. Although very sensitive and irritable, quick to grow feverish and perspire, I do not ever really become ill, and generally recover from any indisposition so quickly that people laugh at me. The only thing that plagues me is my lower abdomen and rectal inflammations. It soon passes the moment that tranquillity of mind and an often explosive cheerfulness are restored. Only in the summer of 1868, after I had returned from the Mastersingers in Munich, was I seized by a persistent and debilitating fever. But I knew where I was with it, and resolved never again to return to Munich (my hell), but to rescue from there what would have perished without me. I have achieved this. And now there will be peace and quiet, for my health as well.

I shall soon have completed my 57th year of life, and I can see now that it was simply *tranquillity* that I lacked in order to have retained my strength until now in its purest and most effective form. Last summer, on the very day on which a handsome son was born to me, overjoyed as I was, I finished composing "Siegfried",[2] which had been interrupted for 11 years. An unheard-of case! No one thought I would ever return to it. But you must hear this final act, Brünnhilde's awakening! The finest thing I've ever done! – And now I have also made a start on the Twilight of the Gods.[3] I need a lot of time, because what I write down is all superlative. But I shall stick at it, and then tell myself (whatever they may say in Munich) "well, I've done it after all." And in years to come – my boy will have to see to what's right. In

1 Isidore von Reutter; see introductory essay, pp. 593–4.
2 The first complete draft of *Siegfried* was in fact finished not on 6 June 1869 (Siegfried's birthday), but on 14 June.
3 The first complete draft of the Prelude to *Götterdämmerung* was begun on 2 October 1869; the second complete draft was begun on 11 January 1870, and the full score on 3 May 1873. Meanwhile Wagner had begun work on the first complete draft of Act I: 7 February – 5 June 1870; the second complete draft was finished on 2 July 1870, and the full score on 24 December 1873. The dates for the remaining acts are as follows. Act II: first complete draft, 24 June – 25 October 1871; second complete draft, 5 July – 19 November 1871; full score (end), 26 June 1874. Act III: first complete draft, 4 January – 10 April 1872; second complete draft, 9 February – 22 July 1872; full score, 10 June – 21 November 1874.

this way I derive new strength from everything. – It is only my young King who still causes me real distress: but it is not so easy to say in what this consists! It was particularly bad with the "Rhinegold" last summer: but he would not let himself be dissuaded. Let anyone try to preach any sense here! But now the word has gone round: everything! everything! as long as it doesn't mean doing without a performance of my new works for any length of time! I am to give the orders, and everyone will obey me. It is all very worrying again. God knows how I shall set about achieving anything of this nature so that it gives me any pleasure. But I shall try my best, and – perhaps – it is possible that I shall perform the "Rhinegold" and the "Valkyrie" next summer. –

But listen here, my dear Anton! Do you, too, not want to be present when it happens? Rietz has burned down your theatre for you,[1] so that he won't have to conduct the Mastersingers any more (for which God be praised!) And so, do come by and by, if ever I set things going again! Best of all, however, would be if you were to come and inspect us here at Tribschen. Can you not manage a Medical Councillor's[2] trip to Switzerland? – You must see, my dear Anton, that you are the *only* person in my life to stand before me in perfect purity and amiability! Believe me, best of friends, I know what I am saying: the only one! – You see, that is why you are the first person this year to whom I have written such a long letter. Now do you believe me? And I hope you will also give my kind regards to your wife and children? Let all of you come here, rather, for I am very fond of you all. You see, two or even three of you can easily be accommodated here in this large farmhouse of mine. You are bound to like it here; and at the same time everything, but everything here & about me will be properly ordered. And so: stop turning it over in your mind, but think instead that it must be so! I'll play you something you'll enjoy.[3] – But enough of this chattering in jest & in earnest! Fare you well! I am and shall always be your loyal and grateful bosom friend

Richard Wagner.

(Call on *Heine*, give him my regards, and tell him
about me, and let me have some news of him!)

RWA (incompletely published in Freunde und Zeitgenossen 506–10).

---

1 The first of Semper's two opera houses in Dresden had burned down on 21 September 1869.
2 A reference to Pusinelli's appointment in Dresden.
3 Nothing came of these plans; but see letter [397], p. 776, note 1.

389. CÄCILIE AVENARIUS, BERLIN [Lucerne, 14 January 1870]

Dear Cecilie,

I still owe you my deepest thanks for a Christmas present of incomparable worth. Only during these last few days have I got into what I considered would be the right frame of mind to read through these letters.[1] You will understand what I mean, since you know how eager I am to collect the family mementoes, and prevent them from being scattered abroad. None of our relations can have remained unaware of this desire of mine, which was first awoken in me some years ago and which has been growing in strength ever since, for they have all expressed their amazement that these mementoes should have been the object of such eager enquiry. I am, accordingly, most grateful to you for having shown such self-sacrifice in copying out these touching documents, whose originals, as you suppose, will one day be of great value to your children, even though they have no personal recollection of the man whose handwriting so touches *us*, since it brings us into immediate contact with people to whom we were once close enough to touch.

The contents of these letters, however, not only touched me, but really shook me. So rarely in domestic life do we find such a clear example of the most total self-sacrifice in pursuance of a nobly conceived end, as is the case here. I can tell you that I am almost inconsolable when I think of this self-sacrifice on the part of our father Geyer, and that especially his letters to Albert straightway filled me with a feeling of bitterness. Particularly moving was the tender, sensitive and highly cultured tone of all these letters, more especially those to our mother. I do not understand how this note of true culture could have become so debased in our family's later dealings with each other. At the same time, however, these same letters to our mother were able to give me a clear insight into the relationship between the two of them at times of great difficulty. I believe I now see it all quite clearly, although I am bound to find it extremely hard to say in what way I see this relationship. It is as though, by sacrificing himself to the whole family, our father Geyer believed he was atoning for some sin or other. –

A printed copy of the "Massacre of the Innocents"[2] arrived at the same time. And so, since the handwritten copy, produced no doubt at the cost of much effort thanks to your sisterly care, is in no way important autographically, but is none the less of value because of its rarity, I would ask you to allow me to return it to you herewith. –

I still owe Eduard a reply to his kind and detailed letter in the matter of the publication of my collected writings. What I have to tell him, however, is desperately little, namely that I see that the time is not yet right for me to

1 To and from Ludwig Geyer.
2 A stage-play by Geyer.

fulfil my wish. This really emerged as the *summa summarum* from the proposals which he put to me. Would you be so kind as to give your kind husband my warmest good wishes, and at the same time simply inform him of this realization on my part?[1]

But now I have a big favour to ask of you: would you apologize on my behalf to your son Richard, of whom – as you know – I think a great deal! – He sent me his philosophical treatise,[2] accompanying it with a letter which I can most emphatically *not* answer until I have managed to study the treatise. But I shall have to *study* it; I am not a trained philosopher: with me the time for such things comes as it once came: at present I do not have that sort of time. In other words, an apology for an apology, and only the assurance of my very real delight at his letter. –

Finally I would ask you to give all your family my sincere good wishes, and to remain assured of the loyal and brotherly affection with which I sign myself

Your

Richard W.

Familienbriefe 276–8.

390. FRIEDRICH NIETZSCHE, BASLE   Lucerne, 14 January 1870

My dear friend,

Your silence surprises me: but I hope you will be able to dispel this feeling. –

But for today – in passing – a request!

From the family letters from times long past that were sent to me as a Christmas present,[3] I see that there is a chronological error in my biography. I hope that the first sheet has not yet been struck off definitively, in which case I would ask you to correct the chronological details on the following pages (in addition to a number of remaining type-setting errors which you will easily spot if you would be so kind as to read through the sheet once again).

pag. 5. (1820)
–   6. (1821)
–   8. (1822)
–   9. (1822)
–   12. (1822–1823.)

1 A collected edition of Wagner's writings in nine volumes was begun the following year and published by Ernst Wilhelm Fritzsch of Leipzig between 1871 and 1873; a tenth volume was added in 1883.
2 On the pantheism of Spinoza.
3 See previous letter.

Do not be angry with me for this![1]–

As the one who was left behind, I had intended not to contact you until such time as you – the one who had gone away[2] – had shown some sign of life. But since the chronology of events has decreed otherwise, I shall report – quite superfluously – that everyone at Tribschen has taken to his or her bed. Coughs, colds, catarrh – or however it is spelt – have left us all prostrate. I have now taken up the Norns again.[3] The King has again shown signs of life – in his usual wild fashion; – it is *possible* that I shall perform Rhinegold and Valkyrie in Munich this year: but that everything will be done as I want it is *not likely*. So much for that.

My Academic appointment has arrived from Berlin: I have told Jacob[4] to admit only those who enquire after the "foreign member in ordinary R.W.". This is my latest title.

But not another word from me, since you are beginning to worry me.

Yours,
R.W.

Nietzsche-Briefe II,2 115–16.

391. FRIEDRICH NIETZSCHE, BASLE   Lucerne, 16 January 1870

Dearest and *least* worrying of friends,

There are people whom I continue to find somewhat worrying. But time will tell. For the present I wish you a painless delivery[5] and, in order to ease your labour pains, am sending you the two latest numbers on "Conducting".[6]

The crest[7] has turned out very well, and we have every reason to be grateful to you for the care you have lavished on it. But it reminded me of my old misgivings about the *vulture*,[8] which everyone is bound to take for an eagle at first glance, at least until some natural historian explains that there is a

1 Nietzsche, who agreed to read the proofs of *Mein Leben*, appears to have responded to this request by removing all reference to specific dates from the opening pages of the text.
2 Nietzsche had visited the Wagners between 24 December 1869 and 2 January 1870.
3 See letter [388], p. 765, note 3.
4 Jakob Stocker, Wagner's man-servant. Wagner had been elected as a foreign member of the Prussian Academy of Arts in Berlin in May 1869, an election which he welcomed at the time as a potential means of establishing himself away from Munich.
5 Nietzsche was currently working on two lectures for the Freie Akademische Gesellschaft in Basle, *Das griechische Musikdrama* (Greek Music Drama) and *Sokrates und die Tragödie* (Socrates and Tragedy).
6 Wagner's essay *Ueber das Dirigiren* (On Conducting) was begun on 31 October 1869 and published in weekly instalments in the *Neue Zeitschrift für Musik* between 26 November 1869 and 21 January 1870. It was republished in pamphlet form by C. F. Kahnt of Leipzig, and taken up into Volume VIII of the *Gesammelte Schriften*, 261–337; PW IV,289–364.
7 On the title-page of *Mein Leben*.
8 The German for "vulture" is *Geier*, a play on the name of Wagner's stepfather.

"cinereous vulture" that is very similar in appearance to the eagle. But since –
because of the allusion – it is important that the "vulture" be instantly
recognizable as such, we would ask you to prevail upon the engraver to avail
himself of the first available picture of such a beast and to hang the vulture's
characteristic ruff around the neck of our bird. Of course it will not be
possible to do this without altering the neck in some way, but it may none
the less turn out a success.

I entirely agree with the paper to be used for *all* the copies, of which,
however, only

twelve

in all are to be struck off.[1] I find this number is exactly right for my purposes
since, apart from my concern with regard to preserving the text, my only
other worry is how to safeguard it from misuse. These 12 copies will then
acquire real significance. –

We have nothing but catarrh and influenza in the house at present; dreadful
weather, with the air like that in a badly aired farmhouse. I am making only
slow and depressing progress on my work.

I am again having trouble with my young monarch: I expect no good will
come of it, and am afraid I shall again have to suffer considerable annoyance.
The Academy has sent me – but you already know about that?[2] As a result I
shall *not* be dedicating "On Conducting" to them.

For the rest I hope for a speedy and satisfactory settlement of a number
of difficult issues at which "the world" will then no longer need to shake its
head. In the meantime Plato has again been of help: we finished the Theae-
tetus yesterday. And in February we plan to take a closer look at Socrates–
Euripedes: I am very much looking forward to it. – And so, be of good cheer,
like a real Prussian cavalryman!

Sincere good wishes!
Yours,
RW.

Nietzsche-Briefe II,2 117–18.

392. FRIEDRICH NIETZSCHE, BASLE   Lucerne, 4 February 1870

Dearest Herr Friedrich,

Yesterday evening I read your treatise[3] to our friend. It took me a long
time to calm her down again afterwards: she found that you had treated the
tremendous names of the great Athenians in a surprisingly modern manner;
I myself thought it necessary to remind her that the nature of public lecturing

---

1 Later increased to eighteen. An extra copy, clandestinely struck off by the printer Bonfantini,
  later found its way into the hands of Mary Burrell.
2 See previous letter, p. 769, note 4.
3 *Socrates and Tragedy*; see also previous letter, p. 769, note 5.

and elegant book-writing nowadays has debased the traditional language used in discussing our great classical models and reduced it to the level of the methods employed in dismissing decidedly modern phenomena. (Mommsen's Cicero as a feuilletonist inevitably came to mind.) This was soon understood as something deriving from a weakness of the age, and, as such, it was excused. For my own part, what I felt most of all was a sense of shock at the boldness with which you impart so new an idea, in such brief and categorical terms, to a public which is presumably not really disposed to be educated, so that, if you want your sins to be absolved, you must reckon upon being totally misunderstood in this quarter. Even those people who are initiated into my own ideas are bound to be shocked when they find how much your ideas conflict with their own belief in Sophocles and even Aeschylus. For myself, of course, I can but say to you: so it is! You have hit the mark, and described the real issue with such acuity that it is with a sense of wonderment that I await your future development, when you attempt to overcome common dogmatic prejudice. – But I am concerned about you, and pray from the bottom of my heart that you do not come to grief. That is why I should like to advise you not to discuss these incredible views of yours in short treatises designed to create an easy effect by raising awkward issues, but, since – as I recognize – you are deeply imbued with these ideas, to collect your thoughts together for a longer and more comprehensive work on the subject. I am sure that you will then find the right word to describe the divine errors of Socrates and Plato, men who were of such overwhelming creative power that, even when turning away from them, we are none the less bound to revere them. Oh my friend! Where shall we find words of praise when we gaze from *our* world upon those inconceivably harmonic beings! And what high hopes and aspirations may we then cherish for ourselves, when we feel deeply and clearly that we can, and must, achieve something that was denied to them! –

Above all things I hope most emphatically that I have left you in no doubt as to *my* opinion of your Socrates and the others, for I have just told you what I think of it. –

Yours,
RW.

Nietzsche-Briefe II,2 137–8.

393. Hermann Levi, Karlsruhe   Lucerne, [28] April 1870

My very dear Herr Kapellmeister,

Your enquiry[1] does you great honour and deserves an equally honest response.

The appeal which came to you from Munich was based upon the assumption that they might eventually find a conductor sufficiently unscrupulous as to perform my work without my personal co-operation. They have not yet succeeded in doing so, since all the most capable conductors who are friendly towards me have refused their help.

If they are now similarly mistaken in their assumption with regard to yourself, their search will no doubt have to continue. My experiences with the Munich Court Theatre during the course of the last two years, and their attitude towards me, have made all contact with them quite impossible, so that there can of course be no question, on my part, of involving myself in a performance of any of my works for which all those arrangements have already been made which, solely and uniquely, should have been ordered by *me* if my co-operation were to have made any sense.

In spite of this somewhat unfortunate state of affairs, my exalted patron, the King of Bavaria, insists upon satisfying a desire of his which I should normally find most flattering, but which consists in the wish to see the "Valkyrie", too, performed as soon as possible.[2] Here, too, I must respect this token of his gracious attitude towards my works, and can never for a moment forget that, without the immeasurable kindnesses shown me by the grace of his royal favour, I should perhaps already have sunk into utter oblivion, and would be taken no further notice of by anyone, least of all by the German people and their theatre directors, As a result, I have also felt obliged to state that, should His Majesty persist in this desire of his, I should certainly raise no objection to a performance of my work, although – since this performance, to my great regret, is to take place in public, I know that I am exposing one of my most difficult and problematical works to the greatest possible vexations in terms of an unsympathetic assessment and totally unclear effect. To avoid these vexations by the only means open to me – my personal co-operation on every aspect of the presentation and execution of the work – has been rendered impossible, as I have lost no opportunity of stating in the appropriate quarter: but instead of obviating this difficulty by removing its causes, the theatre intendancy has fallen back upon an expedient which has involved you, too, in its invitation to Munich.

It grieves me, therefore, to have to explain to you what I have already

1 Levi had been invited to conduct the performance of *Die Walküre* ordered by Ludwig, and had written to Wagner to ask his opinion.

2 The first performance of *Die Walküre*, conducted by Franz Wüllner, was given at the Munich Court Theatre on 26 June 1870.

explained to them in Munich: I have nothing against your conducting my work, provided that any agreement in this regard is made solely between you and the Munich intendancy, and that in no conceivable way are any demands made upon me. –

I am happy to have this opportunity to tell you of my delight at having heard only praise of your performances of my "Mastersingers" in Karlsruhe, and, more especially, that comparisons between the Dresden performance and yours were very much in your favour. How salutary it is for me to be able to welcome a man of real talent as conductor of a German opera-house is something which I probably do not need to affirm. –

Assuring you of my very great respect, I remain

Your most devoted servant
Richard Wagner

P.S. Some considerable time ago Herr Kayser made enquiries of me, in the name of the directors of the Grand Ducal Court Theatre, concerning my fee for the performing rights for my opera Rienzi. I informed him of my demand, and would have thought that I might have expected to have been honoured with the courtesy of a reply: could I now ask you to be so kind as to mediate herein?

RW

I am re-opening this letter to say that, in the event of your seeing in it a way of clarifying the affair in question, I would gladly authorize you to publish the first three pages of today's communication.[1] –

RW.

RWA (published with omission of first postscript in Freunde und Zeitgenossen 515–17).

394. HANS RICHTER, VIENNA   Lucerne, 25 May 1870

Dear Richter,

A few lines to ask a favour of you which I forgot to mention yesterday.

Please call on Herr Dr Egger (co-director of the Vienna Beethoven Committee), and kindly inform him in my name that, if he and many another honest man had wished to persuade me to conduct a special part of the projected Beethoven Festival, they would have done well not to have sent me the list of board members. It is impossible for me even to reply to an invitation which also includes Herr *Hanslick* and Herr *Schelle*. If the good people of Vienna are incapable of understanding this, I shall simply have to let the matter rest there. Let them then revile me all over again. I am used to it, so that it will make no difference to me.

1 i.e. all but the two postscripts. Levi appears not to have made the contents of the letter public.

If *I* were ever to take it upon myself to celebrate Beethoven,[1] I believe I could achieve something, after my own fashion, without having to make claims upon the peculiar powers of the Viennese press, still less to enlist its help.

Please do this for me, and accept my very best wishes.

Yours,
Rich. Wagner.

Richter-Briefe 64–5.

395. ELIZA WILLE, FELDMEILEN　　　　　　　　Lucerne, 25 June 1870

Dear and honoured friend,

I am sure that I scarcely need tell you how pleased we were to receive your letter and invitation! – Of course we shall come, for you must be the first to see us as man and wife.[2] It has cost us a good deal of patience to reach this position: something that has been imperative for years could finally be resolved only through suffering of every description. Since I last saw you in Munich, I have not set foot outside my refuge, a refuge in which she, too, has sought shelter who was to prove that I *could* be helped, and that the axiom of so many of my friends, that "I could not be helped", was untrue. She knew that I had to be helped, and so she helped me: she has borne me a wonderfully handsome and sturdy son, whom I was bold enough to call "Siegfried": he is flourishing, as is my work, and giving me a new and long life, which *has finally found a meaning.* –

And so we have managed without the "world", from which we have withdrawn completely. All that is genuine has proved its worth, and more touching than the acquisition of new friends was the loyalty of old ones. My sister, Ottilie Brockhaus, visited us with her family late last summer: I wish you, too, could have been there. But Midsummer Day has brought you here instead. Our sincere good wishes to you!

But listen now: I hope you will find it right and sensible if we do not accept your invitation until I can bring my son's mother to you as my wedded wife, too. This is no longer far off, and we hope to be in Mariafeld[3] before the leaves start to fall. But you must first prove your own friendship by bringing

1 Wagner's *Beethoven* essay, written between 20 July and 11 September 1870, was published in December 1870 by E. W. Fritzsch of Leipzig. It is reprinted in GS IX,61–126; PW V, 57–126.

2 Confirmation of Cosima's divorce reached Tribschen on 27 July; she and Wagner were married in the Protestant Church in Lucerne on 25 August 1870.

3 The Wagners visited Mariafeld on 28/29 August; there is no record of a prior visit to Tribschen by the Willes.

your splendid family very, very soon and staying with us here at Tribschen. If you have grandchildren, bring them, too; you will find lots of young people here cheerfully gathered around their mother, who is also their teacher and governess. And perhaps many other things besides, which you will like.

How deeply and truly happy it would make us to know that you were coming here very soon! Any day would be acceptable, we are constantly prepared. –

Do you remember prophesying that this would happen, you noble woman, six years ago,[1] when you released me from your hospitality? I was utterly wretched. But you looked at me, and – prophesied – you must recall what you said? Now, my friend, come and convince yourself that you have the true heart of a good prophetess!

Take this my blessing! I pray that all may prosper to which your great and noble heart is attached! This do I wish you in return! –

Yours,
Richard Wagner.

Fehr II,451–2.

396. COUNTESS MARIE D'AGOULT, PARIS [Lucerne, 22 August 1870][2]

Permit me to take your hand today and clasp it to my heart in reverence and gratitude. I approach the mother of the dear woman who, in order to be what she alone could be to me, allowed herself to be swayed by no consideration in the world, but to whom your own great heart has spared the heaviest sacrifice: for she had no need to break with her mother, for her mother understood her and stood by her side with words of sisterly comfort. This was a blessing which was to enfold me, too, in its salutary embrace. And so I may hope that you will not withdraw your hand when I come to you now to thank you for this kindness.

When, in a few days' time, our bond is blessed in the sight of God and the world, I shall feel as though I myself am witness to a human event which, justly considered in all its phases and motives, may revive the observer's oft-wavering faith in a noble destiny for humankind. Of all the afflictions that had to be borne here, not one was tainted with the affliction of selfishness: if, after untold anguish, we could no longer bear it not to belong to each other, it was only the pain of compassion with those whom we had to hurt that really gnawed at our lives. Yet it was a question of saving all of those

1 On 28 April 1864, shortly before Wagner's rescue by Ludwig.
2 Dating from CT.

lives that have a share in ours, that from the dark conflagration of suffering we may soon behold the clear light of consoling reconciliation shine forth.

Whereas I have often had to regard my life and my destiny as the middle of a whirlpool of most painful developments, I may well now gaze with joyful elation upon the meaning of this destiny of mine, now that its luminous ripples have grown quite calm. As a man reborn, I enter upon a life, the noble worth of which I can regard as merited in part only if I may see it as the reward of a life whose torments were undeservedly long, to the point when they could no longer be endured. Within and around me there lives and breathes an element of love whose creative powers enfold me in tender embrace, soaring aloft in order to celebrate the noblest of nuptials with each dawning day.

Thus I bless the mother who bore this unique woman for me, a woman who cast down her eyes sufficiently low to behold the wretch that I am, and who was high-minded enough to dedicate herself to me. And thus do I revere the noble woman who, like-mindedly, countered the high-hearted one with such powerfully inspiriting good-will. May my blessing and gratitude fulfil you with warmth, as praise, however slight, of your great goodness towards him who calls out to you his gratitude and blessing from the depths of his own fulfilled heart!

In true veneration, I am your

obed.
Richard Wagner

Königsbriefe V, 109–10.

397. ANTON PUSINELLI, DRESDEN   Lucerne, 9 November 1870

My dear Anton,

I have kept meaning to inform you of my change of plan with regard to my visit to you. It is kind of you, but shaming for *me*, that you have now anticipated me in this. Various new sets of circumstances have arisen, and persuaded us to postpone our peace mission until next spring.[1] Since I am beginning to become less mobile, I should prefer to combine this trip with the various things or, rather, with *all* the things that relate to my decision to order my affairs once and for all. In order to do so, I must obtain one last insight into certain possibilities necessary to achieving my artistic goals, concerning which my experience leaves me very doubtfully disposed. My ultimate removal to Germany is also bound to depend upon the success of my efforts in this ideal sense.

1 For the reasons behind Wagner's decision to try his luck in Germany, see pp. 597–8. He visited the Pusinellis in Dresden in April 1871, after first calling in at Bayreuth and Leipzig.

Whether I finally settle in the place that can also provide me with a suitable and entirely neutral site for my artistic purposes, or whether, by entirely forgoing these higher objectives, I seek only a domestic hearth for my family (in which case I should definitely choose Dresden) – all this is still to be decided. And in order to see it all in a friendly light, we have just set aside the first fine weeks of next spring for our excursion. –

This by way of a brief indication, and at the same time an inducement to your dear wife to put the leg of mutton in the oven even without us. Your house, after all, is crowded enough already for you to have no difficulty consuming all your provisions. Your brother's fate[1] once more reminds me of the atrocities of the French who, for their part, are complaining that the Germans have been forcing upon them a war between races – but no nation ever thinks of *this* kind of brutality at the outbreak of war. One needs to study the attitude of "Europe" in order to understand the kind of world in which we live. I admit that, if I did not see Moltke and the German army before me, I would see absolutely nothing to inspire me with any hope. For ex., I need only think of a performance of one of my works in Dresden (with Herr Rietz in charge) for me to lose all heart. And – how deeply and intimately all this is bound up together! It is precisely this that has dawned on me, and which makes me so sad, whenever I contemplate the world. –

And yet – I need only look at a friend like you (pleonastically speaking, since you are the only one of your kind!) – and that is enough to cheer me up again, and – much is forgotten! (To forget – ! the ultimate happiness!) But then memory is *also* a source of joy: and that is something we shall take good care to revive. Only a few more months before we see each other again, my dear old Anton! A thousand good wishes from us to you all.

Yours,
R.W.

RWA (incompletely published in Freunde und Zeitgenossen 523–4).

398. HANS RICHTER, SPEISING　　　　Lucerne, 28 November 1870

Dear Richter,

The "antique comedy"[2] I find wholly admirable, and cannot understand how you could doubt for a moment but that it would be worth while setting

---

1 According to CT for 12 September 1870, Louis Pusinelli, "after doing business with shipping firms in Le Havre for 30 years, has now been expelled with his ten children and has to seek a new occupation". The Franco-Prussian War had broken out in July of that year.

2 *Eine Kapitulation* (WWV 102), submitted to Richter under the pseudonym E. Schlossenbach (see postscript). According to CT for 16 December 1870, Richter sketched only a handful of numbers, and plans to stage the work in Berlin came to nothing.

it to music. It goes without saying that the farce belongs in the real folk
theatre, and that you must therefore keep the music light, something which
is in any case indicated by the piece itself: accordingly, it must be a parody
of Offenbach's parodies. But polish it off quickly; for even though the thing
is of interest in itself, its principal effectiveness lies very much in the
immediate present. It must of course come out in Berlin first of all. Unfortunately I can be of absolutely no help to you here, since I have no connections
in Berlin. But it is good of you to draw F. Röder to my attention: I believe
he is an old acquaintance of mine from my Würzburg days of 1833 (!). If he
is prepared to show zeal in taking this business in hand, you will no doubt
fare best. You can be quite open and make use of my honest recommendation
of the piece: I am not afraid of anyone when it comes to giving my word of
approval. Take full advantage of this then with F. Röder. If the farce is well
presented, with suitable skill, it is bound to stand out, to its own incomparable
advantage, from every similar product of the age, and, as such, find favour
with people. You should make certain of this transaction as quickly as possible.
I should prefer it if you were here when you wrote the music: but a start
must be made *quickly*, there is no time to be lost.

And so – that is all for today: I am returning the manuscript which – I can
tell you – I find quite uncommonly appealing. – Give my regards to your dear
mother, and send word soon that you are ready, and that things are making
swift progress. – Best wishes from us all, wife, children, and household!

Cordially yours,
Richard Wagner.

P.S. How long will Schlossenbach have to remain in that hole of his? It is
certainly very sad for such a talented young man! Is there no prospect of his
at least being transferred to Vienna in the near future? I recall him with great
pleasure. Give him my very best wishes for now, and tell him how much I
liked his "Aristophanes".

R.W.

Richter-Briefe 78–80.

399. ALWINE FROMMANN, BERLIN   Lucerne, 1 February 1871

Dear friend,

Your letter brought great joy to our house. The very day before it arrived
we had been talking about you at length: our ears had certainly been burning!
And we were so pleased to receive Werder's good wishes: do give him our
kindest regards in return. We are deeply indebted to you for all your news
concerning yourself, although it all sounds melancholy enough! And yet you
are more active for your age than you like to admit. I, too, am now obsessed

with the curious belief that all who mean well by me will live to see a good deal yet. It is an odd thing really, but I know that I have a long and active life ahead of me, the more so since I have so much still to complete which, as I now realize, no one else can do for me. But now I have been blessed with a son. Who can gauge what this means to me? He is so strong and handsome that I was able to call him "Siegfried", and it was to honour him that I completed my work.[1] He is also called "Helferich", because I intend him to be a useful helper.

I now have to bring up the lad. My wife's four girls are growing up with him, their education and training forming the noble woman's daily task in our peaceful retirement. Everything is prospering. The doctor has not set foot in the house for 5 months now. I am on the point of completing the full score of "Siegfried"; and almost half of the Twilight of the Gods has now been set to music.[2] It will be three years next June since I cut myself off from the world: I have not heard a single note of an orchestra since taking my leave of the King of Bavaria in his royal box at the first performance of the "Mastersingers". But I have also settled my account with the world, since I felt it my duty not to put up with any more jokes, but to call a spade a spade. In addition my life is recorded in detail; I have dictated it to Cosima, who wanted to know all about it; this is something that will outlive me: I am bequeathing it to my son. What Cosima is, and what she is to me, will be recognized by all who see me henceforth.

I know that you love her. – We shall probably come to Berlin in the spring:[3] I intend to discharge my debt of gratitude to the Academy there by lecturing to them on "the Destiny of Opera". From this people will also become acquainted with my plan to get my works properly established. What I am obliged to demand here is in a certain sense similar to Faust's demand that the emperor should grant him enough land as he could dam off from the sea. I shall not come too close to any living soul: and I shall not set foot in the theatre. But I want to try to gain an understanding for myself: without this I have neither the ability nor the desire to achieve anything. – Cosima says I should ask you to keep our plans a secret for the present. – If I could be of use to anyone in Berlin, it would be *Constantin Frantz*. Do you know him? As a person he is immensely unhelpful and unbearable: but – !! Have you read his books "The Restoration of Germany" and "The Science of the State"? – He came into my life at just the right time, and was a great boon to me. But what a pitiful life this man now leads in Berlin! Oh Germany! –

1 But see letter [388], p. 765, note 2.
2 See letter [388], p. 765, note 3.
3 See letter [390], p. 769, note 4. The Wagners were in Berlin between 25 April and 8 May 1871. On 28 April Wagner delivered his lecture *On the Destiny of Opera* to a plenary session of the Prussian Academy of Arts.

Here, for your edification, is my very latest poem.[1] – Cosima advised against sending it to the Nordd. Allg. Zeitung, as I had initially intended. I thought the matter over briefly, and have sent it to Bismarck. – A Leipzig publisher[2] has invited me to write an Imperial Coronation March.[3] Perhaps I shall be inspired with some good ideas.

It would be nice if this piece of music were to be played in beer gardens for example, while, for the actual coronation, you were to parade Taubert and the others like him with their commissions from on high. But we are used to this. God knows what we have done to deserve it! – I hope my son will live to see all this changed! –

My confidence in the future has been revived. It has been granted to me to gaze very, very deeply into the nature of the German spirit: only now can I understand it all, nay – only now do I really admire certain things. Wonderful progress is being made in establishing the new Reich. Everyone here has acted out of a profound instinct and ineradicable aptitudes. Anyone who does not understand figures such as Bismarck, Roon & Moltke around this King Wilhelm – is very much to be pitied. – But enough of this. We may soon be able to chatter about such things in the tranquil warmth of your own apartments. –

Fare you well, kind, dear Alwine! Your two albums are lying here on my music-desk, beautifully bound and displayed beneath the only keepsakes that I have of my great Cosima! – I glance at them daily! –

Her sincere and joyful good wishes accompany mine!

Yours,
Richard Wagner

Otto 337–9.

400. LORENZ VON DÜFFLIPP, MUNICH   Bayreuth, 20 April 1871

Most honoured friend,

Before leaving Bayreuth today I must first let you know, without further delay, the chief result of my investigations, inasmuch that, following our visit to the theatre,[4] it turns out that this theatre is the most fantastical roccoco [*sic*] building that could possibly exist, and that nothing about it can be altered in the least detail. And since this theatre can in no way fulfil the purpose

---

1 *An das deutsche Heer vor Paris* (To the German Army before Paris), written down on 25/26 January 1871.
2 Max Abraham of C. F. Peters.
3 The *Kaisermarsch* (WWV 104) was completed on 15 March 1871 and first heard in Berlin on 14 April 1871.
4 The Margraves' Opera House in Bayreuth.

for which I intended it, I have forthwith abandoned my wish to use it for my stage festival. I say this first and foremost for your information, and perhaps also to reassure those people who have been alarmed by the idea that I might have wished to destroy any part of what, in its way, is a quite unique building. –

In what way this theatre, too, may later be put to some noble use in the event that favourable progress is made on this great undertaking of mine – this is something on which I shall reserve comment until the appropriate time.

For the rest I shall say only that Bayreuth and its surroundings has entirely lived up to my hopes, so that I remain firmly attached to the idea of settling here, and continue to combine with that wish a desire to realize my great enterprise here too. My efforts in this latter direction, however, can continue to relate to Bayreuth only if, on the other hand, I remain assured of my royal benefactor's gracious favour in the event of my settling here. I am therefore anxious to learn from you, my most honoured friend, in what spirit His Majesty deigned to receive the overtures which I made to you in person. It would be safest if you wrote to me in Berlin (Potsdamer Platz, Hôtel du Parc). I intend to arrive there on the 24th inst., having first stayed in Leipzig (with Professor H. Brockhaus, Querstrasse 15), where I hope to recover somewhat from a violent illness which has kept me in bed for half the time I have been here.

With the sincerest good wishes from me and my wife, I would ask you at the same time to accept this assurance of my warmest gratitude for your continuing friendship, and the very real esteem of

Your devoted servant
Richard Wagner

Petzet 808.

401. RUDOLF NOLTE, BERLIN   Lucerne, [18] August 1871

My dear young friend,

Let me begin by congratulating you most warmly upon your safe and honourable return from the War: there is no finer way in which you could have commended yourself to me than by approaching me from this quarter. –

Your decision to give up your University studies in order to devote yourself solely to music depresses me. I have had the saddest experiences in this respect. The fact that music may seem to us more potent than anything else should not persuade us to become exclusively musicians, but rather to grant music entry into every aspect of our lives; in this way it will make life noble and beautiful, whereas only in the very rarest cases shall we ourselves develop into truly beautiful and noble beings if we choose it as our profession.

The able and loyal individual gets into bad company here, a company whose character I have adequately described elsewhere. I know not a single musician whom I could recommend to you for his company or for instruction: I know of no school to which I would care to direct you. A true musician is conceivable only as one who, as a musician, grew up untutored and who knew nothing but music: someone who plays the fiddle or some wind instrument, someone who sings or is a proper bandsman, and who – if it is his calling – will then become a great musician. But no one will become one who has already proceeded to train his mind along exact lines. Music works on the spirit like some wonderful intoxication: if you imprint that spirit upon your life, music will be your redemptress; if you yourself stretch out your hand to touch it, it will be your living hell.

A kindly fate has blessed me with a son in my advancing years. In time to come he will decide his own life according to his own strongest impulses: the only thing I stipulate is that he learns something quite popularly useful; I have arranged with his mother that he should be enjoined to learn what he will need to become a surgeon. If he wants to become a musician, no one shall direct him to a teacher; if he finds one of his own accord, well – he is, after all, his own master.

I hope that you will see from this that I am serious, and that you will remain well-disposed towards me. Assuring you of my best wishes, I remain

Your devoted servant
Richard Wagner

Otto 345–6.

402. FRIEDRICH FEUSTEL, BAYREUTH   Lucerne, 1 November 1871

My esteemed Sir,

I have received from my dear nephew, Clemens Brockhaus of Leipzig, the most gratifying assurance that you would welcome an approach from me if I were to think of appealing to you in the not unimportant matter that has no doubt already come to your attention.

As to the enterprise itself I make so bold as to offer you a more detailed explanation of it in the enclosure which I am sending under separate cover. My reasons for choosing Bayreuth, rather than anywhere else, as the place to carry out my plan will not be difficult for you to guess, even without the further particulars which I am reserving for the moment: they may be found in the demands which I have made upon such a locality. The place ought not to be a capital city with a permanent theatre, nor any of the more popular or larger health resorts which, especially in the summer, would attract quite the wrong sort of audience; it ought to be situated close to the heart of Germany, and be a Bavarian town, since I am also thinking of taking up permanent residence in the place, and think it only right to do so in Bavaria, if I am to continue to enjoy the acts of kindness shown to me by the King of Bavaria. Moreover, this friendly town and its environs left an attractive impression upon me years ago,[1] and the fact that I am still a perfect stranger to its inhabitants ought not to deter me at the outset.

However, I immediately interpreted it as a favourable omen that my dear sister Ottilie Brockhaus was able to tell me of the friendly relations that exist between your own esteemed family and hers, and I set some store by knowing that I have been recommended to you and your good-will on the strength of these family ties.

Permit me therefore to acquaint you forthwith with the matters that concern me.

It is first and foremost various not unimportant points of information which I have to request of you.

I assume that no demands are to be made on the town of Bayreuth in procuring the financial means necessary for my undertaking. Energetic friends of my project are already engaged in collecting the necessary funds, and such is their success that I am already justified in taking the necessary steps to acquire a site on which to build my temporary theatre, although, because of the inclemency of the season, work on this building will have to be postponed for now until next March. For this purpose I intend to come to Bayreuth shortly, and at the latest by the end of this month.[2] I must begin by counting myself fortunate that, with your kind permission, I may turn to you, esteemed Sir, for the purpose of settling important preliminary questions. These concern first and foremost the choice and acquisition of the site itself. What seems to me to be important here is whether, in view of the advantages which my enterprise is able to offer in terms of its reputation and the resultant, not insignificant increase in foreign visitors to the town, the town of Bayreuth might feel persuaded to transfer to me, free of charge, the land on which to build my theatre. I am not saying that the enterprise necessarily requires this support; but it must be clear to all observers that such a privilege would, from the very outset, establish a good and highly commendable working relationship between the town of Bayreuth and my own enterprise. In the event that such willingness be shown, there could of course be no question of my choosing the site myself. On the other hand, if I have to purchase the site, I should welcome your kind suggestion. An area of approximately *Two Hundred* (Prussian) feet square is needed for the building, including projections, and it

1 In July 1835 when Wagner was talent-spotting for Bethmann's opera company.
2 Wagner returned to Bayreuth on 14 December. Building work began in May 1872.

would then depend upon the conditions that were placed on me how much space would be available for the grounds surrounding it. – As regards the choice of the site – if this is to depend upon me in the sense just described – my choice would fall upon the open field interrupted by a road*), which abuts on the end of the Schloss park. – I may also take this opportunity to mention that I have set my thoughts on a long strip of meadowland for my own residence, a plot of land which is situated similarly near to the end of the Schloss gardens, stretching from the left-hand side of the park in the direction of the road that leads to the Eremitage (the Schloss curator who acted as my guide last spring could give you more details.)

For the rest I must mention the chief objection that has been levelled against my choice of Bayreuth on the part of my Patrons. This concerns their anxiety that it will not be possible to find sufficient accommodation in Baireuth for all the visitors. It is a matter of ensuring decent hospitality for 200 persons for a period of several months, with 2000 visitors during the principal month, and of protecting them all against being overcharged. Since I have no suggestions to make here on the basis of my own experience, I leave this matter to your admirable and kind consideration, and should be very pleased if you could enable me to offer my Patrons powerful reassurance on this point. I should also like to be able to reassure them that there will be no shortage of workmen to carry forward the building work with all despatch, and that we shall not find ourselves crippled by strikes etc. The material aspect of the building shall of course be carried out and supervised by Bayreuth's capable Court Architect;[1] but I must insist upon retaining the services of my friend, the Royal Inspector of Buildings in Berlin, W. Neumann[2] to superintend this new plan of mine. –

May I add at once to this recital of my requirements the answer to a further point that was explained to me in Munich, namely that I must obtain the approval of the municipal authorities for the entire undertaking. You will no doubt not lose sight of the fact that we are not concerned here with a money-making theatrical enterprise: the performances will be attended only by invited guests and by patrons of the undertaking; no one can be allowed to pay for admission. At the same time, I have ensured that a sufficient number of seats is placed at the disposal of the inhabitants of Bayreuth to be distributed among them free of charge. –

Having, as I believe, informed you, esteemed Sir, of the main points which I felt encouraged to submit to you for your kind consideration, advice and co-operation, I would now only beg the favour of your gracious reply, and,

---

*) Or, rather: separated from it. – [*Wagner's footnote*]
1 Carl Wölfel.
2 Wilhelm Neumann was later replaced by Otto Brückwald of Leipzig.

at the same time, assure you of the very high esteem with which I have the honour to be

Your most obedient servant
Richard Wagner

RWA (published with minor omissions in Bayreuther Briefe I, 14–18).

403. COSIMA WAGNER, LUCERNE   [Munich, 10 December 1871][1]

Oh my love, my only bliss! Are you as solemn and as quiet as I always imagine you to be? Silent, wistful and hard-working? – When I came out of the hotel and into the "Promenadeplatz" today, and caught sight of these houses and people, – I cried out aloud: "ah! it was this that she had to put up with!!" The royal princess as a goosegirl: falderal! – No! You poor thing! You did not belong in this world! Outcast and banished from a homeland which, sadly, you never saw. "Knowst thou the land?"[2]

Your thoughtful greeting arrived this morning, my belovèd, ever-present one! – I had slept well, helped no doubt by the cold weather that I had survived. Franz[3] did not arrive until long after I had gone to bed: he had still been waiting for me at the railway station when "Schulz"[4] finally reported that I had already been here for 2 hours. But the first person to come to me in bed was – *Lenbach* (!!!) I now realize that it is impossible for me to carry on with my deception any longer: wretch that I am, you have so little trust in me that you undermine all my best-kept secrets! –

Here is a letter for you from M.M.[5] which was passed on to me by Lenbach after he had visited her at her castle the day before yesterday (on his return from Vienna: of course, these lines will tell you all the arrangements that I had already made with Lenbach some time ago. What is the use of going on with this pretence in order to maintain the principle of a birthday surprise? Also, what could I tell you about my day here if I had to conceal from you that I was spending the whole day in Lenbach's studio. You must know then, you poor deceived woman (deceived, that is, about the surprise!) that my entire plan for this journey had long been centred around my correspondence with Lenbach. He went away to Vienna for 8 days at the beginning of December, and everything else was planned in the light of this. (But, as I

1 Wagner had left Cosima the previous day – their first separation in two years – on his way to Bayreuth.
2 The opening hemistich of Mignon's nostalgic lament "Kennst du das Land" from Goethe's *Wilhelm Meister.*
3 Franz Mrazéck, Wagner's man-servant.
4 No details known.
5 Marie Muchanoff, who lived at Schloss Ottensheim near Linz.

say, you trust me in virtually nothing!) – Out with it then. – *Lenbach* came to see me in bed, and did nothing but make lots of sketches. I was with him today in his sumptuous studio from 1 o'clock until 4; of his sketches of you I saw only one fleeting example (a profile) which – although not yet very life-like – I found very moving. All the others he disowns. – I was then subjected to 2 hours' harassment, and made to sit first in one place and then in another, first like this and then like that. Porges[1] had slipped in, and showed himself not at all unskilled at judging the various poses. Finally *Böcklin*[2] arrived; and the most insane sitting began; I was completely torn apart: and then, to cap it all, another young man arrived, whom Lenbach assured me was the greatest living sculptor (but whose name I couldn't catch!)[3] To the sound of regular squeals of ecstasy they finally managed to find the "divinest" pose, swearing to each other that this would be the most remarkable portrait in the whole world. Böcklin would like to bring an easel and paint me as well. The sculptor wants to model me from the other side. – I couldn't conceal this nonsense from you, nor – because of the surprise – could I lie to you about what I have been doing here during this time, and while you would have been inwardly annoyed with me – that is, if you had believed my lies. – I then went with Lenbach to dine at his usual restaurant, and the rest of them came with us for a beer. A strange gathering: I suddenly felt very odd among these childish sculptors! – Then back home, where I had put off all other visitors in order to wait for Düfflipp, who had sent his servant to say that, instead of coming at 6 o'clock, he would not be able to come until after 7. The delay was most welcome to me: with a long sigh I lay down for a brief rest, thought of you, you poor and glorious woman, and then woke up from a deep sleep from which I was torn by D.'s embrace. God forgive me, but I have to regard this curious fellow as my friend! He was deeply moved, nay beside himself, to see me. Curiously enough, he has not yet received any news from H. Schwg.[4] God knows if the parcel[5] arrived in time. I explained the matter[6] at considerable length, and found the most uncompromising willingness to support my request, indeed, I even received his promise to implement the idea. Because of difficulties with train connections I expect I shall now have to remain here a day longer, which will not harm Baireuth but will delight Lenbach. As a result I shall postpone my meeting in Baireuth until the 15th, which may also serve as information for you, my love. However – now that I stop to think about it – it would be safest if your reply to *this* letter were to

1 Heinrich Porges.
2 The Swiss painter Arnold Böcklin.
3 Lorenz Gedon.
4 Hohenschwangau, where Ludwig was currently in residence.
5 A copy of the second complete draft of Act II of *Götterdämmerung*, which Wagner had sent to Ludwig on 4 December 1871.
6 The Bayreuth project.

be sent direct to Baireuth (Sonne). – What D. had to say had an extremely reassuring character in many ways. One thing though: he regretted very much not having insisted more vehemently upon building the theatre 3 years ago; if only he could have foreseen *what* opposition etc! –

For the rest, his news was reassuring more especially on the question of health and morality, and often most tender and heartfelt! Strange! Perhaps there's still room for hope after all. – I am feeling much more cheerful, now that D. has finally left, and I can sit down to write this letter to you. –

The whole of the Mrazek family came to pay their respects this morning: their daughter and son had to sing the "Watch on the Rhine" to me. 3 verses. – Netti looking very well! –

My dear wife! My dear wife!! – Listen now! I shall write to you tomorrow with details of your journey: for (oh joy!) in only a few days' time I shall already have taken you in my arms again. On no account must you leave Lucerne early; but at least spend the night in Basle. – But I shall have much more to say tomorrow, including more good news and favours to ask. –

Now I want to dream that I am with you. Where are you in the evening when the children are in bed? Do you remain downstairs? Probably not. Do go, I beg you, into the Orange Room! – Be good to me, and always forgive me! – Are the children behaving? Has Fidi[1] been wetting the bed again? You know we have a son? A "son"? And such very good daughters, one of whom has finally, finally begun to look like her *mother*! – Kiss them all for me, all that were nurtured in your dear womb! – I love you, as no woman has ever been loved. Blessed, belovèd, marvellous woman! – Fare you well, sleep well, be quietly godlike, as always when you are in your heart's true home! – My greetings to you!

A thousand kisses to her whom I worship!

Yours,
R.

Eger II, 110–12.

404. FRIEDRICH NIETZSCHE, BASLE   [Lucerne, early January 1872][2]

Dear friend,

Never have I read anything more beautiful than your book! How splendid it all is! I am writing to you quickly now because reading it has left me so inordinately excited that I must first await the return of reason before reading

1 Siegfried Wagner.
2 Nietzsche's *The Birth of Tragedy* arrived at Tribschen on 3 January; the Wagners finished reading it on the 6th.

it *properly*. – I told Cosima that you are second only to her: then, some considerable distance behind, comes *Lenbach*, who has painted such a strikingly accurate portrait of me! –

Do as she has written – unimportant though it is in relation to the thing itself.[1] – –

Adieu! Come over and see us as soon as you can, and we'll have a real Dionysian revel!

Yours,
R.W.

Nietzsche-Briefe II,2 493–4.

405. Franz Betz, Berlin   Lucerne, 4 March 1872

Most valued friend and colleague,

Things are now beginning to get fairly serious! My initial concern is Beethoven's 9th Symphony, which I am intending to perform in exemplary fashion in the opera house in Bayreuth on the 22nd of May – to celebrate laying the foundation stone of the provisional festival theatre. You will already have heard about this. But I am turning to you now because I want you to take on the famous baritone solo (together with the solo bass part as a whole) at this ceremony. Many years ago[2] in Dresden I taught Mitterwurzer to sing this exceedingly important "solo" in such a way that he created the most tremendous effect with it. Do not be offended when you *see* it: it is very clumsily done, but – what a marvellous character! The main thing is that *you yourself are there*. *Please* say yes! Only in this way shall we achieve anything worth while.

You need give up only 5 days of your time, i.e. the 19th of May for the journey to Bayreuth, the 20th, 21st and 22nd for your stay here, and the 23rd for the return journey. You *must* be able to do so, and I am sure you will want to. Is that not so?

As for the tenor solo, I have again been thinking of Niemann; I believe he ought to be able to make a success of it, since, essentially, it does not lie very high. But God knows the kind of nettle I may be grasping here, or what I may be bringing down on my head by making a serious approach to a man with whom I have had such unhappy experiences in the past.[3] Perhaps you could let me have some information on this point? I am also – naturally –

---

1 Cosima had written to Nietzsche on 3 January, asking for copies of *The Birth of Tragedy* to be sent to Ludwig II, Marie Muchanoff, Franz Liszt and Hans von Bülow.
2 For the Palm Sunday concert in 1846.
3 See letter [264], pp. 508–14. The four soloists on 22 May 1872 were Marie Lehmann, Johanna Wagner, Albert Niemann and Franz Betz.

still thinking of him for Siegmund in the Valkyrie. But my thoughts always end in a sigh!

Do you know Jäger?[1] in Dresden? I shall have to take a closer look at the whole of Germany's vocal splendours this summer, which is why I shall be moving permanently to the centre of Germany from May onwards.[2] Whatever shall I find there??? Sighs! –

Please send a favourable reply, and remain ever loyal and well-disposed towards

Your sincerely devoted
Richard Wagner

[. . .]

RWA (copy not in Wagner's hand; published with minor omissions in Bayreuther Briefe II, 6–8).

406. FRIEDRICH FEUSTEL AND THEODOR MUNCKER, BAYREUTH

Lucerne, 7 April 1872

My esteemed, dear friends, Herr Feustel and Herr Muncker,

Do not take it amiss if I write to you jointly on this occasion, but such is the information that I have to impart that I should find it difficult to tell what I should have to say to you individually, not least because, as I now recognize, you are but *one* heart and *one* soul as far as I am concerned.

It is also surely unnecessary for me to testify how much your kind letters refreshed and fortified me. For some time I have cherished an even greater desire than that of the success of my artistic activity: it is the desire to settle down to a life of reassuring domesticity in which, to some extent, I might recover my sorely overtaxed mental powers by means of some welcome relaxation; and even more so now that, in old age, I have been granted the supreme blessing of an incomparably happy family life. –

It was this desire above all which guided me in choosing your charming town of Bayreuth, and – since I have got to know you, my dear friends, and, through you, gained an insight into the friendly domestic conditions in your town, – the consideration of settling in your midst has actually outweighed my other consideration, namely the success of my extraordinary artistic undertaking. I have given the King of Bavaria to understand this quite plainly; and this I had a right to do, since the very first assurances which I received from

---

1 Ferdinand Jäger had been recommended by Emil Heckel for the role of Siegfried.
2 Wagner left Tribschen on 22 April, and stayed at the Hotel Fantaisie in Donndorf to the west of Bayreuth from 27 April to 21 September 1872. It was not until 10 November that he and Cosima began their tour of Germany in search of singers for the first festival.

him and which persuaded me to enter into an agreement with him concerned this very point, namely that I should be relieved of all life's cares and allowed to live undisturbed for the free exercise of my art. [It[1] was sufficient for him to know the value that I placed upon settling here and to know, moreover, that He alone could make that move possible, for Him to recognize the point at which He could torment me. Everything that we have planned for Bayreuth and at which the whole world is already gazing with increasing suspense is deeply repugnant to Him: He wants to play with what, to me, is a matter of deadly earnest, and He flies into a rage when prevented from doing so. On this point we must be clear, my friends, and it is fitting that we know with Whom we have to deal. I say to you in all honesty that I am afraid that your friendship for me could be prejudicial to the interests of the town of Bayreuth. If agreement for building the railway that you want to have depends upon the King, I am most concerned lest your sympathies with me prove a hindrance to you in this point. –

Perhaps I am going too far in feeling apprehensive in the way that I have intimated to you here, and] certainly I know from experience that the King always manages to reconcile himself to any given state of affairs, but I still deem it advisable – if I am to stick to my present plans and wishes – to renounce the King's co-operation in settling here. I have said as much recently to Court Councillor Düfflipp, and shall remain steadfast in refusing royal assistance for the purposes of settling in Bayreuth; as a result of which you, my dear Herr Feustel, will finally be entreated to resell the plot of land, when occasion offers, for the benefit of the royal exchequer.

I confess that, as a result of this disappointment in the case of my most ardent wish, I was disposed to renounce all my plans for Bayreuth. But your two splendid letters have persuaded me to change my mind. Let us remain steadfast! The *work* shall flourish, even though its creator be abandoned to his former distress. Even without any property, you will, I am sure, accept me into your midst as one of your fellow-citizens. – – We were moved to tears to learn of the care which you, my dear Herr Muncker, had taken upon yourself in planting the plot of land which had previously been intended for me. Please accept my thanks, as if it really *had* been for me! –

Am I to gather from your intimations, my dear Herr Feustel, that your efforts on behalf of our great undertaking have been crowned with the most heartening success? I pray that I am not mistaken! You will encounter a good deal of indolence and unreliability, but you will presumably manage as I have done, namely by not abandoning your belief that all of us good Germans must and will finally – finally achieve something!

Neumann is dreadful.[2] Two days ago, after receiving your letters, I tele-

1 The section in parentheses has not previously been published.
2 See letter [402], p. 784, note 2; and letter [407], p. 793.

graphed him, very circumstantially and categorically, and hope it may have had some effect. He is just a thoughtless Berliner! Brandt from Darmstadt is quite, quite, different: and he really understands the affair; I only wish we could have left the choice of an architect to him. We may still have to call upon his help. Would you be kind enough to telegraph me at once with news of how N. has conducted himself, so that we may then take whatever steps are necessary. – I fear he will have become engrossed in plans for "my" house, which I regret very much, since this work – at least for the foreseeable future – is now utterly useless! In this connection I am reminded of my previous project, and believe I must ask you in this regard to cancel my agreement with the landlord of the Hotel "Fantaisie", for which I assume that there ought still to be plenty of time.[1] The only purpose that so premature a move could have served would have been to ensure that I was on hand when the time came for my definitive removal (a plan now abandoned), and to provide me with a more immediate point of departure in my efforts on behalf of the future festival. As regards the latter, we are now, I assume, agreed that we cannot be ready by next year, and must therefore set our sights on 1874.[2] On this point I intend to reach an understanding with our Patrons etc. in Bayreuth on the 22nd of May. I must also – as a simple private citizen – take account of my particular circumstances, and find that, while I still have to pay a very high annual rent *here*, summer residence in the "Fantaisie" would tax me unduly heavily. However, I am willing to modify my decision the moment that you, my valued friends, consider that my continuing absence from Bayreuth is detrimental to our undertaking. –

With regard to our festival performance of Beethoven's great symphony, I have discovered a very simple expedient for positioning our large chorus, namely that all the singers who cannot be accommodated on the stage will be placed at the front of the stalls. This will satisfy even my most ideal demands in a quite splendid way, since I am convinced that the actual audience should join in the singing (just like the congregation in church). It is a question here of accommodating the "hosts", in which regard I should like to suggest that those among them who prefer financial compensation to passing artistic enjoyment should be paid in this way. On the whole, I should like to have had the entire stalls, together with the stage, reserved for us mad musicians and singers, while the listening public was relegated to the boxes & galleries. – The question now is how many acceptances were received from the Patrons and well-wishers. For this reason I regret the misunderstanding which led you to believe that the invitation was not to be published until the 15th of April. Could you effect this publication forthwith? So much the sooner

---

1 See letter [405], p. 789, note 2.
2 The first festival did not take place until 1876.

shall we then be clear as to whether the performance is to be well supported, or – as is easily imaginable – has only a moderate appeal. –

As for the rest, I shall write again soon. But for today only the most friendly greetings from the depths of my own and my dear wife's soul to you and your families!

Most truly yours,
Richard Wagner

RWA (incompletely published in Bayreuther Briefe I,67–71).

407. FRIEDRICH FEUSTEL, BAYREUTH   Lucerne, 12 April 1872

My esteemed friend,

Many thanks for your last letter! – It would never occur to me to doubt in the genuine success of our great enterprise as long as you remain loyal to me. But you surely understood me correctly [when[1] you supposed that my displeasure was directed at the locality that has been chosen for our undertaking only insofar that I was bound to feel a sudden sense of renewed disgust at the fact that, precisely because of my choice of locality, I shall again be subjected to the most incomparable, unique and utterly wearying vexations, vexations to which, as I know from experience, every enterprise is necessarily exposed from which it is not possible to exclude all interference on the part of Munich's courtiers and other civil functionaries. That is why I refused from the outset to accept any direct contribution from the King, precisely because I wanted to avoid this interference (in whatever guise). Not to be allowed to achieve even this negative aim, however, drove me to despair as a result of recent experiences, and I thought I would also have to sever the threads of that influential connection as it affected my desire to settle in Bayreuth.] Never for a moment did I believe in any duplicity on the part of my Bayreuth friends, but it alarmed me to think that that appalling system in which all things Bavarian are influenced by Munich [, its Court and its officials] had also insinuated itself into your midst. – On the contrary, had I given up Bayreuth, I should also have had to abandon the entire undertaking. They are both bound up with each other, and inasmuch as my great stage festival excites attention, it is already synonymous with the name of *Bayreuth*. And that is all to the good, and cannot be so quickly replaced.

What pleases me above all else is that you, my dear friend, remain undaunted, and that, on the whole, you even appear to be optimistic about the future. Of course, I can see that all around us things are developing and stirring: and I who had such boundless patience now wish for nothing more

1 The passages in parentheses have not previously been published.

but that we should be given *time* and not rushed [(as is the case, conversely, with my very difficult position with the King of Bavaria.)] – Everything of course is happening; it is prospering and maturing, – however: everything must be kept *pure*. –

I entirely agree with your maxims with regard to the allocation of the financial resources that we require. More specifically, these are as follows:

1.) The theatre building to be *provisional* only; I should be quite content for it to be only of wood, like the halls used for gymnastic displays and choral festivals; it should be no more solid than is necessary to prevent it from collapsing. Therefore economize here, economize – no ornamentation. With this building we are offering only the outline of our idea, and handing it over to the *nation for completion* as a monumental edifice.

2.) Stage machinery and scenery, and everything that relates to the ideal, inner work of art – *perfect* in every way. *No* economies here: everything as though designed to last a long time, nothing provisional. –

3.) Singers and musicians to receive *only* their expenses, no *fees*. Those who do not come for the honour and out of a sense of enthusiasm may as well stay at home. Any singer – be they male or female – who came to me only in return for one of their insane *fees* would be a fat lot of good to me! How could anyone like that satisfy my artistic demands. These, my dearest friend, are *my* miracles, which I shall reveal to the world here and show them how to obtain the people needed to meet such a challenge: and my friends must believe in this. It is different of course when some Court Theatre intendant has to deal with these people: the devil himself takes possession of these poor wretches, but he at least is someone I know how to control. I need about 20 principals and auxiliaries; these should not cost me more than 30,000 ths. for the two months, otherwise – I have no use for them. 100 musicians, with expenses of 50 thrs a month, making 10,000 thalers at most. *I shall answer* for this: for this is *my* empire. It is different when one has to deal with builders, carpenters, wood, canvas, sheet metal, brushes and stage machinery: I have no power here, but must be able only to arrange things and give orders. Here only *money* can achieve anything. – –

[I must say that, in spite of everything, the latest reports about Neumann's reliability have left me dumbfounded. Who could suppose such thoughtlessness! – And so, my dear friend, let us be short and to the point in deciding what to do here. For the time being simply put to one side Neumann's sketches for the house that (some day – perhaps) will be mine! Let us ignore this particular worry for the time being. When things are like *this* – it is best simply to call a truce on *both* sides!] – As for the rest, we can discuss these matters at our convenience when the opportunity presents itself. I am so uncommonly pleased to have found a man like you as a friend, my dear fellow. This is at present more reassuring for my future than if people were already hammering and chiselling away on "my" house today.

Let me know when you need me in Bayreuth: I now consider myself wholly dependent upon you.

We shall stick to our arrangement for the concert whereby the stalls in the auditorium are sacrificed to the singers; the stage is too *narrow* to serve for the mass of performers whom, for very good reasons, I am not prepared to forgo. In the event that the "Patrons" also turn up in large numbers, there will be nothing for it but to perform the symphony *twice*; then everybody will be able to attend, including all my splendid Bayreuth hosts. – – I shall shortly be making a move with a circular letter to my Patrons; something must be done in this regard. –

Sincere good wishes from my dear wife, who is a great admirer of yours! –

Wholly yours,
Richard Wagner

RWA (incompletely published in Bayreuther Briefe I,77–80).

THE BAYREUTH YEARS
1872–1883

INTRODUCTORY ESSAY 1872–1883

For the symbolic ceremony of the laying of the foundation stone of the Festspielhaus, Wagner set great store by the presence of Liszt. The relationship between the two composers had cooled somewhat since Cosima's divorce from Bülow and remarriage in a Protestant church. In his warm invitation to Liszt [408], Wagner characteristically refuses to avoid the touchy subject of Cosima, proclaiming her instead as her father's "innermost being, born anew" and come to deliver him. Liszt did not in fact attend the ceremony, but he assured Wagner of his good will towards the pair of them.

The original plan to hold the first festival in 1873 having proved overoptimistic, Wagner announced that it would be in 1875 instead, and set off with Cosima in search of singers. His determination not to leave the creation of the stage scenery to "routine theatrical scene painters" led him to approach the artist Josef Hoffmann [410], a painter of historical subjects. Hoffmann undertook the commission and in spite of his inexperience produced sketches that were widely admired [426]. It was agreed that since Hoffmann had neither studio nor assistants, the sets would be built and painted by the Brückner brothers (Gotthold and Max) under Hoffmann's supervision. Carl Brandt was engaged to design and construct the stage machinery, and Professor Carl Emil Doepler to design the costumes. Wagner asked Doepler to put out of his mind the classically derived, pseudo-Nordic representations of the Nibelung myths by artists such as Cornelius and Schnorr; rather he should investigate "references to the costumes of the Germanic peoples in Roman authors" and set his imagination to work [427].[1] A further commission was offered to one of Wagner's younger followers, Heinrich Porges, to make a detailed record of the rehearsals in order "to establish a fixed tradition" [415].

Meanwhile, in an attempt to secure a more solid financial foundation for the festival, Wagner arranged to declaim part of his *Ring* poem to an audience of influential statesmen in Berlin; unusually, invitations were not to be extended to people in the literary or theatrical spheres [416]. Bismarck himself was approached [418] and exhorted to support the venture. The two men had met in 1871, two years earlier, at which point Wagner had assured Dülfflipp that it would never occur to him to seek to gain Bismarck's backing.

---

1 Eight of Doepler's costume designs are reproduced in colour, together with his account of the festival, in Peter Cook, *A Memoir of Bayreuth 1876* (London 1979).

Now, however, he was presenting support for the project as the patriotic duty of the architect of the Reich. Bismarck failed to respond and even Ludwig, early in 1874, refused to provide the necessary guarantees for the completion of the theatre. In desperation Wagner turned to the Reich itself, in the person of the Emperor. He now proposed to offer him, through the Grand Duke of Baden, the first performances of the *Ring* as a quinquennial celebration of the victorious conclusion of the Franco-Prussian War in 1871. The *Ring* would surely compare only too favourably, he argued, with the kind of music usually heard on such occasions, and would at the same time "express recognition of an important concept in German culture" [421].

That appeal was rejected before it reached the Emperor, but now Ludwig retracted: "No, no and *no* again: it shall not end like this!" [420, note 2]. On 5 March 1874 Wagner was able to tell Emil Heckel that the King's guarantee of 100,000 thalers had just been confirmed [422]. It was intended to cover the cost of stage equipment, scenery and lighting; everything was to remain the property of the Royal Court Secretariat until such time as the loan was repaid. Wagner was at pains to emphasize that such funds merely allowed the project to proceed; public support was still vital if success was to be achieved. But even this news brought him little cheer, so exhausted and careworn was he by all that had happened. Moreover, that loan was to ensure that admission to the festival had to be paid for, in defiance of the original idealistic plan.

In a long but engrossing letter from October of that year [426] Wagner gives Ludwig a detailed account of the progress of the project as well as of more personal matters. He begins by introducing the technicians contracted and outlining the schedule for preliminary rehearsals in 1875 and final rehearsals from June to August the following year. Unconditional commitment has been demanded of, and promised by, the artists. The singers have all agreed to be paid expenses only; the orchestral players, it is hoped, will continue to draw their regular salaries while on summer leave. Wagner goes on, in this letter to Ludwig, to describe his house Wahnfried, his daily routine, the "Nibelung Chancellery" (his assistants), and the transformation in his prospects effected by the new copyright legislation. Finally he addresses the delicate question of the King's attendance at the festival. A gallery separate from the main auditorium is to be placed solely at his disposal: will he honour the public performances with his presence, or shall a special performance be given for an audience consisting of the King alone?

Generally speaking, Wagner had confidence in his singers, even if his demands were taxing and often unprecedented. Letter [434] contains advice on voice production for the Mime, Max Schlosser: he should assume a false voice for the part, but only once he has mastered it in his natural voice. (There are some similarly interesting instructions for a Beckmesser in [413]:

"The extremely high notes are of course only vehement or ridiculous speech accents, not singing.")

A pair of letters to Brahms from this period [430, 431] require some comment. As champions of the conservative and progressive tendencies respectively in nineteenth-century German music, Brahms and Wagner, and their followers, enjoyed an uneasy relationship. Qualified respect on both sides was frequently subjected to the strains of partisanship, as in the mishandled manifesto of 1860, to which Brahms was a signatory, against the New German School; the allegiance to Brahms of influential critics like Hanslick also helped to polarize opinions. Both musicians and friends of the two composers found themselves drawn into the conflict, often against their will. Hermann Levi's adoption by the Wagner camp in the 1870s cost him his friendship with Brahms, while Bülow's advocacy of Brahms' music, at the same period, was a bitter pill for Wahnfried to swallow. More intriguingly still, Brahms developed a friendly relationship with Wagner's former lover, Mathilde Wesendonck, and was even invited to stay in the vacated Asyl, adjacent to the Wesendoncks' villa.[1] But the pair of letters under present discussion were the result of Brahms' meeting with two of Wagner's personal friends, Peter Cornelius and Carl Tausig, in 1863–4. So close was the rapport established that Brahms, a keen collector, was given precious mementoes, including the autograph of the "Venusberg" music composed for the Paris performances of *Tannhäuser*. The following year (1865), preparations were being made for a production of *Tannhäuser* in Munich. The autograph was needed and Cornelius wrote to Brahms pointing out that Tausig had given away what did not belong to him.[2] Brahms refused to return the manuscript and the matter was dropped. A decade later Wagner returned to the subject [430], this time with success; in exchange for the autograph, he sent Brahms a *de luxe* edition of the full score of *Das Rheingold* [431].

The long-heralded festival finally took place in August 1876. Three cycles of the *Ring* were given before assembled dignitaries, musicians and critics from all over Europe. Ludwig, as ever determined to avoid the public gaze, attended the dress rehearsals and returned immediately to Hohenschwangau. On Wagner's assurance that he would not be subjected to scrutiny [441], he returned for the third cycle. Several aspects of the performances left something to be desired. "There is so much that we shall have to put right next year", he told Lilli Lehmann [443]. The Wotan, Franz Betz, had sung admirably, but his temperamental behaviour had caused difficulties. Apparently piqued that he was forbidden to take curtain-calls, Betz was threatening never to return to Bayreuth. Wagner lavished fulsome praise on his "aston-

1 See Karl Geiringer, "Wagner and Brahms, With Unpublished Letters", *Music Quarterly*, xxii (1936), 178–89.
2 This letter is reproduced, with others, by Karl Geiringer, *loc. cit.*

ishing" performance: "no other achievement known to me comes close to what you achieved in the second act of the Valkyrie"[445]. However, the letter to Lehmann reveals his private annoyance with Betz.

Even more troublesome was the financial burden. The deficit amounted to 148,000 marks and Wagner realized that to repeat the festival the following year was out of the question unless the debt could rapidly be paid off; apart from any other considerations, he knew that the singers could not reasonably be prevailed upon to give their services once more for nothing [444]. In the same letter to Feustel, he spoke of a rescue plan by which the theatre would be acquired and guaranteed by the state, but handed over to the Bayreuth magistracy for administration. Succour was not yet forthcoming and instead of repeating the festival in 1877 a concert tour of London was arranged, with Richter and various Bayreuth singers participating, for the purpose of cancelling the deficit [446]. Eight concerts were given in the Royal Albert Hall between 7 and 29 May. Wagner and his artists were well received but on account of mismanagement by the agents the profit totalled a mere £700 (approximately 14,300 marks).

The effect of all this strain on Wagner's health had been catastrophic: "I am dragging myself from place to place with my entire nervous system in a state of seemingly irrevocable collapse" [444]. He began to be seduced, as occasionally before, by the attractions of America. In May 1877 he told Feustel that he was seriously considering putting up his Bayreuth property for sale, setting sail across the ocean and never returning to Germany. In February 1880 he was again negotiating a permanent relocation [476], this time through Newell Sill Jenkins, an American dentist who had given him treatment. According to this agreement he and his family would be settled in "some climatically beneficial state of the Union", and a sum of one million dollars placed at his disposal; in return America would secure his services for all time and be guaranteed the first performance of *Parsifal*, to be followed by model performances of all his works.

The plan came to nothing, partly because Wagner was unwilling to disrupt his children's life, partly through cooling of interest the other end. But the fact that Wagner could contemplate abandoning Germany at all was symptomatic of his deep disillusionment. His own people had failed to rise to the challenge offered by the "Art-work of the Future". The vision had been realized, but only with the compromise of some fundamental principles: that first audience, as Wagner well knew, was representative of a privileged élite, not of the *Volk* triumphantly embracing the spirit of a newly liberated humanity.

Shortly after the failure of the London fund-raising concerts, Wagner told Wolzogen that he was making "one last attempt to unload the whole affair on to the Munich Court Theatre" [451]. However, when he met Düfflipp in Munich on 20 July 1877 to discuss the matter, he was told that Ludwig had left no instructions as to bailing out Bayreuth. Düfflipp responded to Wagner's despairing reaction by persuading him to confer with Perfall, the Munich intendant, with whom Wagner was scarcely on speaking terms. Wagner's preference was for singers and players from the Munich Court Theatre to give the *Ring* in Bayreuth, but Ludwig wished the 1878 festival to take place in Munich itself. The agreement finally concluded gave Ludwig the right to produce all Wagner's works in Munich without payment; the King, however, voluntarily offered to set aside 10 percent of all such receipts until the deficit was cleared. Wagner further agreed that the first performance of *Parsifal* (either in Bayreuth or Munich) should be given with the orchestra, singers and artistic personnel of the Munich Court Theatre, after which Munich was to have unrestricted rights over the work. It was this clause that was to compel Wagner to accept the Jewish Levi as the conductor of *Parsifal* in 1882.

To return to the year of the first *Ring* festival, it was in July 1876, just a month before the performances started, that a copy of "Richard Wagner in Bayreuth", the fourth part of Nietzsche's *Unzeitgemässe Betrachtungen* (Untimely Meditations), arrived in Bayreuth. The Wagners greeted it rapturously [439], but such a response suggested that they were scarcely aware of the true nature of Nietzsche's current stance with regard to Wagnerism. Nietzsche had been a close friend of the Wagner family and an enthusiastic advocate of the works, but the cryptic ambiguities of "Richard Wagner in Bayreuth" betray his increasing unease about the moral and philosophical content of Wagner's art.[1] Nietzsche was by this time in the grip of the illness – almost certainly syphilis – that was to lead to his insanity and death. Severe headaches, bouts of nausea and frequent fainting fits – Wagner refers to "mental" or "psychic spasms" [466, 474] – had obliged Nietzsche to leave his post as professor at Basle University temporarily in February 1876; he resigned finally three years later. Ignorant of Nietzsche's syphilitic condition, Wagner was convinced that his troubles were the result of habitual masturbation – a belief that would have been supported by a weighty body of contemporary public, and medical, opinion. In an earlier letter, Wagner had playfully suggested to Nietzsche that it was his bachelorhood that was responsible for his malaise. He should either get married or write an opera; if there were no women available, he could always steal one [425]. In 1877, a year after Nietzsche had prematurely walked out of the festival at Bayreuth, Wagner was writing in a more serious vein to Nietzsche's doctor, Otto Eiser [455], urging him to accept his own diagnosis.[2] Remarkable as such an action is, it is less breathtaking than the dogmatic certitude which enabled Wagner to attribute

---

1 For a fuller account of Nietzsche's confrontation with Wagnerism see Roger Hollinrake, *Nietzsche, Wagner and the philosophy of pessimism* (London 1982) and R. J. Hollindale, *Nietzsche: The Man and His Philosophy* (London 1965).
2 See Martin Gregor-Dellin, *Richard Wagner: His Life, His Work, His Century* (London 1983), 451–8.

to masturbation both Nietzsche's weakening eyesight and debilitation, and the blindness of his own youthful friend, Theodor Apel. Apel's loss of sight was in fact a result of injuries sustained when he fell from a horse.

Also present at the first Bayreuth festival was Judith Gautier. She was by now divorced from Catulle Mendès, and the fact that she had formed a close attachment with an amateur composer, Louis Benedictus, did not deter Wagner from pressing his own attentions on her. Unwilling as she was to engage in an affair with him, their intimacy was serious enough to be conducted through a go-between, a local barber by the name of Bernhard Schnappauf, and it continued for some eighteen months, until February 1878. Several of these letters contain requests from Wagner for silks, satins, and exotic perfumes from Paris [453, 458]. Such perquisites and this sexagenarian's passionate protestations of love were apparently inseparable from the mood of creativity conjured for the composition of *Parsifal*. Unable to embrace her physically, he christens his chaise-longue "Judith" – asking for an exceptionally beautiful cover for it – and reclines on that instead. The irony of *Parsifal*, that celebration of renunciation and chastity, taking shape while its creator basked in such sensual indulgence and fantasies, has frequently been remarked upon. Ernest Newman's thesis, that Wagner was in love with *Parsifal* rather than with Judith Gautier,[1] has something to recommend it. But even if Newman's conclusion, that Judith was brusquely dismissed in February 1878 because *Parsifal* was by then "fairly launched", were not already unconvincing, it is now clear from Cosima's Diaries that there was a different ending to the "affair". It appears that she winkled out the full story after she had caught Wagner burning some correspondence in January 1878.[2] She then diplomatically, but resolutely, brought the affair to a conclusion: the abrupt change of tone in [463] – the last surviving letter to Judith – is thus the result of Cosima's intervention rather than of a change of heart on Wagner's part.

One of the consequences of Wagner's disappointment with the artistic standard of the first festival was his return to the idea of a music school. The plan was now to establish it in Bayreuth, to train conductors and singers there [451] and eventually to use it as a basis for the production of model performances – all the mature works to be given over a period of four years, beginning with *Der fliegende Holländer*, *Tannhäuser* and *Lohengrin* in 1880. The public response proved to be inadequate; instead, Wagner put his energies into establishing the *Bayreuther Blätter*, a journal that was to survive under its founding editor, Hans von Wolzogen, from 1878 to 1938. The journal – which was to carry no "correspondence, criticism, reviews, advertisements, etc." [456] – was to be devoted to the Wagnerian cause and written by those

---

1 See *Life*, IV,605–7.
2 See CT for 12 February 1878 and 29 October 1879; also Geoffrey Skelton, *Richard and Cosima Wagner* (London 1982), 226, 230–1, 244–8.

sympathetic to it. Its viewpoint was described (CT for 29 November 1880) as "the decline of the human race and the need for the establishment of a system of ethics". The adoption of such a programme ensured that the *Bayreuther Blätter* was to be identified firmly with the aggressively nationalistic outlook of the Wilhelminian era and with the still more dubious ideology that evolved from it.

Wagner's "system of ethics" was comprehensively expounded in the series of essays, sometimes known as the "regeneration writings", beginning with *Modern* (1878) and reaching an insidious climax with *Heldenthum und Christenthum* (Heroism and Christianity, 1881). The important themes of the essays may be briefly summarized as follows. In abandoning its original, natural vegetable diet, and absorbing the corrupted blood of slaughtered animals, the human race has brought about its own degeneration. A return to natural food is essential if regeneration is to be effected, but it must be accompanied by the observance of a true religion. By partaking – in the Eucharist – of the untainted blood of Christ, even the most degenerate races may be purified. Christ the Saviour has, moreover, been unpardonably identified with the Old Testament God of Israel. In fact, the interbreeding of the Jews with the pure Aryan race is partly responsible for the degeneration of the species.

Wagner's elevation of the New Testament over the Old is apparent in [471], in which he claims that ordinary people would respond better to Christianity if they were "made to forget about God in the 'burning bush' and shown instead only the 'sacred head sore wounded' ". This, Wagner tells Constantin Frantz, is his only quibble with the federalist's latest essay, but it was a quibble serious enough to elicit the observation "how sad it is to see such good minds as C. Frantz's going astray" the following year (CT for 26 November 1880). He is prepared to allow that Christ, the "sublimely simple and true redeemer", be identified with "the historically intelligible figure of Jesus of Nazareth" [475], but only if "cleansed and redeemed of the distortion that has been caused by Alexandrine, Judaic and Roman despotism". Such a de-Judaization of religion, which even prompted Wagner to put forward the idea of an "Aryan Jesus", was, of course, in perfect accord with the new wave of anti-Semitism that was sweeping Germany, and which had, if anything, been intensified by the emancipation legislation of the early 1870s. In spite of the virulence of his anti-Semitism – "I consider the Jewish race the born enemy of pure humanity and all that is noble in man" [489] – and its obsessiveness – see Cosima's Diaries, *passim* – Wagner's apologists have tended to draw exaggerated attention to his attempt to distance himself from the anti-Semitic movement. His refusal to sign Bernhard Förster's "Mass Petition against the Rampancy of Judaism" is often cited in this context, as is his decisive statement to Angelo Neumann: "I have absolutely no connection with the present 'anti-Semitic' movement" [481]. Quite apart from the probably inadvertent anti-Jewish remark just a few lines later in the same letter, one would need to recall only Wagner's private enthusiasm for the gains of the movement and sense of pride in the part he himself had played, to cast suspicion on his present forbearance as opportunistically motivated. The situation was summed up by Bülow in his wry observation: "The master did indeed poke the fire, but he let others burn their fingers in it."[1]

For all his characteristic plain speaking and insensitivity, Wagner could not afford to alienate Jewish musicians indiscriminately; many, as has frequently been remarked, were valued and influential friends and associates. Even so, opportunism was not the only reason for his disavowal of the anti-Semitic movement. To a certain extent, also, Wagner liked to think that he was conducting the argument on a more sophisticated level than the mere agitators, as is evident from an entry in Cosima's Diaries: "In the evening friend Wolz.[ogen] visits us; R. tells him that we cannot champion special causes such as vegetarianism in our *Blätter*, but must always confine ourselves to defining and demonstrating the ideal, leaving those outside to fight for the special cause; for the same reason we cannot join in the anti-Jewish agitation." (CT for 24 February 1881). There were also policy issues over which he took a different view: in particular, the challenge he identified was not that of resisting emancipation, but of resolving the "Jewish question" by more radical means.[2] In this, he was likewise ultimately at odds with the French writer Count Joseph-Arthur de Gobineau, though in the period following their first meeting in 1876 they recognized each other as kindred spirits and delighted in each other's company. Wagner read his writings, notably the *Essai sur l'inégalité des races humaines*, and discovered that Gobineau also propounded a degeneration of the species, but attributed it to miscegenation, i.e. inter-breeding between races, rather than to a change of diet. In [483] Wagner is awaiting a visit from Gobineau with keen anticipation. The Count, "who in every particular has become so valuable an enrichment of our lives" (CT for 8 June 1881), left a month later on the most cordial terms, and as late as May 1882 Wagner was declaring "that he will now read only Gobineau, Schopenhauer, and himself" (CT for 21 May 1882). But a fundamental divergence in their respective philosophies was to become apparent. Gobineau's outlook was a pessimistic one in that he held miscegenation to be both necessary (in some degree) for the continuation of civilization and, at the same time, responsible for the degeneration of the species. Wagner's more optimistic view, that the human race was redeemable by Christ's pure blood,

1 Quoted by Jacob Katz in *The Darker Side of Genius: Richard Wagner's Anti-Semitism* (Hanover, NH, and London 1986), 114. Katz's perceptive study traces the development of Wagner's obsession throughout his life.
2 See Katz, *op. cit.*, 112ff.

was promulgated not only in *Heroism and Christianity* (as mentioned above), but also in *Parsifal*.[1]

Wagner was deeply opposed to the idea of that drama, "in which the most sublime mysteries of the Christian faith are openly presented on stage", ever being given "side by side with an operatic repertory and before an audience such as ours" [479]. For that reason he was determined to confine it to Bayreuth. It is therefore a mark of the confidence and trust he had in the impresario Angelo Neumann that he was prepared at least to entertain the idea of *Parsifal* being given by his touring theatre [488, 498]. In January 1881 Neumann had requested the world performance rights in the *Ring*, proposing to present it in Berlin, London, Paris, St Petersburg and America, and offering Wagner 10 percent of the receipts. That October Neumann also considered the possibility of a permanent Wagner theatre in Berlin; Wagner was lukewarm about the idea but willing to lend his name to such a theatre [488]. A contract for the *Ring* was signed in August 1882 and over the following years Neumann took the work all over Europe. At Wagner's request, *Parsifal* was not included in this arrangement.

The question of the language in which Wagner preferred his works to be given in foreign productions can only be touched on here. He was not opposed in principle to their being translated; indeed, translation was often a prerequisite for performances outside Germany and Austria. But more than that, Wagner realized that audiences would appreciate his works better if they heard them in their own language. Receiving news of an Italian-language production of *Lohengrin* in Australia, Wagner expressed the wish that his works be given in English there for that reason [454]. However, experiences earlier in life had left him with the conviction that "it is impossible even to translate them into French, whereas an attempt to render them into English, Spanish or even Italian may well succeed" [492].

From his largely thwarted idealistic conception of the Bayreuth enterprise Wagner managed to salvage at least one element: a stipendiary foundation which would allow "people without means of their own to attend the performances" [493]. The series of *Parsifal* performances at the 1882 festival passed off to Wagner's qualified satisfaction. There had been complaints from Patrons about the arrangements for food and accommodation [496], but otherwise Wagner was able to regale Ludwig with details of an undertaking carried through with enthusiasm and commitment by all concerned [497]. Having failed to attend *Parsifal* in Bayreuth, pleading ill health, Ludwig was

1 For a fuller account of the "regeneration writings" and the ideological background to *Parsifal*, see Barry Millington, *Wagner* (London 1984), chapters 8, pp. 102–9, and 19, pp. 268–71. For the relationship of "Bayreuth idealism" to the cultural and political history of Germany under the Second and Third Reichs, see *ibid.* chapter 9; Michael Karbaum, *Studien zur Geschichte der Bayreuther Festspiele (1876–1976)* (Regensburg 1976); Hans Mayer, *Richard Wagner in Bayreuth: 1876–1976* (London 1976).

mooting a performance in Munich, a prospect viewed with alarm by Wagner [499]. In a letter written just a month before his death [500], Wagner was maintaining the impossibility of performances in Munich, while looking forward to a repeated festival that year in Bayreuth, offering private performances of *Parsifal* for the King alone. Notwithstanding Wagner's death in February 1883, performances of the work were given at Bayreuth that year. Ludwig eventually achieved his desire the following year, when private performances of *Parsifal* were given in Munich.

408. FRANZ LISZT, WEIMAR   Bayreuth, 18 May 1872

My very dear friend,
   Cosima maintains that you would not come, even if I were to invite you.[1]
That is something we should have to endure, as we have had to endure so
much else! But I cannot forbear to invite you. And what is it that I call out
to you when I say "Come"? You entered my life as the greatest man to whom
I have ever been allowed to address myself on terms of intimate friendship;
you slowly moved away from me, perhaps because I had become less close
to you than you were to me. In your place there came your innermost being,
born anew, and it was she who fulfilled my yearning desire to know you close
to me. Thus you live before me and within me in perfect beauty, and we are
as one beyond the grave itself. You were the first man to ennoble me through
his love; I am now wedded to a second, higher life through her, and can
achieve what I could never have achieved alone. Thus you could be everything
to me, whereas I could only ever be so very little to you: what a tremendous
advantage I have over you!
   If I now say to you: "Come", what I mean by this is: "Come to yourself"!
For you will find yourself here. – Whatever your decision, you have my
blessing and my love!

Your old friend
Richard.

Liszt-Briefe II,307–8.

409. FRIEDRICH NIETZSCHE, BASLE   [Bayreuth], 25 June 1872

Oh friend,
   You really are causing me nothing but worry, but it is because I care so
very much for you! Strictly speaking, you are the only real gain that life has
brought me, and second only to my wife in that respect: fortunately, of course,
I now have Fidi,[2] too; but I need a link between him and me, and only
you can forge that link, much as the son is linked to the grandchild. I am not
worried about Fidi, but about you, and to that extent my worry also affects
Fidi. It is a thoroughly bourgeois concern: I should like nothing more than

---

1 To the foundation-stone laying ceremony. Liszt did not attend, but the Wagners visited him
  in Weimar between 2 and 6 September 1872, and Liszt came to Bayreuth between 15 and
  21 October.
2 Siegfried Wagner.

to see you well like the rest of us, since everything else seems to be perfectly safe with you. I have been carefully rereading the "Birth"[1] on consecutive mornings; and I kept on telling myself: "if only he could get well again and remain so, and if everything else were to go well for him, – for things may not go wrong for him!" How we should like to be able to contribute something here!

But we then stop to think how best to set about doing so, and – it is precisely this that worries us. However: – just hold out a little longer, and all will turn out well in the end. I am growing immensely confident, and my worries always end up as hopes, particularly when I discover that you, too, have confidence in yourself, that you are reassured as to your health, and that you are in good spirits.

I cannot see that I have blazed a trail for you with my "Letter",[2] and am bound to suppose that I have merely hung an additional burden around your neck; nor did I mean to say that you should "ripen" into your task, but only that it would keep you fully occupied for the whole of your life.

But "Tristan" will certainly be of interest to you:[3] only: spectacles off! You must hear nothing but the orchestra. – Adieu! My dear, true friend! Shall we see each other again soon?[4] –

Yours,
Rich. Wagner

Nietzsche-Briefe II,4 29–30.

410. JOSEF HOFFMANN, VIENNA   Bayreuth, 28 July 1872

Dear Sir,

Since a performance of my stage festival: the Ring of the Nibelung, is feasible in practical terms only with support from many quarters, it is my intention to entrust its planned realization in technical matters, too, to a correspondingly varied personnel scattered throughout Germany. With regard to the stage presentation, I have come to the conclusion that nothing worthy of the name of Germany – in the noblest sense of the word – can be achieved here if the relevant work is simply left to our routine theatrical scene painters. It is a question, rather, of my being able to submit designs by genuine artists to the most skilled or experienced scene painters in order to inspire the latter

---

1 Nietzsche's *The Birth of Tragedy.*
2 An Open Letter of 12 June 1872 on the subject of classical education. It was published in the *Norddeutsche Allgemeine Zeitung* of 23 June 1872; also GS IX,295–302; PW V,292–8.
3 Nietzsche attended two performances of *Tristan und Isolde* in Munich, at Bülow's invitation, on 28 and 30 June 1872.
4 The two men next met in Strasbourg between 22 and 24 November 1872.

to produce of their best. With this in mind I have already addressed myself to a number of artists (historical painters). But my particular attention has recently been drawn to your own especial achievements, my dear Sir, the character of which appears to be very close to what I am wanting. Accordingly, what I make so bold as to ask of you now is that you might initially consider it worth your while to acquaint yourself with my poem: the Ring of the Nibelung to the extent of its becoming sufficiently familiar for you to prepare sketches of the principal scenes both as regards the setting of the action and the shape of the dramatis personae, so that these sketches might serve as a model for further elaboration either for you yourself, should you wish to do so, or for such scene painters & costumiers as are still to be chosen.

For the time being it is sufficient for me to have drawn your attention to this matter in general terms, but as soon as you give me the pleasure of more detailed information, I shall at once find an opportunity of coming to an arrangement with you personally on all additional matters.

In the meantime, may I thank you very much for the gratifying asseverations on your part which were conveyed to me by Herr Scharff, and assure you that I have the honour to be

Your respectfully devoted servant
Richard Wagner.

Facsimile in Josef Hoffmann, Bayreuth 1876–1896 (n.d.)
(published with minor variants in Bayreuther Briefe I,97–9).

411. HERMANN LEVI, KARLSRUHE   Bayreuth, 11 August 1872

Most valued friend,
    I am here, and looking forward to seeing you at any time.[1]
    You are most heartily welcome!

Your devoted servant
Richard Wagner

On the eve of the end of the world[2]

Bayreuther Briefe II,29.

1 Levi visited Wagner in Bayreuth on 17/18 August 1872.
2 According to Cosima Wagner's Diary for 12 August 1872, "*Götterdämmerung*, very finely copied out (IIIrd act) by Herr Rubinstein and appropriately completed on the day the world will end [. . .]".

412. FRIEDRICH NIETZSCHE, BASLE   Bayreuth, 23 October 1872

Dear friend,

It was most kind of you to write to me on your birthday, the very day, moreover, on which my wife had written to you about us. What you wrote was most gratifying, since it expressed with pleasant solemnity the frame of mind in which we all seem to be at present. It would almost be called a mood of apprehension following the disgust we feel at everything we see and hear, so that when we finally regain our senses, it is with the question what do we actually have in common with this scandalous world of ours? – Liszt has been staying with us for a week:[1] we have again grown very fond of him; but his departure was bound to leave us with all our old feelings of apprehension. What did he not tell us about the world that we did not already know right down to the very last detail, but which time and again it frightened us to death to hear gone into in this way. There was much he could tell us, since people thought we had fallen out with him, and so he believed he was doing us a favour by telling us of such base behaviour. On the whole I feel increasingly that I know my fellow humans less and less: this may be very necessary if one is to write for posterity. But it is curious how often I feel like a novice under constant supervision! When one is simply working in a vacuum, individual loneliness becomes immense. I can well understand what it was that so often stifled and almost suffocated you: you simply looked around you a good deal. But it is a question now of seeing and not seeing! If one abandons hope, one will no doubt also be rid of one's despair. In the end one feels that the only means of gaining self-consciousness is to set oneself apart, quite emphatically, from one's fellow men, and to do so, moreover, by attacking their vileness. At least I myself have now reached the point where I refuse to mince my words in any way: and if the Empress of Austria herself were to cross my path, she would certainly be well-served! Something must emerge from all this. For one thing is certain, there can be no question of any compromise or private understanding here: to make oneself feared, when one is so very much hated, is the only course that can help. –

I have been thinking more and more about "what is German",[2] and, on the basis of a number of more recent studies, have succumbed to a curious scepticism which leaves me thinking of "Germanness" as a purely metaphysical concept; but, as such, it is of immense interest to me, and certainly something that is unique in the history of the world, its only possible counterpart being Judaism, since Hellenism, for example, does not really fit in here.

But then my gaze falls upon my son, my Siegfried: the boy is growing sturdier and stronger by the day, and is just as quick with his wits as he is

1 See letter [408], p. 809, note 1.
2 The essay *Was ist deutsch?* See letter [334], p. 665, note 1.

with his fist. He is a complete marvel to me, and if I have driven away despair with the support of my wife, the lad is now teaching me what it is to feel hope again. And so the old dance starts up all over again, but this time at the proper speed. The boy now makes me think of you, my friend, and purely for reasons of family egoism inspires me with an inordinate desire to see all the hopes that I have placed in you fulfilled to the very last letter: for the boy – ah! – needs you! –

But I have already told you as much. You know – : in old age people start to repeat themselves! The same is true of me and my outpourings, with which I have been showering the world – and more especially you – in pamphlet form. I expect you have already received "Actors and Singers"?[1] It is yet another way of dealing with the same issue: this time I have approached it directly through actors. In doing so I again had the experience of having already completed it when a great many new ideas struck me that would not have been out of place there, but at least I have a hook on which to hang my next pamphlet. But it is all really only in a vacuum! When I think about it more closely, I simply do not know to whom to send my free copies. Do you want any more for your colleagues in Basle? Rohde shall have one. – Incidentally, your "Basle" colleagues remind me that I must let you and your friends know the dates of our forthcoming visit. We intend embarking upon our voyage of discovery through the German Empire early in November:[2] the first diversion from our main purpose will be a visit to my celebrated dentist in Basle,[3] whose most tender cares can now no longer be avoided. I imagine that this functional visit will last a whole week, and thus provide us with 8 evenings which we would hope to spend in your own and your friends' company, pleasantly consoled for the maltreatment suffered during the day. I imagine that we shall be arriving during the third week of November; we shall then seek to obtain some assurances from you regarding the American's existence and willingness.

Otherwise the life we are leading is now somewhat dissolute, as a result no doubt of our temporary move to the Dammallée.[4] Liszt's visit was the biggest interruption, when the capacity of our "salon" here was put to its severest test. We have now cleared up all misunderstandings with this wonderful man, at least as far as it is still possible to do so, and our only

1 *Über Schauspieler und Sänger* (On Actors and Singers), completed on 14 September 1872, published the following month in pamphlet form, and reprinted in GS IX,157–230, PW V,157–228.
2 See letter [405], p. 789, note 2. The Wagners visited Würzburg, Frankfurt, Darmstadt (twice), Mannheim, Stuttgart, Strasbourg (where they met Nietzsche), Karlsruhe, Wiesbaden, Mainz, Cologne, Bonn, Düsseldorf, Hanover, Bremen, Magdeburg, Dessau and Leipzig. They were back in Bayreuth by 15 December 1872.
3 The American Newell Sill Jenkins. Nothing came of this plan.
4 The Wagners lived at Dammallee 7 from 21 September 1872 to 28 April 1874, when they moved into Wahnfried.

cause for regret was – and is – that we cannot really hope to be of any real help to him in this strangely dissipated life of his. It is possible, however, that he will come and live with us here. After getting to know your New Year's Echoes,[1] he found Bülow's verdict very extreme: even without having heard you play the piece (and it was this that was decisive in our case), he felt that *his* verdict on your "music" must be totally different and certainly more favourable. And so, let us say no more about this B.esque Intermezzo: I feel as though two eccentricities of the most extreme kind had come into violent contact here. This, too, I mention only in passing: for on the whole and in the main everyone must no doubt come to a clearer understanding about himself through *himself*, and not through others. What would become of me, for ex., if I were to set too much store by Herr Edmund Hoefer (see enclosure)?[2] – I reread your book[3] last summer: my wife devoured it again more recently. I imagine your ears must have been pleasantly burning the while, as if you had been listening to some very good music. –

This time you are getting a fairly respectable letter from me: I hope my tittle-tattle cheers you up; you will gather at any rate that in the long run the baseness of people and things cannot affect me, and so I end up by having the advantage of being able to address you, too, in a good mood. –

Best wishes from us all! I hope we shall meet again soon in the city of Erasmus!

Cordially yours,
Richard Wagner.

Feustel's silver-wedding anniversary!

Nietzsche-Briefe II, 4 102–6.

413. Rudolf Freny, Hamburg   Bayreuth, 25 October 1872

Dear Sir,

You are certainly on the right lines with Beckmesser. But don't overdo the man's foolishness; it will take care of itself: he does not need to be old; many people are already old by the time they are forty. Be *deadly serious* in everything: the man never makes jokes, except when pretending to be funny. Great narrowness of intellect and a good deal of spite. Model yourself on some

---

1 *Nachklang einer Sylvesternacht*, written in November 1871. Bülow's criticism had been directed at Nietzsche's *Manfred-Meditation* of 1872.
2 *Cf* CT for 23 October 1872: "R. writes to Prof. Nietzsche, announcing our visit to Basel, and among other things he encloses a little clipping from a newspaper, in which some tasteless extracts from opera texts are quoted and criticized, with the remark, 'This goes even further than R. Wagner'!"
3 *The Birth of Tragedy.*

famous critic or other. Boundless passion, but without the strength to express it: a voice that cracks when he loses his temper. The extremely high notes are of course only vehement or ridiculous speech accents, not singing. Please pay close attention to every instruction, and keep exactly in time with the orchestra when you perform the part.

Your devoted servant
Richard Wagner

Otto 361.

414. ERWIN ROHDE, KIEL   Bayreuth, [28]¹ October 1872

My dear friend,

I find that, with and through Nietzsche, I have got into excellent company. You cannot know what it means for a man who has spent his entire life in bad company, or at least among stupid people, finally to be able to say: God be praised, here is a genus, perhaps even a whole generation, for the sake of which it has been worth my while to have spent half a century shut up in prison! – But this new direction to my life really only began with Nietzsche: my world had previously described a circle no wider than Pohl, Nohl & Porges. No words can express how different it is now! Do not ask for any more news from me; I believe my wife has already written to you? At least I know that she wrote to Gersdorff yesterday evening on the subject, among others, of "Pseudo-Philosophy"² (dreadful word!). We were delighted by your essay: it is a worthy companion piece and counterpart to the "Birth" itself. For us, the main thing was that we were able to learn something from this rebuttal, and also learn to respect and love the "whole man". Something of this nature was bound to be of great help to us all: but I scarcely dare glance any longer into the future morass of the human race. However, this is something we can leave to God to arrange as best redounds to His honour.

Our sincere good wishes, and my especial thanks for the very real honour you have shown us!

Respectfully yours,
Richard Wagner.

RWA (copy not in Wagner's hand; published complete in Elisabeth Förster-Nietzsche, Wagner und Nietzsche zur Zeit ihrer Freundschaft [Munich 1915], 126–7).

1 Although dated 29 October 1872, the letter is postmarked the 28th; Cosima Wagner's Diary confirms the earlier date.
2 Rohde's *Afterphilologie: Sendschreiben eines Philologen an Richard Wagner* (Pseudo-Philosophy: A Philologist's Open Letter to Richard Wagner), published in pamphlet form in Leipzig, had arrived in Bayreuth on 25 October 1872.

415. HEINRICH PORGES, MUNICH   Bayreuth, 6 November 1872

Dear friend,

I have indeed received your gratifying promise, for which I am most grateful to you!

Even before you had written to me, I had already assigned you a particular role in my enterprise which is of the greatest possible importance for the future. I intend to invite you to follow all my rehearsals, just as you did for the 9th Symphony, in order to record and note down all my remarks, however intimate, concerning the interpretation and performance of our work, and in that way to establish a fixed tradition.[1]

I hope this is settled! If you also wished to assist me with the purely mechanical musical rehearsals of the individual singers, your help would be more than welcome. I cannot enter into any actual engagements in this respect, and whatever may have reached your notice in the form of newspaper articles is simply empty boasting, which will do the boasters no good.

With every good wish, I remain

Your sincerely devoted
Richard Wagner.

Bayreuther Briefe II,31.

416. ALEXANDER VON SCHLEINITZ, BERLIN [Cologne,] 3 December 1872

My esteemed benefactor,

There is no one more sensible than I of the debt of gratitude which I owe, more especially, to you, whenever I discover from my dear wife that your own estimable spouse has given yet further proof of her wellnigh self-sacrificial support for my artistic enterprises. And in order that you, too, my esteemed benefactor, may not doubt for a moment in my attitude and feelings in this regard, I make so bold as to appeal to you yourself today in respect of our latest undertaking in order to assure you, above all else, that I am fully conscious of the magnitude of our request.

With regard to Berlin, the capital of the Reich and seat of German politics, I wish to withdraw from all dealings with the city's operatic life, the more so since I know from experience that it is impossible for me to become involved with it in a seemly fashion. Since, moreover, I consider it my duty to devote myself in every respect to the interests of my enterprise this coming winter,

---

1 Published as *Die Bühnenproben zu den Bayreuther Festspielen des Jahres 1876*. Verlag von Ernst Schmeitzner (Chemnitz 1881–2) and Verlag von Siegesmund & Volkening (Leipzig 1896). English translation by Robert L. Jacobs (Cambridge 1983).

I should have avoided Berlin completely if the inestimable gain that your patronage has brought me had not shown me the way by which I might hope to direct consideration of my question into a sphere where I might see it seriously considered as a matter of some importance, and as one which transcended the common interests of theatre-lovers. Whether, in addition and quite apart from this, I shall also achieve anything in terms of the material interests of my undertaking is something that may be left for now to depend upon individual circumstances; but I should at least like to have assured myself of the one advantage that I have just described to you, namely that the matter be brought before the forum of politics and intellect, regardless for the moment of whether material advantages might also accrue to my enterprise as a result.

The idea occurred to me whereby, after a relatively brief introductory lecture, I might read out a substantial part of my Nibelung poem to the kind of influential gathering that it would perhaps only be granted to a highly favoured minister in the royal household to assemble.[1] I should like to see present on that occasion representatives of both actual political power and of the intellectual discipline that Berlin at present comprises: representatives from an artistic sphere would be considered eligible only insofar as they had no immediate contact with the theatre, by which I mean more or less that I should consider a professor of history or even of theology more worthy of my attention than any man of letters or living author, be they never so celebrated.

Since at the same time, however, I am appealing to the sphere of actual political power, by which I mean princes of the royal house and ministers, the question that must now be asked is whether I might not appear over-presumptuous to you, my esteemed benefactor, and whether I might thus be transcending the bounds of decency in claiming this demonstration of your conspicuously kind disposition towards me.

A mere hint from you will suffice to apprise me of your response and make me desist from a request for the temerity of which I should then have the most pressing occasion to pay a brief visit to Berlin in order to entreat your forgiveness in person.

With the greatest reverence, I remain

Your Excellency's
most gratefully devoted servant
Richard Wagner

Otto 362–3.

---

1 On 17 January 1873 Wagner read the poem of *Götterdämmerung* to a group of dignitaries which, according to Cosima Wagner, included "Lepsius, Helmholtz, Delbrück, Moltke, the Crown Prince of Württemberg, Prince Georg of Prussia, and virtually all the ambassadors".

417. ERNST WILHELM FRITZSCH, LEIPZIG   Bayreuth, 25 March 1873

The latest supplement to Brockhaus's Encyclopaedia contains an article belatedly devoted to me which states, amongst other things:

> Following the ending of the Franco-Prussian War, influential friends at the Prussian Court sought to bring Wagner to Berlin to fill the position of General Music Director there, a position that had been vacant since the death of Meyerbeer; they met with no success, since another institution, Joachim's School, had already been summoned into life with the aim of fostering music more effectively. W. thereupon turned back to Bavaria with renewed affection.

Since the authority of the Encyclopaedia could well outlive me, I am protesting in good time against the inaccuracy of the above information: none of my friends could seek occasion to obtain a Prussian appointment for me since all of them know how much I value the lifelong kindness shown me by the King of Bavaria, a boon which consists in my being able to live freely for my art without a fixed appointment, for which reason there could be no conceivable grounds why I should at any time need to "renew" my affection for him who granted me that boon and for whom I feel only gratitude and reverence.

If, in the light of this assurance, my friends should feel some doubt as to the credibility of those scholars who, in matters of art and music, have contributed to Brockhaus's Encyclopaedia, it will not be necessary for me to expose the malicious insinuation contained within the above statements.

Richard Wagner.

SS XVI,54.

418. OTTO VON BISMARCK, BERLIN   [Bayreuth, 24 June 1873]

Most honoured Prince,

Your serene Highness could perhaps obtain the best explanation of why I considered it indispensable at least to attempt to persuade you to take cognizance of my essay[1] if you were to read its final pages. No one will be more understanding than I if Your Highness were unable to show me even this fleeting favour; but many would think it remiss of me if I were to allow myself to be deterred by my apprehension from leaving untried whatever means might be appropriate to acquaint the great reviver of German hopes with the cultural idea which inspires me and which, by virtue of the most strenuous

---

1 *Das Bühnenfestspielhaus zu Bayreuth: Nebst einem Berichte über die Grundsteinlegung desselben* (The Stage Festival Theatre in Bayreuth: With a report on the foundation-stone laying of the same), published in Leipzig in 1873 and reprinted in GS IX,322–44; PW V,320–40.

exertions of my entire life, I now feel impelled to express in terms which the nation will understand. Since any further attempt to persuade Your Highness to take note of this essay is bound to seem as inappropriate as it must be futile, I wish only that these lines may serve to excuse any possible nuisance that this letter may have caused. It may none the less appear to me permissible in your eyes to express my deep anxiety that an undertaking such as that which I am planning should be carried into effect without the participation of the only truly supportive and ennobling authority, a participation that I myself must necessarily consider of the profoundest import; in which case I should have to console myself with the fate that befell the rebirth of the German spirit through the great poets of the second half of the last century, a rebirth to which its true hero, Frederick the Great, remained aloof and indifferent.

With the expression of my boundless respect, I remain

Your Highness's deeply devoted admirer[1]

Richard Wagner.

Freunde und Zeitgenossen 560–1.

419. KING LUDWIG II OF BAVARIA, BERG   Bayreuth, 11 August 1873

My dearly belovèd lord and benefactor,

The revered testimony to my exalted patron's ever-familiar grace and favour which I recently received in the form of your excessively kind letter filled me, as every other attestation of your love and favour has so often filled me, with almost melancholy misgivings as to whether and in what way I might be able to prove myself worthy of such inestimable good fortune. I then turn my mind to this or that means by which to afford you some trifling pleasure. Would it – I then ask myself – give you pleasure to hear good news of my own prosperity and that of my cause? Time and again this question throws me back upon myself, and it requires the expenditure of all my reserves of strength to remain equal to the extraordinary exertions which I must necessarily undergo if I am not to abandon my work, which is as much as to say, if I am not to abandon life itself. What really consumes me in my present situation is the fact that I often have to cancel – nay, often have to deny – these difficulties which it causes me such pain to surmount: there is nothing that people are more eager to descry than an admission on my part that these difficulties exist, for then they may hold out both me and my whole enterprise as a foolhardy venture. This is the support that my fellow men give me! I

---

1 The draft originally read "Your Highness's humble and deeply devoted servant". Bismarck did not acknowledge the letter.

should long ago have turned my back on them if, on the other hand, I had not received such elevating support from a quarter where I had scarcely expected it: hopes now rest upon me which I cannot simply reject with a gesture of cold contempt. But the circles in which this support has been shown me are themselves without real power: the activities of these societies move me, it is true, and place me under an obligation, but their efforts are incapable of raising sufficient funds for me and my enterprise. The princes have shown themselves wholly dismissive, or else their help is sparing to a degree. The richer aristocracy no longer has a soul that is German, and they squander their money on Jewish and Jesuit enterprises. And our stock-market millionaires will have nothing to do with me, unless I transfer my enterprise to Berlin or Vienna, in which case up to a million gulden could be placed at my disposal. The only really effective support has proved to be the untiring efforts of two influentially placed women, the wife of Minister von Schleinitz in Berlin, and Countess Dönhoff (a Neapolitan princess by birth) in Vienna. These two women drew up subscription lists among their own circles of friends, and it is these, almost without exception, which have placed me in the position of being able to keep the enterprise going; but the fact that the Sultan and Khedive of Egypt have had to be enlisted for their support was certainly bound to strike me as curious. However, when it came to carrying out the undertaking in practical terms, I found my chief support in the extraordinary co-operation of the local mayor Herr *Muncker*, and, above all, of the incomparably capable banker Friedrich *Feustel*, whom I have appointed to my committee of management, and to whose honesty and well-tried experience the material supervision and control of the whole undertaking have been entrusted. The paucity of means placed at our disposal did not permit us to begin the building work last year with the energy necessary to expedite it once the workforce could be increased when funds became plentiful. This year alone we could not have brought the building work to the point we still expect to have reached by the autumn if I myself had not set out last winter and, at the cost of personal sacrifices of every description, arranged several concerts in the larger cities[1] which brought in the additional sum of some 40,000 fl. needed for our wholly inadequate building fund. But I cannot continue on this course without wearing myself out prematurely. In these circumstances we are unable to commission the stage equipment and machinery, or to construct the scenery, without raising a loan. My extremely cautious and conscientious friend *Feustel* sees nothing worrying in this, because he recognizes that the announcement that my great undertaking is to take place has already aroused the most wide-reaching interest, and that this will assure the performances an unusually large influx of visitors once

1 Wagner conducted concerts in Hamburg (21 and 23 January), Berlin (4 February), and Cologne (24 April 1873).

they finally do take place. He is not in the least concerned that numerous, not to say over-numerous, applications from intending visitors, at every price moreover, will only be received in the year of the performances themselves; indeed, he even thinks it a good idea to consider increasing the number of seats in the theatre. This optimistic prospect is based not on mere assumptions, but rather on declarations of intent that we have already received from America, for ex., but also from Russia and North Germany, and according to which the people concerned have declared their commitment to applying when the time comes, and of not being deterred by the price. Our most important concern therefore appears to be to keep all of our preparations going without interruption. In this regard our initial consideration must be for the stage technician and scene painter: in view of the long delays in completing the shell of the building, delays exacerbated, moreover, by great local difficulties (including the need to construct a canal), they have had to declare themselves unable to do any preliminary work this year, although these preparations are absolutely indispensable if their work on the production proper is to be completed in time for the performances to take place next year. We had to admit that they were perfectly right, the more so because, in the case of our excellent technician Karl Brandt from Darmstadt, it is a question of entirely new inventions and the careful testing of his innovations. And so, we had to accept this, and postpone the performances for a year, until 1875.[1] Accordingly, next year, 1874, the stage machinery and scenery will be taken in hand and tested; at the same time the singers whom I have chosen will visit me individually in the course of the summer, in order to learn their parts in the first place from the purely musical aspect. On the first of June 1875 everyone involved in the production will then assemble here and spend two months rehearsing every day with the stage machinery, scenery and orchestra, in order to prepare for three complete performances in the month of August.

Only on the basis of these arrangements is there any possibility of our realizing the project in practical terms. But even this is possible only if we start work on the stage equipment late this autumn, and commission both stage machinery and scenery on a fixed contractual tender. In view of the fact that the additional contributions to our funds have almost dried up, more especially during the summer months, and are scarcely sufficient to complete the shell of the building, we are obliged therefore, as already mentioned, to borrow capital which we shall pay back from the Patrons' moneys that are still to come in, and on which we are paying interest out of certain surpluses that have been made possible out of our savings – and all this if we are to stick even to 1875. Herr *Feustel* is of the opinion that there will be no question of any difficulties if we raise a loan, as long as a substantial, but merely

---

1 All these arrangements were subsequently delayed by a further twelve months.

formal, guarantee can be obtained, since our enterprise already represents a demonstrable capital expenditure of 100,000 thalers. Accordingly, my managers cherish the wish that a highly placed patron might be pleased to grant us this formal guarantee, which, as I say, is only of moral, but by no means material, significance.

In the circumstances, therefore, I venture to entreat Your Majesty, as my only true patron and tireless benefactor, to send your Court Secretary, Court Councillor Düfflipp, to Bayreuth, in order that he might then be in a position to scrutinize everything that relates to my great undertaking and, at the same time, gain a precise insight into the strictly businesslike nature of a concern which is entrusted to my committee of management.

It is solely the exceedingly kind exhortation which my exalted protector recently asked Court Councillor Düfflipp to convey to me, and the infinitely salutary assurances with which he was able to accompany that exhortation which encourage me to make this entreaty, just as they have laid me under an obligation to submit to my gracious patron the detailed report included herewith.[1]

I said at the outset that what was so wearing about my present situation is that I have to conceal, and even deny, the difficulties which it involves. Until now I thought I was similarly obliged to show the selfsame reserve towards my exalted friend, for it is his forbearance on which I must make the greatest claim. When I first informed a number of friends of this plan of mine, they expressed the opinion that it must be possible to obtain the sum which I needed in a short space of time, whereupon I promised in turn to bring about the performances within that same space of time, namely as soon as the entire sum that I needed had been placed at my disposal. The extraordinary nature of our undertaking has now had to pass through every stage of practical experience: that this experience has proved the success of our undertaking to be perfectly possible in general terms is, in itself, an outcome of the most encouraging significance; but it is equally undeniable that our plan will have to be modified in terms of the timing of the performances. When the nature of this experience is closely considered, it is clear that our first concern must be to bring forward the timing of the promised performances: for in the light of these same experiences, no one who takes account, for ex., of the unprecedented income brought in by the few concerts which I arranged for the benefit of our enterprise, doubts for a moment but that support for them, and their success, will not amply cover all our costs.

Thus do I turn to my great friend, whose work I myself have now uniquely become, and I do so above all with the heartfelt request for a further extension of his heavenly *forbearance*!

---

1 In reply to this letter Düfflipp wrote to Wagner on 24 September 1873 reminding him of his earlier refusal to accept any further financial support from the King.

Everything else will, and must, take care of itself, as long as I can remain alive and healthy, and, above all, maintain my own forbearance. –

Indeed, my exalted friend, I too have often had serious thoughts about my "Parzival". It will be the pinnacle of all my achievements. How sweetly familiar is the feeling that overcomes me when I think that you yourself share directly in the knowledge of this profound secret, that you are its co-creator! It is as though I am inspired to write this work in order to preserve the world's profoundest secret, the truest Christian faith, nay, to awaken that faith anew. And for the sake of this immense task that it is reserved for me to accomplish, I have felt obliged to use my Nibelung drama to build a Castle of the Grail devoted to art, far removed from the common byways of human activity: for only there, in Monsalvat, can the longed-for deed be revealed to the people, to those who are initiated into its rites, not in those places where God may not show Himself beside the idols of day without His being blasphemed.

Thus, my glorious King, do I proclaim the thoughts that I cherish for our "Parzival"! –

And now I would ask only that you be kind enough to forgive me this long and, in the main, most tiresome letter! It is your kindness, and the heartfelt depth of your sympathy which time and again encourage me to believe that I myself must after all be one of the elect!

With the humblest of greetings my loyal and noble wife prostrates herself at your feet: and with the most abundant prayers for your safe keeping we both gaze up at you in gratitude.

In deepest reverence, I remain unto death my sublime friend's own true one.

Uniquely yours,
Richard Wagner.

Königsbriefe III, 18–22.

420. KING LUDWIG II OF BAVARIA, HOHENSCHWANGAU

Bayreuth, 9 January 1874

My exalted lord and royal benefactor,

By a curious coincidence I have just received word of a distressing incident: Your Majesty will forgive the agitation which I am bound to feel in bringing this matter before its rightful tribunal!

It has been reported to me that Professor F. Dahn of Königsberg has put it about that, upon the strength of a letter which I wrote to him at the time, he approached Your Majesty, my royal benefactor, complaining of my refusal to fulfil my sovereign liege's wish and complaining, moreover, in terms that were probably not to my own advantage. I recall that some considerable time ago F. Dahn sent me a volume of his poems (which I did not have time to read), including an Ode to Your Majesty; with regard to this Ode, he assured me of his belief that my royal benefactor would look upon it most favourably if I were to set the poem to music. I can well understand that F. Dahn might be keen to have one of his poems set to music by me (a man who has so far set only his own poems to music); but that Your Majesty might have expressed the wish to see it set to music struck me as being one of those boasts which I have encountered so often in the past on the part of literary figures and people in general who are unaware of my true situation, with the result that, for the sake of my peace of mind, I have been obliged to accustom myself to ignoring such invitations. Perhaps I judged wrongly in this instance; had I felt any doubt in the matter, however, I should have entreated Your Majesty to allow me to write my own verses for any music that may have been desired of me, since it would have been quite impossible to use the classical metre which Dahn had employed by forcing it artificially upon the German language and to use it for the only kind of music I can write.

If F. Dahn is right and if, by communicating my refusal to Your Majesty, he has really caused you to feel displeasure at me, I should of course regard it as a great misfortune but one which I had earned completely unwittingly, and on this point it would be of inestimable value to me to be reassured by some favourable sign from my royal benefactor. –

At the same time I see myself constrained to inform Your Majesty that, in consequence of your sovereign decisions that have recently reached me,[1] I have had to abandon the projected performances of the Nibelung's Ring; since I am prevented at the present time from issuing instructions for work to begin on the stage machinery and scenery, it is no longer possible to perform the work in 1875, so that in all conscience I can even less reasonably announce a performance for any subsequent year. I shall content myself therefore with having built the theatre with the help of my friends, and with knowing that my work shall one day be performed there for the very first time; and I may relieve my sorrow with the thought that for me, too, the performances had lost all significance since they were incapable of arousing further interest in my royal benefactor, for whose fame and enjoyment I had chiefly desired to summon them into existence.[2]

From the bottom of my heart I repeat the expression of gratitude and most respectful good wishes which I asked Court Councillor Düfflipp to convey in

1 Düfflipp had telegraphed Wagner on 6 January, announcing that Ludwig had refused to underwrite the Bayreuth Festival.
2 Ludwig wrote to Wagner on 25 January 1874, "No, no and *no* again! it shall not end like this! Help must be forthcoming! Our plan must not fail. Parcival knows his calling and will do all that it lies in his power to do" (Königsbriefe III,29).

person to my royal benefactor at the turn of the year. With the most implicit devotion I remain unto death Your Majesty's

Most humble servant
Richard Wagner

Königsbriefe III,27–8.

421. EMIL HECKEL, MANNHEIM   Bayreuth, 19 January 1874

My dear and respected friend,

It is only fitting that I should first address myself to you, the most active and efficient founder and supporter of a society intended to promote my proposed stage festival, now that it is a question of taking a decisive step which may more appropriately be carried out by some sympathetic and well-tried friend of my enterprise than by me myself, who must regard this undertaking as peculiarly his. Powerful assistance has now become necessary if the work that has been begun is to be brought to a swift conclusion; and a swift conclusion is of the essence, because the enterprise depends upon my own soundness of bodily health. In the space of two years we have reached the point where the more immediate friends of my art have raised the sum of one hundred thousand thalers: with this money we have laid a permanent foundation for the entire undertaking by erecting a festival theatre whose structural solidity will ensure that it remains usable for time beyond telling. But now, at the very moment when specific commissions would need to be signed for work to begin on the stage machinery and scenery, the resources of the undertaking's existing supporters have come to an end, progress is necessarily delayed, and the enterprise will enter a critical phase unless some other authority come to our aid in a decisive fashion. –

My local committee of management is of the opinion that the undertaking must be supported at all costs, to the point where it is finally about to be realized, and that we may confidently expect to cover the expenses that have been incurred out of proceeds from the support that will come pouring in for so extraordinary an artistic event. In this sense all that we should have needed was a sufficient guarantee to enable us to raise the necessary loans and ensure the means whereby to continue the work that is already begun. In order to secure such a guarantee I recently approached my exalted benefactor, the King of Bavaria, but for reasons that remain unclear to me His Majesty turned down my request.

You know that we have recently begun to turn to particularly wealthy and well-disposed friends in our search for such a guarantee. But even if help, however fleeting, were to come from this quarter, I am now resolved to seek our salvation in so important a matter in the one place which can impart to it the only truly appropriate dignity.

I am thinking here of the "Reich", although it cannot of course have remained unknown to you that until now I have always recoiled from the thought of seeing my enterprise and the act of cultural volition that lies behind it debated by the members of the Reichstag, since there is not a single man among them whom I thought capable of offering a convincing explanation of the true significance of this undertaking, or of defending it in the face of the shameless disparagement to which it has been subjected by a press which, whether great or small, is as powerful as it is ignorant. – On the contrary, I have now had the idea of offering our victorious Emperor the first performances of this work of mine as a quinquennial celebration to mark the glorious peace concluded with France in 1871. – It would be a question here of comparing my own Nibelung drama – which I should perform along entirely novel lines in a way that matched the uniqueness of the German character – with the festival performances with which, in accord with a less than laudable custom, such sublime occasions are usually celebrated: I should have thought that acceptance of my offer would at the same time express recognition of an important concept in German culture. – But it cannot be my place to hold forth on this subject in a personal and forceful attempt to persuade; rather must I seek advocates among the friends of my art and the patrons of the enterprise, advocates who, armed with the detailed instructions which I myself have drawn up as a guide, would be able to shed the necessary light on the significance of my project, and do so, moreover, in the quarter that matters.

In this context, as in others, it is a source of great encouragement to be able to choose you, my dear and honoured friend, as chief advocate with your own reigning prince, the Grand Duke of Baden, a gentleman for whom I have the highest respect. It was this paragon of German princes who received me and my artistic enterprises with truly enlightened kindness when, after a long period of exile, I first set foot on German soil again in 1861. Since that time I have had no reason to think that the magnanimous sentiments that greeted me then might have grown any cooler, and I believe therefore that you will find His Royal Highness well-prepared and seriously disposed if you approach him now with a request that he negotiate decisive help along the lines already indicated, and do so, moreover, in the name of all who have already lent my undertaking their energetic support, and among whom it gives me particular pleasure to number His Royal Highness himself.

It would not be appropriate for me to indicate more detailed measures which the Grand Duke might adopt in pursuance of this course, in the event that he decides in its favour, since it goes without saying that the co-operation of His Imperial and Royal Highness the Crown Prince of Germany[1] must immediately strike my illustrious patron as the most effective course of action for him to adopt. I should venture only to suggest that the Grand Dukes of Saxe-Weimar and Mecklenburg, together with the Duke of Dessau, all of whom have already taken a personal interest in my enterprise, would presumably be inclined to collaborate here.

If I now wished to describe in detail what I imagine will be the crowning achievement of all my efforts and desires on behalf of so mighty an undertaking, it would be to secure by this means a commission from the German Emperor, under the terms of which I would be granted support in the sum of one hundred thousand thalers, i.e. one third of the total cost, in return for which I would present three complete performances of my stage festival "The Ring of the Nibelung" in the festival theatre specially built for this purpose in Bayreuth, and present them, moreover, during the summer of 1876 as part of the first quinquennial celebrations of the peace that was concluded with France.

Since it ought to be a simple matter for you to indicate in plain figures how many seats the persons concerned would be entitled to in consequence of this, basing your calculations on previous Patrons' entitlements, I need not go into further details in this letter concerning the business aspect of the matter, but would beg you only, in conjunction with our valued friends in Mannheim, to take the first step towards realizing the idea that I have in mind, an idea which I freely admit originated with you.

In respectful friendship, I am

Your devoted servant
Richard Wagner.

Bayreuther Briefe I, 152–6.

422. EMIL HECKEL, MANNHEIM   Bayreuth, 5 March 1874

Dear friend,

The King's signature has just arrived. It guarantees a credit of 100,000 thalers from his own privy purse, and is intended to cover the costs of stage equipment, scenery and gas lighting: during the period of the loan all moneys received from our patrons are to be credited to the royal exchequer until such time as all advances are repaid, and during this period the said acquisitions are to remain the property of the Royal Court Secretariat.

These are the terms of the agreement.

---

1 Friedrich Wilhelm (later Friedrich III). The Grand Duke of Baden, approached by Heckel on the matter, declined to importune his sovereign.

You will see from this that we are simply enabled to go ahead, but that we have not received any additional funds, and therefore remain, as before, dependent upon the support of the general public if the whole undertaking is still to be made possible.

I would beg you therefore to proceed with caution and circumspection in all your announcements and public statements in pursuance of the following two aims:

1. To represent this new facility as a guarantee that the enterprise will take place.

2. Not make people think that nothing more needs to be done now.

We consider it best, therefore, simply to report the facts, namely:

That fixed contracts with the painter Hoffmann in Vienna and the Court Theatre technician Brandt have already been signed, enabling them to produce the scenery and stage equipment as soon as possible.

I think this will be sufficient to allay all fears. I shall now write to my chosen singers in much the same vein, and also issue instructions with regard to the orchestra, all of which will shortly give a different complexion to the affair.

It would please me all the more, my dear friend, if I knew that all this had brought you genuine pleasure, since I, alas, get little enjoyment from this news, so wearied and careworn am I by all that has happened that the outcome leaves me pretty cold, and mindful only of my duties.

Sincerest good wishes to you all from all of us here!

Yours,
Richard Wagner.

Bayreuther Briefe I, 160–2.

423. FRIEDRICH FEUSTEL and THEODOR MUNCKER, BAYREUTH

Bayreuth, 7 March 1874

Gentlemen and friends,

It will always remain an impossibility for me to give adequate expression to my gratitude and recognition of the services you have rendered me in the undertaking that I have instituted. This is the first point that saddens me, now that I have to respond to today's communication from you!

The second is that I am bound to recognize how completely impossible it is for me to discharge my deeply-felt debt by fulfilling your wish to see the performances take place next year.

I thought I had already expressed myself quite clearly enough on this point when we last met, and therefore will only repeat that, the more seriously I feel obliged to contemplate the matter closely, the more I am able to estimate the damage that has been caused by the delay in reaching agreement on a financial guarantee. As a result I am now out of touch with all those people whom I had had in mind for the festival, and must start all over again in securing their services.

For example, it was impossible for me until now to say to any of the singers: "don't agree to any guest performances this summer, so that you can be available for me", and I shall regard myself as fortunate if I can persuade even a handful of them to make themselves available for a few days this year, in addition to their commitments elsewhere.

Believe me, *it is quite impossible* to present this enormous four-part work, each part of which would require three months' preparation in the largest theatres, in a year from now, which is all the time that is left to me.

This is the first point. The second is your suggestion and wish that I myself should raise the necessary funds by means of my own personal activity. Even assuming that I *might* succeed in raising significant funds by constantly travelling around and giving concerts, it grieves me to have to tell you that I could not endure the strain involved, which is why I have had to provide myself with a conductor to assume these duties for me for the festival performances themselves, just as I had to do in Munich, on an earlier occasion, in order to save my energies. I feel more than either of you, my highly esteemed friends, that the ultimate guarantee for the success of our great undertaking lies in my retaining my physical and mental powers, because there is no one, apart from myself, who can judge the extent of the task that I have set myself here. What is more, my experiments last year in this regard have shown me quite clearly that not one of those attempts at personal intervention produced results commensurate with the effort involved. On the contrary, it became clear to me in the light of those experiences that no amount of preaching in advance of the event can arouse people's interest, but only the fact that so extraordinary an achievement is about to take place – even if that interest be tinged with curiosity – for it is this alone which will finally ensure us the necessary funds. Once it is established that the performances really are feasible, this interest can only be increased by delaying people's curiosity, a device that clever people often use to intensify interest; the rehearsals (with scenery etc.) that will be held in the summer of 1875 will intensify that interest to the point where people begin to grow impatient – which is all to the good, and certainly to our own advantage.

On this point I am clear.

But what remains totally unclear to me is how to persuade myself that it will be possible to invite not only my company but 1500 visitors, including the most fastidious of guests, to come to Bayreuth in the present state of what the town can offer by way of accommodation. This, my highly esteemed friends, is so serious a point that I really must ask you to give me some explanation which might serve to reassure me, for I do not believe it will be possible for you to convince me that the funds which have so far been committed here are of a kind to enable 1000 patrons, most of whom are of aristocratic background, together with 500 free seats, to be accommodated in our hotels and private houses so that their visit to Bayreuth does not turn out to be a disagreeable experience which would make it impossible to repeat the festival in some future year.

I therefore consider it my duty to beg my highly esteemed friends to arrange a meeting as soon as possible to discuss this very important issue; and to judge from all that I imagine to be true with regard to solving this problem, you will find, I am sure, that it is certainly not too soon to start thinking seriously about the matter, if we intend to receive our festival visitors in the summer of 1876 in a manner that befits them, so that they will conceive of no obvious aversion to returning in 1877.

I pray that you may receive this response in a friendly and considerate spirit, and as testimony to one who is deeply serious but at the same time oppressed by cares, for the sake of the belief which I would entreat you most sincerely to impute to my great sense of gratitude towards you.

With the truest respect, I am

Yours,
Richard Wagner

RWA (published with minor errors of transcription in Bayreuther Briefe I, 162–6).

424. MORITZ FÜRSTENAU, DRESDEN   Bayreuth, 12 March 1874

Dear Sir,

Could you find out for me how much – i.e. in terms of money – the Uhlig family estimates my letters to my late friend to be worth? It is of course a matter of no mean importance to me to know that letters of such personal intimacy are being kept as merchandise to be sold to the first bidder who comes along, providing only that he pay the highest price, but I have never before had to make an offer in such a matter, and, in any case, am not so comfortably well-off that I could simply give way to my feelings, since I am burdened with obligations in life of the most disparate kind. This by way of explanation in the matter of this friendly favour which I have to ask of you. I should not like to think of these letters to Uhlig being sold off for monetary gain in any other quarter. Within the family circle it must surely be sufficient for them to have copies to remind them of my dearly departed friend, since these at least give the content; but the same is not true of me and my son, who wants to have what belongs to his father. – I look forward to receiving a friendly reply, and remain, with every good wish,

Your old devoted friend,
Richard Wagner.

Adolph Kohut, Der Meister von Bayreuth (Berlin 1905), 179.

425. FRIEDRICH NIETZSCHE, BASLE   [Bayreuth, 6 April 1874][1]

Dear friend,
Your letter has again caused us a great deal of concern on your behalf. My wife will be writing to you in more detail in a day or so. However, today is a public holiday and I have a free quarter of an hour which – perhaps to your annoyance – I should like to devote to you in order to let you know what we have been saying about you. Amongst other things, I found that I myself never had the sort of male company that you keep in Basle in the evenings: if you are all hypochondriacs, such company is scarcely worth having. But it seems to me that what you young men lack is women: of course, as my old friend Sulzer used to say, it is a question of knowing where to get hold of them without stealing them. But you could of course steal one, if need be. My own view is that you ought to get married, or else write an opera; the one would do you just as much good and harm as the other. But, of the two, I prefer marriage. –
    In the mean time I can recommend you a palliative; but you always fill up your medicine chest in advance so that people cannot offer you their own remedies. For example, we are arranging our house etc.[2] in such a way as to be able to offer you accommodation of a kind that was never offered to me even at times of extreme necessity; we intended you to spend the whole summer holidays with us here. But – no sooner had winter set in than you cautiously announced your decision to spend the summer holidays on an extremely high and remote Swiss mountain peak! Does that not sound like careful parrying of a possible invitation from us? We could be of some help to you: why are you so anxious to scorn that help? – Gersdorf and the rest of the Basle crowd could amuse themselves here. There is plenty going on: I shall be reviewing all my Nibelung troops; the scene painter will be painting the sets, and the stage technician fitting up the stage: and we, too, shall be completely involved with it all. – But – we all know about this and various other oddities concerning our friend Nietzsche! –
    I refuse to say any more on the subject, since it obviously does no good!

1 Dating from Colli/Montinari; incorrectly dated 26 December 1874 by Elisabeth Förster-Nietzsche.
2 Wahnfried, which the Wagners moved into on 28 April 1874.

For God's sake, marry a woman of means! Why does Gersdorf have to have been born a man! Then you should travel, and broaden your mind with all the splendid experiences which make Hillebrand so versatile and (in your eyes!) so enviable, and – write your opera, although it is bound to be scandalously difficult to perform. – Who the devil made you a pedagogue? –

You see the radical mood I am in as a result of reading your letter: but – God knows! – I cannot simply stand by and do nothing. –

Incidentally, Dr Fuchs pleased me by quoting a passage from Overbeck which I found so admirable that I am once more devoting my attention to his essay. –

And by the way: full rehearsals (with orchestra) in Bayreuth in the summer of next year: performances in 1876. Not possible before then. –

I am now taking daily baths, since I couldn't bear the pain in my lower abdomen any longer. You should do likewise! And eat meat! – Sincerest good wishes from

Yours faithfully,
R.W.

Nietzsche-Briefe II,4 654–6.

426. KING LUDWIG II OF BAVARIA, HOHENSCHWANGAU
Bayreuth, 1 October 1874

My heaven-sent, dearly belovèd and adored friend!
My lord and most gracious King,

A ray of light has once more pierced the gloom; a dove has descended to bring new strength to my spiritual powers! Yes, all that is shielded by the power of your holy love is now prospering: may this be the thanks that I owe you! My life is prospering, – my work is prospering, for all the difficulties under which they are both intended to prosper fade away before the power of your love, and turn to a tissue of deception easy to dispel. – My thanks for so gracious an answer to my timorous question whether it might seem worth my while to report on the way things stand with regard to our great undertaking, an undertaking which owes not only its outcome but also its rebirth to your grace alone! Deeply gladdened by your affectionate command, I therefore submit my report in the lines which follow.

My King! Only through your infinite goodness was it possible for me to proceed with the necessary commissions for our stage machinery and scenery at the beginning of the second quarter of this year. Since I was obliged to deal with artists employed out of town, I had to arrange a meeting with them and my committee of management, and it was not possible to do so until the last day of April this year. It was with this meeting, and the attendant consultations, that I consecrated my new house, your magnanimous gift to me; my family and I moved in that very same day, and slept our first night there after concluding the various contracts.[1]

In the course of these discussions it emerged that it would now be impossible to meet the necessary delivery dates by the following year, and that not until 1876 could we fix the dates of the performances with any certainty.[2] With regard to the actual work itself, the following distribution of labour has already taken place:

From the very outset my chief assistant and advisor for the entire practical side of the production has been *Carl Brandt*, a brilliant stage technician from Darmstadt; he helped me find an architect to carry out the extraordinarily difficult building work, but from the very first was at a loss as to whom to suggest as a scenery designer, since what we wanted here was a new style of innovatory design, not merely the traditional kind of set-painting, however skilfully done. A chance encounter led me to the right man. In spite of his never previously having painted a theatre set, the Viennese artist J. *Hoffmann* had designed and painted two series of sets for the opening of the new opera-house in Vienna, namely the "Magic Flute" and the "Freischütz" (which were acknowledged on all sides to be quite outstanding), but since that time he has completely withdrawn from the theatre again. As long ago as the beginning of last year I wrote[3] inviting him to produce designs for all four parts of my work, and he completed and submitted these sketches to me by last autumn. Not only I but all who saw them – including the leading connoisseurs to whom he showed them in Vienna – were utterly enchanted by his work: the most difficult challenge of all, the appearance of Valhalla, the citadel of the gods, in the "Rhinegold", we were bound to admire as a truly inspired stroke of genius. However, the artist has no studio or any other assistants to help in painting scenery; since he would have to create everything specially, we agreed that the sets should be built and painted, under his supervision, by the *Brückner* brothers, scene-painters at the Court Theatre in Coburg, for whom *Brandt* was able to give the best possible references. These people have adequate studios, in addition to which we shall also be placing at their disposal a temporary workshop in the vicinity of the festival theatre where they will be able to prepare the larger back-cloths that cannot be divided into sections. They, too, travelled to Bayreuth for our conference,

1 According to Cosima Wagner's diary, the move took place on 28 April, and the consultations with Hoffmann, Brandt, Otto Brückwald, Feustel, Muncker and the Brückner brothers on 28/29 April 1874.
2 Wagner had informed Feustel and Muncker of this decision of 7 March 1874.
3 See letter [410] of 28 July 1872, pp. 810–11. On 29 September 1874 Cosima had noted in her diary, "Great unpleasantness with the painters Brückner and Hoffmann"; and a week later a meeting took place at which Hoffmann was "confronted with all his sins of presumptuousness, obstinacy, and financial greed" (CT for 7 October 1874). By the 12th he had agreed to renounce his participation and accept a golden handshake of 600 thalers.

and agreements were signed with them and the stage technician Brandt; indeed, the existence of these agreements is perhaps not unknown to you following the deposition of the same with your Royal Court Secretariat. Under the terms of these agreements those sets which, because of their technical complexity, are the most difficult to construct will have to be delivered, ready for use, by the 1st of August next year (1875), while the remaining sections must be in position and fully usable by the 1st of May 1876.

I have accordingly drawn up the following plan for the dramatic and musical aspects of the performance, and shall insist that it be strictly adhered to: the singers whom I shall be choosing in the course of 1874 are to assemble here next year for the whole of July and August, in order to spend the first month rehearsing their parts at the piano, and the second on stage with the most important pieces of scenery, so that they will already be sufficiently familiar with their roles to be able to proceed straightaway the following year to the so-called dress rehearsals. I cannot take on any singers who are unable to make themselves unconditionally available not only for the two months indicated in 1875 but also for the three months of June, July and August 1876. For in 1876 an immediate start will be made on complete final rehearsals for all four evenings; during the first two months I intend rehearsing the company, every day, with orchestra, stage machinery and lighting, and hope to reach the point when the three projected complete performances can then be allowed to go ahead in the month of August. These performances will take place during the second, third, and fourth weeks of the month, beginning each Saturday with the prelude: "The Rhinegold" and continuing with the three principal works on each of the following days. Each performance shall begin at 4 o'clock in the afternoon: the second act will follow at 6, and the third at 8, so that between each of the acts there will be a substantial interval which will allow the audience time to walk in the gardens surrounding the theatre, and partake of refreshments in the open air amid such delightful surroundings, so that, at a signal from trombones on the roof of the theatre, they may then reassemble in the auditorium, fully refreshed and as receptive as they were for the first act. I think that the sunset before the last act will induce a particularly elevated mood.

This, then, is a general outline of the performance schedule. What I was able to do last summer in furtherance of this plan was to invite the singers, male and female, to visit me in Bayreuth, according to whether their own commitments allowed them to do so, in order that I might make their closer acquaintance. It was gratifying to discover that every one of them was glad to come; the more famous artists drew my attention to others whom I did not know but whom in turn they persuaded to visit me. In this way I believe that Germany's best dramatic singers have all been introduced to me; I was obliged to ignore only those who did not have sufficient leave at their disposal for the coming years: but all of them declared that they regarded their collaboration solely as a question of honour and would not look for profit or compensation for guest appearances & the like. In this way I have managed to cast almost all the parts in the work with the very best singers, and in doing so was able to take account not only of their vocal and dramatic abilities, but more especially their physical appearance. My gods, giants and heroes are all conspicuously tall, so that whenever one of these giants arrived at the local station, the cry would go up: "here's another Nibelung!". On the other hand, I was fortunate in finding a particularly suitable performer for the uncommonly difficult role of the passionately wild-tempered Alberich: the singer *Hill* from Schwerin will be absolutely outstanding as Mime's brother not only in the dramatic sense but also because of his relatively compact appearance. For *Mime*, on the other hand, I have turned to *Schlosser*, a member of the Munich Opera and my well-tried "David" in the "Mastersingers". The whole tremendous role of *Wotan* has already been performed by *Betz* to my complete satisfaction: *Hagen* will be given an incomparable performance by *Scaria* from Vienna.[1] *Niemann*, who first placed himself at my unquestioning disposal some years ago when he showed a degree of remorse that was truly touching, will be taking the part of *Siegmund*, a role that could have been written for him. A *Siegfried* is not to be found in any of our existing theatres; I shall have to invent one, but in time of greatest need my guardian angel has provided me with the raw material that I need to do so. A young doctor of laws in Pest, one Herr *Glatz*, who has just completed his studies, had himself introduced to me last winter by my loyal friend *Hans Richter*. This handsome young man, whom, because of his appearance, the townsfolk of Bayreuth almost took to be His Majesty the King of Bavaria himself, is the owner of one of the most powerful and noble tenor voices I have ever heard: he is an accomplished equestrian, swordsman and dancer, and also of outstanding intellectual and, more especially, musical training, and is so well-to-do that he is resolved never to set foot in a theatre but to place himself solely at the disposal of my festival. He will be arriving in Bayreuth next month to devote himself uninterruptedly to my instruction and training until the time when the performances themselves take place.[2]

I encountered great difficulties with the women's roles, until the greatest difficulty of all was finally surmounted when friends drew my attention to Frau *Materna* in Vienna, whom I have cast for the part of *Brünnhilde*. She is the only woman with the voice for this tremendous part; in addition she is fiery by nature, heroic in stature and has uncommonly eloquent features, but most of all she is of truly childlike devotion to me and my cause. – As for *Sieglinde*, I have not yet made up my mind, although several capable singers

1 But see letter [436], p. 854, note 3.
2 In his letter to Ludwig of 6 April 1875, Wagner noted merely that "the young man who had offered to sing the part of Siegfried has proved to be utterly incompetent" (Königsbriefe III, 58). The part was finally given to Georg Unger.

have already applied for the part. I shall leave this question in the air for the time being, since I want to see how my relations with the famous Swedish soprano *Nielson*[1] turn out; she has offered me her services through her business manager, the excellent impresario Ullmann, intimating that she would receive 5000 francs a performance from him but that she would sing for me without a fee. She is said to be a singer of the finest quality, significantly superior to the famous soprano *Jenny Lind*, and an enthusiastic admirer of my music. But she has not so far sung in German, and must first learn to do so; in addition her husband is French and is afraid that his wife would never again be allowed to sing in Paris if she had taken part in these festival performances in Germany. And so I am leaving this piece of casting undecided for the moment. But *Fricka* has already found a most admirable exponent in Frau *Sadler-Grün* from Coburg; a Frl. *Oppenheimer* from Frankfurt, a stately and most imposing woman, will sing the part of "Erda", a role of exceptional importance, especially in the third act of "Siegfried".[2] The difficult "Rhine-daughters" will be taken by the two *Lehmann* sisters (leading sopranos in Berlin and Cologne) and by the Berlin contralto *Lammert*: I can rely on the courage and capability of these three singers, whom I shall probably also cast as the "Norns";[3] they will be returning next year to practise the use of their swimming machines. *Gutrune* and *Holda*[4] will be excellently taken by two sisters by the name of *Pauli* (from Dessau and Hanover); and even the voice of the woodbird has found a wholly suitable instrument in a certain Frl. König[5] from Mannheim. All these ladies will also have to appear as "Valkyries" so that I shall be dealing here not with nervous choristers but only with really dramatic singers.

For the orchestra I was forced to limit myself first and foremost to those Court Theatres which suspend their performances for three whole months of the summer and which therefore allow their musicians the necessary leave of absence as a matter of course. I made the relevant enquiries and found these theatres to be the ones at Darmstadt, Karlsruhe, Coburg, Brunswick and Schwerin, together with Meiningen. Of the orchestras of these six theatres I have singled out only the very best musicians in every regard, and plan to build up my orchestra around this nucleus. Kapellmeister *Levi* recently enquired of me why I had not also approached the Royal Court Theatre in Munich: as the reason for this omission I was able to draw his attention to the fact just mentioned, that I have to take account of the musicians' impera-

1 Christine Nilsson [*sic*]. The part of Sieglinde was sung by Josephine Schefsky at the first Festival.
2 Erda was sung by Luise Jaide.
3 The Norns were sung by Friederike Sadler-Grün, Luise Jaide and Josephine Schefsky.
4 i.e. Freia. These two roles were taken by Mathilde Weckerlin and Marie Haupt.
5 The Woodbird was sung by Lilli Lehmann (not Marie Haupt as stated by Newman, *Life* IV, 478).

tive need to take leave of absence, so that there could naturally be no question of my appealing to them: at the same time I assured him that nothing would give me greater pleasure than for him to send me some capable artists from Munich.[1] – However, I have appointed the famous violin virtuoso *Wilhelmy* as leader of the orchestra, after he had begged this formal appointment from me as a special honour: he will be bringing some especially capable violinists from among his pupils. But in order that their remuneration shall not tax my Patrons unduly, I have preferred musicians with a fixed appointment who will continue to draw their salaries during their leave of absence and to whom we shall therefore have to pay only travel and accommodation expenses. My orchestra, moreover, shall be a model for others to emulate: six excellent harpists in the orchestra and one on the stage have already pledged their services. –

I am now overcome by anxiety lest I may have already unduly wearied my gracious lord by rehearsing all the foregoing details in fulfilment of his affectionate order? – But I tell myself: – *He* ordered it so, and so I shall continue! – To begin with a report on the present state of our great undertaking, I may assure my exalted benefactor that his magnanimous example appears in every way to have had an encouraging effect: not that he has found imitators, – this does not seem to have occurred to our German princes! – , but in consequence of the inescapable realization that, contrary to rumour, my sovereign protector is not averse to my undertaking and, indeed, is uniquely resolved to see it realized: people's confidence in its actually taking place had been maliciously undermined, but has now reasserted itself, and my (few!) active friends have met with better success in soliciting support. When approached by a committee founded in Berlin by my most excellent benefactress Frau von Schleinitz, the most eminent German painters declared their readiness to provide paintings and drawings to be auctioned on behalf of the Bayreuth enterprise: the sale will probably take place in November, and all the signs are that the proceeds will be not inconsiderable.[2] Moreover, the number of patrons is imperceptibly increasing, more especially thanks to a quite unique woman, the young Countess Dönhoff, a Neapolitan Princess Campo Reale by birth, so that, under these auspices, the spirits of my much tormented and anxious committee of management are again beginning to rise, although our gaze remains chiefly fixed, as before, upon the magnanimous attitude of our sovereign patron himself. For it is certain that the remaining costs of the enterprise will ultimately be recovered only once the performances have finally been announced and a tremendous sense of curiosity has been aroused in the more well-to-do members of our audience, so that our essential

1 Wagner had written to Levi on 28 August 1874. According to his letter to August Wilhelmj of 4 January 1875, Munich was "reckoning on sending a splendid contingent" (Bayreuther Briefe II,79).
2 The sale brought in 10,000 thalers (see CT for 13 December 1874).

worry now is simply whether we can hold out until then. In this sense, our sovereign patron would offer us the best possible reassurance if he were to empower us to make use, as is indispensably necessary, of the Patrons' moneys that are now being received, so that we can pay for urgent site-work and other work necessary to secure the building. Fortunately, we have no expenses at present in respect of the artists themselves, and (in view of the good will of all concerned) will probably have very few expenses at all here; and the auditorium need not be decorated until all other work is completed; but we shall fall into highly embarrassing arrears with regard to the work that I have just indicated as necessary, if, out of the moneys that are now trickling in from our Patrons, we were now to have to pay back the advance which you so magnanimously granted us, instead of using it for this other work which is now so necessary. It goes without saying that a precise record of all such expenditure will be submitted to your Court Secretariat until such time as the advance itself has been repaid.[1]

Forgive me, my most gracious friend, for having embarked upon so arid a digression! But all that is beautiful on this earth of ours exists only by virtue of its struggle with the inert mass of practical interests! You above all, oh! my incomparable prince!, know with what daemons I have wrestled all my life in order to find space in this leaden world for so aetherial an ideal as mine. The ideal creations that I fashion are infinitely more delicate and finely woven than people demand or require, which is no doubt why I must fight all the more fiercely with material brutality. – But God has made me the kind of man to survive this struggle, – and whenever I have threatened to go under, He sent me His angel! – And now permit me to answer your affectionate question concerning – my life! –

You want to know how I divide up my day? Splendid! For here lies the decision as to the direction that is to be taken by the life which these days fill. In order to characterize my day, I must first describe the aim of my present life: it is to wrest from the daemon of all earthly existence the greatest possible portion of peace and serenity of mind, in order to be able to perform all the tasks allotted to me in the service of the guardian spirit of a world in need of redemption. In view of the way that my life has turned out, I have only a single major regret, namely that I am not ten or fifteen years younger than I am; so much has come to me so late! Of course, I still see a long and active life ahead of me, for there is no sign of any weakness in my vital powers, and all my friends regard me as a marvel in this respect. But I feel as though I am still the same man today as I was ten or fifteen years ago, and this period has now been lost to me since I can no longer exploit it in

1 Ludwig declined to accede to this request, not least because it contravened Article III of the agreement of 20 February 1874, whereby the income from the Patrons was to be paid directly into the royal exchequer. Not until 27 September 1875 was this condition relaxed.

the blissful state I now have reached: in other words, even assuming that I may still be granted a long and creative life, I wish I could enrich it with a further ten or fifteen years. For fate has granted me *a son* after thirty years of sterile marriage. What it means to me to be able to say: I have a son – is indescribable! Like Siegfried he came into the world as destiny's storm raged around him. But he is just as radiantly calm and sunny: and yet, more especially in the expression in his eyes, he resembles the infant Jesus of the Sistine Madonna. It is impossible for this son of mine to remain insignificant. But I am bound to smile when people see me walking with the boy at my side and claim that it is I myself whom they can see walking beside me as a boy. – Of course, my life has acquired a totally new significance: everything I possess, all thought of domicile, citizenship and wealth has now acquired a sense which it never had before. And now I have a wise woman as my wife who orders, enlivens and spiritualizes all this for me. She has relieved the pressure of daily life, and keeps watch over my tranquillity. Her only care is when she becomes aware that not all life's disturbances can be kept at bay, and that it is inevitable that I should often hurl myself into a veritable storm of excitement and exertions. So it was last summer when there was nothing for it but for me to perform what are often tremendous scenes with the most passionate emphasis for each of the singers concerned: in doing so, of course, I became so utterly exhausted that I was finally forced to welcome each interruption as a form of deliverance. Similar, and often superhuman, exertions to which I have often subjected myself for the sake of my calling are no doubt another reason for the constant pains that rack my body, frequently robbing me of my sleep, and obliging me to spend all my time engaged in the search for a cure. This summer was the first occasion I was able to use "my" property for this purpose. "My" garden and "my" house, with its well-equipped bath, provided admirable service in helping me take care of my health. This "property" of mine, as I am able to call it thanks to your act of kindness, will also tell you, if I describe it to you, the daily routine that I follow here. The space of an average, decent-sized dwelling house with an elevated ground floor and a single upper storey has been divided up in such a way as to reduce to a minimum the height of the walls in the first-floor family living-room and to fix the height of the walls of the ground-floor living-room so that, by bringing all the side-rooms together as small guest-bedrooms, I was able to create a large salon which is a source of amazement for all my visitors. Having bathed and attended to my toilet in the small living quarters on the upper floor, I take breakfast with my wife and then go downstairs to the salon at about 10 o'clock. This room holds all my possessions: the panelling around the walls contains my collection of books; our paintings are hung above them, low cupboards around the room contain all our papers and documents; the grand piano is over there, and over here is my large desk with a beautiful Bayreuth marble top; opposite it is a smaller desk for Cosima;

and over there is a large table for portfolios with all our presents and keepsakes, with comfortable chairs around it for receiving our numerous visitors;
the whole room is lit by a bay overlooking the garden. It is here that I work,
as long as I am not prevented by business from doing so. At 1 o'clock the
bell rings for our midday meal; and the door to the "hall" is opened. This
room – which is universally admired – owes its existence to the circumstances
that we did not need a wide staircase leading up to the first-floor rooms,
since visitors never enter these rooms; as a result we were able to move the
narrower staircase, which is all that we need, into a very small projecture
overlooking the street, and use the space intended for a larger stairwell as a
hall that runs the entire height of the house and is lit by a fanlight in the
roof, while at first-floor level there is a balcony leading to the family quarters:
marble is the dominant feature here, i.e. the six statues by Zumbusch which
my gracious benefactor once presented to me, together with marble busts of
my wife and myself: the one of my wife was commissioned from an old friend
in Dresden by the name of Kietz, and has turned out a great success, while
the one of me was made for Cosima by Zumbusch from the model which
you yourself ordered. Beneath the balcony runs a frieze on a gold background
with a Scandinavian snake motif and incorporating Echter's paintings to the
Ring of the Nibelung, the very same ones which my exalted friend once had
copied for me from the frescoes in the Residenz passageway.[1] It is through
this hall that I now pass with Cosima to the modest dining-room where I find
the children around the family table, and where, after they have all been
properly hugged, we take our meal together. It is here that the mood of the day
is decided. Unless serious illness or ill-humour brought about by unpleasant
business has gained the upper hand, a family meal with the children is
generally a source of cheerful high spirits. It is an infinitely salutary feeling
to watch the children of my poor friend Bülow, to whom they were often
little more than a burden, flourishing under their mother's most solicitous
cares, as splendidly as their individual talents allow. My son is adored by all
the other children: they have ear only for his witty and inspired remarks with
which he keeps the little gathering in a state of almost constant amusement.
Nor does this generally fail to have its due effect on me, a glance of deepest
gratitude at his mother then brings the happy meal to an end, after which I
take coffee in the garden, glance through the Bayreuth Tageblatt (the only
newspaper which I allow in the house and which I still read), and generally
discuss with Cosima some stimulating theme on the subject of art, philosophy
or life. After that I have a short rest, and then I glance into the large salon
again to see if any post or anything else has arrived. I am lucky if I do not
find bad news, but only poems sent in for me to set to music, treatises on
the philosophy of art which I am asked to forward to the King of Bavaria,

1 See letter [381], pp. 751–2.

offers of theatrical costumes and knights' armour for the Nibelung theatre, or, most frequently of all, requests for my autograph from English and American music lovers: for, out of sheer necessity, I have made it a rule never, ever to reply to any of these. All other correspondence is dealt with by my dear wife, after she has agreed with me what she is to say, something which, in the majority of cases, is not even necessary. If all is in order, I may now be able to continue the work I had begun in the morning, and work on the instrumentation of perhaps another page of my score. I then go out for a walk, or, if the landlord of the "Sonne" – the only man who hires out carriages hereabouts – has a carriage available, I take the children to the "Eremitage" or "Fantaisie", where what the children call "expeditions of discovery" are organized in the woods. But I often only visit the festival theatre on the charming hill overlooking the town, a place which I had to avoid for a longish period last summer because it was continually being visited by so many strangers that I was forced to keep out of the way. I then take pleasure in the affection shown me by the people of Bayreuth, an affection expressed in all manner of ways since they all recognize what a great commotion my undertaking has caused in the town. I am assured that the strangers who came to visit the theatre this summer could be numbered in their thousands, and that often as many as four or five hundred of them visited the future festival building in the space of a day. – Then evening comes, and with it a simple meal with the children at 7 o'clock. At 8 I withdraw to the salon with Cosima, where we regularly take down a book to read, unless my frequent visitors have been given permission to call on us, in which case conversation and music-making are the order of the day. These soirées are also seen as compensation for the self-sacrificial work which several extremely capable young musicians have already taken upon themselves by copying out the music that we need for the performances. Parcels intended for them are already arriving addressed to: "Nibelung Chancellery in Bayreuth". There are currently four of them: a Saxon, Zumpe, who has already been a Kapellmeister, a Hungarian,[1] a Russian[2] and finally – would you believe it! – a Macedonian.[3] I am also training the four of them to be capable of conducting my work in the future by insisting that they help me in everything now. I then invite these apprentices of mine to make music for us of an evening, and they claim to have learned far more here than in any expensively maintained conservatoire or music school. – This summer, moreover, has brought me so many visits from acquaintances both old and new that it could easily have occurred to me to declare Bayreuth the very centre of the world. At present these visitors, and more especially the citizens of Bayreuth, derive their greatest satisfaction

1 Anton Seidl.
2 Joseph Rubinstein.
3 Demetrius Lalas.

from seeing scaffolding against the front wall of my house, facing the street, since they assume, quite rightly, that "something" is to be added where a blank and windowless wall had previously caused them such keen annoyance.*) In fact, my wife had the excellent idea of having a "scrafito" made by a friend of ours from Weimar, a relatively young painter of historical scenes by the name of *Krausse*, who is admirably competent in this field.[1] It is a monumental representation of the "Art-Work of the Future". The central section is taken up by Germanic myth; since we wanted the figures to have characteristic features, we gave this one the head of the late *Ludwig Schnorr*; Wotan's ravens can be seen flying towards him on either side, while he relates the tidings that he has received to two female figures, one of whom represents classical tragedy in the likeness of Schroeder–Devrient, the other being music, with the head and figure of Cosima; a small boy, armed like Siegfried and with the head of my son, holds her by the hand and looks up at his mother, music, with high-spirited delight. I believe the whole thing will be an outstanding success, and my exalted friend shall be sent a copy of it as soon as it is finished. – An area at the front of the house has been hedged in and planted with flowers, and already contains the granite plinth on which the bronze bust of the owner of all my prosperity and happiness shall be erected. There are still some difficulties in producing it according to my wishes: it emerges from the overall proportions that it will have to be twice life-size. Master Zumbusch explained that the bust would be lighter and less expensive if it were made of marble, whereas, if it has to be cast in bronze, a new model will first have to be made, which will take a good deal of time and incur much greater expense. However, I cannot bear the thought of enclosing the bust in a wooden crate for almost six months of every year to protect it against the bad weather, as would have to be done in the case of marble. As a result I am still undecided, and in the meantime can only gaze sadly at the empty space.[2]

Ah! What happiness it would bring if our most gracious lord were to cast a glance in the direction of his poor Bayreuth! I almost wish that he might indeed do so, since a glance at my house in particular would allow him to recognize the truth of the matter, and see how the facts are always so hideously distorted by the newspapers. We have produced something that, because of its novelty and originality, takes the whole of the world by surprise, and we have produced it, moreover, on very slender means, by omitting all external ornamentation, for ex., and having all the skilled work on the interior of the building carried out by anonymous artisans who have achieved what they have

---

*) May I ask you to be so kind as to inspect the accompanying photograph? [*Wagner's own footnote*]

1 According to Cosima Wagner's diary for 27 October 1874, "Our *Sgraffito* is costing us more than 400 thalers; I would rather have left our house unadorned, but I say nothing about this to R., who is pleased with the ornament".

2 Ludwig took the hint, and made Wagner a present of the bronze bust.

done only by being constantly guided by us in the most painstaking manner. Nevertheless, none of this would have been possible if intellectual property had not received significant protection under recent legislation, as a result of which it is now possible for me to derive a certain income, which would otherwise have been lost to me completely, from the increasing number of performances of my older works which I had previously had to abandon without any form of protection. To this fortunate circumstance I also owe the fact that I can now think of my family's future provision with relative reassurance, since my works are now protected by copyright until thirty years after my death. For now and for the foreseeable future, however, I have my hands full, trying to make good the additional costs of settling here and furnishing my home, and since, whenever the King visits a prisoner, a royal favour always accompanies that act of clemency, I seize this opportunity to beg my exalted lord once again to grant me the financial relief which I need to survive, and allow me to draw, without any deduction, on the annuity which you granted me so magnanimously.[1] When, a number of years ago, I thought I could get by for a time on a reduced annuity, I did not know that I would be granted the great good fortune of having a family to care for. I have a good deal of help in dealing with all the duties that I have taken on, but I could only act with relative freedom after you were gracious enough to allow me to suspend repayment of the said advance. I venture to lay before you the humble request that I may continue to enjoy this magnanimous favour. –

Time and again I am reminded how bitterly I must regret not being some ten years younger: I have so little time left for patient waiting! At the same time I realize that if one is German, one must live to a ripe old age to enjoy even some of the fruits of one's labours; but I am well aware that this fruit is now beginning to ripen within me, and, if heaven has granted me the fullness of years of a Goethe, Gluck or Haydn, it is because I may yet be able to garner a harvest such as no man has ever known. – When the Feustel family first set foot in my recently completed salon, Frau Feustel said: "What will you not be able to write here now!" – I glanced at Cosima, and whispered to her: "Yes, indeed, – I, too, now believe in *Parzival*!" – And this *Parzival*, my belovèd King, I hereby pledge to you! All the preparations for my studies have already been completed. – But, do not think slightingly of the "Twilight of the Gods"! I have now had to work on the instrumentation of this final work with an effort that causes me utter torment, and with the most incessant interruptions, and I often cursed myself for having planned it on such a prodigally lavish scale: it is the tower that rises high into the clouds above the entire Nibelung edifice! Everyone who knows the work has said the same.

1 On 2 March 1869 Ludwig had granted Wagner a loan of 10,000 gulden to be repaid at a rate of 166 florins 40 kreuzers a month. Wagner had already appealed to Düfflipp on 22 August 1871 and again on 8 October 1872 to allow him to suspend repayment of the loan. The request was granted on both occasions, as it was in the present instance.

Oh! my precious and glorious prince! Are you not afraid for its completion? You will regret nothing – nothing, but will learn so many new and unknown things from this work that every reproach will be silenced within you! –

But how fares it with your patience? Had I understood you aright, my dearly belovèd lord, when I flattered myself that you wished me to go into such intimate detail in answering your questions? And there is still so much I could tell you, for knowing that my lips have once been unsealed by you is as much as to cause them to overflow. And so I venture to raise one final point which may almost turn into a humble request, for – it concerns what is perhaps the very difficult question of your royal attendance at the forthcoming festival.

How shall I begin – finally – to broach this question with the modesty that befits me, a question which, from the very outset, might have indicated a serious difficulty that stood in the way of the whole of my enterprise? I know – and have learned from a powerful example – that it is with the utmost seriousness that the enlightened protector of my art has always regarded all performances involving that art, and that, in attending the same, he seeks no superficial or conventional amusement. If I am now offering these performances of my great work to the German public, I do so, my King, in your exalted name; among the patrons of the undertaking are German princes – from the Emperor downwards. Their support for the undertaking has scarcely proved enthusiastic enough to make me think that they were more concerned with the affair itself than with the simple need to come to terms with it. None the less, it is still quite possible that a number of their Serene Highnesses will attend the festival performances. For that reason I have had a gallery built separate from the main auditorium and provided with its own private entrance, but capable of holding at least a hundred persons comfortably. This gallery is at the exclusive disposal of my exalted lord and King: he will admit to it only those whom it pleases him to single out, whereas the purchase of Patrons' certificates will entitle their holders only to good and comfortable seats in the main auditorium. I now come to my anxious question:

> will my King really come here for the festival performances?[1] Will he give them their true festive solemnity through his exalted presence? Or – will he, profound and serious-minded as he is, wish to withdraw from the fellowship of princes who may possibly also come here; and will he prefer to remain away rather than subject himself to – no doubt – many inconveniences which will impede his artistic enjoyment and which he may be made to feel out of his regard for these illustrious visitors?

Of course, I have no right to ask this question, for nothing you have been

---

1 Ludwig attended the dress rehearsals on 6–9 August and the third cycle on 27–30 August 1876.

kind enough to say to me has given me cause to do so. But if, in expressing the concern that I feel, I might have touched on a scruple that causes my exalted friend disquiet in any form, I should beg for nothing more than to know your mind exactly. At all events, I believe that *one* offer at least which I have to make may not be wholly unwelcome, namely my offer to arrange a performance of the entire work – as a final rehearsal, as it were – during the first week of August 1876, at which my exalted lord would be the only spectator in an auditorium completely closed off to the world. What my King may subsequently decide to do – whether, by virtue of his continuing exalted presence, he might deign to grant this festival of German art the true solemnity of a festival marking the birth of a nation – this may perhaps be left to the outcome of the evenings themselves on which the work shall first be presented to him alone.

I venture to allude to this matter in order to acquaint my exalted lord with the possibilities that lie open before him, in order that he may choose among them and inform his most reverentially loyal servant what his instructions may be in the matter. It grieves me only that I was obliged to defer the timing of the performances until so late a date; but I am secure in the knowledge that it was not any lack of enthusiasm on my part which was to blame for this delay; on the contrary, it is my profoundest consolation that, after all I have lived through and witnessed, the ultimate realization of this enterprise of mine must now seem an impossibility made possible. Only a King like you, my exalted friend, and only – perhaps I myself *together with* you could succeed in this.

All hail! All hail to you, my King! All hail to the invisible spirits that watch over our work! The most abundant blessings to the lord of my days, to him who commands my most sacred strength of spirit! –

Thus do I sign myself, eternally true to my most sublime and exalted benefactor,

Richard Wagner

Königsbriefe III,39–53.

427. CARL EMIL DOEPLER, BERLIN   Bayreuth, 17 December 1874

Dear Sir,

I take the liberty of enquiring whether you might be inclined to design the costumes, and superintend the task of making them, for the festival performances of my four-part stage festival "The Ring of the Nibelung" which I am planning to present in the summer of 1876.

To give you some provisional idea as to the nature of the task, I am sending you a copy of the dramatic poem, together with a number of pamphlets relating to its realization. You will see at once that it was my awareness of the difficulties involved here which persuaded me to look around for a distinguished artist with particular experience in the relevant area.

I believe I am more than justified in regarding the task I have set you as a field that is fertile in inventive possibilities. For basically what I require is nothing less than a characteristic portrait made up of individual figures and depicting with strikingly vivid detail personal events from a period of culture not only remote from our own experience but having no association with any known experience. You will soon discover that you have to ignore completely the sort of picture which, following the example of Cornelius, Schnorr & others, artists have tried to put forward in portraying the characters of the medieval Lay of the Nibelungs. At the same time, it will be clear to anyone who has concerned himself of late with attempts to portray the more specifically Norse myths that the artists concerned have merely had recourse to classical antiquity, which they have modified in a way which they deemed to be typically Nordic. Passing references to the costumes of the Germanic peoples in Roman authors who came into contact with these nations do not appear to have received the attention they merit. In my own opinion, the artist who wishes to take up the subject I offer him and make it his own will find a unique field open to him in terms not only of intelligent compilation but also his own inventiveness; and I could wish for nothing more than to know that you, my very dear Sir, had made this task your own.

I would entreat you to let me know your kind decision, and to accept the protestations of especial regard with which I have the honour to be

Your devoted servant,
Richard Wagner.

Bayreuther Briefe I, 187–8.

428. CARL BRANDT, DARMSTADT   Bayreuth, 6 April 1875

Dear Herr Brandt,

You see the sort of people I have to deal with in Darmstadt! I still haven't heard a single word from the Kapellmeister there!!! I believe I shall have to manage without the Darmstadt orchestra!! – But there is something else that bothers me! – I was in the theatre again today, and, if I am not to tell the most dreadful lie, I must finally admit that the architect has built my orchestra pit *completely wrong*. I shall never be able to fit all my musicians into *this* space, it's impossible! There is *nothing* for it but to remove two rows of seats from the auditorium (which is of no importance), then move the dividing wall and rebuild it further back. I shall give Runckwitz provisional notice of this in the morning; but would you be kind enough to get in touch with Herr – Henry

VIII*) in Leipzig? – As far as I recall from what you told me earlier on the subject, moving this wall would present no fundamental difficulties. Given the overall plan, it is a matter of total indifference to me whether 100 spectators fewer are accommodated, or not. What is important is that we should offer a performance that is perfect in every regard – the rest is a matter of indifference.

But your Darmstadt musicians! And no one on whom I can count, except our poor "technician", to whom I extend my most cordial good wishes, while signing myself

Your devoted servant,
Rich. Wagner.

Bayreuther Briefe I, 209–10.

429. ADAM LUDWIG MAZIÈRE, MAINZ   Bayreuth, 18 May 1875

My very dear Sir,
I still have to thank you for your most obliging letter which you recently sent me and to which I can respond only by expressing the hope that you may always remain in charge of what is now so curiously divided a business.[1]

Your wish which was conveyed to me by Herr *Seidl*, whereby I should append my signature to copies of the "Twilight of the Gods" as a form of dedication intended to curry favour with those newspaper editors to whom you are planning to distribute them is impossible for me to fulfil. I have no desire to place the least obstacle in your way by preventing so shrewd and well-considered a move on your part, but I am bound to wish that it be merely the politeness of the firm of *Schott* and not my willingness to engage in acts of homage that is heeded and met by gratitude in that quarter, since I pride myself on having reached the age of 62 without having made the slightest concession to the gentlemen of the press, nor indeed – I am happy to say – have they seduced me into doing so on any occasion whatsoever.

I believe this can all be done without me.

Herr *Seidl* will be sending you more detailed information with regard to the music manuscripts which you require. Everything shall be done according to your wishes!

In sincere friendship,

Your devoted servant,
Richard Wagner

Verleger-Briefe II, 192–3.

---

*) Brückwald, his name has just occurred to me! – [*Wagner's own footnote*]
1 Following the death of Franz Schott in May 1874, the firm was bequeathed to Ludwig Strecker, who appointed Mazière his agent in Mainz.

430. JOHANNES BRAHMS, VIENNA   Bayreuth, 6 June 1875

My dear Herr Brahms,

May I ask you to return my manuscript of the reworked second scene of
Tannhäuser, which I need for an edition of the revised version of the full
score? I admit that it has been reported to me that, on the strength of a present
which Peter Cornelius made you of it, you now claim right of ownership to
this manuscript; but I do not believe I need comply with this claim, since I
had only lent the manuscript to Cornelius, and certainly never gave it to him,
so that there can be no question of his ever having been in a position to
relinquish it to a third party, and, indeed, he assured me in the most solemn
terms that he never did so.

It will presumably not be necessary for me to remind you of this circumstance, nor should it require any further explanation on my part to persuade
you to be so kind as to return this manuscript to me, since it can only be of
value to you as a curiosity, whereas it would be a precious keepsake for my
son to own.

I am, Sir, your most respectful and obedient servant,
Richard Wagner.

Freunde und Zeitgenossen 568–9.

431. JOHANNES BRAHMS, VIENNA   Bayreuth, 26 June 1875

My dear Herr Brahms,

Please accept my thanks for the manuscript which I have just received and
which, you will agree, is not distinguished by any outward elegance, since the
Paris copy was very badly done up at the time; but! – quite apart from any
sentimental reasons – it is of great value to me because it is more complete
than the copy which Cornelius put a thick line through.

I am very sorry not to be able to send you the full score of the Mastersingers
which you asked for, but I have no more copies of it left, in spite of repeated
deliveries from Schott's, so that I can offer you nothing better than a copy
of the full score of the Rhinegold; without waiting for your consent, I am
sending it to you today, since it is distinguished by the fact that it is a de luxe
edition which, in its day, was resplendently displayed at the Vienna World
Exhibition by Schott's. I have sometimes been told that my music is like
theatrical scenery:[1] the Rhinegold must suffer grievously under the weight of
this reproach. None the less, it may not be without interest for you to follow
the remaining scores of the Ring of the Nibelung and see how I have been

1 An allusion to Hanslick's view of Wagner.

able to base all kinds of musical themes upon the foundations of the theatrical scenery that has been set up here. In this sense the Rhinegold may perhaps be found worthy of your kind attention.

I am, Sir, most respectfully,

Your very obedient and grateful servant,

Richard Wagner.

Freunde und Zeitgenossen 569–70.

432. KING LUDWIG II OF BAVARIA, MUNICH Bayreuth, 22 August 1875

Supremely belovèd King and friend,

Only now have I finally found time to meet all my obligations towards my exalted benefactor, obligations that have been piling up in recent months to the point where they threaten to overwhelm me. They are but obligations of gratitude, each one of which is linked to the next, so that there is but one means that offers itself by which to express that gratitude, a means which, on the final evening of those memorable weeks we have all just lived through, inspired me with the words to describe the ideal that I wished to characterize. Permit me therefore to begin at the end in reporting these events.

Once again I invited all my faithful singers and musicians to assemble in my garden for a farewell party; everywhere was illuminated, as it had been for my last birthday; the children had arranged another torchlight procession: I then bade the trumpeter call my guests together, stood on the steps that lead down into the garden from the salon, and addressed my army of guests in terms appropriate to the festive occasion. I explained to them the significance of their action in having assembled here from every corner of Germany, an incomparably select band that had come in response to my appeal to perform so strange a work of art; they could tell themselves with the greatest satisfaction that, in the space of this brief period when, with genuine virtuosity, they had played through the whole of my four dramas in eleven days, they had achieved what had hitherto been unbelievable; but they had also accomplished something far more significant, something of which they themselves were probably scarcely aware: they had set an example which the egotistical world of present-day art now might follow, an example of which we should all be capable if so we chose, and if the right person were to show us the way, namely to offer us proof of the fact that the only truly living art is now music. But – I went on – if I wanted to persuade them to raise a shout of exultation in this same spirit, it would be hard for me to name some abstract entity such as art or music as an object worthy of celebration. When the ancient Greeks wished to celebrate art, they could call on their beautiful god Apollo; we no longer had any gods; and yet I did not know how I could have spoken

to them today without a god, or how, on such a cheerful and festive occasion, I could have placed so sublime an interpretation upon the deed
they had accomplished, and saluted them for it. And so, I concluded, they
would all understand what I wanted to say to them when I called out:
long live the exalted protector of my life: long live the King of Bavaria! –
Inextinguishably the selfsame cry thundered forth from every breast and
soul! –
[. . .]

Königsbriefe III,64–5.

433. FRANZ JAUNER, VIENNA   Bayreuth, 28 September 1875

My very dear friend,
   If I intended giving Tannhäuser in Vienna as an oratorio,[1] we could certainly
have Fr. Wild as Elisabeth – for the sake of her "voice"; but for the theatre
I think that the performer whom you consider so admirable as "Elsa" will
serve us somewhat better for the part of Elisabeth. I suspect I shall have my
hands full trying to accommodate your glass-eyed Swedish Jew as
Tannhäuser. –
   Is it necessary to repeat once again, my dearest friend, that the performances in Vienna are of interest to me *only* on the assumption that they involve
no concessions to the existing company, but that they are models of their
kind, more especially as *dramatic* interpretations?
   Also, the scenery for the Hall of Song is still too operatically "Viennese".
The overall design is very good, but it is too garish and motley in colour. If
you think this is the only way of appearing before a Viennese audience, I
should prefer not to appear there with you. The background should be
somewhat more respectable in colour – there is too much *red* in the decorations which neutralizes the magnificence of the costumes: the chairs must
be made of leather – a dull finish, and the two thrones in particular should
be less colourful. &c. –
   If Fr. Grahn is making life difficult for you, – get rid of her! We shall
never achieve our ideal, and my only wish is that you, at least, are able to
turn the affair to good account.

---

1 The "Paris Version" of *Tannhäuser* was performed in Vienna on 22 November, under
Wagner's supervision. The conductor was Hans Richter, and the cast included the Swedish
tenor Leonard Labatt as Tannhäuser, Bertha Ehnn as Elisabeth, Amalie Materna as Venus,
Louis Bignio as Wolfram, and Emil Scaria as Landgraf Hermann. The choreographer was
Lucile Grahn.

I am returning the sketch herewith. My wife sends you her very best wishes, to which it remains only for me to add my own and assure you that I am

Your most obedient servant

Richard Wagner

Otto 389.

434. GEORG UNGER, MUNICH   Bayreuth, 1 January 1876

My dear Herr Unger,

In order that I may perform at least one friendly act this New Year's Day, I am writing to you at the day's end, in reply to your kind letter which arrived today. –

I can say in all truthfulness that, since our preliminary rehearsals came to an end, I have encountered nothing but unpleasantness. But it is comforting to cast my gaze in your direction. You and Hey are entered in my Book of Hopes. – Ever since Schnorr's death I have known that I was alone and dependent upon new and unknown talent. I never expected to find it ready made, but believed I should first have to nurture and develop it. What I needed to be sure of the right person was not merely a respectable and adequate natural talent, I also had to be able to rely on the character and deeper seriousness of the person whom I was now to acknowledge as having been meant for me. –

Now, you have pleased me greatly in both these respects! But you must never for a moment doubt in me! So – Scherbarth has temporarily faded from the scene?[1] – An admirable thing for him to do! Leave him where he is, he'll cause us no great harm. – How glad I should be to have you here again! But – patience! I am thinking of giving *Tristan* in Vienna with you late next autumn.[2] If our heavenly Hey insists upon studying it with you now, I would ask you not to do so until you are certain of Siegfried right down to the very last muscle. For – – – what you learn from *one* role can then be transferred to every other one in terms of your acting: but you first need to make *this* one fully your own! Once you have mastered Siegfried completely, Tristan will be merely a question of memory for you.

But you could always study smithing with Mime who, as "Locksmith",[3] ought to be fairly conversant with the craft by now. I wish Hey would take

---

1 Karl Scherbarth was opera director in Düsseldorf where Unger had been engaged as tenor before breaking the terms of his contract to study singing with Julius Hey in Munich.

2 Nothing came of this plan. The Viennese première of *Tristan und Isolde* did not take place until 4 October 1883.

3 "Locksmith" = *Schlosser* in German, a reference to the Munich tenor Max Schlosser, who sang Mime at the first festival.

him in hand as well. It emerged recently that he had not yet properly settled into this difficult role of his. He must assume a *false* voice, except that the voice itself must not sound false. It would be good if he could begin by singing this difficult part in his natural voice (as a lyric tenor, let us say): once he has overcome the enormous intonational problems, he may then, as an *actor*, distort his voice in a certain sense, i.e. make it sound rough and hoarse, in order to do justice to the unique dramatic character of the part. But he must not *begin* like this; – that was his mistake at the preliminary rehearsals; he intended it to be dramatically perfect from the outset, – and it was that that made us all laugh. – All right? –

As for my good friend *Seidel*,[1] keep him nice and warm: I don't believe there are many others like him. If he grows full of melancholy, empty his pockets for him at the Orlando Lasso![2] I like your little clique there very much. They also have such good-natured faces! I am sorry that any kind of temporary activity in Munich has been made impossible for me – curious, isn't it? –

By the way, if ever you meet a more admirable singing teacher and person than Hey, do let me know! I should like to know what he looks like! For our splendid Hey has so far proved my ideal in every respect! He can believe it or not!

Fare you well! Every good wish to the smithy! – I have had some splendid insights for which I need you both here!

Happy New Year!

May it repay all your labours!

Your sincerely devoted
Richard Wagner.

[...]

Bayreuther Briefe II, 156–8.

435. KING LUDWIG II OF BAVARIA, HOHENSCHWANGAU
Bayreuth, 26 January 1876

[...] He who wishes to know his age and the spirit of that age should make the same demands upon it as I myself made when I undertook my work! I have recognized our age for what it is, and at the same time have lost all my illusions as to its worth. For how is it possible to go on deluding ourselves as to the shameless wretchedness that lies all around us when every attempt

---

1 Anton Seidl.

2 The "Orlando di Lasso" was an establishment (*Bierwirtschaft*) on the site of the former house of the composer Lassus, who was Kapellmeister at the Bavarian Court in Munich from 1563 to 1594.

to point out the way to salvation is met by open and undisguised abuse? We *want* to be worthless: this has been our motto ever since the Jesuits handed over this world of ours to the Jews. Everything is lost here! The Emperor and his Reich may take as much pleasure as they like in their military regulations: what they are protecting is not worth a straw! –

Yes! My King! I shall complete what I have begun. Had I been a rich man, I should willingly have staked my whole fortune on it; for ultimately it is a question of the material levers that are used to wrest some spirituality from this world. One day my work will exist, in order no longer to exist. For I am not thinking of any lasting influence; in the eyes of the world, those who think of my work as a whim are not mistaken. For, really and truthfully, my work lacks a sure foundation: there is nothing that exists already to which it can attach itself. What we once strove to achieve in Munich has now – like everything else – passed into Jewish hands: I suffer grief upon grief at the utterly degenerate spirit that now informs performances of my work – in the very place where they once flourished to the point of being models of their kind. In Vienna they showed willingness to comply with my principles, and this reawakening of good will on their part encouraged me to go there in order that, over a period of time, I might present correct and unmutilated performances of all my older works (which – curiously enough! – still continue to fill the coffers). I performed wonders, – but at the cost of exertions which I should prefer not to have to submit to again! Miserable singers on tremendous salaries, who openly declared that I was there to their detriment, since I was showing them the bad habits into which they had fallen, without being able to give them the strength to break free from them permanently. They admitted I was right, but what use to them was this sudden conversion since they would inevitably revert to their former faith! The energetic support which the administration gave me served only to incite the press against me, so that I soon had cause to regret having wanted to show these people my works in their proper light! –

[. . .]

Königsbriefe III, 73–4.

436. EMIL HECKEL, MANNHEIM   Bayreuth, 4 February 1876

Dearest and best of friends,

There is much that could be said in reply to the question how we all are! The world, and more especially "Germania", is becoming increasingly repugnant to me!

Our cares are considerable, and I am bound to regard it as utterly foolhardy to allow the performances to go ahead this year. We have sold 490 of our Patrons' certificates, whereas, according to our latest calculations, we need 1300 to break even. In other words, the undertaking that we originally planned is now totally wrecked. We shall simply have to take the risk of seeing what curiosity may finally achieve. Even Feustel believes it is worth taking this risk; but we must anticipate a shortage of funds in June etc when the musicians and singers arrive and want to be paid in cash. I applied for an advance of 30,000 thalers from the Emperor. [But Bismarck has thwarted the affair.][1] I shall see what can still be done when I go to Berlin at the beginning of March, when I shall also be seeing how things are faring with "Tristan", although that, too, is something in which I have little faith.[2] – For the rest, we are putting a brave face on it. Everything will be ready on time (on credit!); the artistic details will be worked out to the highest pitch of perfection. Brandt, as always, is outstanding, – my chief support!

Apart from Scaria,[3] I have encountered no reluctance on the part of the singers: they all seem firmly resolved to remain loyal to our cause. I shall be able to find a remedy for Scaria, – assuming he does not change his mind again at the last minute; the matter is still not entirely settled. Otherwise very little news.

Every good wish from us all to your wife and friends!

If you could conjure up a minor miracle, it would be most welcome to me! But I shall always remain

Your sincerely devoted
Richard Wagner.

RWG (incompletely published in Bayreuther Briefe I,232–3).

437. HEINRICH VOGL, MUNICH   Bayreuth, 24 April 1876

Most valued colleague and friend,

I must confess that, although my initial shock enabled me to put on a brave face at the misfortune which has struck as a result of your own *good*

---

1 The sentence in square brackets has not previously been published.

2 Wagner and Cosima were in Berlin between 4 and 23 March 1876. The local première of *Tristan und Isolde* took place on 20 March, conducted by Karl Eckert, and with Albert Niemann and Vilma von Voggenhuber in the title roles. The proceeds of the performances (nearly 14,000 marks) were made over to Bayreuth after the intendant Hülsen had magnanimously proposed such a course to the Emperor Wilhelm I.

3 Emil Scaria had been obliged, because of his debts, to demand a fee of 7500 marks for the month of August, plus 250 marks for each day he was in Bayreuth during the preceding month. Wagner had no choice but to replace him, firstly by Josef Kögel of Hamburg, and then (on 15 July 1876) by Gustav Siehr of Wiesbaden.

fortune in marital terms,[1] it is becoming increasingly difficult for me to do so now. It was easy for you to say that it would not be hard to find another Sieglinde: it would not have been *easy* at the best of times, but what was already a *difficult* task has now been made even more difficult by the fact that it is now so late in the day, and our better singers are already engaged for the summer. But there is no point in saying anything more on the subject, be it good or bad! Everyone has his cross to bear, including your wife. We must find a remedy, but "formally" I shall be godfather for you. – As for Fräulein Kindermann's kind offer, I could not make up my mind in the end. You see, I cannot accommodate another "soprano" among the Valkyries: all that I am still missing here is the deepest contralto (Schwertleite): since I could find no one else for the part following Frln. Preiss's withdrawal, my niece, Johanna Jachmann-Wagner, finally decided to take over "Schwertleite" as well as the first (lowest) Norn. In consequence, I should need Frl. Kindermann only for the 2nd Norn; but if I find a Sieglinde, as I most certainly must, she will assume the role of this Norn as well, and the 3 Norns will then be taken only by leading singers. I hope Frln. Kindermann will make it easy for me to use her offer of help; she will always be of use to me.

Would you tell Frau Reicher-Kindermann that I was more than pleased to receive her acceptance and also her conditions. – And now the question of "Grane".[2] – If possible, extreme in colour; *black* or *white*, but not some indeterminate chestnut. Large in size, as colossal as possible! It won't be ridden. *Everything exactly as in the vocal score.* At the end of the second act of the Valkyrie, when Brünnhilde gives the impression of lifting Sieglinde on to her horse, the whole group immediately disappears behind a veil of mist which is drawn across in front of them, so that the action – and more especially the impression of riding away – can only be guessed at. – Even if we can manage to persuade Frau *Materna* actually to leap on to the horse at the end of the Twilight of the Gods, there will at least be no question of our seeing her leap on to the funeral pyre, since dense fiery smoke will immediately rise up and conceal the whole of the back of the stage. But the horse must not be afraid of such diabolical goings-on, and it must be possible to lead it down a rocky pathway (Act II, Valkyrie.) My warmest regards to *Menge*, the assistant riding-master! –

And, finally, my most humble greetings and good wishes to your dear wife; I honestly believe she would have been happy to have been with child a few

1 Therese Vogl's pregnancy obliged her to withdraw from the role of Sieglinde. Her husband sang the part of Loge at the first festival.
2 Brünnhilde's horse, which was provided by Ludwig's riding stables.

months earlier, so as not to have had to forgo her artistic triumph on this occasion; but Loge missed his chance![1]

With the most respectful and friendly of sentiments, I remain

Richard Wagner
Godfather to the Wälsungs.

RWA (copy not in Wagner's hand; published with various errors of transcription in Sebastian Röckl, "Zwei unbekannte Briefe Richard Wagners an Heinrich Vogl" in Rheinische Musik- und Theaterzeitung, xii [December 1911]), 707.

438. HERMANN LEVI, MUNICH   Bayreuth, 18 May 1876

Most valued friend,

My sincere thanks for all your exertions and comforting news! Schlosser (for heaven's sake) need only tell me what he requires for his stay here; not a soul (and least of all my "committee", which is certainly in no position to say yea or nay) has demanded that he should not be reimbursed by me! –

I was delighted to hear that you had taken an interest in Frln. Schefzky.[2] I was really on the horns of a dilemma, and couldn't wait until I had had an opportunity to get to know this or that singer. (I have just been informed – belatedly – of a Frl. Hofmeister in Frankfurt, who is said to sing like an angel!) Certainly, it has not escaped my notice that Frln. Schefzky presents us with somewhat raw material; but with almost all my artists I am forced to reckon on their willingness to learn things they did not know previously. The basis, however, is the most painstaking correctness, *especially* in matters of rhythm; from Tannhäuser onwards I have demanded that my singers should ignore all idea of "recitative" and learn to sing the notes correctly and in time, right down to the smallest fraction of their metrical value, because only in that way will they arrive at an understanding of how I intend the role to be sung. But you know all this already, which is why I feel sorry for you having to retrain singers who have been taught by the Ullmanns and Hofmanns of this world. A thousand thanks for doing so! If you can get away in June, so much the better! You will always be welcome. I am most heartily obliged to you, and remain

Yours,
Richard Wagner

RWA (published with minor errors of transcription in Bayreuther Briefe II, 193–4).

1 Wagner's innuendo harks back to Vogl's announcement of his wife's pregnancy, when he humorously suggested that Loge ought to have followed Alberich's example and cursed love.
2 See letter [426], p. 836, note 1.

439. FRIEDRICH NIETZSCHE, BASLE   [Bayreuth, 13 July 1876]

Friend,
    Your book[1] is tremendous! –
    Wherever did you get to know so much about me? –
    Come and visit us soon, and get used to the effects by attending the
rehearsals!

Yours,
RW.

Nietzsche-Briefe II,6/1 362–3.

440. THE ARTISTS OF THE BAYREUTH FESTIVAL, BAYREUTH
Bayreuth, 13 August 1876

Final Request
to my dear fellow artists.

———

!Clarity!
– The long notes will take care of themselves; the small notes and their text
are what matters. –

———

Never address the audience directly, but always the other character; in mono-
logues look up or down but never straight ahead. –
Final Wish:
Remain loyal to me, my dear friends!

Richard Wagner

*Facsimile in Martin Gregor-Dellin, Richard Wagner: Eine Biographie in Bildern
(Munich/Zurich 1982), 181.*

441. KING LUDWIG II OF BAVARIA, HOHENSCHWANGAU
Bayreuth, 13 August 1876

Exalted and glorious friend and lord that has been won back for renewed
veneration,
    Perhaps in these few fleeting lines, that are all I can wrest from my present

1   "Richard Wagner in Bayreuth", Part IV of the *Unzeitgemässe Betrachtungen* (Untimely Medi-
    tations), a copy of which had arrived at Wahnfried on 10 July 1876.

weariness, I may yet succeed in rediscovering that frame of mind which I lost completely in your hurried departure.[1] When I stood on the steps and took leave of my lord and friend who has always made me uniquely happy, I fell prey to a violent fever which constrained me to entrust myself to the tender cares of a number of friends. I still feel a sense of great weariness that overwhelmed me that very same moment when first I was forced to become clearly conscious that my most dearly belovèd of friends had departed. Not until yesterday could I concern myself with certain improvements (in a technical sense) to our performances, and give way to the insistent demands of the whole of my company who were resolved to repair to the railway station and receive their Emperor there, whose visit had been so loudly proclaimed, for they were disposed to regard it as an insult if I were not to be seen at their head. In a few friendly words, the Emperor told me that he had come to the inauguration of my stage festival because he saw it as a matter of "national" importance. Of course he meant well, but his words struck me as somewhat ironical: what has the "nation" to do with my work and its realization? I then repaired to my theatre in order to try out the *head* of my dragon, which had finally arrived from London. Whatever else may have happened has not yet reached my notice. Only one thing about which I had eagerly enquired did I succeed in discovering, namely that Your Majesty would certainly be able to attend the *third performance* without suffering any kind of annoyance. Even the ruling princes among our Patrons have been brought here ultimately only out of curiosity: but their curiosity will be completely satisfied by the first two cycles, and for the third (and even almost for the second) you will certainly find no further claims will be made from that quarter. And so, in my present completely stupefied state and mood, I have but *a single hope*, which is that I may see you again here, my godlike friend and co-creator, to witness *our* work! Everything shall then be better and more beautiful! –

Am I allowed to hope???

A thousand sincere good wishes from your poor and, at present, so sorely tormented and exanimate friend, who may sign himself

Eternally yours to command:
Richard Wagner

All that you wish for shall soon be laid at your feet!

Königsbriefe III, 84–5.

---

1 Ludwig had attended the dress rehearsals of the *Ring* between 6 and 9 August, and then returned to Hohenschwangau at first light on the 10th. He returned for the third cycle (27–30 August).

442. JUDITH GAUTIER, PARIS   [Bayreuth, 2 September 1876]

Chère,

I am sad! There is another reception this evening, but I shall not be going to it!

I reread a few pages of my life which I once dictated to Cosima! She sacrifices herself to her father's habits, – alas!

Could it have been for the last time that I held you in my arms this morning?

No! – I shall see you again – I *want* to see you! because I love you! – Adieu – Be good to me!

R.

Lettres à Judith Gautier 57 (original in French).

443. LILLI LEHMANN, BERLIN   Bayreuth, 7 September 1876

Oh, my dear, kind creature,

How your letter touched me!

I really have no other perception of all that has happened, except the regret that I did not show sufficient gratitude towards you of all people! Otherwise I feel only a dull pain in my soul. When my horses were led away yesterday,[1] I burst into tears! – We are thinking of leaving for Italy in 8 days' time.[2] But I wouldn't like to embark upon anything similar straightaway; the King tried to force us into giving a 4th performance at the end of the month, but of course I had to turn him down.

There is so much that we shall have to put right next year; I hope that most of the performers will be willing to work towards my goal of achieving an increasingly correct production. Only Betz casts a [wholly repugnant][3] shadow upon my memory! The wretch even went so far as to make fun of his part,[4] more especially at the beginning of the last performance of the Valkyrie. I have been thinking more and more about the reasons for his behaviour, and am increasingly confirmed in my belief that he was annoyed at not being allowed to take any curtain calls! I had already suspected as

1 Horses from the royal stables which had been used in *Die Walküre*.
2 The Wagners left Bayreuth on 14 September, and travelled via Verona, Venice and Bologna to Naples, where they arrived on the 29th. A week later the family moved to Sorrento where they met Nietzsche for the last time, before returning to Rome on 7/8 November. Early December saw them in Florence and Bologna; and they were back in Bayreuth on 20 December 1876.
3 The passages in square brackets have not previously been published.
4 The original text had "to deride his part" (*verhöhnen*), but this has been changed to *verspotten* ("to make fun of") in the autograph letter.

much, and questioned him on the subject, whereupon he replied with a dismissive smile to the effect that "he and Niemann scarcely ever went out in front of the curtain in search of applause!" [How deceitful and false these gentlemen mostly are! –]

Well, I think I shall have to take steps to replace him as Wotan next year, since he tells me that in no circumstances would he ever again return to Bayreuth.[1] – What is your own opinion, my dear? –

For the rest, I do not care to concern myself overmuch with the future, it already weighs heavily enough on my soul! –

And yet – and yet – you, my dearest creature, and – let us not forget your sisters, – oh, how brightly you still shine before me, how truly transfigured! Never shall I forget the tremendous force of your prophecy of Siegfried's death! –

And so, may the gods preserve all that is best: thus do I greet you, dear Lilli, from the very depths of my heart as

Your most truly grateful debtor,
Richard Wagner

RWA (incompletely published in Bayreuther Briefe II, 204–5).

444. FRIEDRICH FEUSTEL, BAYREUTH   Rome, 23 November 1876

Most valued friend,

[Not[2] until yesterday evening did I receive the enclosed letter from Herr v. Radowitz (the extraordinary lateness of which you will gather from its contents), so that only now am I in a position to write to you and our esteemed friends on the committee of management in order to express a clearer opinion about the present state of our great undertaking.]

I have received no further information [in this regard] since leaving Bayreuth, other than your announcement that the deficit[3] was turning out to be more and more significant, and that I myself should suggest means of dealing with it. The most obvious solution still seemed to be an appeal to the existing supporters of my enterprise: I drew up such an appeal and forwarded it to you (around the 8th or 10th of October) with the request that you attach it to your report to the Patrons. [On the 14th of last month I wrote to Herr von Radowitz who, during the time that he was in Bayreuth, had expressed his willingness to mediate on our behalf in various quarters.] At the same

---

1 Betz returned to Bayreuth in 1889 when he alternated as Kurwenal and Marke in *Tristan und Isolde*, and also sang Hans Sachs; see also letter [445], pp. 863–4.
2 The passages in square brackets have not previously been published.
3 148,000 marks or 49,300 thalers.

time, however, I also wrote a very detailed letter to the King of Bavaria, [informing him of my wishes as follows:

he should – either – bring the matter to the attention of the Reich by means of his deputy in the Bundestag, i.e. through the Confederation, – or, even better, acquire the entire enterprise, including all that we own, for the Bavarian Crown.

To this] I added the outline of a plan whereby the theatre and all its accessories would be acquired by the state, and transferred to the magistracy of the town of Bayreuth to be administered by them, in return for which the state would stand security for all debts and encumbrances. – I am still awaiting a reply, and may well suppose that, although not lacking the very best of intentions, the King is in some embarrassment as to the right way to satisfy my wishes.

While waiting for a reply from that quarter, I learned from our friend Heckel of his great regret that I myself should have to make an appeal for contributions to cover the deficit, since, in his opinion, this should be left to my friends to do; he had already expressed himself in this vein to our friends on the committee of management. I told him in my reply that he certainly seemed to be motivated by a feeling of great fairness, and that I should indeed welcome it if friends of my cause were to take the matter in hand. With regard to his suggestion that a 4th (extra) performance at increased prices be given to cover the deficit, my only consideration was that the necessary repayment of our debts could not be delayed until then.

[However, I was then still awaiting a reply from Herr v. Radowitz to whom I had written in response to a remark of his concerning a subscription. You will see from his letter not only the incidental reason for the delay in my receiving his reply but also that we can in no way count upon him and his kind. It will also give you a glimpse into the sort of appalling experience I have had to suffer, namely that], while firmly convinced that people exist who are both willing and able to collect together the sum that we need, I know of no one who has it in him to place himself at the head of such an operation. Perhaps this could be achieved by the chairmen of the older Wagner Societies, since it ought to be easier for them to raise their voices now, rather than previously, when the matter was still open to the gravest doubts. At all events, I too regret that the appeal which I sent to you has not been used: its circulation would at least have had the advantage of letting us know where we stood in this regard.

It seems to me therefore that, through no fault of my own, there has been a serious delay here; at the same time I declare my continuing readiness to support any measure that is suggested to me. But at all events it now seems too late to begin preparations to repeat the festival next summer, or even to think of doing so. In order to achieve this goal just *once* and to show the world what was involved, I was prepared to enter this slough of financial confusion and deceit; but to remain bogged down in it, to be always at the mercy of chance, as a result, for ex., of calumnies in the newspapers, and always to end up in the position of seeing myself exposed to anxieties which I ought never to have to experience, inasmuch as I have never sought financial gain here – this is something I must henceforth reject completely. The great shortcomings in the performance of my work can be explained solely in terms of financial uncertainty and the consequent doubts on the part of those responsible for its realization as to whether the whole undertaking would come off on time. Even as I write, we ought to have at our disposal the means for improving and revivifying the production. Moreover, I would not risk inviting certain of my artists who have caused me difficulties of late to work with me again, unless I were able to promise them a fairly substantial fee; but this could only be done if the deficit on this year's performances had already been paid off in full. And even if a 4th (extra) performance were to be inflicted upon my singers and musicians for this purpose, it might easily deter them from taking part, since it would be tempting providence to reckon upon repeating the favourable circumstances which allowed us to give 3 uninterrupted performances, one after the other, in so short a period of time.

As a result I find myself forced to the conclusion that all we can do is wait and see whether, in response to any suggestion that may be made, the money we need to cover the deficit can be found in time. If this cannot be done by the 1st of January, next year's revival of the festival will have to be abandoned, and we shall then have to wait and see whether interest is shown in other quarters, and whether help is then forthcoming. I shall refrain from any further reference to my own person on this occasion, nor shall I draw your attention in any more detail to the state of my health; but I can assure you that even in Italy, under all the impressions that are to be gained here, I am dragging myself from place to place with my entire nervous system in a state of seemingly irrevocable collapse, which, after all that has happened and in view of all the thoroughly disagreeable things that continue to beset me, is scarcely surprising, particularly when one considers that for several years I have been prevented from taking a health cure or such like treatment during the summer. Nevertheless, I cannot regard the undeniable need to repeat the festival next year as binding upon me, unless it takes place in circumstances which at least make the duty of self-sacrifice an agreeable one, i.e. unless I receive some evidence from the friends of my art that they are in some way concerned about me and my cause. I no longer have the ability or the desire to sacrifice my strength to an enterprise that trusts merely to luck.

Since not the slightest blame for this disagreeable state of affairs is to be laid at the door of my estimable friends in Bayreuth, inasmuch as we have jointly achieved something which can arouse only amazement and admiration, it grieves me all the more that I may yet have to cause you a great deal of distress. For I must contemplate the possibility of never being able to hold another festival; this eventuality would become a reality if the deficit could not be covered in time by means of additional contributions, and if repayment could not be postponed any longer, in which case there would be nothing for it but to declare the enterprise bankrupt, and – once a report had been made to the Patrons – transfer all existing property to our creditors. All that belongs to the King of Bavaria would then have to be made over to him; and whatever else there may be of value would be offered to the highest bidder, the proceeds being used to discharge all our remaining debts. I see no other way out, more especially because, for my own part, I am bound to doubt in the success of every one of my independent efforts, and no one who is familiar with the strain I have suffered will expect me to give concerts & the like at present.

Above all, my most valued friend, I must ask you not to interpret this communication as an outburst of ill-humour cruelly intended to cause you discomfort; on the contrary, I have had ample opportunity during these tense last months to consider my real attitude towards my contemporaries, and it is on this basis that I have reached my decision. I have shown them what I can do, and feel justified, but also impelled, to bring to an end my public career as an artist, instead of which it now remains my most pressing concern and obligation to see to the welfare of myself and my family, which I have neglected to do hitherto. –

With my most sincere good wishes to your friends and family, I remain

Your eternally grateful and obedient servant

Richard Wagner

RWA (incompletely published in Bayreuther Briefe I, 247–52).

445. FRANZ BETZ, BERLIN   Rome, 30 November 1876

Dear friend,

The question which I have put to you and Niemann today is one on whose favourable reply depends the possibility of our repeating the performances in Bayreuth, namely whether you can give me another, say, 6 weeks of your time next summer, whereby I accept that, for my part, I shall undertake the said performances only if I can promise to pay you very substantial compensation, the level of which you yourself will specify.

To my most lasting and most grievous regret you were the only person on this occasion who went away without saying goodbye to me! It was the second occasion on which you had robbed me of the purest satisfaction of being able to express, loudly and freely, a recognition and gratitude such as I have had cause to grant to very few people in my life. The first occasion was at the banquet after the first performance[1] when I had intended to speak on the subject of the unique character of German art and its disciples, their energetic enthusiasm and consuming devotion to the task they had been set and by means of which the most talented achievements of other nations could all be surpassed; and I had intended to do so by adducing you and your performance as Wotan as an example of this. But my artists left me in the lurch and I had to comment merely on matters that concerned our patrons. I then hoped to be able to say goodbye to you: how grievously you cheated me of that opportunity!

Believe me, your behaviour continues to remain inexplicable to me, and it is this that really incites my sorrow even now!

God knows what possessed you to act as you did. Let it remain inexplicable, if that is what you wish, unless it depends upon me to clear up some misunderstanding that may have arisen between us. One good deed would dispel all this gloom. Agree to my proposal – and I shall see everything in a better and more friendly light!

Whatever your excuse may be, I can say only one thing to you today:

Our Mastersingers was the best thing I have ever achieved on the stage: I regard your "Hans Sachs" as quite incomparable and unforgettable. – Your "Marke" was perfect. – Your "Wotan" *astonishing*. I keep on coming back to this term; no other achievement known to me comes close to what you achieved in the second act of the Valkyrie, not least because of the unprecedented difficulties caused by its length and range. Let this much be clear between us, even if you should now strive to forget me.

With the most cordial good wishes,

Yours,
Richard Wagner.

Bayreuther Briefe II, 209–11.

446. KARL HILL, SCHWERIN   Bayreuth, 20 February 1877

Dear kind friend Hill,

To be brief! – No Bayreuth this summer: instead we have to go to London, where I shall be giving concerts to cover last year's deficit.[2] I am taking

1 On 18 August 1876. According to Cosima Wagner's diary for that date, "A very, very lovely evening! All the singers absent except for Hill, Frau Grün, Reichenberg, Herr Siehr (outstanding as Hagen)! After working for three months with R., they do not consider it necessary on such an occasion to gather around him; they are said to be angry because we do not allow curtain calls in our theatre".

2 Wagner and Cosima were in London from 1 May to 4 June 1877 for eight concerts at the Royal Albert Hall. The profit on the concerts amounted to £700 (approximately 14,300 marks).

Materna and *Unger* with me, and – as an absolute must – should also like to have – *you*. (Wotan's scenes. Dutchman, Telramund. Wolfram etc.) Time: (the whole of) *May* and (part of) *June*. Keep your expenses down, and think you are returning to Bayreuth, except that on this occasion we have to succeed because of the *deficit*. Will you help in this way to make a free man of me, and place me in a position where I can continue to deal creditably with the festival? Will you?? You shall certainly have no cause to regret it. You may also be able to sing in the theatres there, and earn some extra money. –

You see, best of friends, how things are, and what satisfaction it must give me to be a German.

With the most sincere good wishes, I am

Respectfully yours,
Richard Wagner.

Bayreuther Briefe II,222.

447. FRIEDRICH FEUSTEL, BAYREUTH   London, 13 May 1877

My very dear friend,

I hope that I do not need to repeat the information [which[1] my wife] sent to our friend Adolf[2] concerning the state of our business here: if, in spite of my detailed knowledge of conditions in London, which has always discouraged me from trying my luck here, I none the less thought that such an attempt might ultimately (and unprecedentedly!) succeed on this single occasion, it was less this thought as such, and the hope that was founded upon it, which persuaded me to come to London than the decision to show you and those of my friends who were attracted by the idea that it was not indolence and convenience on my part which made me wish that other means might be found for covering our deficit. It is now time to embark upon an alternative course without any further delay, which is why I would beg you most kindly to send out an invitation at once from the committee of management of the festival enterprise, asking for contributions to cover the deficit; in doing so you should give a brief summary of the present state of affairs, probably also mentioning my eagerness to spare the Patrons this imposition by subjecting myself to such arduous strain, and at the same time opening the subscription list with a contribution of 3000 marks *from me*, to which you yourself, as a generous private citizen, might perhaps be inclined to add your own contribution. I should prefer it if these circulars were not sent to the Wagner Societies as such (on account of their great inability to do anything), but

---

1 The words in square brackets have not previously been published.
2 Adolf Gross, a Bayreuth banker, and Feustel's son-in-law.

urged upon only a few private individuals. My own view is that a list should be sent to Berlin (Davidsohn, Kuschinsky, *Frau v. Schleinitz*), a second one to Vienna (Dr Standthartner for consultation with Countess Dönhof), a 3rd to Munich (Balligand, with an invitation to approach everyone up to and including the King), 4th London (Wagner Society through Dannreuther), a 5th & 6th perhaps to Heckel; and Senator Petersen in Hamburg, and ultimately probably also Dresden, Court Councillor [Dr] Pusinelli, and, above all, Count *Magnis*[1] in Silesia. Each of these copies would have my own contribution of 3000 marks – and perhaps yours as well – placed at the top of the list and entered as a subscription. As soon as the lists were full and sufficiently great to meet our needs, the complete list would then be sent to each subscriber with a request for immediate payment.

If this course, too, should fail, I am resolved to accept Ullmann's American offer, put my property in Bayreuth up for sale, set sail across the ocean with my entire family, and never again return to Germany. –

As far as the local business is concerned, we are afraid we shall not even cover our costs. I should be glad to get back the advances which you paid to the singers on my behalf. You would also place me in your debt if you were to transfer a credit [of 2 to 3000 marks] to me here, so that I can go to Ems at the beginning of June. Whether I shall recover my health there will largely depend upon my receiving reassuring news that a subscription list has been opened and is being put into effect. It is to be hoped that *some* words of comfort should reach me from that quarter!

Please be patient with me and forgive me all the trouble I have already caused you. Please remember me to our friends, to your dear family, and especially to my good Adolf.

In eternal gratitude,
Richard Wagner.

RWA (incompletely published in Bayreuther Briefe 1,261–3).

448. COSIMA WAGNER, BAD EMS   [Bad Ems, around 6 June 1877]

My little wife,
  I believe we must use strong medicine, and am very keen
  1. To use your fortune[2] – (It *will* be made good!!)

---

1 Added in the margin in a different hand, "Ullersdorf of Glatz, Silesia". Count Ullersdorf sent 5000 marks towards the deficit.
2 40,000 francs (about 32,500 marks) which Cosima had inherited from her mother Marie d'Agoult. Wagner accepted her offer of the money as a contribution towards the Bayreuth deficit.

2. To declare that I want *nothing* more to do with the Munich Court Theatre.

Will[1]

Eger II, 126 (including facsimile).

449. FRIEDRICH FEUSTEL, BAYREUTH   Bad Ems, 14 June 1877

My dearest friend,

Here are the two signatures.[2] I hope that these inroads on my family's future existence may at least have the advantage of gaining sufficient time to enable you to discover how things stand and with what kind of people I have had to deal throughout my life. This much at least I have been forced to recognize – and the certainty of this knowledge will remain with me to the end – namely, that it is not my work which has been "judged", but – Bayreuth. My work will be performed everywhere and attract large audiences, but – people will not be prepared to return to Bayreuth. That is the long and the short of it, and the reason why they have grown so coolly indifferent towards my enterprise. I can blame the town only insofar as I *myself* chose it. Yet it was a great idea: with the support of the nation I wanted to create something entirely new and independent in a place which would first achieve importance as a result of that creation – a kind of Washington of art. I had too high an opinion of our upper classes. As a favour to me (and also, in part, out of mere curiosity) they put up for once with the immense inconvenience of Bayreuth, but now recoil from the idea of repeating that experience. Hence, on the whole, their coolness towards my present plight. – A leading firm in London[3] approached me with the suggestion that I should transfer all the Bayreuth stage fittings etc. to a large London theatre, and repeat the festival there in the course of next season. If I really *want* them to, they will rebuild my theatre in Leipzig, and continue my work there. Würzburg or Nuremberg would have had the means to compensate me following last year's great success, and to continue the performances there. Bayreuth could succeed only if my idea for an Academy of Music and Drama were to become a reality along the lines that I recently suggested, resulting in large numbers of people settling there. The town itself, which could expect to reap considerable advantages for many of its inhabitants at least, could ultimately present a petition to the King and the estates, etc. As for myself, all I shall probably

---

1 Wagner and Cosima used the names "Will" and "Vorstell" in their correspondence, a reference to the title of Schopenhauer's *Die Welt als Wille und Vorstellung.*
2 Wagner's and Cosima's, empowering Feustel to draw on their private account in order to pay off the festival's more pressing creditors.
3 No details known.

be able to do is worry about how to cover the deficit, and get rid of – the theatre! –

I was shocked to hear of the terrible way in which the 20,000 marks recently received from Vienna had shrunk to only 7900 marks. [Is[1] this because another of Eysser's bills of exchange has been paid?]

"Dolce far niente." – Yes, indeed! – To do nothing? – No: to *accomplish* nothing! that is my relaxation.

Well, as God wills. I shall always remain beholden unto you!

Sincere good wishes from

Your most obedient servant
Rich. Wagner.

RWA (incompletely published in Bayreuther Briefe I, 268–71).

450. CARL FRIEDRICH GLASENAPP, RIGA   Bad Ems, 25 June 1877

Dear friend,

Please accept my thanks for sending me your recently completed work![2] As you can well imagine, we were deeply touched not only by your aim in writing it but also by the way you have done it. If I am to say briefly what it is that I find to criticize about it, it is less the occasional – and unavoidable – inaccuracy, or even the vagueness in your presentation and arrangement of the facts, than that you were obliged to base so much of your narrative on the accounts of other people, and then generally in their own words, and generally at excessive length, so that these passages stand out all too clearly from your own descriptions based upon personal experience and knowledge. In this way, Nohl & his associates, for example, often give themselves airs, and, more especially, attempt to be far too witty, particularly when it comes to describing me and my remarks or obiter dicta, so that I could easily be put off myself as a person; for all too frequently it is a somewhat insipid and stupid figure that I see reflected in this mirror of theirs.

I should prefer it if the English translation were made on the basis of a rather more concise original: and you might make certain corrections to the first volume in the light of the notes which I sent you. My wife, for ex., has remarked on the omission of Frau v. Muchanoff (Kalergis-Nesselrode.) –

Of course, it would be best if I could find the time and leisure to go through a copy of your book in detail, with a pencil in one hand. But it is impossible for me to do so at present. You can well imagine the difficulties

---

1 This sentence has not previously been published. Eysser was a cabinet-maker in Bayreuth.
2 The second part of Glasenapp's two-volume biography of Wagner had just appeared. The work was later revised in six volumes.

from which I am having to extricate myself at present, simply in order to be able to breathe freely once more, and, indeed, there are times when I despair utterly of ever being able to do so again. Unless you have experienced what I have had to go through, it is impossible to judge the sort of people into whose midst I have been thrown! I recently told my wife as a joke that I was ashamed to be my own contemporary! – What I may yet be able to salvage from the wreck of my festival idea will probably be very little. –

[I[1] had to smile at the fact that you, too, with all the authority that is due to you, had recourse to the "finishing touches which W. is putting to the full score of Parzival". You cannot seriously imagine that I have to compose a little every day in order to enjoy life?] During the early months of last spring, in order to avert my mind forcibly from the most appalling impressions that life then had to offer – I only got as far as working out the poem itself, which had previously existed only as a draft.[2] The poem is now finished, and if you care to visit us in August or September, you may read it for yourself. At all events, you will then be able to convince yourself that Parsifal has nothing whatsoever to do with Lohengrin, in spite of the fact that some people will insist upon seeing it as a postludial prelude to the earlier work. –

Let me conclude by assuring you that you are one of the most deserving people ever to have met me on my way through life. My wife and I regard you and your own wife as utterly devoted to us, and would ask you only to continue to behave towards us in this same spirit.

Sincere good wishes from us both.

Your obedient servant,
Richard Wagner

RWA (incompletely published in Freunde und Zeitgenossen 574–6).

451. HANS VON WOLZOGEN, POTSDAM   Bad Ems, 2 July 1877

Most valued friend,

I have just sought out your letter again, not so much to reply to it but to tell you something in connection with it.

I am at the end of a so-called health cure, although – as such – I am expecting very little from it; nevertheless, I have to think about it to the extent of not subjecting myself to any undue strain.

And so I shall pass over all that I have had to go through ever since discovering that no summons or appeal on my part has succeeded in producing

---

1 The passage in square brackets has not previously been published.
2 A second prose draft of the libretto had been completed on 23 February 1877; the versified text was completed on 19 April 1877. See also letter [221], p. 424, note 1.

even the least inclination on the part of others to relieve me of the burden of last year's festival deficit. I am now struggling under the weight of this burden, and have spent my last remaining savings on it, but – I am filled with a boundless indifference towards all the activities of my so-called Patrons and their societies.

This month I am planning to make one last attempt to unload the whole affair on to the Munich Court Theatre in order that – for the time being at least – I no longer need think of "stage festivals" (in my sense of the word). –

If I fail, I shall go to America, make provisions for my family, and – consider *anything* rather than return to Germany. –

But if the worst does not come to the worst after all, I am planning to use what remains of my life – since I have no alternative in the matter – in carrying out a certain idea of mine. I shall seek, on the most modest basis, to use my presence in Bayreuth to train conductors and dramatic singers. My provisional plan is so practical as to be very straightforward. I need four assistants who will have to be paid next to nothing. My immediate concern is to see that this happens. You are one of the four.[1] My school could be opened as early as the end of this coming autumn. I hope you will find a way of allowing me to persuade you to come and live in Bayreuth – perhaps in the not too distant future.

How much do you need in order to get by – at a pinch? –

(This is all just between the two of us! That goes without saying!)

I shall be leaving here on the 5th of this month, and shall be in Seelisberg (Canton Uri) in Switzerland until the 15th, then Munich, Marienbad Hotel. –

Best wishes from

Your sincerely devoted
Richard Wagner

*Facsimile in Altmann/Bozman, Vol. II, facing page 286
(incompletely published in Bayreuther Briefe II,379–81).*

452. EDWARD DANNREUTHER, LONDON   [Bayreuth,] 22 August 1877

Dear friend,

When I saw myself constrained to sacrifice a considerable part of the receipts of the London concerts that had originally been promised to me, and use that money for the artistic survival of this enterprise of mine, some of my friends had the idea of making good this loss by means of a subscription – since the income was uniquely intended as a contribution towards covering

---

1 Other invitations were sent to Julius Hey, Karl Klindworth, Felix Mottl and August Wilhelmj. Nothing came of the plan.

the remaining deficit on last year's Bayreuth festival, – and you yourself headed that subscription with an appeal to friends of my art in England.

Since that time more obvious ways of covering the deficit have opened up,[1] and I therefore consider it only right to beg the esteemed subscribers whose names were recently sent to me to take back the money which they so generously placed at my disposal, a request which I would ask you to convey to the parties concerned with the assurance that I shall always remain sincerely grateful to them for the support they have shown me.

With all good wishes

Your obedient servant
Richard Wagner

Bayreuther Briefe II, 268–9.

453. JUDITH GAUTIER, PARIS   Bayreuth, 1 October 1877

My love,

Cosima has asked me to write to you about certain errands which I shall entrust to you when the time comes to think about New Year presents, etc.

In the meantime I shall take advantage of this (admirable!) ruse for a very minor matter – *entre nous*, as it were. Our eldest daughter Daniella's birthday falls on the 8th of this month: Cosima tells me that her daughter would be delighted if I included a pretty perfumed sachet with her presents, but she does not want me to spend any money on it. In total disobedience to her wishes I am sending you a postal order for 62 francs, and would ask you to see to a very pretty sachet, filled, and made of silk, etc. Choose a perfume to suit your own taste, entirely to your own taste, and add about half a dozen paper powder-bags, so that I can put them between my own morning linen, which will put me on good terms with you when I sit down at the piano to compose the music of *Parsifal*. –

Address it all to Monsieur Bernard Schnappauf, Barber, Ochsengasse, Bayreuth.

It will serve as a surprise! –

Yes, it's the music to "Parsifal" that is at stake. I couldn't live any longer without throwing myself into a task of this kind. Help me! –

How is your German coming along? Oh! If you really understood my language, how you would like my poem.

And when shall I see you again? You who were so unkind as to not accept my invitation to London? And what was your excuse? All right! I know! Oh, but it was unkind of you! –

---

1 On 20 July 1877 Wagner had met Düfflipp in Munich in order to discuss ways of paying off the outstanding deficit. See also introductory essay, pp. 802–3.

And now, when – how? But so be it! Love me, and let us not wait for a
Protestant heaven: it is bound to be very boring! –

My love! My love! Never stop loving me!

A thousand – from your

Richard Wagner.

(You need to be quick in sending me these things – by post!).

(And our good Benedictus?!)[1]

Lettres à Judith Gautier 59–61 (original in French).

454. EMIL SANDER, MELBOURNE   Bayreuth, 22 October 1877

My very dear Sir,

I was delighted to receive your news,[2] and cannot refrain from thanking
you for it.

I hope you will see to it that my works are performed in "English": only
in this way can they be intimately understood by an English-speaking audience. We are hoping that they will be so performed in London.

We (that is, I and my family) were extremely interested to see the views of
Melbourne which you sent me: since you were kind enough to offer to send
us more, I can assure you that I should be only too delighted to receive them.

Please give my kind regards to Herr Lyster,[3] and, however remote your
part of the world may be, continue to be so well-disposed towards

Your most grateful servant
Richard Wagner

ASM, 150, 153.

455. OTTO EISER, FRANKFURT   Bayreuth, 23 October 1877

My very dear Sir,

I took the liberty of instructing one of my younger friends[4] to write to you,
but was obliged to put your reply to one side until such time as I could read

---

1 Louis Benedictus, an amateur composer and devoted companion of Judith Gautier, who was
   now separated from Catulle Mendès.
2 The Melbourne première of *Lohengrin* had taken place on 18 August 1877. It was sung in
   Italian.
3 William Saurin Lyster was the impresario responsible for the Melbourne performances.
4 At Wagner's request, Hans von Wolzogen had written to Eiser, Nietzsche's doctor, following
   receipt of a letter in which Nietzsche had informed the Wagners of "bad news" concerning
   his health. Eiser, whom Nietzsche had consulted in Frankfurt between 3 and 7 October,
   replied on the 17th.

it with the necessary calm and apprise myself sufficiently of its contents to be able to communicate with you in turn.

In the fateful question that concerns the health of our friend N. I feel an urgent need to inform you, briefly and decisively, of both my opinion and my anxiety – but also of my hope. In my attempts to assess N.'s condition, I have been thinking for some time of identical and very similar experiences which I recall having had with certain young men of great intellectual ability. I saw them being destroyed by similar symptoms, and discovered only too clearly that these symptoms were the result of masturbation. Guided by these experiences, I observed N. more closely and, on the strength of his traits and characteristic habits, this fear of mine became a conviction. I believe it would be wrong of me to express myself more circumstantially on this point, the more so since my only concern is to draw a friendly doctor's attention to the opinion which I have conveyed to you here. It is merely to confirm the great likelihood that I am right that I mention the striking experience I had whereby one of the young friends whom I mentioned, a poet who died in Leipzig many years ago,[1] became totally blind when he was N.'s age, while the other, equally talented, friend,[2] who now ekes out a pitiful existence in Italy, with his nerves completely shattered, began to suffer the most painful eye disease at exactly the same age as N. One thing that struck me as being of great importance was the news that I recently received to the effect that the doctor[3] whom N. had consulted in Naples some time ago advised him first and foremost – to get married. –

I believe I have said enough to enable you to make a serious diagnosis along the lines that I have indicated. It would ill become me to suggest that you should re-examine the symptoms of N.'s illness: it is, after all, clear that the only remedy is to take the greatest possible care of him. But the need to strengthen and regenerate his nerves and his spinal cord seems to me far too important for me to conceal from you my very real wish that something positive be done here. Many years ago an intelligent hydropathist near Geneva[4] cured me completely of erisypelas, of which I had suffered countless attacks until that time but which has not returned to plague me since then:[5] I was utterly demoralized by this illness, to the point where I was afraid of even the slightest draught. My doctor explained that I was simply over-tense, and promised to restore my complete confidence in two months, a promise which he kept. The process he used was extremely successful and had a calmative effect with *light* compresses applied for brief periods, and cold lotions. – When

1 Theodor Apel, whose blindness had been caused by a fall from a horse at the age of twenty-five.
2 Karl Ritter.
3 Otto von Schrön.
4 Dr Vaillant of Mornex.
5 Attacks recurred from 28 July 1880 onwards (see Cosima Wagner's diary for that date).

Minister von Schleinitz paid a relatively lengthy visit here two years ago, he was in a pitiful state of nervous collapse, a condition which, given his addiction to a life of pleasure at an already fairly advanced age, he had no doubt brought upon himself. Six weeks in Gräfenberg set him on his feet again, so that I scarcely recognized him when I saw him again, completely rejuvenated, the following winter and again in the summer of last year. If I were to summarize these various experiences and turn them to the advantage of our poor friend, it would be because I feel so forceful a need to beg you most insistently to give kind and serious consideration to what I have told you. I am firmly convinced that the extremely sympathetic hydropathist at the Gräfenberg Institute will be of fundamental assistance to our friend. I hope you will advise him accordingly, and – if necessary – speak to him in all seriousness, without concealing from him the primary cause of his illness. A friendly *physician* certainly has an authority here which may not be granted to a physicianly *friend.*

I count myself fortunate indeed in having found in you the very man to mediate on N.'s behalf. Forgive me for having allowed the value which you immediately acquired for me as N.'s physician to override the other cause for satisfaction which I can feel at having found in you so intelligent a friend of my poem.[1] However, I do not for that reason fail to appreciate these *two* qualities, but merely reserve for myself the right to clarify the former issue with you *first*, before going into detail in respect of the second.

Respectful good wishes from

Your obedient servant
Richard Wagner

Curt von Westernhagen, Richard Wagner (Zurich 1956), 527–9.

456. Ernst Wilhelm Fritzsch, Leipzig   Bayreuth, 27 October 1877

Most valued friend,

I am most grateful to you for visiting me in Bayreuth, although I am uncertain as to whether the latest turn of events in the matter of our Patrons'

---

1 Eiser submitted two articles, which were later published in the *Bayreuther Blätter*, viz. "Andeutungen über Wagners Beziehung zu Schopenhauer und zur Grundidee des Christenthums" (Notes on Wagner's Relationship to Schopenhauer and to the Basic Idea of Christianity) in *Bayreuther Blätter*, i (1878), 222–9; and "Richard Wagners 'Der Ring des Nibelungen'. Ein exegetischer Versuch" (Richard Wagner's "The Ring of the Nibelung": An Attempt at Exegesis) in *Bayreuther Blätter*, i (1878), 309–17 and 352–66. See letter [457], pp. 876–7.

certificates meets with your wishes or not.[1] In the mean time I still do not know either whether anything will come of the so-called "School", since the invitation asking people to register was seriously delayed, and in any case fell at a bad time of the year, while the claims for support can really only be met by those who are wanting to be appointed. We shall simply have to wait and see. – In the mean time, however, I do not want to give up the "Bayreuther Blätter", and for this reason hope that we shall remain in contact for our mutual benefit. – There have already been enquiries about taking over the "publishing house". However, just as I intend presenting my festival only to a "Society" from now on, so I intend this journal to be available solely to that "Society". The (minimal –) costs will be paid for by contributions from the Society, and the "Blätter" will therefore also belong to the Society, whose members will perhaps have to pay only a small extra charge in order to subscribe to it. Once the courses of study begin, the journal will carry reports on them and on their character, so as to educate our readers, and perhaps also include other Society news, as far as this is of a purely artistic nature. Even if the School cannot be opened until a later date, the journal should publish introductory articles & essays from the 1st of January '78 onwards, albeit in a smaller quantity. Accordingly, I am thinking of beginning in the New Year, in association with Wolzogen, Porges & Pohl, etc., and producing 1 sheet (octavo) every 2 weeks or so. – I should like you to take over the printing, production and distribution of the journal, since it seems to me that you could very easily send it out as a supplement to your M. Wochenblatt, excepting only those (fully subscribed) members of the Society who are not to receive your Wochenblatt. I should very much like to think of your becoming involved in this enterprise – which from a publishing point of view is not in the least speculative – more especially because of our excellent mutual understanding and devotion to the cause; in this way we shall also best succeed in avoiding any competition with your own journal, but, on the contrary, enhance its reputation still further. There will of course be absolutely no question of including any correspondence, criticism, reviews, advertisements, etc., in the Bayreuther Blätter, and if ever we need anything of that kind, I shall always use your own columns. But my enterprise shall always remain an independent undertaking which, financially, belongs to the Society alone.

Please let me know your views on the matter. (I may mention merely in passing that even though you will derive as little profit – i.e. financially speaking – from the Bayreuther Blätter as each of its contributors, you will

---

1 On 15 September 1877 Wagner addressed delegates from the various Patrons' societies and proposed that new statutes be set up enabling a School of Music and Drama to be established in Bayreuth. It soon became clear that the scheme had little support, and on 8 December 1877 Wagner informed the Patrons that the *Bayreuther Blätter* would be inaugurated in "compensation" for the failure of the School.

also have as few expenses as they do, since their expenses in moving to Bayreuth are all to be reimbursed.)

I hope you will understand me, and believe me when I say that it pleases me to recall our good and steadfast relations.

With the most sincere good wishes, I am

Your obedient servant
Richard Wagner

Richard Wagner: "Briefe aus sechs Jahrzehnten" in Die neue Rundschau: XIXter Jahrgang der freien Bühne (Berlin 1908), 996–7.

457. OTTO EISER, FRANKFURT   Bayreuth, 29 October 1877

My very dear Sir,

I have just got round to finishing your article on the "Ring of the Nibelung".[1] Please believe me when I tell you that I was uncommonly touched and delighted by it. At a time when I can think of those days in Bayreuth last year with little but sadness, it fills me with great warmth to know that someone like you was present here then! –

God knows how long I may yet retain my vital strengths; but however long they may last, I can certainly reckon on never finding myself in agreement with my contemporaries; there must always remain something left over which I shall have to leave to a new and younger generation to claim for themselves. Herein lies my consolation and my hope; for what persuades me to enjoy both while I may are occasional signs of life on the part of my fellow men, of the kind which you yourself so splendidly showed me!

Do not expect me to offer any further – or more detailed – criticism of your essay. There is nothing about it to which I would object, and nothing of which I might wish to remind you. I felt only pleasure and deep emotion at all that you said, at your reasons for saying it – and the manner in which you said it. As a curiosity I would remind you only that it was barely a year after completing the poem[2] that I first became acquainted with Schopenhauer's philosophy (and, indeed, with philosophy in general), that it initially repelled me, and that only through a deeply tragic perception of the world – a view which I and Schopenhauer have in common – did I feel powerfully drawn to an understanding of it. –

Not another word about our friend:[3] I know that, thanks to your love, he

1 See letter [455], p. 874, note 1.
2 In December 1852. Wagner first read Schopenhauer's *The World as Will and Representation* in the autumn of 1854; see letter [177], p. 323.
3 Friedrich Nietzsche.

is in the best possible care. I cannot help him now. If he were really to fall on hard times, I could help him then: for there is nothing I would not share with him.

Fare you well, and think kindly of

Your obedient servant
Richard Wagner

Curt von Westernhagen, Richard Wagner (Zurich 1956), 531–2.

458. JUDITH GAUTIER, PARIS   [Bayreuth, 22 November 1877]

There is something which I had forgotten and which *obliges* me to write to you again, oh, my dear Judith! – The slippers *without* heels! . . .

But no! Something else! I want a very beautiful and exceptional cover – for my chaise-longue – which I shall call "Judith"! – Listen! Try and find one of those silk fabrics called "Lampas" or – whatever? Yellow satin background – the palest possible – with a floral pattern – roses; not too large a design, it is not intended for curtains; it is used, rather, for small pieces of furniture. If there is nothing in yellow, then very light blue.*) I shall need six metres! –

All this for mornings well spent on *"Parsifal"*.

This is an Arabian name. The old troubadours no longer understood what it meant. "Parsi fal" means: "parsi" – think of the fire-loving Parsees – "pure"; "fal" means "mad" in a higher sense, in other words a man without erudition, but one of genius ("Fellow", in English, seems to be related to this Oriental root).[1] – You will see (sorry, learn) why this naïve man bore an Arabian name! –

Adieu! my dearest, my "dolcissima anima".

Your

R.W.

I have reclaimed this letter from the servant to whom it had been delivered since Mr Schnappauf has just brought me your latest. – Well! Well – Oh! these letters, these beautiful letters written in your own hand, that warm hand which I held during the *Nibelunges!*

So! Have you understood my French? Oh! I was afraid I might have said something stupid!

– Well! Well! – And so! Now – the errands.

---

*) Same white background, which will be easier to find [*Wagner's footnote*].

1 Wagner's etymology derives from Joseph Görres' edition of *Lohengrin* (Heidelberg 1813), vi. English "fellow" derives from late Old English *fēolaga*, someone who lays down money, or a fee, in a joint undertaking.

I am writing to Félix to send you the Japanese dress! – Slippers, babouches! Agreed! – The gloves – like the sample, chamois I think. –

Nothing else! –

And yet: My dear! My dear!

R.

Lettres à Judith Gautier 65–7.

459. HERMAN ZUMPE, WÜRZBURG   Bayreuth, 4 December 1877

Dear friend,

If you tell me *where* I should recommend you, I shall do so. – Bülow has obtained Hanover – I know of no other posts there. All these intendants have a personal dislike of me. I cannot obtain posts for anyone: I tried it in Munich for Fischer, but they treated him so badly that he couldn't stay, whereas everything has turned out very well for him in Mannheim – why? – because Heckel has gained influence there.

Really, it can only torment me to know that people think I could help them but that I do not wish to do so. Theatres are now a foreign place to me. – What then? Patience! It was just the same for me!

Best wishes.

Yours truly,
R. Wagner.

Bayreuther Briefe II, 278–9.

460. JUDITH GAUTIER, PARIS   [Bayreuth, 18 December 1877]

Dear soul! – Benedictus has fallen substantially in my affection now that I know he writes music – the same thing happens to every new acquaintance that I make, the moment I discover he is another musician who also composes music, but then everyone composes music nowadays, and they are almost always contemptible men, not least because of their weakness and indolence. When I think how much music there is in the world, and for how few works of music I can feel any real affection, to the extent that these few works could be said to contain all that I understand by the name of "music", you would be amazed if I told you. But I am not saying that. The "daring innovations of instrumentation" of which you speak sadden me: when all these young people begin, all that I hear are "daring innovations", either of instrumentation or harmony, – but never of melody!

But Benedictus is your "brother", and consequently my cousin. I am a very bad musician, I read very badly, a new score distracts me, and I feel nothing. In a word, let my "cousin" risk it! –

But now to more *serious* matters: first of all, the two chests which have not arrived. Well! They will arrive, and I shall immerse myself in your generous soul. Cancel the pink satin entirely: there would be too much of it, and it would be good for nothing. Can I expect the two remnants which I mentioned in my last letter? – The brocade can be reserved: I'm inclined to order 30 metres, but perhaps the colours can be changed to flatter my taste even better; in other words: the fawn striped material would be silver-grey, and the blue *my* pink, very pale and delicate. – In the mean time I have intercepted a letter from Félix to C., offering her a black velvet dress at a very reasonable price. I asked for this dress two weeks ago in order to have it before Christmas. Time is short, I don't have Félix's address any longer. Would you call on him, and tell him to hurry? –

Ah! and the Japanese dress: I spend every hour of the day looking at your magnificent painting: with black hair? (Is it you?) You frighten me with all your "oils". I shall make mistakes with them: in general I prefer powders, since they cling more gently to fabrics, etc. But, once again, be prodigal, above all in the quantity of oils to put in the bath, such as the "ambergris" etc. I have my bathtub below[1] my "studio", and I like to smell the perfumes rising.

For the rest, do not think ill of me! I am old enough to indulge in childish pursuits! – I have three years of *Parsifal* ahead of me, and nothing must tear me away from the peaceful tranquillity of creative seclusion.

Come, – Come even if you have to bring my cousin! –

The exhibition? – Oh!, let it come here, and be put on display in my studio!

Oh! belovèd soul, dearly belovèd soul! All is so tragic, all that is *real!* But you will always love me – and I cannot do otherwise, however strong my will.

A thousand kisses.

R.

Lettres à Judith Gautier 78–80.

461. JUDITH GAUTIER, PARIS   [Bayreuth,] 4 January 1878

Judith! oh! what beautiful warmth! I shall love you always! But that is not what concerns me at present:

Your bronchitis? I want to know how it is. And you said nothing about your health? – And the music by my cousin B?[2]

---

1 The original text reads *au-dessus de* (= "above"), but this is clearly an error attributable to Wagner's erratic French. His study was on the top floor at the front of the house, and his bathroom on the mezzanine immediately below.
2 Louis Benedictus.

Now you know everything, I have nothing else to tell you . . .

I like to see you defending your country so valiantly on every occasion, even when it means recognizing that the Madame de Pompadour¹ of 13 years ago was more graceful than that of today. (It was a question only of this when I spoke of an increasing dullness of taste! – Oh! you! wicked detractress!) But I admire you even more for your patriotism, because it is something I lack completely, finding myself the only German amongst this stupid population which is called German!

– And so, you are luckier than I am! But, an end to our quarrels – although they are delightful when they take place between the two of us! –

To be serious! – Since you are obliged to accept other fabrics by way of exchange at a certain shop, I suggest – in the circumstances – that, to make your choice easier (almost impossible), you take a beautiful *white satin*, since in that way we shall avoid any difficulties over shades of colour, and a white satin will always be useful. Well then! after the perfumes etc., count up what remains of the fortune I deposited with you, and spend it on this white satin. Let us reserve the order for brocade until some other time. The question is always whether you have any money left in your account.²

Well, I am always happy to have to wait for the things you send me! – You must send this once again through Schnappauf (!), whereas I would advise you – after this – to write to me directly, *perhaps* – thinking, rather, that I shall not have to hide your charming letters. In case of absolute necessity – (oh!) – all right then – long live *Schnappauf!* –

All my love, my beautiful belovèd, dear and adored soul! My child! my Judith!

Your

Rich.

Parsifal is going well: you shall soon have some new bars!³

Lettres à Judith Gautier 86–7.

---

1 A silk fabric which Wagner had ordered from Judith Gautier.
2 Between 1 October 1877 and 14 January 1878 Wagner sent Judith Gautier 2062 francs (about 1675 marks).
3 The first complete draft of Act I was begun in September 1877 and completed on 29 January 1878; the second complete draft occupied Wagner between 25 September 1877 and 31 January 1878; and the full score between 23 August 1879 and 25 April 1881. The dates for Act II are: first complete draft (end), 30 September [1878]; second complete draft, 13 March – 11 October 1878; full score, 6 June – 20 October 1881; and the dates for Act III: first complete draft, 30 October 1878 – 16 April [1879]; second complete draft, 14 November 1878 – 26 April 1879; and full score, 8 November – 25 December 1881.

462. JUDITH GAUTIER, PARIS   [Bayreuth,] 6 February 1878

Dear Judith,

Your charming letter was scarcely designed to reassure me! – When you were here for the "Festspiele", you seemed so radiant and of so robust a constitution that it only increased my pleasure at the prospect of seeing you again. Try, try to get over these attacks of ill health: there is nothing else you need do to please me!

Press on with the affair of the Chinese dress, and send me the man or woman you are using for this purpose! –

The little bottle of rose-water was completely ruined by cold water; and in my clumsiness I dropped the larger bottle as I was trying to arrange it with the alcohol: it broke, and its contents went all over the carpet; what really surprised me, however, was how little effect the smell had, since I would have expected it to have given me 1000 headaches! –

Send me some more of it. –

And don't forget the Rimmel Bengali rose-powders. – But – above all – be so kind as to let me know *immediately* and in a word if you have found the lilac satin (Ophelia!), since my decision to buy it depends upon your answer.

Dearly belovèd! I have finished the 1st act;[1] you shall have a sample of it as soon as I have dealt with a whole host of other matters which I have neglected of late. The *full score* of the *Idyll*[2] has arrived; I am sending a copy to my cousin Benedictus – in exchange for the score he has *not* sent me! – I am now only waiting for the piano arrangement, which is intended for you.

Cosima continues as ever before to be filled with feelings of admiration and gratitude towards you on account of the Japanese dress and all the other things you have chosen for her. Would to God that our traditional quarrels on the subject of poor *Parsifal* might be over and done with! Believe me, they are not worth the effort.[3]

But – I love to see my address traced by your hand! oh! what – what? – But – that's the way of the world! – Why – in heaven's name – did I not find you during the days that followed the failure of *Tannhäuser* in Paris? – Were you too young at the time? – Let us say nothing! Nothing! – But – let us love! let us love!

Your
Richard

Lettres à Judith Gautier 94–6.

1 Of *Parsifal*; see letter [461], p. 880, note 3.
2 The *Siegfried Idyll* (WWV 103), which Wagner had sold to Schotts the previous autumn.
3 See CT for 24 December 1877.

463. JUDITH GAUTIER, PARIS   [Bayreuth, 15 February 1878]

Dear soul,

I have asked Cosima to take charge of these errands from now on, or rather to make the final arrangements with regard to the various errands with which I have been troubling you for so long.[1] I believe, at the same time, that I do well to entrust these last remaining problems to her (as a woman), since there is no longer any surprise in store! – As for the rest, I am so overwhelmed with work at the moment – work which is not in the least agreeable – that I cannot find time any longer to continue working on *Parsifal*. – Take pity on me! It will soon be over, and I shall rediscover those wonderful moments when I can enjoy talking to you about myself! –

But do not worry about me: the things that annoy me will soon be over and done with! –

Be considerate towards Cosima: write to her properly and at length. I shall be told everything. Do not stop loving me! You will see me often,[2] and, after all, we shall see each other again some day!

Yours,

R.

Lettres à Judith Gautier 96–7.

464. WILHELM TAPPERT, BERLIN   Bayreuth, 8 March 1878

To be used as appropriate!

– When Herr v. Hülsen dined with me, he expressed the wish that he might be allowed to give the "Valkyrie", a suggestion which made such a disagreeable impression upon me that Liszt & my wife were obliged to intervene and intimate to H.E. that he would do well to spare me such importunities. One of the things I let slip in my anger was that, if they wanted to give the "Valkyrie" on its own, they would straightway have to cut half the 2nd act, otherwise it would make no sense at all. It seems that he and Eckert (who was also present) interpreted this as permission to cut the passage in question. –

Since then, Bronsart has expressed a wish to perform the whole of the Nibelung's Ring in Hanover. Hülsen has forbidden him to do so, and issued instructions whereby Hanover, Cassel and Wiesbaden are allowed to perform only those works which he himself has already accepted for Berlin.

---

1 For an explanation of the abrupt change of tone between this letter (the last surviving one to Judith Gautier) and letter [462], see introductory essay, p. 804.
2 "Vous me verrez souvent": perhaps a misreading for "Vous m'écrirez souvent" (You will write to me often).

That was how things stood when Eckert approached me again recently on Hülsen's behalf, repeating his shameless demand that I hand over the "Valkyrie" to him for next autumn. I wanted you to know the answer I sent him – for future use! –

For the rest, *Brunswick* and *Schwerin* – in addition to Hamburg and Leipzig – have now acquired full performing rights to the whole 4-part work.[1]

How are things otherwise, you wicked man? –

Cordially yours,
Rich. Wagner

Otto 418.

465. KING LUDWIG II OF BAVARIA, MUNICH   Bayreuth, 1 April 1878

[...] I may mention in passing that I was recently vouchsafed the most curious experience of breathing new life into a number of youthful compositions of mine which for a time had been lost without trace. It is really my wife whom I must thank for this service, since it was she who showed the most unheard-of zeal and the keenest perspicacity in following every lead in her search for what had been lost. As a result a trunk was recently rediscovered in Dresden containing a small number of bigger instrumental works, but consisting only of their orchestral parts.[2] Well, I now have a young musician here with me, whom I am training as my future conductor;[3] he is having to produce a full score from the rediscovered parts, and in this way each passing week brings with it the surprise of rediscovering another new movement of a great symphony which I wrote and performed in Leipzig over forty years ago. Notwithstanding my intolerance towards these early works and my refusal to have them more widely known, I am bound to concede that this symphony is entirely worthy of me. It has had a remarkable fate. In 1835, in other words 43 years ago, I wanted Mendelssohn (who was then in Leipzig) to look through it for me; in order not to rush him but to leave him ample time, I asked him to keep my manuscript. I often saw him after that, but he never said a word to me about the symphony. He died, and I – moved on. – I told my wife about this at Triebschen. After that she would not rest. Our young

1 Complete performances of the *Ring* were heard in Munich (17–23 November 1878), Leipzig (3–7 January 1879), Vienna (26–30 May 1879), Hamburg (1880) and Berlin, Victoria Theatre (5–9 May 1881). *Die Walküre* was first heard at the Royal Opera House in Berlin (where Hülsen was intendant) on 7 April 1884: the complete cycle was not performed there until 8–17 December 1888, two years after Hülsen's death.
2 According to Glasenapp (VI,66) these were the *Polonia* and *Columbus* Overtures, and the Symphony in C major.
3 Anton Seidl.

friend Nietzsche got to know Mendelssohn's son: enquiries were made through him: not a trace. When the son died in his turn, further enquiries were made of Mendelssohn's old heirs: in vain, the manuscript was and – as it appears – *is* missing. Has it been destroyed? – And then, finally, copies of the orchestral parts were discovered in an old trunk, and – behold! – my youthful work stands before me once again, a source of genuine delight. I may perhaps revise it a little by and by, and believe I shall then be able to offer the world compelling evidence of my youthful talent, from a time when I never composed anything that I was not inspired to write,[1] – a fact which Brahms – my fellow knight – understands so well. –

[. . .]

Königsbriefe III, 120–21.

466. FRANZ OVERBECK, BASLE   Bayreuth, 24 May 1878

My very dear Sir and friend,

How much it pleased me to know that you had remembered my birthday. Please accept my most heartfelt thanks! It also touched me that you should have felt it necessary to speak apologetically about your attempts in Basle to enlist support for Bayreuth. In Basle? – it is extraordinary! My most valued friend, I really think that we are united by more important interests than these – strange-seeming – interests of artistic experimentation!

I gather from your brief allusions that *our old friend Nietzsche* has been holding himself *aloof from you as well*. There is no doubt that very *striking changes* have taken place *in him*: but anyone who observed him and his *psychic spasms* years ago could almost be justified in saying that a long-dreaded and not entirely unpredictable catastrophe had now overtaken him. I have retained sufficient friendship for him *not* to read his book[2] – which I glanced through as I was cutting the pages – and can only wish and hope that he will thank me for it some day.

With the request that you remember me and my wife to your own dear wife, I remain, in friendship and respect,

Your obedient servant
Richard Wagner.

RWA (published without underlinings in Freunde und Zeitgenossen 579).

1 A similar sentiment occurs in the essay *Ueber das Opern-Dichten und Komponiren im Besonderen* (On Opera Libretti and Composition in Particular), first published in *Bayreuther Blätter*, ii (1879), 249–66. Reprinted in GS X,152–75, esp. 172; PW VI,149–72, esp. 169.
2 *Menschliches, Allzumenschliches* (Human, All-Too-Human), two copies of which had arrived in Wahnfried on 25 April 1878.

467. KING LUDWIG II OF BAVARIA, LINDERHOF

Bayreuth, 15 October 1878

My most glorious and most kingly lord and friend,

It was a beautiful day, the eleventh of October! Your heavenly letter arrived, and – the second act of Parsifal was completed right down to the very last note. It was a cause for jubilation and tears of joy in Wahnfried. And I had good reason to celebrate finishing this particular act as though it were some festival. Before I began it, I was afraid of the terrible excitement which the great catastrophe between Parsifal and Kundry would have to offer. In Tristan I had to portray the all-consuming anguish of love's longing, inconceivably intensified to a pitch of the most painful desire for death; the Ring of the Nibelung is replete with raging passion, and Venus and Tannhäuser – in the later revision – know what the terrors of love are. But for Parsifal and Kundry all this is completely new: here are two worlds locked in a struggle for final redemption. How often I told myself that, having lost myself so often before in these various spheres, I could have spared myself that torment on this occasion. But, as the common saying goes, it was a question of "you've made your bed, now you must lie on it!" – I have already complained to my understanding friend that I was disappointed in last summer's expectations concerning my health: it was because of my cure that I interrupted my work at the fatal "kiss"; and now I was supposed to start up again at the very point where only the most high-spirited mood could produce what I need to tend mankind's most critical sufferings with the tenderest possible care. I yearned for an act of the Mastersingers, and thought of my old friend Fischer – now long dead – who was chorus-master in Dresden: I remember once, in 1848, reading out to him a passage from the newspapers that spoke of "noisy scenes" that had taken place somewhere or other, and how he clasped his hands together and cried out: "ah! would that I might hear of *noiseless* scenes!" – Well, I plunged into purgatory, and have re-emerged from it safely. I know – this work, too, has turned out to be worthy of *us*. – I intend going straight on without a break to the third act, which promises me a blessed harvest after the labours of the second act. But I must first introduce it with an orchestral prelude to accompany Parsifal's effortful wanderings up to the point where he rediscovers the realm of the Grail. But this in turn leads to the Good Friday meadow, – and I shall be happy to linger there. – Here, my uniquely belovèd prince, my protector and friend whose radiance illumines me with ever – and ever – greater splendour, here you have the true import of my life. All other events that take place in the world, and, more especially, fate's dallying sport with me and my works, affect me only as much as they would affect a man who was dead and whose spirit gazed down – as though from a cloud – to see what the world would make of all that he had bequeathed to it. I can only shake my head: there is nothing more that can persuade me to feel any interest in such activity. After all, I have my King and my wife! –

Ah! And this King is a source of such great joy! He really intends to have his portrait painted for me! What this means to me is something which he – so great and godlike is he – can, alas, most certainly never imagine! Oh! To be so kind, so infinitely kind as to grant the wretch that I am this boldest of all my entreaties! But – in all seriousness! I trust only Lenbach to requite this most gracious sacrifice of your favour and love. He is a genius among present-day portrait-painters, as the French have once again recognized of late; and he loves his King to distraction, just as he truly understands him with the most innocent inwardness. I am sure that this painting will be something quite splendid! Ah! as long as you remain true to me, my most precious and gracious King! You have always been so, and more and more a match in your kindness, favour – and forbearance! – And so – : I am filled with hope! – It is my only hope, this hope which I place in you, my godlike friend!

In doting love my wife joins me in raising her eyes up to him whom, in awestruck humility, my children behold hovering above them as the guardian angel of their very existence, and to whom I commit my soul with the joyfullest devotion as one who is

uniquely and immortally his
for this world:
"Richard Wagner"

Königsbriefe III, 138–9.

468. ELSA UHLIG, DRESDEN   Bayreuth, 12 December 1878

My dear Fräulein Uhlig,

I was most touched and gratified by your response to my wife's attempts to collect various stray manuscripts of mine by returning with such friendly resignation the manuscript of my essay on "Opera and Drama" which I once dedicated to your father, my faithfully devoted friend who was taken from us at so early an age. You also enclosed the originals of a number of extremely intimate letters to my late friend. In exchange you would like a memento of me. For this purpose I have chosen a silver laurel wreath presented to me some time ago[1] by my friends in Munich, and I would ask you to accept it as a fitting tribute to the memory of a friend who died so young.

I should have preferred it if – at my own expense of course – you could have provided me with copies, duly certified by yourself, of the numerous

---

[1] After the première of *Tristan und Isolde* in 1865. The wreath was not well received by Elsa Uhlig: see CT for 19 December 1878.

letters to your late father which you wish to keep for yourself in order to honour his memory. These letters are no doubt of great value to you in determining the importance which your father had for me, and yet their contents are no less valuable to my own descendants who may one day need to know about this relationship of mine. In this context I should also have valued the return of my transcription of Beethoven's Ninth Symphony. If I gave away these relics to friends, it was out of a kind of passionate concern for them at a time when I stood completely alone in the world, without any children. Fate has now granted me a family and, among my progeny, I also have a son who fills me with hope for the future. When I depart this life, I shall leave no one behind who has so keen an interest in every aspect of my life and work as this son. Only on the basis of what he knows of the rest of my life will he understand the exact circumstances which led me to make a copy of Beethoven's work, and in his hands it will acquire a living significance, whereas for you and your descendants it can never be anything more than a curio of perhaps historical value. I beg you to return this copy for my son.[1]

Although life's hardships have made things exceedingly difficult for me until now, not least because of the attendant inability to be of service to my friends, my situation is now somewhat easier in many respects, inasmuch as I am now able to surrender my works for financial gain. But only now, indeed, am I in a position to be of some service to you in the face of life's hardships. Will you please tell me how I can help you?

With sincere good wishes, I am

Your obedient servant
Richard Wagner

Freunde und Zeitgenossen 580–1.

469. KING LUDWIG II OF BAVARIA, HOHENSCHWANGAU

Bayreuth, 9 February 1879

My most dearly belovèd, exalted and solitary friend,

I must needs seek my only companion on lofty mountain peaks where no one can find him save he who was ever destined to do so! When so heavenly a letter[2] arrives from you, my ineffably precious and glorious friend, and when, in the company of the only woman to share in our beautiful solitude, I weigh up the tender and unfathomable meaning of each of the words you

1 Wagner's arrangement of Beethoven's Choral Symphony (WWV 9) was returned by Elsa Uhlig and presented to Cosima as a birthday present on 25 December 1880. For a history of the Uhlig correspondence, see Appendix B of the Burrell Collection.
2 The letter in question has been lost. Cosima Wagner's diary for 22 January 1879 simply notes, "A nice letter to him from the King".

bestowed on me, we are reminded at times of the sublime symbol of the Holy Trinity that tells how what was once unheard-of has now become real. We then muse on the theme of the "Father", "Son" and "Holy Ghost": and although it brings a smile to our lips, it is also a source of deep renewal and spiritual light. Strengthened and fired by this selfsame renewal, I preface what follows with a greeting of deepest gratitude to my exalted and solitary friend: all hail and God speed to the

all-wise redeemer![1] –

But let me say something straightaway about my son! – A Brahman once withdrew into the loneliness of the forest in order that, free from all earthly fancy, he might live henceforth for inner knowledge alone. A young antelope seeks shelter with him in her wounded state; he tends her; in her gratitude she vows never to desert him. A sigh passes his lips: for once again he feels the cares of love, and is heir to the confusion of man's natural destiny! – How I once cast to one side all that could have served to remind the world of me! A childless marriage had lasted thirty years: to whom could I have left anything during that time? But then I cried out in the house one morning: "a son is there!"[2] How different the world now looked of a sudden! Happy the mother who saw all at once that my past and my future had now acquired a quite different meaning: "you will now live on even after death, continuing to strive and to influence others." All my relics are now being kept: letters, manuscripts, books which I once used, every line that I ever wrote, all have been sought out and collected; my life has been recorded with ever increasing care, and illustrations obtained of all the places I lived and all the houses I inhabited. Though still so young, my son shall know exactly *who* his father was, once he reaches maturity and manhood. Nothing else: it will then be for him to decide. – This, in outline, is our entire system of educating him. The boy is not forced into anything at all; we support him freely and merely direct his natural bent. In no way do we intend him to become an "artist": there is only *one* direction in life that I have assigned to him by giving him the name that I have included with his first name: two names identify him as my son, – Siegfried Richard – Wagner; these, however, I have prefaced with "Helferich", i.e. the "helpful" one. I was persuaded to do so by the following consideration. I told myself: I cannot make an *artist;* but I can instruct a *human being.* Never in my life did I feel a greater sense of despair than on seeing open wounds in men and beasts and not knowing how to help them, while my often distracted cries and rage in seeking help were often met by scorn on the part of the common people. And so I resolved that Siegfried be compelled to learn one thing only, namely how to heal a wound, or at least

---

1 "heilthatvoll Wissenden", a quotation from Act III, Scene 1 of *Parsifal* (GS X,370).
2 A quotation from the dedicatory poem with which Wagner prefaced the *Siegfried Idyll* (SS XII,375).

how to administer first aid; in this way he will at least learn the most basic elements of surgery. This will give him self-confidence, spare me the cruel impressions I have so often suffered, and – if ever it comes to that imaginable extremity in this state-run society of ours – turn him into a useful and popular individual. – How it moved me, on re-reading "Wilhelm Meister", to find Goethe inspired by the same idea in his "Wanderjahre", where he offers his highly irresolute hero a lancet with which to save his son's life! –

And so my Siegfried shall not be lacking in great compassion and deep and heartfelt goodness: and perhaps it will be a good thing to temper his tender-heartedness, which is best done, no doubt, by awakening his self-confidence in lending assistance. But I leave him his head to do with as he wishes. Although I myself am celebrated for my exceptional cranium, my boy's will be found to be quite astonishing: forehead and occiput in perfect harmony. Moreover, his body is supple and well-formed; a temperament that is never less than cheerful, and far removed from all waywardness; great willingness and facility in all things, a friendly pride in tolerating lesser hardships, and total love. His natural wit is often a source of astonishment; all of us, and more especially his sisters, are often amused for hours on end by his sudden sallies of wit which strike him with the speed of lightning and which he expresses with the greatest facility, as though effortlessly. As for his studies, he is enjoined to learn only the basic essentials; but whatever he really wants to know, he will learn for himself soon enough. He has an excellent *ear* for music, but as yet betrays no desire to learn it mechanically. I am pleased to observe that this is so; for there are already enough trained musicians, but of musical souls very few; the eagerness to become an instrumental virtuoso can no doubt be fully satisfied only at the expense of superior natural abilities. And so I want my son to be not only helpful but, more especially *free*, i.e. someone who never feels constrained to lie but who never ceases to be truthful. For this to be so, it is imperative that he should not have to work *for money*, for such a constraint marks the onset of modern slavery. That is why it seems to me important to temper his inclination to think things over, and steel his aversion to all that is not genuine; he shall not be confused if ever he encounters fine furnishings & the like elsewhere, inasmuch as my own fate has granted me a pleasant way of life that I may continue to pursue during the final years of my life, so that he shall not see anything especially desirable in such a life in times to come. But, of course, I must also provide for him to the extent that he does not succumb to the common need of having to earn his living after my death: this possibility has now been granted me by the author's rights on my works, which my heir will enjoy until thirty years after my death as a result of the system of so-called royalties: I intend him to spend half this sum on himself but to convert the other half into capital, so that when my rights expire he will be able to live off the interest on the capital that has been put by. – All this, you see, is aimed at smoothing the paths that a truly free spirit and carefree heart must follow in the active exercise of obligations which, thanks to a more detailed knowledge and more intimate understanding of his father's influence, may one day seem to have been assigned to him.

For this scion of mine, as yet so delicate, is the only help-mate I can still see assigned to me. If I close my eyes today, there is not a single soul in the whole of the world to whom I can confidently entrust responsibility for my works; – not a single soul whom I could entrust with the task of representing me, either today or even tomorrow, at a performance of one of my works for example: I am utterly and completely alone.

Only very recently have I found in Hans von Wolzogen a man who fully appreciates the conceptual significance of my activities and who is firmly committed to advancing their understanding, a commitment which he sees as his one and only task in life. The aesthetic and humanitarian aspect of my artistic activities is very clearly represented by him; I can confidently leave him to function as my "alter ego" in years to come when it is ever a question of preserving my aims. By contrast, I am completely lacking a *musician* and a *dramatist*. I know of no conductor whom I could trust to perform my music correctly, nor any singing actor whom I could count upon to give a correct performance of any of my dramatic characters, unless I first went through the part with him, bar by bar and phrase by phrase. The bungling incompetence that is to be found in every aspect of German art is without equal, and every compromise which I have occasionally sought to enter into with it has led me to the point at which my exalted lord and dearly belovèd friend found me on the evening of the final performance of the Twilight of the Gods in Bayreuth, when I sat behind him, starting up violently on several occasions, so that my most precious friend was moved by his concern for me to ask me what was the matter? But it was too humiliating for me at that very moment to admit what it was that had reduced me to such despair, and to explain that it was my horror at realizing that my conductor[1] – in spite of the fact that I consider him the best I know – was not able to maintain the correct tempo, however often he got it right, because – he was incapable of *knowing why* the music had to be interpreted in one way and not another. – For this is the very heart of the matter: anyone may succeed *by chance* at least once, – but he is not aware of what he is doing, – for I *alone* could have justified it by means of what I call *my* school. – Well, I have been spared the problems of having to maintain a school. This might be a cause for regret, but certainly not for recrimination. The splendid idea I had for Munich really died for me at the moment of Schnorr's death: for I could have relied only upon him, and upon his living example; otherwise I cannot expect any help from pianists and composers of fugues. None the less, it is to be regretted that the Munich

---

1 Hans Richter.

School had to end up in the hands of a man like Rheinberger, who considers it his duty to oblige his listeners at every hour of the day and night with some insulting joke or other at my expense. – But that is how things are! How happy I should be to sing the praises of all these schools of music, whoever their directors, if they could only produce a *single* pupil who was good at something other than merely becoming yet another useless teacher. It is almost impossible to form an idea of how utterly wretched our singers are, both male and female, as they either emerge from these schools of music or else grow up naturally under the guidance of our deeply ignorant bandmasters. In the course of this winter "talented singers" of the kind I have just described – generally highly praised in the newspapers – have announced themselves here, presumably on the assumption that I would immediately engage them for "Parsifal", for example: I generally asked them to sing "Agathe's" aria from the "Freischütz", and had to show them, bar by bar, that they simply had no idea of *what* they were singing, let alone *how* they should sing it. The men are no better: occasionally a singer turns up, and I think: *here's* my man! But as soon as I take a closer look, he botches what he is doing, and if I show him how it should go, he takes fright and declares that he has never heard it like that before, and that it is all new to him. –

In a word, my most precious and dearly belovèd, I venture to think that prospects of performing "Parsifal" are bleak indeed. At a pinch I could cast "Gurnemanz" and "Klingsor", perhaps also "Anfortas"[1] – : but I still do not have the first idea for "Parsifal" and "Kundry"![2] – Ah! We do not need to be so hasty! I and what I write can no longer tolerate haste. What I have created for this age of ours has been much too hasty, much too much, and much too soon: every performance of my works – with the single exception of the one I attended at the side of my exalted lord[3] – has remained a botched affair. But the worst part about it is that I cannot stop blaming myself for it all! I cannot blame ill-fortune or neglect, for I can see well enough that nothing can be done to improve things as they are at present: the present state of affairs is utterly worthless, and only worthlessness can thrive in such a soil. Anyone who has been struck by this thought with the same inconsolable clearness and forcefulness as I have been struck can no longer give himself up to delusion. My Bayreuth "stage festival" was my final question to the "German spirit": I have received my reply: the Grand Duke of Baden even paid for half a Patron's certificate for his son and heir. What more can I ask for?

But where the voice of hope falls silent, that of my daemon – or guardian

1 See letter [242], p. 457, note 1.
2 This dilemma was resolved when Wagner attended a performance of *Der fliegende Holländer* in Dresden on 6 September 1881 with Therese Malten as Senta and Heinrich Gudehus as Erik.
3 The première of *Die Meistersinger von Nürnberg* on 21 June 1868.

angel? – can once again be heard. I feel happier than ever: for me, my work is the source of a life which enfolds me with friendly assurance in a series of ever new mental images. I have a friend such as no other man has, a wife such as has never made her husband so happy, and – now – now I have a son, laughing in high-spirited delight, and bright-eyed as a Wälsung; and over and above all my thoughts and forebodings and wishes there is raised a world not of hope but of *trust*. And how could this trust not grow within me, since my daily round is the birth of a world from within me? Of course! "Parsifal" will succeed! My joy in its success is increasing, just as the work itself continues to grow. Can my dearly belovèd lord and friend tell what my mood is? Well then: "Kundry" has been baptized, and "Parsifal" gazes upon the smiling meadow in gentle rapture: this meadow has already begun to blossom before me; any day now I shall delight in its delicate perfume; and that is why I am so happy today to recall my good fortune and blessings, and to feel the intimate bond that joins me to you, my glorious friend!

Away with all of life's "whims"! – There is a happiness that knows no remorse![1] – Ah! Please, please glance at the first volume of my Collected Writings: "A Happy Evening!" – That was a youthful premonition indeed! It dawns upon me again with the clearest of consciousness whenever I recall the happiness that has been granted me! – You know what I mean: it rests within your great deep soul! It calls down blessings and salvation on the bond that unites us! – Blessings and salvation on him who was sent by God to make me supremely happy – on my exalted and solitary friend!

> In love and loyalty unto death
> Uniquely and eternally yours,
> Richard Wagner

Königsbriefe III, 144–8.

470. HANS VON WOLZOGEN, BAYREUTH   Bayreuth, 18 May 1879

My very dear friend,

I am most grateful to you for communicating C. Schaeffer's letter to me. Whether so long a work as the one he is planning on vocal training would be suitable for our somewhat slender journal I am bound to doubt. I believe that all we can do is criticize the existing system, and offer suggestions and make demands concerning our style in general. On the question of vocal instruction I have become thoroughly sceptical. With the older Italian singers there was nothing for the singing teacher to do except instruct his pupils in music & manner of execution. But we moderns – including us Germans – believe we

---

1 A quotation from *Lohengrin*, Act II, Scene 2 (GS II,89).

can teach untalented singers afflicted with vocal shortcomings to sing properly by means of gymnastic throat exercises. Never in my experience has a singer afflicted with palatal intonation and poor articulation ever really learnt to sing properly. By contrast I have found singers (including some of recent acquaintance) with a naturally sound vocal attack and good articulation whom all I needed to teach was the correct phrasing with sensible breath divisions – at the right *tempo*!! – in order for them to produce the best results that they could ever have been intended by nature to achieve.

I believe it is all a question of practice and of setting a living example!

I at least understand so little about theory that I am utterly incapable of passing judgement on theoretical views etc. –

But – : criticism of our singers' achievements – willingly! But where does one get the necessary authority? Well, ultimately one can claim it for oneself! –

See what you can do, and may God have mercy upon you!

Yours,
R. Wagner.

RWA (published with minor errors of transcription in Bayreuther Briefe II, 383–5).

471. CONSTANTIN FRANTZ, DRESDEN   [Bayreuth, 14 July 1879]

Most honoured Sir and friend,

I am writing to you today immediately after finishing your "Federalism",[1] six copies of which I had already ordered as soon as I received the first copy, in order to present them as gifts to discerning friends of my acquaintance. – You could probably have anticipated my profound admiration for this most outstanding of all your works: with this new gift of yours you have surpassed all that could possibly have been hoped for as a source of salvation. University chairs ought to be established solely for the purpose of studying your book, and – if it were possible to feel any hope – one might indeed hope and expect that your ideas succeed in pervading the minds of all right-thinking persons. – But how similar to my own position I find yours to be! Each in his own sphere, neither of us tires of presenting his ideas to his fellow men in new arrangements, without ever being deterred by the total failure of all our efforts. One ought, no doubt, to be able to identify some higher agency here, except that I fear it is not the agency that makes "history". And this brings me to the one aspect of your theory which causes me misgivings. You locate the realm of history in the sphere of man's "free will", whereas I can see the

---

1 Frantz's *Der Föderalismus als das leitende Princip für die sociale, staatliche und internationale Organisation* (Federalism as the Guiding Principle for Social, State and International Organization), published in Mainz in 1877.

freedom of the will only in the act of denying the world, i.e. in the advent of the "kingdom of grace". If the realm of history were to offer us anything other than the workings of an arbitrary despotism – which certainly does not mean freedom of the will, but rather the will's subjection to blind self-interest – , it would be most surprising if, for ex., ideas like yours had no influence whatsoever on the course of history. This had already become clear to me as a result of the profound doubt which I harboured as to the success of those of your writings which appeared before 1866: that you should ever win over a powerful and capable individual to your cause – one of our princes, ministers or deputies, say, – was bound to strike me as quite out of the question. And how do things stand now? Everything rolls on as though into the pit of madness, and – if this happens of one's own free will – one must at least admit that it is an heroic will which is at work, since it urges the destruction of all that at present exists.

– I believe very definitely that this is the only outcome that now remains open to us; and historical analogies enable me to foresee our return to a state of barbarism around the middle of the next millennium. The man of peace whom you hold out to us presupposes too much reason on the part of the human race; unfortunately, moreover, there is no religion that can guide us along the right path, since – in my own estimation – this must first be revealed to us, and Jesus Christ must first be recognized and imitated by us.

What will give rise to misconceptions in your book is the fact that, among the factors which have contributed to the downfall of the Germans, you really number only feudalism but say nothing of the Catholic Church which has exploited that feudalism. I believe you could have spoken with greater warmth of the German nation's fight for survival at the time of the Reformation. The reasons for the Reformation's lack of achievement and its frailty could be found, with a greater feeling of regret, in Austrian politics, for ex., just as the decline or decay of Spain, Italy and, in a certain sense, even France could have been shown to derive quite clearly from the fact that the Inquisition and other forms of persecuting heretics completely wiped out the country's most talented and capable individuals (as the Huguenots certainly were in France). There is nothing I would say about the *Church* except that, if Christianity had already been a living part of it, the Church has utterly ruined it. As a result it seems to me dangerous and open to the greatest possible misinterpretation to speak in general of "Christianity" today as the supreme authority in life, and I am afraid that you will not escape the – silent or open – reproach that, for reasons that remain unclear, you have held back on this point, showing a reserve into which you could easily have been misled – do not take this amiss! – by the eccentric decision to quote Biblical texts in the Latin translation of the Vulgate. The fact that you are thinking of the Christian religion only in the popular guise of God the Creator and His first revelation to the Jews seems to me the result of your overall plan, which, I admit, appears to be designed to make your ideas more easily accessible; nevertheless, I believe that it is in this area that the most critical point is to be found, when it becomes a question of further developing popular awareness. If the common people were made to forget about God in the "burning bush" and shown instead only the "sacred head sore wounded"[1] they would understand what Christianity is all about, and perhaps this "head" will one day rise up, as the true creator of religion, out of the chaos towards which we are all inexorably hastening.

Let us leave Darwinism alone: I believe little can be achieved here on the basis of feeling. Man evidently begins to exist with the entry of lying (cunning, dissimulation) into the powerful series of the development of beings; God will have revealed Himself with the entry of the most unshakeable truth into every domain of existence: the way from man to Him is *compassion*, and its everlasting name is *Jesus*.

My honoured friend, you see in what an agitated frame of mind you have put me – but it is by no means the worst possible effect that your book could have had! – However, this ought to suffice for today. I shall stop now and repeat only one thing, which I said at the outset, namely that I consider your book the greatest benefit to have been bestowed upon the human race today; let us not ask what use it may be to them, although I can see the "sacred head sore wounded" smiling upon you.

With the most respectful good wishes, I am, Sir,

Your obedient servant
Richard Wagner

Constantin Frantz: Briefe, ed. Udo Sautter and Hans Elmar Onnau (Wiesbaden 1974), 169–70.

472. ERNST VON WEBER, DRESDEN   Bayreuth, 14 August 1879

Most honoured Sir,

I am extraordinarily obliged to you for your kind but far too complimentary letter. I should be deeply flattered to have my name added to those who have been invited to become founder members of your society[2] and would ask you to do this for me.

Your extremely important essay[3] had already reached me, and I must admit to my weakness and say that until now I have not had the courage to read it in detail, since an initial glance at it had moved me beyond measure. But no doubt I should take my courage in both hands. I intend my son to become whatever he wants to be, and to learn whatever he wants to learn: I shall insist only that he learns enough about surgery to be able to administer first

---

1 "O Haupt voll Blut und Wunden" by Paul Gerhardt (1607–76) (EKG 63).
2 An Anti-Vivisection Society.
3 *Die Folterkammern der Wissenschaft* (The Torture Chambers of Science).

aid to both humans and animals, and to steel himself – somewhat better than his father – against the sight of physical suffering. I have greater courage when it comes to moral suffering. Yesterday I officially became a member of the local Society for the Protection of Animals. Until now I have respected the activities of such societies, but always regretted that their educational contact with the general public has rested chiefly upon a demonstration of the *usefulness* of animals, and the *uselessness* of persecuting them. Although it may be *useful* to speak to the unfeeling populace in this way, I none the less thought it opportune to go a stage further here and appeal to their *fellow feeling* as a basis for ultimately ennobling Christianity. One must begin by drawing people's attention to animals and reminding them of the Brahman's great saying, "Tat twam asi" ("That art thou"), – even though it will be difficult to make it acceptable to the modern world of Old Testament Judaization. However, a start must be made here, – since the commandment to love thy neighbour is becoming more and more questionable and difficult to observe – particularly in the face of our vivisectionalist friends.

Everything has to start somewhere, and so I am taking the liberty today of sending you the enclosed sum of 100 marks, and would ask you to be so kind as to pay it into the account of the society which you are planning to set up. If my means allow it, I shall continue with similar contributions in future, which I hope to be able to do every three months. What I must then do will emerge once the society has been established and you are kind enough to inform me how I can be of use to you. May I ask you to extend my most cordial good wishes to Herr *Krausse* – whose cynological significance had escaped me until now – and to accept the sincere respect and deepest regard of

Your most obedient servant

Richard Wagner

P.S. I have just received a most civil letter from Major *von Kochtizky*. No doubt you will be kind enough to convey to this most worthy gentleman both the contents of my present letter and my most humble respects.

R.W.

Bisher ungedruckte Briefe von Richard Wagner an Ernst von Weber (Dresden 1883), 7–8.

473. KING LUDWIG II OF BAVARIA, SCHACHEN

Bayreuth, 25 August 1879

[. . .] Yes! I must have complete freedom with this final work; for, like Tell,[1] I am bound to say that if this *too* slips weakly from my hands, I have no other work to send out into the world. The tremendous effort involved in intro-

1 Schiller's *Wilhelm Tell*, Act IV, Scene 3.

ducing my Nibelung work to the world in the most stylish way possible left me utterly exhausted, not least because it, too, led ultimately only to the birth of an ordinary child of the theatre; I created nothing by doing so, nothing but an empty shell. Even if I *wanted* to risk "Parsifal" in this way – as a new experiment, say! – I feel I *could* not do so since my strength would fail me in the midst of the enterprise, and I should sink to the ground in exhaustion. Worry eats away at my heart, – and what is left is consumed by disgust. The world in which we live does not need my "Parsifal"! – I should be acting in perfect conformity with the world's behaviour towards me if I were to work away gradually at the instrumentation, ensuring in that way that the evening of my life as an artist were pleasantly spent, before sealing the work away under seven seals and bequeathing it complete to my son, so that, when he considers the time to have come, he may present it to the world at an opportune moment, with all the understanding which he will have inherited from me. What good would it do now to release this most Christian of works of art into a world which recoils in its cowardice in the face of the Jews! – But there is one thing – and there is no doubt but that it is this one consideration alone which persuades me to contemplate ways of bringing about a performance during my lifetime – : it is because I am bound to believe that, by desisting entirely from doing so, I should not be fulfilling a certain wish that is close to the heart of my unique and glorious prince, my kingly lord and friend. And – this is a weighty consideration! It is a question here of the stars which once brought me a kingly heart, and which keep us forever united – no doubt, indeed, until the end of the world. Nothing must remain unfulfilled that is traced out there as fulfillable. And so I await a sign from the stars: and I have a good astrologer at my side; my dear wife bids me not lose heart: the "knowing fool"[1] shall appear. – [...]

Königsbriefe III, 158.

474. FRANZ OVERBECK, BASLE   Bayreuth, 19 October 1879

Honoured friend,

Rest assured that I was most comforted to have you remember me on my last birthday and that ever since then it has been my repeated desire to let you know how deep an impression your kind remembrance had left behind. The fact that I do so today – after so long a delay! – is – I freely admit – the result more especially of my remembrance of Nietzsche. How could I ever forget this friend of mine who was driven from me so forcefully? Although I

1 Parsifal.

constantly had the feeling that, at the time of his association with me, Nietzsche's life was ruled by a mental spasm, and although it was bound to strike me as odd that this spasm could have produced so spiritually radiant and heart-warming a fire as was manifest in him to the astonishment of all, and although, finally, the ultimate decision which he reached in the inner development of his life filled me with the utmost horror when I saw how intolerable a pressure that spasm was finally causing him – I must no doubt also admit that in the case of so powerful a psychic process it is simply not possible to argue along moral lines and that one's only response can be a shocked silence.

It saddens me, however, to be so completely excluded from any part in Nietzsche's life and difficulties. Would it be indiscreet of me to ask you to send me news of our friend? I was particularly anxious to beg this favour of you.

Once again – or, rather, for the first time, I would entreat you to accept my deeply felt thanks for your sincere good wishes on the occasion of my last birthday, and at the same time ask you to convey my wife's kindest regards to your own dear spouse and, finally, to accept my own good wishes for your continuing prosperity.

With sincere respect,
Your most obedient servant,
Richard Wagner.

Freunde und Zeitgenossen 583–4.

475. HANS VON WOLZOGEN, BAYREUTH   Naples, 17 January 1880

Dear friend,

I should be sorry if we were to lose Dr Förster because of some displeasure on his part. None the less I must concede that you were right to want to see certain remarks of his removed from so meritorious an essay as the one he wrote for the Bayreuther Blätter.[1] I am almost afraid that we shall have difficulty in reaching an understanding with our friends and patrons on the future meaning and significance of the incomparably and sublimely simple and true redeemer who appears to us in the historically intelligible figure of Jesus of Nazareth, but who must first be cleansed and redeemed of the distortion that has been caused by Alexandrine, Judaic and Roman despotism. Nevertheless, although we are merciless in abandoning the Church and the

---

1 "Richard Wagner als Begründer eines deutschen Nationalstils mit vergleichenden Blicken auf die Kulturen anderer indogermanischer Nationen. Ein Vortrag von Bernhard Förster" (Richard Wagner as the Founder of a German National Style, with Comparative Glances at the Cultures of Other Indo-Germanic Nations) in *Bayreuther Blätter*, iii (1880), 106–22.

priesthood and, indeed, the whole historical phenomenon of Christianity, our friends must always know that we do so for the sake of that same Christ whom – because of His utter incomparability and recognizability – we wish to preserve in His total purity, so that – like all the other sublime products of man's artistic and scientific spirit – we can take Him with us into those terrible times which may very well follow the necessary destruction of all that at present exists. –

In other words, what we are happy to abandon to the most pitiless destruction is all that impairs and distorts this saviour of ours: that is why we ask for sensitivity and care in the way we express ourselves, lest we end up working with the Jews and for the Jews. –

You should none the less suggest some decision!

Cordially yours,
Richard Wagner.

RWA (published with minor errors of transcription in Bayreuther Briefe II,386–7).

476. NEWELL SILL JENKINS, DRESDEN   Naples, 8 February 1880

Dear and respected Sir and friend,

I feel as though my patience will soon run out with regard to my hopes for Germany and her future, and that I may then have cause to regret not having transplanted the seed of my artistic ideas to a fertile and more helpful soil in years long past.

It is not impossible that I may yet decide to emigrate to America with the whole of my family, and take my latest work with me. Since I am no longer young, I should need a very substantial concession from the other side of the ocean. An association would have to be formed that would place a lump sum of one million dollars at my disposal, thus enabling me to settle there and repaying me for all the trouble involved, half of the sum being used to pay for my settlement in some climatically beneficial state of the Union, the other half being deposited in a state bank as a capital investment at 5 per cent. In doing this, America would secure my services for all time. In addition the association would have to raise the funds necessary to enable an annual festival to be held at which I should present all my works by easy stages in model performances: we would make an immediate start with the *first* performance of my latest work, "Parsifal", which I would not allow to be performed elsewhere until that time. Whatever I do in the future, whether as performance manager or as a creative artist, would belong to the American nation, free of charge and for all time, on the basis of the sum that had already been transferred to me.

I was reminded of the fact that, when you last visited me, you kindly and enthusiastically offered to manage my business affairs for me in the event of my deciding to undertake a so-called concert tour of America. I hope you will now understand why it is you, rather than anyone else, to whom I turn in order to acquaint you of this considerably more far-reaching idea? A simple concert tour aimed at earning such & such a sum of money, followed by a return to Germany, is not for me. Only a complete removal would make any sense for me! –

Would you be good enough to think this over a little, and, if it seems to you a good idea, let me know your views?[1]

In the greatest friendship,

Your dutiful and obedient servant
Richard Wagner

Facsimile in K. Liepmann, "Wagner's Proposal to America" in High Fidelity (Dec. 1975), 71.

477. JOSEPH RUBINSTEIN, BERLIN   Naples, 6 April [1880]

Dear friend,

I was sorry to discover from your letter, which I received today, that a letter I wrote to you – following your last communication from Berlin – had not yet arrived. It had been a question of finding out your address there, which I thought I did not know, until I was finally reminded of the old Thiergarten Hotel.

Well, – it was all the kinder of you not to be deterred from writing again! – All praise to you for doing so! And the news you sent me was also of interest of course, since I see you are still protected by the magic enchantment of hope. –

That is because of your faith, and, since you are young, there is still a good deal you can live to see. In my own case, nothing will take root any longer except perhaps the assumption that I may yet be able to produce something that will allow me to forget the misery of the world. As a result, my chief concern is how to work myself up into a good mood and maintain that mood as long as is possible; and in this I shall be helped more especially by an improvement in my health. I am still trying to get acclimatized here:[2] the sea-baths cannot be used until June, but they should finish things off for me. In

---

1 Nothing came of this suggestion.
2 The Wagners had arrived in Naples on 4 January 1880 and remained there until 7 August; they were in Siena between 21 August and 1 October, when they set off for Florence, arriving there on the 4th. They were back in Bayreuth by 17 November, having spent the first half of the month in Munich.

consequence I have provisionally decided to stay here until the end of the autumn, and then spend a whole year settling in at Wahnfried. I shall then finish off the full score of Parsifal – at a single sitting, so to speak. If all goes well, we shall then perform it in the summer of 1882 (with or without a "School"!). –

Are you intending to survive the whole time in Bayreuth? Or are you planning excursions to Kharkov – or Naples? – Wondrous things would you see here, but – only if you put all the Berlin profits into the Bayreuth fund!? – Well, see if you can find some more good news to tell me. Your last article[1] has really caused a furore: Levi was utterly *stupéfait*, and – it seems – genuinely pleased by it. And so: it is still early days! Qui vivra verra!

Sincere regards and every good wish for your continuing prosperity.

Your obedient servant
Richard Wagner.

Bayreuther Briefe II,311–12.

478. HANS VON WOLZOGEN, BAYREUTH   Naples, [6][2] May 1880

Dearest friend,

This time it's me! With regard to our present "situation", I expect my wife will have kept you "au courant" (as the Latins say). For myself there is a great deal I could *say* to you on the subject, but which I would not put into writing. Things look bleak in my German heart, and I am thinking increasingly of removing myself and my children from the German Reich – with an option on America. But it shall first have "Parsifal": I am resolved to leave the matter to inner, rather than outward, circumstances, and present the work in Bayreuth – at all events – in the summer of 1882. [I[3] think the matter can be sorted out – decently – with Munich.

– Now comes the big favour which you will already have guessed on seeing the thick envelopes. I believe once again that my wife has already communicated with you on this point – through Gross. And so: –

Burger is to print the enclosed manuscript – part of the 4th part of "My Life" – in return for his guarantee of the most absolute discretion. The letters, type & paper must be exactly the same as those in the example from the earlier volume of the "Life" which you might care to show him; he can

---

1 "Einige Betrachtungen über den musikalischen Styl der Gegenwart in Deutschland" (Some Observations on Present-Day Musical Style in Germany) in *Bayreuther Blätter*, iii (1880), 61–84; an earlier article, "Ueber die Schumann'sche Musik" (On Schumann's Music), in *Bayreuther Blätter*, ii (1879), 216–29 had elicited a storm of protest.

2 Autograph dated 7 May, but CT dating confirmed by the fact that Ascension Day fell on 6 May in 1880.

3 The long section in square brackets has not previously been published.

obtain the title vignette (an invention of my wife's) from the former printer, who will certainly have kept the die: *Bonfantini*, printer of art prints and books in Basle. I am afraid I must ask you to undertake correction of the first set of proofs, and possibly also edit the headings on each page. For the final corrections, however, I shall have to have the sheets sent to me here. No more than *eighteen* copies are to be run off. –

My most pressing desire is to have a copy ready to send to the King in time for his birthday (25 August). But there is still plenty of time; it will not be a thick volume, today's consignment already contains more than half the manuscript! –

You'll do this for me, won't you?]

The air here is unbelievably good, and it fills me with hope; but I am extremely lazy. My "Affinities"[1] are swelling in my head to the size of a Bible: but the paper – the paper! However, if you continue to be as resourceful as you have been so far, I shall certainly not be missed in the Blätter! – I am looking forward to the May number: I hope there will be something appreciative about me in it? –

You are all so deserving, while I appear so ungrateful; but time will tell: the day will come etc!

Sincerest good wishes to your splendid little wife and dear family! You shall all appear in the "Affinities", – or certainly the two of us will, you, my dear friend, and

Your most loyal
and indolent contributor
Richard Wagner

(Ascension Day – whoopee!)

RWA (incompletely published in Bayreuther Briefe II,390–1).

479. KING LUDWIG II OF BAVARIA, SCHACHEN

Siena, 28 September 1880

[. . .] My trust in the boundless forbearance and grace which my exalted benefactor has always shown me has never been disappointed, and it was in that selfsame spirit that I recently described to him, openly and candidly, the reason why it was impossible for me to work together in common with the musico-dramatic forces that obtain in your Royal Court Theatre, more especially with the aim of bringing about the first performance of my

---

1 Affinities between religion and art, the subject of an essay completed in Naples on 19 July 1880 and published under the title *Religion and Art* in *Bayreuther Blätter*, iii (1880), 269–300. Also GS X,211–53; PW VI,211–52.

"Parsifal". In doing so I was of course too remote from the particular conditions and considerations which have persuaded my generous protector to leave things as they are in the running of that artistic institution – too remote for me to be in a position to judge whether it was an unrealizable demand which I was making in expressing the wish that actual changes be introduced in its administration. In the light of the observations which I have subsequently made in this regard, I believe I should now be acting in a manner both seemly and in grateful accord with my exalted lord's abundant grace, if I declare of my own volition that, in presenting the first performance of my work in Bayreuth, I renounce the co-operation of the Royal Court Theatre as run by its present General Intendant.

A number of considerations and – I may say so quite openly – questions of conscience have persuaded me of late to show serious restraint with regard to this final work of mine. Although conceived in ideal terms, I have had to surrender all of my works to a kind of audience and theatrical practice which I recognize to be deeply immoral, so that I must ask myself in all seriousness whether I should not at least rescue this latest and most sacred of my works from a similar fate, namely that of a common operatic career. I was finally no longer able to deny that the purity of content and subject-matter of my "Parsifal" was the decisive factor here. How, indeed, might it be possible or permissible for a drama in which the most sublime mysteries of the Christian faith are openly presented on stage to be performed in theatres such as ours, side by side with an operatic repertory and before an audience such as ours? I should certainly not blame our Church authorities if they were to raise an entirely legitimate protest against representations of the most sacred mysteries upon the selfsame boards on which, yesterday and tomorrow, frivolity sprawls in luxuriant ease before an audience attracted solely by such frivolity. I was entirely right in feeling that I should entitle "Parsifal" a "*Sacred* Stage Festival". And so I must now try to consecrate a stage for it, and this can only be my solitary festival theatre in Bayreuth. There, and there alone, may "Parsifal" be presented now and always: never shall "Parsifal" be offered in any other theatre as an amusement for its audience: and it is to ensure that this happens that I am uniquely concerned at present and persuaded to consider how and by what means I may safeguard the destiny of this work.[1]

[. . .]

Königsbriefe III, 182–3.

---

1 Ludwig wrote on 24 October 1880, agreeing that *Parsifal* should be given only in Bayreuth. On 14 October Ludwig von Bürkel, his new Court Secretary, had written to Cosima announcing Ludwig's intention of making the Munich orchestra and chorus available to Wagner for two months every summer from 1882 onwards.

480. KING LUDWIG II OF BAVARIA, HOHENSCHWANGAU

Bayreuth, 30 December 1880

[...] – – My belovèd friend, – a gentle and homely spirit stirs at Wahnfried. The children's mother was reborn, and – like all that relates to my precious wife – the event was designed to be commemorated by an artistic spectacle rich in allusions. Under the sensitive guidance of our uncommonly gifted friend, Paul Joukowsky, a tableau vivant was set up depicting a Holy Family. Costumes, disposition, and realization of the individual characteristics were all incomparably beautiful, with the following group being represented: Mary the mother of Jesus (Daniela) in careworn adoration of the infant Jesus (Siegfried), practising with a plane at the carpenter's bench – (Siegfried, I should add, is learning cabinet-making with a local carpenter – it is important for his education!) – , then, behind the Madonna, listening intently to the annunciatory strains of angelic music, Joseph (portrayed by Joukowsky's adoptive son from Naples, Peppino); above them, in the naïve style of the old Italian masters, three angels on musical instruments: Blandine (playing the lute), Eva (playing the flute) and, at the very top, Isolde with a viola. To accompany this scene the opening chorale from the Mastersingers was played on our small household organ. Not only the enthusiastic expressions on the individual faces, but the overall impression, were so overwhelmingly moving that I have persuaded our friend Joukowsky to paint a picture of it, true to life; this will be his next undertaking, and I am sure it will be an outstanding success. – The principal present which I gave my wife was a copy of Beethoven's Ninth Symphony acquired from the estate of a friend[1] long since dead, a copy which I had made as an enthusiastic but far from gifted seventeen-year-old youth exactly fifty years ago (1830) and which I later gave as a keepsake to the friend in question when I left Dresden in 1849. It is an extremely elegant copy, and is now my wife's most prized possession.

However withdrawn our present lives, we none the less receive the occasional visit from some distant friend in the midst of this miserable winter. Heinrich von Stein paid a brief call on us in an attempt to assuage the grief which he feels at not being able to leave his sick old father for some considerable time to come; during the summer months, which his father will be spending on his estates with other relations of his, he plans to stay with us for three months each year and will then organize and take charge of our son's continuing education and development. During his last visit I prevailed upon him to write an article for the Bayreuther Blätter on the subject of "La Renaissance", a very interesting piece by Count Gobineau (which – I believe – we have already made so bold as to recommend for your kind consideration?); this has now been done, much to my great satisfaction, and the article

1 Theodor Uhlig; see also letter [468], p. 887.

will appear in the January number.[1] This young man is of an aristocratic temperament, as is admirably proved by his style. I have great hopes of him. –

If this gossip of mine does not weary my sweet and exalted one, I shall continue and speak of another man who is, however, merely something of a curiosity. He is the opera director of the Leipzig Municipal Theatre, Angelo Neumann, a man of Jewish extraction, and strangely energetic and extremely devoted to me, in a way which – oddly enough! – I find even today is true of the Jews whom I know. He was the first person to put on a complete performance of the "Ring of the Nibelung" in Leipzig, which he did with lasting success; proud of his achievements, he now intends to win the highest renown for himself. The intendant of the Berlin Court Theatre,[2] a man who is exceptionally limited in outlook and who has always detested me, forbade all the Prussian Court Theatres which are subject to his control in Cassel, Hanover and Wiesbaden from performing the Nibelung's Ring there – in spite of their desire to do so – since he himself did not wish to have to make the effort of giving the work in Berlin. Angelo Neumann is now planning to give four performances of the complete cycle next May in Berlin's large Victoria Theatre: he sought my permission to do so, and I did not refuse it to him since, of his own accord, he has formally agreed to engage only the very best singers: Materna, Jäger, the Vogls (husband and wife), Reichmann (Munich) etc. will perform the work under the direction of a conductor whom I myself have trained.[3] Well, when this became known, Hülsen found himself in a terrible dilemma and tried to persuade the Leipzig conductor to give the performance in the Royal Court Theatre; the latter was very attracted by the idea, and sought my agreement, but I firmly refused it, and so the performance will remain, as before, at the neutral Victoria Theatre; this – on top of the Jewish propaganda – should keep Berlin in a state of great excitement for some time to come. – But Angelo is now growing even bolder, and he has asked my permission to visit Petersburg, London and the whole of North America with his army of Nibelungs, and for this purpose – in order to avoid all competition – he has requested exclusive worldwide performing rights for three years. He will pay me one tenth of the gross receipts, and thereby seek to spare me my own trip to America, which I had considered as being necessary. It is quite likely that something will come of this, and – in silence, as it were, – I can observe the wondrous workings of a fate which, having brought the King of Bavaria into my life, cannot decently withdraw now, lest it compromise itself, but which must arrange other circumstances, too, in my favour. Yes, indeed! This has all come about – and much more is to follow –

1 The review appeared in *Bayreuther Blätter*, iv (1881), 13–20.
2 Botho von Hülsen; see also letter [464], pp. 882–3.
3 Anton Seidl; he is the "Leipzig conductor" referred to in the next sentence.

because the miracle was once admitted whereby the heart of a glorious King
was opened unto me! – [. . .]

Königsbriefe III, 196–7.

481. ANGELO NEUMANN, BERLIN   Bayreuth, 23 February 1881

Dear friend and benefactor,

I have absolutely no connection with the present "anti-Semitic" movement:
an article of mine[1] which is shortly to appear in the Bayreuther Blätter will
prove this so conclusively that it will be impossible for anyone of *intelligence*
to associate me with that movement. –

None the less, my advice to you is to give up Berlin and go to London in
May & June. *How* you bring this about is of course your own affair. – It
would be a fine thing if your – and our – enterprise were to be diverted from
its rightful purpose by follies of the kind that now flourish in Berlin.

Our Nibelungs were not made to be hounded by courtiers and Jews – and
that because of some totally absurd misunderstandings!

– I am all in favour of London

– without delay! –

Your most obedient servant
Rich. Wagner

Neumann, Erinnerungen, 139.

482. ADOLF EISENBARTH, BAYREUTH   Bayreuth, 4 March 1881

Dear Sir,

In order to put an end to the situation that has now been going on between
us for a number of years, I would suggest that you address yourself to your
superiors on the Royal Court Authority and obtain their permission to remove,
at least for the duration of the winter months, the sign at the entrances to
the Royal Park forbidding dogs to be taken in without a lead, since the ban
can only make sense during those periods when the park is being dug over
and cultivated. In that way you will oblige all those people whose handsome
and expensive dogs can otherwise wander freely through the town, since dogs
that are kept on a lead are always bad-tempered and given to fighting with
each other. The president of the council, for ex., will also find himself in this

---

1 *Erkenne dich selbst* (Know Yourself), a supplement to *Religion and Art*, published in *Bayreuther
Blätter*, iv (1881), 33–41. Also GS X,263–74; PW VI, 264–74.

same position, since he no longer experiences any unpleasantness when meeting my dogs, now that he allows his own dog to run free.

If you do not intend to apply for the said permission, I shall do so myself, but I cannot guarantee that things will turn out exactly as you wish, since I am not prepared to put up any longer with the kind of disgraceful behaviour that I again had to suffer today at the hands of one of your employees.

I am, Sir, your respectful and most obedient servant

Richard Wagner

Heinrich Schmidt and Ulrich Hartmann, Richard Wagner in Bayreuth: Erinnerungen (Leipzig 1909),49.

483. KING LUDWIG II OF BAVARIA, MUNICH Bayreuth, 16 March 1881

Most gracious lord and dearest of all friends,

How often, deeply moved and then profoundly reassured, have I recalled your royal grace and favour, and listened to the beating of so great and kind a heart! Alas, I was loath to write to you: a King should not see his friend approach in a mood of discontent; and, try as I might, I could not break out of that mood. But then your gracious letter arrived, bringing with it both air and sunlight: I could breathe again freely, and felt raised above myself. And now I must needs thank you from the depths of my soul!

And what is this now? – I was expecting poor weather on returning from Italy:[1] but I looked forward to the pleasures of domesticity and – work – my final work on Parsifal! – they were pleasures which I hoped would help me over my sadness at the gloomy season, but not even my work is a source of much joy; – on the contrary, it leaves me feeling discontented and deeply morose, since I now have to think of performing the piece, and submit to these loathsome experiences all over again, the mere gradual forgetting of which has given me back my sense of calm and serene equanimity in recent years! It is always the same: as soon as a work like this is complete and released by its author, it belongs to the devil! – Recently J. Rubinstein (Wahnfried's supreme court pianist!) played us the first scene of Tannhäuser, which I rewrote in Paris – the "Venusberg"; I had grown so remote from this piece that I listened to the performance as though I were hearing something quite new, written by some other composer; it had the most extraordinary impression upon me, for I was bound to find that this same piece by far surpasses anything that even Berlioz achieved in this dissolute genre, and that it is certainly not inferior to anything that I myself have written. As for the fate that befell this work, I had retained a memory of only the most disheartening

1 See letter [477], p. 900, note 2.

experiences: this tremendous music had to be realized on stage, and it turned out in Paris that such a staging was deemed possible only by transforming it into the most absurd kind of ballet. I then decided to try it out again in Vienna – with the help, I thought, of a ballet-mistress of genius; Lucile Grahn (so I had discovered) was said to have made a tolerable success of the thing in Munich, and so I had her brought to Vienna; but when I got to know her intentions, my only concern was to send the woman back home again, and leave the matter to run its usual – balletic – course. Since then it was always with horror that I thought of this music which – heard now by chance – came to fill me with wonder at what I had written! – And so it is with more or less everything. Not for the world would I wish to go through again what I went through last time with our performances here of the Nibelung's Ring – in spite of the fact that they are still the most correct that have so far been given, – or, if I did, it would only be after my death! – And now – a new work: – it's Parsifal's turn!!! A work for whose characters I am unable to find a single singer in all our opera companies who is truly gifted, let alone suited to his or her part! – Well! It must be so, and – I shall! But: patience! People must be patient with me, since all precautions are in vain. – Yes! I suspect and believe – my most precious and gracious one! – that my best plan will be to cast Jäger¹ as Parsifal: – that is how things stand. In this regard, however, it pains me particularly that my exalted lord has recently heard unfavourable reports about this singer's appearances in Munich; for, to tell the truth, it was the question which I heard my belovèd King put to me in the theatre foyer some months ago,² when he asked why I was not planning to cast Jäger as Parsifal, that remained in my memory as a directive after I had received such distressing news of another tenor³ whom I was then considering for the part. These people are all quite pitiful: a bit of a voice, monstrously overpaid, and – completely untalented, lazy and vain! – And so I am really reduced to getting by with Jäger, but at least hope that I'll make a better Parsifal of him than I did with Unger as Siegfried. But other singers, too, will have to learn the role: perhaps I shall double-cast it! – And the same is true of the women singers: once again I am reminded of your royal question concerning Materna; she is still the "bird in the hand", which I should prefer not to lose for the "two in the bush"! But I may double-cast this part as well!⁴ – Otherwise everything will turn out the sort of ordinary fare that is all I could wish for in the case of such noble characters! Lilli Lehmann, who created my Rhinedaughters, has taken over the task of engaging Klingsor's enchanted

---

1 At the 1882 Festival the role of Parsifal was sung by Hermann Winkelmann, Heinrich Gudehus and Ferdinand Jäger.
2 Perhaps on 12 November 1880, when Wagner had conducted the Prelude to Act I of *Parsifal* in Ludwig's presence.
3 Heinrich Vogl.
4 The role of Kundry was sung by Amalie Materna, Marianne Brandt and Therese Malten.

women: and they have turned out *uncommonly* well! May God give his blessing to this harmless piece of devilry! –

Some time ago I re-engaged the technician K. Brandt, who was my assistant when we equipped the Nibelung theatre. He surprised me, when he came to visit me, by his detailed knowledge of all the demands that are made by the scenery for Parsifal: the arrangements he had made were all so unerringly correct that he was able to tell me that there was insufficient music for the gradual transformation of the forest into the Grail Temple; as a result I was persuaded to add another two to three minutes of music, which, fortunately, has turned out very well.[1] We also agreed that the Brückner brothers would again build the scenery for us, this time to designs by my friend Joukowsky. I much prefer this; for although I have a by no means poor opinion of the abilities of the scene-painters in Munich, I would much rather deal with these modest and no less talented artists from Coburg, since, in my dealings with the former, I am unable to overcome an aversion towards them that is based upon certain far from agreeable experiences, whereas I feel perfectly free in the case of the latter. Joukowsky has completed his work with the most indefatigable zeal and, finally, to our general satisfaction: Klingsor's magic garden, for which everything had to be invented – without any model on which to base the designs[2] – had to be sketched out in full no fewer than seven separate times since it kept on not turning out as I wanted it; but it, too, will be something completely new: it was a strange task for him to design flowers in such a way that the girls can appear to grow out of them. I am expecting the scene-painters to visit me before the month is over, so that I can hand over the sketches to them: if there is still time, I shall take the liberty of submitting them to my exalted friend for his brief perusal. – The "family" portrait,[3] however, has been completely pushed to one side by this work; but I am not permitted to say much about it, since I can see that the others want to surprise me with it on my birthday. As soon as it has turned out a success, it shall be kept in readiness, should my exalted lord be kind and gracious enough to wish to see it. – We were very pleased by our generous benefactor's favourable opinion of Count Gobineau's book, "La Renaissance", which we, too, consider a work of genius. We made the acquaintance of this remarkable man in the course of our visits to Italy, first

1 In the course of the technical rehearsals in June 1882, it emerged that still more music was required. Engelbert Humperdinck duly obliged with some extra bars of connecting music for the first-act transformation scene; his suggestion for repeating the music of mourning for Titurel in order to overcome a similar problem in the third-act transformation (see CT for 28 June 1882) was attempted at the dress rehearsals, but abandoned before the opening night in favour of closing the curtain between the first and second scenes.

2 According to Cosima Wagner's diary for 26 May 1880, "Discovered Klingsor's garden in Ravello": the Wagners had been visiting the park of the Palazzo Rufalo. Joukowsky, who was present, made a number of sketches of the park.

3 See letter [480], p. 904.

in Rome, and now in Naples, and have won him over as our friend. He was the French ambassador to Persia, and then to Sweden, but now lives a life completely cut off from the contemporary situation in France, since, so he claims, there is not a single person there any longer to whom he can make himself understood. A longer work of his, "de l'inégalité des races humaines", appeared as long ago as the 1850s, but was virtually ignored in France because nobody liked it, least of all the so-called democrats, since it depicts the *décadence* of the white race – which alone, however, is destined to achieve mastery over the other races. Neither the book-trade nor Count Gobineau himself was able to obtain this remarkable book for us, since it was sold out, and – now that it has fallen into oblivion – no one is prepared to take on a new edition: finally, Gobineau managed to persuade a professor in Tübingen to lend us the four-volume work for a brief perusal. However, my wife has now advertised for a copy through a Jewish dealer in second-hand books who normally manages to obtain what we want, and – if we get hold of a copy – what pleasure it will give us to present it to our exalted benefactor for his information! I consider Gobineau's ideas to date to be uncommonly daring – but profound! We shall be able to discuss them with him in person since we are expecting him for a relatively long visit, probably arriving in April.[1] So great is his interest in "Bayreuth" that he has already written a fairly long piece for our "Blätter", which my wife will be translating: its theme is apparently very far-reaching, namely, "What we can expect from Asia", a subject on which he has very original views which no one can ignore who is seriously concerned with the question of what is actually likely to become of our civilization.[2] I regard all these and similar questions as not unrelated to the fate and destiny of the uniquely true art which I myself envisage. The sort of misunderstandings to which I, too, am exposed in raising such far-reaching questions is instructive, but also a source of some entertainment. Not a day passes without my receiving some absurd communication or other: vegetarians, Jew-haters, religious sectaries – they all believe they can enlist my support. Recently, however, I received news from Paris of my election as a "membre honoraire de la société des amis du *divorce*": I ask you: "*amis* du divorce!" –

But now at least our trusty swan is continuing his voyage around the world: may he lead to something more noble! – In Naples – fortunately only after I had already left! – "Lohengrin" has aroused unbelievable enthusiasm.[3] It is now going to be given in Madrid, too, to mark the two-hundredth anniversary

---

1 Gobineau arrived in Bayreuth on 11 May and remained until 7 June 1881.
2 "Ein Urtheil über die jetzige Weltlage. Als ethnologisches Resumé vom Grafen Gobineau" (A Verdict on the Present World Situation: An Ethnological Résumé) in *Bayreuther Blätter*, iv (1881), 123–40.
3 *Lohengrin* was first heard in Naples on 26 February 1881; there had already been productions in Bologna, Florence, Milan, Trieste, Turin, Rome and Genoa.

of Calderon's death.[1] The strange part about it is that I am still alive to enjoy such incredibly late fruits! Herr von Hülsen maintains that not a soul will still be talking about the Ring of the Nibelung in twenty years' time: the overhasty man! What did he not say when Tannhäuser and even Lohengrin were initially slow to make an impression in Berlin? He regretted the money that had been spent on them! But a general manager like him never learns; what he fails above all to realize is that if an exalted benefactor gives his word, such an unpopular opera composer can grow God knows how old and live to see all that otherwise – ah! how often! – comes to pass only long after the deaths of great men. – Yes! That is the worst thing for impertinent contemporaries to have to suffer – to be outlived by the other person! –

And so the adventure of another stage festival in Bayreuth awaits me! This time I expect it to last a long time, if I am to present all my works – successively – and give them my seal of approval. Since we intend admitting all who can pay, I have little reason to doubt that the affair will not last, albeit only as long as I myself remain alive, but I trust myself to achieve a fairly respectable old age, particularly when I consider that I shall already have entered upon my seventieth year when Parsifal opens next year. I shall not let this worry me, since years in my case appear not to mean very much: rather would I wish for somewhat more peace of mind and indifference to the interruptions to which I am perpetually exposed, no matter where I may be. In much the same way my physical health is of a kind that no real infirmity seems to set in, but only things that provoke my impatience: I have, for example, been dragging a couple of sore fingers around with me for some months now, and have to have them looked at almost every hour, – which is enough to drive me insane. Fortunately the children in the house then make fun of me, and I and my dear wife have a good laugh. So everything must be possible! –

Today – precisely because – remarkable to tell! – the sun is shining, I intend taking a look at our theatre again, for the first time, in fact, since our return. This curious building is after all an undeniable gain, a reality against which nothing can be said. But steps are now being taken to ensure that our great and glorious and belovèd protector may feel a little more at his ease inside this uncomfortable building: the theatre architect Brückwald is now working on a plan for an extension to the front of the building which will place at our exalted protector's disposal a private entrance, then as decent as possible a room (called the Salon) with direct access to a spacious and entirely self-contained box in the so-called Princes' Gallery. Care must be taken to ensure that this extension is not out of proportion with the rest of the building, so that, when I finally die and the "German nation" begins to stir, to a man,

---

1 *Lohengrin* was produced in Madrid on 25 March 1881; the first Wagner opera to be heard in Spain was *Rienzi*, performed in Italian on 5 February 1876.

behind me, there will be nothing to prevent them from retaining the basic structure – which, after all, is solidly built – if the whole is to be surrounded by massive architecture and got up with monumental decorations: nothing need be altered in the interior of the building – apart from the same kind of monumental decorations which should be executed in some noble material – since it is functional in the highest sense of the word, which is something that unfortunately cannot be said of any other theatre. Only – as I say – a protectorial extension will have to be added! – Oh! Forgive me, my most belovèd and exalted prince! this chatter of mine has taken me on to a third sheet of quarto; what will your patience say to that? But that's how it is, my royal friend makes me so vain and so talkative when he praises my letters with such extravagant grace and goodness. Ah, God! That I might always give you a little – a tiny little – pleasure by dint of all that I do and think – that is something I do indeed take care to aspire to, which is why I prefer to say nothing when things look black or grey inside me. Well, I know of course that my great and merciful lord never escapes entirely without some loud lament on my part, – but God must needs know all! – But the good part about it is that the very frankness with which I may make so bold as to complain to him always does me good and elevates my mood, and that talking to him finally makes me happy and free. And – looked at closely – so it was also today: the fairest smile shows itself only in the midst of tears! –

Well then: my concluding prayer! Whom do I praise? Whom do I thank? It is my saint, my merciful redeemer! To him do all look up to whom he gave me, for whom he saved me, safe and happy and certain, to the astonishment of all the world. They send a thousand heartfelt good wishes of sincerest gratitude to the kindest of men who always remembers them, too, with such gracious benevolence! Thus – through the eyes of others – I look up to him, and worship the God who gave me to him as his own!

In all eternity,
grateful unto death,
Richard Wagner

Königsbriefe III, 200–5.

484. Edward Dannreuther, London   Bayreuth, 1 April 1881

Dearest friend,

I was intending to write to you during the next few days on a business matter. I shall do so now, but first I want to congratulate you – as they say – on the arrival of a new and born Wagnerian – long live Hubert Edward, and may Richard Wagner – significantly – be entered in the parish register as his godfather! Bravo!

I shall leave the London fog in peace, and never again try to drape myself in it: may all that happens be God's handiwork!

Very many thanks for your touching news of Carlyle![1] – But now to business. I am now – for honour's sake – making preparations for the production of Parsifal. Having fared so badly with our English dragon,[2] let us see if we cannot do any better with the Grail *bells*.

Following a discussion with experts on the best way of representing the necessary sound, we agreed after all that it could best be imitated by means of *Chinese tamtams*. In what market are these tamtams to be found in the greatest number and best selection? It is thought to be London. Good! – Who will be responsible for selecting them? Dannreuther, of course. And so, my dearest friend, try to track down 4 tamtams which will produce – at least an approximation of – the following peal.

It should be noted that – in order to produce a deep bell-like sound – these instruments must be struck only *gently* near the rim, whereas if you hit them sharply in the middle they produce a much brighter sound that is quite unuseable. And so, see what you can do! –

I very much enjoyed your article[3] which – as I have only just discovered – was not printed until very late in the B. Bl: it is a real connoisseur's piece, and I was also pleased that the translation had turned out so well, so that you, too, must have been satisfied by it. Very many thanks!

And a thousand good wishes to Chariclea,[4] and my regards to Wolfram.

Assuring you of my loyal friendship, I am

Your devoted servant,

Rich. Wagner.

Bayreuther Briefe II,322–4.

485. KING LUDWIG II OF BAVARIA, BERG   Bayreuth, [16] May 1881

My most dearly belovèd royal lord and merciful friend,

Ever consoled when I raise my eyes to my unique prince, I shall endeavour to collect together my far-scattered thoughts to send you a brief report on

---

1 The historian Thomas Carlyle had died on 4 February 1881.
2 See letter [441], p. 858. The supplier was Richard Keene of Milton Road, Wandsworth. Dannreuther obtained the tamtams as requested.
3 "Die Musik in England. Ein Brief aus London" (Music in England. A Letter from London) in *Bayreuther Blätter*, iv (1881), 76–81.
4 Dannreuther's wife.

my recent adventures. I was in Berlin! My gracious friend knows the reasons for my – merely superficial – involvement in that expedition, which, to a certain extent, could be seen as the starting-point for Angelo Neumann's audacious venture. As a result I attended the dress rehearsals and the first performance of the whole cycle of the Nibelung's Ring: I had set off for Berlin with a very real sense of dread, but was able to return fairly reassured, and even with a certain – relative – satisfaction. The final words which I felt moved to address to the audience there were the truth: I was astonished to witness this success, just as I was astonished at my work. The most extraordinary part about it was that a work which has made such great claims on my life now appeared so completely new to me: I had let it unfold in front of me, in total objectivity, allowing everything to pass before me, pure and clear, as though reflected in the mirror of my soul, and my reaction was one of great satisfaction, mixed with some surprise that such a work could have been written today and – finally – that it could have been presented to the theatre audience of a large city without provoking their actual displeasure and rejection. It is without doubt the Aryan race's most characteristic work of art: no nation on earth could be so clearly conscious of its origins and predisposition than this one tribe from Upper Asia, a tribe which was the last to enter European culture and which until that time had retained its purity better than all the other white races. One could well feel hope on witnessing the success of such a work in our midst!

[. . .]

Königsbriefe III, 208.

486. HERMANN LEVI, BAMBERG   Bayreuth, 1 July 1881

Dearest and best of friends,

Much as I respect all your feelings, you are not making things easy either for yourself or for us! What could so easily inhibit us in our dealings with you is the fact that you are always so gloomily introspective! We are entirely at one in thinking that the whole world should be told about this shit[1] but what this means is that you must stop running away from us, thereby allowing such stupid suspicions to arise. For God's sake come back at once, and get to know us properly! You do not need to lose any of your faith, but merely to acquire the courage of your convictions!

---

1 Wagner had received an anonymous letter on 29 June, accusing Levi of having an affair with Cosima, and demanding that another conductor be found for *Parsifal*. Wagner showed the letter to Levi.

Perhaps some great change is about to take place in your life – but at all events – you are my Parsifal conductor!

So, come on! come on!

Yours,
RW.

Bayreuther Briefe II,326–7.

487. LUDWIG STRECKER, MAINZ   Bayreuth, 30 August 1881

Most honoured Sir and friend,

I think it is now time for me to come to some sensible arrangement with the firm of *Schott & Sons*, whom you yourself now personify.

You are already familiar not only with the difficulties which, from my point of view, have stood in the way of an edition of the music of my latest work "Parsifal", but also with the reasons which persuaded me to consider taking special measures here. It is a question, therefore, of indicating the simplest way of reaching an agreement between us. I shall show you this means without further ado, by making the following proposal.

My chief concern is to prevent a *theatrical* performance of "Parsifal" from taking place anywhere other than *Bayreuth*. Since *France* and *Italy* are in a cartel with *Germany*, and since *Belgium* and *England* are already provided for by your firm, it is more especially *Holland* which worries me, since some impresario there could well permit himself a joke at my expense. I would ask you, therefore, to try to secure the copyright to my works – at least as far as stage performances are concerned – perhaps also having regard for *Denmark* and *Sweden*, in which case there will no longer be any obstacle in the way of your publishing the *full score*, too:[1] in this way I shall be opening up a profitable market to you to the extent that I declare that I should have no objection to performances of individual sections of the work, of whatever length, in the *concert hall*, and, for my own part, would be happy to renounce a fee for the same. In this way I should secure for you unlimited copyright "of the melody", and it seems to me that it could then be left to your ingenuity to safeguard this in the same way, perhaps, as *Fürstner* did in Berlin when he sued the firm of *Breitkopf & Härtel* over a fantasia on "O Star of Eve" from "Tannhäuser" which they had published 37 years previously, and was so successful that I had to come to Härtel's assistance by declaring that *Liszt* had been authorized to publish this piece as a result of my special permission as private publisher of "Tannhäuser".

1 Schott's published Rubinstein's vocal score in April 1882; the full score followed in December 1883.

Of the vocal score I can already offer you the first act, ready for engraving; the whole thing will be finished by the end of the year. We shall need the full score for a short time in order to copy out the parts; nevertheless, this, too, is completely at your disposal up to the time of the performances (at the latest).

I would set the purchase price at one hundred thousand marks, plus cancellation of all my outstanding debts with you. You offered me 40,000 marks for my exclusive account for the rights to the vocal score after it had been marketed for a period of three years. I should now like you to pay me this sum of 40,000 marks at once, upon relinquishment of the copyright, and agree to your paying the balance of 60,000 marks in three instalments from the end of December 1882 onwards.

Lest you consider my demands excessive, I would ask you to consider the example of an *English* publisher[1] who believes it in order to pay Herr *Gounod* 100,000 francs for an oratorio (!). I think that my final and – I believe – my finest work may well compare favourably with that of this somewhat pallid Paris maestro! –

I cannot conclude these lines, however, without thanking you personally, my most honoured Sir and friend, for such manifold demonstrations of the most willing support and kindness, which I wanted to apprise you of here, together with my most sincere good wishes.

Yours respectfully,
Richard Wagner.

Verleger-Briefe II, 226–7.

488. ANGELO NEUMANN, LEIPZIG   Bayreuth, 16 October 1881

But, dearest and best of friends, how you overwhelm me! – How am I supposed to take decisions for you which all of a sudden have become so important? I staked twenty years of my life on founding "Bayreuth", because I envisaged a far-reaching idea with it. A "Wagner Theatre" in Berlin? Nothing could have been simpler: I was offered the means to do so nine years ago. But what I wanted to bring into the world was not possible there. On the other hand, what I created here, in isolation, where people have had to come *to me*, could, if brought to the surface in its purest form, eventually be carried much further afield: but this is a task for *somebody else*: you should be this person, – you have discovered how much I trust you. But this is entirely your own affair, and there is nothing else that *I* can contribute

---

1 Novello, Ewer & Co., who paid Gounod £4000 for his oratorio *La Rédemption*, first heard at the 1881 Birmingham Festival.

here, except to place my works in your hands, preferring you to any other impresario.

What you need is not my money, but my – name? Just as I have given you my works, so you may give my name to the theatre, – but not as part of a list, or even at the head of any such list of interested parties. Berlin must be *your* undertaking, not mine. How much more so if you join together with some artistic consortium with a view to founding this theatre, which, in a practical sense, is something I consider wholly worthy of my approval but which completely excludes me from any financial or sympathetic interest in the affair.

My very dear friend, if you cannot establish a pure (shall we say) "Wagnerian" Theatre – an exceedingly difficult task, I grant you – you would do better to give up the idea altogether.

"Parsifal" is to be performed solely in Bayreuth – for internal reasons which were so clear, for ex., to my exalted benefactor, the King of Bavaria, that he has even given up the idea of reviving the Bayreuth performances at the theatre in Munich.[1] In view of this precedent, how could I do as you suggest with "Parsifal"? I cannot, and may not, allow it to be performed in other theatres, unless – that is – a real "Wagner Theatre" were established, a *sacred* stage theatre which – by touring from place to place – would propagate throughout the world what I have so far nurtured in my own theatre in Bayreuth in purity and fullness. – If we stick firmly and resolutely to this idea for your enterprise, the time may very well come when "Parsifal", too, is handed over, not to any Court or Municipal Theatre, but to your Travelling Wagner Theatre alone.

For today my warmest thanks for so readily and willingly agreeing to my request for an advance! – You should receive the letter for Minister *Ferry*[2] tomorrow at the latest.

Do not be angry, but *think well of me*: then all will be well! –

Cordial good wishes from

Your devoted servant,
Richard Wagner

Neumann, Erinnerungen, 198–9.

---

1 But see letter [499], pp. 929–30.
2 Neumann was hoping to present *Tannhäuser* and *Lohengrin* in Paris in the spring of 1882, and required a letter of introduction to Jules Ferry, the French Minister of Foreign Affairs. Nothing came of the idea.

489. KING LUDWIG II OF BAVARIA, HOHENSCHWANGAU

Palermo, 22 November 1881

[. . .] By a curious quirk of fate I also met here the man who is preparing the vocal score of Parsifal, since considerations of climate had persuaded him, too, to winter in the south.[1] As a result I am, so to speak, playing into his hands, which means that I am making excellent progress on the work. The man in question is the curious figure of Joseph Rubinstein, who first approached me ten years ago while I was at Triebschen, begging me to save him from the Jewishness of which he was a part. I allowed him to have personal dealings with me – he is, in any case, an outstanding musician – although it must be said that he – no less than the good Levi – has caused me a good deal of trouble. What both these unhappy men lack is the basis of a Christian education which instinctively enables the rest of us to appear similar in kind – however different we may in fact be – and the result, for them, is the most painful mental anguish. Faced with these circumstances – and very often having to combat their tendency towards suicide – I have had to exercise the most extreme patience, and if it is a question of being humane towards the Jews, I for one can confidently lay claim to praise. But I simply cannot get rid of them: the director Angelo Neumann sees it as his calling in life to ensure that I am recognized throughout the world.*) There is no longer anything I can say to all this, but simply have to put up with energetic Jewish patronage, however curious I feel in doing so, for – I can explain my exalted friend's favourable view of the Jews only in terms of the fact that these people never impinge upon his royal circle: for him they are simply a concept, whereas for us they are an empirical fact. If I have friendly and sympathetic dealings with many of these people, it is only because I consider the Jewish race the born enemy of pure humanity and all that is noble in man: there is no doubt but that we Germans especially will be destroyed by them, and I may well be the last remaining German who, as an artist, has known how to hold his ground in the face of a Judaism which is now all-powerful. –

[. . .]

Königsbriefe III, 229–30.

---

1 Wagner and his family had arrived in Palermo on 5 November 1881 and remained there until 20 March 1882; three weeks in Acireale and two in Venice completed their winter in Italy, and they were back in Bayreuth on 1 May 1882.

*) Because of their dealings in paintings, jewelry and furniture, the Jews have an instinct for what is genuine and what can be turned to lasting value, an instinct which the Germans have lost so completely as to give the Jews what is genuine in exchange for all that is *not*. [*Wagner's footnote*]

490. JOSEPH-ARTHUR DE GOBINEAU, ROME

Palermo, [10 February 1882]

Dearest and most honoured friend,

I see that I myself must mediate in this matter in order to express my opinion to you as a man between women.

To judge from all that I have been able to gather from various reports, you enjoyed your stay with us and it sounds to have done you good. But I have heard little good concerning the effects of your subsequent changes of address. "O Zeus, why did you create women!" Eteocles exclaims in Aeschylus. In Rome they seem to be raving mad, and elsewhere they are more stubborn than yielding. – Very well then! You do not want to remain in Rome during the coming spring? Excellent! You want to set off next summer for the performances of Parsifal which will take place in August, at a time when neither of us will have time for the other, since the whirlwind of events will snatch us from all our friends even before the beginning of July (because of the rehearsals). We are planning to be back in Bayreuth by the 15th of May at the latest; but we invite you to move into Wahnfried before then; all the servants will already be on hand to wait on you. Joukowsky, too, has offered to place a self-contained apartment at your disposal in his house. And as for female company, your needs will be met, from May onwards, by our numerous daughters. – But – something else! We shall be passing through Rome in mid-April with the single and express purpose of dragging you away from there and abducting you in our saloon carriage; we shall then slowly make our way northwards, and sign a lease in Venice for a splendid and – for you, too, – a spacious apartment which we shall then move into from Bayreuth at the start of the harsh winter season, in order to present another festival the following year in Upper Franconia.[1] Take your choice! But try not to go to Schahnameh (or whatever that place is called in the Auvergne)! "O Zeus" &c.

Be good! It would be best if you could join us straightaway – I can send you Schnappauf!

Yours,
Richard Wagner

Ludwig Schemann, Quellen und Untersuchungen zum Leben Gobineaus (Vol. I: Strasbourg 1914; Vol. II: Berlin/Leipzig 1919), II,290–1.

---

1 Plans to visit Rome did not materialize, but Gobineau – anxious to flee the strains of marriage – returned to Wahnfried on 11 May, remaining there until 17 June. He died in Turin on 13 October 1882.

491. HANS VON WOLZOGEN, BAYREUTH   [Palermo, 22 February 1882]

Dear friend,

On reading through Schemann's "Cherubini",[1] I was struck by the following superficial thoughts, which I am not really disposed to encourage you to elaborate. They are:

1. Tragedy of Rossini, who could write only melodies[2] but not develop them along academic lines.
2. Tragedy of Schumann, who failed to produce a single melody.
3. Tragedy of Brahms, who – in spite of his wealth of ideas – always remains tedious.

The tragedy of Mendelssohn, who was unable to find a truly German libretto – but this has already been dealt with by E. Devrient. –

There are various other tragedies. –

I find it tragic that, for all his eloquence, Schemann feels drawn towards cliquishness and abstruseness for which a lack of determinative impressions may well be to blame. His latest piece contains the most curious things, e.g. the first 10 lines of p. 28 &c. &c. One could, and can, take him to task for a number of odd remarks, such as Cherubini's withdrawal into the Belgian countryside where he ended up because – being a great miser – he found life in Paris too expensive, and because he was never obliged to look out of the window of his Belgian castle. Even though it is not easy to hear Cherubini's church music in Göttingen, I know from experience that the larger Catholic cathedrals in Cologne & Munich for example live off the stuff. – But all this is ultimately beside the point! – It is just that I find the article really belongs elsewhere, [rather than in our journal, which ought to have scarcely enough space for what is correct and important; instead of which you poor devil seem obliged to accept what is incorrect and unimportant! –][3]

Read your own introductory essay with the same deeply satisfied interest that I, for ex., felt on reading it, and then ask yourself what sort of a figure this extremely odd and forgivable – but not entirely understandable – Cherubini cuts immediately after it! – I intend writing you a proper letter some time, but am afraid of making a start on it! For today, only this light relief for my heart! Keep well!

Yours,
RW.

---

1 Ludwig Schemann, "Cherubini" in *Bayreuther Blätter*, v (1882), 16–35; the passage to which Wagner takes exception deals with "the artificial intensification of certain formalistic endings" which, according to Schemann, might be construed as "cheap showmanship" if one did not know that Cherubini was attempting "an artistic revaluation of form".
2 "nur Melodien", not "neue Melodien" as in the printed German edition.
3 This passage has not previously been published.

P.S. I was very glad that Jäger had good weather for his journey back to Hanover!

RWA (published with errors and omissions in Bayreuther Briefe II,400–1).

492. KING LUDWIG II OF BAVARIA, MUNICH   Palermo, 1 March 1882

[...] My "Foreign Minister" (as I call the opera manager Neumann) will soon be starting up his activities in London,[1] after which he plans to tour around with the Nibelungs: it appears the affair is being treated as "season-able". I am very thankful that on this occasion the people in Munich refused the Vogls leave of absence to go to Paris: it was the best way of preventing the whole undertaking from taking place.[2] All the representations which I made to Neumann concerning the impossibility of carrying out this plan were of no avail, since he claimed – not unjustifiably, I grant you – that my works have so many friends in Paris that these latter could no doubt be relied upon to help: but I know that twenty German Jews, considered there to be French patriots, are enough to prevent a single performance of any of my works from taking place there in peace. But in any case, the reason for my reluctance to have my works performed before the Paris public runs much deeper: it is impossible even to translate them into French, whereas an attempt to render them into English, Spanish or even Italian may well succeed. But any attempt to perform them in French simply looks as though it were *I* that was anxious to obtain the approval of this vainglorious nation, whereas it ought to serve them as a salutary confirmation that things of importance can go their own way without having to proceed along the Boulevard des Italiens. I am now working on measures to prevent all performances of my works from taking place in Paris.
[...]

Königsbriefe III,236.

1 Four cycles of the *Ring* were given at Her Majesty's Theatre, London, in May/June 1882, after which Neumann's company visited Breslau, Königsberg, Danzig, Hanover, Bremen, Barmen, Berlin, Amsterdam, Brussels, Basle, Venice, Bologna, Rome, Turin, Trieste, Budapest and Graz; after an interval of six years the company was then reassembled in 1889 to perform the tetralogy in St Petersburg and Moscow.
2 See letter [488], p. 917, note 2.

493. FRIEDRICH SCHÖN, WORMS   Bayreuth, 28 May 1882

Valued Sir and friend,

Your sterling support for my cause I once again had reason to recognize
in the detailed letter in which you entreat me to enumerate my further
requirements, and so, trusting wholeheartedly in your enthusiasm and
perseverance, I am writing to inform you of the result not only of my experiences but of my well-considered view of our present affair.

Regular performances of "Parsifal" in Bayreuth I regard as a school for
the artists taking part, and, since we have had no choice in the matter, these
performances, as before, will have to be reserved for a paying audience. In
consequence, the Society of Patrons, in its present form, must be considered
as having been disbanded. It would be very much after my own heart, however,
if you, my valued friend, were to enlist the support of those whom you thought
most suitable and if – in Worms – you were then to call into existence a
foundation which would make it possible for people without means of their
own to attend the performances. Under your chairmanship, such a foundation
would have to be completely independent of the running of the festival proper;
and it might also be asked to support and promote the "New Bayreuth
Blätter". This seems to me not only the simplest approach, but also the one
that affords the greatest moral and intellectual power, enabling us to perform
real acts of charity and, in a certain sense, to carry out my original idea,[1]
without coming into conflict with the administrative process of the festival, a
conflict which until now has been unavoidable.

My valued friend, please accept with these lines the assurance of my sincere
respect and devotion.

Yours,
Richard Wagner.

Freunde und Zeitgenossen 597–8.

494. KING LUDWIG II OF BAVARIA, BERG   Bayreuth, 8 July 1882

Most precious of men, most dearly belovèd of friends, my royal lord,

A harsher blow could not have befallen me than the news that my exalted
benefactor is resolved to attend not a single performance of my Stage Dedication Drama. *Who* inspired this highest and final outpouring of all my
spiritual powers? In perpetual regard for *whom* did I carry it out in the joyful

---

1 See, for example, letter [129], p. 234. A Stipendiary Foundation was set up by Friedrich
Schön, and continues today, through the Richard Wagner-Verband, to provide bursaries
enabling students to attend the Bayreuth Festival. The present letter was written by Cosima
and signed by Wagner (see CT for this date).

prospect of a successful outcome? What had been pledged as my finest success has now become my life's greatest failure: what is the point of it all if I cannot give joy to *him*?

And – it is the last thing I shall write. The tremendous feeling of weariness which leaves me today with only the strength to pen these few lines tells me where I stand with my powers. *Nothing* more can be expected of me. –

Forgive me, my exalted benefactor, if I cannot acquiesce in my fate with the requisite calm and composure. I do not know at what straw I may yet be able to clutch, since I see it is a question not merely of a private performance (which would have been Your Majesty's to command on any day you had ordered) but that the private performance you want should take place not in the festival theatre in Bayreuth but in the Court Theatre in Munich, – a request about which I should have no misgivings inasmuch as I have in the past been deeply grateful to be able to make such private performances available to my exalted lord in the Munich theatre – but it is quite impossible for these later performances in Munich to present my work to my King in the pure and transfiguring light that can be achieved only through my own preparations in the festival theatre here; my most dearly belovèd lord, let it be performed for you here, by me, at least *once*, for the *first* time. – Otherwise – there is no hope! – Oh, why was this theatre not built in Munich! – then all would have been well! –

But enough, and no doubt more than enough from one who may be hard to forgive! May fate grant me but one final request: to beg for your mercy! – From one who gladly and fervently longs to die *soon*,

My revered lord and master's
most loyal *vassal*
Richard Wagner

Königsbriefe III,244.

495. OTTO LESSMANN, BERLIN   Bayreuth, 10 July 1882

Dear friend,

It amuses me to put your Berlin journal[1] in order on certain matters. Here is another report, not a word of which is true, – which looks particularly impertinent given the tone of great assurance, as though the report were that of a close friend. More than 25 years ago I sketched out a scenario on a single side of paper and gave it the name: the *Victors*. Since conceiving *Parsifal*, I have altogether abandoned this Buddhist project – which is related to the

---

1 According to Cosima Wagner's diary for 10 July 1882, the *Allgemeine Musik-Zeitung* (of which Lessmann was editor) had reprinted the "alleged text for *Die Sieger*".

former only in a weaker sense – , and since that time have given no further thought to elaborating the sketch, still less of reading it aloud.

Your old friend,
R. Wagner

Sammlung Burrell 816–17.

496. THEODOR MUNCKER, BAYREUTH   [Bayreuth, 30 July 1882]

Most honoured friend,

To my great regret I have been forced to gather from the sum total of complaints made by our festival visitors that, although its outstanding artistic success has assured us the permanent footing that we desired, the irredeemable shortcomings in the town's public services threaten to destroy this hope entirely. Although you, most honoured friend, were at pains to see that our visitors were well looked after, their complaints concerning poor accommodation and food, more especially at the three leading hotels, can no longer be ignored. I am told that at the Hotel Sonne a decent piece of meat is not to be had on the fixed-price menu at 7 marks. Since the prevailing bad weather means that the theatre restaurant cannot be patronized, the result is a degree of inconvenience for our visitors which, if taken advantage of by unsympathetic journalists, might well be calculated to bring Bayreuth into fundamental disrepute as a festival town. My own labours have been crowned by artistic success, but if these same labours are insufficient to allow me to continue the festival on an annual footing, I should have cause for the deepest regret that the townspeople's public spirit was to blame. That is why I am now writing to you with the humble request that you do all that it is permitted a man in your privileged position to do in order to put an end to the potentially dangerous shortcomings that I have described to you here.

In constant gratitude and respect, I am,

Your obedient servant,
Richard Wagner

Bayreuther Briefe I,309–10.

497. KING LUDWIG II OF BAVARIA, BERG   Bayreuth, 8 September 1882

My most gracious and revered lord and friend,
                    – Oh! torment of love![1] –
How painfully I suffered at the thought that, on the strength of superficial

---

1 *Parsifal*, Act II (GS X,358).

considerations, my belovèd King had felt obliged to remain away from this year's opening performances of "Parsifal"; for I strove with all my might not to give serious credence to the assumption that any real indisposition might have led him to take this decision. If I *have* to believe otherwise, how much more inconsolable must I then be! What are Parsifal and all the Grail's wonders, what power do they have in the face of such suffering from which I must needs be aloof and to whose relief I can contribute nothing!

There is almost nothing more for me to tell my supremely belovèd lord except to express my anguish at his suffering, since I cannot offset that suffering by recourse to any self-ingratiating doubt. If I could believe that it was the *King* who – through the laws imposed by His Majesty's dignity – felt bound by the force of that dignity, I might rail against fate, and suffer and sigh: but if I am forced to admit that it was the *man*, the most precious of all men, on whom envious nature imposed her constraints, then I shall for ever remain inconsolable. Now I can only wish, I can do nothing but wish: oh, if only I were a magician! –

What shall I tell you about these festive days in Bayreuth that shall seem worthy of being retailed to so exalted a patient? The work was a success, – that much I am bound to say to the honour of the performers. The most touching part about it for me was the splendid enthusiasm of all the participants – from the first to the last: although I have noticed this sort of thing with pleasure before, it seemed on this occasion as though everything was so much more intense. I was often tired and weary when I arrived for one of our performances which followed each other in such rapid succession, and was on the point of commiserating with my singers or musicians on the unremitting strain, but they met me with cries of jubilation, assuring me that their only cause for regret was the inevitable prospect of the end of the festival and their return to the ordinary theatrical and musical round. Many of them were genuinely inconsolable at the end: Fräulein Malten, who had had to leave us on the 15th of August, came back especially from Dresden for the final performance, at which Frau Materna was singing, in order at least to be able to be present as one of the audience. All of them assured me they had stipulated that their managements agree to their appearing only in my own operas for the period immediately after their return. – Theatre managers, amazed at our uncommonly accurate routine, asked me who was in charge, to which I replied by way of a joke that anarchy reigned and that everyone did as he wanted: but since everyone wanted the same thing that I did, everything was always in perfect accord with my own intentions. And that, indeed, is how it was. –

As for the success of the individual singers in solving such great and entirely new tasks, it was a cause for regret that I was too exhausted by the rehearsals to be able, in my resulting poor state of health, to take them through their parts again after each performance. Such rehearsals are really intended to correct points of detail, and there was no one more ready to take part than my singers themselves: they begged me to hold them, but I had to refuse. Yet even the few corrections that I did undertake, more especially with Kundry and Parsifal in the long and crucial scene in the second act, bore excellent fruit: visitors to the festival who had attended the opening performances and who then returned for the final ones were amazed at the progress they were able to note. The good thing here was that the two performers of "Kundry" (Frau Materna and Fräulein Malten), in addition to the singers of "Parsifal" (Herr Winkelmann and Herr Gudehus), were more or less comparable in excellence: the only advantage which Materna and Winkelmann had was that they remained here the whole time and were thus able to gain more practice in performing their parts. – Next to Scaria, the normally outstanding Siehr had a hard fight on his hands as "Gurnemanz": the latter is perhaps the more accurate vocally and musically, and his acting is certainly most dignified, whereas Scaria's performance was marked throughout by a certain *naïveté* which won him the hearts of his audience. The scene with Klingsor's enchanted flowers was utterly unsurpassable, and probably the most masterly piece of direction in terms of music and staging that has ever come my way: it had been a question here of assembling six so-called leading sopranos with equally light, high voices, and of choosing a further twenty-four young leading chorus members with equally good voices and charming appearances. Thanks to the zeal of our admirable conductor, Kapellmeister Levi, whose enthusiasm I cannot praise highly enough, this was a total success: I had singers from five Court Theatres who normally sing Elisabeth, Elsa, Sieglinde and even Brünnhilde (Frl. André from Brunswick). I cannot begin to describe these ladies' engaging enthusiasm; the admirable Porges had played a significant part in rehearsing them, too. If I may mention one major difficulty in performing "Parsifal" in Munich in the event of its being presented to my exalted benefactor there, then I am bound to recognize that it lies in the impossibility of your giving an equally good performance of this scene, unless you succeed in reassembling the same ensemble as before. –

The costumes gave us a good deal of extra work, since the flowermaidens in particular had been designed very sketchily by Joukowsky and had to be almost entirely rethought when it came to running them up: we succeeded in investing them with the most perfect *naïveté*; they really were flowers, just like the giant blooms in the garden itself: the finishing touch consisted simply in their breaking off some of the flowers and placing them on their heads like children, which produced an indescribably charming effect. – The sets were more successful than anything I had previously experienced: in making them the Brothers Brückner were fully initiated as artists. However, the late *Brandt* had incomprehensibly miscalculated the amount of time required for the moving transformations to pass the width of the stage, since they required as much music again as I had already allowed for it; although we were able to get by here by repeating the music, the whole process became so tiresomely distended as to be totally out of keeping with the magical character I had intended. It has already been decided that at future performances the first transformation will be reduced by half, and the second (in the third act), which was not used at all on this occasion, will only be hinted at, and will then lead immediately into the rocky gateway which, shrouded in darkness until that moment, will then split open to lead at once into the Temple of the Grail. –

May my most gracious lord and friend forgive me for this somewhat bungling report with which I really only wanted to give proof of my goodwill, and, in addition to expressing my most painful regret at so deeply distressing a reason for my exalted friend's absence from a festival which owes its existence to him alone, to contribute as best I may to his relaxation of mind. If aught can compare to my pain, it can be only the gratitude which fulfils and inspires me whenever I recall the immeasurable kindness which my most dearly belovèd benefactor has shown to me. All I have asked for, nay, all I have wished for by way of the merest suggestion was granted me with more than kingly grace: the resultant assistance was utterly decisive, just as it was executed by those entrusted with your sovereign command with exemplary zeal and an excellence which can never be adequately acknowledged.

Thus may my gratitude mingle with my pain, that it may be dedicated to my reverend lord as a tragic bloom from the garden of life of the Holy Grail: and thus may I perish at your feet in undying love,

Eternally and for ever your own,
Richard Wagner

Königsbriefe III, 246–9.

498. ANGELO NEUMANN, BREMEN Venice,[1] 29 September 1882

Dear Herr Neumann,

I have heard nothing from you since you left Danzig. I hope that Hanover, too, was a success: did you perform in the Court Theatre there? If so, how did you manage to reach an agreement with Hülsen?[2] You have my approval in advance for all that you do: you know the trust that I place in you, and that if ever I have any misgivings about what you are doing, it is because I have your interests at heart. It is in this spirit that I would advise you to forget about Paris, at least for the time being: not even London will ever reward

---

1 Wagner and his family had left Bayreuth on 14 September, and four days later moved into the Palazzo Vendramin-Calergi in Venice.

2 See letter [464], pp. 882–3. Neumann gave only a concert in Hanover.

your labours, but America certainly would if you follow the system adopted in Germany and announce only *one* cycle in each place.

I set the greatest store by Berlin. I have no doubt but that you could successfully put on a whole winter season there: but it would then be important to pay the greatest possible attention to correctness and general excellence, and to the manner and style of the performances. Nothing cursory or make-shift in the sets; greatest possible care with the staging and acting, where it will not be sufficient to rely upon traditions already existing in Vienna and Leipzig, but where you will have to learn from the lessons that were to be gained from my recent performances of "Parsifal" in Bayreuth.

From what I have heard, you already have an eye on one of the theatres in Berlin for the performances there. The architect *Brückwald* also told me that you had asked him to draw up plans for a genuine Wagner Theatre in Berlin, faithfully modelled on the one in Bayreuth, and I should happily give my consent to his splendid idea of adding a second tier of boxes to the so-called Princes' Gallery in Bayreuth and of slightly raising half the seats in the stalls so as to introduce a differential price structure there.

I am prepared to support you in this undertaking in any way necessary – but this you know already. But I do not know how to reply to your recent and repeated wish that you be allowed to include "Parsifal" in the performances announced by this theatre of yours, since I have already explained my views on the subject in the most explicit terms possible. "Parsifal" can only ever be a part of what I have created in Bayreuth, and my festival theatre there will present this one work alone in a production that is to be repeated there year after year. This isolation is conditioned by the whole conception of the subject itself. My Bayreuth creation stands or falls with "Parsifal". Of course, this creation will pass away with my death, for I know of no one, now or in the future, who could continue my work in the spirit of its creator. If my strength – which on occasions such as these is subjected to the severest strain – fails me before I actually die, so that I cannot concern myself with these performances, I should of course have to think of means of keeping my work as pure as *possible* for the world. If, by then, you and your Wagner Theatre have achieved the necessary standard and can maintain it by dint of constant improvement and the exclusive production of all my earlier works, stage dedication festivals could well be entrusted to this theatre, too, at special periods, and in this spirit "Parsifal", too, might be ceded to your theatre, and to your theatre alone. – On the basis of today's communication you may care to discuss this matter in confidence with such persons as you require to set up your theatre: but I should be compelled to withdraw all I have said, if ever a word of this were made public: you know the worthless and malicious way in which our newspaper reporters avail themselves of such information, and you cannot expect me to throw away my Bayreuth creation, which I have gained at the price of such unspeakable effort, by allowing it to be destroyed by vulgarity. –

———

Would you be kind enough to ask your secretary to let me know briefly how much of my advance has now been paid back out of the receipts you have sent me since then? It is simply a question of ascertaining my present financial position.

———

And now it remains only for me to offer you my very best wishes, my praise and my gratitude! I am still suffering from the effects of nervous exhaustion to which I can hope to put an end only by lasting and undisturbed rest. I am doing all I can to make this possible, but all it needs is a single letter from that insane man Batz, for ex., to throw my entire organism into disarray. – But let us hope for the best!

Every good wish to you and the whole of the Nibelung empire under your sway!

Yours,
Richard Wagner

Neumann, Erinnerungen, 259–61.

499. LUDWIG VON BÜRKEL, MUNICH   [Venice,] 1 October 1882

Dear and most honoured friend and patron,

How anxious and uneasy I feel! My exalted benefactor's non-attendance at the performances of Parsifal (an absence which I must unfortunately interpret as involuntary!), together with the news of his intention of staging a private performance in circumstances which I consider far from promising, leaves me feeling deeply dispirited. It is impossible in this way for my supreme protector to gain the same sort of impression of my work as I believed I had prepared for him with the performances in Bayreuth. If, however, our most gracious lord is satisfied with this, it is more than likely that I shall lose all interest in reviving Parsifal and in continuing to perform the work even in Bayreuth. Why should I make so much effort, if it can all be done so easily without me, in private? –

In your recent kind letter to my wife you intimated that you cherished the hope of perhaps receiving His Majesty's instructions to visit Venice. How desirable it is that this hope should be realized. Perhaps I may be accorded the gracious communication which will relieve me of many of my cares? For I do not see how I can continue the festival without incurring considerable risk, unless I can be given my exalted protector's generous support for another two years and be granted free use of the royal orchestra and chorus. I fully understand, however, the great sacrifice which would have to be made here on behalf of my enterprise, and – how can I cheerfully accept that sacrifice if I cannot give my sovereign benefactor any pleasure by doing so? –

You see, I am in a very real dilemma: is there no word of comfort you could give me? – –

A thousand heartfelt good wishes to Him and His loyal servant!

In eternal gratitude,

Your most obedient servant,
Richard Wagner

Freunde und Zeitgenossen 599–600.

500. KING LUDWIG II OF BAVARIA, HOHENSCHWANGAU

Venice, 10 January 1883

Most merciful font of grace, most royal lord and most friendly of friends,

At last the hour seems propitious for me to satisfy the most glorious need that I am yet able to feel: the spasms which generally hold me in their sway of a morning have passed today somewhat sooner than usual, and I know that my thoughts are now free to express these words of gratitude to him who is lord of my life!

I should like to proceed in a fairly orderly manner in telling you my news, and so, without further ado, shall make haste to correct a mistake. It was not Count Chambord who moved into the Palazzo Vendramin with us, but a relation of his with the title Count Bardi, the son or perhaps the heir of the late Duke of Parma, a nephew of Henri de France through his mother, who was a daughter of the Duc de Berry. He has been joined by various other members of that same deposed royal family, so that the whole palace was full, and we found ourselves obliged to put up my father-in-law Liszt in our own special apartment.[1] But we have had other visitors, too; the faithful Joukowsky, who claims not to be able to live without us, also turned up. The resultant upheaval was made all the worse by a large number of rehearsals which I insisted on holding – in secret at first – with the orchestra of the local Liceo San Marcello, with whom I was rehearsing the symphony[2] which, as one of the more important works of my youth, I had first performed in public in Leipzig almost fifty years ago to the day. I commemorated this half-

---

1 Liszt stayed with the Wagners in Venice from 19 November 1882 to 13 January 1883.
2 Symphony in C major (WWV 29), first heard in Prague in November 1832 under Dionys Weber, but repeated the following month in Leipzig.

century with a family celebration to mark my dear wife's birthday, which falls on Christmas Day. No one was allowed to be present except for our family alone. I have written a short essay for the "Musikalisches Wochenblatt"[1] on the fate of this symphony and on its significance for my development; it may perhaps amuse my exalted benefactor to see it, and in that hope I am taking the liberty of sending a copy forthwith.

For the rest, Grandpapa (as the children call him) brought with him the upheaval that has now become a typical part of his life. He has led so uncommonly turbulent a life that, wherever he goes, he is for ever surrounded by a surging mass of acquaintances who seek him out and call on him, drawing him away to an endless round of matinées, dinners and soirées and in that way prevent us from seeing him, since we ourselves remain away from all these engagements and confine ourselves exclusively to our own company. His latest engagement was a dinner with Don Carlos and a Mexican Duke Iturbide, whom I declared to be a votary of Fitzliputzli, and related to Itztka-huitl and Popocatepetl – which did not, however, deter Papa from appearing at Don Carlos's side in the guise of the Marquis Posa.[2] – From these brief hints my dearly belovèd friend may perhaps gather that I was not exactly in my element here, and that it was only with difficulty that I was able to make the necessary arrangements for preparing for this year's festival.

On this point I had to be perfectly clear in my mind how best to meet the wishes of my revered lord, and the following possibility seems to present itself here.

It is impossible to build any sets that could be used for a performance of Parsifal in Munich *before* they are substantially altered and rebuilt, a process which, after close consideration on my part too, will finally be recognized as feasible only in the festival theatre in Bayreuth. The two moving transform-ations have been cut up for this purpose and are at present unusable. The alterations which made this necessary could not be delayed any further, at least as long as I persist in my resolve to achieve absolute correctness in Bayreuth for this, my farewell work to the world. Since my exalted friend was kind enough to devote his attention to my essay "On the Stage Dedication Festival in Bayreuth",[3] I may hope that my declaration on this point has not remained unappreciated. If my most gracious lord still remains disinclined to grace the actual festival with a transfiguring presence which would in no way expose him to the public gaze, three or even more performances could be made available for my sublime benefactor after the end of the public performances, and given, moreover, by the same company under my personal supervision, in the fullest realization of the artistic ideas I have been aiming

1 Published in GS X,309–15; PW VI,313–21.
2 A reference to the leading figures in Schiller's *Don Carlos*.
3 Dated Venice, 1 November 1882, first published in *Bayreuther Blätter*, v (1882), 321–9. Reprinted in GS X,297–308; PW VI,301–12.

to achieve. Since yet another of these wretched "international" or "world exhibitions" is being held in Munich this year, requiring a certain amount of opera music to amuse its patrons, and since there will be very little time available to use the Court Orchestra and chorus which your boundless generosity has once more placed at our disposal, I must make haste to arrange a greater number of performances this year, lasting, say, until the 15th of August, since this seems to me indispensable if I am to ensure the continuing existence of my undertaking; the whole company may then perhaps remain together for a further week in order for the private performances to go ahead for my revered lord. Of course, these performances will have to take place in Bayreuth itself, since it would be completely impossible to install all the people and equipment necessary to perform the work in Munich sufficiently quickly for the period involved not to extend beyond the time when my singers are free. And since, moreover, the Court Theatre management is desperately looking for operas for the period of the Exhibition, it would be very difficult to reconcile *their* wishes with my exalted benefactor's most gracious desire that private performances, to the total exclusion of the general public, be held in Munich at precisely that time.[1]

I have given much thought to this matter – during sleepless nights, and when feeling unwell – and have come to the conclusion that I should risk one final, submissive assault on my royal lord and friend's so graciously well-disposed heart, begging him to give orders that a work which was created for him alone should finally be performed only under such conditions as alone are necessary if I am to vouch for an accurate impression, whereas any change is bound to produce only a feeling of fatal displeasure within me. – What am I saying here? Perhaps I am sounding my death knell and that of my entire artistic enterprise: for I am bound to fear that even he whom I call the lord of my life will regard all my ideas and entreaties as vain. And yet I know what I am asking for here: it is that selfsame thing for whose sake my lord first took an interest in my shattered life. Let him crown his own work then, just as he raised me aloft with his mercy: may he receive my oath of the most profoundly grateful allegiance as I place at his feet a work that I regard as my farewell to life. I have suffered much to be able to do so! It gave me great pleasure to see from so kind a telegraphic despatch as the one with which my exalted prince deigned to answer my respectful greetings on New Year's Day that our essays in the Bayreuther Blätter have afforded at least some enjoyment. It was most important for me to give a proper account of the essence of my rehearsals with the company, and also the reasons for their success: at all events, this success and more especially the increasing refine-

---

1 Ludwig continued to maintain an obdurate silence on this point. Private performances of *Parsifal* were given in Munich, using the Bayreuth sets and costumes, in May and November 1884, and again in April 1885.

ment of the singers' performances could come about only through perseverance and constantly going back over the rehearsals themselves. What emerged
here under my eyes and continual supervision could not have succeeded so
simply at random. Scaria was perfect; Materna surpassed herself to become
our finest Kundry, not least because she performed the part more frequently
than Frl. Malten, whom I would otherwise consider the best of my singers,
since the latter could obtain leave of absence for only a relatively brief period.
Second only to her was Winkelmann, who made such extraordinary progress
during the performances that great hopes may most certainly be placed in
him. – The memoir of Gobineau[1] strikes me, too, as one of those delicate
and, at the same time, forceful pieces of writing such as perhaps only a woman
might succeed in producing. Countess Latour will be providing a French
translation of it, since there is probably no other Frenchman capable of
understanding and valuing Gobineau sufficiently: he is no longer a part of
the present generation. – There is a further error I should like to correct and
into which my royal lord – very understandably – has fallen: the essay on me
and Parsifal which won your kind approbation is the work of Count Schleinitz's niece, a woman of a profound and enthusiastic temperament. – People
are once again writing a great deal about me, and some of it is assuming a
significant character: I am even told that a French translation of my Collected
Writings is under way in Paris.

While abandoning my works to the march of time to influence them as it
wishes, I rejoice in the splendid hopes aroused and fostered by my son. Until
now it has been almost exclusively architecture which has held his attention
with any force, but music, too, now exercises its powerful sway upon him; he
is eagerly learning harmonic theory; but the theatre, too, and plays, which he
is very keen to see here at the Teatro Goldoni, also interest him to the extent
that he has already written out several tragedies for himself which he plans
to rehearse with his young friends in Bayreuth. He has an excellent mother!
He is on splendid terms with his sisters, all of whom love him dearly, and all
of whom – mother, son and daughters – congratulate their father on the love
of his august protector, his exalted benefactor, and his King whom God has
sent him!

And so for today may I close the circle of my earthly existence by recalling
the favours in whose noble enjoyment I am, unto death, my revered lord and
friend's eternal debtor.

For ever yours,
Richard Wagner

Königsbriefe III, 256–9.

---

1 "Graf Arthur Gobineau. Ein Erinnerungsbild aus Wahnfried" in *Bayreuther Blätter*, v (1882),
341–52. The necrology was written by Cosima.

APPENDIX A

I. MINNA WAGNER'S LETTER TO THEODOR APEL OF 25 OCTOBER 1840
(see introductory essay, p. 54)

My very dear Herr Apel,

I hope you will not be unpleasantly surprised to receive a letter from me, and more especially a letter with *these* contents. As God is my witness, I should have preferred to be able to approach you with words of comfort in your present misfortune than to have to trouble you like this with a request for assistance. Unfortunately, however, I cannot be mistress of my fate, and must now appeal to you to protect myself against despair. – It requires few words to explain my reasons for writing; – Richard had to leave me this morning to go to the debtors' prison; I am still so terribly agitated that my mind is even now reeling from it; the only thing that allows me to collect my thoughts together with any calmness is a letter from Herr Laube which has just arrived and which I have opened in Richard's absence. On the one hand it robs me of every hope of seeing an end to our present misfortune, but, on the other, it gives me the courage to risk one last desperate step – as I readily confess it to be. – In his letter Herr Laube writes to say that it is impossible for you to manage without the sum which Richard had asked for, but, at the same time, Herr Laube declares that you expressed yourself in a friendly and sympathetic vein; if you knew, my dear Herr Apel, how much we are used to the unfriendliness and lack of sympathy of all those people whom we were obliged to turn to for help, you would understand how this news has revived my hopes to a certain extent. What would be left for a poor wretch like me if I could not pin my hopes on an expression of sympathy. Above all, therefore, you should seek *here* what it is that gives me the courage to approach you. – My poor husband, who, as a foreigner, does not even enjoy the advantages granted to the locals in similar circumstances, has fallen into the hands of a German resident here who has shown such obstinacy in taking him to court that I cannot reckon on his relenting sufficiently to release him. I am too confused at the moment to know what I should do: even if I myself had the means to leave Paris, I would never, ever abandon Richard in such a situation, for I know he has not got into it through any thoughtlessness on his part, but that only the noblest and most natural striving on the part of an artist has brought him to the point which anyone could have reached if no special help were at hand. It was only with great reluctance that I agreed to his plan of coming to Paris; but the more I have got to know his intentions here, the more I have come to see that lack of sufficient support will alone be to blame if he goes under and fails to reach the goal he might otherwise be destined to reach. Thanks to his own efforts, he had in fact already got to the point where he could soon lay claim to the fruits of his labours, and it is only the sacrifices it has cost him so far which now stand in his way, he had work, and was bringing in almost enough for me to run his little household for him, however frugally; today's events, however, have destroyed all that. He had finally managed, for instance, to have a work of his accepted for performance at a big concert: the Overture to his Rienzi, which he has just completed[1] and which everyone is convinced will be a great success, was due to be performed in 2 weeks' time; but without his personal presence at the rehearsal, this will not be possible. Is this not reason enough to despair? – What can I do? A poor and abandoned woman like me can achieve nothing by weeping; is it really to end like this? Could you, who have been so kind-hearted towards Richard so often in the past, allow him to be lost to us *both* simply because all that is needed here is an exceptional sacrifice? – May God forgive me, but I cannot imagine it should end like this. – Put it down to the indescribable situation I am in at present, if I may perhaps have overstepped the bounds of decency by expecting things of you which despair alone inspires me to say. I have already discovered to my horror how much Richard owes you; you obtained money for him then thanks to your own credit; – but what was his position then compared to ours now? Would not such a sacrifice be far better made now, since there is now the prospect of our being able to repay such a debt in the course of a year, or two at the most? Believe me, I do not normally share Richard's exaggerated hopes; but I know from the lips of his own acquaintances that he has only to take one more step and he'll reach his goal. – Heaven knows, I have so much more to say to you. I lack the leisure to express myself clearly; I shall make up later for all that I leave unsaid now. The only thing I *can* say is, help, please help! Make a big sacrifice for Richard, try to do so as quickly as possible, and God will reward you if Richard's grateful heart and my own prayer are too weak to do so. – There is nothing more I can add to this; I pray to God that my request is heard, and our gratitude will know no bounds.[2] Sincere good wishes for your own well-being from

Your devoted friend,
Minna Wagner.

SB I, 414–18.

1 The Overture to *Rienzi* was completed in short score on 23 October 1840, but the full score was not finished until 19(?) November 1840; the concert referred to here was almost certainly a figment of Wagner's imagination.
2 Apel wrote to Wagner on 26 October (his letter crossing in the post with Minna Wagner's), announcing that he had given Laube six friedrichsdor (102 marks) to be forwarded to Wagner.

II. Liszt's letter to Wagner of 4 January 1859

(see letters [229] and [230])

In order not to be exposed to the danger of annoying you further with "*emotional* and *serious*" turns of phrase, I am sending the 1st act of *Tristan* back to Härtel, and would ask you not to acquaint me with the remaining ones until they appear in print. –

Since the *Dante* Symphony and *Mass* cannot be treated as bank stock, it will be superfluous to send them to Venice. No less superfluous would it be for me to receive any further telegraphic despatches from there appealing for help, or letters that cannot but wound me. –

In *genuine and truest* devotion, I am,

Yours,
F. Liszt.

Liszt-Briefe II, 245.

III. Ludwig II's letter to Wagner of 10 March 1865

(see letter [318])

Dearly belovèd and most precious of all friends,

Moved by deep anguish, I take up my pen today in order to reply to the letter you addressed to me yesterday. –

I must make a disclosure which will affect you deeply: how hard it will be for me to do so, you can all too well imagine. – Recall the love with which I feel drawn to you, recall the warmth of this everlasting love which, as you have long known, my belovèd friend, can never die nor ever shall; and then judge how profound my grief must be! – I am bound to inform my unique friend that there are circumstances over which I do not have mastery at present, and that the iron grip of necessity makes it my sacred duty not to speak to you, at least for the present. – That my love for you will remain loyal unto death – this, I know, you will never doubt. –

Hope will sustain both you and me, and give us strength & courage; what would man be without this precious gift from God?! – Yes, I firmly hope for happier times, we shall see each other and speak to each other as we did before! –

The terrible grip will weaken! – Courage! – All will be well; o bitter lot; who would have thought it, who foreseen it! – Love is all-powerful; we shall triumph! –

Eternally yours,
Ludwig.

Königsbriefe I, 71–2.

APPENDIX B

The following are the original texts of the various passages omitted from earlier printed editions:

LETTER [57] TO FELIX MENDELSSOHN OF 8 JUNE 1843; see pp. 109–10

Mein verehrtester Herr,
leider traf ich Ihre Karte erst gestern spät am Abend, da ich den Tag über nicht nach Hause kam; somit war ich des Vergnügens beraubt Sie in Dresden sehen und sprechen zu können, und es war mir unmöglich Ihnen Ihre Partitur früher zuzustellen, als es jetzt geschieht.

Mir ist versichert worden, daß die Intention Ihres Liedes vollkommen klargeworden ist u. allgemeines Verständnis erlangt: nur hatte ich zu bedauern, daß trotz der starken Anzahl von Sängern durch die tiefe Lage des *unisono*-Gesanges ziemlich die Hälfte des Chores – die Tenoristen – verhindert wurden durchgreifend mit zu singen, u. deshalb der Gesang vielleicht nicht kräftig genug hervortrat. Waren Sie mit billiger Berücksichtigung dieses Uebelstandes dennoch einiger Maaßen mit der Aufführung zufrieden, so macht es mir große Freude.

Ich darf ja hoffen, Sie nun bald auf längere Zeit in Dresden zu begrüßen, u. kann Ihnen somit zurufen: auf ein wohl freundliches u. dauerndes Wiedersehen!

Mit wahrer Verehrung bin ich

Ihr

Dresden, 8 Juni 1843.

LETTER [188] TO MINNA WAGNER OF 12 JUNE 1855; see p. 350

Von meinen schönen Atlashosen hatte die Königin auch schon gehört: ich muss ihr sie in's Schloss schicken, damit sie dem Pr. Albert welche darnach machen lassen kann. Ich zweifle, dass sie ohne Jungfer *Poseck* gelingen werden.

LETTER [199] TO FRANZ LISZT OF 8 MAY 1857; see p. 367

Und das Bett, auf dem ich einmal verscheiden will, ist auch an der Stelle aufgeschlagen, von der man mich einst hinaustragen soll.

LETTER [209] TO CAROLYNE SAYN-WITTGENSTEIN OF 12 APRIL 1858; see
pp. 384–8

Nun nehmen Sie mir durch Ihre Freundschaft dieses wenige Verdienst, dass
[*sic*] ich mir erworben haben würde, sobald ich Ihnen endlich unaufgefordert
geschrieben; denn – glauben werden Sie meiner Versicherung gewiss nicht,
so eifrig Sie auch sonst im Glauben sind. Nun denn, auch diess werde mir
zu einer Uebung in der Demuth! –

[. . .] und das hätte ich dann so auf meine Weise gethan, dass eben ein
Brief an Sie daraus geworden würde, – ein Brief, wie es mich lange drängte,
Ihnen einen zu schreiben. Eigentlich könnte ich auch sagen, ich hätte Ihnen
nur zu sagen gehabt, warum ich Ihnen so lange nicht geschrieben; damit
wäre ich ungefähr eben so weit gekommen, und Sie hätten mehr von mir
erfahren, als meinen Freunden zu wissen gut thut. Dass Sie mir nun von dem
Konzert im Wesendonck'schen Hause schreiben, ist mir ungemein erwünscht,
denn ich erfahre somit, dass Sie schon davon unterrichtet sind, und stelle
mir vor, dass es mir leicht hätte begegnen können, von dem Konzert Ihnen
keine Sylbe zu sagen, und zwar ganz ohne Absicht, ohne irgend etwas damit
zu wollen. Jedenfalls überhebt mich heute der glänzende Bericht, der Ihnen –
vielleicht aus Herwegh's Feder – zugekommen ist, einer weiteren Schilderung
dieses Ereignisses, und [. . .] Was ich nun an jenem Abende verschwieg,
sagte ich durch meinen Beethoven laut und tönend einer ganzen Gesellschaft:
Ihnen ist berichtet worden, wie man nicht mein Schweigen, sondern nur
mein Tönen verstanden. Und zu diesem tönenden Feste wünschen Sie mir
Glück, wie alle Welt sich daran erfreute. Somit hätte ich Ihnen nur noch zu
sagen, was ich verschwieg: aber das wird eben schwer sein. Versuchen wir's
durch Gleichnisse! Dummes Wort – : Gleichnisse! Was habe ich nur damit
sagen wollen? Es steht da: nun bleibe es geschrieben; denken Sie sich dabei
das Vernünftigste! –

So will ich denn ein wenig erzählen, wie es mir vor und nach diesem
Konzerte ging.

Ungefähr 14 Tage vor diesem Feste, war ich mit mir auf dem Punkte, am
ersten besten dieser Tage meinen Hut zu nehmen, in die Welt zu gehen, und
den Augen dreier Menschen für ewig zu entschwinden. Es schien mir diess
die einzige Lösung einer rein unerträglichen Lage. Was hielt mich zurück? –
das Innewerden, dass ich damit dem einen dieser drei Wesen, vielleicht aber
allen dreien den Tod gegeben haben würde. Und diesen accuten Tod scheut
der Mensch für Andre, wenn er für ihn selbst auch als grösstes Glück
erscheinen müsste. – Ich blieb. Auch brachte ich dann, wie Sie wissen, ein
recht artiges Konzert zu Stande. Diess glänzend heitre Fest griff mich aber
ein wenig an; ich wurde krank, und hatte den Aerger, Ihnen nicht sogleich
darüber schreiben zu können, weil es mit dem besten Willen nicht ging, da
ein mehrtägiges Fieber mich etwas schwächte. Am Tage, wo ich zum ersten

Male etwas an die Luft wieder gehen wollte, erlag meine gute Frau einer Versuchung des Teufels, von der ich nun herzlich wünsche, dass sie sie als Prüfung Gottes glücklich bestehen möge. Für mich erhielt dieser Fall das besonders Treffende, dass die Aermste seit einiger Zeit einem Rückfall eines von länger her rührenden Leidens auf das Bedenklichste unterworfen ist.

Der Genuss unsres Gärtchens, die Beschäftigung mit ihm und die Annehmlichkeit unsrer neuen Häuslichkeit, hatte ihr vorigen Sommer sehr wohlgethan, und die entsetzlich aufgeregten, oft lang andauernden Zustände von Herzbeklemmung mit allerhand andren bedenklichen Symptomen, die sich seit Jahren mit Steigerung bei ihr gezeigt hatten, schienen ganz verschwunden. Von der zweiten Hälfte dieses Winters an stellte sich das Leiden plötzlich, und (seien Sie versichert!) ganz ohne allen bewussten Anlass von aussen (denn sie hat nichts von jener Katastrophe erfahren), so stark und heftig wieder ein, dass die vergangenen Monate schon dadurch uns beiden zur Hölle wurden. Das Charakteristische dieser Herzkrankheiten äussert sich, namentlich durch fortdauernde Schlaflosigkeit, in einer furchtbaren Aufgeregtheit und Heftigkeit, bei Trübsinn, Leichtverletzlichkeit, übelnehmischer Laune und oft gänzlicher Verwirrung alles vernünftigen Gedenkens und Denkens. Alle Mittel des Arztes haben bis jetzt nur das Uebel zu verschlimern vermocht, und da ich seiner Zeit durch Dr. Vaillant bei Genf so gute Resultate für meine Gesundheit gewonnen habe, so suchte ich endlich meine arme Frau zu einer gleichen Kur zu bestimmen. Glücklicher Weise wies mir ein Freund in grösserer Nähe von Zürich eine Wasserheilanstalt nach, die von einem ausgezeichneten Arzte, der einen notorischen Fall, gleich dem meiner Frau (nur bereits noch gefährlicher) glücklich behandelt habe, geleitet würde. Vor zwei Tagen besuchten wir nun gemeinschaftlich diesen Arzt, fassten *Beide* das grösste Vertrauen zu ihm, und meine gequälte arme Frau ist nun entschlossen übermorgen ihre Kur in Brestenberg anzutreten. Diess ist vorläufig der Stillstand im wachsenden Verfalle meiner Lage. Ich werde längere Zeit – wohl gewiss zwei Monate – allein sein, und mindestens im Hause Ruhe, wie hoffentlich auch Musse zur Arbeit gewinnen. Während dem wird sich die Krankheit meiner Frau entscheiden: ich habe gutes Vertrauen, und hoffe auf eine gründliche Beruhigung ihrer Leiden. Wie froh will ich dann sein, wenn sie es mir möglich macht, was ich zu opfern habe, ferner ihrem Gedeihen und ihrer Ruhe der älteren Tage zu widmen! Doch seien *Sie* mir nicht böse, liebe Kapellmeisterin, wenn ich wirklich erst heute dazu komme, Ihnen zu schreiben! –

An Freund Wesendonck will ich Ihre Shakehands ausrichten, doch mich gehörig dabei hüten, nicht ganz Ihren Sinn ihm dabei zu verstehen zu geben; es möchte ihn leicht verwirren, wenn man eine zu vortheilhafte Meinung von ihm hegte. Er ist sehr gutmüthig; sein in mancher Beziehung respectables Verhalten beruht zu meist doch wohl aber nur darauf, dass er sich nicht zu helfen weiss. Zur Höhe einer wirklichen, männlichen Resignation kann er sich unmöglich aufschwingen. Er hat Scheu und Ehrfurcht vor mir; oft zeigt er sogar liebevolle Neigung. Dennoch bleibt der Hauptpunkt meines Verhaltens zu ihm, dass er mir nichts vorwerfen kann. Mit welchen Opfern, nicht nur meinerseits, sondern namentlich auch von Seiten seiner Frau diess erkauft werden muss, denken Sie sich leicht. Sie schwindet, und wird nur durch meinen Blick am Leben erhalten. Doch konnten und mussten wir uns an jenem Festabende gestehen, dass wir mit Niemand tauschen möchten. Das Bewusstsein unsres Leidens ist der Quell unsrer Labung. – [. . .] gegen sehr geringe Geldvortheile; [. . .] nur war mir aber noch keine Arbeit wieder möglich. [. . .] – Beiläufig gesagt, war das Gerücht, ich componire meine neue Oper für eine erste Aufführung in *Prag* wohl so albern, dass es keiner Widerlegung bedurfte; es beruhte auf der Grossthuerei eines Theaterdirectors, der eine scherzhafte Aeusserung von mir so verstehen zu dürfen geglaubt hatte. – Im Uebrigen, beste Freundin, fährt es fort mir miserabel zu gehen! Diess ebenfalls beiläufig! –

So nun haben Sie ein ganzes Bündel guter Nachrichten von mir, auch schon für im Voraus, so dass mir keiner sobald mit besseren bei Ihnen wieder zuvorkom̃en soll. [. . .] nur bin ich seit so langer Zeit dem Gefühle, das ihn leitet, so ganz entfremdet worden, dass ich Allem nur noch wie einem Traum zuschauen kann; feste Realität hat nichts davon für mich, und ich weiss nichts, steht Franz, wenn ich ihm zusehe, im Lichte und ich im Schatten, oder umgekehrt. Es kommt mir alles nur wie ein wesenloses, unhörbares Schweben von Schattenbildern vor, deren sichere Umrisse mir allmählich im̃er unerkennbarer werden. Doch Ihr steht mitten im Feuer, und für Euch ist die Zustimmung der Welt eine bestimmte, vernehmbare Realität die Euch wohlthut. Ich hab' kein Gefühl mehr dafür, desshalb, halten Sie es nicht für Theilnahmlosigkeit, wenn ich meine Freude über Liszt's Triumphe nicht energischer kundgebe; mir versagt die Stimme dazu, wie Einem, der im Traume und zu Traumbildern laut reden will.

Auch Euer verkündigter Besuch will sich in mir noch nicht zu einer realen Hoffnung gestalten: Sie wissen, ich habe keinen Glauben, sondern nur Muth. Belehrt mich Ungläubigen bald: aber dazu muss ich Euch von Angesicht zu Angesicht sehen. Um aber ein Zugeständniss zu machen, will ich *hoffen*. –

[. . .] Könnten Sie sich, liebe Freundin, entschliessen, sie im Voraus, als Pfand Ihres Nachkommens, uns nach Zürich zu schicken, so könnten Sie uns dadurch ein namenlos Gutes erweisen. Im Wesendonck'schen Hause könnte sie recht angenehm wohnen, *und was sie uns sein würde*, das habe ich doch wohl selbst nicht anzudeuten nöthig! Sie sind ja gross, und ungemein in Allem was Sie denken und thun. Thun Sie etwas Ungemeines, denn es handelt sich um nichts Gemeines! – Doch genug auch hiervon! Ich weiss, *mir* begegnet das Ungemeine nur im Schmuck der leidenvollsten Dornenkrone; ein reines, labendes Glück ist mir nicht beschieden. Dann bin ich aber auch religiöser wie Ihr! –

LETTER [231] TO MINNA WAGNER OF 16 JANUARY 1859; see pp. 440–1

Hämmorrhoidal-Beschwerden stellten sich stark wieder ein; um dagegen zu wirken griff ich nun wieder den Magen mit Klystieren an.

LETTER [248] TO ANTON PUSINELLI OF 3 OCTOBER 1859; see pp. 469–71

Ich spreche hier nicht von boshaften Einflüssen, sondern bloss von dem gedankenlosen Gebahren der Weiber überhaupt, und der Weiber von einer gewissen untergeordneten Bildung im Besondren. Sie hat Verkehr mit allerhand alten Jungfern u.s.w., die, wie die Weiber im Allgemeinen ohne eigentliche Vernunft sind, durch das eigentliche Dresdener Element (bekanntlich einem [sic] der elendesten!) auf einem sehr niedren Grade moralischer wie intellectueller Bildung stehen. Bald wird sie durch diess, bald durch jenes allarmirt: Klatsch und aber Klatsch! Da besucht sie Frau Tichatscheck ganz express aus Dresden, um Sie [sic] in meiner Begnadigungs-Angelegenheit von Neuem zu beunruhigen; alle Ruhe, die ich dem entgegensetze und auf meine Frau überzutragen suche, wird da wieder zerstört; man dringt in sie, mich doch wieder von Neuem zu beschwören, diesen oder jenen (ihrer Seits gänzlich unüberlegten) Schritt zu thun. Und so geht es in Einem fort. Oder sie geht nach Dresden zu einer Aufführung meiner Opern: da muss sie denn nun von Einem zum Andren laufen, Jedem 'was Angenehmes sagen, und kommt dann zurück, von Neuem in grösster Herzaufregung. Dazu nun noch die ewige Unruhe über mich, die Erwartung, die Neugier. Somit ersehe ich Eines klar: [. . .]. Dort, liebster Anton, kann sie nicht gedeihen; und das, wessen sie ausser der ärztlichen Hülfe so sehr bedarf, ist eine männliche, stets gegenwärtige Aufsicht, und Versetzung an einen Ort, wo es leicht ist, sie von allem verderblichen Weiberklatsch-Umgang fern zu halten. [. . .] Ich bestehe darauf, dass sie sich eine junge, gebildete Person engagirt, die ihr als Pflegerin, Gesellschafterin und namentlich auch Vorleserin, immer nahe sein soll. Um das Hauswesen soll sie sich in keinem andren Sinne zu bekümmern haben, als dass sie anordnet und befiehlt, was bei der ausserordentlichen Einfachheit und Regelmässigkeit meiner Lebensweise für sie nur ange[ne]hm sein kann. Ich bringe deshalb jedes erdenklich [sic] Opfer, und suche durch meine Unternehmungen ihre Erschwingung möglich zu machen. [. . .] Somit denn, höre meinen Entschluss. Zunächst soll denn meine Frau in Dresden unter Deiner liebenswürdigen Leitung die ihr verordnete, gewiss sehr wohlthätige Traubenkur befolgen. Nach ihrer Beendigung also wohl Ende dieses Monates, fragt es sich dann einfach, soll sie sogleich nach Paris komen, oder erst abwarten, bis ich in Karlsruhe fertig bin? Ich nehme jetzt an, die Aufführung des Tristan werde sich bis zum 3en Dezember hinausziehen, weil man sie für den Geburtstag der Grossherzogin von Baden wünscht. Ist diess der Fall, so rechne ich vor Mitte November nicht nach

Karlsruhe berufen zu werden, und dann könnte meine Frau wohl etwa Anfang November direct nach Paris kommen, wo sie sich sehr freuen wird, in die vollkom̄en fertige Einrichtung mit unsren wohlbekannten Züricher Möblen, einzutreten. Ich wäre dann ungefähr noch 8 Tage mit ihr zusam̄en, und dürfte dann hoffen, sie recht beruhigt und angenehm getröstet, unter der Obhut ihrer Gesellschafterin und eines Dienstmädchens, in ihrer definitiven Häuslichkeit, mit ihren trauten Hausthieren, zurückzulassen, um meine Karlsruher Expedition allein zu überstehen. In Karlsruhe würde ich dann (wenn ich eben allein kom̄e) bei Devrient selbst aufgenom̄en und bestens gepflegt werden. Nach 4 Wochen käme ich dann zu meiner Frau zurück, und Alles wäre wie ein ferner Traum an ihr vorübergegangen. Sollte ich nun aber schon früher nach Karlsruhe müssen, so wäre es allerdings vernünftiger, wenn meine Frau die ganze Zeit noch in Dresden abwartete, und ich mit ihr mir geradeweges erst für meine Rückkehr nach Paris, entweder dort, oder auf dem Wege, also etwa Mitte Dezember, Rendezvous gäbe. Doch halte ich den ersten Plan für vorzüglicher, schon weil ich sie um einen Monat früher in ihre ruhige Pariser Häuslichkeit bringe, den nachtheiligen socialen Einflüssen Dresdens entziehe, und ausserdem es sich Anfangs November besser reisen lässt, als Mitte Dezember.

Hier also mein Plan. [...]

Noch habe ich mich Dir über einen wichtigen Punkt mitzutheilen. Er ist so delicater Art, dass ich kaum dem Freunde, sondern nur dem befreundeten Arzte davon sprechen kann. Ein grosser Beunruhigungsgrund für meine Frau liegt in dem Abbruche meines geschlechtlichen Umganges mit ihr, der sich allmählich einfach aus ihrem leidenden Zustande ganz von selbst ergab. Ich glaube nicht sie einer leidenschaftlichen Sinnlichkeit zeihen zu müssen (wiewohl ich nicht beurtheilen kann, in wiefern ihre ungemäss überreizte Nervosität sie auch in dieser Hinsicht beeinflusst); jedenfalls aber beunruhigte sie von dieser Zeit an die Eifersucht mehr denn je zuvor. Sie kennt mich eben doch zu wenig, und hat von dem wahren Ernste meines Wesens keinen richtigen Begriff. Ich hoffe nun, sie wird mit der Zeit allen Grund gewinnen, ihre Eifersucht für thörig zu erkennen; dennoch hielte ich es, bei dem unzurechnungsfähigen Zustande einer so sehr Gemüthskranken, für wichtig, wenn Du, als Arzt, ihr nach dieser Seite hin – Du kannst es ja halb scherzend gegen mich kehren – ein strenges Verbot auferlegtest, ein Verbot, das sie um sich wie mich besorgt zu machen habe. Lass' Dir das angedeutet sein: leider sind derlei Dinge von unleugbarer Wichtigkeit! –

LETTER [275] TO MINNA WAGNER OF 9 FEBRUARY 1862; see p. 535

[...] nicht nachliess, als ich sehr zurückhaltend über alles diess ihn gut ablaufen liess und [...]

LETTER [276] TO PETER CORNELIUS OF 4 MARCH 1862; see p. 542

(Auch ich fühle mich O. Bach schuldig: er verdient bessere Beachtung, der Unglückliche.)

LETTER [303] TO HANS VON BÜLOW OF 1 JUNE 1864; see p. 610

Grüss' doch Liszt u. sag' ihm von mir. Wenn ich von seinem Grossherzog höre, wird mir es rein übel, wie so von einem herzoglich sächsischen Schwedentränkchen! – Nun, damit *war* ich doch schon fertig! Dingelstedt hat es schwarz auf weiss!

LETTER [310] TO ELIZA WILLE OF 9 SEPTEMBER 1864; see p. 621

[. . .] die bereits ein Jahr nach ihrer Verheirathung, – damals als beide uns in Zürich zum zweitenmale besuchten, – aus Verzweiflung über den begangenen Irrthum ihrer Verheirathung sich das Leben nehmen wollte; seitdem wiederholte Versuche machte, sich absichtlich Todeskrankheiten zuzuziehen, endlich durch eine schwärmerische Wendung zum Erhabenen sich zur Ausdauer und Geduld gestärkt hat. Der Mann, feinfühlend und selbsterkenntnissvoll genug, sieht, wie er steht, und – verwünscht *sich*, dieses Weib an sich gefesselt zu haben; sucht sich durch übertriebene Anstrengungen in der Ausübung seiner Kunst zu betäuben, ja zu ruiniren, um zu vergessen und – zu sterben. – Dies [*sic*] die graunvolle Unterlage, auf welcher sich nun beiderseits die liebenswürdigsten Eigenschaften in der Weise entwickeln und zeigen, dass die rührendste Theilnahme für einander beide verbindet.

LETTER [312] TO ANTON PUSINELLI OF 2 OCTOBER 1864; see pp. 624–5

Lieber theurer Freund!
Es scheint, ich soll nie aufhören es recht schwer zu haben. Die unsinnigsten Gerüchte über meinen plötzlichen Reichthum ziehen mir von jeder Seite her die übelsten Folgen zu. Gegen die neidischen Anfeindungen am Ort hat die offizielle Behörde selbst für nöthig befunden, zu reclamiren: ich habe diese, in einer hiesigen Zeitung gedruckte Berichtigung meiner Frau zugesandt: Aus ihr kannst auch Du ersehen, wie höchst mässig meine äussere Lage bedacht ist: ich habe gerade soviel, um für mich höchst bescheiden auszukommen, was nur dadurch möglich ist, dass der König für meine Wohnung sorgt. Ich habe es mir zur Pflicht gemacht, mein persönliches Interesse auf das bescheidenste Maass zu reduziren, um den vortrefflichen Dispositionen des Königs für die Auffuhrung meiner Werke allein reichen Lauf zu lassen. – Ich bitte Dich nun inständigst, als alter bewährter Freund

mir jetzt zur Beseitigung der hieraus mir entstehenden Schwierigkeiten behülflich zu sein, soweit diess im Terrain Dir gerade nahe liegt. *Erstlich*, habe die Güte, und bedeute die unglückliche *Frau Kriete* über ihren Irrthum; sie verlangt, in der Meinung, ich schwimme hier im Gelde, 1822 Thaler Zinsen für das zurückgezahlte Capital von 2000 Thr. – Es ist Wahnsinn, jetzt so etwas von mir zu verlangen: *es ist* möglich, dass die Zeit einmal kommt, wo ich wirklich für meine Werke und Leiden belohnt werde: um sie herbeizuführen, muss ich jetzt noch grosse Geduld haben. Sollte denn dagegen Hrr. Musikhändler Müller nicht Ehren halber zu bewegen sein, an die Frau Kriete noch etwas herauszuzahlen? – er hat, wie ich erfahre, sich von Flaxland in Paris eine bedeutende Summe für die Pariser Herausgabe (hinter meinem Rücken) auszahlen lassen. Jetzt macht er mit dem fliegenden Holländer brillante Geschäfte. Will er sich anständig benehmen, so will ich ihm auch ohne alle weitere Entschädigung meine neuen Scenen zum Tannhäuser zu beliebiger Ausbeutung übergeben, die ich *sonst* – **nicht** herausgebe. – Diess wäre Eines! –

Nun meine Frau! – Ich beziehe monatlich – ausser freier Wohnung – 100 fl. Damit begnüge ich mich. Das Jahrgeld meiner Frau von 1000 Thalern kann ich natürlich nur durch anderweitige, zufällige Einnahmen bestreiten. Diese werden in der Regel hierfür ausreichen, nur gehen sie nicht regelmässig ein, und es fällt mir schwer, pünktlich zu sein. Wenn doch da *Du*, Liebster, Dich freundschaftlich in das Mittel schlagen wolltest. Nämlich, ich möchte Dich bitten, immer regelmässig alle Vierteljahre die 250 Thaler für meine Rechnung meiner Frau zu übergeben; *ich* dagegen schicke Dir immer sofort zu, was ich auswärts einnehme. Natürlich müssten Deine Auslagen Maass und Ziel haben, und jedenfalls müsstest Du *vor* einem neuen Termine jedesmal den rückständigen alten bereits von mir wiederempfangen haben. Wäre doch eine solche Abmachung möglich: wie viel würde das zu der mir so nöthigen Ruhe beitragen! – Jetzt z.B. hatte ich von *Coburg* für den fliegend. Holländer Zwanzig Louis d'or (110 Thlr) zu beziehen, welche ich meiner Frau direct zu wies. Aus Berlin erwarte ich die Anzüge über meine dortige Tantième, die ich ihr ebenfalls zuweise; aus *Braunschweig* habe ich im Verlauf der nächsten Monate 30 Louis d'or zu erwarten. Sieh, Liebster! diese Einnahmen würde ich sofort direct an Dich weisen, wenn Du z.B. jetzt gleich so gut wärst, meiner Frau noch die fehlenden 140 Thr. zuzustellen.

Gewiss, Du solltest keinen Schaden dabei haben, und – käme ich wirklich einmal in bedeutenden Rückstand – so würde mir (und Dir) in solchen einzelnen Fällen gern denn der König aushelfen. Nur **dies**, so spät wie möglich.

Begreif' das! Und wenn Du irgend kannst, erfülle mir meine Bitte, wogegen Du auf meine ehrenhafteste Gewissenhaftigkeit zählen könntest. –

Nur – Ruhe! Ruhe! – diese ewigen Sorgen untergraben alle Hoffnung, je noch den Geist – wie nöthig – frei zu bekommen!

Also – mach's gut, and lass bald Freundliches hören!
Adressire *München, Briennerstrasse*, 21. –
Adieu! Tausend Grüsse an die Deinigen! Bleibe mir gut, und habe immer
Dank!
Von Herzen

Dein
Richard Wagner

Starnberg,
2 Oct. 1864.

LETTER [323] TO ANTON PUSINELLI OF 6 MAY 1865; see p. 643

Mich verletzt und verbittert endlich jede Berührung mit ihr, die wirklich die
Einzige ist u. bleibt, welche *nie* über mich in's Klare komen wird.

LETTER [335] TO ELIZA WILLE OF 26 SEPTEMBER 1865; see p. 667

Von Ihnen erwarte ich auch noch einmal zu hören, dass Freundin Mathilde
meinen Brief an sie endlich von Ihnen verlangt hat. Sie begreifen doch wohl,
dass ich ihr nie wieder schreiben kann, ehe sie mir diesen – diesen – Brief
nicht beantwortet hat. –

LETTER [356] TO CLARA WOLFRAM OF [15 JANUARY 1867]; see pp. 710–11

Kämen Dir diese Blätter, die bereits ziemlich stark sich vermehrt haben, Dir
noch einmal zur Durchsicht, so würdest Du erkennen, wie lebhaft u. nahe
auch Du, liebe Schwester, in der Erinnerung unserer gemeinschaftlichen
Erlebnisse vor mir stehst, wie innig und gerührt ich Deiner gedenke.
Veröffentlicht könnten diese Blätter natürlich erst lange nach meinem Tode
werden; so oft ich des Abends dazu aufgelegt bin, diktiere ich sie für meinen
jungen Freund, den König von Bayern, der sie schon jetzt stückweise zur
einzigen Aufbewahrung erhält. [. . .] Mein letztes Componir-Instrument
gehört bereits dem König von Bayern.

LETTER [388] TO ANTON PUSINELLI OF [13] JANUARY 1870; see pp. 762–6

Zu dem rechten Auskunftsmittel in diesem Sinne soll nun aber Rath werden:
seit ziemlich 5 Jahren habe ich – in verschiedenen Perioden – einem mir
über Alles vertrauten Wesen meine vollständige Biographie dictirt, an welcher
jetzt nur noch die letzten 10 Jahre fehlen. Der wahrhaftige Sinn dieser Dictate
wird Dir aus der Bestimung erhellen, welche ich nothwendig getroffen habe:

die Dictate selbst könnten erst nur lange nach meinem Tode veröffentlicht werden. Einstweilen aber erhalten sie zuviel Aufklärungen, als dass es meinen Freunden nicht sehr wichtig dünken müsste, ein Document vor Handen zu wissen, aus welchem alle Entstellungen u. Verleumdungen, die über mich, wie über Keinen, cursiren bestimmt zu widerlegen seien. Damit nun ein solches Manuscript nicht dem Untergange ausgesetzt sei, bin ich jetzt daran, auf meine Kosten einige sehr wenige Exemplare durch Druck herstellen zu lassen. Diese sollen zum Theil den Meinigen vermacht werden; Dir, und noch vielleicht zwei jüngeren, gänzlich zuverlässigen Freunden, will ich aber schon bei Lebenszeit je ein Exemplar zustellen, natürlich gegen die treueste Verpflichtung, es nie von sich zu geben, auch nicht nach meinem Tode es zu veröffentlichen. Dagegen wird es diesen Wenigen schon jetzt dazu dienen können, vorkommenden falschen Behauptungen über mein Leben, (namentlich in albernen biographischen Skizzen, welche dann und wann erscheinen) dadurch entgegentreten zu können, dass die nöthig dünkenden Berichtigungen meinen Dictaten selbst entnommen werden.

Für jetzt ist mir von dem Druck ein Probebogen zugestellt worden, welchen ich Dir zugleich freundschaftlichst zustelle. [...] Vollkommen erfüllend und wahrhaft erlösend ist für mich nur das eine Verhältnis geworden, welches andrer Seits die allerschmerzlichsten Leiden mit sich führte. Wenn mir hier die höchste Aufopferung zu Theil wurde, und die traurigsten Opfer gebracht werden mussten, so war es wohl nur Eines, was zu Allem Diesem nöthigte: ein tiefes, unerschütterliches Bewusstsein. [...] Ueber Deinen Irrthum im Betreff des Bräutigam's meiner Nichte Doris Brockhaus bist Du wohl bereits längst aufgeklärt: verursachte er mir (als solcher) ein Lächeln, so hat es mich doch tief gerührt und erfreut, dass er Dir so innige Herzenswünsche für mich eingab. – Fast ging mir so es auch wieder aus Anlass des falschen Gerüchtes meiner vermeintlichen Erkrankung, da ich diessmal das Lächeln der Beruhigung für Dich Guten empfinden konnte. Gott weiss, was die Leute eben immer mit mir treiben müssen! Ich könnte geradesweges eine Zeitung nur für die Widerlegung des Falschen und Schlechten, welches mich täglich betrifft, herausgeben. In Dresden scheint Ihr, wie ich erfahre, in meinem Betreff während des vorigen Sommer's ganz besonders schön unterhalten worden zu sein: die Quelle war mir leicht erräthlich in einer gewissen I. Reuter, welche vor einigen Jahren, als Freundin der Frau Schnorr (welche mich absolut heirathen wollte), sich für ihr Theil in den Kopf gesetzt hatte, ich sollte sie an den König von Bayern bringen. Da das nun Alles nicht ging, habe ich mir den Hass dieser beiden Damen in einem unerhörten Grade zugezogen; dass dieser zum Theil in Dresden, wo die manquirte Königsbraut zu Hause ist, ausgekocht wurde, war zu erwarten. Nun, in diesem Punkte ist noch einiges für die letzten zehn Jahre meiner Biographie nicht uninteressant zu berichten, nur werde ich aus Ekel das meiste zu übergehen haben! – [...] Einzig plagt mich der Unterleib und Aftererhitzungen. [...]

Eigentliche Noth macht mir nur noch mein junger König: worin diese besteht, ist allerdings nicht so leicht zu sagen! Letzten Sommer mit dem "Rheingold" war es schlimm: aber er liess sich nicht davon abbringen. Da predige Einer nun Vernunft! Jetzt heisst es denn: Alles! Alles! nur nicht der Aufführung meiner neuen Werke längere Zeit entsagen! Ich soll befehlen, Alles wird mir gehorchen. Da bangt mir nun denn wieder. Gott weiss, wie ich's anfange, etwas der Art zu Stande zu bringen, dass ich selbst Lust dazu bekomme. Doch will ich's versuchen, und – vielleicht – ist es möglich, dass ich das "Rheingold" und die "Walküre" nächsten Sommer aufführe. –

LETTER [393] TO HERMANN LEVI OF [28] APRIL 1870; see p. 773

P.S. Vor bereits längerer Zeit frug Herr Kayser im Namen der Direction des Grossherzogl. Hoftheaters bei mir wegen des Honorares für das Aufführungs- recht meiner Oper: Rienzi, an. Ich theilte meine Forderung mit, und hätte nun es für zu erwarten gehalten, eines Bescheides hierauf gewürdigt zu werden, welchen Sie, wenn ich darum bitten darf, nun vielleicht gütigst vermitteln wollen?

LETTER [397] TO ANTON PUSINELLI OF 9 NOVEMBER 1870; see p. 777

Das Schicksal Deines Bruders erinnert mich von Neuem an die Scheusslich- keiten dieser Franzosen, die andrerseits sich jetzt beklagen, dass die Deut- schen es zum Raçenkrieg trieben, und keine Nation an diese Brutalität beim Ausbruch des Krieges erinnert. [. . .] (mit Hrn. Rietz à la tête) [. . .].

LETTER [406] TO FRIEDRICH FEUSTEL AND THEODOR MUNCKER OF 7 APRIL 1872; see p. 790

Es genügte nun, dass er wusste, welchen Werth ich auf meine durch Ihn zu ermöglichende Eigen-Niederlassung in Bayreuth legte, um Ihn hierin den Punkt erkennen zu lassen, auf welchem Er mich quälen könnte. Alles, was wir in Bayreuth beabsichtigen, und worauf bereits die ganze Welt mit wachsender Spannung blickt, ist Ihm widerwärtig: mit dem, womit es mir heiliger Ernst ist, will Er spielen, und Er wüthet darüber, dass Ihm diess verwehrt sein soll. Hierüber müssen wir klar sein, meine Freunde, und es geziemt uns zu wissen, mit Wem wir zu thun haben. Ich sage Ihnen aufrichtig, dass ich fürchte, Ihre Freundschaft für mich könne den Interessen der Stadt Bayreuth nachtheilig werden. Hängt die Bewilligung des Baues der von Ihnen gewünschten Eisen- bahn vom König ab, so bin ich sehr besorgt, dass grade Ihre Theilnahme für mich Ihnen in diesem Punkte hinderlich werden könnte. –

Gehe ich vielleicht mit solchen Befürchtungen, wie ich Sie [*sic*] Ihnen hier andeute, zu weit, und [. . .].

LETTER [407] TO FRIEDRICH FEUSTEL OF 12 APRIL 1872; see pp. 792–3

Sie haben mich gewiss aber richtig verstanden, dass meine grosse Misstimmung in sofern dem Lokal unserer Unternehmung galt, als es mich plötzlich von Neuem anwidern musste, eben durch die Wahl meines Lokales in die ganz unvergleichlichen, eigenthümlichen und Nerven verzehrenden Tracasserien zu gerathen, denen mir – nach meinen Erfahrungen – jede Unternehmung ausgesetzt erscheinen muss, auf welches irgend eine Einmischung von Seiten des Münchener Hof- und sonstigen Beamten-Wesens nicht vollständig fern gehalten werden kann. Ich habe deswegen von vornherein eine directen [*sic*] Beisteuer des Königs für unser Unternehmen abgelehnt, um jener Einmischung (unter irgend welcher Gestalt) zu entgehen. Diesen ablehnenden Zweck nun dennoch aber nicht erreichen zu sollen, brachte mich durch die letzten Erfahrungen zur Verzweiflung, und ich glaubte auch die in meiner gewünschten Niederlassung liegenden Fasern jenes Einfluss-Zusammenhanges durchschneiden zu müssen. [. . .] in welchem Alles Bayerische Wesen durch München, seinen Hof und seine Beamten, befangen ist [. . .]. (wie es anderer Seits in meiner sehr schwierigen Lage zu dem Könige von Bayern liegt.) – [. . .]

Die neuesten Berichte über Neumann's Zuverlässigkeit haben mich allerdings trotz Allem noch in Erstaunen gesetzt. Wer kann so etwas Leichtsinniges voraussetzen! – Also, theurer Freund, resolviren wir uns hierüber kurz und bündig. Legen Sie die Neumann'schen Zeichnungen von dem mir (dereinst – vielleicht) bestimmten Hause für jetzt ruhig bei Seite! Wir wollen diesen Theil unserer Sorgen einfach gegenwärtig auf sich beruhen lassen. Wo es *so* hergeht – von der einen, wie von der anderen Seite – da ruft man: "Stillstand!" –

LETTER [436] TO EMIL HECKEL OF 4 FEBRUARY 1876; see p. 854

Bismarck hat die Sache aber hintertrieben.

LETTER [443] TO LILLI LEHMANN OF 7 SEPTEMBER 1876; see pp. 859–60

Nur Betz wirft einen ganz wiederwärtigen [*sic*] Schatten in meine Erinnerung! [. . .] Wie lügenhaft und falsch sind doch meistens diese Herren! –

LETTER [444] TO FRIEDRICH FEUSTEL OF 23 NOVEMBER 1876; see pp. 860–1

Erst gestern Abend bin ich, durch den Empfang des beigelegten Briefes des Herrn v. Radowitz (dessen ausserordentliche Verspätigung Sie aus dem Inhalte entnehmen werden) in die Lage versetzt worden, über den Stand unserer grösseren Angelegenheit mich deutlicher gegen Sie und unsre geehrten Freunde des Verwaltungsrathes äussern zu können.

[...] Am 14 desselben Monates schrieb ich an Herrn von Radowitz, welcher sich mir bei seiner Anwesenheit in Bayreuth, als eifrigen Vermittler nach allen Seiten hin angeboten hatte. Zugleicher Zeit schrieb ich aber auch in sehr ausführlicher Weise an den König von Bayern, indem ich ihm meine Wünsche dahin mittheilte:

er möge – entweder – durch seinen Bundestagsabgeordneten also durch den Bund, die Angelegenheit an das Reich bringen lassen, – oder, besser noch, das ganze Unternehmen mit allem Eigenthum für die Krone Bayern's erwerben.

Diesem fügte ich [...].

Immer noch wartete ich nun aber auf eine Antwort des Herrn v. Radowitz, von welchem ich auch eine Aeusserung im Betreff einer Subscription angesprochen hatte. Sie ersehen nun aus dessen Briefe sowohl den zufälligen Grund der Verzögerung einer Antwort, als auch, dass auf ihn und seines Gleichen in keiner Weise zu rechnen ist. Und hiermit hätte ich denn die schlimmste der gemachten Erfahrungen bezeichnet. Nämlich: [...].

LETTER [449] TO FRIEDRICH FEUSTEL OF 14 JUNE 1877; see p. 868

Ist davon etwa ein neuer Eysser'scher Wechsel bezahlt worden?

LETTER [450] TO CARL FRIEDRICH GLASENAPP OF 25 JUNE 1877; see p. 869

Dass auch Sie, mit aller Ihnen gebührenden Autorität, in die "letzte Hand, welche W. an die Partitur des Parzival legt" gefallen sind, hat mich lächeln gemacht. Gewiss denken Sie doch nicht ernstlich, dass ich so alle Tage immer ein bischen componiren muss, um mich des Lebens zu freuen?

LETTER [478] TO HANS VON WOLZOGEN OF 7 MAY 1880; see pp. 901–2

Ich denke die Sache soll sich – recht anständig – durch München machen. – Jetzt die grosse Bitte, welche Ihnen bereits die dicken Couverts verrathen haben werden. Ich glaube, meine Frau hat ebenfalls bereits – durch Gross – mit Ihnen über dieselbe verkehrt. Also: –

Burger soll das beiliegende Manuscript – ein Theil des 4ten Theiles "meines Lebens" – drucken, gegen Garantie der absolutesten Discretion. Typen, Druck u. Papier muss er genau nach dem Muster, welches Sie ihm mit einem Bande des "Lebens" vorzeigen möchten, ausführen; die Titelvignette (eine Erfindung meiner Frau) kann er sich vom früheren Drucker, der den Stempel gewiss noch aufbewahrt hat, verschaffen. Dieser ist: *Bonfantini*, Kunst- und Buchdrucker in Basel. Eine erste Correctur müssten Sie wohl so gut sein zu übernehmen, vielleicht auch dabei die Ueberschriften der Seiten redigiren. Zur letzten Durchsicht muss ich selbst die Bogen hierher bekommen. Nicht mehr als *Achtzehn* Exemplare sind abzuziehen. –

Mein dringender Wunsch ist, ein Exemplar für den König zu dessen Geburtstag (25 August) fertig zu bekommen. Dafür ist die Zeit durchaus genügend; der Band wird nicht stark, – heute haben Sie bereits über die Hälfte des Manuscriptes! –

Nun, seien Sie so gut! Nicht wahr?

LETTER [491] TO HANS VON WOLZOGEN OF [22 FEBRUARY 1882]; see p. 920

[. . .] als in unsere Blätter: diese sollten kaum Raum für das Richtige und Wichtige haben; statt dessen Sie Aermster genöthigt scheinen, auch das Unrichtige und Unwichtige willkoṁen zu heissen! –

SELECT BIBLIOGRAPHY

Included here are only those autobiographical and biographical sources to which reference is made (with abbreviated titles) in the foregoing annotation. For a more complete bibliography the reader is referred to John Deathridge and Carl Dahlhaus, *The New Grove Wagner* (London 1984), 195–9.

Altmann/Bozman — *Letters of Richard Wagner*, 2 vols, selected and ed. Wilhelm Altmann; trans. M. M. Bozman (London/Toronto 1927)

ASM — Marshall, Jennifer: "Richard Wagner's Letter to Australia" in *The Richard Wagner Centenary in Australia*, ed. Peter Dennison, Miscellanea Musicologica: Adelaide Studies in Musicology, xiv (1985), 149–65

Bayreuther Briefe I — *Bayreuther Briefe von Richard Wagner (1871–1883)*, ed. Carl Friedrich Glasenapp (Berlin/Leipzig 1907); trans. into English by Caroline V. Kerr as *The Story of Bayreuth as told in the Bayreuth Letters of Richard Wagner* (London [1912])

Bayreuther Briefe II — *Richard Wagner an seine Künstler*, ed. Erich Kloss (Berlin/Leipzig 1908)

BB — *Das Braune Buch. Tagebuchaufzeichnungen 1865–1882*, ed. Joachim Bergfeld (Zurich/Freiburg 1975); English trans. George Bird (London 1980)

Bülow-Briefe — *Richard Wagners Briefe an Hans von Bülow*, ed. Daniela Thode (Jena 1916)

Burrell Collection — *see* Sammlung Burrell

CT — *Cosima Wagner: Die Tagebücher 1869–1883*, 2 vols, ed. Martin Gregor-Dellin and Dietrich Mack (Munich/Zurich 1976/7); English trans. Geoffrey Skelton (London/New York 1978–80)

Deathridge — Deathridge, John: "Wagner und sein erster Lehrmeister. Mit einem unveröffentlichten

| | Brief Richard Wagners" in *Bayerische Staatsoper. Die Meistersinger von Nürnberg: Programmheft zur Neuinszenierung* (Munich 1979), 71–5 |

Eger I and II

Eger, Manfred: "Der Briefwechsel Richard und Cosima Wagner. Geschichte und Relikte einer vernichteten Korrespondenz" in *Die Programmhefte der Bayreuther Festspiele 1979: IV – Das Rheingold*, 1–23 and 108–119; *V – Die Walküre*, 1–23 and 108–132

Eger III

Eger, Manfred: "Richard Wagner an Dr. Eduard Liszt. Ein bisher unveröffentlichter Brief" in *Die Programmhefte der Bayreuther Festspiele 1975: III – Die Meistersinger von Nürnberg*, 14–17 and 70–71

Ellis, *Life*

see Glasenapp/Ellis

Familienbriefe

Familienbriefe von Richard Wagner (1832–1874), ed. Carl Friedrich Glasenapp (Berlin 1907); English trans. William Ashton Ellis (London 1911)

Fehr

Fehr, Max: *Richard Wagners Schweizer Zeit*, 2 vols (Vol. I [1849–55] Aarau/Leipzig 1934; Vol. II [1855–72, 1883] Aarau/Frankfurt am Main 1954)

Förster-Nietzsche

Förster-Nietzsche, Elisabeth: *Wagner und Nietzsche zur Zeit ihrer Freundschaft. Erinnerungsgabe zu Friedrich Nietzsches 70. Geburtstag den 15. Oktober 1914* (Munich 1915); trans. into English by Caroline V. Kerr as *The Nietzsche-Wagner Correspondence* (London [1922], repr. 1949)

Frantz

Constantin Frantz: *Briefe*, ed. Udo Sautter and Hans Elmar Onnau (Wiesbaden 1974)

Freunde und Zeitgenossen

Richard Wagner an Freunde und Zeitgenossen, ed. Erich Kloss (Berlin/Leipzig 1909)

Gautier

see Lettres à Judith Gautier

Glasenapp/Ellis

Glasenapp, Carl Friedrich: *Das Leben Richard Wagners*, 6 vols (Leipzig 5/1910–23); English trans. of the third edition by William Ashton Ellis (London 1900–08, repr. 1977) as *Life of Richard Wagner* [vols IV-VI are by Ellis alone]

Gregor-Dellin

Gregor-Dellin, Martin: *Richard Wagner, Eine Biographie in Bildern* (Munich/Zurich 1982)

GS

Richard Wagner: Gesammelte Schriften und Dichtungen, 10 vols (Leipzig 4/1907, repr. 1976)

Hoffmann

Hoffmann, Josef (ed): *Richard und Cosima Wagner an Maler Josef Hoffmann* [1896]

Hölzel-Briefe

"Drei unbekannte Schreiben Richard Wagners an Gustav Hölzel mitgctcilt von Marie Huch in Hannover" in *Die Musik*, xii (1912/13), 171–2

Kapp

Kapp, Julius: *Richard Wagner und die Frauen* (Berlin/Wunsiedel 1951); English trans. of the 1929 German edition by Hannah Waller as *The Women in Wagner's Life* (London 1932)

Kesting

Richard Wagner: Briefe, ed. Hanjo Kesting (Munich/Zurich 1983)

Kohut

Kohut, Adolph: *Der Meister von Bayreuth. Neues und Intimes aus dem Leben und Schaffen Richard Wagners* (Berlin 1905)

Königsbriefe

König Ludwig II. und Richard Wagner: Briefwechsel, 5 vols, ed. Otto Strobel (Karlsruhe 1936–9)

Lange

Lange, Walter: *Richard Wagner und seine Vaterstadt* (Leipzig 1921)

Lenrow

The Letters of Richard Wagner to Anton Pusinelli, ed. and trans. Elbert Lenrow (New York 1932, repr. 1972)

Leroy

Leroy, Maxime: *Les premiers amis français de Wagner* (Paris 1925)

Lettres à Judith Gautier

Richard et Cosima Wagner: Lettres à Judith Gautier, ed. Léon Guichard (Paris 1964)

Liepmann

Liepmann, Klaus: "Wagner's Proposal to America" in *High Fidelity* (Great Barrington, Massachusetts December 1975), 70–2

Liszt-Briefe

Briefwechsel zwischen Wagner und Liszt, 2 vols, ed. Erich Kloss (Leipzig 3/1910); the English trans. by Francis Hueffer, revised by William Ashton Ellis (New York 1897, repr. 1973) is based on Hueffer's incomplete German edition of 1887

Maier-Briefe   *Richard Wagner an Mathilde Maier (1862–1878)*, ed. Hans Scholz (Leipzig 1930)

Mathilde Wesendonck-Briefe   *Richard Wagner an Mathilde Wesendonk: Tagebuchblätter und Briefe 1853–1871*, ed. Wolfgang Golther (Leipzig 44/1914); the English trans. by William Ashton Ellis (London 1905) is based on the first German edition of 1904

MECW   Moulin Eckart, Richard Graf du: *Cosima Wagner. Ein Lebens- und Charakterbild*, 2 vols (Munich 1929–31)

Mein Leben   Wagner, Richard: *Mein Leben*, ed. Martin Gregor-Dellin (Munich 1963, 2/1976); English trans. by Andrew Gray, ed. Mary Whittall (Cambridge 1983)

Meyerbeer   *Giacomo Meyerbeer: Briefwechsel und Tagebücher*, ed. Heinz and Gudrun Becker (Berlin 1960–)

Meysenbug-Briefe   Kohler, Stephan: " 'Die Welt ist mir einmal durchaus conträr!' Richard Wagner und Malwida von Meysenbug: Geschichte einer Freundschaft" in *Jahrbuch der Bayerischen Staatsoper* (Munich 1982), 61–101

Minna-Briefe   *Richard Wagner an Minna Wagner*, 2 vols, ed. Hans von Wolzogen (Berlin/Leipzig 1908); English trans. by William Ashton Ellis (London 1909, repr. New York 1972)

Neumann, *Erinnerungen*   *Erinnerungen an Richard Wagner von Angelo Neumann* (Leipzig 3/1907); trans. into English as *Personal Recollections of Wagner* (London 1909)

Newman, *Life*   Newman, Ernest: *The Life of Richard Wagner*, 4 vols (London 1933–47, Cambridge 1976 [all references are to the later edition])

Niemann-Briefe   *Richard Wagner und Albert Niemann. Ein Gedenkbuch*, ed. Wilhelm Altmann (Berlin 1924)

Nietzsche-Briefe   *Nietzsche: Briefwechsel. Kritische Gesamtausgabe*, ed. Giorgio Colli and Mazzimo Montinari (Berlin/New York 1975–)

Otto   *Richard Wagner: Briefe 1830–1883*, ed. Werner Otto (Berlin 1986)

Otto Wesendonck-Briefe   *Briefe Richard Wagners an Otto Wesendonk*, ed. Wolfgang Golther (Berlin 1905); the English trans. by William Ashton Ellis (London 1899) is based on Albert Heintz's earlier incomplete edition

Petzet   Petzet, Detta and Petzet, Michael: *Die Richard Wagner-Bühne König Ludwigs II.* (Munich 1970)

Putzmacherin-Briefe   *Richard Wagner und die Putzmacherin oder Die Macht der Verleumdung*, cd. Ludwig Kusche (Wilhelmshaven 1967)

PW   *Richard Wagner's Prose Works*, 8 vols, ed. and trans. William Ashton Ellis (London 1892–9, repr. 1972)

Richter-Briefe   *Richard Wagner: Briefe an Hans Richter*, ed. Ludwig Karpath (Vienna/Leipzig 1924)

Ritter-Briefe   *Richard Wagners Briefe an Frau Julie Ritter*, ed. Siegmund von Hausegger (Munich 1920)

Röckel-Briefe   *Richard Wagners Briefe an August Röckel*, ed. La Mara [Marie Lipsius] (Leipzig 1894); English trans. Eleanor C. Sellar (Bristol [1897], repr. Ann Arbor 1969)

Röckl   Röckl, Sebastian: "Zwei unbekannte Bricfe Richard Wagners an Heinrich Vogl" in *Rheinische Musik– u. Theater-Zeitung*, xii/51–2 (23 December 1911), 706–7

Rundschau   Wagner, Richard: "Briefe aus sechs Jahrzehnten" in *Die neue Rundschau: XIXter Jahrgang der freien Bühne* (Berlin 1908), 858–72 and 981–99

RWA   Nationalarchiv der Richard-Wagner-Stiftung Bayreuth

RWG   Richard Wagner Gedenkstätte der Stadt Bayreuth

Sammlung Burrell   *Richard Wagner: Briefe. Die Sammlung Burrell*, ed. John N. Burk (Frankfurt am Main 1953); English trans. *Letters of Richard Wagner. The Burrell Collection* (London 1951)

SB   *Richard Wagner: Sämtliche Briefe*, ed. Gertrud Strobel, Werner Wolf, Hans-Joachim Bauer and Johannes Forner (Leipzig 1967–)

Schemann	Schemann, Ludwig: *Quellen und Untersuchungen zum Leben Gobineaus*, 2 vols (Vol. I Strasbourg 1914, Vol. II Berlin/Leipzig 1919)
Schmidt	Schmidt, Heinrich and Hartmann, Ulrich: *Richard Wagner in Bayreuth: Erinnerungen* (Leipzig 1909)
SS	*Richard Wagner: Sämtliche Schriften und Dichtungen*, 16 vols, 11–16 ed. Richard Sternfeld (Leipzig [1911–16])
Tiersot	*Lettres françaises de Richard Wagner*, ed. Julien Tiersot (Paris 1935)
Uhlig-Briefe	*Richard Wagner's Briefe an Theodor Uhlig, Wilhelm Fischer, Ferdinand Heine*, ed. Hans von Wolzogen (Leipzig 1888); English trans. by J. S. Shedlock (London 1890)
Verleger-Briefe	*Richard Wagners Briefwechsel mit seinen Verlegern. I: Briefwechsel mit Breitkopf & Härtel. II: Briefwechsel mit B. Schott's Söhne*, ed. Wilhelm Altmann (Mainz 1911, repr. Niederwalluf 1971)
Wagner	*Wagner* (New Series): the quarterly journal of the Wagner Society (London 1980–)
Weber-Briefe	*Bisher ungedruckte Briefe von Richard Wagner an Ernst von Weber* (Dresden 1883)
Weissheimer-Briefe	Weissheimer, Wendelin: *Erlebnisse mit Richard Wagner, Franz Liszt und vielen anderen Zeitgenossen nebst deren Briefen* (Stuttgart 1898)
Westernhagen	Westernhagen, Curt von: *Richard Wagner. Sein Werk, sein Wesen, seine Welt* (Zurich 1956)
Wille-Briefe	*Fünfzehn Briefe Richard Wagners mit Erinnerungen und Erläuterungen von Eliza Wille geb. Sloman*, ed. C. F. Meyer (Munich/Berlin/Zurich 1935, repr. Zurich 1982)
WWV	*Verzeichnis der musikalischen Werke Richard Wagners und ihrer Quellen*, ed. John Deathridge, Martin Geck and Egon Voss (Mainz 1986)
Zinsstag	Zinsstag, Adolf: *Die Briefsammlungen des Richard-Wagner-Museums in Tribschen bei Luzern* (Basle [1961])

GLOSSARY OF NAMES

AGOULT, COUNTESS MARIE D' (1805–76). During the course of her 10–year liaison with Liszt (1834–44), she was an important influence on him, both emotionally and intellectually. The second of their three illegitimate children, born at Como on Christmas Eve, 1837, was Cosima – later to become Wagner's companion and wife. After her separation from Liszt, she published, in 1846, under the pseudonym "Daniel Stern", a fictionalized autobiographical novel, *Nélida*, which mercilessly ridiculed him as an artistically impotent egotist. The Countess had no legal claim on the children and, under the influence of Princess Carolyne Sayn-Wittgenstein, Liszt eventually removed them entirely from her sphere of influence.

ANDERS, GOTTFRIED ENGELBERT (1795–1866). Of aristocratic lineage, Anders' original surname is unknown (his adopted name means "Otherwise"). From 1833 he was an employee of the Bibliothèque Royale in Paris. One of Wagner's closest friends in the Paris years (1839–42), he was, similarly, a contributor to Schlesinger's *Revue et Gazette musicale*.

APEL, THEODOR (1811–67). German poet and dramatist. Son of the writer Johann August Apel. Theodor, a reluctant law student, was a contemporary of Wagner's, both at the Nicolaischule and then at the University in Leipzig; the two were close friends. Apel lost his sight after falling from his horse in 1836, in which year the friendship all but terminated as a result of Wagner's departure from Magdeburg. Wagner wrote an overture and incidental music for Apel's play about Christopher Columbus, as well as setting a poem of his to music (*Glockentöne*, 1832).

AUBER, DANIEL-FRANÇOIS-ESPRIT (1782–1871). French composer, chiefly of *opéras comiques*. Auber and his principal librettist, Eugène Scribe, dominated the *opéra comique* for nearly half a century, although only *Fra Diavolo* (1831) remains in the permanent repertory today. *La muette de Portici* (1828), an early performance of which in Brussels precipitated the uprising of the Belgians against the Dutch, ushered in the era of grand opera, but Auber remained most closely identified with the lighter *opéra comique*.

AVENARIUS, EDUARD (1809–85). German publisher who for a time acted as the Paris agent of the Leipzig firm Brockhaus. On Wagner's arrival in Paris in 1839 his half-sister Cäcilie was engaged to Avenarius; they were married the following year. From 1844 his career continued in Leipzig and Berlin.

BAKUNIN, MIKHAIL (1814–76). Russian anarchist who arrived in Dresden in 1849 and there made Wagner's acquaintance. Bakunin's espousal of violent struggle and individual acts of terrorism, in order to bring about the replacement of existing institutions by more equitable forms of social organization, made some appeal to the Wagner of the revolutionary period. For his part in the Dresden uprising, Bakunin was imprisoned in Waldheim, with Röckel, under sentence of death. He was subsequently reprieved and it was his conflict with Marx in 1869–71 that brought about the end of the First International.

BAUDELAIRE, CHARLES (PIERRE) (1821–67). French poet, distinguished also as an art critic. His essay *Richard Wagner et Tannhauser à Paris* (1861) was, in fact, his only venture into music criticism, a discipline in which he had no formal training. Wagner was naturally delighted by the uninhibited eulogy of such an influential critic and they became acquainted during Wagner's second Paris visit (1859–61).

BELLINI, VINCENZO (1801–35). Italian composer, whose successful career was launched in 1827 with his third opera – the first with Felice Romani – *Il pirata*. The soprano Wilhelmine Schröder-Devrient made a profound impression on the youthful Wagner with her assumption of Romeo in Bellini's *I Capuleti e i Montecchi* and Wagner's essay entitled *Bellini* (1837) was an enthusiastic endorsement of the Italianate *bel canto* line. Bellini's technique of melodic sequence has been traced in *Tristan*.

BENEDICTUS, LOUIS [LUDWIG] (d. 1921). Amateur composer, the son of a Dutch diamond merchant. After Judith Gautier's separation from her husband Catulle Mendès in 1874, Benedictus became her close companion. The relationship survived Wagner's intimacy with her in 1876–8. Among his performed works were: *La marchande de sourires* ("drama" in 5 acts, text by Judith Gautier) at the Odéon, Paris, in 1888; and *Une larme du diable* ("mystère", text by Théophile Gautier) at the Galerie Barbazanges, Paris, in 1910.

BERLIOZ, (LOUIS-) HECTOR (1803–69). French composer, regarded today – but not in his time – as the leading French musician of his era. The misunderstanding and neglect Berlioz endured, not least in his frustrated dealings with the Paris Opéra, helped him and Wagner to identify each other as fellow-sufferers, though they failed to sustain an intimate friendship. Berlioz's music contains a number of interesting pre-echoes of Wagner.

BETZ, FRANZ (1835–1900). German baritone. After making his début in Hanover as Heinrich in *Lohengrin*, he took an appointment with the Berlin Court Opera in 1859, remaining with them until his retirement in 1897. Though he initially sang largely Italian and French roles, he later acquired a considerable reputation in Wagner roles, not least those of Hans Sachs, which he sang more than 100 times in Berlin alone, and Wotan/Wanderer, which he sang at the first performance of the *Ring* in Bayreuth (1876).

BILZ (-PLANER), (ERNESTINE) NATALIE (1826–98). Illegitimate daughter of Minna Planer (later Wagner's wife) and a guards captain, Ernst Rudolph von Einsiedel. Minna was seduced and abandoned by Einsiedel at the age of 15. The ensuing child, Natalie, was brought up as Minna's sister, an understandable deception which was sustained throughout Natalie's life. Indeed, for most of it, Natalie also believed the fiction, though she lived with Minna and Wagner intermittently for many years. Natalie did little to improve the already tense marital atmosphere in the household, but both Wagner, and after his death Cosima, made over an allowance to her. She married shortly after Minna's death and outlived her husband. At Wagner's request, Natalie returned a large number of his letters to Minna, but in 1890 Mrs Mary Burrell obtained for her collection 128 more that Natalie had retained.

BISMARCK, OTTO EDUARD LEOPOLD, PRINCE VON (1815–98). Prussian statesman. His career in politics reached its peak when he was appointed chancellor and foreign secretary (September and October 1862 respectively) under Wilhelm I, and subsequently prime minister. The aggressive policies of Bismarck – whose autocratic, ruthless character earned him the nickname the "Iron Chancellor" – led to the Austro-Prussian War of 1866, which established Prussia's hegemony once and for all. Her victory in the Franco-Prussian War of 1870 was followed directly by the foundation of the Second German Empire: Wilhelm I was proclaimed Emperor on 18 January 1871. Though initially repelled by Bismarck and his policies, Wagner came to appreciate, after 1866 – as did many of his compatriots – that their end result would be the long-sought national unification of Germany.

BRAHMS, JOHANNES (1833–97). German composer and pianist. Accompanied the Hungarian virtuoso violinist Eduard Reményi on a concert tour (1853) and subsequently met the even more celebrated player Joseph Joachim, as well as Liszt and Schumann. The latter proclaimed the unknown 20-year-old a genius in the Neue Zeitschrift für Musik (1853) and Brahms remained close to the Schumanns – aesthetically to Robert, and emotionally to Clara. After signing the ill-advised manifesto of 1860 opposing the New German School of Wagner and Liszt, Brahms came to be regarded as a figurehead for the conservative, Classically orientated strain of German music. This predisposition for "absolute music", reinforced by his alignment with the anti-Wagnerite critic Hanslick, gave rise to a grudging and distant relationship with Wagner.

BRANDT, CARL (1828–81). As technical director of the theatre in Darmstadt, Brandt had a high reputation for his abilities, which Wagner drew on in the construction both of the machinery for the Ring and of the Festspielhaus itself. Neither Doepler, the costume designer, nor Fricke, the director of movement, found Brandt easy to work with, but like Wagner they recognized his exceptional talents and he was invited back to Bayreuth to stage-manage Parsifal in 1882.

BREITKOPF & HÄRTEL. German firm of music publishers and printers, established by Bernhard Christoph Breitkopf (1695–1777) in 1719. The firm achieved a considerable reputation under Bernhard's son Johann Gottlob Immanuel (1719–94) but was later (1796) bought by Gottfried Christoph Härtel, at which point the present name was adopted. Härtel's sons Raymund (1810–88) and Hermann (1803–75) entered the business in 1832 and 1835 respectively, and were responsible for its subsequent development and expansion. Under the Härtel brothers the firm acquired a leading position in German music publishing. They published the full scores of *Lohengrin* (1852) and *Tristan* (1860).

BRENDEL, (KARL) FRANZ (1811–68). German music historian, writer and critic. He assumed the editorship of Schumann's periodical *Neue Zeitschrift für Musik* from 1 January 1845 and continued in the post until his death. An influential figure in German musical circles, Brendel used his position to campaign for the New German School of Wagner and Liszt and for the cultural and political unification of Germany.

BROCKHAUS, FRIEDRICH (1800–65). German publisher. With his brother Heinrich he directed the family firm until 1850. In 1828 he married Wagner's sister Luise.

BROCKHAUS, LUISE [née WAGNER] (1805–72). Sister of Wagner who gave up her career as an actress on marrying Friedrich Brockhaus in 1828.

BROCKHAUS, OTTILIE [née WAGNER] (1811–83). Elder sister of Wagner; she married the philologist Hermann Brockhaus in 1836.

BRÜCKNER, GOTTHOLD (1844–92) and MAX (1836–1919). The Brückner brothers were employed by the Coburg Court Theatre when Wagner commissioned them to execute the sets for the first Bayreuth *Ring* (1876) from the designs made by Josef Hoffmann. They similarly prepared the sets for the first *Parsifal* in 1882 from the designs of Paul von Joukowsky.

BÜLOW, BARON HANS GUIDO VON (1830–94). German conductor and pianist. Abandoning his legal studies for a career as a musician, he became an enthusiastic and sometimes aggressive advocate of the New German School. His mentors were Wagner and Liszt, with whom he studied the piano from 1851. Bülow also composed at this time, his works earning praise from both senior composers. But it was as a pianist and conductor that he made his reputation, directing the premières of *Tristan* (1865) and *Die Meistersinger* (1868). Bülow's admiration for Wagner remained undiminished by his wife Cosima's liaison with, and eventual marriage to, him.

BÜRKEL, LUDWIG VON (1841–1903). Successor to Düfflipp as Court Secretary to Ludwig II from 1878. His previous post had been government assessor to the Department of Police. He was favourably inclined towards Wagner and his projects, but was subsequently criticized for his irresponsible management of the treasury.

CALDERÓN DE LA BARCA, PEDRO (1600–81). Spanish dramatist and priest. He was, in his *autos sacramentales*, Spain's principal exponent of religious drama. The extent of Wagner's debt to Calderón's ideas is arguable, and in any case he interpreted them in the light of Schopenhauer's philosophical outlook. Nevertheless he frequently read the plays, notably at the time of the composition of *Tristan* (1857–9), as well as later in life. He and Cosima were dismayed by

Calderón's "Jesuitical hairsplitting", however, and by 1882 Cosima was reporting that "Calderón . . . no longer gives him pleasure".

CERF, KARL FRIEDRICH [real name KARL FRIEDRICH HIRSCH] (1782–1845). German theatre director. Formerly a horsetrader and a member of the war commission (1812–14), he became director of the Königstadt Theatre, Berlin. Cerf made promises to Wagner of a post at the theatre and of a performance of *Das Liebesverbot*, but they came to nothing.

CORNELIUS, (CARL AUGUST) PETER (1824–74). German composer, related to the celebrated artist Peter (von) Cornelius. Having entered the circle around Liszt in Weimar in 1852, he was introduced, the following year, to Wagner. Though a deep admirer of the music of both senior composers, Cornelius was determined to develop his own creative talents as demonstrated in numerous Lieder and his opera *Der Barbier von Bagdad* (1855–8). He lived and taught in Vienna from 1859 to 1865 and it was there that he first came into close contact with Wagner. Cornelius struggled against Wagner's inclination to swamp him, both emotionally and artistically, but his second opera *Der Cid* (1860–62) was to be the last major work he completed. Reluctantly accepting Wagner's invitation to join him in Munich at the end of 1864, Cornelius became initially his musical assistant and then a teacher at the music school re-established by Wagner and Bülow. His third opera, *Gunlöd*, begun in 1866, remained unfinished. Cornelius, who criticized Wagner frankly to friends, took umbrage when he showed too little interest during the composition of it. However, there was a move, blocked by Ludwig, to have *Gunlöd* performed in the Munich theatre, and Wagner himself offered, in 1864, to conduct *Der Cid* in Weimar.

DANNREUTHER, EDWARD (1844–1905). English pianist, writer and teacher. Of German origin, he gradually established himself as a leading figure in English musical life. He was the founder of the Wagner Society in London (1872), was instrumental in obtaining the dragon and other stage props for the first *Ring* in Bayreuth (1876), and then assisted in the organization of Wagner's London tour the following year. His writings and lectures frequently featured Wagner and he also translated three of his essays.

DEVRIENT, EDUARD PHILIPP (1801–77). German theatre historian, librettist and singer. His career as a baritone – he was the Christus in Mendelssohn's celebrated performance of the St Matthew Passion in Berlin in 1829 – was cut short by his partial loss of voice after 1831. He nevertheless took the title role at the première in 1833 of Marschner's *Hans Heiling*, for which he wrote the libretto. He became chief producer and actor at the Dresden Court Theatre (1844–6) and director of the Karlsruhe Court Theatre (1852–70). Among his writings, *Das Nationaltheater des neuen Deutschlands: eine Reformschrift* (1849) is notable for its advocacy of a German national theatre. His reminiscences of Mendelssohn (1869) provoked a spiteful essay from Wagner, entitled *Herr Eduard Devrient und sein Styl*. The soprano Wilhelmine Schröder-Devrient was his sister-in-law.

DIETSCH, PIERRE-LOUIS-PHILIPPE (1808–65). French conductor and composer.

In 1840 he became chorus master at the Paris Opéra, and after a period as *maître de chapelle* at the Madeleine and at the Ecole Niedermeyer teaching harmony, he was appointed conductor at the Opéra in 1860. His and Wagner's paths crossed on two notable occasions. In November 1842 Dietsch's opera *Le Vaisseau fantôme* was given at the Opéra. Wagner's misinformed claim (see p. 53–4) that the libretto, by Foucher and Révoil, was based on Wagner's own scenario for *Der fliegende Holländer*, has often been repeated. It was, however, no more than an unfortunate coincidence that Dietsch's work on a related subject was being staged at precisely the time that Wagner's was entering rehearsal. It was again Dietsch who was conducting *Tannhäuser* at the Opéra in 1861 when the performances were sabotaged by the Jockey Club. Although he was not responsible for the fiasco, Dietsch had already driven Wagner to despair by his incompetent handling of the score.

DINGELSTEDT, FRANZ (1814–81). German writer and critic, who as intendant at the Munich Court Theatre was responsible for the series of performances of *Tannhäuser* there in 1855. From 1857 to 1867 he was intendant at the Weimar Court Theatre, where his professional rivalry with Liszt led to the latter's resignation as Kapellmeister over the issue of Cornelius' opera *Der Barbier von Bagdad*.

DOEPLER, CARL EMIL (1824–1905). Costume designer, born in Warsaw. From 1860 to 1870 he was costume designer for the Court Theatre in Weimar, following which he was based in Berlin as a professor of costume design. In commissioning costumes from Doepler for the first performance of the *Ring* in 1876, Wagner made clear his distaste for the traditional pseudo-Nordic attempts to represent characters from the *Nibelungenlied*. But he did not make his intentions plain enough, and Doepler's costumes were later notoriously described by Cosima as "reminiscent throughout of Red Indian chiefs".

DORN, HEINRICH LUDWIG EGMONT (1804–92). German composer, conductor and writer. As Kapellmeister of the Leipzig Municipal Theatre, he did the young Wagner the dubious favour of bringing about the humiliating performance of his ill-conceived "Drum-beat Overture" in B flat (1830). Their paths crossed again in 1839, when, after a contractual wrangle, Dorn succeeded Wagner as musical director of the theatre in Riga. Dorn subsequently took appointments in Cologne and at the Berlin Opera. His Lieder, in a popular, humorous vein, epitomize his artistic remoteness from Wagner, though his many operas include one based on the Nibelung legend (1854).

DÜFFLIPP, LORENZ VON. Court Secretary to Ludwig II from 1866 to 1877. Though well disposed towards Wagner he had a firmer grasp of political realities than his successor Bürkel was to display.

EISER, OTTO (1834–98). German physician, resident in Frankfurt, where Nietzsche consulted him in October 1877, Wagner offering Eiser his own diagnosis of Nietzsche's malaise. Eiser was also a faithful adherent to the Wagnerian cause, being a representative of the Society of Patrons in Frankfurt, and contributing to the *Bayreuther Blätter*.

FEUSTEL, FRIEDRICH (1824–91). Banker and chair of the town council of Bayreuth. Wagner informed him in November 1871 that he had chosen Bayreuth as the venue for his festival enterprise, and Feustel responded with alacrity, immediately securing the authority of his council to offer Wagner any site he should select. Feustel remained a loyal supporter of Wagner and was a pallbearer at his funeral.

FRANCK, HERMANN (d. 1855). German writer. For a short period edited Brockhaus's newspaper, the *Deutsche Allgemeine Zeitung*. Admired by Wagner for his extensive knowledge and discriminating judgement, an opinion not diminished by Franck's complimentary article on *Tannhäuser* published in the Augsburg *Allgemeine Zeitung* in November 1845. It was shortly before this that Wagner became acquainted with him while Franck was teaching in Dresden. The circumstances of Franck's death in Brighton aroused much interest in the British press. He leapt to his death from a hotel window after, it was alleged, murdering his son. Many felt him to have been incapable of murder, and the inquest left the cause of the son's death open.

FRANTZ, CONSTANTIN GUSTAV ADOLPH (1817–91). German political theorist. Frantz's conservative pan-Germanic views were warmly embraced by Wagner when he encountered them in 1865. Wagner recommended Frantz's writings to King Ludwig, especially his exposition of the principle of federalism, in *Der Föderalismus* (1879).

FRANZ [KNAUTH], ROBERT (1815–92). German composer and conductor. The family name was changed from Knauth to Franz in 1847. As conductor of the Halle Singakademie, Franz helped to re-establish the city's musical reputation, and in 1851 he was offered a teaching appointment by the University there. He was obliged to resign his official positions in 1867 on account of the marked deterioration in his hearing. His compositions, much admired by Liszt, include over 350 songs, gently lyrical in expression and unadventurous in style.

FRENY, RUDOLF [FREYSAUFF VON NEUDEGG] (d. 1894). Buffo bass working in Hamburg.

FRITZSCH, ERNST WILHELM (1840–1902). Publisher in Leipzig, where he edited the journal *Musikalisches Wochenblatt* and published Wagner's collected writings.

FRÖBEL, JULIUS (1805–93). Son of the educational reformer Friedrich Wilhelm August Fröbel. While working in the late 1840s as a journalist in Dresden sympathetic to the democratic cause, he had made the acquaintance of Wagner. Obliged to flee arrest and execution after the events of 1848 in Austria, he went to America, where he remained from 1850 to 1857. Returning to Vienna in the 1860s he was engaged in an advisory capacity by the Austrian government. In 1867 he became, at Wagner's suggestion, the first editor of the *Süddeutsche Presse*. The paper was subsidized by the Bavarian government until the end of 1868, after which Fröbel became its proprietor until he sold it to a Munich banking house in 1873.

FROMMANN, ALWINE (1800–75). The sister of the Jena bookseller Frommann –

who had been an intimate of Goethe – she was an artist who held the post of reader to the Princess Augusta of Prussia (later Queen of Prussia and Empress of Germany). She first wrote to Wagner after hearing *Der fliegende Holländer* in Berlin in February 1844, and again after travelling to Dresden to hear *Rienzi* in October of that year. She continued throughout her life to bring what influence she had to bear on the Court at Berlin on behalf of Wagner.

FÜRSTENAU, MORITZ (1824–89). German writer, flautist and composer. He joined the Court orchestra in Dresden in 1842 as a flautist, succeeding his father as principal flautist in 1852. He became professor of flute at the Dresden Conservatory in 1856, organized various musical activities in the locality, and in later years undertook extensive archival work resulting in a valuable, if not always scrupulously accurate, documentation of musical life in Dresden. It was through Fürstenau's agency that Wagner's letters to Theodor Uhlig were eventually returned to him.

GAILLARD, KARL (1813–51). German writer. Like Alwine Frommann, Gaillard was fired by the Berlin production of *Der fliegende Holländer* in 1844. He too wrote to Wagner in enthusiastic terms, and further promoted the cause in the journal he had established, the *Berliner Musikalische Zeitung* (1844–7). The journal foundered for lack of capital, as did his small music shop. His health declined and within a few years he was dead, much mourned by Wagner who, notwithstanding the slightness of Gaillard's poems and dramas, had a sincere affection for him.

GASPERINI, AUGUSTE DE (1825–69). French doctor and writer on music. An early enthusiast for Wagner's music in France, Gasperini befriended Wagner when he arrived in Paris for the series of three concerts early in 1860 and the production of *Tannhäuser* at the Opéra the following year. He provided much valued moral support and advice, though his plea that Wagner abandon the new music composed for the Paris *Tannhäuser* – on account of the resulting stylistic disparity – was not heeded.

GAUTIER, JUDITH (1845–1917). French author and writer on music; daughter of the writer Théophile Gautier. An enthusiast for Wagner's work from an early age, she met the equally devoted Catulle Mendès in the early 1860s, marrying him on 17 April 1866. Together with the poet Villiers de l'Isle-Adam they visited Wagner at Tribschen in 1869 and again the following year. In 1874 the Mendès couple made a decision to separate, and by the time of the first Bayreuth festival two years later Judith was enjoying the serious attentions of an amateur composer called Louis Benedictus. This, however, did not discourage Wagner from attempting to give vent to his infatuation for her. Their relationship may or may not have been consummated, but they continued to conduct an intimate and clandestine correspondence until February 1878. Wagner claimed that he needed the intoxication of at least her spiritual presence, as well as the silks, satins and exotic perfumes she sent, in order to compose *Parsifal*. She also made an intellectual contribution to Wagnerism, however, with a translation of *Parsifal* into French, various writings on Wagnerian topics, and a three-volume memoir of the composer.

GEYER, LUDWIG (1779–1821). German actor and painter. It has never been conclusively established whether Wagner's father was actually Carl Friedrich Wagner or Geyer. In any case Geyer was a close friend of the family and it was partly at Friedrich's instigation that he took up a career as an actor: from 1809 until his death he was engaged as such in Dresden (from 1814 with the title "Court Actor"). Nine months after Friedrich's death Geyer married Wagner's mother, Johanna (28 August 1814), and the boy grew up bearing his name (until 1827). To the end of Wagner's life, speculation continued not only as to his paternity, but also as to Geyer's possible Jewishness; he was, in fact, of incontrovertible Protestant stock.

GLASENAPP, CARL FRIEDRICH (1847–1915). German writer on music. After studying linguistics, classical philology and the history of art, he taught first in Pernau, and (from 1875) in Riga. His biography of Wagner was begun while Glasenapp was still a student, and completed in its two-volume version in 1876–7 (it was subsequently enlarged and eventually republished in six volumes). The biography was "authorized" in that Glasenapp enjoyed the confidence of Wagner and Cosima and was granted access to much material of significance. However, the merits of its overall factual accuracy were diminished by the "protectionist" approach typical of the inner Bayreuth circle.

GOBINEAU, COUNT JOSEPH-ARTHUR DE (1816–82). French diplomat, novelist and historian. Gobineau's significance for Wagner consisted not in his stylish short stories and other literary works but in his views on miscegenation, particularly as expounded in his *Essai sur l'inégalité des races humaines* (1853–5). The supposed "degeneration of the human species" was an outlook the two men shared, though Gobineau believed that a certain degree of interbreeding – the cause of degeneration – was necessary for the survival of civilization, whereas Wagner held that the pure blood of Christ provided an agent of redemption. Gobineau was a regular visitor at Wahnfried in Wagner's late years, and his views continued to be espoused for long after his death. In 1894 a Gobineau Association was set up by Ludwig Schemann and other members of the "Bayreuth Circle".

GOLDWAG, BERTHA. Viennese milliner and seamstress, who supplied Wagner's wardrobe and furnishings first for his apartment in Penzing (1863–4) and then in Munich (1864–5). In view of the extravagance of the exotic fabrics requested by Wagner, Goldwag travelled to Munich incognito, informing customs officials that her silks and perfumes were for a countess in Berlin. The luxury of Wagner's interiors soon became common knowledge, however, and his embarrassment was maximized when his letters to the *Putzmacherin* were published in 1877, after an unsavoury chain of transactions involving Brahms, among others. According to one source, the letters were at one stage offered to Wagner himself, for a price, but he refused to be blackmailed.

GOUIN, LOUIS. Postal official in Paris; Meyerbeer's personal secretary.

GUTZKOW, KARL FERDINAND (1811–78). German novelist and dramatist. Having broken off his studies at the outbreak of the July Revolution of 1830, he became a political journalist in 1831. Associated with the Young German group of writers, his radical outlook was expressed in various articles and novels until the federal decree of December 1835 caused him to be charged and imprisoned the following year. Turning subsequently to the theatre, he produced a series of plays on social and political themes, and from 1846 to 1848 was dramaturg at the Dresden Court Theatre.

HABENECK, FRANÇOIS-ANTOINE (1781–1849). French violinist and conductor who dominated the Parisian musical scene for many years. At the Opéra he was first director (1821–4), then *premier chef* with Valentino (1824–31), finally holding the post alone (1831–46). He was equally influential as the conductor of the Conservatoire concerts, one of his chief achievements being the introduction of Beethoven's music to France. It was under Habeneck that Wagner heard the Ninth Symphony in Paris (probably early in 1840).

HĀFIZ [*nom de plume* of SHAMS-UD-DIN MUHAMMAD] (d. *c*1388). Persian poet and philosopher. His principal work, the *Dīwān*, is a collection of short odes or sonnets celebrating natural beauties, the pleasures of carousing, and the delights of love. Indeed, Hāfiz was ill suited to the ascetic life of the order of dervishes to which he belonged, a fact which gave rise to contradictions less palatable to his monastic colleagues than to Wagner. Wagner read Hāfiz in a translation by Georg Friedrich Daumer (1846–52); shortly after, a further edition was made by Wagner's brother-in-law, Hermann Brockhaus (Leipzig, 1854–6).

HALÉVY, JACQUES-FRANÇOIS-FROMENTAL (1799–1862). French composer. A fluent composer, especially of *opéras comiques*, he was also an active teacher and administrator in a succession of posts in France. His best-known work is *La Juive* (1835), his first attempt at a serious grand opera, which was an instant success at the Opéra. Another popular work was *La reine de Chypre* (1841), which Wagner reviewed favourably the following year, having laboured over the score in Paris to produce arrangements.

HALLWACHS, REINHARD (1833–72). German stage director, brought from Stuttgart to direct the first performance of *Die Meistersinger* in Munich in 1868. He was also responsible for the première of *Das Rheingold* there the following year.

HANSLICK, EDUARD (1825–1904). German writer on music and aesthetics. A powerfully influential force in 19th-century music criticism, Hanslick was for most of his life implacably hostile to the Wagnerian cause. Hanslick's conservative aesthetic outlook led him to espouse the absolute music of Brahms and his followers as against the progressive notions of music drama and programme music associated with Wagner, Liszt and the New German School.

HÄRTELS. *See* BREITKOPF & HÄRTEL.

HAUSER, FRANZ (1794–1870). Bohemian singer, stage producer and teacher. His appointments in various European cities included that of resident producer at

Leipzig at the time Wagner submitted *Die Feen* to be considered for performance there (1834). After 1837 he became a singing teacher in Vienna; from
1846 to 1864 he was director of the new Munich Conservatory.

HECKEL, EMIL (1831–1908). Music dealer in Mannheim, who was energetic in
raising money for the establishment of the Bayreuth festival. His scheme for a
network of Wagner Societies, whose members might combine to make a joint
subscription to the fund, was adopted, and Heckel himself founded a society
in Mannheim.

HEIM, IGNAZ (1813–80). The conductor of a local choral society, the Harmonie,
in Zurich, where he and his wife Emilie, a singer, were friends of Wagner.

HEINE, FERDINAND (1798–1872). As costume designer and wardrobe manager
at the Dresden Court Theatre from 1819 to 1850, Heine was involved in the
first performances there of *Rienzi* (1842), *Holländer* (1843) and *Tannhäuser*
(1845). He was an enthusiastic advocate of Wagner's works and one of his
firmest friends during the Dresden years. Earlier in his career Heine had been
an actor at Leipzig and an acquaintance of Ludwig Geyer, Wagner's step-
father.

HERWEGH, GEORG (1817–75). German poet and political activist. In 1839 he
escaped court-martial during military service by deserting to Switzerland. There
he quickly established a reputation with the first volume of the revolutionary
Gedichte eines Lebendigen (Poems of a Live Man) (1841), the collection
containing his celebrated broadside against Freiligrath: *Die Partei*. He was
active in the 1848/9 uprisings and subsequently gave shelter to many political
refugees in his house in Zurich. It was there that Herwegh introduced Wagner
to the philosophy of Schopenhauer.

HERZEN, OLGA. Daughter of the radical Russian writer Alexander Herzen and
his wife, Natalie, née Zacharinya. After their mother's death in 1852, Olga and
her sister, also Natalie, were fostered by Malwida von Meysenbug. In 1873
Olga married the French historian Gabriel Monod, an event graced by a
composition of Nietzsche.

HEY, JULIUS (1831–1909). German singing teacher, at the school of music in
Munich. Wagner made his acquaintance at Starnberg in 1864 and subsequently
called upon him for advice on vocal matters during the rehearsals for the *Ring*
in Bayreuth. When Hey gave his opinion that the prospective Siegfried, Georg
Unger, was technically defective, Wagner commissioned Hey with the task of
coaching him for the part.

HILL, KARL (1831–93). German bass-baritone. A postal official prior to his
engagement at Schwerin in 1868. It was his "demonic passion" as the
Dutchman there in 1873 that persuaded Wagner to cast him as Alberich in
the first Bayreuth *Ring*, and he subsequently sang Klingsor in the first *Parsifal*
(1882). He died insane.

HOFFMANN, JOSEF (1831–1904). An academic painter in Vienna who accepted

Wagner's commission to design the scenery for the first Bayreuth *Ring* (1876). Although the sketches he submitted were eminently satisfactory, Hoffmann had neither studio nor assistants to effect their execution, and the task was entrusted to the Brückner brothers. A dispute subsequently broke out when Hoffmann objected to changes made, for technical reasons, in his scenic designs. Wagner was thereafter obliged to minimize Hoffmann's personal involvement in the preparations.

HÖLZEL, GUSTAV (1813–83). Baritone at the Vienna Court Opera. He created the role of Beckmesser in *Die Meistersinger* (Munich, 1868).

HÜLSEN, BOTHO VON (1815–86). German theatre director. In June 1851 he succeeded Küstner as intendant at the Berlin Opera. From 1866 he was responsible also for the theatres at Hanover, Cassel and Wiesbaden.

JÄGER, FERDINAND (1838–1902). Jäger never fully matched Wagner's requirements as a singer. He was recommended by Heckel for Siegfried in the first *Ring*, but passed over by Wagner. He was one of the three Parsifals during the run of first performances in 1882, but he disappointed Wagner and was one of the few singers whom he did not intend to invite back the following year.

JAUNER, FRANZ (1832–1900). Austrian actor and theatre director. Director of the Vienna Court Opera from 1875 to 1880. His determination to capitalize on Wagner's box-office appeal in these years inspired him to negotiate ruthlessly, using the singers he had at his disposal as bargaining counters.

JENKINS, NEWELL SILL. American dentist practising in Dresden. Jenkins, who treated Wagner in Basle and Bayreuth on several occasions, was entrusted with the negotiations involved in his proposed emigration to America (1880).

JOUKOWSKY, PAUL VON (1845–1912). Russian painter. He entered Wagner's circle in January 1880 by presenting himself at the Villa d'Angri in Naples. Wagner responded favourably to him and in due course invited him to design the sets and costumes for *Parsifal*. Joukowsky was regarded as a member of the family and stayed with them, accompanied by his adoptive son Pepino.

KIETZ, ERNST BENEDIKT (1815–92). German painter. He was in Paris, finishing his art studies, at the time Wagner and Minna were there (1839–42). He became a regular visitor at their house and in 1858 (when Kietz was 43) they even offered to "adopt" him. Wagner humorously asserted that Kietz never completed a commission, but his various sketches and portraits of the composer in his early years are invaluable.

KIRCHNER, THEODOR FÜRCHTEGOTT (1823–1903). German organist and composer. After his early organ studies, he became a member of Schumann's circle and was recommended by Mendelssohn for the post of organist at Winterthur. From 1843 to 1862 he played, taught and organized the musical life there and came to the attention of Wagner and Liszt, both of whom admired his talent. During Wagner's years in Zurich, Kirchner was called upon to provide the piano accompaniment for informal play-throughs of his works. His

contacts with Zurich were consolidated in 1862 when he took up a conducting
post there. He lived and worked subsequently in Würzburg (1873–5), Leipzig
(1875–83), Dresden (1883–90) and Hamburg (from 1890).

KLINDWORTH, KARL (1830–1916). German pianist, conductor and teacher. From
1852 he was part of Liszt's circle in Weimar and it was through Liszt's
enthusiastic advocacy that Klindworth met Wagner in London in 1855. Klindworth undertook the arrangement of vocal scores for each opera of the *Ring*,
as well as those for *Die Meistersinger* and *Tristan* (a simpler version than
Bülow's). He remained in London from 1854 to 1868, when he took up a
teaching appointment at the new Moscow Conservatory. On his return to
Germany in 1882, he conducted many performances of Wagner, Liszt, Berlioz
and Brahms. His adoptive daughter, Winifred Williams, became the wife of
Siegfried Wagner.

KÖHLER, LOUIS (1820–86). German pianist. A former pupil of Liszt, he became,
in 1847, director of a school for pianists in Königsberg. His enthusiasm for
Wagner's music drew him to Weimar in 1853 to hear *Lohengrin* there. Wagner
subsequently sent him a copy of the poem of the *Ring*. Like Wagner, Köhler
was concerned with the problems of relating melody to speech, a subject he
investigated in *Die Melodie der Sprache in ihrer Anwendung besonders auf das Lied
und die Oper* (The Melody of Speech, Especially in its Application to Song and
Opera), published in Leipzig in 1853.

KOSSAK, ERNST (1814–80). German philologist and musical journalist, who
founded the Berlin music periodical *Echo* and the *Zeitungshalle*. Wagner made
his acquaintance in Berlin when preparing *Rienzi* for its first production there
(October 1847).

LAUBE, HEINRICH RUDOLF CONSTANZ (1806–84). German writer, critic, and
latterly theatre director. His writing, notably in the three-volume social and
political novel *Das junge Europa* (1833–7), was radical in outlook, and as a
leading member of Young Germany he was constantly persecuted by the
authorities. The strength of his convictions made an impression on the young
Wagner (Laube was a family friend) and as editor of the *Zeitung für die elegante
Welt* he published some of Wagner's earliest essays; in later years, however,
they were estranged. From 1840 Laube was a theatre critic in Leipzig;
subsequently he was director of the Vienna Burgtheater (1849–67), Leipzig
Stadttheater (1869–71) and Vienna Stadttheater (from 1872).

LAUSSOT, JESSIE [née TAYLOR] (*b. c*1829). The English-born wife of the Bordeaux
wine merchant Eugène Laussot. Her passion for Wagner's music and commitment to his ideals led her to offer him, together with Julie Ritter, an annual
allowance of 3000 francs. Wagner's visit to Bordeaux in March 1850 led to a
brief affair with Jessie, but a plan to "elope" to Greece or Asia Minor was
thwarted by the intervention of her mother and husband. Jessie subsequently
separated from Eugène, and went to Florence where she lived with, and
eventually married, the essayist Karl Hillebrand. She was talented musically,

and was active as a conductor and administrator in Florence (see p. 360, note 6).

LEHMANN, LILLI (1848–1929). German soprano. Her early career was spent at the Berlin Opera (1870–85), where she took lyric and coloratura roles. After singing Woglinde, Helmwige and the Woodbird in the first Bayreuth *Ring* (1876), she gradually established herself as a leading dramatic soprano, singing Isolde at Covent Garden in 1884, and in New York in 1886 in America's first *Tristan*. In addition to Wagner she sang in operas by, among others, Verdi, Beethoven, Bellini and Mozart.

LEHRS, SAMUEL (1806–43). German philologist. One of the group of Wagner's close friends in Paris (1839–42). Wagner was indebted to Lehrs for providing him with background material on the Tannhäuser and Lohengrin legends, and for introducing him to intellectual ideas current at the time. The deprivation Lehrs suffered in Paris led to his early death, shortly after Wagner had left for Dresden.

LENBACH, FRANZ VON (1836–1904). German artist. From 1868 he devoted himself to portraiture and became the leading exponent of the genre in the Germany of his day. Many prominent statesmen (including Bismarck (80 portraits), Ludwig I, Moltke and Gladstone) and other celebrities (e.g. Liszt, Duse, Heyse and Bülow) sat for him. He became acquainted both with Cosima and subsequently with Wagner himself, drawing and painting them on several occasions, though not always from life.

LEUTNER, FERDINAND. University lecturer in Vienna and one of the editors of the *Wiener Zeitung*. He wrote to congratulate Wagner on the republication, in 1869, of *Das Judenthum in der Musik*.

LEVI, HERMANN (1839–1900). German conductor. After study in Mannheim and Leipzig, he held conducting posts in Saarbrücken, Mannheim, Rotterdam and Karlsruhe, before becoming chief conductor of the Munich Court Opera (1872–90). Despite his Jewishness and his association with Brahms and his followers, Levi was welcomed by Wagner as a distinguished interpreter of his music, notably *Parsifal*, which he conducted at its première in 1882 and for several years thereafter. Levi's assumption that he would have to undergo baptism in order to conduct *Parsifal* was encouraged by Wagner, but after a disagreeable exchange on the subject, the idea was dropped.

LISZT, EDUARD (1817–79). Uncle of Franz Liszt, though sometimes referred to as "cousin" because he was, in fact, younger than his nephew. He became Imperial Attorney General in Vienna.

LISZT, FRANZ (1811–86). Hungarian composer and pianist. The two men first encountered each other in Paris, in March 1841, when Liszt was already at the height of his fame. But it was not until Liszt had retired from the concert platform to devote himself to composition and to the promotion of other musicians that their friendship blossomed. Their extraordinary but sincere relationship was based on profound mutual admiration and understanding; as the acknowledged leaders of the New German School, each was particularly fascinated by the other's progressive traits, and in terms of influence it is difficult to determine who was the greater beneficiary. The friendship survived occasional periods of coolness, the most serious estrangement being caused by Wagner's liaison with Liszt's daughter Cosima.

LUDWIG II, KING OF BAVARIA (1845–86). The son of Maximilian II and grandson of Ludwig I, he ascended the throne of Bavaria in 1864 at the age of 18. In the Austro-Prussian War of 1866 he took the side of Austria, but in the Franco-Prussian War four years later he supported Prussia, and was eventually reconciled to a German Empire under the Prussian king. His passion for Wagner's music resulted in generous subsidies which transformed the composer's life style. However, public opinion was scandalized by Wagner's affair with Cosima, and by the supposed "exploitation" of the King's munificence; in December 1865 Ludwig was forced to ask Wagner to leave Munich. His support continued and even though the relationship was strained to breaking-point over the following years, Ludwig made a timely contribution to the Bayreuth enterprise and remained fanatically devoted to Wagner's art. His penchant for building fantastic castles of monumental extravagance, combined with his erratic behaviour and progressive lack of interest in his subjects or affairs of state, eventually led to an official declaration of insanity and to his deposition on 10 June 1886. The King and an escorting psychiatrist were found drowned in Lake Starnberg three days later; the precise events of their deaths have never been conclusively established.

LÜTTICHAU, BARON (WOLF ADOLF) AUGUST VON (1786–1863). He began his career as a forestry official, joining the Dresden Court Theatre in 1824, where he remained intendant until shortly before his death. Despite the tensions and disagreements brought about by the disparity in their professional status, he and Wagner each had a certain underlying respect for the other.

LUTZ, BARON JOHANN VON (1826–90). An appeals court judge who replaced Max von Neumayr as cabinet secretary during the course of 1865. He went on to become a minister of state from 1867 to 1871, and prime minister of Bavaria in 1880.

MAIER, MATHILDE (1833–1910). Wagner met Mathilde Maier, the daughter of a notary, at Franz Schott's house in Mainz in March 1862. His overtures to her were discouraged on grounds of incipient deafness. He urged her to join him at Haus Pellet (June 1864) as housekeeper and companion, but hurriedly withdrew the invitation on learning of Cosima's imminent arrival there. A number of passages – probably of a compromising nature – in Wagner's letters to Mathilde of this period have been irrecoverably deleted in the autographs.

MARBACH, ROSALIE [née WAGNER] (1803–37). Elder sister of Wagner. She made her stage début in her stepfather's play Das Erntefest (December 1818), joining the company of the Royal Court two years later. After notable successes in Prague and elsewhere, from 1826, she took up an appointment at Leipzig in

1829. She died prematurely, little more than a year after her marriage to the university professor Oswald Marbach.

MARSCHNER, HEINRICH (AUGUST) (1795–1861). German composer. After a period as musical director at Dresden (1824–6) and Kapellmeister at Leipzig (1827–30), he was appointed Court Kapellmeister at Hanover in 1830, remaining there until 1859. As one of the leading figures in the development of German Romantic opera, Marschner inevitably made a considerable impact on the maturing Wagner, who was exposed to his works in the 1820s and 30s. Many similarities of technique and content between especially Marschner's *Der Vampyr* and *Hans Heiling* and Wagner's *Holländer*, *Tannhäuser* and *Lohengrin* may be discerned.

MATERNA, AMALIE (1844–1918). Austrian soprano. Despite her early career in operetta, she became one of the first of the new breed of dramatic sopranos demanded by Wagner's music dramas. She sang Brünnhilde in the first complete *Ring* (1876) and Kundry in 1882, both at Bayreuth.

MENDELSSOHN (-BARTHOLDY), FELIX (1809–47). German composer, pianist, organist and conductor. After extraordinary early successes as a child prodigy, he eventually took up posts as conductor of the Leipzig Gewandhaus Orchestra (1835–46) and as first director of the newly opened conservatory in that city (from 1843). A handful of operas, including the unfinished *Loreley* (1847), bear witness to Mendelssohn's lifelong struggle for mastery in the medium. But it is primarily for his instrumental and choral works that he is now remembered. The popular view that Mendelssohn's works too rarely rise above superficiality has, over recent years, undergone reappraisal. Wagner's prejudice against him, partly anti-Semitic in origin, did not prevent him from echoing Mendelssohn in his own earlier works.

MENDÈS, CATULLE (-ABRAHAM) (1841–1909). French poet, librettist and critic. He was the founder and editor of the journal *La Revue fantaisiste*, to which he invited Wagner to contribute an article following the *Tannhäuser* débâcle at the Paris Opéra in 1861. His enthusiasm for Wagner was shared by his first wife, Judith Gautier, and they visited Wagner at Tribschen in 1869 (twice) and 1870. Mendès' friendship with Wagner survived the tensions of the last visit (which coincided precisely with the declaration of the Franco-Prussian War), but not the publication, in 1873, of Wagner's crudely jingoistic farce *Eine Kapitulation*. However, Mendès' continuing admiration for Wagner the artist was demonstrated in his full-length biography of him (1886), as well as various other writings, some for the *Revue Wagnérienne* which he co-founded in 1885.

MENDÈS-GAUTIER, JUDITH. *See* GAUTIER, JUDITH.

METTERNICH, PRINCESS PAULINE (1836–1921). Granddaughter of the Austrian statesman; she also married one of his sons, Richard, Prince von Metternich-Winneburg, who became the Austrian ambassador in Paris. It was primarily her influence at the court of Napoleon III that brought about the performance of *Tannhäuser* in Paris in 1861, but it was also her unpopularity in certain

Court circles that was largely responsible for the political demonstrations by the Jockey Club on that occasion.

MEYERBEER, GIACOMO [orig. JAKOB LIEBMANN BEER] (1791–1864). German composer. Meyerbeer began his career as a child prodigy on the piano, but after a series of Italian operas he made his home in Paris, where for many years he dominated French grand opera. Meyerbeer's works are irrevocably associated with triumphal processions and *Grand Guignol*, aspects which made them hugely popular in the Paris of his day, but which appeal less to modern audiences. There have been few opportunities in recent times to judge these works adequately – especially on the stage. Nevertheless, his influentially imaginative orchestration has been appreciated. Wagner's hostile opinion of Meyerbeer was partly a result of his anti-Semitism but was also in tune with the prevailing critical consensus in Germany according to which his works displayed rhythmic monotony and undue eclecticism, elevating contrived effect above genuine dramatic tension.

MEYSENBUG, BARONESS MALWIDA VON (1816–1903). German writer and political activist; a prominent democrat and campaigner for women's rights. Following the 1848/9 uprisings, she was banned from Berlin in 1852 on account of her associations with revolutionaries. As a result she moved first to London, where she became a governess and a newspaper correspondent, and in 1862 to Italy. She was an admirer and friend of Wagner, as well as of Nietzsche, Liszt and a number of radicals such as Garibaldi and Mazzini.

MITTERWURZER, ANTON (1818–76). Baritone at the Dresden Opera. He sang Wolfram in the first performance of *Tannhäuser* (1845) and Kurwenal in that of *Tristan* (1865).

MONNAIS, EDOUARD (1798–1868). French theatre official. For a short period (1839–41) he was associate director of the Paris Opéra, but he continued to wield influence as Commissaire royal près le Théâtre de l'Opéra. He was also editor of and (under the pseudonym "Paul Smith") contributor to various journals.

MRAZÉCK, ANNA (c1834–1914). Housekeeper to Wagner first in Vienna (1863–4) and then in Munich and Starnberg. It was largely Anna Mrazéck's testimony in 1914 that deprived Isolde Beidler of a court ruling that she was indeed Wagner's daughter; she testified that when Bülow visited Wagner at Starnberg in July 1864, Cosima occupied the same room as her husband, not that of Wagner.

MRAZÉCK, FRANZ (d. 1874). Bohemian who acted as manservant to Wagner in Vienna, Munich and Starnberg. He was subsequently employed at the music school in Munich. In her diary entry for 6 August 1874, Cosima records his death, attributing it to ill-treatment by the school's directors in revenge for his loyalty to Wagner.

MUCHANOFF, COUNTESS MARIE [formerly MME KALERGIS, née NESSELRODE] (1823–74). The daughter of the Russian chancellor, Count Karl Robert Nesselrode, Wagner knew her first as Mme Kalergis (she had married a Greek diplomat of that name at the age of 16, separating a year later). During Wagner's 1859–61 stay in Paris, she gave him financial support and also helped to secure conducting engagements for him in St Petersburg in 1863. She married her second husband, a Russian called Muchanoff, in 1864.

MÜLLER, CHRISTIAN GOTTLIEB (1800–63). German instrumentalist and conductor. From 1826 he was a member of the Leipzig Gewandhaus Orchestra, after which he became, in 1831, conductor of the (largely amateur) Euterpe Society in that city. In 1836 he became music director in Altenburg. Wagner studied harmony with Müller for the best part of three years (1828–31).

MUNCKER, THEODOR (1823–1900). Mayor of Bayreuth from 1863. He supported the Bayreuth venture when Wagner first solicited the town's help in 1871, and became a friend as well as a member of the management committee for the festival.

NAPOLEON III, EMPEROR OF FRANCE (1808–73). Nephew of Napoleon I. Louis-Napoleon came to power as president of the Republic of France (1848–52), when he was known as the "Prince-President". He succeeded in presenting the *coup d'état* of 2 December 1851 and dissolution of the Assembly as democratic measures and retrospective approval was given by an overwhelming majority in the plebiscite that followed. Precisely a year later, he made his formal entry into Paris as Emperor Napoleon III.

NEUMANN, ANGELO (1838–1910). Austrian baritone and theatrical producer. From 1876 to 1880 he was director of the Leipzig Opera and he obtained permission from Wagner to mount the *Ring* cycle there in 1878. He contemplated the possibility of a permanent Wagner theatre in Berlin, to which Wagner was willing to lend his name. In August 1882 a contract was concluded enabling Neumann to take the *Ring* on tour with his travelling theatre; in the following years it was performed by them all over Europe.

NIEMANN ALBERT (1831–1917). German tenor. Made his début in Dessau in 1849, and after engagements in Stuttgart, Hanover and elsewhere, became a member of the Berlin Opera (1866–89). He sang Tannhäuser in the Paris performances of 1861 and Siegmund in the first Bayreuth *Ring*. He made his London début also in the latter role (1882) and was the first American Tristan and Siegfried (in *Götterdämmerung*).

NIETZSCHE, FRIEDRICH (1844–1900). German philosopher. In 1869, at the age of 24, he was appointed Professor of Classical Philology at Basle University. From the time of his first visit to Tribschen the same year, he was a frequent and welcome guest at Wagner's house. His literary works were admired by Wagner and Cosima, especially *The Birth of Tragedy*, not least because it appeared to celebrate Wagner's central position in Western culture. For his part, Nietzsche was fascinated by what he regarded as the insidious power of Wagner's music, and overwhelmed by the "horrible, sweet infinitude" of *Tristan*. The ambivalence of Nietzsche's response began to be reflected in his essay "Richard Wagner in Bayreuth" (1875–6), and in subsequent years, as his mental and physical health deteriorated, he took up a bitterly hostile stance towards Wagner's "decadent" art.

NOHL, KARL FRIEDRICH LUDWIG (1831–85). German writer on music, university lecturer and, from 1865 to 1868, professor at the University of Munich. In 1865 he published an edition of Beethoven's letters, which he dedicated to Wagner.

OLLIVIER, BLANDINE (1835–62). Elder sister of Cosima Wagner, born to Liszt and the Countess Marie d'Agoult. She married the French politician Emile Ollivier in 1857, and died in childbirth. Fond as Wagner was of her, there is no evidence to substantiate the rumours that they engaged in an affair.

OLLIVIER, EMILE (1825–1913). French lawyer and politician, the husband of Cosima's sister Blandine. As a young man he was a republican who opposed the Empire. In January, 1870, however, he accepted the invitation to form the first parliamentary government, under Napoleon III. It was thus Ollivier who proclaimed the French declaration of war on Prussia in July 1870.

OVERBECK, FRANZ (1837–1905). Protestant theologian and a professor at the University of Basle, where he was a friend of Nietzsche's.

PERFALL, BARON KARL VON (1824–1907). Intendant of the Munich Court Theatre from 1867 to 1893. Perfall was an influential administrator and his long period of tenure accommodated the musical directorships of Lachner, Bülow, Wüllner and Levi. Strauss was Kapellmeister at the theatre from 1886 to 1889 and from 1894 to 1898.

PFISTERMEISTER, FRANZ SERAPH VON (1820–1912). King Ludwig's cabinet secretary until October 1866, when he submitted his resignation. This was apparently precipitated by his frustration at Wagner's interference in affairs of state. Wagner, for his part, accused Pfistermeister – not unjustly – of scheming against him.

PFORDTEN, BARON LUDWIG VON DER (1811–80). German lawyer and politician. He served as the foreign minister and president of the Bavarian council from 1849 to 1859, and as prime minister from 1864 to 1866. He and Pfistermeister were Wagner's chief antagonists at the Munich Court.

PILLET, LÉON (1803–68). He succeeded Duponchel and Monnais as director of the Paris Opéra officially in 1841 (though in effect the previous year). He was thus the chief administrator with whom Wagner had to deal during his Paris years. He was forced to resign the directorship in 1847.

PLANER, NATALIE. See BILZ (-PLANER), NATALIE.

PORGES, HEINRICH (1837–1900). German editor and writer on music. In 1863 he became co-editor with Brendel of the *Neue Zeitschrift für Musik*, and in 1867 he assumed responsibility, with the editor, Fröbel, of the arts pages of the *Süddeutsche Presse*. He remained in Munich as music critic of the *Neueste*

Nachrichten (from 1880), and in 1886 founded the Porges Choral Society. He came to Wagner's attention in Vienna in 1863, and although he declined to accept Wagner's summons the following year to join him in Munich, he did later act as his assistant, most notably at the rehearsals for the first *Ring* at Bayreuth, which, at Wagner's request, he recorded in detail.

PRAEGER, FERDINAND CHRISTIAN WILHELM (1815–91). German composer, pianist and writer. He settled in London in 1834, where he was much in demand as a teacher. Works by him were performed in France, Germany and England. He befriended Wagner and gave him hospitality during his London visit of 1855, later claiming, falsely, to have been responsible for the invitation. This was only one of countless fabrications in his notorious publication *Wagner as I knew him* (1892).

PUSINELLI, ANTON (1815–78). Wagner's family doctor, and one of his most intimate and trusted friends, from the time of their first acquaintance in Dresden. In the early 1860s, when Wagner's marriage to Minna was on the brink of collapse, Pusinelli was entrusted with the delicate task of acting as intermediary.

RAFF, (JOSEPH) JOACHIM (1822–82). German composer and teacher. He joined Liszt in Weimar from 1850, replacing August Conradi as copyist. In view of Liszt's lack of experience in orchestration, however, Raff's advice and help on many technical aspects of scoring was also sought. From Weimar Raff went to Wiesbaden to teach piano and to compose; many of his works date from the 1860s and 70s. Although associated with the New German School surrounding Wagner and Liszt, Raff's work was occasionally criticized by contemporaries for its eclecticism and triviality. Some of his many salon pieces are based on numbers from Wagner's works. His transcriptions and arrangements include one for large orchestra with strings of the *Huldigungsmarsch*.

REDERN, COUNT FRIEDRICH WILHELM VON (1802–83). As intendant of the Berlin Court Theatre (1828–42) Redern was not unsympathetic to Wagner. Indeed, on Meyerbeer's recommendation he had, early in 1842, accepted *Der fliegende Holländer* for performance there. On Redern's retirement later that year, however, the project fell through, and Wagner demanded the return of his score.

REISSIGER, KARL GOTTLIEB (1798–1859). German composer, conductor and teacher. Kapellmeister at the Court of Dresden from 1828 until his death, Reissiger was present, if sometimes less than fully active, throughout Wagner's time there. In his earlier years Reissiger had justly taken the credit for putting the Dresden Opera in the front rank of German theatres. By the 1840s, however, he was allowing his junior colleague to occupy much of the gap left by his own creeping inertia. Reissiger's compositions, which are competent rather than creatively original, include eight operas.

RELLSTAB, (HEINRICH FRIEDRICH) LUDWIG (1799–1860). German music critic and poet. In 1826 he became music critic for the *Vossische Zeitung*, the outspokenness of his attacks twice causing him to be imprisoned. He was a vigorous proponent of German opera, but his broadly conservative outlook did not incline him favourably towards Wagner's work.

RICHTER, HANS (1843–1916). Austro-Hungarian conductor. After study in Vienna, and experience as a horn player in the Kärntnerthor Theatre there (1862–6), he joined Wagner at Tribschen as a copyist, 1866–7, producing a fair copy of the *Meistersinger* score. He then assisted Bülow in Munich, 1868–9, and went on to conduct Wagner and other operas in various cities, including Brussels, Budapest and Vienna. He conducted the first complete *Ring* at Bayreuth (1876) and maintained a distinguished career thereafter, both in Bayreuth and in England, where he conducted the Hallé Orchestra (1899–1911) and the London Symphony Orchestra (1904–11), as well as giving the first English-language performance of the *Ring* (1908).

RITTER, JULIE [née MOMMA] (1794–1869). After the death of her husband, the merchant Karl Ritter, she took up residence in Dresden, where she became a friend and benefactress of Wagner. In 1850, together with Jessie Laussot, Julie Ritter promised him an annual allowance of 3000 francs. Even after the ignominious "Bordeaux affair", she made over 800 thalers to him annually from 1851 to 1859.

RITTER, KARL (1830–91). Son of Julie Ritter and her husband Karl. Although the parents were German, the sons Karl and Alexander were born in Narva (Estonia) from where the family moved to Dresden after the father's death. It was not until towards the end of Wagner's years in Dresden that he made the acquaintance of the Ritter family. Karl accompanied him into exile in Switzerland and in 1858 went with him to Venice after Wagner was obliged to leave the Asyl.

RÖCKEL, AUGUST (1814–76). German conductor and composer. After training as a répétiteur, and studying in Vienna and Paris, Röckel held posts at Bamberg (1838) and Weimar (1839–43) before being appointed assistant conductor to Wagner in Dresden (1843–9). Their joint involvement in the revolutionary *Volksblätter* (edited by Röckel) and in the uprisings of 1848/9 led to exile for Wagner and a thirteen-year term of imprisonment for Röckel (his death sentence having been commuted). Wagner's letters to Röckel dating from these years contain some revealing passages on his intentions in the *Ring*.

ROHDE, ERWIN (1845–98). German philologist. A friend of Nietzsche who visited Tribschen with him in 1870 and became a close friend of the Wagners.

ROYER, ALPHONSE (1803–75). French man of letters. After writing several novels and travel volumes, he turned to the theatre, becoming the director of first the Odéon, Paris (1853–6), and then the Opéra (1856–62). He was thus in charge at the Opéra over the period of the production of *Tannhäuser* there (1861).

RUBINSTEIN, JOSEPH (1847–84). Pianist born into an affluent Russian Jewish family. He approached Wagner seeking deliverance from his "Jewish deficiencies", and became a regular visitor to Wahnfried. Described as "Wahnfried's supreme court pianist", he played music of all kinds to the Wagners, notably Bach preludes and fugues, and also made piano arrangements of some of Wagner's works. He did not long survive Wagner, committing suicide in Lucerne.

SALIS-SCHWABE, JULIE. The Jewish widow of a Mancunian industrialist. The large deficit from Wagner's three concerts in Paris early in 1860 was partly eased by a gift of 5000 francs (3000, according to *Mein Leben*) from the wealthy Julie Salis-Schwabe. Her intention was to raise a subscription, with Malwida von Meysenbug, to cancel the debt completely. On hearing of Wagner's new-found affluence five years later, she demanded repayment of the loan and legal proceedings were instituted.

SAYN-WITTGENSTEIN, PRINCESS (JEANNE ELISABETH) CAROLYNE (VON) (1819–87). Benefactress and companion of Liszt for many years. After separating from Prince Nikolaus von Sayn-Wittgenstein soon after their arranged marriage, the Princess joined Liszt in Weimar where she exercised a dominant influence over his artistic and emotional life. Her initially warm relationship with Wagner cooled when each began to regard the other as a rival for Liszt's friendship. The Princess co-authored some of the essays on music printed under Liszt's name. She died shortly after completing the twenty-fifth and final volume of her religious tract *Des Causes intérieures de la faiblesse extérieure de l'Église*.

(SAYN-) WITTGENSTEIN, PRINCESS MARIE (1837–1920). Daughter of Princess Carolyne Sayn-Wittgenstein. Wagner was captivated by the 15-year-old princess when she visited him, in the company of her mother and Liszt, in Basle in October 1853. Princess Marie later (1859) married Prince Konstantin zu Hohenlohe-Schillingsfürst, the Master of the Imperial Household in Vienna.

SCHINDELMEISSER, LOUIS ALEXANDER BALTHASAR (1811–64). German composer and conductor, whose career took him to the Königstadt Theatre, Berlin, in 1837, Wiesbaden in 1851, and Darmstadt in 1853. The younger step-brother of Heinrich Dorn, he had been acquainted with Wagner from the latter's student years in Leipzig, and remained a friend and admirer.

SCHLEINITZ, BARON ALEXANDER VON (1807–85). Prussian minister of the Royal Household; an influential and useful ally at the Court in Berlin when Wagner turned to the Reich for support in the early 1870s.

SCHLEINITZ, BARONESS MARIE VON [née VON BUCH] (1842–1912). Wife of preceding. As Marie von Buch, she had been a friend and confidante of Cosima's at the time of Starnberg (1864). During the years of fund-raising for the Bayreuth enterprise, she proved to be an immensely energetic campaigner.

SCHLESINGER, MAURICE [MORITZ] (1797–1871). German music publisher. In 1821 he established a branch of his father's Berlin business in Paris, and was also proprietor and editor of the journal *Gazette musicale de Paris* (from 1835 *Revue et Gazette musicale de Paris*). Wagner earned a modest income from Schlesinger during his Paris years (1839–42). He made arrangements of selections from popular operas of the day, and wrote three novellas for the *Revue et*

Gazette musicale, including *A Pilgrimage to Beethoven*. Several reviews and other journalistic articles were also printed in Schlesinger's journal.

SCHLOSSER, MAX [also known as KARL] (1835–1916). German tenor who sang David in the first performance of *Die Meistersinger* (1868) and Mime in the first *Rheingold* (Munich, 1869, and again at Bayreuth in 1876).

SCHMIDT, JOHANN PHILIPP SAMUEL (1779–1853). German lawyer, Royal Prussian Court Councillor, composer and music critic. As critic of the *Haude und Spenersche Zeitung* in Berlin he wrote about *Rienzi* with considerable enthusiasm at the time of its Dresden première (1842).

SCHNORR VON CAROLSFELD, LUDWIG (1836–65). German tenor. Son of the painter Julius Schnorr von Carolsfeld. After settling in Dresden in 1860, he consolidated his reputation with such roles as Tannhäuser and Lohengrin, subsequently creating that of Tristan opposite his wife Malvina (Munich, 1865). His death only three weeks after the first run of *Tristan* performances was a severe personal blow to Wagner.

SCHNORR VON CAROLSFELD, MALVINA [née GARRIGUES] (1825–1904). Daughter of the Brazilian consul in Copenhagen, where she was born. She made her début in *Robert le diable*, after which she sang in Coburg, Gotha, Hamburg and (from 1854) Karlsruhe. She caused severe embarrassment to Wagner and Cosima by denouncing their liaison to King Ludwig. Subsequently she taught singing in Frankfurt.

SCHÖN, FRIEDRICH (b. 1850). Factory owner in Worms. When, in 1882, Wagner proposed to wind up the Society of Patrons and establish a foundation to enable people of modest means to attend the Bayreuth festival, Schön responded by contributing 10,000 marks to start such a fund. The Stipendiary Foundation – the principle of which still exists today – was thus instituted by Schön.

SCHOPENHAUER, ARTHUR (1788–1860). German philosopher. Wagner was profoundly influenced by Schopenhauer's ideas as expounded in *Die Welt als Wille und Vorstellung* and *Parerga und Paralipomena*. In fact, some of these ideas were already being discussed within Wagner's circle of Zurich friends (notably Herwegh and François Wille) before Wagner himself first read Schopenhauer's *magnum opus* in October 1854. Schopenhauer's elevation of music over the other arts and his philosophy of pessimism had a decisive impact on Wagner's works from the *Ring* onwards. A letter to Schopenhauer on the question of suicide was drafted by Wagner but not sent. The two never met.

SCHOTT'S SÖHNE, B. German firm of music publishers, founded in Mainz in 1770 or 1780 by Bernhard Schott (1748–1809). His sons, Johann Andreas (1781–1840) and Johann Joseph (1782–1855) gave the firm its name "B. Schott's Söhne", expanded the enterprise, and achieved recognition as Beethoven's publishers from 1824. Johann Andreas' son, Franz (1811–74), became the sole proprietor and approached Wagner in the winter of 1859–60. To begin with, he was offered the rights in *Das Rheingold*. Schott subsequently published that work (1873) as well as *Die Walküre* (1874), *Siegfried* (1875), *Götterdäm-merung* (1876), *Die Meistersinger* (1868) and *Parsifal* (1883).

SCHRÖDER-DEVRIENT, WILHELMINE (1804–60). German soprano. Her reputation as one of the leading singers of her day was based on the conviction with which she invested her dramatic portrayals rather than on security of technique. She was particularly acclaimed for her assumption of the role of Leonore in *Fidelio*; among the roles she created were Wagner's Adriano (in *Rienzi*), Senta and Venus. Her marriage to the actor Karl Devrient (brother of Eduard, *q.v.*) was dissolved in 1828.

SCHUMANN, ROBERT (1810–56). German composer, pianist and critic. As founder and first editor of the *Neue Zeitschrift für Musik*, his voice carried some weight in contemporary music criticism. He was encouraging and sympathetic to the young Wagner, though he professed to be perplexed by the through-composed approach to opera. More predisposed to the Classically inclined, absolute music of Brahms, whom he met and befriended in 1853, Schumann would doubtless, had he lived, have been a partisan for him rather than the New German School. However, following a deterioration in his mental health, he spent the last couple of years of his life in an asylum.

SCRIBE, EUGÈNE (1791–1861). French dramatist and librettist. The leading, and certainly most prolific, librettist of his day, his complete works occupying 76 volumes. He thus dominated grand opera in France and wielded enormous influence. Among the many composers for whom he provided librettos were Auber (no fewer than 38), Halévy and Meyerbeer. His texts reflected popular taste in their blend of *Grand Guignol* and historicism, and in the generally liberal, anti-clerical sentiments they express.

SEIDL, ANTON (1850–98). Austro-Hungarian conductor. After studying at Leipzig Conservatory, he assisted in Bayreuth as a member of the "Nibelung Chancel-lery", copying parts and scores. He helped in the production of the 1876 *Ring*, after which, on Wagner's recommendation, he joined Neumann at Leipzig (1879–82), conducting the *Ring* on his European tour, beginning the following year. He made his début at the Metropolitan, New York, in 1885, returning to conduct 340 performances, including the American premières of *Die Meister-singer*, *Tristan* and all the *Ring* operas except *Die Walküre*. His premature death deprived New York of a vigorous champion of Wagner and an authoritative conductor of his scores.

SEMPER, GOTTFRIED (1803–79). German architect. Celebrated as the builder of the Dresden Opera House (the first, opened in 1841, was burnt down in 1869 and eventually replaced by a second Semper building in 1878). He was acquainted with Wagner during his Dresden period and they took part together in the uprising of 1849, Semper taking responsibility for the construction of barricades. To escape arrest he made for first London and then Zurich where he taught and renewed his acquaintance with Wagner. His designs for a festival theatre in Munich – commissioned by Ludwig in the 1860s – were never realized.

SPOHR, LOUIS [LUDWIG] (1784–1859). German composer, violinist and conductor. After a brilliantly successful early career as a travelling virtuoso violinist, Spohr settled at the Court of Cassel (Kapellmeister from 1822, Generalmusikdirektor from 1847). There he was responsible for the production of *Der fliegende Holländer* (1843) and *Tannhäuser* (1853). In spite of his popular success as a composer, Spohr has generally been regarded – both in his own time and the present day – as fluent in technique rather than original in inspiration. Nevertheless, his music anticipated that of Wagner in a number of ways: in his use of chromaticism and leitmotif, in the through-composed construction of his operas, and even in specific chords and modulations.

STAHR, ADOLF (1805–76). German writer and literary scholar. From 1836, professor of Ancient Philology in Oldenburg; from 1854 resident in Berlin, where he wrote on literature and the theatre, as well as novels and memoirs. He wrote enthusiastically about *Lohengrin* in the Berlin *National–Zeitung*, after seeing the work at Weimar in 1851.

STANDHARTNER, JOSEPH (1818–92). Physician resident in Vienna, where he served various members of the Court, including the Empress, and where he made the acquaintance of Wagner. He invited Wagner to occupy his house for six weeks in 1861, while he was away. Standhartner was to remain a firm friend of Wagner's.

STOCKER, JAKOB (1827–1909). Wagner's manservant, who joined the household on his marriage to Vreneli Weidmann (January, 1867).

STOCKER, VRENELI. *See* WEIDMANN, VRENELI.

STOCKS, CHRISTIAN JULIUS DANIEL (1802–81). Beginning his career as a singer at the Schwerin Court Theatre, he went on to become cashier (1843) and chorus-master (1847).

SULZER, (JOHANN) JAKOB (1821–97). From 1847 he was cantonal secretary of Zurich; thereafter, a series of influential posts established him as a leading figure in local and national governmental affairs. He befriended Wagner in his Swiss exile in the 1850s, and provided much valued moral and pecuniary support.

TAPPERT, WILHELM (1830–1907). German critic and writer on music. He settled in 1866 in Berlin where he acquired a reputation as a teacher (at the New Academy of Music) and writer on music. He edited the *Allgemeine deutsche Musikzeitung* (1866–80), and produced a lexicon of anti-Wagner invective. Tappert himself was irreproachably pro-Wagner in his convictions.

TAUSIG, CARL (1841–71). Polish pianist and composer. A prodigious pupil of Liszt in Weimar, he was sent by him in May 1858 to Wagner in Zurich, who was as delighted as he was astonished by Tausig's extrovert playing and personality. He assumed the administration of the scheme of Bayreuth Patrons' certificates in 1871, but fell victim to typhus only a few weeks later.

TICHATSCHEK, JOSEPH (ALOYS) (1807–86). Bohemian tenor. In 1830 hc joined the chorus of the Kärntnerthor Theatre in Vienna; he made his début as a principal in Graz in 1837 and in Dresden the same year. In 1838 he took up an appointment at the Dresden Court Opera, where he helped to elevate the vocal standards to the highest in Germany. He took both lyric tenor and *Spieltenor* roles, but was also widely regarded as an ideal Wagnerian *Heldentenor*, creating and frequently repeating the roles of Rienzi and Tannhäuser. He continued to perform until 1870.

TRUINET, CHARLES (1828–99). French librettist and translator; he wrote under the anagrammatic pseudonym "Nuitter". Founder and director of the archives of the Paris Opéra. He was responsible for revising the French translation of *Tannhäuser* made by others for the performances in Paris in 1861, and subsequently undertook a similar translation of *Der fliegende Holländer* (supervised by Wagner).

UHLIG, THEODOR (1822–53). German violinist, theorist, critic and composer. Illegitimate son of Friedrich August II of Saxony. After joining the Dresden Court orchestra in 1841 he became eventually, though not at first, one of Wagner's closest friends and most dependable supporters. Their friendship, sustained by their similar political outlook, continued into the early years of Wagner's Swiss exile and produced some correspondence revealing as to Wagner's views at that time. Uhlig's writings were admired by Wagner and others, and he had produced an oeuvre of 84 opus numbers by the time of his early death.

UNGER, GEORG (1837–87). German tenor. He made his début in Leipzig in 1867 and was subsequently heard at Mannheim by Richter, who recommended him to Wagner. In order to undertake the role of Siegfried in the first Bayreuth *Ring* in 1876, he had to be coached specially by Julius Hey, on account of his technical deficiencies.

VILLIERS DE l'ISLE-ADAM, COUNT (JEAN-MARIE MATHIAS) PHILIPPE-AUGUSTE (1838–89). French poet. From a family of noble lineage but reduced to impoverishment. His works, written against a background of indigence, are by turns Romantic, mystical, idealistic, and always sensitive to the more visionary tendencies of his age. A friend of Mallarmé, he was influenced by Baudelaire and Poe, and was an admirer of Wagner.

VOGL, HEINRICH (1845–1900). German tenor. He studied in Munich where in 1865 he made his début as Max in *Der Freischütz*. He remained attached to Munich for the remainder of his career, creating the roles of Loge and Siegmund there (1869 and 1870 respectively). Having sung Loge at Bayreuth in 1876, he returned in 1886 as Parsifal, appearing also in Berlin (1881), London (1882), Vienna (1884/5) and New York (1890). He sang all the major Wagner tenor roles with the exception of Walther. His wife, Therese Thoma (1845–1921), created the role of Sieglinde at Munich in 1870 and sang Brünnhilde in the first complete London *Ring* (1882).

WAGNER, ALBERT (1799–1874). Elder brother of Wagner. From 1819 he held appointments as a tenor and actor in various German theatres. From 1857 to 1865 he was a producer at the Berlin Court Theatre.

WAGNER, FRANZISKA (1829–95). Wagner's niece; daughter of Albert Wagner. An actress at the Schwerin Court Theatre, she married Julie Ritter's son, Alexander.

WAGNER, SIEGFRIED (HELFERICH RICHARD) (1869–1930). German composer and conductor; son of Richard Wagner. The birth of his son and heir, regarded as a highly auspicious event by Wagner, was retrospectively celebrated by the composition of the *Siegfried Idyll* (1870). Wagner was not anxious to impose a musical career on his son, and in fact Siegfried pursued architecture for a short time. Then from 1892 to 1896 he became an assistant at Bayreuth, conducting his first performance there in the latter year (*Ring*), and producing *Der fliegende Holländer* in 1906. Assuming directorship of the festival, Siegfried was constrained to a considerable extent in the early years by the conservationist instincts of his mother, Cosima. In his five post-war festivals, however (1924–30), some cautious innovations were made.

WEBER, ERNST VON (1830–1902). Naturalist and founder of an international Anti-Vivisection Society. His pamphlet *Die Folterkammern der Wissenschaft* (The Torture Chambers of Science) met with Wagner's wholehearted approval. Wagner's letter to Weber on the subject of vivisection was developed into an article for the *Bayreuther Blätter* (October, 1879).

WEIDMANN, VRENELI [VERENA] (1832–1906). Vreneli Weidmann first entered Wagner's service in Lucerne in 1859. He appreciated her so much that he re-engaged her, as housekeeper, in Munich (1864), and she remained in his service after his move to Tribschen. She became Vreneli Stocker on her marriage in January 1867.

WEINLIG, CHRISTIAN THEODOR (1780–1842). German organist and composer. Kantor of the Dresden Kreuzschule (1814–17) and of the Thomaskirche, Leipzig, from 1823. Wagner studied counterpoint and composition with him for about six months, beginning in the autumn of 1831. Weinlig's compositions consisted mostly of sacred choral works; he also published a significant treatise on fugue.

WEISSHEIMER, WENDELIN (1838–1910). German conductor and composer. Attended the Leipzig Conservatory in 1856 and subsequently studied with Liszt in Weimar. He became Kapellmeister in various cities, including Mainz, Würzburg, Strasbourg, Baden-Baden and Milan. His friendship with Wagner began in 1862 when the latter was staying in Biebrich. Occasional tensions in their relationship reached a peak in 1868 when Wagner refused to recommend Weissheimer's opera *Theodor Körner* for performance in Munich.

WESENDONCK, MATHILDE [née LUCKEMEYER] (1828–1902). German poet and author. The friendship of Wagner and Mathilde Wesendonck that began in 1852 developed subsequently into a sexual relationship which may or may not have been consummated. The impossible passion of Tristan and Isolde was enacted simultaneously by the composer with Mathilde, until eventually (August, 1858) social propriety dictated his removal. Five of Mathilde's poems were set by Wagner (the *Wesendonck Lieder*); her other works include the five-act drama *Gudrun* (1868), the five-act tragedy *Edith oder die Schlacht bei Hastings* (1872) and the dramatic poem *Odysseus* (1878).

WESENDONCK, OTTO (1815–96). German businessman. After a short but lucrative career as a partner in a New York firm of silk importers, he retired to Zurich in 1851 to enjoy his wealth. Wagner had no scruples about assisting him in this; indeed, it could be argued that Wesendonck needed a struggling artist to patronize as much as Wagner required a generous benefactor. They thus continued to oblige each other even after the marital crisis of 1858.

WIGARD, FRANZ JACOB (1807–85). German professor and doctor. He represented Saxony in the German National Assembly at Frankfurt (1848/9), after which he pursued a career in medicine.

WILLE, ELIZA [née SLOMAN] (1809–93). German novelist. From the years of Wagner's Swiss exile, his friend and confidante. She and her husband François made Wagner's acquaintance after they retired to a small estate at Mariafeld, near Zurich, in 1851. Wagner became a regular visitor to their home.

WILLE, FRANÇOIS (1811–96). German political journalist. He represented Schleswig-Holstein in the German National Assembly at Frankfurt (1848/9). In spite of his political radicalism, and his enthusiasm for Schopenhauer, Wille and Wagner had too little in common to sustain a lasting relationship.

WINKLER, (CARL GOTTFRIED) THEODOR (1775–1856). German poet, impresario and journalist. An old friend of the Wagner family, he became assistant director of the Court Theatre in Dresden. Known professionally as Theodor Hell, he was founder-editor of the Dresden *Abend-Zeitung*, author of the text of Weber's *Die drei Pintos*, and editor of the first collection of Weber's writings (1828).

WITTGENSTEIN, PRINCESS MARIE. *See* (SAYN-) WITTGENSTEIN, PRINCESS MARIE.

WOLFRAM, CLARA [née WAGNER] (1807–75). Elder sister of Wagner; she married the singer Heinrich Wolfram in 1828. Clara herself began an operatic career in a performance of Rossini's *La Cenerentola* in Dresden in 1824, but retired from the stage a few years after her marriage.

WOLZOGEN, BARON HANS (PAUL) VON (1848–1938). German writer on music. After studying comparative philology and philosophy in Berlin (1868–71), he came to Wagner's attention and was invited to Bayreuth in October 1877 as editor of the newly-founded *Bayreuther Blätter*. Wolzogen remained editor from the first issue (published at the beginning of 1878) until his death 60 years later, during which period he became identified as one of the chief guardians of the "Holy Grail" of Bayreuth. He also produced a series of thematic guides to the *Ring* and other works, and edited three volumes of Wagner's letters.

WÜLLNER, FRANZ (1832–1902). German conductor and composer. He held various teaching appointments from 1856 before joining the staff of the music school in Munich (1867), where he directed the choral and orchestral classes. Notwithstanding Wagner's intense disapproval of his decision to accept the offer to conduct the *Rheingold* and *Walküre* premières in Munich (1869 and 1870), Wüllner went on to become principal Kapellmeister of the Court Opera there in 1871, director of the Dresden Conservatory (on Rietz's death in 1877), director of the Cologne Conservatory (1884) and a founder-director of the orchestra that became the Berlin Philharmonic.

ZUMPE, HERMAN (1850–1903). German conductor and composer. After teaching appointments in Weigsdorf and Leipzig, he went to Bayreuth in 1872, to assist Wagner in preparing the score of the *Ring*, becoming a member of the "Nibelung Chancellery". After Wagner's death he consolidated a considerable reputation as a conductor – not least of Wagner's music – and his various stage works also attracted some attention in his lifetime.

INDEX

Compiled by Stewart Spencer

An asterisk refers to the Glossary of Names on pp. 959–87;
the numbers of Wagner's *Letters* are printed in italics.